Std loan.

EMPL

BOW

C·1

WHISTLEBLOWING

Law and Practice

THIRD EDITION

WHISTLEBLOWING

Law and Practice

THIRD EDITION

JEREMY LEWIS
JOHN BOWERS QC
MARTIN FODDER
JACK MITCHELL

OXFORD
UNIVERSITY PRESS

OXFORD
UNIVERSITY PRESS

Great Clarendon Street, Oxford, ox2 6dp,
United Kingdom

Oxford University Press is a department of the University of Oxford.
It furthers the University's objective of excellence in research, scholarship,
and education by publishing worldwide. Oxford is a registered trade mark of
Oxford University Press in the UK and in certain other countries

© Jeremy Lewis, John Bowers, Martin Fodder, and Jack Mitchell 2017

The moral rights of the authors have been asserted

Impression: 1

Published in the United States of America by Oxford University Press
198 Madison Avenue, New York, NY 10016, United States of America

British Library Cataloguing in Publication Data
Data available

Library of Congress Control Number: 2017934736

ISBN 978-0-19-878803-4

Printed and bound by
CPI Group (UK) Ltd, Croydon, CR0 4YY

To our wives, Rebecca, Suzanne, Ali, and Julie
And to the memory of Irene Bowers, Bill and Joyce Fodder, and
Elias and Anne Ellis

FOREWORD

It is a tribute to the authoritative standing of this work that it is now in its third edition only a decade after its first publication. This new edition is timely. Although the total number of cases filed in the Employment Tribunals has fallen dramatically, the graph in relation to whistleblowing cases continues to move in the opposite direction. In 2015, 2449 such cases were filed. Although they undoubtedly include a fair number of misconceived and contrived claims, the underlying trend is plain to see. In the eighteen years since the enactment of the Public Interest Disclosure Act 1998, there has been a palpable change in the workplace. Investigation of a number of public scandals has demonstrated the timidity of the "blind eye, deaf ear, blame the messenger" culture to which the authors refer. That legislation should provide specific protection for whistleblowers is no longer controversial. As they opine, it has become "a crucial part of good corporate governance". Indeed, the controversy has shifted to the more difficult issue of the possible imposition of a legal duty to disclose wrongdoing.

All such issues receive expert consideration in this new edition. It deals comprehensively with the developing jurisprudence and includes detailed coverage of the important changes brought about by the Enterprise and Regulatory Reform Act 2013.

I congratulate the authors on producing once again an invaluable, authoritative and wide-ranging text on this complex and evolving subject.

Sir Maurice Kay
Former Vice President of the
Court of Appeal, Civil Division

PREFACE

At the heart of the legislation protecting whistleblowers is a recognition of the need for protection so as to encourage 'responsible whistleblowing'. The objective is to encourage workers to raise their concerns at an early stage and to an appropriate person, so as to provide an early warning system in the public interest. However, as the volume of cases has increased, tensions have emerged between different interests. There has been a concern to keep whistleblowing protection within what have been seen as its proper public interest bounds. But there has also been a recognition of the desirability of strengthening the protection provided where it is deserved and of the need to avoid placing excessive barriers in the way of those raising public interest disclosures. Those themes were reflected in the amendments effected by the Enterprise and Regulatory Reform Act 2013, which are the principal driver for the new, third, edition of this book. There has been a recasting of the scheme of the legislation, most notably by the introduction of a new public interest requirement which anchors whistleblowing law directly as a protection for those blowing the whistle in the interests of the public and moves away from protecting disclosures relating to purely personal concerns, and also the introduction of provisions for vicarious liability and individual liability of workers and agents. Whilst we refer in this book to 'PIDA' (ie the Public Interest Disclosure Act 1998) as convenient shorthand for the whistleblowing protection contained in the Employment Rights Act 1996, the original PIDA inserted provisions have therefore now undergone significant amendment.

At one stage it appeared that further extensive legislative reforms would follow. That now seems unlikely in the immediate future. There have, however, also been significant developments which are specific to the health and financial services sectors, but which also have implications more widely for good practice in relation to whistleblowing. Those developments are considered in Chapter 12, and we are very grateful to Sir Robert Francis QC and Ivor Adair for their constructive comments on that chapter. The views expressed in that chapter are, however, those of the authors alone.

The European Court of Human Rights jurisprudence on whistleblowing in the workplace has also evolved significantly, and now merits a separate chapter (Chapter 18), in which we also consider the potential implications for the domestic whistleblowing protection.

The flow of appellate level cases has continued apace. We will comment on future judgments touching on the subject matter of this book in the book's comprehensive updater, which will continue to be accessible through the 'publications' page at http://www.littletonchambers.com.

We express our thanks to Sir Maurice Kay for his generous Foreword.

With this edition Cameron Doley has passed the baton to Isabel Martorell to update the chapter on the relationship between whistleblowing law and defamation law, now taking into account the Defamation Act 2013 (which received Royal Assent on the same day as the legislation amending PIDA). We thank them both for their contributions, and Richard Price QC for his chapter on copyright. Public Concern at Work has again provided assistance on this book (and we thank it for its creative and pioneering work on whistleblowing generally). We also pay tribute to the brave people who come forward to blow the whistle in the public interest.

We have been able to take into account at proof-stage some significant recent developments, including the decisions in *Eiger Securities LLP v Korshunova* [2017] IRLR 115 (EAT) and *Kuznetsov v The Royal Bank Of Scotland* [2017] EWCA Civ 43, and the Law Commission's Consultation Paper on Protection of Official Data. Otherwise the law is stated as at 1 December 2016.

J. Lewis
J. Bowers QC
M. Fodder
J. Mitchell

CONTENTS—SUMMARY

CONTENTS

TABLE OF CASES

TABLE OF LEGISLATION

TABLE OF UK STATUTORY INSTRUMENTS

TABLE OF OVERSEAS LEGISLATION

Japan

United States

TABLE OF EUROPEAN LEGISLATION

Directives

Regulations

TREATIES AND CONVENTIONS

TABLE OF INTERNATIONAL TREATIES AND CONVENTIONS

1

INTRODUCTION

In any organization (whether public or private) the people who are 'on the ground' will **1.01** usually be the first to spot trouble or potential trouble or danger, whether these are threats to health and safety or financial corruption or other dangers or wrongdoing. In the whistleblower, companies and public bodies alike possess a valuable resource to discover or uncover risk, although they often will not realize this or see it in this way. They may instead treat whistleblowers in a negative way and penalize them by 'shooting the messenger' for bringing bad news. All too often the culture at work causes staff, through fear of victimization or dismissal, to react by doing and saying nothing (or too little and too late). Further, in cases where an employee has spoken up, the reaction of the employer is often to regard the employee as a troublemaker, to be at best ignored and ostracized ('sent to Coventry'), and sometimes disciplined or even dismissed for speaking up and expressing their concerns. This may be summed up as the approach of 'deny, delay, destroy' that has been adopted by many companies.

An enlightened approach to whistleblowing assists accountability, responsibility, and transpar- **1.02** ency. As such, in addition to providing basic employment rights and protecting a fundamental human right in relation to freedom of expression, protection of those who blow the whistle to an appropriate person may be seen as a crucial part of good corporate governance. There should be a strong speak-up culture in a well-managed company. To that end, the Committee on Standards in Public Life, in its report 'Getting the Balance Right: Implementing Standards in Public Life' CM 6407 January 2005 (at para 4.31), highlighted the role whistleblowing plays 'both as an instrument of good governance and a manifestation of a more open culture'. To similar effect, the Council of Europe recommendation CM Rec 2014/7 on Protection of whistleblowers, in para 1 of its Explanatory Memorandum, states that:

> The Council of Europe recognizes the value of whistleblowing in deterring and preventing wrongdoing, and in strengthening democratic accountability and transparency. Whistleblowing is a fundamental aspect of freedom of expression and freedom of conscience and is important in the fight against corruption and tackling gross mismanagement in the public and private sectors.[1]

---

[1] The appendix 'sets out a series of principles to guide Member States when reviewing their national laws or when introducing legislation'. It states at para 1 that 'The national normative, institutional and judicial

1.03 One aspect of the good corporate governance rationale for whistleblower protection is that such protection may also be regarded as reflecting corporate self-interest in enabling issues to be identified and addressed at an early stage. As the British Standards Institutions Code of Practice on Whistleblowing Arrangements put it:

> Every organization faces the risk that something will go badly wrong and ought to welcome the opportunity to address it as early as possible. Whenever such a situation arises, the first people to know of the risk will usually be those who work in or with the organization. Yet while these are the people best placed to raise the concern they often fear they have the most to lose if they do speak up. … The main reason enlightened organizations implement whistleblowing arrangements is that they recognize it makes good business sense. On the other hand, those few organizations that deliberately engage in wrongdoing to boost profits or that routinely flout the law will not want to encourage whistleblowing.

1.04 The need to engender a change in the pervasive culture, and to strengthen the protection available to the whistleblower, was illustrated and acknowledged in many reports upon numerous tragedies and scandals which could have been prevented, or the impact of which might have been reduced, had people within the relevant organization spoken out or had the warnings of those who did speak out been properly heeded. Usually someone in the organization (often quite low down the pecking order) is found afterwards (often by an inquiry long after the event) to have known of the problem for some considerable period of time. There are many instances where industrial or financial disasters might have been averted had those workers in a position to raise the alarm been encouraged or enabled to speak out at an appropriate time or been heeded when they sought to do so.[2] These multiple cases also demonstrated the pressing need for a change in the workplace culture relating to whistleblowers and the need to bolster the legal protection which is afforded to them. At the risk of over-generalization, various incidents and tragedies, which provided the catalyst for the introduction of the Public Interest Disclosure Act 1998 (PIDA), may usefully be considered as highlighting the following categories or themes; 'turning a blind eye' (by those in a position to raise the alarm), 'turning a deaf ear' (by those able to act upon concerns raised, but who fail to heed the warnings), and 'blaming the messenger' (leading to reprisals against the whistleblower).[3]

1.05 There are a brave few who have managed to succeed in raising their concerns despite facing severe cultural prejudice and practical barriers in doing so. There are undoubtedly many more cases in which whistleblowers have been effective in allowing matters to be addressed internally and as such the matter has not come to public knowledge at all. In too many cases, however, employees witness serious malpractice but are reluctant to report this for fear of blighting their career by appearing 'difficult' or 'disloyal'. There have often enough been good

---

framework, including, as appropriate, collective labour agreements, should be designed and developed to facilitate public interest reports and disclosures by establishing rules to protect the rights and interests of whistle-blowers'. At para 12 it states 'The national framework should foster an environment that encourages reporting or disclosure in an open manner. Individuals should feel safe to freely raise public interest concerns'.

[2] Examples of those issues which led to the legislation include the *Piper Alpha* oil rig disaster in 1988, the *Herald of Free Enterprise* ferry which sunk at Zeebrugge (Belgium) in 1987, information about the sinking of the Argentinian *Belgrano* warship, and the Matrix Churchill employee who warned the Foreign Office that the company was supplying munitions-making equipment to Iraq.

[3] For a consideration of a wider range of events under each heading, see the first and second editions of this book. Recent examples of whistleblowing in the public interest are the Volkswagen emissions scandal, the LIBOR interest rates fixing disclosed by a senior manager at Barclays, problems of abuse in various care homes, and horsemeat adulteration. The Hooper Report for Public Concern at Work highlights the cases of Dr Kim Holt who blew the whistle on procedures prior to the death of Baby P, Dr Bolsin and the Bristol Royal Infirmary, and Nurse Terry Bryan and the Winterbourne View Hospital.

grounds for fears of physical violence, intimidation, or dismissal (or at least ostracization by colleagues) after blowing the whistle.

The reluctance of potential whistleblowers to come forward, however, has not been attributable only to justified fears of reprisals. An additional factor has often been the prevailing 'culture' which exists within many organizations where the whistleblower is contemptuously regarded as a 'grass' or a 'sneak' who is to be shunned and avoided (and the culture of many organizations is very hard to measure from the outside). **1.06**

This culture has sometimes been supported (notably in the NHS) by the use of 'gagging' clauses to restrain employees from voicing their concerns.[4] Indeed, the Nolan Committee in its first report on Standards in Public Life,[5] noted that: **1.07**

> there is a public concern about 'gagging clauses' in public employees' contracts of employment, which prevent them speaking out to raise concerns about standards of public propriety.

The Parliamentary Commission on Banking Standards was set up July 2012 to consider and report on professional standards and the culture of the UK banking sector. In its report 'Changing Banking for Good', it stated 'the Commission was shocked by the evidence it heard that so many people turned a blind eye to misbehaviour and failed to report it. Institutions must ensure that their staff have a clear understanding of their duty to report an instance of wrongdoing, or "whistleblow", within the firm'. **1.08**

This concern has been observed over many decades. Even in the absence of an express gagging clause, the culture of secrecy might be enhanced by the employee's knowledge that the contractual or equitable duty of confidence was owed to the employer[6] and by the example sometimes set by the employing organization in failing to respond to concerns when they have been raised. This culture was further sustained by deficiencies which were perceived to lie within the law which ensured that staff became trapped in an environment breeding inaction and apathy within the workplace despite the presence of dangers and malpractice. In its Second Report, the Committee on Standards in Public Life, noted that: **1.09**

> it is striking that in the few cases where things have gone badly wrong in local public spending bodies, it has frequently been the tip-off to the press or the local Member of Parliament—sometimes anonymous, sometimes not—which has prompted the regulators into action. Placing staff in a position where they feel driven to approach the media to ventilate concerns is unsatisfactory both for the staff member and the organisation.[7]

Academic research has also highlighted that the plight of the whistleblower is often intense and there may be a psychological cost to putting one's head above the parapet and blowing the whistle. Even the strongest-willed individuals may find the burden of standing out from the crowd unbearable over time. C. Fred Alford, Professor of Government at the University of Maryland, discusses the issue in his seminal work *Whistleblowers: Broken Lives and Organizational Power*,[8] concluding that seniority offers little protection, and that there is no difference whether concerns are raised within or outside an organization. Kate Kenny of Queens University Belfast in her article 'Whistleblowing in the Finance Industry' 2013 says that she was surprised by 'the amount of work that goes into being a whistleblower, meaning the constant reading of documents, rebutting of arguments, exposing of lies and learning **1.10**

---

[4] The same issue arose at the BBC, as was made clear by the review of its internal practices following the Jimmy Savile scandal.

[5] Cm. 2850–1 (1995).

[6] This is dealt with in Chapter 14.

[7] Cm. 3270–1 (1996) p 21.

[8] Ithaca, NY: Cornell University Press, 2001.

about the law, all while struggling to hold your personality together; in short by the fact that it's a full time job which, usually without warning, takes over your life'.

A. Momentum for Reform

1.11 A sea change in the cultural perception of the value of whistleblowers was prompted by the Nolan Report which led to the establishment of the Committee of Standards in Public Life, and by the observations of a number of public inquiries, in particular the Cullen and Matrix Churchill Reports.

1.12 It is noteworthy that, along with the legislative developments, the usage of the very term 'whistleblowing' has itself subtly changed over time. A good working definition of 'whistleblower' is found in the Council of Europe Recommendation, Appendix A: 'any person who reports or discloses information on a threat or harm, to the public interest in the context of their work-based relationship. ...' But, beyond this definition, there has to an extent been a shift from a generally pejorative label which often denoted a stance taken against the 'establishment' by a 'sneak', to a word which is synonymous with the values of openness and informed decision-making. This itself reflects changing public attitudes to someone who is prepared to breach confidence in order to bring matters to the wider public attention. It may also say something more generally about the perceived need to bring matters to public attention because of a lesser confidence in the integrity of both public and private administration. By the time that the Public Interest Disclosure Bill was introduced in Parliament, a wide consensus had indeed developed as to the need for such legislation, largely created by the Nolan Commission and the whistleblowing charity Public Concern at Work (PCaW)—an independent consultancy and legal advice centre launched in 1993. The Bill, which became the 1998 Act, was able to sail through Parliament due to cross-party cooperation, which is unusual if not unique on a matter impinging on employment law.

1.13 Reflecting this consensus, it was hoped that PIDA would itself herald a shift in culture and reshape the consensus. To that end, Mr Richard Shepherd MP, who introduced the Private Member's Bill which led to the enactment of PIDA, expressed the important aspiration behind it:

> I hope that the Bill will signal a shift in culture so that it is safe and accepted for employees ... to sound the alarm when they come across malpractice that threatens the safety of the public, the health of a patient, public funds or the savings of investors. I hope that it will mean that good and decent people in business and public bodies throughout the country can more easily ensure that where malpractice is reported in an organisation the response deals with the message not the messenger.[9]

1.14 The legislation was described by Lord Borrie QC, in the House Lords debates on the Bill, as 'the most far reaching piece of whistleblowing legislation in the world'. It was largely a product of the tireless work of the charity PCaW. During the passage of the Public Interest Disclosure Bill in the House of Lords, Lord Nolan commended those behind the Bill 'for so skilfully achieving the essential but delicate balance in this measure between the public interest and the interests of employers.'[10]

1.15 At the heart of the new Act was the aim of identifying which sorts of disclosure required protection, and in which circumstances it would be in the public interest that those making

---

[9] Standing Committee, 11 March 1998, p 4.
[10] *Hansard* HL, 5 June 1998, col 614.

such disclosures should be given protection. Those promoting the Bill emphasized that it was not merely an employee rights bill, but a public interest measure. As Lord Borrie explained (introducing the Bill in the House of Lords for its second reading on 11 May 1998):

> … this measure will encourage people to recognise and identify with the wider public interest and not just their own private position. It will reassure them that if they act reasonably to protect the legitimate interests of others who are being threatened or abused, the law will not stand idly by should they be vilified or victimised.

B. The Public Interest Disclosure Act 1998

1.16 The Act offers protection to the whistleblower, in broad policy terms, provided that the disclosure is proportionate and in relation to one of the specified subjects of public concern, giving rise to the important central concept of a *protected* disclosure. One challenge for those legislating to protect the whistleblower was to encourage disclosure within the structure of the employing organization where the matter can be properly redressed, whilst providing adequate protection in the lesser number of cases where wider disclosure is appropriate. The difficulty faced by the framers of the legislation in seeking to confine protection to appropriate cases of proportionate disclosure may explain the somewhat complex structure of the Act.

1.17 The Act operates by incorporating sections into the Employment Rights Act 1996, and throughout the book we refer to the section as thus incorporated rather than the section of PIDA itself.

C. Moving Forward the Consensus

1.18 PIDA has acted as a catalyst for a whole range of developments of policies in both the public and private sectors. One aspect of this has been the publication of whistleblowing codes developed in particular areas (eg the FCA, the NHS, the Civil Service). To take two important examples: (a) The Civil Service Code, which was issued in 2006, included express reference to PIDA for the first time; and (b) The National Audit Office said in March 2013 that 'The Department of Health should take the lead in making sure that whistleblowers are and feel protected through the NHS. Whistleblowers are a valuable source of intelligence and should feel encouraged to come forward'. PCaW has also published a Code of Practice, and the Council of Europe Recommendation CM Rec 2014/7 on Protection of whistleblowers is also powerful support for the domestic legislation.[11] The Code of Practice and Recommendation are referred to in various parts of the text alongside the legislation.

1.19 In some fields more legislation has further reinforced and gone beyond the general whistleblowing provisions. The Bribery Act 2010, for example, introduced rigorous new anti-corruption regulations that will affect all employers. Employers are most affected by the 'corporate offence', which applies to commercial organizations which fail to prevent acts of bribery which have been committed for the benefit of the organization. A commercial organization is guilty of an offence if it fails to prevent an 'associated person' bribing another with the intention of obtaining or retaining an advantage or business for the organization. 'Associated persons' have been defined widely to include any person who 'performs services' for, or on behalf of, the organization. This may be an employee, agent, or subsidiary,

---

[11] There are many other international instruments, eg The International Civil Aviation Organisation requires whistleblowing procedures as part of mandatory safety reporting systems.

depending on the circumstances. This provides a fresh impetus for effective whistleblowing policies, with a view to being able to rely on a defence (in section 7 of the 2010 Act) that there were adequate procedures designed to prevent persons associated with the company from undertaking bribery (see Chapter 19).

D. Public Awareness and Perception

1.20 Protection by the law is necessary in this area but not by any means sufficient. Legal support for the whistleblower can indeed only go so far; also important is the culture of the particular working environment in which the whistleblower operates and indeed in society more generally. To some extent there is evidence that, over time, and partly because of the passage of PIDA itself, the role of the responsible whistleblower has become much more favourably viewed. An example of this was that *Time* magazine featured whistleblowers on its first front cover of 2003 and dubbed 2003 the 'year of the whistleblower'. Those shown on that cover included the woman who blew the whistle which led to the Enron scandal being exposed. A study by Cardiff University (K. Wahl-Jorgensen and J. Hurr) found that in the period from 1 January 1997 to 31 December 2009, 54 per cent of newspaper stories represented whistleblowers in a positive light, whilst only five per cent were negative in coverage (the remainder were neutral).

1.21 The legislation has achieved one of its goals, in encouraging employees to complain internally rather than outside the employing organization. According to PCaW, 80 per cent of claimants refer their concerns internally first.[12] A report for the Parliamentary Assembly of the Council of Europe (PACE) noted that there is a much more 'whistleblower friendly' climate in the United Kingdom than elsewhere in Europe.[13]

1.22 One (but only one) barometer of public awareness of whistleblowing is the level of claims which have been made to employment tribunals under PIDA. Claims of victimization/dismissal on grounds of a protected disclosure have shown a year-on-year increase since the legislation was introduced, rising from 157 in the first year to 1,761 in 2009, about 2,000 for the period from 1 April 2008 to 31 March 2010, and 2,449 for 2015.[14]

1.23 Of course, whilst the rise in claims suggests improving public awareness of the legal remedies, it may also be one indication of continuing issues of victimization being suffered by those who blow the whistle. Support for that view was provided by a joint University of Greenwich and PCaW study, 'Whistleblowing: the inside story' (14 May 2013), which found that reprisals against whistleblowers included blocking resources (15 per cent), and informal reprisals (20 per cent). The report further found that of the callers to the PCaW helpline 27 per cent were skilled workers and 26 per cent were classed as professionals. In more than one in two cases the employer's response was to deny or ignore the concern. The main issue raised by whistleblowers was financial malpractice (18 per cent), followed by ethical concerns, while more than a fifth (22 per cent) of complaints related to the education sector. The report said 50 per cent of whistleblowers reported being dismissed or resigned after raising their concern. A further 28 per cent were bullied by co-workers or victimized and/or disciplined by their employer.[15]

---

[12] See the study referred to at para 1.23 below, p 6.

[13] Explanatory memorandum of rapporteur Mr Omtzigt, appended to the report of the PACE's Committee on Legal Affairs and Human Rights of 14 September 2009.

[14] PCaW Biennial Review (2011) p 13 and employment tribunal statistics for 2015.

[15] The research based on a review of calls to Public Concern at Work's advice line in 2015 found 1,876 individuals contacted the charity on a workplace whistleblowing matter in 2014, a 15% rise compared to 2012.

Whilst advances have undoubtedly been made with the introduction of whistleblowing legisla- **1.24**
tion, there remain many examples which can be placed broadly in each of the categories of blind
eye, deaf ear, and blaming the messenger (see paragraph 1.04 above) and which emphasize the
continuing importance of whistleblower legal protection and effective whistleblowing policies.
Organizations are still often turning a deaf ear to the whistleblower, as seems to have happened
in the case of abuse at the Winterbourne View care home (featured on the BBC's *Panorama*)
where an employee, Terry Bryan, blew the whistle. There are also still too many examples of
blaming the messenger for the message he or she is giving out. For example, a whistleblower
nurse, Margaret Haywood, was struck off the nursing register because of her involvement in an
undercover *Panorama* film showing apparent abuse at the place where she worked.[16] The PCaW
report entitled 'Where's Whistleblowing Now?' stated that 35 per cent of callers said that they
had suffered reprisals, and a large majority said that they had been ignored. A culture of reprisal
may continue to lead to examples of turning a blind eye. An example was covered extensively
in the Gage Report on the treatment of Baha Mousa in Iraq. This reported on a lack of 'moral
courage' to report abuse, although it seems that the inquiry did hear of one whistleblower.[17]

Whistleblowing has also featured in recent scandals involving alleged phone hacking at **1.25**
the *News of the World* newspaper, and high mortality rates at the Mid Staffordshire NHS
Foundation Trust investigated by Sir Robert Francis QC (discussed in Chapter 12). As a
side issue of the *News of the World* phone hacking imbroglio, the police sought to require the
Guardian to reveal its sources of information[18] (but then pulled back), and we cover these
issues in Chapter 15 on protection of sources. Much more controversial has been the massive
exposure of private emails and diplomatic cables by WikiLeaks. The approach taken there of
wide-scale mass publication may be seen as the antithesis of the carefully graduated approach
encouraged by PIDA, and it is far more controversial for that reason.

A continuing concern as to the way in which whistleblowers are perceived and treated, even **1.26**
within government departments, was evinced in the Public Accounts Committee's Report
published on 1 August 2014.[19] It is worth quoting the summary in full:

> Whistleblowing is an important source of intelligence to help government identify wrongdoing
> and risks to public service delivery. But many concerns go unreported, and the intelligence that
> does exist is not routinely collected and shared. It is essential that employees have trust in the
> system for handling whistleblowers, and confidence that they will be taken seriously, protected
> and supported by their organisations if they blow the whistle. A positive approach to whistle-
> blowing should exist wherever the taxpayer's pound is spent, in private and non-statutory bodies
> as well as public authorities. However, far too often whistleblowers have been shockingly treated,
> and whistleblowers who have come forward have had to show remarkable bravery. Departments'
> own attempts at changing whistleblowing policy and processes for the better have not been
> successful in modifying a bullying culture, or in combating unacceptable behaviour, such as har-
> assment of whistleblowers, within their organisations. The lack of cross-government leadership
> on whistleblowing has resulted in an inconsistent approach across departments.

There is continuing concern at the exposed position of civil servants, who may be in breach of the **1.27**
Official Secrets Act 1989 if they reveal confidential matters (as to which see the Law Commission
consultation paper published in February 2017 referred to in Chapter 14, para 14.163). They
would not then be protected under PIDA (ERA, section 43B(3)).

---

[16] *The Times*, 17 April 2009.
[17] See <http://www.independent.co.uk/news/uk/home-news/british-colonel-blew-whistle-on-abuse-of-iraqi-prisoners-1911328.html>.
[18] *Guardian*, 17 September 2011.
[19] See <http://www.parliament.uk/business/committees/committees-a-z/commons-select/public-accounts-committee/inquiries/parliament-2010/whistleblowing-making-policy-work/>.

E. The Shipman Inquiry Report and Reform

1.28 A further stage in the development of thinking about public interest disclosures after the legislation had been in force about five years came from Dame Janet Smith's Shipman Inquiry report which was published on 9 December 2004.[20] She called for greater public awareness of the role of whistleblowing and the more widespread availability of advice to those raising public interest concerns. Although it was not its primary focus, the report had much to say about whistleblowing because there were individuals who would have been in a position to disclose material about Dr Shipman from an early stage, but were discouraged from doing so by reason of the law as it stood at the time. Had they come forward this might even have saved the lives of some of the victims. The report noted that 'the message that emerges from media reports of whistleblowing cases is in essence a negative one; namely that those who put their heads above the parapet and dare to speak out are liable to be penalised in some way' (para 11.7). There were some natural barriers to raising the alarm by those who had concerns about Shipman, such as being seen as a troublemaker or maverick, fear of recriminations, and 'a feeling of impotence grounded in the belief that even if the report is made nothing will be done about it' (para 11.10). This was in addition to the possibility of a claim for defamation. Further, 'there is a tendency for attention to be focused on the messenger rather than on the message' (para 11.12). The report was also concerned that junior doctors were unwilling to raise concerns about a consultant because of the fear that consultants might block their career progression (para 11.79). Doubts were raised about the good faith test due to motivation of whistleblowers being questioned, and these doubts came to fruition in the reforms referred to below.

F. Reforms

1.29 The legislation is kept under constant review. The Enterprise and Regulatory Reform Act 2013 (ERRA) introduced the first major legislative changes to the whistleblowing provisions, in particular:

(a) A disclosure no longer qualifies for protection unless the worker reasonably believes it is 'made in the public interest'.

(b) Protection no longer depends on the disclosure having been made in good faith. Instead, lack of good faith can lead to a reduction in compensation of up to 25 per cent.

(c) Employers are vicariously liable for whistleblowing victimization by workers and agents, subject to a defence in relation to workers (but not agents) of taking all reasonable steps to prevent this. Liability is also imposed on the worker or agent (though it has been held – we suggest incorrectly – that the legislation appears to provide that the only remedy is a declaration).[21]

(d) Certain healthcare professionals are brought within the scope of whistleblowing protection.

1.30 The amendments may be viewed as having two key strands. Related to the increase in the volume of claims (see paragraph 1.23 above) there was a perception by the Conservative-led coalition Government which was in power at the time that the legislation had moved away from its public interest roots because claims could be brought which were based on

---

[20] Fifth Shipman Inquiry report, Cm. 6394 (2004).

[21] *Royal Mail Group Ltd v Jhuti* [2016] ICR 1043 (EAT) at para 27; s 49(1) ERA. But see Chapter 8 (paras 8.73 to 8.77).

disclosing wrongdoing with no public interest element, based only on a breach of the worker's employment contract. To remedy this, the public interest test was introduced. The relegation of good faith to a remedy issue at the same time reflected concerns that had been raised in the Shipman Inquiry that those who could raise the alarm were being deterred from doing so by having their motives questioned. In addition, the introduction of vicarious liability reduced the scope for employers to have a defence merely on the basis that action had been taken by reason of protected disclosures to meet the exigencies of managing a dysfunctional workforce (see *Fecitt v NHS Manchester* [2012] ICR 372 (Court of Appeal)). To this extent the reforms may be seen as marking an important shifting of the balance between the need to frame legislation which encourages those able to blow the alarm to do so, and concern not to allow remedies such as day-one protection against dismissal and uncapped compensation, to be available in what may, at least viewed in isolation from the broader public interest aims, be seen as undeserving cases. The vicarious liability provisions also place renewed emphasis on the importance of whistleblowing procedures. The reforms are considered in more detail in Chapters 4 and 8, and whistleblowing procedures are reviewed in Chapter 19.

On 12 July 2013 the Department for Business, Innovation and Skills (now renamed) **1.31** launched a Call for Evidence to look at the current whistleblowing laws, and specifically whether there is enough support for people to report wrongdoing. The Government's response to the evidence received as a result of its Call was published in June 2014.[22] This included improved guidance for employers on whistleblowing policies, a duty on regulators to publish annually the number of complaints received and how they have been investigated, adding prescribed persons such as MPs, and additions to the relevant groups covered, such as student nurses.

In addition (and separately) in 2013 PCaW set up a Whistleblowing Commission under **1.32** Sir Anthony Hooper to consider what changes should be made to the legislation.[23] The Commission recommended, inter alia, that

(a) two further categories be added as topics about which disclosures would be protected: gross waste or mismanagement of funds and serious misuse or abuse of authority (these changes have not been implemented).

(b) the licence or registration of organizations which fail to have in place effective whistleblowing arrangements should be reviewed.

The Commission was, however, concerned that a public interest test (which was introduced **1.33** by amendment of ERA for qualifying disclosure in 25 June 2013[24]) would 'lead to uncertainty and unpredictability'.

G. Whistleblowing in the NHS

The area where there has been most intense concern about the operation of the statute has **1.34** been the NHS. On 23 June 2014, in response to a number of reported NHS whistleblowing cases, Ministers appointed Sir Robert Francis QC to lead an independent inquiry (a review) into whistleblowing in the NHS, called 'Freedom to Speak Up'. His report contained

---

[22] See <https://www.gov.uk/government/consultations/whistleblowing-framework-call-for-evidence>.
[23] The details are available at <http://www.pcaw.co.uk/law-policy/whistleblowing-commission/whistleblowing-commission-report>.
[24] See Chapter 4.

wide-ranging proposals designed to change the culture of the NHS, including the creation of whistleblowing 'guardians' in each NHS Trust. He said:

> Reporting of incidents of concern relevant to patient safety, compliance with the law and other fundamental standards or some higher requirements of the employer needs to be not only encouraged but insisted upon. Staff are entitled to receive feedback in relation to any report they make, including information about any action taken or reasons for not taking action.

1.35 In Chapter 9 of his report Sir Robert considered the effectiveness of the existing legal framework, which he described as 'weak'. However, he did not recommend a wholesale review of the ERA provisions, for two reasons:

(a) He believed that legislative change could not be implemented quickly enough to make a difference to those currently working in the NHS; instead there needed to be a change in the culture and mindset of the NHS so that fewer staff would need recourse to the law;

(b) His review was concerned only with the position of disclosures made within one part of the public sector (the NHS), and he considered that different concerns might apply in relation to other parts of the public sector and the private sector (see further Chapter 12).

1.36 He noted that the legislation provides a remedy against past detriment rather than protection against future detriment and regretted that it would, in his view, be extremely difficult to obtain an injunction to prevent detriment occurring. He said there is no evidence that the prospect of an employment tribunal case deters victimization by employers and added that employment tribunals are not the place for patient safety concerns to be heard.

1.37 The Report also pointed out that orders for reinstatement and re-engagement are not available to workers who are not employees and even in the case of employees, an employer cannot be forced to comply with an order to reinstate or re-engage a dismissed employee, in particular if they believe it is not practical to do so.

1.38 The Report rejected suggestions that employers should be forced to reinstate successful claimants because of the need to preserve trust and confidence between the parties. But Sir Robert considered that the provision in relation to blacklisting of trade union activists (Employment Relations Act 1999 (Blacklists) Regulations 2010 and section 104F of the Employment Rights Act 1996) provide a model for the extension of much-needed protection to job applicants who have made protected disclosures in previous employments. His Action point 20.1 was that the Government should review the inclusion of discrimination in recruitment by employers (other than those to whom the disclosure relates) on grounds of having made that disclosure as a breach of either the Employment Rights Act 1996 (ERA) or the Equality Act 2010. As a result of this report the Secretary of State was given power to extend protection to job applicants, but only in the NHS (section 49B ERA). At the time of writing, no regulations have yet been introduced to implement this.

1.39 In an area like whistleblowing it may always be said that protection is weak. A legislative answer will always have limited effect because of, for example, the evidential difficulties in proving the reason that action was taken. So much depends on the culture of the relevant organization and the attitudes of those in management. There is, however, something to be said for the point that the scope for interim relief in the tribunal is too limited, and a related issue as to the scope for injunctive relief in the ordinary courts to plug the gap. The obvious case is where a doctor is suspended and seeks to challenge this as being an irrational exercise of discretion because, it is said, whistleblowing was held against the doctor. It may be little comfort that he or she eventually wins compensation many years after the event, especially if the whistleblower is then blacklisted within their particular area of specialty. We address in Chapter 12 (paragraphs 12.59 to 12.86) whether the protection provided by the PIDA regime in the employment tribunals may be supplemented by injunctive relief for breach of contract (or by way of judicial review) by an action in the ordinary courts. We also address in Chapter 12 the reforms proposed and being implemented in the financial services sector, where the need to foster a more welcoming environment for the raising of public interest concerns has also come under scrutiny.

H. Beyond PIDA

In addition to the central theme of our analysis of PIDA and how it has been interpreted by **1.40** tribunals and appellate bodies, this book also considers the common law, which is relevant to the protection for whistleblowers viewed in the round. In many respects the statute builds on experience gained in common law cases, especially on confidentiality, and adopts some concepts derived from the common law. The question of a public interest defence affects actions for breach of confidence, defamation, and breach of copyright[25]. Indeed, the Act marches along in step with other developments in the common law, such as the development of the public interest defence to claims of breach of confidence, which have facilitated a more sympathetic approach to those acting in the public interest. It is also necessary to take into account the provisions of the European Convention on Human Rights (see Chapter 18).

I. Problems and Dilemmas

(1) A duty to blow the whistle

One general theme running throughout PIDA, and the thinking of those who have pro- **1.41** moted it, is the need to provide support and protection for whistleblowers in order to encourage them to come forward. However, since disclosure by a whistleblower might prevent a disaster or perpetuation of fraud, the question arises as to whether the law should go further and impose a *duty* to blow the whistle, and a correlative responsibility on regulators to investigate the concerns once they have been raised. This has been reflected over the last decade in a number of statutory provisions imposing specific duties of disclosure, such as duties now required of an auditor and duties now imposed for some professional bodies. We consider in Chapter 13 the development of the common law and statutory duties of disclosure, the interrelation of these obligations with the new provisions of the Act, and the competing policy arguments in relation to imposing duties of disclosure. This is, however, a controversial area, as reflected in the differing approaches taken to this in the health sector compared to the financial services sector (see Chapter 12). Requiring a worker to blow the whistle was not recommended by the Hooper Commission set up by PCaW, on the basis that it 'might encourage over reporting, allow scapegoating and lead to organizations focusing on who did not speak up rather than the concern itself or the effectiveness of the whistleblowing arrangements' (para 54). We echo this concern, whilst recognizing that a carefully identified duty of disclosure has a role to play, such as where there is a serious risk to health or safety.

---

[25] For a detailed exposition of the various guises in which a public interest may arise, see Cripps, *The Legal Implications of Disclosure in the Public Interest*, 2nd edn. London: Sweet & Maxwell, 1994.

(2) Interim measures

1.42 Often the procedures for investigation of the subject about which the whistle is blown are long and drawn out. This complaint has focused attention on the need for speedier remedies, especially in the most serious cases. The need for interim measures is referred to in the Council for Europe Memorandum on Protection for Whistleblowers.[26] It stresses that this may cover a range of measures such as 'a provisional measure ordered by the court to stop threats or continuing acts of retaliation, such as workplace bullying or physical intimidation or prevent forms of retaliation that might be difficult to reverse after the lapse of lengthy periods, such as dismissal' (Principle 26, at para 89). The UK Act might be said to be deficient in this respect. The only interim measure provided for at present is interim relief to continue the contract, and this only applies in dismissal cases. Further, the claimant must pass a high threshold in order to succeed at the final hearing by showing a pretty good chance of success, with the effect that the relief is only likely to be available in a narrow set out cases (see Chapter 10, paragraphs 10.46–10.55). There is no interim relief available in cases of detriment other than dismissal. As noted above (paragraph 1.39, and discussed in Chapter 12), the focus is then placed on whether contractual remedies in the ordinary courts can to some extent fill this gap.

(3) The right of the whistleblower to be told the result

1.43 Another area the legislation itself presently does not reach is in communicating the result of any investigation to the whistleblower who prompted it. The PCaW Whistleblowing Code of Practice at para 5e states that the employer's procedure:

> should require that a worker raising a concern
> i.   be told how and by whom the concern will be handled;
> ii. be given an estimate of how long the investigation will take;
> iii. be told where appropriate the outcome of the investigation;
> iv. be told that if the worker believes that he/she is suffering a detriment for having raised a concern, he/she should report this; and
> v.   be told that he/she is entitled to independent advice.

1.44 Further, the employer should conduct periodic audits of the effectiveness of the whistleblowing arrangements and make provision for the independent oversight and review of the whistleblowing arrangements by the Board, the Audit or Risk committee, or equivalent body (paras 7d and 7e).

1.45 The Council for Europe Memorandum at para 75 indeed refers to the approach of 'comply or explain' or introducing a strict liability offence for failing to prevent harm or damage.

(4) Anonymity for whistleblowing

1.46 Another key dilemma remains as to the extent to which anonymity should be encouraged. This is not a straightforward point and we address it in Chapter 19. This is of course different to the question of the protection of confidentiality, ie that the name of the individual who reported or disclosed information is known by the recipient but will not be disclosed without the individual's consent, unless required by law.

1.47 Often and perhaps inevitably anonymous allegations are given less credence by those investigating and are assumed prima facie to be malicious. They may indeed be difficult to investigate and impossible to remedy. It may, however, be said that blowing the whistle anonymously is better than not blowing it at all. It can be countered that anonymity impedes the pursuit of truth. Probably the most famous anonymous source of all time was so-called Deep Throat,

---

[26] Recommendation CM/Rec(2014)7 and explanatory memorandum (available at https://www.coe.int/t/dghl/standardsetting/cdcj/CDCJ%20Recommendations/CMRec(2014)7E.pdf).

who played the major part in the Watergate scandal involving President Nixon. He unmasked himself just before his death. It is of course more difficult to investigate anonymous charges, because there are liable to be difficulties in testing the information with the informant. That said, anonymity does allow individuals to come forward who might otherwise remain silent for fear of reprisals. The current Government guidance, of March 2015, which takes the view that it is good practice to cater for anonymous whistleblowing, suggests that some of the challenges of obtaining follow-up information could be overcome by using telephone appointments or through an anonymized email address.

J. International Perspective

Notwithstanding the issues identified above where the UK protected disclosure regime may be regarded as providing incomplete protection, the scope of protection in the UK generally compares favourably to that available in other countries. The legislation has attracted praise by PACE, and in large part has been held as a model for other EU countries to follow.[27,28] The number of other countries with dedicated whistleblowing laws has however grown significantly in recent years. **1.48**

More international efforts to support whistleblowers are to be welcomed, but as set out in the Council of Europe report dated 14 September 2009[29] there are 'deeply engrained cultural attitudes which date back to social and political circumstances, such as dictatorship and/or foreign domination, under which distrust towards "informers" of the despised authorities was only normal'. Clear standards are set out in the Council of Europe Recommendation as already mentioned. The public interest may differ between states, and this is recognized in the ECHR jurisprudence; in *Former King of Greece and Others v Greece* no 25701/94, at para 87, the court was 'of the opinion that because of their direct knowledge of their society and its needs, the national authorities are in principle better placed than the international judge to appreciate what is "in the public interest"'. The ECHR jurisprudence is considered in chapter 18. **1.49**

One important overseas development of particular note is the Dodd–Frank Wall Street Reform and Consumer Protection Act 2010, which may have an effect on US-based finance houses trading in the United Kingdom. The Act was passed after various US financial scandals, including the Madoff and Alan Stanford schemes, creates a whistleblower cause of action[30] that allows individuals to bring claims directly in federal courts up to ten years after the alleged retaliatory conduct, including double back pay, and to receive from 10 up to 30 per cent of the sanctions imposed by the Securities and Exchange Commission or the CFTC (the Commodity Futures Trading Commission), by civil penalties, as long as the SEC or CFTC recovers a minimum of $1 million.[31] This affects 'any subsidiary or affiliate whose financial information is included in the consolidated financial statements' of a publicly traded company, and this may be anywhere in the world. It is also worth noting that the US Whistleblower Protection Act includes an office of Special Counsel which **1.50**

---

[27] See Council of Europe Resolution 1729 (2010), referring to PIDA as 'forward-looking'.

[28] See Tom Devine, in 'Developments in whistleblowing research 2015', David Lewis and Wim Vandekerckhove (eds), International Whistleblowing Research Network, listing 29 countries with dedicated whistleblowing laws.

[29] Report of the Committee on Legal Affairs and Human Rights.

[30] This followed The False Claims Act 1986 which created liability for fraud against the US Government and included robust whistleblower (qui tam) provisions and allows for non-discretionary awards to qualified whistleblowers.

[31] One award has been for $30 million.

investigates retaliation complaints and may seek relief on their behalf. As we discuss further in Chapter 12 (paragraphs 12.113 and 12.114), the approach is in stark contrast to that under the UK legislation which does not offer rewards for making protected disclosures and instead focuses on encouraging disclosure in the public interest.

1.51 This book inevitably concentrates on the protection of the worker and the concomitant restriction on employers. There are, however, other perspectives in the area which make striking the balance in the legislation more difficult and add to the complexity. These relate, for example, to the position of the co-worker who may be the subject of allegations (perhaps incorrectly but based on a reasonable belief) which may reasonably appear to the worker to be defamatory and, as is particularly liable to arise in such a case, the position of the employer dealing with allegation and counter-allegation within the workforce. Further, there is the public interest in ensuring that wrongdoing is brought to light and can be dealt with by the regulators. Indeed, one of the fascinating aspects of whistleblowing is to identify the interplay between the public and private interests which arise and between legislation and organizational culture.

Part I

PROTECTING WHISTLEBLOWERS—THE PUBLIC INTEREST DISCLOSURE ACT 1998

2

STRUCTURE OF THE PUBLIC INTEREST DISCLOSURE ACT 1998

A. Introduction

During the passage of the Public Interest Disclosure Bill in the House of Lords,[1] Lord **2.01**
Nolan stated that his Committee on Standards in Public Life had been persuaded of the
urgent need for protection for public interest whistleblowers. He commended those behind
the Bill:

> for so skillfully achieving the essential but delicate balance in this measure between the pub-
> lic interest and the interests of employers.[2]

At the heart of the Act, therefore, was the aim of identifying which sorts of disclosure required **2.02**
protection, and in which circumstances it would be in the public interest that those making such disclosures be given protection. Those promoting the Bill emphasized that it was
not merely an employee rights bill, but a public interest measure. As Lord Borrie explained
(introducing the Bill in the Lords for its second reading on 11 May 1998):

> … this measure will encourage people to recognise and identify with the wider public inter-
> est and not just their own private position. It will reassure them that if they act reasonably
> to protect the legitimate interests of others who are being threatened or abused, the law will
> not stand idly by should they be vilified or victimised.

Since then there have been major reforms introduced by the Enterprise and Regulatory **2.03**
Reform Act 2013 (ERRA), notably in relation to introducing a new test that there must
be a reasonable belief that the disclosure is made in the public interest, relegating the good
faith condition to a remedy issue and introducing vicarious liability and personal liability for
workers and agents in relation to detriment claims. The stated purpose of those amendments
was, however, to reinforce the original purpose as set out by Lord Borrie.

In this chapter we outline the scheme adopted to achieve this ambitious aim. The measures **2.04**
are then analysed in more detail in the following chapters of this book.

---

[1] The substantive provisions of PIDA came into force on 2 July 1999, a year after it received Royal Assent.
The Act applies only to England, Scotland, and Wales.

[2] *Hansard* HL, 5 June 1998, col 614.

B. The Scheme of the Legislation

2.05   At the heart of the legislation were the new concepts of 'qualifying disclosure' and 'protected disclosure'. These brought together a number of different criteria by which to identify whether protection was merited. Only a 'qualifying disclosure' is a candidate to be a 'protected disclosure', and only a 'protected disclosure' attracts the special protection of the measures introduced by PIDA, principally through amendment to the Employment Rights Act 1996 (ERA).

2.06   There is a 'protected disclosure' if:

(1)   the disclosure is a 'qualifying disclosure' as defined in ERA, section 43B; and
(2)   there is compliance with one of ERA, sections 43C–43H, which set out different requirements depending on to whom the disclosure is made, becoming more demanding as the recipient of the disclosure becomes more remote from the employer or with a less obvious legitimate interest in receiving the information.

The flow chart at the end of this chapter outlines this process.

2.07   The test for a 'qualifying disclosure' is set out in section 43B ERA, as supplemented by section 43L ERA. It consists of the following essential elements:

(1)   A disclosure of 'information' (which means conveying facts). Where the person receiving the information is already aware of it, a 'disclosure' encompasses bringing the information to that person's attention (section 43L ERA).
(2)   In relation only to disclosures made on or after 25 June 2013 (by virtue of amendments introduced by ERRA), a reasonable belief on the part of the worker making the disclosure that it is made in the public interest.
(3)   A reasonable belief on the part of the worker making the disclosure that the information disclosed tends to show one or more of six categories of 'relevant failures'.
(4)   The making of the disclosure must not of itself be a criminal offence (for example due to breach of official secrecy legislation).

2.08   The first five categories of failure concern a past, ongoing, or likely future (a) criminal offence, (b) breach of a legal obligation, (c) miscarriage of justice, (d) danger to health or safety, or (e) damage to the environment. The last category relates to cover-ups—that information tending to show that matters falling in one of the previous categories has been or is likely to be deliberately concealed.

2.09   This initial hurdle of establishing a 'qualifying disclosure' therefore focuses on two elements: the nature of the information being disclosed and the threshold requirements as to the 'reasonable belief' of the worker making the disclosure, and, in relation to disclosures since 25 June 2013, a further element of reasonable belief that the disclosure is made in the public interest. These threshold requirements are a key regulator of the level of protection offered by the legislation. We consider this in more detail in Chapters 3 and 4.

2.10   The legislation then provides various levels of protection for which different hurdles must be cleared. In outline, these relate to disclosure:

(1)   to the employer (ERA, section 43C(1)(a), (2));
(2)   to anyone other than the employer legally responsible for the situation in respect of which the disclosure is made or to whose conduct the disclosure relates (ERA, section 43C(1)(b));
(3)   in the course of obtaining legal advice (ERA, section 43D);
(4)   to a Minister if the individual is appointed under any enactment by the Minister (ERA, section 43E);

(5) to a regulator as prescribed in Regulations (ERA, section 43F);

(6) to any other person when it is reasonable to do so according to set criteria (ERA, section 43G); and

(7) where the disclosure is of exceptionally serious matters (ERA, section 43H).

Broadly, these levels of protection can be separated into what was referred to by Auld LJ in **2.11** *Street v Derbyshire Unemployed Workers' Centre* [2005] ICR 97 at para 5 as a 'three tiered disclosure regime':

(1) The first tier consists of sections 43C–43E. As originally enacted, a distinction was drawn between section 43D where a qualifying disclosure was to be treated as a protected disclosure without any further hurdles, and sections 43C and 43E where there was a further requirement that the disclosure must be made in good faith. That remains applicable to qualifying disclosures made prior to 25 June 2013. For disclosures since that date, the distinction is removed, so that, provided the recipient of that disclosure is someone falling within section 43C or 43E, or the disclosure is made in the course of obtaining legal advice within the meaning of section 43D, a qualifying disclosure is also a protected disclosure without need to meet any further conditions. The low first tier threshold is at the heart of the legislation in encouraging disclosures to the employer, or otherwise to someone accountable for the relevant failure.

(2) The second tier consists of regulatory disclosures under section 43F. Here the threshold is set a little higher than first tier disclosures. As with first tier disclosures, in relation only to disclosures made prior to 25 June 2013 there is a requirement that the disclosure be made in good faith. But in addition there was and remains a further requirement that the worker must reasonably believe that the information which was disclosed, and any allegation contained in it, are substantially true. The threshold is, however, still deliberately lower than for wider disclosures, in recognition that a disclosure to a prescribed regulator is more likely to be in the public interest.

(3) The third tier comprises wider disclosures under section 43G or 43H. Here the threshold for protection is at its highest, although the threshold is lower for section 43H (exceptionally serious failures) than for section 43G (other wider disclosures). As with section 43F, for both sections there is a requirement that the worker held a reasonable belief that the information disclosed (and any allegation contained in it) was substantially true and, in relation only to disclosures made prior to 25 June 2013, that the disclosure was made in good faith. For both sections 43G and 43H there is also a requirement to satisfy a general test of whether, in all the circumstances, it was reasonable to make the disclosure. The worker opting to make a third tier disclosure therefore has a significantly greater degree of uncertainty as to whether the disclosure will be protected, and is encouraged first to make a first or second tier disclosure. In addition, under section 43G, the worker must comply with one of subparagraphs (2)(a), (b), or (c). Essentially these deal with whether it is reasonable for the worker to believe that s/he will be victimized if the disclosure is made to the employer or that evidence will be concealed (where there is no prescribed person under section 43F) or where the disclosure has previously been made to the employer or under section 43F to a prescribed regulator (section 43G(1)(d), (2)).

Whilst the concept of a protected disclosure was a new one which was introduced by PIDA, **2.12** the mechanisms for protection are based principally upon structures that were already in place, although there has been a significant departure with the introduction of the vicarious/personal liability provisions. Essentially there are now three types of protection which are provided:

(1) Protection from being subjected to a detriment on the ground of having made a protected disclosure (section 47B ERA). This may include a detriment which was sustained during or after employment, but in the case of employees does not include dismissal

(where the remedy is unfair dismissal). This is one of a number of rights not to suffer detriment contained in Part V ERA, with common enforcement mechanisms and provisions for remedy in sections 48 and 49. However, in significant respects the protection goes beyond most other rights in this Part of the Act. Protection is available to an extended category of 'workers' (sections 43K, 43KA ERA). In addition, in relation only to protected disclosures made on or after 25 June 2013, employers are made vicariously liable for detriments on the grounds of making a protected disclosure inflicted by another worker in the course of their employment or by an agent with the employer's authority, subject, in relation to workers, to a defence if the employer shows that it took all reasonable steps to prevent the worker form doing the thing in question or anything of that description: section 47B(1), (1D) ERA. There is also provision for such a worker or agent to be personally liable, subject to a defence if acting in reliance on a statement by the employer that doing the act or failure to act in question does not contravene the ERA provided it is reasonable to rely on that statement (section 47B(1A), (1E) ERA). In the EAT it has been held that there is only provision for compensation to be awarded against the employer (section 49(1) ERA); *Royal Mail Group Ltd v Jhuti* [2016] IRLR 854 (EAT). The provisions for vicarious and individual liability mark the legislation apart from the other detriment provisions in Part V ERA.

(2) In the case of employees, protection by virtue of dismissal being automatically unfair where the reason or principal reason for dismissal was a protected disclosure (section 103A ERA). This includes where the reason or principal reason for selection for dismissal on grounds of redundancy was the making of a protected disclosure (section 105 ERA). The minimum qualifying employment (section 108(3)(ff) ERA) and the exclusion for taking part in industrial action (sections 237(1A) and 238(2A) of the Trade Union and Labour Relations (Consolidation) Act 1992 (TULRCA)) are disapplied. There are also differences in the remedies available; the limit on the compensatory award is disapplied (ERA, section 124(1A)) and the provisions for claiming interim relief in the ERA, sections 128–132 extend to protected disclosure dismissal cases.

(3) Agreements not to make protected disclosures are rendered void (section 43J). Workers therefore have protection against allegations of having acted in breach of contract by having made protected disclosures.

C. Some Initial Observations

2.13 The following features of the legislation are noteworthy at the outset:

(1) The legislation does not amend the common law, save to the extent that ERA, section 43J renders void a provision in an agreement prohibiting a worker from making a protected disclosure. Instead, as noted above, the legislation draws upon the existing statutory framework for unfair dismissal and protection against detriment.

(2) The legislation specifically refers to confidentiality only in relation to determining whether a third tier disclosure under section 43G is protected. In determining whether it is reasonable for the worker to make such a disclosure, one of the relevant criteria is 'whether the disclosure is made in breach of a duty of confidentiality owed by the *employer* to any other person' (section 43G(3)(d) ERA, emphasis added). The issue of duty of confidentiality owed *to the employer*, which is the subject matter of most common law claims (and is covered in Chapter 14 of this book), is not specifically referred to as something that must be taken into account.

(3) There is no residual class of protection in addition to the six specific defined categories of 'relevant failure'. It is therefore not open to the courts to determine on a case-by-case basis

that there are other disclosures which should be protected under the legislation in the public interest. In this respect the legislation differs from some other jurisdictions which have legislated to protect whistleblowers.

(4) It does not follow that a whistleblower who falls outside the ambit of the Act will have no protection at all. The worker might still be able to rely upon the general unfair dismissal protection under section 98 ERA and may have a contractual claim for wrongful dismissal. Clearly though, the extent of the remedy which is available is liable to be significantly more restricted.

(5) PIDA generally operates by amendment of other legislation, primarily the ERA. Its provisions are more easily followed by a review of the legislation which has been amended, rather than PIDA itself.

(6) Some of the provisions of PIDA as originally enacted have been repealed or amended. Section 8 PIDA set out provisions for compensation for unfair dismissal, but was repealed without ever coming into force and instead it was provided that there is no limit on the compensatory award. Section 12, which related to work outside the United Kingdom, has been repealed. Section 13, which excluded police officers, has been repealed and replaced with a new section 43KA introduced into the ERA, which extends the application of the protected disclosure provisions to police officers. As noted above, the original requirement that the disclosure be made in good faith, which applied to all disclosures other than to those made in the course of obtaining legal advice, has been relegated to being a factor relevant to the remedy stage—where it can lead to a reduction of up to 25 per cent of the award or of compensation for detriment.

(7) The extent of the protection made available to workers is exceptional compared to most individual employment rights, which reflects the public policy underlying the legislation. That is reflected in the provisions for uncapped compensation, protection from the start of employment, the availability of interim relief, the extended category of workers protected, and the provisions for vicarious and personal liability.

D. Policy Considerations and 'Responsible Whistleblowing'

2.14 In a number of cases it has been emphasized that the legislation should be construed purposively having regard to its underlying objectives. To that end in *BP plc v Elstone and Petrotechnics Ltd* [2010] IRLR 558 the EAT commented that:

> the legislation should if possible be construed so as to advance the purpose of the legislation, which is seen as to provide protection for those who 'blow the whistle' in the public interest.

2.15 Similarly, in *Babula v Waltham Forest College* [2007] ICR 1026 at para 81, Wall LJ summarized the aims of the legislation as being 'to encourage responsible whistleblowing'. This supported the construction that a worker could reasonably believe that information tended to show a past, present, or likely future breach of a legal obligation if the obligation did not in fact exist but was reasonably believed to exist.

2.16 Again, in *Croke v Hydro Aluminum Worcester Ltd* [2007] ICR 1303 (EAT) a purposive approach was taken in determining the scope of workers covered by the legislation (see Chapter 6). In *Boulding v Land Securities* (EAT/0023, 3 May 2006)[3] the EAT went a step further, in the context of a submission by the employer of no case to answer, where it was said (at para 24) that in protected disclosure claims, 'there is a certain generosity in the construction of the statute

---

[3] Considered further in Chapter 3, paras 3.101, 3.102.

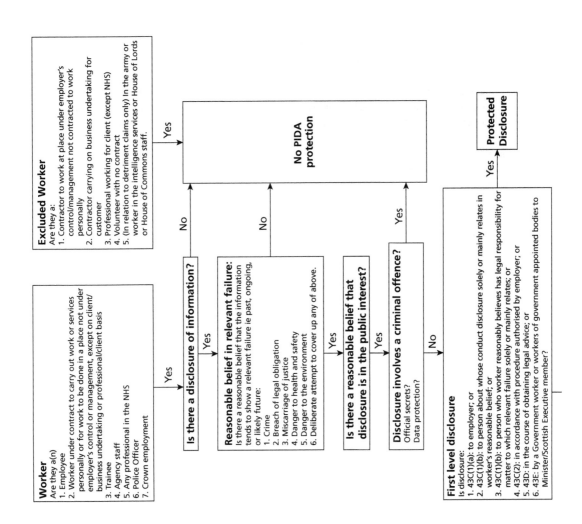

Worker
Are they a(n)
1. Employee
2. Worker under contract to carry out work or services personally or for work to be done in a place not under employer's control or management, except on client/business undertaking or professional/client basis
3. Trainee
4. Agency staff
5. Any professional in the NHS
6. Police Officer
7. Crown employment

Excluded Worker
Are they a:
1. Contractor to work at place under employer's control/management not contracted to work personally
2. Contractor carrying on business undertaking for customer
3. Professional working for client (except NHS)
4. Volunteer with no contract
5. (In relation to detriment claims only) In the army or worker in the intelligence services or House of Lords or House of Commons staff.

Is there a disclosure of information?

Reasonable belief in relevant failure:
Is there a reasonable belief that the information tends to show a relevant failure ie past, ongoing, or likely future:
1. Crime
2. Breach of legal obligation
3. Miscarriage of justice
4. Danger to health and safety
5. Danger to the environment
6. Deliberate attempt to cover up any of above.

Is there a reasonable belief that disclosure is in the public interest?

Disclosure involves a criminal offence?
Official secrets?
Data protection?

First level disclosure
Is disclosure:
1. 43C(1)(a): to employer; or
2. 43C(1)(b): to person about whose conduct disclosure solely or mainly relates in worker's reasonable belief; or
3. 43C(1)(b): to person who worker reasonably believes has legal responsibility for matter to which relevant failure solely or mainly relates; or
4. 43C(2): in accordance with procedure authorised by employer; or
5. 43D: in the course of obtaining legal advice; or
6. 43E: by a Government worker or workers of government appointed bodies to Minister/Scottish Executive member?

No PIDA protection

Protected Disclosure

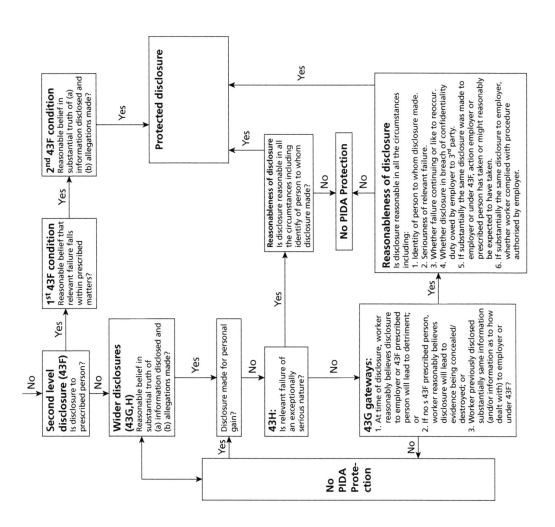

and in the treatment of the facts'. That approach would suggest that, having regard to the underlying policy considerations, the conditions for protection should not be too stringently applied, and that this extends to factual issues, such as the assessment of whether there was a reasonable belief. As against that, the scope of the legislation has been carefully delineated and as such those limits have to be respected (see eg *Day v Lewisham and Greenwich NHS Trust* [2016] IRLR 415 at para 35[4]).

2.17 However, in some situations the concept of 'responsible whistleblowing' gives rise to competing policy considerations. To some extent these were recognized in *ALM Medical Services Ltd v Bladon* [2002] ICR 1444, [2002] IRLR 807 at para 2, where Mummery LJ commented:

> The self-evident aim of the provisions is to protect employees from unfair treatment (i.e. victimisation and dismissal) for reasonably raising in a responsible way genuine concerns about wrongdoing in the workplace. The provisions strike an intricate balance between (a) promoting the public interest in the detection, exposure and elimination of misconduct, malpractice and potential dangers by those likely to have early knowledge of them, and (b) protecting the respective interests of employers and employees. There are obvious tensions, private and public, between the legitimate interest in the confidentiality of the employer's affairs and in the exposure of wrong.[5]

2.18 The concept of 'responsible whistleblowing' may in some cases be in tension with the legislative objective of encouraging those in a position to sound the early alarm to come forward and do so to an appropriate person. It involves confining protection to those with a sufficient basis for believing that information tends to show a past, present, or likely future relevant failure and to those who have a reasonable belief that disclosure is in the public interest. The more stringently those and other requirements are applied, the greater the risk of a chilling effect due to workers fearing that they will not be protected. The conundrum was previously most clearly illustrated by the concept of good faith. Given the emphasis on 'responsible whistleblowing' and the heightened protection which the legislation provides—such as in terms of removing limits on compensation—it is understandable that the legislation was construed such that those who act for an ulterior motive may be denied protection on the basis of not having acted in good faith. Yet the consequence was that any worker in a position to sound an early alarm was at risk of being portrayed as having done so for an ulterior motive. The relegation of the good faith requirement to the remedy stage goes some way to ameliorating that risk. But to some extent similar considerations are likely to apply in determining the approach to the public interest test which was introduced by the ERRA amendments, and in relation to the other elements of the reasonable belief test for a qualifying disclosure. Workers may delay raising the alarm due to concern as to whether the sufficiency of the basis for their belief could be challenged. It is this tension, between confining protection to cases of 'responsible whistleblowing' and the practical impact of the arguments which are therefore left open in order to challenge whether a worker is protected, that underlies many of the controversies in the construction of the legislation.

---

[4] But as to the decision in *Day*, see also *McTigue v University Hospital Bristol NHS Foundation Trust* [2016] ICR 1155 (EAT), where, applying a purposive construction to the legislation, the EAT (at para 27) adopted a more inclusive approach as to the meaning of 'worker'. These decisions are considered in detail in Chapter 6 (at paras 6.20–6.29).

[5] This passage was followed in *Chesterton Global Ltd (t/a Chestertons) v Nurmohamed* [2015] ICR 920 (EAT) at para 16 in considering the public interest test introduced by ERRA.

3

PROTECTABLE INFORMATION

A. Overview of Employment Rights Act 1996, section 43B

The starting point in establishing protection for a disclosure is based on the concept of a **3.01** 'qualifying disclosure'. This focuses on the nature of the information which may attract protection if other conditions set out in the Employment Rights Act (ERA) as modified by PIDA are satisfied in the particular case. But it has also been interpreted as involving threshold requirements in relation to the basis for belief in the information disclosed.

Section 43B(1) ERA provides that: **3.02**

> In this Part a 'qualifying disclosure' means any disclosure of information which, in the reasonable belief of the worker making the disclosure, is made in the public interest and tends to show one or more of the following—
>
> (a) that a criminal offence has been committed, is being committed or is likely to be committed,
>
> (b) that a person has failed, is failing or is likely to fail to comply with any legal obligation to which he is subject,
>
> (c) that a miscarriage of justice has occurred, is occurring or is likely to occur,

(d) that the health or safety of any individual has been, is being or is likely to be endangered,

(e) that the environment has been, is being or is likely to be damaged, or

(f) that information tending to show any matter falling within any one of the preceding paragraphs has been, or is likely to be deliberately concealed.

3.03   Each of the categories of information in subparagraphs (a) to (f) is referred to as a 'relevant failure'.[1] Together, the 'relevant failures' extend to a very wide range of information. Protection is not tied to whether the information is confidential or to whether a common law defence to breach of confidence can be established. Indeed, only in very exceptional circumstances would a disclosure within the employing organization constitute a breach of the duty of confidentiality at all, whether express or implied in the contract of employment. Equally, there is no requirement that the person to whom the disclosure is made is not already aware of the information from other sources: section 43L(3). The whistleblower need not be telling him/her something which she did not already know.[2] There must, however, be some 'information' which is drawn to the attention of the person to whom disclosure is made.

3.04   In approaching the question of whether there is a qualifying disclosure, a sequenced approach is appropriate. This was emphasized by the EAT in *Easwaran v St George's University of London* (UKEAT/0167/10, 24 June 2010). The EAT (at paras 18 and 19) suggested breaking down the test into three key elements:

(1)   Did the worker disclose any information?

(2)   If so, did the worker believe that the information tended to show at least one of the relevant failures (and, we would add, if so, which relevant failures)?

(3)   If so, was this belief reasonable?

In effect the third step (reasonable belief) involves a consideration of the sufficiency of the connection between (a) the information disclosed and (b) the relevant failure which the worker believed that the information disclosed tended to show. In addition, for disclosures made on or after 25 June 2013, there is a further element: whether there was a reasonable belief that the disclosure is made in the public interest (see Chapter 4).

B. Disclosure of Information

(1) The disclosure must contain 'information'

(a) The Geduld guidance

3.05   In order for there to be a qualifying disclosure, there must be a 'disclosure of information'. In some cases this has led to issues as to whether a bare allegation or expression of concern as to a relevant failure involves any disclosure of information. The requirement is controversial, because it may operate to place barriers in the way of workers promptly raising concerns. To that end, the Whistleblowing Commission, established by Public Concern at Work and chaired by Sir Anthony Hooper, criticized it as being artificial and liable to undermine the purpose of the law, and recommended its removal.[3]

3.06   Whilst the requirement has become associated with the decision of the EAT in *Cavendish Munro Professional Risk Management Ltd v Geduld* [2010] ICR 325 ('*Geduld*'), it was foreshadowed by the EAT's decision in *Everett Financial Management Ltd v Murrell* (UKEAT/

---

[1] ERA, s 43B(5).

[2] But see the discussion of *Cavendish Munro Professional Risk Management Ltd v Geduld* [2010] ICR 325 at para 3.29 below.

[3] Whistleblowing Commission Report (November 2013), para 112 and recommendation 19.

552, 553/02 and EAT/952/02, 24 February 2003). The claimant was one of nineteen dealers who signed a petition seeking a written assurance from the directors that they were not engaged in any unlawful activity. The employment tribunal concluded by a majority that this constituted a protected disclosure, but the EAT disagreed. It concluded that merely expressing a concern and seeking reassurance that there was no breach of a legal obligation did not involve any disclosure of information within section 43B.

3.07 This approach was given greater prominence by the decision of the EAT (Slade J) in *Geduld*, which has become the leading guidance on this issue. The claimant was removed as a director of his employer, CPMR, following the breakdown of his relationship with the other two directors. His solicitors wrote a letter stating that they had 'given full advice' to the employee regarding his rights as a shareholder, director, and employee, including in relation to a 'purported agreement between the parties signed immediately before the Christmas break but 'back dated'. They said that there were issues as to the validity of a shareholders' agreement and as to unfair prejudice of the claimant, reserving his rights and putting forward settlement proposals. They added that they had advised him that such arguments were significant and very likely to be successful in court. In response, he was dismissed. The employment tribunal upheld his claim under section 103A but the EAT allowed the appeal.

3.08 The EAT emphasized that 'information' involves 'conveying facts' and is different from making an allegation or stating a position. It noted that the distinction between 'information' and 'an allegation' is apparent from the reference to both of these terms in ERA, section 43F. That 'information' was different from 'an allegation' was said also to be clear from the victimization provisions in the Sex Discrimination Act 1975 and in the Race Relations Act 1976 (now consolidated in the Equality Act 2010), which set out different ways in which an individual could assert victimization, by giving 'information' and making 'an allegation'. The EAT explained that a complaint or allegation might not necessarily convey facts and as such may not involve a disclosure of 'information'. By way of illustration of the point, the EAT offered the following example (at para 24), which has been cited in several subsequent decisions:

> Communicating 'information' would be: 'The wards have not been cleaned for the past two weeks. Yesterday, sharps were left lying around.' Contrasted with that would be a statement that: 'You are not complying with health and safety requirements.' In our view this would be an allegation not information.

3.09 The EAT proceeded (at para 25) to further illustrate the distinction between a disclosure of information and a statement of position, saying this:

> In the employment context, an employee may be dissatisfied, as here, with the way he is being treated. He or his solicitor may complain to the employer that if they are not going to be treated better, they will resign and claim constructive dismissal. Assume that the employer, having received that outline of the employee's position from him or from his solicitor, then dismisses the employee. In our judgment, that dismissal does not follow from any disclosure of information. It follows a statement of the employee's position. In our judgment, that situation would not fall within the scope of the Employment Rights Act section 43.

3.10 Therefore, merely to complain of constructive dismissal only involves asserting an allegation. If a solicitor complains to the employer that, if an employee is not treated in a better manner, the employee will resign and claim constructive dismissal, that is only the stating of a position, which is all the solicitor's letter had done in this case. Applying this analysis, the EAT therefore held that the employment tribunal was wrong. Mr Geduld's solicitor's letter set out a *statement of his position*, and did not *convey information* as contemplated by the legislation, let alone *disclose* information (see paragraphs 3.27–3.32 below). It was a statement of position which was quite naturally and properly communicated in the course of negotiations between the parties.

(b) Information as to omissions

3.11 As noted by the EAT in *Millbank Financial Services Ltd v Crawford* [2014] IRLR 18, the disclosure of information may relate to an omission. In that case Ms Crawford, a chartered accountant, was employed by MFS as financial director designate, subject to a six-month probationary period. Shortly before the expiry of the probationary period, she was told that it was being extended and that MFS had some concerns about her performance, but there was no suggestion that she was going to be dismissed. She sent a letter to senior management stating that she had received no feedback during her probationary period, that she had not had a consultation with HR or a director, and that she had not been told how long her probationary period was to last. After receipt of the letter, MFS cancelled a meeting that was to have been held on the following day, and a week later she was dismissed. MFS applied to strike out the claim on the basis that the letter contained no information in the *Geduld* sense. Ms Crawford's case was that the letter contained information which, in her reasonable belief, tended to show a failure by MFS to comply with legal obligations, in the form of the implied term of trust and confidence, director's statutory duties, and director's duties under the FCA (Financial Conduct Authority) Code.

3.12 The ET refused to strike out the claim and the EAT upheld that decision. It noted that one of the examples given in *Geduld*, of the wards not having been cleaned, was an instance of a disclosure as to an omission. Here the letter went far beyond simply making an allegation or stating a position. It set out the factual basis of the complaint in considerable detail. This included asserting omissions (such as the failure to provide feedback), which took for granted the known fact that MFS had extended her probationary period when it had no contractual right to do so. Once it was established that the letter conveyed facts, it was a matter for the ET hearing the case whether there was the requisite reasonable belief.

(c) Information distinguished from seeking advice or information

3.13 A further distinction drawn in some cases has been between conveying information and seeking advice or information. But it is important not to place form over substance. An employee concerned to soften the message may well put forward the information in tentative terms, or in the form of a question, whilst still conveying information. The issue is illustrated by the decision in *Blitz v Vectone Group Holdings Ltd* (UKEAT/0253/10/DM, 29 November 2011). The claimant, an accountant, was employed as European Financial Controller for the respondent (the holding company of a group providing mobile phone services throughout Europe). He was only employed for four weeks and the EAT commented that he behaved in an 'extraordinary way' during that time. In early September 2008, he travelled to Italy in connection with the respondent's Italian operations. He claimed that whilst there he was told by an employee of the Italian subsidiary that he had to collect cash and travel great distances all over Italy and that he sometimes slept by the roadside and operated on little sleep. On 5 September 2008 he sent an email about this to the Head of HR and to the Head of the Legal Department, saying that he had a question about the duty of care for IT employees, especially since they needed to arrange insurance. The email went on to say that an employee in the Italian office had mentioned that he often had to sleep on the road or only for a few hours as he covered a large territory, and that there was an added concern that cash was in transit. In relation to this aspect of the case, the ET held that the email of 5 September 2008 was not a qualifying disclosure, on the basis that it was seeking advice rather than making a statement of fact. That conclusion was upheld by the EAT which commented that it could not fault the ET's decision that the claimant was seeking rather than supplying information. It added (at para 140) that the claimant did not assert that there was serious malpractice because he did not know what the facts were, and noted that the claimant had accepted this in cross-examination and that he did not know how long the employee had driven for or what distances. But this appears an unduly restrictive approach. On any view the claimant had disclosed information that he had been informed by the employee in the Italian office that he often had to sleep on the road or only for a few hours, that he covered a large territory, and that there was a concern that cash was in transit. This did not cease to be information conveyed because there was also a question about the duty of care. That the claimant had not found out details of how long the employee had driven or what distances was a factor that could go to the issue of reasonable belief, but again did not negate the conveying of information.

(d) *The importance of the context*

Subsequent decisions have emphasized the importance of context, which may make it inappropriate to determine whether there was a bare allegation before hearing evidence. That was the conclusion of the EAT in *Greenly v Future Network Solutions Ltd* (UKEAT/0359/13/JOJ, 19 December 2013). Greenly claimed that he made protected disclosures to his employer in relation to failure to pay sums due under his contract and under the National Minimum Wage (NMW) Regulations, and later complained to HMRC of a breach of NMW Regulations. The ET struck out the claims except that which was based on the disclosure to HMRC on the basis that there was no disclosure of information. The EAT held that the ET had erred in doing so prior to hearing evidence of the context at a full hearing. HHJ Eady QC commented (at para 40) that: **3.14**

> While the distinction between the 'disclosure of information' and the making of 'an allegation' is a valid one, it can require the drawing of quite fine distinctions as between different statements, in circumstances where the broader context may be all important. A disclosure of information may well contain an allegation (as, arguably, does the statement 'the wards have not been cleaned for the past two weeks') and vice versa. The raising of a grievance might, thus, amount simply to the making of a complaint or allegation but it might also—depending on the circumstances—be disclosing information.

To similar effect, in *Kilraine v Wandsworth LBC* [2016] IRLR 422 (EAT), Langstaff J (at para 30) cautioned as to the need for some care in the application of the principle in *Geduld*. He commented that:

> The dichotomy between 'information' and 'allegation' is not one that is made by the statute itself. It would be a pity if tribunals were too easily seduced into asking whether it was one or the other when reality and experience suggest that very often information and allegation are intertwined…. The question is simply whether it is a disclosure of information. If it is also an allegation, that is nothing to the point.

On the facts, though, the EAT upheld the employment tribunal's finding that where the claimant had complained that there had been 'numerous incidents of inappropriate behaviour towards me, including repeated sidelining', this did not convey any information, given that it did not disclose anything at all specific. The EAT added that even if it did convey information, it did not tend to show a relevant failure, since 'inappropriate' might 'cover a multitude of sins' and was 'simply far too vague'. Conversely, applying the above dicta in *Kilraine*, the EAT in *Eiger Securities LLP v Korshunova* [2017] IRLR 115 accepted that there had been a disclosure of information where the claimant, who was employed in the respondent broking business, had told the managing director that it was wrong to trade from her personally designated computer without identifying himself and referred to what her clients thought of this behaviour. The EAT accepted that an allegation and information may be intertwined. Whether the words used amounted to a disclosure of information was context-dependent, and essentially a question of fact for the tribunal.

(e) *Statement of opinion may involve disclosure of facts*

HHJ Eady QC again reiterated the importance of context, and the fact-sensitive nature of the assessment of whether there is a disclosure of information rather than a mere allegation **3.15** or statement of position, in *Western Union Payment Services UK Ltd v Anastasiou* (UKEAT/ 0135/13/LA, 21 February 2014). She noted that it was possible to envisage circumstances where the statement of position could involve the disclosure of information and vice versa, and that whether there was a disclosure of information in a particular case will always be fact-sensitive. Mr Anastasiou claimed that he had been subjected to detriments as a result of disclosures alleging that misleading statements had been made during two earnings calls, in February and April 2010. He was employed in a senior sales role in a team formed to develop opportunities from the Payment Services Directive (PSD). The employer, Western Union, had an opportunity to provide terminals with software to facilitate money transfers via retail outlets, and to earn commission from this. In the two telephone earnings calls, statements were made to the effect that Western Union expected to have an additional 10,000 retail agent locations operational by the end of 2010. Further, in the second call it was also stated that they would provide an additional 700 agents locations in relation to the Martin McColl convenience stores. Concerns were raised by Mr Hanna, the leader of Mr Anastasiou's team, about whether the expectation of 10,000 locations being achieved by end 2010 was realistic. Mr Hanna later complained that he was being sidelined for raising this. Mr Anastasiou was interviewed during an investigation into Mr Hanna's complaint. The ET found that he said that it was unlikely (with a 30 per cent likelihood) that the 10,000 location target would be achieved, if there was not a change of approach, and a 70 per cent chance if sales were outsourced, and that the McColl accounts should not be counted towards that target. The ET found that the claimant was subjected to detriments as a result of what he had said in the investigation.

3.16 Mr Anastasiou provided evidence to the investigation as to whether the information given in the conference calls had been correct or whether it had been misleading. Although to some extent Mr Anastasiou had been asked to provide his opinion, this was not just as to whether he considered the statements should have been made, but also as to the actual sales position as he understood it. The ET concluded that he had provided information—derived from his experience and knowledge of what was happening—as to the likelihood of meeting the sales target and as to the appropriateness of including the McColl locations. His evidence was capable of protection as a disclosure of information. These were findings open to the ET, and the EAT agreed that that they involved a disclosure of information.

(f) Disclosures as to state of mind

3.17 Once it is accepted, however, as in *Anastasiou*, that an opinion may itself disclose facts, this may be regarded as undermining the force of the distinction between an allegation and disclosure of information. An allegation, if honestly made, will invariably at least entail a statement of belief, and it may be said that the real issue ought to be whether this belief, together with any other facts disclosed, was reasonably believed to tend to show a relevant failure.

3.18 The distinction is illustrated by two employment tribunal decisions. In *Maini v Department for Work and Pensions* (ET, Case No 2203978/01, 15 October 2002) the claimant was employed by the Department for Work and Pensions (DWP). His role involved visiting those claiming benefits to discuss their individual cases with them. He made allegations of corruption to the Chief Executive Officer of the Benefit Agency and to the National Audit Office. Although he alleged that there was 'a huge amount of corruption', and urged the need to investigate the Benefit Agency in London, he failed to provide any further details. The employment tribunal held that these were not qualifying disclosures as they merely made allegations rather than containing any information tending to show one or more relevant failures.

3.19 However, an alternative analysis is that the bare allegation of corruption in the *Maini* case at least involved the disclosure that the claimant believed that there was indeed corruption. That was the approach taken by the employment tribunal in *McCormack v Learning and Skills*

Council (ET, Case No 3104148/01, 5 December 2002). The tribunal rejected a submission that a bare allegation of 'financial irregularities' would not have disclosed information. The tribunal commented that it could not see how a person could disclose his/her belief without thereby disclosing information.

This issue was addressed by the EAT (Wilkie J) in *Goode v Marks and Spencer plc* (UKEAT/ 0442/09, 15 April 2010). The respondent employer, Marks and Spencer (M&S), had put forward proposals to the staff representative body to reduce the discretionary enhanced redundancy terms. The claimant (G) complained about the proposals to his line manager (R), saying that he thought they were 'disgusting'. He later sent an email to *The Times* newspaper, claiming that M&S proposed drastically to reduce redundancy benefits, that the consultation body would be unable to resist, and that the result would be that staff would be made redundant in a cost-cutting exercise in which their redundancy packages would be reduced. G was summarily dismissed by M&S for sending the email to *The Times*. The employment tribunal found that there was no qualifying disclosure. In upholding that decision the EAT commented that the disclosure to R was at its highest only 'information' in the sense of being a statement of G's state of mind, namely that he was disgusted with the proposals (applying *Geduld*). Even viewing this in the context of the proposals to consult with the representative staff bodies over changes to a discretionary scheme, there was no information which anyone could reasonably believe tended to show a likely failure to comply with a legal obligation. In any event there was no reasonable belief in a likely breach of a legal obligation given that the scheme was discretionary and there was to be consultation as to proposed changes to the scheme, and nothing to indicate that the consultation would be a sham. **3.20**

The EAT's approach, therefore, was to deal with the possibility that disclosure of the worker's state of mind might of itself be a disclosure of information on the basis that little turned on this because it was not information which could sustain a reasonable belief as to a relevant failure. We suggest, however, that this will not always be the case. The enquiry will necessarily be fact specific. Having regard to the purposes of the legislation, there may be circumstances where a bare allegation tends to show a relevant failure. Where a worker initially raises a concern it may be that a bare allegation of the relevant failure is made in the expectation that there will then be an opportunity given to discuss and expand on the concerns with a view to them being investigated by the recipient of the disclosure. A further important consideration may be the identity of the person making the disclosure. To take an extreme example, suppose that, having been responsible for carrying out an audit for a client, an employee reports to her employer that she believes that there is a serious fraud being perpetrated by that client and asks to meet to discuss this further. She expects to be able to develop this and to show supporting evidence at a meeting with the employer but is dismissed before being given the opportunity to do so because the employer is concerned that this will damage relationships with the client. In that scenario, it would be most surprising if the employer could say that there was no qualifying disclosure and therefore no protection on the basis that all that was disclosed was a bare allegation and that there was no disclosure of information. The better analysis would be that there was a disclosure of information as to the employee's state of mind as to the belief in the wrongdoing, and that the employee could reasonably believe that this of itself would tend to show the relevant failure. The reasonable belief would be founded upon (a) the fact that the employer would be expected to know that she was well placed to make the assessment having carried out the audit and (b) the early stage at which the matter was raised before having yet had the opportunity to develop this further at the expected meeting. **3.21**

Although on one view this might be considered an extreme example, the point is one of more general application. The legislation is designed to encourage workers who may potentially be able to act as an early warning of danger or wrongdoing to feel secure in coming forward with their concerns. The worker may well expect to be able to raise those concerns in the first **3.22** instance in fairly general terms in the expectation of being given the opportunity to explain the basis for the concerns more fully. It would sit uneasily with the purposes of the legislation if in those circumstances the employer, rather than investigating the allegation or seeking further details, could subject the worker to a detriment. In that context, and applying the purposive approach[4] that 'there is a certain generosity in the construction of the statute and in the treatment of the facts',[5] the bare allegation or concern as to the relevant failure might be said to be information tending to show a relevant failure. This may, however, be contrasted with the situation where, when details of the basis of the belief are sought, the worker declines or is unable to provide these. It may also be contrasted with a case where, as in *Goode*, there was no reason to believe that the worker was in a special position of knowledge in relation to alleged wrongdoing and so his state of mind could not of itself support the requisite reasonable belief. These factors are, of course, wholly consistent with both the recognition in *Anastasiou* that an opinion may amount to a disclosure of information, and with the requirement for a fact-sensitive approach, taking into account the context, when determining whether there has been a disclosure of information.

(g) Disclosure of information and issue of reasonable belief must be kept distinct

3.23   Further, it is important not to elide the distinct issues of whether there is a disclosure of information, and whether the reasonable belief test is satisfied. The question of whether information has been disclosed merely involves consideration of whether facts have been conveyed, irrespective of whether the alleged facts are true, or the basis for the belief in them (if any) is reasonable. In *Easwaran v St George's University of London* (UKEAT/0167/19, 24 June 2010) the employment tribunal's reasoning was criticized for having run these different elements together. This appeared to have led the tribunal into error in finding that there had been no disclosure of information. The claimant was a medical demonstrator. He worked largely in a dissecting room, which he complained was excessively cold. The windows in the room were kept open to counteract a risk of fumes building up. The claimant had an altercation with the dissecting room technician, Mr Dennis, who refused to close the windows. He then wrote a letter to management in which he complained that the dissecting room was freezing and that this was a breach of basic health and safety requirements and that this could affect his health adversely, in particular due to a risk of pneumonia. Apparently influenced by the conclusion that this was not a reasonable belief, some passages in the employment tribunal's decision suggested a finding that there was no disclosure of information but merely an allegation. That was not correct, in that there had at least been disclosure of the information that the room was very cold and that Mr Dennis was not prepared to close the windows. However, the employment tribunal's decision was upheld on the basis of the finding that the claimant lacked the requisite reasonable belief.

(h) Decisions illustrating the allegation/statement of position/information distinction

3.24   Notwithstanding this guidance, the distinction drawn in *Geduld* between an allegation and a disclosure of information has given rise to some difficulty in application. These problems are illustrated by three further cases in which it has been argued that there was a mere allegation rather than a disclosure of information. The argument failed in *Royal Cornwall Hospital NHS Trust v Watkinson* (UKEAT/0378/10, 17 August 2011). The respondent's chief executive disclosed to the respondent's board that an opinion had been obtained from counsel stating that the respondent Trust and the Primary Care Trust would be acting unlawfully if they did not conduct public consultation before relocating the provision of 'upper GI' services. The

---

[4]   See Chapter 2, paras 2.14–2.18 in relation to the appropriateness of adopting a purposive approach.
[5]   *Boulding v Land Securities Trillium (Media Services) Ltd* (UKEAT/0023/0306, 3 May 2006) discussed at para 3.101 below.

EAT rejected a submission that this was merely an allegation rather than the disclosure of information. It involved conveying information as to what had to be done by the respondent and the Primary Care Trust to comply with their duty.[6]

The argument again failed in *The Learning Trust and others v Marshall* (UKEAT/0107 11/ZT, **3.25** 18 July 2012). Here the claimant, a primary school teacher, had raised a grievance in January 2007, alleging unequal treatment on ground of race. The grievance was dismissed. She also complained in a letter of 6 June 2007 that the head teacher was acting in a discriminatory manner by failing to deal with the issue of her progression to UPS3 on the pay scale. She later raised a complaint to the head teacher (by letter of 10 July 2007) and then a further grievance (by letter of 13 July 2007) in relation to failure to be appointed to a role she had applied for, and complained of aspects of the advertising and selection process and of race discrimination. The head teacher then sent an email to the school's governing body referring to the need to manage her exit on the basis that she had become unmanageable. Ultimately she was dismissed. The ET upheld claims of dismissal and detriment by reason of protected disclosures (in relation to her suspension). The EAT then upheld findings that the letters of 6 June and 10 and 13 July 2007 were protected disclosures rather than merely allegations. The letter of 6 June did allege that the head teacher was acting in a discriminatory manner by failing to deal with the issue of progression to UPS3. But it also said the matter had been going on 'for the longest time', that the issue had been raised in a meeting with him, that he said he was busy, and that when she raised it the next week he said he would see to it but did not act on the concerns. As such it set out facts in relation to the delay in dealing with a pay progression claim. The letter of 10 July 2007 also set out a series of respects in which it was said that the recruitment process for the post was in breach of equal opportunities policies, including failure to advertise internally, failure to provide a job description, failure to provide a person specification for the job, short notice of interview, and lack of clear selection process. It was therefore not a mere allegation. Finally, the letter of 13 July appended the other two letters and expressly alleged discrimination on grounds of sex and race. It therefore repeated the information conveyed in the previous letters. In each case the ET was entitled to find that the facts were linked to and capable of supporting complaints of discrimination. The ET's findings on the issue of dismissal were, however, remitted to the tribunal due to deficiencies in reasoning, in placing reliance on grievances without determining whether they were protected disclosures.

However, the submission that there was only an allegation rather than a disclosure of informa- **3.26** tion succeeded in *Smith v London Metropolitan University* (UKEAT/0364/10, 21 July 2011). Dr Smith was employed by the respondent as a senior lecturer in the theatre studies department. Following a confrontation with colleagues she was moved to the English Literature department. She was concerned that she was then required to take on teaching responsibilities that were beyond her qualifications and which she claimed she was not contracted to teach. She raised a grievance in which she made this complaint. This was dismissed, and appeals were also rejected. She raised a further grievance in which she claimed that she was feeling harassed and stressed by constant criticism, attempts to undermine her professionalism, and the time being taken to deal with each of the problems that were being created. Ultimately, the claimant was dismissed for failing to carry out her duties. The claim of detriment and dismissal by reason of protected disclosures failed on the basis that her misconduct, rather than her grievances, were the reason for her treatment and dismissal. However, the EAT also accepted that

---

[6] See also *Freeman v Ultra Green Group Ltd* (UKEAT/ 0239/ 11, 9 August 2011) (ET erred in finding there was only a mere allegation despite the claimant (a financial planner) disclosing that he had been directed to prepare models on an incorrect basis, he was not willing to do so, and it would mislead investors); *Gebremariam v Ethiopian Airlines Enterprise* [2014] IRLR 354 (EAT), paras 61-64 (ET erred by inadequate reasoning; information was arguably intertwined with allegations).

there was no qualifying disclosure because the grievances amounted to allegations rather than a disclosure of information. Yet the grievances had conveyed information that the claimant lacked qualifications to carry out work that she was being required to do, that her contract did not permit this (or at least the fact that this was her belief), that she was feeling stressed and harassed, and that resolution of problems was taking a long time. As indicated by the reasoning in *Easwaran*, whether or not there was a reasonable belief that those matters were well founded and tended to show a past, present, or likely future breach of a legal obligation (or endangering of health and safety[7]) was a separate question from whether they conveyed information (even if in some cases only information as to how the claimant was feeling).

(2) Information disclosed need not be unknown to the recipient

3.27 The information disclosed need not have been previously unknown to the recipient of the information. Section 43L(3) ERA provides expressly that, in a case where the person receiving the information is already aware of it, the references to disclosure of information must be treated as referring to bringing the information to that person's attention. Without this provision workers could be discouraged from making public interest disclosures because, not knowing what information the employer already had, they could not be confident of being protected.

3.28 In *Everett Financial Management*, the EAT recorded that it was common ground between (leading) counsel in that case that there could be no disclosure of information if the provider of the information was aware that the recipient already knew of the information. A similar view was expressed in *Aspinall v MSI Mech Forge Ltd* (UKEAT/891/01, 25 July 2002). Mr Aspinall arranged for a colleague to make a video of how certain factory equipment worked as evidence in support of the claimant's personal injury claim. Although the video could have been said to convey information tending to show that health and safety was or was likely to be endangered, the EAT said that it was unconvinced that the making of the video by a fellow worker to whom nothing new was disclosed could amount to a protected disclosure.

3.29 However, section 43L(3) does not exclude cases where the worker did not know that the employer was already aware of the information. A more nuanced approach to limiting the meaning of a disclosure was advanced by the EAT (Slade J) in *Cavendish Munro Professional Risk Management Ltd v Geduld* [2010] ICR 325. The EAT noted that the natural meaning of disclosure is to reveal something not already known to the recipient of the information. That meaning is extended by section 43L(3) so as to encompass bringing information to a person's attention even though the person is already aware of it. However, the EAT reasoned that the term 'disclosure' is not synonymous with a communication. The EAT explained (at paras 28 and 29) that:

> 28. On the facts of this case, the solicitor's letter of 4 February 2008 was written as part of an ongoing unresolved dispute between the parties. It in effect was alleging that Mr Geduld was an oppressed minority shareholder and, in summary terms, stated the basis of that position. It did not disclose any facts; it merely summarised the basis of a position adopted by Mr Geduld.

> 29. If an employee is feeling badly treated, the solicitor may write to say that the employer is in breach of contract. There may be allegations over allocation of work or that the employee has been overlooked for a promotion. The solicitor may say, 'If the situation does not improve, we have advised our client that he can resign and claim constructive dismissal'. In those circumstances, in our judgment, no protected disclosure is made in such a letter. Similarly, if the individual met the employer without the intervention of

---

[7] It is not clear, however, whether it was asserted that it was believed that the health and safety of the claimant was being endangered. Contrast *Fincham v HM Prison Service* (UKEAT/0925/01 and EAT/0991/01, 19 December 2002).

the solicitor and made the same points, there would be no protected disclosure by that employee to the employer.

On one reading, this may be viewed as essentially reiterating the requirement to identify **3.30** some 'information' as having been disclosed, rather than only a statement of position or an allegation. To that end, the EAT again emphasized that the letter from the claimant's solicitors had not disclosed any facts, but merely summarized the position he had adopted. However, an alternative reading of the EAT's reasoning was that because the solicitor's letter was summarizing the matters relied upon as part of an ongoing dispute, it could not be said to be drawing those matters to the employer's attention. On this view, the extended defin- ition in section 43L(3) has the effect that a worker who reveals information in circumstances where so far as he is aware the recipient of the information (eg the employer) is not or may not be aware of it does not lose protection merely because the employer is in fact aware of it. But it does not cover the situation where the worker knows full well that the employer is already aware of the facts in question, because in those circumstances it cannot be said that anything is being drawn to the employer's attention.

At first blush, this distinction might be thought to have some force. There will indeed be **3.31** circumstances where it is straining language to say that information which the employer (or other recipient of the information) already knows is being brought to his/her attention. That may be the case for example if the worker repeats back information recently given to him/her in the first place by the employer. Further, it may be said that part of the underlying rationale of the legislation was to encourage workers to provide an early warning of a relevant failure, whereas it cannot be said that this is being done if the worker knows full well that s/he is not revealing anything not already known by the recipient of the communication.

However, this distinction gives rise to some serious difficulties. These may be illustrated by **3.32** the following scenarios:

(1) First, imagine a situation where a worker overhears his line manager discussing that certain machinery is dangerous but proposing not to take any action about it for the time being. The worker then confronts the line manager about this. The information discussed is the dangerous state of the machinery, and the worker reasonably believes that this tends to show that health and safety is being endangered. Since the information has come from the line manager, it cannot be said to be drawing the information to the line manager's attention in any ordinary sense. But it would run contrary to the policy of the legislation if this meant that the worker was not protected. As the Court of Appeal put it in *Babula v Waltham Forest College* [2007] EWCA Civ 174, [2007] ICR 1026 at para 80 (per Wall LJ), the purpose of the statute is 'to encourage responsible whistleblowing'. That policy is promoted by encouraging the worker to raise the disclosure internally with an appropriate person in the first instance.

(2) A second scenario is where the worker, having made a disclosure, repeats the same dis- closure to the same person. For example a worker might disclose the same information to the employer on a second occasion and indeed on subsequent occasions because of a concern that the matter is not being adequately investigated. Because of those con- cerns the second disclosure might be put in more strident language, but it would not be consistent with the aims of the legislation if an employer, who took exception to the second disclosure and subjected the worker to a detriment as a result, could say that the worker was not protected because the same information had previously been disclosed and the worker knew that the employer was well aware of the information. There may be cases where the fact that it is known that the recipient of the information is already aware of the information is material to the assessment of whether there was a reasonable belief that the disclosure was made in the public interest. But we suggest that the terms

of section 43L(3) should not provide a basis for saying there was no disclosure of information at all. An alternative approach to repeated disclosures, with support from *Eiger Securities LLP v Korshunova* [2017] IRLR 115 (EAT), at para 35, is to regard detrimental action which is materially influenced by a repetition of a disclosure as falling within ERA, section 47B(1), even if the repetition is not separately relied upon as protected disclosures. That may though be more difficult to apply to employee dismissals, where a significant influence on the decision is not sufficient. The EAT's decision (see paragraph 3.14 above) also illustrates a difficulty in focusing on whether there is new information. The EAT accepted that there might have been a mere allegation if the claimant had said only that it was wrong for the managing director to trade from her personally designated computer without identifying himself. But this was to be read together with the 'new information' she provided about the client reaction. We suggest that this creates unnecessary uncertainty. Although the managing director was already aware that he was using the claimant's computer, his attention was being to the fact (in the claimant's view) that it was wrong for him to do so. Consistently with section 43L(3), that ought to have been sufficient to constitute a disclosure of information.

(3) Extent to which the disclosure must spell out the relevant failure and why it is shown by the information disclosed

3.33 The legislation does not specify the extent to which the disclosure must spell out that there has been a relevant failure, or which relevant failure the information disclosed tends to show. In our view (a) there is no necessary requirement for a disclosure to contain an allegation as to any relevant failure, and (b) there is no single requirement applicable to all cases as to the extent to which the relevant failure in question must be specifically identified. Instead, the legislative language entails a fact-specific enquiry, having regard to the context. In some cases it will be obvious from what has been said that the information tends to show a relevant failure and, where concerned with breach of a legal obligation, the nature of the legal obligation. Where the position is less obvious, there may need to be some signpost in what has been said to give an indication of the relevant failure in question. The context of a disclosure, which can sometimes be lost before a tribunal, may require careful consideration. Previous correspondence, specific verbal communications, or, if necessary, information pertaining to a specific sector may each be relevant.

3.34 In *Korashi v Abertawe Bro Morgannwg University Local Area Health Board* [2012] IRLR 4 (at paras 65 and 66), the EAT observed that section 43B contains no obligation to make any allegations. Consistently with this, sections 43F, 43G, and 43H, require a reasonable belief that '*any allegations*' contained in the disclosure are substantially true. The reference to 'any allegations' indicates that there is no requirement for allegations to be made. The person making the disclosure may have no positive view as to whether the relevant failure in fact occurred. As the EAT emphasized in *Dr Y-A-Soh v Imperial College of Science, Technology and Medicine* (UKEAT/0350/14/DM, 3 September 2015), at para 47, a worker may pass on to an employer information provided by a third party that the worker is not in a position to assess, yet reasonably believe that the information tends to show a relevant failure. There would then be no allegation made, but the issue remains as to the extent to which the relevant failure in question needs to be spelled out. If a third party is responsible for the information, tribunals will consider whether that source is of sufficient quality to attract the reasonable belief. 'Tittle tattle' overheard at the water cooler will be treated differently to information disclosed by an outgoing member of staff who is responsible for the area that concerns the disclosure. Greater difficulty may arise with an anonymous allegation, where nothing is known of the source.

3.35 Support for this view may be found in a number of decisions which followed the guidance initially given by the EAT in *Fincham v HM Prison Service* (UKEAT/0925/01 and EAT/

0991/01, 19 December 2002). Ms Fincham made various complaints about the conduct of other members of staff (who were not her managers) which she alleged amounted to harassment. She contended that these tended to show a breach of the implied trust and confidence term in their contracts of employment. The tribunal decided that it was not permissible to look at the various disclosures collectively to determine whether, taken together, they tended to show a breach of a legal obligation. As to this aspect of the decision, and conflicting subsequent authority, see further paragraphs 3.45–3.51 below. It further decided that none of the disclosures individually tended to show such a breach, on the basis that an employer cannot be taken to have acted in breach of contract every time when one employee behaves badly to another. The decision and reasoning on this issue was upheld by the EAT. It emphasized (at para 33) that, whilst there could be a series of acts that collectively gave rise to a breach of the trust and confidence term:

> … there must in our view be some disclosure which actually identifies, albeit not in strict legal language, the breach of legal obligation on which the employers are relying.

This might be read as indicating that there has to be a reference to the particular legal **3.36** obligation which the employee has in mind, albeit that precise legal language need not be used. However, it is doubtful whether the EAT intended to set out any such general rule. First, the difficulty in *Fincham* was not a failure to identify the relevant legal obligation, but a failure to set out in one disclosure the facts which collectively might have indicated a breach of that legal obligation. Identifying the legal obligation in the letter, without referring to the earlier series of complaints which the tribunal considered needed to be taken together to show a breach of a legal obligation, would not have been sufficient.[8] Second, the legislation does not provide, as it could easily have done, that the particular relevant failure must be identified. In some cases, identifying the relevant failure may be important in order to explain the significance attached to the other information disclosed so that it does tend to show a relevant failure. In other cases, it will be apparent that the information disclosed tends to show a relevant failure without having to spell this out. Indeed, in *Fincham* the EAT accepted that there was a qualifying disclosure as a result of Ms Fincham having complained that she was under pressure and under stress. Contrary to the decision of the employment tribunal, the EAT considered that this could not be anything other than a statement that her health and safety was being, or at least was likely to be, endangered. The EAT therefore accepted that (subject to the reasonable belief test) it was sufficient that the relevant failure was identifiable from the information disclosed, notwithstanding that the particular failure (in this case health and safety being endangered) was not mentioned expressly.

Subsequently, in *Western Union Payment Services UK Ltd v Anastasiou* (UKEAT/0135/13/LA, **3.37** 21 February 2014), the decision in *Fincham* was explained on the basis that all it required was that the employer (or other recipient of the disclosure) should have some idea of what obligation is in issue. It follows that the extent to which there is any need to spell out the obligation is necessarily dependent on the context. In that case the obligation was said to be apparent to all involved as a matter of common sense. As noted above (paragraph 3.15), the claimant had made his disclosures in the context of an investigation concerning whether misleading statements had been made in an earnings call. It was in that context that he had provided information as to the likelihood of meeting sales targets, and the appropriateness of including certain stores in the sales figures, which tended to show that the information

---

[8] But compare *Flintshire v Sutton* (EAT/1082/02, 1 July 2003), where the EAT held that there was no need to distinguish between four memoranda to members of a council raising concerns, where the memoranda made up a series.

given in the sales call was misleading. As such, when the claimant disclosed information in the investigation which supported the view that what was said in the earnings call should not have been said, the reason why the claimant believed it should not have been said was readily apparent; ie that it had been misleading in that it had given a more favourable picture to potential investors than was truly apparent.

3.38 Other decisions since *Fincham* have similarly taken a more relaxed approach to what is required in order to identify the relevant failure than that case might be thought to have required, and can similarly be explained by the need for a contextual and fact-specific assessment of what the information disclosed tends to show. One instance of this was in *Douglas v Birmingham City Council and others* (UKEAT/0518/02, 17 March 2003). The claimant, Mrs Douglas, was a staff governor of a local education authority school. She initially raised concerns in confidence with a fellow governor (C) about her perception of a lack of equal opportunities at the school. C, however, reported the discussion to the head teacher. Mrs Douglas then wrote to the chair of governors complaining about C and the attitude of the head teacher. She complained that in the head teacher's eyes speaking up about equality was worse than discrimination and that staff were expected to ignore discrimination. The EAT construed the disclosure as a complaint that the head teacher was not carrying out policies relating to equal opportunities and equal rights. Mrs Douglas did not identify a specific policy but the EAT noted that realistically there must have been a policy to implement equal opportunities. The EAT held that an allegation that the head teacher was acting in a manner which was contrary to equal opportunities policies tended to show a breach of contract insofar as the policies were apt for incorporation in contracts of employment, as well as a breach of the anti-discrimination legislation. It was not a bar to this conclusion that Mrs Douglas had not expressly alleged a breach of contract.

3.39 Similarly, in *Odong v Chubb Security Personnel* (UKEAT/0819/02, 13 May 2003) the EAT did not require that a specific legal obligation be identified. Mr Odong was employed as a security officer by Chubb at an American Express site. The tribunal found that he was removed from the site because he failed to obey a reasonable instruction to conduct temperature checks. The tribunal rejected his case that his removal was due to a protected disclosure in relation to health and safety. It decided that his refusal to enter the room to carry out the checks was not due to health and safety concerns, nor was that the reason for removal. Allowing the appeal, the EAT accepted that on the employment tribunal's own findings of fact there could be, in the alternative, a protected disclosure under section 43(1)(b) of failing or being likely to fail to comply with a legal obligation. Mr Odong had stated that he was not prepared to enter the room to carry out the checks because the room was marked 'no entry' and he did not accept that the person instructing him to do so had authority to give that instruction. Mr Odong did not further identify any legal obligation as being in play. However, the EAT accepted that his disclosure raised issues in relation to a breach of his own contract if he entered the room without proper authority or if he was given an unauthorized instruction and a breach of obligations owed to American Express which had designated the room as 'no entry'.

3.40 Again in *Bolton School v Evans* [2006] IRLR 500, the EAT was willing to find that there had been a qualifying disclosure notwithstanding that the disclosure itself did not identify the particular relevant failure. Mr Evans disclosed that he was going to break into the computer system of the school where he was employed in order to demonstrate that the system was insecure and would too readily lead to unauthorized disclosures. He also told the headmaster, after the event, what he had done. The EAT accepted that this amounted to a qualifying disclosure in relation to a breach or likely breach of a legal obligation. It was noted that Mr Evans did not in terms identify any specific legal obligation. However, the EAT considered that this did not matter as, similarly to the situation in *Anastasiou*, it would have been obvious to all that the concern was that private and sensitive information about pupils could get into the wrong hands and it was appreciated that this could give rise to a potential liability. This was sufficiently shown by the information disclosed without the need to specify any particular legal obligation.

A danger in dispensing with the need for the particular relevant failure to be spelt out is that **3.41** an employer may not appreciate that a protected disclosure has been made. Whilst it might appear obvious what particular obligation was in question when a disclosure is in focus in employment tribunal proceedings, the position may be less apparent at the time when the disclosure was made. It may be that the fact of making an allegation, or at least identifying the relevant failure in question, signals to an employer that a protected disclosure is being made. Lack of clarity as to this may be said to be inconsistent with good corporate governance because the employer may not be alerted to the need to treat the disclosure seriously, or to the need to be vigilant to protect against victimization. A failure to specify the relevant failure, at least in general terms, may also create later evidential difficulties for the worker. It may make it more difficult to establish that, at the time of making the disclosure, the worker held a genuine (and reasonable) belief that the information tended to show the relevant failure. An employer may be able to argue that if the worker had held such a belief it would indeed have been spelled out at the time so as to ensure that it was taken seriously. Further, the worker may be exposed to the risk that a tribunal will find that rather than having raised genuine concerns which were believed to show a relevant failure, the employee has been engaged in searching after the event for something on which to found a claim in litigation.

As against that, the approach in *Korashi* and *Anastasiou* accords with the ordinary language **3.42** of the legislation, which does not require the making of an allegation and frames the test as being one of reasonable belief as to what the information tends to show. Further, in some cases, whilst it may be apparent that the information disclosed is likely to breach some legal obligation or amount to a criminal offence, the worker might not have knowledge of the specific obligations. In such circumstances it would be surprising if the employee was unprotected in bringing the information to the employer's attention, or was required to delay in doing so, due to the need first to obtain legal advice as to the specific legal obligation engaged.

Indeed, as the decision in *Odong* illustrates, concerns as to wrongdoing may be raised in a **3.43** range of contexts within the workplace, and it may be unrealistic to expect specific legal obligations to be identified. Where the relevant failure is a breach or likely breach of a legal obligation or commission of a criminal offence, the underlying purposes of the legislation might be undermined by a requirement to specify the particular legal obligation or offence. The need to refer to a specific legal obligation or offence might discourage workers from raising concerns. For example, a worker might identify financial irregularities and recognize them as indicators of fraud, but also be reluctant to allege in terms that the information tended to indicate a fraud. Instead, the worker might prefer simply to draw the information to the employer's attention so that it can be properly investigated. It would not be consistent with the purpose of the legislation if the worker could be victimized for so doing.

However, especially where there is no express allegation, there may be a need for particular **3.44** care in order to ascertain what in context the worker reasonably believed the information tended to show. The importance of proper regard being paid to the relevant context is illustrated by the decision in *Royal Cornwall Hospital NHS Trust v Watkinson* (UKEAT/0378/10, 17 August 2011). As noted above (paragraph 3.24), the chief executive disclosed to the respondent's board that an opinion had been obtained from counsel stating that the respondent Trust and the Primary Care Trust (PCT) would be acting unlawfully if they relocated the provision of 'upper GI' services without public consultation. On its face this disclosure identified a legal obligation without indicating expressly that there was a likelihood of a future failure to comply. However, the context was that the strategic health authority and the PCT had made clear their determination to avoid public consultation on the proposed changes. In that context, the disclosure was of information showing that there was not only a duty to consult, but also a likely future breach of that obligation.

(4) Aggregating disclosures

3.45 Is it possible for separate disclosures to be read together with the result that the later disclosure may be regarded as a qualifying disclosure, even though read by themselves neither would be a qualifying disclosure? As a matter of appellate authority, the position may be viewed as confused, with different EAT panels taking diverging approaches without citing the earlier decisions. In our view, however, the different decisions may be understood by having regard to, and distinguishing, the different senses in which it may be said that disclosures should be read together. As to this:

1. A previous disclosure may provide context which is relevant to understanding what is conveyed by the later disclosure. That is wholly consistent with authority to the effect that what has been said or written is properly to be understood in its context (see *Greenly* and *Anastasiou*, considered at paragraphs 3.14 and 3.15 above), and is supported by the decision in *Norbrook* considered below at paragraph 3.47. Whether a previous communication properly forms part of the context against which a later disclosure is to be understood, and how it impacts on what is conveyed by the later disclosure, is a fact-specific issue for the determination of the tribunal in each case.

2. A previous disclosure may provide context to the later disclosure in a different sense. When considering whether the disclosure tends to show a relevant failure, it will be relevant to have regard to the implications of the information disclosed against the context of what is reasonably believed to have already been known by the recipient of the disclosure. Thus where disclosure is made to someone to whom previous disclosures have been made, in assessing whether it was reasonable to believe that the information disclosed tends to show a relevant failure, it may be expected that this could be assessed against the context of what by reason of those past disclosures the recipient could reasonably be expected already to know. By way of example, suppose X discloses to his manager that a colleague (B) had a serious allergy to nuts. Then on a further occasion, X discloses to the same manager, that another colleague had put some nuts in the colleague's packed lunch as a joke. It would be absurd to suggest that the earlier disclosure must be ignored in considering whether, when making the second disclosure, X held a reasonable belief that the information tended to show that health and safety of the colleague was likely to be endangered.

3. A previous disclosure might be regarded as incorporated by reference in a subsequent disclosure. Again, where there is an express or implied reference to the previous disclosure in this way, we suggest that taking the two together should be controversial, and this is supported by the decision in *Norbrook* (see below, paragraph 3.47).

4. A further possibility is that there are simply disclosures about different conduct on different occasions which cumulatively might be regarded as showing a breach of a legal obligation but where no disclosure incorporates any other disclosure by reference. As noted below, the EAT's decision in *Fincham v HM Prison Service* suggests this is not permissible. This may on occasion be difficult to distinguish from the second category above, since there may come a point at which it might be said that the information disclosed in the latter disclosure falls to be evaluated in the context of what was already known. But ultimately the contextual relevance of previous disclosures when evaluating whether there

was a reasonable belief that the information tends to show a relevant failure is a matter for the tribunal.

5. A final possibility is where there is an attempt to include subsequent conduct or disclosures as part of a previous disclosure by reason of the close association with them. This is illustrated by the EAT's decision in *Barton v Greenwich LBC* (UKEAT/0041/14/DXA, 1 May 2015), which is discussed at paragraphs 3.50–3.51 below. It is clear that disclosure by association in this sense is not permissible.

6. More controversial is any attempt to read two or more disclosures together so as to take the information conveyed collectively and then assess collectively whether it tends to show a relevant failure, even though that conclusion cannot be reached as a matter of construing the later disclosure in context. But here too what has been said previously may be an important context in the different but still important sense of providing the background information which is relevant to assessing whether the further information conveyed in the alleged qualifying disclosure tends to show a relevant failure. After all, to some extent most disclosures will assume some background knowledge. Thus, to take an extreme example, a disclosure that the bow doors of a ship may be left open may be said to assume knowledge that if the bow doors are left open the ship will be unsafe. As such it may be questioned why the relevant background information against which to assess what is shown by a subsequent disclosure cannot derive from an earlier disclosure. But as against this, to seek to group together different disclosures may be regarded as likely to give rise to uncertainty. Hence this has proved controversial.

As to the third of these categories, as noted above (paragraph 3.35) in *Fincham v HM Prison Service* the EAT (presided over by Elias J) concluded that it was not permissible to look at various disclosures made by the claimant to see whether, taken collectively, they tended to show (in the claimant's reasonable belief) a breach of a legal obligation—in that case the implied term as to trust and confidence. Here on the facts it was not simply a matter of referring to the previous disclosures to provide context in the sense of what information was conveyed in the later disclosures. Instead it was a matter of seeking to rely on various complaints made separately as collectively tending to show that there was a breach of the implied term of trust and confidence. This was regarded as impermissible. **3.46**

Without citing the decision in *Fincham*, in *Norbrook Laboratories (GB) Ltd v Shaw* [2014] ICR 540 the EAT took the view that a disclosure could be read together with a previous disclosure or disclosures. Norbrook sold and distributed pharmaceuticals. The claimant managed a team of territory managers. In winter 2010, after heavy snowfall, territory managers raised with the claimant that they were having difficulty getting to their appointments and were concerned that they should still be paid. The claimant sent an email to Norbrook's health and safety manager asking to be provided with advice on what territory managers should do as to driving in the snow, and asking whether there was a company policy and whether a risk assessment had been done. The employment judge held that by itself this was not a disclosure of information. It was simply an inquiry asking for information and in response he was told that there was no company policy or risk assessment. The claimant then emailed the health and safety manager again, saying that he had been hoping for some formal guidance and that the team were under a lot of pressure to keep out on the road and that it was dangerous. A week later, as a result of the territory managers asking for clarification about their pay if they were snowed in, he sent a further email, this time instead to the HR department, saying that he was after a simple policy statement to help build morale and goodwill within the team, and that he had a duty of care for their health and safety. He said that having spent two days driving through the snow he knew how dangerous it could be. **3.47**

3.48 The employment judge held that the three emails, taken together, were capable of amounting to a qualifying disclosure as the claimant was informing his employer that the road conditions were so dangerous that health or safety of his team was being put at risk. The EAT upheld that conclusion, and specifically held that a prior communication could be taken into account as 'embedded' in the later disclosure. On that basis the employment judge was entitled to conclude that, in the later emails, the claimant was drawing attention to the danger of driving in snowy conditions, and was communicating information rather than just expressing an opinion or making an allegation. Further, the EAT concluded that the same applied to the third communication even though it was sent to a different department, since it was clear that he was referring to his earlier communications.

3.49 In support of its conclusion, the EAT cited the decision in *Goode v Marks and Spencer plc* (see paragraph 3.20 above) as authority for the proposition that an earlier communication can be read together with a later one. However, in *Goode* (at para 36), the EAT merely proceeded on the basis that even if this was possible, a qualifying disclosure had not been established. Notwithstanding this, as noted above, we suggest that the approach is appropriate at least in the way that it was applied in *Norbrook*. This was principally the use of the previous disclosure to give context to what was conveyed in the subsequent disclosure. Thus the second disclosure referred to the team being under pressure to keep out on the road and that it was dangerous. Given the context of the previous email, that plainly referred to the roads being dangerous because of the snowy conditions. It was not a case, as in *Fincham*, of the previous email containing some quite distinct information which was sought to be grouped together. Similarly, in relation to the third disclosure, there was express reference to driving through the snow being dangerous, and a clear reference to what had been said previously by virtue of the claimant saying he was after a simple policy statement to help build morale and goodwill within the team.

3.50 A subsequent decision of the EAT in *Barton v Greenwich LBC* (UKEAT/0041/14/DXA, 1 May 2015), may at first blush be seen as following the *Fincham* line of cases, though neither that case nor *Norbrook* was cited. The EAT commented that it was not possible to convert a disclosure that does not qualify into a qualifying disclosure by associating it with a disclosure that does qualify, and nor is it possible to aggregate two emails so as to create a protected disclosure. However, seen in context the decision may be regarded as addressing a narrower issue, identified in the fifth category set out above. The claimant had initially made a disclosure to the Information Commissioner's Office ('ICO') by a letter of 22 December 2011 alleging, based on a report to him from a colleague, that the colleague's line manager had emailed 'hundreds' of documents to her home which he believed contained confidential or personal data about himself, and that her personal email was neither part of a secure system nor encrypted. The claimant considered that this was a significant breach of the Data Protection Act 1998. The council told the claimant that he should have referred the matter to his line managers before raising concerns with the ICO. He was specifically instructed not to contact the ICO or other external bodies in relation to the matter without the prior authority of his line manager and he was told that the council would investigate the concerns promptly. The claimant then telephoned the ICO on 11 January 2012 to seek advice as to what he should do about the instruction not to communicate with the ICO. The tribunal concluded that the letter of 22 December 2011, although a qualifying disclosure, was not a protected disclosure under section 43F ERA as the claimant did not have a reasonable belief that the information disclosed and any allegations contained within it were substantially true. So far as the second disclosure was concerned, the tribunal found that the only information conveyed was the instruction given not to contact the ICO. The ET concluded that although the claimant believed that his employer did not have the power to issue the instruction, this was not a reasonable belief, as he had taken no steps to evaluate the legality of the instruction before calling the ICO, there had been no urgency to call the ICO before checking this, and the claimant had made no request when he did call the ICO to speak to anyone with experience in employment matters.

On the appeal it was argued that disciplining the claimant for the second call was a detriment, **3.51** but that there was an 'associative connection' between that call and the first email. It was in that context that HHJ Serota QC concluded that it was not possible to aggregate or associate the disclosures so as to give rise to a protected disclosure. Put in those terms the position was similar to that considered in *Bolton School v Evans* [2007] ICR 641, where the Court of Appeal rejected an argument that detrimental treatment by reason of conduct associated with a protected disclosure—in that case hacking into a school's computer system to bear out what had been said by the claimant as to the system being insecure—could be regarded as a detriment by reason of the protected disclosure. The Court of Appeal emphasized that 'disclosure' bears its ordinary meaning and that it was not possible to regard the whole of the conduct associated with the disclosure as being part of it. Equally it was not possible to regard the telephone call made to the ICO on 11 January 2012 as itself part of the initial disclosure by association. As such the EAT's reasoning did not address the question as to the scope for a previous disclosure to be the relevant context for a subsequent disclosure in any of the senses identified above; whether to cast light on what was conveyed by the disclosure, or as embedded within the disclosure (as with the third disclosure in *Norbrook*), or as identifying factual matters which could be taken already to be known by the recipient of the disclosure so as to be material in assessing whether the further information disclosed would tend to show a relevant failure.

C. Reasonable Belief

(1) Overview

For there to be a qualifying disclosure, the worker must have a 'reasonable belief' that the **3.52** information disclosed 'tends to show' one or more of the relevant failures. In summary, and as developed below, the following key principles apply in relation to this test:

(1) The test involves both a subjective test of the worker's belief and an objective assessment of whether that belief could reasonably have been held (*Babula v Waltham Forest College* [2007] EWCA Civ 174, [2007] ICR 1026 at paras 75, 81, and 82).

(2) The worker can be wrong, yet still hold a reasonable belief (*Darnton v University of Surrey* [2003] ICR 615 at paras 31 and 32; *Babula* at paras 41 and 75).

(3) The test of reasonable belief applies to all elements of the test of whether the information disclosed tends to show a relevant failure, including (in the case of section 43B(2) (a), (b)) whether the relevant criminal offence or legal obligation in fact exists (*Babula* at paras 75–84).

(4) It is not sufficient for the worker to have a reasonable belief that what s/he is saying on its face (ie if true) tends to show a relevant failure. Reasonableness of the belief is to be tested having regard not only to what was set out in the disclosure, but also to the basis given for that information and any allegation made (*Darnton* at para 29; *Babula* at para 82, p 1045E–F).

(5) What is reasonable depends on all the circumstances assessed from the perspective of the worker at the time of making the disclosure, and is for the tribunal to assess (*Darnton* at para 33; *Babula* at para 41). This may include consideration of the circumstances in which the disclosure was made, to whom the disclosure was made, the context and extent to which the worker claims to have direct knowledge of the matters disclosed, and a comparison with how the worker would be expected to have behaved if s/he genuinely and reasonably believed in the truth of the matters disclosed and that they tended

to show a relevant failure (*Darnton* at paras 28–32; *De Haney v Brent Mind and Lang* (UKEAT/0054/03, 19 March 2004); *Muchesa v Central & Cecil Housing Care Support* (EAT/0443/07, 22 August 2008).

(6) Whilst reasonableness must be assessed from the standpoint of the person making the disclosure at the time the disclosure was made, rather than considering the facts as found with the benefit of hindsight, the truth or falsity of the information disclosed and whether or not the relevant failure in fact occurred may be relevant when assessing reasonable belief (*Darnton* at paras 29 and 31; *Sir Robert McAlpine v Telford* (EATS/0018/03, 13 May 2003); *Aryeetey v Tuntum Housing Association* (UKEAT/0070/07, 12 October 2007); *Muchesa v Central & Cecil Housing Care Support* at para 31; *Dr Y-A-Soh v Imperial College of Science, Technology and Medicine* (UKEAT/0350/14/DM, 3 September 2015) at para 46). There is some authority that the truth of the information disclosed will always be relevant (*Sir Robert McAlpine v Telford*), but dicta in *Darnton* (at para 29, p 625D–E), *Babula* (see per Wall LJ at para 79), and *Dr Y-A-Soh* (at para 42) indicate to the contrary. But the tribunal must not lose sight of the legislative test of whether the information was reasonably believed to show the relevant failure, rather than whether the worker reasonably believed there was a past, present, or likely future relevant failure: *Dr Y-A-Soh* at para 46.

(7) The worker must exercise a judgement consistent with the evidence and resources available, including the expertise and seniority of the worker, their ability to investigate further, and whether it is appropriate in all the circumstances instead to refer the matter to someone else to investigate (*Darnton* at paras 31 and 32).

(8) The standard to be applied has to take into account that it is only necessary to have a reasonable belief that the information 'tends to show' the relevant failure, rather than that it positively establishes that failure (*Babula* at para 79). This distinguishes the test for a qualifying disclosure from that for establishing protection under sections 43F to 43G where there is a requirement for a reasonable belief that the information disclosed and any allegation contained in it are substantially true. A worker may recognize that further investigation may well establish that information disclosed is untrue (eg if it has been reported by a third party and is not within the worker's direct knowledge) or the relevant failure did not occur (or is not occurring or not likely to occur). Notwithstanding this, the worker may still hold a reasonable belief that the information disclosed, on the basis of the part of the evidential picture available at that time, points towards a past, ongoing, or likely future relevant failure (*Darnton* at para 30; *Bolton School v Evans* [2006] IRLR 500, EAT).

(9) The burden is on the worker making the disclosure to establish the requisite reasonable belief (*Babula* at para 74).

(2) The *Darnton* guidance

3.53 Guidance as to the appropriate approach for assessing reasonable belief was laid down by the EAT in *Darnton v University of Surrey* [2003] ICR 615, which was substantially endorsed by the Court of Appeal in *Babula v Waltham Forest College* [2007] EWCA Civ 174, [2007] ICR 1026. Mr Darnton was a senior lecturer at Surrey University's European Management School. During his short period of employment with the university he clashed on a number of occasions with the head of the School, Professor Gamble. In June 1999, two months after the start of his employment, he sent a memorandum to Professor Gamble stating that he felt threatened and harassed and that he was seeking professional advice. Following further clashes, it was agreed between Mr Darnton and Professor Gamble that Mr Darnton's full-time employment would end on 8 September 1999. A compromise agreement was entered into after Mr Darnton had taken legal advice. Pursuant to the agreement, Mr Darnton was to continue working for the School on the basis of a twelve-month associate lectureship for which he was to be provided with £20,000 worth of work. Having found another permanent job, Mr Darnton resigned from the teaching part of his lectureship. The university then regarded the obligation to provide £20,000 worth of work as at an end. Mr Darnton disagreed. Mr Darnton wrote a letter to the vice-chancellor of the university, and copied it to the chancellor. It was this letter which was relied upon as containing protected disclosures. The EAT described it as being 'full of intemperate language and complaints about Professor Gamble'. It included allegations of harassment and intimidation and a claim that Mr Darnton had been coerced into signing a compromise agreement. The School then wrote to Mr Darnton saying that his services were no longer required. Mr Darnton contended that this amounted to automatically unfair dismissal by reason of his having made protected disclosures.

3.54 The employment tribunal held that there was no qualifying disclosure and also that the disclosures were not made in good faith. In relation to whether there was a qualifying disclosure, the EAT held that the employment tribunal had erred in law by considering whether the allegations were in fact true and then considering in the light of this whether there was a reasonable belief in them. Instead, whether there was a reasonable belief must be assessed on the basis of the facts as understood by the worker (or as the worker ought reasonably to have understood them).

3.55 The EAT (at para 31) also endorsed the commentary in the first edition of this book as follows:

We have derived considerable assistance from *Whistleblowing: The New Law* by John Bowers QC, Jeremy Lewis and Jack Mitchell. The learned authors write, at p.19, under the heading 'Reasonable belief in truth':

'To achieve protection under any of the several parts of the Act, the worker must have a "reasonable belief" in the truth of the information as tending to show one or more of the six matters listed which he has disclosed, although that belief need not be correct (s 43B(1)). This had led some to criticise the statute as giving too much licence to employees to cause trouble, since it pays no regard to issues of confidentiality in this respect. Nor need the employee actually prove, even on the balance of probabilities, the truth of what he is disclosing. This is probably inevitable, because the whistleblower may have a good "hunch" that something is wrong without having the means to prove it beyond doubt or even on the balance of probabilities ... The notion behind the legislation is that the employee should be encouraged to make known to a suitable person the basis of that hunch so that those with the ability and resources to investigate it can do so.

The control on abuse is that it must have been reasonable for the worker to believe that the information disclosed was true. This means, we think, that the following principles would apply under the Act:

(a) It would be a qualifying disclosure if the worker reasonably but mistakenly believed that a specified malpractice is or was occurring or may occur.[9]

(b) Equally if some malpractice was occurring which did not fall within one of the listed categories, the disclosure would still qualify if the worker reasonably believed that it did amount to malpractice falling within one of those categories.

(c) There must be more than unsubstantiated rumours in order for there to be a qualifying disclosure. The whistleblower must exercise some judgement on his own part consistent with the evidence and the resources available to him. There must additionally be a reasonable belief and therefore some information which tends to show that the specified malpractice occurred ...

(d) The reasonableness of the belief will depend in each case on the volume and quality of information available to the worker at the time the decision to disclose is made. Employment tribunals will have to guard against use of hindsight to assess the reasonableness of the belief in this respect in the same way as they are bound, in considering liability in unfair dismissal cases, to consider only what was known to the employer at the time of dismissal or appeal ...'

---

[9] But see the comments in *Kraus v Penna* [2004] IRLR 260, EAT, considered at para 3.93 below, emphasizing that 'likely' means 'probable' or 'more probable than not'.

Summarizing this commentary, the EAT observed (at para 32) that:

> we agree with the authors that, for there to be a qualifying disclosure, it must have been reasonable for the worker to believe that the factual basis of what was disclosed was true and that it tends to show a relevant failure, even if the worker was wrong, but reasonably mistaken.

3.56 It is relevant, we suggest, to distinguish two different senses in which it might be said that the worker must believe that the factual basis of what was disclosed is true. Suppose that a nurse reports having been informed by a patient of information which led to concerns as to a consultant's competence. The facts disclosed would be that this had been reported by the patient, and the nurse must reasonably believe that this was indeed what the patient had told him. That is clear from the EAT's rejection of the submission that it was sufficient for the worker to have a reasonable belief that what s/he is saying on its face (ie if true) tends to show a relevant failure. There is, we suggest, no additional requirement to believe that what the patient had said was true. The nurse may not know one way or the other whether that was the case, yet it would remain important to report the concern so that it could be investigated.

3.57 The EAT's conclusion that it is not sufficient to have a reasonable belief that the information disclosed on its face tends to show a relevant failure may be further illustrated by the following scenario:

> An employee (Ms X) develops concerns that another employee (Ms Y) has been making fraudulent expenses claims. If true this would be a criminal offence and a breach or likely breach of Ms Y's contractual duties to the employer. Ms X's suspicions are based on her analysis of Ms Y's expenses claims and receipts. Ms X reports her concerns and the basis for them to a senior manager (Ms Z). However, her allegations were based on a careless and incorrect, albeit honest, analysis of the expenses claims.

3.58 Viewed at face value, the information (that an analysis of expenses and receipts indicated false expenses claims) would indeed tend to show a relevant failure. It would also be reasonable for Ms X to believe that the disclosure would tend to convey to the recipient of the report (Ms Z) that there had been a relevant failure. It would not be necessary to consider further whether the investigation was careless. However, since, as decided in *Darnton*, a tribunal may have regard not only to what was set out in the disclosure, but also to the basis for that information, the tribunal would need to consider whether Ms X lacked the requisite reasonable belief in the light of her carelessness in analysing the receipts and expenses.

3.59 How may this be reconciled with the differing tests in section 43C ERA (internal disclosures) and sections 43F, 43G, and 43H (disclosures to a prescribed body or wider disclosures)? In relation to sections 43F, 43G, and 43H, the worker must reasonably believe that the information disclosed, and any allegation contained in it, are substantially true. There is no equivalent requirement for section 43C disclosures, and it cannot therefore have been the legislative intention that such a requirement is imposed under section 43B. This difficulty would not arise if reasonable belief were to be assessed on the basis of what the information on its face tends to show. This would enable a clear distinction to be drawn between a qualifying disclosure as being concerned with identification of the subject matter which is capable of being protected, and the further requirements set out in sections 43C to 43G. It would also be consistent with the policy of encouraging workers to make known their concerns internally so that they can be properly investigated by those best able to do so.

3.60 The EAT in *Darnton* acknowledged (at para 30) that section 43B must not be construed in such a way as to import an obligation akin to the requirement in sections 43F, 43G, and 43H for a reasonable belief that the information disclosed, and any allegation contained in it, are substantially true. It grappled with this, in part, by stressing the lower standard to be applied in order to satisfy the section 43B reasonable belief test. It emphasized (at para 30) that the required standard of belief in the truth of what has been disclosed cannot be such as to require the employee in all cases to believe that both the factual basis for the belief and what it tends to show are substantially true. The EAT's essential point was that the standard of what is reasonable must depend on all the circumstances.[10] Thus (at para 28) the EAT noted that:

> circumstances that give rise to a worker reporting a protected disclosure will vary enormously from case to case. The circumstances will range from cases in which a worker reports matters which he claims are within his own knowledge, or have been seen or heard by him. At the other extreme will be cases where the worker passes on what has been reported to him, or what has been observed by others.

In each case, as the EAT emphasized, the worker must exercise judgement consistent with the evidence and resources available, as to the credibility of the information and as to what it tends to show, such that in the circumstances it was reasonable to hold that belief. But the standard required will depend on the circumstances. This approach affords to tribunals the flexibility to distinguish circumstances where the employer will be best able to investigate from, at the other extreme, allegations that the worker ought to have realized were untrue or where the employer has provided an adequate explanation which is unreasonably rejected by the worker. **3.61**

In the ordinary course this exercise will require the worker to have some grounds for believing that the information disclosed is true. However, as noted in *Dr Y-A-Soh v Imperial College of Science, Technology and Medicine* (UKEAT/0350/14/DM, 3 September 2015), at para 47, there will be circumstances in which a worker passes on to an employer information provided by a third party that the worker is not in a position to assess. The EAT commented that so long as the worker believes that the information tends to show a state of affairs identified (falling within one of the relevant failures), the disclosure will be a qualifying disclosure. Clearly in this scenario the worker may have no positive view as to the truth of the information supplied. Indeed the worker may be sceptical about it, yet it may still be important that the information be passed on so that it can be properly investigated. A worker who receives a call as to a bomb threat may believe it is likely to be a hoax, but it would be strange if the passing on of that information so that it can be properly investigated was not a qualifying disclosure. In such a case, where the worker is not in a position to assess the information and it is appropriate instead to pass it on to the employer (or other appropriate person) to assess, the position is similar to the proposition rejected in *Darnton*, that the reasonable belief is properly to be assessed on the basis of what the information on its face tends to show. **3.62**

Further, if tribunals apply too stringent a test of reasonable belief, there is a risk that this will encourage workers either not to make the disclosure or to delay making disclosures which are best investigated by the employer whilst they seek to firm up their suspicions. As noted above, the EAT in *Darnton* (at para 31) endorsed the view that where the whistleblower has a good 'hunch' that something is wrong without the means to prove it, s/he should be encouraged to make known to a suitable person the basis of that hunch so that those with the ability and resources to investigate can do so. **3.63**

The reasonable belief test has both a subjective and an objective element: see *Babula v Waltham Forest College* [2007] EWCA Civ 174, [2007] ICR 1026 at paras 81 and 82. As the EAT put it in *Welsh Refugee Council v Brown* (UKEAT/0032/02, 22 March 2002) at para 9: **3.64**

> … a finding that Mrs Brown had a reasonable belief for these purposes necessarily connotes two component matters; thus it necessarily connotes that she *did* in point of fact believe what she was saying, that is, it necessarily connotes a subjective finding to that extent. Second and

---

[10] Endorsing a passage in the first edition of this book.

further, it connotes a finding that that belief was reasonable, that is, it was a tenable belief neither eccentric nor fanciful, it is a belief that withstands objective assessment.

3.65 In relation to the objective element, the EAT therefore suggested that the belief must be 'tenable', but the degree of scrutiny involved will necessarily be dependent on the circumstances. Those circumstances are likely to include the basis or source of the information and whether the person making the disclosure is in a position where s/he ought to investigate further, or could reasonably leave it to the recipient of the disclosure to investigate further. In this case Mrs Brown was employed as the regional coordinator of a project run by the respondent, which was an organization set up to assist refugees. The respondent's finance officer raised with Mrs Brown concerns that a director of the respondent had been submitting expenses claims and then reclaiming the expenses from the city council, and had also been submitting false expenses claims. Mrs Brown reported these concerns to the respondent's management committee. She claimed that this was a protected disclosure and that she was subjected to detriments, culminating in her dismissal, as a result of her disclosures. She succeeded before the employment tribunal, and its decision was upheld on appeal. The EAT dealt with the question of whether Mrs Brown's belief was reasonable by a series of rhetorical questions as follows (at para 13):

> How could the grounds be other than reasonable as a basis for further disclosure, given the source of the information? What else should Mrs Brown as regional coordinator have done, other than pass the material forward? Should she have kept silent pending her own investigation before passing the matter forward?

3.66 The EAT therefore placed emphasis on the fact that the information came from an apparently credible source and that the standard of reasonable belief was properly to be viewed in the context of the fact that it would not have been appropriate to do other than to make the information available to the employer. This is in keeping with the purpose of the legislation.

3.67 As the EAT emphasized in *Korashi v Abertawe Bro Morgannwg University Local Health Board* [2012] IRLR 4, the effect of the objective element of the test is that those whose disclosures more naturally demand respect may also need to do more to demonstrate that the belief is reasonable. As the EAT noted (at para 62):

> … many whistleblowers are insiders. That means that they are so much more informed about the goings-on of the organisation of which they make complaint than outsiders, and that that insight entitles their views to respect. Since the test is their 'reasonable' belief, that belief must be subject to what a person in their position would reasonably believe to be wrong-doing.

3.68 The EAT illustrated this by contrasting the position of a lay observer and a consultant surgeon who each learn that an apparently healthy young man was taken to hospital after an athletics injury and died on the operating table. Whilst it may be reasonable for the layperson to believe that the death indicates a breach of duty, the same might not be true of the surgeon. It would be necessary to have regard to his knowledge of what was involved in the operation, and/or to the fact that he may be expected to look at all the material including the records (if available to him) before making a disclosure.

3.69 As above, the reasonable belief test also entails a subjective element. But some care is needed with the formulation in *Welsh Refugee Council v Brown* that the worker must believe what s/he is saying. If a worker claims to have seen something personally, and knows that this is untrue, then clearly there could be no reasonable belief in the disclosure. In those circumstances the worker would be unlikely in any event to meet the requirement for a reasonable belief that the disclosure was made in the public interest (or the good faith requirement for disclosures made prior to 25 June 2013). If the worker has been provided with information second hand, it may be that the worker is sceptical as to whether it is true but still recognizes that it requires further investigation by the employer, and (as discussed further in the next section in relation to the 'tends to show' test) the worker may still have the requisite reasonable belief on the basis of a judgement exercised on the limited part of the evidential picture available to the worker.

In considering the subjective element of the reasonable belief test, one available approach is **3.70** to compare how the worker acted with what would have been expected if the worker had genuinely believed the matters disclosed. In *Muchesa v Central & Cecil Housing Care Support* (UKEAT/0443/07, 22 August 2008) the senior night carer at a residential care home made allegations to a daughter of a resident of seriously defective care of that resident. She also made calls to the police and social services alleging serious neglect. The allegations related to matters which she claimed to have witnessed personally. The EAT noted that, in concluding that she lacked the requisite reasonable belief, and also had not been acting in good faith, the employer had been entitled to take into account various objective factors which together indicated that she had not behaved in the manner to be expected had she reasonably (or indeed genuinely) believed in the truth of the complaints. These factors included a failure to use the whistleblowing policy despite being aware of it, a failure to ask another member of staff to witness the conduct of which she was complaining, failing to ask the police to attend, failure to write up the incident which she reported, and spending time photocopying rather than dealing with the incident.

Further, as indicated by the EAT in *de Haney v Brent Mind and Lang* (UKEAT/0054/03, **3.71** 19 March 2004), relevant factors may extend to the circumstances in which the allegation is raised before the employment tribunal. Mrs de Haney alleged that in a meeting with her line manager she had complained about the appointment of a colleague which she claimed was in breach of her employer's equal opportunity policy. The claimant had raised a concern about the appointment in writing prior to her dismissal, but the allegation that her concerns in relation to this amounted to a protected disclosure was not contained in the originating application or the claimant's further particulars of her claim, but was first made in her witness statement. In those circumstances the EAT held that the tribunal had been entitled to find that the allegation was put in as a 'makeweight' and as such was not a qualifying disclosure (in that she did not hold the requisite reasonable belief).

(3) Tends to show

There is no need to hold a reasonable belief that the information disclosed actually establishes **3.72** a relevant failure. It is sufficient if it 'tends to show' (rather than 'shows') a relevant failure. As Wall LJ emphasized in *Babula v Waltham Forest College* [2007] EWCA Civ 174, [2007] ICR 1026 at para 79, this is an important qualification. It lies at the heart of the distinction drawn between the reasonable belief requirement in section 43B and the requirement under section 43F, 43G, and 43H that the worker must have a reasonable belief that the allegations are substantially true. Especially in relation to internal disclosures, the legislation recognizes that the worker may only have access to part of the evidential picture. The information available to the worker might indeed tend to show a relevant failure, in the sense of being one piece of evidence which merits a concern being raised. It might, however, not be reasonable to hold the belief that the allegation is substantially true prior to an investigation of the matter by the employer.

There may be a variety of reasons for the worker only having part of the picture. It might be **3.73** that this arises because the information is only received second-hand. Thus, for example, if a worker hears from a colleague that another colleague has been stealing from the company, that might well be sufficient to found a reasonable belief that this was information that tended to show that that colleague had been stealing. But it might be premature to hold a belief that the allegation is substantially true without investigation as to the reliability of the source, or further details of the circumstances of the alleged thefts or the explanation provided by the person alleged to have been stealing. The employer might be best placed to investigate those matters. As such it is appropriate that the further requirement of a substantial belief in the truth is not applied to an internal disclosure (ie within the employing organization or otherwise within section 43C), but is required only for an external disclosure.

3.74 This was reflected in the reasoning of the EAT in *Bolton School v Evans* [2006] IRLR 500. Mr Evans disclosed that he was going to break into the school's computer system in order to demonstrate that the system was insecure and would too readily lead to unauthorized disclosures. The employment tribunal found that Mr Evans had a reasonable belief that his employer was likely to breach the seventh Data Protection principle. This principle requires that appropriate technical and organizational measures be taken against unauthorized or unlawful processing of personal data and against accidental loss or destruction of, or damage to, personal data. The Data Protection Act 1998 (Schedule 1, Part 2, paragraph 9) contains principles of interpretation relating to this, providing that, having regard to the state of technological development and the cost of implementing any measures, the measures to be taken must ensure a level of security which is appropriate to the harm that might result and the nature of the data to be protected. On behalf of the respondent school, it was argued that Mr Evans could not have held a reasonable belief that the seventh Data Protection principle would be infringed without appreciating what that principle obliged the employer to do, and that this required him to weigh up the considerations set out in the principles of interpretation in order to determine whether or not the information tended to show a likely breach. In rejecting this argument the EAT held (at paras 51 and 52) that:

> we do not think that the protection is lost merely because the employer may be able to show that, for reasons not immediately apparent to the employee, the duty will not apply or that he has some defence to it. The information will still, it seems to us, tend to show the likelihood of breach. It is potentially powerful and material evidence pointing in that direction even although there may be other factors which ultimately would demonstrate that no breach is likely to occur.
>
> There may indeed be cases where a relatively detailed appreciation of the relevant legal obligation is required before an employee can establish that he reasonably believed that the information tended to show that a breach of a legal obligation was likely. But it would undermine the protection of this valuable legislation if employees were expected to anticipate and evaluate all potential defences, whether within the scope of their own knowledge or not, when deciding whether or not to make that disclosure.

3.75 The EAT recognized therefore that the legislation is constructed to cater for the fact that the employee may only be aware of part of the evidential picture. What matters is that the employee reasonably believes that the disclosure points in the direction of a breach being likely to occur, even though there might ultimately be other considerations that are raised which indicate that this is not the case.

3.76 The distinction between a reasonable belief in the state of affairs (the past, present, or likely future relevant failure) and the statutory test of a reasonable belief that the information tended to show a relevant failure was again emphasized in *Dr Y-A-Soh v Imperial College of Science, Technology and Medicine* (UKEAT/0350/14/DM, 3 September 2015). Here the claimant, a college lecturer, raised a grievance alleging that the reason that she had low feedback scores was because her lectures were more challenging than other lecturers and that she did not spoon-feed her students. She later passed on information which she had received from students to the effect that one of her colleagues, Dr McPhail, had told them what would be in the exams. An investigation acquitted Dr McPhail of malpractice. Disciplinary proceedings were then brought against the claimant in part on the basis of bringing vexatious allegations. Her defence was that she had only said that he had spoon-fed students and was repeating what she had been told by students in the context of defending herself in relation to the feedback and was not implying that there had been improper practice by him. That was rejected and she was dismissed.

In subsequent proceedings, the claimant relied on her comments about students being **3.77** spoon-fed, and her allegations about Dr McPhail, as being protected disclosures. She contended that she believed that there was a legal obligation upon lecturers not to undermine the integrity of the examination system, and that the information given by the students that she relayed tended to show that Dr McPhail had done so by giving specific information about what would be in an examination question. The tribunal concluded that she lacked the requisite reasonable belief. It found that she did not believe that Dr McPhail was undermining the integrity of the exam system, and accepted that she was not directly alleging this. It held that she believed only that it was wrong and unfair to call him a good teacher and her a bad teacher because he received good feedback scores, but that this was not a breach of a legal obligation. However, the EAT concluded that the tribunal had erred in that it had asked whether the claimant reasonably believed that the wrongdoing had occurred, rather than whether there was a reasonable belief that the information tended to show the wrongdoing. The EAT noted that the question of whether the claimant reasonably believed that the examination system was being undermined was not the same as asking whether she had a reasonable belief that the information tended to show this was the case. Where the claimant's state of mind was of critical importance, as here, it was essential to focus on the correct statutory question. Whether or not the claimant reasonably believed that Dr McPhail was undermining the examination system might be relevant to the overall assessment, but it was not the statutory test. There may be circumstances where an employee passes on information from a third party which s/he was not in a position to assess, but on the basis of that information could still have a reasonable belief that it tends to show a breach of a legal obligation. Whether that was the case was remitted to a differently constituted tribunal to assess.

The 'tends to show' formula provides a means of dealing with the case of a worker who **3.78** passes on information but is simply not in a position to assess its accuracy. As such, it avoids pushing workers into extreme positions in order to attract the protection of the legislation. It is easy to envisage that the worker might be reticent about making allegations, yet believe that the information is indicative of a relevant failure and therefore it needs to be investigated. Thus, for example, if an internal accountant discovers various irregularities which are reasonably believed to be indicators of fraud, there is no additional requirement for him/her to believe that once the matter has been fully investigated it will be found that there has in fact been a fraud. The irregularities may be powerful and material evidence tending to show a fraud even though ultimately there will be sufficient countervailing evidence to demonstrate that there has been no fraud. This may also be seen as an application of the principle set out in *Darnton* that all the relevant circumstances must be taken into account in determining whether there is the requisite reasonable belief. One important circumstance may be that the worker only has part of the evidential picture and it is reasonable in the circumstances not to require further investigation. Plainly, however, this can only apply where the worker does not have the full evidential picture and the evidence available or which ought to be ascertained could reasonably be regarded as indicating a relevant failure. If in the above example the internal accountant discovered the various irregularities, but also knew that there was an innocent explanation, there could be no question of the requisite reasonable belief existing, even though, taken in isolation, the irregularities could be regarded as an indicator of potential fraud.

(4) Truth or falsity as a useful evidential tool

3.79 The EAT in *Darnton* noted that although the issue of whether the information was disclosed was true might not be determinative of whether there was a reasonable belief, it will often be evidentially relevant. It explained (at para 29) that:

> in our opinion, the determination of the factual accuracy of the disclosure by the tribunal will, in many cases, be an important tool in determining whether the worker held the reasonable belief that the disclosure tended to show a relevant failure. Thus if an employment tribunal finds that an employee's factual allegation of something he claims to have seen himself is false, that will be highly relevant to the question of the worker's reasonable belief. It is extremely difficult to see how a worker can reasonably believe that an allegation tends to show that there has been a relevant failure if he knew or believed that the factual basis was false, unless there may somehow have been an honest mistake on his part. The relevance and extent of the employment tribunal's enquiry into the factual accuracy of the disclosure will, therefore, necessarily depend on the circumstances of each case. In many cases, it will be an important tool to decide whether the worker held the reasonable belief that is required by s 43B(1). We cannot accept Mr Kallipetis' submission that reasonable belief applies only to the question of whether the alleged facts tend to disclose a relevant failure. We consider that as a matter of both law and common sense all circumstances must be considered together in determining whether the worker holds the reasonable belief. The circumstances will include his belief in the factual basis of the information disclosed as well as what those facts tend to show. The more the worker claims to have direct knowledge of the matters which are the subject of the disclosure, the more relevant will be his belief in the truth of what he says in determining whether he holds that reasonable belief.

3.80 Similarly, in *Muchesa v Central & Cecil Housing Care Support* (UKEAT/0443/07, 22 August 2008), where the worker claimed personally to have seen misconduct, the EAT noted that the employment tribunal were:

> entitled, in reaching their decision, to consider whether the complaints were in fact true … and to regard their view of their truth or untruth as an important tool to the resolution of the issue before them of reasonable belief.

3.81 In *Sir Robert McAlpine Ltd v Telford* (EATS/0018/03, 13 May 2003) the EAT went a step further and suggested that the truth of the information disclosed will always be material. The issue arose in the context of an interim appeal against the refusal of a tribunal to bar the claimant from making allegations of fraud in his oral evidence. Following *Darnton*, the EAT noted that circumstances which related to the claimant's belief at the time when s/he made the disclosures, and in particular whether there were reasonable grounds for the belief, were relevant even if it turned out that the allegations of fraud were unfounded. The EAT explained (at para 9(iv)) in its summary of the legal principles that:

> always of assistance in order to decide the question of reasonable belief, would be included the question as to whether, in fact, it was happening; because, if it was happening, then that would assist the Tribunal in deciding that his belief that it was happening was a reasonable one, although it would not of itself be determinative of that aspect, one way or the other.

3.82 This dictum was followed in *Aryeetey v Tuntum Housing Association* (UKEAT/0070/07, 12 October 2007). The claimant, who was the respondent's finance director, made disclosures as to fraudulent conduct by the chief executive. He then made a disclosure to the housing corporation in which he also alleged that his investigation had been obstructed. He complained of detriments in being required to apologize, and then being suspended, disciplined, and ultimately dismissed. A report for the respondent found that there were financial irregularities, and to that extent vindicated the claimant, although it also found that there was no dishonesty. The report was not provided to the claimant, but the EAT concluded that the employment tribunal had still been entitled to refer to this in support of the conclusion that the claimant had the requisite reasonable belief that the matters he disclosed tended to show a breach of a legal obligation. The employment tribunal found that he had made protected disclosures by reason of which the claimant had been subjected to detriments and then dismissed.

Conversely, in *Babula v Waltham Forest College* [2007] EWCA Civ 174, [2007] ICR 1026, **3.83** Wall LJ (at para 79) commented that the fact that a worker may prove to be wrong was 'not relevant' provided that the belief was reasonable and (as was required at that time) the disclosure made in good faith. However, the Court of Appeal was not directly addressing the issue as to whether the truth of the allegation could be a useful evidential tool. Wall LJ (at para 38) cited without criticism the passage in *Darnton* in which it was noted that factual accuracy of the allegation will in many cases be an important tool.

We suggest that it remains permissible to have regard to this, particularly in a case where **3.84** the worker claims to rely on matters witnessed first hand, but that *Sir Robert McAlpine Ltd v Telford* took a step too far insofar as it suggested that the truth or falsity of the allegation will *always* be material. The extent, if at all, to which the employment tribunal may derive assistance from a consideration of whether or not the allegations were in fact well founded will be a matter for the employment tribunal's assessment in all the circumstances. In some cases, it may not be a proportionate use of the tribunal's time for there to be detailed evidence as to this, having regard to the fact that the worker may hold a reasonable belief yet in fact be wrong. This may, for example, be the case where it is unclear and would require detailed evidence as to whether the allegations were in fact true, and where the worker was not making the disclosure on the basis of information which s/he witnessed directly.

The prospect that a tribunal may be invited to make findings as to the truth or falsity of the **3.85** underlying allegations may, however, have important implications for the conduct of litigation. It impacts on the extent to which disclosure of documents may be considered relevant and proportionate where it bears on the truth of the allegations, even where it concerns matters which the worker could not have taken into account in forming the requisite belief. More broadly, and taken together with other lines of defence that may be available (for example in relation to causation), it may impact on whether an employer chooses to put reasonable belief in issue, knowing that this may invite close consideration of potentially sensitive issues associated with the substance of the protected disclosures. The need to consider all the evidence on the question of whether the allegation was true or false, including that which might be available from an employer, also bears on considerations as to whether the case should be halted before the employer's evidence is called.[11]

(5) Test applies to existence of a legal obligation or criminal offence

As decided by the Court of Appeal in *Babula v Waltham Forest College* [2007] EWCA Civ **3.86** 174, [2007] ICR 1026, the reasonable belief test applies to all elements of the requirement of a belief in the information as tending to show a relevant failure. This includes whether or not, in the case of a belief in a past, ongoing, or likely future criminal offence or breach of legal obligation, that offence or obligation in fact existed at the relevant time. As explained by Wall LJ (at para 75):

> Provided his belief (which is inevitably subjective) is held by the tribunal to be objectively
> reasonable, neither (1) the fact that the belief turns out to be wrong, nor (2) the fact that the

---

[11] *Boulding v Land Securities Trillium (Media Services) Ltd* (EAT/0023/0306, 3 May 2006). For further discussion of this case see paras 3.101–3.102 below.

information which the claimant believed to be true (and may indeed be true) does not in law amount to a criminal offence, is, in my judgment, sufficient, of itself, to render the belief unreasonable and thus deprive the whistleblower of the protection afforded by the statute.

3.87 Mr Babula, an American citizen, was employed by the respondent college as a business studies lecturer. He was told by his students that his predecessor had used lesson time to teach religious studies, dividing the class into Islamic and non-Islamic groups, and had told the Muslim students that he wished a September 11 type incident would occur in London. Mr Babula raised the matter with a supervisor, who took the view that no action was required. Concerned that there might be a threat to national security and believing that, at the least, an offence of incitement to racial hatred had been committed, and that the college had failed to comply with a legal obligation to report it, Mr Babula contacted the CIA and FBI and informed the college that he had done so. The disclosure led to a series of actions by the college which Mr Babula felt left him with no choice but to resign. The employment tribunal struck out his claim as having no reasonable prospect of success, on the ground that, on the basis of the facts asserted by Mr Babula, any incitement was to religious, not racial, hatred, which was not an offence at the time, and, therefore, the disclosure was not a qualifying disclosure complying with ERA, section 43B(1). The employment tribunal said that it reached this conclusion reluctantly, since it recognized that Mr Babula had acted reasonably, viewing his actions through the eyes of an American with the events of September 11 in mind. However, the employment tribunal felt driven to this conclusion by the decision of the EAT in *Kraus v Penna plc* [2004] IRLR 260, where it had been held that a worker could not have the requisite reasonable belief in relation to a criminal offence or legal obligation if that obligation did not exist at the time. This was explained on that basis that there would then be nothing by reference to measure the reasonableness of the belief.

3.88 In rejecting this view, the Court of Appeal emphasized that if a worker reasonably believed that a criminal offence had been committed, was being committed, or was likely to be committed, and provided his/her belief was found by the tribunal to be objectively reasonable, neither the fact that the belief turned out to be wrong nor the fact that the information which s/he believed to be true did not in law amount to a criminal offence, was sufficient, of itself, to render the belief unreasonable. The court emphasized (at paras 75, 81, and 82) that the reasonable belief test involves both a subjective and an objective element. The worker must genuinely believe that the information disclosed tends to show one of the relevant failures and that belief must be objectively reasonable. A belief—including a belief as to the existence of the legal obligation—may be reasonable but turn out to be wrong. Equally, as noted by the EAT in *Bolton School v Evans* [2006] IRLR 500, there may be a reasonable belief notwithstanding that for some reason not immediately apparent to the employee the duty alleged to have been breached does not apply or there is some defence to it.

3.89 The Court of Appeal in *Babula* noted that this approach was also supported by policy considerations:

> The purpose of the statute, as I read it, is to encourage responsible whistleblowing. To expect employees on the factory floor or in shops and offices to have a detailed knowledge of the criminal law sufficient to enable them to determine whether or not particular facts which they reasonably believe to be true are capable, as a matter of law, of constituting a particular criminal offence seems to me both unrealistic and to work against the policy of the statute. (Wall LJ at para 80)

3.90 The force of these policy considerations is reinforced when the further provisions of the scheme for protection are considered. ERA, section 43D relates to a disclosure made in the course of obtaining legal advice. Thus, if an employer intercepted a communication from an employee seeking advice in relation to legal obligations, and disciplined the employee, it would be open for the employer to argue that there was in fact no legal obligation. Even though the employee had acted wholly reasonably, and was properly seeking legal advice as to the legal obligations in play, the disclosure would then be unprotected. Similarly, the approach in *Kraus* would have enabled the employer to penalize an employer who genuinely raises concerns internally with the employer in relation to legal obligations which the employee reasonably, but incorrectly, believed to exist.

The value of the approach in *Babula* is illustrated by the earlier decision of the EAT in *Felter* **3.91** *v Cliveden Petroleum Company* (UKEAT/0533/05, 9 March 2006). Dr Felter was appointed as director and executive chairman of an oil company, Cliveden SA, which owned eight geological basins, known as the 'Chad Convention'. These were to be explored for oil. Fifty per cent of Cliveden's interest in the Chad Convention was sold to a Canadian corporation, Encana (the respondent). Subsequently, 50 per cent of Cliveden's shares were sold to two Chinese companies. Dr Felter alleged that he had made a protected disclosure by advising Cliveden that it was obliged to tell Encana of the share sale before it took place or immediately afterwards. The tribunal held that there was no such express or implied obligation under the agreement with Encana to do so. Following *Kraus*, this was decisive of the issue despite the difficult legal issues which arose as to what obligations should be implied under the agreements which the EAT referred to as 'impenetrable'. Following *Babula* these difficulties are lessened as, consistent with the aims of the legislation in encouraging workers to raise their concerns internally, the focus instead would be on the reasonableness of Dr Felter's belief. That is subject to two related caveats. First, whether or not the legal obligation in fact exists is likely to be relevant when assessing whether the belief is reasonable (paragraphs 3.79–3.85 above). Second, identification of the alleged obligation, its source and the basis for the belief as to a breach or likely breach has been held to be 'a necessary pre-requisite' to the tribunal's assessment of reasonable belief (see *Eiger Securities LLP v Korshunova* [2017] IRLR 115 (EAT), discussed at paragraph 3.118 below).

(6) Disclosures in relation to likely future failures

Each of the categories caters for concerns in relation to the future. There may be a disclosure **3.92** about a criminal offence which is 'likely to be committed', or about a likely failure to comply with a legal obligation, or that a miscarriage of justice is likely to occur, or that health and safety or the environment are/is likely to be endangered or damaged, respectively. In each case this raises issues as to the degree of likelihood that is required. In evaluating whether it was reasonable to believe that the relevant failure was likely, a tribunal might not be able simply to assume that an existing state of affairs will continue. There might be a need to consider whether the circumstances giving rise to the concerns are likely to be rectified before there is a relevant failure. For example, if there is a disclosure by an in-house accountant as to inadequacy in accounting records kept by the company, a tribunal will need to consider not only whether the information *tends to show* that the records did not satisfy statutory requirements, but also whether there is evidence tending to show that this *would be likely to be the case* by the time at which the records must be compliant.

This issue arose in *Kraus v Penna plc* [2004] IRLR 260, EAT. Mr Kraus's services were provided **3.93** to Syltone by Penna plc for human resources advice in relation to Syltone's proposed reorganization and redundancy programme. Kraus alleged that he had been told that a representative of Syltone had made it clear that he intended to reduce the workforce significantly beyond the number identified as being redundancies likely to result from the reorganization, and then to recruit back at a later date. He asserted that he had warned Syltone that it 'could breach employment legislation and would be vulnerable to claims for unfair dismissal in pursuing this course of action'. Shortly afterwards, Syltone dispensed with Kraus's services. He alleged that this was in response to his disclosures warning of possible breaches of employment legislation.

The employment tribunal struck out the claim on the basis that it had no reasonable prospect of success. The EAT upheld this decision. It emphasized that the word 'likely' means 'probable' or 'more probable than not'. Thus, in relation to a future breach of a legal obligation: 'The information disclosed should, in the reasonable belief of the worker at the time it is disclosed, tend to show that it is probable or more probable than not that the employer will fail to comply with the relevant legal obligation'. Since, on Kraus's own case, he had only warned that Syltone 'could' breach employment legislation and be vulnerable to unfair dismissal claims, the EAT concluded that 'Mr Kraus's belief was limited, at this early stage, to the possibility or the risk of a breach of employment legislation, depending on what eventually took place'.

3.94 As noted in the previous section, the Court of Appeal in *Babula v Waltham Forest College* [2007] EWCA Civ 174, [2007] ICR 1026 rejected the view in *Kraus* that the reasonable belief test does not apply to whether there is a legal obligation. However, the Court of Appeal (at para 77) sidestepped the question as to whether the EAT's interpretation of the word 'likely' was correct, as it did not affect the conclusions as to the meaning of reasonable belief. Wall LJ (at para 74) did express the view that *Kraus* was correctly decided on its facts. There are, however, some difficulties with the EAT's analysis. First, the decision was made at a pre-hearing review without hearing any evidence. It does not necessarily follow that because the disclosure is couched in cautious terms (such as referring only to a possibility of a breach) the worker could not have subjectively believed that there was a likely failure to comply. A worker may well be concerned to couch the disclosure in moderate terms, perhaps for fear of the reaction of management if more serious allegations are made. In each case there must therefore be consideration of the substance of the information disclosed, and of the worker's own case as to his/her state of belief and of the circumstances in which that stated belief is asserted. The decision in *Kraus* might be supportable on the basis that not only was the disclosure couched in terms of possibility rather than probability of breach, but that it was, as the EAT noted, merely a proposed course of conduct, in its preliminary stages, on which Mr Kraus had been engaged specifically to advise. As such, the tribunal could have concluded that even if Mr Kraus did believe that Syltone would have failed to comply, there was no reasonable basis for the belief at the time of the disclosure. However, rather than adopting this approach, the EAT (at para 21) founded its decision on the conclusion that, based on the terms of the disclosure, Mr Kraus did not himself believe the information tended to show a likely breach, so that the issue of the reasonableness of the belief did not arise.

3.95 Second, a line of high authority supporting the proposition that 'likely' does not necessarily mean 'more probable than not' was not cited to the EAT. This line of authority was considered by the House of Lords in *In re H and others* [1996] AC 563. It was noted that 'likely' in ordinary language may mean probable or might include what might well happen. The meaning therefore has to be considered in the light of the particular context. The case concerned care and supervision orders where a child was 'likely to suffer significant harm'. In that context 'likely' meant 'a real possibility, a possibility that cannot sensibly be ignored'. Similarly, in *Cream Holdings Ltd v Banerjee* [2004] UKHL 44, [2005] 1 AC 253 the various possible shades of meaning of the word 'likely' were considered in the context of the test for granting interim relief in freedom of expression cases. Section 12(4) of the Human Rights Act 1998 provides that relief should not be granted to restrain publication before trial unless the court is 'likely' to be satisfied that the applicant is likely to establish that publication should be allowed. In context the House of Lords concluded that 'likely' did not mean that it was necessary to establish in every case that success at trial was more likely than not. Further, Lord Nicholls, who gave the only substantive speech, noted (at para 12) that:

> as with most ordinary English words 'likely' has several different shades of meaning. Its meaning depends upon the context in which it is being used. Even when read in context its

meaning is not always precise. It is capable of encompassing different degrees of likelihood, varying from 'more likely than not' to 'may well'. In ordinary usage its meaning is often sought to be clarified by the addition of qualifying epithets as in phrases such as 'very likely' or 'quite likely'. In section 12(3) the context is that of a statutory threshold for the grant of interim relief by a court.

However, the decision in *Kraus* contains no acknowledgment that the term 'likely' may have **3.96** more than one ordinary meaning. Nor does it set out any explanation as to why the context indicates that the meaning 'more probable than not' should be applied. Instead, reliance was placed on cases in other contexts where 'likely' has been interpreted as more probable than not.[12] However, given the high judicial recognition that 'likely' can have more than one meaning, this reveals nothing as to why the context requires the more limiting interpretation to be applied in the context of section 43B.

As discussed in Chapter 10, consideration has also been given to the meaning of the term **3.97** 'likely' in the context of applications for interim relief in whistleblowing cases. In that context, it has been reaffirmed that 'likely' means a significantly higher degree of likelihood than simply being more likely than not: see *Ministry of Justice v Sarfraz* [2011] IRLR 562 at para 16, EAT; *Raja v Secretary of State for Justice* (UKEAT/0364/09, 15 February 2010); *Dandpat v The University of Bath and another* (UKEAT/0408/09 and others, 10 November 2009).[13] However the considerations which apply in that context are quite different from those applicable to whether there is a qualifying disclosure under ERA, section 43B. A greater degree of certainty is required in relation to interim relief because, notwithstanding the interim and predictive nature of the assessment, if the relief is granted the employer must continue paying the employee to the conclusion of the proceedings, and does not recover those payments if the claim ultimately fails.

By contrast the context in relation to section 43B may be said to support the construction **3.98** of 'likely' as meaning only a real possibility that cannot be ignored. This would sit well with the aim of the legislation in encouraging workers to come forward, and thereby provide an early warning of a relevant failure. Conversely, the implication of *Kraus* is that, if a worker discloses information in order to prevent wrongdoing, the disclosure will be unprotected if the worker believes the wrongdoing will be avoided. Indeed, this was the conclusion of the employment tribunal in *Owalo v Galliford Try Partnership Ltd* (Case No 3203344/03, 2 April 2004). Mr Owalo was a design and build contractor employed by a construction company. Acting in good faith, he disclosed that the design for a proposed building would be in breach of building regulations. The employment tribunal held that there was no qualifying disclosure precisely because on his own evidence he made the disclosure 'in order to rectify a problem before it arose'—although on the facts the dismissal was found not to be by reason of the disclosures.

As this illustrates, the logic of the reasoning in *Kraus* is that if a worker identifies a real risk of **3.99** serious wrongdoing, but is not confident that the information s/he discovered renders it more likely than not that the wrongdoing will take place, the worker will act at his/her own peril in bringing this to the attention of the employer to be investigated. It would be strange if a worker

---

[12] *Bailey v Rolls Royce (1971) Ltd* [1984] ICR 688 (CA), relating to legislation setting out restrictions on lifting, carrying, or moving a heavy load 'likely to cause injury'; *Taplin v C Shippam Ltd* [1978] IRLR 450, EAT, concerning the power of a tribunal to grant interim relief continuing a contract, and dicta of Lightman J in *BCCI v Ali (No 3)* [1999] IRLR 528 as to the meaning of 'likely' to destroy or seriously damage trust and confidence.

[13] Applications for permission to appeal were rejected: [2010] EWCA Civ 305 (Arden LJ) and 785 (Smith LJ).

who has the courage to come forward and report concerns should be unprotected because s/he believes that if s/he had not come forward someone else would probably, though not certainly, have done so, and thereby prevented the future wrongdoing. It would be all the more strange if the worker believes that the result of reporting concerns to the employer is likely to be that the employer will prevent the future wrongdoing, that as a result the worker cannot be said to have the requisite belief in a likely failure to comply with a legal obligation and be protected.

3.100   There is also a particular difficulty in factoring in the employer's likely response to the disclosure. The EAT in *Kraus* placed some emphasis (at para 20) on the fact that Mr Kraus had been engaged specifically to advise on the proposed course of conduct. The implication is that because he was to advise on the proposals, and there was nothing at that early stage to indicate that his advice would not be followed, it could not be said that there was a likely failure to comply with a legal obligation. However, there is a risk of absurd results if it is necessary to take account of the employer's likely reaction to the disclosure in order to ascertain whether a future relevant failure is likely. Take the example of an employee who has reasonable grounds to believe that a colleague, who is working out notice, is likely to copy unlawfully and take away the employer's confidential database unless prevented from doing so. If the employee simply says nothing, the database is likely to be stolen. However, if s/he makes a report to the employer, there will not be a likely breach because the colleague will immediately be placed on garden leave and will not have the opportunity to remove the database. It would be anomalous, and wholly contrary to the underlying policy of the legislation, if the employer could contend that there was no qualifying disclosure because, by reason of making the disclosure, the worker could not reasonably have believed that there was a likely relevant failure. Indeed, this would suggest that a worker who has no faith in his/her employer's ability or willingness to prevent a relevant failure may make a qualifying disclosure, but a worker who does have faith in the employer's willingness and ability to act appropriately may not. This is hardly conducive to the legislative aim of encouraging internal disclosures to the employer.

3.101   The danger of reaching a conclusion contrary to the policy of the legislation was recognized by the EAT in *Boulding v Land Securities Trillium (Media Services) Ltd* (EAT/0023/0306, 3 May 2006). Mr Boulding was a senior engineer who was responsible for monitoring compliance with regulations for safety of equipment. He raised concerns that certain certificates, known as 'CE markings', which indicated safety compliance, were missing from some of the equipment. This did not indicate a present breach of regulations, but there would be a breach if the equipment was supplied to a customer without the CE markings. At first instance, the tribunal dismissed the claim at the completion of the claimant's evidence, and before hearing the respondent's evidence. It held that although Mr Boulding had made the disclosure to his employer in good faith, it was clear on his own evidence that he did not have a reasonable belief in a likely failure to comply with a legal obligation. The tribunal relied in part on a finding that the equipment would not be supplied unless Mr Boulding agreed that compliance was complete, and also that on the evidence the employer's response to the concerns raised by Mr Boulding indicated that it intended to obtain the documentation.

3.102   The EAT allowed the appeal on the basis that the claimant should have been allowed to test the respondent's evidence. It emphasized that once a subjective belief in the likely failure is established, an objective standard is then to be applied to the finding of fact as to what was believed. This required consideration of the employer's evidence bearing on what was likely to happen, rather than just looking at the evidence of the employee. However, the EAT appears to have been willing to contemplate that there may be a likely failure to comply with the obligation to supply the equipment with CE markings even though Mr Boulding's own evidence was that he was confident that documentation would be obtained. Whilst the *ratio* of the decision may be limited to the conclusion that the case should not have been stopped without hearing full evidence, this does not sit easily with the emphasis in *Kraus* that a 'likely' failure is one that is probable or more probable than not. The approach taken by the EAT reflected an expressly purposive approach to the legislation and the facts. The EAT emphasized (at para 24) that in whistleblowing cases 'there is a certain generosity in the construction of the statute and the treatment of the facts. Whistleblowing is a form of discrimination claim'. In assessing whether the disclosure was protected, the EAT noted (at para 31) that, given that Mr Boulding had acted in good faith in raising appropriate compliance issues, and had done so after obtaining appropriate advice, it would be 'out of step with the regime of protection for an employee in such a situation not to have the statutory protection, as he saw it, although steps were being taken to provide documentation'.

(7) Reform? Reasonable suspicion or concern

The requirement for a reasonable belief in the truth of the information and that it tends to **3.103** show a relevant failure has given rise to some controversy as to whether it sets the threshold for protection too high. It might well be that the worker does not and cannot know, or have any belief, as to whether the information is true or reliable. The worker might still have a concern that appropriate investigation is needed to identify whether or not the information is true. The policy of the legislation is for the concerns to be reported internally, without risk of reprisal, so that they can be investigated. Reflecting these considerations, in her Fifth report,[14] Dame Janet Smith concluded, in relation to the reasonable belief test in section 43B, that:

> it seems to me that this requirement ... may operate against the public interest, especially in cases where the worker has access to incomplete or secondhand information. I am concerned that, in order to make a disclosure even to his/her employer, a worker has to be in the position where s/he could say, for example, 'I believe that this disclosure tends to show that a crime has been committed and my belief is reasonable'.... if this threshold were applied to workers having the state of mind of [various people who could have raised early concerns about Shipman], I doubt that they would confidently have been able to cross that threshold. Moreover, I do not think that anyone answering a call on the PCaW[15] helpline could confidently have assured any of those persons (had they been 'workers') that their state of mind was such that they were guaranteed protection.
>
> The onus should not, in my view, be on an individual to establish 'reasonable belief' in the case of internal disclosures and disclosures to external regulators. The public interest would, in my view, be best served by substituting 'suspicion' for 'belief'.

The response proposed by Dame Janet Smith was that it should be sufficient to show a **3.104** 'reasonable suspicion', rather than requiring a 'reasonable belief' that the disclosure tends to show a relevant failure. However, a worker might be sceptical of the information received, yet sufficiently concerned to believe that the matter needs to be properly investigated. It may therefore be more appropriate to refer to a 'reasonable suspicion or concern' that the disclosure tends to show a relevant failure. Whilst this formulation may be clearer, it is suggested that the legislation as currently framed is capable of being construed consistently with this. Once it is accepted, as emphasized in *Darnton*, that the standard of belief will vary according to the circumstances, and that due consideration must be given to the implications of the 'tends to show' test, the legislation is capable of being purposively construed so that the reasonable belief requirement is satisfied where an employee, though sceptical of information, reasonably believes that it has sufficient credence to warrant further investigation, and that this information if true would tend to indicate a breach of an obligation (albeit that there may be other factors or explanations that ultimately show this not to be the case).

---

[14] Fifth Shipman Inquiry report, Cm. 6394 (2004), paras 11.110 and 11.111.
[15] Referring to Public Concern at Work—the whistleblowing charity.

D. The Six Categories

3.105 There are six defined categories of protectable disclosure which are described by ERA, section 43B(1) as 'qualifying disclosures'. There is scope for considerable overlap between the six categories in particular cases. Damage to the environment may, for example, fall within subsections (a), (b), and (e) of section 43B(1).

3.106 It is also noteworthy that there is no necessity for a link between the matters disclosed and the actual employment of the worker: see *Hibbins v Hesters Way Neighbourhood Project* [2009] ICR 319, Silber J. The discloser might simply be acting as a concerned employed citizen.

3.107 The six categories of relevant failure constitute a complete statutory regime. There is no concluding catch-all provision to give flexibility to the concept of protected disclosure. Tribunals therefore have no licence to go outside the parameters of these six protected areas. There is also no specific reference to financial irregularities, although these will usually fall within the rubric of criminal offences of one sort or another, such as fraud, theft, or false accounting. The Whistleblowing Commission set up by Public Concern at Work suggested the addition of two further categories: gross waste or mismanagement of funds and serious misuse or abuse of authority.[16] The report noted that equivalent legislation in Australia and in the United States includes these categories. Thus in the United States the Whistleblower Protection Act 1989 covers disclosures of 'gross mismanagement', 'gross waste of funds', and 'abuse of authority'. These are more elastic concepts in the hands of the courts. The Whistleblowing Commission suggested, though, that these categories be limited to operations rather than policy issues. More broadly, the Commission's report (para 76) favoured having a non-exhaustive list of categories of wrongdoing, allowing scope for wrongdoing not included in the list to be covered. Indeed, to some extent the approach of having a comprehensive list of relevant failures may reflect the approach to the legislation prior to the amendments made by ERRA, in that there was no provision regulating the importance of the subject matter of the disclosure other than that it fell within one of the six categories. That is changed with the introduction of the public interest test.

3.108 As the legislation is presently formulated, however, it remains necessary to show that one of the six categories of relevant failure is engaged. We now consider in turn the scope of each of the categories of information referred to in the statute.

(1) Criminal offence

3.109 The first of the relevant failures is that 'a criminal offence has been committed, is being committed or is likely to be committed'. This involves a criminal offence of whatever degree of seriousness, and may include breach of a minor regulation. There is no specific geographical scope placed on where the crime may be committed or whether it is a crime under the law of the United Kingdom or any other country or territory (ERA, section 43B(2)). As noted above (paragraph 3.86), the test of reasonable belief applies whether or not the criminal offence exists, so that a worker might reasonably, but incorrectly, believe that there was such an offence (*Babula v Waltham Forest College* [2007] EWCA Civ 174, [2007] ICR 1026).

3.110 In *Milne v The Link Asset and Security Company Ltd* (UKEAT/0867/04, 26 September 2005) it was argued that a decision was flawed due to a failure to draw the distinction between section 43B(1)(a) relating to a criminal offence and section 43B(1)(b) relating to legal obligations. The claimant was a broker and manager of the respondent brokerage firm. He signed up for the respondent's employee benefit trust tax scheme (EBT). He raised concerns about the EBT

---

[16] Whistleblowing Commission report (November 2013) para 77.

which, after his dismissal, he sought to rely on as protected disclosures. Disciplinary proceedings were brought against Mr Milne. He resigned claiming constructive dismissal. Although not mentioned in his resignation letter, he later claimed that concerns which he had raised about the EBT amounted to protected disclosures and he had been dismissed by reason of them. The employment tribunal found this was not the case and that the respondent had genuine concerns as to his conduct and performance. It also held that whilst he had genuine concerns about the EBT, he did not have a genuine belief in the illegality of the scheme. It was argued that the employment tribunal had only made findings relevant to section 43B(1)(a), whereas the claim was under section 43B(1)(b) (legal obligation). This was said to be significant due to the different mental elements. Thus, the employment tribunal referred to whether there was tax evasion, whereas it was sufficient for section 43(1)(b) if the scheme was unlawful. The employment tribunal also contrasted a belief in illegality with a concern as to Mr Milne's own financial position, whereas there could be a breach of a legal obligation in relation to his own tax position. The EAT acknowledged that distinction, and that the language indicated that there were errors made by the employment tribunal in using language appropriate for a claim under section 43(1)(a). Ultimately, however, it concluded (at para 58) that the employment tribunal probably did appreciate that it was dealing with a section 43(1)(b) claim. Whilst in some cases the distinction may be significant, nothing turned on this in Milne's case. The employment tribunal found that Milne lacked a genuine or reasonable belief in the illegality and had acted opportunistically in bringing the claim to put pressure on the employer through litigation. A costs order against Milne was therefore upheld.

(2) Legal obligation

3.111 Failure to comply with a legal obligation includes a breach of any statutory requirement, contractual obligation, common law obligation (eg negligence, nuisance, defamation), or administrative law requirement.

3.112 This might include a legal obligation imposed by a different jurisdiction. This was the case in *Bhatia v Sterlite Industries (India) Ltd and another* (ET, Case No 2204571/00, 2 May 2001). Mr Bhatia was employed in London by a company listed on the National Stock Exchange of India, which also had operations in Australia and, through a subsidiary company, in the United States. His role involved responsibility for documentation in relation to mergers and acquisitions. It was decided that the respondent's optical fibre cable division should be listed on the New York Stock Exchange via an initial public offering (IPO). While preparing for a presentation in relation to this, the claimant was told by the respondent's chairman to include reference to a particular product as an existing business line. But the claimant knew that this was untrue. He told the chairman that if the IPO documentation included the product as being an existing business line this would be illegal under American legislation. The claimant later also had occasion to inform the chairman that proposals in relation to conversion of preference shares in the Australian subsidiary into ordinary shares would be in breach of Australian law. The tribunal concluded that the claimant had a reasonable belief that the disclosures tended to show likely criminal offences and likely breaches of legal obligations under American and Australian law.

3.113 There is no requirement that the disclosure must relate to breach of a legal obligation by another person. It may relate to disclosure by a worker of his/her own breach of an obligation: see *Odong v Chubb Security Personnel* (UKEAT/0819/02, 13 May 200)3[17] and *Bolton School v Evans* [2006] IRLR 500.[18] However, where the disclosure relates to a worker's own

---

[17] See para 3.39 above.
[18] See paras 3.40 and 3.74 above.

wrongdoing, the employer may well be able to show that detriment was not on grounds of the disclosure, but due to the breach of the obligation. It would not be sufficient for the worker to show that the wrongdoing would not have been discovered but for the protected disclosure: see *Harrow LBC v Knight* [2003] IRLR 140 and Chapter 8.

3.114 There is no requirement that the obligation must reach a minimum level of seriousness. However, in relation to trivial concerns, the worker may face difficulty in establishing a reasonable belief that the disclosure was made in the public interest (see Chapter 4). But the reasonable belief test allows scope to respect the value judgement made by the worker making the disclosure. Thus, for example, what to some may seem a minor health and safety issue, might reasonably be seen differently by an employee who takes the view that there is a wider importance in strict compliance with health and safety requirements.

3.115 The issue as to the scope of what may constitute a 'legal obligation' was considered in *Parkins v Sodexho* [2002] IRLR 109. Commenting on the approach taken in *Parkins*, in the subsequent decision of *Douglas v Birmingham City Council and others* (UKEAT/0518/02, 17 March 2003), the EAT noted that:

> Judge Altman gave a wide meaning to the term 'legal obligation', which we have cited. The Tribunal adopted a passage in the *Encyclopaedia of Labour Relations Law Eds Hepple O'Higgins and Upex* as follows:
>
> > 'This includes a breach of any statutory requirement; contractual obligation; common law obligation for example negligence, nuisance, defamation or an administrative law requirement.'

3.116 The EAT in *Parkins* (Judge Altman) specifically held that the term 'legal obligation' was wide enough to cover obligations under the claimant's contract of employment.[19] It held (paras 15 and 16) that:

> it is obviously not sufficient under Section 43B that there should simply be a breach of contract but what has to be shown is first a breach of the employment contract as being a breach of a legal obligation under that contract. Secondly, there must be a reasonable belief that this has, is, or is likely to happen on the part of the worker. Thirdly, there must be a disclosure of that which is alleged to be the reason for dismissal. In other words, where it is a breach of the contract of employment, the worker is bound to make his case on the basis that the reason for dismissal is that he has complained that his employer has broken the contract of employment.
>
> Subject to that as being the necessary basis for the whole complaint, under the protection from protected disclosures, we can see no real basis for excluding a legal obligation which arises from a contract of employment from any other form of legal obligation. It seems to us that it falls within the terms of the Act. It is a very broadly drawn provision.

3.117 The decision now falls to be considered in the light of the requirement to hold a reasonable belief that the disclosure was made in the public interest, which we consider further in Chapter 4.

3.118 As to the approach to reasonable belief in relation to legal obligations, important guidance was set out in *Eiger Securities LLP v Korshunova* [2017] IRLR 115 (EAT). The EAT in *Eiger* (at para 47) held that, save in obvious cases, identification of the nature of the legal obligation the claimant believed to apply and how it was believed there had been (or more precisely, tended to show)

---

[19] Approved by the EAT in *Fincham v HM Prison Service* (EAT/0925/01/RN, 19 December 2001) (para 24); *Kraus v Penna plc* [2004] IRLR 260 at para 30. In *Felter v Cliveden Petroleum Company* (EAT/0533/05, 9 March 2006) the EAT noted (at para 12) that counsel had reserved the right to argue on appeal that *Parkins v Sodexho* was wrongly decided and that 'legal obligations' refers only to statutory, not common law, obligations. There is no proper basis for implying any such limitation.

a failure to comply, is 'a necessary precursor' to the assessment of whether the claimant held a reasonable belief. Slade J explained (at para 46) that 'identification of the obligation does not have to be detailed or precise but it must be more than a belief that certain actions are wrong'. That allows for varying circumstances in which the issue may arise (see paras 3.65 to 3.68). But the application to the facts in *Eiger* indicates a difficulty in application. As noted at para 3.14 above, the claimant worked on a broking floor and took issue with the managing director (and others) using her computer terminal for trading without identifying themselves. The EAT held that the ET had erred in failing to determine what legal obligation the claimant believed to have been breached. But the ET accepted that the claimant genuinely believed that what she was disclosing was a breach of the regulations governing the industry, and in contravention of what she believed to be a legal obligation on the respondent to be transparent with clients and not to mislead them as to who was conducting communications. As such on its face she identified, albeit not in a detailed or precise way, the nature of the obligation and what was believed to be the source. We suggest that the better approach, rather than a requirement for the legal obligation to be further defined, is to take into account as part of the assessment of reasonable belief, what at the time of making the disclosure the claimant understood to be the nature of the legal obligation (here believed to be a breach of regulatory requirements as to transparency), why it was understood to be a legal obligation and why the information tended to show a relevant failure. Any vagueness in relation to this would be one factor in the assessment of reasonableness of belief, to be weighed in all the circumstances. If it was established that there either was or was not such an obligation that could also bear on reasonableness (see paras 3.79 to 3.85).

The EAT's decision in *Eiger* might be explained on the basis that, in relation to reasonableness of belief, rather than focussing on a breach of a legal obligation the ET said only that it was reasonable to believe that what she was saying was true and applicable in the industry. The EAT concluded that it was not obvious that this entailed a breach of a legal obligation. It was insufficient that she believed the conduct was 'wrong'; that was also consistent with only being 'immoral, undesirable or in breach of guidance without being in breach of a legal obligation' (para 46). Consistently with this, it has been held that, without more, a mere generalized statement that the employee is 'concerned with financial probity' will not suffice: *Sim v Manchester Action on Street Health* (UKEAT/10085/01, 6 December 2001) at para 4.

3.119 Similarly, a 'professional obligation' will not suffice unless the worker reasonably believes that it amounts to a legal obligation. This was one of the bases for rejecting a protected disclosure dismissal claim in *Butcher v Salvage Association* (UKEAT/988/01, 21 January 2002). Mr Butcher, was employed by the respondent as chief financial officer. He raised a concern internally that, in being asked to adopt the chief executive's preferred approach to presentation of financial reports, he was being invited to change figures and monthly management reports to the board in a way which he believed would be misleading. The ET heard expert evidence on the point, concluded that Mr Butcher's concerns were about acting professionally and that it was 'contrived to seek to promote an issue as to professional ethics into a legal obligation'. Nor were professional ethics requirements incorporated into his contract since the accounts were only internal (so there was no question of misleading a third party or the board—who were aware of the issues), and in preparing the accounts in the way required he was acting on the instructions of the board and the governing committee. The appeal on this issue was dismissed by the EAT at a preliminary hearing, and permission to appeal was refused by the Court of Appeal ([2002] EWCA Civ 867). The decision is, however, now to be read subject to the decision of the Court of Appeal in *Babula* that a reasonable belief in the existence of a legal obligation, even if wrong, is sufficient.

3.120 Whether disclosure of a breach of a self-regulatory code qualifies for protection will turn upon whether there is reasonably believed to be a legal obligation to comply with the rule.

This might give rise to difficult issues of construction. Whilst a breach of a code of conduct might enable the self-regulatory organization to take disciplinary action, it may in some contexts be difficult to identify a *legal* obligation which has been flouted. But the absence of a clear distinction between a legal and a regulatory obligation indicates that a subjective belief that a regulatory requirement entails a legal obligation would readily be viewed as reasonable. In many cases the regulatory obligations will be imposed in pursuance of a statutory power to do so. Taking as an example the rules contained in the handbook of the Financial Conduct Authority (FCA), these are made pursuant to the statutory power to do so under s139 of the Financial Services and Markets Act 2000 (FSMA). Although a breach of the FCA's Principles is not 'actionable' in the sense of giving rise to an individual cause of action in a court of law, it is still capable of giving rise to obligations as between firms and customers including requirements to pay compensation: see *R (British Bankers Association) v Financial Services Authority* [2011] Bus LR 1531 at para 71. It is far from apparent why this, although no doubt a regulatory obligation, should not also be regarded as a legal obligation, particularly having regard to the wide definition approved in *Parkins v Sodexho* and *Douglas*. Indeed, this is reinforced by the other potential consequences of breach including public censure (section 205 FSMA), financial penalties (section 206 FSMA), injunctive relief on application of the FCA or Secretary of State to prevent further breach (section 380 FSMA), and a restitution order (sections 382 and 384 FSMA). Further, aside from the FCA context, even where regulatory provisions have no statutory foundation, they will often be founded on implied contractual obligations between members and those subject to regulatory governance: see eg *Modahl v British Athletic Federation Ltd* [2002] 1 WLR 1092 (CA). Conversely, as highlighted in *Eiger* (paras 38, 46), a breach of what is (or is only believed to be) only industry guidance would not suffice.

(3) Miscarriage of justice

3.121 The third heading of relevant failure is 'that a miscarriage of justice has occurred, is occurring, or is likely to occur'. This would include all interference with the proper judicial process, such as perjury or failure to disclose evidence.

3.122 'Miscarriage of justice' is not a widely used term of art, although it is mentioned in section 2 of the Criminal Appeals Act 1968. As such, there is little case law to guide tribunals and they can be expected to adopt a common-sense, broad-brush approach to this term. An instructive case in this context, which shows the potential ambit of the term, is *Lion Laboratories v Evans* [1985] 1 QB 526 (CA). Two employees of Lion Laboratories disclosed to the press information casting doubt on the reliability of breathalyser equipment produced by the employer company. These machines were used by the police to measure levels of intoxication in drink-driving cases. The Court of Appeal decided that, because of the public interest in the matter, wide disclosure was justified since it related to potential miscarriages of justice. An injunction was therefore refused.

3.123 One potential difficulty inherent in the 'miscarriage of justice' category is that it may involve revisiting previous decisions and therefore be in tension with the interest of finality of litigation. This issue was addressed in *Parker v Northumbrian Water* [2011] IRLR 652. Mr Parker had brought proceedings which concerned his complaint relating to changes made by his employer to the treatment of hours not worked on days when employees had been rostered to work. The proceedings were initially for unlawful deduction of wages. They were recast as a claim for a declaration of particulars of employment. Various declarations were duly made. After Mr Parker was dismissed he brought various new claims including one of unfair dismissal. He sought by amendment to add claims of detriment and dismissal by reason of protected disclosures. The dismissal claim was permitted, but the detriment claim was rejected. Following a review, one ground for rejecting the claim was that, in effect, the protected disclosure relied upon amounted to a collateral attack on the decision in the first proceedings. This was because the alleged disclosure involved an allegation that the employer had lied to the employment tribunal and EAT and that, as a result of misleading them, there had been a miscarriage of justice. Allowing the appeal, HHJ Hand QC accepted that Parliament must have intended that a case could be raised in which the reasonable belief related to the incorrectness of a previous decision. The protection against abuse was the reasonable belief test. Even though there had been an unsuccessful appeal against the decision in the first proceedings that did not mean that the protected disclosure claim should be barred as an abuse of process. Clearly, it could be highly relevant to the reasonableness of the belief, although that would depend on all the circumstances. But if the employment tribunal ultimately concluded that the belief was not reasonable, that would be a determination of the claim on the merits. That was in contrast to an estoppel or abuse of process argument which prevents a claim from proceeding on the merits at all.

(4) Health and safety risks

The fourth category is that the health or safety of any individual has been, is being, or is likely to be endangered. This is potentially a very wide category, covering health risks to customers, employees, the person making the disclosure, or any other person. Thus, as noted above (see paragraph 3.35), in *Fincham v HM Prison Service* (UKEAT/0925/01 and EAT/0991/01, 19 December 2002),[20] the EAT considered that the claimant's complaint that she was under pressure and under stress could not be anything other than a statement that her health and safety was being or was at least likely to be endangered. **3.124**

Nor, prior to the requirement for a reasonable belief that the disclosure was made in the public interest, was there any express provision excluding trivial concerns. This issue was raised in the Parliamentary debates in Standing Committee. Ian McCartney, the Minister of State, Department of Trade and Industry, commented[21] that: **3.125**

> we would not want the full protection of the law to apply to, for example, a worker who discloses that his boss smokes, drives a car, or quite legitimately manufactures hazardous chemicals. If, however, his boss smokes in a munitions factory, that might be a different matter, as might the fact that the firm pollutes a river by discharging poisonous waste into it, or that the manufacturing process cuts corners on safety, or that the disposal of dangerous chemical by-products is unregulated. Disclosures about such matters will be covered by the Bill.

However, Mr McCartney explained that the government was not in favour of a proposed amendment specifically to address this on the basis that: **3.126**

> … it could have deterred people from raising issues of proper concern and led to legalism and complex case law.

> The Government are satisfied that the Bill contains sufficient safeguards to ensure that workers will not be encouraged to disclose trivial matters or concerns. Individuals must act in good faith if they are to attract protection. External disclosures are protected only if a worker acts reasonably.

As this indicates, whilst trivial concerns are not in terms excluded, if the concerns are trivial that would be liable to raise questions as to whether it was genuinely believed that there was a danger to health and safety and whether that belief was reasonable. But in any event the issue is now addressed by the public interest test introduced in 2013. Indeed, whether trivial concerns may be raised featured prominently in the Hansard debates leading up to the introduction of that public interest test by the Enterprise and Regulatory Reform Act **3.127**

---

[20] See paras 3.35 and 3.36, above.
[21] Standing Committee D: Wednesday, 11 March 1998.

2013. Additional limits may also arise from the nature of the particular allegation. That was the case in *Easwaran v St George's University of London* (UKEAT/0167/10, 24 June 2010) where, as discussed at paragraph 3.23 above, the claimant complained that a medical demonstration room was 'freezing' and that this breached basic health and safety requirements as it could cause pneumonia. The claim failed as the claimant lacked a reasonable belief, given that pneumonia is not a condition caused by working in cold temperatures. Nor had the room temperature otherwise fallen below a level such as to endanger health and safety.

3.128 The ERA (in sections 44 and 100) already provides some protection on victimization for health and safety matters, being protection against detriment and dismissal if the employee is (in summary) disadvantaged or dismissed for carrying out health and safety activities or because the employee is a member of a works safety committee or refuses to work in circumstances of danger which the employee 'reasonably believed to be serious and imminent and which he could not reasonably have been expected to avert'. This test is naturally a difficult one to satisfy. However, it also includes disclosures as to future health and safety risks to the employer which is in some respects more widely drawn than section 43B, as interpreted in *Kraus*. Employees are protected from detriments other than dismissal (by ERA, section 44(1)(c)) and are to be regarded as automatically unfairly dismissed (pursuant to ERA, section 100(1)(c)) if:

> (c) being an employee at a place where—
>
> > (i)   there was no such representative or safety committee, or
> > (ii) there was such a representative or safety committee but it was not reasonably practicable for the employee to raise the matter by those means,
>
> he brought to his employer's attention, by reasonable means, circumstances connected with his work which he reasonably believed were harmful or *potentially harmful* to health or safety. (emphasis added)[22]

3.129 In this context, therefore, the bar is set at a lower level than 'likelihood' of danger to health and safety. Potential harm is sufficient. As against that, protection is confined to employees, rather than the wider class of workers who are covered under the protected disclosure provisions: see *Smith v Carillion (JM) Ltd* [2015] IRLR 467 (CA).

(5) Damage to the environment

3.130 The fifth category is 'that the environment has been, is being, or is likely to be damaged'. This would cover a wide range of matters. Examples might be potential oil spills, toxic waste emissions, or other pollution risks. In *Schaathun v Executive & Business Aviation Support Ltd* (UKEAT/0226/12/LA, 30 June 2015), the claimant purportedly made numerous disclosures, including one to the Environment Agency, about the storage of hazardous substances.

In many cases there will be an overlap with other relevant failures such as in relation to legal obligations or endangering health and safety, as in *Collins v National Trust* (ET, Case No 2507255/05, 17 January 2006), which is considered in Chapter 5 (paragraph 5.119).

(6) Cover-ups

3.131 The final category of relevant failure is 'that information tending to show any matter falling within any of the preceding paragraphs has been, or is likely to be deliberately concealed'.

---

[22] See *Masiak v City Restaurants (UK) Ltd* [1999] IRLR 780 where it was held that ERA, s 100(1)(e) is not confined to concerns as to the health and safety of other employees but covers concerns as to the health and safety of the general public.

It is one of the first reactions (and perhaps a natural reaction) in those about whom the whistle is blown to seek to restrict information about the malpractice. If that is done deliberately, disclosures about the cover-up are as well protected as would be the original information about the malpractice itself. This would not, however, cover accidental or unintended concealment. **3.132**

E. Criminal Disclosures

(1) Exclusion for disclosures that are criminal offences

There is special provision (ERA, section 43B(3)) that where the disclosure of the information is itself a crime (eg it breaches the Official Secrets Act 1989) it does not qualify as being a 'qualifying disclosure' under the Act. This is especially controversial since it might be said that one area where the whistle might most usefully be blown in the public interest is in the Civil Service or the security services where to do so would often amount to a breach of the Official Secrets Act, and therefore be a crime. **3.133**

Of more general application, particular difficulties may arise in relation to offences under the Data Protection Act 1998 (DPA). In particular, section 55 of the DPA provides for an offence in the following terms: **3.134**

    (1) A person must not knowingly or recklessly, without the consent of the data controller—

        (a) obtain or disclose personal data or the information contained in personal data, or

        (b) procure the disclosure to another person of the information contained in personal data.

On its face this is potentially of wide application. The word 'data' is widely defined. It includes any information which 'is being processed by means of equipment operating automatically in response to instructions given for that purpose' or which is 'recorded with the intention that it should be processed by means of such equipment' (DPA, section 1(1)). It also includes non-automated records where these are part of a 'relevant filing system' as defined in DPA, section 1(1). 'Personal data' is widely defined as data which relates to living individuals who can be identified from the data. There are also certain categories of data identified in DPA, section 2 which constitute 'sensitive personal data'. These include matters such as the racial or ethnic origin of the data subject (ie the person who is the subject of the personal data) or his 'physical or mental health or condition'. However, the offence under DPA, section 55 is not restricted to this narrower category, but includes personal data generally. Subject to the defences which are set out in section 55, where a person obtains information relating to one or more identifiable individuals from the employer's electronic records and knowingly discloses that information without the permission of the employer (as the data controller), section 55(1) would apply. Since the disclosure would involve the commission of a criminal offence, it could not be a qualifying disclosure. **3.135**

DPA, section 55(2) sets out circumstances where disclosing the personal data is not an offence. It provides: **3.136**

    (2) Subsection (1) does not apply to a person who shows—

        (a) that the obtaining, disclosing or procuring—

            (i) was necessary for the purpose of preventing or detecting crime, or

            (ii) was required or authorised by or under any enactment, by any rule of law or by the order of a court,

        (b) that he acted in the reasonable belief that he had in law the right to obtain or disclose the data or information or, as the case may be, to procure the disclosure of the information to the other person,

(c) that he acted in the reasonable belief that he would have had the consent of the data controller if the data controller had known of the obtaining, disclosing or procuring and the circumstances of it, or

(d) that in the particular circumstances the obtaining, disclosing or procuring was justified as being in the public interest.

3.137 The issues raised by section 55(2) will be in play in most cases where there would be a qualifying disclosure but for ERA, section 43B(3). In many cases section 55(2)(b) will apply, since the scheme of PIDA is to encourage disclosure to an appropriate person, and having regard to the further tests for protection where there is a wider disclosure. Nevertheless, the test of a reasonable belief in the right to obtain or disclose the data or information is conceptually different from the test of a reasonable belief in information tending to show a relevant failure. An employee who does not believe that s/he has any right to disclose information consisting of personal data may opt to make the disclosure in spite of this because of a belief that it tends to show a relevant failure.

3.138 In those circumstances the employee may still be able to fall back on the exceptions in section 55(2)(a) and (d). In neither case is reasonable belief part of the test. It may be argued, therefore, that this connotes that a court must make an objective assessment of whether the disclosure is in fact in the public interest or necessary to prevent crime. We suggest, however, that a court would be entitled to have regard to the protected disclosure legislative scheme as providing an indication of whether the disclosure is justified in the public interest. Thus, if an employee makes a disclosure which (apart from ERA, section 43B(3)) would be a qualifying disclosure and would be protected, this of itself will often be a compelling basis for determining that the disclosure is justified in the public interest.[23]

3.139 By way of an illustration of the difficulties which might arise, suppose an employee believes that his/her employer has been defrauding HMRC by under-declaring amounts paid by way of salary to employees. The employee provides information which is the basis for the concerns to HMRC (the Commissioners for HMRC being the relevant prescribed persons under ERA, section 43F), but the information supplied is from the employer's tax records relating to its employees. Authorization from the employer to make the disclosures is neither provided nor sought. If the employee had a reasonable belief that the information disclosed tended to show a criminal offence, and a reasonable belief that the information disclosed and any allegations contained in it were substantially true, then, subject to section 43B(3), the disclosure would be protected under section 43F. We suggest that this should also be a sufficient basis to demonstrate that the disclosure was justified in the public interest under DPA, section 55(2)(d), even if on investigation the concerns proved not to be correct.[24] Similarly, it would be likely that the employee could show a reasonable belief in the right to disclose the information to the appropriate authorities.

(2) Consequential procedural issues

3.140 Because of ERA, section 43B(3) there may be an overlap of jurisdictions dealing with a particular disclosure. Where the disclosure is alleged to constitute a criminal offence and proceedings are in progress or (possibly) anticipated,[25] the employment tribunal might be willing, upon

---

[23] But see the discussion in Chapter 4 of *Street v Derbyshire Unemployed Workers' Centre* [2005] ICR 97 (CA) at para 4.80 where the Court of Appeal regarded the opening words of PIDA as requiring the worker to act in the public interest rather than denoting that disclosures made in accordance with the PIDA requirements were thereby to be regarded as having been made in the public interest.

[24] See by analogy *In re a Company* [1989] 1 Ch 477, discussed in Chapter 14.

[25] But see *Halstead v Paymentshield Group Holdings Ltd* [2012] IRLR 586 (where the Court of Appeal concluded that it was not appropriate for there to be a stay of tribunal proceedings on the basis of threatened or anticipated High Court proceedings) and *Asda Stores Ltd v Brierley* [2016] ICR 945 (where the Court of Appeal

application by either party, to postpone the tribunal proceedings. There is no overriding right for a party in criminal proceedings to have them stayed pending the conclusion of criminal proceedings in connection with the same matters: *Guinness plc v Saunders* 17 October 1988, unreported (CA). In relation to whether to grant a postponement the tribunal has a broad discretion taking into account what the interests of justice require: *Carter v Credit Change Ltd* [1979] IRLR 361 (CA). In considering whether to allow an adjournment the tribunal will ordinarily consider the degree of similarity between the issues before the tribunal, the extent of the delay likely to be caused, how late the application is made, and the reasons for the delay in making an application for an adjournment. Relevant considerations that may point in favour of postponing the employment tribunal proceedings in the event of a substantial overlap in issues include whether there are complex factual or legal matters to determine and voluminous documentation to be considered, and whether more of the issues could be determined in the criminal or high court proceedings: see *Mindimaxnox LLP v Gover* (UKEAT/0225/10/DA7, 7 December 2010) (concerning a stay pending concurrent civil proceedings in the High Court).

The arguments in favour of a postponement are likely to be more powerful where, as in the case **3.141** of section 43B(3), the tribunal has directly to consider whether the disclosure constituted an offence, than when the issue of criminal conduct arises in ordinary unfair dismissal proceedings. This is illustrated by the leading case of *Bastick v James Lane (Turf Accountants) Ltd* [1979] ICR 778. Mr Bastick was dismissed from his employment in a betting office for dishonestly paying out on losing bets. There were also criminal charges of theft arising out of the same activities. It was argued that if the tribunal proceedings took place first, Mr Bastick would be prejudiced either because he might lead evidence in the employment tribunal proceedings which would prejudice him in the criminal trial, or by being inhibited in advancing evidence in the tribunal proceedings. Despite this, his application for a postponement of the employment tribunal proceedings was refused and the decision was upheld by the EAT as a legitimate exercise of discretion. In refusing the postponement the employment tribunal placed emphasis on the unacceptable delay that would result from postponement, since the issues before the criminal court and the tribunal were different. The issue in the criminal court would focus on whether Mr Bastick had acted dishonestly, whereas the focus in the tribunal proceedings was on what the employer knew and on the reasonableness of the decision to dismiss. That consideration would not apply, however, where the issue of criminality is directly raised, as where section 43B(3) is in issue.

(3) Standard of proof

During the Parliamentary debates on the Public Interest Disclosure Bill 1998, at the House **3.142** of Lords committee stage on 5 June 1998, an unsuccessful attempt was made to introduce an amendment limiting the exclusion in section 43B(3) to where the worker acted knowingly or recklessly in some way. It was argued that the exclusion could otherwise work unfairly, especially as it could apply to strict liability offences. In rejecting this argument, Lord Borrie QC emphasized that protection is intended to apply to disclosures in the public interest and that 'it is very difficult to say that the commission of a criminal offence by a discloser can nonetheless be in the public interest'.[26]

Lord Nolan[27] and Lord Borrie QC,[28] speaking on the Bill in the House of Lords, opined **3.143** that where no such proceedings were in prospect but the employer alleges that the disclosure

---

emphasized the significance of there being parallel proceedings on foot, and concluded that there was no power to stay equal pay proceedings in the employment tribunal merely because the High Court was considered to be a more appropriate forum for such claims). But no issue arose in those cases as to prospective criminal proceedings.

[26] *Hansard* HL, 5 June 1998, col 616.
[27] ibid, col 614.
[28] ibid, cols 616, 617.

constituted a crime, the standard of proof which the tribunal should apply would be effectively a criminal one. Both based their comments on the decision in *In re A Solicitor* [1992] 2 All ER 335. The government spokesman, Lord Haskell,[29] while pointing out that the effects of such a finding would not be the same as in a criminal court, stated that a 'high standard of proof' would be required. However, subsequent authorities have emphasized that it is not appropriate to refer to a higher standard of proof: see *In re S-B* [2010] AC 678 at para 13; *In re B* [2009] AC 11; *In re D* [2008] 1 WLR 1499. The standard of proof remains the balance of probability. In some cases the unusual nature of what is alleged may, as a matter of good sense, bear on the inherent likelihood of it occurring. However, there is no necessary connection between seriousness and inherent probability: see eg *In re B* per Lord Hoffmann at para 15 and per Baroness Hale at paras 72 and 73; *In re S-B* at paras 12–14.

F. Legal Professional Privilege

3.144 ERA, section 43B(4) makes special provision to prevent a legal adviser claiming protection under the Act if s/he discloses information which was supplied by a worker, if the worker could have claimed legal professional privilege in relation to such information. The legal adviser will not be able to assert that s/he has made a qualifying disclosure if s/he discloses the information without authority from the worker client.

3.145 On a literal reading of section 43B(4), it might be argued that if the lawyer then discloses the privileged information to the employer on the client's instructions to do so, this is not a qualifying disclosure. Section 43B(4) states in terms that disclosure of the privileged information by a person to whom it was given in the course of obtaining legal advice is not a qualifying disclosure. There is no express mention of an exception if the disclosure was authorized by the client. However, it would be wholly inconsistent with the approach of the legislation to deny a worker protection for a disclosure to his employer which otherwise satisfies the requirements of a qualifying disclosure, merely because the disclosure is made through the solicitor. The better view therefore is that section 43B(4) does not affect the lawyer's ability to make disclosures to others on the express instructions of a worker who is his/her client, in which case there would be a disclosure as agent for the worker client and that would be judged in the normal way. This can be reconciled with the wording of section 43B(4) on the basis that once the client has given authority to the lawyer to disclose the information, and that information is duly disclosed, there could no longer be a claim to legal privilege in relation to that information.

G. Geographical Scope

3.146 To fall within the Act, the relevant failure or malpractice may occur or be anticipated to occur either inside or outside the United Kingdom (ERA, section 43B(2)). Thus, an employee in the United Kingdom might raise concerns about the felling of rainforests in South America, or human rights violations in East Timor, provided that this is reasonably believed to amount to a crime or other breach of a legal obligation (see paragraph 3.112 above). Nor does it matter what law applies to the disclosure as a matter of private international law (section 43B(2)). Separate consideration may, however, need to be given to the issue of territorial jurisdiction of the tribunal to hear the dispute where the employment is outside the United Kingdom (see Chapter 6, paragraphs 6.96–6.143).

---

[29] ibid, col 616.

4

THE PUBLIC INTEREST TEST

A. Evolution of the Public Interest Test

The introductory wording of the Public Interest Disclosure Act 1998 provided that it was: **4.01**

> An Act to protect individuals who make certain disclosures of information in the public interest …

The public interest purpose which is intended to be served by the legislation is reflected in **4.02** the exceptional nature of the protection provided when compared to most other individual employment rights. In particular:

1. A worker making a protected disclosure is able to claim uncapped compensation both in detriment and dismissal cases (sections 47B, 103A, 124(1A) ERA).
2. It is a day one right; there is no qualification period (section 108(3)(ff) ERA).
3. There is a remedy for detriment other than dismissal, in contrast to the ordinary position in relation to other allegations of unfair treatment during employment (section 47B ERA).
4. There is an additional remedy of interim relief (section 128 ERA).
5. There is an extended category of those who are protected, beyond employees and extending beyond the usual category of workers (sections 43K, 43KA ERA).

As originally enacted, however, despite its title, the 1998 Act included no express require- **4.03** ment that disclosures be made in the public interest. Pursuant to amendments to section 43B ERA introduced by section 17 of the Enterprise and Regulatory Reform Act 2013 (ERRA), that has now been remedied in relation to disclosures made on or after 25 June 2013[1]. In addition to the requirement for the worker to have a reasonable belief that the information disclosed tends to show one or more of the relevant failures, it must also entail:

> any disclosure of information which, in the reasonable belief of the worker making the disclosure, is made in the public interest …'

---

[1] Section 103 ERRA.

4.04 At the same time as introducing this amendment, and of relevance to how it is to be construed, the legislation was further amended to remove the requirement that the disclosure be made in good faith in relation to qualifying disclosures made on or after 25 June 2013. Instead, good faith was relegated to being a factor which could lead to a reduction in compensation.[2] Prior to the amendment, the good faith requirement had applied to all disclosures other than those made for the purposes of legal advice (section 43D ERA).

4.05 The amendments thus entailed a marked shift in approach. As originally enacted the public interest element was left to emerge as a consequence of the definition of protected disclosures. The essential concept was that the definition of what sorts of disclosures could be qualifying disclosures, together with the graduated approach to protection depending on the person to whom the disclosure was made, would have the result that a disclosure which met the requirements for protection would be one which was made in the public interest. That was reinforced by the good faith requirement, which was construed by the Court of Appeal in *Street v Derbyshire Unemployed Workers' Centre* [2005] ICR 97 (CA) so as to permit a finding that a disclosure was not made in good faith if the predominant purpose was an ulterior motive (ie other than preventing, remedying, or facilitating investigation into the relevant failure[3]). Relying on the introductory wording to PIDA, that was said to accord with the purpose of the legislation. The interpretation of good faith is considered in more detail in Chapter 10 on Remedies.

4.06 This approach to the legislation was controversial in two respects. One aspect was that it became apparent that it was ineffective to ensure that the legislation was confined to disclosures which are made in the public interest, at least unless there was a very wide meaning to be given to the public interest as encompassing for example employers honouring their contractual obligations. In *Street v Derbyshire Unemployed Workers' Centre*, in addressing the good faith test, Wall LJ suggested (at para 71) that:

> The primary purpose for the disclosure of such information by an employee must, I think, be to remedy the wrong which is occurring or has occurred; or, at the very least, to bring the section 43B information to the attention of a third party in an attempt to ensure that steps are taken to remedy the wrong. The employee making the disclosure for this purpose needs to be protected against being victimised for doing so; and that is the protection the statute provides.

4.07 However, protection could apply to a worker making a disclosure entirely in their own self-interest, for example if a worker were to raise a breach of their own employment contract. As established in *Parkins v Sodexho* [2002] IRLR 109 (EAT), such a matter may properly amount to a protected disclosure under the pre-amendment provisions. The breadth of the protection, however, risked undermining the credibility of the legislation as a whole, rendering the exceptional protection available for protected disclosures as inappropriate given the absence of any public interest.

4.08 The second area of controversy concerned the good faith test. There was an inherent tension in the approach. On one hand, the immediate justice of a particular case may lead to the conclusion that those who have acted for an ulterior motive, such as to gain an employment advantage, should not benefit from the exceptional remedies available in a protected

---

[2] Section 18 ERRA deletes the reference to good faith as a requirement of protection for a disclosure in ss 43C, 43E, 43F, 43G, and 43H in relation to any disclosure made after that section came into force on 25 June 2013 (s 103(2)(b) ERRA).

[3] But as discussed in further detail in Chapter 10 at para 10.127, a different motive would not necessarily lead to a finding of a worker not acting in good faith (see *Dr Y-A-Soh v Imperial College of Science, Technology and Medicine* (UKEAT/0350/14/DM, 3 September 2015) at para 58).

disclosure claim. Yet, against that, a disclosure may be 'in the public interest' even if it is not made with the motive of promoting the public interest. Any approach which focuses on motive entails the risk of encouraging employers to 'shoot the messenger'—in the sense of challenging their motives—rather than listening to their message. The employer is encouraged to search for ulterior reasons for the blowing of the whistle and it might seek to do so even in the case of an internal disclosure. This undermines the good corporate governance aims underlying PIDA. It also risks employees being discouraged from raising concerns due to the fear that in response they will come under suspicion and their reason for doing so will be challenged.

The concern that the focus on good faith was not conducive to encouraging those who could **4.09** blow the whistle to come forward was one theme of the Shipman Inquiry conducted by Dame Janet Smith DBE, in relation to the circumstances surrounding Harold Shipman's murder of a large number of his patients. If an employee had given early warning of Shipman's actions, this would plainly have been in the public interest even if it was done out of personal antagonism towards him. As this illustrated, the public policy in encouraging the disclosure of concerns may be no less compelling merely because there are ulterior motives. Wrongdoing may be brought to light by someone who is motivated by personal antagonism as well as by public-spirited individuals. As Dame Janet Smith put it in her report:

> If employers are able to explore and impugn the motives of the 'messenger', when trying to justify having taken action against him/her, many 'messages' will not come to light because organisations like PCaW will have to advise those who come to them for advice that, if their motives can be impugned, they may not be protected by the PIDA. The Court of Appeal emphasised that someone in Mrs Street's situation was not totally without remedy; she lost the 'automatic protection' of the PIDA but retained the right to argue that, in all the circumstances, her dismissal had been unfair. That is undoubtedly so, but anyone advising her before she made her disclosure would have had to give very cautious advice. The effect of receiving that cautious advice might well have meant that she would have kept quiet. This would be unfortunate if the information affected, for example, patient safety in a healthcare setting. It is clear that, prior to the decision in *Street* at least, PCaW did not advise those who sought its advice that the presence of mixed motives would defeat a claim to automatic protection under the legislation.[4]

As Dame Janet Smith DBE noted, the effect of *Street* may be that where a potential whistle- **4.10** blower's situation at work means that his/her motives may be impugned, those advising him/ her will need to draw attention to the risk that his/her claim may fail on that basis. Worse still, s/he might need to be advised of the risk of a costs order against him/her if found not to have acted in good faith (see eg *Clark v Clark Construction Initiatives Ltd* [2008] ICR 635 (EAT)). The circumstances of the Shipman Inquiry placed into sharp focus the adverse public policy consequences in terms of the 'chilling effect' if workers are deterred from coming forward due to concern that their motives will be questioned, and the public interest in serious disclosures being made irrespective of the motivation.

The Court of Appeal in *Street* reasoned that even if PIDA did not apply, this did not pre- **4.11** vent employees bringing an ordinary unfair dismissal claim. But this may not apply either if the worker is not an employee, or lacks sufficient qualifying service, or the detriment does not take the form of dismissal. Ordinary unfair dismissal may also be of little comfort if an employee is to face character assassination for bringing a claim. Automatic unfairness and uncapped compensation is required precisely because of the need to encourage whistleblowers to step forward, not least as an early warning system for revealing concerns. One of the key reasons why whistleblowers have historically been reluctant to disclose concerns is the

---

[4] Fifth Report, Cm. 6394 (2004) at para 11.106.

worry that they will be seen as troublemakers, disloyal, or as attacking the employer.[5] The decision in *Street* may be seen as offering unwarranted encouragement for employers to take that course.

4.12 In the light of these considerations, Dame Janet Smith DBE[6] recommended that the good faith requirement should be removed altogether, commenting that:

> … if disclosure is in the public interest, it should not matter whether the person making the disclosure has mixed (or, possibly, even malicious) motives.

> … I think that there should be public discussion about whether the words 'in good faith' ought to appear in the PIDA. In my view, they could properly be omitted. The three tiered regime of the PIDA, with its incrementally exacting requirements, should afford sufficient discouragement to those minded maliciously to raise baseless concerns. I think that it would be appropriate also if the preamble to the PIDA made it plain that the purpose of the PIDA is to protect persons disclosing information, the disclosure of which is in the public interest. That would serve to focus attention on the message rather than the messenger. The public interest would be served, even in cases where the motives of the messenger might not have been entirely altruistic.

4.13 As initially framed, the amendments sought only to address the concerns arising out of the *Parkins v Sodexho* issue so as to bring out the public interest element expressly and to the forefront. The later decision also to relegate the good faith test to the remedy stage may be regarded in part as a response to the concerns that it could encourage an attack on the messenger rather than listening to the message, though it was also explained on the basis that to have both a good faith test and a public interest test would entail excessive complexity and as such might deter potential whistleblowers from speaking up. To this end, the amendment was linked to the introduction of the public interest test and explained at the House of Lords Report stage in the following terms by Lord Younger (BIS Parliamentary Under-Secretary of State):

> I note the argument that by introducing a public interest test the Government have inadvertently created a double hurdle for potential whistleblowers to navigate. To succeed, a claimant would need to show that they reasonably believed that the disclosure was in the public interest and that it was made in good faith. It is not the Government's intention to make it harder for whistleblowers to speak out. It remains a government commitment that they have the right protection in law. However, I can see that by fixing the legal loophole created by *Parkins v Sodexho* in the way that the Government propose, there is a risk that some individuals may be concerned that it is too hard to benefit from whistleblowing protection, and therefore they will decide not to blow the whistle. We have listened to the arguments made by noble Lords on this point, but the Government remain unconvinced that the good faith test should be removed in its entirety. There are instances where it is important that the tribunal is able to assess the motives of a disclosure, even where it was in the public interest.[7]

4.14 The move away from a focus on motive, to focus directly on the public interest, may also be said to reflect an emerging international consensus, at least across the EU, as reflected in the Council of Europe Recommendation on 'Protection of Whistleblowers', and accompanying Explanatory Memorandum, adopted by the Council of Ministers on 30 April 2014.[8] The proposal sets out twenty-nine principles for whistleblower protection. For these purposes, a 'whistleblower' is defined as 'any person who reports or discloses information on a threat or harm to the public interest in the context of their work-based relationship, whether in the

---

[5] ibid, para 11.10.
[6] ibid, paras 11.105 and 11.108.
[7] HL Report Stage, 26 February 2013, *Hansard*, col 1008.
[8] Recommendation CM/Rec (2014) 7.

public or private sector'. Protection is framed by reference to the concept of a 'public interest report or disclosure' which is defined as meaning 'the reporting or disclosing of information on acts and omissions that represent a threat or harm to the public interest', where 'report' refers to either internal disclosure or reporting to an outside authority and 'disclosure' refers to making the information public. The first principle is framed in general terms as requiring a national framework designed to facilitate public interest reports and disclosures by rules to protect the rights and interests of whistleblowers. But the Explanatory Memorandum (at para 37) explains further that a national review would enable the legislator to determine how national rules 'facilitate or hinder the honest communications of warning or reports of threats or harm to the public interest'. In relation to this it further explains that:

> 'Honest' or 'bona fide' means 'without fraud or deceit'. It does not mean the individual is right nor does it mean he or she has no other ulterior motive. This distinction is important in whistleblowing as it means that only someone who reports or discloses information which he or she knows to be untrue or false should lose the protection of the law.

The public interest test therefore now lies at the heart of the legislation. But much of the debate which was focused on good faith can now be applied to the public interest test. Too lax an approach to the public interest test risks undermining the rationale for the wider protection and risks discrediting the legislation. That issue was given particular focus by the approach of the EAT in *Chesterton Global Ltd v Nurmohamed* [2015] ICR 929, which as we discuss below contained dicta suggesting that the public interest test did no more than prevent a worker from relying on a breach of their own contract of employment where the breach was of a personal nature and there were no wider public interest implications. As against that, too strict an approach to the test, or one which reintroduces a focus on motive or which is too uncertain in application, might risk a chilling effect and encouragement to focus on attacking the whistleblowing messenger rather than heeding the message of the whistleblowing. Against that context, we turn to the construction of the public interest test. **4.15**

B. *Chesterton Global v Nurmohamed*

The approach to the public interest test was first considered at appellate level in *Chesterton Global Ltd (t/a Chestertons) v Nurmohamed* [2015] ICR 920 (EAT). The decision raised directly the issue of whether a disclosure could be regarded as made in the public interest, notwithstanding that (a) the worker making the disclosure had a self-interest in doing so and (b) the only class directly affected by the alleged wrongdoing were employees of the employer. **4.16**

In *Chesterton* the Claimant worker, Mr Nurmohamed, had been the Director of the Mayfair office of Chestertons, a firm of estate agents. He was responsible for sales from that office. The context of his disclosures was his concern that a new commission structure introduced by Chestertons would entail a reduction in his income. He contended that he had made three protected disclosures, two to the Area Director for the Central London area and one to Chestertons' Director of Human Relations. Mr Nurmohamed said that he believed Chestertons was deliberately misstating £2–3 million of actual costs and liabilities through the entire office and department network. He believed that this misstatement affected the commission earnings of 100 senior managers, including himself, whilst benefiting Chestertons' shareholders who received the enhanced profits by way of dividend. Mr Nurmohamed's claim succeeded in the ET. **4.17**

The ET found that the gist of the disclosure was that management were manipulating the company's accounts to the benefit of the shareholders. As to whether the disclosure in relation **4.18** to this was in the public interest, the tribunal set out its approach to the meaning of 'public interest' in the following terms (at 924H–925A):

> It is clear to us that it [i.e. 'the public interest'] cannot mean something which is of interest to the entirety of the public since it is inevitable from the kind of disclosures which arise from time to time such as disclosures about hospital negligence or disclosures about drug companies that only a section of the public would be directly affected. With this in mind, it is our view that where a section of the public would be affected, rather than simply the individual concerned, this must be sufficient for a matter to be in the public interest.

4.19   On this analysis, therefore, the crucial issues were (a) who did the claimant have in mind, other than himself, as being affected by the subject matter of the disclosure (or, in the claimant's belief, in whose interest was it that the disclosure be made)? (b) was that belief reasonable? and (c) was that group sufficient to constitute a section of the public?

4.20   The tribunal identified that there were two groups who were potentially affected; (a) the 100 senior managers whose commission was likely to be affected, and (b) anyone who relied on Chestertons' accounts, such as a potential vendor. The tribunal rejected the case which was made that Mr Nurmohamed had the latter group in mind. However, the tribunal accepted that, whilst the person about whom Mr Nurmohamed was most concerned was himself, he did also have the 100 senior managers in mind and reasonably believed that the disclosure was in their interests. In particular, it noted that the over-inflation of costs set against the office budgets would have decreased profits and potentially reduced bonuses for all the senior managers. The tribunal also accepted that the 100 senior managers were a sufficient group of the public to amount to this being in the public interest.

4.21   An appeal to the EAT was dismissed. On behalf of the employer it was argued that the tribunal should have examined the subject matter of the disclosures to determine whether, objectively, they were of real interest to the public in general or to a sufficient section of the public. In response the EAT first highlighted that the test is focused on reasonable belief, such that it is sufficient if the belief is objectively reasonable. The EAT further rejected the contention that the group of 100 senior managers could not be a sufficient section of the public by reason of having a common characteristic of the mutuality of obligations with the employer. It also rejected the contention that whether the disclosures were in the public interest turned on whether the employer was a private or public company. However, the EAT also emphasized the particular nature of the information disclosed, involving alleged manipulation of the accounts and a belief that the employer, a well-known firm of estate agents, was deliberately mis-stating £2–3 million of actual costs and liabilities through the entire office and department network.

4.22   At the time of writing, an appeal in *Chesterton* is due to be heard in 2017, and will be covered in updates to this book available online.[9]

C. Analysis and Implications of the Decision in *Chesterton*

(1) Overview

4.23   The decision in *Chesterton* makes clear at least that it is not necessarily a bar to a tribunal finding that disclosure is in the public interest either that (a) self-interest is the worker's principal reason for making the disclosure, or (b) that the disclosure concerns a dispute between

---

[9] Updates are at http://www.littletonchambers.com/lib/articles%20pdf/whistleblowing%206th%20supplement.pdf.

employer and employees, and the only people that the worker has in mind as affected are fellow employees.

Elements of the reasoning might be viewed as going further, and indicating that a worker **4.24** who reasonably believes that the disclosure is to the benefit of others, at least if they can be viewed as sufficient to be a section of the public, is to be taken as having made the disclosure in the public interest. Indeed the EAT commented (at para 36) that:

> … the sole purpose of the amendment to section 43B(1) of the 1996 Act … was to reverse the effect of *Parkins v Sodexho* [2002] IRLR 109. The words 'in the public interest' were introduced to do no more than prevent a worker from relying on a breach of his own con-tract of employment where the breach is of a personal nature and there are no wider public interest implications.

This approach would have the advantage of certainty. In that respect it is consistent with **4.25** the approach taken by the Council of Europe in its Recommendation on the Protection of Whistleblowers[10] which emphasizes the need for the scope of whistleblower protection to be clearly specified so that any member of the public can be reasonably expected to understand what is covered and what is not, and make an informed decision accordingly.[11]

However, as discussed further below (paragraphs 4.33–4.35), the view that the only purpose **4.26** of the amendment was to exclude a worker's reliance on a breach of that worker's own employ-ment contract (subject to the breach not being only personal in nature) is directly contrary to what was said on behalf of the Government in explaining the amendments and rejecting an alternative opposition amendment. In any event, it is apparent from other aspects of the EAT's reasoning, that it was not indicating that a disclosure was to be regarded as made in the public interest in every case where a worker has in mind that the disclosure is also in the inter-ests of some other person(s). That is apparent from the tribunal's approach to the assessment of whether the group whom a claimant considers to be affected constitutes a sufficient group to be regarded as a section of the public. As to this, the EAT commented (at para 25) that:

> a relatively small group may be sufficient to satisfy the public interest test. *What is sufficient is necessarily fact-sensitive.* (emphasis added)

No specific guidance was given as to what factors might bear on the 'fact-sensitive' assessment **4.27** of whether the group can be regarded as a 'section of the public' in any particular context. But the very recognition that the issue is fact-sensitive is inconsistent with an across-the-board approach that the public interest is engaged whenever the worker has in mind some other person(s) as benefitting from the disclosure. On the facts in *Chesterton* an important part of the context which was regarded as material to that 'fact-sensitive' assessment was the overall picture, including not only the large number of employees affected but the serious nature of the wrongdoing which it was found that the claimant reasonably believed had occurred. We return below to the potential value, or otherwise, of the 'section of the public' test, given the fact-sensitive analysis that is required (see paragraphs 4.53–4.60).

We suggest in summary that: **4.28**

1. The decision in *Chesterton* is properly to be understood having regard to the particular content of the disclosure in that case. It should not be taken as meaning that disclosure is necessarily to be regarded as made in the public interest wherever it was reasonably believed (by the worker making the disclosure) to benefit someone other than the worker,

---

[10] Recommendation CM/Rec (2014) 7, adopted by the Committee of Ministers on 30 April 2014.
[11] Para 44 of the Explanatory Memorandum.

and nor should this turn on a vague test of whether those affected are to be regarded as a section of the public.

2. In each case, the reasonable belief test requires first the identification of what factors the worker had in mind as the basis for believing that disclosure was in the public interest or which might be regarded as equating to a belief that disclosure was in the public interest in the sense at least of serving some wider good beyond the personal interests of the worker. In determining whether the belief was reasonable, one factor to which a tribunal may have regard is whether the worker had in mind others who would also benefit from the disclosure. But whilst this factor may be important, it is neither a necessary requirement for the disclosure to be in the public interest nor a necessarily sufficient factor.

3. Whilst a disclosure may reasonably be believed to be in the public interest despite only being to the benefit of fellow employees, consideration is still required of the basis for believing that the disclosure furthers the public interest rather than just being a matter of furthering private interests, albeit on a collective basis.

4.29 The above considerations are supported, we suggest, by (a) the statutory context, (b) the legislative purpose as gathered from the *Hansard* material, and (c) the ordinary meaning of 'the public interest' which Parliament can be taken to have had in mind when legislating to provide this unique protection.

(2) The statutory context

4.30 Having regard to the statutory context, we suggest that the following considerations in particular are important:

1. The plain purpose of the amendment was to place emphasis on the public interest in the disclosure. It is the fact that disclosures are to be, in the worker's reasonable belief, made in the public interest, which explains and is central to the exceptional nature of the relief provided by the legislation as summarized at paragraph 4.02 above. The test serves the crucial function of drawing the distinction between those disclosures with a sufficient public interest element to justify this heightened level of protection from a private dispute or grievance with the employer, whether individual or collective. This tends to suggest that there should be some reasonable belief as to some wider importance, or matter of wider public concern or public interest, beyond the private dispute between employee or employees and employer. Although it may be 'ordinarily' unfair to dismiss an employee for making a disclosure which is not protected,[12] it is the public interest nature of the disclosure which explains the disapplication of the usual qualification requirement and compensation limits.

2. Given that a central theme in making the amendment was to re-assert the public interest nature of disclosures, it would therefore be surprising if, without more, the new test had the effect that it was necessarily met in the case of a collective grievance merely on the basis that the disclosure also related to others and not simply to the worker making the disclosure. Whilst the worker might regard some aspect of the collective grievance as raising some matter of wider public interest, the key distinction drawn is between matters only of private interest and those furthering some wider public interest, such as the public interest in safeguarding against a serious health and safety threat or exposing serious wrongdoing.

3. The reasonable belief test entails a recognition that views may differ as to what is in fact in the public interest.

---

[12] This was a point specifically highlighted by Auld LJ (at 99C–D) in *Street v Derbyshire Unemployed Workers' Centre* [2005] ICR 97 (CA) when considering the previous good faith requirement.

4. The legislation has to be capable of applying in a wide range of differing circumstances, including to those who may not have taken legal advice, and must serve its primary purpose of encouraging those able to raise an early alarm as to relevant failures to do so. That suggests that technicality needs to be avoided. A worker may in substance believe that he or she is acting in the public interest without specifically formulating a view in those terms. Thus a worker who is making a disclosure of a likely criminal offence because it is the right thing to do, or so that the offence can be prevented, is no doubt to be regarded as acting in the belief that disclosure is in the public interest unless there is something else to show the contrary, irrespective of whether the belief is specifically formulated in those terms.

5. The relegation of the good faith test to the remedy stage may be relevant in two respects:

   5.1 Consistently with the approach in *Chesterton*, it indicates that the focus is not on motive. Lack of good faith falls to be considered only at the remedy stage, where the effect is limited to a reduction in compensation of up to 25 per cent (sections 49(6A) and 123(6A) ERA). The effect of relegating the good faith requirement to a remedy issue is that a worker may make a protected disclosure in the belief that making it is in the public interest, even though there is some ulterior reason for making the disclosure (such as personal gain) and as such it is not made in good faith. Otherwise it would not be possible for issues as to good faith to arise at the remedy stage.

   5.2 But this in turn places still greater weight on the importance of the public interest test. It contemplates that the importance of the subject matter is such that, as a matter of public policy, it is appropriate to grant relief even to a claimant who was not acting in good faith when making the disclosure. That in turn would make it all the more surprising if a worker raising a collective complaint as between workers and employers was necessarily to be regarded as acting in the public interest, by reason of colleagues amounting to a section of the public, without reference to what public interest is believed to be furthered.

6. The ERRA amendments also extended the scope of liability beyond the employer and imposed liability on agents and individual employees (even if they are subject to allegations made in the disclosures which they reasonably—or indeed correctly—believe to be unfounded): section 47B(1A) ERA. Workplace disputes often include allegation and counter-allegation of some alleged unfair treatment or other conduct that might be regarded as a breach of contract. These may be allegations as between a manager and subordinates, or between colleagues at a similar level of seniority. An excessively broad view of what may be regarded as the public interest, focusing only on who the disclosure is regarded as benefitting rather than considering whether, more broadly, the disclosure was reasonably regarded as in the public interest, risks commonplace grievances concerning personal disputes being converted into protected disclosures merely on the basis that the adverse treatment is alleged to also affect other colleagues. There is the consequent heightened risk of claims of personal liability being deployed where a worker, who is subject to such an allegation, is alleged to have reacted in a manner which involves some detrimental treatment to the person who made the allegation. That would apply even if the allegation was false, provided it was based on a reasonable belief.

7. The categories of relevant failure can be taken as providing some guidance as to what is meant by the public interest. Leaving to one side the broad category of non-compliance with a legal obligation, each of the other categories naturally suggest a broader public interest or public good associated with disclosure, irrespective of the number of individuals directly affected. Disclosure of information exposing a likely criminal offence, miscarriage of justice, or danger to the environment would also naturally be regarded as being in the public interest.

(3) *Hansard* and the legislative history

4.31 The above considerations are reinforced by reference to express explanations of the Government's intention in passing the amendment legislation. Unsurprisingly, considerable emphasis was placed on reverting to the original public interest objectives of the legislation. The fullest explanation was provided for the Government by Norman Lamb MP, the Employment Minister, during discussion in the House of Commons Public Bill Committee on 3 July 2012, where he stated:[13]

> Setting out the issue that the Government seek to address might be helpful. The original aim of the public interest disclosure legislation was to provide protection to individuals who made a disclosure in the public interest—otherwise known as blowing the whistle. The clause seeks to make that public interest clear, and the hint is in the title of the original legislation, which was designed to deal with public interest disclosure—that is what we are talking about.
>
> …
>
> The intention that any disclosure should be in the public interest was apparent on Second Reading as well as from the heading of the legislation. The Bill's sponsor, Lord Borrie, said in the House of Lords that
>
>> 'the tribunal must be satisfied that that disclosure was reasonable, having regard, among other things, to the seriousness of the threat to the public interest.'
>
> That is how that was defined by the Bill's sponsor, who also said:
>
>> As I hope I have made clear, this measure will encourage people to recognise and identify with the wider public interest and not just their own private position.(Official Report, House of Lords, 11 May 1998; Vol. 589, c. 891.)
>
> Under that legislation, if it is found that the public interest disclosure rules have been breached and that someone was dismissed for that reason, compensation is unlimited. That is a day one right, so it is right that that is limited to the small number of cases that the legislation was originally designed to address.
>
> …
>
> To return to my explanation of the purpose of the clause and of why the Government have designed it in such a way, the decision in the case of *Parkins v Sodexho Ltd* has resulted in a fundamental change in how the Public Interest Disclosure Act operates and has widened its scope beyond what was originally intended. The ruling in that case stated that there is no reason to distinguish a legal obligation that arises from a contract of employment from any other form of legal obligation. The effect is that individuals make a disclosure about a breach of their employment contract, where this is a matter of purely private rather than public interest, and then claim protection, for example, for unfair dismissal.
>
> The ruling has left the Public Interest Disclosure Act open to abuse and is creating a level of uncertainty for business. Concerns have been expressed, underpinned by anecdotal evidence, which I appreciate is a dangerous word to use in this Committee, from lawyers—that is an even more dangerous word—that it is now common practice to encourage an individual to include a Public Interest Disclosure Act claim when making a claim at an employment tribunal, regardless of there being any public interest at stake. That has a negative effect on businesses, which face spending time preparing to deal unnecessarily with claims that lack a genuine public interest element. It also has a negative effect on genuine whistleblowers, by encouraging speculative claims. Furthermore, by widening the scope of the Public Interest Disclosure Act to allow claims of a personal nature, the effectiveness and credibility of the legislation is, in my view, called into question. It is common ground between all Committee members that those issues need to be dealt with.

---

[13] *Hansard*, HC Public Bill Committee, 3 July 2012, at cols 385–89.

The clause will amend part IVA of the Employment Rights Act 1996 to close the loophole that case law has created. The clause emphasises the need for there to be an issue of public interest involved when an individual is pursuing a public interest disclosure case. The Government support protection for genuine whistleblowers. The clause in no way takes away rights from those who seek to blow the whistle on matters of genuine public interest.

…

The clause will make it clear that, when the individual is raising their concern at work, or otherwise, under the terms of the legislation, they must reasonably believe that they are making their concern known as a matter of public interest. That is the original purpose of the Public Interest Disclosure Act, as Lord Borrie said in Parliament, and that is what was intended when the legislation passed through Parliament.

The clause will remove the opportunistic use of the legislation for private purposes. It is in the original spirit of the Public Interest Disclosure Act that those seeking its protection should reasonably believe that their raising an issue is in the public interest.

…

In essence, the real issue here is the opportunistic use of part IVA for personal reasons rather than in the public interest.

…

I have quoted Lord Borrie, who made it clear when he was promoting the Bill that it was designed to deal with public interest issues. The Government seek to legislate now to bring that Act back to its original purpose.[14]

4.32 Emphasis was therefore placed on the exceptional nature of the relief provided (noting that it was a day one right), such that it should be reserved for cases which (in the worker's reasonable belief) raised matters of wider public interest. That was contrasted with disclosures for private purposes.

4.33 During the passage of the Bill, an Opposition amendment was tabled which would instead have excluded only private contractual obligations owed solely to the worker making the disclosure. This was resisted both on the basis that there might be cases where a breach of such an obligation does give rise to a wider public interest, and that there would be other cases which were not concerned with a breach of contract which, without more, raised a personal dispute rather than any wider public interest. As explained by Norman Lamb before the House of Commons Public Bill Committee:

Including a public interest test in the Bill deals with the *Parkins v Sodexho* case in its entirety. Therefore there is no need to disallow claims based on an individual's contract, as suggested in the amendment. Indeed, although our aim is to prevent the opportunistic use of breaches of an individual's contract that are of a personal nature, there are also likely to be instances where a worker should be able to rely on breaches of his own contract where those engage wider public interest issues. In other words, in a worker's complaint about a breach of their contract, the breach in itself might have wider public interest implications.

The blanket restriction of claims involving breaches of an employee's contract, which the Opposition amendment would introduce, could have unintended adverse consequences for individuals who are legitimately concerned about a breach of their contract that has wider public interest implications. Such a restriction would not reflect the intention or the spirit of the legislation and would unfairly and unduly restrict the number of cases in which an individual could bring a public interest disclosure case. Public Concern at Work—and I believe this is also the spirit in which amendment 69 is intended—has suggested that the approach of disallowing contractual claims could be an alternative to introducing a public interest test.

---

[14] *Hansard*, 3 July 2012, cols 385–89.

However, as well as potential unintended consequences for individuals, this approach would not in itself achieve the aim of addressing the issues raised by the *Parkins v Sodexho* decision. For example, the issue in that case could have been reframed as a health and safety issue, with similar issues then arising in relation to disclosures of minor breaches of health and safety legislation, which are of no interest to the wider public.

Furthermore, a worker has many more rights than those contained in his contract of employment, such as rights derived from common law and statute. To use wording related to personal work contracts would still leave much of the loophole open. An example here could be that the claim under the Public Interest Disclosure Act is based on an employer's failure to follow the statutory process for dealing with a flexible working request. This is a breach of a legal requirement—the right to request flexible working—but it is clearly an issue of purely personal interest and not what the Public Interest Disclosure Act was all about. Yet the phraseology used in the suggested amendment, if taken on its own as an alternative to what the Government are suggesting, could still allow an employee, who claims a breach of a right to request flexible working and gets sacked as a result, to bring it within the terms of the legislation, which is entirely against what was originally intended.[15]

4.34 A similar explanation was provided by another Government Minister, Jo Swinson,[16] during the subsequent House of Commons debate on 17 October 2012. She commented on the proposed Opposition amendment in the following terms:

> Amendment 94 seeks to address a point we covered in Committee. I understand that its aim is to prevent a disclosure relating to a breach of a private contract from being a qualifying disclosure for the purposes of a whistleblowing claim, unless it is clearly in the public interest.... We believe that such an approach would have the potential for unintended consequences and would not in itself address the concerns raised by the *Parkins v. Sodexho* decision. For example, the issue in that case could have been reframed as a health and safety issue, with similar issues then arising in relation to the disclosures of minor breaches of health and safety legislation, which are of no interest to the wider public. Not only are we closing the loophole identified in the *Parkins v. Sodexho* case, but by introducing the public interest test we are removing the potential for the opportunistic use of the protection. That will prevent any cases similar to the *Parkins v. Sodexho* case in the areas that would otherwise be uncovered by the amendment.
>
> …
>
> I think that it will do what the Government intend it to do—basically what it says on the tin. It is about making sure that the public interest disclosure regime has to have a public interest test. That is what was meant when the legislation was initially framed and formed. The case law that has come up since then has showed that there was a loophole, and I think, to be fair, that the Opposition have accepted that it needs to be closed.[17]

4.35 The EAT's dicta in *Chesterton*, to the effect that the amendment was intended to do no more than prevent workers from relying on a breach of their own contract as being a protected disclosure, was wholly inconsistent with the rejection of the Opposition amendment which would have been expressed in those terms, and the reasons for doing so. In support of its view of the purpose of the amendment, the EAT in *Chesterton* (at para 36) placed reliance on the dictum in *ALM Medical Services v Bladon* [2012] IRLR 807 (CA) that the aim of the legislation is to protect employees from unfair treatment for reasonably raising in a responsible way genuine concerns about wrongdoing in the workplace. But that decision preceded the introduction of the public interest test, which makes clear that the legislation applies only to

---

[15] *Hansard*, 3 July 2012, cols 388–89.
[16] Parliamentary Under-Secretary of State for Employment Relations, Consumer and Postal Affairs and for Women and Equalities.
[17] *Hansard*, HC Debates, 17 October 2012, cols 346, 347.

the narrower category of disclosures which are reasonably believed to be made in the public interest. Nor is the protection confined to disclosures about wrongdoing in the workplace.

(4) Meaning of 'the public interest' in other contexts

On the same date as the legislation introducing this amendment received Royal Assent (25 **4.36** April 2013), the Defamation Act 2013 was also given Royal Assent. Section 4 of that Act also contained a provision concerned with the public interest, in the context of a defence to a defamation claim. Section 4(1) of that Act provides:

(1) It is a defence to an action for defamation for the defendant to show that—

    (a) the statement complained of was, or formed part of, a statement on a matter of public interest; and

    (b) the defendant reasonably believed that publishing the statement complained of was in the public interest.

Again, the legislation contained no definition or express guidance as to what was meant by 'a **4.37** matter of public interest'. The reason for that approach was set out in the Consultation Paper on the draft Defamation Bill[18] (at para 13) in the following terms:

> The draft Bill does not attempt to define what is meant by 'the public interest'. We believe that this is a concept which is well-established in the English common law and that in view of the very wide range of matters which are of public interest and the sensitivity of this to factual circumstances, attempting to define it in statute would be fraught with problems. Such problems include the risk of missing matters which are of public interest resulting in too narrow a defence and the risk of this proving a magnet for satellite litigation adding to costs in relation to libel proceedings.

Given that this concerned legislation passed on the same date, it might be assumed that there **4.38** was a similar expectation in relation to public interest in the protected disclosure context that reference would be made to the use of that term in the common law in other contexts. However, Supperstone J, sitting in the EAT in *Chesterton*, concluded that he was not assisted by considering how the words 'in the public interest' had been construed in the context of other legislation. To some extent, there is good reason for this caution. In particular:

1. Typically in other contexts, reference to the public interest is by way of a defence in response to prima facie interference with a right. That is the context in which it arises under section 4 of the Defamation Act 2013, and by way of defence to a claim of interference with privacy or confidentiality or copyright (see Chapters 14, 16, 17). By contrast, typically a protected disclosure does not interfere with any other right (though it may do if for example the disclosure is prima facie defamatory). On the contrary, the legislation is framed around safeguards which are geared to encouraging the raising of relevant failures with an appropriate recipient.

2. Related to the above, the interests in encouraging workers to come forward and disclose information in relation to relevant concerns militates against adopting a test which is excessively uncertain or otherwise sets the bar too high.

3. For protected disclosures, the principal route which workers are encouraged to follow is disclosure to the employer. Ordinarily (though not necessarily) the disclosure relates to concerns arising in the workplace. No doubt the EAT had that in mind in *Chesterton* in commenting (at para 36) that the objective is to protect employees from unfair treatment when they reasonably (and in a responsible way) raise genuine concerns about wrongdoing in the workplace (albeit that the subject of the disclosures could also be relevant failures

---

[18] Consultation Paper CP3/11 (March 2011).

arising outside the arena of the workplace). In raising such matters, ordinarily the worker is entitled to expect confidentiality. Further, whilst there can be wider disclosures made, there are other safeguards in place which are applicable to those such as in relation to section 43G that the disclosure be reasonable in all the circumstances of the case. It may be said that given that the disclosure will typically be to a limited audience (the employer) it would be surprising if there was a requirement that the concerns must relate more broadly to being of concern to the public generally. In that respect the context is quite different from that which typically (but not always) arises for example in considering a defence to a defamation claim.

4. It is important to take into account the specific statutory context. Notably, it is significant that the good faith requirement is no longer part of the test for liability, but is retained as a factor at the remedy stage, indicating that a disclosure may be regarded as having been made in the public interest despite not having been made in good faith.

5. It is not in any event the case that there is a single accepted definition of public interest. On the contrary, there tends to be an emphasis on the need for flexibility in dealing with the many different factual scenarios that may arise. To that end, in the Law Commission's Working Paper on Breach of Confidence, it commented in respect of the public interest defence in breach of confidence claims that:

> the range of circumstances in which the defence might properly be used is so wide and so variable that it is not practicable to define in general terms all the criteria to be used and … it would be misleading to single out particular issues (such as the existence of misconduct) for consideration…. The public interest is a developing concept which changes with the social attitudes of the times: many things are regarded as being in the public interest today which would not have been so regarded in the last century, or even twenty years ago, and it would be unrealistic to suppose that the concept will not undergo further changes in the years ahead…. There is, of course, a substantial public interest in the preservation of confidences and the task of the court would therefore be to balance this against the public interest in disclosing the information to which a confidence related.[19]

4.39 However, whilst it is necessary to take account of the specific context of the protected disclosure legislation, we suggest that the way in which the term public interest is ordinarily used, and has been adopted in other contexts, provides some assistance in relation to what Parliament can be taken to have intended in specifically introducing the test with a view to re-emphasizing the public interest element in the legislation.

4.40 The *Oxford English Dictionary* suggests the following definition of 'the public interest':

> the benefit or advantage of the community as a whole; the public good.

4.41 To similar effect, a report of the Joint Parliamentary Committee on Privacy and Injunctions (27 March 2012) suggested in the Executive Summary, that:

> Although definitions of public interest change from time to time, an overarching definition of public interest is the people's general welfare and well being; something in which the populace as a whole has a stake. It is not the same as that which is of interest to the public.

4.42 A similar approach is also adopted in detailed guidance provided by the Information Commissioner's Office (ICO) on the public interest test set out in the Freedom of Information Act 2000 (FOIA).[20] By way of overview, the guidance states that:

> The public interest here means the public good, not what is of interest to the public, and not the private interests of the requester.

---

[19] No 58, 1974, at para 93.
[20] See https://ico.org.uk/media/for-organisations/documents/1183/the_public_interest_test.pdf.

The guidance adds (at para 9) that: **4.43**

> The public interest can cover a wide range of values and principles relating to the public good, or what is in the best interests of society…. the public interest can take many forms.

The ICO guidance notes (at para 13) that disclosures under the FOIA are in effect to the **4.44** world at large. In that sense the position is very different to that usually applicable to protected disclosures. But a common feature of each of these definitions is a focus on the concept of the public good or general welfare. That is also reflected in the Explanatory Memorandum to the Council of Europe's Recommendation on 'Protection of Whistleblowers', which comments in general terms (at para 41) that:

> Throughout Europe, the public interest is understood as the 'welfare' or 'well-being' of the general public or society. Protecting the welfare and well-being of the public from harm, damage or breach of their rights is at the heart of this recommendation…. The purpose of a national framework is to facilitate the reporting or disclosing of information about wrongdoing or risk to the public interest as it is in the public interest to prevent and punish such acts.

The Recommendation does not expressly set out a distinction between different types of **4.45** 'wrongdoing'. It also states that 'public interest' is intentionally not defined because there is scope in some areas for a difference of appreciation between Member States. That is subject to the provision in Recommendation 2 that it should expressly cover 'violations of law and human rights, as well as risks to public health and safety and to the environment'. Again, that begs a question as to the scope of protection which is envisaged by 'violations of the law', read in the light of the general prescription that public interest connotes something having an impact on the welfare of the general public or society. Equally, reference to human rights law is perhaps indicative of a consensus that complaints as to a breach of certain employment legislation, such as equality legislation, is readily susceptible to a belief that preventing or challenging this furthers the public interest even if the worker raising this is the only person directly affected. Indeed, in *Chesterton* the respondent conceded that a complaint by an employee about an employer operating a racially discriminatory policy may be made in the public interest because public policy is directed against discrimination in society at large on grounds of race.

A focus on the wider public good or general welfare might be said, as the employment tri- **4.46** bunal noted in *Chesterton*, to be open to the objection that many disclosures that would be regarded as being made in the public interest will only benefit and be of interest to a limited number of people. We suggest that the answer to this is twofold. First, whether a disclosure is in the public interest is not necessarily to be calibrated by reference to the number of people affected (although that may be a relevant consideration). Second, and related to this, what may be regarded as in the public interest is not the same as what is of interest to the public, as reflected in Lord Wilberforce's commonly cited dictum in *British Steel Corporation v Granada Television Ltd* [1981] AC 1096 (HL) at 1168G that:

> … there is a wide difference between what is interesting to the public and what it is in the public interest to make known.

Depending on the nature of the disclosure, a matter which only directly affects a single per- **4.47** son, and is of direct interest to a small group, may nevertheless be regarded as in the public interest in the sense of furthering the wider public good. That is also the sense in which the term is commonly used. Thus the public interest in freedom of expression is not calibrated by the number of people who directly benefit in any particular case but as being a public good in itself. Similarly the public interest in disclosing serious wrongdoing is not ordinarily viewed as dependent on the number of people affected but as being of itself a public value. If a victim of a violent crime reports the offence, it is no less in the public interest that this should be reported merely because no one else was directly affected by the attack. Indeed, it is because what is in the public interest requires a value judgement that, as noted in the passage cited above from the Law Commission Working Paper, the public interest is a developing concept that varies with social attitudes; hence also the importance of framing the test in terms of reasonable belief.

4.48 This approach accords closely with the structure of the legislation as viewed in the round and also with the purpose of the amendment. The starting point is that it is implicit in the list of relevant failures that prima facie there is recognized to be a public interest in disclosing information which tends to show a past, ongoing, or future criminal offence, breach of a legal obligation, danger to health and safety, damage to the environment, miscarriage of justice, or cover-up of those matters. That also accords with the view taken of the UK legislation in the Explanatory Memorandum to the Council of Europe Recommendation on 'Protection of Whistleblowers' (see paras 41 and 43). It is also consistent with dicta in *Street v Derbyshire Unemployed Workers' Centre* [2005] ICR 97 (CA). Thus Auld LJ, having identified that the purpose of the legislation was to protect those 'who make certain disclosures in the public interest', identified the public interest aims as being 'those specified in section 43B' (para 47). In essence that identified a public interest in addressing the categories of relevant failure, or as Wall LJ put it (at para 71), 'to remedy the wrong which is occurring or has occurred; or, at the very least, to bring the section 43B information to the attention of a third party in an attempt to ensure that steps are taken to remedy the wrong'. But from that general category, the public interest test then carves out those matters where either the worker does not believe, or it is not reasonable to believe, there is any wider significance or public good beyond a private dispute between worker (or workers) and employer. In each case it is for the tribunal to give careful consideration to the basis on which there was a belief as to some wider public interest (or, to cater for the possibility that the view might not be specifically formulated in those terms, equates to a belief in a wider public interest) and to assess whether that belief was genuinely held at the time and was reasonable. That might still arise in the context of what is essentially a collective dispute between workers and employer, but it calls for a consideration of what the worker had in mind which indicates that the disclosure was seen as in some wider public interest, whether arising from exposing the serious nature of wrongdoing or otherwise.

4.49 In *Chesterton*, reliance was also placed by the employer on the observations of Baroness Hale (at para 147, at 409C) in *Jameel (Mohammed and another v Wall Street Journal Europe Sprl* [2006] UKHL 44, [2007] 1 AC 359 (in the context of the 'Reynolds defence' of disclosure in the public interest for the purposes of qualified privilege in the law of defamation) that:

> First, there must be a real public interest in communicating and receiving the information. This is, as we all know, very different from saying that it is information which interests the public—the most vapid tittle-tattle about the activities of footballers' wives and girlfriends interests large sections of the public but no-one could claim any real public interest in our being told all about it. It is also different from the test suggested by Mr Robertson QC, on behalf of the Wall Street Journal Europe, of whether the information is 'newsworthy'. That is too subjective a test, based on the target audience, inclinations and interests of the particular publication. There must be some real public interest in having this information in the public domain. But this is less than a test that the public 'need to know', which would be far too limited.

4.50 Insofar as this was relied upon to support the point that the public interest is not the same as what is of interest to the public, that is pertinent (though perhaps trite). But beyond that we suggest that the EAT in *Chesterton* were right to regard this as adding little in the protected disclosure context. Ordinarily the issue is whether a more limited disclosure is protected, rather than whether the matter should be put in the public domain. Reference to 'a real public interest' reveals little as to how that is to be assessed beyond the considerations noted above, and does not take into account the reasonable belief test which contemplates that the worker's view may be reasonable even if the tribunal disagrees that there is indeed a 'real public interest'.

Reliance was also placed by the employers in *Chesterton* on detailed guidance on the dual **4.51** aspects of 'public' and 'benefit' produced by the Charity Commission. For the purposes of the 'public' aspect, the guidance provides that:

> To satisfy this aspect the purpose must:
> - benefit the public in general, or a sufficient section of the public—what is a 'sufficient section of the public' varies from purpose to purpose
> - not give rise to more than incidental personal benefit—personal benefit is 'incidental' where (having regard both to its nature and to its amount) it is a necessary result or by-product of carrying out the purpose.[21]

Again, we suggest that this is of limited assistance in the protected disclosure context. It is a **4.52** definition which is framed with the need to establish charitable purposes in mind. The first limb reflects the approach in *Chesterton* of focusing on who is affected, which we address further in the following section. So far as concerns the second limb of this test, we suggest that this is an instance of the need to have regard to the particular context; in this case a definition for identifying charitable purposes. It does not follow that the same requirement is appropriate in the context of protected disclosure legislation. On the contrary, the relegation of the good faith requirement to a remedy issue reflected a recognition that disclosure may merit protection and properly be regarded as in the public interest, notwithstanding that a worker is acting for an ulterior motive or principally to benefit his own ends in making the disclosure.

(5) 'Section of the public' test

Against this context, we return to the approach applied in *Chesterton* of considering whether **4.53** those whom a worker has in mind as affected/benefitted can be regarded as a sufficient group to be a section of the public. We suggest that, in the context of the reasonable belief test, this approach may be a useful evidential tool, but that its limits should also be recognized.

The EAT in *Chesterton* recognized (at para 25) that what is sufficient to amount to a 'section **4.54** of the public' is fact sensitive. That in turn begs the question as to what factors might bear on that assessment, and indeed whether the same group could be regarded as a section of the public for some purposes but not for others. That assessment can only properly be made, we suggest, by keeping in mind that the statutory test remains one of whether the disclosure is made in the public interest, rather than whether it is of interest to or of benefit to some members of the public, and that the plain purpose of the amendment was to focus protection on cases where the disclosure was reasonably viewed as advancing some wider public interest as opposed to being solely a private grievance. Unless that is kept in mind, and there is a consequent consideration of the full factual context, the focus on identifying the group directly affected may lead a tribunal into error in two important respects.

First, it might still be reasonable for a worker to believe that a disclosure which directly affects **4.55** only that worker is made in the public interest. The same might apply where the worker makes the disclosure out of a sense that it is the right thing to do without giving specific consideration to which individuals or groups are directly affected. If that is the basis which is

---

[21] Public benefit: rules for charities. The Charity Commission (First published:14 February 2014).

put forward for the reasonable belief, seeking to identify which particular groups the worker had in mind as being directly interested or affected is likely to be at best a red herring. That is clear from the categories of relevant disclosure. To take one example, the legislation plainly contemplates that there is a public interest in reporting or preventing crime. As noted at paragraph 4.47 above, a worker who reports that, for example, she has been the subject of a violent crime, may reasonably believe that it is in the public interest to disclose this even if she is the only victim or indeed the only likely victim, on the basis that there is a broader public interest in such conduct being dealt with.

4.56   Second, even where a dispute concerns other workers, and the claimant has this in mind, it may still not be reasonable to regard it as other than an essentially private dispute, rather than a matter engaging the public interest. It was plainly not the intention of the legislature, in seeking to re-emphasize the public interest element of the legislation, to permit every private collective dispute to be capable, without more, of being framed by reference to protected disclosures wherever there is a reasonable belief that the employer's stance entailed a breach or likely breach of a legal obligation.

4.57   As such we suggest that the 'section of the public' test needs to be approached with some caution. In each case it is necessary to have regard to the relevant set of beliefs at the time of making the disclosure. That may entail that there are different considerations which are relevant to the issue of whether it was made in the public interest than whether there was a 'section of the public' which the worker specifically had in mind. Equally, the fact that the worker had others in his thoughts as sharing an interest in the disclosure does not necessarily entail that disclosure is in the public interest. A 'fact-sensitive' analysis is necessary. Indeed, in that sense the question of whether the group that the worker had in mind constitutes a 'section of the public' may be better regarded as a conclusion which follows from the overall circumstances.

4.58   With those caveats, however, we suggest that consideration of whether the worker had in their thoughts others as being affected by the subject matter of the disclosure provides a useful evidential tool, whilst not being the end of the enquiry. It provides one starting point for indicating that the worker had in mind considerations beyond their own circumstances, albeit it does not necessarily follow that disclosure was believed to be in the public interest. Further, the protected disclosure legislation has to serve the purpose of providing protection to those making public interest disclosures, who may well not have taken any legal advice before doing so. The considerations that could legitimately be regarded as rendering the disclosure in the public interest will often not be formulated in those terms. Instead, in applying the reasonable belief test, a tribunal may have to piece together what set of beliefs or considerations the worker had in mind and whether that set amounted to a belief that disclosure was made in the public interest (and if so whether that belief was reasonable). In some cases that might have little to do with identifying any particular group affected, and might instead be founded on a more general belief that making the disclosure is the right thing to do. As noted above, in such a case identifying the group that the worker had in mind as being affected is likely to be less helpful. But in other cases, as in *Chesterton*, one part of the set of beliefs held at the time of making the disclosure may be that it is also in the interests of others. Depending on all the circumstances, a single issue, such as the seriousness of wrongdoing, may be highly material in taking the matter outside the realm of only being a private dispute such that it can be said that there was a reasonable belief that it was in the public interest. The assessment of whether those affected constitute a section of the public is then the consequence of that assessment of the circumstances in the round.

4.59   In *Chesterton* the context against which the fact-sensitive assessment was made was that the employee held a reasonable belief that deliberate manipulation of company accounts, misstating some £2–3 million of actual costs and liabilities throughout the entire office and department network, would cause a large number of employees, including himself, to suffer loss. Taken together that was found to be a sufficient basis for the claimant to hold a reasonable belief that the disclosure was in the public interest. It does not necessarily follow, we suggest, that the same group of managers would be regarded as a 'section of the public' if the alleged wrongdoing was, say, simply an alleged unreasonable exercise of discretion in relation to bonus. If placed in the full factual context, the conclusion in *Chesterton* accords with an uncontroversial view that there is a public interest (and in any event it is reasonable to believe that there is a public interest) in exposing or challenging dishonest conduct of that nature: see eg *KGM v News Group Newspapers Ltd* [2010] EWHC 3145 at [39] (where the Court commented that there is a potential public interest in the exposure of wrongdoing such as, for example, breach of fiduciary duty or the misappropriation of corporate funds, which might override an otherwise legitimate expectation of privacy).

The position may be further illustrated by reference to the example given in the Explanatory **4.60** Notes to section 17 of ERRA (introducing the public interest test). This suggests that if a worker does not receive the correct amount of holiday pay, which may be a breach of the terms of his/her contract of employment (and, it might have been added, a failure to comply with a statutory obligation), this is a matter of personal rather than of wider interest. We suggest that, without more, the mere fact that a group of workers raises this collectively, and that the claimant has others in the group in mind as well as himself, does not necessarily change a private dispute into a disclosure which is made in the public interest. However, the worker may have in mind not only the dispute between worker or workers and employer but also the wider importance or public interest in employers complying with their holiday pay obligations. That might be because if holiday pay is not paid it could lead to working excessive hours or financial hardship, or simply on the principle that there is a public interest in all employers complying with their legislative obligations. The nature and basis of the belief would be a matter for the employee to explain in any particular case, and it would be the tribunal's duty to make an assessment of whether this amounted to a belief that disclosure was made in the public interest and the reasonableness of that belief. In assessing whether it is reasonable to regard this as a disclosure in the public interest, it is likely to be useful for the tribunal to consider whether the employer had in mind others as being directly affected by the subject matter of the disclosure, or the number of others affected. But, depending on the subject matter of the disclosure, we suggest that is neither a necessary nor a necessarily sufficient basis for the conclusion that the disclosure was in the public interest.

D. Reasonable Belief and Need for Fact-Sensitive Assessment

(1) Reasonable belief

In each case, in determining whether there was a reasonable belief that disclosure was made **4.61** in the public interest, the necessary starting point is to identify what factors the worker had in mind, at the point in time when it was made, which are said to be the basis for any such belief. In some cases that may be self-evident from the nature of the disclosure. But in others, where on its face the disclosure may be regarded as advancing the worker's own interests, it will be necessary to identify any respects in which it was believed that the disclosure furthered some wider interest, and whether on that basis there was a reasonable belief that the disclosure was made in the public interest. As noted in *Chesterton,* a fact-sensitive approach is required. Further, it is important to have regard to the particular context. Thus, the nature of the worker's role, or the service being delivered, may be such that in some fields the public interest test will readily be satisfied. As is discussed in Chapter 12 (paragraph 12.45), the position in that respect is illustrated by the approach in the Francis report concerning speaking up in the NHS, emphasizing the interdependence of the different elements of delivery of a good service, and that concerns about oppressive or bullying and dysfunctional relationships are to be considered safety issues.

4.62 Two other decisions at EAT level have further emphasized that the fact-sensitive nature of the enquiry is likely to make it inappropriate to determine without hearing evidence, at least where some matter or material is put forward which might be said to engage the public interest. Applying this approach led to the conclusion that a claim had been wrongly struck out in *Morgan v Royal MENCAP Society* [2016] IRLR 428 (EAT). The alleged protected disclosures were in effect complaints about the conditions in which the worker was being required to work. She asserted a belief that they represented a danger to her health and safety. Although the employment judge accepted that these matters were highly relevant to the worker, he concluded that they were not a matter of public interest and on that basis struck out the claim. Moreover, he did not believe that the worker could have had a reasonable belief that these matters amounted to 'ones within the public interest'.

4.63 In the EAT, Simler J emphasized, following Maurice Kay LJ in *North Glamorgan NHS Trust v Ezsias* [2007] IRLR 603 (see Chapter 11 at paragraph 11.49), that it is in an exceptional case that an application to an employment tribunal in a whistleblowing claim would be struck out as having no reasonable prospect of success when the central facts were in dispute. Simler J noted that it was not necessary for an ET to determine what was in fact in the public interest; rather, it was for the ET to determine whether the worker's subjectively held belief that the disclosures were in the public interest was, when objectively viewed, reasonable. That, she said, was a fact-sensitive question. What was reasonable in one case might not be regarded as reasonable in another. The facts in a particular case might show that the worker's complaint about a matter affecting his or her contract or working conditions may have wider public interest implications.

4.64 Here the ET had failed to take the facts at their highest, as it was required to do on a strike-out application. The ET had rejected the worker's case that she held the subjective belief for which she contended. While her disclosures were about her own predicament and the fact that she had an earlier injury that made her working conditions dangerous in her view, she also asserted a belief that others might be affected by the working conditions, and made other contentions that were not tested by evidence and should have been accepted at the strike-out stage. Simler J was unpersuaded that this was a case where it could be said that no reasonable person could have believed that the matters which the worker was raising engaged the public interest. As HHJ Richardson said when dealing with the case on the EAT sift, it was reasonably arguable that an employee might consider health and safety complaints—even where the worker making the disclosure was the principal person affected—to be made in the wider interests of employees generally. Indeed, this was a point noted by the Minister in the course of the debates in Parliament about the amendment to the whistleblowing regime.[22] Whether such a belief was reasonably held in a particular case was, Simler J noted, a question of disputed fact which was not capable of determination without hearing the evidence and without resolving one way or another the factual disputes. Accordingly, Simler J concluded that the employment judge had erred in law in striking out this case on the basis of legal argument only and without resolving the potential factual disputes.

4.65 The fact-sensitive nature of the assessment of reasonable belief was again emphasized in *Underwood v Wincanton plc* (UKEAT/0163/15/RN, 27 August 2015). Mr Underwood was one of four lorry drivers who collectively submitted a complaint that overtime at Wincanton's

---

[22] See *Hansard*, 3 July 2012, col 388, set out at paras 4.33 and 4.34 above.

depot was being dealt with unfairly and in breach of contract. He contended that the complaint also affected other lorry drivers at the same depot and that this was one of a number of protected disclosures he claimed to have made. At a preliminary hearing the employment judge made an unless order requiring the claimant to show cause why the claim should not be struck out, and ultimately a strike-out order was made. The decision to do so preceded the EAT's decision in *Chesterton*. The employment judge placed emphasis on the fact that the complaint concerned a dispute between the claimant and the employer with reference to the terms and conditions of employment and also a dispute between fellow employees and the employer. He reasoned that it could not be said to be 'in the public interest' since:

> it falls squarely within the provisions of the *Parkins v Sodexho* case in that it is a dispute between the Claimant and the Respondent with reference to the terms of employment existing between the Claimant and the Respondent. How can that be said to be in the public interest? It is not something which the public are affected by, directly or indirectly. The Claimant appears to argue that because other employees are affected by the dispute they are members of the public and therefore the disclosure is in the public interest. However the reason the dispute resonates with the claimant's fellow employees is only because those fellow employees are in the same employee/employer relationship as is the Claimant with the Respondent. There is no 'Public interest'. It does not 'relate to or concern the people as a whole'. (Definition of the meaning of 'Public' contained in the Collins English Dictionary, Fifth Edition, 2000). In those circumstances it cannot be said to be in the *reasonable* belief of the Claimant to be in the public interest. It is the interest of the Claimant who is in dispute with the Respondent over his terms and conditions of employment and the allocation of overtime but does not satisfy the statutory definition and cannot be said to be a 'reasonable' belief in all the circumstances.

The EAT allowed the appeal. By the time the matter came before the EAT, the decision of **4.66** the EAT in *Chesterton* stood in the way of this line of reasoning. The EAT (Recorder Luba QC) concluded that in the light of (a) the *Chesterton* decision, and (b) the wording of the complaint relied upon as being a protected disclosure, it could not be said that the case met the high threshold of there being no reasonable prospect of success required for a strike out. The EAT emphasized the need for a careful factual determination to be reached in each case as to whether the particular aspects of the case were sufficient to meet the public interest test. In that respect it was relevant that the complaint letter was written in opaque terms, but at para 37 it was stated that, on one reading, it:

> possibly suggested that a cohort of drivers were being mistreated and being deprived of overtime (which they might otherwise have legitimately expected to receive, or at least legitimately have expected to be treated fairly in consideration for) for reasons which include, at least tentatively, the possibility that they are being too onerous in detecting defects in their vehicles or carrying out checks.

That, in the view of the EAT, '… might be thought to be a matter of some public interest to other road users …'. Whilst the claimant had been given an opportunity to show cause why this part of the case should not be struck out, and had not specifically raised this, given the terms of the complaint letter, the EAT was not satisfied that it could be said that there were no reasonable prospects of success before evidence was heard. The EAT considered that it was appropriate to follow the decision in *Chesterton*, albeit that Recorder Luba QC commented (at para 43) that, at least as a matter of first impression, he had some sympathy with the submission that the EAT in *Chesterton* missed the point by focusing too closely on the question of who was affected by the matter in question. The decision of the EAT in *Chesterton* was inconsistent with concluding that the fact that the dispute was a matter between employer and employees, and was liable to resonate with other workers only by reason of being fellow employees, necessarily prevented it being made in the public interest. Whether the claimant did hold a reasonable belief that it was made in the public interest was a matter to be determined after a full hearing.

(2) Must the worker have actually formed a belief as to the public interest?

4.67 It follows from the reasonable belief requirement that the worker who has given no thought either way to whether the disclosure involves a public interest element, or to something which can properly be regarded as equating to the public interest, cannot succeed. We suggest, however, that this is subject to the following important caveats:

1. The legislation has to be framed in terms which provide suitable protection for those acting in the public interest who may well not have taken legal advice and as such may not have framed a view formulated specifically in terms of public interest. To that end it must be sufficiently flexible to cover a situation where a worker's set of beliefs amount to a belief that that disclosure is in the public interest without the worker having precisely formulated a view in those terms. A worker who reports information tending to indicate a danger to health and safety might do so with a view to avoiding harm to others. That might not have been formulated in terms of whether this is furthering a public interest. But it would seem open to a tribunal to conclude that it is plainly in the public interest to protect the health and safety of others, and that as such a belief that the disclosure would prevent such harm amounts to a belief that disclosure is in the public interest.

   The position can be illustrated by reference to the view put forward by Sir Robert Francis QC in his report, 'Freedom to Speak Up' (February 2015) that concerns about oppressive or bullying and dysfunctional relationships were to be considered safety issues in the NHS context.[23] Suppose a nurse reports a concern as to being bullied by his line manager. If no consideration is given to any implications of the bullying other than the impact on the nurse raising the concern, it could not be said that there was a belief that disclosure was in the public interest. But suppose also that the nurse believes that the bullying is detrimental to his ability to care for patients and that addressing the concern would remedy this. It would seem open to a tribunal to conclude that this (a belief that the disclosure would facilitate improved patient care) is in substance a belief that making the disclosure is in the public interest.

2. Closely related to this, the framing of the relevant failures might itself be taken as an indication of what may be regarded as in the public interest. Thus, it may be said to be implicit in the legislation that generally, in the absence of some factor indicating otherwise, disclosure of information which is reasonably believed to tend to show criminality, serious wrongdoing, a miscarriage of justice, or danger to the environment is to be regarded as in the public interest. As such, in the absence of factors pointing to the contrary, it may be expected that a worker who satisfies the requirement for a qualifying disclosure of showing a reasonable belief that the information tends to show a past, present, or likely future criminal offence, serious wrongdoing, danger to health and safety, etc may be taken to have held a belief that disclosure was in the public interest irrespective of whether the worker subjectively formulated matters in these terms.

3. The position becomes more difficult where there are factors indicating a private interest in the disclosure, where it is less self-evident that disclosure is in the public interest even if there is a reasonable belief that the information tends to show a relevant failure. In those circumstances closer focus is required as to the basis on which it is said that it was believed that disclosure was in the public interest.

4. By analogy with the approach in *Korashi v Abertawe Bro Morgannwg University Local Health Board* [2012] IRLR 4 (EAT), the extent to which the worker may be expected to have formulated a view specifically in terms of identifying the public interest may also be affected by the particular circumstances of the worker and the resources available. More might be expected of somebody with expertise in the area or with the ability and resources to assess the significance of the information.

---

[23] See Chapter 12, para 12.47.

Thus as set out above, in *Morgan v Royal MENCAP Society*, the EAT noted that the claimant **4.68** had stated a view that others may be affected by the poor working conditions that were the subject of her disclosure. A tribunal might infer that implicit in this was a belief that raising a health and safety concern was to the benefit of others. In those circumstances, it would be open to a tribunal to regard the belief, that disclosure would enable the health and safety concerns to be addressed and thereby to protect others, implicitly to entail a reasonable belief that disclosure was in the public interest even if not formulated in the those terms.

Similar reasoning might be applied to the circumstances in *Chesterton*. It is noteworthy that **4.69** the ET made factual findings as to Mr Nurmohamed's reasons for making his disclosure: in part his personal position but also what he thought was the effect of the matters he was raising on the earnings of his colleagues. To the extent that the reasoning proceeded solely on the basis that it was determinative that the claimant had in mind that that disclosure was also to the benefit of other senior managers, it could be that this failed to grapple with why this was regarded as a dispute which engaged the public interest, or why the managers were regarded as sufficient to be a section of the public, rather than there being a private dispute between employees and employer. But the decision might be explained on the basis that in the context of the serious nature of the wrongdoing (in the claimant's reasonable belief), the belief that disclosure to expose that wrongdoing was to the benefit also of the other senior managers affected could properly be regarded as indicating a belief that disclosure was in the public interest.

E. Is the Public Interest Test Material to Relevant Failures other than Non-compliance with a Legal Obligation?

Having regard to the nature of the relevant failures other than in relation to legal obliga- **4.70** tions, ordinarily it will be self-evident that a worker who reasonably believes that information tends to show a past, present, or likely future relevant failure (other than in relation to legal obligations) will also hold a reasonable belief that disclosure is made in the public interest. Exceptions may, however, arise where the public interest test requires more careful consideration. Indeed, that is inherent in the necessarily general terms in which the relevant failures are framed. Thus, the first category of relevant failure includes disclosure of information tending to show that a criminal offence has been committed. There is no limit on how long ago or how serious or minor the criminal offence in question must be. Disclosure to an employer of information which is believed to show that a colleague committed some minor offence many years ago may give rise to a substantial question as to whether the worker believed this was in the public interest and if so whether any such belief was reasonable.

More generally, the public interest test may be of considerable importance in relation to **4.71** some disclosures within the category that health or safety has been, is being, or is likely to be endangered. The issue is illustrated by the decision in *Fincham v H M Prison Service* (EAT/ 0925/01/RN, 19 December 2002), which is considered in more detail in Chapter 3 (at paragraphs 3.35, 3.36). Ms Fincham made various complaints about the conduct of other members of staff (who were not her managers) which she alleged amounted to harassment. She complained that she felt under constant pressure and stress awaiting the next incident. The EAT concluded that the tribunal had erred in finding that this did not amount to a qualifying disclosure. It commented (at para 30) that:

> We found it impossible to see how a statement that says in terms 'I am under pressure and stress' is anything other than a statement that her health and safety is being or at least is likely to be endangered. It seems to us, therefore, that it is not a matter which can take its gloss from the particular context in which the statement is made. It may well be

that it was [a] relatively minor matter drawn to the attention of the employers in the course of a much more significant letter. We know not. But nonetheless it does seem to us that this was a disclosure tending to show that her own health and safety was likely to [be] endangered ...

4.72 On its face, the disclosure was made in the context of an essentially personal grievance of the nature that was intended to be excluded by the amendment to introduce the public interest test. At minimum, if the complaint had been made after the introduction of the new test, it would have been necessary to show that she believed that the disclosure raised some wider concern or issue of public interest, and the reason for that belief, and an assessment would have been required as to whether it was reasonable.

4.73 Certainly, in introducing the public interest test the Government viewed it as being capable of applying in cases falling within the health and safety category. As set out in paragraphs 4.33 and 4.34 above, in opposing the alternative Opposition amendment which focused only on the category of legal obligations, the point was made both in Committee on 3 July 2012 and in the Second Reading on 17 October 2012, that the claim in *Parkins v Sodexho* [2002] IRLR 109 (EAT):

> could have been reframed as a health and safety issue, with similar issues then arising in relation to the disclosures of minor breaches of health and safety legislation, which are of no interest to the wider public.

4.74 In *Parkins*, Mr Parkins claimed that he had made a protected disclosure in that he had complained that he did not have supervision on site in respect of his use of a buffing machine. He alleged that this tended to show a breach of his employment contract and also an infringement of health and safety legislation and policy. His claim was brought both on the basis of dismissal by reason of his protected disclosure and a claim under section 100(1)(c) ERA in relation to raising health and safety issues. However, the issue came before the EAT on an interim relief application, which was only available in relation to the protected disclosure claim. As such, whilst the EAT disagreed with the reasoning of the tribunal that a breach of the contract of employment was not a legal obligation within the spirit of the legislation, the case proceeded both under the legal obligation and endangering health and safety criteria for a relevant failure.

4.75 However, whilst the *Fincham* decision illustrates the potential for disclosures within the health and safety category to be made within essentially personal disputes, we suggest some care is needed in relation to the apparent view (see paragraph 4.73, above) that 'minor breaches of health and safety legislation' would not be covered. Ultimately, the test remains one of reasonable belief. There is no exception on the grounds of triviality as such. If a worker in fact believes that there is a public interest in strict compliance with health and safety legislation, and that health and safety has been, is being, or is likely to be endangered, it would seem most unlikely that this would be regarded as other than reasonable.

F. Is the Worker's Motive Relevant?

4.76 The test of whether a disclosure was 'made in the public interest' might, shorn of other context, be seen as focusing on the motive in making the disclosure. Indeed, in order to avoid any ambiguity as to this, the legislation could instead have simply provided that the requirement is for a reasonable belief that making the disclosure is in the public interest. That would have mirrored the language used in section 4 of the Defamation Act 2013 which requires a reasonable belief that the statement 'was in the public interest'. Similar language is used in the Data Protection Act 1998, section 32(1)(b), referring to a reasonable belief that publication 'would be in the public interest'. In each case that phrase focuses clearly on the effect of the disclosure (ie whether it is believed to be in the public interest) rather than the reason for making it.

However, in context it is apparent that a worker may act in bad faith or for ulterior motives **4.77** and yet be able to show a belief that the disclosure is made in the public interest. That is apparent from the removal of the good faith requirement as part of the test for a protected disclosure, and its retention at the remedy stage. Taken together with the introduction of the public interest test, the clear legislative intention is to encourage and provide protection for disclosures which are reasonably believed to be in the public interest, irrespective of whether there is some ulterior reason for making them. A worker may reasonably believe the disclosure to be made in the public interest despite being made in bad faith. By way of example, a worker who makes a disclosure that a drug which is produced by the employer is dangerous might act in bad faith if the reason for raising this is to negotiate an improved exit package, and yet still reasonably take the view that disclosure of such information is in the public interest.

During the passage of the Enterprise and Regulatory Reform Bill, in response to a pro- **4.78** posed amendment to remove the good faith requirement, and at a stage when this was being opposed by the Government, a point expressly made on behalf of the Government was that despite the public interest test, removal of the good faith requirement would mean that malicious disclosures could still be protected. Jo Swinson (the then Parliamentary Under-Secretary for Business Innovation and Skills) said of the proposed amendment that:[24]

> It proposes the removal of the good faith test, which has been in place since the legislation was introduced. That would mean that individual whistleblowers would retain the benefit of employment protection even if their reasons for blowing the whistle were malicious, if they deliberately set out to cause commercial damage, or if they acted out of a desire for personal revenge.

> There is clearly a balance to be struck. We are conscious of the recommendations of Dame Janet Smith's inquiry into the tragic circumstances of the Shipman case. She suggested that the good faith test be removed to encourage more whistleblowers to come forward. We also recognise that the motivations of whistleblowers are not always clear-cut. Personal feelings, particularly when a relationship has broken down, sometimes make it difficult to understand the intentions of the person who is making a disclosure. Having said that, I should add that, as we have already made clear, we believe that the legislation is working well overall, and that the good faith test serves an important purpose.

Consistently with the distinction between the motive for making the disclosure and whether it **4.79** was believed that making it was in the public interest, in *Chesterton* although the employment tribunal found that the person about whom the claimant was most concerned in making the disclosure was himself, that did not entail that he failed the public interest requirement. If the question had been whether the motive or predominant reason for making the disclosure was his own personal interest, it would seem that the claim may have failed. But that was not the question addressed. Irrespective of the fact that the claimant was principally concerned about his own situation, given that he had the other senior managers in mind, the public interest test was satisfied. Given the absence of any analysis as to why the disclosure was made, but only of what was in the claimant's mind as to who was affected by the content of the disclosure, that appears to indicate a focus on whether the claimant held a belief that making the disclosure was in the public interest, rather than a focus on the motive for making the disclosure.

---

[24] HC 2nd reading, 17 October 2012, *Hansard*, cols 330–31.

4.80 The implications of this approach may be illustrated by the decision in *Street v Derbyshire Unemployed Workers' Centre* [2005] ICR 97 (CA), the leading case on the meaning of the good faith test. Ms Street made disclosures which plainly had a public interest element. These included allegations that, in effect, her manager had engaged in fraud in order to obtain funding for the Centre at which she worked by setting up a secret account so as to conceal the true level of the Centre's assets. Even though she was found to have had an honest and reasonable belief that her allegations were substantially true, her claim failed because her principal reason for making the disclosures was found to be personal antagonism for her manager. Applying the public interest test, it would be available for her to say that she reasonably believed that making the disclosure was in the public interest, because there was plainly a public interest in revealing the fraud. There was no inconsistency between making the disclosure out of personal antagonism, yet also regarding the making of the disclosure as in the public interest. Instead, lack of good faith would be a matter for the remedy stage.

4.81 Whilst the public interest test does not therefore turn upon the motive for the disclosure, motive may well still be evidentially important. Where a tribunal finds that a worker has acted out of ulterior motives, rather than with the predominant motive of exposing, preventing, or addressing wrongdoing, it may well be difficult to persuade a tribunal that it was believed that making the disclosure was in the public interest, particularly where the disclosure is not obviously a matter of wider public interest.

4.82 Further, factors which under the previous test may have been relied upon to support an inference that a disclosure was not made in good faith may now be liable to be relied upon to challenge whether the disclosure was made in the public interest. One instance is that the time of raising the issue may bear both on whether it was made in good faith and whether it was genuinely believed to be made in the public interest. In *de Haney v Brent Mind and Lang* (EAT/0054/03, 19 March 2004) it was said that relevant factors in relation to whether a disclosure was made in good faith may extend to the circumstances in which the allegation is raised before the employment tribunal. Mrs de Haney alleged that in a meeting with her line manager she had complained about the appointment of a colleague which she claimed was in breach of her employer's equal opportunity policy. The claimant had raised a concern about the appointment in writing prior to her dismissal, but the allegation that her concerns in relation to this amounted to a protected disclosure was not contained in the claim form or the claimant's further particulars of her claim, but was first made in her witness statement. In those circumstances, the EAT held that the tribunal had been entitled to find that the allegation was put in as a 'makeweight' and as such was not a qualifying disclosure (in that she did not hold the requisite reasonable belief). Now the same point would be framed on the basis that the very fact that the matter was raised as an afterthought indicated that there was no belief at the time of making the disclosure that it was made in the public interest.

G. Are the circumstances of the disclosure relevant to whether it is made in the public interest?

4.83 The public interest test requires not only that in the worker's reasonable belief the disclosure is on a matter of public interest, but that it is (in the worker's reasonable belief) made in the public interest. The potentially distinct issues as to whether the disclosure (a) involves a matter of public interest and (b) whether making it is in the public interest, is reflected in these elements being separately expressed in the public interest defence contained in the Defamation Act 2013. As set out at paragraph 4.36 above, section 4(1) of that Act specifically requires that, in order to provide a defence to a defamation claim, both (a) the statement complained of was or formed part of a statement on a matter of public interest, and (b) the defendant reasonably believed that publishing the statement complained of was in the public interest. The new statutory provision replaced the common law *Reynolds* privilege defence[25] which focused on 'responsible journalism', and reflects the emphasis on considering not only the public interest content, but also whether the publication was appropriate in the particular circumstances. Indeed, in *Reynolds* ten non-exhaustive factors were listed as meriting consideration in this respect, including the seriousness of the allegation, the nature of the information, the source, steps taken to verify the information and timing.

Clearly, the considerations relevant in the context of protected disclosures are different. **4.84** Ordinarily the disclosure does not entail infringing any other right in a way which is at all comparable with the public interest defences for defamation or breach of confidentiality. As such ordinarily there is not the same need for balancing competing public interests as to whether there should be disclosure. Nor ordinarily is there the same sensitivity as to the timing of disclosure to be taken into account in considering whether disclosure at that time is in the public interest. Further, the defence under section 4 Defamation Act 2013 is most likely to be invoked in the context of disclosure to the public generally. That is to be contrasted with the carefully constructed framework for protected disclosures, with its differing conditions depending on to whom the disclosure is made. Bearing that structure in mind, it can be said that, where a disclosure is reasonably believed to involve the public interest, it would be inappropriate to impose on workers the further hurdle of having to establish a reasonable belief that in all the circumstances it was in the public interest that the disclosure be made. Instead, the appropriate further conditions to be applied are those precisely provided by sections 43C to 43H, depending on to whom the disclosure is made.

The same argument can be put in another way. Even if there is an additional requirement for **4.85** a value judgement as to whether disclosure not only involves but serves the public interest, that could only realistically be of any significance in first-level disclosures (ie within sections 43C, 43D, or 43E). For wider disclosures (sections 43G or 43H) there is a requirement that it was reasonable in all the circumstances to make the disclosure (see Chapter 5 for a discussion of these provisions). On any view that is a more stringent test than that of a reasonable belief that the disclosure is in the public interest, since it applies an objective standard rather than a standard of reasonableness as viewed from the worker's perspective. It is therefore difficult to conceive that a worker who believes that a disclosure is on a matter of public interest could meet all the requirements of sections 43G and 43H and yet fail to establish a reasonable belief that the disclosure was made in the public interest by reason of the circumstances in which the disclosure is made.

The same can be said of a disclosure to a prescribed person (usually but not always the appro- **4.86** priate regulator). In that instance (as for wider disclosures) a worker must hold a reasonable belief that the disclosure and any allegation contained within it is substantially true. Again, it may be difficult to conceive of a case where, despite satisfying that requirement and holding a reasonable belief that the disclosure involves the public interest, a worker's claim would fail on the basis that in all the circumstances he or she did not reasonably believe that making the disclosure to a regulator was in the public interest.

That then only leaves first-level disclosures. The policy of the legislation is very much to **4.87** encourage the making of such disclosures as an early-warning signal. Further, in relation to such disclosures it is rather less likely that there will be strong countervailing public

---

[25] Following the decision in *Reynolds v Times Newspapers* [2001] 2 AC 127 (HL).

considerations which make it unreasonable to believe that making the disclosure is in the public interest despite a reasonable belief that it involves the public interest.

4.88 Nevertheless, it is possible to conceive of situations where it will be argued in relation to first level disclosures that, even if a worker reasonably believed that disclosures involved matters of public interest, it could not reasonably have been believed that that the particular disclosure or disclosures in issue was or were made in the public interest. One scenario that may arise is illustrated by the decision in *Phipps v Bradford Hospitals NHS Trust* (EAT/531/02, 30 April 2003). Here the claimant wrote a letter to the medical director raising concerns as to treatment of patients with breast cancer. It was held that the disclosure was not made in good faith. An inference was drawn that he had sent the letter to put a marker down that his position was not to be lightly challenged by the medical director. In particular the tribunal took into account that (a) the issue had already been the subject of a report and discussion with the employer and (b) there was a failure to set out sufficient information in the letter, or subsequently, to enable the matter to be investigated. Following the amendments introduced by ERRA the good faith argument would no longer be available on the issue of liability. Instead it might now be argued that, even if the letter was on a matter of public interest, the claimant could not reasonably have believed that making disclosure at that time was in the public interest where the matter had already been the subject of a report, particularly if he was not going to provide sufficient information to enable it to be investigated.

4.89 The decision in *Ezsias v North Glamorgan NHS Trust* [2011] IRLR 550 may provide a further illustration of where arguments along these lines might now be pursued, given that lack of good faith is no longer a defence to liability. Mr Ezsias was a surgeon who held concerns as to the clinical competence of colleagues. His complaints were described by an internal inquiry panel as 'excessively frequent, unacceptably detailed, and unrelenting to an extreme degree'. In turn, complaints were made against him by colleagues who were the subject of his complaints. Ultimately, he was suspended and then dismissed on the basis of an irretrievable breakdown of relationships with his colleagues. He contended that his complaints amounted to protected disclosures, and that his dismissal was automatically unfair. In his skeleton argument he claimed that there were seventy-five topics that he complained about. The employment tribunal concluded that it did not need to deal with each of these matters because the complaints were part of Mr Ezsias' 'campaign' against certain colleagues and that the real reason why he made the complaints was to further that campaign, and the disclosures were therefore not in good faith. That reasoning was specifically approved by the EAT (at paras 24 and 37).

4.90 Whilst there were other grounds on which the claim failed, without further explanation the reasoning rather begs the question as to what the purposes of Mr Ezsias' campaign(s) were. To assert that a campaign was being pursued does not without further explanation address whether it is a campaign to have the relevant failures prevented or dealt with, or whether there is some other ulterior objective of the 'campaign'. But the question now arises as to whether, in the absence of good faith as a barrier, a tribunal could say that there came a point in Mr Ezsias' unrelenting campaign where it could no longer reasonably be seen as furthering any public interest and instead amounted to a campaign of harassment.

4.91 Repeated disclosures may still be qualifying disclosures because of section 43L ERA, which provides that a reference to the disclosure of information shall have effect in relation to any case where the person receiving the information is already aware of it, as a reference to bringing the information to his attention. But suppose that, knowing that the matter is under investigation at an appropriate level of management, the worker insists on escalating it to Board level, cutting across reporting lines. As illustrated by the situation in *Ezsias,* the issue then arises whether it can then be said that the continued insistence on disclosing the same matters, and cutting across lines of investigation before they have been concluded, does not serve and could not reasonably be believed to serve any public interest. There might be an argument that it will be detrimental to the efficient administration of the company or public body that its board is distracted by a disclosure which could and should be raised at a lower level—at least unless and until the worker has a reasonable basis for concluding that he or she is not being taken seriously—or that management is engaged in a cover-up, or that the serious nature of the information or the urgency of any threat explains the need for escalation.

As against that line of argument, it can be said that allegations may well be repeated or **4.92** escalated by a worker if s/he is not satisfied that they have been resolved. It does not follow from the persistent nature of such disclosures that they should be regarded as not having been made in the public interest even though they are reasonably believed to involve disclosures of information which tends to show a relevant failure, and to involve matters of public interest. Indeed, perseverance and a determination to be heard and heeded may well be the hallmark of a worker who is genuinely concerned as to matters which are the subject of the disclosure. Experience indicates that all too often it is precisely that determination and resilience which is required before the disclosure is heeded, if it is heeded at all.

H. Summary

Pulling together the strands of the above discussion, we suggest in summary that the follow- **4.93** ing considerations are relevant to the approach to the public interest test:

1. As the decision in *Chesterton* makes clear, it is not necessarily a bar to a tribunal finding that disclosure is in the public interest either that (a) self-interest is the worker's principal reason for making the disclosure or (b) that the disclosure concerns a dispute between employer and employees, and that the only people that the employee has in mind as affected are fellow employees.
2. The reasonable belief test emphasizes that it is not for the court to assess what is in the public interest, but only whether the claimant held that view and it was a view which could reasonably be held. But that is subject to the qualification that the tribunal may be required to consider whether the factors the worker had in mind are properly to be regarded as equating to the public interest (eg improved patient care in the example at paragraph 4.67, subpara 1, above).
3. The test is required to be sufficiently flexible to take into account the different circumstances of the worker to whom it must be applied. That may mean applying the test in circumstances where the worker's state of mind amounts to a belief that disclosure is in the public interest even though the worker may not have formulated a view in precisely those terms.
4. The essential purpose of the test is to distinguish what are essentially private complaints from those engaging a wider public interest. But there may be an overlap. A disclosure concerned with an essentially personal complaint (whether individual or collective) may also be believed to be in the public interest because of some wider implications, or because, for example, addressing or exposing wrongdoing may be believed to further the public interest.
5. The starting point is to identify the set of beliefs that are relied upon by the worker as indicating that the disclosure was made in the public interest. In many cases it may be useful in that respect to focus on whom the worker had in mind as affected by or benefitting from the disclosure. That may be indicative of the disclosure being made in a wider

public interest. But it may still be important to have regard to all the circumstances, such as whether the belief as to the nature of the wrongdoing or harm to others indicates that the disclosure is reasonably believed to be in the public interest rather than, say, a collective grievance without any wider public interest.

6. In other cases, focusing on whom the worker had in mind as being directly affected by the disclosure may be unnecessary or unhelpful. Some disclosures will be self-evidently in the public interest by reason of their subject matter or to whom they are made. In other cases the worker may not have specifically given consideration to who else is affected but yet reasonably consider that addressing the relevant failure, depending on its nature and context, is in the public interest.

7. The decision in *Chesterton* is properly to be understood having regard to the particular content of the disclosure in that case. It should not be taken as meaning that disclosure is necessarily to be regarded as in the public interest wherever it is reasonably regarded as benefitting someone other than the worker, or doing so on the basis of a vague test of whether those affected should be regarded as a section of the public.

8. A worker may still reasonably believe that a disclosure is made in the public interest (in the sense that it is in the public interest that the disclosure be made) even though the disclosure is not made in good faith. However, motive may still be relevant in that evidentially it may bear on whether the tribunal accepts that the worker genuinely believed that making the disclosure was in the public interest.

9. In theory, a belief that the disclosure is made in the public interest entails a view not only to be taken on whether the subject matter is of public interest, but also whether making the disclosure at a particular time or in a particular way is in the public interest and possibly whether it outweighs any interest in not making the disclosure at that time. In practice, these considerations are likely to be less important in the protected disclosure context, in the light of the structure of the protected disclosure legislation, with the greater hurdles which in any event need to be overcome for wider disclosures.

5

THE THREE TIERS OF PROTECTION

A. The Three Tiers

At the heart of the scheme of the protected disclosure legislation are the differing thresholds **5.01** for protection dependent on to whom the disclosure is made. The scheme was described in *Street v Derbyshire Unemployed Workers' Centre* [2005] ICR 97 as setting out a 'three tiered disclosure regime':

(1) The first tier was said to include disclosures under ERA, sections 43C (employer or other responsible person), 43D (disclosures in the course of legal advice), and 43E (Minister of the Crown). These set the lowest threshold for protection. They are sometimes referred

to by way of shorthand as 'internal disclosures'. This reflects the fact that the most significant category of disclosures within this group are disclosures to the employer. However, it also encompasses other disclosures which may be outside the employing organization, including disclosures to those whose conduct is in question or who have legal responsibility for the relevant failure. We therefore prefer to refer to disclosures within this category (sections 43C, 43D, and 43E) as 'first tier disclosures'. In each case the legislation acknowledges that the recipient of the disclosure is likely to be an appropriate choice for raising concerns in the first instance, and a low threshold is therefore set for protection. In relation to disclosures made on or after 25 June 2013, there are no further requirements over and above those to establish a qualifying disclosure. The same applied to section 43D disclosures made prior to that date. Otherwise, for disclosures made prior to 25 June 2013, the only additional requirement was for the disclosure to be made in good faith.

(2) The second tier is disclosures to a prescribed body under ERA, section 43F. We refer to these as 'regulatory disclosures'. The threshold for protection is set higher than for first tier disclosures, but still at a level which reflects the fact that the recipient is likely to be an appropriate person to whom to make the disclosure.

(3) The third tier comprises wider disclosures under ERA, section 43G or 43H. For these disclosures the thresholds for protection are set at their highest. For ease of reference we refer to these as 'third tier disclosures'.

5.02 Broadly, therefore, the stringency of the requirements in each tier of disclosure relates to whether the recipient of the disclosure has a direct interest in receiving the information, or is readily identifiable as a party well placed to investigate or address the relevant failure. In this chapter we consider in turn each of the heads of protection within each of the three tiers.

B. First Tier Disclosures: Section 43C

(1) Overview

5.03 ERA, section 43C provides:

Disclosure to employer or other responsible person

(1) A qualifying disclosure is made in accordance with this section if the worker makes the disclosure …—
    (a) to his employer, or
    (b) where the worker reasonably believes that the relevant failure relates solely or mainly to—
        (i) the conduct of a person other than his employer, or
        (ii) any other matter for which a person other than his employer has legal responsibility, to that other person.

(2) A worker who, in accordance with a procedure whose use by him is authorised by his employer, makes a qualifying disclosure to a person other than his employer, is to be treated for the purposes of this Part as making the qualifying disclosure to his employer.

5.04 This was described by Lord Borrie QC (one of the promoters of the Public Interest Disclosure Bill) as being 'absolutely at the heart' of the Act.[1] Similarly, Lord Haskell, speaking for the government at the House of Lords committee stage, said:[2]

When my noble friend Lord Borrie spoke to the first amendment, he reminded us that we want to encourage the use of proper internal procedures. That is why the purpose of Section

---

[1] *Hansard* HL, 19 June 1998, cols 1801–02, during the Lords report stage.
[2] *Hansard* HL, 5 June 1998, col 621.

43C in Clause 1 of the Bill is to encourage workers to raise their concerns with the employer first, whether directly or through proper internal company procedures. They need only act in good faith in doing so, which is deliberately not an onerous condition.

The Bill is therefore very much in line with the Government's partnership approach, which seeks to encourage greater co-operation between employers and workers and trade unions.

For disclosures on or after 25 June 2013, no additional evidential test applies in this section **5.05** beyond the requirement, by virtue of the need to establish a qualifying disclosure, that the worker 'reasonably believes the information tends to show' the malpractice or misconduct. For earlier disclosures there is an additional requirement that the disclosures were made in good faith.

(2) Section 43C(1)(a): disclosure to the employer

Where a disclosure is made internally within the employer's organization an issue may **5.06** arise as to whether this constitutes disclosure to the employer. Some guidance can be drawn from the decision of the EAT in *Douglas v Birmingham City Council and others* (EAT/0518/02, 17 March 2003). As summarized in Chapter 3 (paragraph 3.38), the claimant, Mrs Douglas, was a staff governor of a local education authority school. She raised concerns in relation to a perceived lack of equal opportunities at the school. Her concerns were initially raised in confidence with a fellow governor (G). A subsequent disclosure was made to the chair of the governing body of her school, which was to be regarded as her employer within the extended meaning in ERA, section 43K(1). The EAT held that the initial disclosure to a fellow governor did not fall within section 43C(1)(a) because the disclosure was made to G 'in a confidential manner and not to her *qua* employer'. The EAT also noted that Mrs Douglas had consulted G for advice only and indicated that she would herself pursue the matter and did not want it to be handled on her behalf by G. In that context the EAT commented (at para 30) that a statute which is designed in the public interest to protect disclosures ought not to apply to a private conversation between two governors. The subsequent disclosure to the chair of governors was, however, a disclosure to Mrs Douglas' employer since he led the governing body which was to be treated as her employer.

The test of whether the disclosure is made *qua* employer provides a helpful yardstick. It **5.07** indicates that the concept would ordinarily include a disclosure to any person senior to the worker, who has been expressly or implicitly authorized by the employer as having management responsibility over the worker. But it also indicates that there might be circumstances where even a disclosure to someone more senior in the hierarchy will not be a disclosure to that person *qua* employer. Thus, if the disclosure is made to a more senior colleague but on the basis of confiding confidentially in a friend, it may be that the disclosure was not made to the colleague *qua* employer.

In *Premier Mortgage Connections Ltd v Miller* (EAT/0113/07, 2 November 2007), in the **5.08** context of an employee who was less senior than director level, the EAT commented that the term 'employer' is wide enough to cover a disclosure made by a worker to the employing company by presenting the complaint to a single serving director. Unsurprisingly, the EAT noted that disclosure to an ex-director did not constitute disclosure to the employer.

Equally, section 43C(1)(a) does not cover a disclosure to a more junior colleague unless that **5.09** person has a particular role in receiving complaints such as pursuant to a special policy. Nor would it ordinarily cover disclosure to a colleague on the same level.

Further, the question as to whether the disclosure is to the employer is to be determined at **5.10** the time the disclosure is made rather than when the alleged detriment (or dismissal) occurs. It is possible therefore for there to be a disclosure within section 43C(1)(a) made to one employer, but for the act or failure to act (or dismissal), by reason of making the disclosure, to be by a subsequent employer. That was the situation in *BP plc v Elstone and Petrotechnics Ltd* [2010] ICR 879, EAT. The claimant employee was previously employed by P, but subsequently became a consultant with BP. He made an alleged protected disclosure to P whilst he was in its employment. He alleged that when employed by BP he suffered a detriment in that BP withdrew proposed further consultancy engagements on the grounds of the disclosure previously made to P. The EAT concluded that the legislation was broad enough to cover an unlawful detriment imposed by BP, on the grounds of a protected disclosure made to the previous employer, P.

5.11   The scope of the persons to whom the disclosure can be made might be covered expressly in a whistleblowing procedure, and it is best practice for the employer to do this, although there is no such statutory requirement. An employee who wholly fails to abide by the terms and conditions of that policy may be more likely to be found not to have held a reasonable belief that the disclosure was made in the public interest, just as for disclosures prior to 25 June 2013 this may have made a finding of lack of good faith more likely (see eg *Muchesa v Central & Cecil Housing Care Support* (EAT/0443/07, 22 August 2008[3]) and *Smith v Ministry of Defence* (ET, Case No 1401537/04 26 April 2005[4])).

(3) Section 43C(1)(b)

(a) Centrality of promoting accountability

5.12   Section 43C(1)(b) ERA provides that if the worker reasonably believes that the relevant failure relates solely or mainly to the conduct of a person other than the employer or to matters for which that other person has legal responsibility, there is a protected disclosure (subject also to the requirement if the disclosure was prior to 25 June 2013, that it was made to that person in good faith). As the EAT (HHJ Richardson) succinctly put it in *Premier Mortgage Connections Ltd v Miller* (EAT/0113/07, 2 November 2007) (at para 28):

> … we think the legislative purpose of section 43C is reasonably clear. It is to provide workers with a high level of protection where they make disclosures to their own employers or to those whom they reasonably believe to be responsible either by their conduct or by virtue of the law for the matter they are disclosing.

5.13   The worker may therefore have a choice of to whom to make the disclosure (and may do so to each or any of them). The EAT proceeded to illustrate this with an example of a teacher, employed by a school, who takes his children on an adventure holiday, organized by a specialist firm.[5] The teacher hears that an employee of the specialist firm had told a child to ignore a safety precaution. The teacher may, subject to the requirement for a reasonable belief that the information tends to show a relevant failure (in this case that health and safety has been, is being, or will be endangered), do any or each of the following:

(1)   report the matter to his own school (section 43C(1)(a)); or
(2)   complain about it to the employee of the specialist firm whom he believes told the child to ignore the safety precaution, so long as the teacher reasonably believes that the matter is solely or mainly about his conduct (section 43C(1)(b)(i)); or
(3)   report the matter to the specialist firm provided he reasonably believes that the matter solely or mainly relates to health and safety and that the firm has legal responsibility for this (section 43C(1)(b)(ii)).

---

[3] Discussed at para 5.65 below.
[4] Discussed in Chapter 10 at para 10.132.
[5] See, to similar effect, *Ross v Eddie Stobart Ltd* (EAT/0085/10, 16 May 2011) at [38].

At the Lords report stage of the Public Interest Disclosure Bill, Lord Borrie (a promoter of the **5.14** Bill) emphasized that section 43C(1)(b) was central to the scheme of the legislation in that it encourages disclosure to those accountable for relevant failures, and encourages accountability within employing organizations. He explained[6] that:

> Subsection (b) demonstrates that the 'other responsible person' refers to the person responsible for the malpractice because it is his misconduct which is in issue or because he has a legal responsibility for the malpractice.

> This clause is absolutely at the heart of the Bill because this is the provision which will assert and help to ensure that those who are responsible for the concern or malpractice—be it crime, other kinds of illegality, danger to health or safety—are made aware of the concern and can investigate it.

> The effect is that if the concern proves well-founded and there is concern on behalf of the public interest, the employer will, in law, be accountable for the response. Your Lordships will all recall the tragic loss of life in connection with the Zeebrugge ferry. Even though the official inquiry found that on five occasions staff had voiced concerns that the ferries were sailing with their bow doors open, the company was not liable in criminal law, as the board—known in law as the controlling heart and mind of the organisation—had not been informed on those concerns and was unaware of the resultant risk.

> By contrast, when four schoolchildren were killed during a canoeing expedition at Lyme Bay, the managing director of the Outward Bound centre was gaoled for two years because a member of staff had written to him with a clear and graphic warning about the grave risk to life if safety standards were not dramatically and considerably improved. Unable to give good reason as to why he had ignored that warning, the managing director was the very first person in the United Kingdom to be gaoled for what is called corporate manslaughter. Therefore, what will be Section 43C of the 1996 Act signals that concerns should be raised with those who, in law, are responsible for the matter—normally the employer. However, where someone else is legally responsible, then it will be that person.

> In practical terms the clause as it stands, unamended, is right to emphasise the vital role of those who are in law accountable for the conduct or practice in question.

The provision encourages disclosure to those who are best able to investigate concerns or are **5.15** responsible for addressing them. It highlights accountability in two senses. First, it places an onus on those who are in law accountable to take appropriate action in relation to disclosures as to relevant failures. Second, it promotes and fosters accountability, by helping to ensure that those who have a legal responsibility for relevant failures are properly held accountable and do not escape appropriate censure for failing to take action on the basis of professed ignorance of the relevant failures. The provision is therefore an important part of the scheme for encouraging good corporate governance.

The objective of fostering accountability cannot, however, be read as requiring any implicit **5.16** limitation on what can properly be disclosed to the employer under ERA, section 43C(1)(a). A protected disclosure may be made to the employer concerning a relevant failure notwithstanding that the disclosure has nothing to do with the employer, and in relation to which there is no question of the employer being accountable in any way: see *Hibbins v Hesters Way Neighbourhood Project* [2009] ICR 319, EAT, Silber J.

(b) Section 43C(1)(b)(i)

Conduct of a person other than his employer   Section 43C(1)(b) has two limbs which are **5.17** alternatives. The first limb is where the worker reasonably believes that the relevant failure relates solely or mainly to the conduct of someone other than the employer and the disclosure

---

[6] *Hansard* HL, 19 June 1998, cols 1801–02.

is made to that person. There is a very substantial overlap with the second limb of ERA, section 43C(1)(b). In many, perhaps most, cases, if there is a relevant failure which relates solely or mainly to the conduct of a particular person, that person will have a legal responsibility in relation to the matter.

5.18   A potential complication arises where the conduct is of an employee or director of the employer. Can it be said that this person's conduct is properly attributable to the employer and therefore that it does not relate wholly or mainly to a person *other than the employer*? We suggest not. It would be inappropriate to construe the legislation narrowly so as to restrict the ability of an employee to take up concerns with the individual whose conduct is at the heart of the relevant failure.

5.19   **Solely or mainly conduct of the other person**   Where more than one person is involved in the relevant conduct, ERA, section 43C(1)(b)(i) may involve a comparison of the degree of involvement of that person in the relevant failure with that of the employer or others. The issues which may arise can be illustrated by the following example. Suppose an employee (A) suspects that his employer has been conspiring to distort market prices and that a third party (T) has also been involved in this. It may be that the employee could not make a disclosure under section 43C(1)(b)(i) to T. Although the disclosure relates in part to the conduct of T it might not relate 'solely or mainly' to T's conduct. On the contrary, it might relate at least equally to the conduct of the employer or the employer's employees. The appropriate and safer course would be to make the disclosure to the employer.

5.20   This indicates a potential difficulty where there are several people other than the employer involved in the relevant failure. It may be difficult to say that the relevant failure relates wholly or mainly to the conduct of any one person. But if T also has a legal responsibility for causing the market distortion, a disclosure could be made to T under section 43C(1)(b)(ii). Further, the reasonable belief test applies, so that a worker may reasonably believe that the conduct related solely or mainly to the conduct of a person, notwithstanding that the belief ultimately turns out to be incorrect: see *Premier Mortgage Connections Ltd v Miller* (EAT/ 0113/07, 2 November 2007) (at para 36).

(c) Other responsible persons: section 43C(1)(b)(ii)

5.21   **Legal responsibility**   The second limb of section 43C(1)(b) contemplates disclosure to someone with 'legal responsibility' for the relevant failure. The phrase 'legal responsibility' needs to be construed in context. We suggest that it encompasses someone who may be responsible, in the sense of being held responsible or being accountable, for the wrongdoing. This is consistent with the aims of the provision in promoting accountability. It does not extend to disclosure to any person who has a legal responsibility for investigating another person's wrongdoing. Otherwise the distinction between section 43C and section 43F ERA would collapse. It would be difficult to conceive of a case where a disclosure to a prescribed body would not be to a person legally responsible for the relevant failure. That could not be the statutory intention. As the EAT noted in *Ross v Eddie Stobart Ltd* (EAT/0085/10, 16 May 2011) (at para 38), it is clear from the structure of the legislation that disclosure to regulatory authorities is not within section 43C(1)(b). Equally, it would mean that any disclosure to the police would fall within section 43C(1)(b) if there was a qualifying disclosure relating to a criminal offence. This would be inconsistent with the scheme of the legislation in encouraging the investigation of matters internally.

5.22   The importance of accountability also explains the decision in *Premier Mortgage Connections Ltd v Miller* (EAT/0113/07, 2 November 2007) that there must be legal responsibility for dealing with the relevant failure at the time of disclosure. The EAT concluded that it is not sufficient that the recipient of the disclosure had legal responsibility for the wrongdoing at the time it took place. For that reason, subject to the latitude afforded by the reasonable belief test, disclosure to a former director in relation to accounting irregularities which took place when s/he was still a director would not be covered. Whilst a former director might still be sued or prosecuted for wrongdoing whilst previously a director, there would not in those circumstances be a continuing legal responsibility to deal with the complaint. Further, the EAT was sceptical as to whether reliance on the reasonable belief test would help. As the EAT put it (at para 38), an ex-director is not generally legally responsible for errors and omissions prior to ceasing to be a director, and the EAT could see no reason why an employee should generally think otherwise.

The concept of accountability also assists in explaining the approach in *Douglas v Birmingham City Council and others* (EAT/ 0518/ 02, 17 March 2003).[7] Following the initial confidential disclosure, Mrs Douglas made a further disclosure to the chair of the governing body in relation to failure to carry out policies relating to equal opportunities. The EAT concluded that this constituted a disclosure to the employer, but accepted that if this was not correct, it fell within section 43C(1)(b)(ii) as disclosure to 'another responsible person'. The reasoning in support of this conclusion was not set out, but it can be explained on the basis that the governors were responsible for ensuring the proper implementation of the equal opportunities policy, and they were accountable for a failure to do so. **5.23**

Consistently with the emphasis on accountability, Public Concern at Work (PCaW) has suggested on its website[8] (and we agree) that section 43C(1)(b) would entail protection in the following circumstances:

(a) A nurse employed by an agency who, in the care home where she works (ie where she is placed by the agency), raises a concern about malpractice in that home. The care home might have vicarious liability for the malpractice and therefore this might be regarded as conduct of the care home or a matter for which it has legal responsibility.

(b) A worker in an auditing firm who raises a concern with the client (in relation to a matter for which the client would be legally responsible, such as a potential liability for inadequate accounts).

(c) Someone who works for a local authority highway contractor who raises a concern with the local authority that the performance of the contract exposes the authority to negligence claims from injured pedestrians.

Difficulties may arise, however, in distinguishing between whether there is legal responsibility in the sense of accountability for a relevant failure, or simply a responsibility to investigate or address another's failure without being accountable for that failure. The distinction may be illustrated by reference to the employment tribunal's decision in *Azzaoui v Apcoa Parking UK Ltd* (ET, Case No 2302156/01, 30 April 2002). A parking attendant disclosed that undue pressure was being placed on parking attendants to meet production targets, thereby forcing them into the position of issuing false parking contravention notices (PCNs) and making inaccurate reports which were used as evidence against motorists in appeals. The disclosure was made both to the claimant's employer and to the local council, which was the employer's client and on behalf of which parking fines were levied. The tribunal concluded that the disclosure to the council fell within section 43C(1)(b)(ii). This finding was not further explained. It is understandable that the tribunal concluded that the council was legally responsible, given that the alleged wrongdoing involved the council (albeit unwittingly) in the wrongdoing by relying on inaccurate reports as evidence against motorists in appeals. **5.24**

---

[7] See para 5.06 above.
[8] See http://www.pcaw.co.uk.

Indeed, on this basis it would have been open to the tribunal to find that the disclosure fell within section 43C(1)(b)(i) as it related to the conduct of the council. The tribunal did not, however, rely on this provision. We suggest that in order to rely on section 43C(1)(b)(ii) it was necessary for the tribunal to address further the issue of whether the council could be held responsible for the failures of employees of its clients. This issue was not directly addressed.

5.25 **Solely or mainly to any other matter for which another person has legal responsibility** Although the phrase 'solely or mainly' applies to both limbs of ERA, section 43C(1)(b), there may be an important difference in how it applies to the two limbs. In relation to the second limb of section 43C(1)(b) the phrase 'solely or mainly' is not applied to the degree of responsibility for the matter to which the relevant failure relates. The issue is instead whether the relevant failure relates solely or mainly to a particular matter, rather than whether the recipient of the disclosure has sole or main responsibility for that matter. As the EAT put it in *Premier Mortgage Connections Ltd v Miller* (EAT/0113/07, 2 November 2007) (at para 40):

> The test is not whether the failure relates to a matter for which the person has sole or main responsibility, but whether the failure relates solely or mainly to a matter for which he has responsibility.

5.26 It is possible that the relevant failure might be solely or mainly about something for which a number of people, including the recipient of the disclosure, have legal responsibility. Thus, in the market distortion example referred to at paragraphs 5.19–5.20 above, there might be a number of people and entities involved with various degrees of culpability but all with some legal responsibility. If the disclosure relates solely or mainly to the market distortion, the disclosure could be made to each person with legal responsibility without need for further consideration of who has greatest legal responsibility.

5.27 Conversely, if the disclosure related only in small part to something for which the recipient of the disclosure had a legal responsibility, the disclosure could not be made under section 43C(1)(b)(ii). Thus, suppose that a worker makes a disclosure that the employer has been damaging the environment by dumping excessive pollution into a local river and that some of the pollutant material has been leaking from pipes en route to the river. The construction company which built the pipes might have a legal responsibility for flaws in the construction giving rise to the leaks, but the disclosure would not be solely or mainly about a matter for which the construction company had legal responsibility. It would not be a disclosure solely or mainly about defective pipes, but about the employer's conduct in causing the pollution.

5.28 **A person other than his employer** The phrase 'other than his employer' may be thought to contain an ambiguity. Does it mean simply that the recipient of the disclosure is not the employer, or does it connote that the employer does not have a legal responsibility for the matter? It might be argued that the policy of the legislation indicates that it only applies where the employer has no legal responsibility, so that where the employer does have legal responsibility the employee is encouraged to raise the matter internally with the employer. We suggest, however, that the better view is that the phrase 'other than his employer' simply means that the recipient of the disclosure is not the employer—and does not preclude the employer also having a legal responsibility for the matter. As to this:

(a) The phrase 'other than his employer' appears in both limbs of section 43C(1)(b). In the first limb, section 43C(1)(b)(i), it plainly does not connote that the employer has no involvement in the relevant failure. The employer may have some involvement provided the failure does not relate mainly to the employer's conduct rather than that of the person to whom the disclosure is made. The same phrase in section 43C(1)(b)(ii) does not, we suggest, have a wholly different connotation as requiring that the employer have no legal responsibility.

(b) If the intention was that the disclosure could only be made to a third party where the employer did not have a legal responsibility, clear language could have been used to indicate this. It could readily have been stipulated as a requirement that the employer have no legal responsibility for the relevant failure.

(c) Those with a legal responsibility for a relevant failure have a proper and compelling interest in receiving a disclosure in relation to it, and this is recognized in the scheme of the legislation.

(d) Reasonable belief

In relation to both limbs of section 43C(1)(b), the requirements that the failure relate solely **5.29** or mainly to the conduct of another person, or another matter for which another person has legal responsibility, are qualified by the 'reasonable belief' test. The guidance in *Darnton v University of Surrey* [2003] IRLR 133 as to the meaning of 'reasonable belief' in relation to a qualifying disclosure (discussed in Chapter 3) is likely also to be material here. The worker must not only have a genuine belief but also, objectively, there must be some reasonable basis for holding that belief.

(4) Disclosures to employer and disclosure under section 43C(1)(b) compared

Whilst ERA, section 43C encompasses disclosures to someone other than the employer, **5.30** this does not have all the same consequences as a disclosure to the employer. The following aspects about disclosure under section 43C(1)(b) should be noted:

(a) Subject to section 43C(2) (see below) this does not amount to raising the matter with the employer for the purposes of a subsequent wider disclosure (under section 43G), when it is in some cases possible to build on the failure to act on one disclosure to make another.

(b) The Act does not place any obligation on the person responsible to respond to the concern or to investigate it in any way (though nor does the statute expressly place such an obligation on the employer when disclosure is made to it).

(c) If the worker is victimized for making a disclosure under this subsection, any claim which s/he may have cannot be made against the person to whom s/he made this disclosure unless that person is an agent or worker of the employer.

(5) Section 43C(2): whistleblowing and other authorized procedures

Section 43C(2) ERA expressly provides that where the organization has a whistleblowing **5.31** procedure which involves raising the concern with someone other than the employer, a disclosure to that person will be treated as if it were a disclosure to the employer. Typically this would apply to a procedure authorizing a disclosure to a health and safety representative, a union official, its parent company, a retired non-executive director, its lawyers or external auditors, or to a commercial reporting hotline.

However, section 43C(2) is not limited to a procedure which is specifically designated as a **5.32** whistleblowing procedure. It applies wherever the employer has authorized a procedure for raising matters other than with the employer and the disclosure is made in accordance with that procedure. In *The Brothers of Charity Services Merseyside v Eleady-Cole* (EAT/0661/00, 24 January 2002) the claimant was employed by a charity in a hostel run by his employer. The respondent employer engaged another company (PPC) to run a confidential telephone report service by which employees could raise and discuss concerns. PPC would then report on concerns to the employer where the circumstances so required. The claimant reported his concerns to this telephone service, and the EAT held that this fell within section 43C(2). The EAT specifically rejected a submission that section 43C(2) applied only to a situation where an employer set up a specific procedure for employees to make qualifying disclosures, or where the employer set up another person or body with some authority to take specific action in consequence of whatever a worker discloses to him/her or it. The EAT declined to provide an exhaustive definition of the kind of procedures to which section 43C(2) would apply. However, it emphasized (at paras 19–21) that in the reporting procedure in that case, all employees had access to the service and that in the event of a disclosure of criminal activities within the employers' homes or organization, a disclosure of that fact would in turn be made by PPC to the employer, albeit preserving the anonymity and confidentiality of the informant.

5.33 It is not, however, a prerequisite of section 43C(2) for the procedure to provide for the report ultimately to be passed on to the employer. It might also apply for example where, under a procedure authorized by the employer, a complaint is made about the employer to a third party with a view to that party investigating the employer. Thus, in *Chubb and others v Care First Partnership Ltd* (ET, Case No 1101438/99, 13 June 2001) it was conceded that section 43C(2) applied to a complaint made to a local authority about alleged mistreatment of residents at the respondent care home. The disclosures were made in accordance with the employer's complaints procedure. One significant consequence is that, notwithstanding the separate provision made in section 43F ERA for disclosures to regulators, where the internal procedure authorizes disclosure to the regulator, as is required in some fields, the disclosure may then fall within section 43C(2) with its lower thresholds for protection: see Chapter 12, paragraphs 12.57 and 12.111.

5.34 Further, there is no requirement for a standing procedure, or one of general application, for reporting concerns. It is sufficient if there is an ad hoc procedure which may be set out for a particular occasion or disclosure. This was the case in *Speyer v Thorn Security Group Ltd and others* (ET, Case No 2302898/03, 20 August 2004).[9] Here an employee was specifically requested to assist in an investigation by the Manhattan District Attorney. As such, disclosures made in a specific meeting with the District Attorney fell within section 43C(2).

5.35 The Act does not require employers to set up whistleblowing procedures. However, a worker who makes a wide, public disclosure is more likely to be protected if there was no such procedure or it was not reasonable to expect him/her to use it (section 43G(3)(f)).

C. First Tier Disclosures: Section 43D

(1) Overview

5.36 Section 43D ERA, as inserted by PIDA, is a short section which covers a disclosure made in the course of seeking legal advice about a concern. It provides that:

> a qualifying disclosure is made in accordance with this section if it is made in the course of obtaining legal advice.

5.37 The legal advisers, in turn, cannot of their own volition make a protected disclosure of the information if it would be covered by legal professional privilege (section 43B(4)). They can make only such disclosure as the client instructs them to make on the client's behalf. If the legal advisers disclose the privileged information without authority, they will be unable to assert that they made a qualifying disclosure. If the disclosure is authorized by the client, this will be judged as having been a disclosure made by the client, and it will only be protected if it is made in accordance with the other provisions of the Act.

---

[9] See Chapter 10 at para 10.132.

(2) From whom can the legal advice be sought?

Section 43D is headed 'disclosure to legal adviser'. However, the section itself does not refer **5.38** to a 'legal adviser'. It merely requires that the disclosure is made in the course of obtaining 'legal advice'. As such, there is no express limit on the categories of people from whom that advice might be sought. Thus, on its face it would apply to obtaining legal advice not only from a lawyer, but also a union representative, the CAB, or a lay adviser. Further, it would apply where legal advice is being obtained from other professionals who are not lawyers, such as if an accountant advises on tax law or an auditor advises in relation to whether accounts are compliant with company law obligations. It would also apply if advice is obtained from PCaW. However, in *Audere Medical Services Ltd v Sanderson* (UKEAT/0409/12/RN, 29 May 2013), in the context of a disclosure to PCaW, the EAT appear to have assumed, though without argument, that section 43D is confined to legal advisers. The EAT noted (at para 11) that no issue had been taken as to whether PCaW is a legal adviser and that it was assumed that it was (though the ET had also noted that PCaW's website says that it is a legal advice centre designated by the Solicitors Regulation Authority). The disclosure to PCaW for the purposes of obtaining legal advice was found to be a qualifying disclosure under section 43D ERA.

The issue therefore arises as to whether the apparently wide scope of section 43D is, as a mat- **5.39** ter of construction, properly to be cut down by virtue of either the reference to 'legal adviser' in the heading, or the context or purpose of the legislation or by reference to *Hansard*. In principle, the heading of section 43D is properly to be taken into account in construing the section, but only subject to the caveat that it may be an inaccurate guide to the meaning. The applicable principle is summarized in Bennion, *Statutory Interpretation*[10] as follows:

> A sidenote, marginal note or heading to a section is part of the Act. It may be considered in construing the section or any other provision of the Act, provided due account is taken of the fact that its function is merely to serve as a brief, and therefore possibly inaccurate, guide to the content of the section.[11]

This passage was cited by the Court of Appeal in *R v Okedare (No 2)* [2014] 1 WLR 4088 (at **5.40** paras 21–23) in the context of adopting a construction of the scope of the statutory power to make a confiscation order which it recognized could be seen as being at variance with the subheading for the relevant section. The court proceeded on the basis that it was consistent with the observation of Lord Reid in *R v Schildkamp* [1971] AC 1 (HL), at p 10, that a side-note is 'a poor guide to the scope of a section, for it can do no more than indicate the main subject with which the section deals'. Especially as the heading is a 'necessarily inaccurate' guide to the meaning, we suggest that the heading to section 43D is an insufficient basis to override the plain wording of the section so as, for example, to exclude legal advice given by an accountant or union official. As a short and inaccurate guide to the content of section 43D, the heading is capable of being reconciled with the wording of the section on the basis that someone who provides advice, irrespective of whether s/he is a lawyer, is in that specific respect regarded as a 'legal adviser'.

An argument might be constructed to cut down the scope of section 43D by reference to the **5.41** purpose of the legislation. If the scope of section 43D were too wide, it might undermine the structure of encouraging internal disclosures. Further, the fact that even for disclosures made prior to 25 June 2013, a disclosure could be made under section 43D without any need to comply with the good faith requirement which applied to all other categories of protected disclosure

---

[10] Sixth edn, London: LexisNexis, 2013, at pp 696–97.
[11] This passage was applied by Henry LJ in *Oyston v Blaker* [1996] 2 All ER 106 at 104 (CA).

made prior to that date, is strongly indicative that the section is intended to be of limited ambit. As against this, however, irrespective of who is a legal adviser, the scope of section 43D is limited by the fact that it only applies to a disclosure in the course of obtaining legal advice.

5.42 A further argument for limiting the scope of section 43D to legal advice from a lawyer may be founded on the interrelation with section 43B(4), which makes specific provision for the situation where there is a disclosure in breach of legal professional privilege of information obtained in the course of legal advice. This was emphasized during the progress of the Public Interest Disclosure Bill through Parliament. The issue arose in the context of proposed amendments, at the Lords committee stage (on 5 June 1998) and again at the Lords report stage (on 19 June 1998), to provide for disclosures to trade union officials. In opposing the proposed amendments both Lord Haskell (for the Government) and Lord Borrie (a proposer of the Bill) emphasized the distinction between lawyers and union officials in relation to legal professional privilege and, specifically, the obligation under section 43B(4) restricting unauthorized disclosure by the lawyer. It was canvassed that one possibility would be to make similar provision in relation to disclosures to union officials, but it was noted that this was problematic because the information might be required for the officials' collective role. Lord Borrie commented:[12]

> Where a member makes a disclosure to his union in the course of obtaining legal advice—and here, if you like, I am talking about the union solicitor—then, irrespective of whether the union is recognised at the workplace, if there is such a disclosure and a seeking of legal advice on how to raise the matter, that disclosure to the union solicitor will be protected under Section 43D.
>
> …
>
> Where a person is approached for confidential legal advice, protection under Section 43D will apply. As with all disclosures for legal advice, Section 43B(4) ensures that the lawyer cannot do as he pleases with the information. That is a most important point. As it stands, the amendment would not impose on advice agencies and unions the linked obligation under Section 43B(4). Unless the advice agency or union accepts that the information is subject to clear obligations of confidence, it will be free to do as it pleases with the information.
>
> It is possible that certain advice agencies—or, indeed, unions—will accept as a matter of practice strict obligations of confidence. However, the amendment does not deal with that aspect of the matter…. One solution would be to say that the disclosures to unions under the provision should be subject to obligations of confidence. Therefore, that would make it the same as disclosures to lawyers. But to do so would have a significant effect on the role of unions in labour relations. It would mean that the information could be used for no other purpose than the one to which the client had agreed. It could not be used in the course of general negotiations with the employer. More significantly, if the information related to some safety risk, but the whistle blower decided that he did not want to raise it or pursue it, it would not be open to the union to take up the matter itself even though the well-being of some of its members might well be affected.
>
> Without such an obligation of confidence as a *quid pro quo* to trade union officials being equated with lawyers, one possible effect of the amendment would be to give irresponsible whistle blowers a potential passport to media and more public disclosures if they were to find an individual union member or officer who would brief the media. The publication would be effected by that person on his own behalf. The employer would have no recourse against the employee whose disclosure would be protected.

5.43 The scope of section 43D was therefore expressly linked to that of section 43B(4). The consequent restriction on further disclosure being made, at least without permission from the

---

[12] *Hansard* HL, 5 June 1998, cols 624–26.

person obtaining the legal advice, may be regarded as an important consideration in explaining the absence even of a good faith requirement in such a case even for disclosures made prior to 25 June 2013. But section 43B(4) relates specifically to disclosure of information which could be subject to a claim of legal professional privilege. This would include only a subset of the communications which might be covered by the phrase 'made in the course of obtaining legal advice'. It covers members of the legal profession when exercising professional skill as a lawyer in a relationship of lawyer and client, including foreign lawyers[13] and in-house lawyers.[14] But privilege does not apply where someone who does not have formal legal professional qualifications performs the functions of a legal adviser, such as a personnel consultant in an industrial dispute.[15] Nor does it apply where legal advice is given by other non-lawyer professionals such as accountants.[16]

Whilst section 43B(4) provides a further indication that section 43D is more limited in scope than its literal wording suggests, it can be said that there is no necessity for section 43B(4) and section 43D to be similar in scope. If section 43D was not limited in scope to legal professional advisers, it would still have been appropriate to provide that a disclosure in breach of legal privilege information would not be a qualifying disclosure. Further, if section 43D was intended to apply only in circumstances giving rise to legal professional privilege, this could readily have been stated in the section. It would not only serve to exclude other professionals (eg accountants) who give legal advice but also others such as a personal consultant who performs the function of a legal adviser. This would therefore go further even than is suggested by reference to the heading to section 43D.

An attempt might also be made to rely directly on the comments made during the passage of **5.44** the Bill through Parliament, and specifically the above comments by Lord Borrie, as showing that section 43D has a more limited ambit and applies only in circumstances giving rise to legal professional privilege. However, there are significant obstacles to reliance on *Hansard* for this purpose. Reference may only be made to *Hansard* as an aid to construction so as to remove ambiguity in rare cases,[17] and if three conditions are satisfied. These are '(a) legislation is ambiguous, obscure or leads to an absurdity; (b) the material relied upon consists of one or more statements by a minister or other promoter of the Bill together if necessary with such other Parliamentary material as is necessary to understand such statements and their effect; (c) the statements relied upon are clear.': *Pepper v Hart* [1993] AC 593 at 640B–C, per Lord Browne-Wilkinson; *R v Secretary of State for the Environment, Transport and the Regions, ex p Spath Holme* [2001] 2 AC 349 at 391E, 392D–E. Further, the statement must be directed to the very issue which is in question in the litigation: *Pepper v Hart* at 617A–B, per Lord Bridge; *Melluish (Inspector of Taxes) v BMI (No 3) Ltd* [1996] 1 AC 454 at 481F–482A, per Lord Browne-Wilkinson. It has been emphasized that ministerial answers to questions should only be admitted under the *Pepper v Hart* rule in the plainest of cases: *R (Brown) v Secretary of State for the Home Department* [2015] 1 WLR 1060 (SC) per Lord Toulson (with whom Baronnes Hale, Lord Sumption, and Lord Carnwath agreed) at para 27. Even then, whilst the statement in *Hansard* is able to be taken into account as an aid to construction as part of the background to the legislation, it is not necessarily determinative; it does not control the meaning of the Act: *Wilson v First County Trust Ltd (No 2)* [2004] 1 AC 816 per Lord Nicholls at para 58.

---

[13] *Great Atlantic Insurance v Home Insurance* [1981] 1 WLR 529 at 536A (CA).
[14] *Alfred Compton Amusement Machines v Customs & Excise Commissioners (No 2)* [1972] 2 QB 102 at 129 (CA).
[15] *New Victoria Hospital v Ryan* [1993] ICR 201 (EAT).
[16] *Chantrey Martin v Martin* [1953] 2 QB 286 at 293–94 (CA).
[17] *Pepper v Hart* [1993] AC 593 at 617A–B, per Lord Bridge.

5.45   Whilst the above statement by Lord Borrie was by a promoter of the Bill, we suggest that the other conditions for reliance on the statement are not satisfied. Even if it could be said, despite the apparently plain wording of section 43D, that it was ambiguous (by reference to the considerations outlined above), Lord Borrie was not directly addressing the issue as to the breadth of section 43D and in what circumstances legal advice would be covered. Instead, he was opposing an amendment directed at providing specific reference to unions.

5.46   Taking the above arguments together, there is a possibility that the courts will determine that section 43D is to be construed as containing an implicit limit as to the categories of persons from whom legal advice must be sought, and that it applies only to a legal adviser in circumstances where the advice would give rise to legal professional privilege. Certainly, the safer course is to seek legal advice from a lawyer. However, we suggest that the better view of the construction of section 43D is that it is not appropriate to cut down the plain meaning of the words 'made in the course of obtaining legal advice'. Where the disclosure is to someone who does not ordinarily provide legal advice, there will be a question of fact in each case for a tribunal where the issue is raised as to whether the advice being obtained is legal advice. Thus, if a worker approaches a trade union official who is not legally qualified and seeks guidance as to what to do in relation to concerns as to a relevant failure, the natural interpretation might be that the worker is not specifically obtaining legal advice but guidance generally as to what to do in relation to the concerns. However, the worker may have asked the official for advice as to his/her legal rights or obligations in the event that s/he makes a wider disclosure. The union official might then be expected to make appropriate enquiries within the union organization so as to be able to provide appropriate legal advice. We suggest that section 43D is of ample scope to cover such a disclosure, and it is not appropriate to construe the section purposively so as to deny protection under it to a worker in such circumstances. The position might be otherwise if the worker makes a request for legal advice from someone who cannot reasonably be expected to provide, and does not provide, any legal advice. In such a situation we suggest that it could not be said that this was in the course of obtaining (rather than merely requesting) legal advice.

(3) Capacity in which the legal advice is sought

5.47   Further, section 43D does not expressly state in what capacity the advice must be sought. It is therefore not (at least expressly) limited to the situation where workers seek advice on their own behalf from their own lawyer. It would on its face cover a situation where a worker seeks advice, at the employer's expense, on behalf of the employing company from the employer's lawyers. There remains a lack of appellate authority as to whether the section is properly to be construed in this way. The arguments for a narrower construction may be regarded as having been stronger when, as now only applies in relation to disclosures made prior to 25 June 2013, there was a lower threshold for protection under section 43D than for other first tier disclosures due to the absence of a good faith requirement. Where workers seek legal advice from their own lawyer it would plainly be an unacceptable infringement of client–lawyer confidentiality for such communications to be subjected to scrutiny to identify whether they are made in good faith. It may also be seen as appropriate that if an employee does have in mind to make a disclosure for ulterior motives, s/he should be able to obtain advice as to this, and to ascertain that it would not be covered, without losing protection. But these considerations do not necessarily apply with the same force where the worker seeks legal advice from the employer's lawyers rather than taking his/her own advice. It may be questioned why, prior to the amendments made by ERRA in relation to disclosures made on or after 25 June 2013, there should have been a lower threshold for protection in such circumstances than for a disclosure to the employer.

We suggest, however, that the better view is that section 43D may still apply notwithstanding that the disclosure is to the employer's rather than the employee's own legal adviser. There may be circumstances where the presence of an ulterior motive might indicate that the disclosure to the employer's lawyers was not in fact in the course of obtaining legal advice. But there will also be circumstances where the worker turns to the employer's lawyers as the most immediate, and in some cases appropriate, source of advice in relation to concerns encountered in the course of employment. If a disclosure with a view to obtaining advice in such circumstances were to be excluded from the ambit of section 43D, clearer words of exclusion would be required.

D. First Tier Disclosures: Section 43E: Ministers of the Crown and Government-Appointed Bodies

Subject to the good faith requirement, which applies only in relation to disclosures made prior to 25 June 2013, section 43E ERA provides that workers are protected if they disclose their concerns to a Minister of the Crown provided that their employer is: **5.48**

  (i) an individual appointed under any enactment ... by a Minister of the Crown or a member of the Scottish Executive; or
  (ii) a body any of whose members are so appointed.

This therefore applies to government employees. It would also apply to, amongst others, employees of utility regulators such as OFWAT, OFCOM, and OFGEM and to NHS trusts, tribunals, and all kinds of non-departmental public bodies whose members are appointed by a Minister of the Crown. The section refers to disclosure to a Minister as, legally, this is taken to be the effect of a disclosure to a Department. **5.49**

This provision is based on the recommendations that the Committee on Standards in Public Life made in its First[18] and Second[19] Reports. An employee may be more comfortable making the disclosure to the Department since it is at one remove from the work relationship, and thus disclosure may not be seen so directly as diminishing trust and confidence in the relationship with the employer. The Department may also have far greater ability to put matters right in response to the concerns expressed. **5.50**

As under section 43C(1)(b), a disclosure under this section is not treated as one to the employer for the purposes of any subsequent, wider disclosure (section 43G). In addition, if the worker is victimized for making a disclosure under this section, any claim s/he may have is made against the employer and not against the Minister to whom s/he made this disclosure. **5.51**

E. Regulatory Disclosures: Section 43F

(1) Overview

The second tier of disclosure identified by Auld LJ in *Street* was disclosure to a prescribed person under ERA, section 43F. Section 43F(1) provides: **5.52**

  (1) A qualifying disclosure is made in accordance with this section if the worker—
    (a) makes the disclosure to a person prescribed by an order made by the Secretary of State for the purposes of this section, and

---

[18] Cm 2850–I (1995), pp 60 and 91–92.
[19] Cm 3270–1 (1996), p 22.

    (b) reasonably believes—
        (i) that the relevant failure falls within any description of matters in respect of which that person is so prescribed, and
       (ii) that the information disclosed, and any allegation contained in it, are substantially true.

5.53 In addition, for disclosures made prior to 25 June 2013 only, the good faith requirement also applies. Irrespective of when the disclosure was made, the worker must therefore reasonably believe that the malpractice falls within the matters prescribed for that regulator and 'that the information disclosed, and any allegation in it, are substantially true' (section 43F(1)(b)). Thus, although the worker must meet a higher evidential burden than in section 43C relating to first tier whistleblowing, where a regulator has been prescribed, there is no requirement:

(a) that the particular disclosure was reasonable;
(b) that the malpractice was serious; nor
(c) that the worker should have first raised the matter internally.

5.54 The favoured position of the whistleblower who makes disclosure to a regulator is explicable on the basis that:

(a) the list of prescribed persons and of the matters in relation to which there can be disclosure to them is designed to ensure that the regulator is an appropriate person to who to raise the concern. Further, the regulators may have a statutory duty to investigate such matters and they can only perform their role if members of the public are prepared to come to them with information. Workers will be deterred from doing so if there is inadequate protection against retaliation in the workplace for perceived disloyalty;
(b) the regulator can usually be relied upon to maintain confidentiality of the material once it is in his/her domain, whether the allegation is right or wrong;
(c) the motivation of anyone revealing material to a regulator is likely to be one of concerned public interest because the regulator will not pay money for the material (although someone who makes such a disclosure may qualify for a Crimestoppers Trust award).

5.55 These considerations have also been persuasive in forging a preferential position under the common law of confidence for disclosures made to prescribed regulators over other external disclosures. In *In re A Company* [1989] 1 Ch 477, where an employee reported an internal matter to the Financial Intermediaries, Managers and Brokers Regulatory Association (FIMBRA) which was then the relevant regulator under the Financial Services Act 1986 (and whose functions are now performed by the Financial Conduct Authority), Scott J said:

> it may be the case that the information proposed to be given, the allegations to be made by the defendant to FIMBRA and for that matter by the defendant to the Inland Revenue, are allegations made out of malice and based upon fiction or invention. But if that is so, then I ask myself what harm will be done. FIMBRA may decide that the allegations are not worth investigating. In that case no harm will have been done. Or FIMBRA may decide that an investigation is necessary. In that case, if the allegations turn out to be baseless, nothing will follow from the investigation. And if harm is caused by the investigation itself, it is harm implicit in the regulatory role of FIMBRA.

5.56 Notwithstanding these considerations, even where the disclosure is made to a prescribed regulator it may be important to consider whether it can also be characterized as a first tier disclosure. Where there is a prescribed regulator, it is often the case that the employing organization will provide, whether in a whistleblowing policy or otherwise, that disclosure to the prescribed regulator is permitted. The effect is that where the disclosure is made in accordance with a procedure deployed by the prescribed regulator, it can be said that section 43C(2) applies, which entails a lower threshold for protection than under section 43F: see Chapter 12, paragraphs 12.54 and 12.107. Whilst this may be seen to undermine the structure of the legislation, there are strong policy reasons for this approach. The requirement that the worker must reasonably believe that the information disclosed and any allegation contained in it are substantially true may be problematic, since there may be good policy reasons for workers to be confident in disclosing concerns based on information they have heard which they are not able to verify.

(2) Prescribed persons

5.57 The Public Interest Disclosure (Prescribed Persons) Order (SI 2014/2417)[20] sets out a list of the persons who are prescribed for the purposes of this section. In each case there is a corresponding description of the matters in respect of which the person is prescribed. In respect of a Member of the House of Commons, there is a catch all, in that they are prescribed for anything falling within the description for any other prescribed person. A list of the prescribed persons and the corresponding description of matters in respect of which they are prescribed, and contact details, is set out in the BIS document 'Blowing the Whistle to a Prescribed Person: List of prescribed persons and bodies' (February 2016).[21] There has been one further amendment to the list since that publication, SI 2016/968.[22]

(3) Reasonable belief that relevant failure falls within a relevant description

5.58 The worker must make the disclosure to a prescribed person and reasonably believe that the relevant failure falls within any description of matters in respect of which that person is prescribed. It is to be noted that the reasonable belief test does not qualify the requirement in section 43F(1)(a) that a person or body is prescribed. If, for example, a disclosure is made to the police, not being a prescribed body, there is no scope to argue that there was a reasonable but mistaken belief that the police were prescribed.

5.59 As illustrated by the decision in *Barton v Greenwich LBC* (UKEAT/0041/14/DXA, 1 May 2015), the requirement for a reasonable belief that the disclosure falls within the description of matters in respect of which the relevant body is prescribed may in some cases provide a trap for the unwary. The facts of this case are set out in more detail at paragraph 5.66 below. However so far as is material here, Mr Barton raised concerns with the Information Commissioner's Office (ICO) in relation to the manager of a colleague having sent a large number of emails home. He was then instructed by his employer not to contact the ICO without the prior authority of his line manager. He then called the ICO to seek advice as to what he should do about the instruction not to communicate with the ICO. In relation to this call, the ET concluded that there was no qualifying disclosure on the basis that Mr Barton did not hold a reasonable belief that the information tended to show a breach of a legal obligation, since there had been no urgency about calling the ICO and he could have looked into this. But the ET also held that even if there was a qualifying disclosure it did not fall within section 43F since the Information Commissioner was only a prescribed person in respect of matters specified in the schedule to the Order. This related to data-protection compliance, and not to employment law advice on whether the enquirer's contract of employment had been breached.

---

[20] As amended by a series of subsequent amendment orders.

[21] Available at https://www.gov.uk/government/uploads/system/uploads/attachment_data/file/510962/BIS-16-79-blowing-the-whistle-to-a-prescribed-person.pdf.

[22] The additions, not included in the February 2016 BIS document, are the Commissioners nominated under s 15(6) of the Local Government Act 1999 (for matters relating to functions of a best value authority), Food Standards Scotland, Older People's Commissioner, Qualifications Wales, and the Wales Audit Office.

5.60 Nor does the reasonable belief test apply to what matters are prescribed in relation to a particular body or person. Thus, suppose a worker has a reasonable and genuine but mistaken belief that the relevant failure amounts to fraud by a company. If the worker made a disclosure to the Secretary of State for Business, Innovation and Skills he could then be said to hold a reasonable belief that the relevant failure falls within the description of 'Fraud, and other misconduct, in relation to companies', which applies to that prescribed person. However, if the worker was mistaken as to the description of matters for which the Secretary of State was prescribed, and made a disclosure in relation to a matter for which the Secretary of State was not prescribed, that would not fall within section 43F. As such, it would be a good precaution, if there is any uncertainty as to whether the matter is appropriately raised with a prescribed person, for the worker or his/her adviser first to contact the particular regulator informally to discuss the nature of the concern in order to establish whether it is within the regulator's remit and to explore what action the regulator considers appropriate.

5.61 This may be particularly important in cases where more than one body is identified in the Public Interest Disclosure (Prescribed Persons) Order 1999 as being responsible for the same matter. This arose in *Dudin v Salisbury District Council* (ET, Case No 3102263/03, 20 February 2004). Mrs Dudin was employed as a tenant participation officer by a district council. She became convinced that bullying was endemic in the council. She raised concerns and allegations about this with the council's scrutiny committee, which was a committee charged with reviewing and scrutinizing decisions made and actions taken in connection with discharge of council functions. She argued that this was a disclosure within ERA, section 43F. The Health and Safety Executive (HSE), and also local authorities with responsibility for enforcement of health and safety legislation, are both prescribed in the Public Interest Disclosure (Prescribed Persons) Order 2014 (and its predecessor in force at the time[23]) in relation to matters which may affect the health or safety of any individual at work and matters which may affect the health and safety of any member of the public, arising out of or in connection with the activities of persons at work. On its face, therefore, the disclosure to the council fell within the description of prescribed matters in the Order. However, although not specified in the Order, the relevant enforcing authority for employees of the local authority was the HSE rather than the local authority.[24] On this basis the tribunal held that section 43F did not apply. The decision may be doubted on the basis that it added a gloss to section 43F(1)(a). On the face of that provision it should have sufficed to have a reasonable belief that the concerns related to health and safety at work, and so fell within the description of matters in respect of which the council was prescribed. As against this, the decision may be explained as being consistent with the underlying rationale that section 43F is concerned with disclosure to an appropriate body.

(4) Time at which the recipient must be prescribed

5.62 In *Miklaszewicz v Stolt Offshore Ltd* [2002] IRLR 344 (Court of Session) the issue arose as to whether, for the purposes of section 43F, it was necessary that the recipient of the disclosure had to be prescribed at the time of the disclosure or at the time of the detriment. In 1993, six years before PIDA came into force, Mr Miklaszewicz reported to the Inland Revenue that his employer had engaged in unlawful tax evasion in changing his employment status to self-employed when that was a false description of his status. As a result he was dismissed later that year. However, he continued to work in the same industry and, by virtue of transfers of undertakings, in December 1999 he came to be employed again by the same employer. He was dismissed purportedly on grounds of redundancy but claimed that the real reason was

---

[23] Public Interest Disclosure (Prescribed Persons) Order 2014, SI 2014/2418.
[24] Pursuant to reg 4 of the Health and Safety (Enforcing Authority) Regulations 1998 (SI 1998/494).

his disclosures in 1993. The employment tribunal decided that it did not have jurisdiction because the protected disclosures were made before PIDA came into force, but the EAT and Scottish Court of Session disagreed. As the EAT had decided in *Meteorological Office v Edgar* [2002] ICR 149, the court held that there could be a claim if the detriment or dismissal was after PIDA came into force. However, the more difficult issue related to section 43F. It was argued that its plain wording made clear that there could not have been a protected disclosure under section 43F in 1993 since the Inland Revenue was not at that stage a prescribed body. The Court of Session held that since the claim under the legislation is triggered by the dismissal (or other detriment), 'the making of the disclosure requires to be considered at that point in time; and it is then that the criteria for treating it as a protected disclosure are applicable, on a proper construction of the relevant statutory provisions'. On that basis, since by the time of dismissal the Inland Revenue was a prescribed person, and the disclosure was in relation to matters for which it was prescribed, that was sufficient.

In adopting this approach, the Court of Session followed a purposive construction of the **5.63** legislation. At the heart of section 43F is the principle that a lower threshold for protection should apply where there is a disclosure to an appropriate prescribed body, as identified in the relevant order. On the facts in *Miklaszewicz* the result was consistent with this in that the Inland Revenue was plainly the appropriate body with which to raise concerns about tax evasion. The emphasis on assessing whether there is a protected disclosure by reference to the position at the date of dismissal is, however, problematic. First, principles of certainty require that a person should know at the time of making a disclosure whether they are doing so in a manner such as to be protected under section 43F. The decision cannot therefore entail that a person who made the disclosure in accordance with section 43F could lose protection in the event that the person was subsequently removed from or replaced on the list or the relevant description of matters narrowed subsequent to making the disclosure.

At most, therefore, the decision in *Miklaszewicz* might be regarded as adopting a purposive **5.64** approach so as to extend protection in order to additionally include cases where at the time of detriment or dismissal the disclosure would have been within section 43F. It is not generally the case that the criteria for a protected disclosure are assessed at the time of the detriment. Thus, in relation to whether there is the requisite reasonable belief for the purposes of a qualifying disclosure, the position must be assessed on the basis of the circumstances of the worker, and what he knew, at the time of making the disclosure, rather than the worker's knowledge at the time of being subjected to a detriment.[25] The decision in *Miklaszewicz* might be reconciled with this on the basis that the worker must still have had a reasonable belief, at the time of making the disclosure, that it involved a relevant failure within the description of matters which were subsequently prescribed for the Inland Revenue. Thus, it was sufficient that, at the time of the disclosure, he had a reasonable belief that the disclosure related to a relevant failure in relation to National Insurance and income tax, being matters in relation to which the Inland Revenue (and then HM Revenue and Customs) was subsequently prescribed. The decision did not necessitate assessing what he reasonably believed at the time of dismissal. It is not to be regarded as supporting any wider principle that a worker's state of mind or belief is to be assessed at a time subsequent to the making of the protected disclosure.

(5) Reasonable belief that the information disclosed and any allegation contained in it are substantially true

In each of sections 43F, 43G, and 43H, the worker must reasonably believe that (a) the infor- **5.65** mation disclosed and (b) any allegation contained in it, are substantially true. In Chapter 3

---

[25] See *Darnton v University of Surrey* [2003] IRLR 133, in Chapter 3, paras 3.53ff.

we discussed how the reasonable belief test for a qualifying disclosure has been construed, notably in the cases of *Darnton v University of Surrey* [2003] ICR 615 (EAT) and *Babula v Waltham Forest College* [2007] ICR 1026. In *Muchesa v Central & Cecil Housing Care Support* (EAT/0443/07, 22 August 2008) the EAT acknowledged that there are differences in wording as compared to section 43B. As the EAT accepted (at para 26), 'the subject matter of the belief, ie what the employee had reasonably to believe if he is to obtain protection, is different'. Notwithstanding this, the EAT concluded that the guidance in *Darnton* and *Babula* applies also to the test under sections 43F, 43G, and 43H. Having regard to this, we suggest that the following considerations are relevant:

(a) As in the case of the reasonable belief test for a qualifying disclosure, the worker's belief must be tested by reference to the circumstances as they were understood, or ought to have been understood, by the worker, rather than simply by the facts as ultimately found to have existed by the tribunal.

(b) It must be reasonable for the worker to believe both (i) that the factual basis for what was disclosed was true (in the sense explained at paragraph 3.56) and (ii) that it tends to show a relevant failure (see *Muchesa* at para 27). In relation to a qualifying disclosure, the extent to which the worker is expected to investigate and hold a belief in the truth of what is disclosed will depend on the circumstances. Indeed there may be cases where a worker can only pass on information from a third party and is not in a positon to assess whether it is true: *Dr Y-A-Soh v Imperial College of Science, Technology and Medicine* (UKEAT/0350/14/DM, 3 September 2015). But in relation to a disclosure under sections 43F, 43G, and 43H, the statutory language makes expressly clear that a reasonable belief is required that (i) the information disclosed and (ii) any allegation contained in it, are substantially true.

(c) The worker will not lose protection if his/her belief was mistaken, provided it was reasonable for him/her to hold it. But, as with the test for reasonable belief in section 43B, whether the allegation was in fact true is likely to be relevant in ascertaining the reasonableness of the belief. This was emphasized in *Muchesa*. The claimant was employed as a senior night carer at a residential care home. She made allegations to a daughter of a resident of seriously defective care of that resident. She also made calls to the police and social services alleging serious neglect. The claimant was subsequently suspended. She then lodged grievances alleging sexual harassment and race discrimination. She also made very serious allegations about care of residents. It was not disputed that the reports to the patient's daughter, police, social services, and the Council for Social Care Inspection (CSCI) were qualifying disclosures. The employment tribunal found that the claimant did not have a reasonable belief that the disclosures made to the external recipients were substantially true. The EAT concluded that the employment tribunal was entitled to consider whether the complaints were true and to regard its view of this as an important tool in the resolution of the reasonable belief issue, especially as the claimant was complaining of matters of which she claimed to have direct knowledge. The tribunal was also entitled to have regard to objective factors such as failure to use the whistleblowing policy and failure to ask another member of staff to witness the conduct of which she was complaining, failure to write up the incident, and spending time photocopying rather than dealing with the incident. In all, she had not behaved in the manner to be expected had she reasonably (or indeed genuinely) believed in the truth of the complaints.

(d) Again, as in the reasonable belief test for a qualifying disclosure, and as illustrated by *Muchesa*, all the circumstances must be considered in order to ascertain whether the belief was reasonable. However, the standard to be applied in relation to whether it was reasonable to hold the belief is likely to be higher than that for a qualifying disclosure.

In particular the worker may be required to have done more to look into the matter, or have had it looked into, than at the first tier of disclosure. Thus, in relation to a disclosure to the employer (or other first tier disclosure) there may be a reasonable belief even though the worker has done little to investigate the matter, because the policy of the legislation is to encourage workers to raise their concerns with the employer who may be best placed to investigate. Under section 43F, there is no obligation first to raise the matter with the employer. However, if it was raised with the employer it will be relevant to take into account any response by the employer, or any failure to respond or inadequacies in the response, in relation to how this affects the reasonableness of the belief.

(e) The differing considerations which are likely to apply to a disclosure under section 43F are indicated by the fact that the phrase 'tends to show', which appears in section 43B, does not appear in section 43F (or 43G or 43H). As discussed in Chapter 3, the phrase is important in the context of section 43B. It accommodates the possibility that the worker may only have access to part of the evidential picture. As such, it might be premature to require, prior to making a disclosure to the employer (or other first tier disclosure), that the worker hold a reasonable belief that the allegation is substantially true. It might be sufficient that the worker has come across, and disclosed, information which tends to show a relevant failure, even though it is possible that on further investigation the full evidential picture may show this not to be the case. By contrast, for the purposes of sections 43F (and 43G and 43H), the worker cannot merely say that the information disclosed tends to point in the direction of a relevant failure, and needs further investigation. The worker must reasonably believe that the allegations are substantially true.

(f) Notwithstanding the degree of leeway built into the 'substantially true' test, it does not follow that the worker can make any allegations that are known to be false, even if those allegations are only peripheral. In *Korashi v Abertawe Bro Morgannwg University Local Area Health Board* [2012] IRLR 4 it was argued that where there were a number of allegations made as part of a disclosure, it would be sufficient if the gist of the complaint was reasonably believed to be substantially true. However, the EAT expressed the view that, whilst there is no obligation to make any allegation, the statutory formulation requires that in relation to each allegation made there must be a reasonable belief that it was substantially true. The effect is that scattergun allegations will not be protected if they include some wild allegations known to be false. Tribunals will still need to exercise care not to overlook the degree of leeway afforded by the term 'substantially'. There is a public interest in concerns as to relevant failures being raised with the appropriate prescribed body. It would be unfortunate if those with the courage to come forward and raise such concerns were to lose protection because of a degree of lack of circumspection in the terms in which the concerns are raised.

5.66 The potential impact of the differing standards for a qualifying disclosure and for protection under section 43F ERA are illustrated by the decision in *Barton v Greenwich LBC* (UKEAT/0041/14/DXA, 1 May 2015). Mr Barton was employed by Greenwich LBC, and had formerly been an elected shop steward and health and safety representative. He received a concern from a work colleague (Mr Oree) that the colleague's line manager had emailed 'hundreds' of documents to her home which he believed contained confidential or personal data about himself and that her personal email was not part of a secure system nor encrypted. Mr Barton considered that this was a significant breach of the Data Protection Act 1998 ('DPA'). He did not report the matter to his line managers but instead reported his concerns, and what he had been told, to the ICO, and sought advice from the ICO advice line as to whether there was any urgent action that could be taken to retrieve this material and to prevent the line manager accessing it. He then reported the matter to his line managers. The information that Mr Barton provided to the ICO (and which had been provided to him) was wrong. In fact the manager had emailed only eleven documents to her home email and that email was password protected, and it was not inappropriate for her to have sent them to the home email address.

5.67 The Council told Mr Barton that he should have referred the matter to his line managers before raising concerns with the ICO. He was specifically instructed not to contact the ICO or other external bodies in relation to the matter without the prior authority of his line manager. He was told that the Council would investigate the concerns promptly, and in fact the Council then did so. However, Mr Barton then telephoned the ICO to seek advice as to what he should do about the instruction not to communicate with the ICO. The ICO confirmed to him that the respondent had no authority to tell him not to contact them. He later relayed this to the Council.

5.68 The Council took the view that Mr Barton's second contact with the ICO in breach of the instruction given to him was a serious breach of duty. He was already subject to a final written warning in relation to an unrelated matter. He was dismissed for breach of the instruction in relation to contacting the ICO and another matter. The employment tribunal dismissed the claim on the basis that there were no protected disclosures, and an appeal to the EAT was dismissed. So far as concerned the first disclosure to the ICO, the employment tribunal accepted that it was a qualifying disclosure. It disclosed information based on what Mr Barton had been told by his colleague, Mr Oree. Mr Barton had not sought to verify this at the time before contacting the ICO, and was aware that there was no immediate urgency as to contacting the ICO. The ET accepted that Mr Barton had a long association with Mr Oree acting as his representative and on the face of it he had no reason to doubt Mr Oree's complaint. Mr Oree had indeed presented to him as very concerned about the matter. In all, the ET concluded that the belief was a reasonable one in the circumstances, albeit the point was quite finely balanced.

5.69 However, in relation to section 43F the ET reached a different conclusion. The ET accepted that the enquiry raised an issue relating to DPA compliance and so the ICO was a prescribed person for the purposes of the communication. It also accepted that the disclosure was made in good faith, and that, as to section 43F(1)(b) ERA, Mr Barton had a reasonable belief that the breach alleged fell within the ICO's prescribed role given that the focus was on DPA compliance. However, the ET concluded that Mr Barton did not have a reasonable belief that the information disclosed and the allegations contained within it were substantially true. The ET directed itself that this required a higher threshold than the test for a qualifying disclosure. As such, relying on the same circumstances as had been taken into account when assessing the qualifying disclosure issue, the ET held that the belief as to the truth of the information and any allegation made was not reasonable since Mr Barton had 'jumped the gun' in circumstances where he knew and/or could fairly easily have found out there was no real urgency and that there was time to seek some verification of the allegation made by Mr Oree before contacting the ICO.

5.70 The decision of the employment tribunal in *Holden v Connex South Eastern Ltd* (ET, Case No 2301550/00, 15 April 2002) further illustrates the potential interrelation between internal disclosures and regulatory disclosures when it comes to assessment of the worker's reasonable belief. Mr Holden was a train driver employed by Connex and was appointed as a health and safety representative. He had a track record of raising a number of genuine and legitimate concerns. Mr Holden became concerned about measures to be introduced by his employers which he believed would be in breach of regulations prohibiting train operators from undertaking safety-critical work for such long hours as to cause them fatigue. By a code of practice his employers were required to carry out suitable and sufficient assessment before introducing the changes. Mr Holden raised his concerns with the managing director of Connex as to a breach of the regulations and requested a copy of the risk assessment. He was refused a copy and, after the restructure was implemented, his concerns were reinforced when he received a number of complaints from other drivers who felt increasingly tired. He carried out his own investigations which led him to believe that many of the incidences where a signal had been passed at danger could be attributed to tiredness or fatigue. He then reported his finding to HM Railway Inspectorate. He later also sent a second report to the Inspectorate and provided copies to his members. The tribunal decided that the two reports constituted protected disclosures under section 43F. It concluded that even if it had not been established that all the allegations made were true, Mr Holden held a reasonable belief that they were true. In so concluding the tribunal emphasized that it was the employers who held all the detailed information, and it was as a result of their failure to provide Mr Holden with the necessary health and safety information which he sought that he had needed to investigate the matter himself. Thus, the fact that he had raised concerns with his employer (albeit not the specific findings which he then reported to the Inspectorate in his first report), and had requested and been denied information and documentation which the employer possessed, and by reference to which the concerns could have been verified, played an important part in demonstrating that his belief was reasonably held.

(6) Evidential issues

5.71 Where the disclosure is made to a prescribed body, it will be important to give careful consideration to the evidence which may be relevant arising from this, including identifying issues in relation to disclosure of documents. There might be an issue as to whether the employer was aware of the disclosure to the prescribed body prior to the alleged detriment or dismissal. The approach taken by the prescribed body might also be material to the issue of whether the worker had the requisite reasonable belief that the information and the allegations were substantially true. Just as the truth of the allegations was recognized in *Darnton* as being a material consideration, so if the prescribed body has treated the allegations as raising sufficient concerns to merit serious investigation, a tribunal may regard this as persuasive on the issue of the reasonableness of the belief. If the prescribed body has not pursued the concerns, or has rejected them, the respondent employer may seek to place reliance on this in challenging the reasonableness of the belief. Thus, if the employer has had no or minimal contact from the prescribed body, the employer might point to this as indicating a lack of substance in the allegations made. Conversely, it may be important for the worker to ascertain in such circumstances why an investigation has not been progressed. In some cases it may be, for example, that the prescribed body is awaiting the outcome of the employment tribunal proceedings.

It will therefore be important to consider not only any disclosure from the employer in relation to its dealings with the prescribed body, but also what evidence might be gathered from the prescribed body itself. This may include consideration of whether relevant documentation or information in relation to communications with the employer can be obtained from the prescribed body. The employment tribunal has power to order the provision of information and documentation from a third party in Great Britain: see Employment Tribunals (Constitution and Rules of Procedure) Regulations 2013 (SI 2013/1237), Schedule 1, para 31.

(7) Section 43FA: regulator annual reports and role in encouraging whistleblowing

5.72 Section 43FA ERA, which was inserted by section 148 of the Small Business, Enterprise and Employment Act 2015, provides the Secretary of State with a power to require prescribed persons (under section 43F) to produce an annual report in relation disclosure of information made to it. At the time of writing, no regulations have yet been made under this provision. As explained in the Explanatory Notes to the 2015 Act, the provision was introduced taking into account that the response to the Government's call for evidence on whistleblowing highlighted a lack of consistency in the approach taken by section 43F prescribed bodies and a lack of communication by them. The provision is discussed further in Chapter 12, paragraph 12.119, in the context of the FCA's annual reports.

In addition, in March 2015, the Government published Guidance for prescribed persons on their role in relation to whistleblowing. The guidance is in quite general terms. It highlights that insofar as statutory functions permit, prescribed persons can look into a disclosure and recommend how an employer could rectify the problems it finds either in relation to the employer's whistleblowing policies and procedures or in the relation to the issues which form the substance of the report. The guidance also emphasizes the importance of giving feedback to the whistleblower, and noting that if only limited feedback can be given, the reasons for this should be explained. However, no obligation is placed on regulators to investigate matters reported.

The guidance also notes the role prescribed persons can play in encouraging organizations they oversee to have whistleblowing policies in place and assisting in ensuring the arrangements are effective. The Whistleblowing Commission,[26] set up by PCaW, recommended that the licence or registration of organizations which fail to have in place effective whistleblowing arrangements should be reviewed. That is not, however, specifically mentioned in the Government's guidance, which instead suggests that the prescribed person could draw attention to the benefits of an open whistleblowing culture and lead by example in the prescribed bodies' own whistleblowing arrangements.

The Whistleblowing Commission also recommended (recommendation 23) that referral of PIDA claims to prescribed regulators by the employment tribunal service should be mandatory, subject to individuals being given the option to opt out of the referral process. That recommendation has not been taken up. Instead, the tribunal is given a discretion, with the claimant's consent, to send a copy of any accepted claim to a section 43F regulator: reg 14 of Schedule 1 to the Employment Tribunals (Constitution and Rules of Procedure) Regulations 2013 (SI 2013/1237).

F. Wider Disclosures under Section 43G

(1) Overview

5.73 Sections 43G and 43H set out the circumstances in which other disclosures, including those to the media, may be protected. These provisions give the tribunal much more scope for determining the reasonableness of aspects of the employee's behaviour than the earlier provisions. Section 43G provides (omitting the good faith requirement which applies only to disclosures made prior to 25 June 2013):

Disclosure in other cases

(1) A qualifying disclosure is made in accordance with this section if—

...

    (b) he reasonably believes that the information disclosed, and any allegation contained in it, are substantially true,

    (c) he does not make the disclosure for purposes of personal gain,

    (d) any of the conditions in subsection (2) is met, and

    (e) in all the circumstances of the case, it is reasonable for him to make the disclosure.

(2) The conditions referred to in subsection (1)(d) are—

    (a) that, at the time he makes the disclosure, the worker reasonably believes that he will be subjected to a detriment by his employer if he makes a disclosure to his employer or in accordance with section 43F,

---

[26] Report on the effectiveness of existing arrangements for workplace whistleblowing in the UK (November 2013), Recommendation 3.

(b) that, in a case where no person is prescribed for the purposes of section 43F in relation to the relevant failure, the worker reasonably believes that it is likely that evidence relating to the relevant failure will be concealed or destroyed if he makes a disclosure to his employer, or

(c) that the worker has previously made a disclosure of substantially the same information—

    (i) to his employer, or

    (ii) in accordance with section 43F.

(3) In determining for the purposes of subsection (1)(e) whether it is reasonable for the worker to make the disclosure, regard shall be had, in particular, to—

    (a) the identity of the person to whom the disclosure is made,

    (b) the seriousness of the relevant failure,

    (c) whether the relevant failure is continuing or is likely to occur in the future,

    (d) whether the disclosure is made in breach of a duty of confidentiality owed by the employer to any other person,

    (e) in a case falling within subsection (2)(c)(i) or (ii), any action which the employer or the person to whom the previous disclosure in accordance with section 43F was made has taken or might reasonably be expected to have taken as a result of the previous disclosure, and

    (f) in a case falling within subsection (2)(c)(i), whether in making the disclosure to the employer the worker complied with any procedure whose use by him was authorised by the employer.

(4) For the purposes of this section a subsequent disclosure may be regarded as a disclosure of substantially the same information as that disclosed by a previous disclosure as mentioned in subsection (2)(c) even though the subsequent disclosure extends to information about action taken or not taken by any person as a result of the previous disclosure.

The approach of the legislation is therefore to build additional requirements on top of those **5.74** which apply for regulatory disclosures. In addition to the requirement of reasonable belief in the substantial truth of the information and allegations, there are three further requirements. The first additional requirement relates to motive; the disclosure must not be for purposes of personal gain. The second (section 43G(2)) sets out three preconditions, one of which must be met if the disclosure is to be capable of protection. Finally, to be protected the disclosure must be reasonable in all the circumstances (section 43G(1)(e) and (3)). If the concern has been raised internally beforehand or with a prescribed regulator, the reasonableness of the worker's belief in the substantial truth of the information disclosed will be assessed having regard to what happened in a first tier disclosure and any response which s/he may have received from management or the prescribed regulator to the original complaint. Thus, if the response was a stony silence or an ineffectual remedy, the employee may be justified in escalating the concern and taking the matter further to a wider audience.

(2) 'Personal gain'

A disclosure under section 43G or 43H does not qualify for protection unless the disclosure **5.75** is not made for purposes of personal gain.[27] As to this:

(a) Although the provision is primarily aimed at the grosser excesses of 'chequebook journalism', it is not expressly limited to financial gain. In *Kajencki v Torrington Homes* (ET, Case No 3302912/01, 30 September 2002) the employment tribunal expressed the view that it was capable of encompassing other forms of personal advantage. Mrs Kajencki worked as manager of a residential care home. She raised concerns with the

---

[27] ERA, s 43G(1)(c); s 43H(1)(c).

council's Joint Inspection Unit about standards of food hygiene and staff training. The tribunal decided that the disclosure was made for the purposes of personal gain in that Mrs Kajencki had made the disclosures with the objective of leading her employer to give her effective control over running the home. The contrary view was however taken by the employment tribunal in *Wright v Merseyside Passenger Transport Authority* (ET, Case No 2100417/08). The tribunal rejected an argument that a disclosure was for personal gain because it was directed at seeking to avoid having to go on a driving course. The ET noted the exclusion of rewards in section 43L(2), and took that as an indication that only financial gain is covered. That would, however, seem to be a non sequitur, and if it was intended to confine the exclusion to financial gain that could readily have been stated in the legislation.

(b) We suggest that, consistently with the rationale of the exception for personal gain, the provision would also catch a situation where the benefit did not go directly to the worker but to a member of his/her family, provided that its purpose was personal gain. The position would, we suggest, be otherwise if the payment was to be made to charity, and as such could not be regarded as direct or indirect personal gain for the worker making the disclosure.

(c) The concept of personal gain does not, however, catch any reward payable by or under any enactment (section 43L(2)), such as a payment made by HMRC for information received.[28] The exception does not cover private rewards of any sort, such as an award by the charity Crimestoppers. The effect of section 43L is that where a reward is made by a regulator whether or not prescribed under section 43F, it is not a bar to protection that the disclosure was made for the purposes of obtaining such a reward if the power to make the award is provided by statute. Such rewards are occasionally made by statutory agencies in return for information supplied. Banks also sometimes provide rewards for such information.

(d) Protection is not lost merely because the worker receives a payment or otherwise benefits from the disclosure. The focus is on the *purposes* for which the disclosure was made.

(e) Section 43G(1)(c) does not specify how it applies in a case of mixed motives, as often occurs. As discussed in Chapter 10 (at paragraphs 10.115 and 10.116), it has been held in *Street v Derbyshire Unemployed Workers' Centre* [2005] ICR 97 (CA) that an ulterior motive may only negative good faith if it is a predominant motive. It might be argued that the same should apply in relation to personal gain, as it would be unfortunate if a worker who satisfies the other requirements of section 43G, including acting reasonably, and who acts primarily in the public interest (eg to prevent a relevant failure), could be subjected to a detriment for so doing. There are also dicta in *Street* which support this view. Thus, Auld LJ noted that 'whether the motive of personal gain was of such a nature or strength as to 'make the disclosure for the purposes of personal gain' is for the tribunal to assess.[29] Nor is it necessarily an answer that this approach would involve considerable overlap with the good faith test which still applies to disclosures made prior to 25 June 2013. The good faith test only had the effect that a predominant ulterior motive could lead to good faith being negatived; it did not require this and the test ultimately remains one of good faith: see *Dr Y-A-Soh v Imperial College of Science, Technology and Medicine* (UKEAT/0350/14/DM, 3 September 2015) (discussed at paragraph 10.127 et seq). Further, it has been stressed that the various elements of the tests for a protected disclosure involve overlapping requirements. In *Street* (at para 51), Auld LJ referred to the 'large but not total overlap, or of "overkill", or sheer untidiness of drafting on the part of

---

[28] Parliamentary Debates HC, Standing Committee D, 11 March 1998.
[29] At para 53; see para 5.01 above.

the parliamentary draftsman of section 43G'. Overlap between good faith and personal gain requirements is therefore less surprising.

We suggest, however, that it is more likely that the personal gain requirement will be satisfied if personal gain is one of the purposes of making the disclosure. The legislation does not expressly distinguish between a principal or subsidiary purpose in this context. Elsewhere in the legislation, where the requirement is for a principal reason or purpose, that is expressly stated. The position may be compared to the difference between the causation test for unfair dismissal and for other detriments. For unfair dismissal, the focus is on the reason or principal reason for the dismissal (section 103A ERA), therefore clearly signalling that in cases of mixed reasons the focus is on the principal reason. No such distinction is drawn for detriment (section 47B ERA), with the effect that a significant influence is sufficient (see Chapter 7). We suggest that similarly it is more likely that the test in section 43G(1)(c) will be construed as meaning that if one of the purposes which materially influences the making of the disclosure was personal gain, protection under sections 43G and 43H does not apply. Conversely, if personal gain was not a material influence, it cannot be said that this was a purpose of the disclosure. However, the issue awaits appellate authority. There remains a possibility that, just as policy considerations led to the introduction of the predominant purpose threshold in relation to the good faith test, applying a purposive approach a similar narrow construction may be applied in relation to the personal gain requirement. That may be said to be in keeping with the relegation of the good faith requirement to being a remedy issue, which reflects a greater recognition of the importance of facilitating public interest disclosures, notwithstanding the motives for making them.

(3) The section 43G(2) preconditions

Even where an allegation is not made for personal gain, and it is reasonably believed to be **5.76** substantially true, a third tier disclosure will still only qualify for protection under section 43G if one or more of the three further preconditions (sometimes referred to as gateways to protection) are met. These conditions are that the worker reasonably believes that he will be victimized by the employer if he makes the disclosure (section 43G(2)(a)); that he reasonably believes that there is likely to be a cover-up such that 'evidence relating to the relevant failure will be concealed or destroyed if he makes a disclosure to his employer' (section 43G(2)(b)); or that the matter or substantially the same matter had previously been raised internally or with a prescribed regulator (section 43G(2)(c)). It is only necessary to meet one of these three preconditions. Also, though not raised as a specific condition, there is clearly, underlying these preconditions, the presumption that, before any wider disclosure is protected, there should ordinarily be a first tier or regulatory disclosure and that only if this has not addressed the problem should the matter be taken outside the organization. Even if the precondition is met, the tribunal must still consider whether the worker acted reasonably in all the circumstances of the particular case.

(a) Precondition 1: reasonable belief in victimization; subsection (2)(a)

The first of the alternative preconditions which may be met is that the worker reasonably **5.77** believes that s/he will (not may) be subjected to a detriment by his/her employer were s/he to raise the matter internally or with a prescribed regulator. The relevant belief must exist at the time when s/he makes the external disclosure and must be objectively reasonable. As such, if the worker does not address his/her mind to the question of whether to make a disclosure to the employer, neither of the first two preconditions in section 43G can be satisfied.

Relevant considerations may include:

(a) the nature of the relevant failure. Thus, if disclosure involves an allegation of a breach of a legal obligation or a criminal offence by the employer it is likely to be easier to establish the requisite reasonable belief than if the concern is about a risk to health and safety which the employer could remedy;

(b) the identity of the person alleged to have been responsible for the relevant failure. Thus, if there is an allegation of wrongdoing made against the most senior levels of the employing organization, the reasonable belief might be more readily established than if it relates to a more junior employee or relates to an allegation against someone other than the employer;

(c) whether there is an effective whistleblowing policy which makes clear to whom the concern should be addressed, and that workers will not be subjected to detrimental treatment for honestly raising concerns;

(d) the employer's culture, internal policies, and track record in relation to responding to the raising of concerns;

(e) in relation to regulatory disclosures, whether it would be necessary for the employer to be informed of the identity of the employee making the disclosure, and whether this would be apparent in any event to the employer;

(f) the employer's response if the concern was raised internally in the first instance, or if the employer had otherwise learnt of earlier disclosures. In *Korashi* [2012] IRLR 4 the EAT noted the absence of detriment suffered following earlier disclosures. In the light of this it accepted that, in relation to subsequent disclosures to the police, the claimant could not have had a reasonable belief that he would suffer detriment.

5.78 In order to reduce the risk of wider disclosures, it is therefore important that there be an effective whistleblowing policy, that staff are made sufficiently aware of it, that victimization of those honestly raising concerns is regarded as unacceptable within the employing organization, and that a disclosure to a prescribed regulator is a permissible option.

(b) Precondition 2: reasonable belief in a cover-up; subsection (2)(b)

5.79 The second precondition deals with circumstances where the worker reasonably believes that a cover-up of the malpractice is likely to occur if s/he makes the disclosure at the first tier.[30] It can only be satisfied where there is no regulator prescribed under section 43F to whom the reporting of that malpractice should be made. Accordingly, where there is a prescribed regulator, a concern about a cover-up should be raised with that regulator before any wider disclosure might be capable of protection unless the matter is exceptionally serious (section 43H). However, in contrast to section 43G(2)(a), which requires a belief that the worker 'will' be subjected to a detriment, section 43G(2)(b) requires only that concealment is 'likely'. This therefore connotes a lesser degree of certainty. However, if construed in the same way as section 43B(1)(b), this would still require a belief that the concealment or destruction of evidence is more likely than not to occur: see *Kraus v Penna* [2004] IRLR 260, EAT (considered in Chapter 3, paragraphs 3.93 to 3.102).

(c) Precondition 3: previous internal disclosure; subsection (2)(c)

5.80 The third approach is that the wider disclosure may be protected where the matter has previously been raised internally or with a prescribed regulator. It should be noted that the disclosure at this third tier does not have to be of *exactly* the same information as was disclosed at the first, provided it is *substantially* the same. Typically the employee will build into the third tier disclosure additional information identified since the disclosure to the employer, and also specifically cover the failure of the employer to respond to the initial concerns. Indeed,

---

[30] See eg *Shepherd v Phoenix Contracts (Leicester) Ltd* (ET Case No 1902593/2008, 16 March 2010), where s 43G(2)(b) was satisfied because when the disclosure was made to the employer, the response was 'I didn't hear that'.

the brush-off or contemptuous response to the first disclosure will often light the touchpaper for more explosive and wider disclosure. Section 43G(4) specifically deems a disclosure to be 'substantially the same' where the subsequent disclosure 'extends to information about action taken or not taken by any person as a result of a previous disclosure'.

The EAT decision in *Bladon v ALM Medical Services Ltd* (EAT/709/00 and EAT/967/00, 19 **5.81** January 2001)[31] supports a particularly broad approach to the meaning of 'substantially the same'. The decision needs to be treated with a degree of caution as it was a preliminary hearing attended only by the appellants, although the EAT did say (at para 21) that its comments might give assistance to tribunals. In relation to the phrase 'substantially the same', the EAT explained (at para 31) that:

> it would, in our judgment, be wholly inappropriate for tribunals to embark upon an exercise of nice and detailed analysis of the disclosure to the employer, compared with the disclosure to the outside body, for the purpose of deciding whether the test in section 43G(2) (c) has been made out. The correct approach, in our judgment, is for tribunals to adopt a commonsense broad approach when deciding whether or not the disclosure is 'substantially the same'.

Mr Bladon was employed in a nursing home. He raised concerns about patient welfare and **5.82** care with his employer and then also with the Nursing Home Inspectorate within the local authority. Because both the concerns raised internally and with the Inspectorate related to concerns about patients being put at risk by failures of care, the EAT held that the disclosures satisfied the requirement under section 43G of being 'substantially the same'. This was so irrespective of whether the examples given by Mr Bladon of lack of care were similar or the same in both cases or if additional examples were given in the disclosure to the employer or to the Inspectorate.

Notwithstanding the broad approach in *Bladon*, ultimately the issue of whether the infor- **5.83** mation is substantially the same raises a question of fact. As such, where further information is added, this entails a risk that the information will be viewed as not merely being a further example of the same matter, but as raising information which is not substantially the same. That is apparent from contrasting the conclusion in *Bladon* with that in *Korashi* [2012] IRLR 4. Dr Korashi was appointed to a post in the obstetrics and gynaecology department of an NHS Trust. He made disclosures to his employer that a consultant colleague (Mr A) had been guilty of negligence in the treatment of patients. He later raised allegations to the General Medical Council in relation to this, identifying allegations in relation to six patients. He subsequently made an allegation to the police in which he contended that Mr A was associated with the deaths of four patients as a result of his gross negligence. However, two of these cases had not been the subject of earlier disclosure and allegation. In those circumstances, the EAT upheld the conclusion that there had not been an earlier disclosure to the employer of substantially the same information.

Further, the previous disclosure must itself have been a qualifying disclosure. This require- **5.84** ment was set out by the EAT in *Goode v Marks and Spencer plc* (EAT/0442/09, 15 April 2010) (Wilkie J). As set out in Chapter 3 (paragraph 3.20), the claimant (G) had complained to his line manager that he thought the employer's proposals to reduce the discretionary enhanced redundancy terms were 'disgusting'. He later sent an email to *The Times* saying that the employer proposed to reduce redundancy benefits drastically, that the consultation body would be unable to resist, and that this would result in staff redundancies with reduced

---

[31] The decision was overturned by the Court of Appeal ([2002] EWCA Civ 1085, [2002] ICR 1444) but this issue as to the meaning of 'substantially the same' was not addressed.

redundancy packages. He was summarily dismissed for sending this email. The employment tribunal found that there was no qualifying disclosure and its decision was upheld on appeal. The EAT concluded that even if the disclosure to *The Times* was a qualifying disclosure it was not protected under section 43G. G's contention that he had previously made disclosure of substantially the same information to his employer (within section 43(G)(2)(c)(i)) was rejected. The internal disclosure was not a qualifying disclosure, there having been no disclosure of information, other than possibly a statement of G's state of mind that he was 'disgusted'. If the external disclosure was a qualifying disclosure, but the previous internal disclosure was not, the previous disclosure could not be regarded as a disclosure of substantially the same information. The previous expression of disgust at the proposals was therefore insufficient to meet the requirement of a previous disclosure of substantially the same information.

5.85 Where this precondition applies, it is specifically provided that, in assessing whether it was reasonable to make the disclosure, the tribunal must have particular regard to whether the worker, in raising the matter with the employer, had complied with the terms of any authorized procedure for raising such concerns. This need not be an expressly agreed procedure since the statute refers to 'any procedure whose use by [the worker] was authorized by the employer'. Thus, for example, if the whistleblowing procedure provides a right to appeal against the conclusions reached in response to the concerns, but the employee makes a third tier disclosure before exhausting the internal appeal process, this might be a factor pointing against it being reasonable to make the third tier disclosure.

(4) Reasonableness: subsection (3)

5.86 The final requirement under ERA, section 43G is that it must be reasonable in all the circumstances of the case for the worker to have made the disclosure. Subsection (3) expounds some of the factors in determining reasonableness. The tribunal is obliged to take into account each of these factors: the identity of the recipient, the seriousness of the relevant failure and whether the relevant failure is continuing or is likely to occur in the future, any duty of confidentiality to a third party, and the nature of previous disclosure(s). However, section 43G(3) does not purport to set out a comprehensive list of all the relevant considerations. Whilst a tribunal must take into account the factors identified in section 43G(3), as emphasized by Auld LJ in *Street*,[32] in accordance with section 43G(1)(e) the tribunal is required to take into account 'all the circumstances of the case'.

5.87 The particular considerations identified can be seen as drawing on factors that have been recognized as important in the context of the common law of confidentiality and in particular whether confidentiality has been overridden in the public interest. During the passage of the Public Interest Disclosure Bill, Richard Shepherd MP (a promoter of the Bill), referring to the relationship with the common law of confidentiality, commented[33] that:

> in consultations, the Minister and I agreed that any cross-reference to the law of confidence in the Bill was inappropriate for a number of reasons. First, we were keen to make the public interest in all disclosure of wrong-doing the pre-eminent factor. Secondly, we feared that it would not be sufficiently clear to employers and employees how this area of case law might apply if there were some umbilical link. Thirdly, we recognised that workers who reported a serious wrong-doing should not forfeit protection because it later transpired that that information was not[34] in law confidential. When the courts have granted or refused an injunction to stop the disclosure of that same confidential information, the view of the Minister,

---

[32] At para 28.
[33] Parliamentary Debates HC, Standing Committee D, 11 March 1998.
[34] The word 'not' appears to have been a typographical error or to have been mis-spoken.

with which I acquiesced, was that those decisions should be relevant, but not binding on the tribunal. As such, no reference was made to the law of confidence in the Bill.

The common law of confidence, and whether confidentiality has been overridden in favour of **5.88** disclosure in the public interest, is therefore not determinative of how the issues arising under sections 43G and 43H, and in particular the issue of reasonableness, would be resolved.[35] In some instances, however, it helps to illustrate the considerations which might arise, and we make some reference below to cases drawn from the common law of confidence for that purpose. We discuss this in more detail in Chapter 14.

(a) Identity of the person to whom the disclosure is made: subsection (3)(a)

The tribunal must have regard to 'the identity of the person to whom the disclosure is made'. **5.89** There is no limit on the range of people to whom such a disclosure might be made. It could include the police, a professional body, a non-prescribed regulator, a union official, the relatives of a patient at risk, a contracting party whose rights were being flouted, colleagues who cannot be regarded as the employer (such as where more junior colleagues are informed of concerns so that they can assist in investigating the concerns), shareholders (who have a role as stakeholders in the business), friends and neighbours, members of voluntary groups, or the media, amongst others. However, whilst the list of potential recipients is vast, in each case it will be important to show why this was an appropriate person to whom to make the disclosure and it will be relevant whether there was a more appropriate recipient of the disclosure.

In any given case it may be possible to identify a hierarchy in terms of the most appropriate **5.90** recipients of a disclosure. This might, for example, be as follows: internal within the organization; to a regulator with power to redress the concern; to a trade union; to the responsible Minister; to a Secretary of State-appointed body; to an MP; to shareholders; to interested third parties, eg to a concerned citizens group; to the local or trade media; to the national media. In each case, however, this will turn on all the circumstances, including the other express factors identified in section 43G(3).

An illustration of some of the considerations that may be material in relation to the identity **5.91** of the recipient is provided by decisions in relation to the public interest defence in respect of duties of confidentiality (see Chapter 14). Disclosures of confidential information to the media were held to be justified in *Initial Services v Putterill* [1968] 1 QB 396, where a disclosure to the *Daily Mail* about price-fixing was held to be lawful by the Court of Appeal because the public were being misled. Lord Denning MR (at pp 405G–406B) observed that ordinarily any disclosure should be to a person with a 'proper interest to receive the information' but that there might be cases 'where the misdeed is of such a character that the public interest may demand, or at least excuse, publication on a broader field, even to the press'. Similarly, in *Lion Laboratories v Evans* [1985] 1 QB 526 the Court of Appeal held that the press was an appropriate recipient of the information in relation to suspect roadside breathalysers as it was important that people had the information needed to challenge criminal charges and it seemed that the Home Office—which had approved the breathalyser—was an interested party. In *Cork v McVicar* (1985), *The Times*, 31 October 1985 the High Court allowed the *Daily Express* to publish allegations of corruption in the Metropolitan Police.

However, the Court of Appeal in *Francome v Daily Mirror* [1984] 1 WLR 892 held that the **5.92** *Daily Mirror* could not publish confidential information which suggested that a jockey had

---

[35] See also *Street*, para 5.01 above, where the Court of Appeal held that cases drawn from the common law of confidence were not material to the proper construction of the 'good faith' requirement which at that time applied in the context of protected disclosures.

been engaged in misconduct as the public interest would be just as well served by a disclosure to the police or the Jockey Club. This position was explained in *A-G v Guardian Newspapers Ltd (No 2)* [1990] 1 AC 109 at 268, per Lord Griffiths:

> In certain circumstances the public interest may be better served by a limited form of publication perhaps to the police or some other authority who can follow up a suspicion that wrongdoing may lurk beneath the cloak of confidence. Those authorities will be under a duty not to abuse the confidential information and to use it only for the purpose of their inquiry.

5.93 *W v Egdell* [1990] 1 Ch 359 (CA) provides a further illustration of a disclosure to the particular recipient being regarded as permissible, whereas a wider disclosure would not have been reasonable. The claimant suffered from paranoid schizophrenia and was detained in a secure hospital after killing five people. He applied to a mental health review tribunal and, to support his application, sought a report from the defendant who was an independent consultant psychiatrist. The defendant's report revealed that the claimant had a continuing interest in home-made bombs and expressed the opinion that the claimant was a continuing danger to the public. The claimant then withdrew his application and refused to consent to the defendant disclosing the report. However, the defendant disclosed the report to the medical officer at the secure hospital and a copy was sent to the relevant Secretary of State. Whilst there would have been an obvious breach of confidence if the medical report had been disclosed to the public, the Court of Appeal held that there was no such breach where the report was made available to the authority concerned with deciding whether the claimant should be released from a secure hospital.

(b) The seriousness of the failure: subsection (3)(b)

5.94 A further consideration in assessing reasonableness is 'the seriousness of the relevant failure'. Thus, if the matter is very serious, that may justify a wider disclosure than would otherwise be the case. A lower level of seriousness would, for example, be expected where a third tier disclosure of confidential information was made to the police or a non-prescribed regulator, than if the same information was disclosed to the media.

(c) Whether the relevant failure continues: subsection (3)(c)

5.95 The third matter which must be weighed in the balance of reasonableness is 'whether the relevant failure is continuing or is likely to occur in the future'. This is closely connected with the question of the seriousness of the concern. The sense of this provision is that it is more likely that the disclosure will be reasonable if it is about a continuing or future threat as opposed to something which has blown over, in the sense that it has already happened and it is not considered likely that it will happen again.

5.96 Conversely, disclosure to the media is likely to be more difficult to justify where the concern has already been satisfactorily addressed, whether within the employment organization or otherwise. This picks up on a theme in the jurisprudence on the law of confidence (see Chapter 14). This has been touched on in, for example, *Weld-Blundell v Stephens* [1919] 1 KB 520; *Initial Services v Putterill* [1968] 1 QB 396 at 405; and *Schering Chemicals v Falkman* [1982] QB 1 at 27. Where the threat has passed, there must be a particularly clear public interest in any confidential information being disclosed.

(d) Duty of confidentiality owed to a third party: subsection (3)(d)

5.97 This provision was inserted in the House of Commons at committee stage in order to ensure that tribunals took account of the interests of a third party to whom a duty to maintain confidentiality of information was owed. In introducing the amendment, the sponsoring Minister, Ian McCartney, commented that it was necessary in order to deal with information which was subject to particular confidence, such as arising out of a banker–client or doctor–patient relationship. He explained[36] that:

> … the amendment would ensure that tribunals take into account the damage that may occur to a third person by disclosure. The tribunal may already take that into account, but it is not obliged to do so. One example might be that of a doctor's receptionist who disclosed medical records in good faith and in accordance with information available to her. But she could be wrong and the patient might have suffered an irreversible invasion of privacy.
>
> Another example might arise out of a business relationship. A bank employee might disclose that one of the bank's clients appeared to be insolvent. That could be very damaging to the client, who trusted the bank's duty of confidentiality to protect him. It would certainly damage his relationship with the bank and there might be damage to the bank's wider reputation and future business. Any potential damage might be justified by the circumstances, but the amendment has neither the intention nor the effect of suggesting that a duty of confidence to a third party will override all other factors. It would merely ensure that the tribunal will take that and any damage caused into account.

The effect of the reference to the duty of confidentiality to third parties is therefore not to set **5.98** an absolute bar to protection where such confidentiality is infringed. Rather, it is one matter which is expressly declared to be material in determining the reasonableness of the particular disclosure. This was also stressed by Richard Shepherd MP, one of the promoters of the Bill, who commented[37] that:

> … during consultation, the point was made that there are some particularly important obligations of confidence, for example those owed by a doctor to his patient or a bank to its customer. A fear was expressed that the Bill as drafted might unwittingly permit or encourage a secretary in a doctor's surgery or a clerk in a bank to disclose a concern about malpractice or misconduct without regard to the fact that that information was subject to an important obligation of confidence owed by the employer to a third party. The amendment has been tabled simply to allay those fears. Its purpose is not to thwart protection simply because the information was subject to a routine claim of confidentiality. It covers those exceptional cases in which there is a particularly important duty of confidence, as between doctors and patients, when a worker's disclosure breaches that duty and harms the third party. In such cases, it is right that the tribunal should consider the breach and the degree of any harm that it causes in deciding whether the disclosure was reasonable.

Again, therefore, it was emphasized that not all obligations of confidentiality would have **5.99** the same weight, but rather that tribunals were expected to be able, when assessing reasonableness, to recognize certain obligations of confidentiality as being of particular importance. Further, this subparagraph does not refer to confidentiality obligations owed by employees to their employer—though there is scope to take account of this in considering all the circumstances of the case.

An example of circumstances meriting disclosure of information despite confidentiality obligations owed to a third party is provided by the decision in *W v Egdell* [1990] 1 Ch 359 (CA), **5.100** summarized at paragraph 5.93 above. A further example would be the position of a doctor who carries out a blood test on an individual and becomes aware that s/he is HIV-positive. The doctor could not plausibly argue that it is in the public interest to inform the public about this through the media. In the event that the patient had a partner, and the doctor has reason to suspect that s/he will not be informed of the position, the disclosure to that person might be reasonable.

---

[36] Parliamentary Debates, HC Standing Committee D, 11 March 1998.
[37] ibid.

(e) Previous disclosures: subsection (3)(e)

5.101   In a case where the worker has previously made a disclosure of substantially the same information to his/her employer or to a prescribed person under section 43F, the tribunal must also take into account action which the employer or prescribed person took or might reasonably be expected to have taken. This may be a factor pointing either in favour of or against the disclosure being reasonable. Thus, if the employer has investigated the concern and taken all reasonable action in respect of it, the further disclosure is unlikely to be reasonable unless, perhaps, the whistleblower does not know that the action has been taken and could reasonably believe that it had not been taken. It is also likely to be a strong factor against the disclosure being reasonable if the worker jumped the gun and made a wider disclosure before awaiting a response from the employer and without having afforded the employer sufficient time to act. Conversely, if action taken by the employer was inadequate and fell short of the action which the employer or prescribed person could reasonably be expected to have taken, or indicated that the concerns were not being treated seriously, this might point strongly in favour of a wider disclosure being reasonable.

5.102   The provision therefore makes clear that it is important that the worker who made the disclosure is kept informed as to the outcome of any investigation which has taken place into the concern s/he has expressed and what action has been taken if the allegation is found to be substantiated. If the employer investigates and does not report back any outcome or reasons for the outcome to the worker, it might be reasonable for the worker to take the matter further, perhaps even to the media (depending on other considerations such as the nature of the matters disclosed). Conversely, should the employer openly investigate and report back to the worker, with a thorough explanation as to why the allegation is not substantiated, it might be unreasonable for the worker to proceed further down the line of disclosure.

(f) Whistleblowing procedures: subsection (3)(f)

5.103   Where a third tier disclosure is to be made on the basis that the worker has previously made a disclosure of substantially the same information to the employer, in determining reasonableness the tribunal must consider whether the worker complied with any whistleblowing procedure authorized by the employer. Thus, in *Korashi* [2012] IRLR 4 (at para 80) it was noted that the whistleblowing procedure required disclosure in the first instance through that procedure, and the failure to comply with that requirement was relevant in indicating that disclosure to the police was not reasonable in all the circumstances.

5.104   However, it is suggested that it will not be enough simply to introduce such a procedure in a workplace. Reasonable steps should also be taken to promote the whistleblowing procedure amongst the workforce. Ideally, once such a procedure is introduced, its use should be monitored and its role explained to the workforce, for example (depending on the size of the organization), through team briefings, newsletters, or posters. We discuss in Chapter 19 what would be appropriate to put in these procedures.

5.105   It should be noted that a grievance procedure is different from a whistleblowing procedure—a point made by Lord Borrie[38]—in that under a grievance procedure it is for the worker to prove his/her case, whereas under a whistleblowing procedure the worker raises the matter so that it may be investigated. This may be significant in relation to the extent of any evidence which the worker must adduce.[39]

---

[38] *Hansard* HL, 5 June 1998, col 627.

[39] This was also reflected in the specific distinction which was drawn between whistleblowing procedures and grievance procedures in para 15 of Sch 3 to the Employment Act 2002 relating to the scope of statutory grievance procedures (now repealed). This provided that the standard grievance procedures were only applicable to a protected disclosure if the information disclosed related to a matter which could have been raised

(g) Assessment of all the circumstances

Provided that the tribunal does take into account each of the factors in section 43G(1)(e), **5.106** and properly directs itself as to the need to take into account all relevant circumstances, its judgment as to whether it was reasonable to make the disclosure is likely to be difficult to disturb on appeal. It will be for the tribunal to determine which circumstances in addition to the specific factors in section 43G(3) are relevant, and what weight to give to each of the factors taken into account, including the factors in section 43G(3). Whilst, as indicated above, consideration of how the public interest defence has been applied in the context of confidentiality may provide an illustration of some of the relevant considerations, decisions in that different context are in no way binding and each case must be considered on its own facts by the tribunal against the touchstone of reasonableness.

The following two cases are examples of how the tribunals have taken account of the compet- **5.107** ing considerations in first instance decisions which have considered questions of reasonableness specifically in the context of section 43G.

In *Staples v Royal Sun Alliance* (ET, 2001) the claimant was a part-time negotiator in the **5.108** respondent's estate agency division. Concerns were raised internally by the claimant about the health and safety of customers and the way financial services were being sold. But the claimant also subsequently mentioned one concern to a customer. The tribunal held that the raising of the concern with the customer fell within section 43G as (a) it concerned a breach of consumer law, (b) the claimant had already raised it internally, and (c) it was reasonable to tell the customer, as to which the tribunal noted that it could understand why the claimant felt obliged to inform potential customers so they would not be deceived.[40] The nature of the concern, together with the fact that the disclosure was made to those with a proper interest in receiving the information, was therefore determinative.

In *Kay v Northumbria Healthcare NHS Trust* (ET, Case No 6405617/00, 29 November **5.109** 2001) the employment tribunal found that a disclosure fell within section 43G even though made to the press, having regard in particular to the response when the issues were raised internally, and the issues of serious public concern which were raised. Mr Kay was a ward manager employed by an NHS Trust. He managed a ward for the elderly. He raised internally concerns he had as to bed shortages, but it was made clear to him that there were no resources available to address this. The situation deteriorated and some elderly patients were moved to a gynaecological ward. As a means of highlighting his concerns, he then wrote a satirical letter, framed as an open letter to the Prime Minister, which was published in his local paper. As a result he was disciplined for unprofessional conduct. The employment tribunal found that there was a protected disclosure. Kay had a reasonable belief that the disclosure tended to show a danger to health and safety in that elderly patients were being directed from a ward dedicated to their needs to one not so dedicated, and he was entitled to take the view that this would compromise their health care. In concluding that it was reasonable to make the disclosure to the press, the tribunal took into account (a) the previous internal disclosure, (b) the fact that it had been made clear that no action would be taken due to lack of resources, (c) that Kay was not aware of any authorized procedure for raising concerns within the meaning of section 43G(3)(f), (d) that it was a matter of serious public concern that elderly patients should be moved around in the way described, and (e) that it was in the public interest that the information and concerns be raised.

---

as a grievance with the employer and it was the intention of the worker that the disclosure should constitute the raising of a grievance.

[40] This summary is drawn from summaries of cases published by PCaW. Ultimately, the claim failed on the basis that the protected disclosure was not the reason for dismissal.

(5) Disclosure to a trade union

5.110 There is no express provision relating to disclosure to a trade union. An attempt was made during the passage of the Protected Information Disclosure Bill to make specific reference to such disclosure. In favour of the amendment it was argued that union officials (who will often not be employed by the same company as the whistleblower) were in reality in a similar position to legal representatives, and would often be the first port of call, especially in relation to a health and safety issue. In rejecting a proposed amendment to refer to unions in section 43C, it was said that this would not be consistent with the scheme of the legislation in encouraging concerns to be raised first internally with the employer or the person legally responsible for the failure.[41] It was also noted that disclosure to a trade union solicitor would be covered under section 43D, and that it can be expected that where there is a whistleblowing procedure it will provide for disclosures to trade union officials so that there would be protection under section 43C(2).

5.111 There remains an issue, however, as to the adequacy of coverage in relation to union officials. If an employee approaches a union official (other than a union lawyer) for initial guidance as to how to address concerns, this will not fall within section 43C unless such a disclosure is authorized under the employer's procedures. Nor will it fall within section 43D unless the disclosure is in the course of obtaining legal advice.[42] But there will also not be protection under section 43G unless the employee could satisfy one of the preconditions in section 43G(2). If the union official is the first port of call for initial guidance, it will not be possible to show that substantially the same information has been disclosed to the employer. If the gateway requirements of section 43G(2) are not satisfied, and it is not an exceptionally serious failure falling within section 43H, the employee will not have protection for making a protected disclosure.

G. Wider Disclosures of Exceptionally Serious Matters: Section 43H

5.112 Section 43H provides an alternative basis for protecting disclosures relating to matters of an exceptionally serious nature. It provides (leaving aside the good faith requirement that applies only to disclosures made prior to 25 June 2013):

Disclosure of exceptionally serious failure

(1) A qualifying disclosure is made in accordance with this section if—

 ...

    (b) he reasonably believes that the information disclosed, and any allegation contained in it, are substantially true,

    (c) he does not make the disclosure for purposes of personal gain,

    (d) the relevant failure is of an exceptionally serious nature, and

    (e) in all the circumstances of the case, it is reasonable for him to make the disclosure.

(2) In determining for the purposes of subsection (1)(e) whether it is reasonable for the worker to make the disclosure, regard shall be had, in particular, to the identity of the person to whom the disclosure is made.

5.113 The essential difference between section 43H and section 43G, therefore, is that in place of the three alternative preconditions in section 43G(2), under section 43H it is sufficient to

---

[41] *Hansard* HL, 19 June 1998, cols 1800–01, per Lord Haskell; cols 1801–02, per Lord Borrie.
[42] See paras 5.38–5.46 in relation to whether section 43D is to be construed as limited to seeking advice from lawyers.

establish that the relevant failure is exceptionally serious in nature. As in section 43G, there is still a requirement that the worker must possess a reasonable belief that the information disclosed is substantially true, must not be acting for personal gain, and it must be reasonable for him in all the circumstances to make that disclosure. Even where the relevant failure is 'exceptionally serious', therefore, the disclosure is not protected unless it was reasonable in all the circumstances for the worker to make it. However, in relation to reasonableness the only factor which *must* be taken into consideration is the identity of the person to whom the disclosure is made. The other factors listed in section 43G(3) in relation to reasonableness *may* still be taken into account but there is no express statutory requirement to do so.

The requirements as to the identity of the recipient of the disclosure and the requirement for reasonableness in all the circumstances (section 43H(1)(e), (2)) were inserted by a government amendment in committee in the Commons.[43] The Minister said: **5.114**

> The Government firmly believe that where exceptionally serious matters are at stake, workers should not be deterred from raising them. It is important that they should do so, and that they should not be put off by concerns that a tribunal might hold that they should have delayed their disclosure or made it in some other way. That does not mean that people should be protected when they act wholly unreasonably: for example, by going straight to the press when there could clearly have been some other less damaging way to resolve matters.

> The amendment will encourage people to act reasonably even in serious matters, but it should not make them afraid that they will lose protection when they do so. It restores the balance between the need to make a disclosure and the need to do so in an effective and reasonable manner. Such disclosures should not be made in an offhand, rushed way to the press, as if that were the first or only way to raise the complaint or allegation. The amendment re-tilts the balance to an even keel by recognising employers' needs as well as the dangers of discouraging urgent and serious disclosures.[44]

During the passage of the Public Interest Disclosure Bill through the House of Lords, an attempt was made to amend clause 43H so as to replace the 'exceptionally serious' requirement with the words 'very serious'. In support of the amendment it was argued that the 'exceptionally serious' test set the threshold too high, and might lead tribunals down a cul-de-sac in considering whether a small enough percentage of failures was of a particular type.[45] In rejecting the proposed amendment it was emphasized that the 'exceptionally serious' test deliberately set a very high threshold, with the intention that it would apply only in rare circumstances. Lord Haskell (for the Government) explained[46] that: **5.115**

> … the new section is meant to apply only in very rare cases. The purpose of inserting 'exceptional' is to indicate that the case is indeed a rare case. Nobody wants individuals disclosing confidential information to other bodies unless the circumstances are exceptional.

> However, we all recognise that there will be concerns that are rare, but so grave that they need to be disclosed and dealt with as soon as possible. We believe that the current wording conveys that very clearly.

> …

> We believe that the best way to convey the order of seriousness under new Section 43H is by referring to failures that are objectively judged to be exceptionally serious. There may be disclosures which are very serious, but hardly exceptional, and such disclosures would be protected under other provisions in the Bill.

---

[43] Parliamentary Debates, HC Standing Committee D, 11 March 1998.
[44] ibid, col 10.
[45] *Hansard* HL, 5 June 1998, col 629, per Lord McCarthy.
[46] *Hansard* HL, 5 June 1998, cols 629–30.

5.116 It was intended, therefore, that the term 'exceptionally serious' would connote a very high standard, meaning something more than 'very serious'. The scope of what is 'exceptionally serious' is a matter of fact and degree for the tribunal. It is a matter on which there may be legitimate room for disagreement, and not much room for appeal to the EAT since this is pre-eminently a matter for assessment by the tribunal hearing all the evidence.

5.117 In some cases it will be apparent from the nature of the failure itself that it is exceptionally serious. Thus, in *Herron v Wintercomfort for the Homeless* (ET, Case No 1502519/03, 11 August 2004), section 43H was found to apply where the relevant failure was that there had been a murder. The claimant met with a client (B) who displayed signs of bruising and said that her partner had threatened to set fire to her. B was later admitted to hospital with serious burns and subsequently died from her injuries before she was able to give any information to the police. The claimant was contacted by the police and told them about her meeting with B. She was pressed by the police to hand over the file. She initially resisted because she wanted to contact her superior first. After she had been unable to contact her superior she handed the file over. Her employer regarded her disclosures as a breach of confidentiality. She was already serving out her notice at the time of the events, but she was subjected to detriments including being required to attend a disciplinary hearing and then being told that she was no longer trusted to work at the same office and would be relocated. This was found to be a detriment on the grounds of protected disclosures under section 43H. Since the relevant failure related to a murder it was indeed exceptionally serious in nature. Further, the disclosure was regarded as reasonable even if made in breach of an obligation of confidentiality in the light of the fact that it was made to the police and in response to approaches by them. The serious nature of the relevant failure, and the fact that it was made to an appropriate body (the police), were also regarded as material in relation to whether there was a qualifying disclosure. The file handed over contained much material which did not amount (if taken separately) to a disclosure within section 43B, but a more broad-brush approach was regarded as appropriate given that the police required to see the whole file in relation to a murder investigation and would not have allowed her to select individual parts of the file to hand over.

5.118 Again, in *Bolkovac v DynCorp Aerospace Operations (UK) Ltd* (ET, Case No 3102729/01) the tribunal was satisfied, based on the nature of the relevant failure, that section 43H applied. Kathryn Bolkovac worked as a police monitor, under the control of the United Nations, in Bosnia. She sent a memo to about fifty people working for her employer and for the UN setting out details of her concerns as to trafficking of women and girls for prostitution by organized criminal gangs and that the problem was not being taken sufficiently seriously by police monitors and their superiors. She implied that many of the recipients of her email attended brothels. She was then dismissed. The tribunal upheld her claim that her dismissal was automatically unfair, having been by reason of protected disclosures contained in her memo. It concluded that the disclosure fell within section 43H, given that her concerns were to be set in the context of a grave humanitarian situation involving the exploitation and enslavement of women by criminals, and the exceptionally serious nature of the failure by some elements of the UN administration to take an adequate grip on the situation. In relation to whether it was reasonable in all the circumstances of the case to make the disclosure, the tribunal noted that Ms Bolkovac had not continued to raise the matter with her employer or with senior officials in the UN's International Police Task Force because they had already been alerted to her concerns or had indicated that they did not share her view as to the seriousness of the matter. In the circumstances it had been reasonable to make the disclosure to a wide audience. Compensation of £110,000 was subsequently awarded.[47]

In other cases, there might be a combination of factors which, taken together, lead a tribunal **5.119** to conclude that the failure is exceptionally serious. This was the case in *Collins v National Trust* (ET, Case No 2507255/05, 17 January 2006), which concerned disclosure to the press of a draft report relating to contamination on land owned and managed by Mr Collins' employer, the National Trust. Mr Collins genuinely and reasonably believed that the draft report showed (a) that the environment was likely to be damaged and (b) that health and safety were likely to be endangered, as the contamination had potential to cause damage to workers and the public, including children. Further, he reasonably believed that information about this was being concealed, in that the report was not disclosed by the local council to the National Trust for over a year and was to be kept confidential pending further investigation. Mr Collins was dismissed purportedly on the grounds that he had disclosed the report to the press in breach of a lawful instruction that queries about the report should be referred either to his employer's press officer or its property manager. The tribunal, however, held that the real reason for dismissal was the disclosure of the content of the report to the press.

In relation to the requirement that the disclosure be of an 'exceptionally serious nature', the **5.120** tribunal accepted that to gain protection the relevant failure must be 'very serious indeed'. In concluding that this test was satisfied it took into account in particular that:

(1) there were three relevant failures: damage to the environment, endangerment of health and safety to the public, and concealment of information;
(2) the public were invited onto the land for recreational purposes; children played there and were identified in the report as especially at risk; and
(3) the respondent (the National Trust) was a well-known and well-respected conservation charity in which the public place special trust and confidence, and the disclosure related to land which the Trust owned and managed.

The tribunal accepted that the respondent may have acted reasonably in adopting a strategy **5.121** of further consultation before disclosing the report. However, it stressed that the fact that the respondent may have been acting reasonably did not necessarily entail that Mr Collins had been acting unreasonably. In this case the tribunal concluded that he had been acting reasonably in the light of his genuine and reasonable concerns about public safety, that there was reason to believe that disclosure of the report would be delayed, and that the public should be able to obtain their own advice on the risks indicated in the report. Accordingly, Mr Collins' claim succeeded.

Whilst ultimately the tribunal will be required to make a broad-brush assessment in all the **5.122** circumstances, we suggest that the following considerations are likely to be significant in the assessment of whether something is 'exceptionally serious':

(a) By their nature, and by virtue of the requirement for a reasonable belief that the disclosure is made in the public interest, most disclosures falling within section 43B will often be of quite serious matters. Section 43H connotes something of a different order, which can properly be regarded as exceptional.

---

[47] This paragraph draws on the summary in IDS Employment Law Supplement, 'Whistleblowing at Work', p 75. Kathryn Bolkovac's experiences form the basis of the film *The Whistleblower* (2011), starring Rachel Weisz as Ms Bolkovac.

(b) Taking a purposive approach in assessing whether the failure is exceptionally serious in nature, it may be helpful to consider whether the seriousness justifies making a wider disclosure without satisfying any of the gateways to protection in section 43G(2).

(c) The seriousness of the harm caused is fundamental. A danger to public safety, as in *Collins*, may be more likely to qualify than financial concerns.

(d) Whether it is an ongoing or imminent failure is important—although *Herron* illustrates that if the matter is serious (in that case murder) it may still qualify.

(e) The decision in *Collins* indicates that the number of failures may cumulatively affect whether, taken together, they can each be regarded as exceptionally serious.

(f) The number of potential victims may be important.

(g) The nature of the person responsible for the failure may be relevant, as was the case in *Collins*.

6

WHO IS PROTECTED UNDER PIDA?

A. Introduction

The scope of person protected by the protected disclosure provisions is set out in the follow- **6.01**
ing provisions:

(a) section 230 ERA, which contains the definitions of employee and worker which are of
general application for the purposes of the ERA;
(b) section 43K ERA, which sets out an extended definition of worker for the purposes of
the protected disclosure provisions;
(c) section 43KA ERA, which brings police constables and police cadets within the scope of
the protected disclosure provisions; and
(d) Part XIII (sections 191 to 195) which deals with the application of provisions of the ERA
to certain types of employment or quasi-employment relationships: Crown employment, armed forces, Parliamentary staff).

The same provisions also apply to determine those individuals who are workers for the purposes
of establishing personal liability for acts of detriment, other than dismissal of an employee (as
considered further in Chapter 7).

6.02 By way of broad overview, in *Bates van Winkelhof v Clyde and Co LLP* [2014] UKSC 32 [2014] 1 WLR 2047 (para 31) Lady Hale suggested that employment law could be regarded as essentially covering three types of people:

- those employed under a contract of employment,
- those self-employed people who are in business on their own account and undertake work for their clients or customers, and
- an intermediate class of workers who are self-employed but do not fall within the second class.

The protection of individuals from action taken against them by their employer on the ground that they have made a protected disclosure is afforded not only to an 'employee' but also to the wider class of those who come within the intermediate class which is often called 'limb (b)', as its definition is contained in section 230(3)(b) ERA set out below (paragraph 6.08).

6.03 However, under section 43K ERA whistleblowing protection is also extended part way into Lady Hale's second type, to persons in other relationships, by defining them as workers where they would not otherwise fall within the intermediate limb (b) class. That extended class can be divided into four subcategories:

(1) Individuals who are introduced or supplied by a third person; the person for whom the individual works may in certain circumstances be constituted as their employer even though there is no contract between the individual and that person.

(2) Individuals who contract with a person for the purposes of that person's business but not in a place under that person's control or management and where the work is not necessarily to be done personally by the individual.

(3) Individuals being provided with work experience pursuant to a training course or programme, or with training for employment (or both).

(4) Individuals in other miscellaneous relationships within the health sector.

6.04 This chapter considers the various protected categories of relationship where one of the parties is to be regarded as a 'worker' and thus protected. It also notes particular relationships which would appear to fall outside the scope of the scheme of protection. It concludes by considering the extent of protection afforded to those whose employment is not confined to England and Wales.

B. Employees

6.05 An 'employee' is defined by ERA, section 230(1) as:

> … an individual who has entered into or works under (or, where the employment has ceased, worked under) a contract of employment.

6.06 A 'contract of employment' is defined as:

> … a contract of service or apprenticeship, whether express or implied, and (if it is express) whether oral or in writing.

6.07 The following principles are applicable in relation to whether there is a contract of employment:[1]

(a) The first essential prerequisite for 'employment' is that there must be a contractual relationship, express or implied, between the worker and the employer. The need to consider whether there is an implied contract is particularly important where there is a 'triangular'

---

[1] See eg *Autoclenz Limited v Belcher and others* [2011] UKSC 41, [2011] ICR 1157 (Supreme Court) at paras 18–21.

relationship, such as where a worker is supplied by an agency to an end user/client. There are typically written contracts between the end user and the agency, and the worker and the agency, but there needs to be an assessment of whether there is an implied contract directly between the worker and the end user. A contract can be implied if it is necessary to give business reality to the relationship and arrangements between the worker and the end user and to establish the enforceable obligations that one would expect to see between them: *Cable & Wireless plc v Muscat* [2006] EWCA Civ 220, [2006] ICR 975 at para 51.[2]

(b) Second, there must be mutuality of obligation.[3] The obligations must relate to the personal provision of work for remuneration and an obligation to perform it, though the remuneration need not be paid directly by the employer.[4]

(c) There must also be a sufficient degree of control to be consistent with an employment relationship.[5]

(d) In addition, it is necessary to identify whether the other provisions of the contract[6] indicate that it is a contract of service.[7] It is necessary to paint a picture from the accumulation of detail: *Hall v Lorimer* [1994] ICR 218 at 226 (CA), [1992] ICR 739 at 744–45, EAT.[8]

(e) The court must give 'appropriate weight' to how the parties themselves categorize their relationship: *Stringfellow Restaurants Ltd v Quashie* [2012] EWCA Civ 1735, [2013] IRLR 99, Elias LJ at para 52 citing *Massey v Crown Life Insurance* [1978] IRLR 31, 32 and Lord Justice Ralph Gibson in *Calder v H Kitson Vickers Ltd* [1988] ICR 232, 251. In a case where the position is uncertain the parties' categorization can be decisive.

C. Workers under Section 230(3)(b) ERA

The ordinary meaning of 'worker' contained in ERA, section 230(3) is someone who is either **6.08** an employee or someone who is not an employee but is:

> an individual who has entered into or works under (or, where the employment has ceased, worked under)—
>
> ...
>
> (b) any other contract, whether express or implied and (if it is express) whether oral or in writing, whereby the individual undertakes to do or perform personally any work or services for another party to the contract whose status is not by virtue of the contract that of a client or customer of any profession or business undertaking carried on by the individual.

---

[2] There has been a degree of retrenchment in this area: *James v London Borough of Greenwich* [2008] EWCA Civ 35, [2008] ICR 545; *Muschett v HM Prison Service* [2010] IRLR 451. See also *Evans v RSA Consulting Ltd* [2010] EWCA Civ 866, [2011] ICR 37.

[3] See eg *Clark v Oxfordshire Health Authority* [1998] IRLR 125 (CA).

[4] *Cable & Wireless plc v Muscat* [2006] EWCA Civ 220, [2006] ICR 975 at para 35; *Cotswold Developments Construction Limited v Williams* [2006] IRLR 181 at paras 48 and 49, EAT.

[5] See eg *Bunce v Postworth Limited t/a Skyblue* [2005] IRLR 557 where there was insufficient control for there to be an employment relationship between an agency worker and the agency.

[6] As to the scope for looking beyond the terms of the written document (or terms implied into the written document), see para 6.10(f) below.

[7] *Cable & Wireless plc v Muscat* [2006] EWCA Civ 220, [2006] ICR 975 at paras 31 and 32.

[8] There is, of course, a plethora of authority on the distinction between a contract of service and a contract which is not a contract of service. The principles are set out in more detail in *Chitty on Contracts*, 32nd edn. London: Sweet & Maxwell, 2015, Vol 2, Chapter 40, paras 40-010 to 40-031; and Bowers, *A Practical Approach to Employment Law*. Oxford: Oxford University Press, 2017.

6.09 There are three elements to the limb (b) definition. They were set out by Elias P in *James v Redcats (Brands) Limited* [2007] IRLR 296, [2007] ICR 1006 at para 6:

> First, there must be a contract to perform work or services. Second, there must be an obligation to perform that work personally. Third, the individual will not be a worker ... if the provision of services is performed in the course of running a profession or business undertaking and the other party is a client or customer. In practice the last two are interrelated concepts ...

6.10 In more detail:

(a) There must be an express or implied contract. It has been said on many occasions that there must be 'mutuality of obligations', but in *Cotswold Developments Construction v Williams* [2006] IRLR 181 the EAT held that there is no such requirement in relation to the definition of a worker over and above the mutuality required to establish a contract. Further, where the worker has been engaged on discrete separate assignments, there is no need to establish some umbrella contract, or that there was some obligation to offer further assignments. The claimant could be a worker in relation to each assignment. But it does not follow that the absence of mutuality of obligation outside the specific assignments is irrelevant to the assessment of whether there was a worker relationship. It might shed light on the character of the relationship; the fact that services are only supplied on an assignment-by-assignment basis may tend to indicate a degree of independence or lack of subordination in the relationship whilst at work, that may point against a worker relationship: *Windle v Secretary of State of Justice* [2016] ICR 721 (CA).

(b) It must be a contract 'whereby the individual undertakes to do or perform personally any work or services for another party to the contract'. There must be a contractual obligation to do work personally. It does not necessarily follow from the fact that the work is in fact done personally that there was a contractual obligation to do so.[9]

(c) The question whether or not a contract provides for the performance of personal services is essentially a matter of construction. The court is concerned with construing the contract, rather than with general policy considerations.[10]

(d) The right or obligation to employ a substitute will not necessarily mean that there is no obligation on the part of the 'contractor' to perform personal services, unless that right to employ a substitute is unfettered. The authorities were reviewed in *Pimlico Plumbers Ltd v Smith* [2017] EWCA Civ 51 (at para 84), where Sir Terence Etherton MR, provided the following summary:

> 'Firstly, an unfettered right to substitute another person to do the work or perform the services is inconsistent with an undertaking to do so personally. Secondly, a conditional right to substitute another person may or may not be inconsistent with personal performance depending upon the conditionality. It will depend on the precise contractual arrangements and, in particular, the nature and degree of any fetter on a right of substitution or, using different language, the extent to which the right of substitution is limited or occasional. Thirdly, by way of example, a right of substitution only when the contractor is unable to carry out the work will, subject to any exceptional facts, be consistent with personal performance. Fourthly, again by way of example, a right of substitution limited only by the need to show that the substitute is as qualified as the contractor to do the work, whether or not that entails a particular procedure, will, subject to any exceptional facts, be inconsistent with personal performance. Fifthly, again by way of example, a right to substitute only with the consent of another person who has an absolute and unqualified discretion to withhold consent will be consistent with personal performance.'

---

[9] *Redrow Homes (Yorkshire) Limited v Wright* [2004] EWCA Civ 469, [2004] ICR 1126 at para 21.
[10] *Pimlico Plumbers Ltd v Smith* [2017] EWCA Civ 51 at para 73, following *Redrow*.

(e) In cases where the 'contractor' is unable, as opposed to unwilling, to carry out specified services and has accepted an obligation to perform those services, but is unable to do so, and where he himself does not bear the costs of employing a substitute, a limited or occasional power of delegation may not be inconsistent with a contract to provide personal services: *Carmichael v National Power plc* [1999] ICR 1226 (HL).

(f) Unless the parties to the agreement have agreed that a document or series of documents was intended to constitute an exclusive record of their agreement, any question arising as to the nature or terms of the contract is a question of fact to be determined from a consideration of all the evidence, including written documents, oral statements, and conduct, including what happened in practice: see *Cable & Wireless plc v Muscat* [2006] EWCA Civ 220, [2006] ICR 975 at para 33. Where the written terms of the contract provide that there is no obligation to carry out the work personally, there is no scope to imply a term inconsistent with that express term. However, it may be possible to show that the written terms do not properly reflect the reality of the relationship. Having regard to inequalities of bargaining power, there is greater scope in the employment field than in commercial disputes, to find that, having regard to all the circumstances, the true agreement between the parties is different to that set out in the written agreement: *Autoclenz Limited v Belcher and others* [2011] UKSC 41, [2011] ICR 1157 (Supreme Court).

(g) The status of the other party (ie the 'employer') must not be that of 'a client or customer of any profession or business undertaking carried on' by the putative worker. The meaning of a 'business undertaking' was considered in *Byrne Brothers (Formwork) Limited v Baird* [2002] ICR 667, EAT, where (at para 17) Mr Recorder Underhill QC provided guidance in relation to this provision:

...

(2) '[Carrying on a] business undertaking' is plainly capable of having a very wide meaning. In one sense every 'self-employed' person carries on a business. But the term cannot be intended to have so wide a meaning here, because if it did the exception would wholly swallow up the substantive provision and limb (b) would be no wider than limb (a). The intention behind the regulation is plainly to create an intermediate class of protected worker, who is on the one hand not an employee but on the other hand cannot in some narrower sense be regarded as carrying on a business. ... It is sometimes said that the effect of the exception is that the 1998 Regulations do not extend to 'the genuinely self-employed'; but that is not a particularly helpful formulation since it is unclear how 'genuine' self-employment is to be defined.

(3) ... Possibly the term 'customer' gives some slight indication of an arm's-length commercial relationship ... but it is not clear whether it was deliberately chosen as a key word in the definition or simply as a neutral term to denote the other party to a contract with a business undertaking.

(4) It seems to us that the best guidance is to be found by considering the policy behind the inclusion of limb (b). That can only have been to extend the benefits of protection to workers who are in the same need of that type of protection as employees *stricto sensu*. ... The reason why employees are thought to need such protection is that they are in a subordinate and dependent position vis-à-vis their employers: the purpose of the Regulations is to extend protection to workers who are, substantively and economically, in the same position. Thus the essence of the intended distinction must be between, on the one hand, workers whose degree of dependence is essentially the same as that of employees and, on the other, contractors who have a sufficiently arm's-length and independent position to be treated as being able to look after themselves in the relevant respects.

(5) Drawing that distinction in any particular case will involve all or most of the same considerations as arise in drawing the distinction between a contract of service and a contract for services—but with the boundary pushed further in the putative worker's

favour. It may, for example, be relevant to assess the degree of control exercised by the putative employer, the exclusivity of the engagement and its typical duration, the method of payment, what equipment the putative worker supplies, the level of risk undertaken, etc. The basic effect of limb (b) is, so to speak, to lower the passmark, so that cases which failed to reach the mark necessary to qualify for protection as employees might nevertheless do so as workers.

6.11 This guidance has been followed in several cases.[11] It was supplemented in *Cotswold Developments Construction*, where the EAT said (at para 53):

> The distinction is not that between employee and independent contractor. The paradigm case falling within the proviso to 2(b) is that of a person working within one of the established professions: solicitor and client, barrister and client, accountant, architect etc. The paradigm case of a customer and someone working in a business undertaking of his own will perhaps be that of the customer of a shop and the shopowner, or of the customer of a tradesman such as a domestic plumber, cabinet maker or portrait painter who commercially markets services as such. Thus viewed, it seems plain that a focus upon whether the purported worker actively markets his services as an independent person to the world in general (a person who will thus have a client or customer) on the one hand, or whether he is recruited by the principal to work for that principal as an integral part of the principal's operations, will in most cases demonstrate on which side of the line a given person falls.

6.12 In *James v Redcats (Brands) Limited* [2007] ICR 1006 (EAT) Elias J added that the client or customer of a business exception could apply even though there was no pre-existing business or one which is independent of the contract alleged to give rise to the worker relationship. Drawing upon the approach in the slightly differently worded definition of 'employer' in discrimination legislation,[12] he suggested (paras 52–69) that, whilst it is necessary to analyse all elements of the relationship, it may assist to assess whether an obligation of personal service is the dominant feature of the contractual arrangement. If so, that would indicate a worker relationship.[13] As Elias J explained (at para 59):

> The dominant purpose test is really an attempt to identify the essential nature of the contract. Is it in essence to be located in the field of dependent work relationships, or is it in essence a contract between two independent business undertakings? The test does not assist in determining whether a contract is a contract of service or of services; it does not, in other words, help in discriminating between cases falling within limbs (a) and (b) of the definition of worker. Its purpose is to distinguish between the concept of worker and the independent contractor who is in business on his own account, even if only in a small way.[14]

6.13 In *Clyde & Co LLP and another v Bates van Winkelhof* [2014] UKSC 32 [2014] 1 WLR 2047, [2014] IRLR 641, the Supreme Court considered the application of the statutory test to a case of a limited partner, but also provided guidance of wider application. Ms Bates van Wilkelhof (BvW)

---

[11] See *Cotswold Developments Construction v Williams* [2006] IRLR 181 at para 33, listing the cases that have followed *Byrne Bros v Baird*. Thereafter in eg *Plastering Contractors Stanmore Ltd v Holder* EAT, 07 July 2014; *Yorkshire Window Co Ltd v Parkes* EAT, 27 May 2010; *Autoclenz Ltd v Belcher*, EAT, 4 June 2008; *Consistent Group Ltd v Kalwak* [2007] IRLR 560.

[12] Referring to 'a contract personally to execute any work or labour'. See *Mingeley v Pennock and another* [2004] EWCA Civ 328, [2004] IRLR 373 (CA).

[13] A submission that this approach was wrong was rejected in *Yorkshire Window Company Limited v Parkes* (UKEAT/0484/09, 27 May 2010), EAT (Serota J) at para 84.

[14] For elaboration and consideration of this passage see paras 36 and 37 of the judgment of Lord Clarke in *Hashwami v Jivraj* [2011] UKSC 40, [2011] ICR 1004 where there was an extensive consideration of the authorities. The principal purpose of the contract is now regarded as being a relevant but not a decisive consideration. See also *R v CAC, ex p BBC* [2003] EWHC 1375 (Admin) [2003] ICR 1542, where the meaning of 'profession' was considered, and it was held that the existence of a regulatory body may be relevant but is not necessarily determinative.

was a solicitor and a member of the respondent LLP. The LLP had two categories of members, 'equity members' and 'senior equity members': the rights of the latter were more extensive than those of the former. BvW was in the former category. She brought claims against the LLP and one of its senior equity members claiming that she had been subjected to detriment for having made protected disclosures. The ET held that BvW was not a limb (b) worker because she was in business in her own right, receiving a share of the profits in relation to the work carried out. The EAT allowed an appeal but the Court of Appeal held that under section 4(4) of the Limited Liability Partnerships Act 2000,[15] if Clyde & Co had not been registered as an LLP, then BvW would have been a partner in an 1890 Act partnership. For this reason she was not a 'worker' within the meaning of section 230(3)(b) of ERA and therefore could not pursue a whistleblowing claim.

6.14 The Supreme Court allowed BvW's appeal. Lady Hale (with whom Lord Neuberger and Lord Wilson agreed) said that the 2000 Act was a UK-wide statute and that there was doubt about whether partners in a Scottish partnership can also be employed by the partnership. It was that feature which explained why section 4(4) had been included in the 2000 Act. There was no need to give 'a strained construction' to section 4(4). All that it was saying was that, whatever the position would be were the LLP members to be partners in a traditional partnership, then that position is the same in an LLP. That was how section 4(4) was to be construed. Once the section 4(4) point was dealt with the result in favour of worker status became, if not a foregone conclusion, at least one to which there lay a fairly clear path. Lady Hale opened her discussion of the point by remarking that it was striking 'how much hard work has to be done in order to find that a member of an LLP is *not* a worker within the meaning of section 230(3)(b) of the 1996 Act.' It was common ground before the Supreme Court that BvW worked 'under a contract personally to perform any work or services', that she provided those services 'for' the LLP, and that the LLP was not her 'client or customer'. Thus the EAT's approach had been correct. BvW was a limb (b) worker.

6.15 Turning to considerations of more general application beyond that of limited partners, Lady Hale set out the three categories noted at paragraph 6.02 above. Lady Hale proceeded to endorse the view of Maurice Kay LJ in *Hospital Medical Group Ltd v Westwood* [2013] ICR 415 (CA) that there is not one single test to be applied, though integration in the business and the degree of subordination may each be relevant factors in applying the statutory language. In *Hospital Medical Group* the claimant was engaged in practice as a GP for the NHS but also provided services to a private clinic for which he carried out transgender work and also for the respondent for whom he performed hair restoration surgery. The Court of Appeal held that he was a limb (b) worker. Maurice Kay LJ pointed out, at para 18, that neither the *Cotswold* 'integration' test nor the *Redcats* 'dominant purpose' test (ie whether personal service is the dominant feature of the contractual arrangement) purported to lay down a test of general application. Maurice Kay LJ also said that there was not a single key with which to unlock the words of the statute in every case, albeit that the 'integration' test would often be appropriate (and was in that case).[16] Lady Hale said that she agreed with Maurice Kay LJ: there could be no substitute for applying the words of the statute to the facts of the individual case. The difficulties could not be avoided 'by adding some mystery ingredient of 'subordination' to the concept of employee and worker.' While subordination might sometimes be an aid to distinguishing workers from other self-employed people, it was not a freestanding and universal characteristic of being a worker.[17] BvW fell within the express words

---

[15] Section 4(4) of the 2000 Act provides that: 'A member of a limited liability partnership shall not be regarded for any purpose as employed by the limited liability partnership unless, if he and the other members were partners in a partnership, he would be regarded for that purpose as employed by the partnership.'

[16] At para 19.

[17] But see also *Halawi v WDFG UK Ltd t/a World Duty Free* [2015] IRLR 50 (a race discrimination claim), where the Court of Appeal, whilst assuming that the guidance in *Bates van Winkelhof* also applied to

of section 230(3)(b) and could not market her services as a solicitor to anyone other than the LLP, of which she was a member. She was an integral part of their business and in no sense was the LLP her client or customer.

6.16 In *Pimlico Plumbers Ltd and another v Smith* (UKEAT/0495/12/DM, 21 November 2014) Judge Serota QC provided (at para 116) the following helpful analysis of the law as to worker status post the *Bates van Winkelhof* case:

1. In considering whether a person is a limb (b) worker the starting point must be the words of the statute and that there is no one formula or characteristic that can be said to be determinative.
2. The court or tribunal must take a holistic approach and may take account of matters such as the degree of subordination of the worker to the 'employer' and the degree of his integration into the 'employer's' business and also whether the contract between employer and 'worker' was in essence a contract between two independent business undertakings; the extent to which the 'worker' carried out work other than for the 'employer' and his right to do so.
3. The employer of a person integrated into the 'employer's' workforce and carrying out work for that employer is in no sense his customer or client.
4. If a 'worker' carries out work for more than one 'employer' he can nonetheless be a limb (b) worker of one or more such employers if the statutory criteria are met.

D. Workers under the Extended Definition in Section 43K ERA

6.17 Under the heading 'Extension of meaning of "worker"' section 43K(1) provides:

For the purposes of this Part 'worker' includes an individual who is not a worker as defined by section 230(3) but who— ...

And it then sets out under subsections (a) to (d) a disparate range of persons/relationships, before concluding that

and any reference to a worker's contract, to employment or to a worker being 'employed' shall be construed accordingly.

Section 43K(2) then makes provision as to who is the worker's employer for the purposes of each of the relationships.

6.18 In *Day v Lewisham and Greenwich NHS Trust and another* [2016] IRLR 415 (EAT), at para 36, Langstaff J said that section 43K provides

a list of particular extensions of the meaning of worker. Broadly they may be seen as follows. By sub-s (1)(a) s 43K makes provision for agency workers, who though not employees nor workers in most cases would be placed in a similar position to those of employees or limb (b) workers in respect of the work they were engaged to do. Arden LJ saw it that way in *Sharpe*.[18] Subsection 1(b) is concerned with contractors; (ba)–(cb) provide for diverse

---

discrimination claims, commented (per Arden LJ at para 44) that since independence was not a necessary feature of the claimant's work, there was no necessity to modify the requirement for subordination. Here a beauty consultant who provided her services through a limited company and an employment agency, was held not to be a worker. She was found not to be subject to control of the putative employer (WDF) in the way she carried out her work (other than control over the workplace). The lack of subordination was also consistent with her lack of integration in WDF's business. In addition, she had a right to substitute performance, which she had exercised (and so it was not a sham). For both these reasons, the court held that on the facts she was not a worker.

[18] Referring to *Sharpe v Bishop of Worcester* [2015] EWCA Civ 399 [2015] IRLR 663 (CA), discussed at para 6.34 below.

categories of persons involved with health service bodies, and (d) is concerned with a person who might be such as an intern, or possibly on a sandwich course, though both these suggestions are hesitant ones, or someone who could be described as an 'atypical worker'... there is no general principle which unites them.

In *Croke v Hydro Aluminum Worcester Limited* [2007] ICR 1303, the EAT held that in con- **6.19** struing the extended definition of a worker in ERA, section 43K, it is, by analogy with other statutory provisions relating to discrimination or victimization, appropriate to apply a purposive construction. The legislation is therefore to be construed, where this can properly be done, so as to provide protection rather than to deny it.[19]

(1) Can an individual be a worker under section 230 for one employer whilst at the same time being a worker under section 43K for a different employer?

This is of particular relevance to relationships that possibly engage section 43K ERA. The **6.20** focus here is on the wording at the outset of section 43K, that the provision covers an individual who is not otherwise a worker under section 230(3) ERA. There are currently conflicting views at EAT level. Dicta in *Day v Lewisham and Greenwich NHS Trust and another* [2016] IRLR 415 (EAT)[20] indicate that the effect was indeed to prevent reliance on section 43K in relation to Employer A, if the worker was an employee (within the meaning of section 230(3) ERA) of employer B. But in *McTigue v University Hospital Bristol NHS Foundation Trust* [2016] ICR 1155, the EAT adopted a different construction. In the view of Mrs Justice Simler (President), the exclusionary wording (that section 43K ERA did not apply if the individual was not already a worker within section 230(3) ERA) was to be applied in respect of each potential respondent. As such if the individual was a worker of Employer A within section 230(3) ERA there would be no need to rely on section 43K as against Employer A. But this would not prevent reliance on section 43K in relation to a claim against Employer B. The position is illustrated by the early case of *Hayes v Reed Social Care & Bradford MDC* (ET, Case No 1805531/00). Here the claimant was held to be employed both by the agency who supplied his services and by the local authority for whom he worked and which substantially determined the terms of the engagement. That was consistent with the approach in *McTigue*, but on the approach in *Day* only the agency could have been liable.

We consider the reasoning in *Day* and *McTigue* in more detail below in paragraphs 6.22– **6.21** 6.29. We suggest that, having regard to the purpose of the legislation and the role of section 43K in extending protection, and bearing in mind the differing claims that may arise against differing employers (such that having a right against one employer may still leave a significant gap in protection), the reasoning in *McTigue* is to be preferred. However, since at the time of writing *Day* is proceeding on appeal, the issue is likely to be the subject of a definitive ruling by the Court of Appeal.

In *Day v Lewisham and Greenwich*, Dr Day applied nationally to the predecessor of Health **6.22** Education England (HEE) to train in emergency medicine. He entered into a training contract, which was expressed not to be a contract of employment with what later became HEE. That body was responsible for organizing training programmes of and posts for postgraduate trainee doctors. He was placed by HEE with Lewisham (and Greenwich NHS Trust) (Lewisham), where he worked as a specialist registrar in Acute Care Common Stem Emergency Medicine. Whilst working at the Queen Elizabeth Hospital, Dr Day complained

---

[19] The limits of the purposive approach were reached in *Day v Lewisham and Greenwich NHS Trust and another* [2016] IRLR 415 (EAT) which we discuss below in paras 6.22–6.26.
[20] *Day* will be heard by the Court of Appeal later this year and the result will be noted in the updater to this book at http://www.littletonchambers.com/publications/books-241/.

that patients' safety was compromised by serious under-staffing. The complaints were made not only to the hospital, where he worked under a contract of employment with Lewisham, but also, he claimed, at meetings with HEE held to review his progress in training.

6.23 Dr Day made a claim in the ET that he had suffered detriment in consequence of these concerns which, he claimed, were protected disclosures. Other respondents to his claims fell away leaving just Lewisham and HEE. HEE applied to the employment tribunal to strike out the claim against it and the ET acceded to that application. Dr Day contended that he was a worker and that HEE was his employer within the meaning of section 43K, albeit that (at the same time) Lewisham was his employer under ERA section 230(3)(a). During the preliminary hearing, his argument was advanced only on the basis that subsection 43K(1)(a) applied. This is considered in more detail below (at paragraph 6.30 et seq), but it provides that an individual will be a worker under section 43K if he or she

> works or worked for a person in circumstances in which—
>
> (i) he is or was introduced or supplied to do that work by a third person, and
> (ii) the terms on which he is or was engaged to do the work are or were in practice substantially determined not by him but by the person for whom he works or worked, by the third person or by both of them.

6.24 In considering this the ET accepted that it was arguable that Dr Day had been supplied by HEE to do the work he did for Lewisham in a training post as specialist registrar in ACCS Emergency Medicine. However, it held he did not meet the terms of section 43K(1)(a)(ii), and we deal with that aspect below in paragraph 6.44.

6.25 HEE argued that the opening words of section 43K(1) meant that where an individual was a section 230(3) worker, none of the separate situations in which the meaning of 'worker' might be extended by section 43K could apply. In effect, they were extensions to be adopted where needed. They were not additional rights to sue in respect of a complaint which would already be answered by an employer under section 230(3). For Dr Day it was argued that the purpose of section 43K was to extend the meaning of 'worker', which already encompassed a wide range of situations in which one person worked for another. A relationship with a second possible employer under section 43K was not excluded by the existence of a relationship with an employer under section 230(3). The intention was 'to encompass all those in an economically subordinate position bar limited exceptions'. It was urged that a purposive approach should be taken to the interpretation of these whistleblowing provisions.[21] Doctors, and in particular doctors in training, were professionals and public servants whose entitlement—indeed, duty—to speak out on matters of concern was well recognized. If HEE were correct in their construction of the statue, then HEE could penalize Dr Day in a way which affected the continuation of his training, without being called to account. That, it was argued, was a lacuna. Dr Day's counsel referred to Article 10 of the European Convention of Human Rights and the whistleblowing cases decided by the European Court of Human Rights.[22] If protection were not provided to doctors in training it would amount to a breach of their Article 10 rights. Whilst there was no free-standing remedy under Article 10, it underpinned the width which should be given when reading section 43K purposively. It was incumbent upon an employment tribunal to read the legislation compatibly with the Convention.[23] A wide latitude should be given to what was possible: see *Ghaidan v Godin-Mendoza* [2004] 2 AC 557 (HL) at paras 41, 118–119, and 121.

---

[21] The purposive approach is referred to in *Croke v Hydro Aluminium Worcester Limited* [2007] ICR 1303 and *BP PLC v Elstone* [2010] IRLR 558. See Chapter 2, paras 2.14–2.18 for a fuller consideration of this point.

[22] Considered in detail in Chapter 18. See in particular in relation to the approach to the ECHR in *Day v Lewisham and Greenwich,* the discussion in paras 18.54–18.56.

[23] Reference was made to paras 57 and 58 of the judgment of Mummery LJ in *X v Y* [2004] EWCA Civ 662, [2004] ICR 1634 (CA).

Langstaff J accepted that a purposive approach should be taken to interpreting relevant pro- **6.26** visions. However, that did not mean that a court was entitled to ignore the words of the legislation because the purpose would be better served if they did not appear. The prohibition against detriment or dismissal for making a public interest disclosure was set out with particularity in ERA. The diverse categories contained in section 43K(1) had no general principle which united them, save that the words 'who is not a worker as defined by section 230(3)' meant that those to whom section 43K applied could not also be a worker as defined by section 230(3). Those words had to be given meaning. The intention was that those who are workers within section 230(3) should adopt the route of complaint set out in sections 43C–43H. They did not need additional protection against those who are more peripheral to their employment. In Langstaff J's view the purpose of this part of ERA was to extend the meaning of worker to a limited category of other relationships. The inclusion of the reference to trainee midwives,[24] together with the references to others with particular relations to health service bodies,[25] demonstrated that the draughtsman of the statute had in mind a variety of specific health service relationships. The omission of specific reference to the relationship of a trainee doctor with HEE (or to the deaneries which preceded HEE) was strongly suggestive that Parliament deliberately did not intend to include it.

In *McTigue*[26] the respondent relied on that reasoning to submit that the opening words **6.27** of section 43K(1) mean that the extended protection only applies where someone is not otherwise a worker under section 230(3), irrespective of the identity of the respondent and the identity of the person with whom the worker has a section 230(3) worker relationship. Accordingly, if an agency worker had a section 230(3) limb (b) worker contract with the agency, the agency worker was excluded from the extended protection available under section 43K(1)(a) vis à vis all others, including the end user. It was accepted that this interpretation substantially reduced the protection which the provision appeared to have been intended to afford, but it was argued that Parliament had specifically delineated the extended protection afforded and that for purposes of clarity and certainty it is important that a worker knows who their employer is for the purposes of making a protected disclosure.

Simler J said she did not consider that this is what Langstaff J had intended. In her view **6.28** the opening words in section 43K(1) mean that the provision is only engaged where an individual is not a worker within section 230(3) in relation to the respondent in question. If he or she is such a worker there was no need to extend the meaning of worker to afford protection against that respondent. However, an important purpose of section 43K is to extend cover to agency workers in relation to victimization for protected disclosures made while working at the end user. McTigue's case exemplified that situation. Although an employee of Tascor, McTigue was supplied to work at the respondent's centre with the respondent's employees who were thus in a position to subject her to detriments after she made protected disclosures. It was against that treatment (if it was established) that she required protection. The extended definition of worker in section 43K(1)(a) potentially provided it in respect of her claim against the respondent. The fact that she had worker status in relation to the agency under section 230 and could not accordingly rely on section 43K against the agency was irrelevant in relation to her claim against the respondent. She was not a section 230(3) worker in relation to the respondent. The extended definition of 'worker' provided a potential route to a remedy the claimant would not otherwise have had as an agency worker who is neither an employee nor a limb (b) worker in respect of the respondent end user for whom she carries out the work. That construction gives meaning to

---

[24] Section 43K(1)(cb).
[25] Section 43(ba), (bb), and (c).
[26] See para 6.47 below for the facts of this case.

the introductory words of section 43K(1) which apply to all categories of worker identified at subsections (a) to (d) and is entirely consistent with the stated purpose of the provision. There is no resulting uncertainty or lack of clarity. An agency worker may complain to both the end user and the agency about matters of concern, as the claimant did here, as both are potential employers for protected disclosure purposes. The construction of section 43K(1) gives effect to Parliament's intentions as evidenced by the language of the provision, having regard to the statutory and social context. It was unnecessary to resort to a purposive construction that would give an extended meaning of 'worker' beyond the legitimate reach of the subsection (whether because it is thought that the broad objective of the statute would be better effected by that approach or on some other basis).

6.29 As noted above, we suggest the reasoning of Simler J in *McTigue* is to be preferred. It is more consistent with the purposes of the legislation. There is little reason to exclude the protection merely because someone else who may have nothing to do with the detriment in question may be also be capable of being regarded as the employer. However, clarification by the Court of Appeal would be welcome and is likely to be provided on the appeal in *Day*.

(2) The section 43K(1)(a) and 43K(2) definitions

6.30 Section 43K(1)(a) ERA provides that a worker includes a person who:

> (a) works or worked for a person in circumstances in which—
>
>> (i) he is or was introduced or supplied to do that work by a third person, and
>> (ii) the terms on which he is or was engaged to do the work are or were in practice substantially determined not by him but by the person for whom he works or worked, by the third person or by both of them.

6.31 Section 43K(1)(a) therefore makes special provision to cover agency workers, where the agency introduces workers or finds them the post and the terms of engagement are substantially determined by the agency or the organization where they perform the work. This provision needs to be read together with the corresponding definition of an employer for these purposes set out in section 43K(2), which provides that the employer is: 'the person who substantially determines or determined the terms of the engagement'. This widening of scope represents a somewhat different provision to that introduced (controversially) into the Working Time Regulations 1998 which treats as the employer the body which actually pays the worker. The person or body determining the terms of engagement seems to denote the person or body who or which provides the details of the work to be performed and the level and terms of remuneration. In some cases, however, workers in this category will fall within the narrower category of employee on the basis that it is necessary to imply a contract in order to give business reality to the relationship.[27]

6.32 Although section 43K(1)(a) is principally directed at agency workers, it is capable of applying in other cases, as illustrated by the decision in *Douglas v Birmingham City Council* (EAT/ 0518/02, 17 March 2003), also discussed in Chapter 3 at paragraph 3.38 and Chapter 5 at paragraph 5.06. The claimant was a paid classroom assistant. Her contract of employment was with the local authority. The EAT upheld the ruling of the employment tribunal that the claimant was not deemed, for the purposes of the whistleblowing legislation, to be an employee of the governors (contrary to the more general position under Article 3(1) of the Education (Modification of Enactments Relating to Employment) Order 1999 (SI 1999/2256)). However, it concluded that she was a worker within the extended definition given by section 43K(1)(a) because she was supplied by a contract of employment, effected by the

---

[27] See para 6.07(a) above.

city council, to do work for the governing body of the school and the terms on which she was engaged to do that work were in practice determined not by her, but by the governing body or by the council or both. She thus fell within section 43K(1)(a) as a 'worker'.

In *Croke v Hydro Aluminum Worcester Ltd*, Croke, an engineer, had formed a company of **6.33** which he was the sole director. That company entered into a contract with a recruitment consultancy by which it agreed to provide the services of Croke. Hydro requested the consultancy to supply engineers. Croke provided his CV to the consultancy which forwarded it to Hydro which, following an interview, entered into an agreement with the consultancy by which the latter would provide Croke's services via Croke's company. When Hydro terminated the contract Croke made a complaint that he had suffered a detriment because of making a protected disclosure. The EAT held that the tribunal could conclude that he was a 'worker' vis à vis the end user for the purposes of ERA, section 43K(1)(a). This was subject to satisfying the statutory requirement that the terms upon which Croke worked were substantially determined not by Croke (as the putative worker) but by the person for whom he worked (Hydro as the end user), or by a third person (which might be the employment agency) or both.[28]

A qualification to *Croke* emerged from *Sharpe v Bishop of Worcester* [2015] EWCA Civ 399 **6.34** [2015] IRLR 663 (CA). The Reverend Sharpe was the rector of Teme Valley South. He resigned and brought claims that he had been unfairly dismissed and subjected to detriment for making protected disclosures. This raised the issue of whether he had been an employee or a worker in relation to the respondent. The primary focus of the appeal to the Court of Appeal was on the question of whether there was a contract at all and if so whether it was a contract which fulfilled the requirements of section 230 or section 43(K)(1) between the respondent and Reverend Sharpe. Reverend Sharpe argued in the alternative that section 43(1)(a) did not require a contract between him and the respondent; the respondent contended that section 43K(1)(a) did require such a contract. The employment judge found as a matter of fact that there was no contract, express or implied, between Reverend Sharpe and the bishop. The Court of Appeal held that there was no basis for setting aside this finding; even if there was a contract it was not a contract of employment. The Court went on to deal with the worker issue raised by Reverend Sharpe's alternative reliance on section 43K(1). Lady Justice Arden said (at para 113) that the conclusion that there was no contract meant that there was no contract for the purposes of section 43K(1)(b) either. The only question is whether there also needed to be a contract for the purpose of section 43K(1)(a). The EAT had held that on the true interpretation of this provision there was no requirement for a contract. The argument for Reverend Sharpe was that the reference to 'the terms on which he is or was engaged to do the work terms' in section 43K(1)(a) did not entail the need for a contract. If Parliament had intended that a contract was required then the term 'contract' would have been used. Lady Justice Arden (with whose judgment Davis LJ agreed) rejected this contention. It inevitably followed from the statutory reference to 'terms on which he is or was engaged to do work' that there must be a contract.

---

[28] Compare *Finlay v Worcestershire County Council* (ET 1305546, noted at IDS Brief 884 p 18). Finlay was employed under a contract of employment with an agency which assigned him to work for the county council. During the assignment Finlay made disclosures to the county council to the effect that his working arrangements involved potential breaches of the Data Protection Act and he argued that these were disclosures to his 'employer'. The county council terminated the assignment and Finlay made a claim in the employment tribunal against it. The county council successfully argued that it was not 'the employer', ie 'the person who substantially determines or determined the terms on which [the worker] was engaged': Finlay had a contract of employment with the agency and it was the agency which was his employer because the amount of the remuneration received by Finlay was subject to agreement between Finlay and the agency.

6.35   The decision in *Sharpe* begs a question as to the application of section 43K(1)(a) to a tri-partite situation, such as where a worker is supplied by an agency. Typically the contractual relationships will be between worker and agency, and between agency and end user, but not between worker and end user. The issue then arises as to whether section 43K(1)(a) can be relied upon against the end user in the absence of a direct contractual relationship. We suggest that the better view is that section 43K(1)(a) can apply. In *Sharpe* there were no relevant contractual terms governing the relationship. That may be distinguished from the situation where there is a contractual matrix, and contractual terms that in effect determine the terms on which the worker will be employed, but not directly with the end user. It may well be that no contract can be implied directly between the worker and end user because the relevant obligations can be adequately explained by the other contracts.[29] But it remains the case that the worker's services in that case are provided pursuant to a contract. Section 43K does not provide that the employer in that situation must be the other party to the contract. It may be that although the end user is not a party to the contract between agent and worker, it can still be regarded as determining the terms on which the worker is engaged, on the basis that those terms reflect and are determined by the end user's requirements, and indeed may be imposed pursuant to the contract between the agent and the end user. Whether that will be so raises a fact-sensitive question in each case. But, in contrast with the position in *Sharpe*, in that situation meaning can realistically be given to the statutory reference to the 'terms on which he is or was engaged to do work'. Further, the typical tripartite situation involving agency, worker, and end user is precisely the sort of situation which the provision was designed to address, and as such it would be highly surprising if Parliament intended to exclude most claims against the end user by virtue of the typical contractual matrix.

6.36   *Keppel Seghers UK Ltd v Hinds* [2014] IRLR 754 (EAT), which was decided between the judgments of the Employment Appeal Tribunal[30] and the Court of Appeal in the *Sharpe* case, provides an illustration of the potential significance of the issue as to whether a direct contractual relationship is needed, and we suggest the EAT's reasoning supports the view expressed above as to the scope of the decision in *Sharpe*. Hinds was a health and safety consultant in the construction industry. The ET accepted that it was a prerequisite for obtaining work that he provided his services through a company. Hinds accordingly set up Crown. Crown never employed anyone else and the only purpose of establishing Crown was to meet the industry requirement. Keppel, a construction contractor, approached a recruitment agency ('First') with a specification for a consultant. The ET found that First sourced the individual consultant in accordance with Keppel's specifications and put Hinds forward for interview by Keppel. There was no direct contractual relationship between Hinds and Keppel. In considering how Hinds had been introduced to Keppel and how his services were then supplied, the ET found that it was:

> ... Hinds himself that was introduced to and supplied to do work ultimately for the respondent and not his company, Crown.... [T]he interview that he had with [Keppel] ... was with him personally. It was clearly [Hinds] himself who was being engaged by [Keppel].

The contract between Keppel and First contained the requirement that any individual contractors providing services to Keppel would have to do so through intermediary companies. It also envisaged that the contractors (rather than the companies via which they were required to supply their services) would be subject to suitability checks. The ET found that it was not in the parties' contemplation that any intermediary company could substitute anyone else

---

[29]   See *James v Greenwich LBC* [2015] EWCA Civ 209, [2008] ICR 545 (CA); *Smith v Carillion (JM) Limited* [2015] IRLR 467 (CA).
[30]   UKEAT/0243/12/DM, 28 November 2013 Cox J.

for the individuals who had thus been assessed. Whilst the terms on which First engaged Crown allowed for a substitute, the ET found that the terms of the end user (Keppel) did not envisage this.

The ET expressly rejected Keppel's argument that Hinds was in fact employed by Crown and **6.37** he was able to determine his own terms through that entity: Keppel substantially determined the terms of Hinds' engagement and was the employer for section 43K(2) purposes. Keppel set the specification for the work; Keppel authorized changes to Hinds' hours—he could not dictate his hours; Hinds was obliged to report regularly to Keppel's manager and was generally subject to Keppel's control, though as a health and safety professional he worked on his own much of the time and was not micromanaged. Hinds' evidence that it was Keppel that decided that he should leave and determined the terms of his departure (ie his period of paid notice) was not challenged.

HHJ Eady said it was notable that section 43K put the focus on the way in which the rela- **6.38** tionship had arisen and had been governed: the introduction or supply and the 'in practice' substantial determination of the terms of the engagement. That reflected the fact that the whole purpose of this statutory extension to the definition of 'worker' and 'employer' was to go beyond the normal contractual focus of those terms for statutory purposes in the employment field. That reasoning, we suggest, is pertinent in relation to the scope of the decision in *Sharpe*, as to the need for a contractual relationship. HHJ Eady referred to the recognition by the EAT in *Sharpe*[31] that the phrase 'terms on which he is or was engaged to do the work' did not imply the existence of a contract (as to which, as noted above, the Court of Appeal in *Sharpe* took a different view), and that absence of actual day-to-day control would not be determinative. Regard would need to be had to the totality of the contractual provisions and all the circumstances of the relationship. The focus of section 43K is on what happened in practice rather than on the contractual agreement, albeit the contracts provide a useful starting point.

HHJ Eady held that the ET had not lost sight of section 43K(1)(a) or reached conclusions **6.39** inconsistent with the contractual provisions in question. What happened in practice was that there was a focus on the suitability of Hinds as an individual (not on Crown): Hinds was 'sourced' at an individual meeting and was interviewed as such and not as a representative of Crown. That provided sufficient basis for the ET's conclusion that Hinds was introduced as an individual for section 43K(1)(a)(i) purposes. It was 'perhaps unhelpful' that the ET did not expressly separate out its consideration of the issue of 'supply' from that of introduction, but there might be some degree of overlap in terms of the relevant findings of fact in respect of these terms. In any event the judgment had to be read as a whole and the ET clearly kept in mind the important point in each respect: was it Hinds as an *individual* who had been introduced or supplied? In respect of supply, the ET was again entitled to rely on the same matters as those in relation to the question of introduction. There was force in Hinds' submission that a contractual right to provide a substitute need not exclude the application of section 43K. The focus of the definition at 43K(1)(a)(i) is on the factual question as to whether or not the complainant has been supplied; it does not include a requirement that no one else can be supplied in their place. The existence of a right of substitution might point to the fact that it was not, in truth, the complainant who was being supplied, but this might not necessarily be so. However, that was not a point that arose for determination.

As to the issues raised on the question of determination of the terms of Hinds' engagement, **6.40** Keppel's submission was that a distinction was to be drawn between section 43K(1)(a)(ii)

---

[31] At para 237.

(which refers to the terms on which the worker 'is or was engaged to do the work'), and section 43(2) which refers to the terms on which the worker 'is or was engaged'. In essence the respondent's argument was that section 43K(1)(a)(ii) was broader in that it could encompass in the round how the worker was engaged to do the work, which entails determination not only by the contract between agency and worker, but also by the contract between end user and agency. The respondent argued that by contrast, under section 43K(2) there was a narrower focus on who determined the terms on which the worker was engaged, which, it was argued, focused on the specific terms agreed with worker and would exclude the self-employed as they would substantially determine those terms.

6.41 The EAT rejected this contention. As explained by HHJ Eady, *both* provisions allow that the terms of the engagement might have been determined by more than one entity. Section 43K(1)(a)(ii) simply distinguishes between (a) terms substantially determined by the worker themselves and (b) terms substantially determined by others (which might be both the end user and agency). Section 43K(2)(a) then takes the assessment further forward to define the employer as being the party (which, by this stage, cannot be the worker) who *substantially* determines or determined those terms. Insofar as there was any distinction between the phrases in section 43K(1)(a)(ii) and section 43K(2) it was too subtle to be of any use and in any event had no application on the facts in *Keppel*.

6.42 Keppel had contended that Crown substantially determined the terms on which Hinds was to do the work he did. Because Hinds was the sole director of Crown, that really meant that Hinds had determined them. The ET had disagreed: Crown was simply a vehicle through which Hinds' services were supplied. In the EAT's view the ET was entitled to focus on the specific terms of the engagement in question and it had found that Keppel was in the position of determining Hinds' terms of engagement both at the outset ('the terms on which he was engaged *to do* the work') *and* during the course of the agreement's operation. Given that the ET had found that it was Keppel which had laid down the specification for the engagement and had interviewed Hinds personally to see if he was suitable, it was entirely consistent for the ET to conclude that Keppel had also determined the initial terms of the engagement. The ET was entitled to look at the various contracts relevant to the relationship and to see how these worked in practice. Although the ET referred to 'control', this was not irrelevant to the question as to who determined the terms on which work was to be done. The ET was plainly influenced by the fact that the requirements of the work were laid down by Keppel and that Hinds was obliged to report to Keppel's manager. Those findings of fact supported its conclusion as to both the initial determination of the terms on which Hinds was 'to do the work' and as to the continuing determination of those terms (ie that it was the respondent which was the employer for section 43K(2)(a) purposes). The ET had regard to Keppel's ability to determine (or control) the terms of Hinds' engagement through the question of hours and shift arrangements as examples of how this worked in practice. That disclosed no error of law.

6.43 Although the EAT in *Keppel* proceeded on the basis of its decision in *Sharpe* that there was no need for a contractual relationship, which was subsequently overturned by the Court of Appeal, as noted above (paragraph 6.35) we suggest that the reasoning (save for reliance on the EAT's decision in *Sharpe*) still survives.

6.44 The EAT returned to the meaning of the test of who substantially determines the terms in *Day v Lewisham and Greenwich NHS Trust and another* [2016] IRLR 415. As we have noted (at paragraph 6.22 et seq above, the ET accepted that it was arguable that Dr Day had been supplied by HEE to do the work he did for Lewisham and Greenwich NHS Trust in a training post as specialist registrar in ACCS Emergency Medicine. To bring HEE within section 43K, HEE had to be 'the person' who 'substantially determines or determined' the terms on which Dr Day is or was engaged. Consistently with the reasoning in *Keppel*, the EAT (Langstaff J) emphasized that section 43K(1)(a)(ii) invites a comparison. Essentially, the question is as to who determines the terms more as between (a) the worker and (b) the other parties (typically, the agency and end user). That leaves no room for the application of any exception to apply where the influence is no more than trivial. Further, as in *Keppel*, the EAT agreed that the result under section 43K(1)(a)(ii) could be that more than one person, in combination, determines the terms. So here it could be HEE and Lewisham.

However, for liability to arise against a respondent, it would also need to be found that it was **6.45** the employer under section 43K(2)(a) on the basis of having substantially determined the contractual terms. In that respect the claim against HEE failed on the facts. Though HEE plainly made the decision as to where Dr Day was to work, and it kept his training under review and supplied much of his salary, these factors did not mean that the ET was obliged to hold that it had determined 'the terms on which [Dr Day] ... was engaged to do the work', let alone done so substantially. In essence this upheld the ET's finding of fact. The terms on which Dr Day was engaged to work had been governed by what was known as the *Gold Guide*, (the 2013 Reference Guide for Postgraduate Specialty Training in the UK) which governed the training of doctors. It had not been suggested that HEE was responsible for the *Gold Guide*. Accordingly, insofar as what he did was training, the terms relating to that aspect of his work were not determined by HEE. Insofar as it was the performance of clinical duties, Lewisham was the body substantially responsible for determining Dr Day's terms and conditions of work.

The EAT proceeded to note (at para 42) that the disclosures made arose out of and in relation **6.46** to the work for Lewisham. The work in issue was work as a specialist registrar at the hospital where Dr Day performed his services under contract with Lewisham. The relationship which Dr Day had with HEE was a relationship distinct from the relationship of employee/employer which he had with Lewisham. On the arguments advanced there was nothing about Dr Day's relationship with HEE in the form of employment or worker status which could fall within the legislation. The *detriment* Dr Day complained about arose in the course of his relationship with HEE, and not in respect of the work he did for Lewisham; and in this respect the position of HEE was little different from any third party who might have acted detrimentally towards him as a whistleblower and was not covered by the ERA's protected disclosure provisions. That reasoning might suggest that in assessing who substantially determines the terms, it is relevant to have regard to the particular disclosures and the context in which they are made. We suggest, however, that this element of the reasoning is to be read in the context of the EAT answering the argument that there should be a purposive construction in favour of HEE being treated as employer. The EAT concluded (at para 44) that Parliament had carefully delineated the scope of protection against detriment; it did not apply in relation to someone in respect of whom the claimant was neither an employee nor worker. But that did not entail that it is necessary to have regard to the particular disclosures as part of the anterior assessment of who substantially determined the terms.

The most recent case to tackle the proper approach to who substantially determines the **6.47** terms (in sections 43K(1)(a) and 43K(2)) is *McTigue*.[32] On this issue the decision closely tracked that in *Keppel* and *Day* in emphasizing that comparison under section 43K(1)(a) (ii) is between (a) the worker and (b) the other parties taken together. McTigue was an employee of an agency, Tascor. She was engaged to work as a Forensic Nurse Examiner at a sexual assault referral centre, the Bridge, which was operated by the respondent (among

---

[32] [2016] ICR 1155 (EAT).

others). She had a written contract of employment with Tascor's predecessor in a standard form which dealt with remuneration and other aspects: the ET found that it painted a picture of a normal contractual arrangement as between employer and employee. McTigue was also issued with an honorary appointment by the respondent, and a standard form contract. It authorized her to carry out the duties of, and practise as, a forensic nurse examiner at the Bridge. It identified the named supervisor or professional practitioner under whose supervision she would work at the Bridge, requiring her to inform the named supervisor of any absence by 9am on the first day of absence. It required her to cooperate with the respondent (among other things) in relation to issues of health and safety, clinical governance, and working time. Significantly, it reserved the respondent's right to terminate the honorary contract in case of any reason or cause for concern that might jeopardize the continuity of quality of care offered to patients.

6.48 The dispute centered on the meaning and proper application of subsection 43K(1)(a)(ii). The employment judge concluded that for a party to 'substantially determine terms' it would have to decide the majority of the terms or the more significant ones. On this approach the respondent trust emphatically did not 'substantially determine' terms. The trust did not contribute or determine more than a minority of them. In the EAT it was contended that the judge erred in law in holding that to substantially determine the terms on which the claimant was engaged, the respondent would have had to determine the majority of the terms or the more significant ones. Section 43K(1)(a)(ii) expressly recognized that there can be more than one party who substantially determines the terms, so a definition based on who determined 'the majority of the terms' cannot be correct. Moreover, the language of the statute does not require focus on a qualitative assessment of the terms but focuses on whether or not they were determined by the party in question and the extent to which they were so determined. The proper approach was to ask whether the terms of employment were 'in large part' (as held in *Day*) determined by the party in question, focusing on the act of determining the terms and entailing questions of fact and degree as to whether the influence of the party was sufficient to mean that party substantially determined the terms.

6.49 Simler J agreed: as determined in *Day*, a comparison must be made between the extent to which on one hand the individual determined his or her terms of engagement to do the work, and on the other hand somebody else determined those terms, in order to ascertain whether the terms of the worker extension in section 43K(1)(a)(ii) were fulfilled. If the individual substantially determined his or her terms in comparison with the others, they would not be a worker under section 43K(1)(a)(ii). If the other person or persons substantially determined the terms, the individual was a worker for these purposes. A comparison between the supplier and the end user was not invited by the provision.

6.50 Section 43K(1)(a)(ii) expressly envisaged that there might be two persons who substantially determined the terms on which the individual is engaged to do the work (the person who supplies the individual and the person for whom he or she works), and the EAT was of the view that the same must inevitably be true in relation to section 43K(2)(a) which defined the 'employer' for these purposes. The EAT explained that the provision defines employer as the 'person' who substantially determines or determined those terms. Since as a matter of ordinary statutory interpretation the singular included the plural, if both the supplier of the individual and the person for whom the individual worked substantially determined the terms on which the individual was engaged to do the work then both are the 'employer' of the worker for the purposes of this subsection. That view, though consistent with the EAT's view in *Keppel*, was more controversial than the conclusion in relation to section 43K(1)(a)(ii), since section 43K(2)(a) might be read as inviting comparison between the potential employers. But it is consistent with a purposive approach which treats the test as setting a threshold for liability rather than requiring a choice between different potential employers who each may have carried out different acts of detriment.

Simler J reasoned that both the supplier and the end user could substantially determine **6.51** the terms, and the subsection did not invite any comparison between how substantially the supplier of the individual determined the terms compared with how substantially the end user did so, there was no room for an interpretation of section 43K(1)(a)(ii) based on who determined 'the majority of the terms' or 'the most significant terms' as between the agency supplier and the end user. Where two parties (other than the individual) have between them determined the terms upon which an individual worked but have done so to different extents, each might nevertheless have substantially determined the terms.

Nobody suggested that McTigue determined the terms of the contracts under which she **6.52** worked. She had (at least) sets of contractual terms, and two parties other than herself had determined the terms of the written contracts under which she worked. Although in practice each might have done so to a different extent, that extent was nonetheless plainly capable of being substantial in both cases. The ET's decision was set aside.

Simler J suggested (at para 38) that in determining whether an individual is a worker within **6.53** section 43K(1)(a) the following questions should be addressed, and this forms a useful guide to the state of the law on that section:

(a) For whom does or did the individual work?
(b) Is the individual a worker as defined by s. 230(3) in relation to a person or persons for whom the individual worked? If so, there is no need to rely on s. 43K in relation to that person. However, the fact that the individual is a s. 230(3) worker in relation to one person does not prevent the individual from relying on s. 43K in relation to another person, the respondent, for whom the individual also works.[33]
(c) If the individual is not a s. 230(3) worker in relation to the respondent for whom the individual works or worked, was the individual introduced/supplied to do the work by a third person, and if so, by whom?
(d) If so, were the terms on which the individual was engaged to do the work determined by the individual? If the answer is yes, the individual is not a worker within s. 43K(1)(a).
(e) If not, were the terms substantially determined (i) by the person for whom the individual works or (ii) by a third person or (iii) by both of them? If any of these is satisfied, the individual does fall within the subsection.
(f) In answering question (e) the starting point is the contract (or contracts) whose terms are being considered.
(g) There may be a contract between the individual and the agency, the individual and the end user and/or the agency and the end user that will have to be considered.
(h) In relation to all relevant contracts, terms may be in writing, oral and may be implied. It may be necessary to consider whether written terms reflect the reality of the relationship in practice.
(i) If the respondent alone (or with another person) substantially determined the terms on which the individual worked in practice (whether alone or with another person who is not the individual), then the respondent is the employer within s. 43K(2)(a) for the purposes of the protected disclosure provisions. There may be two employers for these purposes under s. 43K(2)(a) ERA.

---

[33] See the discussion at paras 6.20–6.29 above.

(3) The section 43K(1)(b) definition

6.54 As we have seen, the ordinary definition of a worker under ERA, section 230(3) covers an independent contractor who *personally* provides services other than in a professional–client or business–client relationship. The definition is a wide and flexible one which includes the self-employed.[34] This definition is further extended by ERA, section 43K(1)(b) to an individual who:

> ... contracts or contracted with a person, for the purposes of that person's business, for the execution of work to be done in a place not under the control or management of that person and would fall within s. 230(3)(b) if for 'personally' in that provision there were substituted '(whether personally or otherwise)'.

6.55 Accordingly, the requirement of personal service is removed but *only* if the work is not to be done at a place under the control or management of the employer. This would therefore encompass a homeworker, irrespective of whether that homeworker engages others to carry out the work.

(4) The NHS

6.56 Subsection (1) of section 43K (as amended[35]) brings within the category of 'worker' for the purposes of PIDA protection in England and Wales a person who:

> (ba) works or worked as a person performing services under a contract entered into by him with the National Health Service commissioning Board ... or with a local health board ...
>
> (bb) works or worked as a person performing services under a contract entered into by him with the health board under ... the National Health Service (Scotland) Act ...
>
> (c) works or worked as a person providing services in accordance with arrangements made
>   (i) by the National Health Service commissioning Board ...
>
> (cb) is or was provided with work experience provided pursuant to a course of education or training approved by, or under arrangements with the Nursing and Midwifery Council in accordance with Article 15(6)(a) of the Nursing and Midwifery Order 2001.

6.57 The intention would appear to be that PIDA protection applies across virtually the whole of the NHS. Doctors, dentists, ophthalmologists, and pharmacists in the NHS are usually independently contracting professionals and would appear to be intended to be covered under section 43K, although they would not necessarily otherwise come under the definition of employee or worker in the ERA. However, points of concern have been expressed by Public Concern at Work (PCaW).[36] In any event, the scope of protection will turn substantially on whether the approach to the opening words of section 43K(1) adopted in *McTigue* is preferred to that suggested by the dicta in *Day*, as discussed at paragraphs 6.20–6.29 above.

(5) Applicants for employment, etc in the health service

6.58 Section 49B ERA, inserted by section 149 of the Small Business, Enterprise and Employment Act 2015, empowers the Secretary of State to make regulations prohibiting an NHS employer

---

[34] For a review of the case law see *Cotswold Developments Construction v Williams* [2006] IRLR 181.

[35] With effect from 25 June 2013 (ERRA s 103(2)).

[36] PCAW's concerns were set out in paras 20–28 of its briefing for Members of the Parliamentary Health Select Committee: see http://www.pcaw.org.uk/law-policy/policy-papers/category:National+Health+Service+%28NHS%29+and+Care. In *Suhail v Herts Urgent Care* (UKEAT/0416/11/RN, 14 November 2012), the EAT upheld a tribunal's finding that the claimant, who worked as an out of hours GP for the respondent, was not a 'worker'. Cf *Hospital Medical Group Limited v Westwood* [2013] ICR 415 (CA), where the doctor was integrated into the employer organization and properly regarded as a worker, and *Abertawe Bro Morgannwg University Health Board v Ferguson* (UKEAT/0044/13/LA, 24 April 2013), where it was accepted that a GP was a worker employed by a health board.

from discriminating against an applicant because it appears to the NHS employer that the applicant has made a protected disclosure. An 'applicant', in relation to an NHS employer, means an individual who applies to the NHS employer for—

(a) a contract of employment,
(b) a contract to do work personally, or
(c) appointment to an office or post.

It is provided that an NHS employer discriminates against an applicant if the NHS employer **6.59** refuses the applicant's application or in some other way treats the applicant less favourably than it treats or would treat other applicants in relation to the same contract, office, or post. Regulations made under the section may in particular—

(a) make provision as to circumstances in which discrimination by a worker or agent of an NHS employer is to be treated, for the purposes of the regulations, as discrimination by the NHS employer;
(b) confer jurisdiction (including exclusive jurisdiction) on employment tribunals or the Employment Appeal Tribunal;
(c) make provision for or about the grant or enforcement of specified remedies by a court or tribunal;
(d) make provision for the making of awards of compensation calculated in accordance with the regulations;
(e) make different provision for different cases or circumstances;
(f) make incidental or consequential provision, including incidental or consequential provision amending specified primary and other legislation.

'NHS employer' means an NHS public body prescribed by regulations to be made under the **6.60** section, and 'NHS public body' means—

(a) the National Health Service Commissioning Board;
(b) a clinical commissioning group;
(c) a Special Health Authority;
(d) an NHS trust;
(e) an NHS foundation trust;
(f) the Care Quality Commission;
(g) Health Education England;
(h) the Health Research Authority;
(i) the Health and Social Care Information Centre;
(j) the National Institute for Health and Care Excellence;
(k) Monitor;
(l) a Local Health Board established under s. 11 of the National Health Service (Wales) Act 2006;
(m) the Common Services Agency for the Scottish Health Service;
(n) Healthcare Improvement Scotland;
(o) a Health Board constituted under s. 2 of the National Health Service (Scotland) Act 1978;
(p) a Special Health Board constituted under that section.

For the purposes of the regulation-making power, 'worker' has the extended meaning given **6.61** by section 43K ERA, and a person is a worker in relation to an NHS employer if that NHS employer is the worker's employer within the extended meaning given by that section. The definitions contained in section 230(6) of employees and workers are extended accordingly.

Section 49B came into force on 26 May 2015.[37] As yet, no regulations have been made in **6.62** exercise of the powers granted by it. The provision is considered in more detail in Chapter 12 (paragraphs 12.32–12.46).

---

[37] See SI 2015/1329, reg 2(e).

(6) Trainees

6.63 A trainee on work experience or on a vocational scheme receives protection, if s/he is a person who is (ERA, section 43K(1)(d)):

> ... provided with work experience pursuant to a training course or programme or with training for employment otherwise than (i) under a contract for employment or by an educational establishment on a course run by that establishment.

6.64 For such trainees the person providing the training is deemed to be the employer for the purposes of the Act (see section 43K(2)(c)). This does not, however, cover trainees or students in education. It would probably cover a student on a sandwich year (ie a year spent gaining work experience in the relevant field) since the training is not run by the educational establishment. Whilst this is supported by and often set up by, or with the help of, an educational establishment, the work during the year out does not possess the necessary integration with the educational establishment to fall within the relevant words 'run by'.

E. Police Officers and the Problem of Judicial Immunity

6.65 Until 1 April 2004 section 13 of PIDA extended section 200 ERA to, and thereby excluded, police officers from protection under the PIDA-inserted provisions. This did not affect the rights of civilian staff in the police service to claim protection. The exclusion of police officers from protection was criticized by the Police Complaints Authority, the Association of Chief Police Officers, and other consultees, in particular given that miscarriages of justice are one of the specified malpractices expressly covered by the Act (see section 43B(1)(c)).

6.66 When the proposed public interest disclosure legislation was before Parliament, the Government gave an absolute commitment that police officers, whilst they would be outside the coverage of the Act, would be given equivalent protection by regulation. The Police (Conduct) Regulations were indeed amended to permit the making of an internal grievance complaint where a police officer complains of victimization as a result of a disclosure. However, subsequently a different and much more effective mechanism was adopted. Section 37 of the Police Reform Act 2002[38] inserted a new section 43KA into ERA which provides that, for the purposes of the PIDA-inserted provisions,[39] a person who holds, otherwise than under a contract of employment, the office of constable or an appointment as a police cadet shall be treated as an employee employed by the 'relevant' officer under a contract of employment; and any reference to a worker being 'employed' and to his 'employer' shall be construed accordingly.

6.67 By section 43KA(2) the 'relevant officer' is defined in relation to members of a police force or special constables as the chief officer of police. In relation to a member of a police force seconded to the Serious Organized Crime Agency to serve as a member of its staff, *that* agency is the relevant officer. In relation to any other person holding the office of constable or an appointment as police cadet, the relevant officer is the person who has the direction and control of the body of constables or cadets in question.

6.68 Where the effective dismissing agent is a disciplinary panel, a complaint in respect of that dismissal runs up against the doctrine of judicial immunity. The issue has been considered

---

[38] The Police Reform Act 2002 (Commencement No 8) Order 2004 (SI 2004/913) brought into force s 37 on 1 April 2004.

[39] Part IVA and s 47B, and ss 48 and 49 so far as relating to that section, and s 103A and the other provisions of Part X so far as relating to the right not to be unfairly dismissed in a case where the dismissal is unfair by virtue of s 103A.

most recently by the Court of Appeal in *P v Commissioner of Police for the Metropolis* [2016] EWCA Civ 2, [2016] IRLR 301. P, a serving Police Officer, was assaulted in 2010. As a consequence she suffered post-traumatic stress disorder (PTSD). She complained in an application to the employment tribunal that she did not have support at work to help her cope with the consequences of that condition, aggravated by the fact that just prior to 12 September 2011 she had worked excessively long hours. On that date, whilst 'in drink', as the EAT put it, she was involved in an incident which led to her arrest and dismissal. She asserted that her behaviour was heavily affected by her PTSD. An investigation led to a disciplinary charge before the Police Misconduct Board. She substantially accepted that she had been culpably guilty of the misconduct alleged, but relied on her good record as a police officer and her condition in mitigation. The Board nonetheless decided that she should be dismissed from the Force without notice. A claim of (ordinary) unfair dismissal was struck out because P had no right to bring such a claim. However, P also claimed that she had been subjected to disability discrimination contrary to section 15(1) of the Equality Act 2010 (EqA) and failure to make reasonable adjustments contrary to section 20 and 21 EqA. In the Court of Appeal, Laws LJ noted that generally police officers enjoyed no protection under employment legislation but that protection was extended to officers who made protected disclosures. He went on to consider the provisions of the EqA which, under section 39, forbids employers to discriminate against employees in various respects as regards their employment. Under section 42 EqA the office of constable is treated as employment by the chief officer of police for the purposes of Part 5 of the Act. That was the avenue to the ET followed by P. However, P's claim had been struck out: the ET accepted that the Metropolitan Police Misconduct Board was a judicial body which enjoyed immunity from suit. On appeal to the EAT there was extended discussion of two decisions of the Court of Appeal: *Heath v Commissioner of Metropolitan Police* [2005] IRLR 270 and *Lake v British Transport Police* [2007] ICR 1293.

Heath was a civilian employee of the Metropolitan Police. She made a complaint of sexual **6.69** assault by a police inspector in the workplace. A disciplinary panel was convened under the Police (Discipline) Regulations which comprised three male police commanders. The claimant gave evidence and responded to questions by a male advocate instructed to prosecute the charges. She was cross-examined by a male counsel, instructed on behalf of the inspector. The inspector also gave evidence. Subsequently she issued proceedings before the employment tribunal alleging sexual discrimination by members of the panel. As Auld LJ put it (para 5), '[s]he claimed: (1) that she had felt intimidated because the membership of the Board was entirely male; (2) that her union representative, a woman, had to plead with the Board to allow her to sit at the back of the hearing room so as to give her female support; and (3) that the inspector's male barrister, in asking her in cross-examination to demonstrate (while she was in close proximity to the inspector concerned) how the inspector had sexually assaulted her, humiliated her by asking her to open her jacket and squeeze her right breast with her left hand—without any objection from the Board members.' The ET held that the police disciplinary hearing was a judicial proceeding in respect of which members of the panel had an absolute immunity in respect of complaints of unlawful sex discrimination. The EAT upheld the decision as did the Court of Appeal. The Court of Appeal referred in particular to *Trapp v Mackie* [1979] 1 WLR 377 (HL). There Lord Diplock identified four indicia of judicial proceedings whilst emphasizing the need for flexibility and that failure to meet any one condition would not necessarily be fatal:

> (1) whether the tribunal is 'recognised by law', (2) whether the issue is 'akin to' that of a civil or criminal issue in the courts; (3) whether its procedures are akin to those in civil or criminal courts; and (4) whether the result of its procedures leads to a binding determination of the civil rights of a party or parties.

The Court of Appeal in *Heath* concluded that the ET and the EAT were justified in finding that the Board, in its consideration of Heath's allegations against the inspector, was a judicial body acting judicially: 'the essential features of the disciplinary hearing rendered it closely analogous to a judicial proceeding before a court of justice.'

6.70 In *Lake* the claimant was a constable in the British Transport Police. He faced disciplinary charges including allegations that he had made false accusations against a sergeant and that he had incited another officer to make a false statement. He was found guilty and it was directed that he be dismissed from the force under the police regulations. Lake exercised his right (Regulation 40) to request the Chief Officer of the Force to review the finding and the sanction imposed. The appeal was substantially dismissed. Lake brought ET proceedings, but he also brought a further appeal to the Police Appeal Tribunal, under section 85 of the Police Act 1996. In a determination after the decision of the ET, the Police Appeal Tribunal again substantially dismissed Lake's appeal. Lake's claim in the ET was brought against the Chief Constable on the ground that he had been unfairly dismissed because the reason for his dismissal was that he had made a protected disclosure. It was argued for the Police respondent that Lake had been dismissed by the Police Disciplinary Board and that *Heath* meant that the board was fulfilling a quasi-judicial function and, as a consequence, its proceedings and its decision were immune from suit. The ET agreed. So did the EAT. The Court of Appeal allowed Lake's appeal and struck out the part of the ET's order (made following the pre-hearing review) that had directed that the proceedings before the police disciplinary board and the decision of the board could not form the basis of the section 103A claim because those proceedings and that decision were immune from suit.

6.71 However, as Laws LJ explained in *P* (at para 8), the purpose and intention of that order was only to make clear that in considering the claim of automatic unfair dismissal under section 103A against the Chief Constable, the tribunal was not bound by the findings of fact made by the disciplinary panel. The chairman of the disciplinary panel had judicial immunity. But that did not mean that the Chief Constable's decision to dismiss was immune, or that in the claim against the Chief Constable the tribunal was constrained to accept the findings of the disciplinary panel. On the contrary, *Heath* was applied by the Court of Appeal in dismissing the claimant's appeal in *P.* Laws LJ added that he was 'troubled' that it appeared that claims of discriminatory dismissal brought by police officers, where the effective dismissing agent was a disciplinary panel such as was the case in *P*, would not be viable in the employment tribunals yet Parliament had legislated to allow such claims to be made. He noted that Parliament had passed the EqA in the knowledge of the *Heath* judgment, and yet had included no provision to remove the cloak of immunity from such disciplinary panels. He therefore thought it might be 'fruitful to give some thought to the terms of the Regulations under which such panels are constituted', contrasting the position where (as *in Lake*) the effective dismissing officer was the Chief Constable (in which case a claim could be brought based on the dismissal) with cases where the dismissal was by the disciplinary panel, in which case it could not.

6.72 Applying the criteria in *Heath,* the impact of the doctrine of judicial immunity is not limited to police cases. The broader application is illustrated by the decision in *Engel v The Joint Committee for Parking & Traffic Regulation Outside London (PATROL)* [2013] ICR 1086. Here the EAT held that a decision by the Chief Adjudicator of the Traffic Parking Tribunal not to allocate cases to a fee-paid Parking Adjudicator could not amount to a detriment for the purpose section 47B ERA because it fell within the scope of judicial immunity. Engel was a parking adjudicator authorized to hear appeals against decisions of local enforcement authorities to uphold the imposition of penalty charges in respect of certain road traffic contraventions. It was common ground that the Chief Adjudicator was a judicial office holder and that, in the discharge of her judicial functions, she was entitled to judicial immunity; and that, in respect of her discharge of those functions, the Joint Committee could not have vicarious responsibility. It was common ground, too, that the Chief Adjudicator, in addition to being a judicial office holder discharging judicial functions, was an employee of the Joint Committee and did perform administrative or 'ministerial' functions. The employment judge had, however, concluded that the decision not to allocate personal or postal cases to Engel was made in the performance of her duties as a judicial office holder. It was common ground that in appointing and reappointing an adjudicator, the Chief Adjudicator would not be exercising a judicial function. It was also common ground that a decision by the Joint Committee not to reappoint a person as an adjudicator or to remove him from office under reg. 17(3) of the relevant Regulations[40] would not be made in the exercise of judicial functions, by whomsoever it was made.

The EAT said that the concession was correctly made that the taking of disciplinary steps **6.73** by the Chief Adjudicator against an adjudicator, other than a decision not to allocate personal or postal cases or both, would not be in the exercise of her judicial functions. Disciplinary proceedings had nothing to do with the resolution of disputes between parties to an appeal by an adjudicator. They concerned only the position of the adjudicator. This was contrasted with a listing or allocation decision, which would be the exercise of a judicial function. It was submitted on behalf of Mr Engel that the decision not to allocate him any personal or postal cases was not a listing decision, but a decision to suspend him from work. The EAT accepted that the decision had that effect: if Engel was not allocated any cases to determine, he could not work and so could earn no fees. But the EAT rejected the proposition that it was necessary to look at the purpose of the decision not to allocate. Even if the decision was taken as a free-standing disciplinary measure and even if it was taken for the improper purpose alleged by Engel of subjecting him to a detriment because of his protected disclosure, the decision would still be covered by judicial immunity. The principle of immunity for the exercise of judicial functions was ultimately a policy decision, which must be upheld even in extreme circumstances, as Lord Denning MR had explained in *Sirros v Moore* [1974] 3 All ER 776 at 781J–782D. The employment judge was entitled and right to find that the Chief Adjudicator's decision not to allocate further personal or postal cases to Engel was a decision taken in the exercise of judicial functions in her capacity as a judicial office holder. It would not be open to an employment tribunal to determine that, in consequence, the Joint Committee subjected Engel to a detriment contrary to section 47B ERA.

F. Crown Employees

Except as described below (that is in relation to the armed forces and national security per- **6.74** sonnel) the PIDA-inserted provisions of the ERA apply in relation to Crown employment and persons in Crown employment in the same way as they have effect in relation to other employment and other employees or workers (ERA, section 191(1) and (2)(aa)). 'Crown employment' means 'employment under or for the purposes of a government department or any officer or body exercising on behalf of the Crown functions conferred by a statutory provision' (section 191(3)).

---

[40] The Civil Enforcement of Parking Contraventions (England) General Regulations 2007 SI 2007/3843.

G. Partners and Members of Limited Liability Partnerships

6.75 Section 1 of the Partnership Act 1890 defines partnership as 'the relation which subsists between persons carrying on a business in common with a view of profit'. A partner in that sense is not an employee.[41] The distinction between a partnership and an employment relationship was explained by Lord Donaldson MR in *Cowell v Quilter Goodison* [1989] IRLR 392 (CA) as follows:

> The firm was not a corporate entity. It had no separate identity. His relationship with the other partners was governed by the concept to which the Partnership Act applies, namely of people who are carrying on business in common with a view to profit, a very well known and well understood relationship in law, and one which is wholly different from the employment relationship.[42]

6.76 However, what purports to be a partnership arrangement may take various forms, including so described 'salaried partners' or 'fixed-share partners'. Whether these are 'true' partners, in the sense of falling within the definition in section 1 of the 1890 Act, or are employees, depends on the substance of the relationship rather than on the label.[43] Section 2(3) of the 1890 Act provides that the receipt by a person of a share of the profits of the business is prima facie evidence of being a partner, but it is not necessarily determinative.[44] Equally, the absence of a direct link between the level of payments and the profits of the firm is usually a strong pointer against a true partnership but is not necessarily determinative. Other relevant features may include:

- whether there is provision for a contribution to the working capital of the firm,
- whether the partnership agreement provides expressly or impliedly that not only will the acts of the claimant within authority bind the other partners but also that their acts bind him,[45]
- whether there has been a purported change from employment status, and
- how clearly the partnership status is expressed.[46]

---

[41] *Palumbo v Stylianou* (1966) 1 ITR 407; *Cowell v Quilter Goodison* [1989] IRLR 392; *Tiffin v Lester Aldridge LLP* [2011] IRLR 105 (EAT).

[42] As noted in *Reinhard v Ondra* LLP [2015] EWHC 26 at para 42, some doubts about this reasoning were expressed in *Clyde & Co LLP and another (Respondents) v Bates van Winkelhof (Appellant)* [2014] UKSC 32 [2014] 1 WLR 2047, but the Court in *Reinhard* accepted that it remains binding at least at first instance.

[43] *Stekel v Ellice* [1973] 1 All ER 465 at 473; *Williamson & Soden Solicitors v Briars* (EAT/0611/10/DM, 20 May 2011) at para 30; *Cobbetts LLP and another v Hodge* [2010] 1 BCLC 30 at para 84. In *Stekel v Ellice* [1973] 1 All ER 465 where Megarry J noted that if there is a contract of employment and the only qualification of that relationship is that the employee is being held out as being a partner, the name 'salaried partner' was 'perfectly apt' and no relationship of partnership was created. At 'the other extreme' there might be a full partnership deed under which all the partners save one take a share of the profits, with that one being paid a fixed salary not dependent on profits, in which case that person could be a partner. See *Cobbetts LLP and another v Hodge* [2010] 1 BCLC 30 (person held out as partner not a partner); and, similarly, *M Young Legal Associates Ltd v Zahid Solicitors (a firm) and others* [2006] EWCA Civ 613.

[44] See eg *Williamson & Soden Solicitors v Briars* (EAT/0611/10/DM) (the claimant was in fact an employee despite accepting remuneration calculated as a profit share which was in part guaranteed and in part dependent on net profits of the firm. The claimant took no risk of loss, and was subject to control by the firm, with important matters in the hands of the equity partners). Cf *Tiffin v Lester Aldridge LLP* [2011] IRLR 105, upholding the employment tribunal's decision that a person who agreed to be a 'fixed-share partner' when an LLP was created out of a partnership was not an employee.

[45] *M Young Legal Associates Ltd v Zahid Solicitors (a firm) and others* [2006] EWCA Civ 613 at para 33.

[46] See *Williamson & Soden Solicitors v Briars* (EAT/0611/10/DM, 20 May 2011) where it was common ground that the claimant had been an employee before the alleged change in status, and the fact that the paperwork did not clearly express a change to being a partner, combined with the onerous responsibilities that rest upon a partner, were persuasive against a finding of a change from employment status.

There is no minimum share of profit that a person has to receive to be a partner.[47] Whether the claimant is under the direct control of the other partners may be relevant[48] but is not necessarily determinative.[49]

So far as concerns limited liability partnerships, section 4(4) of the Limited Liability Partnerships Act 2000 provides that: **6.77**

> A member of a limited liability partnership shall not be regarded for any purpose as employed by the limited liability partnership unless, if he and the other members were partners in a partnership, he would be regarded for that purpose as employed by the partnership.

That provision has been held to have the effect that, at least as a matter of English law,[50] a **6.78** person who is a member of an LLP cannot also be an employee: see *Reinhard v Ondra* LLP [2015] EWHC 26 at paras 33–45.[51] However, different considerations apply in relation to whether the relationship of partnership or membership of an LLP could be brought within even the extended definition of a worker. The Supreme Court resolved these issues in *Clyde & Co LLP and another v Bates van Winkelhof* [2014] UKSC 32, [2014] 1 WLR 2047, [2014] IRLR 641, reversing *Bates van Winkelhof v Clyde & Co* LLP [2012] EWCA Civ 1207, [2012] IRLR 992. As noted above (at paragraphs 6.13–6.15) the Supreme Court concluded that nothing in section 4(4) of the Limited Liability Partnerships Act 2000 prevents a finding that a limited liability partner may also be a worker within the meaning of section 230(3)(b) ERA. On the facts in *Winkelhof* the claimant was both a limited liability partner and a worker. It was common ground before the Supreme Court that the claimant worked 'under a contract personally to perform any work or services', that she provided those services 'for' the LLP, and that the LLP was not her 'client or customer'. As such she was a limb (b) worker.

H. Non-executive Directors

A non-executive director (NED) is a member of the board of a company who does not have **6.79** responsibility for daily management or operations, and is not an employee of the company. They are office holders, with the same directors' duties under the Companies Act 2006 as executive directors. They are appointed to bring independent, impartiality, wider experience, special knowledge and/or personal qualities to the Board.[52] Their role is particularly relevant in the financial services sector, given the regulatory requirement for a non-executive director in each regulated firm to take on the role of whistleblowing champion (see Chapter 12, paragraphs 12.108–12.110). Whilst NEDs are not employees, we suggest that they can fall within the definition of a worker. This was the conclusion of an employment tribunal in *Osipov v International Petroleum Ltd and others* (Case No 2200944/2015, 23 March 2016 (EJ Lewzey)). The issue arose in the context of concluding that two NEDs were liable for protected disclosure detriment claims under the individual liability provision in section 47B(1A) ERA. The tribunal expressly proceeded on the basis of applying the same test of a worker as would apply

---

[47] *Tiffin v Lester Aldridge LLP* [2011] IRLR 105 at para 10.
[48] *Williamson & Soden Solicitors v Briars* (EAT/0611/10/DM) at para 31.
[49] See eg *Tiffin v Lester Aldridge LLP* [2011] IRLR 105 at para 34.
[50] The position is less clear under Scottish law as it is not settled whether it is possible to be both a partner and an employee: see *Clyde & Co LLP and another v Bates van Winkelhof (Appellant)* [2014] UKSC 32 [2014] 1 WLR 2047 per Lady Hale at para 42.
[51] Considering the effect of the decision of the Court of Appeal in *Tiffin v Lester Aldridge LLP* [2011] IRLR 105 and *Clyde & Co LLP and another v Bates van Winkelhof (Appellant)* [2014] UKSC 32, [2014] 1 WLR 2047 (SC).
[52] Institute of Directors factsheet (http://wci-ined-information-bank.co.uk/wp-content/uploads/2015/03/IoD-Factsheet.pdf).

for a claimant. One of the NEDs was found in substance to be an executive director. For the other it was noted that the services he provided included attending board meetings, signing the claimant's terms of appointment, and also exercising managerial functions in intervening in a dispute between the claimant and an adviser. But more generally, the tribunal commented that it was unlikely that it would have been Parliament's intention not to include NEDs.

6.80 We suggest that, whilst the conclusion is correct, it is not necessary to revert to a purposive construction to reach that conclusion. As emphasized in *Bates van Winkelhof v Clyde and Co LLP* [2014] UKSC 32, [2014] ICR 730, there can be no substitute for applying the words of the statute, section 230(3)(b) ERA, to the facts of the individual case. Typically the letter of appointment will provide that the NED is appointed under a contract for services.[53] The NED will undertake to perform services personally, including at least attendance at board meetings. There will typically be other responsibilities such as sitting on a remuneration committee. Undertaking the role of whistleblowing champion would itself entail the provision of services. The exception for a client or customer or any profession or business undertaking carried on by the individual would not apply.

I. Limits of the Definition of 'Worker' and the Power to Extend Coverage

6.81 Whilst the category of 'workers' under the PIDA provisions is a wide one, it is not all-embracing. We address below categories of individuals who carry out work but are not (or may not be) covered either because they do not fall within the general definition of 'worker', even as extended, or they are specifically excluded. The Secretary of State has a power to amend section 43K so as to extend the categories of individuals who count as workers for the purposes of Part IVA. This power was set out in a new section 43K(4) ERA, inserted by section 20 ERRA. An order under subsection (4) cannot make an amendment that has the effect of removing a category of individual unless the Secretary of State is satisfied that there are no longer any individuals in that category. No amendments have, as yet, been proposed.

(1) Volunteers

6.82 Although section 43K ERA provides for an extended definition of the term 'worker', there must be a contractual relationship to which the worker is a party: see *Sharpe v Bishop of Worcester* [2015] EWCA Civ 399 [2015] IRLR 663 (CA), discussed at paragraphs 6.34 and 6.35 above. That is subject to the issue, discussed at 6.35 above, as to whether for the purposes of section 43K(1)(a) ERA, that must be a contract with the alleged employer. In order for there to be a contractual relationship there must be an agreement supported by consideration, an intention to create legal relations, and reasonable certainty of terms. Where a person works as a volunteer it may be that the requirements for consideration and for an intention to create legal relations are not satisfied. The tribunal will have regard to the reality of the situation.

6.83 As to the requirement of consideration, one common feature of a volunteering relationship is the absence of any obligation to provide the volunteer with work and of any minimum commitment of time from the volunteer. If so there will not be an umbrella or global contract of employment linking each occasion on which the volunteer has worked for the 'employer'.[54] However, on the facts, it might be that there is an obligation to offer and accept work, even

---

[53] See PLC standard letter of appointment for Non-Executive Directors.
[54] *Clark v Oxfordshire Health Authority* [1998] IRLR 125 (CA).

if the work is only of a sporadic or casual nature.[55] Even where there is no minimum commitment of time, the volunteer may be a 'worker' as a result of entering into a contractual relationship on the occasions when work has in fact been done by the volunteer.[56]

A further common feature of a volunteering relationship is the absence of any payment for **6.84** the work done except in respect of expenses incurred. Payments made to workers will not constitute consideration if they are genuinely *ex gratia* (although tribunals may be sceptical of this if the payments are made as a matter of course). Nor will payments made genuinely by way of reimbursement of expenses constitute consideration. In these cases, even where there may be a right to terminate the volunteer relationship which is akin to a dismissal, and even though the volunteer may gain status and skill from acting as a volunteer, the volunteer is unlikely to be a 'worker', at least where there is no mutual time commitment and no other mutual obligations such as an obligation to provide training.[57] However, whilst it may be that expenses have merely been estimated in broad-brush terms to save administrative costs, in a series of cases flat-rate payments made to volunteers have been a crucial factor leading to a finding that the volunteer was in employment (either under a contract of services or personally providing work or labour). The fact that the payment is low is irrelevant since the tribunal is not concerned with assessing the adequacy of the consideration.[58] Further, where there is no or no immediate payment, it may be that other mutual obligations are accepted such as an obligation to train, supervise, and provide a safe system of work.[59]

A series of cases against Citizens' Advice Bureaux, arising out of claims under the Disability **6.85** Discrimination Act 1995 (DDA) and then the EqA, explored the extent and circumstances in which 'volunteers' may be said to be employed. They culminated in *X v Mid Sussex CAB* [2012] UKSC 59, [2013] IRLR 146, [2013] ICR 249, where the Supreme Court held that the Equality Directive (2000/78/EC) did not cover voluntary activity.

In *Sheffield CAB v Grayson* [2004] IRLR 353, Mr Grayson, who was accepted to be an **6.86** employee of the CAB, claimed discrimination contrary to the DDA. The CAB raised the defence which at that time applied under section 7 DDA, that there were only eleven paid employees. The issue was whether volunteers at the CAB in question fell within the definition of employment in section 68 DDA (which included a contract personally to do any work), thus raising the headcount above fifteen. They were engaged pursuant to a 'volunteer agreement' which was construed by the employment tribunal which also heard oral evidence. The EAT said that the central question for the employment tribunal was whether the CAB's volunteer workers were subject to a contract under which they were obliged to work for the Bureau. Rimer J, giving the judgment of the EAT, said (at para 12) that:

> ... it would appear to us surprising if the answer to that question were yes, since it is of the essence of volunteer workers that they are ordinarily under no such contract. As volunteers, they provide their services voluntarily, without reward, with the consequence that they are entitled to withhold those services with impunity. However that starting position is not necessarily also the finishing point. In every case, including this one, if a question arises as

---

[55] Though see *Carmichael v National Power plc* [1999] 1 WLR 2042 (HL).

[56] *Clark v Oxfordshire Health Authority* [1998] IRLR 125 (CA); *McMeechan v Secretary of State for Employment* [1997] ILRR 353 (CA); *Asila Elshami v Welfare Community Projects and Leema* (Case No 6001977/98).

[57] *Gradwell v Council for Voluntary Service, Blackpool, Wyre & Fylde* (Case No 2404313/97); *Alexander v Romania at Heart Trading Co Limited* (Case No 310206/97).

[58] *Migrant Advisory Services v Chaudri* (EAT/11400/97); *Asila Elshami v Welfare Community Projects and Leema* (Case No 6001977/98); *Rodney Harrambeen Organisation Limited* (Case No 36684/86).

[59] See *Armitage v Relate* (Case No 43238/94) where there was a minimum time commitment and a provision for recouping training expenses if obligations were not met.

to the legal relationship between an alleged employer and a so-called voluntary worker, it is always necessary to analyse that relationship to see exactly what it amounts to. But if the proposition is that the volunteer worker is in fact an employee under a contract of service, or under a contract personally to do work, for the purposes of s. 68 of the 1995 Act, then in our view it is necessary to be able to identify an arrangement under which, in exchange of valuable consideration, the volunteer is contractually obliged to render services to or else to work personally for the employer.

6.87 The EAT noted that the CAB required its volunteers to sign the volunteer agreement, the stated purpose of which was 'to clarify the reasonable expectation of both the volunteer and the Bureau'. In the EAT's view the agreement was:

> directed at clarifying each side's 'reasonable expectations' and this was not the language of contractual obligation. Respective contractual obligations were not usually expressed in terms of 'reasonable expectation'. They would ordinarily be expressed in terms of unqualified obligation, or at any rate the primary obligations will be so expressed, in particular those relating to the employee's hours of work and his reward for it.

The EAT went on to consider various aspects of the volunteer agreement and came to this conclusion (at para 18):

> We are prepared to accept that this element of the Agreement, and also the provision in it to the effect that the Bureau will indemnify advisers against negligence claims by disgruntled clients, probably do, or at least may, evidence a binding contractual relationship between the Bureau and the volunteer, namely a unilateral contract in the nature of what is sometimes referred to as an 'if' contract, one which can be expressed as follows: 'if you do any work for the Bureau and incur expenses in doing so, and/suffer a claim from a client you advise, the Bureau will indemnify you against your expenses and any such claim'. But that contract is still not one which imposes on the volunteer any obligation actually to do any work for the Bureau.

6.88 The EAT concluded that 'the contract imposed no obligation on the volunteer to do anything'. The provision requiring the volunteer to undertake training did not constitute consideration (at para 21). The 'crucial question' was not whether any benefits flowed from the Bureau to the volunteer in consideration of any work actually done by the volunteer for the Bureau, but whether the volunteer agreement imposed a contractual obligation upon the Bureau to provide work for the volunteer to do and upon the volunteer personally to do for the Bureau any work so provided, being an obligation such that, were the volunteer to give notice immediately terminating his/her relationship with the Bureau, the latter would have a remedy for breach of contract against him/her. The volunteer agreement imposed no such obligation. It was open to a volunteer at any point, either with or without notice, to withdraw his/her services from the Bureau, in which event the Bureau would have no contractual remedy against him/her. It followed that the advisers and other volunteers were not employed by the Bureau.[60]

6.89 Even where there is an agreement supported by consideration this will not be binding unless there is an intention to create legal relations, rather than an agreement which is 'purely voluntary or is binding in honour only'.[61] The label placed on the agreement by the parties, such as whether the worker is referred to as a 'volunteer', may be relevant but it is not determinative as to whether there was an intention to create legal relations. The tribunal can also have regard to the context in which an agreement was made in order to ascertain whether there

---

[60] See also *Murray v Newham CAB* [2001] ICR 708; *Bruce v Leeds CAB* (EAT/1355/01); and *X v Mid Sussex CAB* [2012] UKSC 59, [2013] ICR 249, [2013] IRLR 146.

[61] See Stuart-Smith LJ in *R v Lord Chancellor's Department, ex p Nangle* [1991] IRLR 343 at para 23 (DC).

was the requisite intention. On this basis, in *Rogers v Booth* [1937] 2 All ER 751 the Court of Appeal held that an officer of the Salvation Army had no contract because the relationship was a purely spiritual one. This was so even though she was paid a maintenance payment. The payment was expressly stated to be purely hardship money since the officer had no other means of earning a living.[62] However, in *Percy v Church of Scotland Board of National Mission* [2005] UKHL 73, [2006] 2 AC 28 it was emphasized that there is no necessary inconsistency between there being a contract and the obligations being exclusively spiritual, and that the issue now needs to be considered in the modern context of statutory protection provided for workers and employees (per Lord Nicholls at paras 25 and 26). Where the agreement lacks precision and is informal this may be consistent with an absence of intention to create legal relations.[63] The mere fact that there is a recognized practice of using volunteers and an informal relationship may not, however, be sufficient to persuade a tribunal of an absence of an intention to create contractual relations.[64]

(2) Members of the armed forces and those involved in national security

There are various exclusions from the scope of protection offered under the ERA which broadly mirror those found in other parts of employment legislation. As we have noted, the Act applies to people who are employees of, work for, or are in the service of the Crown (ERA, section 191). However, it is not extended to those in the armed forces (section 192). **6.90**

Nor does it extend to those involved in national security (section 193). The general rule in section 193 applies, to the effect that a Crown servant is protected under the Act, unless the worker is the subject of a ministerial certificate that his/her work safeguards national security. This is a conclusive answer to a claim and would not be open to review by the employment tribunal. **6.91**

A worker in the security service or at GCHQ will therefore not be protected by the Act even where s/he raises a concern only internally. Concern was expressed in the House of Commons committee debate as to whether the scope of the definition of security service was clear enough. A proposed amendment sought to apply the Act to non-operational employees, for example office cleaners and messengers who might come across waste or maladministration which did not impinge on sensitive and secret matters. This proposal was withdrawn. **6.92**

(3) Parliamentary staff

Sections 194 and 195 apply provisions of the ERA to House of Lords and House of Commons staff respectively but do not include an application of Part IVA or section 47B (detriment as the grounds of a protected disclosure). Part X (unfair dismissal) is applied and section 103A is not expressly excluded. It might be argued that a member of Parliamentary staff falls within the definition of a worker, and that it was for this reason that there was no need to refer specifically to section 47B in relation to the list of detriment claims which are listed in sections 194 and 195. That does though beg a question as to why section 45A (relating to detriment suffered by workers in working time cases) is amongst the detriment claims listed where the ERA has effect in the same way as for other employment. **6.93**

(4) Holders of Judicial Office

In *Gilham v Ministry of Justice* (UKEAT 0087/16/LA, 31 October 2016) the EAT addressed the issue of whether a holder of judicial office was also worker. The claimant was a district **6.94**

---

[62] See also *Diocese of Southwark v Coker* [1998] ICR 140 (assistant curate in Church of England not an employee as no contractual intention).

[63] *Chitty on Contracts*, 30th edn. London: Sweet & Maxwell, 2008, p 211, para 2-176.

[64] See eg *Asila Elshami v Welfare Community Projects and Leema* (Case No 6001977/98).

judge, who sought to bring a detriment claim under section 47B ERA. It was common ground that she was an office holder, but the issue was as to whether she was also a worker within the meaning of section 230(3) ERA.[65] Following *Sharpe*,[66] and subject to an argument based on the Human Rights Act (HRA), it was not disputed that for ERA section 230(3) to apply there had to be a contract between the parties. However, the claimant argued that the relationship between district judges and the Ministry of Justice had the typical features of a contract that would fall within section 230(3); that is, offer, acceptance, consideration, mutuality of obligation, and exchange of promises. Simler J rejected this argument. She noted that case law on the status of religious office holders and, in particular, Lord Sumption JSC's judgment in *Preston v President of the Methodist Conference* [2013] 2 AC 162, showed that the status of office holder and employment are not mutually exclusive. Since the typical features of an employment contract are also often features of appointed office, focus on such features did not assist in determining whether there was a contract of employment or for services. Whether or not there was such a contract was a question to be determined by reference to the manner in which the individual was engaged and the character of the rules, or terms, governing their service. Simler J did not consider that the principle of judicial independence prevented there being a worker relationship. But she concluded that there were no features of the method of the claimant's appointment, the duties or functions of her role, or the means by which she could be removed from it, which supported the existence of a contract between her and the Ministry of Justice in addition to the office which she held. On the contrary, a district judge's appointment was by the Crown (an Instrument of Appointment signed by the Lord Chancellor) and on appointment she was placed on a reserve list until a vacancy arose; the duties, functions, and authority of a district judge are defined by statute and by rules made under statutory authority, and to the extent that the terms of service went beyond this they were incidental to the terms made by or under statute (and were not at all determined by private negotiation). Responsibility for welfare arrangements, training and guidance, and deployment of the judiciary rests with the Lord Chief Justice (rather than the Ministry of Justice or Lord Chancellor), and the Ministry of Justice had no power to end the relationship. Equally, Simler J accepted that these features provided a clear and complete explanation for the relationship between the parties, and that as such there was no necessity to imply a contractual relationship. The relationship was fully explained by and referable to the claimant's appointment as an office holder, and the availability of whistleblowing protection did not justify a different conclusion.

6.95 Simler J also rejected the third and final ground of appeal. It was argued that the qualified right to freedom of expression under Article 10 of the Convention, which extends to whistleblowing protection at work, can and must be given effect by reading section 230(3) ERA in a way that is compatible with those rights. It was contended that this is the effect of section 3 HRA and that, accordingly, the definition of worker in section 230(3)(b) ERA can and should be read so as to include those in an 'employment relationship' but who do not have a contract for services. Whilst the strong interpretive obligation in section 3 HRA may require a court to read in words which change the meaning of legislation so as to make it Convention compliant, courts cannot adopt a meaning that is inconsistent with a fundamental feature

---

[65] See *Ministry of Justice (formerly Department of Constitutional Affairs) v O'Brien* [2013] ICR 499 in which, following a reference to the CJEU, the Supreme Court had held that recorders are in an 'employment relationship' within the Framework Directive on Part-Time Work (97/81/EC), and they must be treated as 'workers' for the purposes of the Part-time Workers Regulations 2000. No argument based on this authority was pursed in the EAT because, unlike in *O'Brien*, the claim was not based on rights derived from EU law. In *O'Brien* the rights invoked did derive from EU law and extended to those with an 'employment relationship' so that the word 'worker' had to be read as having that effect.

[66] See paras 6.34–6.35 above.

of the legislation being construed. Simler J accepted that a fundamental feature of section 230(3) ERA is to define those within the scope of protection by reference to the existence of a contract, whether a contract of service or a contract for services. Parliament had extended the meaning of 'worker' (and associated terms) for the purposes of whistleblowing protection beyond that otherwise provided by section 230(3) ERA under section 43K(1). This extended protection afforded was carefully identified and delineated, preserving the general rule that a contractual relationship is required for 'worker' status, save only in a limited number of circumstances (for example agency and NHS arrangements), where the requirement to have a contract was replaced by a requirement to work for a person in particular circumstances or performing particular services. Parliament was or would have been entitled to conclude that extended protection is unnecessary to give effect to the claimant's Article 10 rights. Judicial office holders had a range of protections[67] for the right not to suffer whistleblowing detriments. A district judge's position was therefore quite different from that of a worker or employee who did not benefit from such protections: in many respects, a district judge is protected to a greater degree than other workers. Where adequate safeguards were in place there could be no necessity to rewrite section 230(3)(b) so as to permit the specific route to a remedy provided by section 47B ERA. Further, Simler J considered that extension of the meaning of worker in section 43K(1) is properly a question for Parliament.

J. Workers whose Employment is not Confined to England and Wales

(1) Three aspects

In considering whistleblowing claims with an extraterritorial element, it is necessary to give consideration to the following issues:[68] **6.96**

(a) the forum: the jurisdiction of the tribunal in terms of international rules of jurisdiction; this is governed principally by EU Regulation No 1215/2012 (the recast Brussels Regulation) or, in a non-EU case, the ET Rules of Procedure 2013, rule 8;
(b) the applicable law;
(c) the territorial scope of the relevant legislation (ie section 47B, and section 103A ERA); this is often, though arguably inaccurately, referred to as an issue of 'jurisdiction'.

(2) The forum: territorial jurisdiction—the EU regime

(a) Overview

The recast Brussels Regulation applies in relation to proceedings issued on or after 10 January 2015. It supersedes Council Regulation (EC) No 44/2001, which continues to apply to proceedings issued prior to that date.[69] It principally applies where the respondent is domiciled in an EU Member State.[70] If the respondent is not domiciled in a Member State then the general **6.97**

---

[67] In this respect Simler J referred to (a) s 3 of the Constitutional Reform Act 2005 which guarantees judicial independence, (b) s 11 of the County Courts Act 1984 which guarantee's a district judge's tenure, (c) statutory protection of a district judge's salary, and (d) a district judge's ability to make a complaint about another judicial office holder under the Judicial Discipline (Prescribed Procedures) Regulations 2014 and the Judicial Grievance Policy.

[68] *Simpson v Intralinks Ltd* [2012] ICR 1343 EAT, at para 5; *Powell v OMV Exploration & Production Ltd* [2014] ICR 63, at para 3.

[69] There are also similar provisions in the 2007 Lugano Convention, which applies where the respondent is domiciled in Iceland, Norway, or Switzerland.

[70] Denmark was not initially included, but subsequently notified the European Commission of its decision to implement the Regulation.

rule is that when a claim is sought to be brought in a Member State, that own state's rules of jurisdiction apply (as to which see paragraphs 6.111–6.112 below).[71] Where the respondent is domiciled in a Member State, the general rule (set out in Article 4(1)) is that the person shall be sued in the courts of that Member State (and not elsewhere). In addition, section 5 (comprising Articles 20 to 23) contains specific provisions relating to individual contracts of employment.[72] It provides (so far as is relevant to claims brought by employees) as follows:

Article 20

1. In matters relating to individual contracts of employment, jurisdiction shall be determined by this Section, without prejudice to Article 6,[73] point 5 of Article 7,[74] and, in the case of proceedings brought against an employer, point 1 of Article 8.[75]

2. Where an employee enters into an individual contract of employment with an employer who is not domiciled in a Member State but has a branch, agency or other establishment in one of the Member States, the employer shall, in disputes arising out of the operations of the branch, agency or establishment, be deemed to be domiciled in that Member State.

Article 21

1. An employer domiciled in a Member State may be sued:
    (a) in the courts of the Member State in which he is domiciled; or
    (b) in another Member State:
        (i) in the courts for the place where or from where the employee habitually carries out his work or in the courts for the last place where he did so; or
        (ii) if the employee does not or did not habitually carry out his work in any one country, in the courts for the place where the business which engaged the employee is or was situated.

2. An employer not domiciled in a Member State may be sued in a court of a Member State in accordance with point (b) of paragraph 1.

Article 23

The provisions of this Section may be departed from only by an agreement: (1) which is entered into after the dispute has arisen; or (2) which allows the employee to bring proceedings in courts other than those indicated in this Section.

6.98 Subject to specific exceptions set out in Article 20.1, where section 5 applies, the other rules are therefore excluded. As it was put by Gross LJ in *Bosworth and Hurley v Arcadia Petroleum Ltd and others* [2016] EWCA Civ 818, at para 30, where section 5 applies 'it is at or very near the top of "the hierarchy of jurisdictional rules" ... it "trumps" everything (or nearly everything) else'. The general effect is to enable the employee to sue in the UK if (a) that is where

---

[71] This is subject to exceptions in Articles 18(1) (relating to consumer claims), 21(2) (set out below), 24 (certain provisions relating to exclusive jurisdiction) and 25 (where the parties have agreed that a court or courts of a Member State are to have jurisdiction).

[72] For a further and more detailed analysis see Adrian Briggs, *Civil Jurisdiction and Judgments*, 6th edn. (Abingdon: Informa Law from Routledge, 2015), pp 150–60.

[73] Article 6 provides that as against a defendant who is not domiciled in a Member State, the jurisdiction of the courts of each Member State shall, subject to limited exceptions including Article 21(2), be determined by the law of that Member State, and any person domiciled in a Member State may, whatever his nationality, avail himself in that Member State of the rules of jurisdiction there in force.

[74] Article 7(5) provides that a person domiciled in a Member State may be sued in another Member State as regards a dispute arising out of the operations of a branch, agency, or other establishment, in the courts for the place where the branch, agency, or other establishment is situated.

[75] Article 8(1) provides that a person domiciled in a Member State may also be sued where he is one of a number of defendants, in the courts for the place where any one of them is domiciled, provided the claims are so closely connected that it is expedient to hear and determine them together to avoid the risk of irreconcilable judgments resulting from separate proceedings.

the employer is domiciled[76] (or deemed to be domiciled) but also (even where the employer is not domiciled in a Member State); (b) where the work under the contract is or was[77] habitually carried out in the UK; or (c) if the employee does or did not carry out work in any one country, if England was the place where the business which engaged the employee is or was situated. The employee is free to choose between these alternatives: *Simpson v Intralinks Ltd* [2012] ICR 1343 (EAT) para 32. But other exceptions to the requirement to sue in the place where the employer is domiciled, such as the right under Article 7(2) in matters relating to tort to bring a claim in the place where the harmful event occurred, have no application if section 5 applies. Jurisdiction agreements are permitted but limitations are placed on their effectiveness; principally in that they can not exclude jurisdiction unless entered into after the dispute has arisen.

The habitual place of work is where the employee mainly carries out his or her obligations **6.99** towards the employer or has established the effective centre of his or her working activities. Where the respondent is domiciled abroad in a Member State, and the worker does not habitually work in the UK (irrespective of whether the habitual place of work is where the respondent is domiciled), the consequence is that the tribunal will lack jurisdiction irrespective of the territorial scope of the legislation. In *Powell v OMV Exploration & Production Ltd* [2014] ICR 63 (EAT), where the employer was domiciled in Austria, and although the employee was resident in the UK, his employee's habitual place of work was Dubai. He worked in Dubai for three weeks in every four. The fourth week was spent in England, where he did some work. The employer had no presence in Great Britain (an associated company had offices in England and Scotland). There was an express choice of law in favour of Manx law. The EAT upheld the ET's decision that the claimant had to sue his employer in Austria, which was its domicile. The place where he habitually worked was Dubai, not Great Britain. For good measure the EAT also agreed with the ET that there was an insufficiently close connection with Great Britain for the claim of unfair dismissal to be within the territorial scope of ERA.

(b) 'Individual contract of employment'

Section 5 only applies in matters 'relating to individual contracts of employment'. That in **6.100** turn begs the question of whether the provisions apply to a worker, including the extended category of worker within section 43K ERA. If section 5 does not apply, then, in the event that the respondent was not domiciled in the UK, it would be necessary to bring the case within one of the general exceptions, notably under Article 7(2) where, in matters relating to tort, the claim is brought in the place where the harmful event occurred. As set out further below, the meaning of an 'individual contract of employment' also potentially arises in relation to determining the applicable law (see paragraphs 6.114–6.116), though it may be of less importance in that context due to the nature of the ERA as containing mandatory provisions.

It is clear the term 'individual contract of employment' is not to be construed simply by **6.101** reference to its domestic meaning. But there remains a lack of authoritative guidance as to the extent to which it covers the range of worker relationships encompassed by the protected disclosure legislation. Some indicia were suggested by the Court of Appeal in *WPP Holdings Italy Srl v Benatti* [2007] 1 WLR 2316 (CA). The court cited with approval the judge's

---

[76] For an analysis and application of the requirement of domicile or deemed domicile albeit under Council Regulation (EC) No 44/2001, see *Olsen v Gearbulk Services Ltd and another* (2015) UKEAT/0345/14, [2015] IRLR 818, at paras 15–18.

[77] Briggs (at p 154) points out that no case has held that section 5 is inapplicable if there is no longer an employment relationship.

summary of the following features of a contract of employment for the purposes of section 5 of Council Regulation (EC) No 44/2001:

> (ii) the provision of services by one party over a period of time for which remuneration is paid; (ii) control and direction over the provision of the services by the counterparty; and (iii) integration to some extent of the provider of the services within the organizational framework of the counterparty.

6.102 The court upheld the finding, applying those criteria, that a management consultant engaged on a non-exclusive basis to come up with proposals and strategies to improve performance of the corporate group was not employed under an individual contract of employment. The emphasis on the element of control in particular might suggest a narrower approach than permitted by the test for a worker. However, on the facts in *Benatti*, the exception for being a client or customer of a profession or business undertaking carried on by the individual may have applied.[78] More broadly, caution is needed in applying the *Benatti* criteria because of the need to give a purposive effect to the provisions. This was emphasized by the Court of Appeal in *Petter v EMC Europe Ltd* [2015] IRLR 847. Whilst accepting that the indicia set out in *Benatti* were helpful, the court stated that it was equally important to bear in mind that the underlying policy of section 5 (of Council Regulation (EC) No 44/2001, and the recast Brussels Regulation) is 'to protect employees because they are considered from a socio-economic point of view to be the weaker parties to the contract' (per Moore-Bick LJ at para 17). In *Petter* the claimant was employed as a director of an English company (EMC Europe), but a significant part of his total remuneration came from a share distribution scheme under agreement with EMC Europe's ultimate parent company, EMC Corporation, which is a Massachussets company. The court accepted that a dispute concerning the agreements with EMC Corporation relating to remuneration under the share distribution scheme related to an individual employment contract. Those agreements would not amount to a contract of employment with the parent company under UK law. But the parent company was to be regarded as an employer for the purposes of section 5. The decision suggests scope for a broad approach to construction of the requirement for an individual employment contract, although on the facts of that case there was no doubt that there was a contract of employment (in UK terms) at least with EMC Europe, and that the dispute related to this. It did not therefore directly address the extent to which other worker relationships are covered.

6.103 The issue as to meaning of an 'individual contract of employment' in the context of territorial jurisdiction was addressed by the CJEU in *Holterman Ferho Exploitatie BV v Spies von Bullesheim* [2016] IRLR 140. The court reiterated that 'contract of employment' in this context has an independent meaning which must be common to all Member States. Here Mr von Buellesheim was a German national and resident, who had been appointed as a director of Holterman, and performed duties as a manager of the company and was also a minority shareholder in that company. The company brought proceedings against him, and he sought to rely on the provisions in section 5 of Council Regulation (EC) No 44/2001, which (as with Article 22 of the recast Brussels Regulation), provided in relation an individual contract of employment that the employer can only bring proceedings in the courts of the Member State in which the employee is employed. The court identified the following elements:

- Contracts of employment have 'certain particularities: they create a lasting bond which brings the worker to some extent within the organizational framework of the business of the undertaking or employer, and they are linked to the place where the activities are pursued, which determines the application of mandatory rules and collective agreements.' (para 39)
- '[I]t presupposes a relationship of subordination of the employee to the employer.' (para 40)

---

[78] See Briggs, pp 152–53.

- '[F]or a certain period of time one person performs services for and under the direction of another in return for which he receives remuneration.' (para 41)
- 'With regard to the purpose ... the Regulation aims to provide the weaker parties to contracts, including contracts of employment, with enhanced protection by derogating from the general rules of jurisdiction.' (para 43)

Drawing together these strands, the CJEU concluded that it was for the national court to assess **6.104** whether Mr von Buellesheim, in his capacity as a director and manager of Holterman, performed services for and under the direction of that company in return for remuneration, whether there was a lasting bond which brought him to some extent within the organizational framework of the business, and whether in all the circumstances there was a relationship of subordination. In *Aslam & Others v Uber BV and others* (Case No. 2202550/2015, London Central Employment Tribunal), the respondent sought to place reliance on those dicta in support of an argument that Uber drivers were not to be regarded as working under an 'individual contract of employment'. The issue arose in the context of the meaning of Article 8(1) of the Rome 1 Regulation concerning the law of the contract (see paragraph 6.114 below). In particular a requirement of acting under the direction of the putative employer and having been brought within the organizational framework might have been problematic. Having held that the claimants were workers within the meaning of section 230(3)(b) ERA,[79] the employment tribunal also found that they were employed under an individual contract of employment within the meaning of Article 8 of the Rome 1 Regulation. The tribunal relied in particular on *Allonby v Accrington and Rossendale College* [2004] ICR 1328, where the ECJ had said that the term 'worker' had a Community meaning which 'cannot be interpreted restrictively',[80] and that a worker was 'a person who, for a certain period of time, performs services for and under the direction of another person in return for which he receives remuneration',[81] and 'formal classification of a self-employed person under national law does not exclude the possibility that a person must be classified as a worker ... if his independence is merely notional, thereby disguising an employment relationship.'[82] In the view of the employment tribunal the 'critical distinction for Community law purposes' (and therefore Rome 1) was that 'between the dependent worker (who was seen as meriting protection) and the independent contractor in business on his own account (who is not)'. Whether those in the former category were working under a contract of service 'or under some looser legal relationship' was 'unimportant, provided that the individual has a dependent (or "subordinate") status'. In the employment tribunal's view, the 'key question in every case is whether or not he or she is operating an independent profession or business'.[83]

The decision in the *Uber* case is likely to be the subject of an appeal. But the approach **6.105** adopted at first instance would indicate an alignment of the test for an individual contract of employment in the recast Brussels Regulation and the Rome 1 Regulation, with the test which applies for 'employment' in the context of the EqA and for worker status in section 230 ERA. However, the decision in *Allonby* was in a different context (equal pay) and also concerned with a Treaty provision which referred to 'workers' rather than 'contracts of employment'. The tribunal's approach does derive support from the emphasis (eg in *Holterman* and *Petter*) on the underlying purpose in protecting the weaker party to the contract, and it supports the expansive approach to the question of whether there is an individual contract of employment. But as yet there is a lack of authoritative guidance to that effect.

---

[79] See above paras 6.08 et seq.
[80] *Allonby* para 66.
[81] *Allonby* para 67.
[82] *Allonby* para 71.
[83] The employment tribunal referred to *Bates van Winkelhof* (see paras 6.13–6.15 above) and *Hashwani v Jivraj* [2011] ICR 1004.

6.106 Whilst the CJEU in *Holterman* placed some emphasis on subordination, as noted above (paragraph 6.15), in *Bates van Winkelhof* the Supreme Court stated that this was not a universal characteristic of being a worker under section 230 ERA, and that the specific statutory language needed to be applied. Indeed, one potential difference was suggested by the observation in *Holterman* that, whilst it was for the national court to assess the position applying the above criteria, it would be necessary to establish who had authority to issue Mr von Bullesheim with instructions and to monitor their implementation. The court noted that if his ability to influence that body was not negligible, it would be appropriate to conclude that there was no relationship of subordination. That might suggest a narrower approach than under UK law, where a director and controlling shareholder of a company may also be an employee: see, for example, *Secretary of State for Business, Enterprise and Regulatory Reform v Neufeld* [2009] ICR 1183 (CA).

(c) 'Relating to' an individual contract of employment

6.107 A separate question arises as to whether, assuming the claimant is to be treated as employed under an 'individual contract of employment', a protected disclosure claim is to be regarded as a claim 'relating to' that contract. A protected disclosure claim is in effect a statutory tort, rather than a claim of breach of contract. But the presence of a worker contract is a necessary ingredient in establishing the right to bring a claim (subject to the issue referred to above at paragraphs 6.34 and 6.35 as to whether a contract is required under section 43K(1)(a) ERA). To that end it might be thought that such a claim plainly relates to the contract of employment. We suggest that is indeed the better view. But the approach to this issue has been developing and the issue awaits clear judicial clarification.

6.108 Prior to the decision in *Alfa Laval Tumpba AB and another v Separator Spares International Ltd and others* [2013] ICR 455 (CA) a test had been applied of whether the contract of employment was of 'legal relevance' to the claim. That approach was rejected in *Alfa Laval*. Although it had not consistently been applied in this way,[84] the Court of Appeal regarded the legal relevance test as entailing a restriction to claims under the contract, which the court emphasized was not the correct approach. The court concluded that instead there should be a broad test applying the actual words by asking if the claim relates to the contract of employment. The court suggested (at para 25) that it might be helpful to ask whether the acts complained of, whether formulated in contract or not, would amount to a breach of the contract of employment. If so, the claim would relate to the individual contract of employment; and if not, it would not. Here the allegations of breach of copyright and misuse of confidential information would amount to allegations of breaches of the employment contract and as such section 5 of Council Regulation (EC) No 44/2001 applied.

6.109 The rejection of a requirement that the claim be brought under the contract cleared a path for protected disclosure claims to be regarded as relating to the contract. But an approach of focusing on whether the claims, whether or not framed in contract, would amount to a breach of contract, suggested a further complication. The employment tribunal would not ordinarily be called upon to determine if a protected disclosure claim could amount to a breach of contract. That may well be the case in most detriment claims, as victimization for making a protected disclosure is liable to entail a breach of duties of good faith and possibly the implied term of trust and confidence. But the position might be more difficult in a dismissal claim due to the exclusion of those implied terms (see Chapter 12, paragraphs 12.64 et seq). Given

---

[84] See *CEF Holdings Ltd v Mundey* [2012] IRLR 912, where the test of legal relevance was treated as encompassing all cases where the status of the employee was legally relevant to the claim rather than only covering claims under contract. That would clearly apply to protected disclosure claims, but the Court of Appeal in *Alfa Laval* nevertheless said that the line of cases including *CEF Holdings* was not to be followed since it applied the erroneous 'legal relevance' test.

that the approach in *Alfa Laval* was expressly intended to be 'comparatively easy to apply' (per Longmore LJ at para 25), it may be questioned whether such a complication was intended.

Some further light was cast on this in *Bosworth and Hurley v Arcadia Petroleum Ltd and others* **6.110** [2016] EWCA Civ 818.[85] The court emphasized that it was not necessarily sufficient if the claim could have been pleaded as a breach of the contract of employment. The correct approach is to consider whether the reality and substance of the conduct related to the employment contract (per Gross LJ at para 65). That was not the case in *Bosworth*; the conspiracy claim involved conduct amounting to a breach of contract but it would have been wrongful irrespective of the employment contract.[86] It might be argued that having regard to the underlying social purpose (providing a more favourable jurisdictional regime for employees), detriment and dismissal claims should be treated "relating to" the individual employment contract since they are concern employment rights, capable of being brought only by virtue of the worker relationship. But this would essentially entail reverting to the rejected legal relevance test as interpreted in *CEF Munday*; even if the particular conduct amounted to a breach of contract, the substance of the claim is a statutory one and could only be brought as such. The position is likely to be reviewed by the Supreme Court, permission to appeal having been given in *Bosworth*. In the meantime, if section 5 does not apply, jurisdiction would still be established under Article 7(2) of the Recast Brussels Regulation, if the detrimental act occurred in the UK.

(3) The forum: the ET Rules of Procedure 2013, rule 8

Where the respondent is not domiciled in an EU Member State or in Iceland, Norway, or **6.111** Switzerland, the domestic law in relation to jurisdiction applies. Those rules are based on where proceedings are served. Prior to the amendment of the employment tribunal rules in 2013, tribunals had a power to stay proceedings on the basis of *forum non conveniens*: see *Crofts v Cathay Pacific Airways Ltd* [2005] ICR 1436 (CA) at paras 48 and 49. The 2013 rules do not contain an express power to order a stay, but the tribunal has an implicit power to make such an order, in order to apply principles of private international law, pursuant to rule 29 of Schedule 1 to the 2013 rules: *Asda Stores Ltd v Brierley* [2016] ICR 945 (CA) at para 19. However, in *Lawson v Serco Limited* [2006] ICR 250 (HL), at para 24, Lord Hoffmann stated that it would be contrary to principle to stay an unfair dismissal claim on the grounds of *forum non conveniens* because no other tribunal has jurisdiction to hear an unfair dismissal claim under section 94 ERA. The same would seem to apply to claims under section 47B and section103A ERA. In a case not governed by the European regime, limits on the jurisdiction are instead set by rule 8 of the ET Rules of Procedure 2013[87] (in addition to the limits on the geographical scope of the legislation considered at paragraphs 6.122 et seq below).

So far as material, rule 8 provides: **6.112**

> (2) A claim may be presented in England and Wales if—
>
>> (a) the respondent, or one of the respondents, resides or carries on business in England and Wales;
>>
>> (b) one or more of the acts or omissions complained of took place in England and Wales;

---

[85] See also *Petter EMC Europe Ltd* [2015] IRLR 847 (CA), where the court focused on the substantive relationship with the contract of employment in concluding that a claim against the employer's parent company in relation to stock awards related to the contract of employment (being part of the remuneration and a means of retaining employees) and the parent company was to be regarded as an employer for these purposes.

[86] Of relevance to claims against workers and agents, Gross LJ suggested that claims between parties not in a contractual relationship could not be said to be 'matters relating to a contract'. But the court was not dealing with claims where the presence of a worker's contract was a necessary ingredient in establishing a claim.

[87] Employment Tribunals (Constitution and Rules of Procedure) Regulations 2013.

(c) the claim relates to a contract under which the work is or has been performed partly in England and Wales; or

(d) the Tribunal has jurisdiction to determine the claim by virtue of a connection with Great Britain and the connection in question is at least partly a connection with England and Wales.

(3) A claim may be presented in Scotland if—

(a) the respondent, or one of the respondents, resides or carries on business in Scotland;

(b) one or more of the acts or omissions complained of took place in Scotland;

(c) the claim relates to a contract under which the work is or has been performed partly in Scotland; or

(d) the Tribunal has jurisdiction to determine the claim by virtue of a connection with Great Britain and the connection in question is at least partly a connection with Scotland.

6.113 In addition to setting the relevant limits of territorial jurisdiction where the European regime does not apply, these provisions determine which of the rival forums of England and Wales on one hand, and Scotland on the other, shall have jurisdiction in relation to a claim. They do not expand on the territorial grasp of the relevant substantive legislation (ie ERA for whistleblowing claims), or under the recast Brussels Regulation: see *Jackson v Ghost Ltd* [2003] IRLR 824, and *Financial Times Ltd v Bishop* (EAT/0147/03). A purposive approach was applied to the construction of the predecessor of rule 8[88] to avoid it limiting the territorial grasp of legislation that would otherwise have applied. To that end, in *Pervez v Macquarie Bank Ltd (London Branch)* [2011] IRLR 284, Underhill (P) construed the test of whether the respondent was 'carrying on business' in England or Wales as being satisfied where the claimant employee was seconded there. The same issue does not arise under the 2013 Regulations, which are in less restrictive terms, in that it is sufficient if the claim relates to a contract under which the work is or has been performed partly in England or Wales (or Scotland).

(4) Applicable law

6.114 So far as the applicable law question is concerned,[89] this is determined in relation to contractual obligations by the Rome I Regulation[90] (applicable to contracts made on or after 17 December 2009[91]) and for non-contractual obligations by the Rome II Regulation[92] (with effect from 11 January 2009). Whilst the Rome I Regulation does not apply to non-contractual obligations, the rights conferred by the ERA are only applicable where there is a contract of employment or a worker. Proof of such a contract is thus a necessary step in any claim, and in relation to this the relevant provisions are contained in the Rome I Regulation.[93] The provisions most relevant to employment are as follows:

Article 3 *Freedom of choice*

1. A contract shall be governed by the law chosen by the parties. The choice shall be made expressly or clearly demonstrated by the terms of the contract or the circumstances of the

---

[88] Reg 19 of the Employment Tribunals (Rules of Procedure) Regulations 2004.

[89] For a further and more detailed analysis see Dicey, Morris, and Collins, *The Conflict of Laws* 15th edn, Chapter 9, section 9.

[90] Regulation (EC) No 593/2008 of the European Parliament and of the Council of 17 June 2008 on the law applicable to contractual obligations.

[91] The predecessor was the Rome Convention on the law applicable to Contractual Obligations 80/934/EEC (OJ 1980 L266, p 1). In *Republik Griechenland v Nikiforidis* (Case C-135/15, 18 January 2016), the CJEU concluded that the Rome I Regulation could apply to an employment contract entered into before 17 December 2009 if it was varied on or after that date, but only where the variation was of 'such magnitude that a new employment contract must be regarded as having been concluded on or after that date'.

[92] Regulation (EC) No 864/2007 on the law applicable to non-contractual obligations.

[93] See per Langstaff P in *Simpson v Intralinks* [2012] ICR 1343 at para 16, a case discussed below in para 6.102 on claims under the Sex Discrimination Act 1975 and the Equal Pay Act 1970.

case. By their choice the parties can select the law applicable to the whole or to part only of the contract.

2. The parties may at any time agree to subject the contract to a law other than that which previously governed it, whether as a result of an earlier choice made under this Article or of other provisions of this Regulation. Any change in the law to be applied that is made after the conclusion of the contract shall not prejudice its formal validity under Article 11 or adversely affect the rights of third parties.

3. Where all other elements relevant to the situation at the time of the choice are located in a country other than the country whose law has been chosen, the choice of the parties shall not prejudice the application of provisions of the law of that other country which cannot be derogated from by agreement.

4. Where all other elements relevant to the situation at the time of the choice are located in one or more Member States, the parties' choice of applicable law other than that of a Member State shall not prejudice the application of provisions of Community law, where appropriate as implemented in the Member State of the forum, which cannot be derogated from by agreement.

5. The existence and validity of the consent of the parties as to the choice of the applicable law shall be determined in accordance with the provisions of Articles 10, 11 and 13.

Article 8 *Individual employment contracts*

1. An individual employment contract[94] shall be governed by the law chosen by the parties in accordance with Article 3. Such a choice of law may not, however, have the result of depriving the employee of the protection afforded to him by provisions that cannot be derogated from by agreement under the law that, in the absence of choice, would have been applicable pursuant to paragraphs 2, 3 and 4 of this Article.

2. To the extent that the law applicable to the individual employment contract has not been chosen by the parties, the contract shall be governed by the law of the country in which or, failing that, from which the employee habitually carries out his work in performance of the contract. The country where the work is habitually carried out shall not be deemed to have changed if he is temporarily employed in another country.

3. Where the law applicable cannot be determined pursuant to paragraph 2, the contract shall be governed by the law of the country where the place of business through which the employee was engaged is situated.

4. Where it appears from the circumstances as a whole that the contract is more closely connected with a country other than that indicated in paragraphs 2 or 3, the law of that other country shall apply.

Article 9 *Overriding mandatory provisions*

1. Overriding mandatory provisions are provisions the respect for which is regarded as crucial by a country for safeguarding its public interests, such as its political, social or economic organisation, to such an extent that they are applicable to any situation falling within their scope, irrespective of the law otherwise applicable to the contract under this Regulation.

2. Nothing in this Regulation shall restrict the application of the overriding mandatory provisions of the law of the forum.

3. Effect may be given to the overriding mandatory provisions of the law of the country where the obligations arising out of the contract have to be or have been performed, in so far as those overriding mandatory provisions render the performance of the contract unlawful. In considering whether to give effect to those provisions, regard shall be had to their nature and purpose and to the consequences of their application or non-application.

---

[94] As to the meaning of an 'individual employment contract', see paras 6.100–6.110 above.

6.115 The Rome II Regulation similarly makes provision, in Article 16, for overriding mandatory provisions, in the following terms:

> Nothing in this Regulation shall restrict the application of the provisions of the law of the forum in a situation where they are mandatory irrespective of the law otherwise applicable to the non-contractual obligation.

6.116 Section 204 ERA provides expressly that for the purposes of the Act it is immaterial whether the law which governs any person's employment is UK law. As such it falls squarely within the scope of a mandatory provision within Article 16 of the Rome II Regulation. That was also the view expressed by the employment tribunal in *Aslam and others v Uber BV and others* (Case No 2202550/2015). The tribunal held that the protected disclosure provisions in the ERA amounted to 'overriding mandatory provisions' for the purposes of Article (2) of Rome I. Parties could not contract out of the relevant protections and section 204(1) ERA provided that it was immaterial whether the law which otherwise governed the relevant employment was the law of the United Kingdom or not. That, in the view of the employment tribunal, signalled the importance which Parliament had attached to the rights which it sought to guarantee. It was a 'crucial measure to safeguard public [interest]'.

The protected disclosure provisions therefore cannot be excluded by a foreign choice of law, though applicable foreign law may be relevant for constituent elements of a protected disclosure claim such as whether there is a contractual relationship between the worker and putative employer.

(5) Interrelation of territorial jurisdiction and applicable law issues

6.117 An issue as to the interrelation between territorial jurisdiction and choice of law, in the context of a choice of law clause, arose in *Simpson v Intralinks* [2012] ICR 1343 (EAT). Here the claimant brought claims under the Sex Discrimination Act 1975 (SDA) and the Equal Pay Act 1970 (EqPA). She was a German national and resident in Frankfurt. She worked for some of her time in Great Britain but mainly in Germany. Her employer was UK registered (and, accordingly, UK domiciled). Her contract was stated to be governed by the laws of the Federal Republic of Germany. There was an exclusive jurisdiction clause in her contract in favour of the Frankfurt court. Under section 10(1) of the SDA she was regarded as working at an establishment in Great Britain because she worked (at least) partly in Great Britain and not 'wholly or mainly outside Great Britain'. She was therefore within the territorial scope of that SDA and the EqPA.[95]

6.118 The employment tribunal concluded that it had no jurisdiction. The employment judge said that the parties had chosen German law to be the proper law of the contract for the purposes of Article 3.1 of the Rome Convention. For the purposes of Article 6.2 of that Convention,[96] in the absence of a choice of law clause Germany would be the country in which the claimant habitually carried on her work and so the employment contract would be governed by the law of Germany. The tribunal concluded that the claimant therefore could not rely on the provisions of the SDA and the EqPA to bring a claim in the United Kingdom courts or tribunals but had to rely upon German law.

6.119 The EAT (Langstaff P) allowed the claimant's appeal. The fundamental point was that the claimant had a choice under Article 19 of Council Regulation (EC) No 44/2001 (now replaced by

---

[95] Such claims would now lie under the Equality Act 2010 which contains no express territorial limitation but there is a similar implied limitation to that applicable in relation to the Employment Rights Act 1996: See *R (on the application of Hottak) v Secretary of State for Foreign and Commonwealth Affairs* [2016] EWCA Civ 438, [2016] IRLR 534.

[96] Article 6 of the Rome Convention was the predecessor to Article 8 of the Rome I Regulation set out at para 6.115 above. Article 6(1) of the Rome Convention is to materially the same effect as Article 8.1 of the Rome I Regulation, and Article 6(2) to materially the same effect as Articles 8.2 to 8.4 of the Rome I Regulation.

Article 21 of the recast Brussels Regulation) to sue her employer either in the country of the employer's domicile (Great Britain) or the country in which she habitually worked (Germany). It was for the claimant to choose between these forums. The Article contains no hierarchy as between those choices. The 'exclusive jurisdiction' clause was ineffective because it was agreed prior to the termination (and thus ineffective under what would now be Article 23). Article 19 (now Article 21) permitted the respondent employer to be sued in the United Kingdom.[97]

6.120 That left a further question: was the applicable law such that the employment tribunal had no jurisdiction? The applicable law was governed by the Rome Convention.[98] Article 6(2) of the Rome Convention (now Article 8.2 to 8.4 of Rome I) applied in order to determine what mandatory rules of law would apply in the absence of choice. Paragraph (2) required a court to look to the law of the country in which the employee habitually carries out his/her work in performance of the contract. The employment tribunal had found as a fact that that was Frankfurt. There was a proviso to apply a different applicable law if it appeared from the circumstances as a whole that the contract was more closely connected with another country. Langstaff P held that insight into how such a question might be resolved was given by the case law referred to in paragraph 6.122 et seq below, namely *Lawson v Serco Ltd* [2006] ICR 250 (HL), *Duncombe v Secretary of State for Children, Schools and Families (No 2)* [2011] ICR 1312 (SC), and *Ravat v Halliburton Manufacturing and Services Ltd* [2012] ICR 389 (SC). The *Lawson v Serco* line of jurisprudence should not simply be read across from the ERA, but it was 'informative, even if not decisive' (para 41). That the parties themselves agreed that German law would be the applicable law also had 'some relevance in determining the closeness of connection', albeit mediated by the fact that Article 6.2, which contained the test of being 'more closely connected with another country' followed Article 6.1 which qualified the parties freedom to choose the applicable law.

6.121 However, whilst it followed that German law applied for the purposes of construing the employment contract, or determining if there was an enforceable contract, it did not follow that this had the effect of excluding (in that case) the discrimination legislation. That would be to overlook Article 7 of the Rome Convention (now Article 9 of Rome I). That provision is concerned with all situations in which in forum A the law of a state other than that which constitutes forum A is to be applied. The EAT concluded that the provisions of the EqPA and of the SDA were mandatory provisions by definition, because they stated that they could not be derogated from by agreement. As noted above (paragraph 6.116), the same would apply to the protected disclosure provisions of the ERA. The employment tribunal may though still be called upon to determine, as a question of fact, issues of foreign law arising within such a claim, such as in relation to the proper construction of the worker contract or indeed whether there was a contractual relationship between worker and putative employer.

(6) The territorial scope of ERA, sections 47B and 103A

(a) Sufficient connection test

6.122 The question of the territorial reach of the protected disclosure legislation is a matter of statutory constructions which is distinct from and additional to the question considered above as to whether, as a matter of conflict of laws, the tribunal has territorial jurisdiction to hear a protected disclosure claim. When PIDA was enacted there were express limits to the territorial reach of the ERA. Section 196(3) ERA provided that the right to claim unfair dismissal did not apply 'to any employment where under his contract of employment the employee ordinarily works outside Great Britain'. Further, section 12 PIDA provided for the insertion of a new

---

[97] Article 21 would have the same effect on the facts of the case.
[98] See now the Rome I Regulation.

section 196(3A) into the ERA to the effect that section 47B ERA would similarly not apply to employment where under the worker's contract s/he ordinarily works outside Great Britain. However, these substantive provisions of PIDA, including section 12, had been in force for little more than three months[99] when section 196 ERA was repealed.[100] Instead, the implicit territorial scope of the legislation was left to be determined as a matter of statutory construction.[101]

6.123 In *Lawson v Serco Ltd* [2006] ICR 250 the House of Lords (Lord Hoffmann giving the only substantive speech) concluded that there are indeed implicit territorial limits to the scope of unfair dismissal legislation. In *Burke v The British Council* (UKEAT/0125/06, 14 December 2006) (at para 23) the principles to be derived from *Lawson* were summarized as involving five gateways to jurisdiction:

(a) The standard case—the employee is working in Great Britain at the time when he is dismissed, with the focus on that time rather than on the time the contract was made.

(b) The peripatetic employee—the employee's base, that is, the place where he is ordinarily working, as judged not so much by the terms of the contract but by the conduct of the parties, is in Great Britain.

(c) The expatriate (1)—the employee who works and is based abroad and who is the overseas representative, posted abroad by an employer for the purposes of a business carried on in Britain, for example foreign correspondent of the *Financial Times* (see Lord Hoffmann para 38).

(d) The expatriate (2)—the employee who works in a British enclave abroad; jurisdiction will be established provided the employee was recruited in Britain; this was the position of Mr Botham (Germany) and Mr Lawson (Ascension Island) but not of Ms Bryant (British Embassy, Rome) who was engaged in Rome.[102]

(e) The expatriate (3)—the employee who has equally strong connections as the above two with Britain and British employment law.

6.124 In relation to the first category (the standard case), the focus is on where the employee was working at the time of dismissal, rather than when the contract was first entered into. It is not sufficient if the employee happened to be in Great Britain on a working visit, however fleeting. Lord Hoffmann contrasted an employee who is really working in Great Britain with someone who is merely on a casual visit, even if working on that visit, for example in the course of peripatetic duties based elsewhere. Similarly, in *Pervez v Macquarie Bank Ltd* [2011] ICR 266, EAT, it was noted that whilst in that case the employee, who worked on secondment on a settled and indefinite basis, fell within the first category (a standard case), the position could be otherwise if the secondment was for a shorter time or the employee was less integrated into the business of the company to which he was seconded. Further, when the employee was not working at the time of dismissal, as where the employee was on sickness absence or garden leave, a broader factual enquiry is needed to determine the factual position at the time of dismissal. In *YKK Europe Ltd v Heneghan* [2010] IRLR 563, at para 56 the EAT suggested the following non-exhaustive list of relevant factors:

• why the employee was absent from work, and the length of his absence before dismissal; where the employee was ordinarily working, or based, and for how long, before his absence from work began;

• where the employee would have been working at dismissal, if he had not been absent from work; whether there was an active employment relationship between the date of his absence from work and the date of dismissal;

---

[99] The substantive PIDA provisions came into force on 2 July 1999: SI 1999/1547.
[100] By s 32 of the Employment Relations Act 1999, in force from 25 October 2009: SI 1999/2830.
[101] There remains an express provision in relation to mariners in ERA, s 199(7), (8).
[102] *Bryant v Foreign and Commonwealth Office* (EAT/174/02, 10 March 2003).

- from where the contract was being operated at dismissal; and
- whether the tribunal would have had territorial jurisdiction as at the date on which the claimant became absent from work.

Subsequent case law has considerably developed the principles laid down in *Lawson*. The **6.125** employees in *Ministry of Defence v Wallis* [2011] ICR 617 did not neatly fit into either of Lord Hoffmann's exceptional categories; they were employed wholly outside Great Britain by the Ministry of Defence in the British Section of International Schools and purely because they were spouses of members of the Armed Forces who were posted abroad. Their contracts were governed by English law and their terms and conditions were essentially English. They paid national insurance contributions. Their contracts were found by the employment judge to have sufficient connection with Great Britain to permit the tribunal to exercise jurisdiction. The EAT and the Court of Appeal (Mummery, Etherton, and Elias LJJ) agreed.

In *Duncombe v Secretary of State for Children, Schools and Families (No2)* [2011] UKSC 36; **6.126** [2011] ICR 1312 the claimants were teachers who were employed by the British Government under a contract governed by English law to work in European schools. The Supreme Court held that the tribunal could hear their claims. Baroness Hale of Richmond, giving the judgment of the court, said (para 8):

> It is therefore clear that the right will only exceptionally cover employees who are working or based abroad. The principle appears to be that the employment must have much stronger connections, both with Great Britain and with British employment law than with any other system. There is no hard and fast rule and it is a mistake to try and torture the circumstances of one employment to make it fit one of the examples given, for they are merely examples of the application of the general principle.

Developing this further, at para 16, Baroness Hale referred to the need, in expatriate cases, for the employment to have 'such an overwhelmingly closer connection with Britain and with British employment law than with any other system of law that it is right to conclude that Parliament must have intended that the employees should enjoy protection from unfair dismissal'.

In *Ravat v Halliburton Manufacturing Services Ltd* [2012] UK SC 1; [2012] ICR 389 the **6.127** Supreme Court also eschewed too rigorous an emphasis on the specific examples given by Lord Hoffmann in *Serco* in favour of a broader test. In particular a distinction emerged between 'true expatriates' and those who either partly live or work in Great Britain. In *Ravat* the claimant was employed by a company based in Aberdeen which had associated companies in the USA and Germany. He lived in Great Britain but travelled to and from his employment in Libya, working for twenty-eight days at a time. The work he did was for the German associated company. His employer paid travel costs. Salary was in sterling and paid in the UK with income tax and national insurance deducted. His employer had assured the claimant that he had UK employment rights. He was dismissed for redundancy. The Court of Session held that the tribunal had jurisdiction. The Supreme Court dismissed a further appeal. Lord Hope said that the fact that the relationship was 'rooted and forged' in Great Britain, whilst never unimportant, was not sufficient in itself to take the case out of the general rule that the place of work is determinative of jurisdiction. He continued (paras 27–29):

> I agree that the starting point needs to be more precisely defined. It is that the employment relationship must have a stronger connection with Great Britain than with the foreign country where the employee works. The general rule is that the place of employment is decisive. But it is not an absolute rule. The open-ended language of section 94(1) leaves room for some exceptions where the connection with Great Britain is sufficiently strong to show that this can be justified. The case of the peripatetic employee who is based in Great Britain is one example. The expatriate employee, all of whose service is performed abroad, but who had nevertheless very close connections with Great Britain because of the nature and circumstances of employment, is another.

It will always be a question of fact and degree as to whether the connection is sufficiently strong to overcome the general rule that the place of employment is decisive. The case of those who are truly expatriate because they not only work but also live outside of Great Britain requires an especially strong connection with Great Britain and British employment law before an exception can be made for them.

But it does not follow that the connection that must be shown in the case of those who are not truly expatriate because they are not both living and working overseas must achieve the high standard that would enable one to say that their case was exceptional. The question whether on given facts the case falls within the scope of section 94(1) is a question of law, but it is also a question of degree. … The question of law is whether section 94(1) applies to this particular employment. The question of fact is whether the connection between the circumstances of the employment in Great Britain and British employment law was sufficiently strong to enable it to be said that it would be appropriate for the employee to have a claim for unfair dismissal in Great Britain.

In para 32 he summarized the test as follows:

The question whether the tribunal has jurisdiction will always depend on whether it can be held that Parliament can reasonably be taken to have intended that an employee in the claimant's position should have the right to take his claim to the employment tribunal.

6.128 A further refinement was identified in *Bates van Winkelhof v Clyde and Co* [2012] IRLR 992, in which Elias LJ, at para 98, contrasted a case where an employee was employed wholly abroad, with one where a claimant lived and/or worked for at least part of the time in Great Britain. In the former case there is a strong connection with the jurisdiction abroad, and Parliament can be assumed to have intended in the usual case that that jurisdiction, rather than that of Great Britain, should provide the appropriate system of law. In such circumstances it is necessary to identify factors which are sufficiently powerful to displace the territorial pull of the place of work abroad. That entails a comparative exercise between factors pointing towards a connection with Great Britain compared to factors pointing to another jurisdiction. By contrast, that is not necessary in the second case (where the claimant lived and/or worked for at least part of the time in Great Britain), since the territorial attraction is:

… far from being all one way, and the circumstances need not be truly exceptional before the connection with the system of law in Great Britain be identified. All that is required is that the tribunal should satisfy itself that the connection is, to use Lord Hope DPSC's words:[103] 'Sufficiently strong to enable it to be said that Parliament would have regarded it as appropriate for the tribunal to deal with the claim.'

6.129 As explained in *CreditSights Ltd v Dhunna* [2014] EWCA Civ 1238, [2014] IRLR 953, [2015] ICR 105, at para 40, where a comparative exercise is required, it is not as to the relative merits of competing systems of law. As it was put by Rimer LJ (at para 40, and with whom the other members of the Court of Appeal agreed):

The object of the exercise is simply to decide whether an employee is able to except himself from the general rule by demonstrating that he has sufficiently strong connections with Great Britain and British employment law.

6.130 To similar effect, in a passage cited with approval in *Dhunna* (at para 34), in *Powell v OMV Exploration and Production Ltd* [2014] IRLR 80, the EAT (at para 51) explained that:

The starting point which must not be forgotten in applying the substantial connection test is that the statute will have no application to work outside the United Kingdom. Parliament

---

103 In *Ravat* at para 29.

would not have intended that unless there were a sufficiently strong connection. 'Sufficiently' has to be understood as sufficient to displace that which would otherwise be the position.

Further, where an employee is autonomous, and able to negotiate his own contract as at least **6.131** an equal party without any pressure being placed upon him, the free choice of law and jurisdiction which would apply, and hence that which would not, should in general be respected.[104] Where the choice is of English law, that is not of itself sufficient to establish a sufficient connection with the UK. But taken together with other factors, it is liable to be an important consideration, as illustrated by the decision in *Jeffery v The British Council* [2016] IRLR 935 (EAT). Amongst the various claims brought by the claimant were those of protected disclosure detriment and dismissal (based on constructive dismissal), though it was accepted that the same principles applied to these as to ordinary unfair dismissal claims (as to which see 6.134 et seq below). The EAT described his situation at the time of his resignation as being 'truly expatriate'—he worked and lived abroad in Bangladesh at the time of his resignation claiming constructive dismissal. The employer was a public corporation established by Royal Charter, which described itself as the UK's 'international organization for cultural relations and educational opportunities'. Its staff were not government employees. As part of its work it ran teaching centres in many parts of the world. The claimant was a UK citizen, recruited in the UK, but since his engagement in 1994 he had almost always worked abroad within teaching centres. He did not ordinarily live or have a home in the UK, though he owned properties there which he let, and he hoped to retire there. His employment contract provided that it was subject to the laws of England and Wales, and he was entitled to membership of the Civil Service Pension Scheme. From August 2012 he was a teaching centre manager in Bangladesh. He ultimately resigned in protest at a decision to close that teaching centre, albeit after that decision was reversed. At first instance the employment judge concluded that the tribunal did not have jurisdiction. But that conclusion was reversed on appeal.

The EAT noted that, given the claimant was 'truly expatriate', applying the approach in *Bates* **6.132** *van Winkelhof*, it was necessary for him to show an especially strong connection with Great Britain and British employment law, or as it was put in *Duncombe*, an overwhelmingly closer connection with Britain and British employment law, in order to establish that the tribunal had jurisdiction. The EAT (HHJ Richardson) also noted that (as explained in *Ravat* at para 27 per Lord Hope) it was not sufficient that an expatriate employee is a UK citizen and recruited in the UK by a British company, though these factors would 'never be unimportant'. HHJ Richardson also noted that in *Dhunna* (at para 43) Rimer LJ had said that the fact that English law applied was 'not compelling'. But this was taken to mean that it could not on its own compel the conclusion that territorial jurisdiction was established. He noted that it would always be significant if a contract was governed by English law as it would bear on the connection with British employment law and, as explained by Lady Hale in *Duncombe* (at para 16), it would be relevant to the expectation of each party as to the protection which the parties would enjoy.

The EAT accepted that the claimant had established an overwhelmingly closer connection **6.133** with Great Britain and with British employment law than any other system. It was important, though not sufficient, that he was a UK citizen recruited in the UK to work for a UK organization, and the contract provided that English law applied. But on top of that (a) he was entitled to a Civil Service pension, granted by a UK Act of Parliament; (b) his salary was subject to a notional deduction for UK income tax; and (c) the nature of the respondent was important—it described itself as a 'non departmental public body' and belonged to a list of organisations which, whilst not directly part of government, were recognized as playing such a part in the life of the nation that there was a right afforded to a Civil Service pension.

---

[104] *Olsen v Gearbulk Services Ltd and another* (2015) UKEAT/0345/14, [2015] IRLR 818, at para 43.

Conversely, there was very little to establish any connection with Bangladeshi employment law and the stay in Bangladesh was always intended to be short term. Although the claimant worked in a business carried on in Bangladesh (ie the teaching centre) which was managed locally, it was not a profit-making business, and was part of the operation of the respondent (a UK charity and public body), and was part of a broader operation intended to be the UK's international organization for cultural relations and educational opportunities. A further factor was that the claimant's contract said that he was subject to the Official Secrets Act 1989. In fact it had limited application to him, but the reference to it in his contract drew his attention to the fact that even when serving abroad, as a British citizen working for a public body he might come within its scope. However, the EAT did not consider it necessary to rely on this factor in order to reach its conclusion that this was an exceptional case where there was an overwhelmingly stronger connection with Britain and British law.

(b) Do different principles apply in whistleblowing cases?

6.134 Can it be argued that different principles should apply to claims under section 47B ERA, or that the test for whistleblowing dismissals is different to that for ordinary unfair dismissal? Arguments to that effect have not so far met with success. In *Serco* it was only the scope of the unfair dismissal right that was directly under consideration.[105] Lord Hoffmann did comment (at para 38) that there was no reason why all the various rights included in the ERA should have the same territorial scope. However, Lord Hoffmann also noted that uniformity of application would be desirable in the interests of simplicity.

6.135 In *Olsen v Gearbulk Services Ltd and another* [2015] IRLR 818 Langstaff J accepted that it might be that the nature of the employment law right being asserted was 'also of significance' to the issue of whether the ET had jurisdiction and that when considering the analogous question of jurisdiction which arose under EqA there might be

> a stronger case for supposing that Parliament intended peripatetic workers with an international role in a global business to be governed by the law which they had agreed to adopt as to their contract, and, hence, dismissal from contract, and therefore those rights which related centrally to the contract, as opposed to matters which more obviously involve the assertion of a fundamental civil wrong, in which society more generally has an interest, such as the elimination of discrimination.

However, though it might have been thought that whistleblowing claims also related to a fundamental civil wrong, Langstaff J also held that the *Lawson* test was the correct one to apply to Mr Olsen's whistleblowing claims. On that basis he upheld the ET's decision that it could not entertain those claims.

6.136 In *Smania v Standard Chartered Bank* [2015] ICR 436 (EAT), Mr Smania, who was employed by the respondent bank, made allegations of financial malpractice. He was subsequently dismissed. Mr Smania was Italian. He lived and worked in Singapore. The contract under which he worked was subject to Singaporean law. The only connection with the United Kingdom was that the case concerned a UK bank headquartered in London. Mr Smania accepted that if his claim had been one of 'ordinary' unfair dismissal he could not meet the *Serco* test. He unsuccessfully contended in the ET that a more generous test should apply in the case of a whistleblower. Mr Smania's appeal to the EAT was dismissed. The EAT (Langstaff J (President)) accepted that in principle it was possible for some rights secured by the ERA to have wider territorial application than others. But this required a reasoned basis, and no adequate basis for this had been shown in relation to the whistleblowing provisions.

---

[105] Directive 96/71/EC of the European Parliament and of the Council of 16 December 1996 concerning the posting of workers in the framework of the provision of services (OJ 1997 L18/1).

Langstaff J rejected the contention that, given the importance of the banking sector, a differ- **6.137** ent and wider approach should be taken when considering the territorial scope of protection. In this respect he drew a distinction between the construction of the legislation as to the test for its territorial grasp, and the application of that test. The words of the legislation could not be interpreted as having a different meaning for one sector alone. Nor was there any distinction between different types of disclosures, or based on whether it concerned an activity that was subject to regulation in the UK. That approach did, however, leave open scope for arguments that in applying the sufficient connection test, it may be relevant to argue that the subject matter of the disclosure was of particular public interest in the UK. As Langstaff J put it (at paras 38 and 39):

> I accept that there may be scope for distinguishing between disclosures only of interest to the public local to where they are made, and those which if true may be of considerable interest to the public within the United Kingdom, when applying the same test to determine whether the statute has extraterritorial effect: but the approach of purposive construction is the approach taken in order to assist in identifying what that test is, not in considering its application to the facts of a particular case. No question as to the proper test arises when the process is not one of identifying, by construction, what that test is, but rather is the process of applying that test to different circumstances. Applying a test appropriately to the circumstances must not be confused with construing the statute purposively: there is one statute, with one meaning (whatever the appropriate construction is), though there are many circumstances to which that construction may then apply, which inevitably will differ.
>
> Mr Milsom's arguments may be good ones—if the test properly to be applied permits this—when deciding whether in the particular circumstances of a given case the statute has extraterritorial reach: but this is a process of application of a given test, and (if adopting a purposive approach) Parliament's intention is relevant only to deciding what the test should be, not in determining its application in any particular case.

Langstaff J also rejected a submission that the ET should have applied the approach taken in **6.138** *Bleuse v MBT Transport Limited* [2008] IRLR 264 (EAT)[106] to protect the right to freedom of expression guaranteed by Article 10 ECHR as part of UK law and through the EU Charter (Article 11 of which adopted Article 10 ECHR). As to this, Langstaff J noted that neither the ECHR nor EU law applied in Singapore; nor did the claim involve a directly effective right. The decision therefore left open arguments that may arise in the event of a claim where the extra-territorial effect concerns another EU Member State.

So far as concerned detriment claims, Langstaff J concluded that the test was no less stringent **6.139** than that applicable for claims of unfair dismissal by reason of a protected disclosure. As he explained (at para 43):

> The rights are to some extent distinct, but in practical terms the most serious of all detriments in the employment context is that of suffering dismissal. It is more likely that the threat of dismissal for making an unwelcome disclosure exerts a chilling effect on potential whistle-blowers than that the threat of a lesser detriment does. I would therefore hold that, albeit the rights are distinct, no less stringent a test should apply when asking whether a claim to have suffered detriment short of dismissal is within the scope of the 1996 Act as applies when asking whether a claim to have been unfairly dismissed because of the disclosure is covered.

---

[106] In *Bleuse* the EAT held that the ET had jurisdiction in respect of a claim by a German national who was a lorry driver employed primarily in Germany and Austria (and never in the UK) under the Working Time Regulation. This was because it was necessary to give full effect to the Working Time Directive. A combination of the choice of English law to govern the contract, and the need to ensure that rights conferred by EU law was properly given effect to confer jurisdiction. The correctness of *Bleuse* remains to be tested in a higher court and some doubt was implicit in Lady Hale's judgment in *Secretary of State for Children, Schools and Families v Fletcher* [2011] UKSC 14, [2011] IRLR 498, [2011] ICR 495.

6.140 In this respect, the conclusion was consistent with the general direction of travel, which has been to apply the same test to all employment rights whatever their statutory source. Thus in *R (on the application of Hottak) v Secretary of State for Foreign and Commonwealth Affairs* [2016] EWCA Civ 438, [2016] IRLR 534 the Court of Appeal upheld the judgment of the Divisional Court that the principles applicable to claims for unfair dismissal by employees engaged abroad, as explained in the authorities referred to above, provide the relevant guidance for cases brought under the EqA. Although short-lived, the provisions inserted by PIDA, section 12 (excluding protection against detriment where the worker ordinarily worked outside Britain) may also be regarded as showing a legislative intention that the territorial scope of the right to be protected from victimization for whistleblowing would be the same as for unfair dismissal.

6.141 A submission that there should be a different test for territorial grasp in whistleblowing dismissal cases was again rejected by the EAT in *Fuller v United Healthcare Services Inc & Anor* (UKEAT 0464/13/0409, 4 September 2014). Here the claimant was a US citizen, employed by a US company and paid in US dollars. He travelled extensively for his work, and undertook an international assignment which involved his working in London for about half of his time. Whilst there he lived in accommodation rented for him by the respondent, though he also retained his home in Texas. He was informed of the termination of his assignment to London during a telephone call whilst he was in the USA. The assignment therefore ended before the employment ended, as he was effectively recalled to the USA, and then subsequently dismissed when no suitable post could be found. The employment judge found that overwhelmingly the strongest connection, both in the deliberate intention of the parties as expressed in the contract (which referred to a base in the US) and in where in fact the claimant worked, was with the USA, and that there was not a sufficiently strong connection with the UK, and UK employment law, to fall within the grasp of unfair dismissal protection. The contractual position had not been overtaken by events when the claimant took up the assignment in the UK. The employment judge found that the claimant had not moved to the UK and given up his base in the USA, despite carrying out some work in the UK and in other countries. Further, he had been dismissed in the USA. The EAT upheld the employment judge's assessment. It accepted that, in essence, the employment relationship was overwhelmingly American in nature and that the work carried out in the UK did not alter that, and there was no reason to apply a different test for section 103A ERA.[107]

6.142 As noted above, *Smania* was concerned with a claimant who was a Singapore resident, who worked and paid tax in Singapore, and with respect to events in Singapore. *Fuller* similarly concerned a non-EU resident and a dismissal in the USA. As such the decisions left over an issue as to whether reliance might be placed on Article 10 of the ECHR where the act of detriment or dismissal occurred in the UK (albeit in relation to a worker resident and ordinarily working abroad) or where detriment or dismissal concerned a worker in another EU Member State. Nor did the EAT rule out taking into account the nature of the protected disclosure or detriment in applying the sufficient connection test. We suggest that one respect in which Article 10 may be of significance, notwithstanding the decisions in *Smania* and *Fuller*, is where the detrimental act takes place whilst the worker is in the UK. In those circumstances, even though the worker lives and ordinarily works abroad, an argument might proceed on the following lines:

1. Where a worker is subjected to a detriment or dismissal for making a protected disclosure, a failure to provide an effective remedy may amount to an infringement of the freedom of

---

[107] See also *Strickland v Kier Ltd and others* (UKEAT/0062/15/DM, 23 September 2015), where the EAT (in the context of a claimant who worked in Dubai and Saudi Arabia) followed *Smania* and *Fuller* to the effect that in relation to territorial grasp there is no wider test for whistleblowers than for ordinary unfair dismissal.

expression rights under Article 10 ECHR. This may be so even where the employer is not a public authority on the basis of the state's obligation to provide freedom of expression: see *Heinisch v Germany* (Application No 28274/08, 21 July 2011), ECtHR, and the line of cases following that decision, discussed further in Chapter 18.

2. The PIDA-inserted provisions of ERA are the domestic means by which freedom of expression rights in relation to protected disclosures are protected. Accordingly, so as to provide an effective remedy and to comply with the positive obligations on the state to secure the protection of Convention rights (where within the territorial scope of HRA and Article 10), insofar as ERA permits of such a construction, the territorial scope of those provisions (ERA, sections 47B, 103A, and 105) should be construed so as to be no less wide than the territorial scope of the HRA.

3. The territorial scope of the obligations under HRA is coextensive with Article 1 of the Convention, which imposes an obligation on Member States to 'secure to everyone within their jurisdiction the rights and freedoms' in the Convention. Other than in exceptional circumstances where there may be extraterritorial reach, this imposes an obligation on members states to secure the Convention rights within their territory: see *R (Al-Skeina) v Secretary of State for Defence* [2007] UKHL 26, [2008] 1 AC 153; *Bankovic v Belgium* (2001) 11 BHRC 435, ECtHR; and *Ismail v Secretary of State for the Home Department* [2016] 1 WLR 2814 (SC) at paras 32–35. As it was put in *Ismail* (at para 32):

   It is well settled … that a person who is physically present in a country which has acceded to the Convention is entitled to the protections enshrined in the Convention. Moreover, such a person may invoke his or her rights where the actions of the Member State would expose them to consequences in a non-contracting foreign state which would amount to a violation of Convention rights.

4. That would suggest that no assistance is to be gained from reference to Article 10 in relation to acts or failures to act whilst abroad. But it can be argued that the position is otherwise where the act or failure to act takes place in the United Kingdom, notwithstanding that, on a *Serco* analysis, the act may be unprotected (for example where it occurs on a casual visit to the United Kingdom by an employee working abroad).

5. Following the approach in *Smania*, there is no need in such a situation to depart from the test of whether there is a sufficiently strong connection to the UK. Indeed, the approach in *Bates van Winkelhof* illustrates the extent to which that test is sufficiently flexible to take into account the different circumstances in which it may be applied. There is ample scope for a tribunal to conclude that there is a sufficiently strong connection in circumstances where the detrimental act occurs in the UK and, as such, whistleblowing protection is required so as to comply with the obligation to secure Article 10 rights for those within the jurisdiction. Further, the principle of effectiveness is of relevance, since Article 13 of the European Convention imposes an obligation to afford everyone whose rights and freedoms in the Convention are violated 'an effective remedy before a national authority': see eg *R (Al-Skeini) v Secretary of State for Defence* (above) at paras 147–49, per Lord Brown.

This line of argument may be of particular significance in relation to a worker who ordinar-   **6.143**
ily works outside the United Kingdom, but is subjected to an act of victimization within the United Kingdom. The position may be illustrated by the following example. Assume a worker is engaged by a UK company to provide security services in Iraq. The worker raises concerns to his employer as to backhanders and other corruption relating to security contracts. The concerns amount to protected disclosures. He returns to the United Kingdom during two weeks' holiday leave. Whilst in the United Kingdom, by way of reprisal for making the protected disclosures, the employee is notified that he is to receive no bonus and is asked to resign. When he fails to do so he is dismissed by reason of the protected disclosures.

Applying *Serco* principles, there could be no claim even though the actions amounting to detriment (cancellation of the bonus) and the dismissal both occurred in the United Kingdom. But, it might be argued, the positive obligation to protect freedom of expression rights is engaged in such circumstances. Since the victimization occurred in the United Kingdom, it can be argued that the obligation to secure the protection of rights under Article 10 arises, being within the territorial scope of HRA, and that there would not be an effective remedy for breach of the Article 10 right unless the territorial scope of sections 47B and 103A was construed so as to permit the claim to be brought. That said, separate consideration may need to be given to territorial jurisdiction of the tribunal. That would not be a problem if the respondent was domiciled in the UK, and nor would it be a bar if domiciled outside the EU. But there would be no jurisdiction if the employer was domiciled in another Member State and the employee habitually worked outside the UK: see *Powell v OMV Exploration & Production Ltd* [2014] ICR 63 (EAT).

7

THE RIGHT NOT TO SUFFER DETRIMENT

A. ERA, Section 47B: Overview

Protection against detriment on grounds of a protected disclosure is provided by section 47B **7.01** ERA. Prior to amendment by the Enterprise and Regulatory Reform Act 2013 (ERRA), the legislation provided only for claims to be brought against the worker's employer. Those claims were and continue to be provided for in section 47B(1):

> A worker has the right not to be subjected to any detriment by any act, or any deliberate failure to act, by his employer done on the ground that the worker has made a protected disclosure.

7.02   The ERRA introduced a major extension to the scope of protection which applies in relation to qualifying disclosures made on or after 25 June 2013. In summary it now enables claims to be made of detriment by a worker against:

(1)   the worker's co-workers; or
(2)   an agent of the worker's employer; or
(3)   the employer as being vicariously liable for a co-worker or an agent.

These provisions, together with associated defences, are set out in section 47B(1A) to (1E) ERA and are considered in detail in Chapter 8. They do not apply to claims of dismissal by an employee.

7.03   The correct approach to the application of section 47B was explained by the EAT in *London Borough of Harrow v Knight* [2003] IRLR 140.[1] The EAT said that once the making of one or more protected disclosures had been established there were three steps:

(1)   Has the worker suffered an identifiable detriment or detriments?
(2)   Has there been an act or deliberate failure to act by the respondent by which the worker has been subjected to the identified detriment or detriments? This focuses on the link between the detriment and the act or omission.
(3)   Was the act or deliberate failure to act 'done on the ground that' the worker made the protected disclosure or disclosures? This focuses on the reason for the act or omission.

7.04   Subsequently, in *Pinnington v Swansea City Council and another* [2004] EWCA Civ 135, [2005] ICR 685 at para 27 Mummery LJ identified four elements of the cause of action under section 47B (once the making of a protected disclosure was established):

> It is a necessary ingredient of her cause of action under section 47B(1), first, that she was subjected to 'detriment,' secondly, she was subjected to detriment 'by any act, or any deliberate failure to act,' and, thirdly, that it was by the employer, and, fourthly, that it was on the ground that 'the worker has made a protected disclosure'.

7.05   The four-step approach in *Pinnington* separates out two issues implicit in the second step of the *Harrow v Knight* approach.

7.06   Section 49(2) sets out a provision marking the boundary between detriment and unfair dismissal claims in the following terms:

> (2)   This section does not apply where—
>   (a)   the worker is an employee, and
>   (b)   the detriment in question amounts to dismissal (within the meaning of Part X [ERA]).[2]

7.07   Employee dismissal claims can therefore only be brought under section 103A and/or 105(6A) ERA. The unfair dismissal and detriment regimes are intended to be complementary. Compensation awarded under Part X ERA is limited to compensation for loss sustained in consequence of the dismissal (section 49(7) ERA). It will not include compensation for loss

---

[1]   See to similar effect, in a post-ERRA decision, *Vairea v Reed Business Information Ltd* (UKEAT/0177/15/BA, 3 June 2016) at para 71.

[2]   Section 47B(2) was amended by the Employment Relations Act 1999 to reflect the repeal of provisions for contracting out of unfair dismissal protection in relation to fixed-term contracts. As originally enacted subsection (2) made provision that where an employee was on a fixed-term contract of more than one year and had agreed in accordance with the then section 197 ERA to waive any claim for unfair dismissal if the contract was not renewed, the employee could bring a claim under section 47B that his/her contract was not renewed because s/he had made a protected disclosure.

sustained prior to the dismissal. Claims by an employee in respect of dismissal are considered in Chapter 9.

There is no reason why an employee cannot claim both in respect of victimization before **7.08** dismissal and in respect of the dismissal itself, and indeed this is often done.[3] The relationship between a section 47B claim and a section 103A claim was considered by the Court of Appeal in *Melia v Magna Kansei Ltd* [2005] EWCA Civ 1547, [2006] IRLR 117 and touched on briefly by Langstaff P in the EAT in *Romanowska v Aspirations Care Ltd* (UKEAT/0015/14/SM, 25 June 2014), and we deal with those cases and that relationship in Chapter 9 at paragraphs 9.13–9.17.

There is no qualifying period or age limit for protection under section 47B. **7.09**

B. Deployment of the Pre-existing Models of Protection

Prior to PIDA, Part V of the ERA provided a set of categories in which employees, and in **7.10** some cases workers, had a right not to suffer detriment. The addition of protection in relation to the making of protected disclosures has been part of a trend towards substantially expanding the categories in which protection against detriment applies. When the ERA was enacted the protection encompassed employees who had been designated to carry out health and safety duties or were members of health and safety committees (section 44), those who declined to work on a Sunday (section 45), trustees of occupational pension schemes (section 46), and employee representatives (section 47). In addition to the protected disclosure provisions it has now been expanded to include victimization in relation to jury service (section 43M), working time (section 45A), employees exercising the right to time off work for study or training (section 47A), leave for family and domestic reasons (section 47C), tax credits (section 47D), flexible working (section 47E), study and training (section 47F), and employee shareholder status (47G). For each of the categories of protection in Part V, section 48 sets out common provisions in relation to enforcement and section 49 sets out common provisions for remedies, subject to specific provision in relation to compensation in protected disclosure dismissal cases covered by section 103A.

The original model for this mechanism was the forerunner of what is now section 146 of **7.11** the Trade Union and Labour Relations (Consolidation) Act 1992 (TULRCA). The formula initially used in that context gave employees the right not to have 'action short of dismissal' taken against them for the purposes of preventing or deterring them from being or seeking to become a member of an independent trade union, or penalizing them for so doing. However, in ERA Part V the protection is instead framed as the 'right not to be subjected to any detriment as an individual by any act, or any deliberate failure to act' on specified grounds, including on the ground that the worker has made a protected disclosure. Section 146 of TULRCA[4] itself has been amended to adopt this formula following the decision in *Associated Newspapers Ltd v Wilson; Associated British Ports v Palmer* [1995] ICR 406 (HL), to the effect that the previous formula did not cover omissions.

To some extent, therefore, helpful guidance as to the approach to section 47B ERA, and **7.12** the enforcement and remedy provisions, can be drawn from cases in the other categories

---

[3] A claim of unfair dismissal, including for automatically unfair dismissal contrary to s103A ERA can be heard by an employment judge sitting alone. However if the claimant's claim includes a claim of detriment contrary to s 48 ERA it will have to be heard by an employment judge sitting with members: this is the effect of the Employment Tribunals Act 1996 s 4.

[4] As amended by Sch 2 to the Employment Relations Act 1999.

of protection in ERA, Part V, and in section 146 TULRCA. This is, however, subject to two qualifications. First, the phrase 'action short of dismissal', formerly found in the old section 146, was an inadequate description of the entitlement under ERA, section 47B in two important respects. It did not cover deliberate omissions to act, and also carried the implication that the focus was only on events up to but not including dismissal itself. As we shall see, section 47B entitlement also covers post-termination detriment. The second qualification in relation to cases under TULRCA, section 146 is that the worker's right not to be subjected to any detriment under that provision is limited to situations where the employer's act, or deliberate failure to act, was for the 'sole or main purpose' of preventing, etc the worker's union activities. Under section 47B it is sufficient that the whistleblowing is a material influence (ie a 'more than trivial' influence) on the act which causes the detriment. See paragraph 7.69 et seq, below.

7.13 In addition, guidance as to the meaning of ERA, section 47B is to be drawn from long-standing anti-discrimination legislation. The Equality Act 2010 (section 39(2)(c), (d)), in keeping with its predecessor discrimination legislation,[5] provides that it is unlawful to discriminate by dismissing an employee or 'subjecting him to any other detriment'.

C. Meaning of 'Detriment'

(1) The general approach

7.14 'Detriment' is not defined in the ERA (nor in the Equality Act 2010 or the predecessor discrimination legislation where it also featured). Guidance as to its meaning has largely been developed in the context of discrimination legislation, but several decisions have confirmed the applicability of that guidance to the protected disclosure context: see *Coats v Strathclyde Fire Board* (EATS/0022/09/BI, 3 November 2009) at paras 22 and 28; *Korashi v Abertawe Bro Morgannwg University Local Health Board* [2012] IRLR 4 at para 69; *Woodward v Abbey National plc (No. 1)* [2006] EWCA Civ 822, [2006] IRLR 677 (per Ward LJ at para 59); *Blackbay Ventures Ltd (t/a Chemistree) v Gahir* [2014] IRLR 416, paras 84–86; *Vairea v Reed Business Information Ltd* (UKEAT/017/15/BA, 3 June 2016) at paras 14 and 71. As Ward LJ explained in *Woodward* at para 59 (giving the only substantive judgment of the Court):

> the context [of discrimination and protected disclosures] is not different. Victimisation is established by showing inter alia the discrimination of the employee by 'subjecting him to any other detriment'—see section 6(2) of the Sex Discrimination Act 1975 and section 4(2) of the Race Relations Act 1976 and the Disability Discrimination Act 1995. Under section 47B of the Employment Rights Act 1996 a worker likewise has the right 'not to be subjected to any detriment'. Although the language and the framework might be slightly different, it seems to me that the four Acts are dealing with the same concept, namely, protecting the employee from detriment being done to him in retaliation for his or her sex, race, disability or whistle-blowing. . . . All four Acts are, therefore, dealing with victimisation in one form or another. If the common theme is victimisation, it would be odd indeed if the same sort of act could be victimisation for one purpose, but not for the other.

7.15 In *Moyhing v Barts and London NHS Trust* [2006] IRLR 860 (EAT), Elias J set out a helpful synthesis of relevant principles, drawing on the guidance in two House of Lords decisions, *Chief Constable of West Yorkshire Police v Khan* [2001] UKHL 48, [2001] ICR 1065 and

---

[5] eg the Sex Discrimination Act 1975 (section 6(2)) and the Race Relations Act 1976 (section 4(2)).

Shamoon v Chief Constable of Royal Ulster Constabulary [2003] UKHL 11, [2003] ICR 337, as follows:

> 15. ... In *Chief Constable of West Yorkshire Police v Khan* [2001] UKHL 48, [2001] ICR 1065, a case of victimisation discrimination, Lord Hoffmann observed (para 53):
>
>> '... bearing in mind that the employment tribunal has jurisdiction to award compensation for injured feelings, the courts have given the concept of the term "detriment" a wide meaning. In *Ministry of Defence v Jeremiah* [1980] ICR 13, 31 Brightman LJ said that "a detriment exists if a reasonable worker would or might take the view that the [treatment] was in all the circumstances to his detriment". Mr Khan plainly did take that view ... and I do not think that, in his state of knowledge at the time, he can be said to have been unreasonable.'
>
> 16. A similarly broad analysis was adopted in *Shamoon v Chief Constable of Royal Ulster Constabulary* [2003] UKHL 11, [2003] ICR 337. The Northern Ireland Court of Appeal in that case had held, following a decision of the EAT in *Lord Chancellor v Coker* [2001] ICR 507, that in order for there to be a detriment there had to be some physical or economic consequence arising as a result of the discrimination which was material and substantial. The House of Lords rejected that approach. Lord Hope said this (at paras 34–35):
>
>> '... The word "detriment" draws this limitation on its broad and ordinary meaning from its context and from the words with which it is associated. *Res noscitur a sociis*. As May LJ put it in *De Souza v Automobile Association* [1986] ICR 514, 522G, the court or Tribunal must find that by reason of the act or acts complained of a reasonable worker would or might take the view that he had thereby been disadvantaged in the circumstances in which he had thereafter to work.
>>
>> 'But once this requirement is satisfied, the only limitation that can be read into the word is that indicated by Brightman LJ. As he put it in *Ministry of Defence v Jeremiah* [1980] ICR 13, 30, one must take all the circumstances into account. This is a test of materiality. Is the treatment of such a kind that a reasonable worker would or might take the view that in all circumstances it was to his detriment? An unjustified sense of grievance cannot amount to "detriment": *Barclays Bank plc v Kapur (No 2)* [1995] IRLR 87. But contrary to the view that was expressed in *Lord Chancellor v Coker* [2001] ICR 507 on which the Court of Appeal relied, it is not necessary to demonstrate some physical or economic consequence.'
>
> 17. Lord Hutton (at para 91) and Lord Scott (at paras 103–105) both expressly approved this analysis. Lord Scott said that 'if the victim's opinion that the treatment was to his or her detriment was a reasonable one to hold, that ought ... to suffice'.

Elias LJ (with whom Floyd and Sullivan LJJ expressed agreement) revisited this area in *Deer v University of Oxford* [2015] IRLR 481, noting (at para 25) that: **7.16**

> The concept of detriment is determined from the point of view of the claimant: a detriment exists if a reasonable person would or might take the view that the employer's conduct had in all the circumstances been to her detriment; but an unjustified sense of grievance cannot amount to a detriment: see *Derbyshire v St Helens Metropolitan Borough Council (Equal Opportunities Commission intervening)* [2007] ICR 841, para 37 per Baroness Hale of Richmond reciting earlier authorities.

As these decisions make clear, 'detriment' has a wide meaning. A detriment exists if a reasonable worker would or might take the view that the treatment was, in all the circumstances, to his detriment. It is not necessary for there to be some physical or economic consequence arising as a result of the discrimination which was material and substantial. This is a test of materiality, taking into account all the circumstances but from the perspective of the worker bringing the complaint. **7.17**

7.18 The limitation identified by Lord Hope in *Shamoon* at paras 34–35, that the detriment must arise in the employment field, does not mean that the detriment must be imposed *during* employment: see *Woodward*. Similarly, although Lord Hope in *Shamoon* made reference to detriment involving the worker being 'disadvantaged in the circumstances in which he had thereafter to work', this is properly to be regarded as only one example of a detriment. It also encompasses a detriment imposed by the employer *after* the employment has terminated, such as in relation to the provision of a reference. We consider below in more detail the implications of the decision in *Woodward*, and the scope of the limitation to detriment in the employment field, both (a) in relation to the post-termination of employment protection and (b) in relation to detriments covered during the employment relationship.

7.19 In *De Souza v Automobile Association* [1986] ICR 514 at 524G, the Court of Appeal held that there would only be a detriment if the employee was disadvantaged and a reasonable employee would consider s/he was disadvantaged. The test is an objective one by reference to a reasonable person in the shoes of the particular worker. However, what has to be considered is the impact of the act or omission from the employee's point of view. This point was made by the EAT in considering how to apply *Shamoon* in the context of whether a 'substantial change' was to the 'material detriment' of an employee under regulation 4(9) of the Transfer of Undertakings (Protection of Employment) Regulations 2006 (SI 2006/246) (TUPE) in *Tapere v South London & Maudsley NHS Trust* [2009] ICR 1563 at para 54. In that case the change of location of employment on transfer meant potential disruption to childcare arrangements and a longer journey or an altered journey, involving travelling on the M25, which the employee did not find attractive. The EAT held that the questions that ought to have been asked were whether the employee regarded those factors as detrimental and, if so, whether that was a reasonable position for the employee to adopt. In determining the matter by weighing the employee's position against that of the employer and deciding that the employer's position was reasonable, the employment tribunal had looked at the matter from the wrong standpoint and thus misdirected itself as to the correct approach to regulation 4(9).[6] It follows that if a worker is the subject of banter for having made a protected disclosure then, notwithstanding that a hypothetical reasonable worker might find the banter offensive, there would not be a detriment if the particular worker was not at all bothered by it. The perspective of the particular worker is highly material to whether the act is detrimental or disadvantageous at all.

7.20 Conversely, if the worker is subjected to objectively detrimental treatment, such as being treated with unwarranted suspicion by the employer, this might be a detriment even though the worker is unaware of this treatment. This is apparent from the decision in *Garry v Ealing LBC* [2001] EWCA Civ 1282, [2001] IRLR 681 where the Court of Appeal held, in the context of the Race Relations Act 1976, that a worker had been subjected to a detriment when an investigation into her activities was continued longer than an ordinary investigation would have been. This was held to be a detriment even in relation to the period during which the claimant was unaware that the investigation was going on.[7]

7.21 In *Shamoon*, the House of Lords rejected the requirement that the detriment must be 'substantial'. Notwithstanding this, in *Moyhing* it was accepted on behalf of the claimant, with apparent approval by the EAT (at para 20), that a *de minimis* difference in treatment could

---

[6] See also Lord Neuberger's speech in *St Helens MBC v Derbyshire and others* [2007] UKHL 16, [2007] ICR 841 at para 67, including his quotation from Lord Scott in *Shamoon* at para 105: 'if the victim's opinion that the treatment was to his or her detriment is a reasonable one to hold, that ought, in my opinion, to suffice'.

[7] As explained by Pill LJ at para 29.

not amount to a relevant detriment. The EAT noted that this exception was recognized in *Jeremiah*, approving, on this ground only, the earlier decision of the Court of Appeal in *Peake v Automotive Products Ltd* [1977] ICR 968.[8] In relation to a section 47B claim, in *Pinnington v The City and County of Swansea and another* [2004] EWCA Civ 135, [2005] ICR 685, on an application for permission to appeal, a panel of the Court of Appeal (Keane and Neuberger LJJ) also contemplated a *de minimis* exception in a post-*Shamoon* case. However, the substantive appeal was upheld on other grounds without considering it necessary to determine whether there was a detriment (at paras 46 and 47). A *de minimis* exception does not sit easily with the emphasis in *Shamoon* that, once the detriment was established as being in the employment field, the only limitation was one of materiality. Nor, in the light of the objective element in the test for detriment, and the opportunity to reflect lower levels of detriment in the size of any award for injury to feelings, is there any necessity to construe the legislation so as to exclude detriments which might be regarded as trivial or *de minimis*. The answer, in practice, may be that a *de minimis* or trivial detriment is unlikely also to be adjudged 'material'.

(2) Unjustified sense of grievance

One aspect of the test of for detriment is that, as Lord Hope noted in *Shamoon*, 'an unjusti-fied sense of grievance will not suffice' to constitute a detriment. In context, having regard to the general principles set out above, whether the grievance is unjustified is to be deter-mined by reference to what could reasonably be considered to be the case from the claim-ant's perspective. **7.22**

This principle was applied by the employment tribunal in *Pinnington*. The claimant made disclosures including that the special needs school in which she was employed as a nurse was implementing a policy of non-resuscitation of terminally ill children at the school. An inquiry was ordered by the local council which found no basis for the allegations. The claimant fell ill, but the tribunal held that she had an 'unjustified sense of grievance' and if that caused her ill health it could not amount to a detriment for the purposes of PIDA. The decision was ultimately upheld on other grounds by the Court of Appeal, as we discuss below (paragraphs 7.51–7.55).

It is a common complaint of whistleblowers that their disclosure has not been investigated properly or indeed at all. In *Deer* the claimant contended that she had been treated less favourably in respect of a grievance and an appeal that she had brought and this less favour-able treatment was by reason of the fact that she had previously brought proceedings against Oxford University. The claims of victimization were struck out on the basis that the claim-ant had not suffered a detriment as her grievance had had no merit. The Court of Appeal reversed that ruling. Elias LJ, with whom Floyd and Sullivan LJJ agreed, considered that the mere fact that the grievance was bound to fail did not exclude the possibility of there being a detriment. There could still be a detriment in relation to the way that grievance pro-cedures had been applied, or in delay in allowing the procedure to be pursued, irrespective of whether the complaint was substantively well founded. This could give rise to a legiti-mate sense of injustice. Whether that is so would be a question of fact for the tribunal. To some extent the reasoning in *Deer* proceeded on the basis of considerations relevant to the discrimination context that the very fact of being treated less favourably by reason of race **7.23**

---

[8] See also *Porcelli v Strathclyde Council* [1986] ICR 564, Court of Session, referring (at p 573G) to gen-der-based unpleasant conduct being sex discrimination unless the harm inflicted was 'a mere scratch'. Also, in *Jiad v Byford* [2003] EWCA Civ 135 (at para 43) the Court of Appeal accepted that a trivial disadvantage would not suffice. But this was in the context of following the test in *Lord Chancellor v Coker* [2001] EWCA Civ 1756, [2002] ICR 321 in the Court of Appeal—since rejected in *Shamoon*—that the detriment must be substantial and material.

or sex could give rise to a sense of grievance (para 26). But we suggest that the underlying reasoning that procedural failings may themselves be capable of amounting to a detriment, given the broad meaning of that term, is self-evidently correct, albeit that the application of this is fact sensitive. Indeed the very fact of being treated less favourably by reason of having blown the whistle might similarly contribute to a justified sense of grievance.[9]

7.24 The potential significance of differential treatment is illustrated by the decision in *Theatre Peckham v Browne* (UKEAT 0154/13/2RN, 24 June 2014). The respondents sought, in a situation of stalemate between two employees, to seek to persuade the claimant to bring her employment to an end by agreement. In concluding that the employment tribunal was entitled to find that that treatment was of such a kind that a reasonable worker might regard it as a detriment, the EAT emphasized that the tribunal had not acted in the same way towards the other employee who had not made a protected disclosure (see paras 30–31 of the judgment).

7.25 The fact-sensitive nature of the enquiry is illustrated by the decision in *Cordant Security Ltd v Singh & Anor* [2016] IRLR 4 (EAT), another claim based on the Equality Act 2010. The claimant's uninvestigated allegation was found by the ET to have been fabricated and it was further found that if the allegation had been investigated there would have been no substantive benefit to the claimant as it would have been found to be untrue. The ET expressly found that the claimant did not suffer any injury to feelings as a result of the failure to investigate the fabricated complaint. Any injury to feelings arose from other circumstances and not the way in which his allegation of misconduct had been dealt with. The EAT said that this was one of the cases where the claimant employee did not suffer any sense of grievance or injustice as a result of the less favourable treatment: there had been no discrimination because one of the necessary elements of a finding of a contravention of section 39(2)(d) of the Act, namely detriment, was not present. The EAT went on to say that it was necessary to bear in mind the range of circumstances in which complaints by employees are made. Those circumstances may range from a complaint which turns out to be unsubstantiated (although genuinely believed), through to those complaints that are exaggerated or partially true, to those which are entirely fabricated. Whether or not a person had a real sense of grievance or injustice arising out of less favourable treatment involving the failure to investigate a particular complaint was a matter for the ET to decide having regard to all the circumstances of the case.

7.26 It follows from this approach that the reason for a particular act or omission may bear on the question of whether it could be regarded, objectively, as detriment. As a result there may be some overlap between issues as to detriment and whether protected disclosures (or discrimination) were the reasons for the treatment. This point was made in *St Helens MBC v Derbyshire and others* [2007] UKHL 16, [2007] ICR 841 (HL), where the council, which was a respondent to equal pay claims brought by Mrs Derbyshire and other employees, sent out two letters to Mrs Derbyshire and her colleagues which warned of the economic consequences of their equal pay claims succeeding. The claimants claimed that these letters were acts of victimization on the part of the council and that the letters had been written on the ground that the claimants had done protected acts by bringing equal pay proceedings. In the course of his speech Lord Neuberger said this (at para 68):

> In my judgment, a more satisfactory conclusion, which in practice would almost always involve identical considerations, and produce a result identical, to that in *Khan*, involves focusing on the word 'detriment' rather than on the words 'by reason that'. If, in the course of equal pay proceedings, the employer's solicitor were to write to the employee's solicitor

---

[9] See also *Vairea v Reed Business Information Ltd* (UKEAT/0177/15/BA, 3 June 2016), where an argument based on *Deer* was pursued in a protected disclosure context but failed on the facts (at para 98), but there was no suggestion that it was inapplicable in principle in the whistleblowing context.

setting out, in appropriately measured and accurate terms, the financial or employment consequences of the claim succeeding, or the risks to the employee if the claim fails, or terms of settlement which are unattractive to the employee, I do not see how any distress thereby induced in the employee could be said to constitute 'detriment' for the purposes of sections 4 and 6 of the 1975 Act, as it would not satisfy the test as formulated by Brightman LJ in *Jeremiah*, as considered and approved in your Lordships' House. An alleged victim cannot establish 'detriment' merely by showing that she had suffered mental distress: before she could succeed, it would have to be objectively reasonable in all the circumstances. The bringing of an equal pay claim, however strong the claim may be, carries with it, like any other litigation inevitable distress and worry. Distress and worry which may be induced by the employer's honest and reasonable conduct in the course of his defence or in the conduct of any settlement negotiations, cannot (save, possibly, in the most unusual circumstances) constitute 'detriment' for the purposes of sections 4 and 6 of the 1975 Act.

Accordingly, even though the worker may regard the employer's response to his/her protected disclosure as 'detrimental', the employer may be able to show that its action (or for that matter inaction) was only an 'honest and reasonable' reaction to that disclosure which may in turn bear upon whether the worker could reasonably consider him/herself to have been subjected to a detriment. **7.27**

However, the dicta to the effect that an unjustified sense of grievance is not to be regarded as a detriment should not be elevated to a principle which obscures the statutory language. It is intended to be an application of the principle that there is no detriment if a reasonable person in the position of the worker would not consider him/herself to have been disadvantaged: see *Barclays Bank plc v Kapur (No 2)* [1995] IRLR 87 at paras 43–44 (CA). It is not intended to connote that detrimental treatment does not constitute a detriment if the worker ought to have appreciated that the treatment was justified. This is confirmed by the guidance provided by the EAT in *Moyhing v Barts and London NHS Trust* [2006] IRLR 860. The claimant was a male student nurse who complained of discrimination in that male nurses had to be chaperoned when carrying out intimate procedures on female patients, whereas the same did not apply where female nurses carried out intimate procedures on male patients. The claimant felt that this stigmatized him as being someone who was likely to attack a female patient, but the employment tribunal held that there was no detriment because there was good reason for the chaperoning policy and the claimant's objection to it was unjustified. The EAT, however, held that there was a detriment: the employment tribunal's approach had, impermissibly, effectively introduced a defence of justification to direct discrimination. The objective element in the test of detriment required consideration of whether the claimant could reasonably have perceived the treatment to be detrimental. The reason for the treatment was a relevant circumstance because the perception of a reasonable employee will often be affected by this. But ultimately, however justified the respondent's policy, it was not unreasonable for the claimant to feel demeaned and irritated by it. **7.28**

This reasoning is potentially of significance in protected disclosure cases. Suppose, modifying the facts in *Pinnington*, a potential protected disclosure is made which raises issues as to an apparent breach of confidentiality. It might be reasonable for the employer to investigate and, further, in order to facilitate the investigation, it might be reasonable for the worker to be suspended on full pay for a short period during the investigation. In considering whether a reasonable worker would regard this as a detriment, one of the relevant circumstances is that a reasonable worker might recognize the need to investigate and therefore not regard the suspension as indicating a lack of trust on the part of the employer. Yet the worker might still reasonably consider that being suspended is detrimental, perhaps on the basis that it might lead to stigma among colleagues. It does not follow from the fact that the suspension might be justified that it cannot amount to subjecting the worker to a detriment. **7.29**

7.30 Ultimately there is no substitute for applying the statutory language. But in the assessment of whether the worker could have regarded the act or relevant failure to act as detrimental, considerations such as whether the worker ought to have appreciated that the treatment was reasonable or justified, the reason for the treatment, the adequacy of the response to the disclosure and whether the worker was affected for an extended period of time, and whether the conduct involves positive action or only mere inaction, may be relevant considerations. Several of these considerations were illustrated by the decision in *Blackbay Ventures Ltd (t/a Chemistree) v Gahir* [2014] IRLR 446 (EAT). The claimant's role as 'responsible pharmacist' involved overseeing compliance with statutory requirements. The ET held that she had made protected disclosures, principally on 31 August, prior to her dismissal on 3 September. In addition to upholding her s103A unfair dismissal claim, the ET upheld a claim of detriment by virtue of the stress she suffered in continuing in her role despite the serious concerns raised. The EAT allowed an appeal against the detriment decision and remitted the issue to the ET. The EAT noted that, it was hard to see how the claimant could reasonably have held a justified sense of grievance or suffered a detriment from simple inaction given that her job necessarily involved drawing attention to breaches of obligations, the short period of time between the disclosure and dismissal (which could not found a detriment claim) and the ET's finding that the complaints were being promptly addressed.[10]

(3) The threat of a detriment

7.31 The legislation does not expressly cover threats of detrimental treatment. However, it is unlikely that there could be a threat of a detriment which does not itself amount to a detriment. That certainly seems to have been the government's thinking. Speaking on behalf of the government during the Lords committee stage of the Public Interest Disclosure Bill, Lord Haskell explained that:

> an employee who has made a disclosure to his employer could be threatened with relocation to a remote branch of a company, for instance, where promotion prospects are poorer. That kind of threat is a detriment and even though the worker can be assured that the employer could not lawfully carry out the threat, the fear of the threat may well amount to detrimental action. Any threat which puts a worker at a disadvantage constitutes in itself detrimental action.[11]

7.32 Lord Haskell further explained the Government's reluctance specifically to include reference to threats of detriment. Such a provision would have cast doubt on whether threats were covered in the other cases (contained in ERA, Part V) where there is protection against suffering a detriment.

7.33 During the debate[12] Lord Wedderburn had expressed concern that the then recent decision of the Court of Appeal in *Mennell v Newell & Wright (Transport Contractors) Ltd* [1997] IRLR 519 would lead to a construction of the proposed legislation that would not regard threats of a detriment as being detriments. However, this case related to a claim of dismissal for asserting a statutory right. In relation to that cause of action, it was held that there could be no claim until the statutory right had been asserted. The closer parallel is therefore with a separate point which was made during the same debate: that threats to prevent disclosures being made would not be covered as there would not be protection until the disclosure was made. In response it was said that whilst what was merely in somebody's head could not be

---

[10] See also *Chattenton v City of Sunderland Council* (ET, Case No 6402938/ 99, 18 July 2000) (Claimant was locked out of his office after disclosing concern over the downloading of pornography from the internet onto a shared computer that he used. But this was not a detriment as the respondents explained that they had changed working practices to prevent access to the internet and porn sites and the change applied to everyone).

[11] *Hansard* HL, 5 June 1998, col 634.

[12] *Hansard* HL, 5 June 1998, col 631.

covered, if it was mentioned to someone in the position of employer that a disclosure was going to be made, that would itself constitute a disclosure. It was accepted that, whilst it might be possible to imagine cases not covered, ordinarily a disclosure made to the employer or via internal procedures was likely to get through rather than merely be attempted.[13]

This did not fully meet the concern, however. One potential difficulty arises because of **7.34** the need for there to be a disclosure of information, rather than simply a statement of concern (see Chapter 3, paragraphs 3.05–3.26). As we discuss in Chapter 3 (at paragraphs 3.14–3.22), unless a broad contextual view is taken of this requirement, there is scope for absurd results. An employer could dismiss a worker who had only got as far as intimating that s/he wished to raise a concern: the employer would be able to avoid liability for acting contrary to the PIDA-inserted provisions as long as the employer could show that no information (reasonably believed as tending to show a relevant failure) had yet been disclosed by the worker prior to the dismissal. Further, because of the need to establish the requisite reasonable belief for a qualifying disclosure, there might in some cases be a stage where an employee is engaged in conducting his/her own investigations in relation to a suspected relevant failure. If an employer got wind of this and made threats to discourage the worker from continuing the investigation or making allegations arising from those investigations, this would not be covered if the worker had not yet made a disclosure or did not yet have the requisite reasonable belief for a qualifying disclosure. Consistently with this, in *Bolton School v Evans* [2006] IRLR 500 the EAT commented (at para 68) that:

> putting it simply, it seems to us that the law protects the disclosure of information which the employee reasonably believes tends to demonstrate the kind of wrongdoing, or antici-pated wrongdoing, which is covered by section 43B. It does not protect the actions of the employee which are directed to establishing or confirming the reasonableness of that belief. The protection is for the whistleblower who reasonably believes, to put it colloquially if inaccurately, that something is wrong, not the investigator who seeks either to establish that it is wrong or to show that his concerns are reasonable.

(4) Post-termination disclosures and post-termination detriment

(a) *The decision in Woodward v Abbey National plc*

As noted above, in the guidance set out in *Shamoon*[14] as to the meaning of 'detriment' it **7.35** was identified that the detriment must be 'in the employment field'. This analysis was based on considerations material to the specific statutory context of the Sex Discrimination Act 1975 and the Race Relations Act 1976. The material provisions were contained in a part of those Acts headed 'Discrimination in the Employment Field', and the reference to detri-ment came at the end of a series of provisions identifying unlawful discriminatory treatment in relation to offering employment and during employment. However, in *Rhys-Harper v Relaxion Group plc* [2003] UKHL 33, [2003] ICR 867 (HL), in the context of the anti-dis-crimination legislation,[15] it was determined that there could also be post-termination com-plaints of discrimination. Similarly, section 47B ERA is contained in a part of ERA headed 'Protection from Suffering Detriment *in Employment*' (our emphasis). But in *Woodward v Abbey National plc (No. 1)* [2006] EWCA Civ 822, [2006] IRLR 677 the Court of Appeal followed *Rhys-Harper* and concluded (per Ward LJ at para 64) that there could be a det-riment imposed after the end of the employment contract. The term 'in employment' was

---

[13] *Hansard* HL, 5 June 1998, col 635, per Lord Haskell.

[14] See above, para 7.18.

[15] See now the Equality Act 2010 s 108 which prohibits discrimination where the discrimination arises out of and is closely connected to a relationship which used to exist between the claimant and the respon-dent, and conduct of a description constituting the discrimination would, if it occurred during the rela-tionship, contravene the Equality Act.

properly to be construed as meaning 'in the employment relationship' and this could survive the termination of the contract itself.

7.36 In *Woodward* the claimant claimed that, some years after the termination of her employment, she was caused detriment by her ex-employers, including by their not providing a reference for her, and that this was because she had made protected disclosures. She made claims pursuant to ERA, sections 47B and 48. The Court of Appeal[16] reversed the EAT[17] and the Court of Appeal's own earlier decision in *Fadipe v Reed Nursing Personnel* [2001] EWCA Civ 1885, [2005] ICR 1760. In *Fadipe*, ERA, section 44, which is in the same terms as section 47B, had been held not to apply where the alleged detriment was inflicted and suffered after the employee had ceased to be employed. In *Woodward* the Court of Appeal held that, although it had not been expressly overruled, *Fadipe* could not stand with the decision in *Rhys-Harper*.

7.37 Ward LJ, giving the only substantive judgment in *Woodward*, rejected the primary submission for the employer that *Rhys-Harper* had no application at all to claims under the ERA because different statutes were in play. As noted at paragraph 7.14 above, he emphasized that the context was not materially different. Although the language and the framework were slightly different, the discrimination and ERA detriment legislation dealt with the same concept, namely protecting the employee from detriment being done to him/her in retaliation for his/her sex, race, disability, related protected act, or whistleblowing. This was made explicit by the long title to PIDA, which provides that it is to allow whistleblowers 'to bring action *in respect of victimisation*'. It would be odd if the same sort of act could be victimization for one purpose but not for the other. Second, as Lord Nicholls had said in *Rhys-Harper*, no sensible distinction could be drawn between giving a reference the day before employment ends and giving a reference the day after. In *Fadipe* Mummery LJ was clearly confining the 'employment relationship' to the duration of the contract, but that approach could not stand with the wider scope of an employment relationship given to the concept in *Rhys-Harper*.

7.38 This conclusion was supported by the general definition in ERA, section 230,[18] which covers the whole spectrum of the ERA. Thus, 'worker' means not only an individual who currently works under a contract of employment but one who formerly worked under such a contract. Although a provision framed in this way served the purpose of giving a former employee the right to bring his/her claim under section 48 (or a claim for unfair dismissal), it did not follow that this is its *only* purpose, and if that was the intention one would have expected the point to have been more clearly made in a provision explaining that a right accruing during the currency of a contract of employment can be enforced by the victim after the contract is at an end. Drafted as it was, it was an omnibus definition of 'employee, worker, etc' and it was accordingly more likely that the legislature intended the purpose to be served and the meaning to be ascribed to take colour from the context of the section in which 'worker' appears. Under section 47B, 'worker', in its ordinary meaning, was just as naturally to be construed as including a former employee.

7.39 The Court of Appeal emphasized that the underlying purpose of section 47B would be sold short if it allowed the former employer to victimize his/her former employee with impunity. It made no sense at all to protect the current employee but not the former employee. If it was

---

[16] [2006] EWCA Civ 822.
[17] [2005] ICR 1750.
[18] Section 230 reads: '(1) In this Act "employee" means an individual who has entered into or works under (or, where the employment has ceased, worked under) a contract of employment'. And similarly for 'worker' in subs 3.

in the public interest to blow the whistle, then the whistleblower should be protected when s/he becomes victimized for doing so, whenever the retribution is exacted.

(b) Further issues as to the scope for post-termination detriment claims

Whilst establishing the principle that there could be a claim based on detriment after the **7.40** termination of employment, the Court of Appeal left a number of issues unresolved. Indeed, it did not even proceed to decide whether the particular allegations and facts of *Woodward* would lead to a remedy being afforded to her. The reason for this was, first, that there had been no argument on this point, but, second, because of the diversity of the ways in which those constituting the majority in the House of Lords in *Rhys-Harper* had described the test. It was not appropriate to resolve this without determination of the facts in the case and without hearing argument on the facts.

The various tests suggested in *Rhys-Harper* in relation to whether relief should be **7.41** afforded after termination of employment[19] were summarized by Ward LJ in *Woodward* (at para 53):

(1) for Lord Nicholls, the employment relationship triggered the employer's obligation not to discriminate in all the incidents of the employment relationship whenever they arise, provided the benefit in question arises between the employer or former employer as such and the employee or former employee as such (paras 44, 45);

(2) for Lord Hope the test was whether there is still a continuation of the employment relationship (paras 114, 115);

(3) for Lord Hobhouse the test was one of proximity: does the conduct complained about have a sufficient connection with the employment (para 139) or a substantive and proximate connection between the conduct complained of and the employment by the alleged discriminator (para 140);

(4) for Lord Rodger, one must look for a substantive connection between the discriminatory conduct and the employment relationship, with the former employer discriminating *qua* former employer (para 205);

(5) for Lord Scott, it depends on whether the relationship between employer and employee brought into existence when the employee entered into the employer's service is still in existence (para 200) or is still continuing notwithstanding the termination of the employment (para 204).

In other words Lord Hope and Lord Scott seem to tie the application of the Act to the **7.42** continuance of the employment relationship whereas the majority look for a connection (variously described) between the former employee as such and the former employer as such.

Lord Nicholls (at para 45) further expanded in *Rhys-Harper* on his preferred test, **7.43** explaining that:

to be an 'incident' of the employment relationship for this purpose the benefit in question must arise between employer or former employer as such and employee or former employee as such. A reference is a prime example. Further, save perhaps in exceptional circumstances which it is difficult to envisage, failure to provide a non-contractual benefit will not constitute a 'detriment', or discrimination in an opportunity to receive a 'benefit', within the meaning of the anti-discrimination legislation unless the non-contractual benefit in question is one which normally is provided, or would be provided, to others in comparable circumstances. This is so with regard to current employees. It is equally so with former employees. But I stress this is not to say that an employer's practice regarding current employees is to be treated as equally applicable to former employees. This is emphatically

---

[19] See now s 108 of the Equality Act 2010.

not so. The two situations are not comparable. What is comparable is the way the employer treats the claimant former employee and the normal way he treats or would treat other former employees in similar circumstances.

7.44 As this indicates, it is fairly clear that an employer who victimizes a whistleblower by declining to give an appropriate reference after the termination of employment would now be vulnerable to a claim. The weaker the connection between the claims and the former employment relationship, the more problematic such claims become.

(c) Post-termination disclosures

7.45 In *Woodward* the Court of Appeal expressly left open the question as to whether the protected disclosure had to precede the termination of employment. The EAT subsequently held, in *Onyango v Berkeley (t/a Berkeley Solicitors)* [2013] IRLR 338, that claims may be made based on post-termination disclosures. HHJ Clark reiterated that 'worker' and 'employer' are defined in section 230 ERA and the definition applies to those who have ceased to be in the relevant contractual relationship. Since the detriment might arise post termination there could be no warrant for limiting the disclosure to the duration of the employment. As a matter of pure construction of the statute, post-termination disclosures may be relied on if they lead to detrimental treatment. That is in line with the underlying policy of the legislation to encourage responsible whistleblowing. Indeed it may be in some cases that it is only after employment has terminated that a worker will feel free to raise concerns. Whether there is a sufficient connection with the employment would then be a question of fact in each case.[20]

(5) Limitation of detriment claims to the employment field during employment

7.46 The limitation of detriment claims to the employment field is reflected in the test for vicarious liability introduced by the ERRA, which is considered in Chapter 8. Thus, for example, where, in response to a worker's protected disclosure, his managers continue to deal with him as normal at work but cold-shoulder him socially outside work, the issue of sufficiency of connection will ordinarily be answered by applying the test of whether the manager was acting in the course of employment (see section 47B(1A) and Chapter 8 of this book). The issue is liable to cause greater difficulty in relation to claims based on qualifying disclosures prior to 25 June 2013 where it raises issues as to whether a colleague's conduct is to be attributed to the employer (see paragraphs 8.83–8.86) or where the detriment was inflicted outside of work.[21]

D. 'Act or Deliberate Failure to Act'

7.47 An employer subjects a worker to a detriment both by *acts* to the worker's detriment and also by *deliberately failing to act* so as to cause detriment. Examples would include refusing promotion, not giving a pay rise, failure to look into or deal fairly with a grievance, or failure to provide facilities or training which would otherwise have been made available, provided in each case that the failure was 'deliberate'.

7.48 The requirement that the failure be 'deliberate' connotes that there must be a decision rather than merely an oversight leading to a failure to act, and as such the line between

---

[20] On an application for permission to appeal, the Court of Appeal in *Ali v Washwood Heath Technology College & Ors* [2014] EWCA Civ 97 left open the question of whether a post-termination disclosure would be protected, it being unnecessary to determine this in order to refuse permission.

[21] Cf *Sidhu v Aerospace Composite Technology Ltd* [2001] ICR 167 where the employer organized a family day out to which employees, their families and friends were invited. The majority in the ET held that the racial attack perpetrated by an employee was not within the course of his employment and this conclusion was held by the Court of Appeal, reversing the EAT, to be one open to the tribunal on the evidence.

an act and a deliberate failure may be a fine one. The implicit requirement for a decision is further indicated by the statutory context. First, this involves consideration of the reason for the failure to act. Second, ERA, section 48(4)(b) provides that 'a deliberate failure to act shall be treated as done when it was decided on'. However, section 48(4) provides that:

> in the absence of evidence establishing the contrary, an employer shall be taken to decide on a failure to act when he does an act inconsistent with doing the failed act or, if he has done no such inconsistent act, when the period expires within which he might reasonably have been expected to do the failed act if it was to be done.

A prima facie case of a failure to act can therefore be made out in the absence of identifying **7.49** a specific decision. But this is only 'in the absence of evidence establishing the contrary'. Thus, for example, where information leaks out of an investigation into a disclosure which embarrasses the worker who made the disclosure, prima facie a decision to leak the information is deemed to have been made when the information was leaked. But the employer might be able to show that the leak was due to an oversight or organizational error rather than a decision to disseminate the information.

In *London Borough of Harrow v Knight* [2003] IRLR 140 a complaint was made that the **7.50** claimant suffered stress as a result of the way in which his protected disclosures were handled. There was a failure by the employer to keep the matter confidential, resulting in the claimant being cold-shouldered by colleagues. However, the EAT emphasized (at para 12) that there was no finding that the failure to act was ' "deliberate", as opposed to merely insensitive or careless'. The position would have been otherwise if the lack of support had been deliberate and due to an adverse perception of the employee by reason of his having made the disclosure. That was found to be the case in *Flintshire v Sutton* (EAT/1082/02, 1 July 2003), where a failure to support was due to a perception that the claimant was a problem because he had made the relevant protected disclosures. Further, as emphasised in *Blackbay Ventures Ltd (t/a Chemistree) v Gahir* [2014] IRLR 446 (see para 7.30 above), it is essential for the ET to address the question of when any deliberate decision to take no action was taken, since any detriment could only run from that point. The ET had erred in failing to making findings as to this, and indeed the EAT noted it was difficult to square any such deliberate decision with the finding that the claimant's concerns appeared to have been addressed promptly.

The absence of an act or 'deliberate' failure to act was crucial to the Court of Appeal's reason- **7.51** ing in *Pinnington v Swansea City Council and another* [2005] EWCA Civ 135, [2005] ICR 685. Mrs Pinnington was a nurse at a special needs school. From 1997 she made allegations that a policy of non-resuscitation of terminally ill children was being implemented at the school. An inquiry was ordered by the local council which found no basis for the allegations. Mrs Pinnington was away from work on certificated sick leave from 17 September 1997 to 31 March 1998, suffering from stress and anxiety. She returned to work for a short period between 31 March and 29 April 1998 but then went sick again and did not return prior to her dismissal. On 2 July 1998, that is after she had begun the second period away sick, she was suspended by the employer for breach of confidence about records relating to children at the school. There was then a second inquiry, which was carried out by the governors following further complaints of the same kind that the claimant had made before: again, it was found that there was no evidence of the policy of non-resuscitation of the kind the claimant alleged. Following a capability hearing (and thereafter an appeal) the claimant was dismissed with effect from 3 July 1999. PIDA only came into effect on the previous day, 2 July 1999.

The tribunal held that the dismissal of the claimant was fair and that the principal reason **7.52** for the dismissal was incapability due to illness. The reason for her dismissal was *not* (as she alleged) that she had made protected disclosures about the alleged policy of non-resuscitation.

The tribunal also held that the employer was entitled to suspend the claimant in July 1998 because of disclosures she had made in breach of confidence. The tribunal identified, as the only relevant period in which detriment *could* have been suffered, the two days, 2 and 3 July 1999. No period earlier than that was relevant, because the protected disclosure provisions did not come into effect until 2 July 1999. Even in that short period the claimant was prevented by ill health from going to work.

7.53 For Mrs Pinnington it was argued that there was a 'deliberate failure to act' by the employer after the PIDA provisions came into force on 2 July 1999, the deliberate failure being *not* terminating the suspension, which had been in force since 2 July 1998. This was rejected by the Court of Appeal on the basis that whilst there was a failure to act, in the sense of the failure to terminate the suspension, this was not a *deliberate* failure. There was neither any evidence of a deliberate failure nor any basis upon which one could be inferred. There was no question of needing to make a decision because prior to 2 July 1999 the employers had already decided that they were going to dismiss her on grounds of incapability and it was unrealistic in those circumstances to expect that they should have considered, on 2 July, terminating the suspension.

7.54 Mummery LJ did say (at para 45) that:

> if she was to remain in employment, then I can see the argument that there might have been, I say no more than that, some duty on the part of the employers to revisit the question of continuing her original suspension in the light of the provisions relating to protected disclosure which had come into force on 2 July 1999. But that is not this case.

7.55 In context this was not a suggestion that there could be a deliberate failure to act in the absence of any decision having been made. Rather, it was said in the context of considering whether there was any basis for inferring that a decision had been made.

7.56 There does not have to be a duty on the employer to act in order for a complaint of a failure to act to be made. It is sufficient that there was a discretion or power to act and this discretion or power was deliberately not exercised because of the protected disclosure. In *Abertawe Bro Morgannwg University Health Board v Ferguson* [2013] ICR 1108 (EAT), the claimant GP disclosed concerns to the respondent Health Board that one of her partners in the practice of which they were both members had acted wrongly in relation to prescribing a drug. The provisions in section 43K(1)(ba) (discussed above in Chapter 6) constituted the GP as a worker vis-à-vis the respondent health board. The detriments complained of were that the health board had:

- failed properly to investigate the GP's concerns, preventing her from fulfilling her obligations to the General Medical Council;
- failed to treat the GP's identity as whistleblower with due confidentiality, releasing her name and her report to her GP partners;
- failed to act in accordance with its own whistleblowing policy so as to prevent the GP from being subjected to reprisals from her colleagues in her GP practice;
- forced the GP to take voluntary leave as an alternative to suspension and had inappropriately maintained that enforced voluntary leave;
- forced the GP to be subjected to an investigation.

7.57 The health board's application to strike out the claim was rejected by the ET, and the EAT upheld that rejection. It was argued for the health board that there had to be an obligation or duty to act in the way in which it was alleged there had been a failure to act. The EAT disagreed. It expressed the view that the statute did not necessarily extend so far as to cover a failure to fulfill a mere expectation that the board would act in a particular way. It would do so only if the board had the ability or power to do something, but there need not be an obligation to do it. If there was such an ability or power, the health board would have a choice as to how it behaved. If it chose to exercise that choice by not taking action when it otherwise could have done so legitimately then that was capable of being a deliberate failure to act. If it were established as a deliberate failure which, applying the words of the section, subjected the claimant doctor to any detriment, she would succeed in a claim if it were also shown that the health board had deliberately decided not to act as it did on the ground that she had made a protected disclosure. These were fact-sensitive questions that could not be determined on a strike-out application. They involved considering both the contractual and statutory context, since, on the facts, the relationship created between a doctor and a health board was one which was regulated by a contract, but might also be governed by the statutory provisions which relate to the actions and activities of the health board.

E. Subjection by the Employer

(1) *London Borough of Harrow v Knight*

The cause of action requires that something must be done or omitted to be done which **7.58** subjects the worker to a detriment. This requirement was considered in *London Borough of Harrow v Knight* [2003] IRLR 140.[22] Mr Knight, a technical officer in the council's environmental services department, made a report to the council's chief executive and director of finance, Mr Redmond, in accordance with the provisions of the council's whistleblowing procedures. He raised concerns that his immediate superior might have been complicit in breaches of regulations by a business that was under investigation. It was conceded by Harrow that this was a protected disclosure. Harrow had commenced an investigation into Mr Knight's allegation but this took a long time and, whilst it was ongoing, Mr Knight wrote several letters complaining of the time that was being taken and contending that he was being victimized because of his disclosure. Harrow did not reply to those letters and Mr Knight said that this had caused him to have a nervous breakdown. The tribunal found that the exacerbation of Mr Knight's medical condition was 'related to the disclosure'. It accepted that he had suffered over the months, especially when his letters were ignored both by the chief executive and the investigators. He had suffered a detriment which was 'directly related to the protected disclosure that he has made'. The tribunal concluded that the complaint succeeded. The appeal succeeded in part because the tribunal had not properly applied the test that any detriment be 'on the ground that' the worker had made a protected disclosure. We discuss this further below.[23] But the EAT also commented on the need to consider whether Mr Knight had been 'subjected to' the detriment by the employer.

The EAT noted that in some cases the doing of the act and the suffering of the detri- **7.59** ment are essentially two sides of the same coin. This will be so, for example, where the detriment consists of being subject to disciplinary action by the employer. However, this was not so in the present case. The alleged detriment was the claimant's ill health. It was therefore an important part of the analysis to identify the act or deliberate failure to act and on what basis this was said to have subjected the claimant to the detriment.

---

[22] See para 7.03 above.
[23] At paras 7.73–7.76.

The tribunal had failed to set this out and had instead asked simply whether Mr Knight suffered a detriment 'related to' his having made a protected disclosure; and found that 'the applicant's medical condition [was] related to the disclosure'. The EAT was, however, satisfied that in two respects—the failure by the chief executive to respond to his letters and the failure to look after him—the tribunal had properly found that the claimant had been subjected to a detriment. It should be noted that the EAT followed the test in *Burton and Rhule v De Vere Hotels Ltd* [1996] IRLR 596, which has since been disapproved (see paragraph 7.60 below).

7.60   The meaning of 'subjecting' in this context was more recently considered by the EAT in *Abertawe Bro Morgannwg University Health Board v Ferguson* which we have referred to in paragraphs 7.56–7.57. There the EAT rejected the health board's contention that the phrase 'subjected to' entails an element of willfulness. That concept was unnecessary given the requirement that the act or failure to act be by reason of a protected disclosure. Nor did it have to be shown that the Health Board could control what happened to the claimant. That was inconsistent with what the House of Lords had said in *Macdonald v Ministry of Defence; Pearce v Governing Body of Mayfield Secondary School* [2004] 1 All ER 339 (HL).[24] Instead the phrase 'subjected to' merely connotes an element of causation. The words are used instead of the phrase 'caused by' so as to encompass deliberate failures to act. The EAT made this observation (at para 18):

> If a course of events, harmful to a worker, was ongoing, then to fail to stop it could amount to a deliberate failure to act. Yet it might be difficult to talk of the failure to act as having 'caused' the ongoing detriment, since that was being caused by the ongoing course of events, and not by a failure to stop it. Linguistically—to convey a sense of causation capable of operating both in respect of a (positive) act, and a (negative) failure to act—'subjecting to' better conveys the sense of that which the legislature wished to achieve.

(2) Liability for the acts of employees and agents

7.61   Before the amendments introduced by the ERRA, the victimization provisions of the ERA did not expressly impose liability on anyone other than the employer. In that respect the landscape was altered fundamentally, so far as concerns qualifying disclosures, by the introduction of vicarious liability, and of personal liability for workers and agents. We consider this in detail in Chapter 8.

(3) Action by prospective employers and other third parties

7.62   Subject to any regulations made pursuant to the recently enacted section 49B ERA (concerning applicants for employment in the NHS), the ERA does not confer a right of action against any third party other than the employer (as widely defined by the statute) who victimizes the worker. As such there may not be a claim under the Act against clients of the employer (unless that third party comes within the extended definition of employer in section 43K(2) ERA). Nor can a prospective employer be liable for discriminating against a whistleblower by declining to employ him/her on that ground. The Act does not provide protection against a refusal to offer employment. Thus a prospective employer who declines to employ a whistleblower by reason of the whistleblowing can do so with impunity.[25] A whistleblower may therefore still run the risk that if s/he speaks out then future job

---

[24] At paras 26, 29, 37, 98, 103, 105, 122, 145, 204, and 205, disapproving *Burton v De Vere Hotels*.

[25] It should, however, be noted that a worker who *does* manage to obtain employment after having blown the whistle is protected from detriment or dismissal visited upon him/her on the ground of a disclosure made in previous employment: *BP plc v Elstone* [2010] IRLR 558 (CA).

prospects will be damaged. The failure to offer protection against this contingency contrasts with the position under discrimination law in relation to protected characteristics under the Equality Act 2010.

The Small Business, Enterprise and Employment Act 2015, section 149 amended the ERA **7.63** to create a new regulation-making power in relation to job applicants in the NHS in accordance with the recommendation made by Sir Robert Francis QC.[26] Section 49B ERA is inserted, to provide that the Secretary of State may make regulations prohibiting an NHS employer from discriminating against an applicant who applies to the NHS employer for a contract of employment, a contract to do work personally, or appointment to an office or post if the discrimination occurs because it appears to the NHS employer that the applicant has made a protected disclosure. Under such regulations an NHS employer will discriminate against an applicant if the NHS employer refuses the applicant's application or in some other way treats the applicant less favourably than it treats or would treat other applicants in relation to the same contract or office. This provision is given further consideration in Chapter 12 of this book at paragraphs 12.32–12.46.

If an employer fails to take reasonable steps to protect a whistleblowing employee from **7.64** consequential adverse action by others, and this exacerbates the consequences of a breach by the employer, the failure to act may lead to the employer being saddled with the consequences of this failure. This is illustrated by *The Trustees of Mama East African Women's Group v Dobson* (EAT/0219/05/ and UKEAT/0220/05/TM, 23 June 2005) where the tribunal was concerned with a claim by a whistleblowing teacher. The tribunal found that the teacher had been dismissed for making a protected disclosure. The respondent employer submitted that the period of loss to be compensated should be restricted to take account of the fact that there had been a loss of confidence in the claimant on the part of her students. As a result of this, it was argued, she could not have carried on teaching anyway. In rejecting this line of argument, the tribunal concluded that, assuming that the employer's students were not prepared to be taught by the claimant, then that situation was itself caused by the employer's mishandling of the inquiry following the claimant's disclosure. That situation was unlikely to have arisen if the employer had dealt with the matter properly. Even if it had occurred, it would in any event have been for the employer to manage the situation. The employer would have had a duty to protect the claimant.

The EAT agreed. To allow the employer's submission would be to allow the employer to **7.65** save itself money on compensation by relying upon its own wrongful acts: that could not be correct.[27] It should be observed that the employer's failure to handle the inquiry, with the resulting leakage of information to the students, would not necessarily have to be 'on the ground of' or 'by reason of' the whistleblowing in order for the conclusion to follow that it could not be relied upon to limit compensation (indeed, it does not appear to have been expressly suggested that it was). It appears to have been considered to be sufficient that the failure to protect the employee was a breach of duty toward the employee and so a wrongful act. That was enough to provide an answer to the arguments as to compensation, though it would not have been a sufficient basis of itself to establish liability for victimization on the grounds of a protected disclosure.

---

[26] The independent review 'Freedom to Speak Up'. http://webarchive.nationalarchives.gov.uk/20150218150343/ http://freedomtospeakup.org.uk/the-report/ p 193 para 9.19.

[27] In *Prison Service v Beart (No. 2)* [2005] EWCA Civ 467, [2005] ICR 1206, at paras 29 and 30, the Court of Appeal ruled to similar effect.

F. 'On the Ground That'

(1) Overview

7.66 In order to establish victimization the detriment must have been inflicted 'on the ground that' the worker made a protected disclosure. This involves identifying the reason or reasons for the act or deliberate failure to act. In many, if not most of the whistleblowing claims that come before tribunals, the key, and difficult, issue is not whether there was a protected disclosure but whether that disclosure was the ground of the conduct complained of (in the case of a detriment) or the reason or principal reason (in the case of a dismissal). Where there is more than one protected disclosure, it is not essential to work out what causative effect each of those disclosures had. Where the disclosures operate cumulatively the focus is on the cumulative impact: see *El-Megrisi v Azad University (IR) in Oxford* (UKEAT/0448/08/MAA, 5 May 2009), discussed in Chapter 9 at paragraphs 9.22–9.24. Equally, a tribunal may be able to conclude that protected disclosures were a material influence without being able to identify which of a number of disclosures influenced which particular detriments: see, for example, *Chief Constable of West Yorkshire Police v B & C* (UKEAT/0306/15/RN, 3 August 2016), at para 23.

7.67 The expressions 'on the ground that' and 'by reason that' raise the same question: the need to focus on the reason or reasons why the employer acted or failed to act.[28] In summary, as explained in *NHS Manchester v Fecitt and others* [2011] ICR 476 (EAT) and [2011] EWCA Civ 1190, [2012] ICR 372 (Court of Appeal), the test to be applied is whether the protected disclosure was a significant influence on the act or deliberate failure to act. The test is drawn from high authority in the context of discrimination law. An influence is significant provided only that it is more than trivial,[29] which entails at least that it is a material influence.[30] The focus is on the mental processes, conscious or subconscious, of the person whose act or deliberate failure to act is in question. As such, it is to be distinguished from a test of causation, which focuses on the consequences attributable to an act or failure to act. On that basis it is sometimes referred to as the 'reason why' test.

7.68 At first blush, the reason why test is a wide one in that, in contrast to the test in relation to dismissal (where it is necessary to identify *the reason* or the *principal* reason), any *material influence* will suffice. However, as the decision in *Fecitt* itself illustrates, that apparent width is qualified in an important respect by case law which appears to permit a distinction between the protected disclosure itself and its consequences (such as causing conflict between work colleagues). Other distinctions may also be made—albeit that tribunals are urged to be circumspect in doing so—such as between the disclosure and the manner of the disclosure or the steps (such as conducting an investigation) associated with the disclosure. We expand below on general principles as to the formulation of the reason why test, before turning to the way in which it has been qualified through the distinctions which authority indicates it is permissible to draw.

---

[28] For an example of what can go wrong where this prescription is not followed, see *El-Megrisi v Azad University* (EAT/0448/08, 5 May 2009), Underhill J. It is important that the claimant's case as to the detriments and the reason for them is properly particularized: *Secretary of State for Work and Pensions (Jobcentre Plus) v Constable* (UKEAT/0156/10/JOJ, 30 June 2010).

[29] *Igen Ltd v Wong* [2005] EWCA Civ 142, [2005] ICR 931 at para 37, per Peter Gibson LJ; *Fecitt* (EAT) at para 65 and *Fecitt* (CA) at para 45.

[30] *Villallba v Merrill Lynch & Co Inc* [2007] ICR 469 at para 82, EAT; *Fecitt* (EAT) at para 59.

(2) The significant influence test: 'causation' and 'reason why' distinguished

7.69 In *Fecitt* the EAT (HHJ Serota QC) identified four alternative ways of formulating a 'causation' test as follows (at para 28):

> (a) The 'but for' test; neither counsel has suggested that is the appropriate test so I need say no more about it. (b) The claimants need to prove that the protected act was a material or significant factor in the detriment they suffered. (c) The claimants need to prove that the prohibited act was the direct or proximate cause or principal cause of the detriment they suffered. (d) The respondent must show, where claimants have suffered a detriment, that it is 'in no sense whatever' associated with the protected disclosures.

7.70 Of these alternatives, it was, as HHJ Serota QC noted, common ground that the first alternative (the 'but for' test) was not applicable. The third alternative (direct or proximate cause) was rejected by both the EAT and subsequently by the Court of Appeal. The EAT opted for the fourth alternative (the 'no sense whatever' test), whereas the Court of Appeal favoured the second alternative (the 'no material influence' test). However, both the EAT (at para 65) and the Court of Appeal (at para 43) viewed these tests as not being materially different.

7.71 The rejection of the 'but for' test reflected the crucial distinction between an approach which focuses solely on legal consequences and one which focuses on the reasons for an act or deliberate failure to act. In *Chief Constable of West Yorkshire Police v Khan* [2001] UKHL 48, [2001] ICR 1065 at para 29, Lord Nicholls explained that:

> contrary to views sometimes stated, the third ingredient ('by reason that') does not raise a question of causation as that expression is usually understood. Causation is a slippery word, but normally it is used to describe a legal exercise. From the many events leading up to the crucial happening, the court selects one or more of them which the law regards as causative of the happening. Sometimes the court may look for the 'operative' cause, or the 'effective' cause. Sometimes it may apply a 'but for' approach. For the reasons I sought to explain in *Nagarajan v London Regional Transport* [1999] ICR 877, 884–885, a causation exercise of this type is required either by s 1(1)(a) or s 2. The phrases 'on racial grounds' and 'by reason that' denote a different exercise: why did the alleged discriminator act as he did? Unlike causation, this is a subjective test. Causation is a legal conclusion. The reason why a person acted as he did is a question of fact.

7.72 As we consider further below (at paragraphs 7.161–7.162), a causation test *does* apply in relation to linking an act or deliberate failure to act to an alleged detriment. However, so far as concerns whether an act or deliberate failure to act was on the grounds of a protected disclosure, the focus is on the mental processes of those responsible for the act or deliberate failure to act in question. In that respect the same applies whether applying the 'on the ground that' test within ERA, section 47B, or looking at the reason for dismissal (section 103A), although the reference only to a 'principal' reason in relation to dismissal of an employee does introduce a very important distinction which we discuss in more detail in Chapter 9 at paragraphs 9.19–9.24 As Lord Nicholls explained in *Nagarajan v London Regional Transport* [1999] ICR 877, at 886, in the context of comparing the language for direct race discrimination and victimization:

> 'On racial grounds' in section 1(1)(a) and 'by reason that' in section 2(1) are interchangeable expressions in this context. The key question under section 2 is the same as under section 1(1)(a): why did the complainant receive less favourable treatment? The considerations mentioned above regarding direct discrimination under section 1(1)(a) are correspondingly appropriate under section 2. If the answer to this question is that the discriminator treated the person victimised less favourably by reason of his having done one of the acts listed in section 2(1) ('protected acts'), the case falls within the section. It does so, even if the discriminator did not consciously realise that, for example, he was prejudiced because the job applicant had previously brought claims against him under the Act.

7.73 The difference between a 'but for' test of causation, and a focus on the (conscious or sub-conscious) 'reasons why' the act or deliberate failure to act took place, is critical. It presents a potentially difficult hurdle for the claimant. The distinction between the applicable test for causation and that for reason or ground is starkly illustrated by *London Borough of Harrow v Knight* [2003] IRLR 140.[31] Mr Knight reported allegations that his line manager had condoned breaches of food regulations by a food business in the borough. The report also criticized Mr Esom, the chief environmental health officer, to whom his line manager reported. It took nine months to produce a final report. In the interim Knight wrote to the chief executive (Mr Redmond) expressing concerns as to the progress of the investigation and alleging victimization as a result of having made the original disclosure. On the findings of the employment tribunal, the case turned on the allegation that Mr Redmond had failed to respond to letters from Mr Knight and that there had been a failure to look after him so as to protect him from (amongst other things) being cold-shouldered by colleagues, including Mr Esom, and that as a result he sustained an illness of a depressive nature. The ET expressed themselves thus:

> the exacerbation of the applicant's medical condition is related to the disclosure . . . . We accept that the applicant suffered over the months especially when his letters were ignored both by the chief executive and the investigators. He has not gained from this disclosure; rather he has suffered a detriment which is directly related to the protected disclosure that he has made.

7.74 In allowing the respondent council's appeal and remitting the case, the EAT commented (at para 16) that:

> on any view the failure of Mr Redmond to answer Mr Knight's letters was *related to* the protected disclosure: after all, the disclosure was the fundamental subject matter of the letters and they would never have been written but for the fact that the disclosure had been made. Likewise any failure on the part of the Council to look after Mr Knight *related to* the disclosure: the awkward situation created by the disclosure was the very reason why he needed help. But that does not answer the question whether that formed part of the motivation (conscious or unconscious) of Mr Redmond or Mr Esom. Mr Redmond, for example, might have failed to answer the letters because he was annoyed by the original report and regarded whistleblowers as disloyal and a nuisance: that would indeed be a deliberate omission 'on the ground that' he had made the protected disclosure. But he might in principle equally have failed to do so for one of a number of other reasons.

7.75 Accordingly it would not be sufficient to say that but for the disclosures there would not have been a train of events, including a failure to respond promptly to Mr Knight's letters, which led to him becoming unwell. It was necessary to consider the reason for the failure to respond to his letters. Indeed, the EAT commented that here, by applying a test of whether the detriment 'related to' the protected disclosure, the tribunal had erred in importing an even lower threshold than the 'but for' test: 'it merely connotes some connection (not even necessarily causative) between the act done and the disclosure'.

7.76 As the passage from the EAT's judgment quoted above points out, the focus on mental processes does not confine the scope to conscious motivation but can extend to the subconscious. This was explained in *Nagarajan* (in the context of race discrimination victimization) by Lord Nicholls.[32] An employment tribunal may decide that the proper inference to be drawn from the evidence is that, whether the relevant officer(s) realized it at the time or not, the protected disclosure was the reason for the act complained of. In a protected disclosure case, it may be important for a tribunal to be alive to the possibility of subconscious as

---

[31] Also discussed at para 7.58 above.
[32] At pp 885–86.

well as conscious motivation. The nature of stereotypical assumptions is of course likely to be different from the context of race discrimination, but may still be present. It may be that the organizational culture is such as to indicate the presence of stereotypical assumptions that those who speak up or reveal wrongdoing are regarded as disloyal or troublemakers.[33]

In his speech in *Khan* Lord Nicholls drew upon and clarified the guidance he gave in *Nagarajan*. Addressing the role of consideration of the mental processes leading to a decision, in *Nagarajan* Lord Nicholls had explained (at p 884) that: **7.77**

> to be within section 1(1)(a) the less favourable treatment must be on racial grounds. Thus, in every case it is necessary to inquire why the complainant received less favourable treatment. This is the crucial question. Was it on grounds of race? Or was it for some other reason, for instance, because the complainant was not so well qualified for the job? Save in obvious cases, answering the crucial question will call for some consideration of the mental processes of the alleged discriminator. Treatment, favourable or unfavourable, is a consequence which follows from a decision. Direct evidence of a decision to discriminate on racial grounds will seldom be forthcoming. Usually the grounds of the decision will have to be deduced, or inferred, from the surrounding circumstances.
>
> The crucial question just mentioned is to be distinguished sharply from a second and different question: if the discriminator treated the complainant less favourably on racial grounds, why did he do so? The latter question is strictly beside the point when deciding whether an act of racial discrimination occurred.

In short, the focus on mental processes is directed to identifying the reasons for an act or failure to act. **7.78**

Lord Nicholls also dealt in *Nagarajan* (at p 886) with the appropriate approach where there are mixed reasons for action or a failure to act: **7.79**

> Decisions are frequently reached for more than one reason. Discrimination may be on racial grounds even though it is not the sole ground for the decision. A variety of phrases, with different shades of meaning, have been used to explain how the legislation applies in such cases: discrimination requires that racial grounds were a cause, the activating cause, a substantial and effective cause, a substantial reason, an important factor. No one phrase is obviously preferable to all others, although in the application of this legislation legalistic phrases, as well as subtle distinctions, are better avoided so far as possible. If racial grounds or protected acts had a significant influence on the outcome, discrimination is made out.

However, a narrower approach was suggested by Lord Scott in *Khan* (at para 77), who expressed the view that: 'The words "by reason that" suggest, to my mind, that it is the real reason, the core reason, the causa causans, the motive, for the treatment complained of that must be identified'. This dicta was at the heart of the issue in *Fecitt* as to the correct approach to the 'reason why' test. It was relied upon by the respondent in support of a contention that it was insufficient if the protected disclosure was a subsidiary influence on the act or relevant failure to act. In particular, the reference by Lord Scott to a 'core reason' would bring the test most closely into line with the principal reason test in the context of unfair dismissal. That would in turn avoid anomalous results flowing from the distinction between the test for victimization and dismissal. **7.80**

However, that contention failed in *Fecitt* both in the EAT and the Court of Appeal. Giving the leading judgment in the Court of Appeal, Elias LJ accepted (at para 43) that there could be **7.81**

---

[33] *Geller and another v Yeshurun Hebrew Congregation* (UKEAT/0190/15/JOJ, 23 March 2016) contains (in the context of alleged sex discrimination) a useful analysis of the law on subconscious discrimination and the duties of a tribunal to consider the possibility that it has occurred.

anomalous results but concluded that this was the consequence of placing dismissal for a protected disclosure into 'the general run of unfair dismissal law'. He therefore concluded (at para 45) that:

> In my judgment, the better view is that section 47B will be infringed if the protected disclosure materially influences (in the sense of being more than a trivial influence) the employer's treatment of the whistleblower. If Parliament had wanted the test for the standard of proof in section 47B to be the same as for unfair dismissal, it could have used precisely the same language, but it did not do so.

7.82 The particular anomaly referred to by Elias LJ was the risk that a non-employee worker whose contract was terminated would be able to succeed in establishing a victimization claim on the basis that the protected disclosure was a significant influence, even though it was not the sole or principal reason for dismissal. This indicates that a worker could succeed whereas an employee's claim would fail on the same facts. [34] The apparent purpose of section 49(6) ERA was to avoid this by ensuring that the non-employee worker should not receive any greater compensation than an employee in the same situation. But the wording adopted is ineffective to achieve that aim. It does not provide, as it could have done, that the worker whose contract is terminated will receive no greater compensation than if that worker was an employee. Instead it proceeds on the express hypothesis of comparing with a worker dismissed 'for the reason specified in section 103A'. Therefore, in the case of a worker whose dismissal is significantly influenced by protected disclosures, the comparison is expressly with an employee in relation to whom the reasons or principal reason for dismissal was a protected disclosure (the section 103A reason), rather than an employee in relation to whom the protected disclosure was only a significant influence but not the principal reason. That is an anomaly, but Elias LJ was clear, in *Fecitt*, that it is for Parliament to rectify this.

7.83 Further, this is not the only anomaly that may arise by virtue of the difference between the tests for unfair dismissal and detriment. The difference may be particularly acute in a constructive dismissal context. Suppose a worker complains of adverse treatment by his manager in that by reason of a lack of trust, s/he is not afforded access to opportunities at work by his/her manager and as a result has lost and is continuing to lose the ability to earn commission or a higher bonus. If a tribunal were to find that the loss of trust was influenced by having made protected disclosures, but that this was not the principal reason, and that this was an influence in the acts or deliberate failures to act in withholding access to various opportunities, the employee would be able to claim compensation for unlawful detriment. Yet if the employee accepted this conduct as a repudiatory breach bringing the contract to an end, there could be no basis for a claim of constructive unfair dismissal by reason of a protected disclosure since the protected disclosures were only a subsidiary influence on the act or failure to act relied upon as constituting the repudiatory breach. The same treatment would be unlawful for the victimization provisions, but not as a basis for protected disclosure liability for unfair dismissal. The pre-dismissal detrimental acts may still give rise to a claim under section 47B ERA if they entailed detriments other than dismissal. But compensation in relation to those detriments might not then include losses consequential on termination if protected disclosures were only a significant influence.[35] Yet, as Elias LJ emphasized in *Fecitt*, that is the consequence of the structure of the legislation. It provides an insufficient basis for watering down the extent of the protection for victimization.

---

[34] See eg *Westminster Drug Project v O'Sullivan* (UKEAT/0235/13/BA, 11 March 2014), where the claimant (a non-employee worker) succeeded on the basis that the dismissal was materially influenced by her protected disclosure; there were other factors taken into account but it was not necessary to decide if the protected disclosure was the principal reason.

[35] But see the discussion of *Roberts v Wilsons Solicitors LLP* [2016] ICR 659, [2016] IRLR 586, in Chapter 10 para 10.61 in relation to the issues liable to arise in relation to whether loss could be attributed to the detriments rather a subsequent termination of employment.

It is therefore now clear, following the Court of Appeal's decision in *Fecitt*, that the test of **7.84** no significant (or material) influence applies to ERA, section 47B detriment claims. It is also clear that in this context, a significant or material influence simply means one which is more than trivial: *Fecitt* (CA) at para 45. In that respect the EAT and Court of Appeal followed the decision in the discrimination context in *Igen Ltd v Wong* [2005] EWCA Civ 142, [2005] ICR 931 at para 37, per Peter Gibson LJ. The Court of Appeal in *Fecitt* (at para 45) referred to a 'material' influence, whereas the test as derived from *Nagarajan* (at para 37, per Lord Nicholls) refers to a 'significant' influence. However, this is a distinction without a difference in this context since in both cases it is used to describe an influence that is more than trivial, and an influence which is not material is to be regarded as trivial.[36]

The EAT in *Fecitt* considered that it was appropriate to apply the formulation derived **7.85** directly from the Burden of Proof Directive 97/80, that the act or failure to act should be in no sense whatsoever on the ground of the protected disclosure. The Directive does not apply to protected disclosure claims, and the Court of Appeal reverted to the no significant influence test. However, this was not a material difference in approach. In *Igen* Peter Gibson LJ noted (at para 37) that the 'no discrimination whatsoever' formula was not in substance different from the no significant influence test. This was noted by the EAT in *Fecitt* (at paras 52 and 65). In the Court of Appeal, whilst adopting the no material influence formulation, the court viewed this as derived from the same EU principles that no discriminatory influence should be tolerated. As Elias LJ explained (at para 43):

> I agree with Mr Linden that *Igen* is not strictly applicable since it has an EU context. However, the reasoning which has informed the EU analysis is that unlawful discriminatory considerations should not be tolerated and ought not to have any influence on an employer's decisions. In my judgment, that principle is equally applicable where the objective is to protect whistleblowers, particularly given the public interest in ensuring that they are not discouraged from coming forward to highlight potential wrongdoing.

(3) Distinction between the disclosure and matters which form part of the background to or are incidental to the disclosure

We have already observed that, as a matter of first impression, the 'no significant/material **7.86** influence' test may appear to be of encouragingly wide ambit from the claimant's point of view. This is all the more so when, as we discuss in more detail below, statute provides that on a complaint of detriment it is for the respondent employer to show the ground on which any act, or deliberate failure to act, was done.[37] However, it is essential to keep in mind that the focus remains (a) on the mental processes of those said to be responsible for the act or deliberate failure, and (b) on whether this was influenced by the fact of the protected disclosure. That said, in many cases a key issue is as to the extent to which it can be said that although what influenced the detrimental act or failure to act was related to the protected disclosure, it was 'separable' or distinct from it. This has arisen in various different forms, being increasingly controversial the closer the issue which is said to be 'separable' from the fact of making the disclosure itself becomes, including:

- something done which is related to or associated with or in preparation for making a protected disclosure, such as investigating matters in relation to the subject matter of it (eg *Bolton School v Evans* [2006] IRLR 500 (EAT) [2007] IRLR 140 (CA)); or

---

[36] See *Fecitt* in the EAT at paras 52, 59, and 65 and *Villallba v Merrill Lynch & Co Inc* [2007] ICR 469 at para 82 (EAT).
[37] See paras 7.191–7.201 below.

- a fact or matter which is consequential on the protected disclosure having been made, such as a breakdown in working relationships and the need to deal with a difficult working environment between colleagues (*NHS Manchester v Fecitt and others* [2011] EWCA Civ 1190, [2012] ICR 372 (CA), *Vivian v Bournemouth BC* (EAT/0254/10, 6 May 2011), or consequential procedural requirements arising in investigating the issues raised (*Shinwari v Vue Entertainment Ltd* (UKEAT/0394/14/BA, 12 March 2015); or
- inadequacies in the way in which the employer responds to the disclosure (*Salisbury NHS Foundation Trust v Wyeth* (UKEAT/0061/15/JOJ, 12 June 2015); *Price v Surrey County Council and Governing Body of Wood Street School* (EAT/0450/10, 27 October 2011); or
- something which is revealed or evidenced by the protected disclosure, such as an underlying health concern or lack of aptitude of the worker for the job, or some prior misconduct of the worker revealed by the information provided (*Martin v Devonshires Solicitors* [2011] ICR 352; *Hossack v Kettering BC* (UKEAT/1113/01, 29 November 2002); or
- the manner or form in which the disclosure was made, such as the use of intemperate language, or the manner in which a 'campaign' of protected disclosures has been pursued (*Panayiotou v Chief Constable of Hampshire Police and another* [2014] IRLR 500 (EAT)); or
- distinct wrongdoing associated with the disclosure, such as a breach of confidentiality (*Aspinall v MSI Mech Forge Ltd* (UKEAT/891/01, 25 July 2002)).

7.87 This lies at the heart of the difficult issues liable to arise in the application of the 'reason why' test. Indeed, as we discuss further at paragraphs 7.100–7.106 below, it was on the basis of drawing a distinction between the protected disclosure and the consequences of it (giving rise to a dysfunctional work environment) that, despite the adoption of the material influence test, the Court of Appeal in *Fecitt* concluded that the employment tribunal had been entitled to find that the test was not satisfied on the facts.

(a) Conduct associated with or in preparation for the disclosure

7.88 The PIDA regime protects disclosure: it does not protect the employee from the consequences of acts which might be regarded as connected to the disclosure but are not disclosures in themselves. Thus, in *London Borough of Harrow v Knight* [2003] IRLR 140 the EAT emphasized that the tribunal had erred in applying a test of whether the detriment suffered by the claimant (ill health) was 'related to' the protected disclosures (see paragraphs 7.73 to 7.75 above). It is plainly not sufficient that disclosures form part of the historical background or context for the act or omission complained of. Rather, they must operate as the reason (or a part of the reason) for that act or omission. Whilst the delay in dealing with his disclosures (and the failure to respond to his enquiries) *might* conceivably have been in conscious or unconscious response to what might have been an unwelcome disclosure by Mr Knight, it did not necessarily follow that it was. Those responsible for dealing with Mr Knight's complaint *might* simply not have got round to acting as they should have done through pressure of other work, indolence, or even, perhaps, because they did not like Mr Knight for reasons entirely unconnected with his protected disclosure.

7.89 One important aspect of the distinction between the disclosure itself and conduct that might be regarded as associated with it, is that it is not a sufficient basis for protection that the detrimental treatment was in response to investigations carried out with a view to gathering or verifying evidence in relation to a prospective protected disclosure. This was brought into sharp focus in *Bolton School v Evans* [2006] IRLR 500 (EAT), [2007] IRLR

140 (CA). Mr Evans, a technology teacher at the respondent school, was concerned that the school's new computer system was insecure, and that information might be obtained from it by pupils in breach of the Data Protection Act. This concern arose out of the school having adopted a single network for educational and administrative purposes. In order to test his concerns, and to demonstrate that they were well founded, Mr Evans hacked into confidential information on the network from a computer used by pupils in the technology department. He gave prior warning of his intention to the member of staff designated by the headmaster as the individual to be contacted in relation to any concerns about the system (Mr Edmundson), and also to the head of computing. After he had hacked into the system he informed Mr Edmundson, the head of computing, and the headmaster of what he had done. He was disciplined, the headmaster having reached the decision that the claimant had deliberately hacked into the network. It was accepted that Mr Evans was acting in good faith and, further, that he might have been justified in his belief that he was not being properly listened to in relation to his security concerns. A written warning was nevertheless issued. Mr Evans appealed, but the appeal was dismissed. Mr Evans decided that his position was untenable and he resigned. He felt that he had been victimized for highlighting security concerns and was aggrieved that the school had focused on his conduct rather than tackling what he considered to be the much more important question of why the system had been established in what he perceived to be an insecure way.

In the ET hearing of his claim for compensation for detriment and constructive dismissal **7.90** Mr Evans argued that the warning (a detriment) had been imposed contrary to ERA, section 47B, in that it had been imposed because he had made a public interest disclosure. He further contended that the imposition of the warning in those circumstances amounted also to a breach of the duty of trust and confidence and that he had resigned in response to that breach. It followed, he contended, that he had been automatically unfairly dismissed contrary to ERA, section 103A.

The ET did not accept that it was reasonable for the school to take the view that the **7.91** hacking into the computer was unauthorized, but it did not doubt that the school had genuinely taken that view. The school believed that Mr Evans had committed an act of misconduct. The tribunal held that there had been a protected disclosure and it reasoned that it was wrong to treat Mr Evans' conduct in hacking into the system as distinct from the disclosure of information itself. The tribunal considered that it would emasculate the public policy behind the legislation to accept the school's submission that Mr Evans was the subject of disciplinary action not because he had blown the whistle on a suspected failure to comply with the legal obligation, but rather because he had hacked into the school's computer system without authority. It said that to allow an employer to defeat a PIDA case in this way would be to drive a coach and horses through the intention of the legislature that whistleblowers should have employment protection. In order to obtain sufficient evidence to found a reasonable belief, Mr Evans had to do more than simply express misgivings. The investigation undertaken by Mr Evans to found his reasonable belief could not be divorced from the disclosure itself. Accordingly he had established that the reason that disciplinary action was taken against him was because he made a protected disclosure.

The EAT disagreed. It concluded that the statute protected disclosures but did not pro- **7.92** tect other conduct by the employee even if that conduct was connected in some way to the disclosures. It contrasted this with the wider scope of the victimization provisions under the Race Relations Act 1976, as reflected in the decision in *Aziz v Trinity Street Taxis Ltd* [1988] IRLR 204. The law only protected a claimant if s/he had reasonable grounds for his/her belief and it did not allow him/her to commit what would otherwise be acts of misconduct in the hope that s/he might be able to establish the justification for the belief to the employer. The law protects the disclosure of information which the employee reasonably believes tends to demonstrate the kind of wrongdoing, or anticipated wrongdoing, which is covered by section 43B. It does not protect the actions of the employee which are directed to establishing or confirming the reasonableness of that belief.

7.93 In giving permission to appeal ([2006] EWCA Civ 710), Sedley LJ noted the public importance of the point, in that:

> there are likely to be few cases where a whistle-blower has not been dismissed for what the employer genuinely believes to be misconduct; so that the purpose and effectiveness of the 1998 Act may themselves be in question.

7.94 However, the Court of Appeal dismissed Mr Evans' appeal, ([2006] EWCA Civ 1653, [2007] IRLR 140). It held that it was wrong to give a special purposive meaning to the term 'disclosure' so as to encompass Mr Evans' act of hacking into the system. It was not sufficient that the school had found out about the misconduct as a result of the disclosure. Mr Evans was dismissed for his misconduct in hacking into the system, not for making a disclosure that the system was vulnerable. Although the tribunal should look with care at arguments that a dismissal was because of acts related to the disclosure rather than because of the disclosure itself, in Mr Evans' case there was no reason to attribute ulterior motives to the employer.[38]

7.95 It was argued that there were two aspects to Mr Evans' decision to hack into the school's computer network. It was in part to test his concerns and as such was part of the investigation in order to establish reasonable belief. But it was also to demonstrate the validity of his concerns as to security weaknesses. In relation to this, it was argued that the conduct of breaking into the system might be regarded as part and parcel of the disclosures which Mr Evans made. By hacking into the computer system Mr Evans was communicating, and evidencing by his conduct, that the system was inadequate. Further, he did so in the context of having raised these concerns expressly both before and after having hacked into the system. Nothing in the legislation expressly requires that the disclosure has to be by words or in writing.[39] This argument was rejected on the facts: breaking into the computer system did not involve communication with anyone. If, however, a disclosure could be by conduct (which was not the finding in *Bolton School*) it is plain that it must be permissible in some circumstances for an employer to assert that it is disciplining the employee by reason of that conduct rather than for the message which the conduct is intended to convey. Otherwise, to adapt the facts in *Bolton School*, Mr Evans would have been insulated against disciplinary action even if he had caused wholly disproportionate damage to the computer network, and acted precipitately when there was no reason to believe that his concerns were not being heeded. See also *Eiger Securities LLP v Korshunova* [2017] IRLR 115 (EAT), at paras 49–54 (discussed at para 3.118 above), where the ET erred in failing to consider if detrimental treatment was due not to the alleged protected disclosure, but instead to acting consistently with the objection raised in the alleged protected disclosure (by repeated objection to sharing passwords and changing the use of passwords so as to frustrate the use of her Bloomberg chat handle by others).

7.96 The decision in *Bolton School* may be contrasted with the slightly earlier decision of the EAT in *The Trustees of Mama East African Women's Group v Dobson* (UKEAT/0219/05 and EAT/0220/05, 23 June 2005). Mrs Dobson was employed as an English teacher by the respondent, a small charity whose aim is to support Somali women in Sheffield and to

---

[38] Buxton LJ at para 18.
[39] See Chapter 3, para 3.28, discussing the decision in *Aspinall v MSI Mech Forge Ltd* (EAT/891/01, 25 July 2002).

provide them with training in English as a second language. She received information from a student that a former student had mistreated children at a crèche which the respondent operated. The former student was the sister of the manager (S) to whom the claimant would normally have first reported the allegation. For this reason Mrs Dobson first reported the matter to another employee or ex-employee of the respondent, but she was advised to report it to S and then did so. S purported to investigate the allegations and found them unfounded. Following a disciplinary hearing Mrs Dobson was then dismissed on three grounds: (1) making a false allegation, (2) not following the procedure thereby damaging the reputation of the respondent, and (3) breach of confidentiality (referring to the report to a colleague or former colleague). The tribunal found that Mrs Dobson had a reasonable belief for her report, based on the information she had received, and it amounted to a protected disclosure. The tribunal also found that the reason for dismissal was the protected disclosure. Of the reasons given in the dismissal letter, the fact that the disclosure was false did not prevent it being protected and the other matters were intimately connected with the protected disclosure.

In the appeal it was argued that the reasons given in the letter were indeed distinct from the disclosure itself. This was rejected by the EAT, primarily on the basis that the tribunal had made a finding of fact which was open to it, being that it was the protected disclosure that was the principal reason for dismissal. However, the EAT also made clear that fine distinctions between the disclosure and matters associated it with it were unlikely to be successful in the context of the legislation (at paras 19 and 25): **7.97**

> There is a very strong public interest in the vindication of whistle blowers so that their action is protected. This does not mean that all of their claims and allegations have to be supported. They have to be investigated and provided the disclosure meets the terms of the Employment Rights Act 1996, action against them is unlawful. See for the social policy behind the Act and its application in employment cases *ALM v Bladon* [2002] ICR 1444, *Street v Derbyshire* above, our judgment in *Lucas v The Chichester Diocesan Housing Association* EAT/0731/04, and the approach of Dame Janet Smith in the Shipman Enquiry which adopted evidence given to it by Public Concern at Work.
>
> . . .
>
> . . . it cannot be right for an employer to assert a non-tainted reason and yet in the social context of this legislation avoid its connection to the protected activity. The reason or the principal reason the Tribunal found was that the Claimant had raised a disclosure.

This reasoning had considerable force in relation to the attempt to draw a distinction between the disclosure and its falsity. However, it was more problematic in relation to the other two grounds set out in the letter of dismissal. As regards failing to follow the correct procedure, this related to a contention that Mrs Dobson ought to have obtained the assistance of an interpreter to clarify what had been said. The tribunal rejected the need for this. Insofar as an inference was drawn that this was not the real reason, this was unexceptional. However, insofar as it was rejected as the reason because it was associated with the disclosure, this was problematic. What mattered for the purposes of section 103A was the respondent's reasons for dismissal rather than whether they were reasonable. The obtaining of an interpreter was an aspect of the investigation which preceded the disclosure. Insofar as this was drawing a distinction between the disclosure and the manner of the disclosure, we consider that distinction further below (paragraph 7.125 et seq), but again in summary that is a distinction that has been recognized as permissible in principle, but to be approached with caution. Similarly, the allegation of breach of confidentiality related to a matter preceding the disclosure consisting of the (unprotected) disclosure to the colleague. **7.98**

7.99 In the context of the legislation it is indeed appropriate that tribunals should be wary of too readily drawing a distinction between a disclosure and the way it is made.[40] However, it is apparent, not only from the wording of section 47B but also the structure of the legislation, that there is a distinction to be drawn between the steps to investigate concerns as to relevant failures, and the disclosures themselves. Thus, the EAT and the Court of Appeal in *Bolton School* were, in our view, right to conclude that the employment tribunal had adopted an incorrect approach in construing the legislation purposively so as to conclude that 'the investigation undertaken by the employee to found his reasonable belief should not be divorced from the disclosure itself'.[41] Equally, in *Trustees of Mama* if the employer's principal reason for dismissal had been a previous breach of confidentiality in what was not a protected disclosure (as opposed to breaching confidentiality by making a protected disclosure) that ought not to have been found to infringe ERA, section 103A. As to this:

(a) The employment tribunal's approach in *Bolton School v Evans* [2006] IRLR 500 would potentially produce absurd results. Plainly, for example, where one employee bullies and assaults a colleague in order to obtain information to sustain a protected disclosure, an employer must be free to take disciplinary action for such conduct. It could not be an answer to say that the bullying was part of an investigation for the purposes of making a protected disclosure. A somewhat analogous point was considered in *Serco Ltd v Redfearn* [2006] EWCA Civ 659, [2006] IRLR 623 (CA), in the context of the Race Relations Act 1976. It was argued by a claimant who had been dismissed due to being a member of the British National Party, which had a 'whites only' membership policy, that 'racial grounds' encompass grounds that are 'significantly informed by racial considerations or racial attitudes' or 'referable to race'. Just as it is insufficient for protection under PIDA that conduct (eg the worker's previous investigation) is referable to the disclosure, so being referable to race was identified as being far too wide a test under the Race Relations Act. Mummery LJ drew attention to the absurd consequences if this was taken to its logical conclusion, including that an employee could not be disciplined for discriminatory conduct.

(b) As in *Redfearn* there is a policy background. If all investigatory action or other steps associated with but previous to the protected disclosure were deemed to be protected as part of the disclosure, this would fatally undermine the structure of the legislation. There is a low threshold for protection for disclosures to an employer precisely because employees are encouraged to raise concerns with an appropriate person who may be better placed to investigate them further. If all investigatory steps by the employee were also protected, however disruptive, a significantly higher threshold would be appropriate in some cases, even in first tier disclosures under section 43C.

(d) The structure of the legislation is premised on there being a reasonable belief for a qualifying disclosure. In many cases the investigatory steps will precede there being such a belief, and be carried out in order to gather the information for such a belief. The logic of the employment tribunal's position in *Bolton School v Evans* would be to provide protection to workers where it turns out that there is information to sustain a reasonable belief and where the worker then makes a disclosure, but not for those who satisfy themselves from their investigations that the concern is not well founded and so do not make the disclosure. Yet there is no strong reason why the two cases, each relating to

---

[40] As noted by the Court of Appeal in *Bolton School*: see para 7.94 above.
[41] It was argued in *Bolton School v Evans* in the Court of Appeal that breaking into the system was itself a disclosure by conduct insofar as it was designed specifically to demonstrate the weakness in security. This was rejected on the facts (see paras 7.89–7.95 above).

workers investigating genuine concerns which may merit further investigation by them, should be treated so differently.

(e) There remains a difficulty that workers might be discouraged from raising concerns if they are advised that there must be a reasonable belief sufficient to satisfy the qualifying disclosure test, yet that investigations to substantiate that belief will not be specially protected. The risk of this is, however, mitigated in two ways:

(i) A tribunal can be expected to analyse critically the reasons for the disciplinary action or dismissal and to regard an assertion by the employer that the real reason was the worker's conduct preceding or associated with the disclosure rather than the disclosure itself with appropriate circumspection: see *Fecitt* [2011] EWCA Civ 1190 [2012] ICR 372 at para 51. This is a process which tribunals are accustomed to undertaking in the context of other discrimination cases, where employers will rarely admit to having taken discriminatory action and it is necessary to assess whether the alleged non-discriminatory reason is true or sufficient.

(ii) As discussed in Chapter 3, in *Darnton v University of Surrey* [2003] ICR 615 the EAT stressed the need to have regard to all the relevant circumstances in deciding whether the requisite belief was held for the purposes of a qualifying disclosure, and in *Bolton School v Evans* it was emphasized that an employee might only have part of the evidential picture. As such, in assessing whether a worker held a reasonable belief that information tends to show a relevant failure, there is scope to take into account potential difficulties in investigating further the basis for a concern, and also to take into account the policy consideration that workers are to be encouraged to make concerns known at an early stage to those best placed to investigate.

(b) Distinction between the disclosure and its consequences

Just as a distinction may in principle be drawn between steps prior to the disclosure and **7.100** the disclosure itself, so there may in principle be a distinction between treatment by reason of the disclosure and by reason of its consequences. Whilst tribunals may be expected to examine carefully whether an employer seeking to draw such a distinction was not significantly influenced by the disclosure itself, the legitimacy in principle of the distinction was confirmed by the Court of Appeal in *NHS Manchester v Fecitt and others* [2011] EWCA Civ 1190, [2012] ICR 372. The claimants in the *Fecitt* case were registered nurses with many years of clinical experience who worked at a walk-in centre run by the respondent Trust. Mrs Fecitt was a clinical coordinator for walk-in centres, with managerial responsibility for the nursing staff at the walk-in centre. Mrs Woodcock was a primary care nurse who worked there principally and Mrs Hughes was a bank nurse who worked shifts at the centre. Mrs Woodcock became concerned that a colleague working as a general nurse, Mr Swift, was making what she believed to be false statements to other members of staff about his clinical experience and qualifications. She expressed her concerns to Mrs Fecitt who carried out some research and discovered that Mr Swift was only qualified as a children's nurse. Mrs Fecitt raised concerns about Mr Swift's lack of his professed qualifications to her line manager, Mrs Coates, and was supported by Mrs Woodcock and Mrs Hughes. It was accepted that these concerns were protected disclosures. Mr Swift acknowledged to Mrs Coates that he had exaggerated his qualifications to colleagues, although not to the trust itself. He apologized and confirmed that there would be no repetition of his behaviour. Although Mrs Coates was prepared to leave it at that, the claimants were not satisfied with this response and sought to pursue the matter further, causing dissatisfaction amongst some of their colleagues, who considered that they were subjecting Mr Swift to a 'witch hunt'. The workforce divided into three groups: those supporting Mr Swift, those siding with the claimants, and those remaining neutral.

7.101 Mr Swift was interviewed again as a result of Mrs Fecitt's persistence, this time by a different manager, Mrs Kerwin, who took a similar view to Mrs Coates: the matter should not be taken any further. However, Mr Swift became extremely distraught and there were concerns about his mental state. He lodged a bullying and harassment complaint against Mrs Fecitt (the employment tribunal rejected the suggestion that management encouraged Mr Swift to make this complaint). A hearing took place at which it was concluded that Mrs Fecitt had not been guilty of bullying or harassment, although questions were raised about her management style.

7.102 Mr Swift was suspended from duty. Mrs Fecitt made a formal complaint under the trust's whistleblowing policy. The tribunal found that the claimants were subjected to certain hostile and unpleasant acts as a result of continuing to pursue the matter. Although senior management tried to encourage the staff to work professionally with each other, the employment tribunal concluded that no real attempt was made to identify the adverse behaviour to which the claimants had been subjected. Nor did management consider whether it might be necessary to threaten disciplinary sanctions to prevent the situation from escalating. Mrs Fecitt, however, had her management functions removed from her. The trust's medical director produced an interim report concluding that there were no concerns about Mr Swift's competence and his suspension was then lifted. In his final report the medical director said that no further action should be taken against Mr Swift, but he also found that Mrs Fecitt had been justified both in initially raising the matter and also in pursuing it to senior management level. Management was criticized for not being sufficiently robust.

7.103 All three claimants lodged grievances although only that of Mrs Hughes was ultimately pursued to a hearing, at which it was found that she had been subjected to treatment which had resulted in her being 'isolated and prejudiced' by her colleagues, and that management could have done more to prevent this. The tribunal concurred in that analysis and said that it was true of all three claimants. Mrs Fecitt and Mrs Woodcock were removed from the centre and redeployed elsewhere. Mrs Hughes ceased to be offered shifts and the tribunal concluded that this was, at least in part, related to the 'dysfunctional' situation that existed at the centre and which had also resulted in Mrs Fecitt and Mrs Woodcock being redeployed.

7.104 The claimants alleged that the actions taken against them were because they had made protected disclosures and were therefore in breach of their rights under ERA, section 47B. The tribunal held that the trust was not liable under section 47B. It was not sufficient to establish liability that management either did not do as much as it could have done or was simply unsuccessful in its attempts to resolve matters. In any event any failure by the trust to take appropriate steps was not because the claimants had made a protected disclosure. Furthermore, neither Mrs Fecitt nor Mrs Woodcock had been redeployed away from the centre because they had made a protected disclosure. The redeployment was because the centre had been rendered 'dysfunctional' and removal appeared to management to be the only feasible method of resolving the problem. It was not done 'on the ground that' such protected disclosures had been made. As Elias LJ put it in the Court of Appeal, the trust was plainly satisfied that it was management's genuine view that it was necessary to remove Mrs Fecitt and Mrs Woodcock rather than those who were subjecting them to adverse treatment. A similar conclusion was reached by the tribunal with respect to Mrs Hughes, notwithstanding that Mrs Lake, the manager who had ceased to offer Mrs Hughes her shifts, had, when taking advice as to whether she could do this, described Mrs Hughes as a 'trouble causer'.

An appeal was allowed by the EAT and the matter remitted to the tribunal. This was in part **7.105** by reason of a failure to consider vicarious liability—as to which the EAT was found by the Court of Appeal to have been in error (see Chapter 8, paragraphs 8.02–8.04). However, the EAT also considered that the tribunal had applied the wrong 'reason why' test, in that it appeared to have applied a test of direct and proximate cause of the detriment. The tribunal's decision was then restored by the Court of Appeal. Although concluding that the appropriate test was that the protected disclosure must not be any material influence on the act or failure to act, on the tribunal's findings of fact the respondent had succeeded in establishing this. The tribunal's decision showed that it was satisfied that the reasons given by the trust for acting as it did were genuine, and demonstrated that the fact that the claimants had made protected disclosures did not influence those decisions. The tribunal had explained that it was satisfied that although the respondent was open to criticism for not protecting the claimants more effectively than it did, the failure to act more robustly was not a deliberate omission and was not because the protected disclosures had been made. The redeployments had appeared to be the only feasible method of dealing with a dysfunctional situation and that the claimants, the victims of harassment, had been redeployed was obviously not a point lost on the tribunal. The tribunal was satisfied that the respondent had genuinely acted for other reasons; and once an employer satisfies a tribunal that he has acted for a particular reason—here being to remedy a dysfunctional situation—that necessarily discharged the burden. It was only if the tribunal considered that the reason given was false (whether consciously or unconsciously) or that the tribunal was being given something less than the whole story that it would be legitimate to infer victimization. Since the tribunal was satisfied that in redeploying Mrs Fecitt and Mrs Woodcock the respondent had acted in order to resolve the dysfunctional situation, there was no basis for going behind that finding of fact. Similar reasoning applied in the case of Mrs Hughes.

The Court of Appeal therefore drew a crucial distinction between acting by reason of a **7.106** protected disclosure, and acting by reason of the dysfunctional situation which was a consequence of the protected disclosures. The fact that the situation was the result of the protected disclosures did not mean that the employer was influenced in its decision by the protected disclosures. The position would have been otherwise if, for example, the reason that Mrs Fecitt had been redeployed was not simply because of the dysfunctional situation but was influenced by the fact that she had made protected disclosures. Whether that was the case was a question of fact for the tribunal.

A similar approach was taken by the ET and EAT in *Vivian v Bournemouth BC* (UKEAT/ **7.107** 0254/10, 6 May 2011). Mrs Vivian raised a grievance against her line manager, alleging she had been bullied. The conclusion of the grievance panel (and the appeal panel) was that there was insufficient evidence to uphold her complaint. Management decided to separate Mrs Vivian from her line manager. She was placed in a redeployment pool. She refused to cooperate in the redeployment process, contending that it was the perpetrator of the alleged bullying who should have been moved. Since it was therefore not possible to find her alternative employment Mrs Vivian was dismissed. The employment tribunal accepted that Mrs Vivian's grievance against her line manager amounted to a protected disclosure. Mrs Vivian argued that a policy under which a person who claimed she had been bullied could be put in a redeployment pool and ultimately dismissed was inherently contrary to ERA, section 47B. Rejecting this contention the EAT concluded that the tribunal was entitled to find that:

(1) Mrs Vivian was placed in the redundancy pool not by reason of having made a protected disclosure but because it was concluded that Mrs Vivian and the alleged perpetrator needed to be separated; and

(2) none of those dealing with the matter were motivated by the fact that Mrs Vivian had made a protected disclosure.

7.108 The fact that the perceived need for separation arose following a protected disclosure had been made did not prevent reliance on that need as the reason for removing the claimant from working with the manager she had complained about. Indeed, if it was not open to the employer to act in this way, this could result in considerable injustice since either the need for separation would be ignored, or otherwise it would necessarily have to be those who were the subject of complaint who would have to move even though the complaint had not been upheld.

7.109 Like the *Fecitt* case, the decision in *Vivian* illustrates the limits of protection for those making public interest disclosures. The disclosure may set in train events leading to circumstances which require management action which may be adverse to the whistleblower, but that action will not necessarily be by reason of the protected disclosure.

7.110 The principle that the consequences of a disclosure may be distinguished from the disclosure itself is not limited to dealing with a potentially dysfunctional workforce. A further illustration is provided by the decision of the EAT in *Shinwari v Vue Entertainment Ltd* (UKEAT/0394/14/BA, 12 March 2015). After a review of leading authorities from the discrimination context,[42] the EAT confirmed that a tribunal is entitled to draw a distinction between the fact of making a protected disclosure and the consequences of it, and further rejected a suggestion that this was only permissible in an exceptional case. Mr Shinwari was employed as a customer assistant for a cinema operator. He witnessed a colleague selling complimentary tickets to members of the public in contravention of the respondent's rules. The colleague then offered Mr Shinwari a £5 bribe to buy his silence. Mr Shinwari took the money but only as evidence to hand to managers and not as a bribe. His complaint as to his employer's subsequent conduct included a failure (a) to keep confidential that he was the source of information about the wrongdoing of another employee (Mr Ali); (b) to protect him and keep him safe in the workplace; (c) to move him to a safe working environment other than simply to nearby Shepherd's Bush, which was too closely located to the Westfield cinema location where he had been based, and (d) to stop bullying and harassment he suffered at the hands of colleagues, resulting in him being ostracized and isolated. He also complained that his hours of work had been reduced. The EAT concluded that the tribunal had been entitled to find that there were legitimate reasons for the respondent's acts, and those reasons were not his disclosures. In relation to the alleged failure to keep the information confidential, the reason for disclosing the claimant's witness statement to Mr Ali was the legitimate reason, consistent with the respondent's disciplinary policy, that an individual who was to be disciplined should be provided with the evidence on which the disciplinary action would be based.

7.111 The safeguard, as the EAT noted in *Shinwari* (at para 58), is that the tribunal must be astute to ensure that the factors relied on (a) are genuinely separable from the fact of making the protected disclosures, and (b) are in fact the reasons why the employer acted as it did.[43] To similar effect, albeit focusing only on the second of these elements—the reason for the employer's actions—the Court of Appeal noted in *Fecitt* (per Elias LJ at para 51) that:

> where the whistleblower is subject to a detriment without being at fault in any way, tribunals will need to look with a critical—indeed sceptical—eye to see whether the innocent

---

[42] *Woodhouse v North West Homes Leeds Ltd* [2013] IRLR 773 and *Martin v Devonshires Solicitors* [2011] ICR 352, which are considered at paras 7.135–7.145 below.
[43] See to the same effect: *Panayiotou v Chief Constable of Hampshire Police and another* [2014] IRLR 500 (EAT) at para 52.

explanation given by the employer for the adverse treatment is indeed the genuine explanation. The detrimental treatment of an innocent whistleblower necessarily provides a strong prima facie case that the action has been taken because of the protected disclosure and it cries out for an explanation from the employer.

Ultimately, however, whether detrimental treatment was significantly influenced by the protected disclosure itself rather than the simply the situation which it created raises a question of fact for the tribunal.

7.112 Whilst these decisions indicate limits of protection, they also illustrate that considerable difficulties would be likely to arise if a distinction of this nature cannot be drawn. Employers must in principle be able to manage the difficult situations that may arise where protected disclosures impact upon working relationships. As discussed in Chapter 3, an important aspect of the protected disclosure legislation is that a disclosure may be protected notwithstanding that it includes allegations that are found to be incorrect, but where the worker reasonably believed at the time that information tending to show a relevant failure was being conveyed. Where that involves allegations made about colleagues it is unsurprising if it leads to serious tensions requiring management action, such as separating the workers involved, notwithstanding that this may reasonably be regarded as detrimental treatment. As noted above (para 7.108), it would challenge basic concepts of fairness if, given such a situation, it necessarily had to be someone who was the subject of a false allegation, rather than the worker who made the allegation, who had to be moved away. Indeed there may have been allegation and counter-allegation, each properly treated as conveying information and amounting to a relevant failure.

7.113 The scope for the employer to avoid liability by relying on this distinction has, however, to some extent been narrowed by the introduction of vicarious liablity. Thus, whilst an employer may, as in *Fecitt*, take action in response to the need to deal with a dysfunctional workforce, that will not provide an answer to vicarious liablity for the acts of victimization of a co-worker which may arise from that dysfunctional situation. Indeed, it was in part on that basis that the EAT in *Fecitt* allowed an appeal (proceeding on the then incorrect basis that there was vicarious liability prior to the amendments made by the ERRA): [2011] ICR 476. Similarly if, as in *Shinwari*, an employer fails to keep the identity of a whistleblower confidential, it would in turn be exposed to the risk of liability by reason of the alleged perpetrator treating the worker detrimentally by reason of the disclosure.

(c) Distinction between the disclosure and inadequacies in dealing with it

7.114 In *Salisbury NHS Foundation Trust v Wyeth* (UKEAT/0061/15/JOJ, 12 June 2015), at para 29, HHJ Eady QC noted that a further distinction has been recognized between the protected disclosure itself and the way in which the employer responds to it. That was a distinction drawn in *Price v Surrey County Council and another* (EAT/0450/10, 27 October 2011), where a failure in one aspect of the investigation of the matters raised by the protected disclosure was not by reason of the disclosure (see Chapter 9, paragraphs 9.31 and 9.32).[44]

7.115 As illustrated by the decision in *Shinwari* (paragraph 7.110 et seq above) this is closely related to the distinction between the disclosure and its consequences. Indeed, we suggest it can properly be regarded as being one instance of that distinction. In each case the key

---

[44] See to similar effect *Ibekwe v Sussex Partnership NHS Foundation Trust* (UKEAT/0072/14, 20 November 2014), where a managerial failure to deal with a grievance (containing a protected disclosure) was not on the grounds of the protected disclosure.

is to focus on what the reason was for the conduct of which complaint is made, and it requires a critical analysis of any explanation provided for the detrimental conduct. In *Wyeth* the claimant, who was a nursing assistant, had made protected disclsosures as to concerns that an operating department practitioner on his team (ODP1) was misusing anaesthetic drugs. He raised the concerns initially in 2011 and made a further disclosure in 2012, in each case to the General Manager of Main Theatres, Mrs Hope. The 2012 disclosure resulted in a conflict with another ODP (ODP2), who had acted aggressively towards the claimant after being told by Mrs Hope to stop his own investigation into the allegations. After the claimant complained about this to Mrs Hope, he was moved temporarily from night shift to day shift. He was told this was to avoid the hostile situation with ODP2, but he found it humiliating and embarrassing. The respondent investigated the allegations against ODP1, and it was concluded that there was no direct evidence to support the allegation of anaesthetic drug misuse. However, that conclusion was reached without interviewing the claimant, whose name was not put forward to the investigator by Mrs Hope. The claimant was notified of the outcome of the investigation by letter, which is when he realized that he had not been called to be part of the investigation. The letter was also sent to other members of staff and ended with the comment that 'unfounded gossip undermining [ODP1's] return to work' would not be tolerated, which the claimant took as a veiled warning to him. On returning to work after the Easter holiday, it was apparent that the outcome of the investigation was generally known and being discussed. The claimant felt that he had been made to look a liar, and therefore tendered his resignation.

7.116 The ET found that he had been constructively dismissed, and as no fair reason for dismissal was put forward it followed that the dismissal was unfair. But it also inferred that the reason for dismissal was the claimant's protected disclosures. The EAT allowed an appeal in relation to that finding and remitted the issue to a (differently constituted) tribunal. Whilst the ET identified six elements to the detrimental treatment (amouting to repudiatory conduct) in response to which the claimant resigned, a reasonable reading of its decision was that the principal elements were the move onto the day shift and the exclusion of the claimant from the investigation. Whilst the employer had not put forward a fair reason for the dismissal, in relation to section 103A ERA (and the same would apply for section 47B ERA), it was still necessary to consider the explanation for the conduct and whether it was distinct from the protected disclosure itself, given that the respondent had put forward some evidence by way of explanation of its conduct. So far as concerned the shift move, there was evidence that Mrs Hope was concerned about a volatile situation and took the view that there was a need for an experienced ODP to work on the night shift. Since ODP1 was likely to be suspended, she did not want to move ODP2 as well. That potentially provided an explanation based on the consequences of the dislosure/the way the employer responded to it rather than the disclosure itself, but the ET failed to engage with that explanation, or to state whether it was accepted or rejected, and if rejected why.

7.117 In relation to the claimant's exclusion from the investigation process, it appears that the ET had identified the explanation as being Mrs Hope's desire to save face by avoiding disclosure of the 2011 disclosure and how she had failed to deal with it. That was not laudable conduct on Mrs Hope's part. But there still needed to be an assessment of whether it amounted to detrimental treatment not by reason of the protected disclosure itself, but as a consequence of it and which was to be regarded as distinct. It was not possible to ascertain from the tribunal's reasoning how it addressed this and how it impacted on its assessment of the reason or principal reason for dismissal. The appeal was therefore allowed on the basis that the ET had failed to conduct the necessary critical analysis of the respondent's reason for its conduct and failed properly to explain its finding and reasons in that regard.

(d) Distinctions more closely connected to the disclosure itself

7.118 The above categories entail identifying some element which is plainly distinct from the disclosure, such as the investigation prior to it or the working relationship that may be consequential upon it. But it is far more problematic where the employer contends that something about the disclosure itself, such as the fact that it was a breach of confidence or as to the manner of the worker's disclosure, was a legitimate basis for disciplinary action or dismissal. The decisions considering this issue may be broadly considered under the following heads:

(1) Breach of confidentiality or other wrongdoing (short of a criminal offence) involved in making the disclosure.
(2) The manner of the disclosure.
(3) Other matters evidenced by the disclosure that may be regarded as separable from it.

7.119 Although we consider each of these in turn, there is an overlap between them (in particular in relation to the second and third categories) and the considerations that are relevant to them.

7.120 ***Breach of confidentiality*** Where a disclosure involves a criminal offence, section 43B(3) ERA expressly provides that it is not a qualifying disclosure. There is no express provision as to the position where the disclosure entails a tort such as breach of confidentiality or breach of copyright. Clearly that does not of itself prevent the disclosure being a protected disclosure. But is it open to an employer to contend that it was not the fact of the disclosure itself, but the fact that for example it involves a breach of confidentiality that was the reason for the detrimental treatment or dismissal.

7.121 The decision in *Aspinall v MSI Mech Forge Ltd* (UKEAT/891/01, 25 July 2002) might be regarded as providing some support for such a submission. Mr Aspinall arranged for a colleague to make a video of how certain factory equipment worked as evidence in support of Aspinall's personal injury claim. Mr Aspinall passed the video to his solicitor, and the ET held that this amounted to a protected disclosure in relation to health and safety. When the employer discovered that the video had been handed over in this way, Mr Aspinall was subjected to disciplinary proceedings and put under pressure to name the person who made the video. He was told that if he named the person he would be given a final written warning and if he did not, there would be further discussion as to action to be taken. He resigned in response. The EAT disposed of his claim that he had been constructively dismissed on the basis that he had not been threatened with dismissal and had instead resigned of his own accord.[45] However, it also commented on the protected disclosure issues. It expressed reservations as to whether making the video amounted to a protected disclosure—and this was subsequently cited in *Bolton School v Evans* as support for the distinction that it drew between a protected disclosure and the investigation.

7.122 The EAT also held that even if making the video had amounted to a protected disclosure, the allegedly repudiatory act on the part of the employer—the demand to name the colleague who had taken the video—was not by reason of a protected disclosure, but solely because of the perceived breach of confidentiality as to the employer's manufacturing process. The

---

[45] The EAT in *Aspinall* did not apply a test that it was sufficient if the protection disclosure was a significant influence. Instead (as noted by the EAT in *Fecitt*), it followed the test propounded by Lord Scott in *Chief Constable of West Yorkshire Police v Khan* [2001] UKHL 48, [2001] ICR 1065 at 1082 of whether the protected disclosure was 'the real reason, the core reason, the causa causans, the motive for the treatment complained of'. As the Court of Appeal's judgment in *Fecitt* was to show, this is not the correct test in detriment cases (see paras 7.69–7.72 above).

perceived breach of confidentiality appears to have related to the employer's misapprehension that the video might have been made by an outside third party—whereas in fact the claimant had said that it was made by a colleague (EAT decision, para 6).

7.123 One difficulty with the brief reasoning in *Aspinall* is that it does not directly address what was alleged to be the breach of confidentiality and whether, if the breach consisted of the making of a protected disclosure, it would still have been regarded as permissible for the employer to discipline the claimant on the grounds of that breach. Ordinarily it would not, we suggest, be acceptable for a tribunal to permit an employer to draw a simple distinction between the information conveyed in a protected disclosure and a breach of confidence in making it. This would permit a coach and horses to be driven through the legislation. The structure of the legislation carefully identifies the requirements for protection at each stage. That protection would be illusory if an employer could argue that, for example, although all the requirements of section 43G are satisfied (including that disclosure is reasonable in all the circumstances), the employee could be disciplined for making the disclosure in breach of confidence. This would be particularly unsatisfactory since the legislation deliberately avoids tying protection to the law of confidentiality. Indeed, in *Street v Derbyshire Unemployed Workers' Centre* [2004] EWCA Civ 964, [2005] ICR 97, the Court of Appeal specifically drew attention to the differing tests for protection that apply in relation to the law of confidentiality.

7.124 It is possible, however, to imagine some situations that may give rise to more difficult issues, and which suggest a fact-sensitive enquiry may be required as to whether, exceptionally, confidentiality can be distinguished from the fact of the disclosure. Suppose the disclosure is made under section 43C(1)(b) to someone who is not the employer, on the basis that the worker reasonably believes that the failure relates solely or mainly to the conduct of that person or a matter for which that person has legal responsiblity. Unlike section 43G ERA there is no safety valve for the tribunal to assess whether the disclosure is reasonable in all the circumstances of the case, and nor is there any requirement that the disclosure must first have been made to the employer (though in some cases failure to do so may bear on whether there was a reasonable belief in the relevant failure). It may be said that the protected disclosure provisions cannot be read as giving carte blanche to disclose any confidential information, subject only to it being part of what was reasonably taken into account in forming the reasonable belief as to a relevant failure. Difficult questions might also arise as to whether the confidential information was a necessary element of the information which was the basis of the reasonable belief as to a relevant failure. Suppose, for example, that suspected wrongdoing consists of information which is reasonably believed to show that senior managers are seeking to persuade staff to defect en masse to a competitor and have been disclosing trade secrets to that competitor. The belief that the competitor was complicit in this may be reasonable but wrong. The particular trade secret information held by the senior managers may be relevant, for example in forming a belief that the conduct tends to show a likely breach of an obligation or as to the seriousness of the breach and the engagement of the public interest. Suppose also that the worker confronts the competitor with the information tending to show that it has been encouraging the senior managers to reveal confidential information, but in so doing carelessly reveals the secret information which she is concerned the senior managers have or are likely to disclose, but that the worker is mistaken and that this information has not been disclosed, and its disclosure could have been prevented. It would be surprising if the worker was insulated from any action taken by the employer on the basis that what was disclosed was part of a protected disclosure. But the employer would have to persuade a tribunal that it was this breach of confidentiality, and not the protected disclosure, which was the reason for the disciplinary action.

Distinction between the disclosure itself and the manner of the disclosure or matters **7.125**
evidenced by disclosure An alternative line of reasoning is to seek to draw a distinction
between the fact of making disclosures and the manner in which they are made. Since long
before the enactment of protection for whistleblowers, tribunals had grappled with the distinction between retribution for doing protected acts or activities and action taken against
an employee because of the manner in which protected acts or activities had been performed.

In principle it is plain that the legislation cannot be construed as providing protection for **7.126**
workers to make disclosures in any manner or form they wish subject to meeting the conditions for a qualifying disclosure. To take one extreme example, if a worker communicates
a disclosure in the form of graffiti daubed on the wall of the manager's office, it must in
principle be available for the employer to take appropriate disciplinary action. To similar
effect, in *Panayiotou v Chief Constable of Hampshire Police and another* [2014] IRLR 500 at
para 49, the EAT commented that an example of a case where a distinction may be drawn
is where a worker discloses information using racist or otherwise abusive language. But as
against that, as noted in *Boulding v Land Securities Trillium (Media Services) Ltd* (UKEAT/
0023/0306, 3 May 2006), public policy underlying the legislation requires that 'there is a
certain generosity in the construction of the statute and the treatment of the facts'.[46] That is
particularly apposite in this context. Disclosures may often be advanced in strident terms.
Strong feelings may be aroused by the very fact the worker is raising concerns about relevant
failures, and all the more so where the worker is concerned that previous warnings have
not been heeded. A low threshold for the distinction between the disclosure and manner of
disclosure may risk undermining the protection of the legislation.

The approach taken has been that whilst it may be permissible to draw such a distinction, for **7.127**
example by relying upon the intemperate language used, tribunals should be cautious about
doing so. This approach was first taken in relation to victimization for carrying out health
and safety or trade union duties. The dangers of permitting too fine a distinction to be drawn,
based on the way in which a protected activity is carried out, were emphasized in *Goodwin
v Cabletel UK Ltd* [1997] IRLR 665.[47] Mr Goodwin was employed by the respondents as a
construction manager and a health and safety representative. He raised concerns about the
safety record of one particular firm of subcontractors. He wanted to take a strong line against
the firm but his employers favoured a more conciliatory approach. Ultimately, his employer
decided that he should be removed from direct dealings with the firm in question and his job
was changed to that of assistant construction manager reporting to a manager who was formerly his equal. In the light of the demotion, he resigned and claimed constructive dismissal.
He claimed he had been dismissed automatically (constructively) unfairly for carrying out or
proposing to carry out his health and safety duties. The EAT held that the tribunal had erred
in law in dismissing his claim on the basis that it was the way in which he carried out his
health and safety activities, rather than the actual doing of them, which led to his dismissal.
The EAT commented (at para 40) that:

> the protection afforded to the way in which a designated employee carries out his health
> and safety activities must not be diluted by too easily finding acts done for that purpose to
> be a justification for dismissal; on the other hand, not every act, however malicious or irrel-
> evant to the task in hand, must necessarily be treated as a protected act in circumstances
> where dismissal would be justified on legitimate grounds.

---

[46] See Chapter 3, paras 3.101–3.102.
[47] The EAT purported to follow the Court of Appeal's decision in *Bass Taverns Ltd v Burgess* [1995]
IRLR 596, relating to dismissal for union activities, although the policy considerations were set out less
firmly in that case, and it turned largely on a finding as to the scope of union activities in the context.

7.128 The EAT (at para 39) cited with approval the judgment of Phillips J in *Lyon v St James Press Ltd* [1976] IRLR 215, where he said (at paras 16 and 20), in relation to the protection for trade union activities, that:

> . . . trade union activities must not be allowed to operate as a cloak or an excuse for conduct which ordinarily would justify dismissal; equally, the right to take part in the affairs of the trade union must not be obstructed by too easily finding acts done for the purpose to be a justification for dismissal. The marks are easy to describe, but the channel between them is difficult to navigate.
>
> . . .
>
> We do not say that every such act is protected. For example, wholly unreasonable, extraneous or malicious acts done in support of trade union activities might be a ground for a dismissal which would not be unfair.

7.129 The tenor of these cases is therefore to recognize the caution required before allowing a tribunal to draw a distinction between the manner in which union or health and safety activities are carried out (and by extension the manner in which a disclosure is made) and the activities themselves, whilst recognizing that drawing such a distinction may be permissible. That has also been the approach adopted in the protected disclosure context. To that end, in *Hossack v Kettering BC* (UKEAT/1113/01, 29 November 2002)[48] the EAT accepted (at para 41) that whilst it was in principle permissible to differentiate between the content of a disclosure and the manner in which it is made, such a distinction could emasculate the legislation and any tribunal approaching a protected disclosure would need to be alert to that danger.

7.130 The manner of the disclosure may be relevant in part in that it may give rise to consequences which are themselves capable of being regarded as separable from the fact of disclosure. As the EAT noted in *Korashi v Abertawe Bro Morgannwg University Local Health Board* [2012] IRLR 4 (EAT), at para 98, there is a distinction between a protected act and the manner in which it is done, but, citing *Vivian*, the distinction is particularly important where the manner reflects on the management of the working environment. However, it is clear that the potential distinction between the disclosure and the manner of the disclosure is not confined to situations where there is some consequential effect, such as an impact on relationships, which may be identified as a distinct reason for the detrimental treatment. Further, whilst in *Lyon v St James Press Ltd* the EAT referred to the exception applying in extreme circumstances such as 'wholly unreasonable, extraneous or malicious acts' as discussed further below (paragraph 7.146), there is no principle of law or requirement that the distinction can only be drawn in exceptional cases. Such a requirement was rejected by the EAT, in *Panayiotou v Chief Constable of Hampshire Police and another* [2014] IRLR 500 in the context of drawing a distinction between the fact of having made disclosures and the manner in which a 'campaign' of disclosures was pursued.[49] We return to this in the following section, in relation to consideration of how the case law has developed.

7.131 That said, the less extreme the manner of the disclosure, the greater may be the evidential hurdle in demonstrating that the treatment was indeed due to the manner of the disclosure and not influenced to a significant extent by the fact or content of the disclosure. For that reason, whilst not required as a matter of law, it is to be expected that a defence based only

---

[48] Discussed further at para 7.134 below.
[49] See also *Shinwari v Vue Entertainment Ltd* (UKEAT/0394/14/BA, 12 March 2015), considered at para 7.110, where the EAT similarly rejected an exceptionality test, but not in the context of drawing a distinction based on the manner of disclosure.

on a distinction between disclosure and the manner of the disclosure without more, will indeed ordinarily be met with healthy scepticism. But ultimately, once it is accepted in principle that the distinction is capable of being made, the issue of whether it is established is one of fact for the tribunal. Further, even where a tribunal rejects the contention that the act or failure to act was by reason of the manner of disclosure, insofar as the manner of the disclosure was an influence in the decision this may be taken into account in order to reduce compensation. We consider this further in Chapter 10.[50]

Distinction between the disclosure and other separable matters evidenced by it   A further **7.132**
distinction considered in the cases has been between the disclosure itself and something which is evidenced by the disclosures but which the tribunal is entitled to regard as distinct from it. Again, this raises the problematic issue of a distinction not based on a situation or act which is clearly distinct from the disclosure, such as the investigation or the breakdown in working relationships, but adverse consequences flowing directly from the disclosure itself, perhaps because of what it reveals. It is the very fact of the disclosure or its content, and in turn what it evidences, that is relied upon.

It is plain that in principle the distinction must be capable of being drawn between a **7.133**
disclosure and matters evidenced by a disclosure. To take an extreme example, if a worker discloses (confesses) to having been involved in planning a robbery, clearly the employer is entitled to dismiss and report the worker to the police. The fact the wrongdoing is evidenced by the disclosure provides no protection from that course. Yet whilst the principle is clear that a distinction may properly be drawn between the disclosure and what it evidences, the practical application of that principle is fact sensitive and may be fraught with difficulty.

The EAT's decision in *Hossack v Kettering BC* (UKEAT/1113/01, 29 November 2002) pro- **7.134**
vides an instance of a protected disclosure decision falling within this category. Ms Hossack was dismissed from her position as policy research officer to the Conservative group on the council after writing a letter to the district auditor with allegations of wrongdoing against officers of the council and Labour councillors. The EAT held that the tribunal had been entitled to find that the reason for Ms Hossack's dismissal was not the protected disclosure she made, but her inability to distinguish her role as a research officer employed by the council, from a political role as an elected member of the Conservative group. That inability had resulted in a loss of confidence in Ms Hossack as an employee. The tribunal had found that the councillor who dismissed her had no difficulty with the information in the disclosure itself. However, the disclosure, and the comments by Ms Hossack within it, such as that the Conservative group was her group, showed Ms Hossack's inability to understand the limits of her advisory role. The claim failed not on the basis of a distinction based on the manner of the disclosure but because the fact of making it demonstrated that she was not suitable for her role.

In *Hossack* the employer's focus was on the fact of having made the disclosures rather than **7.135**
the merits or accuracy of what was said. In *Martin v Devonshires Solicitors* [2011] ICR 352, albeit in the context of a claim of victimization for doing protected acts under sex discrimination legislation, it was the content of the disclosures and the falsity of that content which were relied upon as evidencing separable matters. The protected acts were said to be contained in grievances brought by the claimant which complained of harassment and

---

[50] See Chapter 10, paras 10.26–10.40 in relation to contributory fault in the event of dismissal. Contributory conduct may also be taken into account in assessing which loss is to be regarded as attributable to the victimization for the purposes of ERA, s 49(2).

victimization. Her allegations were found to be false and medical evidence later indicated that the allegations were likely to have arisen from a mental illness and there could be further similar allegations if the claimant returned to work. The claimant was dismissed on the grounds that the relationship with the employer had irretrievably broken down. The EAT concluded (at p 363F–G) that it was the fact that the claimant was mentally ill and the management problems to which that gave rise which were the reasons for the dismissal. Her complaints were only evidence of that condition. Accordingly the employment tribunal had been entitled to find that there were a series of features or consequences of the complaint that were properly and genuinely separable from the making of the complaint itself: the falseness of the allegations, the fact that she was unable to accept that they were false, and that both these features were the result of mental illness and the risk of further disruptive and unmanageable conduct as a result of that illness. The EAT noted that whilst such a line of argument may be abused, employment tribunals can be trusted to distinguish between features which should and should not be treated as properly separable from the making of the complaint.

7.136 *Martin* might be distinguished from cases of protected disclosure victimization on the basis that an important part of the employment tribunal's reasoning in *Martin*, in distinguishing the protected act from the other features that were the reason for the decision, was that it was necessary to discern whether or not the fact that the grievance alleged unlawful discrimination played any material part in the employer's reasons (at p 362B–C). The employment tribunal accepted evidence that the fact that the grievances made reference to discrimination had no material bearing on the decision (at p 362G). On the facts it was therefore possible in *Martin* to identify features that were distinct and separable from the protected act. But in practice, whilst the facts may be regarded as having been fairly extreme, the decision has been regarded as supporting more broadly that a fact-sensitive distinction may be drawn between a protected act or protected disclosure and separable factors or consequences following from or evidenced by it.

7.137 An attempt to curtail the scope for such a distinction was made by the EAT in *Woodhouse v West North West Homes Leeds Ltd* [2013] IRLR 773. Again this was a protected act (as opposed to protected disclosure) case. The respondent, WNW, managed part of the housing stock of Leeds City Council. Mr Woodhouse was working for WNW as a project officer and because of this he had a working relationship with a Mr Chapman, a principal surveyor employed by Leeds. Mr Woodhouse alleged that Mr Chapman had told him that he had 'an attitude problem'. Mr Woodhouse, who is of black ethnicity, regarded this as 'a racist remark'. He made no formal complaint at the time. He later came to the view that his manager had not given him adequate support against Mr Chapman and was also guilty of racist attitudes. Mr Woodhouse raised a grievance which included an allegation of racial discrimination. Subsequently a colleague told Mr Woodhouse that she had heard Mr Chapman saying that Mr Woodhouse 'had only got his job because he was black'. It was also said that Mr Chapman had a habit of calling colleagues by offensive nicknames. Mr Woodhouse raised a further, second, grievance in respect of those matters. A further eight grievances against WNW followed. There were complaints of delay in dealing with Mr Woodhouse's previous grievances and complaints of victimization and harassment which he said were due to his having made previous complaints. Mr Woodhouse's sixth grievance was based on a belief that he had been racially discriminated against in relation to an incident with a colleague. The conduct of management in relation to the sixth grievance was the subject of the seventh grievance. The eighth grievance included an allegation that West North West Homes had manoeuvred him into being selected for redundancy because of his previous allegations. A ninth grievance complained that after returning to work after being off sick, Mr Woodhouse was refused a phased return to work and not paid at the correct rate. The final, tenth, grievance complained about the content of a letter written to Mr Woodhouse concerning voluntary severance.

Mr Woodhouse's first grievance was upheld in part, although not as to his complaint of **7.138** discrimination. The other nine grievances were each in turn investigated and dismissed. Mr Woodhouse was subsequently suspended and then dismissed by WNW. The chair of the panel that dismissed him said that Mr Woodhouse had 'lost all trust and confidence' in West North West Homes and that that had been the position for some considerable time; it was not considered that there could be a sustainable working relationship going forward because it was clear from Mr Woodhouse's statements and occupational health advice that his view of WNW would only change if his allegations of discriminatory conduct were accepted. It was noted that Mr Woodhouse's numerous allegations of discrimination had 'been taken seriously, but were ultimately not upheld following thorough investigations'.

Mr Woodhouse presented nine ET complaints. The complaints of race discrimination, **7.139** harassment, and victimization against WNW were dismissed. The ET concluded that the claim was 'on all fours' with *Martin v Devonshires*. They identified 'separable factors' as follows:

- The grievances were not just repeatedly made but they were unfounded.
- In the vast majority of cases, apart from the first two grievances ... they were 'substantially without any significant evidential basis'.
- Allegations of racism 'were scattered around in circumstances where, in the majority of cases, there was clearly no basis for suggesting a racial element'.
- There was 'a repeated pattern of grievances ... which were thoroughly and exhaustively investigated and objectively demonstrated to be false'.
- Each time Mr Woodhouse's grievances were resolved, it fueled his belief (accepted as sincere), that WNW and its managers were racist.
- WNW had decided that Mr Woodhouse's loss of trust and confidence in them meant that his employment could no longer be continued. If it did then there would be at some future date further allegations, themselves damaging and taking up considerable time.

The EAT allowed Mr Woodhouse's appeal. At para 88 the EAT noted that section 27(2)(d) of **7.140** the Equality Act 2010 does not stipulate that a 'protected act' must be objectively justifiable; it simply refers to 'making an allegation' of a contravention. To a limited extent the Equality Act provides protection to an employer from the consequences of taking action against an employee who has done a protected act which does not apply in PIDA cases. In particular, section 27(3) provides a bad faith defence where the evidence, information or allegations is 'false'. 'False' means wrong or incorrect or, in the terms used by the employment tribunal 'ill-founded', 'substantially without any evidential basis', 'unfounded', and 'objectively demonstrated to be false'. However, no contention of bad faith had been advanced and the employment tribunal had accepted Mr Woodhouse's sincerity.

The employment tribunal had found that Mr Woodhouse had not been dismissed because **7.141** of his protected acts but because of his loss of trust and confidence in WNW. The EAT said that evidence related to the impact made on fellow employees by the repeated allegations of race discrimination and also to WNW's need to avoid future repetition had been referred to by the tribunal as an integral part of its reasoning that there had been no victimization of Mr Woodhouse. However, the relevant question was whether Mr Woodhouse's conduct had played any significant part in WNW's decision to dismiss. The employment tribunal itself recognized the need to exclude the raising of grievances as a cause of the decision to dismiss and had 'regarded *Martin* as an analogue' of Mr Woodhouse's case. Indeed they had said that the latter was 'a stronger case'. The EAT disagreed: in *Martin* the incidents alleged by the employee to have occurred had in fact *never* occurred and were very likely paranoid delusions caused by the employee's mental illness. Further, it was not apparent to the EAT what the 'separable feature' was found by the tribunal that heard Mr Woodhouse's complaint to have been, even though the employment tribunal appreciated that they had to identify such a feature. The EAT said that *Martin* could not be 'regarded as some sort of template into which the facts of cases of alleged victimisation can be fitted'. Whilst there were 'exceptional cases', the EAT emphasized that they would indeed have to be 'exceptional'. Measuring cases against the yardstick of *Martin* was dangerous:

> One person's conviction that they have been discriminated against is very likely to generate the polar opposite, ie that the complainant is irrational, in the person or organisation complained about. Experience of this type of litigation teaches that grievances multiply and so the fact that there are a series of them is not unusual. It is a slippery slope towards neutering the concept of victimisation if the irrationality and multiplicity of grievances can lead, as a matter of routine, to the case being placed outside the scope of s. 27 of the EA. All the more so when the origin of the problem is established, as here, to have been a real, as opposed to imaginary, race discrimination.

7.142   In the view of the EAT the facts of *Woodhouse* were but a 'pale pastiche of the situation in *Martin*' and employment tribunals 'would do well to start from the proposition that very few cases will be like *Martin*'. The conclusion that Mr Woodhouse had been dismissed because he had lost trust and confidence in WNW and WNW wished to avoid further repetition of grievances by ending the employment relationship was, in reality, a conclusion that Mr Woodhouse had been dismissed if not because of past protected acts then because of the belief of the likelihood of future protected acts. It was an error to reach any other conclusion. The only proper conclusion was that Mr Woodhouse had been victimized by his suspension and dismissal and the ET's decision was therefore reversed.

7.143   To some extent the reasoning in *Woodhouse* may be distinguished from that in protected disclosure cases because of the reference to the likelihood of future protected acts. The restriction on victimization in the Equality Act 2010 encompasses not only action taken because a person had done a protected act, but also by reason of a belief that a person had done or would do a protected act (section 27(1) EqA 2010). By contrast, in the protected disclosure provisions there is protection only where the detrimental act or failure to act was done on the ground that the worker had made a protected disclosure.[51] As such it does not cover a detriment by reason of a belief that the worker is likely in future to make a protected disclosure, though often where this follows a previous protected disclosure, the tribunal may be able to infer that it was that disclosure which tainted the employer's view of the worker and led the employer to believe that the worker was likely to make a further disclosure, and as such the previous disclosure was, at least, a significant influence in the detrimental treatment.

7.144   In any event, despite this distinction from the victimization provisions in the Equality Act, the decision in *Woodhouse* illustrates the difficulty of drawing a bright-line distinction between the cases where the principle of separabilty will be applied and those where it will not. Just as in *Fecitt* the dysfunctional work relationships were regarded as something distinct from the fact of the disclosure, so in *Woodhouse* the fact that the employee had lost confidence in the employer might have been regarded as a distinct feature. It may be doubted why it should matter whether that is a consequence of the disclosure (for example

---

[51] As to whether this is capable of covering the case where the employer wrongly believes that the employer had made a protected disclosure, see Chapter 12, paras 12.43–12.46.

because of dissatisfaction with steps taken to investigate it) or something evidenced by and manifested in the disclosure. On that basis, the issue of whether a distinction can properly be drawn, as well as the identification of factors that were a significant influence on the employer, can be said to be matters of fact and degree for the assessment of the tribunal. That does not sit easily with the EAT's approach in *Woodhouse*.

As against this, the decision in *Woodhouse* starkly highlighted the difficulties in distin- **7.145** guishing between a disclosure and what the making of the disclosure evidences. The protection offered by the protected disclosure legislation would be seriously undermined if an employer, when faced with a worker raising issues as to wrongdoing in the employer organization, could readily say that detrimental treatment or dismissal was due to the fact that disclosure showed the worker had lost confidence in the employer rather than the fact of the disclosure itself.

However, dicta in *Woodhouse*, to the effect that it is only in exceptional cases that a distinc- **7.146** tion may be drawn between a protected disclosure or protected act and separable factors or consequences of it, have not been followed. As noted above (at paragraph 7.110) in *Shinwari v Vue Entertainment Ltd* (UKEAT/0394/14/BA, 12 March 2015) the EAT (at para 58) expressed its disagreement with this suggestion. A similar view was expressed in *Panayiotou v Chief Constable of Hampshire Police and another* [2014] IRLR 500 (EAT). In both *Panayiotou* (at para 52) and *Shinwari* (at para 58), it was emphasized that the tribunal must be astute to ensure that the factors relied on (a) are genuinely separable from the fact of making the protected disclosures, and (b) are in fact the reasons why the employer acted as it did. But ultimately these are issues of fact for the tribunal. The decision in *Woodhouse* was explained on its facts in *Panayiotou* (at para 53) on the basis that the factors relied upon were not in fact properly separable from the protected acts: they involved a view of the employee's subjective state of mind and the possibility that he might make further complaints in future.

Whilst *Shinwari* may be regarded as an instance of the category of cases, akin to *Fecitt*, of a **7.147** distinction based on something consequential on the disclosure, *Panayiotou* was more controversial in that it applied the principle to what was said to be the manner or way in which the whistleblowing worker went on pursuing the issues raised in the disclosures.

Mr Panayiotou, a former police officer, claimed that he had been subjected to various det- **7.148** riments and then dismissed from Hampshire Police because he had made protected disclosures. He made protected disclosures to senior officers concerning the attitude of certain other officers in respect of the treatment of race and the treatment of victims of rape, child abuse, and domestic violence on the Isle of Wight where he was stationed. There was an investigation and Mr Panayiotou was found to be largely correct in his concerns. The ET found that while Mr Panayiotou had raised matters correctly, he had not been happy with the outcome of the investigations that resulted from his disclosures. He began to campaign for the Hampshire police to take the actions that he believed appropriate. When this did not happen be formed the view that matters were being covered up and this made him more determined to try other channels to secure redress.

A number of things then occurred which caused the ET 'concern'. First, the permission **7.149** previously granted for Mr Panayiotou to be involved in his wife's businesses was revoked and the police declined to consider an application for that permission to be restored. The ET was critical of the way in which these matters were dealt with and considered that the reasons given by the Chief Constable for these decisions were 'not genuine'. Second, whilst he was on sick leave Mr Panayiotou was arrested at his home, the alleged offence being that he was receiving sick pay whilst working without authorization in his wife's business. The

ET was very critical of this episode. Third, two officers carried out surveillance, in their own time, of the market stall run by Mr Panayiotou's wife. This was approved at a senior level and was undertaken to establish whether Mr Panayiotou was working in his wife's business. The ET found that the two officers involved were not impartial and the conclusion reached that Mr Panayiotou was involved in a business was not sustainable. Finally, a decision was made to recommend that Mr Panayiotou be dismissed using regulation 7 of the Police Regulations 2003, which allowed dismissal on the basis that a police officer had an incompatible business interest. That regulation provided that the Chief Constable did not have to discuss the matter with the officer concerned. The adoption of this process avoided the procedural safeguards and appeal rights that would have applied if the route of dismissal for misconduct had been taken.

7.150   The ET concluded that Mr Panayiotou's protected disclosures were 'the genesis of' these detriments but only in the sense of 'If I had not taken the M5 and travelled on the A303 instead I would not have had the car crash'. Rather, it was the actions taken by Mr Panayiotou *subsequent* to the disclosures which made the police hostile to him. This hostility was coupled with an exasperation with Mr Panayiotou for having worked so little while seeking to be involved with his wife's businesses. Mr Panayiotou 'had become a one-man industry for the force, taking up huge amounts of management time'. The ET concluded that:

> There comes a point where the fact of a disclosure is overtaken by the campaign of the discloser to vindicate himself and champion those about whom those grievances were raised, and that point came far into the past. It is why the actions of the force are in no sense whatsoever connected with the public interest disclosures.

7.151   The ET concluded that the police were determined to rid themselves of Mr Panayiotou and did so in a manner that was not fair. However, the dismissal was not in any sense whatsoever connected with the public interest disclosures he had made. It was the manner in which he pursued those disclosures that caused the force to act as it did. The ET dismissed the claims.

7.152   In the EAT it was contended that the ET made an error of law in finding that the claims of detriment, victimization, and whistleblowing failed because the 'fact of a disclosure [was] overtaken by the campaign of the disclosure'. In particular, it was incorrect to have treated the continuing disclosures as a campaign: they were still disclosures and were protected. The EAT agreed that if that was what the ET had done it would have been in error. Later qualifying disclosures of information would not cease to be protected disclosures merely by reason of the fact that a claimant had made earlier protected disclosures. However, the real issue was whether or not the tribunal did make that error.

7.153   The EAT concluded that, reading the decision of the ET as a whole, the ET was seeking to draw a distinction between the fact of making protected disclosures and the manner or way in which Mr Panayiotou subsequently pursued the issues raised as one aspect of its finding that the employer's actions were not by reason of the protected disclosures. On the ET's findings Hampshire Police was motivated by the fact that Mr Panayiotou would campaign relentlessly if he were not satisfied with the action taken following his protected disclosures. It was the fact that Mr Panayiotou would never accept any answer save that which he sought, and the sheer effort required to deal with the correspondence which he generated and the further complaints he made if he were not satisfied with the action taken, together with his long absence from sickness from which he would not be returning, which explained why the employer acted as it did. The ET was not saying that disclosures of information, made as part of a campaign, could not be protected disclosures. Its key finding was that Mr Panayiotou 'had become completely unmanageable'.

Accordingly Mr Panayiotou's appeal failed. The distinction between the fact of making **7.154** the protected disclosures and other features of the situation which were related to, but were separable from, the fact that Mr Panayiotou had made protected disclosures was a valid one. There was therefore no error on the part of the tribunal in their consideration of why the respondents acted as they did.

The approach in *Panayiotou* raises some significant difficulties. Experience indicates that **7.155** those who blow the whistle may need to be persistent and determined for the message to be heard. The protection provided by the legislation may be seriously undermined if such determination, reflected in relentlessly pursuing disclosures, may be regarded as a separable and permissible reason for dismissal. However, it is plainly arguable that in the more extreme cases an employee's persistence and refusal to let matters lie (especially if the employer believes it has done all that it reasonably can to investigate the concerns raised by that employee) may mean that the employment cannot continue because the employee is simply unmanageable. The difficulty in knowing where a tribunal will draw that distinguishing line gives rise to substantial uncertainty. There is a risk that workers may be deterred from persisting in pursuing important public interest disclosures to an employer whom the employee thinks is not taking those disclosures sufficiently seriously.

(e) Conclusions on 'separability'

Drawing together a number of strands, we suggest that: **7.156**

(1) In principle it is permissible for a distinction to be drawn between a protected disclosure and something which is associated with that disclosure, done in preparation for it, which is consequential on it, or is evidenced by it. It is also permissible to distinguish the manner of the disclosure and how it is pursued.

(2) For analytical purposes it may be useful to consider these separate categories, though the distinction between the disclosure and the adequacy of the response to it may be better viewed as one aspect of the distinction between the disclosure and the consequences of it. But they share a common theme that consideration must be given to whether what is relied upon is indeed properly separable. That is a matter for the assessment of the tribunal.

(3) A distinction is likely to be more easily made (subject to evidence as to the employer's true reasons) where it is not based on something about the disclosure itself, such as where it is concerned with the investigation in preparation for the disclosure or with consequences of the disclosure such as a breakdown in relationships.

(4) The distinction is liable to cause greater difficulty where it is based on something to do with the disclosure itself, such as the manner of the disclosure; but ultimately the issue is one for the assessment of the tribunal.

(5) The issue is fact sensitive. Tribunals need to be astute to ensure that they are satisfied that what is relied upon is indeed separable from the fact of disclosure and that the fact of disclosure is not a significant influence in the treatment (or the principal reason for dismissal in employee dismissal cases). Further, there is a need to focus on any explanation for the conduct put forward by the employer (or which the tribunal identifies as arising from the evidence) and to address whether that explanation is accepted, if not why not, and whether if accepted it is a reason which is properly separable from the disclosure itself.

(6) Whilst there is no requirement that such distinctions can only be drawn in extreme cases, at least when considering distinctions based on the disclosures themselves, such as the manner in which the disclosures are made or pursued, the less extreme the matters relied upon are, the less likely a tribunal is to accept that the factor being relied upon is indeed separable or formed the reasons for the treatment.

(7) Notwithstanding the dicta in *Aspinall,* ordinarily it is unlikely that the fact that a protected disclosure was made in breach of confidence (or breach of copyright) could of itself be a separable reason for detrimental treatment, though it is possible that there may be exceptional situations where this becomes more plausible (see 7.124 above). But breach of confidence committed in the course of investigating the disclosure, rather than involved in the disclosure itself, or otherwise provided as superfluous information rather than a necessary part of the disclosure, could be separable.

(8) A wide range of evidential factors may have an impact on the inferences a tribunal is liable to draw. One factor that may be evidentially relevant, *Fecitt* being perhaps the best example, is where the decision-maker takes action which (a) is adverse to the worker but (b) does so from a position of what might be described as neutrality and in order to deal with the fallout that has arisen from the disclosure rather than the disclosure itself. As against that, where there is a dispute in the workforce, and action is taken only against the whistleblower and not others with whom that worker has fallen into dispute, a tribunal may infer that the protected disclosure was the reason for the differential treatment.

(9) Conversely, although *Panayiotou* indicates that separability may still be accepted in such a case, a tribunal may be more likely to draw adverse inferences in cases, such as *Woodhouse*, where the worker's disclosure is in relation to apprehended relevant failures by the employing organization (or managers within it) itself rather than by the whistleblower's co-workers. In those circumstances there may be a strong basis to infer that the management of the employing organization might be hostile to the worker because of his or her disclosures. Contentions that it was not the worker's disclosures that were the problem but a collapse of trust and confidence between employer and worker that has led to the detriment or dismissal call for particularly anxious consideration, as indicated by *Woodhouse*. Cases not concerned with whistleblowing, in particular *Perkin v St Georges Healthcare NHS Trust* [2005] IRLR 934 and *Jefferson (Commercial) LLP v Westgate* (UKEAT 0128/12/1907, 19 July 2012), recognize that a breakdown in trust and confidence between employer and employee may, even in the absence of any misconduct on the part of the employee, render dismissal fair for 'some other substantial reason'. However, it would be unfortunate if tribunals were too easily persuaded that such a breakdown of trust and confidence between a whistleblowing worker and his/her employer was the reason for the dismissal or detriment, rather than the whistleblowing itself, because it will very often be the case that trust and confidence is damaged on both sides when a relevant failure is drawn to the attention of management.

(10) Having said that, the decision in *Panayiotou* might suggest that an employer who only takes action against a whistleblower following:
   - a thorough and, so far as is reasonably possible, impartial investigation of the concerns raised and a reporting of the results of those investigations to the whistleblower;
   - a refusal by the whistleblower to accept that the relevant failure has either been cured or shown not to have existed in the first place;

may be better able to persuade a tribunal that the action taken was not because of the whistleblowing but due to a separable set of facts. But we suggest that there are considerable perils in this line of reasoning. The tribunal in *Panayiotou* appear to have regarded it as an exceptional case in that the employee had become 'completely unmanageable'. There is a serious tension with the public policy underlying the legislation if persistence and robustness in pursuing disclosures, which the worker reasonably believes are made in the public interest, could of itself be a basis for detrimental treatment.

(4) Failure in the investigation of the discloser's concerns

7.157 Whilst it is possible for a failure to investigate to give rise to a claim under the ERA,[52] section 47B (or section 103A), there are likely to be a number of significant hurdles to overcome.

(a) Detriment

7.158 An employer will be under a duty to investigate disclosures where these amount to grievances and, accordingly, a failure to investigate a disclosure which also amounted to a grievance is likely to amount to a detriment. It may also be a breach of the term of trust and confidence because it might indicate that the employer condones wrongdoing or the continuance of a hazard. If the employee's disclosure relates to a matter which does not concern the employee's own job then in some cases it may be arguable that a failure to investigate that disclosure would not amount to a detriment. Given the wide meaning of the term 'detriment', however, this is unlikely. The worker might be caused considerable anxiety by the failure to investigate serious concerns and the implication that the employer is either unwilling to address them or does not treat them seriously: see eg *Local Government Yorkshire and Humber v Shah* (UKEAT/0587/11/ZT, 19 June 2012), considered in Chapter 10, paragraph 10.82.

(b) Act or deliberate failure to act

7.159 Where the objection is to a specific step taken in the investigation, such as disclosing information which involves failing to respect a request for anonymity, there is no difficulty in establishing an act by the employer, though there might be substantial difficulty in showing that detrimental treatment was by reason of the protected disclosure: see eg *Shinwari* (paragraph 7.110 above). The position is less straightforward where there is a failure to take steps, such as a delay in commencing the investigation. It will be necessary to establish that this is a 'deliberate' failure. In *Lingard v HM Prison Service* (ET, Case No 1802862/04, 16 December 2004) the claimant prison officer complained of a large and wide-ranging number of detriments visited upon her on the ground that she had made protected disclosures about practices in the prison where she was working. The detriments included failures in the investigation in relation to her concerns. The employment tribunal concluded that it was a detriment to a whistleblower to fail, deliberately or by maladministration or negligence, to investigate legitimate concerns which directly affected the duties the whistleblower had to carry out and which she was contractually obliged to disclose. However, this formula, referring to maladministration or negligence, does not take into account the need for the failure to be deliberate.

(c) Reason why question

7.160 In many cases, however, the principal difficulty will be in showing that a failure in the investigation was 'on the ground that' the worker made the protected disclosure, rather than merely that the failure 'relates to' the disclosure and would not have happened 'but for' the disclosure. Clearly, failings in the investigation of a protected disclosure will relate to the disclosure and would not have happened but for it. But that is not of itself sufficient. If an employer who receives a disclosure of a relevant failure regards the employee as causing trouble in making the disclosure, and for that reason decides to put off or otherwise avoid dealing with the concerns, and the employee suffers stress due to the failure to deal with the concerns, it can be said that there has been a detriment on the ground

---

[52] *Salisbury NHS Foundation Trust v Wyeth* (UKEAT/0061/15/JOJ, 12 June 2015) is an example, albeit the case was remitted because the EAT was not satisfied that the ET had carried out the necessary critical analysis of the explanation put forward by the employer, and, in relation to one aspect, whether the reason was properly separable from the disclosure (see para 7.114 above).

of the making of the disclosure. If, on the other hand, the employer does not investigate because of a pre-existing dislike of the employee, or because s/he simply fails to make time to do so, then the pre-existing dislike of the employee or perhaps just apathy, rather than the protected disclosure, would be the reason for the failure to act. There may be other respects in which the reasons for failing to investigate are not laudable, but yet not be by reason of the disclosure (see paragraph 7.114 above, and the EAT's analysis of the explanation for the detrimental treatment in *Wyeth*). The detriment sustained by the worker might still be due to having raised protected disclosures, for example because making the disclosure or the absence of a satisfactory response is highly stressful and upsetting. But the test is not whether the detriment is on the grounds of the protected disclosure, but whether the act or deliberate failure to act is on those grounds. This focuses on the employer's reasons, rather than on the reason for the employee considering that s/he is disadvantaged.

(5) Causation test for detriment and for act/deliberate failure to act distinguished

7.161 The 'reason why' test, which applies to whether an act or deliberate failure to act was on the grounds of a protected disclosure, is to be distinguished from the causation test to be applied in determining whether that act or deliberate failure gave rise to an alleged detriment. This distinction was highlighted by the EAT in *Vivian*, where it was noted (at para 80) that:

> The linkage between the act and the disclosure does not raise a question of causation but of conscious or unconscious reasoning. This is to be contrasted with the link between 'act' and the 'detriment' which is a question of causation.

7.162 The distinction may be illustrated by supposing (adapting the facts and findings in *Vivian*) that it had been found that the selection for redeployment had been on the grounds of a protected disclosure. Suppose further that in the period that followed, the claimant (a) lost earnings (eg due to not being able to earn overtime whilst redeployment was sought) and (b) was ultimately dismissed. The loss of earnings would then be a detriment to which the claimant would have been subjected by the act of being placed in the redeployment pool. The causal link with the relevant act (being placed in the redeployment pool) would be sufficient. Provided that that act of being placed in the redeployment pool was on the ground of a protected disclosure, it would be no answer to say that the loss of pay (a detriment) was not motivated by the protected disclosure. There may, however, be arguments as to a break in the chain of causation if the loss of pay was prolonged due to a refusal to contemplate redeployment. In relation to dismissal, however, section 103A of the ERA would apply, and so the issue would be whether the reason or principal reason for the dismissal was the protected disclosure.

(6) Tainted information and tainted decisions

7.163 In an organization of any size it may be difficult for the employee to identify when and by whom a decision adverse to him has been taken. It may be clear that a protected disclosure has been made but the linkage between that disclosure and subsequent detrimental treatment or, indeed, dismissal may be much less clear. In many cases that will be because there is, potentially, more than one reason for the detriment or dismissal. That issue is considered above. But there may be a further problem of identifying the role played by a protected disclosure in a chain of events which led eventually to dismissal or detriment. The person or persons who actually took the decision adverse to the worker might not themselves have been influenced by the fact that the worker made a protected disclosure and indeed they might not even have known about it. But can that decision be said to be on the grounds of/ by reason of the protected disclosure if it was procured by someone who acted as they did because of the protected disclosure, perhaps by the giving of information upon which the decision-maker bases his or her decision?

A key question in addressing this issue is as to whether the claim can only be based (if at all) **7.164** on the act or failure to act of the procurer/ influencer, or whether there can be a claim on the basis of the decision of the person who may have been unwittingly influenced. The issue can be illustrated by the following scenarios:

1. Suppose a manager's decision to issue a written warning to an employee is based on false complaints by colleagues. Unbeknown to the manager, the complaints are in response to the employee's protected disclosures. Indeed, the manager may be unaware that protected disclosures have been made. So far as concerns individual liability it would plainly be inappropriate for the manager to bear liability (under section 47B(1A)) for having acted on the ground of a protected disclosure. The identification of the relevant acts or failures to act said to have been on the ground of the protected disclosure may also be relevant in terms of the evidence that requires to be called at the hearing in the event that there is no pleaded case against the colleagues. If their influence on the decision could lead to a claim succeeding despite the manager being innocent, there would then still be a need to call their evidence in response to the claim.

2. Suppose that, instead of deciding to give a warning, the manager's decision is to dismiss the employee. That distinction is pertinent in the protected disclosure context because of the different regimes that apply for employee dismissals and other detriments. For dismissals the specific vicarious liability provision in section 47B(1B) ERA does not apply, and the claim will only succeed if the protected disclosures were the reason or principal reason for dismissal rather than merely an influence. There are also different remedy regimes. If the correct analysis was that because the manager was unaware of the protected disclosures, his decision to dismiss was not by reason of such disclosures, that would have consequences in terms of available remedies. Despite the dismissal having been procured by reason of protected disclosures, there would be no remedy of reinstatement or re-engagement available, and no interim relief. It would also raise the issue of what remedy could lie based on the separate act of procurement, given the exclusion in section 47B(2) ERA of detriment claims where the detriment consists of dismissal of the employee.

3. A third scenario perhaps brings these issues into sharper focus. Suppose the manager's decision is influenced not by another worker, but by a third party for whose acts or deliberate failures to act the employer does not have liability because they are not an agent or worker of the employer. The third party might be a customer who complains about the employee because of the employee's protected disclosure. If an unwitting decision by the manager to dismiss or issue a warning can be regarded as being by reason of a protected disclosure if procured by another employee, that begs the question of why the same reasoning should not apply if the influence is by a third party. Yet that may be said to extend the protection of the legislation beyond its proper boundaries by imposing liability on an employer who may have no knowledge or even any reason to suspect that the third party was influenced by protected disclosures.

In the context of claims of discrimination under the Equality Act 2010, a clear response **7.165** to this issue has been given in *CLFIS (UK) Ltd v Reynolds* [2015] IRLR 562 (CA). The Court of Appeal concluded that it is necessary to focus on the specific act or failure to act that was on discriminatory grounds. In the above scenarios, the claim would only be for the acts of the colleagues who influenced the unwitting manager. If those colleagues made a complaint on discriminatory grounds, that complaint would be the relevant act of discrimination. There would be no claim based on the manager's decision (other than to the extent that it affected loss flowing from the discriminatory act of the colleagues). However, in the protected disclosure context, decisions both prior to the decision in *Reynolds*, and also since that decision (notably, in *Royal Mail Group Ltd v Jhuti* [2016] ICR 1043 (EAT)), have suggested a different conclusion. We address first the earlier decisions, before turning to consider more closely the decisions in *Reynolds* and *Jhuti* (a dismissal case), and also (though *Reynolds* was not expressly considered) in *Dr Brito-Babapulle v Isle of Wight NHS Trust* (UKEAT/0090/16/DM, 10 June 2016) (a detriment claim).

(a) *The pre-*Reynolds *approach*

7.166   In *Western Union Payment Services UK Ltd v Anastasiou* (UKEAT/0135/13/LA, 21 February 2014) the appeal was concerned with claims of detriment other than dismissal, consisting of sidelining the claimant in relation to certain accounts, making enquiries into his expense claims, referring the results of those enquiries and other alleged financial irregularities to a disciplinary hearing, and intervening in his bankruptcy petition. There was no evidence that those employees who had actually directly subjected the worker to the pleaded detriments had been aware of the making of the protected disclosure by him. Indeed, they were not aware of the protected disclosures. Despite this, although the EAT allowed an appeal against the ET's decision to uphold the detriment claims, rather than simply reversing the ET's decision it remitted the issue to the tribunal in the light of the worker's case that those employees who had directly subjected him to detriments had been instructed to do so. The EAT said (at para 74) that they could see that—hypothetically—there might be cases where there was an organizational culture or chain of command such that the final actor might not have personal knowledge of the protected disclosure but where it nevertheless still materially influenced the treatment of the complainant worker. However, in such cases it would still be necessary for the ET to explain how it had arrived at the conclusion that this is what had happened and the EAT concluded that that explanation had not been given in that case: accordingly the case was remitted.[53]

7.167   The issue arose in the context of a protected disclosure dismissal claim in *The Co-Operative Group Ltd v Baddeley* [2014] EWCA Civ 658 (CA). The claimant was employed by the Co-Op as a Quality Assurance Manager. He was dismissed on the basis of disciplinary charges related to his alleged role in, or failure to report, irregularities in relation to dealing with stock, referred to as 'amnesty stock' which was returned to one of the Co-Op's sites when it was nearing its sell-by date. The claimant's case was that he had done nothing wrong, and that his dismissal was by reason of concerns, amounting to protected disclosures, which he had himself raised in relation to amnesty stock. The ET upheld the claimant's claims, both of ordinary unfair dismissal and dismissal by reason of protected disclosures. The EAT upheld the decision despite being critical of the ET's reasons, but the Court of Appeal allowed the appeal, and remitted the case to a differently constituted tribunal, on the basis that the decision was inadequately reasoned. The ET had found that the employees who made the decision to dismiss and to uphold the appeal had done so not because they believed the claimant to be guilty of the misconduct, but to give effect to the wish of the claimant's line manager, Mr Berne, to dismiss him because he had made protected disclosures. Underhill LJ (with whom Ryder LJ and Laws LJ agreed) accepted that there could be a protected disclosure dismissal in what he referred to as 'an Iago situation': where the decision–makers, though not themselves acting by reason of protected disclosures, were procured to act by another

---

[53] For the disposal hearing judgment which expands the EAT's reasoning on this point see UKEAT 0135/13, 12 May 2014.

employee who was acting by reason of a protected disclosure. To that end, he explained as follows (at paras 41 and 42):

41. The starting-point is that section 103A uses the formulation 'the reason (or, if more than one, the principal reason) for the dismissal' which also appears in section 98(1) and has been central to the concept of unfair dismissal from its first introduction. That phrase was, classically, explained by Cairns LJ in *Abernethy v Mott Hay & Anderson* [1974] ICR 323 as referring to the 'set of facts known to the employer, or it may be of beliefs held by him, which cause him to dismiss the employee'. . . .. Cairns LJ's exact language may not be wholly apt in every case, but the essential point is that the 'reason' for a dismissal connotes the factors operating on the minds of the person or persons who made the decision to dismiss. The same approach applies to the 'ground' for a putative detriment contrary to section 47B.

42. That requires the identification of the decision-maker(s). It was accepted before us, and appears to have been accepted by the ET, that the relevant decision-makers— that is, the persons with whose motivation we are concerned—are Mr Atkinson and Mr Logue.[54] In principle, therefore, it is immaterial what Mr Berne may have thought or wanted *except* to the extent that that operated on their minds. There was some discussion before us whether that approach was applicable in all cases or whether there might not be circumstances where the actual decision-maker acts for an admissible reason but the decision is unfair because (to use Cairns LJ's language) the facts known to him or beliefs held by him had been manipulated by some other person involved in the disciplinary process who has an inadmissible motivation—for short, an Iago situation. Mr Carr accepted that in such a case the motivation of the manipulator could in principle be attributed to the employer, at least where he was a manager with some responsibility for the investigation; and for my part I think that must be correct.

On the facts, therefore, this was not a case where the decision-makers had followed Mr Berne's agenda. It was not, therefore, a case of being procured to act without knowledge that Mr Berne was victimizing the claimant by reason of protected disclosures. As such, the court's observations in relation to the effect of such procurement were obiter.

Again, in *Ahmed v City Of Bradford Metropolitan District Council & Ors* (UKEAT 0145, 27 **7.168** October 2014), the EAT proceeded on the basis that determination of the grounds for the detrimental act or failure to act did not depend solely on the decision-maker; it could be affected by an earlier act or deliberate failure to act which infected the later decision. Mr Ahmed was employed by Bradford Council. During a redundancy exercise he was offered an alternative post subject to a CRB check and an internal reference, both of which were regarded as formalities. The tribunal found that Mr Ahmed had previously made what were held to be protected disclosures of information tending to show a serious breach of contract by Bradford in relation to a scheme funded by the European Development Fund. Mrs Baker, the second respondent, had taken against Mr Ahmed as a result of the making of those disclosures and put herself forward to write the reference, even though she had no knowledge of Mr Ahmed's work. Mrs Baker wrote a reference she knew to be negative and in a sense misleading and that would affect Mr Ahmed's ability to secure the new post. She did so to ensure that he was forced out of Bradford's employment. The employee who was considering the appointment of Mr Ahmed to the new post, Mr Rashid, formed the (incorrect) view that Mr Ahmed had misled him about sickness absence. Mrs Baker did not disabuse Mr Rashid. Mr Rashid withdrew the offer of the new post to Mr Ahmed and in doing so relied to a substantial degree on the reference given by

---

[54] Respectively, the employees who decided to dismiss and to uphold the appeal.

Mrs Baker. That led to Mr Ahmed being made redundant. The employment tribunal put it this way (para 144):

> The decision to reject the Claimant for the SCDO post was taken by the Fourth Respondent, Mr Rashid. We were satisfied that Mr Rashid took his decision because he unreasonably but honestly believed the Claimant to be lying about sickness absence and *because of the reference* [emphasis added]. We do not consider Mr Rashid's acting on the reference to deny the Claimant the job renders Mr Rashid's action on the ground of protected disclosure although the underlying reference was written and delivered to him on that ground. The Second Respondent's motivation in writing the reference and the Fourth Respondent's motivation in acting on the reference as received were different and the latter was not caused, in a sufficient sense, by the Claimant's protected disclosure. It was not Mr Rashid's real reason for rejecting the Claimant.

7.169 In the EAT it was argued on behalf of Mr Ahmed that the ET had impermissibly severed the relationship between Mrs Baker's motives and those of Mr Rashid. They had incorrectly ignored the fact that the detriment that was suffered by Mr Ahmed—that is, the withdrawal of the offer of the SCDO post—was as a result of something accepted by the ET to be a detriment that had been caused, or was as a result of, protected disclosures made by Mr Ahmed. On the findings of the ET Mrs Baker had deliberately set out to secure Mr Ahmed's employment with the council coming to an end by scuppering his chances of redeployment. The EAT agreed. HH Judge Clark said that in those circumstances it was almost impossible to argue that, from the findings of the employment tribunal, by reason of the protected disclosure her act in particular in relation to the reference could *not* be regarded as having had a 'material influence, being more than a trivial influence' on the treatment meted out to Mr Ahmed. The employment tribunal applied the wrong test for causation and applied too strict a test; they should have applied the test formulated in *Fecitt*. Mrs Baker's reference was a means of manipulating the redeployment process and the motivation for writing the reference should not have been separated from the reliance on the reference by Mr Rashid. The fact that Mr Rashid did not realize he was being misled by the reference did not sanitize the effect of the reference and did not exonerate Bradford as the employer from a decision that ultimately was significantly influenced by an infected reference that came into existence as a result of a protected disclosure. In summarizing the law, the EAT put it thus:

> Where an employee X does an act which amounts to a detriment to employee Y by reason of a protected disclosure, such as by giving an unfair and negative reference, with the intention that it should lead to the Claimant suffering a further detriment at the hands of employee Z, or might reasonably be found to have been so intended, the employer will be liable for the second detriment if it can be shown to have been infected by the first discriminatory act and had materially influenced the imposition of the second detriment imposed by Z upon Y.

(b) Reynolds—the Equality Act approach

7.170 The judgments in *Western Union, Ahmed,* and *Baddeley* each preceded the decision of the Court of Appeal in the age-discrimination case of *CLFIS (UK) Ltd v Reynolds* [2015] IRLR 562 (CA) reversing [2014] ICR 907. Dr Reynolds was employed by Canada Life FS and was in her seventies. Her contract was terminated by Canada Life after rumblings of discontent with her performance within management. Mr Gilmour was the dismissing officer. Dr Reynolds' claim that she had been discriminated against on the ground of her age was dismissed by the ET. The ET had said that the decision-maker was Mr Gilmour and no one else and it acquitted Mr Gilmour of being influenced by Dr Reynolds' age.

7.171 The EAT remitted the case to the ET. It accepted the argument advanced on Dr Reynolds' behalf that, even if the sole decision-maker was Mr Gilmour, his decision might have been shaped and informed by others within CLFS. If the actual decision to terminate an employee's contract was taken by a senior manager, that senior manager might have no personal knowledge of the employee and might have to rely entirely on reports which had been prepared by others, for example about an employee's performance or conduct. Dr Reynolds' contention was that if the mental processes of those who prepared such reports were based on discriminatory grounds, then in principle the tribunal had to examine those mental processes and could not confine itself to the mental processes of the eventual decision-maker alone. Singh J agreed with this proposition. The employment tribunal had found, as a matter of fact, that the views of others *did* play a part, but it failed to examine the mental processes of those other persons to see if *they* were based on the prohibited ground of age.

The Court of Appeal reversed the decision of the EAT. Underhill LJ gave the substantive **7.172** judgment of the Court. He reasoned that the ET had focused solely upon Mr Gilmour and his reasons for acting as he did, because it had not been suggested on behalf of Dr Reynolds that anyone else discriminated against her. The burden of proof provisions in the Equality Act 2010 did not place a blanket obligation on CLFS as respondent to prove the absence of discrimination in respect of every act of every employee that had formed part of the chain of events leading to the dismissal. Dr Reynolds had to establish a prima facie case that the dismissal had been because of her age. Whether that case was made out had to be decided by reference to the case that she had advanced. Since that case only referred to Mr Gilmour, the ET had not erred in only considering Mr Gilmour's motivation. Underhill LJ explained that in a case such as this, where it was contended that one employee of the respondent had been influenced by another employee into acting in a way detrimental to the claimant, an ET should treat the conduct of the person supplying the information—who we will call the 'influencer'—as a separate act from that of the person who acted on the information supplied—the 'influencee'. The alternative—namely a 'composite approach' which seeks to bring together the influencee's act with the influencer's motivation—was unacceptable in principle. This was because under the relevant provisions of the Equality Act 2010, liability could *only* attach to an employer where an individual employee, or agent for whose act the employer was responsible, had done an act which satisfied the definition of discrimination.[55] That meant that the individual employee who did the act complained of must him or herself have been motivated by the protected characteristic. On the facts as found in *Reynolds* there was no basis on which the influencee's act—that of Mr Gilmour—could be said to be discriminatory because Mr Gilmour was unaware of the basis of the influencer's motivation. In other words, it would be quite unjust for the person influenced—Mr Gilmour in this case—to be liable to a claimant where he personally was innocent of any discriminatory motivation.

The court's conclusion was that the solution in such cases was to ensure that the claim spe- **7.173** cifically raised the conduct of or act of the influencer and cited that influence either as the detriment or as contributing to the risk of a dismissal or detriment. This would ensure that the tribunal would then evaluate that specific claim and the extent to which the influencer caused or contributed to the risk of dismissal or detriment on a loss of a chance basis—that is to say to what extent the influencer's influence contributed to the risk to the claimant of their dismissal or a detriment. Underhill LJ acknowledged some practical difficulties arising from this approach. Because evidence would need to be produced and facts determined, such an allegation needed to be put clearly and notice of it given so that the respondent could call the necessary evidence. However, the fact that the apparent decision-maker had been influenced by another might not become clear to the claimant until well into the proceedings, or even at trial. Underhill LJ did, however, consider that these practical difficulties

---

[55] Section 109 of the Equality Act 2010.

could be surmounted, if need be by an amendment being sought at the appropriate time. Underhill LJ also noted that reference had been made to his remarks in *Baddeley* (to which we have referred), but that there had been a consensus that the difference in the statutory provisions as between the discrimination legislation and the unfair dismissal legislation meant that it was unsafe to read across from one type of case to the other.

(c) Jhuti *and protected disclosure dismissals*

7.174 The issue of whether the approach in *Reynolds* should be applied to the protected disclosure context was addressed, at least in relation to claims under section103A ERA, by the EAT in *Royal Mail Group Ltd v Jhuti* [2016] ICR 1043. The claimant was employed as a probationary media specialist in the respondent's sales division. The ET found that she had made protected disclosures to her manager, a Mr Widmer, regarding the misuse of tailor-made incentives (TMIs) to some customers to trial new or more expensive mail services. For regulatory reasons, TMIs could not be used solely for the purpose of reducing the price of a Royal Mail service: the respondent's own policy stated that to do so would be a serious regulatory breach. The claimant's disclosures were to the effect that she believed that the TMIs were being given out in breach of that policy and contrary to Ofcom regulations. The ET that heard her claim held that she had thereafter been subjected a series of detriments by Mr Widmer because she had made those disclosures. Importantly, the tribunal found that this included 'setting up a paper trail which set her to fail', through the ever-changing and unobtainable requirements which he set her (paras 21 and 35) The claimant had then gone off sick. She was made subject to a performance procedure and this resulted in her dismissal. The ET found that the dismissing officer, Mrs Vickers, believed that she was dealing with a 'bona fide performance procedure' because she believed what Mr Widmer told her, because she had not been provided with copies of certain documents, and because the claimant's illness meant that Mrs Vickers had no opportunity to interview her. The tribunal's conclusions were expressed thus:

> 345. Given the information that was before her, it was not only not surprising but was in fact inevitable that Ms Vickers would choose to dismiss the claimant and would choose to do so for the reasons she sets out in her letter of 21 July 2014 at paragraph 3, essentially on the grounds of performance. We find that, in terms of her own reasoning, the fact that the claimant had made protected disclosures was not part of her reasoning and that she genuinely believed that the claimant was a poor performer. In this context, we note that she had not even seen any of the written disclosures which we have found to be protected disclosures (the emails of 8 and 12 November 2013). Following the case of *CLFIS (UK) v Reynolds* [[2015] ICR 1010], Ms Vickers must herself have been motivated by the protected disclosures and, notwithstanding that the evidence before her was hugely tainted as a result of Mr Widmer and others, there is no basis on which her decision can be said to be based on the disclosures on the basis of someone else's motivation. Therefore, the principal reason for the decision was not the making of the protected disclosures and the complaint of automatically unfair dismissal under section 103A of the Employment Rights Act 1996 fails.

> 346. However, given Mr Widmer's actions, including the treatment which he meted out to the claimant as a result of her protected disclosures, the email trail that he prepared in this context, and his other actions as set out in these reasons above, it was inevitable that Ms Vickers would, as she did, dismiss the claimant.

7.175 The claimant (cross-) appealed against the decision to reject the section 103A claim. Mitting J noted that the employment tribunal appeared to have believed that it could treat the earlier acts of victimization as giving rise to a claim for compensation for losses flowing from dismissal subject only to proof of causation. He considered that approach to be erroneous because section 47B(2) ERA expressly excludes from consideration the detriment of dismissal and so, of necessity, the financial and other consequences of dismissal, whatever the causative link. Mitting J said he believed that the ET's conclusion was based on a misunderstanding or misapplication of Underhill LJ's judgment in *Reynolds* in which (as explained above), Underhill LJ had explained that, in a discrimination claim under the Equality Act 2010, it was possible for compensation (for detriment visited on an employee by a co-worker) to be awarded when dismissal followed acts of unlawful discrimination, subject only to proof of causation. However, in Mitting J's view there was no read-across from discrimination principles and the discrimination scheme, which contained no equivalent to section 47B(2).[56] In a whistleblowing dismissal claim the starting point was 'the reason (or, if more than one, the principal reason) for the dismissal'. In the vast majority of cases, all that it was necessary to discern was the set of facts known to the person who made the decision to dismiss.[57] He or she would be the sole, or, where the decision was a joint one, they would be the joint human agents of the employer who determine the decision.

In Mitting J's view there was no binding statement in the authorities that the mind of that **7.176** person or those persons must in all circumstances be equated with that of the employer. Mitting J referred to what Underhill LJ had said in *Cooperative Group Ltd v Baddeley* [2014] EWCA Civ 658 (as set out at paragraph 7.167 above). It had been submitted on behalf of the respondent, the Royal Mail, that Underhill LJ's observation only applied to the fairness of the decision and not the reason for the decision. Mitting J rejected this: there could be no reason why the reason held by the manipulator of an ignorant and innocent decision-maker could not be attributed to the employer anymore than the unfairness of his motivation, and nothing in the words of Underhill LJ suggested that he intended to draw a clear distinction between the two. Nor was there any reason of principle why any such clear distinction should be drawn. Accordingly:

> as a matter of law, a decision of a person made in ignorance of the true facts whose decision is manipulated by someone in a managerial position responsible for an employee, who is in possession of the true facts, can be attributed to the employer of both of them.[58]

The principle applied in the more nuanced circumstances' of *Royal Mail v Jhuti* for the following reasons (set out by the EAT at para 35):

> First, Mr Widmer was the Claimant's line manager responsible for induction and supervision and for allocating duties to her and, in due course, for reporting upon her performance. Secondly, she made protected disclosures to him, disclosures which he realised were serious and of significance to him, to those in positions senior to him and to the Respondents generally. Thirdly, she was deliberately subjected to detriments by him from the moment that she made the disclosure until he ceased to be her line manager. Fourthly, his temporary replacement, Mr Reed, displayed no difference in approach from that adopted by Mr Widmer. Fifthly, Mr Widmer 'was setting up a paper trail which set her to fail'. Sixthly, he succeeded. Seventhly, he lied to Ms Vickers about the disclosures made by the Claimant by 'explaining disingenuously that this was an issue which had been raised but that the Claimant had told him that she had got her wires crossed' and by giving her email to him of 13 November 2013 to Ms Vickers, but not the earlier emails of 8 and 12 November 2013. Eighthly, Ms Vickers was deprived of information for unexplained reasons by Human Resources who did not give her copies of the emails of 6 February and 25 and 26 February 2014 and by the decision to separate the grievance from performance issues.

---

[56] Mitting J referred to *Kuzel v Roche Products Ltd* [2008] IRLR 530 at para 48 where Mummery LJ said that the statutory structure of the unfair dismissal legislation is so different from that of the discrimination legislation that an attempt at cross-fertilization or legal transplanting runs a risk of complicating rather than clarifying the legal concepts.

[57] This referenced Cairns LJ in *Abernethy v Mott, Hay and Anderson* [1974] ICR 323 but noted that the test was put in slightly different words by Mummery LJ in *Kuzel* at paras 54 and 56.

[58] *Royal Mail v Jhuti* per Mitting J at para 34.

In those circumstances, it was not only the mind of Ms Vickers which needed to be examined to discern the respondent's reasons for dismissal. The reason and motivation of Mr Widmer had also to be taken into account. Once it was, as the employment tribunal found, it was inevitable that dismissal would occur and it did occur on the tribunal's findings by reason of the fact that the claimant had made prohibited disclosures principally to Mr Widmer. The automatically unfair dismissal case should therefore succeed.[59]

7.177 The reasoning in *Baddeley* and *Jhuti* may be thought to sit uncomfortably with the approach of the majority of the Court of Appeal in *Orr v Milton Keynes Council* [2011] IRLR 317. In that case Mr Orr was dismissed for misconduct. The findings of the tribunal (as explained in the Court of Appeal) regarding the incident which had led to Mr Orr's dismissal for behaving in an abusive and insubordinate manner, were that Mr Orr's manager, Mr Madden,

> was not entirely blameless, first, because he had gone behind Mr Orr's back in seeking to engineer by devious means a reduction in his working hours and, second, because in the course of their discussion he had said to Mr Orr, who in the heat of the moment had lapsed into Jamaican patois, 'You lot are always mumbling on and I cannot understand a word you lot are saying.'

7.178 The respondent council accepted that the use of those words constituted an act of direct unlawful discrimination. However (like the employee in *Jhuti*), Mr Orr did not attend the hearing that led to his dismissal by a Mr Cove. Mr Madden did attend but he did not tell Mr Cove the details of what had happened between him and Mr Orr. The ET found that the level of investigation was reasonable in the circumstances and that the conduct of the disciplinary process had been reasonable and fair. It found that, on the basis of the evidence before it, the council (ie Mr Cove) genuinely and reasonably believed that the allegations made against Mr Orr were well founded. Dismissal fell within the band of reasonable responses and accordingly was not unfair. It is right to say that the ET did not make an express finding that Mr Madden's remark had provoked the outburst from Mr Orr which led to his dismissal. It is also right to say that there were other allegations against Mr Orr. However, in the Court of Appeal the question was whether Mr Madden's knowledge of what led to the meeting and then to the exchanges between him and Mr Orr was to be imputed to the council as his employer. For Mr Orr it was argued that since Mr Cove failed to take this into account when he formed his view of Mr Orr's behaviour on that occasion the council had therefore failed to act reasonably when reaching the decision to dismiss him.

7.179 Sedley LJ considered that the argument advanced on behalf of Mr Orr was correct. Any relevant facts known to any person within the organization who in some way represented the employer in its relations with the employee should be taken to be known by the employer. However the majority, Moore-Bick and Aikens LJJ, disagreed. In their view this would be to impose a more onerous duty on the employer than that provided for by section 98 ERA. The extent of that duty was explained in the authorities on that section: *Post Office v Foley* [2000] IRLR 827 CA and *London Ambulance Service NHS Trust v Small* [2009] IRLR 563 (CA). Those cases made it clear that the tribunal's task is confined to deciding whether in the light of the information available to him at the time of the

---

[59] The EAT in *Jhuti* also expressed the view that remedies against an individual worker are limited to a declaration. But, as discussed further in Chapter 8 (paras 8.73–8.77), that appears erroneous since it overlooks section 48(5) ERA. It does not appear to have been central to the EAT's reasoning, though it may have added to the emphasis on differences from discrimination legislation, and so supported the view that a read-across from that legislation is not appropriate.

employer's decision was reasonable, in the sense of being one that a reasonable employer could have made. The obligation to carry out a reasonable investigation as the basis of providing satisfactory grounds for thinking that there had been conduct justifying dismissal, necessarily directed attention to the quality of the investigation and the resulting state of mind of the person who represented the employer for that purpose. If the investigation was as thorough as could reasonably have been expected, that would support a reasonable belief in the findings, whether or not some piece of information had fallen through the net. There was no justification for imputing to the dismissing officer knowledge that he or she did not in fact have and which (ex hypothesi) he or she could not reasonably have obtained. Accordingly, for the purposes of deciding (in accordance with the approach in *Meridian Global Funds Management Asia Ltd v Securities Commission* [1995] 2 AC 500 (HL) as to attribution) whose knowledge was to be imputed to the employer for the purposes of section 98 ERA, it was the person deputed by the employer to hear the case against the employee (and no one else).

The issue then arises as to how the approach in *Jhuti* may be distinguished from the **7.180** decision in *Orr*. Both cases concern an omission by an employee's manager to present all the facts he knew to the employer's appointed officer who was considering the employee's dismissal. In both cases the employee did not attend the hearing and therefore the undisclosed facts were unlikely to come out. Whereas in *Orr* the court concluded that the focus was on the dismissing officer, in *Jhuti* the conclusion was that it was necessary to consider not only the mind of the dismissing officer but also that of the respondent's manager. The important distinction lies, we suggest, in the consideration of who really brought about the dismissal, being a consideration which lies at the heart of the concept suggested in *Baddeley* of an 'Iago' situation. In *Orr* the manager's conduct was a potentially important part of the context if the dismissing officer had been aware of it. But it was not the case that the manager had in effect set out to procure the employee's dismissal. The court was faced with determining whether the employer was to be treated as having all the knowledge of those in relevant managerial positions irrespective of whether there was a reasonable investigation, and concluded that was not the case. That may be distinguished from a case where the manager had set out to procure the employee's dismissal by setting her up to fail by imposing unobtainable targets. In that situation it is artificial to regard the manager as somehow acting outside the disciplinary process. On the contrary the manager, Mr Widmer in Ms Jhuti's case, was an integral part of that process. Indeed, he had expressly informed human resources that if things did not change they would need to look at removing Ms Jhuti from the business (para 12), and on the tribunal's finding he had in effect achieved that. To suggest that it was only the mind of the ultimate dismissing officer that was relevant in determining the reason for dismissal would, in those circumstances, fly in the face of reality. On the contrary, in reality in such a situation the manager (the manipulator in an Iago situation) brings about the dismissal of the employee, even if it is someone else who, in ignorance of this conduct, pulls the trigger. A parallel might be drawn with the line of authorities in relation to the distinction between an actual or constructive dismissal, where a tribunal is required to ask who really terminated the employment.[60] To similar effect, to deal with an Iago situation such as contemplated in *Baddeley*, the tribunal might ask who really brought about the dismissal.

The alternative solution, if following the approach in the *Reynolds* case, would be to ensure **7.181** that the dismissed worker's claim specifically raises the conduct of or act of the influencer

---

[60] See eg *Jones v Mid-Glamorgan County Council* [1997] ICR 815 (CA).

and cites that influence either as the detriment contributing to the risk of a dismissal or as a distinct act of detriment. In other words the claim that the ET appears to have allowed in *Jhuti*—that the employer could be liable for Mr Widmer inflicting a detriment by effectively procuring the dismissal of the claimant—would on that view be the correct legal route. However, in the following respects that may be said to be unsatisfactory:

(1) First, the approach in *Royal Mail Group v Jhuti* has the advantage of placing substance over form and meeting the reality of the situation that the manipulator is an integral part of the dismissal process. Where, as an act of whistleblowing victimization, the manager has sought to manage a claimant out of the business, and succeeded, it would be to ignore reality to say that the dismissal is not by reason of the protected disclosures merely because the means adopted involved an innocent manager as the dismissing officer.

(2) Second, there are remedies which are specific to dismissal cases, notably reinstatement and interim relief, and it would be an injustice for those to be unavailable to the employee in such a situation. These were not relevant considerations in *Reynolds*, because the remedies for unlawful discrimination do not distinguish between dismissal and other detriments.

(3) Further, as Mitting J emphasized, there would be difficulties arising by virtue of the operation of section 47B(2) ERA, if the claim could only be framed on the basis of a separate act of detriment by the person procuring the dismissal. Whilst the detriment might be framed as being the act of procurement or victimization rather than the dismissal itself, the scheme of the legislation is to exclude from the detriment provisions losses which are consequential on the dismissal: see *Melia v Magna Kansei* [2005] EWCA Civ 1547, [2006] IRLR 117. That difficulty is overcome if, in a case of dismissal procured by reason of protected disclosures, the dismissal is regarded as being principally by reason of the protected disclosures.

(4) Put in terms of the reasoning in *Meridian Global*, it may be said that there is no greater difficulty than that which arises in a case of constructive dismissal. Suppose in *Royal Mail* the employee had left in response to the acts of victimization by the manager. The manager was the person within the organization with the authority to carry out the managerial acts which constituted victimization. If those acts were by reason of protected disclosures, there would be little difficulty in saying that the reason or principal reason for dismissal was the protected disclosures. It may be questioned why the position should be any different where, instead, managerial authority or the managerial position is abused so as to procure that there is a dismissal, notwithstanding that the dismissing officer is ignorant of this.

7.182 No doubt some difficulties of application arise in the approach suggested in *Jhuti*, and by the dicta in *Baddeley*. The position appears straightforward in a flagrant Iago case such as outlined above, where the dismissal is procured by the abuse of managerial authority. It is, however, not difficult to imagine more nuanced cases. The dismissing officer's decision may be influenced by a number of sources and considerations. But these are factual decisions which flow from the test of whether the reason or principle reason for dismissal, rather than a mere influence on it, is the protected disclosure. In a straightforward Iago situation where the dismissing officer merely pulls the trigger and the dismissal is plainly brought about by another (the manager), there may be little difficulty in focusing on the knowledge of the manager who is pulling the strings. In other cases the influence of the manager may need to be weighed against other factors so as to determine the principal reason for dismissal.

7.183 One further complication in applying the reasoning in *Jhuti* arises where those who in effect procure the dismissal are colleagues but cannot be said to be acting in a managerial position or otherwise acting with the delegated authority of the employer. Indeed, as noted in the third scenario at paragraph 7.164 above, it may be that the person who procures the decision is a third party, such as a customer, for whom the employer has no responsibility. If it can be said that a decision-maker who has no knowledge of a protected disclosure can nevertheless be said to have acted on the grounds of or by reason of the protected disclosure as a result of the decision being (to use the terminology in *Ahmed*) infected by the influence of a third party who was influenced by the protected disclosure, that begs a question as to why the same reasoning does not apply to input from any third party. The issue did not directly arise in *Jhuti,* where the detrimental conduct was by the claimant's line manager essentially setting her up to fail as part of managing her out of the business. But the reasoning (at paras 33–35), contemplated that the answer lies in focusing on whose acts or omissions can properly be attributed to the employer. In those circumstances, applying the reasoning in *Meridian Global*, the manager could readily be seen as the directing mind of the business for dismissal claims arising from the way in which he exercised his managerial role and authority. That provides a basis for distinguishing the position where the influence is from a third party such as a customer, since there would be no question of their reasons for acting being attributed to an employer who was unaware of them. In relation to the intermediate situations, such as the influence by fellow workers, it can be said that the question it begs as to whether the acts or motivations of those employees are to be attributed to the employer is in principle no different from that which potentially arises in a constructive dismissal situation where an employee resigns in response to the dismissal (and which we consider further in Chapter 8).

The need to identify whose acts are to be attributed to the employer for these purposes can, **7.184** however, be said to introduce an element of uncertainty and complexity which would be avoided by adopting the *Reynolds* approach. So, for example, it does not necessarily follow that the wide test for vicarious liability for detriment purposes set out in section 47B(1A) should also apply for the purposes of deciding whether those acts are to be attributed to the employer, at least in the context of determining whether they infect an employee dismissal decision. Statutory attribution of liability based on a worker acting within the course of employment is applied only to detriment claims and is balanced by the introduction of the statutory defence based on taking all reasonable steps to prevent the detrimental act or detrimental acts of that description (section 47B(1D) ERA). This in turn raises the prospect of anomalous results. An employer who may be able to succeed in the statutory defence if, for example, faced with a claim that colleagues made false allegations against the claimant by reason of protected disclosures would have no defence if acting on those disclosures by dismissing for reasons, so far as the employer is aware, that have nothing to do with protected disclosures. Further refinement may be needed to avoid such a result. One possibility may be that the colleagues' conduct should not be attributed to the employer in circumstances where the statutory defence would have been made out.

(d) Application to detriment claims

Whilst in *Jhuti* the issue of indirect influence on the decision-maker arose in a dismissal **7.185** claim, the decision in *Dr Brito-Babapulle v Isle of Wight NHS Trust* (UKEAT/0090/16/DM, 10 June 2016) provides some support for its application, post-*Reynolds*, in a detriment claim (though neither *Reynolds* nor *Jhuti* were cited). Here the claimant held a locum position with the respondent NHS Trust. The employment tribunal accepted that some (though not all) of the matters she relied upon amounted to protected disclosures. She asserted two detriments: failure to pay her on-call hours after 28 October 2013, and failing to afford her a hearing prior to dismissal. The tribunal accepted that these were detriments, but concluded that neither of them was on the grounds of the protected disclosures. So far as concerned the on-call hours, the tribunal accepted that the explanation for the decision to withhold payment was that the decision-maker was given incorrect HR advice to the effect that it was not the policy to pay for on-call time which had not actually been worked. The ET stated that it could not accept the basis for that advice, but nonetheless it provided a reason (which it accepted) which was not the protected disclosure. Indeed, the evidence of the decision-maker (K) was unchallenged as to the reason for her decision. However, the EAT held that it was not sufficient to focus on K's mental processes. In order to ascertain whether the protected disclosures were a significant influence, it was also necessary to consider the mental processes of the individual within HR who had given the erroneous advice which in turn led to the decision to refuse the on-call payments. The issue was therefore remitted. Although neither *Reynolds* nor *Jhuti* were mentioned in the decision, in effect this appears to have been an application of the *Jhuti* approach. Applying the *Reynolds* approach, the detrimental act relied upon (K's decision to withhold the payments) would not have been treated as on the grounds of a protected disclosure. The relevant detrimental act would have been the giving of the erroneous advice.

7.186 We suggest, however, that, at least in relation to section 47B ERA detriment claims, the *Reynolds* approach is to be preferred, and that the approach in *Jhuti* is properly to be confined to employee dismissal claims (which is the context in which it was applied in that case). First, it is only in relation to claims by employees that the particular difficulty arises from section 47B(2) ERA that claims of detriment are excluded where the detriment amounts to dismissal. As such, the *Reynolds* approach has the advantage of clarity and certainty in focusing on the reasons of the persons making the particular decision or carrying out the relevant act or omission in question, without the complication that a claim against the perpetrator may be barred by section 47B(2) ERA. Indeed in *Brito-Babapulle* if there had been consideration of the distinct acts liable to constitute detrimental treatment, the ET may not have fallen into the error which the EAT found it had made. Equally, that would be conducive to certainty in identifying the issues, and in clarifying the matters on which evidence needs to be produced.

7.187 Second, this reflects the distinction between detriment and dismissal provisions in that, as HHJ Eady QC put it in *Salisbury NHS Foundation Trust v Wyeth* (UKEAT/0061/15/JOJ, 12 June 2015), at para 24: 'A shorthand way of describing the difference is to say that the detriment protection mirrors the language of discrimination protection whereas section 103A mirrors that of unfair dismissal.'

7.188 Third, and perhaps most significantly, the operation of the individual and vicarious liability provisions in detriment claims gives rise to the same key difficulty which was found to be persuasive in *Reynolds*. Underhill LJ's judgment in *Reynolds* was, as we have noted above, founded on the proposition that liability under the anti-discrimination legislation could *only* attach to an employer where an individual employee or agent for whose act the employer was responsible had done an act (in the course of his or her employment) which satisfied the definition of discrimination treatment in this regard. It was therefore said to be inappropriate to combine the innocent duped dismissing officer's action in dismissing with the procurer's malign motive to produce a discriminatory dismissal. That led to the concern that the dismissing officer might be liable for discrimination even though he or she is innocent of discrimination. That difficulty does not arise in claims of dismissal of an employee, since only the employer is liable. Nor did it arise in *Dr Brito-Babapulle* where the only respondent was the employer. But it clearly does arise in detriment claims where individual workers or agents are also made a respondent. Following the amendments made by the ERRA, ordinarily the more straightforward basis for imposing liability on an employer will be on the basis that an act done by the another worker of the employer in the course of employment is attributed to the employer (section 47B(1A) ERA). But it necessarily follows when that provision is relied upon that if the employer is liable, the worker is also liable, subject only to the narrow defence in section 47B(1E) where the worker relied upon the employer's statement. In an Iago situation, where an innocent disciplining officer (X) had been manipulated into acting by another manager (M) who was influenced by protected disclosures, no difficulty arises if (as suggested in *Reynolds*) vicarious liability arises for the employer based on the act by M, and individual liability also arises for M. But if, following the reasoning in *Jhuti*, the decision by X is itself taken to be on the grounds of a protected disclosure, liability for that act under section 47B(1B) would also entail and be parasitic upon liability of the innocent manager under section 47B(1A).

Applying that to the facts in *Dr Brito-Babapulle*, on the EAT's analysis the refusal to pay **7.189** on-call payments was an act done by K in the course of her employment. If it was to be treated as done on the ground of protected disclosures, albeit unwittingly so far as K was concerned, that would seem to result in personal liability for K, which could not be the legislative intention. The alternative would be to construe section 47B(1A) so that liablity only arises for the worker if that worker personally acts by reason of the protected disclosure, yet to impose liability on the employer by reason the motivation of the influencer. Whilst the legislation might be strained to seek to reach that result, the approach in *Reynolds* provides a more straightforward answer.

(e) Conclusion

At the time of writing, the decision in *Jhuti* is proceeding on appeal to the Court of Appeal. **7.190** For the reasons set out at paragraph 7.181 above, the decision avoids some unsatisfactory aspects of applying the *Reynolds* approach to a dismissal decision in an Iago situation, and may be said to reflect the legislative structure in relation to the different approach and remedies to be taken in dismissal claims. But whilst the approach has some attraction for claims under section 103A ERA, at least in detriment claims under section 47B ERA, the approach in *Reynolds* is to be preferred. We therefore suggest that claimants who bring whistleblowing dismissal or detriment claims should carefully consider whether it is necessary to plead that the dismissal or other matter complained of was procured or influenced by someone other than the person who took the actual decision or committed the actual act which impacted upon the claimant. It may also be appropriate to consider whether the procurer or influencer should be joined as a respondent, though vicarious liability of the employer is not dependent on doing so. Furthermore, it will be necessary to review these matters as the case progresses, and even during the hearing.

(7) The burden of proof in relation to the 'reason why' question

In general terms the burden is on the claimant to prove the facts constituting the protected **7.191** disclosure. There are two exceptions. The first exception now relates only to qualifying disclosures made prior to 25 June 2013, in relation to which the good faith requirement applies as a liability stage issue (other than in relation to section 43D ERA). The second exception relates to establishing the grounds for an act or deliberate failure to act. Workers may face particular difficulties in establishing why an employer acted, or deliberately failed to act, in a manner alleged to have caused detriment. It will be the employer who is best placed to adduce evidence in relation to this and to explain its conduct. In recognition of this, ERA, section 48(2) provides that 'on [a complaint of victimization to a tribunal by a worker] it is for the employer to show the ground on which any act, or deliberate failure to act, was done'. By virtue of ERA, section 48(5), the reference here to the employer also encompasses a respondent worker or agent.

7.192   In *Harrow v Knight* (referred to in paragraph 7.58 above) Mr Knight cited section 48(2) in defence of the tribunal's approach in his case. The EAT noted that it had not been referred to any authority as to the effect of this subsection and that it did not appear to have any equivalent in the 'victimization' provisions of other statutes (eg section 4 of the Sex Discrimination Act 1975, section 2 of the Race Relations Act 1976, and section 146 of TULRCA).

7.193   The EAT considered that the subsection might seem to be intended to have the same effect as section 98(1) of the 1996 Act, which requires an employer in a claim of unfair dismissal to prove what the reason for the dismissal was and that it was within one of the categories of admissible reasons: if the employer fails to establish either of those matters the dismissal is generally unfair. But the EAT reasoned that the concept of 'unfair dismissal' did not require the tribunal to be satisfied of anything save that the section had not been complied with and in that sense it had no positive content. By contrast, 'victimization' requires the ingredient that the employer had acted on the prohibited ground. The EAT thought that there was no reason in principle why the statute could not have provided that the employer be deemed to have so acted where he did not prove any other reason, but would have expected such a provision to be clearly spelt out. Furthermore, if section 48(2) were construed as having such a deeming effect, the result would appear to be that an employer who could not prove his 'ground' could be liable to a series of claims under each (and, they might have added, *all*) of the anti-victimization provisions of ERA, Part V. That would no doubt be highly unlikely to happen in practice, but even the theoretical possibility cast doubt on the correctness of the approach.

7.194   The employer (Harrow LBC) contended that all that ERA, section 48(2) did was to make it clear to employers that they have to be prepared to say in the tribunal why they acted in the respect complained of, with the result that if they failed to do so they might find inferences drawn against them (though only if such inferences are justified by the facts as a whole). Whilst stating that it did not need to resolve this issue, the EAT indicated that it found this submission persuasive.

7.195   The EAT's tentatively expressed views on the issue have attracted criticism.[61] It is suggested that the EAT was not correct insofar as it indicated that the burden of proof could not be dispositive. However, we suggest that the essential point made by the EAT was not that the burden of proof could never ultimately be dispositive, but that failure to positively establish the reason for the treatment does not meant the claimant succeeds. There is not simply a binary choice between two alternatives, as in the choice between fair and unfair dismissal. It may be that the employer is unable to establish the reason for the adverse treatment and yet still be able to satisfy the tribunal that it is not the protected disclosures. That accords with the approach adopted in relation to the burden of proof for unfair dismissal by reason of a protected disclosure as explained in *Kuzel v Roche Products Ltd* [2008] EWCA Civ 380, [2008] ICR 799. As in the case of ERA, section 103A, so also in relation to section 48(2) the employer may discharge the burden of proof either by establishing a legitimate reason for dismissal or simply by proving that the reason for dismissal is not the protected disclosure. The approach in *Harrow v Knight* therefore correctly identified that a failure to establish positively a legitimate reason was not necessarily determinative. That view was confirmed by the Court of Appeal in *Dahou v Serco Ltd* [2016] EWCA Civ 832, [2017] IRLR 81. Laws LJ noted (at para 40) that no doubt it would usually follow that a respondent employer's failure to show its reasons would entail that the employee's case was right. But that was not a necessary conclusion. An employer may still show that the protected disclosure was not the reason—as

---

[61]   *Harvey on Industrial Relations and Employment Law*, para DII R[631].

could be done, for example, by showing a lack of knowledge of the protected disclosure. Further, as the Court of Appeal emphasized in *Kuzel*, most cases are decided on the basis of positive findings rather than on the burden of proof. But if the employer does not discharge the burden upon it to establish either a legitimate reason or that the protected disclosures were not the reason, the claim will succeed. Consistently with this, in *Fecitt and others v NHS Manchester* [2010] ICR 476 the EAT said (at para 37)[62] that it was 'clear . . . that the burden of proof is on the employer to prove, in effect, where there has been a detriment that the claimant was not victimized'. The possibility of disproving the unlawful reason (even if a legitimate reason cannot be established) substantially reduces the risk highlighted in *Harrow v Knight* that an employer who provides no evidence could be found to have acted for all the impermissible reasons in Part V.

As with the approach in *Kuzel*, there is an initial evidential burden on the claimant to **7.196**
adduce some evidence to show the prohibited reason: see *Dahou v Serco Ltd* [2016] EWCA Civ 832, [2017] IRLR 81 per Laws LJ at paras 29 and 37.[63] In relation to this, it may well be that the fact of the protected disclosure being followed by adverse treatment will suffice for this purpose. As Elias LJ noted in *Fecitt* (at para 51):

> The detrimental treatment of an innocent whistleblower necessarily provides a strong prima facie case that the action has been taken because of the protected disclosure and it cries out for an explanation from the employer.

We suggest though that it may be putting matters too high to say this 'necessarily' provides a strong prima facie case. This will depend on a fact-sensitive assessment, including issues such as the proximity between disclosure and adverse treatment and the employer's knowledge of the disclosure.

Further clarification, which supports this construction of section 48(2) ERA, was pro- **7.197**
vided by the EAT in *Ibekwe v Sussex Partnership NHS Foundation Trust* (UKEAT/0072/ 14/MC, 20 November 2014). Here the claimant contended that her employer's failure to deal with a complaint by her, set out in a letter of 5 April 2012, was causatively linked to the fact of a previous protected disclosure that she had made. The ET concluded that there was nothing to suggest that any managerial failure had anything to do with protected disclosures, and indeed positively found that this was not the case. Referring to section 48(2) ERA, the ET stated that this did not assist the claimant as she did not win by default if the respondent failed to establish a reason and there remained an evidential burden on the claimant. On appeal the employee submitted that the ET failed to apply the burden of proof laid down in section 48(2) ERA. HHJ Peter Clark rejected this contention and approved the ET's approach. He emphasized that few cases turn on the burden of proof. Failure by the respondent to show positively why no action was taken on the employee's letter did not mean that the section 47B complaint succeeded by default. Ultimately it was a question of fact for the ET as to whether or not the 'managerial failure' to deal with the claimant's letter of 5 April was on the ground that she there made a protected disclosure. Their clear and unequivocal conclusion, having considered the whole of the evidence, was that it was not. That was a finding of fact with which the EAT would not interfere. There is clearly a close connection between the application of the burden of proof and the extent to which the fact-finding tribunal is persuaded to draw inferences, discussed in the next section.

---

[62] See also para 48.
[63] Applying the similarly worded provision relating to detriment for taking part in trade union activities in s 148(1) of the Trade Union and Labour Relations (Consolidation) Act 1992.

7.198 The EAT's decision in *Phoenix House Ltd v Stockman & Anor* [2017] ICR 84 demonstrates the dangers of focusing to an excessive degree on the burden of proof in victimization cases instead of engaging with the task of fact finding, and falling back on the burden of proof only where it has not been possible to resolve relevant issues of fact before the tribunal. In *Phoenix* the claimant had received a twelve-month written warning for misconduct from the respondent's manager, Ms Taylor. The employment tribunal had held that this was a detriment which had been influenced by the claimant having made a protected disclosure. Ms Taylor had not given evidence but Ms Bond of the respondent's HR department had told the tribunal that she had advised Ms Taylor that a twelve-month sanction (as opposed to the previous norm of six months) was appropriate because that was to be the new normal practice based on her own experience with employers and in tribunals elsewhere than with the respondent. The employment tribunal noted that Ms Taylor did not explain why she accepted the advice of Ms Bond and observed that Ms Bond's account of her application of a twelve-month sanction 'was uncorroborated by supporting evidence'. The tribunal concluded that because the sanction imposed lasted longer than the normal period set out in the respondent's disciplinary policy, the relevant facts from which an inference that the sanction had been influenced by the making of the protected disclosure or the protected act were established. It then went on to find that because Ms Taylor had not given evidence and because Ms Bond's account was uncorroborated, the respondent had not discharged the burden of proof imposed on them of demonstrating the absence of a connection between the two.

7.199 The EAT (Mitting J) said (at para 30) that this was not an appropriate way of addressing this question. The crucial issues were whether (a) Ms Taylor had accepted the advice of Ms Bond (which by inference the employment tribunal found she had) and (b) whether or not that advice was given for the reasons stated by Ms Bond. There was no necessary requirement for corroboration of Ms Bond's evidence. If the tribunal accepted Ms Bond's evidence as to her reason for giving the advice, it followed that it was not affected by the making of protected disclosures (or undertaking a protected act). That was the key factual question which the tribunal needed to address. Instead, the employment tribunal had 'ducked the single most important question to answer' in the context. It was not permissible to do so.

7.200 In relation to a second detriment—the sending of a meeting invitation letter from Ms Bond to the claimant—the EAT held that a similar error had been made. The tribunal had concluded that Ms Bond's evidence did not discharge the respondent's burden of proof and show that the disclosure itself did not materially influence Ms Bond's decision to send the meeting invitation letter to the claimant. Again, the EAT emphasized that what the employment tribunal had to decide was whether or not Ms Bond was telling the truth. It was not possible to decide an issue which depended on the truthfulness or otherwise of a single witness by falling back on the burden of proof rather than deciding that question (and still less so where, as here, the claimant had not put in issue whether Ms Bond was telling the truth in this respect). By again ducking that issue, the employment tribunal did not adequately discharge its duty to find relevant facts about the supposed detriment.[64]

7.201 It is to be noted that one consequence of ERA, section 48(2) is that a worker (whatever the length of his/her employment) would appear to be in a more advantageous position as

---

[64] See to similar effect the remarks of the Court of Appeal in *Dahou v Serco Limited* [2016] EWCA Civ 832, [2017] IRLR 81 (per Laws LJ at para 36) on the requirement for the tribunal to 'enter into a reasoned adjudication on the employer's case' and to 'grapple with the essentials of the employer's case' because the claimant's case 'involved the conclusion that the respondent had concocted a false basis for [the claimant's] suspension and dismissal and maintained that false story before the Employment Tribunal'.

regards the burden of proof than an employee who has not qualified for the right not to be unfairly dismissed under ERA, section 98. By way of exception to the ordinary burden on an employer where an employee has qualifying service for an ordinary unfair dismissal claim, such an employee will bear the burden of proving that a protected disclosure was the reason or principal reason for dismissal,[65] and if unable to establish this will not be able to fall back on a claim in respect of the dismissal under section 47B. By contrast, under section 48(2) the employer will bear the burden of proof in relation to a worker who is not an employee, but whose contract is terminated.

(8) Drawing inferences

Before statute intervened,[66] tribunals hearing discrimination claims applied the approach stated by Neil LJ in *King v Great Britain–China Centre* [1992] ICR 516 at 529 (CA). The outcome of a claim of discrimination would usually depend on what inferences it was proper to draw from the primary facts found. The tribunal would have looked to the employer for an explanation of the conduct complained of and, if no satisfactory explanation was put forward, from that conduct it would be legitimate for the tribunal to infer that the conduct was on racial grounds. This, as Neil LJ put it, was not a matter of law but 'almost common sense'. It did not help to think in terms of shifting evidential burdens; instead, the tribunal would have to make findings as to the primary facts and draw such inferences as it considered proper from those facts. This guidance was built on by Sedley LJ in *Anya v University of Oxford* [2001] EWCA Civ 405, [2001] ICR 847, where he stressed the importance of the tribunal making proper findings of primary fact and setting out their reasoning from those findings. **7.202**

Whilst, in relation to other forms of discrimination, the guidance in *King* has been displaced by the intervention of statute, it might be argued that the guidance remains of assistance in relation to consideration of the reasons for acts or failures to act alleged to be on grounds of protected disclosures. Claims under ERA, sections 47B and 103A are a species of discrimination claim: *Virgo Fidelis Senior School v Boyle* [2004] IRLR 268 at para 44(b) (EAT); *Felter v Cliveden Petroleum Company* (UKEAT/0533/05, 9 March 2006) at para 15. The *King* guidelines have also on occasion been suggested as having wider application. In *Neckles v London United Busways Ltd* (UKEAT/1339/99, 10 February 2000) the EAT, at a preliminary hearing, held (at para 12) that a tribunal had directed itself correctly in applying the *King* guidelines by analogy in a case of alleged refusal to offer employment on grounds related to union membership contrary to section 137 of TULRCA. **7.203**

It may be suggested that the process of fact-finding might be unduly complicated by referring to the *King* guidelines which were framed in a context where there was no equivalent of ERA, section 48(2). In *Nicholson and others v Long Products* (UKEAT/0166/02, 19 November 2003) the EAT rejected a submission that the approach endorsed in *King* was applicable in the case of a dismissal for trade union reasons. The EAT explained (at para 20) that the guidance in *King* had been deemed necessary in the specific context of alleged discrimination which required a tribunal to consider whether there was differential treatment and the adequacy of the explanation for it. This was not to suggest that the drawing of **7.204**

---

[65] See *Jackson v ICS Group of Companies Ltd* (EAT/499/97, 22 January 1998). But see also the discussion in Chapter 9, para 9.47 as to whether this is open to challenge in the light of the reasoning in *Kuzel*.

[66] Section 136 of the Equality Act 2010 and predecessor legislation; Arts 2 and 7 of the EC Equal Treatment Directive 76/207 (as amended); Arts 1, 2(1), and 4(1) and (2) of the EC Burden of Proof Directive 97/80; Arts 8(1) and (2) of the EC Race Discrimination Directive 2000/43; Art 10(1) and (2) of the EC Framework Employment Directive 2000/78; for an analysis, see *Igen Ltd v Wong* [2005] EWCA Civ 142, [2005] IRLR 258.

appropriate inferences as secondary findings of fact was not an important part of the fact-finding process, but that:

> what a Tribunal is, of course, required to do . . . is to scrutinise the evidence and, so far as is relevant and necessary, to find the primary facts and then to proceed, again insofar as it is necessary to do so to inform the parties as to why they have won or lost, to reach factual conclusions or secondary findings of fact based on the primary findings of fact.

7.205 In any event, inevitably in considering the nature of any inferences it is appropriate to draw where a detriment has been sustained after making a protected disclosure, the tribunal will need to focus on the adequacy of the explanation provided by the employer for the conduct in question. We have referred in paragraph 7.111 to the comments of Elias LJ in the Court of Appeal in *Fecitt* (at para 51) in this regard.

7.206 Further, given the need in a detriment case to consider not only the principal reason for any act or deliberate failure to act, but also whether the protection disclosure was a material influence, it will be particularly important for the tribunal to set out clearly its findings of primary facts, and how its secondary findings flow from those primary facts. The need for such findings to be clearly set out was emphasized by the EAT in the context of a protected disclosure dismissal claim in *The Brothers of Charity Services Merseyside v Eleady Cole* (UKEAT/0661/00, 24 January 2002). The tribunal had drawn an inference that the real reason for the dismissal of the claimant was not his poor performance (as the employers contended), but his having made a protected disclosure. The EAT allowed an appeal on the basis that the decision was insufficiently reasoned. It observed (at para 31) that there was force in the submission that:

> under Section 103A where a finding of unfair dismissal in circumstances such as those in this case necessarily involves a finding that the reasons put forward by the employer were not genuine and that evidence given before the Tribunal was untruthful, it is incumbent on the Tribunal to base its conclusions on clear findings as to the primary facts about which of the persons before it were responsible for what happened, and to explain clearly how those findings lead causally to the conclusion that the protected disclosure had been the true reason for the employee's dismissal.[67]

7.207 The decision in *The Brothers of Charity* also raised an issue as to the extent to which inferences can properly be drawn from the fact of unreasonable conduct. The tribunal had drawn inferences from the fact that it regarded the criticisms of the claimant's performance as trivial and not sufficient to justify terminating the claimant's employment. The EAT regarded this as indicating that the tribunal was focusing on the reasonableness of the decision to dismiss, rather than whether the complaints as to the claimant's performance were in fact the reason for dismissal—whether or not reasonably so. The EAT emphasized that issues as to reasonableness were relevant for ordinary unfair dismissal under ERA, section 98, but that under section 103A, the focus was on the reason for dismissal.

7.208 The extent to which the unreasonable nature of behaviour might give rise to adverse inferences has been considered further in the context of race and sex discrimination. A tribunal cannot draw an inference of discrimination from the mere fact of unreasonable treatment. However, an inference may be drawn where there is no explanation for the unreasonable treatment: *Bahl v The Law Society* [2004] EWCA Civ 1070, [2004] IRLR 799 at para 101. Further, in considering whether to accept an employer's explanation for an act or deliberate failure to act by which an employee was subjected to a detriment, a tribunal is more likely

---

[67] *Redcar and Cleveland Borough Council v Scanlon* (UKEAT 0088/08/2005, 20 May 2008) contains an endorsement of an ET's approach to primary fact-finding and inference-drawing in a whistleblowing case.

to regard the explanation with suspicion if the explanation relies on unreasonable conduct: *Bahl v The Law Society* [2003] IRLR 640 at paras 99–101 (EAT).[68]

As this indicates, positive findings will often turn not only on the findings of primary **7.209** fact, but also on the inferences which can properly be drawn from those findings, such as in relation to the adequacy of the explanation for the employer's acts or deliberate failures to act.[69]

G. Time Limits for Claims of Victimization

(1) Section 48(3), (4) ERA

Section 48(3) provides that a tribunal shall not consider a complaint under section 48 (that **7.210** is to say a tribunal will have no jurisdiction to entertain such a complaint) unless it is presented before the end of the period of three months beginning with the date of the act or failure to act to which the complaint relates or, where that act or failure is part of a series of similar acts or failures, the last of them, or within such further period as the tribunal considers reasonable in a case where it is satisfied that it was not reasonably practicable for the complaint to be presented before the end of that period of three months.[70]

Section 48(4) ERA provides that where an act extends over a period, the 'date of the act' **7.211** means the last day of that period, and a deliberate failure to act shall be treated as occurring when it was decided on. In the absence of evidence establishing the contrary, an employer is to be taken to decide on a failure to act when s/he acts in a way inconsistent with doing the failed act or, if no such inconsistent act has occurred, when the period expires within which s/he might reasonably have been expected to carry out the failed act if it was to be performed.

The application of time limits in a protected disclosure detriment case was considered by the **7.212** EAT in *Vivian v Bournemouth BC* (UKEAT/0254/10, 6 May 2011). The EAT emphasized that all four elements identified by the EAT in *Harrow v Knight* [2003] IRLR 140 at para 5 (see paragraph 7.03) had to be established in order to succeed in a claim under ERA, section 47B. As such, a claim could not be brought until the act complained of had caused a detriment. This gave rise to the conundrum that time runs from the date of the act or deliberate failure to act, but a detriment caused by an act done on the grounds of a protected disclosure might be suffered more than three months after the act and therefore when the primary time limit had already expired. In such circumstances it could be said that it was not reasonably practicable to present a claim to an employment tribunal within three months of the act. If the claim was brought within a reasonable period thereafter it could be held to be in time by application of ERA, section 48(3)(b). However, section 48(3)(b) was not relied upon in the *Vivian* case itself.

---

[68] For more recent summaries of the relevant principles, see eg *Tower Hamlets PCT v Ugiagbe* (UKEAT/0068/09/ZT, 13 May 2010) at paras 27–33, *Rudd v Eagle Place Services Ltd* [2010] IRLR 486, and *CP Regents Park Two Ltd v Ilyas* (UKEAT/0366/14/MC, 16 June 2015).

[69] See eg *Everett Financial Management Ltd v Murrell* (EAT/552/02, 24 February 2003) where in para 23 the EAT referred to the following passage in the employment tribunal's decision: 'the Respondent did not in their evidence produce any plausible explanation for their conduct and the majority of the Tribunal thus infers a link between the Applicant's signature of the petition and his later treatment'. The EAT made this reference without criticizing this approach (although the employer's appeal was allowed for other reasons).

[70] For a more detailed exposition of the law relating to time limits in unfair dismissal and victimization cases, see *Blackstone's Employment Practice* (Oxford: Oxford University Press, 2017), Chapter 3.

7.213 The need to focus on the act causing the detriment rather than the detriment was also the focus of *Flynn v Warrior Square Recoveries Ltd* [2014] EWCA Civ 68, where the Court of Appeal (Maurice Kay LJ giving the substantive judgment) proceeded on assumed facts as follows. Mr Flynn was employed by WSRL as a senior broker. At the material time, WSRL was owned by Kennedys. In December 2005 Mr Flynn supplied information to the senior partner of Kennedys and he amplified the information at a meeting in March 2006. Mr Flynn alleged that two directors of the company had misappropriated a large sum of money. The response of WSRL was to subject him to disciplinary proceedings on the ground that he had breached trust and confidence by making an untrue allegation. On the same day in October 2006 Kennedys wrote to Mr Flynn on behalf of the two directors alleging that he had defamed them and seeking certain undertakings not to repeat the allegations. A meeting was arranged for 31 October but it was adjourned. In September 2007 Mr Coates of Kennedys wrote to Mr Flynn stating that he had completed his investigation. Time passed and in November 2009 Mr Flynn was informed by letter that the allegations against him were withdrawn. The disciplinary proceedings were withdrawn subsequently. Throughout this time Mr Flynn remained an employee of WSRL but he was on sick leave from March 2006 until May 2010 when he resigned. The company paid him his sick pay for more than four years. Mr Flynn commenced proceedings in the ET on 22 September 2010. WSRL applied to strike the claim out on the grounds, amongst others, that it was out of time. The ET concluded that the proceedings were commenced in time but the EAT allowed an appeal: the ET had fallen into legal error because it had failed to identify the act or deliberate failure to act which had caused the detriment and had 'confused a continuing detriment with a continuing cause'. The latest point in time at which any identified act, or deliberate failure to act, could have occurred either as alleged in the proceedings before the ET or found by the ET could be 18 March 2010. This was because in a letter dated 10 March 2010, Mr Flynn had been told that the disciplinary action initiated against him in 2006 was withdrawn and that there were no 'live' allegations against him. No defamation proceedings were ever issued against Mr Flynn. In dismissing the appeal Langstaff P gave the following guidance (at para 5):

> in any case that considers a question of whether a complaint is out of time, it is incumbent upon an Employment Tribunal to identify carefully the act, or the deliberate failure to act, that the Claimant identifies as causing him a detriment. The date of that act, or the date of that failure to act, must then be established. If at the latest the act, or the deliberate failure to act, is prior to the issue of Employment Tribunal proceedings by more than three months, it is only where the Claimant can show that it was not reasonably practicable for him to present a complaint before the end of that period of three months that he will be permitted to continue. A Tribunal otherwise must not (that is the meaning of the words 'shall not') consider his complaint. The Tribunal has no discretion in the matter, having found the facts, except that which is inherent in the judgment as to reasonable practicability which is called for by section 48(3)(b). Such a judgment must be based upon some evidential material. If a Tribunal has no submissions made to it nor evidence that may persuade it that it was not reasonably practicable to make a complaint earlier than was done, then it cannot exercise its power to prescribe a further period under section 48(3)(b), because it has no basis for doing so. It is for the person seeking to avoid the harsh impact of time limits to put that material before the Tribunal.

7.214 Mr Flynn appealed to the Court of Appeal. One of his contentions was that the threat of defamation proceedings was never withdrawn before the commencement of the proceedings in the ET, notwithstanding requests for assurances that it had been. However, the finding of the ET was that whilst Mr Flynn may have held the view that the threat was continuing, on an objective assessment it was not. As the Court of Appeal said, it was in any event a flawed analysis because it expressly concentrated on the alleged detriment rather than specific acts or deliberate failures to act. It was plain that the threatened disciplinary proceedings and defamation action had the identical factual substratum, namely the allegedly false allegation made by Mr Flynn against the two directors. It was fanciful to suggest that the same 'withdrawn' allegations continued to support a continuing threat of defamation actions. On any objective view, the threat of a defamation action (which, in any event, would have been statute-barred by October 2007, subject to a highly improbable extension of time) had disappeared by 30 November 2009. Once the EAT had correctly identified the legal error on the part of the ET in focusing on detriment rather than on the act or deliberate failure to act in relation to the issues of time, it was inevitable that it would be driven to the conclusion that the relevant acts or failures to act, in the form of the threats and the failure to withdraw them, had ceased to exist long before June 2010, that is three months before the commencement of proceedings.

A similar point arose in *McKinney v London Borough of Newham* [2015] ICR 495. Mr **7.215** McKinney was employed by Newham in their Finance Department from 29 July 1985 until termination of the employment on 31 July 2012. He brought a complaint alleging detrimental treatment short of dismissal on the grounds that he had made protected disclosures. The principal question before the employment tribunal was whether the three-month primary limitation period began to run for the purposes of the whistleblowing complaint when the respondent reached the decision to reject Mr McKinney's third-stage grievance on 8 October 2010, following a hearing on 6 October, or when Mr McKinney learned of that decision on 14 October, on receipt of Newham's outcome letter dated 8 October. The EAT upheld the ET's ruling that the earlier date was the correct one. On behalf of Mr McKinney it was submitted that since Mr McKinney did not receive his grievance outcome letter until 14 October, time for his whistleblowing claim began on that day, by analogy with the Supreme Court construction of the effective date of termination in *Gisda Cyf v Barratt* [2010] IRLR 1073. However, EAT authority was to the effect that a detriment is suffered for the purposes of the anti-discrimination legislation when the detrimental act is done, not when the complainant has knowledge of it: *Mensah v Royal College of Midwives* (EAT/124/94, 17 December 1996), Mummery J and *Virdi v Commissioner of Police of the Metropolis* [2007] IRLR 24 (Elias J). In *Virdi*, Elias J had declined to follow the contrary view expressed by Morison P in *Aniagwu v London Borough of Hackney and Owens* [1999] IRLR 303, that time did not begin to run until the claimant was aware of the detrimental treatment. HHJ Clark said there was no material difference between the detrimental treatment provisions under ERA and EqA as far as limitation was concerned. That accorded with the approach of the Court of Appeal in *Flynn v Warrior Square*. The concept of effective date of termination, considered by the Supreme Court in *Gisda Cyf v Barratt*, under section 97(1)(b), differed from the detriment provisions in the ERA and EqA. Whilst the current state of the authorities was less than satisfactory, in HHJ Clark's view a clear thread was now emerging (*Mensah*; *Virdi*; *Garry v Ealing LBC*;[71] *Flynn v Warrior Square*) which pointed towards the counter-intuitive position that time begins to run against the claimant relying on a detriment, both under ERA and EqA, whether or not he is aware that a detriment has been suffered. The ET had been right to treat time as running from the date of the respondent's grievance decision.

---

[71] [2001] EWCA Civ 1282, [2001] IRLR 681.

7.216   Section 48(4A) ERA applies section 207B ERA to a complaint of victimization contrary to section 47B ERA. The effect is that the period between the complainant contacting ACAS before instituting proceedings and the date of receipt of a certificate of early conciliation does not count for the purposes of working out the time limit. These provisions are considered in more detail in more general works.[72]

(2)   An act extending over a period

7.217   The issue as to whether an act can be said to 'extend over a period' is essentially an issue of fact and degree. There is an equivalence with the discrimination statutes in the use of the concept of a continuing act. The Equality Act 2010, section 123[73] provides that 'any act extending over a period shall be treated as done at the end of that period'. In *Hendricks v Metropolitan Police Commissioner* [2002] EWCA Civ 1686, [2003] IRLR 96, the Court of Appeal accepted that a female police officer who contended that numerous alleged incidents of sex discrimination over an extended period were linked to one another might be able to demonstrate that those incidents were 'evidence of a continuing discriminatory state of affairs covered by the concept of "an act extending over a period"' (Mummery LJ at para 48). Having referred in para 51 to earlier authorities from *Owusu v London Fire & Civil Defence Authority* [1995] IRLR 574 through to *Derby Specialist Fabrication Ltd v Burton* [2001] IRLR 69, Mummery LJ said this (at para 52):

> The concepts of policy, rule, practice, scheme or regime in the authorities were given as examples of when an act extends over a period. They should not be treated as a complete and constricting statement of the indicia of 'an act extending over a period'. I agree with the observation made by Sedley LJ, in his decision on the paper application for permission to appeal, that the Appeal Tribunal allowed itself to be sidetracked by focusing on whether a 'policy' could be discerned. Instead, the focus should be on the substance of the complaints that the Commissioner was responsible for an ongoing situation or a continuing state of affairs in which female ethnic minority officers in the Service were treated less favourably. The question is whether that is 'an act extending over a period' as distinct from a succession of unconnected or isolated specific acts, for which time would begin to run from the date when each specific act was committed.

7.218   Accordingly, a continuing act is not merely the maintenance of a rule, practice, scheme, or regime, but may also consist of the 'act' of being responsible for an ongoing situation in which the less favourable treatment occurs. The 'act' or 'acts' in *Hendricks* were not the alleged individual acts of the officers for whom the Commissioner was responsible but the alleged responsibility of the Commissioner for an ongoing situation or continuing state of affairs in which female ethnic minority officers were treated less favourably.

7.219   The starting point is to determine what is the specific act of which complaint is made (see Auld LJ in *Cast v Croydon College* [1998] IRLR 318 at para 24). This was the approach in *Unilever UK plc v (1) Hickinson (2) Sodexho* (UKEAT/0192/09/RN, 24 February 2009). Mr Hickinson was employed by Sodexho in security at the premises of Unilever. Unilever required Sodexho to remove Mr Hickinson after he was discovered making covert recordings of Unilever's staff. Sodexho did not have an alternative position for Mr Hickinson and dismissed him. Mr Hickinson alleged that he had been subjected to a detriment by Unilever on the ground of the making of a protected disclosure. He made his complaint

---

[72] *Blackstone's Employment Practice* (Oxford: Oxford University Press, 2017) (n 73) paras 5.08–5.14.
[73] Similar provision was made by the Race Relations Act 1996, s 68(7), the Sex Discrimination Act 1975, s 76(6), and the Disability Discrimination Act 1995, Sch 3, para 3(3).

to the employment tribunal more than three months after Unilever required his removal from site but less than three months after his dismissal by Sodexho. The EAT held that his complaint was out of time. The detriment was the requirement of removal, and the subsequent dismissal by Sodexho could not be said either to be an act or deliberate failure to act by Unilever or part of a continuing act. The employment tribunal had erred in saying that there was a continuing single act, namely the email of 4 July 2008 from Unilever, as a result of which Mr Hickinson had suffered detriment in that he was removed from the site together with the consequences. The detriment was the removal, not the 'continuation' of the removal. There was no evidence to suggest a continuing dialogue between Unilever and Sodexho in relation to Mr Hickinson after his removal.[74]

In *Tait v Redcar and Cleveland BC* (UKEAT/0096/08/ZT, 2 April 2008) it was held (in the context of a whistleblowing claim) that a disciplinary suspension is an act which extends over a period and accordingly the last day on which the act of suspension is deemed to take place is the date on which the employee was informed that the suspension was at an end. **7.220**

(3) A series of similar acts or failures

An alternative possibility, which does not feature in the discrimination statutes, is that an act or failure to act was 'part of a series of similar acts or failures'. The similarly worded section 147(1) of TULRCA provides the time limit for a complaint under section 146 of that Act in relation to victimization for trade union activities. In relation to section 147(1), in *Yewdall v Secretary of State for Work and Pensions* (EAT/0071/05, 19 July 2005), Burton J, giving the judgment of the EAT, said this (at para 28): **7.221**

> What is required to be shown is a series of similar acts. Mr Powell made the submission, by reference to *Group 4 Night Speed Ltd*, that when one is addressing in similar legislation (in that case under what was then the Wages Act), where there are so many different kinds of unlawful deductions of wages that can be found, the need for the series of deductions to be similar indicates that it is not simply their unlawfulness which is going to create the similarity, and we agree. Thus, acts which are all capable of amounting to breaches of section 146 are not, for that reason or, indeed, for the reason that they cause detriment, similar. They must be, in our judgment, similar by way of nature.

Accordingly, the EAT considered that it was not sufficient to establish 'similarity' by reference to the underlying reason for the acts or failures. It will be a question of fact as to whether the acts or failures to act are sufficiently alike to be 'similar'. **7.222**

However, a different approach was taken by the Court of Appeal, in a PIDA context, in *Arthur v London Eastern Railway Ltd (trading as One Stansted Express)* [2006] EWCA Civ 1358, [2007] IRLR 58. The employment tribunal (which did not hear any evidence) said that for the acts to be 'part of a series' required 'a significant degree of linkage', and rejected the claimant's contention that it was sufficient that there was a common motive for the acts or failures to act. The EAT endorsed this approach but the Court of Appeal remitted the issue for a rehearing. Mummery LJ said that the employment tribunal erred in law in determining the important time limit point without hearing any evidence or making any findings of fact. He emphasized (at para 35) that some evidence was needed to determine what link, if any, there is between the acts within the three-month period prior to presentation of the claim and the acts outside the three-month period. He explained (at para 31) that the purpose of the provision was to deal with cases where, although there could not be said to **7.223**

---

[74] *Nageh v David Game College Ltd and another* (UKEAT/0112/11/DA, 22 July 2011) and *St John Ambulance v Mulvie* (UKEAT/0129/11/DA, 1 July 2011) were concerned with similar points.

be a continuing act, there was some link between the separate acts or omissions which made it just and reasonable for them to be treated as in time. As such it was necessary to look at all the circumstances surrounding the acts, including:

> Were they all committed by fellow employees? If not, what connection, if any, was there between the alleged perpetrators? Were their actions organised or concerted in some way? It would also be relevant to inquire why they did what is alleged.

He also said that, 'depending on the facts', he would not rule out the possibility of a series of apparently disparate acts being shown to be part of a series of similar acts by reason of them all being on the ground of a protected disclosure. Lloyd LJ disagreed on this point on the basis that it would give no meaning to the requirement that the acts or failures to act be 'similar'. However, he was in a minority on this issue. Sedley LJ offered the example that there could be a series of acts made up of different acts of harassment, such as putting chewing gum on a chair and salt in tea, where the only link between different acts by different aggressors might be the perpetrators' inferred reasons for their actions. The emphasis on considering the sufficiency of linkage in all the circumstances, like the approach in *Hendricks*, places emphasis on a fact-sensitive approach which, as the EAT emphasized in *Canavan v St Edmund Campion Catholic School* (UKEAT/0187/13/1302, 13 February 2015) (at para 56), puts difficulties in the way of a respondent employer who seeks to obtain the striking out of a claim on a series of acts issue at an interim stage. Whilst there might be cases in which the facts are clear enough for a decision to be made at that stage, they are not likely to be frequently met.

8

VICARIOUS AND INDIVIDUAL LIABILITY

A. The Pre-amendment Position

The Enterprise and Regulatory Reform Act 2013 (ERRA) made sweeping changes to **8.01** section 47B ERA in relation to a claim based on qualifying disclosures made on or after 25 June 2013[1] by introducing co-worker and agent liability for detriment, and a special form of vicarious liability. Prior to the amendment, only the employer owed an obligation not to subject a worker to detrimental treatment by reason of a protected disclosure. As such liability could only be founded on acts or omissions which could be attributed to the employer as being the employer's own act/omission so as to be a breach of the obligation on the employer.

The position before the amendment was made clear by the Court of Appeal's decision in **8.02** *NHS Manchester v Fecitt and others* [2011] EWCA Civ 1190, [2012] ICR 372. Prior to that decision the EAT in *Cumbria County Council v Carlisle-Morgan* [2007] IRLR 314 had concluded that vicarious liability could apply. However, as explained in *Fecitt*, this overlooked the fact that vicarious liability is by its nature a form of secondary liability by which wrongs of the employee (in an employee/employer context) are attributed to the employer. Therefore, for vicarious liability to arise in relation to detriment for making a protected disclosure, there first would have to be a relevant obligation imposed on the worker/employee. Prior to the amendments made by the ERRA there was no such obligation imposed on workers or agents. The only obligation was imposed on the employer. As such there was no scope for vicarious liability to operate. Even if the acts of an employee did amount to a legal wrong, such as unlawful harassment, that would only provide a basis for applying vicarious liability for *that* wrong. It would not be a justification for making the employer liable under the protected disclosure provisions (*Fecitt* at para 33).

---

[1] See Enterprise and Regulatory Reform Act 2013 (Commencement No 1, Transitional Provisions and Savings) Order 2013, SI 2013/1455.

8.03   The facts in *Fecitt* are considered in detail in Chapter 7 (at paragraphs 7.100–7.106). In summary, the claimants were registered nurses employed at a walk-in centre run by the respondent trust which was their employer. They raised concerns that a colleague, Mr Swift, had made false statements about his clinical experience and qualifications, and it was accepted that in so doing they had raised protected disclosures. The workforce divided into those siding with the claimants, those who believed that they were subjecting Mr Swift to a witch hunt, and those who were neutral. The employment tribunal was satisfied that, as a direct result of the disclosures, the claimants were subjected to unpleasant behaviour by other staff at the walk-in centre. The EAT had remitted the case to the employment tribunal to consider the issue of vicarious liability, including as to the reason for the unpleasant treatment and whether the acts complained of were so closely connected with the employment of those responsible so as to make the employer vicariously liable. But the Court of Appeal concluded that no such claim was available. The only claim that could be made was against the employer based on any conduct that could be attributed to the employer. That claim failed because the employer's action was by reason of the dysfunctional state of the workforce rather than by reason of any protected disclosures.

8.04   The Court of Appeal acknowledged in *Fecitt* (at para 61) that the absence of vicarious liability might be regarded as exposing a significant weakness in the protection which is afforded to whistleblowers, certainly by comparison to the discrimination legislation. An employee who makes a protected disclosure may well be at risk of adverse treatment by colleagues without any remedy under the legislation. But the Court of Appeal regarded that as a necessary conclusion from the terms of the legislation. That view was reinforced by the absence of any statutory defence covering situations where the employer has taken reasonable steps to prevent the wrongdoing.

8.05   The decision begged a question as to the circumstances in which the conduct of directors or employees would be attributed to the employer so as to give rise to primary liability. Notwithstanding the introduction of vicarious liability that issue may still arise. Notably it may have to be considered in the context of constructive dismissal claims and as such is discussed further below in that context.

B. The Amended Section 47B ERA

8.06   Section 47B ERA sets out provision for worker/agent liability, and liability of the employer as principal, in the following terms:

> (1A)   A worker ('W') has the right not to be subjected to any detriment by any act, or any deliberate failure to act, done—
> > (a)   by another worker of W's employer in the course of that other worker's employment, or
> > (b)   by an agent of W's employer with the employer's authority, on the ground that W has made a protected disclosure.
>
> (1B)   Where a worker is subjected to detriment by anything done as mentioned in subsection (1A), that thing is treated as also done by the worker's employer.
>
> (1C)   For the purposes of subsection (1B), it is immaterial whether the thing is done with the knowledge or approval of the worker's employer.
>
> (1D)   In proceedings against W's employer in respect of anything alleged to have been done as mentioned in subsection (1A)(a), it is a defence for the employer to show that the employer took all reasonable steps to prevent the other worker—
> > (a)   from doing that thing, or
> > (b)   from doing anything of that description.
>
> (1E)   A worker or agent of W's employer is not liable by reason of subsection (1A) for doing something that subjects W to detriment if—
> > (a)   the worker or agent does that thing in reliance on a statement by the employer that doing it does not contravene this Act, and
> > (b)   it is reasonable for the worker or agent to rely on the statement.

But this does not prevent the employer from being liable by reason of subsection (1B).

(2) This section does not apply where—
   (a) the worker is an employee, and
   (b) the detriment in question amounts to dismissal (within the meaning of Part X).
(3) For the purposes of this section, and of sections 48 and 49 so far as relating to this section, '*worker*', '*worker's contract*', '*employment*' and '*employer*' have the extended meaning given by section 43K.

Broadly, these provisions track the pre-existing legislation in the Equality Act 2010 (EqA), **8.07** sections 109 and 110, providing for a form of vicarious liability in relation to discrimination claims. As such the legislation in that field provides a source of guidance as to how the provisions are to be applied. The principal differences from the discrimination legislation are the following:

(1) Although it does not appear to be a difference in substance, in some ways the legislation follows a more natural sequence than the discrimination provisions. The discrimination provisions start by imposing the primary liability on the employer for the relevant acts or omissions of the employee or agent (in section 109 EqA), and proceed to provide that where the relevant act or omission is treated as having been done by the employer it is also a contravention by the employee or agent (section 110 EqA 2010). By contrast section 47B ERA first sets out the primary obligation upon the worker/agent of the employer not to subject that employer's workers to detriment by reason of such a worker making a protected disclosure. The liability of the employer is then founded on a breach by the worker/agent of that primary liability, subject to the employer's statutory defence, and with the qualification that employer liability may still arise despite the worker having a defence under section 47B(1E). That in turn more closely tracks the usual position at common law (though, as addressed below, not following the common law test) that vicarious liability is a secondary liability founded upon a primary wrongdoing of the worker/agent.
(2) Unlike the discrimination legislation there are no provisions specifically relating to instructing, causing, inducing, or aiding a contravention of the legislation, equivalent to sections 111, 112 EqA.
(3) The provision in section 47B(2) ERA, excluding operation of the victimization provisions where the detriment amounts to dismissal of an employee, also has no equivalent in the EqA. This is needed to keep detriment and dismissal distinct.

The vicarious liability provisions apply to two categories of person: (a) workers of the same **8.08** employer and (b) agents of the same employer. The circumstances in which liability may be attributed to, or avoided by, the employer differ depending on which of these categories apply. We address first the more common position relating to vicarious liability for other workers, before turning to the position in relation to agents of the employer.

C. Liability of and for Workers

(1) Restriction to workers of the same employer

The first category of person who may be subject to personal liability (and for whom the **8.09** employer may be vicariously liable) is another worker of the same employer as the worker who made the disclosure. Section 47B ERA provides for the term 'worker' to have the same extended meaning as applies for other purposes in relation to the protected disclosure provisions, which is discussed in Chapter 6. Section 47B(3) ERA refers to the extended meaning in section 43K. It does not, however, expressly refer to the extended meaning in section

43KA relating to police officers. But section 43KA itself expressly provides that it applies to section 47B ERA.

8.10 Ordinarily the provision only applies to another worker who shares the same employer as the worker who made the disclosure. The only exception arises by virtue of the fact that employment has been construed so as to cover former employment: *Onyango v Berkeley (t/a Berkeley Solicitors)* [2013] IRLR 338 (EAT); *Woodward v Abbey National Plc (No 1)* [2006] ICR 1436 (CA). There would not seem to be anything in the legislation which requires the worker made liable to have been employed at the same time as to the worker who made the disclosure.[2] The provisions would therefore apply where the worker held liable joined the employer's employment after the worker making the disclosure had left that employment. But since the worker held liable must have been acting in the course of employment, there could be no liability unless that worker was in the employer's employment at the time of the detrimental act which was alleged.

8.11 Problems in the application of the legislation may arise in circumstances where workers work alongside each other with different employers. That typically arises because workers employed by a different legal entity within a group of companies are assigned to work with a group entity which is different from their employer. Alternatively, it may happen as a result of workers being supplied by an agency to supplement the permanent work-force. One such scenario could be various subcontractors working on a building project. In such circumstances, unless it can be established that the employer of the worker who made a protected disclosure is in fact the employer of the wrongdoing worker, or to be regarded as the employer (eg under section 43K(1)(a) and (2)), there can be no personal liability of the worker, and hence no vicarious liability for the worker, unless the worker falls to be regarded as an agent of that employer. As we discuss below, recent authority in the context of discrimination legislation has suggested a restrictive view as to whether someone is to be regarded as an agent if employed by a different employer, but this is an area where there is scope for future development: see paragraphs 8.48 et seq below and in particular the discussion of *Ministry of Defence v Kemeh* [2014] EWCA Civ 91, [2014] ICR 625 (CA).

8.12 The risk of an anomalous result in such a situation is stark. Assume a situation where three workers work together as a team. Two are permanent employees of the same employer and one is an agency worker supplied to their employer by an employment business, and whose only contractual relationship is with that business. One of the permanent employees (W) makes a protected disclosure revealing a serious fraud. The other permanent employee (P) and the agency worker (A) then react adversely and together freeze him out of team discussions and carry out other steps amounting to victimization by reason of the disclosure. A would not be regarded as a worker employed by the same employer as W (see section 43K(2)(a) ERA). Nor are there any provisions in the legislation, in contrast to the discrimination provisions, for imposing liability on the basis of aiding a contravention. As such, despite working together as a part of a team and being jointly engaged in the acts of victimization, only P would be personally liable unless A could be regarded as covered by the agency provisions (ie section 47B(1A)(b)). Even if the agency provisions did apply there would be the potential anomaly arising from the differing tests for vicarious liability as between workers and agents (see below) and the fact that the statutory defence available to the employer applies only to vicarious liability for workers (but again, see the discussion below (at paragraphs 8.62 et seq) of the dicta in *Wijesundera v*

---

[2] See *BP plc v Elstone* [2010] IRLR 558 where the EAT held that the disclosure made by a worker need not have been made during the course of the employment with the respondent employer (as long as it was made when he enjoyed worker status with an employer).

Heathrow 3PL Logistics Ltd [2014] ICR 523 (EAT) and *Victor-Davis v Hackney LBC* (UKEAT/ 1269/01/MAA, 21 February 2003) as to how an effect which is similar to the statutory defence might be achieved in agency cases).

(2) In the course of employment

(a) Everyday, not common law, meaning

In the context of race discrimination, the Court of Appeal made clear in *Jones v Tower Boot* **8.13** *Co Ltd* [1997] ICR 254 that the common law principles for establishing vicarious liability do not apply. Instead the statutory words are to be given their everyday meaning. As explained in the EHRC Code of Practice on Employment (at para 10.46):

> The phrase 'in the course of employment' has a wide meaning: it includes acts in the workplace and may also extend to circumstances outside such as work-related social functions or business trips abroad. For example, an employer could be liable for an act of discrimination which took place during a social event organised by the employer, such as an after-work drinks party.

> **Example:** A shopkeeper goes abroad for three months and leaves an employee in charge of the shop. This employee harasses a colleague with a learning disability, by constantly criticising how she does her work. The colleague leaves the job as a result of this unwanted conduct. This could amount to harassment related to disability and the shopkeeper could be responsible for the actions of his employee.

The broad view of the 'course of employment' is consistent with the fact that, in contrast to **8.14** the common law position, employers have a statutory defence based on taking all reasonable steps to prevent the detrimental acts or detrimental acts of that description. A wide ambit for liability therefore serves the policy purpose of securing good practice by encouraging preventative measures. As such, acts which have little or no connection with what the workers were employed to do may still be regarded as done in the course of employment. That was the case in *Tower Boot*. Mr Jones, who was aged sixteen and of mixed ethnic parentage, was employed as an operative at a shoe factory. During his brief employment he was physically and verbally racially abused by two fellow operatives. That abuse included burning his arm with a hot screwdriver, throwing metal bolts at his head and calling him racially abusive names. Applying the ordinary layperson's meaning, these were all held to be acts done in the course of employment. The court noted (per Waite LJ at 265C) that there could be scope for disagreement as to what was regarded as done in the course of employment depending on whether it occurred in or out of the workplace, in or out of uniform, or in or out of rest-breaks. But this was a matter for the industrial jury.

Despite the broad ambit, there may be scope for different tribunals to reach different con- **8.15** clusions. One relevant fact in borderline cases may be whether the wrongdoing employee was deploying seniority or authority connected to the workplace, even if not in a formal supervisory position. That was the case in *Thomas Honda Ltd v Purkis* (UKEAT/0265/ 13/RN, 10 January 2014). Here the claimant was employed at a Honda dealership. She complained of sexual harassment by a colleague with whom she had had a relationship. He hit her once outside of work and four times at work. The tribunal found that the four occasions on which he hit her at work were in the course of his employment. He did not have supervisory responsibility over her but he was more senior than her by reason of his age, the time he had spent with the company, and his status within it, and was regarded as such by her. He called her into his office and then physically assaulted her. When he gave this instruction he did so as someone in a position of seniority to her at work. The EAT held that, applying the *Tower Boot* test, this was a conclusion that the employment tribunal was entitled to reach.

8.16   Again, the scope for differing views is illustrated by the decision in *UK Insulation Ltd v Cook* (UKEAT/0605/04/DA, 8 November 2004). Here the claim was of sexual harassment by a colleague (Mr Holliday). He had previously made unwanted sexual advances outside work which were not in the course of employment. The employment tribunal found that on 12 August 2003, whilst he was on sick leave, Mr Holliday attended the work premises to deliver a sick note and at the same time handed a letter to a colleague for him to give to the claimant. He did so. She found the letter threatening and it was adjudged by the ET to be an act of sexual harassment. The ET further held that this act was in the course of employment, taking into account that the letter had been handed to a work colleague to deliver to her whilst he was on the premises delivering a sick note, ie it was delivered taking advantage of work time, premises, and a colleague. The EAT allowed an appeal as the ET had made an error of fact in that there was no evidence that Mr Holliday had attended work on that date. The majority determined that subtracting the fact of having attended work, the question of whether this was in the course of employment did not admit of only one possible answer and so the case was remitted to the ET to determine. The minority concluded that the ET's critical finding was that Mr Holliday took advantage of work time, premises, and colleagues and so the act complained of was in the course of employment.

(b) Identifying the culprit

8.17   One difficulty that sometimes arises in victimization cases is in establishing the identity of those responsible for the act of victimization.[3] Notwithstanding this, without identifying the particular colleague responsible it may still be possible to infer that the detrimental act was carried out by a colleague in the course of employment and by reason of a protected disclosure, so as to be able to establish employer liability. That might for example be the case where an anonymous threat is left at work which alludes to the fact of the protected disclosure having been made. In the discrimination context, vicarious liability was established in *Commissioner of Police of the Metropolis v Maxwell* (UKEAT/0232/12/MC, 14 May 2013), [2013] Eq LR 680, despite the act of victimization (on grounds of race and/or sexual orientation) being an anonymous leak to *The Sun* newspaper. Without being able to identify the source of the leak, it was possible to infer from the content that it was someone for whom the employer was vicariously liable.

8.18   In other cases, however, the inability to identify the culprit may have the effect that the necessary inference cannot be drawn. The potential difficulty is illustrated by the decision, in the context of considering common law vicarious liability for tort, in *Allen and others v The Chief Constable of the Hampshire Constabulary* [2013] EWCA Civ 967, 30 July 2013. Here the claimant alleged that after she had begun a relationship with a police officer (L) she had been subject to a campaign of harassment by another police officer (R). Part of her complaint was that she had been sent anonymous letters that became increasingly derogatory and abusive. In striking out the claim, the Court of Appeal noted that, being anonymous, by their nature the letters did not purport to be from a police officer and so there was no sufficient connection to that role. The same reasoning would have applied under the statutory test of being in the course of employment.

---

   [3] See Chapter 7, paras 7.174–7.190 for a discussion of in particular *Royal Mail Group Ltd v Jhuti* [2016] ICR 1043 (EAT), *The Co-Operative Group Ltd v Baddeley* [2014] EWCA Civ 658 (CA), and *Reynolds v CLFIS (UK) Ltd* [2015] EWCA Civ 439, [2015] ICR 1010, which deal with the issue of 'procured' dismissals and the possibility (though not followed in *Jhuti*) that a claimant needs to plead the case against the colleague of the claimant employee who procured that dismissal.

(c) Acts outside working hours

Given the broad test of whether conduct was 'in the course of employment', disputes over **8.19**
the application of the concept have tended to focus substantially around its application
outside working time. Again, guidance may be drawn from decisions in the context of discrimination claims.

The fact that the detrimental act occurs outside of working time does not necessarily entail **8.20**
that it is to be regarded as not in the course of employment. Applying the layperson's test of
that phrase, it has been held to extend to off-duty conduct and work-related social events,
at least where they can be regarded as an extension of the work environment, being an issue
of fact for the tribunal. To that end, in *Chief Constable of Lincolnshire Police v Stubbs* [1999]
ICR 547 (EAT) alleged sexual harassment by a fellow police officer which occurred when
attending a pub immediately after work and at a leaving party for a colleague was found
to be within the course of employment. In each case the incidents occurred during social
gatherings of police officers, and did not entail socializing only with the harasser. The EAT
distinguished this from, say, a chance meeting at the supermarket. It emphasized that the
questions of whether the claimant and harasser were on duty, or whether they were on the
employer's premises, were considerations for the tribunal to take into account, but were
not the only relevant factors. Ultimately, it was for the employment tribunal to assess as
a matter of fact whether the incidents fell on the side of the line of being in the course of
employment.

A work-related social occasion was again regarded as merely an extension of work in *Livesey* **8.21**
v Parker Merchanting Ltd (UKEAT/0755/03, 13 January 2004). Here the claim concerned
sexual harassment by a colleague which had started at a work Christmas party, but which
had then continued in a car when they were given a lift home after the event. In the employment tribunal the lay majority had taken the view that the element of harassment that had
continued in the car was not conducted in the course of employment. That conclusion was,
however, overturned by the EAT, on the basis that there was no justification for a distinction
between events at the party and in the car immediately afterwards. It was a continuation of
the same course of conduct.

There is, however, no rule that all work-related events are to be regarded in the same **8.22**
way. There is scope for tribunals to regard matters differently depending on factors such
as whether it is an official work event, or whether, in the case of a social gathering,
it is mainly work colleagues in attendance or the gathering follows immediately after
work. Further, because of the fact-sensitive nature of the assessment, there is scope in
borderline cases for different tribunals to reach different, but equally valid, conclusions,
as was emphasized by the Court of Appeal in *Sidhu v Aerospace Composite Technology
Ltd* [2000] EWCA Civ 183, [2001] ICR 167 (CA). The claimant was subjected to violence and racial insults by a colleague during an employer-organized family day out. The
claimant responded by brandishing a chair. Both he and the colleague were dismissed.
The claimant was found to have been unfairly dismissed, but a majority of the tribunal
found that the racial attack was outside the course of employment. Although the day
was organized by the employer, this was outweighed by a combination of other factors,
including that (a) the day out was at a public theme park, rather than at work, (b) it
was outside working hours, and (c) most of those who participated in the incident were
friends and family, rather than employees. In restoring the tribunal's decision (which the
EAT had overturned) the Court of Appeal commented that the decision had been open
to the employment tribunal notwithstanding that a different tribunal may well have
reached a different conclusion.

8.23 The mere fact that an employee could be disciplined as a result of conduct outside of work is not sufficient of itself to render it in the course of employment. An argument based on the fact that disciplinary proceedings had been initiated arising from the conduct at the family day out was rejected in *Sidhu*. A similar argument also failed in *HM Prison Service v Davis* (UKEAT/1294/98, 29 March 2000), where an employment tribunal was held to have erred in finding that alleged sexual harassment had occurred in the course of employment. The claimant and the colleague were both prison officers. The alleged incident began when the colleague visited the claimant at home whilst they were off duty. The alleged harassment took place at a pub and again on returning to her flat. The EAT noted that the colleague had not pulled rank on the claimant or given her orders or threatened that he would cause difficulties for her at work unless she gave in to him. The only connection with work was the fact was that they had originally met at work and the colleague might have obtained her address through unauthorized access to information at work. That was insufficient. Nor was it relevant that it was a disciplinary offence for officers to engage in conduct outside work that would bring discredit on the Police Service under the employer's code of conduct. Further, the tribunal had also erred in relying on how the employer acted after the incident. That could have no bearing on whether the conduct was in the course of employment.

8.24 Off-duty conduct was again found not to be in the course of employment in *Waters v Metropolitan Police* [1997] ICR 1073 (CA). Again, the claim concerned sexual harassment. It was alleged that a policewoman had been sexually assaulted by a fellow officer while they were both off duty. Although the alleged assault occurred at a police section house where she had a room, that was not sufficient on the facts for the matter to be treated as being in the course of employment. The alleged assailant lived elsewhere, and he had visited the claimant in circumstances which placed him in the same position as a social acquaintance with no working connection.

(d) Comparison with and assistance from common law vicarious liability cases

8.25 As noted above, in *Jones v Tower Boot* the Court of Appeal emphasized that the statutory test of whether conduct is 'in the course of employment' is distinct and different from common law principles.[4]

8.26 The common law of vicarious liability has been and remains in a constantly developing state. In relationships which it is established are capable of giving rise to vicarious liability, the test is whether the connection between (a) the relationship of the primary wrongdoer and the person alleged to be liable, and (b) the wrongful act or default of the primary wrongdoer, is such as to make it just and reasonable to hold the person legally responsible to the claimant for the consequences of the wrongdoer's conduct. The test was set out by the House of Lords in *Lister v Hesley Hall Ltd* [2002] 1 AC 215 (HL) and has been revisited by the House of Lords in *Dubai Aluminium Co Ltd v Salaam and others* [2002] UKHL 48, [2003] 2 AC 366 and *Various Claimants v Catholic Child Welfare Society and others* [2012] UKSC 56, [2013] 2 AC 1 (SC), and subsequently by the Supreme Court in *Mohamud v Wm Morrison Supermarkets Plc* [2016] UKSC 11, [2016] AC 677. The principle developed in *Lister* was a departure from the previous long-established approach that an act was carried out in the course of employment, and therefore subject to vicarious liability, if it was either authorized by the employer, or a wrongful and unauthorized mode of doing an act authorized by the employer.

---

[4] For an in-depth consideration of the common law tests of vicarious liability, see Practical Law practice note on 'Vicarious Liability' (Jeremy Lewis).

The change in the law brought about by and since the decision in *Lister* has the effect that **8.27** there is less likely to be a different result when compared to the statutory test in section 47B ERA. But it remains the case that the tests are distinct. The statutory test is to be regarded as at least as wide as, if not wider than, the *Lister* test: *Livesey v Parker Merchanting Ltd* (UKEAT/0755/03, 13 January 2004). That is unsurprising given the public policy underlying the legislation and the availability of the statutory defence. As such in borderline cases, common law decisions on similar facts might provide a sense check. If vicarious liability has been established applying the common law test it is unlikely that the statutory test would not (subject to the statutory defence) be satisfied.

However, the value of referring to decisions on the common law test remains limited given **8.28** the fact-specific nature of the assessment and the different test to be applied. The common law test requires a focus on whether what was done was sufficiently closely connected to what the employee/worker was authorized to do (*Dubai Aluminium Co Ltd v Salaam* [2002] UKHL 48, [2003] 2 AC 366, per Lord Nicholls at para 23), or, put another way, with their job or field of activities (*Mohamud v Wm Morrison Supermarkets Plc* [2016] UKSC 11, [2016] AC 677 per Lord Toulson at para 44). The potential for a different outcome at common law is illustrated by the following decisions:

- In *Vaickuviene v Sainsbury plc* [2013] IRLR 792, Mr Romasov was killed by a fellow employee (Mr McCulloch) on the employer's premises. Albeit obviously an extreme case, the circumstances might also have founded claims of race victimization and protected disclosure detriment. Mr McCulloch had previously told Mr Romasov that he did not like immigrants and that he should go back to his own country. Mr Romasov had written a letter of complaint which, subject to satisfying the public interest test, would be likely to have contained protected disclosures. It was alleged that Mr McCulloch had learnt of the complaint and taken exception to it. On the night of the killing there had been a couple of arguments between them at work, and then Mr McCulloch had taken a knife from the kitchenware section of the supermarket and stabbed Mr Romasov. The court held that the mere bringing together of employees was not a sufficient basis for imposing vicarious liability. Both Mr Romasov and Mr McCulloch were employed to stack shelves. Mr McCulloch had no supervisory responsibility for Mr Romanov. There was no connection between what the employee was engaged to do (stacking shelves) and the wrongdoing. But applying the statutory course of employment test, a different conclusion might be expected. The assault occurred whilst Mr Romasov and Mr McCulloch were at work, and it appears was in response to a complaint made at work. The question of whether in layperson's terms the attack was in the course of employment could be answered without having to be satisfied of the connection with stacking shelves.
- In *Graham v Commercial Bodyworks Ltd* [2015] ICR 665 (CA) an employee had been 'mucking around' at work and had deliberately splashed flammable liquid onto the claimant's overalls, apparently as a prank. The claimant then suffered serious injuries when the colleague used a cigarette lighter in his vicinity. The Court of Appeal accepted that this was reckless conduct but was not in the course of employment since, in the court's view, the highly reckless act of splashing the flammable liquid onto the overalls and then using a cigarette lighter in the vicinity was not sufficiently closely connected with the wrongdoing employee's job or anything which he was authorized to do. But, given that this reckless behaviour had occurred whilst the employees were at work, it would seem to have fallen squarely within what, in layperson's terms, would be regarded as in the course of employment so as to satisfy the statutory test.
- In *Wilson v Exel UK Ltd t/a* Exel [2010] CSIH 35, as a prank a supervisor forcibly pulled an employee's head back by her hair. The Court of Session concluded that, despite the fact that the incident happened whilst at work and during working hours, there was no

vicarious liability as the conduct was not connected with anything he was employed to do. The court emphasized that the fact that the employment provides the opportunity for the act to occur is not necessarily sufficient. Here there was found merely to have been an incidental or random attack by an employee that happened to take place on the employee's premises during working hours. The supervisor was not purporting to do anything connected with his duties. Yet, given that this occurred at work and during working hours, it would be surprising if it was not regarded as falling within the statutory test of being in the course of employment.

- In *G B v Stoke City Football Club Ltd and Fox* [2015] EWHC 2862 an apprentice footballer was assaulted by one of the senior professional players, F, who was the first-team goalkeeper and club coach. It was alleged that the assaults took the form of 'gloving', whereby a gloved finger was covered in a hot rubbing ointment and inserted into his rectum. This was said to have been commonly used against apprentices as a form of punishment by the professional players for failing to perform menial tasks for them. Although the claim failed on the facts, the court held that the club would in any event not have been vicariously liable, as F had no power, duty, or discretion conferred upon him by the club to train, discipline, or chastise the apprentices. There was thus no sufficient connection for common law vicarious liability to apply. Whilst the decision may be dubious even as authority on common law vicarious liability (and it relied on the Court of Appeal's subsequently overturned decision in *Mohamud*), it is in any event likely that the conduct would have been regarded as in the course of employment applying the statutory test, given that it was alleged to have occurred at work, as a form of work-related punishment.

(3) The employer's statutory defence

8.29 Following the discrimination model, now contained in section 109(4) EqA, it is a defence if the employer can show that it took all reasonable steps to prevent the worker from doing the detrimental act or omission, or from doing anything of that description.

8.30 For the defence to be available it is first necessary to identify whether the employer took any steps at all to prevent the employee from doing the acts in question (or acts of that description). If any such steps were taken it is then necessary to consider whether there were any further steps that it was reasonable to take to prevent the particular detrimental act in question or acts of that description; *Canniffe v East Riding of Yorkshire Council* [2000] IRLR 555 and *Croft v Royal Mail Group plc* [2003] ICR 1425 (CA).

8.31 A step may be a reasonable step even though it would not actually avoid the discrimination: see *Canniffe*. However, an employer is entitled to consider whether the time, effort, and expense of the suggested measure are disproportionate to the result likely to be achieved. As explained by Pill LJ in *Croft* at para 63:

> Steps which require time, trouble and expense, and which may be counterproductive given an agreed low-key approach, may not be reasonable if, on an assessment, they are likely to achieve little or nothing.

8.32 On this basis, in *Croft* the court accepted that a tribunal was entitled to conclude that there were no further steps that it was reasonable to take to prevent harassment of an employee who was undergoing gender reassignment to become a woman. The employer had taken a number of steps including agreeing with the claimant that she would be known as and dealt with as a woman, changing all her records to reflect this, and telling the workforce that she was now to be seen and addressed as a woman, stressing the harassment policy and using a low-key approach to avoid problems. The further steps which it was contended on behalf of the claimant should be taken were educating the workforce and amending the harassment policy to refer to transsexuals. But these would not have had any more than a marginal effect on employees. The court accepted that the concept of what is reasonable permits the employer to consider whether the time, effort, and expense of the suggested measures are disproportionate to the result likely to be achieved. That was found to be the case here.

Since the focus is on reasonable preventative steps, subsequent events (such as whether the **8.33** perpetrator was then disciplined) are not relevant, albeit that subsequent acts may shed light on any steps which precede the discrimination: see *Al-Azzawi v Haringey Council* (UKEAT/ 158/00, 3 December 2001) and *Fox v Ocean City Recruitment Ltd* (UKEAT/0183/11, 13 June 2011). Applying that principle, disciplinary steps taken after the event against the perpetrator would not be relevant. But evidence to show that the employer actually only paid lip service to a whistleblowing policy would be relevant.

Again, because it is necessary to focus on preventative steps, it is important for a tribunal **8.34** properly to identify the acts of detrimental treatment. This was emphasized in a discrimination context in *Marks and Spencer plc v Martins* [1998] ICR 1005 (CA). The discrimination claim arose from the claimant's treatment in a job interview. This resulted in her not being offered a job, but it was the interview rather than the refusal to offer employment that was the act of discrimination. As a result of failing to focus on the correct act, the tribunal erred in rejecting the statutory defence.

In assessing what steps could reasonably have been taken, an important issue is whether any **8.35** other employee had any knowledge of any particular risk that an employee would act in the way that the perpetrator had done (*Canniffe*). If the act in question was a one-off act and there was nothing to alert any other employee to the particular risk, then it might well be sufficient for there to be an adequately promulgated whistleblowing policy making clear that the conduct in question would not be condoned or encouraged by the employer, together with requisite training and publicizing of the policy. Support for that view derives from decisions in the discrimination context. In *Caspersz v Ministry of Defence* [2006] (UKEAT/ 0599/05, 3 February 2006), the EAT accepted that a tribunal was entitled to conclude that the statutory defence was satisfied in the case of alleged harassment of a police officer by the Assistant Chief Constable to whom she reported. The respondent had a dignity at work policy and it had been conscientiously implemented. The EAT did, however, caution that this should not be taken as carte blanche for employers simply to adopt a policy and do no more. Particularly if there was good reason to think that an employee was being subjected to harassment (and by extension good reason to suspect other detrimental treatment), an employer could not simply rely on the policy, no matter how seriously the employer takes it.

Similar reasoning was applied in *Livesey v Parker Merchanting Ltd* (UKEAT/0755/03, 13 **8.36** January 2004). Here the employer's equal opportunities and harassment policy was given a high profile and adhered to, and the perpetrator had been given training in equal opportunities and made aware of the importance attached to the equal opportunities policy. In upholding a tribunal's finding that the statutory defence was made out, the EAT placed particular emphasis on the specific finding that senior management did not have any knowledge of the perpetrator's conduct until after the sexual harassment had occurred.

As Burton J explained (at para 22) in *Canniffe* (again in the discrimination context), the **8.37** position is liable to be different if there was 'knowledge or suspicion in relation to a particular employee of his own predilections or temperament, and certainly if there was an awareness of a risk that he might commit inappropriate acts towards a particular employee or particular employees'. In *Canniffe* there was a suggestion that the employee had confided some concerns to her line manager, but she had only done so as a friend on a confidential basis. The circumstances in which she had confided in him were relevant, but not a complete answer. There were still other reasonable steps that might have been taken, such as warning the perpetrator or at least subjecting him to closer supervision, and notifying other managers of the need for vigilance.

8.38 Again by analogy with the position in discrimination cases, guidance as to what may be regarded as reasonable steps may be derived from the EHRC's Code of Practice on Employment.[5] The guidance suggests (at para 10.52) — with our further comments in brackets — that reasonable steps might include:

(1) implementing an equality policy (or, in the protected disclosure context, a whistleblowing policy);

(2) ensuring workers are aware of the policy;

(3) providing equal opportunities training (or by analogy, training in relation to the importance of the whistleblowing policy and so as to avoid detriment by reason of protected disclosures);

(4) reviewing the policy as appropriate; and

(5) dealing effectively with employee complaints (although as noted above, steps taken subsequent to the discriminatory act or acts of detriment are irrelevant except insofar as they cast light on whether the employer merely paid lip service to a policy without implementing it in practice or are relevant in relation to subsequent acts of detriment or discrimination).

(4) The worker/agent's statutory defence

8.39 Section 47B(1E) ERA provides a narrow defence for a worker/agent who subjects a worker to a detriment but does so in reliance on a statement made by the employer that so acting (or failing to act) does not contravene the Employment Rights Act 1996 (ERA), and that it was reasonable to rely on that statement.

8.40 The provision is modelled on section 110(3) EqA. However, in the protected disclosure context, the importance of the defence is likely to lie in the fact that it will typically be the employer who will conduct the investigation arising from a protected disclosure. Further, the investigation of this will often be conducted separately from the ordinary line management. That investigation may lead to the conclusion that what was disclosed did not amount to a protected disclosure, eg because the discloser had no reasonable belief that the information disclosed tended to show a relevant failure. A line manager who, in relation to the worker, then proposes to take action which is influenced by the disclosure having been made may therefore need to rely on the conclusion of that investigation.

8.41 The position may be illustrated by a situation where one worker (A) makes an allegation that another worker (B) has been engaged in a fraud. The information disclosed is investigated and the manager is informed that the allegation was made without any reasonable basis. The manager faced with the breakdown in relationship between A and B may decide that they need to be separated and that, since A made an allegation without any reasonable basis, A should be the person to be moved. If what was said by A was found to be a protected disclosure, the manager may need to rely on the defence in section 47B(4) ERA. Before taking such action the manager should obtain a statement from his employer.

8.42 In practice, an important issue may then arise as to how specific that statement must be. Is it necessary to state in terms that doing the act/omission in question would not contravene the Act? Is it sufficient that there is a statement (such as that an investigation has revealed that what was said was not a protected disclosure) from which it could reasonably

---

[5] See further the discussion of whistleblowing policies and procedures in Chapter 19.

be concluded that doing the act/omission would not contravene the Act? Does the statement by the employer have to make reference to the act in question? For example, is it sufficient that the employer has communicated that there was no protected disclosure made, or is it necessary for the employer's statement to be that, in the example above, moving the worker who made the disclosure would be permissible?

The wording of the legislation appears to suggest that it is not sufficient that the statement **8.43** provides a reasonable basis for the worker/agent to believe that the proposed move (the relevant act) does not contravene ERA. Instead, the statute appears to require that this must be stated in terms. Indeed, the legislation does not merely require that there is a statement that the act does not contravene the whistleblowing provisions. Rather, it requires a statement that the conduct would not contravene ERA (as a whole). But it may be doubted whether the provision will be construed in that literal way. If the purpose of the provision is at least in part to recognize the fact that it may be the employer who is best equipped to determine whether what was said amounts to a protected disclosure, then there is little basis for taking a formalistic, literal interpretation to what must be said. Given that in practice the worker/agent taking action will not normally have contemplated in advance the engagement of section 47B(1E), it is unlikely they or their employer will have taken legal advice, so it will be rare for them to insist on first receiving a statement formally recording that their action would not be a breach of ERA. More likely is that the worker/agent will rely on feedback in broader terms as to the outcome of the employer's investigations.

In the context of the equivalent provision in EqA (section 110(4)), the guidance in the EHRC **8.44** Code provides some support for a less literal view of what is required. Paragraph 10.56 of the EHRC Code offers as an example, that the provision might apply if a line manager asks a company director if she needs to make reasonable adjustments for a machine operator with multiple sclerosis, and the director wrongly replies that she does not think the person is covered by the EqA because he is not in a wheelchair. Clearly, the gist of that statement is that the worker would not be contravening the obligation under the Act related to disabled persons by not making reasonable adjustments. A statement by the employer that after investigation there was found to be no protected disclosure would appear to be to similar effect.

In any event, even where the requisite statement is made, there will be a fact-specific issue **8.45** as to whether it is reasonable for the worker (or agent) to rely upon it. This mirrors, to some extent, the test imposed on workers for their reasonable belief for a disclosure to qualify. In relation to whether there is a qualifying disclosure, the worker is expected to exercise a judgement which is consistent with the resources available to that worker. Similar considerations may apply for the purposes of section 47B(1E). If the employer indicates that the matter has been investigated and the worker (or agent) relying on the defence has no reason to believe that the employer's conclusion is wrong, then the application of the reasonableness test will be straightforward. The position may be otherwise if the worker/agent seeking to rely on the defence knows or believes that the employer has not adequately investigated the disclosures.

D. Liability of and for Agents

In addition to vicarious liability for employees, under section 47B(1A)(b) ERA an employer **8.46** of the person who made the protected disclosure is also liable for anything done by an agent of that employer with the employer's authority. The provision therefore requires focus on two questions:

(1) Who is to be regarded as an agent?
(2) What test applies for whether that person was acting 'with the employer's authority'?

8.47 These two elements to some extent overlap, in that the question of whether the person was exercising the employer's authority is relevant to whether the person was an agent as well as whether liability arises.

(1) Agency relationship

8.48 In contrast to the position in relation to workers, the legislation contains no definition of an agent. The approach taken has been to adopt the ordinary common law meaning (*MoD v Kemeh* [2014] ICR 625; *May & Baker Ltd v Okerago* [2010] IRLR 394.) In *Yearwood v Commissioner of Police of the Metropolis* [2004] ICR 1660, the EAT (at para 35) applied the definition of agency as being:

> the fiduciary relationship which exists between two persons, one of whom expressly or impliedly consents that the other should act on his behalf so as to affect his relations with third parties, and the other of whom similarly consents so to act or so acts.

8.49 That approach was approved by the Court of Appeal in *Ministry of Defence v Kemeh*, with the qualification that it is not an essential requirement for agency that the agent should be able to affect the principal's relations with third parties. It was noted that an estate agent is a typical example of where an agent introduces or canvasses custom on behalf of the principal without having the power to bind the principal contractually. The person could be an agent by virtue of standing in the shoes of the employer in relation to independent third parties, without being able to enter into contracts for the employer.

8.50 On that basis Elias LJ (with whose judgment Lewison LJ and Kitchin LJ agreed) doubted (at para 39) whether there was any substantive distinction from the alternative formulation contended for in *Yearwood* of an agent as a person who acts on behalf of another person with their authority. However, although concluding that ability to effect the principal's relations with third parties is not essential, Elias LJ appeared to proceed to treat it as an important indication of an agency relationship. To that end he commented (at para 40) that:

(1) An employer's employees would not ordinarily be treated as agents, though they might be depending on the particular obligations cast upon them such as where a senior manager is authorised to contract on behalf of the employer with third parties.

(2) Equally, where an employee of a third party carries out work for the benefit of another employer, that of itself would not be sufficient to render that employee an agent of the third-party employer.

8.51 In *MoD v Kemeh* the claimant claimed that whilst working as a cook in the British Army in the Falklands he was subjected to racial abuse by a subcontractor's employee (Mr Ausher) who was providing facilities management services to the MoD. The court rejected the contention that Mr Ausher could be regarded as in an agency relationship with the MoD. Giving the leading judgment, Elias LJ said that merely performing work for a third-party employer was not of itself sufficient to make the performer an agent of that employer. Elias LJ accepted that the fact that someone was employed by another person (A) would not automatically prevent that person being an agent of a different employer (B). But Elias LJ emphasized that cogent evidence would be required to show that the duties which the employee was obliged to carry out as an employee of A were also being performed as an agent of B. At minimum, for an agency relationship the worker would need to be acting on behalf of the employer. But here, whilst Ms Ausher was working for the benefit of the third-party employer (the MoD), she was not acting on that employer's behalf. Whilst the MoD had the right to veto the presence of Ms Ausher, that fell far short of constituting an authority to her to act on its behalf with respect to third parties. She would not be standing in the shoes of the employer in relation to independent third parties.

It was argued for the Claimant in *Kemeh* that there would be an agency relationship if (a) there was a degree of direction by the putative principal, (b) there was a degree of integration with the principal's employees, and (c) there was a degree of proximity. This proposed test was rejected.

The decision in *Kemeh* may be contrasted with that in *Unite the Union v Nailard* [2017] **8.52**
ICR 121. Here a union was held liable for the acts of sexual harassment by two full-time union officials, notwithstanding that the two officers were employed by a third party—the employer of the workforce represented by the union. The officials were clearly acting on behalf of the union in representing its members, and in this case taking part in negotiating meetings with the employer, during which the harassment of the claimant (also a union official) took place. Nor was it any answer that the union had limited control over what the officials did since, as the EAT noted (at para 54), that would often be true of a principal who commissions an agent to undertake tasks on his behalf.

In *Kemeh* there was no suggestion that Mr Ausher exercised any management authority **8.53**
over the claimant. By contrast, an agency relationship is liable to arise where someone other than a worker of the employer exercises management authority on behalf of the employer. That situation was considered in a series of cases in the context of discrimination/victimization claims concerning police officers. In *Cumbria Police v McGlennon* [2002] ICR 1156, the EAT considered that agency liability would apply in relation to what were essentially management decisions on such matters as recruitment and posting, which were part of the functions of the direction and control of a police force vested by statute in a chief constable, but in fact carried out under his authority by other officers at the appropriate level of the chain of command. In *Chief Constable of Kent County Constabulary v Baskerville* [2003] ICR 1463, the Court of Appeal confirmed that the *Cumbria Police* case was rightly decided.

In *Commissioner of the Police of the Metropolis v Weeks* (UKEAT/0130/11/JOJ, 22 November **8.54**
2011), the EAT accepted that an officer from another police force could, by virtue of the management responsibilities undertaken, have responsibility as an agent. Here the claimant was a civilian employee in the Metropolitan Police. She was line managed by an officer of the City of London Police. He was responsible for assessing her performance and making decisions which could have an impact on her prospects for promotion and career advancement. The EAT upheld the tribunal's decision rejecting the contention, at a preliminary hearing, that the Chief Constable could not be liable, on an agency basis, for alleged sex discrimination by the line manager. On the facts in *Weeks* the line manager was able to bind the Chief Constable contractually in that he was able to reach a binding agreement with her as to her supervisory responsibility and her pay. As accepted in *Kemeh*, however, that is not to be regarded as a necessary ingredient for an agency relationship.

As illustrated by the above decisions, whilst in *Kemeh* Elias LJ's reasoning placed some **8.55**
emphasis on interaction on behalf of the principal with third parties as an indication of an agency relationship, interaction with the employer's employees may suffice for this purpose.

For there to be an agency relationship, the agent must, however, be exercising authority on **8.56**
behalf of the employer. In *McGlennon* and *Weeks*, the management functions in question plainly derived from the management powers residing in the Chief Constable and delegated through the hierarchy to be exercised on his behalf. The position is different where the person alleged to be an agent is exercising powers which never resided in the employer. To that end in *Yearwood v Commissioner of Police of the Metropolis* [2004] ICR 1660, the EAT held that there could be no question of an investigating officer, appointed under the Police Regulations to investigate disciplinary action against a police officer, being in that capacity an agent of the Chief Officer. The powers were conferred directly on the investigating

officer (even if he was appointed by the Chief Officer) and as such there was no question of exercising authority delegated by and on behalf of the Chief Officer.

8.57 Particular care may be needed in assessing whether the alleged agent is acting on behalf of the employer where, instead of someone coming into the employer's organization to manage the employer's staff (as in *Weeks*), the employee is placed into another employer's workforce. That was the case in *Remploy Ltd v Campbell and Redbridge LBC* (UKEAT/0550/12/JOJ, 19 November 2013). The employer had placed the claimant with a local authority (Redbridge LBC), working in its CCTV operations. Redbridge terminated that placement. It was found to have discriminated on grounds of race in doing so. The issue arose as to whether it had been acting as Remploy's agent. Redbridge had power to terminate the placement under the arrangements with Remploy, and in that sense had the consent or authority of Remploy to do so. It did not, however, follow that it had been acting *on behalf* of Remploy in doing so, and that issue was remitted to the employment tribunal.

8.58 The EAT in *Remploy* also accepted that the requisite authorization from the principal could be provided by ratification after the event, but only if the claimant employee (who was subjected to the alleged discrimination or victimization) perceived that the agent was acting in the name of or on behalf of the principal. In this case the EAT held that the tribunal had been entitled to find that Remploy had adopted the decision of the local authority to terminate the placement, albeit that the issue of whether the employee perceived that the decision had been made by the local authority in the name of or on behalf of Remploy still needed to be decided.

8.59 The circumstances in *Remploy* may be contrasted with those in *Lana v Positive Action Training in Housing (London) Ltd* [2001] IRLR 501 (EAT). Here the claimant, Ms Lana, was placed by the respondent with a firm (Walker Management) as a trainee quantity surveyor. There was a tripartite relationship, effected by contracts between the claimant and respondent, and between the respondent and the end user, Walker Management, where the respondent had agreed to provide the claimant with training and was to fulfil that obligation by the placement with Walker Management. The EAT concluded that Walker Management was to be regarded as the agent of the respondent for the purposes of fulfilling the training obligations which the respondent had entered into with the claimant. Whereas in *Remploy* the alleged principal was a public body which assisted disabled people to find work and it was unclear whether the alleged agent was carrying out any function on its behalf (which was an issue remitted to the tribunal), in *Lana* the putative agent, Walker Management, was found to be providing the training on behalf of the respondent.

As emphasized in *Blackwood v Birmingham and Solihull NHS Trust* [2016] ICR 903 (CA), at para 59, it does not follow that the relationship between a training provider (with whom there is a placement) and a training company will always be that of principal and agent. In that case a university student undertook a vocational placement with the respondent trust, which was arranged by the university as part of her diploma of higher education in mental health training. But, in the context of a sex discrimination claim, the relationship between the university and the NHS trust was found to be one of two principals operating at arm's length, rather than principal and agent. Whilst the university would have agreed to certain parameters with the provider (the NHS trust) as to what work would be provided, it would ordinarily have no involvement in, or control over, the student's day-to-day working environment.

8.60 At common law a key distinction is drawn between an independent contractor and others who may be regarded as agents. Whilst there may be vicarious liability for an agent acting on behalf and within the scope of authority conferred by the principal (*Heatons Transport* *v TGWU* [1973] AC 15 (HL) at 99), there is no vicarious liability for the wrongdoing of an independent contractor. That issue does not arise in the same way under section 47B ERA. If the person is to be regarded as an agent, then the vicarious liability provisions apply. But it may be that the same result is achieved in many cases by focusing on the requirement that the purported agent act on behalf of the employer.

(2) Requirement of agent acting with authority of the principal

Although liability arises only where the agent acts with the employer's authority, it is **8.61** expressly provided that it is immaterial whether the detrimental treatment is done with the knowledge or approval of the employer (section 47B(1C) ERA). The phrase 'knowledge or approval' is used in the EqA, section 109(3) and it has a clear statutory provenance.[6] Consideration of how the equivalent discrimination provisions using this phrase have been determined is therefore particularly relevant. It has been held that it does not confine liability to the narrow category where the principal has authorized the agent to discriminate. In a series of decisions the EAT has instead applied a test of whether the discriminator was exercising authority conferred by the principal (*Bungay v Saini* [2011] Eq L R 1130; *Lana v Positive Action Training in Housing (London) Ltd* [2001] IRLR 501 (EAT); *Victor-Davis v Hackney LBC* (EAT/1269/01/MAA, 21 February 2003); *Mahood v Irish Centre Housing Ltd* (UKEAT/0228/10/ZT, 22 March 2011)). To similar effect, in *Ministry of Defence v Kemeh* [2014] ICR 625, Elias LJ formulated the test (at paras 11 and 12) as being whether the discriminatory act (or, in the context of protected disclosures, the detrimental treatment by reason of the protected disclosure) was done in the course of carrying out the functions which the agent is authorized to undertake. Applying that test it has been emphasized that it is sufficient if the discriminatory act (and so by analogy the act of detrimental treatment) would have fallen within the acts which the agent had authority to carry out lawfully on behalf of the employer.

A potentially wider test was suggested by the EAT in *Wijesundera v Heathrow 3PL Logistics* **8.62** *Ltd* [2014] ICR 523, in the context of a sex discrimination/harassment claim. The EAT emphasized (a) that a broad view of the scope of the agency is necessary, and (b) that this is subject to there being a sufficiently close connection between the treatment complained of and what agent was authorized to do. Both these elements appear to have been drawn from common law principles of vicarious liability. As noted above, in that context a test applies of whether the wrongful conduct was so closely connected with what the agent was authorized to do that it may be regarded as just and reasonable for it to be regarded as done in the course of the employer's business and for there to be vicarious liability: see *Lister v Hesley Hall Ltd* [2002] 1 AC 215 (HL); *Dubai Aluminium Co Ltd v Salaam* [2002] UKHL 48, [2003] 2 AC 366, Lord Nicholls at para 23; *Mohamud v Wm Morrison Supermarkets Plc* [2016] UKSC 11, [2016] AC 677 (SC). Further, in that context it had been emphasized that there needs to be a broad view of what of what the alleged wrongdoer was authorized to do, or their job or field of activities, rather than just focusing on the wrongful act.

It was on that basis that a broad view was needed of the employee's field of activities that **8.63** in *Mohamud v Wm Morrison Supermarkets Plc* [2016] UKSC 11, [2016] AC 677 there was found to be vicarious liability for an employee (Mr Khan) who worked in the kiosk at the supermarket's petrol station and for no good or apparent reason committed a brutal and

---

[6] 'knowledge or approval', for example, also appeared in s 58(1) of Disability Discrimination Act 1995; Regulation 11 of Part-time Workers (Prevention of Less Favourable Treatment) Regulations 2000/1551 and s 13(1) of the Race Relations Act 1968.

unprovoked attack on a customer. Mr Khan had responded to an inquiry by the customer, Mr Mohamud, about printing some documents, by ordering Mr Mohamud to leave the shop, and using threatening and racist language. He had then followed Mr Mohamud to his car, told him never to come back and punched and kicked him. In the Supreme Court it was emphasized that it was not appropriate to focus on whether the assault was authorized. Viewed more broadly, Mr Khan's job was to attend to customers and respond to their inquiries. He did so with a foul-mouthed rant and by ordering the customer to leave the shop: when he followed the customer out of the kiosk and then assaulted him, this was adjudged to be part of the same seamless episode.

8.64 No difficulty arises where the detrimental treatment occurs in the course of undertaking a management function which the agent was authorized to carry out. That was the case in *Bungay v Saini* [2011] Eq L R 1130, which concerned a claim of religious discrimination against an advice centre, and against its chairman and director as agents of the centre. The EAT applied a test of whether the discriminator was exercising authority which was conferred by the principal. The EAT's starting point was therefore to ascertain the authority conferred by the centre on the chairman and director. As members of the centre's board, they had been managing the centre as part of their authority as directors. They had operated and encouraged a discriminatory, anti-Hindu policy at the advice centre and the centre's mistreatment of the claimants, who were Hindus, resulted from that policy. As such the employment tribunal had been entitled to find that they were liable, and the centre was liable for their acts as its agents, notwithstanding that the duties were performed in a discriminatory manner.

8.65 However, beyond the context of exercising management authority, some caution may be needed in deploying the suggested approach in *Wijesundera* of applying agency liability based on a close connection to authorized acts. The statutory language, both in the discrimination and protected disclosure legislation, expressly requires that the agent acts with the employer's authority, not that this authority extends to other matters which are sufficiently closely connected with authorized acts. There may be a fine line between asking whether the acts in question were sufficiently closely connected with what was authorized that they are to be regarded as within the scope of authority, which appears to have been the EAT's approach in *Wijesundera*, and extending liability to acts which are outside the scope of authority on the basis of a sufficient connection to that which is authorized.[7] However, it is a distinction which appears to be demanded by the statutory language, requiring a focus on whether the agent was acting within the scope of the agent's express, implied, or ostensible authority. That is subject to the limitation, implicit in the legislation, that the mere fact that the agent was acting for an illicit reason (ie by reason of the protected disclosure) does not itself take the treatment outside the scope of authority.

8.66 Practically, should a worker consider s/he has suffered a detriment by a possible agent, the worker should consider raising this with the employer. Conversely, in receipt of such a request, an employer will have an opportunity to expressly state whether it does or does not authorize the prohibited conduct, and/or to explain the basis for the conduct (for instance to confirm it is not for a prohibited reason). The response may also shed light on whether the perpetrator was acting on the employer's behalf.

---

[7] See also *So v HSBC* [2009] EWCA Civ 296, [2009] 1 CLC 503; *Playboy Club London Ltd v Banco Nazionale Del Lavoro Spa* [2014] EWHC 2613, rejecting an argument that in negligent misrepresentation claims the close connection test was displaced by a narrower test based on authority, and in that respect distinguishing the decision in *The Ocean Frost* [1986] 1 AC 717 (HL) as concerned with deceit.

(3) No statutory defence

One reason for caution as to the breadth of the test for agency liability is that the statutory defence **8.67** in section 47B(4) ERA does not apply to the liability of an agent for a principal where there is no employment relationship (see also *Ministry of Defence v Kemeh* [2014] EWCA Civ 91, [2014] ICR 625, at para 13). As set out below, some EAT decisions have suggested that the legislation can be construed so as to reach a result which is similar to the statutory defence. However, that approach is difficult to reconcile with the statutory language and is inconsistent with more recent authority.

In *Victor-Davis v Hackney LBC* (UKEAT/1269/01/MAA, 21 February 2003), the EAT **8.68** expressed the view that a discriminatory act done by a person without the knowledge or approval of a principal cannot be deemed to have been done as an agent of that person and with their authority where the principal has taken such steps as are practicable to prevent the person from doing the act. This was viewed as having the same effect as the statutory defence. However, it is difficult to reconcile a test based on reasonable practicable steps with the statutory language which focuses on the scope of authority. That would appear to place the focus on whether the authority was in fact restricted, rather than whether reasonably practicable steps were taken. Indeed in *Wijesundera v Heathrow 3PL Logistics Ltd* [2014] ICR 523, the EAT suggested (at para 49), without this having been tested in argument, that it was open to an employer to expressly restrict the authority of the agent and that an agent was only entitled to do that which was within his lawful authority.

That suggestion, however, begs some further questions as to what is sufficient to restrict author- **8.69** ity. Clearly, it is insufficient simply to prohibit victimization. That would be inconsistent with the approach that the employer may be liable for acts which would be authorized if done lawfully. Essentially this point was emphasized in context of a claim of sexual harassment by elected officers of a trade union in *Unite the Union v Nailard* [2017] ICR 121. The EAT rejected a submission that the respondent union could not be responsible for the harassment by its officials because such harassment was contrary to union policy, since the officials had been carrying out tasks (speaking at meetings concerning matters to be negotiated with the employer of the workers they represented and corresponding about this) within the scope of their authority. As the EAT explained (at para 58):

> A principal cannot avoid responsibility for acts done with his authority merely by saying to his agent 'Of course you must not do anything illegal' or (in the context of the Equality Act) 'Of course you must not do anything against equality law'. Such a statement does not limit the scope of the agent's authority to act on the principal's behalf. It merely spells out the obvious: the principal does not approve if he carries out authorised functions in an unlawful manner. But the fact that the principal would disapprove does not prevent the agent's act being treated as done by the principal: section 109(3) [EqA].[8]

The approach begs the question of what would have been sufficient to limit authority. In **8.70** *Nailard* the acts of harassment principally related to the way the officials spoke to the claimant during meetings. The EAT's approach made clear that, so far as the officials were authorized to conduct those meetings, the acts did not cease to be done with the authority of the principal merely because it was impermissible to carry out the meetings in that way. The reasoning suggests that the position would have been different only if the officials' authority to act on behalf of the union in those meetings had been removed, so that harassing the claimant would no longer have been an unauthorized means of carrying out an authorized act. To some extent this mirrors the approach at common law where a distinction is drawn between (a) a prohibition that limits the sphere of the agent's employment and (b) merely

---

[8] Section109(3) EqA is in materially the same terms as s 47B(1C) ERA.

forbidding conduct within the sphere of employment: see *Ilkiw v Samuels* [1963] 1 WLR 991. It is only in the first of these two classes that vicarious liability is excluded. In *Ilkiw* there was an express prohibition on permitting anyone else to drive the lorry which the employee was employed to drive to transport sugar. This was conduct within the sphere of employment rather than limiting the scope of employment.

However, the line between something which limits the sphere of the agent's employment and something which only limits the way in which the agent is permitted to carry out authorized acts may not always be easy to draw, and in any event risks giving rise to anomalies. The position may be illustrated by the instance of an agent who is given managerial authority over an employee and, by way of victimization for a protected disclosure, issues a first written warning. Clearly it would not be sufficient to take this outside of being something done with the authority of the principle that it was made clear that there was no authority to engage in acts of victimization. The position would be otherwise, however, if it had been made clear that issuing of disciplinary warnings was not within the scope of the agent's authority. But that gives rise to a practical difficulty, as the employer may have no forewarning that a restriction of that kind is needed. As such an employer may be liable for the acts of an agent despite having taken all reasonably practicable steps to prevent this, whereas such reasonable steps would provide a defence to a claim by an employee.

E. Remedies against Individual Employees or Agents

8.71 A worker (W) can present a claim against another worker, employee, or agent of W's employer individually. The employer's vicarious liability is dependent on the various elements of the claim (detrimental act or deliberate failure to act on the grounds of a protected disclosure) being established against the worker or agent, but is not dependent on that worker or agent being found to be personally liable. The worker or agent may escape personal liability either because no claim is brought against them or because they establish a defence that the employer authorized their conduct (see section 47B(1E)). That same defence is found in section 109(4) EqA.

8.72 It will often be important to give careful consideration at the outset to whether to include a claim against the worker/agent where there is a detriment claim. It may be important to do so by reason of the prospect that the employer may be able to establish a defence under section 47B(1D) ERA, with the effect that only the worker/agent would be liable for the detrimental act or failure to act. It may also be important where there is a risk of the employer avoiding liability by entering into insolvency.

(1) Is the remedy limited to a declaration?

8.73 In *Royal Mail Group Ltd v Jhuti* [2016] IRLR 854, the EAT (at para 27) suggested that a declaration is the only remedy available where a claim succeeds against a worker or an agent. That view was *obiter*, since the only claim was against the employer, and we suggest that it was plainly wrong. The EAT's reasoning proceeded by reference to the terms of section 49(1) ERA, which refers to section 48(1A) (which in turn sets out the right to bring a claim of unlawful detriment on the grounds of a protected disclosure under section 47B ERA) and provides:

> (1) Where an employment tribunal finds a complaint under section 48(1), (1ZA), (1A) or (1B) well-founded, the tribunal—
> (a) shall make a declaration to that effect, and
> (b) may make an award of compensation *to be paid by the employer* to the complainant in respect of the act or failure to act to which the complaint relates. (emphasis added)

The EAT (Mr Justice Mitting) noted that the power to make an award of compensation was **8.74** therefore expressed to be as against the employer. However, this appears to have overlooked section 48(5) ERA which provides:

In this section and section 49 any reference to the employer includes—

. . .

(b) in the case of proceedings against a worker or agent under section 47B(1A), the worker or agent.

This provision therefore makes clear that, in line with the model that is familiar in dis- **8.75** crimination legislation, compensation can also be awarded against the individual worker or agent. That also accords with the Explanatory Memorandum to the ERRA, which provided (at para 113), in relation to section 19 ERRA (which introduced the vicarious and individual liability provisions), that:

The effect of this section is to introduce a vicarious liability provision so that where a worker is subjected to a detriment by a co-worker done on the ground that the worker made a protected disclosure, and this detriment is done in the course of the co-worker's employment with the employer, that detriment is a legal wrong and is actionable against both the employer and the co-worker.

To similar effect, in introducing the provisions during the passage of the bill which led to **8.76** the ERRA, the Government minister stated that the provisions mirrored the provisions in the EqA on vicarious liability for discrimination (where there is no such exclusion of compensation as a remedy),[9] and he added as follows:

The equivalent provision in the Equality Act does allow for claims against co-workers and we think that it is right that the legislation is the same here.

Before I conclude, let me explain this thinking, particularly in view of the comments made by the noble Lord, Lord Low of Dalston. Individuals have a personal responsibility to make sure that they act in the right way towards people with whom they interact. The law recognises this in many different ways. For example, the law of negligence makes you personally liable if you crash your car into someone and contract law makes you liable if you misrepresent an item that you are selling to somebody. If you are a taxi driver and you crash your car into someone, or a salesman and you misrepresent an item you are selling, the principle of vicarious liability means that your employer will be liable, too. We think that the same should be true in whistleblowing. If you cause a co-worker a detriment after they blow the whistle, perhaps by bullying them, you should be liable for that conduct and your employer should be liable, too. This amendment therefore will encourage workers to behave appropriately to each other and will encourage employers to have the right processes in place to protect whistleblowers.[10]

From that statement it may be inferred that the Government minister would have been sur- **8.77** prised to find that the effect of the provision was to limit liability against a co-worker only to a declaration. Section 48(5) ERA makes clear that is not the case.

(2) Causation

On the basis (as we suggest is the case) that section 49(1) ERA permits a compensation **8.78** award against an individual agent or worker, some potentially difficult issues may arise as to causation of loss. Where several workers are involving in the acts of victimization, the position

---

[9] *Hansard*, HL Report Stage, 26 February 2013, col 1001 per Viscount Younger.
[10] ibid, col 1004 per Viscount Younger.

as against the employer might be simplified on the basis of vicarious liability for each of the employees concerned. On that basis there may be no need against the employer to identify what loss or harm was caused by each employee's acts separately, as it may be possible to stand back and consider the cumulative picture. That approach is not available if each employee may be liable to pay compensation individually. In that event, it would be necessary to consider the potentially awkward question of the loss or harm caused by each employee individually, save perhaps to the extent that they can be regarded as having acted in tandem.

(3) Joint and several awards and contributions

8.79 In the context of discrimination claims, where it is well established that there can be awards of compensation against individual employees,[11] one issue addressed has been the scope for the tribunal to apportion the share of liability between individual employee and employer where both are liable. Clearly, where there are discrete acts of detriment, and the worker is not found liable for all the acts in relation to which there are adverse findings against the employer, it will be necessary for there to be discrete awards against employer and worker so that the remedy against the worker is properly tied to the detrimental acts for which he or she is liable. However, in relation to detrimental acts (or deliberate failures to act) for which the employer and the respondent employee are both liable, the tribunal has no power to apportion liability as between the employer and the respondent employee or to order a contribution from the respondent employee (see *Hackney LBC v Sivanandan* [2013] ICR 672 (EAT) and *Brennan and others v Sunderland City Council* [2012] ICR 1183). The EAT in *Brennan* also expressed the tentative view (*obiter*) that a contribution could not be claimed in the ordinary courts under the Civil Liability (Contribution) Act 1978. This provides (in section 1(1)) that:

> any person liable in respect of any damage suffered by another person may recover contribution from any other person liable in respect of the same damage (whether jointly with him or otherwise).

8.80 By section 2(1) of the 1978 Act, the contribution is the amount which is 'just and equitable having regard to the extent of that person's responsibility for the damage in question'. However, section 1(6) of the 1978 Act provides that references to a person's liability in respect of any damage are to such liability which has been or could be established in an action brought in England and Wales by or on behalf of the person who suffered the damage. The EAT in *Brennan* preferred the view that the reference to an action was to a claim justiciable in the ordinary courts, with the result that there could be no contribution claim in relation to a tribunal award.

8.81 Some similar arguments may be applied in the context of the protected disclosure provisions. Indeed the issue may arise, even if the claim in the tribunal was only brought against the employer, as to whether, having established a breach of the right founded on vicarious liability for the worker or agent, a contribution could then be obtained in the ordinary courts under the 1978 Act. The reasoning in *Brennan* at present stands in the way of that course. Given the exclusive jurisdiction of the employment tribunal to deal with protected disclosure claims, it can be said that this should not be circumvented under the guise of a contribution claim. It might also be said that if that is the position where there was no claim brought against the worker, the position should in principle be no different where the claim was brought against both worker and employer and the award made against both.

---

[11] As set out above (paragraphs 8.73–8.77), we suggest that is also the case in protected disclosure detriment claims, notwithstanding the view expressed to the contract in *Jhuti*.

That does, though, have the potential to lead to injustice due to one party being left to shoulder the full liability, and the point has yet to be the subject of binding authority. The view expressed on this issue in *Brennan* rests largely on a narrow approach to the meaning of 'action' (which is not expressly defined in the legislation), and the EAT itself recognized that, if correct, this would result in an unsatisfactory lacuna.

Particularly given the uncertainty as to availability of a contribution claim, it may be a **8.82** sensible course for employers to include an express contractual provision in contracts of employment for an indemnity in the event that the employer is found liable to make any payment of compensation by reason of the vicarious liability provisions of section 47B ERA. That also has the benefit of certainty, whereas even if a contribution claim under the 1978 Act was available, there would still be the need for assessment of the contribution. Such a term might also be highlighted within the whistleblowing policy.

F. Attribution and Constructive Dismissal

The provisions for vicarious liability set out in section 47B ERA do not apply in relation **8.83** to dismissal of an employee. That gives rise to a potential complication in cases of constructive unfair dismissal. The conduct in response to which the employee resigns might separately give rise to a detriment claim under section 47B ERA to which the vicarious liability provisions apply (see the discussion of *Melia v Magna Kansei* [2005] EWCA Civ 1547, [2006] ICR 410 in Chapter 9 at paragraphs 9.13–9.18). But that leaves an issue as to whether the detrimental treatment can be attributed to the employer for the purposes of founding a constructive dismissal claim. If a worker (A) is bullied by a colleague (B) for making a protected disclosure, that may give rise to a detriment claim. But if A resigns in response to bullying, can she say this was by way of acceptance of repudiatory breach *by the employer*, and can B's reason for the bullying be attributed to the employer?

In the context of discrimination claims, the approach taken at EAT level has been to apply **8.84** the common law approach to vicarious liability: see *Hilton International Hotels (UK) Ltd v Protopapa* [1990] IRLR 316 (EAT); *Livesey v Parker Merchanting Ltd* (UKEAT/0755/03/DA, 13 January 2004). However, as explained in *Fecitt*, vicarious liability operates to make an employer liable for breach of some duty or obligation owed by the employee. In a constructive dismissal case the relevant obligation (ie not to dismiss unfairly) is owed by the employer rather than the employee. That would suggest that instead of considering vicarious liability, which is founded on secondary liability for breach of the employee's obligations, an analysis is required of whether the employee's conduct and reasons are to be regarded as conduct and reasons of the employer.

This in turn requires an assessment as a matter of statutory construction as to whose **8.85** conduct and state of mind is to be attributed to the employer (*KR v Royal & Sun Alliance plc* [2006] EWCA Civ 1454, [2007] 1 All ER (Comm) 161 (CA)). The question of whether the employee was acting within authority is liable to be relevant but not necessarily determinative when applying this approach. As explained by Lord Hoffmann in *Meridian Global Funds Management Asia Ltd v Security Commission* [1995] 2 AC 500 (PC) at 511–12:

> But their Lordships would wish to guard themselves against being understood to mean that whenever a servant of a company has authority to do an act on its behalf, knowledge of that act will for all purposes be attributed to the company. It is a question of construction in each case as to whether the particular rule requires that the knowledge that an act has

been done, or the state of mind with which it was done, should be attributed to the company. Sometimes, as in *In re Supply of Ready Mixed Concrete (No 2) [1995] 1 AC 456* and this case, it will be appropriate . . . .. On the other hand, the fact that a company's employee is authorised to drive a lorry does not in itself lead to the conclusion that if he kills someone by reckless driving, the company will be guilty of manslaughter. There is no inconsistency. Each is an example of an attribution rule for a particular purpose, tailored as it always must be to the terms and policies of the substantive rule.

8.86 As discussed in Chapter 7 (at paragraph 7.177 et seq), these principles were applied in *Orr v Milton Keynes Council* [2011] EWCA Civ 62, [2011] ICR 704 in relation to unfair dismissal legislation. In that case it was concluded that as a matter of construction, it is the knowledge of the dismissing officer, and not of other managers in the employer organization, which is relevant in considering the fairness of the dismissal, where the dismissal is not of a constructive variety. As discussed at paragraphs 7.163 to 7.190, that is subject to the issue as to whether the knowledge of a worker or agent who procures the dismissal can be attributed to the employer. So far as constructive dismissal is concerned, applying a similar approach to that adopted in *Orr* would entail liability for alleged detrimental conduct consisting in taking a managerial disciplinary decision or grievance decision. Conversely, where management authority is not being exercised a different result might be expected. The decision in *Wallbank v Wallbank Fox Designs Ltd* [2012] EWCA Civ 25, [2012] IRLR 307 (CA) provides an illustration of this. Here the employer was vicariously liable for the act of an employee in responding to lawful instructions by assaulting his supervisor. But this was not the exercise of managerial authority. Instead, it was a violent refusal to accept such authority. As such, it would make little sense to regard it as conduct attributable to the employer so as to establish a repudiatory breach of contract by the employer.

G. Concluding Comments

8.87 The vicarious liability provisions were introduced at a relatively late stage during the passage of the Bill which became the ERRA without any prior public consultation. The amendments were an understandable response to the issues raised in the Mid Staffs enquiry and highlighted by the decision in *Fecitt*. But there was a marked lack of discussion of the practical issues likely to result. The focus during the Hansard debates was on the legislative lacuna which arose on facts such as those applicable in *Fecitt*, where those who blew the whistle could be subject to reprisals from colleagues without there being a remedy. However, the facts in *Fecitt* also illustrate the complication of importing individual and vicarious liability. Detrimental treatment in response to the making of a protected disclosure may take various different forms ranging from, on one hand, extreme harassment to, on the other, giving the cold shoulder or being unwilling to work alongside a colleague who has made the disclosure. From the perspective of a worker who is the subject of allegations of wrongdoing, the latter reaction may be natural and understandable, particularly where the allegations are unfounded (though based on a reasonable belief). Indeed, from the perspective of the person who is the subject of the allegations, they may appear defamatory. The further risk then arises of allegation and counter-allegation, as occurred in *Fecitt*, which may now in each case possibly be backed by the threat of legal action. In *Fecitt* the Court of Appeal was able to sidestep that problem on the basis that action taken in response to there being a dysfunctional workforce was not by reason of a protected disclosure. But that is no longer an answer where the claim arises from vicarious liability for the actions of colleagues. Faced with such issues, greater importance is necessarily placed on the statutory defence, and the importance of effective implementation of a whistleblowing policy backed by effective training, which we consider further in Chapter 19.

9

DISMISSAL FOR MAKING A
PROTECTED DISCLOSURE

A. Comparison with the Pre-PIDA Position

9.01 In relation to protection against dismissal, the PIDA provisions improved the protection for employees dismissed for the reason or principal reason that they have made a protected disclosure in the following principal respects:

(a) there is no minimum service qualification;
(b) compensation is not capped;
(c) an application for interim relief may be made; and
(d) dismissal is automatically unfair.

9.02 Protection previously applied only to employees under a contract of employment rather than the wider class of worker. Workers who are not employees now also have protection against detriment even where this takes the form of dismissal of the worker. But the separate provision for dismissal cases still applies only to employees, other than a provision in relation to remedy in section 49(6) ERA, which is considered in Chapter 10, paragraphs 10.104–10.107.

B. The Relationship between a Dismissal of an Employee for Making a Protected Disclosure and an 'Ordinary' Unfair Dismissal

(1) Overview

9.03 The legislation makes dismissal by reason or principal reason of the making of a protected disclosure a prohibited reason for dismissal under ERA, sections 99 to 103A. In summary, the structure of the legislation is as follows.

(a) Section 94 gives an employee the right not to be unfairly dismissed.

(b) Section 98(1) requires an employer facing a claim of unfair dismissal to show the reason or principal reason for the dismissal and that it falls within the potentially fair reasons set out in section 98(1) and (2).

(c) If a potentially fair reason is shown, then in an ordinary unfair dismissal case the question of whether the dismissal is fair would depend on the test in section 98(4) of whether in the circumstances the employer acted reasonably or unreasonably in treating it as a sufficient reason for dismissing the employee.

(d) However, section 98(6) provides that this is subject to the various provisions for automatic unfairness including section 103A. The effect is that a tribunal is not to consider whether or not the employer's actions were reasonable (although reasonableness may conceivably become relevant to the amount of compensation).

(e) Section 103A provides that:

> an employee who is dismissed shall be regarded for the purposes of this Part as unfairly dismissed if the reason (or, if more than one, the principal reason) for the dismissal is that the employee made a protected disclosure.

(f) If there were a number of reasons for the dismissal then the dismissal will be automatically unfair only if the protected disclosure was the principal reason.

9.04 In *Butcher v The Salvage Association* (EAT/988/01, 21 January 2002), [2002] EWCA Civ 867 (CA), the EAT (at a preliminary hearing) held that where an ET makes a finding of unfair dismissal on one basis, there is no separate right to complain that the decision should have been reached on another basis (in this case the making of a protected disclosure). In refusing permission to appeal, the Court of Appeal did not appear to take a different view. We would respectfully suggest that the EAT was incorrect. An employee is entitled to a determination of the claim brought and the decision in *Butcher* is better explained on the basis that there were findings of fact made to the effect that the alleged protected disclosures were not in fact the principal reason for dismissal. If there is an arguable error of law in the finding of a protected disclosure dismissal, this can be appealed even though the claimant has succeeded in relation to ordinary unfair dismissal. That was the view of the EAT in *El-Megrisi v Azad University (IR) in Oxford* (UKEAT/0448/08/ MAA, 5 May 2009), where it was accepted that it was a matter of 'potential practical value' for the appellant claimant to obtain a finding not simply that she had been unfairly dismissed for 'being a nuisance' but that the reason why she had been perceived as a nuisance by her previous employer was that she had raised matters of concern about what appeared to be serious possible irregularities. The EAT added that in any event the claimant was entitled as a matter of right to have the totality of her claim adjudicated. There might be exceptional cases where for some particular reason it is an abuse for a claimant to pursue an aspect of a claim which can have no conceivable benefit for him/her. However, *El-Megrisi* was not a case in that category.[1]

(2) Amendment to add an ordinary unfair dismissal claim to a protected disclosure dismissal claim

A related point as to the nature of the relationship between ordinary unfair dismissal and dismissal contrary to section 103A has arisen in various cases dealing with applications to amend existing claims. In *Street v Derbyshire Unemployed Workers' Centre* [2004] ICR 213[2] the claim had been (at least primarily) pleaded on the basis that the protected disclosure was the reason for the dismissal. During the hearing the claimant sought to run a claim of 'ordinary' unfair dismissal as well, it having initially been conceded that no claim of ordinary unfair dismissal was pleaded. One of the issues for the EAT was whether the tribunal was correct in declining to entertain the ordinary unfair dismissal claim (it had gone on to dismiss the PIDA-based claim). **9.05**

The EAT said that this raised an issue of construction in relation to the originating application, to see whether it contained the basis of a claim so that this could be adduced. This was a technical issue, involving a pure point of law and not the assessment of the reality of the circumstances.[3] *Selkent Bus Co Ltd v Moore* [1996] ICR 836[4] laid down the guidelines upon which a decision about raising a new or additional claim might be made.[5] Amongst the considerations were whether the amendment sought was a substantial alteration by pleading a new cause of action. If a new complaint or cause of action was proposed to be added by way of amendment, it was essential for the tribunal to consider whether that complaint was out of time and, if so, whether the time limit could be extended under the applicable statutory provisions (but as to this, see the reasoning in *New Star* and in *Kuznetsov* at paragraphs 9.10 and 9.11(2) below). The EAT then analysed the originating application. In box 1 Mrs Street had described the 'type of complaint' as 'Unfair Dismissal—Right not to be dismissed or victimized following disclosure of wrongdoing by employer under PIDA 1998'. Under the 'details of complaint' she had written: **9.06**

> I conclude that I have been disciplined and dismissed unfairly, that I was protected under PIDA and the allegations I made were made in good faith at the time and were made to organisations . . . because I feared victimisation and eventual dismissal, which has come to pass.

The EAT's analysis was that on this wording there *was* within the originating application the basis of a claim for ordinary unfair dismissal. It went on (in paras 36–39) to say this: **9.07**

> We accept . . . [the] submission that there is what we described as a single channel, that is, one complaint is made under the sole basis which is section 94, a complaint of unfair dismissal. It may take different forms and different facts will be relevant to different specific forms . . .

---

[1] In *Hamer v Kaltz* (UKEAT/0502/13/BA, 4 August 2014), at para 21, HHJ Richardson said that, where an employment tribunal was faced with claims of unfair dismissal which relied on a provision such as s 103A and also on ordinary unfair dismissal, it made sense first to consider the s 103A issue: if an ET finds the principal reason is proscribed, it makes no sense to rule separately on ordinary unfair dismissal unless it is done expressly on an alternative basis in case the ET is wrong about s 103A.

[2] The decision in the Court of Appeal ([2004] EWCA Civ 964; [2005] ICR 97) is discussed in detail in Chapter 10, paragraphs 10.112–10.129.

[3] *Bryant v Housing Corporation* [1999] ICR 123 at 130, per Buxton LJ.

[4] See now the summary of the applicable principles in the cases reviewed in some detail by Underhill J in *TGWU v Safeway Stores Ltd* (UKEAT/0092/07, 6 June 2007), at paras 7–13; followed in *Enterprise Liverpool Ltd v Jonas* (UKEAT/0112/09, 24 July 2009), at paras 14–20; *Smith v Lehman Bros* (EAT/0486/05, 13 October 2005); *2 Sisters Food Group Ltd v Abraityte* (UKEAT/0209/15/MC, 13 November 2015), deciding that the balance of hardship and injustice test applies even to new claims brought out of time, though consideration of time limits remains important.

[5] See the principles set out at p 842 of the judgment.

If what was thought to be advanced was a completely new ordinary unfair dismissal claim, *Selkent* would have been directly relevant. In *Selkent* it is not decided whether or not such a change constitutes a new cause of action. The principal basis upon which *Selkent* was decided was that new facts, not previously pleaded, would have to be put in evidence and it was unfair to allow that to be done at the stage that had then been reached. . ... we have come to the conclusion that the Employment Tribunal focused incorrectly on section 111 and did not focus upon the other factors in *Selkent* and did not correctly analyse the Originating Application as containing in itself a claim for ordinary unfair dismissal which simply needed particularisation. It will be borne in mind that the onus then would fall on the employer to produce reasons. As it happens, the Respondent did so, for it met a claim of ordinary unfair dismissal by its answer that the dismissal was nothing to do with public interest disclosure, was to do with gross misconduct and was fair; and it demonstrated the procedure adopted.

9.08   The decision might be explained on the basis that Mrs Street had said that she had been 'disciplined and dismissed unfairly' (ie 'simple unfair dismissal') before going on to refer, separately and additionally, to PIDA. However the EAT's approach seems to have been that claims of 'ordinary' unfair dismissal and a dismissal contrary to section 103A indeed concern the same 'cause of action' as each other—the cause of action being unfair dismissal. In any event, irrespective of whether there is a new cause of action, to the extent that the amendment seeks to introduce new legal and factual issues (including the issue as to whether dismissal was reasonable within section 98(4) ERA), that is highly relevant to the discretion as to whether to permit the amendment.

(3) Amendment to add a protected disclosure dismissal claim to an ordinary unfair dismissal claim

9.09   The focus on the substance of whether new legal and factual issues are raised, rather than the narrow question of whether there is technically a new cause of action, was highlighted in *New Star Asset Management v Evershed* [2010] EWCA Civ 870. The issue arose in the context of an application by the claimant, Mr Evershed, to add a whistleblowing claim to an existing ordinary unfair dismissal claim. The unamended grounds of claim were characterized as 'somewhat discursive and general' with 'few particulars . . . given' and:

> Apart from the references . . . to a breach of 'the duty of trust and confidence' entitling the Claimant to claim constructive dismissal, there is no attempt to formulate the claim of unfair dismissal by reference to s. 98 of the Employment Rights Act 1996 or any other provision of the statute.

9.10   The application was made to include a claim under section 103A on the basis that Mr Evershed's suspension (which was relied upon as the culminating act entitling him to resign) was in response to the lodging of a grievance by him, and that that grievance constituted a protected disclosure. This was rejected for various reasons, including that it was an attempt to raise a new cause of action which would require wholly different evidence to that envisaged in the claim as originally pleaded. In the EAT Underhill J said that it was clear that the amendment did indeed raise a new basis of claim, since there was nothing in the original pleading to indicate that the Mr Evershed intended to rely on section 103A. He added that it might be possible to quibble with the phrase 'cause of action' since section 103A was a form of unfair dismissal; but that was 'not a point of any significance'. The weight to be attached to the fact that there was a new basis of claim depended on the extent of the difference between the original and the new bases of claim, since 'mere re-labelling' is much more likely to be permitted than an amendment which introduces very substantial new areas of legal and factual inquiry.[6]

---

[6] Referring to para 13 of the EAT's judgment in *Transport and General Workers Union v Safeway Stores Ltd* (UKEAT/0092/07, 6 June 2007).

Underhill J then considered the areas of factual inquiry raised by the proposed amendment and whether they were already raised in the previous pleading. He concluded that the amended claim would not require the adducing of wholly different evidence from that required by the original claim. The Court of Appeal agreed: the allegations in the pleadings were not identical but the thrust of the complaints in both was essentially the same.[7]

An 'ordinary' unfair dismissal case will require the employer to establish the reason for the dismissal which operated in its directing mind, and as such it may well be that there will be considerable overlap in practice between the exercise thus required and the additional necessity of considering whether one or more protected disclosures was or were the reason or principal reason for dismissal. That may have a significant bearing on the assessment of whether an amendment should be permitted. But the tribunal will need to consider in the round the issues bearing on the balance of prejudice. Relevant factors are likely to include the extent of factual overlap and what has already been set out in the pleadings, together with issues such as how late the issue is raised, the reason for the timing of the application, any impact on the length and cost of the hearing, and applicable time limits. The position in further illustrated by two decisions where opposite conclusions were reached as to whether to permit a protected disclosure dismissal claim to be added to an ordinary unfair dismissal claim: **9.11**

(1) In *Makauskiene v Rentokil Initial Facilities Services (UK) Ltd* (UKEAT/0503/13, 29 April 2014), the claimant was a cleaning operative. Her case was that at a consultation meeting in relation to reducing her hours of work, she had raised a grievance as to bullying and harassment. She was later dismissed for having contacted the client directly about certain concerns, when on the respondent's case she had been warned not to contact them. She brought claims of ordinary unfair dismissal and race discrimination. There was a hearing which (though it had been listed for a final hearing) was then used to identify the issues in the case. This resulted in the discrimination claim being identified. But it was only after that hearing that an application was made to add claims of dismissal and detriment by reason of protected disclosure. The application relied upon the fact that the claim form had substantially incorporated the terms of a letter which set out a timeline and included various matters relied upon as disclosures and detriments. The detriment claim would have relied upon a large amount of disclosures and detriments that were not at the heart of the unfair dismissal claim. Although the various disclosures and detriments were referred to in the letter, the claim did not draw a causative link between the disclosures and the detriments other than dismissal. In those circumstances the ET's decision not to permit the detriment claim to be added was upheld. However, the EAT reversed the decision not to allow the section 103A claim, taking into account that there was already an extant unfair dismissal claim which had been brought in time, that the matters already pleaded (albeit without having put this under the protected disclosure label) already drew the link between specified detrimental treatment and the dismissal, that the reason for dismissal was bound to be in play at the final hearing, and that the amendment would not materially increase the amount of evidence required for the final hearing.

(2) By contrast, permission to amend to add a protected disclosure dismissal claim was refused in *Kuznetsov v The Royal Bank Of Scotland* (UKEAT 0089152907, 29 July 2015,

---

[7] See the guidance, albeit not in a case involving protected disclosures, of Underhill LJ in *Abercrombie & Ors v Aga Rangemaster Ltd* [2013] EWCA Civ 1148, [2014] ICR 209 (at para 48):

> [T]he approach of both the Employment Appeal Tribunal and this court in considering applications to amend which arguably raise new causes of action has been to focus not on questions of formal classification but on the extent to which the new pleading is likely to involve substantially different areas of inquiry than the old: the greater the difference between the factual and legal issues raised by the new claim and by the old, the less likely it is that it will be permitted.

[2017] EWCA Civ 43). The claimant was employed in RBS's Global Banking and Market division. He was dismissed purportedly on grounds of redundancy, and initially, in March 2012, brought a claim of ordinary unfair dismissal. At the time of presenting the initial claim, the claimant was acting in person and the claim lacked particularity. Over two and a half years later, and after two preliminary hearings, in a draft list of issues a complaint was raised that the dismissal was by reason of making a protected disclosure regarding non-payment of bonus and proposed relocation. In relation to the ordinary dismissal claim, the EAT allowed an appeal against the ET's refusal to permit the claimant to argue that the real reason for his dismissal was not redundancy but was a reason connected with the wish to avoid paying the claimant a bonus, taking into account that there had been no concession made that there was a fair reason for dismissal. As such no amendment was required in relation to that claim. But the ET refused to allow the claim of dismissal by reason of a protected disclosure to proceed and this was upheld both by the EAT and the Court of Appeal. That claim did require permission to amend. In the Court of Appeal, Elias LJ (at para 26) expressly rejected a submission that adding a whistleblowing claim was no more than particularization of an existing unfair dismissal claim. The EAT noted that exercising the discretion the employment judge had been bound to take into account that if brought as a new claim the protected disclosure claim would have been out of time and there was no basis for saying it was not reasonably practicable to bring the claim in time. The employment judge had also been able to take into account the procedural background, including that the claimant had earlier clarified that he was not raising any further claims, and had not mentioned the possibility at any earlier stage, including at the preliminary hearings. The degree of overlap with the issue as to whether there was a fair reason for dismissal on the unfair dismissal claim did not require a different conclusion. Raising matters as background evidential points was a different matter to pursuing a separate head of claim. In any event, the whistleblowing claim raised other legal and evidential issues, which would add to the time and cost of the hearing, including issues as to what disclosures were made. Further, by contrast with *Makauskiene* where the factual basis for the claim was already incorporated into the claim form (via the terms of a letter), in *Kuznetsov* the claim as to protected disclosures was still unparticularized. It was also all the more unfair for the respondent to have to deal with this after such a long delay. In all, the employment judge's conclusion that the balance of prejudice was against allowing the amendment was a wholly permissible conclusion. The Court of Appeal agreed. Elias LJ emphasized (at para 25) that a claim is not simply something to set the ball rolling, to be augmented as a party thinks fit. Delay in the tribunal proceedings was no answer to failing to include the claim at the outset.

C. The Boundary Line between Dismissal and Detriment

9.12   Two cases at appellate level have considered the demarcation line between detriment and dismissal claims.[8] For convenience we set out section 47B insofar as it is relevant to the issues discussed in this section.

(1)   A worker has the right not to be subjected to any detriment by any act, or any deliberate failure to act, by his employer done on the ground that the worker has made a protected disclosure.

---

[8] It should be noted that a detriment claim under s 48 ERA, unlike an unfair dismissal claim (whether under s 98 or s 103A) is not one of the claims that can be heard by an employment judge sitting alone because it is not included in the list in s 4 of the Employment Tribunals Act as amended.

(1A) A worker ('W') has the right not to be subjected to any detriment by any act, or any deliberate failure to act, done—

   (a) by another worker of W's employer in the course of that other worker's employment, or

   (b) by an agent of W's employer with the employer's authority,

on the ground that W has made a protected disclosure.

(1B) Where a worker is subjected to detriment by anything done as mentioned in subsection (1A), that thing is treated as also done by the worker's employer.

(2) . . . this section does not apply where—

   (a) the worker is an employee, and

   (b) the detriment in question amounts to dismissal (within the meaning of [Part X]).

In *Melia v Magna Kansei Ltd* [2005] EWCA Civ 1547, [2006] ICR 410 the ET upheld Mr   **9.13**
Melia's claims that in May 2001 he had made a protected disclosure about working practices and because of this he had been subjected to detriment over the period between May and November 2001 by being

- bullied
- subjected to an investigation for alleged misuse of his employer's computer system
- suspended.

The ET also upheld Mr Melia's claim that he had been constructively dismissed for whis-   **9.14**
tleblowing: he had resigned on 9 November 2001 in response to these detrimental acts which were also breaches of contract by the employer. Mr Melia claimed compensation for injury to his feelings occasioned by the detrimental acts and argued that the assessment of that compensation should take account of everything that had been done to him from the making of the disclosure up to and including his suspension and then resignation. The ET only awarded compensation for injury to feelings for detriment in the period up to the date by which, in its view 'the conduct [of the employer] moved from being a detriment to being a matter of dismissal'. They decided that that date was late June 2001 and assessed compensation at £6,000. In the EAT Mr Melia submitted that had the ET extended its consideration of the events which occurred up until November 2001 it would have arrived at a larger figure. The EAT upheld the ET's decision: section 47B was intended to apply to anything short of dismissal (including constructive dismissal) and the detriment which was excluded from section 47B was thus not only the actual dismissal, but also the behaviour of the employer which effectively gave rise to a dismissal (or more accurately a repudiatory breach which the employee could accept, giving rise to constructive dismissal), within the meaning of section 95. In those circumstances the ET was correct in its approach.

The Court of Appeal allowed Mr Melia's appeal and remitted the case to the ET to assess   **9.15**
compensation for the period up to the date of Mr Melia's' resignation in November 2001. Chadwick LJ (with whom Smith and Wilson LJJ agreed) said that sections 47B and 103A spring from the same root; PIDA. They were parallel elements in the protection which Parliament had decided to give to whistleblowers, and these were intended to be complementary. Parliament did not intend to confer a right under Part V of the 1996 Act for the protection of whistleblowers in circumstances where the worker (being an employee) would have a right under Part X of that Act in relation to the same loss or detriment. In a case where compensation was to be awarded under Part X it was limited to compensation for loss sustained in consequence of the dismissal and would not include compensation for loss sustained prior to the dismissal. Loss sustained prior to the dismissal could not be loss sustained in consequence of the dismissal. When the two sections were read together, the proper meaning to be given to the phrase 'the detriment in question amounts to dismissal' was that it excluded detriment which can be compensated under the unfair dismissal provisions. If the detriment could not be compensated under the unfair dismissal provisions—for

the reason that it is not a loss sustained in consequence of the dismissal—then there was nothing to take it out of section 47B; and the provisions in section 49, which required compensation for that detriment, should be applied. The meaning of 'dismissal' in Part X was that dismissal occurred when the employment was terminated, which, in Mr Melia's case, was 9 November 2001, and not at some earlier date.

9.16 In *Romanowska v Aspirations Care Ltd* (UKEAT/0015/14/SM, 25 June 2014), the ET had struck out 'on the papers' Ms Romanowska's claim that she had been dismissed from her employment in a care home following an incident when she was accused of dragging a resident back to his room. Ms Romanowska appeared to have accepted that she had 'pulled' the resident but said she did so only because he was being caused distress by agency workers employed by his employer. During the disciplinary proceedings which followed (and an appeal which followed her dismissal) Ms Romanowska had raised concerns about the use of agency workers. The employment judge who considered her claim of automatically unfair dismissal appeared to accept that these expressions of concern could amount to the making of protected disclosures. The Employment Appeal Tribunal (Langstaff P) held that the claim should not have been dismissed summarily. Langstaff P also considered the interrelationship between the claim of unfair dismissal that was advanced, and a detriment claim which was apparently not advanced. The point appears to have arisen because the claimant's case (possibly in the alternative) was that in the ordinary course she should, at the most, have received only a final written warning for the incident involving the resident and that what appeared to have tipped the balance toward dismissal was the making of the supposed protected disclosure(s). Langstaff P said this:

> It seems to me a difficult issue whether, if a protected disclosure makes the difference between a final written warning and dismissal in the eyes of the employer, (as a question of causation within context, and taking into account whether a purposive approach to the legislation is appropriate,) that should not be regarded as meaning that the principal reason for the dismissal is the protected disclosure. If it were not, then (depending on the width given to the words '[dismissal] within the meaning of Part X' in section 47B) there might be a lacuna, in that a real wrong would be done to an employee without any opportunity of redress, despite the statute appearing to single out dismissal for particularly effective remedy. I note that this the decision of the Court of Appeal in *Melia v Magna Kansei* could be argued to be decisive, but this also arguably remains an issue of law which may still need to be determined, if it arises, upon consideration of all of the facts and more detailed submissions than I have had here.

9.17 It is, with respect, a little difficult to follow the reference to *Melia* as being (at least potentially) decisive of this issue. *Melia* establishes that an act (or omission) can be at once a repudiatory breach (or one of a number of such breaches) for the purpose of establishing a employee's claim that he or she was constructively dismissed and also a detriment for the purposes of establishing a section 47B claim. Ms Romanowska's claim was concerned with the employer's decision to dismiss her and the reason for it. On one view of the hypothetical situation posited by Langstaff P in the passage quoted above, the reason or principal reason for dismissing the employee would be the protected disclosure because it is crucial in turning what would otherwise only have been a final written warning into a dismissal. On another view, taken as a composite whole, the principal reason for the decision to dismiss would be the employee's alleged misconduct, not her protected disclosure. As discussed at paragraph 9.34 below, a similar issue has been considered by the EAT in the context of constructive dismissal. The approach adopted in that context suggests that, while the causative relevance of the protected disclosure as tipping the balance in favour dismissal may be regarded as an important consideration, ultimately the weight to be given to this is a matter for the assessment of the tribunal.

9.18 A further area in which the relationship between dismissal and detriment claims needs to be considered are those involving what we have described as tainted information or tainted decision cases. In short, is a 'procured' dismissal to be dealt with under the detriment regime or the dismissal regime? More detailed consideration is set out in Chapter 7 at paragraphs 7.163–7.190 and also below at paragraph 9.27.

D. Identifying the Principal Reason in Dismissal Cases

Once a protected disclosure is established, the focus is on the reason for the subsequent dismissal. In an ordinary dismissal context, the law as to and test for the reason for dismissal were summarized by Elias J in *ASLEF v Brady* [2006] IRLR 576: **9.19**

> 51. In *Devis v Atkins* [1977] ICR 662 at 677–678 Viscount Dilhorne addressed the reason for dismissal in the following terms:
>
>> The decision of the Court of Appeal in *Abernethy v Mott, Hay and Anderson* [1974] IRLR 213, was on the 1971 Act. Lord Denning MR said that the reason shown for the dismissal "must be a reason in existence at the time when he is given notice. It must be the principal reason which operated on the employer's mind." He went on to say that it must be made known to the man before he is given notice or told to him at the time. I do not see anything in the Act which makes it a condition of fair dismissal that the man dismissed must know before he is given notice or told at the time that he is given notice the reason for it. I prefer the view of Cairns LJ, who said:
>>
>>> "A reason for the dismissal of an employee is a set of facts known to the employer, or it may be of beliefs held by him, which cause him to dismiss the employee. If at the time of his dismissal the employer gives a reason for it, that is no doubt evidence, at any rate as against him, as to the real reason, but it does not necessarily constitute the real reason. He may knowingly give a reason different from the real reason out of kindness . . ."
>
> 52. So the question is: why did the employers dismiss him? If the principal reason was the act or acts of misconduct, then the requirements of section 98(1) are met. If, on the other hand, there was some other reason, they will not be.

This indicates that the test of the reason for dismissal therefore involves the same considerations as arise in the 'on the ground that' test in section 47B (see Chapter 7). Both focus on the mental processes of the employer. Indeed, as noted in Chapter 7, in *Nagarajan v London Regional Transport* [1999] ICR 877, Lord Nicholls emphasized that the tests of 'on racial grounds' and 'by reason that' in the context of the Race Relations Act 1976 were the same. In the context of protected disclosures, in *Felter v Cliveden Petroleum Company* (EAT/0533/05, 9 March 2006) it was accepted (at para 15) that 'the words "on the ground that" in section 47B and "the reason . . . for the dismissal" in section 103A require the same approach'. **9.20**

However, although they call for a similar exercise, there is a significant distinction between the approaches in section 47B and in section 103A. Following the guidance in *Fecitt and others v NHS Manchester* [2011] EWCA Civ 1190 (CA), section 47B will be infringed if the protected disclosure materially influences (in the sense of being more than a trivial influence) the employer's treatment of the whistleblower.[9] That does not, however, suffice in the context of unfair dismissal. In a case where there are mixed reasons for dismissal, section 103A only applies where the protected disclosure was (at least) the principal reason. This also contrasts with the United States' Whistleblower Protection Act 1989 which merely requires the employee to demonstrate that the whistleblowing was a contributing factor in the dismissal or other action taken against the whistleblower. **9.21**

---

[9] See Chapter 7 at para 7.66 et seq for a full discussion of this point. See also *Eiger Securities LLP v Korshunova* [2017] IRLR 115 (EAT), at paras 55 to 65 (discussed at para 3.118 above), where the ET was found to have failed to distinguish between the dismissal and detriment tests when, in upholding a s 103A complaint, it found that the employer had the protected disclosure 'in mind' when reaching the decision to dismiss.

9.22   The employer's reaction may be in relation to a series of disclosures rather than just one. An example of a tribunal having failed to give proper consideration to the mental processes of the employer in such a situation is provided by the case of *El-Megrisi v Azad University (IR) in Oxford* (UKEAT/0448/08/MAA, 5 May 2009). The respondent did not dispute that the claimant had made what amounted to three protected disclosures over the period between November 2005 and December 2006. She was given four weeks' notice of dismissal in January 2007, ostensibly on grounds of redundancy. The tribunal stated that 'the professed 'redundancy situation' was a manufactured means to disguise the real reason for the claimant's dismissal. It noted that it was 'significant' that the perceived redundancy situation arose immediately after the latest and perhaps most formal representation by the claimant of her continuing concerns. In relation to the respondent's submission that a *Polkey*[10] deduction should be made, the tribunal said:

> no Polkey deduction can arise where we find, as we do, that the Respondent dismissed the Claimant because they thought she was a nuisance who would not willingly undertake the questionable tasks, amongst others, that were assigned to her.

9.23   Further, in deciding to award a 50 per cent uplift for failure to follow the then statutory disciplinary procedures, the tribunal recorded that:

> In our judgment, the Claimant was dismissed because the Respondents thought that she was an obstructive nuisance and a trouble maker.

9.24   However, and notwithstanding those findings and conclusions, the tribunal dismissed the claim of unfair dismissal contrary to section 103A. Its reasoning appears to have been that it was not appropriate to view the disclosure which immediately preceded the dismissal in isolation and hold that whistleblowing was the principal reason for dismissal. The EAT held that in a case where a claimant had made multiple disclosures, section 103A did not require that the contributions of each of them to the reason for the dismissal be considered separately and in isolation. Where the tribunal found that they operated cumulatively, the question was whether that cumulative impact was the principal reason for the dismissal. On the tribunal's own findings that clearly was the case. The EAT said that not only had the tribunal misdirected itself but that if it had given itself the correct direction there was only one answer to which it could have come on its own findings of fact, namely that the principal reason for the claimant's dismissal was that she had made protected disclosures.

(1) Dismissal at the behest of third parties

9.25   An issue in respect of which there appears to be, as yet, no direct appellate authority is whether a dismissal comes within section 103A or, in the case of a worker who is not an employee, section 47B, where the employer has dismissed at the behest of a third party who makes the request or demand for the reason or principal reason that the employee made a protected disclosure. As described by Underhill J in *Henderson v Connect (South Tyneside) Ltd* [2010] IRLR 466 (EAT), in a typical case of this kind a client of the employer, for whom the employee is working, takes against the employee for some reason—good or bad—and tells the employer that he is not willing to have the employee work at his premises, or on his business, any longer: he may or may not insist on the dismissal of the employee, but the employer may have no other work that the employee can do, so that dismissal is an inevitable consequence of the client's stance. The client, not being the employer, is under no statutory obligation to follow any procedure to allow the employee to put his case and will not generally do so. The employer may; but that will be of limited value since he is not the real decision-maker. The employee

---

[10] *Polkey v Dayton AE Services Ltd (formerly Edward Walker (Holdings) Ltd* [1987] IRLR 503.

thus suffers a clear 'procedural' injustice. If the client's decision is unreasonable, the injustice will also be substantive. Underhill J commented that cases of this kind are not very comfortable for an employment tribunal but observed that it had long been recognized that the fact that the client who procures, directly or indirectly, the dismissal of an employee may have acted unfairly, and that the employee has thus suffered an injustice, does not mean that the dismissal is unfair within the meaning of the statute because the focus of section 98 ERA is squarely on the question whether it was reasonable *for the employer* to dismiss. If the employer has done everything that he reasonably can to avoid or mitigate the injustice brought about by the stance of the client—most obviously, by trying to get the client to change his mind and, if that is impossible, by trying to find alternative work for the employee—but has failed, any eventual dismissal will be fair: the outcome may remain unjust, but that is not the result of any unreasonableness on the part of the employer. Underhill J recognized that that may seem a harsh conclusion; but it would be equally harsh for the employer to have to bear the consequences of the client's behaviour: Parliament had not chosen to create any kind of mechanism for imposing vicarious liability or third-party responsibility for unfair dismissal.

The case law on dismissals at the behest of third parties reviewed by Underhill J in *Henderson* **9.26** establishes that third-party pressure to dismiss can constitute a substantial reason justifying the dismissal of the employee so as to fall within the terms of section 98(1)(b)ERA and that an employer cannot be held to have acted unreasonably even if the third party's motive for seeking the removal of the employee was suspect, albeit that the requirements of section 98 (4) still needed to be satisfied. In *Dobie v Burns International Security Services (UK) Ltd* [1984] ICR 812 the Court of Appeal held that in deciding whether the employer acted reasonably or unreasonably, a very important factor of which the employer has to take account, on the facts known to the employer at that time, is whether there will or will not be injustice to the employee and the extent of that injustice. None of this case law directly answers the point we are considering here, but, in making it clear that it is the employer's reason that matters and not that of the third party, then, provided the tribunal is satisfied that the employer's reason or principal reason was the perceived need to comply with the third party's request or demand, then a claim under section 103A would fail. Where the worker is not an employee then the tribunal would need to be satisfied that the whistleblowing was not even significant influence in the employer's decision, but if so satisfied then, again, the protected disclosure claim would fail.

(2) Tainted information and tainted decisions to dismiss

We have considered this issue at some length in Chapter 7 at paragraphs 7.163–7.190 and **9.27** will therefore only note it here. As explained in those paragraphs, the issue (so far as dismissal is concerned) is whether a dismissal can be for the reason or principal reason that the employee made a protected disclosure if the person who actually takes the decision to dismiss is not personally affected, consciously or unconsciously, by the whistleblowing—or does not even know that the employee has made a protected disclosure. If the decision can be said to have been tainted because it was reached on the basis of information or an instruction from another person (at least if a worker or agent of the same employer) who was acting by reason of protected disclosures, will the employee have a claim under section 103A? Or does the route to compensation lie in making a claim in detriment for the acts of the person who supplied the information or gave the instruction, as would follow from the reasoning of Underhill LJ in the *CLFIS (UK) Ltd v Reynolds* [2015] ICR 1010 (CA) (which concerned a claim under the Equality Act)? Since *Reynolds*, the EAT in *Royal Mail Group Ltd v Jhuti* [2016] ICR 1043 has concluded that there could be a claim against the employer where the dismissing officer was unwittingly manipulated by another employee acting by reason of a protected disclosure. At the time of writing, the decision is proceeding to the Court of Appeal.

E. Constructive Dismissal

9.28 Section 95(1)(c) ERA provides that for the purposes of Part X ERA an employee is dismissed by his employer if the employee terminates the contract under which he is employed (with or without notice) in circumstances in which he is entitled to terminate it without notice by reason of the employer's conduct. It is well settled that to be 'entitled' the employee has to be 'entitled' in accordance with the law of contract. Thus it is only where the employer is guilty of conduct which goes to the root of the contract of employment or which shows that the employer no longer intends to be bound by one or more of the essential terms of the contract that this entitlement arises.[11] In cases of constructive dismissal, the burden is on the employee first to show that s/he resigned in response to a repudiatory breach of contract. As clarified by the Court of Appeal in *Buckland v Bournemouth University Higher Education Corporation* [2010] EWCA Civ 121, [2010] ICR 908, a range of reasonable responses test forms no part of the exercise of deciding whether the employer was in (a necessarily repudiatory) breach of the trust and confidence term. The court also held that, unlike an anticipatory breach which can be cured up to the moment of acceptance, a completed breach cannot be cured in this way, although if there is a delay, especially after steps to make amends, the employee may be taken to have affirmed the contract and so lost the opportunity to claim constructive dismissal. However, if the employee had more than one reason for resigning, it is sufficient that the employee resigned at least in part by reason of some or all of the conduct constituting a repudiatory breach: *Frenkel Topping Ltd v King* (UKEAT/0106/15/LA, 21 July 2015) at para 29. If detrimental treatment is by reason of a protected disclosure, that is of itself liable to be at least an important factor in relation to whtether there is a repudiatory breach (*Frenkel* at para 36).

9.29 Having established the dismissal within ERA, section 95(1)(c), it remains necessary to identify the reason for dismissal. As explained by Browne-Wilkinson LJ in *Berriman v Delabole Slate Ltd* [1985] ICR 546 (CA):

> in our judgment, even in a case of constructive dismissal, [section 98(1) ERA] imposes on the employer the burden of showing the reason for the dismissal, notwithstanding that it was the employee, not the employer, who actually decided to terminate the contract of employment. In our judgment, the only way in which the statutory requirements of [ERA] can be made to fit a case of constructive dismissal is to read [section 98(1)] as requiring the employer to show the reasons for their conduct which entitled the employee to terminate the contract thereby giving rise to a deemed dismissal by the employer.

9.30 The focus is therefore on the reason for the conduct which the employee has shown amounted to a repudiatory breach of contract. The issues considered in Chapter 7 in relation to whether an act or deliberate failure to act was on the grounds of a protected disclosure are therefore also liable to arise here. Again, it is important to consider whether the conduct was by reason of the protected disclosure rather than merely related to it. As such, where an employee resigns in response to a failure to deal adequately with a protected disclosure, even if the employer's failures give rise to a constructive dismissal claim, that is insufficient to establish a section 103A claim unless it can also be established that the failures were by

---

[11] *Western Excavating (ECC) Ltd v Sharp* [1978] ICR 221 (CA). Employees who are arguing that they were constructively dismissed by virtue of acts or deliberate failures to act by reason of a protected disclosure would be well advised to make an additional claim in respect of the matters complained of and contend that they were detriments. In the event that the constructive dismissal claim fails for some reason that may leave an entitlement to recover compensation for detriment: further and in any event compensation can be awarded for injury to feelings for the detriment. See on this aspect *Melia* discussed at paras 9.13–9.15.

reason of the protected disclosures. The following guidance as to constructive dismissal claims was given by HHJ Eady in her judgment in *Salisbury NHS Foundation Trust v Wyeth* (UKEAT 0061/15/JOJ, 12 June 2015) at para 31:

> In such a case, the ET will have identified the fundamental breaches of contract that caused the employee to resign in circumstances in which she was entitled to claim to have been constructively dismissed. Where no reason capable of being fair for section 98 purposes has been established by the employer, that constructive dismissal will be unfair. Where, however, the reason remains in issue because there is a dispute as to whether it was such as to render the dismissal automatically unfair, the ET then has to ask what was the reason why the Respondent behaved in the way that gave rise to the fundamental breaches of contract? The Claimant's perception, although relevant to the issue why she left her employment (her acceptance of the repudiatory breach), does not answer that question.

It was because of this requirement that a protected disclosure constructive dismissal claim failed **9.31** in *Price v Surrey County Council and another* (EAT/0450/10, 27 October 2011). Mrs Price, who worked as an office assistant in the respondent school, raised a complaint as to bullying which was accepted as containing protected disclosures. After a long delay she was told by the chairman of the governors that her grievance was rejected. An independent investigation was then carried out by the local authority. Mrs Price was informed by letter from the governors that the outcome of this investigation was that there was no evidence to substantiate her allegations. In fact that was not a fair reflection of the investigation, which had noted that the question as to whether there had been bullying or heavy-handed management was a finely balanced decision. The EAT upheld a finding that this gave rise to a breach of the implied term of trust and confidence in response to which the claimant had resigned and been constructively dismissed. Although Mrs Price had resigned only after her appeal against the rejection of the grievance was dismissed, and her complaints about the appeal were not upheld, she had not affirmed the contract and the repudiatory breach could not be cured (following in this respect *Buckland v Bournemouth University Higher Education Corporation* [2010] EWCA Civ 121, [2010] IRLR 445 (CA)).

However, the claim under section 103A failed. The argument for Mrs Price was that the whole **9.32** process which led eventually to her resignation arose from the protected disclosure. Her forced resignation was, as the tribunal accepted, a justified response to the fundamental breach represented by the governors' letter notifying her of the results of the investigation. In the EAT's view that approach reflected a misunderstanding of the statutory scheme. It is the 'making' of the protected disclosure which is the focus of attention, and which had to be the principal reason for the dismissal. In this case, by contrast, Mrs Price's forced resignation came about not because of the making of her complaint as such, but because of the inadequacy in one important respect of the authorities' response to it. There was no finding that the inadequate handling was by reason of the protected disclosures. On the contrary, the tribunal made findings that this was *not* the case. Following *Berriman*, the important question was not simply why the employee resigned but, crucially, what the reason was for the conduct in response to which she resigned.

An additional potential complication in dismissal cases, by contrast with detriment cases, lies **9.33** in identifying the principal reason for dismissal where there are competing influences. This may be straightforward enough where there is only one act or omission of the employer which is relied upon by the employee as constituting 'the conduct' amounting to a repudiatory breach, or where there has been a practice of detrimental treatment due to protected disclosure.[12] But what if the employee establishes that s/he terminated the contract because of a series of acts and

---

[12] See also *Flintshire v Sutton* (EAT/1082/02, 1 July 2003), where there was a continuing failure to provide support to which the claimant was entitled due to a 'perception of the Applicant as a problem because he had made the relevant protected disclosures'.

omissions of the employer which cumulatively was such as to lead to a breach of the implied term of trust and confidence in the employer? Do *all* of those acts or omissions have to have been done for the reason or principal reason that the employee made a protected disclosure? The last action of the employer which leads to the employee leaving need not itself be a breach of contract; the question is, does the cumulative series of acts taken together amount to a breach of the implied term? Whilst the final act might not be blameworthy or unreasonable it has to contribute something to the breach even if relatively insignificant, and the matters relied upon must, viewed objectively, be capable cumulatively of breaching the implied trust and confidence term.[13] Is it sufficient to ground a case of constructive dismissal contrary to section 103A that the last 'relatively insignificant' act by the employer was a response to or by reason of the protected disclosure having been made when the rest of the chain of events upon which the employee relies had nothing to do with it, indeed perhaps preceded it having been made?[14]

9.34 As explained by HHJ Eady QC in *Salisbury NHS Foundation Trust v Wyeth* (UKEAT/0061/15/JOJ, 12 June 2015), at para 34, in each case it will be for the employment tribunal to identify the acts (or deliberate failures to act) which give rise to the repudiatory breach in response to which the employee resigned, and to assess the weight to be given to each of these elements. As discussed in Chapter 7 (paragraph 7.114), in *Wyeth* the claimant was a nursing assistant who resigned in response to the respondent's conduct in the wake of her protected disclosures. There were various aspects to this: (a) moving the claimant without consultation from the night to the day shift, (b) ignorning the difficulties that had arisen from the sudden move, (c) failing investigate and resolve his complaint of bullying, (d) leaving him 'temporarily' working on the day shift, (e) not including him in the investigation into the operating department practitioner about whom he made the protected disclosures (ODP1), and (f) sending letter to the claimant and other staff about ODP1's return, which might have been read as a veiled threat. However, from these it was possible to discern from the employment tribunal's reasoning that the principal influences were the move onto the day shift and the exclusion of the claimant from the investigation. The focus was therefore on those elements in assessing the respondent's explanation for the conduct and whether there had been a sufficient critical analysis of that explanation and the reason or principal reason for dismissal.

Ultimately, it will be a matter for the tribunal, as a question of fact, to assess in all the circumstances the weight to be given to the various aspects of the conduct comprising the repudiatory breach of contract, and whether the protected disclosure(s) was/were the principal reason. We suggest, however, that in such cases it will assist to take into account three aspects of the matter. First and foremost, there will need to be a qualitative assessment of how important the protected disclosure was in the erosion of trust and confidence. But together with this, or as part of it, there may need to be a quantitative assessment of how much of the matter complained about can be identified as by reason of the protected disclosure, and also a temporal assessment, in that those events that come later in the story, especially the 'last straw', may thereby be regarded as more important.

---

[13] See Glidewell LJ in *Lewis v Motorworld Garages Ltd* [1985] IRLR 465; *Omilaju v Waltham Forest LBC* [2005] EWCA Civ 1493, [2005] ICR 481 at para 20, Dyson LJ; *Wishaw and District Housing Association v Moncrieff* (EATS/0066/08, 22 April 2009).

[14] The question discussed here is of course distinct from the issue as to whether the repudiatory breach (or breaches) by the employer are the cause of the employee leaving. As to this, see *Jones v F Sirl & Son (Furnishers) Ltd* [1997] IRLR 493 (noting that the repudiatory breach need not be the sole cause), and *Nottinghamshire County Council v Meikle* [2004] EWCA Civ 859, [2004] IRLR 703 and *Frenkel Topping Ltd v King* (UKEAT/0106/15/LA, 21 July 2015) at para 29, which set an even lower threshold (the resignation being, at least in part, due to the repudiatory breach of the employer).

F. Selection for Redundancy

Specific provision is made in relation to redundancies so as to stop employers using redundancy as a way of ridding themselves of whistleblowing employees. If the reason for the dismissal was a redundancy affecting more than one employee then, by ERA, section 105(1), it is unfair to select a particular employee for dismissal for redundancy on the ground that he made a protected disclosure. A dismissal will be unfair if (a) the principal reason for it was redundancy, (b) other employees in a similar position (ie potentially subject to redundancy) were not dismissed 'in the same circumstances', and (c) the reason or principal reason for the selection of the complainant employee was because s/he had made a protected disclosure. However, section 105 only applies where there is a genuine redundancy situation, rather than one created by reason of a response to a protected disclosure. If, conversely, an employer decides that he wishes to dismiss an employee for having made a protected disclosure, and for that reason creates a redundancy situation, then section 103A ERA, rather than section 105, applies: see *Bombardier Aerospace v McConnell* [2008] IRLR 51 (NICA) at para 10. **9.35**

G. Unofficial Industrial Action

Whilst section 237(1) of the Trade Union and Labour Relations (Consolidation) Act 1992 (TULRCA) provides that generally an employee who is taking part in unofficial industrial action at the time of his/her dismissal cannot bring a claim for unfair dismissal, this bar will not apply where the employee was dismissed or made redundant because s/he had made a protected disclosure (section 237(1A)). **9.36**

H. The Burden of Proof

It is for the employee to prove that s/he was dismissed and that s/he made a protected disclosure.[15] By contrast, at least in relation to 'ordinary' unfair dismissal, the burden is on the employer to show the reason for dismissal and that it is a reason falling under section 98(2) or is for some other substantial reason (ERA, section 98(1), (2)). This is subject to an exception where an employee has not accumulated one year's continuous employment prior to dismissal. **9.37**

The issue as to how this applies in the context of there also being a claim under ERA, section 103A, at least where there is sufficient qualifying service, was addressed in *Kuzel v Roche Products Ltd* [2008] EWCA Civ 380, [2008] ICR 799. As with ordinary unfair dismissal, the burden of proof is on the employer. The proper approach was summarized as follows (at para 47 of the EAT judgment: [2007] ICR 945 in a passage which the Court of Appeal specifically approved (at para 30) as being 'a helpful analysis': **9.38**

(1) Has the claimant shown that there is a real issue as to whether the reason put forward by the employers ... was not the true reason? Has she raised some doubt as to that reason by advancing the section 103A reason?

---

[15] There is an exception relating only to qualifying disclosures made prior to 25 June 2013, that in relation to the good faith requirement applicable to such disclosures the burden of proof is on the employer: see Chapter 10, paras 10.108–10.154.

(2) If so, have the employers proved their reason for dismissal?

(3) If not, have the employers disproved the section 103A reason advanced by the claimant?

(4) If not, dismissal is for the section 103A reason.

9.39 In answering those questions it follows:

(a) that failure by the respondent to prove the potentially fair reason relied on does not automatically result in a finding of unfair dismissal under section 103A;

(b) however, rejection of the employer's reason, coupled with the claimant having raised a prima facie case that the reason is a section 103A reason, entitles the tribunal to infer that the section 103A reason is the true reason for dismissal; but

(c) it remains open to the respondent to satisfy the tribunal that the making of the protected disclosures was not the reason or principal reason for dismissal, even if the real reason as found by the tribunal is not that advanced by the respondent;

(d) it is not at any stage for the employee (with qualifying service) to prove the section 103A reason.

9.40 As to the limited initial evidential onus on the employee to raise an issue as to the real reason for dismissal, the court emphasized that this did not detract from the fact that the legal burden of proof remained throughout on the employer. It followed the approach of the Court of Appeal in *Maund v Penwith District Council* [1984] IRLR 24. The employee was dismissed by the council on the grounds of redundancy but claimed that the true reason for his dismissal was not redundancy but the council's dislike of his trade union activities, which would have been an automatically unfair reason. In relation to the onus of proof, Griffiths LJ explained (at p 149):

> it is not for the employee to prove the reason for his dismissal, but merely to produce evidence sufficient to raise the issue or, to put it another way, that raises some doubt about the reason for the dismissal. Once this evidential burden is discharged, the onus remains upon the employer to prove the reason for the dismissal.

9.41 To similar effect, Purchas LJ commented (at pp 154–55) that:

> the onus that rests upon the employee is to show that there is an issue which warrants investigation existing, against which an alternative reason, or competing reason, may be established. I emphasise that the onus resting upon the employee is not to prove, on a balance of probabilities, that his contending reason is the principal reason, but he must prove, on the balance of probabilities, that the issue exists. The gravity of the accusations, if any, involved in raising the issue will reflect upon the quality of the evidence necessary to establish the existence of the issue. Once the employee has adduced evidence to establish, on the balance of probabilities, the existence of the issue, the onus of showing which of the two competing reasons, or more if there are more, is the principal reason, remains as it always had been, on the shoulders of the employer.

9.42 Stephenson LJ stated (at p 157) that:

> the legal burden is placed by the statute on the employer and it remains there. If the employee raises on the evidence before the industrial tribunal an issue as to another reason being the real one, he has not to go further and prove that other reason to be the real one, even if it is an inadmissible reason and to disguise it would be very wrong for any employer and even more serious misconduct on the part of a public authority like the respondent council.

9.43 Whilst the legal burden of proof remains throughout on the employer, as the decision in *Kuzel* made clear, this does not mean that the employee will necessarily succeed if the employer fails to establish a fair reason. The burden may be discharged either by showing a principal reason for dismissal (whether or not a fair reason) other than a protected disclosure, or even, if no reason can be shown, by establishing that the protected disclosure was not the principal reason. An employer who cannot satisfy the tribunal of its reason for dismissal may for example be able to demonstrate that the protected disclosure could not have been the reason because the dismissing officer was not aware of the protected disclosure having been made. Alternatively it may be able to persuade the tribunal that the sympathetic and appropriate way in which it responded to the protected disclosure makes it unlikely that the protected disclosure was the principal reason for dismissal.

In *Kuzel* itself the employer failed to demonstrate a potentially fair reason for dismissal. Dr **9.44** Kuzel was summarily dismissed from her role as head of regulatory affairs of Roche having previously raised issues of regulatory compliance with her employer. The tribunal rejected Roche's argument that there was 'some other substantial reason' for dismissal, consisting of a breakdown in relationships. But it also rejected the contention that the protected disclosures were the reason for dismissal. Instead it found that the reason was the 'catastrophic loss of temper' by the manager who dismissed her, together with his failure to follow advice as to the procedures to be followed. The EAT remitted the matter to the tribunal on the basis that the language of the tribunal, in stating that the protected disclosure reason had not been 'made out', indicated that it had placed a burden on the employee. But the tribunal's decision was restored by the Court of Appeal which noted that this merely indicated that the reason had not been made out because Roche had disproved it. On the tribunal's findings, Roche had been able to do so through its evidence that the dismissing officer had encouraged and supported Dr Kuzel in the actions she was taking in relation to regulatory concerns, and the absence of evidence of Roche criticizing her for pursuing those issues.

A tribunal will therefore err if, having rejected the employer's reason for dismissal, it pro- **9.45** ceeds directly to find that the dismissal was for a prohibited reason without addressing whether the employer has shown otherwise. Although not in a whistleblowing context, the employment tribunal was found to have fallen into this error in *University of Bolton v Corrigan* (UKEAT 0408/14/RN, 21 December 2015). The ET had incorrectly proceeded from having found that the respondent had not established that the sole or principal reason for the claimant's dismissal was that he was redundant, directly to being satisfied that the claimant's competing claim that she was dismissed for trade union activity was made out.

The approach in *Kuzel* also requires in the first instance that there is a focus on the employer's purported reason for dismissal, and whether that is rejected. A tribunal was found to have fallen into error by not doing this in *Croydon Health Services NHS Trust v Beatt* (UKEAT 0136/15/JOJ, 19 January 2016). The EAT held that instead of determining 'the set of facts known to the employer, or it may be beliefs held by him, which cause him to dismiss the employee', the ET embarked on its own assessment of the conduct charges upheld against the claimant at the dismissal and appeal stages, found them less than compelling, and then moved to the conclusion that conduct was not the reason for dismissal, but that the protected disclosures were the reason. Judge Clark said that what was 'signally missing' was an analysis leading to the conclusion that the evidence from the chairs of the dismissal and appeal panels 'was false and a deliberate attempt to mislead the Employment Tribunal as to the true reason for dismissal'.[16]

The decision of the Court of Appeal in *Kuzel* did not directly address any issue as to **9.46** the burden of proof in a case where the employee does *not* have sufficient qualifying service for a claim of unfair dismissal. In *Smith v Hayle Town Council* [1978] ICR

---

[16] See also the discussion of the proper approach in detriment cases in paras 7.195–7.200 of Chapter 7 and the discussion in those paragraphs of the *Dahou* and *Phoenix House* cases.

996, the Court of Appeal concluded that in such a case the burden of proof was upon the employee to show that the reason for the dismissal was the proscribed ground. The majority's decision and reasoning in *Smith* was followed by the EAT in *Tedeschi v Hosiden Besson Ltd* (EAT/959/95, 2 October 1996). Further, in *Jackson v ICS Group Ltd* (EAT/499/97, 22 January 1998), the EAT rejected a claimant employee's argument that the position was altered by changes in the wording of the statute to the wording now contained in ERA, section 108(3).[17]

9.47 These authorities preceded the decision in *Kuzel*. Whilst not directly addressed by the decision in *Kuzel* (although the issue was canvassed in argument before the Court of Appeal), that line of argument might be thought to be open to challenge in the light of, or in any event read subject to, the Court of Appeal's reasoning in *Kuzel*. In concluding that the burden of proof lay on the employer (at least in a case where there was sufficient qualifying service), the court emphasized that the reason or principal reason for dismissal consists of a set of facts operating on the mind of the employer and as such are within the employer's knowledge (per Mummery LJ at para 54). The same of course remains true in a case where an employee lacks sufficient qualifying service. However, an argument to this effect was considered and rejected in the post-*Kuzel* case of *Ross v Eddie Stobart Ltd* (UKEAT/0068/13/RN, 8 August 2013). The EAT concluded that it was not open to the EAT to depart from the majority opinion of the Court of Appeal in *Smith v Hayle* which had been consistently followed and applied at both Court of Appeal and EAT level. There was no material distinction between the trade union protection afforded by TULRCA and that afforded to dismissed claimants in health and safety, working time, and whistleblowing cases.

9.48 Whilst the legal burden of proof is therefore on the employee who lacks qualifying service to establish an ordinary unfair dismissal claim, in practice a tribunal is likely to look to the employer for an explanation of the reason for dismissal, since it is the employer who is able to directly put forward the set of facts operating upon its mind which are said to constitute the reason for dismissal. As Mummery LJ noted in *Kuzel* (at para 53) the reason for dismissal is a question of fact to be determined as a matter either of direct evidence or of inference from the primary facts established by the evidence. In practice therefore, irrespective of the legal burden of proof a tribunal may draw appropriate inferences from any inadequacies in the explanation given.[18] Indeed, in *Kuzel* the Court of Appeal stressed, and the EAT reiterated in *Ross v Eddie Stobart*, that in most cases the issue as to the reason for dismissal should be resolved on the basis of the tribunal's findings of fact (including the drawing of any appropriate inferences) rather than being left to be resolved by reference to the burden of proof.

---

[17] See also *Nicholson and others v Long Products Ltd* (UKEAT/0166/02, 19 November 2003), at para 2, again placing the burden on the employee to establish an inadmissible reason (dismissal for trade union reasons) due to lack of qualifying service.

[18] For further criticism of the approach of placing the burden of proof on an employee lacking qualifying service in a whistleblowing context, see David Lewis. 'Is it time to blow the whistle on the burden of proof?' (2002) 31 ILJ 79, who argued that it should be considered whether the Human Rights Act 1998 (HRA) and the requirement to give effect to Art 10(1) of the European Convention on Human Rights enable a different approach to be taken and proposes that tribunals could adopt the position that, irrespective of length of service, where a claimant produces evidence to suggest that the reason for dismissal fell within ERA, s 103A or 105(6A), the HRA requires the employer to show that this was not in fact the reason or principal reason. The author argues that this would put the approach in dismissal cases more in line with that taken by ERA, s 48(2) in cases of detriment, and also deal with the anomaly that workers who are not employees are more favourably treated in this regard by virtue of the reversal in the burden of proof.

One line of argument specifically rejected by the EAT in *Kuzel* (and not pursued before **9.49** the Court of Appeal) was that the approach to the burden of proof in discrimination cases, as set out in *Igen v Wong* [2005] EWCA Civ 142, [2005] ICR 931,[19] should be applied in the context of a whistleblowing claim. The EAT said that there was a danger in taking a broad view that, because the protection afforded to 'whistleblowers' is protection against a form of discrimination (more particularly victimization), the statutory regime applied to those unlawfully discriminated against on grounds of sex, race, disability, religion, sexual orientation, or now age, can simply be grafted onto the provisions of the ERA under which the protected disclosure protection is provided. The differences between the parallel elements in the whistleblowing protection must be borne in mind. The 'reverse burden of proof' introduced into the discrimination statutes, eg section 63A of the Sex Discrimination Act 1975 (SDA), leading to the *Igen* guidance, had not been incorporated into ERA, Part IVA, and the burden of proof is provided in ERA, section 48(2). There was no room to import some different formulation of the burden of proof from another statute. The EAT added, however, that 'some assistance' could be derived from *King v Great Britain–China Centre* [1992] ICR 516 in relation to the drawing of inferences, in particular in the event that the employer's explanation for the subjecting to detriment was found to be inadequate or unsatisfactory. In our view direct invocation of *King* is probably unnecessary, but it may not be objectionable as long as the ET is not swayed from following the steps set out in *Kuzel*, which provide a clear path to follow. The Court of Appeal, which heard Dr Kuzel's appeal, was not asked to consider whether *Igen* applied.

Whilst the decision in *Kuzel* rejected the application of the discrimination test for burden **9.50** of proof, this therefore left open a question as to whether useful guidance could be drawn from that context in relation to the approach to drawing inferences. That issue was further considered by the EAT in *Nunn v Royal Mail Group Ltd* [2011] ICR 162. In that case the claimant had been the subject of a disciplinary investigation. No disciplinary action resulted but management formed the view that the claimant had deliberately misled his manager during the investigation and a second investigation was held. As a result of that second investigation the claimant was demoted, his pay was reduced, and a 'suspended dismissal' was imposed. The claimant responded by bringing a claim for unlawful deduction from wages. He was then dismissed, the employer's case being that he refused to accept his demotion. The claimant brought a claim of unfair dismissal and alleged that he had actually been dismissed for making a protected disclosure (by contending that he had been treated unlawfully); alternatively for asserting a statutory right. The employment tribunal found that the reason for the claimant's dismissal was his failure to accept the downgrading, rather than being by reason of a protected disclosure. The EAT upheld the decision as being a finding of fact that was open to the tribunal.

In the EAT the claimant contended that the tribunal should have directed itself in a manner similar to that to be followed in discrimination cases, and as such should have directed itself in accordance with the following:

> (i) that it is rare for there to be direct evidence of dismissal occurring on account of there having been a protected disclosure; (ii) that the outcome of the case will usually depend on the inferences from the primary facts (which facts may include events occurring both before and after the event complained of); (iii) that the tribunal must make findings in relation to all the primary facts alleged by a claimant and consider the whole picture; (iv)

[19] See the discussion of the decisions of the EAT ([2011] IRLR 111) and the Court of Appeal in *Fecitt and others v NHS Manchester* [2011] EWCA Civ 1190 in Chapter 7.

that there may, however, be cases where the facts found are such as to suggest action has been taken by reason of a protected disclosure; and (v) that in such a case a tribunal will look to the employer for an explanation and if the explanation is inadequate or incomplete may find against the employer. This approach to discrimination cases can be seen in a number of cases such *Anya v University of Oxford* [2001] ICR 847.

It was further argued that the tribunal should not look at the employer's reasons for dismissal in isolation but should be prepared to draw inferences from primary facts which suggested the employer's stated reason for dismissal was not correct.

9.51 This argument was rejected. The EAT said that different considerations arise in discrimination claims where it is necessary to exercise a degree of care in relation to the establishment of primary facts and in order to see whether the burden of proof should shift. As such in a discrimination case the court is urged to look carefully in relation to what inferences can be drawn from the primary facts, particularly as the basic information will often be in the hands of the employer rather than the employee. In unfair dismissal claims, the burden is on the employer,[20] there being no need for the employee to set up sufficient facts to impose that burden. In assessing what reasons the employer is putting forward a tribunal will have in mind what the employee is saying about the reason, and will need to test the employer's witnesses in relation to those matters which point to a reason other than that which the employee is putting forward. However, it was a matter for the tribunal to come to a view as to whether, on the balance of probabilities, the employer had satisfied it as to the (true) reason. The EAT said that, in this particular case, the question very much turned on the credibility of the dismissing officer and the tribunal was in the best position to assess him and his state of knowledge at the material time.[21]

9.52 Although the EAT in *Nunn* placed emphasis on the different approach to the shifting burden of proof in discrimination cases, we suggest that a more convincing distinction lies in the requirement to identify the principal reason for dismissal. In a discrimination claim the tribunal must consider whether the decision or act was in any sense whatever on the prohibited ground. Similarly, in relation to section 47B ERA, a tribunal must consider whether the protected disclosure is a significant influence (in the sense of being more than trivial), whether conscious or unconscious. That necessitates a closer examination to identify the various influences upon a decision. By contrast, in a dismissal case the focus is only on identifying the principal reason. That said, ultimately the decision in *Nunn* turned on the findings of fact by the tribunal. It should not, we suggest, be taken in any way as detracting from the need for the tribunal to identify carefully the relevant primary facts and to consider the inferences that can properly be drawn from those primary facts, taking into account any inadequacies in the explanation given.

9.53 Consistently with the approach in *Nunn*, the importance of focusing on the reasons of the dismissing officer was again emphasized by the EAT in *Whitelock & Storr and others v Khan* (UKEAT/0017/10/RN, 26 October 2010). The claimant had been dismissed by his employers, a firm of solicitors. The dismissal was stated to be on the grounds that the claimant had used the employers' facilities in an endeavour to set up a rival firm, the claimant's unwillingness to confirm duty solicitor slots or deal with them by transfer elsewhere, a failure by the claimant to attend a court hearing, and his persistent unauthorized absences. The claimant contended that he had actually been dismissed for making protected disclosures in a grievance submitted two days before disciplinary proceedings against him were commenced.

---

[20] At least where the employee has accumulated two years' continuous service: see paras 9.46–9.48 above.
[21] An application for permission to appeal was refused: [2011] EWCA Civ 244.

That grievance had included contentions that the employers were in breach of contract by failing to make payments due to the claimant. The employers had asked for forbearance in view of financial stringencies they were under.

In its reasons for judgment in favour of the claimant as to the reason for dismissal, the **9.54** employment tribunal said that it had 'no doubt that the indignation and fear of possible bankruptcy' carried through into the respondent's reaction to the protected disclosures and the tribunal was 'reinforced in that conclusion considering the circumstances by which the [employers] came to discipline and then dismiss the Claimant'. The employment tribunal referred to its 'misgivings' as to the disciplinary process and its result and concluded that 'the Respondents' evidence left the Tribunal in no doubt that the reason for the Claimant's dismissal was that he had made the protected disclosures'. The 'misgivings' were set out in detail and the tribunal went on to say that even if it was wrong in its conclusion that the employers had dismissed the claimant for having made protected disclosures then it was satisfied that the dismissal was an 'ordinary' unfair dismissal, because 'the whole process by which [the claimant's] dismissal was brought about was defective' since there had been no proper investigation of the grounds upon which the employers purported to find gross misconduct. The tribunal also said that the conclusion that the claimant was guilty of misconduct in relation to the transfer of slots rested on a fundamental misconception.

In the EAT the employers argued, in reliance on the staged approach set out in *Kuzel*, **9.55** that the employment tribunal should first have considered the reason for dismissal being advanced by the employers rather than going direct to a consideration of the true reason for dismissal. On the basis that the claimant had produced some evidence supporting a case for protected disclosure dismissal, the tribunal should then have considered the employers' reason for dismissal and either accepted it or rejected it before moving on to considering the protected disclosure issue as put forward by the claimant in more detail. Simply dismissing the employers' case on the basis of 'misgivings' and because of a dismissal letter being sent two days after the grievance letter (although many of the grievances had been raised orally previously) was an impermissible way of dealing with the employers' case.

The EAT agreed. The tribunal was obliged to consider first the potentially fair reason being **9.56** advanced by the employers, albeit that in considering the employers' reason, the tribunal would need to have regard to the contention that this was a 'put up job' in response to the claimant's grievance complaint. It followed from the burden on the employer that the tribunal needed to consider the employers' reason first, before it was required to move on to consider the alternative reasons for dismissal, including particularly that being advanced by the claimant. The tribunal had erred in its approach and the case was remitted to a different tribunal for rehearing on the issue of the reason for dismissal.

A respondent that does not call the person who took the decision to dismiss to give **9.57** oral evidence and be cross examined will not necessarily fail to prove the reason or reasons for dismissal; see for example the protected disclosure claim of *Blitz v Vectone Group Holdings Ltd* (UKEAT/0253/10/DM, 29 November 2011), where the EAT was satisfied that the ET was 'well aware of the need for special care in a case where the Employment Tribunal was placing reliance upon the witness statement of someone who was not called'.[22]

---

[22] Para 122.

I. Unfair Dismissal Protection for Non-Protected Disclosures

9.58　Notwithstanding a finding that a disclosure did not amount to a protected disclosure, there might still be an issue as to whether a dismissal by reason of the disclosure was (procedurally or substantively) unfair. This was a point stressed by Auld LJ in *Street v Derbyshire Unemployed Workers' Centre* [2005] ICR 97 at 112.[23] He commented that:

> it has to be remembered that even if a worker might be deterred from making a relevant disclosure because of concern that his employer might raise against him a suggestion of bad faith in the sense of a mix of motives, including personal antagonism, or fails in his section 103A claim on that account, all is not lost. His automatic protection provided by that section is lost, but he can still maintain an 'ordinary' claim for unfair dismissal against his employer in which a mix of motives may not be fatal to his claim.

9.59　Whilst there remains the possibility of an ordinary unfair dismissal claim, the fact that a disclosure does not meet the requirements for a protected disclosure, and the reasons that it fails to do so, may be material to the decision as to whether dismissal was a reasonable sanction.

9.60　Further, even in pre-PIDA cases, the factors which would now be material to whether there was a protected disclosure can be seen at play in the determination of whether a dismissal was fair. In *Cornelius v Hackney LBC* (EAT/1061/94, 18 January 1996), Mr Cornelius, who was employed by Hackney Council as an internal auditor, discovered that a stores officer also employed by Hackney had acted illegally and in a manner detrimental to his employers' interests. He reported on these matters to his employers but became concerned about what he perceived to be an unwillingness amongst senior management to deal with corrupt practices. He passed on details of his concerns, and of documentary evidence in support, to his trade union and to the chairman of the performance review subcommittee. The employment tribunal held that the dismissal was procedurally unfair. However, even though Mr Cornelius had genuinely been seeking to address a perceived cover-up of corrupt practices, the tribunal held that he was substantially to blame for his dismissal by reason of having disclosed his concerns to his trade union and to the chairman of the performance review subcommittee, especially as his report was annotated with unflattering remarks about his colleagues. Compensation was therefore reduced by 50 per cent. On appeal, however, the EAT concluded that the decision to reduce compensation was perverse. As the EAT explained:

> there is a high duty upon local government officers in the Appellant's position to report dishonesty in any form, and to persist if need be in ensuring that it is brought to the attention of those in authority and that appropriate action is taken. . . . It is difficult to see how the Appellant could be criticised for passing the documents in his possession, all of which related to his duty to uncover corruption, to the Chairman of the Committee which was concerned in investigating the matter, and who had expressly requested to see them.
>
> Equally we are at a loss to understand why the Appellant should be criticised for sending documents to his Union in order to obtain advice from them, if he was unable to resolve the matter satisfactorily by other means.

9.61　Although the tribunal had proceeded only on the basis of procedural unfairness, the EAT plainly regarded the dismissal as substantively unfair. It is likely that an employee in Mr Cornelius' position would now be able to succeed under the ERA. Reliance could now be

---

[23]　See paras 9.05–9.08 above.

placed on section 43G ERA in light of the fact that the concerns had previously been raised with management. Having done so it was then reasonable to make the wider disclosure in the light of the genuine concern that there was a cover-up, together with the fact that the disclosure was made to those with a genuine and legitimate interest in receiving the information either to provide assistance and advice (in the case of the union) or to investigate the handling of corruption (in the case of the councillor).

In *Byford v Film Finances Ltd* (EAT/804/86, 23 March 1987), there were again echoes of **9.62** reasoning that would be material in a post-PIDA case. Although the claimant had a genuine belief in serious allegations against her employer, other considerations led to a finding that dismissal was fair. Mrs Byford was a long-serving employee who felt that she owed obligations of loyalty not only to the company that employed her, but also to its former chairman who was a minority shareholder in the company and had been ousted from a role in managing the company by the majority shareholders. Out of loyalty to the former chairman, Mrs Byford was persuaded to spy on the activities of the company for the minority shareholders. She discovered what she genuinely believed was evidence of improper and fraudulent conduct by the directors of the employing company (who were associated with the majority shareholders), including conduct constituting a fraud on the minority. She reported her findings to the minority shareholders and, as a result, unfair prejudice proceedings were commenced. Upon discovering Mrs Byford's role, the respondent company dismissed her.

The EAT upheld the employment tribunal's finding that the dismissal was fair. The dis- **9.63** missal had been for 'some other substantial reason' in that there was a breakdown in trust in Mrs Byford as a result of her having gone behind the directors' backs to report her findings to the minority shareholders. Further, the EAT considered that not only was the decision to dismiss within the range of reasonable responses but there was really no other alternative since Mrs Byford plainly could not be trusted.

Neither the employment tribunal nor the EAT resolved the issue as to whether the alle- **9.64** gations made by Mrs Byford were true. As such, the decision proceeded on the basis that the employer was entitled to demand loyalty irrespective of the truth of the serious allegations. In a post-PIDA decision a key consideration would have been that the disclosure was made to minority shareholders, and that was also important to the tribunal's reasoning. Although the minority shareholders might be said to have had a legitimate interest in the information as to a fraud on them, the EAT emphasized that if there was to be a disclosure of the concerns it would have been more appropriate to make disclosure to the auditors or if, as Mrs Byford alleged, they too could not be trusted, to the Department of Trade and Industry (as it was then known). In the post-PIDA world this would no doubt have been reflected in a finding that the disclosure was not protected under section 43G ERA.

The employer's entitlement to expect loyalty was similarly emphasized in *Thornley v Aircraft* **9.65** *Research Association Ltd* (EAT/669/76, 11 May 1977). Mr Thornley raised concerns about the aircraft design of the Tornado aircraft. He was not satisfied with the response. Ultimately, he sent a letter to the *Guardian* and was then dismissed. The EAT was unimpressed with the argument that unless Mr Thornley publicized his concerns, the aircraft would be sold with flaws. It was not for him to denigrate his employer's product. On the facts, the matters Mr Thornley disclosed might have fallen within the health and safety, or, possibly, the relevant failures relating to likely breach of legal obligation now enacted within ERA, section 43B. But in any event it is most unlikely that disclosure to the press would have fallen within section 43G, unless it could be shown that there was no more appropriate recipient of the information. Again, the factors which would be likely to take the case outside a protected disclosure also led to the finding that dismissal was not unfair.

9.66 The considerations relevant to whether there was a protected disclosure are therefore likely to be of importance where the issue of reasonableness under section 98 needs to be addressed. Further, one of the aims of the promoters of PIDA was to encourage a change in culture so that there would be a different and more sympathetic attitude to those who raise concerns in a reasonable way. One corollary of this may be that those who do not meet the requirements of a protected disclosure attract less sympathy. For example, one consequence of the protected disclosure legislation has been to encourage much more widespread adoption of whistleblowing procedures. Where there is such a procedure, and despite this a disclosure is made without making use of it and which does not meet the requirements for a protected disclosure, an employer may be on stronger ground in contending that dismissal fell within the range of reasonable responses.

9.67 Despite the above considerations, each case will turn on its facts. A dismissal may well not fall within the range of reasonable responses despite not being automatically unfair. The circumstances that may arise vary widely and the reasons for not amounting to a protected disclosure may be crucial. At one extreme a disclosure may simply not qualify because, though raising genuine concerns, it does not disclose information. At the other extreme may be cases of making false allegations with no reasonable or even genuine belief in the truth of what is said, or that information disclosed tends to show a relevant failure. Again, whether the disclosure was made externally or to an appropriate person, and whether if not protected there was a breach of confidentiality, may be important. If to an outside source, the factors set out in section 43G ERA, even if not all satisfied, may be relevant. By way of example, if a worker reports suspected fraud by a colleague to the police, but fails to report this first to the employer, this would fall outside ERA, section 43G if it did not meet the gateway requirements in section 43G(2). But if the employee held an honest and reasonable belief in the fraud and had merely failed to follow correct procedures internally, an employer would no doubt have difficulty in persuading a tribunal that dismissal fell within the range of reasonable responses. The employer is entitled to expect loyalty from the employee, but, to take an extreme, the duty of fidelity could not extend to requiring an employee to conceal fraud.

9.68 In considering the substantive fairness of the decision to dismiss, we suggest therefore that the factors material to whether there was a protected disclosure are likely to be important but not necessarily determinative. The important considerations are likely to include the nature and seriousness of the allegation, whether the person receiving the information had a proper interest in receiving it, whether there are others to whom the information could more appropriately have been communicated, the motive for the disclosure, the extent to which the employer can legitimately regard it as showing disloyalty, and the evidential basis for the disclosure.

J. Time Limit

9.69 An unfair dismissal claim must be brought within three months of the effective date of termination (ERA, section 111(2)(a)). This is subject to the provisions for suspension of running of time and extension of the time limit by reason of the ACAS notification provisions (ERA, section 207B). The only other basis for extending time is if it was not reasonably practicable for the employee to claim within the period of three months and then only if the time within which the claim was actually made was a reasonable one (ERA, section 111(2)(b)).

Where dismissal is with notice, time begins to run from the expiry of the notice period: *Lupetti* **9.70**
v Wrens Old House Ltd [1984] ICR 348 (EAT). A claim can, however, be brought during the
notice period (ERA, section 111(3)). Similarly, in a constructive dismissal claim, time begins
to run from the date on which the repudiatory breach is accepted as bringing the employment to an end (or the expiry of any period of notice given to terminate the contract), rather
from the date of the repudiatory breach (*Meikle v Nottinghamshire County Council* [2005]
ICR 1 (CA)). Care may, however, be needed if there are also potential detriment claims, to
ensure that delay in bringing an unfair dismissal claim, even if that claim is still in time,
does not result in the detriment claims being out of time.

10

REMEDIES IN DISMISSAL AND DETRIMENT CLAIMS

A. Introduction

10.01 A feature of the protected disclosure regime is the availability of more extensive remedies, including uncapped compensation and the availability of interim relief. Following the amendments introduced by the Enterprise and Regulatory Reform Act 2013 (ERRA), a further distinctive feature is the provision for a reduction in compensation where a protected disclosure was not make in good faith. Because good faith was previously a liability-stage issue (and still is in relation to qualifying disclosures made prior to 25 June 2013) it has received a degree of judicial attention which may otherwise appear disproportionate given the more limited role it now plays as a remedy-stage consideration. Because of this, and because it applies both to unfair dismissal and detriment claims, and remains a liability-stage issue in relation to qualifying disclosures made prior to 25 June 2013, we deal separately with 'good faith' in Section D below.

B. Unfair Dismissal Remedies

(1) Overview of remedies

The primary remedies for unfair dismissal are provided for in ERA, section 112. Where an **10.02** employment tribunal finds that the grounds of complaint are well founded, the tribunal must explain to the complainant what orders may be made under section 113 for reinstatement or re-engagement and in what circumstances they may be made, and ask the claimant whether s/he wishes the tribunal to make such an order. If the claimant expresses such a wish, the tribunal may make an order under section 113. If no order for reinstatement or re-engagement is made under section 113 then the tribunal *shall* make an award of compensation for unfair dismissal, which is to be calculated in accordance with sections 118 to 126. The requirements of section 113 are mandatory and a failure to explain the orders amounts to an error of law (*Pirelli General Cable Works Ltd v Murray* [1979] IRLR 190 (EAT)).

Section 118 ERA provides that where a tribunal makes an order of compensation for **10.03** unfair dismissal under section 112(4) (ie where no order is made for reinstatement or re-engagement), the award is to consist of:

(a) a basic award (calculated in accordance with sections 119 to 122 and 126), and
(b) a compensatory award (calculated in accordance with sections 123, 124, 126, and 127).

(2) Reinstatement and re-engagement

An order for reinstatement is an order that the employer shall treat the complainant in all **10.04** respects as if he had not been dismissed (ERA, section 114). An order for re-engagement is an order, on such terms as the employment tribunal may decide, that the complainant be engaged by the employer, or by a successor of the employer, or by an associated employer, in employment comparable to that from which s/he was dismissed or other suitable employment (section 115).

In exercising its discretion whether to make a re-employment order, the tribunal must first **10.05** consider whether to make an order for reinstatement, and in so doing the tribunal must take into account (section 116(1)(a)):

(a) whether the complainant wishes to be reinstated;
(b) whether it is practicable for the employer to comply with an order for reinstatement; and
(c) where the complainant caused or contributed to some extent to the dismissal, whether it would be just to order his reinstatement.

If the tribunal decides not to make an order for reinstatement, it must then consider whether **10.06** to make an order for re-engagement and, if so, on what terms (section 116(2)). In so doing the tribunal must take into account (section 116(3)):

(a) any wish expressed by the complainant as to the nature of the order to be made;
(b) whether it is practicable for the employer (or a successor or an associated employer) to comply with an order for re-engagement; and

(c) where the complainant caused or contributed to some extent to the dismissal, whether it would be just to order his re-engagement and (if so) on what terms.

(a) Practicability of compliance

10.07 In deciding whether such an order should be made, the tribunal generally reviews the practicability of the employer reinstating or re engaging given the circumstances at the date the order would take effect (usually the remedies hearing or later, on receipt of the last relevant written submission (*Rembiszewski v Atkins* UKEAT/0402/11/ZT, 10 October 2012). The practicablity criterion may be of particular concern for whistleblowers given the degree of resistance to them by other workers. This may be reviewed again at the stage of the enforcement of the order (*Port of London Authority v Payne and others* [1994] IRLR 9 (CA)). It is also the case that many whistleblowers would prefer compensation to going back to the environment which caused them to blow the whistle in the first place.

10.08 The key test for the tribunal is whether, having regard to the employment relations realities of the situation, the order is capable of being successfully put into effect (per Stephenson LJ in *Coleman and Stephenson v Magnet Joinery Ltd* [1974] IRLR 343 (CA)). This is not the same as what is 'possible'. The case of *Meridian Ltd v Gomersall and another* [1977] IRLR 425 (EAT) states that the tribunal may take into account the impact the order is expected to have on other staff. It is not however enough to say that it is not expedient to re-employ (*Qualcast (Wolverhampton) Ltd v Ross* [1979] IRLR 98 (EAT)).

10.09 When initially deciding whether to make a re-employment order, the tribunal only makes a provisional determination of practicability. It need not pre-judge future eventualities, but due weight is given to the commercial judgment of management unless disbelieved: *Port of London Authority v Payne*. Practicability means capable of being carried into effect with success: *Lincolnshire County Council v Lupton* [2016] IRLR 576 (EAT). There is not necessarily a duty to create a vacancy; this a question of fact and degree for the tribunal: *Lupton* at para 18. Loss of trust and confidence in the claimant, if genuine and founded on a rational basis, may negate practicability: see *United Lincolnshire Hospitals NHS Foundation Trust v Farren* (UKEAT/0198/16/LA, 14 November 2016) at para 40. Significantly in the whistleblowing context, allegations by an employee indicating a loss of confidence in the employer may show that re-employment is not practical (*Nothman v London Borough of Barnet (No 2)* [1980] IRLR 65 (CA); *Wood Group Heavy Industrial Turbines Ltd v Crossan* [1998] IRLR 680 (EAT)). It is relevant if the issue would impact on close working relationships (*Enessy Co SA t/ a the Tulchan Estate v Minoprio* [1978] IRLR 489 (EAT)) or, conversely, there could be re-engagement at a different workplace (*Oasis Community Learning v Wolff* (UKEAT/0364/12/MC, 17 May 2013). The way proceedings have been conducted may also be taken into account (*Central and North West London NHS Foundation Trust v Abimbola* (UKEAT/0542/08/LA, 3 April 2009); *Rembiszewski*), albeit allowing for reactions in the heat of litigation: *Oasis Community Learning* at para 18; *Cruickshank v Richmond LBC* (EAT/ 483/ 97).

(b) Contributory fault

10.10 The employee's contributory conduct must be taken into account, provided it is 'blameworthy' (*The Boots Company Ltd v Lees-Collier* [1986] ICR 728, (EAT)). The same test must be applied as for the compensatory award under ERA, section 123(6). The greater the degree of blameworthiness, the less likely that an order will be made (*Nairne v Highlands and Islands Fire Brigade* [1989] IRLR 366).

(c) Other factors

The tribunal, in exercising its discretion, can weigh up all manner of features of the **10.11** case. The cases have shown that this may include poor personal relationships with other employees (*Intercity East Coast Ltd v McGregor* (EAT/473/96) and the impact on employment relations generally (*Coleman v Magnet Joinery Ltd* [1974] ICR 46 (CA)). In the former case the acrimonious relationship between employee and supervisor, to which the employee had contributed, was enough to render an order unworkable.

(d) Permanent replacements

Reinstatement or re-engagement is not off the table where a permanent replacement has **10.12** been hired. Section 116(5) ERA provides that where an employer has engaged a permanent replacement, this shall not be taken into account in deciding whether or not to make a re-employment order unless 'it was not practicable for [the employer] to arrange for the dismissed employee's work to be done without engaging a permanent replacement' or the employer engaged the replacement 'after the lapse of a reasonable period without having heard from the dismissed employee that he wished to be reinstated or re-engaged', and at the time the replacement was taken on, 'it was not practicable for [the employer] to arrange for the dismissed employee's work to be done without engaging a permanent replacement' (section 116(6)).

(e) Reasons

The tribunal must, if requested, give reasons for the decision, including the basis on which it **10.13** has decided whether re-employment is practicable or not (*Port of London Authority v Payne and others* [1994] ICR 555 (CA); *Clancy v Cannock Chase Technical College* [2001] IRLR 331 (EAT)).

(f) Terms of re-engagement

The tribunal must make an order for re-engagement on such terms which are, so far as is rea- **10.14** sonably practicable, as favourable as reinstatement (ERA, section 116(4)). The order should specify the place of employment and the nature of the employment to be provided (*Rank Xerox (UK) Ltd v Stryczek* [1995] IRLR 568 (EAT)), together with the date for compliance (*Pirelli General Cable Works Ltd v Murray* [1979] IRLR 190 (EAT)). A tribunal cannot order an improved re-engagement (*Stryczek*).

(g) Compensation and back pay in re-employment cases

In a section 103A unfair dismissal claim there is no statutory limit on the amount the **10.15** tribunal can award in this regard (ERA, section 124(3)). The tribunal may order the full amount of back pay which has accrued between dismissal and the date when the order will take effect. The claimant can be compensated for any improvements in such terms and conditions between the date of dismissal and the date on which the order takes effect.

ERA, section 114(4) sets out the appropriate reductions (see generally *Butler v BRB* **10.16** EAT/510/89):

(a) where the employee receives an ex gratia payment or wages in lieu of notice for the period between their termination date and re-employment, this should be deducted;
(b) any payments received by the employee in respect of employment with another employer in the same period; and
(c) such other benefits as the tribunal thinks appropriate in the circumstances.

10.17   The EAT in *City & Hackney Health Authority v Crisp* [1990] ICR 95 (EAT) decided that it was inappropriate to make any deduction from this sum for either contributory fault or a failure to mitigate.

10.18   The statutory provisions distinguish between partial compliance with the tribunal's order and non-compliance. Partial compliance occurs if the employee is reinstated or re-engaged but there is not full compliance with the terms. The tribunal then cannot make an additional award (see paragraph 10.19 below) but can order compensation for the loss sustained by non-compliance (s.117 ERA).

10.19   The tribunal does not have power to enforce its own awards of re-employment. Section 117(3) thus provides that if the claimant is not reinstated or re-engaged, the tribunal is required, subject to the defence of impracticability, to make an additional award of between twenty-six and fifty-two weeks' pay as well as a standard award of compensation for unfair dismissal calculated in accordance with ERA, sections 118–127. If a reinstated employee is placed on terms different to those ordered by the tribunal, this will not be compliant with the order (*Artisan Press Ltd v Strawley and Parker* [1986] ICR 328 (EAT)).

(3) Compensatory award

10.20   Section 123 ERA directs that the amount of the compensatory award shall be such as the tribunal considers just and equitable in all the circumstances, having regard to the loss sustained by the complainant in consequence of the dismissal insofar as that loss is attributable to action taken by the employer. Whereas the compensatory award for ordinary unfair dismissal claims is subject to a ceiling, there is no ceiling on compensation for a dismissal where the reason or principal reason was that the employee made a protected disclosure (ERA, section 137(1)).[1]

10.21   The detailed principles as to recovery of financial loss may be found in *Blackstone's Employment Law Practice 2017* (Oxford: Oxford University Press, 2017), Chapters 32–36. Very large awards are often made for pecuniary loss in whistleblowing cases because employees can more readily convince the tribunal that because they have blown the whistle they will find it very difficult to work in the particular industry in which they operate:

- In *Fernandes v Netcom Consultants UK Ltd* (ET Case No 22000060/00, 24 January 2000) Mr Fernandes, a fifty-eight-year-old chief financial officer, was awarded £293,441 on the basis that he would not secure similar work in the future.
- In *Watkinson v Royal Cornwall NHS Trust* (UKEAT/0378/10), the respondent's chief executive was dismissed by reason of protected disclosures and the detriments suffered were found to include libellous publicity. Having regard to the damage to his career, he received compensation of £1.2m, reduced to just over £800,000 on review.
- In *Montgomery v Universal Services Handling Ltd* (ET Case No 2701150/03) the employee successfully showed that the reason he could not gain security clearance to work in the security industry as he wished was because of his dismissal and his subsequent period of unemployment.[2]

---

[1] This provision was introduced at the report stage of the Bill on 30 March 1999. When introducing the amendment the then Secretary of State for Trade and Industry, Stephen Byers, explained that 'we must send out a clear message underlining how seriously we regard this issue'.

[2] See also *Bhatia v Sterlite Industries (India) Ltd* (ET Case No 2204571/00, 2 May 2001), discussed in Chapter 3, para 3.112, where there was an award of £805,384.

- In *Best v Medical Marketing International Group Plc (in voluntary liquidation)* (ET Case No 1501248/2008, 2 July 2013) the claimant was latterly the Executive Chairman and Group managing director of the respondent, which was a pharmaceutical company. There was no attendance by the respondent at the hearing. He was found to have made protected disclosures with a view to exposing the 'fraud, misfeasance and unlawful activities' of the other directors and others and taking legal advice as to his concerns. The tribunal made a compensatory award in relation to his dismissal of £2,259,088, reflecting two years and two months' pay. This was uplifted by a further 50 per cent under the then applicable provisions relating to non-compliance with the statutory disciplinary and dismissal procedures, resulting in a total compensatory award of £3,402,245 (though the respondent was in voluntary liquidation).

- In *Osipov v International Petroleum Ltd and others* (ET Case No 2200944/2015, 23 March 2016) the claimant was employed by IPL—an Australian-domiciled oil and gas exploration and production company listed on the Australian stock exchange. He was later appointed as CEO of IPL. He made what were found to be protected disclosures in relation to failure to conduct a competitive tendering process in relation to exploration operations in the Niger. The tribunal found that he suffered detriments (including being removed from a business trip to the Niger), and ultimately was dismissed by reason of his protected disclosures. The tribunal made an award of £563,462 in relation to unfair dismissal which was uplifted by 12.5 per cent for failure to comply with the ACAS code.[3]

10.22 In general, an employer may rely upon evidence that an employee would or may have left employment in any event in order to limit compensation payable, usually referred to as a *Polkey* reduction.[4] That is subject to two exceptions that are liable to be relevant in a whistleblowing context. First, an exception where the circumstances in question arise from the employer's own wrongdoing: see *Prison Service v Beart (No 2)* [2005] ICR 1206 (CA). In the PIDA context, the decision in *The Trustees of Mama East African Women's Group v Dobson* (EAT/0219/05 and UKEAT/0220/05/TM, 23 June 2005), which is discussed at paragraphs 7.64–7.65 in Chapter 7, may be regarded as an example of this principle.

10.23 Second, notwithstanding that employment would or may have ended anyway, a whistleblower may suffer a continuing handicap in obtaining new employment due to the stigma associated with being seen as a whistleblower in the eyes of some potential employers and/ or from having brought a tribunal claim. It is open to the worker to claim for such losses. This was the subject of consideration in *Small v Shrewsbury and Telford Hospitals NHS Trust* (UKEAT/0300/14/LA, 19 May 2015). Here the claimant worked on an agency basis as a project manager for the respondent NHS Trust. He succeeded in his claim that he lost his agency employment, in July 2012, by reason of having made protected disclosures in relation to health and safety considerations. The ET found that he would have been dismissed in any event on 14 November 2013. He argued before the EAT that the tribunal should still have considered his case as to continuing losses beyond that date on the basis that he suffered a stigma or disadvantage on the labour market due to having been dismissed for raising a health and safety matter. However, this had not been argued in the ET, and the EAT refused to permit it to be argued on appeal. The EAT emphasized that it was necessary to produce evidence to support a claim for stigma damages; it could not simply be assumed that this was so due to being a protected disclosure case. Although stigma damages did not

---

[3] The award was said to be provisional to allow the parties liberty to apply if they were unable to agree the tax position for grossing-up purposes. At the time of writing, the case is under appeal to the EAT.

[4] Following the decision in *Polkey v AE Dayton Services* [1988] AC 344 (HL).

need to be formally pleaded, it was not something to which the tribunal had automatically to refer if not raised by the parties. Here the point could not be taken on appeal because it had not been laid before the ET.

10.24 The tribunal will also consider the percentage likelihood of gaining another job at a specific time and at a specific rate (eg *MOD v Cannock* [1994] ICR 918 (EAT)).[5]

10.25 It is often appropriate, in assessing what income the employee would have earned if s/he had not blown the whistle, for the claimant to focus on a comparison with another otherwise similarly placed employee who has not blown the whistle and to consider what has happened to his/her career path by way of comparison with the claimant (eg *Acikalin v Phones 4u Ltd* (ET Case No 3302501/04). This may be particularly important in predicting what bonus the employee would have received if s/he had not blown the whistle.

(4) Unfair dismissals and contributory fault

10.26 Pursuant to section 123(6) ERA, a tribunal is required to reduce the compensatory award to the extent it considers just and equitable where the dismissal was to an extent caused or contributed to by any action of the claimant. A reduction may also be made to the basic award on this basis. The conduct in question must have been culpable/blameworthy. In relation to the compensatory award the conduct must have had some causative influence on the dismissal. In relation to the basic award there is no requirement for the conduct to have contributed to the dismissal, but it must have occurred before dismissal (or if on notice, before notice of dismissal: *British Gas Trading Ltd v Price* (UKEAT/0326/15/DM, 22 March 2016)).

10.27 As noted in Chapter 7, there has been some judicial recognition that the legitimate protection against victimization could be undermined by too readily allowing employers to draw a distinction between the protected activity or disclosure and the manner in which it was carried out or made. These considerations are also apposite in relation to the extent to which awards may be subject to deductions for contributory fault due to, for example, the intemperate way in which a disclosure was made.

10.28 In the pre-PIDA unreported case of *Friend v CAA (No. 1)*[6] an employment tribunal held that a whistleblower had contributed 100 per cent to his dismissal. Captain Friend was employed by the CAA as a flight operations inspector. As a result of expressing strong views as to safety matters, he enjoyed a poor relationship with some of his colleagues. Ultimately, following allegations made against him by some of his colleagues, he was dismissed. The employment tribunal held that the dismissal was procedurally unfair but that his compensation should be reduced by 100 per cent due to his contributory fault. In upholding this decision, the Court of Appeal explained that there was no need for the tribunal to have investigated whether Captain Friend's safety concerns were well founded since in relation to compensation:

> the question for the industrial tribunal . . . was not whether he was right or wrong, reasonable or unreasonable, in the views he expressed; but whether his way of expressing them, and the steps he took, or omitted to take, as a means of emphasising them, amounted to action which caused or contributed to his dismissal . . . [F]or the purpose of answering that question it was unnecessary to enlarge the ambit of an already long hearing by going into the rights and wrongs of the controversy engendered by the helicopter safety issue.

---

[5] On career loss awards in cases not involving whistleblowing see *Wardle v Crédit Agricole Corporate & Investment Bank* [2011] IRLR 604 (CA); *Abbey National plc v Chagger* [2010] IRLR 47 (CA).

[6] Cited in [1998] IRLR 253.

The issue arises as to whether the approach in the *Friend* case could be applied in the case **10.29** of someone automatically dismissed under ERA, section 103A. Could it thus be argued that the manner of disclosure in a particular case contributed to the employee's dismissal and accordingly that compensation ought to be reduced under section 123(6) on the ground that the dismissal was to an extent 'caused or contributed to by [an] action of the complainant'?

On one level it is difficult to see how contributory fault has any part to play in assessment of **10.30** compensation where the tribunal has concluded that the dismissal was *automatically* unfair because the reason or principal reason for the dismissal was the making of a protected disclosure. How can the employee ever be said to have contributed to a dismissal which is for that reason, save in the sense that s/he made the disclosure which is itself the subject of protection? Further, the protected conduct cannot be the ground of a reduction for contributory fault. This point was established in *Property Guards Ltd v Taylor and Kershaw* [1982] IRLR 175 (EAT). The employees, who were security guards, were dismissed because they had failed to disclose 'spent' convictions. This was argued to constitute contributory action. By section 4(3)(b) of the Rehabilitation of Offenders Act 1974, however, it was provided that 'a conviction which has become spent or any circumstances ancillary thereto, or any failure to disclose a spent conviction or any such circumstances, shall not be a proper ground for dismissing or excluding a person from any office, profession, occupation or employment'. Accordingly, the dismissals were effectively automatically unfair. The EAT said (at para 13) that no question of contribution could arise because there was no obligation to disclose, and there was no question of any fault by either of the claimants, which could form the subject matter of a claim that there was contribution to their dismissal.

However, it is clear that contributory fault *can* be found in a case of automatic unfair dismissal. **10.31** This is shown by the terms of other provisions for automatic unfair dismissal. Section 152 of the Trade Union and Labour Relations (Consolidation) Act 1992 (TULRCA) makes dismissal of an employee on grounds related to union membership or activities automatically unfair. Section 155 of TULRCA specifies certain matters which are to be disregarded in assessing contributory fault. It therefore follows that conduct other than those specified matters may lead the tribunal to conclude that the dismissal was caused or contributed to by the action of the complainant. This is also consistent with the express provision that contributory fault can be taken into account in whistleblowing detriment claims (ERA, section 49(5)). There is no inconsistency with the finding that the principal reason for dismissal was a protected disclosure because it is sufficient if contributory conduct played a material part in the dismissal, albeit that it was not the principal reason: see *Robert Whiting Designs Ltd v Lamb* [1978] ICR 89, EAT. Notwithstanding this feature, whilst in principle the way in which a worker behaves when making a protected disclosure might properly be blameworthy conduct justifying a reduction in compensation, such as due to being unnecessarily abusive, a good deal of leeway is to be permitted. This is consistent with the policy, as noted in *Boulding v Land Securities Trillium (Media Services) Ltd* (EAT/0023/06, 3 May 2006) at para 24, that, having regard to the public interest in the legislation, 'there is a certain generosity in the construction of the statute and in the treatment of the facts'.

A related issue was highlighted by the decision of the EAT in *Melia v Magna Kansei* [2005] **10.32** ICR 874.[7] In addition to the deductions that can be made on the grounds of contributory

---

[7] This decision (at Court of Appeal level) is considered further below (at 10.72–10.76) in relation to the scope of injury to feelings awards.

fault, the tribunal may reduce compensation on the basis of the likelihood that a fair dismissal would have occurred in any event or that it is just and equitable to do so.[8] One potential difficulty arising from this point is if it encourages a search for evidence to hold against the person who has blown the whistle. This was found to have occurred in the case of *Melia* itself. The claimant complained that, having made a disclosure in May 2001 in respect of alleged bullying by a manager, he was subjected to various detriments by his employer over the succeeding months and up to November 2001. He was then suspended pending an investigation of an allegation of gross misconduct. He said that this confirmed to him that his employer was not capable of performing, nor willing to perform, his contract of employment, nor its legal duties under various statutory instruments including the Health and Safety at Work Act. He purported to accept the repudiatory breaches and terminated the contract with immediate effect. As Chadwick LJ put it in the Court of Appeal,[9] 'In short, he alleged that he was forced to resign because he was a "whistleblower"'.

10.33 The tribunal upheld Mr Melia's complaints of victimization and that the principal reason for his constructive dismissal was that he had made a protected disclosure. However, it also ruled that, prior to and unconnected with his dismissal, Mr Melia had seriously misused the respondent's computer system; an act for which he might, but not necessarily would, have been fairly dismissed in any event. An award of £6,000 was made for the detriment and the respondent had to pay a compensatory award of £11,601.87. There was a reduction of 50 per cent in both the basic and compensatory award on the grounds that it was just and equitable to do so in the light of Mr Melia's misconduct prior to dismissal. This reduction was made notwithstanding the tribunal's finding that the evidence of wrongdoing was:

> discovered after a concerted effort to find material which—as a result of the protected disclosure—could be used to ensure the termination of the claimant's employment, if possible without the need for any form of negotiated settlement.

10.34 The EAT (at para 55) noted the force of the submission that the employer should not be permitted 'to scrabble around after a protected disclosure to try to find some misconduct which it could then use as a justification or excuse for dismissal, or at any rate by way of self-defence to claim against it'. Indeed, this in itself would appear to have been an unlawful detriment under ERA, section 47B. Notwithstanding this, the EAT considered that there was no basis to interfere with the tribunal's decision on this issue.

10.35 Subsequent decisions have similarly proceeded on the basis that contributory fault reductions can be made notwithstanding the dismissal being automatically unfair. In *Kaltz Ltd v Mrs B Hamer* (UKEAT/0198/11/RN, 24 February 2012), it was agreed that such a deduction could be made. Again, in *Audere Medical Services Ltd v Sanderson* (UKEAT 0409/12/RN, 29 May 2013) the EAT could see no reason in principle why there could not be a reduction for contributory fault in a case of automatically unfair dismissal by reason of a protected disclosure.

10.36 The point was revisited in detail in the somewhat complex case of *Arriva London South Ltd v Graves* (UKEAT/0067/15/DA), by HHJ Clark on 3 July 2015. Mr Graves was employed by Arriva as a bus driver until his dismissal by Mr Gary Smith, operating

---

[8] *Devis & Sons Ltd v Atkins* [1977] AC 931 (HL). See also *Aryeetey v Tuntum Housing Association* (EAT/0324/08, 8 April 2009) (considered below, at paras 10.144 and 10.145), where (a) further disclosures, made subsequent to those which triggered a disciplinary hearing and which contained allegations of dishonesty made for an ulterior motive, justified a reduction for compensatory fault; and (b) conduct in making disclosures not in good faith subsequent to dismissal was relied upon at a remedies hearing to limit the award on the basis that the claimant could have been fairly dismissed.

[9] [2005] EWCA Civ 1547, [2006] IRLR 117.

manager for the Norwood Garage at which Mr Graves was then based, on 26 September 2013. Graves was a member of the RMT, although Arriva recognized Unite and not RMT. In 2011 Graves and an RMT colleague, Mr Farr, brought proceedings complaining of trade union detrimental treatment contrary to section 146 of TULRCA. Those complaints were upheld by the ET in finding that Graves had been disciplined by Mr Smith for wearing an unauthorized 'hi vis.' vest. The evidence showed, however, that another employee, Mr Diplock, had in the past worn unauthorized vests, ie those not showing the Arriva logo, without being disciplined. The difference, the tribunal found, was that Graves' vest had the legend 'RMT' on the back. The tribunal found that a Mr Hall also subjected Graves to detrimental treatment for the prohibited purpose under section 146. Mr Hall was the operations manager at the South Croydon Garage at which Graves then worked.

No action was taken against Messrs Hall and Smith following the tribunal's decision and no **10.37** training was provided consequent upon that tribunal's judgment. On Arriva's case Graves was dismissed for going off route and then seeking to cover up that fact by putting in a false occurrence report ('OR'). As a result, and following a complaint by a member of the public, he was interviewed by Mr Hudgell (deputy operations manager). Mr Hudgell suspended the claimant. The interview by Mr Hudgell which formed the basis of the detriment (short of dismissal) claim was found by the tribunal to have been held for a proper motive. That part of the claim failed.

In 2013 Mr Gary Smith held a disciplinary hearing and then dismissed Graves for breach **10.38** of trust amounting to gross misconduct. Mr Graves' appeal was heard by Mr Halligan and Mr Hall (who featured in the earlier claim) and dismissed by them. The ET had taken into account the history of dealings between Mr Graves and Messrs Smith and Hall, his less than perfect disciplinary record, his falsifying a company document (the log card), and treatment of other disciplined employees and concluded that Arriva had failed to disprove the prohibited reason/s notwithstanding Mr Graves' admitted misconduct: the complaint under sections 152 TULRCA (dismissal on grounds of union activities) and 104 ERA (dismissal for assertion of a statutory right) was made out. The Tribunal said that they found 'that as the real reason for dismissal was a prohibited reason . . . no reduction for contributory fault is appropriate'.

Judge Clark said that it was plain that the employment tribunal considered that as they had **10.39** found inadmissible reasons for dismissal contrary to section 152 TULRCA and section 104 ERA, no reduction for contributory fault was appropriate. It was quite clear that a tribunal's power to reduce a claimant's compensatory award by reason of contributory conduct was directed to the effect of that conduct on the dismissal, not the employer's reason for dismissal; *Steen v ASP Packaging Ltd* [2014] ICR 56 (EAT), paras 11–15.

In Mr Graves' case the ET had appeared to conclude that no contribution enquiry was **10.40** necessary because it had found that dismissal was for the prohibited reasons. That was not correct. Given that Graves was, on his own admission, guilty of blameworthy conduct, the question was whether that conduct caused or contributed to the dismissal to any extent and, if so, to what extent (applying the slightly different tests under sections 123(6) and 122(2) ERA)? That question was remitted for determination.

(5) Good faith reduction

In relation to claims relating to qualifying disclosures made on or after 25 June 2013, sec- **10.41** tion 123(6A) ERA (introduced by the ERRA) makes specific provision that there can be a reduction of up to 25 per cent of the compensatory award if the disclosure was not made in good faith. There is a similar provision in relation to detriment claims in section 49(6A)

ERA, again limited to claims arising from disclosures made on or after 25 June 2013. We consider these provisions, and their relationship with reductions for contributory fault, in paragraphs 10.141–10.147 below.

(6) Failure to follow the ACAS code

10.42 Under section 207A TULRCA and section 124A ERA, the compensatory award may be increased or decreased by up to 25 per cent where either the employer or an employee fails to comply with a statutory code if that failure was unreasonable. In practice this refers to the ACAS Code on Disciplinary and Grievance Procedures ('the Code').

10.43 So far as concerns disciplinary procedures, it applies to procedures relating to allegations of misconduct or culpable poor performance.[10] The risks of ignoring the Code are illustrated by the first instance decision in *Clark-Harris v Chelmsford Mencap* (ET Case No 3201402/ 10). Here, in response to the claimant raising a protected disclosure with the employer's board, she received a letter criticizing her for not first raising the matter with her supervisor and stating that she should regard this as a first written warning for failing to adhere to procedures. She was later dismissed and succeeded in claims of automatic unfair dismissal and detriment by reason of protected disclosures. She was awarded compensation of £6,000 for injury to feelings which was increased by 25 per cent to reflect what the tribunal described as the employer's comprehensive failure to comply with the ACAS code, having not held any disciplinary hearing prior to the disciplinary sanction.[11]

10.44 Some difficulty may arise in relation to the application of the Code in relation to grievances, which are liable to arise either in constructive dismissal claims or in detriment claims. Grievances are defined as being 'concerns, problems or complaints that employees raise with their employers'.

As discussed in Chapter 4, notwithstanding the requirement for a reasonable belief that a disclosure is made in the public interest, that does not necessarily exclude disclosure of information where the worker's primary concern is his or her own position. In any event, on its face the definition does not exclude 'concerns' or 'problems' in relation to matters of public interest, or provide that the concern has to be in relation to, or only in relation to, the employee's own position. There is an exception for collective grievances (para 47 of the Code), but only where they are raised by a representative of a recognized trade union or other appropriate workplace representative. Nor does the Code on its face restrict its application by reference to the way in which the concern is raised, so as only to apply if raised under a grievance procedure rather than under a whistleblowing procedure.

Under the now repealed statutory grievance procedures, the statutory grievance procedure appended to the Employment Act 2002 provided expressly (at para 15) that the grievance procedures were only applicable to the kind of disclosure dealt with by Part IVA ERA (concerning protected disclosures) where the information related to a matter which the employer could raise as a grievance and it was the employee's intention that the disclosure should constitute the raising of the matter with the employer as a grievance. That reflected a recognition that some different considerations apply. Some support for the non-applicability of the Code might also be derived from the reasoning in in *Phoenix House Ltd v Stockman v Lambis* (UKEAT/0264/15/DM, 17 May 2016). In concluding that the Code did not apply

---

[10] *Holmes v Qinetiq Ltd* [2016] IRLR 664 (EAT). See also *Phoenix House Ltd v Stockaman and Lambis* [2017] ICR 84—concluding that the adjustment under s 207A TULRCA does not apply to a dismissal for some other substantial reason (arising in that case from a breakdown in relationships).

[11] Case summary drawn from IDS Employment Handbook on Whistleblowing.

to a dismissal for some other substantial reason (SOSR) arising from a breakdown in relationships, Mitting J reasoned (at para 21) that clear words were needed for the Code to apply due to its punitive effect and emphasized that whilst there were overlaps in the requirements for a fair dismissal, some of the provisions applicable to a misconduct dismissal (for example in relation to investigation) might not be of full effect for an SOSR dismissal. By analogy it might be argued that the procedures set out in the grievance procedures—essentially designed around the key steps of a meeting, decision, and possible appeal—are framed to deal with resolving a complaint concerning the worker's own situation. There are parallels in the good practice approach to public interest disclosures, which involves ascertaining details of the concern, giving feedback to the extent the situation permits, and a further level of recourse if the concern is unresolved (see Chapter 19). But there may be some differences of approach and emphasis—such as in relation to provision for a decision and appeal—where the worker is raising a matter for the employer to look into in the public interest rather than a complaint as to their own situation.

However, in the absence of clear authority, and given the terms of the definition of a grievance, employers would be well advised to abide so far as possible with the procedural requirements of the Code even where a concern is raised under a whistleblowing procedure, which as noted above will ordinarily accord reasonably closely with good practice in relation to eliciting details of the concern, and providing recourse to a hearing and at least one level of escalation if the concern is not resolved. Further, even if it is found that there is technically a breach of the Code, there is no jurisdiction to make an adjustment unless this is found to have been unreasonable.

10.45 Given the potentially substantial sums that may be awarded in the light of compensation being uncapped, the adjustment of up to 25 per cent could be a substantial sum. However, under the previous legislation concerning statutory grievance procedures it was held to be appropriate to have regard to the overall size of the compensatory award (as well as the degree of culpability) when assessing the appropriate extent of any adjustment.[12] A similar approach is likely to apply under the present provisions.

(7) Interim relief

10.46 Pursuant to ERA, section 128(1)(b) (as amended by PIDA, section 9) employees (but not other workers) who are dismissed because they have made a protected disclosure are able to seek interim relief pending the main hearing. This emphasizes the importance of protecting those who make protected disclosures. If a tribunal finds that the employee is likely to win at the full hearing, it will order that the employee is re-employed or, if the employer is not willing to accept this, make an order for the continuation of the employment contract so that the claimant will receive his/her pay and normal benefits. If after the full hearing the tribunal finds for the employee, such an interim order is likely to increase the chances that the tribunal will find that it is practicable for the employer to comply with any re-employment order made at the full hearing.[13]

10.47 An application for interim relief must be made within seven days of the dismissal (ERA, section 128(2))—that is to say that the normal three-month time limit is abrogated. The tribunal must determine the application as soon as possible thereafter (section 128(4)) and cannot postpone the hearing of the application unless there are exceptional circumstances

---

[12] *Abbey National plc v Chagger* [2010] ICR 397 (CA); *Wardle v Crédit Agricole Corporate and Investment Bank* [2011] ICR 1290 (CA).
[13] An order for interim relief was made in *Fernandes v Netcom Consultants UK Ltd* (ET Case No 22000060/00, 24 January 2000): see para 10.21 above.

(section 128(5)). A claim cannot be made if the complaint is only of selection for redundancy by reason of a protected disclosure under ERA, section 105: see *McConnell v Bombardier Aerospace (No 1)* [2007] NICA 27, [2008] IRLR 51 and *McConnell v Bombardier Aerospace (No 2)* [2008] NICA 50, [2009] IRLR 201.

10.48 If at the interim relief hearing the tribunal considers that it is likely that, at a full hearing, it will find that the reason or principal reason for the dismissal was on the ground of whistleblowing, then a series of provisions apply (ERA, section 129(1)). In the parallel provisions in respect of interim hearings in trade union activities cases, the term 'likely' has been interpreted as meaning a 'pretty good chance of succeeding', which equated to better than 'more likely than not'.[14] This test has been approved in the context of protected disclosures.[15] It is a high threshold, involving a significantly higher degree of likelihood than the phrase 'more likely than not': *Ministry of Justice v Sarfraz* [2011] IRLR 562 (EAT). As the EAT explained in *Parsons v Airplus International Ltd* (UKEAT/0023/16/JOJ, 4 March 2016) (at para 7):

> This interpretation is justified because if the employee satisfies the test the Tribunal must make an Order for interim relief and, if it does so, the employer is obliged to pay the employee pending the determination of the complaint and there is no provision for re-payment in the event that she ultimately fails on the merits.

10.49 However, the statutory touchstone is likelihood of success. There does not have to be some other factor (or factors) such as a requirement to show that the case was sufficiently exceptional for interim relief to be appropriate: *Raja v Secretary of State for Justice* (EAT/364/09). Nor is there any requirement that the claimant is seeking reinstatement or re-engagement.[16]

10.50 In determining an interim relief application the employment tribunal is engaged on a predictive exercise as to the likely outcome at the full hearing. This involves making a summary assessment, on the basis of the material then before the tribunal, of whether there is a 'pretty good chance' of the claim succeeding (*Parsons* at para 8). It is therefore not appropriate to seek to make a summary determination of the factual issues as if it was a final determination of the matter: *Raja* (above) at para 25; *Parkins v Sodexho Ltd* [2002] IRLR 109 (EAT) at paras 23–29; *Parsons* (at para 8). Related to this, it is sufficient for the tribunal, when giving reasons, to indicate the essential gist, since (a) the decision will inevitably be based to an extent on impression and therefore not be susceptible to detailed reasoning, and (b) it is better not to say anything which might pre-judge the final determination on the merits: *Parsons* (at para 8).

10.51 An application should not be dismissed merely because it is complex or due to the scale of the paperwork to be considered: *Raja*. But the employment tribunal has considerable discretion as to the case management of such claims. The parties may be required merely to draw attention to key points (*Raja*) and there is no error of law in refusing to admit oral evidence: *Dandpat* (n 14) at para 12.

---

[14] *Taplin v C Shippam Ltd* [1978] IRLR 450 (EAT).

[15] *Raja v Secretary of State for Justice* (EAT/364/09); *Dandpat v The University of Bath and another* (EAT/0408/09 and others, 10 November 2009) (applications for permission to appeal were rejected: [2010] EWCA Civ 305 (Arden LJ) and 785 (Smith LJ)); *Ministry of Justice v Sarfraz* [2011] IRLR 562 (EAT); *Parsons v Airplus International Ltd* (UKEAT/0023/16/JOJ, 4 March 2016) (refusing interim relief despite there being a 'good arguable case').

[16] For an example of a continuation order made where neither re-engagement nor reinstatement were sought, see *Kowalska v NKG Ltd and Binning* (ET Case No 2329687/2008 and another, 7 November 2008): (continuation order made where claimant was dismissed after raising complaints re late payments and non-payment of holiday pay, taking into account proximity of dismissal and letters of complaint).

If the tribunal finds that on determining the substantive hearing it is likely to be found that **10.52** the reason or principal reason for the dismissal was a protected disclosure, the tribunal will first explain its powers to the parties (ERA, section 129(2)) and ask the employer if it will re-employ the employee pending the full hearing (section 129(3)). If the employer is willing to do so then an order is made to that effect (section 129(4)–(6)). If the employee does not accept re-engagement (that is, a different post though on terms no less favourable: section 129(3)(b)) the tribunal will decide whether that refusal is reasonable. If it is reasonable the employee's contract is deemed to continue until the full hearing. If the refusal is not reasonable no order is made pending full hearing (section 129(8)). Salary payments made pursuant to an interim relief order are not emoluments from employment, as they are paid consequent on termination of employment, and as such payments up to £30,000 are tax free: *Tutillols v Revenue and Customs Commissioners* [2014] UKFTT 672 (First-Tier Tribunal (Tax Chamber).

If the employer fails to attend the hearing or says that s/he is unwilling to re-employ the **10.53** employee (section 129(9)) the tribunal will (if the test for interim relief is satisfied) make an order, under section 130, that the employee's contract is deemed to continue until the full hearing. Even if the employee does not actually return to work, such an order will strengthen the employee's bargaining position in negotiations and may have some influence on the tribunal's decision whether to grant a re-employment order at the full hearing and on whether it was practicable for the employer to comply with it. Interim relief has rarely been awarded, but seeking interim relief will frequently cause the tribunal to put the case down for an earlier hearing than it would otherwise achieve.

There are sensitive tactical considerations in deciding whether to pursue an interim relief appli- **10.54** cation. From the claimant's perspective:

(a) the hearing gives the chance to obtain continuing pay that will not have to be repaid whatever happens at the main hearing (which may be many months afterwards);

(b) an interim relief hearing may give an early chance to test the respondent's evidence and whether the respondent is really willing to have the protected disclosures aired in a public tribunal (which is often a major consideration for the employer in deciding whether to settle a claim); and

(c) an early hearing, especially on a sensitive matter, may bring forward the pressure for settlement before the litigation has become such a drain on resources.

However, such a hearing may: **10.55**

(a) lead to weaknesses in the claimant's case being exposed at an early stage,

(b) lead to costs being expended that are needed to prepare for the substantive hearing, and

(c) embolden the respondent if the application fails, notwithstanding the high threshold of showing the claim is likely to succeed.

C. Detriment Claims

(1) Overview

So far as detriment complaints are concerned, ERA, section 49 provides that, where an **10.56** employment tribunal finds that a complaint under section 48 is well founded, the tribunal *shall* make a declaration to that effect, and *may* make an award of compensation to be paid by the employer to the complainant in respect of the act or failure to act to which the complaint relates. References to the employer in this context include a worker or agent who is a respondent to the claim (s.48(5))[17]. The amount of the compensation awarded shall be such as the tribunal considers just and equitable in all the circumstances, having regard to (s 49(2)):

(a) the infringement to which the complaint relates, and

(b) any loss which is attributable to the act, or failure to act, which infringed the complainant's right.

10.57 Section 49(3) specifically provides that the loss shall be taken to include:

(a) any expenses reasonably incurred by the complainant in consequence of the act, or failure to act, to which the complaint relates, and

(b) loss of any benefit which he might reasonably be expected to have had but for that act or failure to act.

10.58 Reductions to the award can be made on the following grounds:

(a) That it appears to the tribunal that the disclosure was not made in good faith (section 49(6A) ERA). We consider this further in Section D below.

(b) Contributory fault: that the act or failure to act was to any extent caused or contributed to by action of the claimant: section 49(5) ERA. The principles discussed at paragraphs 10.26–10.40 above will apply. The contributory conduct must be blameworthy/culpable and have had some causative influence on the detrimental treatment. However, tribunals will need to approach this with caution and sensitivity to the whistleblowing context before, for example, regarding the manner in which a protected disclosure issue is raised as giving rise to contributory fault: see *Boulding* v *Land Securities Trillium (Media Services) Ltd* (EAT/0023/06, 3 May 2006).

(c) A reduction for failure to follow an ACAS code. This is discussed at paragraphs 10.42–10.45 above. This only applies to claims by employees. It therefore does not apply to detriment claims by other workers: see section 207A(1) TULRCA and *Local Government Yorkshire and Humber v Shah* (UKEAT/0587/11/ZT, 19 June 2012).

10.59 Substantial pecuniary losses in detriment cases (absent claims of dismissal) are less common than in unfair dismissal claims for the straightforward reason that in most cases they relate to a period when the employee remained in employment (though, as discussed in Chapter 7, the detriment might also be inflicted after the employment has ended).[18] There might still be substantial financial loss, however, in such cases as where the detriment consists of the impact on discretionary bonus payments, or where it has resulted in being passed over for a promotion, or where a detrimental reference results in the loss of other employment.

10.60 In contrast with unfair dismissal claims, compensation for detriment claims invariably includes non-pecuniary losses. Recent EAT authority has called into question whether that is consistent with the statutory language (see paragraphs 10.66–10.69 below). It is also subject to section 49(6) ERA, where the detriment consists of termination of a contract which is not a contract of employment. In such a case, compensation is limited to that sum which would be available in an unfair dismissal claim. We consider this further below.[19]

---

[17] As discussed in Chapter 8 (paras 8.73–8.77) we suggest that the view expressed, *obiter*, in *Royal Mail Group Ltd v Jhuti* [2016] ICR 1043 (EAT), to the effect that a declaration is the only remedy against a worker or agent who is a respondent to a protected disclosure detriment claim, is wrong.

[18] *Woodward v Abbey National plc (No. 1)* [2006] EWCA Civ 822, [2006] IRLR 677.

[19] At paras 10.104–10.107.

(2) Whether loss is attributable to the act or failure to act

The test of whether the loss is 'attributable to' the act or failure to act was considered **10.61** by the EAT in *Roberts v Wilsons Solicitors LLP* [2016] ICR 659. The claimant had been a member of the respondent LLP. He had purported to accept a repudiatory breach of contract by virtue of treatment alleged to be a detriment under section 47B ERA. Notwithstanding that he then refused to provide any service, the respondent insisted that he remained a member of the LLP until, by letter of 30 April 2015, the respondent gave him notice expelling him from the LLP with immediate effect. The ET struck out a constructive dismissal claim on the basis of authority that the doctrine of repudiatory breach does not apply to LLPs.[20] It also struck out the claim to losses flowing from termination. That aspect of the decision was successfully appealed. The EAT rejected an argument that the fact of a lawful termination had the effect of excluding any claim in relation to post-termination losses. Addressing the test of attribution of loss, the EAT concluded that this raises a question of fact in each case. It neither sets a 'but for' test, nor does it require that the infringement or unlawful act must be the proximate cause of loss. As the EAT explained (at para 24):

> Depending on the circumstances, a loss may be attributable to a particular act whether that act is closest in time to the loss or not, and two or more consecutive (or concurrent) acts may combine to bring about a particular consequence or loss. Proximity by itself is not the determining factor, though it is obviously relevant, and the further away in time a loss is from the infringement to which it is said to be attributable, the harder in practice it is likely to be to prove that case. Rather, it is a question of fact and judgment in every case for the tribunal whether a particular consequence or loss is attributable to a particular unlawful act or infringement or to something else or both and if so, to what extent. The mere fact that an infringement is less close in time to the loss or consequence than something else to which it is also said to be attributable, does not inevitably or necessarily negate the infringement as also having relevant contributing attribution.

The EAT added that 'attributable' is an ordinary English word and is 'capable of being **10.62** applied flexibly . . . on a broad common sense basis.' Here the claim should not have been struck out as there was a question of fact to determine. If there was unlawful victimization which led the claimant to withdraw his labour, which in turn led to him being expelled, it would be open to the tribunal to regard losses following termination of employment as the natural and likely consequence of the unlawful detriment, and to regard such losses as attributable to those detriments. The tribunal would need to consider whether he acted reasonably and justifiably in withdrawing his labour or, conversely, whether it was wrongful conduct which amounted to an intervening act. These were issues of fact, not law, for the tribunal.

(3) Injury to feelings

(a) Can injury to feelings be claimed?

Following *Norton Tool Co Ltd v Tewson* [1972] IRLR 86, it had been almost universally **10.63** accepted that unfair dismissal compensation could not include compensation for injury to feelings[21] occasioned by the dismissal. Following Lord Hoffmann's remarks in *Johnson v Unisys Ltd* [2001] IRLR 279 (HL), to the effect that they had the power to do so, however, various employment tribunals began to make awards for injury to feelings in unfair dismissal cases. The issue reached the House of Lords again in *Dunnachie v Kingston upon*

---

[20] *Flanagan v Liontrust Investment Partners LLP and others* [2015] EWHC 2171(Ch).
[21] Or for personal injury.

Hull City Council [2004] UKHL 36, [2005] 1 AC 226, and it was held that tribunals could not do this.[22]

10.64 Whilst injury to feelings awards cannot be made in dismissal cases, until called into question by recent EAT authority, it was accepted such awards could be made in detriment claims. Section 49(2) ERA, which applies to each of the various types of detriment claims under ERA rather than being specific to protected disclosures, provides:

> (2) [Subject to . . . (6)[23] the amount of the compensation awarded shall be such as the tribunal considers just and equitable in all the circumstances having regard to—
> (a) the infringement to which the complaint relates, and
> (b) any loss which is attributable to the act, or failure to act, which infringed the complainant's right.

10.65 Leaving to one side section 49(2)(a) ERA, this provision is in strikingly similar terms to the provision for unfair dismissal compensation under section123(1) ERA. This provides that the compensatory award is to be such amount as the tribunal considers is just and equitable 'having regard to the loss sustained by the complainant in consequence of the dismissal in so far as that loss is attributable to action taken by the employer'. Section 49(2) ERA additionally provides for the tribunal to have regard to 'the infringement to which the complaint relates'. The House of Lords in *Dunnachie* determined that this permitted only an award of financial loss. That suggests that the key issue of statutory construction is whether a different approach is indicated in the context of detriment claims by reason of the requirement to have regard to the infringement to which the complaint relates. In the context of detriment for trade union activities, in *Cleveland Ambulance NHS Trust v Blane* [1997] ICR 851 the EAT concluded that this wording did indicate that non-pecuniary loss, including injury to feelings, could be awarded. That was followed specifically in a protected disclosure context in *Virgo Fidelis Senior School v Boyle* [2004] IRLR 268, where the EAT held that guidelines adopted in discrimination claims should also apply in protected disclosure claims.[24]

10.66 The view that there can be injury to feelings awards might be questioned by reference to the decision of the EAT in *Santos Gomes v Higher Level Care Ltd* [2016] ICR 926. Although not a protected disclosure case, the provision directly under consideration in *Santos Gomes*—regulation 30(4) of the Working Time Regulations 1998 (WTR)—is in materially the same terms as section 49(2) ERA. Just as section 49(2) provides for the tribunal to have regard to the infringement to which the complaint relates, so regulation 30 WTR provides for the amount of the compensation to be such as the tribunal considers just and equitable having regard not only to the loss sustained by the worker but also, under regulation 30(4)(b) to 'the employer's default in refusing to permit the worker to exercise his right'. Having regard to the construction of section 123(1) ERA in *Dunnachie*, it was accepted on behalf of the claimant that injury to feelings could not be awarded under regulation 30(4)(a) which provides for the award to have regard to any loss. Reliance was placed on regulation 30(4)(b) (the employer's default). But in relation to this, the EAT noted that an award of injury to feelings is compensatory. Therefore it was said that a provision which focuses on seriousness of default is not apt to cover such an award. As to the comparison with the approach to discrimination claims, the EAT highlighted the differing wording under the Equality Act 2010 (EqA). In that context, there is the same power to award compensation as available to a county court judge who, it is expressly provided, may make an award of damages including

---

[22] But financial losses flowing from damage to health are recoverable in an unfair dismissal claim: see eg *Devine v Designer Flowers Wholesale Florist Sundries Ltd* [1993] IRLR 517, EAT.
[23] Subsection (6) is discussed at paragraphs 10.104–10.107 below.
[24] Followed eg in *Commissioner of Police of the Metropolis v Shaw* [2012] ICR 464 (EAT).

compensation for injury to feelings. The EAT noted that, unlike in relation to the Part Time Workers Regulations 2000, Fixed-Term Employees Regulations 2002, and Agency Workers Regulations 2010,[25] there is no express exclusion of an award for injury to feelings, but concluded that this did not indicate that such an award could be made.

Some modest further support for the view that no injury to feelings award is available may be garnered from dicta of the EAT in a protected disclosure context in *Roberts v Wilsons Solicitors LLP* [2016] ICR 659, [2016] IRLR 586. There was no challenge to the power to award injury to feelings and was not directly in issue.[26] But in passing the EAT noted (at para 21) that although courts had treated the compensation principles applicable to unlawful discrimination claims as also being applicable in whistleblowing detriment claims, the language of section 49 ERA is different from the language providing for the compensation for the statutory tort of unlawful discrimination under the EqA. The EAT noted that it was closer to section 123(1) ERA dealing with compensation for unfair dismissal. **10.67**

However in *Santos Gomes* (at para 56) the making of injury to feelings awards in trade union detriment cases was explained on the basis that such claims are a form of discrimination. That is equally applicable in whistleblowing cases, as expressly stated in *Virgo Fidelis* (albeit that it was noted in *Santos Gomes* that no issue as to the power to award injury to feelings arose in *Virgo Fidelis*). By contrast the claim under the WTR was viewed (at paras 59, 69) as being akin to a claim for breach of contract. That distinction was also highlighted in *obiter* comments of the EAT in *Rowe v London Underground Ltd* (UKEAT/0125/16/JOJ, 17 October 2016). On that basis, Eady J commented (*obiter*, at para 42) that she saw no reason not to follow the decisions in *Cleveland Ambulance* and *Virgo Fidelis* which had 'given rise to a general understanding that injury to feelings awards are available in detriment cases other than those involving protected characteristics under the EqA'. She noted (at para 45) that this led to different conclusions based on very similar statutory wording, but this was explicable by the differing contexts. **10.68**

We suggest that the better view is indeed that injury to feelings awards are available for detriment claims. Taking section 49(2) ERA as a whole, and allowing for the context that the claim has been held to be akin to a discrimination claim, the requirement to have regard to the infringement to which the complaint relates provides a clear indication that there is not an intention to restrict the award to pecuniary loss. The requirement to have regard to the loss is to be read in that context. Further, although the award for injury to feelings is compensatory, the seriousness of the infringement is likely to have an impact on this as the more serious the infringement, the greater the impact on the claimant is liable to be. To that end, the EAT noted in *Virgo Fidelis* (at para 44(a)): **10.69**

> Clearly, the nature of the offence or its repetition may have an impact on the level of the award for injury to feelings and indeed the *Vento* guidelines set out in para 65 of Mummery LJ's judgment [2003] ICR 318, 335 are primarily based on the nature of the discrimination or its repetition, the argument being that the worse the offence the more likely it is that the victim will suffer injury to feelings. Indeed, the reference in section 49(2)(a) of the 1996 Act to the tribunal having regard to the 'infringement' to which the complaint relates, appears to us to be no more than a reminder to tribunals to have some regard to the nature of the complaint when assessing the resulting loss, simply to state what might be regarded as the obvious, namely the more serious the offence, the more likely it is that feelings have been injured.

---

[25] Equality Act 2010 (ss119(4) and 124(6)); Part-time Workers (Prevention of Less Favourable Treatment) Regs 2000, reg 8(11); Fixed-Term Employees (Prevention of Less Favourable Treatment) Regulations 2002, reg 7(10); Agency Workers Regulations 2010, reg 18(15).

[26] Indeed it suited the respondent for the purposes of the arguments in that case to say that injury to feelings could be awarded (see at para 39).

10.70 We therefore discuss the position below on the basis that injury to feelings awards are available, but with the caveat that, having regard to some of the reasoning in *Santos Gomes* and the contrast with the wording set out in the Equality Act 2010, this is an issue which may yet be subject to challenge.

(b) The boundary between detriment and dismissal

10.71 The dividing line between detriment and dismissal is a narrow one. It is quite common for dismissed employees (or workers) to allege (successfully) that prior to their dismissal on the ground of their having made a protected disclosure they were subjected to victimization on that ground which caused a pre-existing detriment. The dismissal may of course take the form of straightforward dismissal or a constructive dismissal. Because there can only be an injury to feelings award for detriment claims, it becomes important to identify what is regarded as part of the dismissal claim, and what constitutes detriment. Thus, if a disciplinary hearing is conducted in a vindictive manner, compensation for this could only be claimed if the case could be brought under ERA, section 47B, rather than regarding the disciplinary proceedings as part and parcel of the dismissal.

10.72 Similarly, in a constructive dismissal case, the issue arises as to whether the repudiatory conduct can lead to a section 47B detriment claim or whether it is part of the dismissal. This issue was addressed in *Melia v Magna Kansei* [2005] EWCA Civ 1547, [2006] IRLR 117, making it clear that in both of these instances the claim could proceed as a detriment claim, alongside a claim of unfair dismissal for losses arising out of the dismissal itself.

10.73 As noted above,[27] Mr Melia succeeded in claims that he had been subjected to a detriment by reason of protected disclosures, and also that he had been constructively unfairly dismissed under section 103A in that he resigned in response to being victimized for having made protected disclosures. In reaching its conclusion as to the appropriate compensation for being subjected to detriment, the tribunal only compensated him for the detriment up until June 2001, rather than for the whole period to his resignation in November 2001. It took the view that section 47B(2) meant that it had to separate from the dismissal and effectively discount such of the treatment (and thus its consequences) as effectively amounted to the unfair dismissal. This was because it could not award within the scope of compensation for unfair dismissal a sum of money to reflect the injury to feelings caused by the manner, still less the fact, of that dismissal. Accordingly, the tribunal would only compensate for detriment up to the point at which the treatment of Mr Melia became so serious that it amounted to a fundamental breach of contract. In the tribunal's view, that point was not the date by which Mr Melia decided that his employment had to end, but the date, which the tribunal decided was late June 2001, by which the conduct moved from being a detriment to being a matter of dismissal.

10.74 The EAT supported this approach but the Court of Appeal allowed Mr Melia's appeal. It decided that the proper meaning to be given to the phrase 'the detriment in question amounts to dismissal' is that it excluded detriment which could be compensated under the unfair dismissal provisions. If the detriment could not be compensated under the unfair dismissal provisions because it was not a loss sustained *in consequence of the dismissal*, then there was nothing to take it out of section 47B; and the provisions in section 49, which require compensation for that detriment, should apply. An employee who was dismissed, whether expressly or constructively, was entitled to recover in respect of detriment right up to the point of dismissal. 'Dismissal' in section 47B should be construed to have the same

---

[27] At paras 10.32–10.34.

meaning as the meaning given to it in Part X of the ERA—which was the point in time when the employment was terminated. Chadwick LJ said:

> When the two sections are read together, the proper meaning to be given to the phrase 'the detriment in question amounts to dismissal' is that it excludes detriment which can be compensated under the unfair dismissal provisions. If the detriment cannot be compensated under the unfair dismissal provisions—for the reason that it is not a loss sustained in consequence of the dismissal—then there is nothing to take it out of section 47(B); and the provisions in section 49, which require compensation for that detriment, should apply.[28]

10.75 In a constructive dismissal case, it is not in fact the repudiatory breach itself that constitutes the dismissal, but the acceptance of that repudiatory breach by the employee, thereby terminating the contract.[29] Mr Melia was therefore entitled to compensation for injury to feelings right up to 9 November 2001. Equally, in a case of dismissal by the employer it would be open for the employee to assert that the manner in which disciplinary proceedings were conducted amounted to a detriment for which there could be an injury to feelings award, notwithstanding that the proceedings culminated in dismissal. Thus, in *Virgo Fidelis* (above) an injury to feelings award was made arising in part from deficiencies in the disciplinary steps leading up to dismissal for whistleblowing. It is only injury to feelings consequential on the dismissal itself which is excluded.

10.76 This approach considerably simplifies the issue as to where a detriment amounts to dismissal thereby excluding an injury to feelings claim. One residual issue, however, relates to the case of appeals made against the dismissal decision. Clearly, a detriment in relation to the conduct of an appeal can be taken into account in calculating injury to feelings. What of the decision to uphold the dismissal itself? Strictly, the dismissal might already have taken effect by that time and so the decision on appeal may be said not to amount to dismissal. However, it would be bizarre if injury to feelings were unavailable for a detriment consisting of the fact of the dismissal but were available for a detriment consisting of the fact of the dismissal being upheld. Nor would this be consistent with the reasoning in *Melia*, which emphasizes that the scheme of the legislation is to draw a distinction between detriments which can be compensated by an unfair dismissal claim (albeit restricted to financial losses) and those which cannot. We think the better view, therefore, is that there cannot be an award of injury to feelings in respect of a detriment consisting of the upholding of an appeal on the grounds of a protected disclosure, but we recognize that there is no direct authority on the point.[30]

(c) Injury to feelings—the appropriate amount

10.77 As Mummery LJ noted in *Vento* (at para 50), it is an artificial exercise to seek to translate into hard currency hurt feelings such as upset, frustration, worry, anxiety, mental distress, fear, grief, anguish, humiliation, unhappiness, stress, depression, and so on. In *HM Prison Service v Johnson* [1997] ICR 275 (EAT) Smith J (at 283B-E) set out the following synthesis of relevant principles:

> (i) Awards for compensation for injury to feelings are compensatory. They should be just to both parties. They should compensate fully without punishing the tortfeasor. Feelings of indignation at the tortfeasor's conduct should not be allowed to inflate the award.

---

[28] This closely paralleled the approach taken in *Eastwood v Magnox Electric plc* [2004] UKHL 35, [2004] ICR 1064 (HL) to the scope of what is excluded by the decision in *Johnson v Unisys Ltd* [2001] ICR 480 (HL), that damages are not recoverable at common law for the manner of dismissal. In that context also, the '*Johnson* exclusion area' has been drawn by distinguishing between breaches of contract prior to dismissal and the termination of the contract itself.

[29] See now *Geys v Société Générale, London Branch* [2013] ICR 117 (SC).

[30] See further Bowers and Lewis, 'Non-economic Damage in Unfair Dismissal Cases: What's Left After *Dunnachie*?' (2005) 34 ILJ 83.

(ii) Awards should not be too low, as that would diminish respect for the policy of the anti-discrimination legislation. On the other hand, awards should be restrained, as excessive awards could ... be seen as the way to "untaxed riches."

(iii) Awards should bear some broad general similarity to the range of awards in personal injury cases. ...

(iv) In exercising their discretion ... tribunals should remind themselves of the value in everyday life of the sum they have in mind. This may be done by reference to purchasing power or by reference to earnings.

(v) Finally, tribunals should bear in mind ... the need for public respect for the level of awards made.

10.78   In *Vento v Chief Constable of West Yorkshire Police (No 2)* [2002] EWCA Civ 1871, [2003] IRLR 102, the Court of Appeal gave guidance with regard to the level of awards for injury to feelings in discrimination cases.[31] At paras 65–68 Mummery LJ said this:

Employment tribunals and those who practise in them might find it helpful if this court were to identify three broad bands of compensation for injury to feelings, as distinct from compensation for psychiatric or similar personal injury.

(i)   The top band should normally be between £15,000 and £25,000. Sums in this range should be awarded in the most serious cases, such as where there has been a lengthy campaign of discriminatory harassment on the ground of sex or race. This case falls within that band. Only in the most exceptional case should an award of compensation for injury to feelings exceed £25,000.

(ii)   The middle band of between £5,000 and £15,000 should be used for serious cases, which do not merit an award in the highest band.

(iii)   Awards of between £500 and £5,000 are appropriate for less serious cases, such as where the act of discrimination is an isolated or one-off occurrence. In general, awards of less than £500 are to be avoided altogether, as they risk being regarded as so low as not to be a proper recognition of injury to feelings.

10.79   In *Da'Bell v NSPCC* [2010] IRLR 19, the EAT updated these guidelines in line with the Retail Prices Index so that the top of the bottom band would be £6,000, the middle band £18,000, and the higher band £30,000.[32] In *Local Government Yorkshire and Humber v Shah* (UKEAT/0587/11/ZT, 19 June 2012) (considered further at 10.82 below), the EAT suggested that with inflation and the passage of time, the bands may need to be revised upwards again. With effect from 1 April 2013, civil claims for general damages, including for pain and suffering and mental distress, have been increased by 10 per cent following the decision in *Simmons v Castle* [2013] 1 WLR 1239 (CA). Different panels of the EAT have differed as to whether this applies to discrimination (and by extension detriment) claims.[33] At the time of writing, the issue is due to be resolved by the Court of Appeal.

10.80   Mummery LJ added in *Vento* that there was within each of these bands 'considerable flexibility, allowing tribunals to fix what is considered to be fair, reasonable and just compensation in the particular circumstances of the case'.

10.81   This guidance was followed in the context of a section 47B protected disclosure detriment claim in *Virgo Fidelis Senior School v Boyle* [2004] IRLR 268. The EAT reduced the award made by the tribunal for injury to feelings from £42,500 to £25,000. The EAT did, however, draw attention to the fact that under the *Vento* guidelines the seriousness of the offence is an

---

[31]   In *Miles v Gilbank* [2006] EWCA Civ 543, [2006] IRLR 538, however, the Court of Appeal reminded litigants that *Vento* provided guidance and is not a rule of law.

[32]   See also *Bullimore v Pothecary William Weld* [2011] IRLR 18 (EAT).

[33]   In favour of applying the 10 per cent increase: *Sash Window Workshop Ltd and another v King* [2015] IRLR 348 (EAT); *Beckford v Southwark LBC* [2016] IRLR 178 (EAT). Against applying the 10 per cent increase: *Chawla v Hewlett Packard Ltd* [2015] IRLR 356 (EAT); *Pereira de Souza v Vinci Construction UK Ltd* [2015] ICR 1034 (EAT).

important factor in assessing the impact in terms of injury to feelings and the level of award. In relation to this, the EAT commented (at para 45) that 'detriment suffered by "whistleblowers" should normally be regarded by tribunals as a very serious breach of discrimination legislation'. However, although serious, whistleblowing victimization is not to be regarded as inherently more serious than other forms of discrimination prohibited under EqA such as race or sex discrimination; see *Commissioner of Police of the Metropolis v Shaw* [2012] ICR 464 (EAT).

Further, it is important to keep in mind that the award remains compensatory. The relevance **10.82** of seriousness of the conduct is not in terms of punishing the employer but in the likely impact on the claimant. The focus is on the impact on the particular claimant. That is illustrated by the approach in *Local Government Yorkshire and Humber v Shah* (UKEAT/0587/11/ZT, 19 June 2012), where the EAT upheld an injury to feelings award of £25,000. The claimant, who was employed by a primary care trust, was seconded for a two year period to the respondent as a project director in relation to the 'Get-Connected' project which was designed to set up a Muslim women's network, and which received public funding. She raised concerns, which were found to amount to protected disclosures, in relation to governance, financial probity, and controls, including the level and propriety of expenses paid to expert advisers and consultants. In summary she was found to have been forced out of her role by reason of her disclosures. Her concerns were not investigated until after her resignation, and there was then a whitewash. She was found to have suffered detriments principally consisting of the failure to investigate her concerns, giving her work to someone else (Mrs Arshad-Mather) and by ending the secondment agreement (through constructive dismissal). In relation to the injury to feelings award, the tribunal took into account that her professional background in commissioning meant that she had experienced the need for financial sound judgement and probity in the management of public funds. The fact that her concerns were not investigated went 'right to the core of her professional experience'. She was distressed on returning to work after leave and seeing her work being carried out by Mrs Arshad-Mather (about whom she had raised concerns in relation to expenses). She felt profound feelings of humiliation, moving from being programme director with a good salary to having no job. She found it distressing to be financially dependent on her husband but felt unable to contemplate a role with another employer rather than being self-employed. The tribunal described a 'perfect storm of a respondent failing to investigate and take seriously the claimant's concerns and belief about a lack of financial probity, against a background of a claimant whose career to that date had been engaged in promoting exactly that: the appropriate commissioning and spending of public money'. She was found to be suffering from ongoing symptons of mental distress, some of which was directly due to the detriments. But the tribunal did not accept that she was suffering from post-traumatic stress disorder caused by the detriments and declined to make a separate award for psychiatric injury. The ET concluded that the respondent's actions had an ongoing 'devastating effect' on the claimant and her family, domestic, private, and professional life, and this had not been lessened by the respondent's robust defence to her claims and response since the liability judgment. Having regard to the *Vento* bands and *Da'Bell*, and the need for the award to be compensatory rather than punitive, it made an injury to feelings award of £25,000. Against those findings, the EAT rejected the contention that the award of £25,000 for injury to feelings was excessive. It emphasized that the ET was entitled to have regard to the claimant's distress at her concerns being ignored by the respondent, and that this went to the core of her professional experience and to her ongoing distress. Further (at para 65) the EAT expressly endorsed the ET's self-direction that 'detrimental action against whistleblowers should always be regarded as a very serious breach of discrimination legislation'.

Loss of congenial employment can be taken into account as part of an injury to feelings **10.83** award, and is not a separate head of award (*Ministry of Defence v Cannock* [1994] ICR 918

(EAT) at 942B-943B). Conversely, in England and Wales, aggravated damages are a separate head of award (*Scott v Commissioners of Inland Revenue* [2004] IRLR 713 (CA), and see para 10.100 below).

(d) Medical evidence

10.84 The claimant will need to lead evidence as the basis for an award for injury to feelings, explaining the impact of the detrimental treatment on the claimant; it is not made automatically (see *MOD v Cannock* [1994] ICR 918 (EAT)). Whilst medical evidence may be relevant if asserting that health has been damaged or personal injury suffered, the evidence in support of an injury to feelings claim need not be medical evidence. In *Vento* Mummery LJ emphasized that injury to feelings is not a medical term. In includes '[s]ubjective feelings of upset, frustration, worry, anxiety, mental distress, fear, grief, anguish, humiliation, unhappiness, stress, depression and so on and the degree of their intensity are incapable of objective proof or of measurement in monetary terms'.

(e) Knowledge

10.85 *Skyrail Oceanic v Coleman* [1981] ICR 864 (CA) appeared to decide that injury to feelings could only be made where the treatment was known to be discriminatory and this knowledge caused the injury (and see to this effect *Alexander v Home Office* [1988] ICR 685 (CA) (per May LJ at 693C-D)). There was no statutory basis for that requirement and it was rejected in *Taylor v XLN Telecom Ltd* [2010] IRLR 499 (EAT). *Skyrail* was explained as requiring only that the injury to feelings must be caused by discriminatory treatment, and dicta in *Alexander* were held to be obiter. The EAT added that no doubt the injury to feelings would be greater where the discrimination was overt or the discriminatory motivation known to the claimant.

10.86 These principles apply as follows:

(a) If a tribunal is considering more than one act of detriment, an injury to feelings award can be assessed on a global basis, looking at matters in the round, rather than making separate awards for each act or omission (*Tchoula v ICTS (UK) Ltd* [2000] ICR 1191 (EAT)).

(b) The EAT has held that, where employment is lost, it is permissible to take into account the nature of the employment (eg that it is only an evening job), provided the tribunal is wary not to make generalized assumptions: *Orlando v Didcott Power Station & Sports Social Club* [1996] IRLR 262. That is though necessarily subject to the principle that ultimately the award is focused on the impact on the particular claimant.

(c) Subject to avoiding double-recovery for the same loss, there can in principle be separate awards for injury to feelings and injury to health: *HM Prison Service v Salmon* [2001] IRLR 425 (EAT)).

(d) Pursuant to *MOD v Cannock* [1994] ICR 918 (EAT), the fact that a claimant receives interest on an award should be ignored (although note there is distinct statutory provision for interest on discrimination claims (SI 1996/2803) which does not apply to protected disclosure claims).

(4) Personal injury—psychiatric damage

10.87 Compensation can be awarded in respect of personal injury resulting from discrimination under the race, sex, and disability statutes (or, now, the EqA): see *Sheriff v Klyne (Lowestoft) Ltd* [1999] IRLR 481 where the Court of Appeal ruled that the tribunal (or the county court) can award compensation by way of damages for physical or psychiatric injury consequent upon or caused by the statutory tort of discrimination, since the claimant is entitled to be compensated for the loss and damage actually sustained as a result of the statutory tort. On the basis that the *Virgo Fidelis* line of authority is correct (see paragraphs 10.66–10.70

above), such a personal injury claim could also be made arising out of an ERA, section 47B protected disclosure detriment claim. Stuart Smith LJ in *Sheriff* said that care needed to be taken in any complaint to an employment tribunal under this head where the claim includes, or might include, injury to health as well as injury to feelings. Obtaining a medical report would be well advised especially since the time within which to make a complaint was limited and an adjudication might follow shortly afterwards.

An issue which might need to be addressed is whether the psychiatric damage was fore- **10.88**
seeable. This was the subject of the Court of Appeal's decision (by a majority) in *Essa v Laing Ltd* [2004] EWCA Civ 2, [2004] IRLR 313, a case of direct racial discrimination by the use of racist words. The employment tribunal concluded that the claimant was not entitled to compensation for psychiatric loss suffered in that case because it was not reasonably foreseeable. This was overturned on appeal. A victim of direct discrimination—at least in the form of racial abuse—is entitled to be compensated for the loss which arises naturally and directly from the wrong. Pill LJ said (at para 39) that it is possible that different considerations will apply where the discrimination takes other forms than that in the *Essa* case.

We have seen how the appellate courts have tended to assimilate the principles from sex, **10.89**
race, and disability discrimination law into the protections afforded to whistleblowers, most notably in *Woodward v Abbey National plc (No. 1)* [2006] EWCA Civ 822, [2006] IRLR 677[34] and in *Virgo Fidelis*. It is difficult to find a rational distinction between a victim in the position of Mr Essa and a whistleblower who can show a direct (but not reasonably foreseeable) link between the treatment meted out to him/her and ensuing psychiatric illness. The approach to attribution of loss is discussed further at paragraph 10.61 above.

It is for the claimant to prove both that injury to health has been suffered and that it **10.90**
was caused by the relevant detrimental act or deliberate omission. Medical evidence is not required for an award. In its absence tribunals may make an award based on the 'comparatively minor instances of upset or distress, typically caused by one–off acts or episodes'. But this might instead be dealt with under the heading of injury to feelings as 'in practice the two types of injury are not always easily separable': *HM Prison Service v Salmon* [2001] IRLR 425 (EAT) at para 29.

The most common form of personal injury claim in discrimination cases involves psychi- **10.91**
atric injury. Awards are often made with reference to the *Judicial College Guidelines* (13th edn, Oxford: Oxford University Press, 2015) by which relevant factors to be taken into account in valuing such damage include the injured person's ability to cope with life and work, the effect on the injured person's relationships, the extent of treatment and future vulnerability, prognosis, whether medical help is being sought, and the nature of the abuse and its duration.

There are within these Guidelines four categories of award for psychiatric injury (in each **10.92**
case showing the 10 per cent *Simmons v Castle* uplift for awards post 1 April 2013):[35]

- severe (£41,675 to £88,000 or with a 10 per cent uplift £45,840 to £96,800) where the claimant has marked problems with the above factors and the prognosis is poor;
- moderately severe (£14,500 to £41,675 or with a 10 per cent uplift £15,950 to £45,840) where there are significant problems in relation to the above factors but where the prognosis is more optimistic;

---

[34] Discussed in Chapter 7, paras 7.35–7.39.
[35] See para 10.79 above.

- moderate (£4,450 to £14,500 or with a 10 per cent uplift £4,900 to £15,950) where there has been a significant improvement and the prognosis is good; and
- less severe (£1,170 to £4,450 or with a 10 per cent uplift: £1,290 to £4,900) which will take into account the length of the period affected and the extent to which daily activities and sleep were affected.

10.93 Where the injury is caused in part by the detrimental treatment on the grounds of a protected disclosure, and in part for other reasons, an assessment must be made, albeit on a broad basis, apportioning the extent of the contribution and discounting the award accordingly. On this basis in *HM Prison Service v Salmon* [2001] IRLR 425 (EAT) a psychiatric injury award was reduced by 25 per cent.

(5) Aggravated damages

10.94 Aggravated damages were another issue in the appeal in *Virgo Fidelis* where the tribunal had decided that it did not have the power to make a separate award for aggravated damages. The EAT disagreed and made an award of £10,000 in this respect. In *HM Prison Service v Johnson* [1997] ICR 275, the EAT had held (after citing *Rookes v Barnard* [1964] AC 1129 (HL), and in particular p 1221, per Lord Devlin) that, as a matter of principle, aggravated damages ought to be available to claimants for the statutory torts of sex and race discrimination: the commission of the torts might be sufficiently intentional as to enable the claimant to rely upon malice or the defendant's manner of committing the tort or other conduct as aggravating the injury to feelings.

10.95 Subsequently,[36] the Court of Appeal appeared to have assumed that aggravated damages were available in discrimination cases. In *Virgo Fidelis* the EAT said this:

> The decision whether or not to award aggravated damages and, if so, in what amount must depend on the particular circumstances of the discrimination and on the way in which the complaint of discrimination has been handled. Common sense requires that regard should also be had to the overall magnitude of the sum total of the awards of compensation for non-pecuniary loss made under the various headings of injury to feelings, psychiatric damage and aggravated damage. In particular, double recovery should be avoided by taking appropriate account of the overlap between the individual heads of damage.

10.96 The EAT considered that the extent of overlap would depend on the facts of each particular case. It referred to what Carswell LCJ said in *McConnell v Police Authority for Northern Ireland* [1997] IRLR 625 at para 19, that an award of aggravated damages should not be an extra sum over and above the sum which the tribunal of fact considers appropriate compensation for the injury to the claimant's feelings. Any element of aggravation ought to be taken into account in reckoning the extent of the injury to his/her feelings, for it is part of the cause of that injury. It should certainly not be treated as an extra award which reflects a degree of punishment of the respondent for his/her behaviour. This approach had been followed in *Tchoula v ICTS (UK) Ltd* [2000] ICR 1191. Judge Peter Clark in the EAT had remarked that tribunals sometimes include an element of aggravated damages in their award for injury to feelings and sometimes the awards were expressed separately. However, that was a matter of form rather than substance. The first question must always be, 'do the facts disclose the essential requirements for an award of aggravated damages?'.

10.97 Finally, in *Vento*, where the decisions in *Johnson* and *Tchoula* appeared to have been cited with approval (although *McConnell* was not referred to in the judgment), the Court of

---

[36] *Alexander v Home Office* [1988] ICR 685 (CA); and *Noone v North West Thames Regional Health Authority* [1988] IRLR 195 (CA).

Appeal had stated (at para 67) that the decision whether or not to award aggravated damages depended on the particular circumstances of the discrimination and the way in which the complaint of discrimination had been handled. An award was made of £5,000 for aggravated damages. There must be misconduct of sufficient gravity in the way litigation was conducted: *Ministry of Defence v Fletcher* [2010] IRLR 25 (EAT).

In *Virgo Fidelis*, the EAT rejected the argument that the element of aggravation can be included in the compensation for injury to feelings, as was the *McConnell* approach. The tribunal was in error in coming to the conclusion that it did not have the authority to make an award of aggravated damages, and the EAT decided that a figure of £10,000 should be awarded by way of aggravated damages.[37]   **10.98**

The EAT reviewed the principles applicable to awards of aggravated damages, in a protected disclosure context, in *Commissioner of Police of the Metropolis v Shaw* [2012] ICR 464. The EAT emphasized the compensatory nature of such awards. They may be made on the basis of (a) the manner in which the wrong was committed, or (b) the motive for it, or (c) the respondent's conduct subsequent to the wrongdoing but in relation to it. In each case these matters may add to the degree of distress caused, but as such they are only relevant to aggravated damages if the claimant was aware of them. The EAT also noted that, in relation to conduct subsequent to the wrongdoing, tribunals should be aware of the risks of awarding compensation in respect of conduct which has not been properly proved or examined in evidence, and allowing the scope of the hearing to be disproportionately extended by considering distinct allegations of subsequent misconduct.   **10.99**

The EAT was concerned that making separate awards for aggravated damages rather than including them as part of injury to feelings could 'sometimes if only subconsciously lead tribunals to treat them as punitive'. However, the EAT concluded that a distinct figure could continue to be attributed to aggravated damages since that would make it easier to continue to apply the *Vento* guidelines to the non-aggravated element of the injury to feelings award. Aggravated damages should, however, be a distinct subheading within injury to feelings so as to emphasize the compensatory element. Tribunals should assess whether the totality of the injury to feelings award, including aggravated damages, was fair and proportionate in relation to the totality of suffering caused to the claimant. Tribunals should identify the main considerations which have led them to make the overall award for injury to feelings, specifying any aggravating or mitigating features to which they attach particular weight.   **10.100**

In *Vento* an award had been made of £17,000 for injury to feelings and £20,000 for aggravated damages. The EAT concluded that this was out of line with the conventional scale of aggravated damages awards, which were mainly in the range of £5,000 to £7,500, and it was also exceptional for the aggravated damages to exceed the ordinary injury to feelings. The claimant police officer had been subjected to a false allegation, and disciplinary proceedings had been brought by reason of having raised a protected disclosure about the conduct of other officers. He suffered loss of faith in the Metropolitan Police to whom he had devoted his career. There was a loss of congenial work as he felt the need to move to a different unit, and he continued to feel ostracized and stigmatized as an outsider. However, this fell short of being in the category of the worst cases. It was not a case of prolonged bullying, and the   **10.101**

---

[37] For cases where the employer behaved in a misguided way but not one deserving of aggravated damages, see *Herron v Wintercomfort for the Homeless* (ET Case No 1502519/03), discussed in Chapter 5 (para 5.117) and *Niekrash v South London Healthcare NHS Trust* (UKEAT/0252/11/JOJ, 7 March 2012) (complaints and exclusion of consultant urologist found not to be malicious, though an apology ought to have been more fulsome and made earlier).

false allegations had been dropped rather than proceeding to any disciplinary sanction. The EAT reduced the total award to £30,000, of which £22,500 was attributed to 'core' injury to feelings and £7,500 to aggravation of it.

(6) Exemplary damages

10.102 The EAT also considered the question of exemplary damages in *Virgo Fidelis*, although these damages were not granted in that particular case. The EAT started its discussion with *Rookes v Barnard* (above) where the House of Lords identified the two circumstances in which exemplary damages might be available, namely:

(1) oppressive, arbitrary, or unconstitutional action by the servants of the government; and
(2) where the defendant's conduct had been calculated by him/her to make a profit for him/herself.

10.103 The object of an award of such damages is to punish or deter. Lord Devlin said (at p 412D–I) that the fact that the injury to a claimant had been aggravated by the malice or by the doing of the injury would not normally be justification for an award of exemplary damages; aggravated damages would be sufficient in that type of case. In *Cassell & Co Ltd v Broome* [1972] 1 All ER 801 at 838C, the class of 'servants of government' was extended to 'those who by common law or statute are exercising functions of a governmental character' (per Lord Reid). Finally, the decision in *Kuddus v Chief Constable of Leicester Constabulary* [2002] 2 AC 122 clarified that the availability of exemplary damages was not confined to cases where the tort in question existed prior to 1964 and that 'once the cause of action test no longer exists and the *Rookes v Barnard* test becomes fact-sensitive rather than cause-of-action-sensitive', the EAT could 'see no reason why in principle exemplary damages could not be awarded, provided that the other conditions are made out'. However, 'in the majority of cases aggravated damages would be sufficient to mark the employer's conduct'. The decision in *Kuddus* was applied to a protected disclosure claim in *Virgo Fidelis*, where it was decided that the tests for making such an award were not satisfied. Subsequently, in *Ministry of Defence v Fletcher* [2010] IRLR 25, the EAT held that exemplary damages were only available where the wrongdoing was conscious and contumelious.

(7) Victimization by dismissal of a worker who is not an employee

10.104 By ERA, section 49(6) where a complaint is made under section 48(1A), and the detriment to which the worker is subjected is the termination of his/her worker's contract, and that contract is not a contract of employment, any compensation must not exceed the compensation that would be payable under ERA, Chapter II of Part X if the worker had been an employee and had been dismissed for the reason specified in section 103A (ie on the ground that s/he made a protected disclosure). However, since there is in fact no limit on the compensation that is payable to such an employee this subsection bites only in one important respect. It operates to limit any sums that can be recovered for non-pecuniary damage since these could not be recovered in an unfair dismissal claim (see *Roberts v Wilsons Solicitors LLP* [2016] ICR 659, [2016] IRLR 586, at para 39).

10.105 It does not follow that no sums can be recovered for injury to feelings in a termination of contract case. But any such award would be limited to sums which an employee could receive as 'compensation' in the unfair dismissal claim. It is relatively clear that the basic award should be taken into account as part of the 'compensation' that would be received for unfair dismissal. Although it does not consist of compensation for financial loss, the introductory words of ERA, section 118 make clear that it is part of the award of compensation for unfair dismissal. It is also notable that in the Court of Appeal in *Dunnachie v Kingston* *upon Hull City Council* [2004] EWCA Civ 84, [2004] ICR 481, Sedley LJ expressed the view (at para 48) that:

> for the ordinary case of unfair dismissal, assuming that there is no reinstatement or re-engagement, it is the basic award which is there to compensate for the unfairness.

It might be argued that compensation in an unfair dismissal case could also include the sum **10.106** of between twenty-six and fifty-two weeks' pay by way of an additional award for failing to comply with a re-employment order. However, it is most unlikely that this could be taken into account. There would be no way of assessing in the case of a non-employee whether, if s/he had been an employee, the employer would have failed to comply with such an order, and such a claim flows from the refusal to comply with the order, rather than otherwise being payable by reason of the unfair dismissal.

In substance, therefore, in the case of a non-employee dismissal, the non-pecuniary damage **10.107** award made in respect of a detriment consisting of termination of the worker's contract has a ceiling equivalent to the basic award that would have been payable to an employee in the position of the claimant, since the financial loss would also be recoverable by an employee through the compensatory award.

D. Good Faith

(1) Overview of the good faith provisions (as amended)

As originally enacted the requirement that the disclosure be made in good faith in order **10.108** to be protected played a prominent role in the protected disclosure legislation. It applied to all disclosures other than those made for the purposes of legal advice. Following the amendments by ERRA, the good faith requirement has been substantially downgraded. In relation to qualifying disclosures made on or after 25 June 2013 it is now limited to being a factor falling to be considered at the remedy stage, as a basis for reducing compensation, applicable both to dismissal and detriment claims. As discussed in more detail in Chapter 4, the change reflected in part a recognition that focus on motive, as a basis for removing protection altogether, ran the risk that those in a position to make public interest disclosures would be deterred from doing so on the basis that their motives might be attacked, and that employers would be encouraged to attack the motives of whistleblowers rather than heeding what they had to say.

In relation to detriment claims, the right to bring a claim of detriment (other than dismissal **10.109** of an employee) is provided by section 48(1A) ERA. Section 49(6A) ERA (as amended by the ERRA) then provides:

> (6A) Where—
>   (a) the complaint is made under section 48(1A), and
>   (b) it appears to the tribunal that the protected disclosure was not made in good faith, the tribunal may, if it considers it just and equitable in all the circumstances to do so, reduce any award it makes to the worker by no more than 25%.

The equivalent provision in relation to unfair dismissal claims is set out in section 123(6A) **10.110** ERA, as part of the provisions relating to the compensatory award, as follows:

> **123 Compensatory award**
>   (1) Subject to the provisions of this section and sections 124, 124A and 126, the amount of the compensatory award shall be such amount as the tribunal considers just and equitable in all the circumstances having regard to the loss sustained by the complainant

in consequence of the dismissal in so far as that loss is attributable to action taken by the employer.

...

(6) Where the tribunal finds that the dismissal was to any extent caused or contributed to by any action of the complainant, it shall reduce the amount of the compensatory award by such proportion as it considers just and equitable having regard to that finding.

(6A) Where—

(a) the reason (or principal reason) for the dismissal is that the complainant made a protected disclosure, and

(b) it appears to the tribunal that the disclosure was not made in good faith,

the tribunal may, if it considers it just and equitable in all the circumstances to do so, reduce any award it makes to the complainant by no more than 25%.

10.111 In relation to disclosures made prior to 25 June 2013, the previous test still applies, including the liability-stage good faith requirements. As such where disclosures have been made over a period of time, dating back prior to 25 June 2013, there will be a dual regime, with different tests applied as to whether the disclosure is protected, depending on when it was made.

(2) The Meaning of good faith

(a) Good faith is not synonymous with honesty

10.112 The leading case on the meaning of 'good faith' in the context of protected disclosures is still *Street v Derbyshire Unemployed Workers' Centre* [2004] EWCA Civ 964, [2005] ICR 97, which was decided when good faith was required for liability. The Court of Appeal rejected a submission that good faith merely connoted that the disclosure was made 'honestly' or with 'honest intention'. Instead, in context, good faith focuses on the motive of the person making the disclosure, so that it is open to a tribunal to find that a disclosure was not made in good faith if it was made for some ulterior purpose. Second, however, the Court of Appeal accepted that, in a case of mixed motives, protection is not to be denied merely because there was some ulterior motivation unless that was the dominant or predominant purpose of the disclosure.

10.113 Mrs Street worked as an administrator for the Derbyshire Unemployed Workers' Centre. She was dismissed after making a series of allegations against the manager, which she claimed fell under ERA, section 43G (being made to the treasurer of one of the borough councils that funded the centre) and under section 43C (being made to a councillor who sat on the centre's management committee, and therefore being a disclosure to her employer). Her disclosures included that the manager had committed fraud in setting up a secret account so as to conceal the true level of the centre's assets for the purposes of obtaining funding which was means tested. She also alleged that the manager had made trips abroad for the benefit of other organizations during his working time, that he had frequently instructed the claimant to work for other organizations in her working time for the centre, and that he had shown double standards in the implementation of the centre's equal opportunities policy. At the instigation of the centre's management committee, an investigation was carried out into each of the allegations other than the allegations of fraud (which were believed to be for another body—the local TUC—to look into). Mrs Street refused to cooperate with the investigation by being interviewed because, she said, she did not regard the investigation as truly independent. The internal investigation found the allegations to be unfounded. Following a disciplinary interview, she was dismissed on the grounds that she had made unfounded and libelous allegations and had then refused to cooperate with the investigation. The employment tribunal found that Mrs Street satisfied all the requirements of sections 43C and 43G except good faith. The tribunal therefore found that she had reasonably believed that the information disclosed and the allegations contained in it were substantially true, that she had reasonably believed that she would be subjected to a detriment if she made the disclosure to her employer, and that she had not made the disclosure for the purposes of personal gain. It also found that in all the circumstances it was reasonable for her to make the disclosures. However, the tribunal found that the disclosures had not been made in good faith because Mrs Street had been motivated by personal antagonism to the manager against whom she made the allegations. This decision was upheld by the Court of Appeal.

Auld LJ (giving the leading judgment) questioned the validity of the finding that the disclosure was reasonable in all the circumstances. He noted that this sat uneasily with the finding that it was not made in good faith, and there were indications that the tribunal had focused on the identity of the recipients of the disclosure rather than considering all the circumstances. Notwithstanding this, the findings raised in stark terms the meaning of good faith. The Court of Appeal upheld the conclusion that, even though Mrs Street disclosed what she honestly and reasonably believed constituted serious wrongdoing (in this case including fraud), and was subjected to detrimental treatment as a result, the disclosure had not been made in good faith by reason of her ulterior motive (personal antagonism). **10.114**

(b) Ulterior motive must be the predominant or dominant motive to negative good faith

The Court of Appeal in *Street* acknowledged one potential difficulty in relation to the negativing of good faith on the basis that the worker was actuated by personal antagonism. It was noted that the very fact of the belief that someone has been guilty of a relevant failure, or dissatisfaction with the way a disclosure is handled, may itself lead to hostility or antagonism on the part of the worker. Auld LJ referred to the dictum of Lord Diplock in *Horrocks v Lowe* [1975] AC 135 at 150 (a defamation case), in which he commented that: **10.115**

> A defendant's dominant motive may have been to obtain some private advantage unconnected with the duty or the interest which constitutes the reason for the privilege. If so, he loses the benefit of the privilege despite his positive belief that what he said or wrote was true.
>
> Judges and juries should, however, be very slow to draw the inference that a defendant was so far actuated by improper motives as to deprive him of the protection of the privilege unless they are satisfied that he did not believe that what he said or wrote was true or that he was indifferent to its truth or falsity. The motives with which human beings act are mixed. They find it difficult to hate the sin but love the sinner. Qualified privilege would be illusory, and the public interest that it is meant to serve defeated, if the protection which it affords were lost merely because a person, although acting in compliance with a duty or in protection of a legitimate interest, disliked the person whom he defamed or was indignant at what he believed to be that person's conduct and welcomed the opportunity of exposing it.

To similar effect in *Street* Wall LJ noted that motivation is a complex concept and a person making the disclosure is hardly likely to have warm feelings for the person about whom or the activity about which the disclosure is made. Auld LJ noted that the parallel with qualified privilege in defamation claims is not exact, and that there is a higher threshold of proof to establish malice than might be required for other or lesser forms of bad faith. Notwithstanding this, drawing on the analysis of Lord Diplock, the Court of Appeal concluded that it should only be if the ulterior motive was the dominant or predominant purpose that it could operate to negative good faith. If the dominant or predominant purpose **10.116** of the disclosure was in the public interest then personal antagonism or hostility would not be a basis for removing protection. That said, as noted by the EAT in *Meares v Medway Primary NHS Trust* (EAT/0065/10, 7 December 2010) (at paras 25–34), there is no necessary requirement for a tribunal to spell out all various motives that may impact on a decision. It is open to a tribunal simply to find that a disclosure was not in good faith by reason of an ulterior motive that it identifies as being the sole or predominant motive. This was followed in *Korashi v Abertawe Bro Morgannwg University Local Area Health Board* [2012] IRLR 4 (at para 67), where the EAT noted that the essentially factual nature of the assessment had been highlighted by Rimer LJ in refusing permission to appeal in *Meares* ([2011] EWCA Civ 897).

(c) Legitimate and illegitimate purposes

10.117 The Court of Appeal in *Street* referred to the 'public interest purpose' of the protected disclosure legislation[38] and emphasized that protection is for those making the disclosure 'in the public interest'.[39] This did not mean that there must be some wider public significance of the disclosure, such as to exclude, for example, disclosures by workers as to a breach of their own contracts of employment (as now is intended to be provided for by the requirement for a reasonable belief that disclosure is made in the public interest). It connoted that the motive must be consistent with the aims of the legislation, being principally to remedy, prevent, or facilitate investigation in relation to a relevant failure.

10.118 To this end, Wall LJ commented (at para 71) that:

> the primary purpose for the disclosure of such information by an employee must, I think, be to remedy the wrong which is occurring or has occurred; or, at the very least, to bring the s 43B information to the attention of a third party in an attempt to ensure that steps are taken to remedy the wrong. The employee making the disclosure for this purpose needs to be protected against being victimised for doing so; and that is the protection the statute provides.

10.119 Similarly, Auld LJ (at para 55) noted that resentment against the person who was the subject of the disclosure should not necessarily negative good faith 'if, when making the disclosure, the worker is still driven by his original concern to right or prevent a wrong'.

10.120 The Court of Appeal, however, did not purport to set out a comprehensive list of what could be a legitimate or proper purpose. It left scope for there to be argument (on the facts of a particular case) not only as to what constitutes the dominant purpose, but as to what constitutes a legitimate purpose. Wall LJ emphasized (at para 74) that it would 'be folly to attempt to list what could constitute ulterior motivation or bad faith'.

10.121 In many cases it may be apparent that particular purposes are not legitimate. There might be various reasons for this, such as the pursuance of a grudge, retaliation against a colleague who has in some way harmed the person making the disclosure, general resentment against the employer's policy, a desire for publicity, or deployment of the disclosure as a tactic to obtain some personal advantage.[40] *Street* itself provides an example of personal antagonism as an ulterior motive which was inconsistent with having made the disclosure in good faith. One indication that personal antagonism is the predominant motive may be the intemperate terms in which the disclosure is made. Similarly, if the disclosure is liable to be seen as in response or retaliation to action taken or threatened against the claimant, this may assist in

---

[38] Per Auld LJ at para 56.
[39] Per Auld LJ at para 47.
[40] See also eg *Bleasdale v Healthcare Locums plc* (UKEAT/0324/13/LA, 15 April 2014) (claimant who was herself implicated in wrongdoing made disclosures primarily to further her own cause).

identifying an ulterior motive. Both factors are illustrated by the EAT's decision in *Meares v Medway Primary Care Trust* (EAT/ 0065/ 10, 7 December 2010). The claimant was a nurse who reacted angrily when issues were raised as to turning up late to work. She wrote a letter in response which raised allegations of bullying and harassment, but this letter was found by the tribunal to have been written in a rude and aggressive tone which was indicative that the claimant had been motivated by personal antagonism. The disclosure was therefore found not to have been made in good faith.

There might also be particular suspicion as to the claimant's motives for making a disclo- **10.122** sure where the claimant has some other claim or dispute with the employer. The disclosure might then be seen or portrayed as seeking to procure a personal employment advantage rather than being made in the public interest. In *Bachnak v Emerging Markets Partnership (Europe) Ltd* (EAT/0288/05, 27 January 2006) the claimant was employed by an infrastructure investment adviser. He made disclosures which included allegations that investors had been misled. Some of the disclosures were made after Mr Bachnak had been given notice of termination of his employment and whilst he was serving out his notice. Another was made after he had been summoned to a meeting for copying documents without permission, and yet another after his suspension but before his dismissal. The EAT upheld the tribunal's findings that the disclosures had primarily been made by Mr Bachnak to strengthen his hand in negotiations for a new contract with the respondent or to put pressure on the respondent not to dismiss him. The EAT held that the tribunal had therefore been entitled to find that he had not acted in good faith because he had acted in his personal interest rather than in the public interest.

A potentially more problematic approach, which has occasionally been taken in the face of **10.123** repeated disclosures, has been to assert that the worker was pursuing his own campaign. This was found to be the case in *Morrison v Hesley Lifecare Services Ltd* (EAT/0262/03 and EAT/0534/03, 19 March 2004), where the disclosures relied upon were preceded by disciplinary action taken against the claimant. Mr Morrison resigned from his position as a special support assistant in a school for children exhibiting challenging behaviour. He claimed that he had been constructively dismissed for a reason connected with protected disclosures. Prior to the alleged protected disclosures he had been disciplined for using inappropriate language to colleagues. He had received a further verbal warning in respect of his language and had received a written warning after his line manager had complained of harassment. Mr Morrison in turn made threats through his solicitors against the respondent alleging serious violations of his rights under the Data Protection Act, libel, and slander. After the written warning was administered he made allegations to the Social Services Directorate (9 April and 2 May 2001) and the police Child Protection Unit (10 July 2001), followed by a disclosure to his employer on 11 July 2001. The employment tribunal found that he had latched onto the complaint of whistleblowing after being advised by counsel that a constructive dismissal claim would not succeed. The tribunal concluded that Mr Morrison had not acted in good faith, but had instead sought to deploy the protected disclosure legislation as part of a campaign he had waged against the respondent. The finding was upheld by the EAT, which commented (at para 32) that:

> we bear in mind that this legislation is designed to protect people who no doubt would be regarded as officious at best, and bloody minded at worst. It is in the public interest that people be protected if they make disclosures meeting the specific conditions, and do so in good faith reasonably believing the material before them. It is not Parliament's intention to protect those who simply wage a campaign against their employer.

In context it was not the mere fact of a campaign which drove the tribunal to its conclusion **10.124** of bad faith, but the nature of the campaign and the way the legislation was being deployed.

Thus, mere persistence in pursuing an allegation, or waging a campaign out of a determination to have the employer investigate or remedy a relevant failure, would not negative good faith. The disclosures were not being made for their own end but as a tactical ploy. Essentially the protection provided by the legislation was being abused.

10.125　However, an employee concerned to prevent or address wrongdoing or health and safety concerns may well be expected to pursue the matter determinedly unless assured that the issue is being addressed. There is a danger in that very determination being viewed as waging a 'campaign'. The issue is illustrated by the decision of the EAT in *Ezsias v North Glamorgan NHS Trust* [2011] IRLR 550. Mr Ezsias was a surgeon who held concerns as to the clinical competence of colleagues. His complaints were described by an internal inquiry panel as 'excessively frequent, unacceptably detailed, and unrelenting to an extreme degree'. In turn complaints were made against him by colleagues who were the subject of his complaints. Ultimately he was suspended and then dismissed on the basis of an irretrievable breakdown of relationships with his colleagues. He contended that his complaints amounted to protected disclosures, and that his dismissal was automatically unfair. In his skeleton argument he claimed that there were seventy-five topics that he complained about. The employment tribunal concluded that it did not need to deal with each of these matters because the complaints were part of Mr Ezsias' 'campaign' against certain colleagues and that the real reason why he made the complaints was to further that campaign, and the disclosures were therefore not in good faith.[41] That reasoning was specifically approved by the EAT (at paras 24 and 37). Whilst there were other grounds on which the claim failed, without further explanation this begs the question as to what the purposes of the campaign were. To assert that a campaign was being pursued does not without further explanation address whether it is a campaign to have the relevant failures prevented or dealt with, or whether there is some other ulterior objective of the 'campaign'.

(d) Does a predominant non-public interest motive necessarily negative good faith?

10.126　The decision in *Street* makes clear that once it is established that a worker's predominant motive for making a disclosure was something other than preventing or remedying the relevant failure, or facilitating investigation into it, it is at least open to a tribunal to consider whether the disclosure was made other than in good faith. Some dicta, subsequent to the decision in *Street*, appeared to suggest that an ulterior motive such as personal antagonism would necessarily negative good faith. Thus in *Bachnak v Emerging Markets Partnership (Europe) Ltd* (EAT/0288/05, 27 January 2006) (at para 24), the EAT commented that:

> the statutory protection is afforded to those who make disclosures in the public interest; thus where the predominant purpose is the employee's personal interest, or in the case of *Street*, personal antagonism against a manager, the disclosure will not be made in good faith.[42]

10.127　The better view is that if a tribunal finds that the predominant motive was not the protection of the public interest, it may still find that the motive was not sufficiently illegitimate as to render the disclosure made other than in good faith. In this respect the position was clarified by the EAT's decision in *Dr Y-A-Soh v Imperial College of Science, Technology and Medicine* (UKEAT/0350/14/DM, 3 September 2015). Here the claimant was employed

---

[41] See the EAT's judgment at para 24.

[42] See also to similar effect *Lucas v Chichester Diocesan Housing Association Ltd* (EAT/0713/04, 7 February 2005) at para 39: 'an Employment Tribunal must consider all the evidence and decide for itself whether the dominant or predominant motive is an ulterior one in which case it will not attract the protection.'; *Roberts v Valley Rose Ltd* (EAT/0394/06, 31 May 2007) at para 7.

by the respondent college as a full-time lecturer until her dismissal on 11 January 2012. Following adverse feedback about her lectures she was given a performance warning as to the need to improve. She continued to be rated poorly in feedback. In February 2011 she raised a grievance against the Head of Department (Professor Alford) after being warned she might fail her probationary period. In a probationary review, one of her two academic advisers (Dr McPhail) exaggerated the extent to which he had met the claimant to discuss her teaching. He described one of the two lectures he attended as one of the worst lectures he had ever seen. The panel recommended that her appointment not be confirmed. The claimant then raised a grievance against Dr McPhail. At a subsequent review it was recommended that the claimant's probation be extended and there was criticism of Dr McPhail's supervision. However, after an investigation had cleared Dr McPhail of malpractice, disciplinary proceedings were brought against the claimant for making vexatious allegations. This related to her allegation that he spoon-fed his students, and her having indicated that by this she meant that he had given his students the exam questions. The claimant contended that her comments about students being spoon-fed were protected disclosures and contended that she believed that there was a legal obligation upon lecturers not to undermine the integrity of the examination system, and that the information given by the students that she relayed to the respondent tended to show that Dr McPhail had done so by giving specific information about what would be in an examination question. The EAT overturned a finding that that she had lacked the requisite reasonable belief that she had disclosed information tending to show a breach of a legal obligation. It also upheld the tribunal's finding that the disclosure had been made in good faith. Although the disclosure had been made to defend herself, rather than to prevent, remedy, or cause investigation of the wrongdoing, that did not equate to it being made in bad faith. As the EAT explained (at para 58):

> The fact that a disclosure of information was made by a worker seeking to defend herself against an adverse assessment of her performance does not necessarily mean that the disclosure was made other than in good faith. There is no halfway house between 'good faith' and 'bad faith'; the one is the converse of the other. 'Bad faith' connotes some degree of impropriety in the making of the disclosure. On the ET's findings the disclosure was not made out of spite towards Dr McPhail but rather to illustrate why some lecturers might be more popular with students than others, hence rendering the SOLE [system of online evaluation] marks an unfair way of assessing a lecturer's performance. The ET correctly applied the words of the statute; it had regard to the guidance in *Street*, and we do not think it erred in law.

10.128 As the decision illustrates, if an employee primarily acts in his or her own personal interest, *Street* does not compel a tribunal to find that this necessarily negatives good faith. Indeed, that issue did not arise in *Street*. It was only necessary to determine whether a tribunal had been entitled to find that Mrs Street had not acted in good faith due to having acted out of personal antagonism, not to conclude that it was bound to find this. *Street* was not a case in which the court was faced with a tribunal having found that an employee had acted in good faith despite primarily acting in her own personal interest.

10.129 Consistently with this, in *Street* Auld LJ (with whom Jacob LJ agreed), in the context of comparing the good faith requirement with the requirement in section 43G ERA that the disclosure must not be for personal gain, commented (at para 50) that whilst there was scope for motivation of personal gain to negative good faith, there might still be a sufficiently justified motivation to pass the good faith requirement. He also noted (at para 53) that:

> in considering good faith as distinct from reasonable belief in the truth of the disclosure, it is clearly open to an employment tribunal, where satisfied as to the latter, to consider nevertheless whether the disclosure was not made in good faith because of some ulterior

motive, which may or may not have involved a motivation of personal gain, and/or which, in all the circumstances of the case, may or may not have made the disclosure unreasonable. Whether the *nature or degree of any ulterior motive* found amounts to bad faith . . . is a matter for its assessment on a broad basis. (emphasis added)

10.130 As this emphasizes, ultimately the tribunal must apply the statutory test of whether the disclosure was made in good faith. Whilst, having regard to the underlying purposes of the legislation, motive is relevant to good faith, the tribunal must still consider not only the degree of any ulterior motive (including whether it is the predominant motive), but also the nature of the ulterior motive, and whether this is such that, in all the circumstances, good faith is negatived. Similarly, whilst in his concurring judgment, Wall LJ observed that the primary purpose of the disclosure must be to remedy the wrong or cause it to be remedied, he also added (at para 72) that:

it will, of course, be for the tribunal to identify those different motives, and nothing in this judgment should derogate from the proposition that the question for the tribunal at the end of the day as to whether a person was acting in good faith will not be: did the applicant have mixed motives? It will always be: was the complainant acting in good faith?

10.131 Similarly, in *Meares v Medway Primary Care Trust* (EAT/0065/10, 7 December 2010), the EAT concluded that an employment tribunal had not erred in finding that a disclosure was not made in good faith because it was instead motivated by personal antagonism. However, the EAT disapproved of the formulation that if the main motive for the disclosure *was* personal antagonism to the claimant's manager then it *could not* be regarded as in good faith. The EAT stated (at para 40) that:

we would prefer the formulation that a Tribunal was entitled to hold it was not in good faith, because plainly, as it seems to us, every case must depend upon its own facts and this must particularly be so when it comes to issues as complex as motivation. [43]

10.132 Several employment tribunal decisions illustrate (a) the proposition that a disclosure might be made in good faith even though there is no predominant motive of remedying or preventing the relevant failure, or facilitating its investigation; and (b) the need to stand back and consider directly the statutory test of 'good faith' rather than focusing only on the question of whether there is a predominant ulterior motive. The following provides some examples.

• *Speyer v Thorn Security Group Ltd and others* (ET Case No 2302898/03, 20 August 2004) concerned disclosures made by the claimant in the course of an investigation by the Manhattan District Attorney into potential fraud and financial irregularity by the parent company of the claimant's employer. Mr Speyer was asked by his employer to assist it in cooperating with the investigation. A meeting was held with the District Attorney, which his employers attended, when information relied on as being protected disclosures was provided by Speyer. The disclosures were treated as made under ERA, section 43C(1)(a) as the employers were represented at the meeting with the District Attorney, and under section 43C(2) as they were made in accordance with a procedure authorized by the employer, albeit on an ad hoc basis. The tribunal found that the disclosures were made in good faith, notwithstanding that Mr Speyer had emphasized that he was only acting on instructions in making the disclosures. Although (since the decision preceded the Court of Appeal's decision in *Street*) the tribunal equated good faith with honest intention, it was apparent from the tribunal's findings that this did not affect the decision. In

---

[43] This was specifically approved by Rimer LJ (at para 16) in refusing permission to appeal in *Meares* [2011] EWCA Civ 897.

particular, although the tribunal found that Mr Speyer had used the opportunity to seek to establish his own innocence of any illegality, the tribunal regarded this as incidental only. However, even if the predominant purpose had been to establish Mr Speyer's own innocence, or if his predominant purpose had been to act in accordance with instructions to cooperate, that would not necessitate a finding of bad faith, especially when set against the tribunal's finding that he disclosed all that he knew that might be of interest to the enquiry.

- *Green v First Response Training and Development Ltd* (ET Case No 250542/03, 13 April 2002): Mr Green was employed by a company which provided training and education services, and which was partly funded by the local council. He became concerned that the employer was invoicing for more hours of training than were being provided to the students. He raised concerns with the employer, in the form of the sole director and shareholder (E), but there was a failure to provide him with documentary evidence to allay his concerns. Subsequently, Mr Green's employment was terminated, but he was allowed to continue working whilst he sought alternative employment. Whilst still working for the respondent he raised further concerns. These included concerns raised with the relevant examination body about E's conduct of examinations and, having looked at the employer's paperwork and records, concerns raised with the principal of the funding college that E had submitted exaggerated and fraudulent claims for funding. The tribunal was satisfied that Mr Green had been dismissed for making a protected disclosure under section 43G. It rejected the employer's contention that the disclosures had not been made in good faith. However, the tribunal noted that Mr Green had been 'rightly concerned about the impact upon his own reputation and that of his colleagues, had the wrongdoing come to light in other circumstances'. The tribunal plainly regarded this as a legitimate motive for the disclosure. If the issue is considered in terms of whether there was an ulterior motive, it might be argued that in those circumstances Mr Green would have been acting in his own personal interest rather than in the public interest. But that did not entail that he was not acting in good faith.

- The decision of the employment tribunal in *Smith and others v Ministry of Defence* (ET Case No 1401537/04, 26 April 2005) also illustrates the difficulties which may arise in applying a test of predominant motive, rather than considering whether there is bad faith. The claimants were part of the Ministry of Defence Guard Force (known as MGS) stationed at a base in Bristol. Their concerns arose because a colleague (T) was permitted to return to work after a period of suspension and investigation following his conviction for indecent assault on an eight-year-old girl. Outside the base, about fifty metres from one of the guard points, there was a nursery used by children of the staff engaged at the base. The team initially raised internally their objections to T being permitted to return to work. They were told that the decision was final and that disciplinary action would follow if they did not abide by this and work alongside T. The claimants then raised their concerns both with the local MP and with the press. There were further steps that could have been taken to pursue the matter internally with higher levels of management or through the whistleblowing procedure but this was not done. The claimants were dismissed for gross misconduct following the press reports. It was argued that they had made protected disclosures to the press consisting of information tending to show that the health and safety of the children in the nursery had been, was being, or was likely to be endangered. The tribunal held that there was no qualifying disclosure as the requisite reasonable belief was lacking. It also held that the disclosure was not made in good faith. The proximity of the nursery was part of the claimants' concerns, but, in the tribunal's view, their principal motivation was their 'strongly held revulsion' at having to work with T due to the crime for which he had been convicted. The concerns expressed in relation to the nursery, though genuine, were (the tribunal held) the vehicle through which the claimants sought to justify their instinctive feelings of revulsion towards T and their objections to working with him.

The employment tribunal therefore drew a distinction between the concern as to health and safety at the nursery (which it regarded as a genuine but subsidiary and unreasonable concern) and the revulsion towards T due to his crime and the consequent objection to working with him (which it considered to be an ulterior motive). But it is notable that the tribunal directed itself, purporting to follow *Street*, that 'the disclosure will not be made in good faith if an ulterior motive was the dominant or predominant purpose of making it'. It therefore did not go on expressly to consider whether, on the basis that it had identified an ulterior motive, this meant that the disclosure was made in bad faith having regard to both the nature of the identified ulterior motive and the fact that the concerns in relation to health and safety were genuine. Applying the test of whether there was a predominant ulterior motive may not necessarily have led to the same conclusion as might have been reached if the tribunal had then asked whether the fact that the primary motivation was revulsion at T's crime meant that the (genuine) concerns had not been raised in good faith.

(3) 'Appears to the tribunal . . .'

10.133 In both section 49(6A) and section 123(6A) ERA, the legislation does not simply provide that a reduction falls to be made where the disclosure was not made in good faith. Instead there is reference to whether it 'appears to the tribunal' that the disclosure was not made in good faith. We suggest that phrase serves to make clear that this is not an issue which the tribunal is compelled to address in any event, irrespective of whether it was raised by the parties. But it permits an adjustment based on an assessment from the material before the tribunal. In that respect it may be compared to the use of a similar phrase in section 207A TULRCA in respect of the effect of failure to follow a statutory code.[44]

(4) Burden of proof and drawing of inferences

10.134 Prior to the amendments introduced by the ERRA, when good faith was a condition for protection (except in relation to section 43D ERA), the burden of proving that a disclosure was not made in good faith was on the employer: *Bachnak v Emerging Markets Partnership (Europe) Ltd* (EAT/0288/05, 27 January 2006) (at para 25);[45] *Lucas v Chichester Diocesan Housing Association Ltd* (EAT/0713/04, 7 February 2005). We suggest that is still the case under the amended provisions. The reasoning which previously led to that conclusion at liability stage continues to apply. If it is not shown that the disclosure was not in good faith, the provision for a reduction in the award does not arise.

10.135 In *Lucas* the EAT emphasized that the evidence as a whole must be cogent in order to establish absence of good faith. This was said to be because absence of good faith is a serious allegation and an unusual and surprising feature in an employment relationship. In part, that reasoning is unconvincing. First, the EAT relied upon the dictum of Lord Nicholls in *Re H (Minors) (Sexual Abuse: Standard of Proof)* [1996] AC 563 (HL) for the proposition that the more serious the allegation, the more cogent the evidence is required to be to prove it. Subsequent authorities have clarified that this is a misinterpretation of what Lord

---

[44] A similar phrase is used in the context of interim relief (s.129(1)), where the tribunal are engaged in an assessment as a matter of impression (see para 10.50 above). However we suggest that limited help is derived from that comparison given the very different context, since in relation to interim relief the tribunal is not engaged in a final determination of the issue.

[45] See para 10.122 above.

Nicholls said in *Re H*: see *Re S-B* [2009] UKSC 17, [2010] 1 AC 678 at para 13; *Re B* [2008] UKHL 35, [2009] AC 11; *Re D* [2008] UKHL 33, [2008] 1 WLR 1499. The standard of proof remains the balance of probability. In deciding a case on the balance of probabilities a court or tribunal will need to take into account, to the extent appropriate on the particular facts, the inherent probabilities. In some cases the unusual nature of what is alleged may, as a matter of good sense, bear on the inherent likelihood of it occurring. However, that is necessarily dependent on the particular circumstances, and there is no necessary connection between seriousness and inherent probability: see eg *Re B* per Lord Hoffmann at para 15, per Baroness Hale at paras 72 and 73; *Re S-B* at paras 12–14.

It is not necessarily the case that acting for an ulterior motive must be regarded as an **10.136** unusual and surprising feature in an employment relationship. Various factors will bear on how likely or surprising it would be for the worker to have made the disclosure for an ulterior motive. If the disclosure is in the context of a strained relationship or where a worker has some other apparent grounds for dissatisfaction, such as where the worker has been passed over for a promotion or a pay rise, it may be far from surprising that there is an ulterior motive.

In other respects, however, we suggest that there is force in the approach of requiring cogent **10.137** evidence before making a finding of lack of good faith, and that this should not be affected by the test of what 'appears to the tribunal'. It is indeed the case that, notwithstanding relegation of the good faith issue to a remedy matter, a finding that a worker has not acted in good faith in making the disclosure is a serious allegation. It may have ramifications for the worker's reputation beyond its immediate impact on the compensation. There remains a temptation for an employer to attack the messenger rather than to listen to the message, and it would be unfortunate if that were to be encouraged by too readily accepting allegations of lack of good faith.

As to the evidential basis for inferring that a disclosure was not made in good faith, a wide **10.138** range of factors might be relevant as a basis for drawing appropriate inferences. Relevant considerations are likely to include the following.

- The potential ulterior motives arising out of the personal circumstances of the employee. Thus, if the employee has reason to be resentful of the employer, or has an opportunity to gain an employment advantage, an employer may seek to identify this as the predominant motivation for the disclosure.
- The means by which the disclosure is made—which may be regarded as telling in relation to the true motivation. Thus, in the case of *Smith and others v Ministry of Defence* (see paragraph 10.132 above), the fact that disclosure was made to the press was influential in the employment tribunal's decision. The tribunal's view was that if the safety of the children in the nursery had been the claimants' primary concern, they would not have broadcast this to the public at large, but would have used the respondent's whistleblowing procedure or approached the nursery or the relevant regulator (Ofsted) or the appropriate Minister.
- The timing of the disclosure. Thus, if the disclosure is made long after the employee became aware of the alleged relevant failures despite opportunities to raise the matter earlier, this may, if unexplained, be regarded as material. This was regarded by the tribunal as significant in *Mehdaoua v Demipower* (ET Case No 2201602/04, 11 January 2005) where an allegation of fraud was made by the claimant's manager. The unexplained delay between the alleged wrongdoing and the disclosure, taken together with the fact the disclosure was made when a colleague had been or was about to be dismissed, was treated by the tribunal as indicating an absence of good faith and that the disclosure had in fact been made in support of the colleague.

- Whilst pursuant to ERA, section 43L there can be a disclosure of information not-withstanding that the recipient of the information is already aware of it on the basis of drawing it to his/her attention,[46] if the worker was aware that the matter was already being addressed that may impact on the assessment of good faith. This was a consideration in *Phipps v Bradford Hospitals NHS Trust* (EAT/531/02, 30 April 2003). The claimant was a consultant surgeon. He wrote to the hospital's medical director raising concerns as to treatment of breast cancer patients, and referring to his obligation to raise this under General Medical Council guidelines. However, the EAT upheld a finding that the letter was written with a view to establishing his position and making clear to the respondent that it was not to be lightly challenged. In support of that finding the employment tribunal noted that the issue raised had already been the subject of a report and discussion within the respondent. Other factors also indicating a lack of good faith were (a) that immediately prior to writing the letter Mr Phipps had had a meeting with the medical director following an investigation of interpersonal relationships and was suspicious as to whether the chief executive was, in his words, 'trying to shaft him', and (b) a failure to set out information in the letter or subsequently to enable the respondent to investigate.

- The worker's conduct after making the disclosure. An ulterior motive might (as in *Street* and *Phipps*) be indicated by a refusal to cooperate with the investigation or to provide further details without good reason, thereby undermining the policy of enabling the matter to be investigated. Similarly, in *Nese v Airbus Operations Ltd* (UKEAT/0477/13/DA, 27 January 2015), the EAT held (at para 59), that it was permissible to look at what happened after a disclosure was made for evidence as to the claimant's motivations at an earlier stage. In that case, the EAT commented that, given that the claimant continued to repeat the same points (relating to concern as to safety risks) even after there was no reasonable basis for so doing, and after various relevant assurances had been given, it was open to the employer and an ET to draw the inference that he never really believed those matters originally and had a different motivation for making the allegations. Here the ET had not made clear findings as to this, but nothing turned on that as the reason for dismissal was the repetition of concerns without any reasonable basis after relevant assurances were given, which was found to be not in good faith but instead motivated by anger and mistrust of managers.

- Generally, a tribunal may consider the claimant's conduct in the round to assess whether the claimant has acted in the way to be expected if the disclosure was being made for a legitimate purpose: see eg *Muchesa v Central and Cecil Housing Care Support* (EAT/0443/07, 22 August 2008), discussed in Chapter 3 (at paragraph 3.70).

(5) Allegations of lack of good faith need to be clearly advanced

10.139 The EAT in *Lucas v Chichester Diocesan Housing Association Ltd* (EAT/0713/04, 7 February 2005) also emphasized that if an allegation of improper motivation is to be made this should be made explicit in advance and put squarely to the claimant in cross-examination. This has, however, been qualified in two subsequent EAT decisions, *Roberts v Valley Rose Ltd* (EAT/0394/06, 31 May 2007) and *Meares v Medway Primary Care Trust* (EAT/0065/10, 7 December 2010). In *Lucas* allegations as to an ulterior motive were first raised in closing submissions. The tribunal decided that the disclosures (as to financial irregularities) were made out of spite because Ms Lucas' hours had been reduced. Not only was this not an allegation

---

[46] But see the discussion of *Cavendish Munro Professional Risk Management Ltd v Geduld* [2010] ICR 325, EAT in Chapter 3 at paras 3.29–3.30 as to the meaning of disclosure.

that had been trailed in the notice of appearance, but the relevant allegation was not put to her in cross-examination.[47] *Lucas* was distinguished in *Roberts*, where (a) a broad allegation of lack of good faith had been set out in the Grounds of Resistance and therefore put the claimant on notice that she would have to defend an allegation of bad faith, (b) the materials relevant to the allegation were exchanged in standard disclosure, (c) the allegation was set out in a witness statement (albeit served only five days before the hearing), and (d) there was then cross-examination on the point. As such there was an opportunity to rebut the allegation, and an attempt to do so.

In *Meares* the EAT posed itself the question of what was meant by the requirement that the allegation be clearly made 'in advance'. It noted that this begged the question: in advance of what? The EAT concluded that, provided a reasonable opportunity is made available for the claimant to rebut a suggestion of lack of good faith, the critical time before which the allegation must be made is before the tribunal begins to consider the decision after the end of evidence and submissions. In *Meares* the EAT noted that if the claimant had been put at a disadvantage by such an allegation being raised for the first time in submissions, it would have been open to the claimant to ask for an adjournment or to call for further evidence to deal with the point, and indeed the EAT commented that it would have been expected that the claimant's counsel would have done so.[48] Notwithstanding that observation, if the issue is first raised in submissions the respondent would be at risk of a tribunal refusing to permit the allegation to be pursued if evidence could have been called which would have affected the issue. In *Meares* itself, although express reference to want of good faith was first made in submissions, questions had been put in cross-examination to the claimant as to her motives for making the disclosure. The EAT noted that given that this was the substantive basis for challenging want of good faith, this was far more helpful than simply asking about good faith, which may have simply begged the question as to what was meant by this. The claimant had therefore been given a fair chance to answer the allegation in evidence, and had also had the final word in submissions, so there was said to be no procedural unfairness. Further, as Rimer LJ noted in refusing permission to appeal ([2011] EWCA Civ 897), the failure to plead the good faith defence was not surprising in the particular circumstances in *Meares* because of the highly imprecise way in which the protected disclosure point had been set out in the claim form.

10.140

(6) Unfair dismissal remedies and good faith

(a) Relationship with reduction for contributory fault

The power to reduce the compensatory award for want of good faith is separate and additional to the general provision under section 123(6) ERA to make a reduction for contributory fault. It differs from the contributory fault provision in that there is no requirement to show any causation of or contribution to the dismissal. That in turn begs a question as to whether the tribunal could circumvent the limit of 25 per cent on the reduction for good faith by making a further reduction in relation to lack of good faith under the heading of contributory fault. One argument against this is that it would be contrary to the statutory scheme. By placing a limit on the extent of the reduction for not acting in good faith, a

10.141

---

[47] *Lucas* was followed by the EAT in *Doherty v British Midland Airways Ltd* (2006) IRLR 90 at para 39. The EAT emphasized the need clearly to put allegations of malice by the claimant in the context of a claim of constructive dismissal on the ground of trade union activities.

[48] See to similar effect the comments of Rimer LJ in refusing permission to appeal in *Meares*: [2011] EWCA Civ 897 at para 34.

balance is struck between (a) not overcompensating those who act for an ulterior motives, and (b) seeking not to deter workers from raising the alarm for fear that their motives will be attacked. The counter-argument is that there is no inconsistency in allowing a further reduction for contributory fault, since a reduction can be made to the compensatory award under the heading of contributory fault only if the ulterior motive was causatively relevant to the dismissal. The extent of the influence on the decision, in a case where the employer dismisses in part because of the belief that the worker is acting in bad faith, might be regarded as justifying a larger reduction.

10.142 There is, however, a further hurdle to making a reduction related to good faith under section 123(6) ERA. The reduction for contributory fault under section 123(6) only applies to any 'action' by the claimant. But where the reduction relates to a protected disclosure not being in good faith, the relevant action is the protected disclosure itself. The making of the disclosure otherwise than in good faith is not of itself a separate 'action' of the claimant. Without more, the 'action' is the making of the protected disclosure itself and it would be inconsistent with the legislation to treat this as 'blameworthy' conduct.

10.143 We suggest therefore that the better view is that there can only be a further reduction in relation to good faith under the heading of contributory fault if this manifests itself in some blameworthy conduct other than the making of the disclosure itself. But in a case where there is found to be a lack of good faith it may well be the case that there is some such conduct. Indeed the lack of good faith might be inferred from some other conduct of the claimant. In those circumstances there would seem to be nothing to prevent a further reduction provided that the tribunal stands back to have regard to the whole picture and to determine that as a whole the extent of the reduction for contributory fault and lack of good faith is appropriate.

10.144 The scope for related conduct to lead to a reduction is illustrated by the decision in *Aryeetey v Tuntum Housing Association* (EAT/0324/08, 8 April 2009), which preceded the amendment to the legislation to relegate good faith to a remedy-stage issue. In *Aryeetey* the claimant was the respondent's finance director. He made disclosures, initially internally, alleging breach of internal financial procedures by the chief executive. He then, on 11 April 2005, made a disclosure to the housing corporation, repeating the allegations and also alleging interference with his investigation into these matters. This was found by the ET to be the trigger which led the respondent first to require the claimant to apologize to the chief executive, then to suspend the claimant, later to discipline him, and eventually to dismiss him.[49] The respondent did dismiss him, notwithstanding that prior to completion of the disciplinary process it had received a report which vindicated the claimant's concerns as to financial irregularities, although it also exonerated the chief executive of any dishonesty. The ET found that the claimant had made protected disclosures, with the disclosure to the housing corporation having been made pursuant to ERA, section 43F. He had been subjected to detriments (being required to apologize and suspension) and then dismissed by reason of his protected disclosures. However, after being suspended the claimant had made a further disclosure to the housing corporation which went beyond his previous disclosures in that it made an allegation of dishonesty on the part of the chief executive for an ulterior motive. As the ET noted, this was a response to being victimized. The ET commented that:

> As to what motivates the Claimant in terms of these disclosures: by now he was beleaguered and had been unfairly treated and could see his dismissal round the corner. He

---

[49] See the summary of Smith LJ in refusing permission to appeal to the Court of Appeal: [2010] EWCA Civ 1088 at para 3.

threw caution to the winds in what was an attempt to get the Housing Corporation to investigate; the aim obviously being that this would ward off his dismissal. Nevertheless he should not have effectively accused Mr Renwick of dishonesty.

This did not prevent a finding of unfair dismissal, because it was the earlier protected **10.145** disclosures that had been the trigger. However, taking into account this conduct, there was a 25 per cent reduction for contributory fault.[50] Further, at a subsequent remedies hearing, the ET found that following his dismissal the claimant had engaged in a sustained campaign to show that the respondent's chief executive was dishonest. After the liability hearing, the claimant pressurized the housing corporation for an inquiry. It found no evidence of dishonesty. He then wrote to the police (with copies to other bodies) alleging that the respondent was guilty of fraudulent accounting and possibly of theft. The police found no evidence of any criminal practices. The ET held at the remedies hearing that the claimant's motive was a vendetta and that the claimant could not have had a reasonable belief in the truth of the accusation that the chief executive was dishonest. Instead, he had become unreasonably obsessed and 'gone over the borderline from good faith into bad faith in persisting with his allegations'. Therefore, the ET considered that if the claimant had remained in the respondent's employment he would have been dismissed at least by the time of a letter he wrote to the police of 16 April 2007. The respondent would not have been acting unfairly in dismissing him for persisting in making the disclosures as he had written to the police showing 'his obsession to destroy [the chief executive of his employers]'. Therefore, he was awarded no compensation for the period after 16 April 2007.[51] Yet, especially in light of the findings as to what led to the disclosures which prompted a reduction for contributory fault, it would seem doubtful that the further disclosures would have been made if the claimant had remained in employment and not been victimized. The reduction for want of good faith by the claimant after he had been dismissed appears to have been unwarranted.

Any deduction under section 123(6A) ERA is applied after calculating the net loss, includ- **10.146** ing after offsetting any contractual or ex gratia termination payments (other than redundancy payments): *Digital Equipment Co Ltd v Clements (No 2)* [1997] ICR 237 (EAT), [1998] ICR 258 (CA), *MoD v Wheeler* [1998] 1 WLR 637 (CA). That would indicate that any *Polkey* reduction for the chance that the employment would have terminated in any event should also be made prior to other deductions (see *Allen v Queen Mary University of London* (UKEAT/0265/15/JOJ, 11 April 2016)).

Where there are percentage reductions to be made under section 123(6A), or for contribu- **10.147** tory fault, or any adjustment for non-compliance with the ACAS code, it makes no difference to the calculation in which order the deductions are made. But care will be needed to avoid double counting where there is an overlap, as may be the case if making a reduction both for lack of good faith, and in relation to contributory conduct which may be a manifestation of the lack of good faith.

(b) Good faith and the basic award

Although section 123(6A) refers to a power to reduce 'any award', in context and given that **10.148** it has been placed within section 123 ERA, it would seem to refer specifically to the compensatory award. There is no separate provision permitting a reduction on the grounds of

---

[50] An appeal by the employer against the liability finding was rejected. There was no appeal by the claimant against the finding of contributory fault: EAT/0070/07, 12 October 2007.

[51] Permission to appeal was refused by Mummery LJ ([2009] EWCA Civ 974 at 1374), and an attempt to reopen the case was also refused by Smith LJ ([2010] EWCA Civ 1088).

lack of good faith in respect of the basic award. It might be argued that there may be scope for this to be taken into account under section 122(2) ERA, which provides a power for the tribunal to reduce the amount of the basic award where it would be just and equitable to do so having regard to any conduct of the claimant prior to dismissal. The absence of any express provision for a reduction for good faith might be explained on the basis that, unlike in relation to the compensatory award, there is no requirement under section 122(2) ERA for the pre-termination blameworthy conduct to be a cause of the dismissal: see *British Gas Trading Ltd v Price* (UKEAT/0326/15/DM, 22 March 2016). As discussed at paragraph 10.142 above, however, one difficulty with that argument is that lack of good faith is not of itself conduct. That is not a difficulty insofar as the lack of good faith manifests itself in some conduct distinct from making the disclosure by reference to which a reduction in the award is considered appropriate. But so far as making the protected disclosure itself is concerned, it may be said that this should not be a basis for reducing the award given that the conduct must be culpable or blameworthy: *Langston v Department for Business, Enterprise and Regulatory Reform* (UKEAT/0534/09/ZT, 9 March 2010). It can be said that there would be an inconsistency in treating the disclosure as a protected disclosure, yet to treat the making of it as culpable or blameworthy. Further, the legislative decision not to make a comparable provision about the basic award may be regarded as indicating a legislative intention that a reduction on this basis should be confined to the compensatory award.

(c) Good faith and re-employment orders

10.149 There is also no express provision for taking into account lack of good faith in assessing whether an order for reinstatement or re-engagement should be made. There is, however, scope to take into account lack of good faith, either where this caused or contributed to the dismissal (section 116(3)(c) ERA) or because it has an impact on practicability of the order (section 116(3)(b) ERA), perhaps due to loss of trust and confidence in the employee or because of the consequent acrimony in working relationships (although in a large employer consideration would need to be given as to whether this could be overcome by re-engagement in a different area[52]), or as part of the general discretion as to whether to make such an order (see paragraphs 10.10 and 10.11 above). The scope for such considerations is illustrated by the decision in *Nothman v Barnet LBC (No 2)* [1980] IRLR 65 (CA), albeit preceding the protected disclosure legislation, where it was considered impracticable to reinstate the employee in the light of her allegations that there had been a longstanding conspiracy from her colleagues to remove her from her job. Ormrod LJ commented (at para 4) that:

> It is only right to say that anyone who believes that they are a victim of conspiracy, and particularly by their employers, is not likely to be a satisfactory employee in any circumstances if reinstated or re-engaged.

10.150 Whilst those comments need to be treated with caution given the change of environment brought about by the introduction of the protected disclosure legislation, they may still be particularly pertinent in a case where disclosures have been made in bad faith.

10.151 If, notwithstanding lack of good faith, the tribunal makes a re-employment order, it can only order a reduction in the amount of back pay to be ordered if the claimant caused or contributed to the dismissal. There is no provision equivalent to section 123(6A) ERA permitting a reduction due to lack of good faith irrespective of whether this contributed to the dismissal.

---

[52] See eg *Lincolnshire County Council v Lupton* (UKEAT/0328/15/DM, 19 February 2016).

(7) Case management

Now that good faith is a remedy issue only, it is likely to be important to clarify whether   **10.152**
it is a matter to be addressed during the liability stage of any hearing. In most cases where
good faith is in issue, it is likely that there will also be an issue as to whether there was a reasonable belief that disclosure was made in the public interest. Given that the public interest
test entails focusing on the claimant's set of beliefs, there is likely to be a close overlap in the
evidence considered on that issue with the matters relied upon in relation to whether disclosure was in good faith, and as such ordinarily the appropriate course will be for evidence
to be heard and tested relevant to the good faith issue at the same time as dealing with the
liability issues.

(8) Costs and good faith

Prior to the amendments relegating lack of good faith to a remedy issue, where a tribunal   **10.153**
found that a disclosure was not made in good faith, but instead for an ulterior motive, there
was liable to be a substantial risk of an adverse costs order on the basis that the claimant acted
unreasonably in bringing or conducting the proceedings.[53] In *Clark v Clark Construction
Initiatives Ltd* [2008] ICR 635, the EAT (at para 114) held that the tribunal was entitled
to conclude that it was unreasonable to bring the particular protected disclosure claim that
had failed because the disclosure had been shown not to have been made in good faith;
rather, it had been raised as a negotiating tactic (para 24). The EAT said that the claimant
was in a position to know that he had not made the complaint to the employers in good
faith, in the sense that it was not for a purpose which the law is willing to protect. That was
not something that would only have become obvious after the evidence had been heard, and
it followed that the claimant was seeking to recover compensation notwithstanding that he
ought to have known that the claim would not succeed. In the EAT's view, that justified the
tribunal in concluding that the claimant's conduct was unreasonable.[54]

Following the amendments introduced by ERRA rendering good faith a remedy issue only,   **10.154**
this line of argument focusing solely on good faith is no longer available. However, it may
still be adapted, and remain persuasive if, alongside a finding of lack of good faith, a tribunal
also finds that the worker did not hold a genuine belief that the disclosure was made in the
public interest.

---

[53] Now set out in Employment Tribunals (Constitution and Rules of Procedure) Regulations 2013 (SI
2013/1237), Sch 1, rule 76.
[54] See also *Milne v The Link Asset and Security Company Ltd* (EAT/0867/04, 26 September 2005), where
a costs order was upheld by the EAT in the light of the tribunal's finding that the claimant made allegations
of illegality without any genuine belief in them and had brought the claim in order to put pressure on the
employer.

11

EMPLOYMENT TRIBUNAL PROCEDURE AND ALTERNATIVE DISPUTE RESOLUTION

11.01 General questions of procedure are dealt with in other texts to which the reader is referred.[1] We consider here those points that are or may be peculiarly apposite to whistleblowing cases. We begin with tactical considerations as to what should go into claim forms and responses in such cases, then move to points about the hearing, and conclude with alternative dispute resolution.

A. Claim Forms

11.02 A claim must be made by an employee to an employment tribunal within three months of the effective date of the dismissal (ERA, section 111(2)(a)) or detrimental act or deliberate failure to act (or the last in a series of such acts or failures) complained of, save when time is extended. It is mandatory under the Employment Tribunals (Constitution and Rules of Procedure) Regulations 2013/1237, rule 8(1) to use the claim form as set out in those Rules. Rules 8 and 10 require the claimant to set out the details of a claim and the respondent to

---

[1] Such as *Blackstone's Employment Law Practice* (Oxford: Oxford University Press, 2017).

state the grounds for resisting a claim. The claim must be accompanied by the prescribed fee; rule 11. The tribunal staff should reject the form if it fails to comply with various requirements laid down in the Rules: rule 12, but the claimant may in such a case ask that the rejection be reconsidered.

It is important that claimants state in their application precisely and in a clear and logi- **11.03** cal manner what disclosures are relied on, to whom they were made (especially whether internally or externally and which of ERA, sections 43C to 43H are said to apply), and why they fall within the six statutory categories of relevant failure. If possible, the making of each disclosure should be linked in the claim to the precise detriment (or dismissal) which is said to have been the result of each disclosure, though where there are multiple disclosures it may be appropriate to refer to the cumulative impact: see *El-Megrisi v Azad University (IR) in Oxford* (UKEAT/0448/08/MAA, 5 May 2009), discussed in Chapter 9, paragraphs 9.22–9.24. Each cause of action which is relied on should thus be stated as precisely as possible. Careful consideration should also be given to whether to bring the claim against an individual worker or agent alleged to be responsible for acts of victimization (other than dismissal of an employee)—see Chapter 8, at paragraphs 8.71 et seq. Although many employment tribunals will give some leeway for employees to refine their cases as matters progress, some will not, with potentially calamitous results for claimants. It is not worth the employee running that risk and seeking leave to amend at a later stage (see Chapter 9, paragraphs 9.03–9.11).

In practice, however, at the start of proceedings the employee may not know with certainty **11.04** which disclosure was the actual reason for the detriment or dismissal and will often be relying on the drawing of inferences from the evidence to make the case. It may therefore be necessary instead to put the case in the alternative in relation to which of the disclosures was the reason for the detriment. The employee has to prove that s/he made disclosures and thus should know precisely what is relied on by him/her. The employee also has to prove that the disclosures were protected. But on the element of good faith (now relegated to the issue of remedy rather than being a substantive requirement for the disclosure to be protected) and in relation to establishing that the dismissal was not by reason of the protected disclosure or the detriment was not on the ground of a protected disclosure, the respondent[2] has to satisfy the burden of proof.[3]

Setting out each cause of action will render it easier to decide what evidence must be led at **11.05** the hearing and to found any application for disclosure, which is often very important in PIDA cases. It is also useful at this early stage to sketch out the precise extent of any injury to feelings which is alleged to have been caused.

Whilst taking care to address the various elements of the cause of action, however, it is **11.06** important that the essential overall 'story' or narrative is not lost. The claim form and response form will probably be the first documents that an employment tribunal reads when dealing with an interim application or at the main hearing. It is not the role of the pleadings to set out the detailed evidence which will ultimately be heard, but it is to the claimant's advantage if the initial claim conveys in a logical and persuasive way the claimant's essential case. In some claims, such as where the contentions as to the existence of protected disclosures are complicated or cover a protracted period, it may help for there to be a summary section at the outset clearly identifying the causes of action and the essential nature of the claim.

---

[2] See Chapter 7, paras 7.191 et seq, and Chapter 9, paras 9.37 et seq.
[3] See Chapter 10, paras 10.134–10.138.

B. Responses

11.07 Frequently, respondents find the applications in PIDA cases to be unclear, and will straight away seek further information or written answers about precisely what is alleged against them as a case management order; rule 29. It is important that cases do not reach the stage of the employment tribunal hearing without the issues being properly specified. A response may be rejected if the basic conditions and procedures are not complied with or it is presented late; rule 17 or 18. The respondent may in this situation seek a reconsideration of that rejection; rule 19.

11.08 We suggest that the following factors are borne in mind by employers' representatives (and respresentatives of worker/agent respondents) in framing their response:

(a) If it is contended that no disclosure of information within the meaning of the statute was in fact made, this should be stated in clear terms.

(b) If it is to be submitted that any disclosure was not made in good faith, or if it is disputed that the worker held a reasonable belief that disclosure was made in the public interest or that the information tended to show the relevant failure, this should be spelt out and the basis for the contention should be given. In relation to good faith this point now only goes to compensation and not to liability. But a contention that the worker not only lacked a reasonable belief as required by section 43B ERA, but also did not genuinely hold that belief, may raise similar issues. Clearly, in any event representatives should only plead bad faith if they have good grounds for doing so. Indeed, asserting this without good grounds may result in discipline by professional bodies and/or an order for costs in serious cases.

(c) In many PIDA cases, the parties are seeking to gain the 'moral high ground' before the tribunal, whatever the legal niceties of the respective positions may be. As with the claim form, this may involve the response painting the general picture sought to be portrayed at an early stage in trenchant terms. The response can thus legitimately be used to tell the story from the respondent's point of view and to rebut the adverse atmosphere which the worker is sometimes seeking to cultivate.

11.09 There are many tactical issues surrounding what matters the employer wishes to put in issue in a PIDA case. For example, if reasonable belief is disputed (eg in relation to a qualifying disclosure) the impact may be that the tribunal will need to hear evidence about the underlying allegation—which the employer may wish to avoid in a public forum (especially given what is said in *Darnton v University of Surrey* [2003] ICR 615, discussed in Chapter 3 that it is relevant whether the allegations made by the claimant are in fact true). There may be a number of reasons why the employer might choose not to fight on that ground. One might be an issue as to costs and proportionality, since a point taken as to whether there was a 'reasonable belief' for the purposes of a qualifying disclosure may substantially widen the scope of the hearing and it may be held unreasonable to have put it in issue. The strength of other parts of the case, such as the 'reason why' the detriment or dismissal took place (see Chapter 7), may affect the assessment. Another might be that the employer wants to avoid going into all the details of each of the allegations (and in a serious case the tribunal may refer matters to appropriate authorities for investigation, such as HM Revenue & Customs, which could be highly detrimental to the employer's overall interests; ET Rules rule 14 and see 11.77). That said, if other elements of the protected disclosures are in issue, this still might not be effective in wholly excluding consideration of the issue, since the truth of the allegation may be argued to be relevant to reasonable belief that disclosure was made in the public interest.

C. Case Management

A judge must, after acceptance of the response, 'confirm whether there are arguable complaints and defences within the jurisdiction of the tribunals'; rule 26(1). If (s)he considers that the tribunal has no jurisdiction to consider the claim (or part of it) or that it has no reasonable prospect of success, that claim or part may be dismissed: rule 27(1). Similar provisions relate to the response, rule 28(1). In *ALM Services Limited v Bladon* [2002] EWCA Civ 1085, [2002] IRLR 807 the Court of Appeal said that there should be directions hearings (now renamed preliminary hearings) in protected disclosure cases in order to identify the issues and to ascertain what evidence the parties intend to call on those issues. In *Price v Surrey County Council and another* (UKEAT/0450/10, 27 October 2011), the EAT encouraged the formulation of a list of issues in each case and set out guidance as to their formulation, whilst also stressing that the list drawn up by the parties should not be accepted uncritically by the employment tribunal at the case management stage. The judge has a supervisory role in this important endeavour. The EAT emphasized that the list of issues should identify clearly the central issues (eg unfair dismissal and detriment due to a protected disclosure) and should avoid mixing these (and indeed the relevant sub-issues) with the detailed factual allegations in relation to the case. **11.10**

In addition, the EAT (at para 25) criticized the list of issues which had been prepared in that case for a 'lack of discrimination between the significant and the "utterly trivial"' factual issues in the case. The EAT commented (at para 59) that the emphasis on a long list of individual detriments, together with the inclusion of many allegations that were peripheral, exaggerated, or unsustainable, had added considerably to the length of the case and to the difficulty for the tribunal in seeing the wood for the trees. Those representing parties in such a case are expected to cooperate in avoiding such a scenario. **11.11**

The EAT's observations were consistent with those of Mummery LJ in *St Christopher's v Walters-Ennis* [2010] EWCA 921 (CA) at para 14, in which he commented that: **11.12**

> The real issues would have been clearer, the hearing shorter and the judgment of the ET more focussed, if there had been drastic pruning at the pre-hearing Case Management Discussion to exclude peripheral and minor issues from the list agreed by the parties.

Those remarks, although made in the context of a race discrimination claim, were reiterated by the EAT in a case involving protected disclosure claims in *Korashi v Abertawe Bro Morgannwg University Local Area Health Board* [2012] IRLR 4 at para 31. **11.13**

Rule 29 of the Employment Tribunals (Constitution and Rules of Procedure) Regulations 2013/1237 provides the tribunal with various general powers to manage tribunal cases: these powers may be exercised in or out of a preliminary hearing, which is often held by telephone or could be by other 'electronic communication'; rule 46. At a preliminary hearing itself, the employment judge may conduct a preliminary consideration of the claim and make a case management order; determine any preliminary issue; consider whether a claim or response should be struck out; make a deposit order; and explore the possibility of settlement or alternative dispute resolution; rule 53. **11.14**

In *Blackbay Ventures Ltd (t/a Chenistree) v Gahir* [2014] IRLR 416, the EAT (at para 98) provided a helpful summary of particulars to be elicited from the claimant (set out in case 133 of Appendix 2). Drawing on that guidance, we suggest the tribunal (and the respondent) will be concerned to elicit from the claimant at this stage by way of further information (if these details are not already clearly pleaded) such matters as: **11.15**

(a) when, where, and to whom each disclosure was made and which of sections 43C to 43H are relied upon;

(b)   precisely what information is alleged to have been disclosed;

(c)   each alleged relevant failure should be separately identified, together with which of section 43B(1)(a)–(f) is relied upon, and what matters are said to indicate that it was reasonable to believe that the information tended to show that relevant failure. In relation to non-compliance with a legal obligation, save in obvious cases, in order to facilitate an assessment of reasonable belief, the nature and source of the obligation should be identified and how it was believed the information tended to show a past, ongoing, or likely future relevant failure: *Blackbay* (para 98); *Eiger Securities LLP v Korshunova* [2017] IRLR 115 (see Chapter 3 paragraph 3.118);

(d)   where the claim is one of detriment under section 47B ERA, what act(s) or omission(s) of on behalf of the employer is/are relied upon as being on the grounds of a protected disclosure and where and when they occurred and by whom they were done and (if any workers or agents have been joined as a party) against whom each claim is made;

(e)   what detriments are alleged to have been caused by the acts or deliberate failures to act relied upon;

(f)   what facts and matters are relied upon by the claimant in support of the allegation that the acts or deliberate failures to act and/or (as the case may be) dismissal were on the ground of or by reason that s/he had made a protected disclosure;

(g)   if reliance is placed on section 43G, which of the gateways in section 43G(2) are relied upon and on what basis.

It is, however, important that each case should be considered on its own merits and in particular that there is a balance to be struck between seeking necessary further information, and making requests which give a claimant an opportunity to improve or expand on the pleaded case.

11.16   Similarly, the tribunal (and the claimant) will wish to elicit from the respondent:

(a)   whether it is accepted that (a) qualifying disclosure(s) was/were made as alleged by the claimant, and if not what are the areas of dispute;

(b)   whether it is accepted that the qualifying disclosure(s) is/are (a) protected disclosure(s) and if not, why not, and, in particular, whether, and if so in reliance on what facts and matters, the respondent intends to dispute that the disclosure(s) fall within whichever of section 43C to 43H is relied upon by the claimant;

(c)   what the respondent contends is the reason or principal reason for dismissal or the ground for the detrimental act or failure to act, and whether it is disputed that the act or failure to act was done, and amounted to a detriment.

(1) Preliminary hearings

11.17   At preliminary hearings, the central issues which should be determined at the hearing are defined (which is a particularly important matter for PIDA cases) and any outstanding procedural matters can be dealt with before the main hearing commences. It is part of the overriding objective of the Employment Tribunal Rules to deal with cases justly (Rule 2). Dealing with a case justly includes by the rules, so far as is practicable these principles:

(a)   ensuring that the parties are on an equal footing;

(b)   dealing with cases in ways which are proportionate to the complexity of the issues;

(c)   avoiding unnecessary formality and seeking flexibility in the proceedings;

(d)   avoiding delay so far as compatible with proper consideration of the issues; and

(e)   saving expense.

This is largely a replication of the overriding objective in the Civil Procedure Rules which apply in the county court and High Court (CPR, rules 1.1–1.3), and a tribunal or judge must seek to give effect to the overriding objective either when exercising any power given to it or him/her. There is also an obligation on the parties, which ought not to be overlooked, to assist the tribunal to further the overriding objective (rule 2).

A preliminary hearing is held by an employment judge sitting alone and is held in private save where a preliminary issue is being determined: rule 56 in which case it must be in public. **11.18**

Interim orders may commonly include: **11.19**

(a) that a party provide additional information—for example because the claim or response is not clear or because a schedule of loss should be provided; this may be particularly important in such hearings;

(b) requiring the attendance of any person in Great Britain either to give evidence or to produce documents or information; rule 32;

(c) requiring any person in Great Britain to disclose documents or information to a party to allow a party to inspect such material as might be ordered by a county court (or, in Scotland, by a sheriff); rule 31;

(d) requiring the provision of written answers to questions put by the tribunal or employment judge;

(e) staying (in Scotland, sisting) the whole or part of any proceedings;

(f) that part of the proceedings be dealt with separately—this may cover a split liability and remedy hearing; rule 57;

(g) that different claims be considered together and that the decision in one shall be binding on others; rule 36;

(h) that any person whom the employment judge or tribunal considers might be liable for the remedy claimed should be made a respondent in the proceedings; rule 35;

(i) dismissing the claim against a respondent who is no longer directly interested in the claim; rule 34;

(j) postponing or adjourning any hearing;

(k) giving permission to amend a claim or response;

(l) that any person whom the employment judge or tribunal considers has an interest in the outcome of the proceedings may be joined as a party to the proceedings; rule 34

(m) that a witness statement be prepared or exchanged; rule 43; or

(n) gaining information as to the timetabling of the hearing; rule 45.

The employment tribunal at this stage may also decide to send the papers to the relevant regulatory body for investigation; rule 14 (see below). **11.20**

The employer may also want to adjourn the hearing so that s/he can investigate the concern which has been raised by the employee, but tribunals are likely to be reluctant to break a fixture which has been laid down for a hearing. **11.21**

(2) How to apply for an order

A party may apply for an order to be issued, varied, or revoked at any stage in the proceedings; rule 29. **11.22**

The application should identify the precise orders which are being sought there. It should also set out a brief explanation as to why they are sought and how the order will be likely to assist the employment judge in dealing with the proceedings efficiently and fairly. **11.23**

An order which has been made or refused by one employment judge cannot simply be revisited by another. If there is a subsequent application, tribunals should ordinarily follow the same principles as are applicable under the CPR and only set aside or vary such an order where there has been a change in the circumstances since it was made or a material omission or misstatement **11.24** or some other substantial reason for doing so: see *Serco Ltd v Wells* [2016] ICR 768 (EAT).[4] As explained in *Serco*, at para 43(d), rule 29 of Schedule 1 to the ET Rules 2013 which provides that a case management order can carry, suspend, or set aside an earlier case management order 'where that is necessary in the interests of justice', is to be interpreted consistently with this principle. In *Serco* an employment judge had ordered a preliminary hearing to determine whether the claimant had sufficient length of service to bring an ordinary unfair dismissal claim. The order was revoked at a subsequent case management order, on the basis that in the interim there had been a list of issues drawn up which went beyond those envisaged by the previous judge and that the preliminary issue would resolve only a few of the issues. The EAT allowed an appeal on the basis that a fresh list of issues was not a material change of circumstances and that, as such, there had been no jurisdiction to revisit the earlier case management order.

D. Additional Information

11.25 Requests for further information or for written answers may be particularly important in protected disclosure cases—where claims are frequently poorly drafted yet there are a number of stages through which the claim must pass to succeed and where it is vital that the parties know each others' respective cases if the final hearing is to be kept within reasonable bounds.[5] The general principles applied in relation to requests for such orders are as follows:

(a) a tribunal may order a party to provide further details of the allegations in a claim or response;

(b) the tribunal can so order at the request of a party or at the tribunal's own motion either before or at a hearing;

(c) parties should try to avoid long and complicated requests, and the earlier requests are made the more likely they are to be granted;

(d) the purpose of such a request is to inform the other side of the case that they have to meet, to prevent parties from being taken by surprise by enabling them to prepare rebutting evidence and to define the issues in dispute for the tribunal; and

(e) a party who fails to comply with an order to provide further information may find his/her claim or response, or relevant parts, dismissed or struck out.

11.26 Tribunals are, in general, anxious that cases do not become a complex battle of pleadings reminiscent of some cases in the High Court. In *Stone v Charrington & Co Ltd* [1977] ICR 248 the EAT stated that:

> industrial tribunals were set up with the purpose of operating cheaply, quickly and informally and as far as possible therefore it is desirable that the formalities of the regular courts should be avoided. To introduce a formal system of discovery and inspection, interlocutories [now known as interim orders] and so forth might in the abstract produce more perfect justice but it would be at such great cost in time, money and manpower that the whole machine would grind to a halt.

---

[4] Affirming the line of cases following *Goldman Sachs Services Ltd v Montali* [2002] ICR 1251, where a case management order to determine a limitation issue as a preliminary issue was held to have been wrongly reversed by a later case management order because there had been no material change of circumstances.

[5] See eg *Secretary of State for Work and Pensions (Jobcentre Plus) v Constable* (UKEAT/0156/10/JOJ, 30 June 2010) where, reversing the employment judge's decision, the claimant was ordered to give particulars of (a) what the protected disclosure was that the claimant claimed to have made, (b) to whom and how he made the protected disclosure, and (c) how the disclosure was alleged to have led to dismissal, since without this information the respondent would not know which witnesses would be called and what documents would be necessary.

Important guidance on the proper scope of orders for further information under the old **11.27** Rules (but still relevant to the new) was given in *White v University of Manchester* [1976] ICR 419 at 423 by Phillips J, who said:

> It is just a matter of straightforward sense. In one way or another the parties need to know the sort of thing which is going to be the subject of the hearing. Industrial tribunals know this very well and, for the most part, seek to ensure that it comes about. Of course, in the end, if there is surprise they will ordinarily grant an adjournment to enable it to be dealt with, but by and large it is much better if matters of this kind can be dealt with in advance so as to prevent adjournments taking place. …

In *Honeyrose Products Ltd v Joslin* [1981] IRLR 80, Waterhouse J pointed out the essential **11.28** principles to be applied, which still hold good. Claims should be sufficiently simple to enable the employers (and worker/agent respondents) to identify with reasonable clarity the case that they have to meet and the range of argument that is likely to occur before the tribunal. That said, it would be 'most unfortunate if it became the general practice for employers to make requests when the nature of the case is stated with reasonable clarity'.

An order for further information will, however, be refused where it is unnecessary or overly **11.29** burdensome or oppressive. Part of the overriding objective provides for proportionality in any event. Thus, a request for details of incidents that occurred many years ago might be refused as both unnecessary and burdensome since the witnesses are unlikely to recall the relevant matters which are in issue. Requests that are very detailed and relate to statistical or other matters might also fail on the grounds that they are too burdensome.

A request for evidence, as opposed to facts, may be ordered since the request is not limited to **11.30** the pleadings but might encompass any issue in the case. More typically, however, a request for evidence will not be ordered, being unnecessary for the other party to respond to the case, and on the basis that the evidence is a matter for witness statements and disclosure.

Well-targeted requests for further information are likely to be of particular importance in **11.31** relation to those parts of the other side's case where only the other party has full access to the information. From the employer's perspective, in considering the approach to take in the litigation on issues such as whether the claimant had the requisite reasonable belief for a qualifying disclosure, it may be particularly important to hone in on the information and evidence which was available to the worker at the time of making the disclosure so that this can be tested at the hearing. For the employee, it will be important to consider what information might be available to test the employer's contentions as to the reasons for alleged detrimental action. In some cases, for example, it may be appropriate to seek information as to how comparators were treated in a comparable situation in order to support an inference that the difference in treatment was due to a protected disclosure. Similar considerations are also applicable when identifying documents which may need to be sought.

E. Disclosure

(1) Applicable principles

Each party may need (a) document(s) which is or are in the possession of the other to prove **11.32** its case. In PIDA cases, it is necessary to consider carefully what are the categories of documentation which are likely to exist and which may be relevant, in particular so as to obtain evidence in relation to those parts of the case which are not within a party's own knowledge. In relation to the reason for treatment (eg dismissal or detriment) it will be important to identify who might have been party to or consulted about the decision and to ensure that there is disclosure of internal emails bearing on the reaction to the disclosure(s) made. In relation to whether the claimant held a reasonable belief that the information disclosed tended to show a relevant failure, documents bearing on whether that relevant failure in fact occurred may be relevant and necessary for a fair trial: see for example *Gray v Merrill Lynch, Pierce, Fenner & Smith Ltd* (UKEAT/0058/16/DM, 16 March 2016).[6]

11.33   On the application of a party or of its own motion, a tribunal may order a party to grant disclosure or inspection of a document to another party; rule 31. Such orders are not limited to documents as strictly so called, so that digital material, photographs, and video evidence may also be obtained in this way. In contrast with the position under CPR 31, there is no general duty on the parties to give disclosure in tribunal proceedings. Tribunals are nevertheless directed by rule 31 to adopt the same principles as the county court does in making orders. The principles of standard disclosure under the CPR (by which county courts are governed) require a party to disclose those documents on which s/he relies, any documents which support or adversely affect his/her or another party's case, and any other documents which a party is required to disclose pursuant to a relevant practice direction. CPR 31APD, para 5.4 states that in deciding whether to make an order for specific disclosure the court will take into account all of the circumstances of the case and, in particular, the overriding objective (especially in this respect to deal with cases justly and in a cost-effective manner).

11.34   The general rule is that a document is relevant which:

> it is reasonable to suppose contains information which may, not which must, either directly enable the party either to advance his own case or to damage the case of his adversary (including) a document which may fairly lead him to a train of inquiry which may have either of these two consequences.[7]

The documents which are sought to be disclosed must be relevant and necessary for the fair disposal of the proceedings[8] and the fact that they are available and would be disclosed normally is not the correct approach for the tribunal to take in refusing the application.

11.35   In *Copson v Eversure Accessories Ltd* [1974] ICR 636, Sir John Donaldson said:

> cases are intended to be heard with all the cards facing upwards on the table. The tribunal's power of ordering further and better particulars, discovery or issuing witness orders will be of little value in the pursuit of justice if the parties do not know they exist. Tribunals should therefore be vigilant to ensure that their existence is known in appropriate cases.

11.36   In *Birds Eye Walls Ltd v Harrison* [1985] IRLR 47 Waite J stated the important general principle that:

> no party is under any obligation, in the absence of an order upon the Industrial Tribunal, to give discovery in the Tribunal proceedings. That is subject, however, to the important qualification that any party who chooses to make voluntary discovery of any documents in his possession or power must not be unfairly selective in his disclosure. Once, that is to say, a party has disclosed certain documents (whether they appear to him to support his case or for any other reason) it becomes his duty not to withhold from discovery any further documents in his possession or power (regardless of whether they support his case or not) if there is any risk that the effect of withholding them might be to convey to his opponent or to the tribunal a false or misleading impression as to the true nature, purport or effect of any disclosed document.

---

[6] See further Chapter 3 at paras 3.79–3.85 in relation to treating truth or falsity of an allegation as an evidential tool in relation to reasonable belief.

[7] (*Compagnie Financière v Peruvian Guano Co* (1882) 11 QBD 55; see *also Ballantine (George & Sons) v FER Dixon* [1974] 2 All ER 503).

[8] *Dolling Baker v Merrett* [1990] 1 WLR 1205; *Canadian Imperial Bank of Commerce v Beck* [2009] EWCA Civ 619, [2009] IRLR 740; *Plymouth City Council v White* (EAT/UKEAT/0333/13/LA, 23 August 2013).

There are two principles to be borne in mind in this area so that no party should suffer **11.37** injustice. The first is that the duty of every party not to withhold from disclosure any document whose suppression would be likely to render the disclosed document misleading is a high duty which the tribunals should interpret broadly and enforce strictly. The second is that the tribunal should use its wide and flexible powers as master of its own procedure to ensure that if any party can be shown at any stage of the proceedings to have been at risk of having his/her claim or defence unfairly restricted by the denial of an opportunity to become aware of a document in the possession or power of the other side material to the just prosecution of his/her case, s/he does not suffer any avoidable disadvantage as a result. Further, the parties owe a continuing duty to the tribunal so that if they become aware during the proceedings of documents which are relevant those should be disclosed.

In making any orders, the tribunal will take into account considerations of proportionality, **11.38** and in certain circumstances an application for an order for disclosure will be refused if to grant it might lead to such significant expenditure of time and cost to a party as to be oppressive (see *Wilcox v HGS* [1975] ICR 306; and *Perera v Civil Service Commission* [1980] ICR 699).

(2) Disclosure by non-parties

It may be especially important in PIDA cases for a party to gain some documents from **11.39** people or institutions who are not party to the action, for example statutory regulators ('prescribed persons') to whom a disclosure has been made. A tribunal may make an order, either on application or of its own motion, requiring a person in Great Britain who is not a party to disclose documents or information (rule 31) or to attend and to produce any document relating to the matter to be determined (rule 32). In the case of *Chubb and others v Care First Partnership Ltd* (ET Case No 1101438/99B) Mrs Chubb and the other claimants were care assistants who made an external disclosure of abuse at a care home where they worked. The tribunal ordered third-party disclosure from the local authority of its notes of the initial allegations and copies of reports made following investigations into the allegations.

(3) Form of application

The party requiring the information should initially approach the other side by letter, with **11.40** a copy being sent to the tribunal. If the other side refuses a reasonable request, an order for disclosure should be sought from the tribunal (in accordance with rule 31). The letter should set out clearly the documents (or class of documents) which are being sought[9] and the request may be facilitated by a schedule or draft order identifying the documents sought so that the employment judge who is considering the application can tick off the documents to be disclosed.

(4) Restrictions on disclosure

The following general restrictions on disclosure may be particularly relevant in PIDA cases. **11.41**

(a) Confidentiality

In *Science Research Council v Nassé* [1979] IRLR 465, it was held that where a party **11.42** claims that it is not appropriate to disclose a document, the tribunal may inspect the

---

[9] See *Mace v Ponders End International* [2014] IRLR 697 (EAT), emphasizing the importance of spelling out precisely what the other party is required to do, rather than there being a general order to give disclosure of documents.

document and decide whether the claim is valid. Confidentiality is only a consideration to be taken into account, not a determinative factor, and the overall test is whether discovery is necessary for the fair disposal of the proceedings (see paragraph 11.34 above). That there is no rule whereby confidential documents are excluded from discovery merely because they are confidential was emphasized in *Alfred Compton Amusement Machines Ltd v Customs and Excise Commissioners (No 2)* [1974] AC 405, where it was stated that, in the absence of some additional factor, such as the fact that the claimant is exercising a statutory function which would be impeded by disclosure, confidentiality would not justify the non-disclosure of a document where the disclosure is necessary for the fair disposal of the proceedings. But the tribunal should consider whether there are alternatives which would protect confidentiality, such as by redacting the confidential material: see *Plymouth City Council v White* (UKEAT/0333/13/LA, 23 August 2013).

(b) Self-incrimination

11.43 Section 14 of the Civil Evidence Act 1968 provides that a party does not have to give disclosure if it would tend to incriminate him/her or his/her spouse or expose them to proceedings which might lead to a penalty.[10] Mere assertion of the privilege will not, however, necessarily be accepted. The tribunal must decide from the circumstances of the case and the nature of the evidence whether there are grounds to invoke the privilege. The privilege must be claimed before the evidence is supplied or it will be too late.[11]

11.44 Where does this leave a respondent who has evidence that s/he has committed a criminal act and a claim in regard to a disclosure of that act? First, if the respondent has to rely upon asserting the privilege against self-incrimination, that does not bode well for the defence of the claim and the view the tribunal is likely to form of him/her. Second, consideration will need to be given as to whether it is (a) possible and (b) tactically advantageous to dispute that there is a qualifying disclosure, having regard to the fact that whether the allegation is true may be a relevant consideration in assessing reasonable belief (*Darnton v University of Surrey* [2003] ICR 615). In theory, it might be possible to assert that the claimant had no reasonable belief at the time. But in practice this is unlikely to carry any force in a case where it is necessary to plead the privilege against self-incrimination.

F. The Power to Sit in Private

11.45 Where the subject matter of the disclosure which is in issue consists of information that is still sensitive, as it often will be, the respondent employer may consider applying for an order that the hearing or part of it be conducted in private. The general principle is that hearings of claims are to be held in public. Rule 50 of the Employment Tribunals (Constitution and Rules of Procedure) Regulations 2013/1237, however, provides that a hearing or part of a hearing may be conducted in private. The tribunal must in making this decision 'give full weight to the principle of open justice and to the Convention right of freedom of expression'; rule 50(2).

---

[10] See Hollander, *Documentary Evidence*, 12th edn. London: Sweet & Maxwell, 2015, Chapter 21.
[11] *IBM UK Limited v Prime Data* [1994] 1 WLR 719.

G. Striking Out, Deposit Orders, and Submissions of No Case to Answer

(1) Submissions at the close of the claimant's case that there is no case to answer

In PIDA claims tribunals are only likely to accede to a submission of no case to answer by a **11.46** particular party in exceptional cases. In *Boulding v Land Securities Trillium (Media Services) Ltd* (EAT/0023/06, 3 May 2006) the EAT held that the employment tribunal had erred in acceding to a 'half-time' submission of 'no case to answer' made in a whistle-blowing claim. The claimant alleged that he had been unfairly dismissed for having blown the whistle on what he said was the respondent's wrongdoing. Since he had less than one year's continuous employment, the burden was on the claimant to show that the reason or principal reason for dismissal was a protected disclosure. For this reason the claimant's case was heard first. As discussed in Chapter 3 (paragraphs 3.101–3.102), the claimant raised concerns with his employer that some of the employer's equipment lacked certain markings as was required. This would have led to a breach of the employer's obligations had the equipment been supplied to a customer without this being rectified. However, the tribunal decided that, although the claimant had made a disclosure to his employer in good faith, it was clear on his own evidence that he did not have a reasonable belief that his employer was likely to fail to comply with a legal obligation, and that there was therefore no qualifying disclosure.

The EAT reasoned (following *Lucas v Chichester* (EAT/0713/04, 7 February 2005) that a **11.47** whistleblowing claim is in the nature of a contention that discrimination has occurred and it should normally be heard in full. In *Logan v Commissioners of Customs and Excise* [2003] EWCA Civ 1068, [2004] IRLR 63 the Court of Appeal approved the statement of principle by Judge Clarke in *Clarke v Watford Borough Council* (4 May 2000) that:

(1) There is no inflexible rule of law and practice that a tribunal must always hear both sides, although that should normally be done.
(2) The power to stop a case at 'half-time' must be exercised with caution:
  (a) it may be a complete waste of time to call upon the other party to give evidence in a hopeless case;
  (b) even where the onus of proof lies on the claimant, as in discrimination cases, it will only be in exceptional or frivolous cases that it would be right to take such a course;
  (c) where there is no burden of proof, as under s 98(4) of the Employment Rights Act 1996, it will be difficult to envisage arguable cases where it is appropriate to terminate the proceedings at the end of the first party's case.

The EAT said that the question posed under ERA, section 43B of the likelihood of the **11.48** employer not responding to the claimant's allegation of wrongdoing, and stopping uncertified electrical equipment being used, did not depend solely on the claimant's appreciation of the matter. The employment tribunal should have considered, by examining evidence from the respondent, what its response was likely to be. At first blush this might seem to be a contrived conclusion. The fact that the statutory protection accorded to whistleblowers is akin to a discrimination statute is of relevance where the issue is why the respondent acted in the way it did. In such cases it is usually unwise to stop a case before the respondent's evidence on that issue has been heard. However, the issue on which the EAT focused in *Boulding* was the reasonableness of the claimant's belief that wrongdoing would be likely to occur. That might be thought to depend on the claimant's appreciation of what he knew (or thought) at the time. Unless his own evidence as to what he thought and believed and why he did so persuaded the tribunal that there was a triable issue in that regard then it was unlikely that he would win the case.

(2) Striking out for no reasonable prospect of success

11.49 In *Ezsias v North Glamorgan NHS Trust* [2007] EWCA Civ 330, [2007] ICR 1126, the Court of Appeal stressed the rarity of it being appropriate to strike out whistleblowing claims. The doctor employee alleged that he had been dismissed by reason of having made protected disclosure, whereas the trust said that the dismissal resulted from a complete lack of confidence in him and from his responsibility for a breakdown of the relationships in his department. The court decided that whilst tribunals should be alert to providing protection to respondents from claims that had little or no reasonable prospect of success, they had to exercise appropriate caution before making an order that would prevent an employee from proceeding to trial in a case which involved serious and sensitive issues. Where the parties raised factual issues which revealed diametrically opposed cases it would be legally perverse to strike out a claim.[12] In *Sood v The Governing Body of Christ the King School* (UKEAT/0449/10/ZT, 20 July 2011), the EAT identified a further question as being whether a strike-out order would save time and expense given the possibility that allegations which were arguably out of time might still be relied upon as background evidence. Whilst that statement was made with reference to allegations of race discrimination, the same could apply to allegations of detriment on grounds of protected disclosures.[13]

11.50 Further, in *Pillay v Inc Research UK* (EAT/0182, 9 September 2011), the EAT confirmed that the same principles apply notwithstanding that a claimant lacked sufficient qualifying service to bring an unfair dismissal claim unless he established a dismissal by reason of a protected disclosure. There would still need to be an investigation of why the claimant had been dismissed. The tribunal had struck out a claim at a pre-hearing review on the basis that there was no evidence from which it could be inferred that the dismissal was by reason of the alleged protected disclosures, and that the claim therefore had no reasonable prospect of success. It had been wrong to do so.

11.51 In *Abertawe Bro Morgannwg University Health Board v Ferguson* (UKEAT/0044/13/LA, 24 April 2013), the EAT again stressed (at para 33) that the circumstances in which it will be possible to strike out a fact-sensitive protected disclosure claim are likely to be rare and that:

> In general it is better to proceed to determine a case on the evidence in light of all the facts. At the conclusion of the evidence gathering it is likely to be much clearer whether there is truly a point of law in issue or not.

11.52 It does not follow that it is never appropriate to strike out where there is a relevant dispute of fact. The correct approach is to take the allegations in the claim at their highest unless than can be conclusively disproved or be shown to be demonstrably untrue.[14] The relevant principles were reviewed by Simler J in *Daly v Northumberland and Tyne and Wear NHS Foundation Trust* (UKEAT/0109/16/JOJ, 7 July 2016). She endorsed the approach established in *Ezsias* that it is only in exceptional cases in whistleblowing claims that a claim would be struck out as having no reasonable prospect of success where the central facts are in dispute. But she also noted that there are cases where, even taking the central facts at their highest, it is clear that the claim cannot succeed on the legal basis on which it is advanced.

---

[12] See also *Balls v Downham Market High School* [2011] IRLR 217.

[13] See also *Morgan v Royal MENCAP Society* [2016] IRLR 428 (EAT), considered in Chapter 4 at paras 4.62–4.64, applying the same approach in relation to the fact-sensitive question of whether there was a reasonable belief that a disclosure was made in the public interest.

[14] *Ukegheson v Haringey LBC* [2015] ICR 1285 (EAT).

There may also be circumstances where the facts sought to be established by the claim are totally and inexplicably inconsistent with the undisputed and contemporaneous documents, such that it may be open to the tribunal to strike out the claim.[15] Even where the threshold for striking out proceedings is reached, the tribunal should consider alternatives to striking out, including the possibility of ordering further particulars to be given. In *Daly* there was a dispute of fact at the heart of the case in relation to whether the alleged detriment (refusal to cooperate in relation to a reference) was on the ground of a protected disclosure.[16]

(3) Deposit orders

By rule 39(1) of the 2013 ET Rules it is provided that: **11.53**

> Where at a preliminary hearing (under rule 53) the Tribunal considers that any specific allegation or argument in a claim or response has little reasonable prospect of success, it may make an order requiring a party ('the paying party') to pay a deposit not exceeding £1,000 as a condition of continuing to advance that allegation or argument.

In addition rule 39(5) provides that if after a deposit order has been made the tribunal   **11.54** decides the allegation or argument against the paying party substantially for the reasons given in the deposit order, (a) the paying party is to be treated as having acted unreasonably in supporting that allegation unless the contrary is shown (meaning that the tribunal must consider making a costs order), and (b) the deposit is forfeit and paid to the other party.

An application for a deposit order may be useful particularly where there are scattergun   **11.55** allegations (bearing in mind that there can be £1,000 for each claim and a heightened risk of an adverse costs order if the claim in respect of which the deposit order was made is pursued). On the other hand the tribunal must be alive to the danger of stifling claims and producing a chilling effect by virtue of the cumulative orders and the fear of costs. In *Wright v Nipponkoa Insurance (Europe) Ltd* (UKEAT/0113/14/JOJ, 17 September 2014) the EAT held that, if making a number of deposit orders, the ET should have regard to the question of proportionality in terms of the total award made. The ET is not restricted to considering purely legal questions. It is entitled to have regard to the likelihood of the party being able to establish the facts essential to their case (para 34).

The test for a deposit order is more easily satisfied than for a strike out of a claim, because   **11.56** it is satisfied if there is little, rather than no, reasonable prospects of success. In *Sharma v New College Nottingham* (UKEAT/0287/11/LA, 1 December 2011) it was suggested that the approach set out in *Ezsias* to determining disputed issues of fact also applied in considering whether a deposit should be ordered. But in *Spring v First Capital East Ltd* (UKEAT/0567/11/LA, 1 December 2011), the EAT (Wilkie J) said that the *Sharma* decision provides no support for any submission that the test for a deposit is the same as that for striking out. Whilst there is more leeway on a deposit order, there must of course still be a proper basis for doubting the likelihood of being able to establish facts essential to the claim or response: *Van Rensburg v The Royal Borough of Kingston upon Thames & Others* (UKEAT/

---

[15] See also *Robinson v Royal Surrey County Hospital NHS Foundation Trust and others* (UKEAT/0311/14/MC, 30 July 2015) where the EAT accepted that the whistleblowing case was so implausible that it was permissible to strike it out. The EAT took into account how the case had developed, not having been initially pleaded, then being said that protected disclosures were first made in 2009, then later that they were first made in 2011, but the claimant had been unable to identify her protected disclosures.

[16] See also eg *Romanowska v Aspirations Care Limited* (UKEAT 0015/14/2506, 25 June 2014) where a whistleblowing claim was wrongly struck out as having no reasonable prospects of success: the employment judge had held that the claimant might well establish that she had made protected disclosures and it was not appropriate to strike out a claim the result of which would turn on evidence from the employer as to the reasons for dismissal.

0095/07/MAA, 16 October 2007). Again, though, the danger is of too lax an approach stifling valid claims.

H. Costs

11.57 An important distinction between proceedings in the courts and those in the tribunal is that the tribunal's powers to award costs to a successful party are more limited. Given the passions aroused, and often the very great effort that goes into preparing a PIDA case, and (as we discuss below) due to the ingredients in the cause of action, costs are more likely to be sought and to be awarded than in some other areas of employment law. In other words, it might be said that when a PIDA claim or response falls flat it really falls flat, and it is easier to establish that the losing party has behaved in an unreasonable manner. A costs order may be made, and indeed the tribunal is obliged to consider making a costs order, when: a party or his/her representative 'has acted vexatiously, abusively, disruptively or otherwise unreasonably in either the bringing of the proceedings (or part) or the way the proceedings (or part) have been conducted'; 'any claim or response had no reasonable prospect of success'; or where a hearing has been postponed or adjourned on the application of a party made less than seven days before the hearing was to begin: rule 76(1). The tribunal may also make a costs order, but is not obliged to consider doing so where a party has been in breach of any order or practice direction or where a hearing has been postponed or adjourned on the application of a party: rule 76(2). In addition there is a different provision for orders to recover tribunal fees from the other party. This can be ordered where the claim is decided in whole or in part in favour of the party who paid the fee: rule 76(4).

11.58 In order to show that there was no protected disclosure, an employer might press hard the argument that the worker lacked the requisite reasonable belief for a protected disclosure. Again, although the questions are not precisely the same, a tribunal which is persuaded that a worker has made the disclosure without any reasonable belief, especially if a third-tier disclosure was made, might be open to arguments that the worker acted unreasonably in so doing. However, as the EAT emphasized in *HCA International Limited v May-Bheemul* (EAT/0477/10, 23 March 2011), there is no general principle that a costs order should be made merely because a central allegation which has been made by a losing party—in that case being subjected to detriments on the grounds of protected disclosures—had been untrue. The EAT upheld a tribunal's refusal to make a costs order where the claimant had held an honest belief in the truth of her disclosures alleging fraud and financial irregularities, but that belief was held not to be objectively reasonable. The EAT emphasized (at para 42) that:

> the objective unreasonableness of genuine belief, and a consequent failure on a Claimant's part to establish the necessary legal elements of the claim, does not equate to unreasonable conduct of the proceedings.

11.59 A costs order is more likely to be made if the tribunal also finds that there was no genuine belief in the disclosure on the part of the employee: see eg *Milne v The Link Asset and Security Company Limited* (EAT/0867/04, 26 September 2005). On the basis of such a finding there should be little difficulty in concluding that the claim had no reasonable prospect of success.[17]

---

[17] *Sharma v London Borough of Ealing* (UKEAT/0399/05, 5 January 2006) at paras 9 and 29. See also the decisions on whether lying necessarily leads to a cost order: *Arrowsmith v Nottingham* [2012] ICR 159, and *Kapor v Governing Body of Barnhill* (UKEAT/0352/13).

Furthermore, in the hope of achieving a settlement, the respondent may fight on all points **11.60** until a time which is close to the hearing and then make late admissions so as to avoid going into the details of the protected disclosures in a public forum. This might be appropriately visited in an order for costs in a serious case if it wastes costs.

The power to award costs is, however, a disciplinary power and not a compensatory one.[18] **11.61** There are thus two stages to be considered before making an order, namely a finding of such conduct as to entitle costs potentially to be awarded and the exercise of discretion in making an order for costs. The tribunal then considers the appropriate amount of the award or refers it to the county court for assessment.

An application which is made at the end of a hearing (as is normally, but not necessarily, the **11.62** case) can either be oral or in writing. Any application must be made within twenty-eight days of the date on which the judgment finally determining the proceedings was sent to the parties (not the date when it is actually received): rule 77 of the 2013 ET Rules. Before a costs order is made, the party subject to the order must be given a reasonable opportunity to make representations, whether in writing or at the hearing. The party seeking the order must also be given a reasonable opportunity to put the case for a costs order.[19]

In *Health Development Agency v Parish* [2004] IRLR 550, the EAT held that the conduct of **11.63** a party prior to proceedings, or unrelated to proceedings, cannot form the basis of an order for costs. It follows that it would be an error for a tribunal to treat an employer's failure to have in place or to abide by a whistleblowing policy prior to the start of proceedings as itself amounting to unreasonable conduct for the purposes of the costs provision.

In *McPherson v BNP Paribas* [2004] IRLR 558, the Court of Appeal held that there is **11.64** no requirement for a precise causal link between the party's unreasonable behaviour and the costs incurred by the receiving party. But in *Yerrakalva v Barnsley MBC* [2012] ICR 420 (CA) Mummery LJ recognized that the *McPherson* case had created some confusion. He clarified what he had meant by saying that the ET should look at the whole picture of what happened in a case and identify the conduct found to be unreasonable and what effects it had (para 41). It was not necessary to establish a precise causal link between the unreasonable conduct in question and the specific costs being claimed. But this did not mean that causation was irrelevant. Here it was reasonable for the employers to question the claimant's credibility and to incur costs in doing so. See also *Sud v Ealing LBC* [2013] ICR D39 (CA) and *Scott v Russell* [2013] EWCA Civ 1432, where the Court of Appeal in each case resisted 'inappropriate over analysis' and called for a broad-brush approach to be taken.

(1) Vexatious

In the form of the rules as they were before 1993, the formulation required for a costs award **11.65** had to merit being described as 'frivolous and vexatious' and the classic description of this was given by Sir Hugh Griffiths in *Marler (ET) Ltd v Robertson* [1974] ICR 72 at 76D:

> If the employee knows that there is no substance in his claim and that it is bound to fail, or if the claim is on the face of it so manifestly misconceived that it can have no prospect of success, it may be deemed frivolous and an abuse of the procedure of the tribunal to pursue it. If an employee brings a hopeless claim not with any expectation of recovering compensation but out of spite to harass his employers or for some other improper motive or acts vexatiously and likewise abuses the procedure [his action is vexatious].

---

[18] *Scott v Commissioners of Inland Revenue* [2004] IRLR 713.
[19] *Onyx Financial Advisors Ltd v Shah* (UKEAT/0109/14, 26 August 2014).

These considerations, and in particular the focus on an improper motive,[20] may be of particular significance where a tribunal concludes that a protected disclosure claim has been brought not because of any genuine belief in its merits, but in order to strengthen the claimant's negotiating position due to the absence of a statutory cap.

(2) Unreasonable conduct

11.66 This categorization which was introduced in 1993 extends not only to a party who knows that there is no merit in the case but also to one who ought to have known that the case had no merit. In *Cartiers Superfoods Ltd v Laws* [1978] IRLR 315, the EAT held that a tribunal should enquire as to what a party knew or ought to have known had s/he gone about the matters sensibly. The question of whether a party knew or ought to have known that a claim was without merit should be considered throughout the hearing and not just at its commencement so that, while it might be reasonable to begin proceedings, it may later become clear that it is unreasonable to take them further, for example because further information or documents become(s) available. In *Beynon v Scadden* [1999] IRLR 700 at para 28, the EAT suggested that it may be unreasonable conduct to fail to seek further information, written answers, or disclosure in order to assess the merits of a case.

11.67 The fact that a party has sought legal advice is a relevant factor but is not determinative of itself against costs being awarded. The tribunal ought, however, to be wary of the dangers of hindsight entering the picture. The fact that a party loses before the tribunal does not mean that the case was unreasonably brought or conducted, still less that there was vexatious behaviour. What becomes clear to the parties (eg after cross-examination) at the end of the proceedings may not have been foreseeable at the start or even part way through the process. In this area, tribunals need to be sensitive to the general challenges which are faced by whistleblowers if they feel their concerns are not being heeded. What may be seen by some as the waging of a campaign or repetitive allegations may reflect lack of feedback or a zealous determination to be heard. This may be material, both in relation to assessing whether the conduct was unreasonable, and in deciding whether, if it was unreasonable, it is appropriate to exercise the discretion to make an order of costs. It is an error to move straight from a finding of unreasonable conduct to making an order for costs, rather than considering in all the circumstances whether a costs order is appropriate: see *Oni v UNISON* (UKEAT/ 0370/14, 17 February 2015). That may be relevant where the claimant whistleblower has, for example, become convinced of conspiracies or has made wild allegations or unreasonably wide and frequent information requests, but where this has been influenced by the person feeling that concerns were not being heeded or the employer not having followed a whistleblowing policy. This is a difficult and sensitive area and the tribunal has to decide where the line is to be drawn between appropriate but challenging behaviour and unreasonable conduct.

11.68 There are specific issues which arise when a party makes an offer to settle which is not accepted. In proceedings in the civil courts a winning party who fails to do better than an offer which has been made to him/her by the losing party will usually expect to pay the losing party's costs from the date of the offer (see generally CPR Part 36). The use of so called *Calderbank* letters is common—that is, an offer to settle without prejudice, save as to costs. Such a letter is not revealed to the court until the end of the trial. Initially, the practice of issuing *Calderbank* letters was not looked upon favourably in tribunals (see Lindsay J in *Monaghan v Close Thornton Solicitors* (EAT/3/01, 20 February 2002)). In *Kopel v Safeway*

---

[20] As to the focus on motive, see also *Sharma v London Borough of Ealing* (UKEAT/0399/05, 5 January 2006) at para 29.

Stores [2003] IRLR 753, it was held that a failure by a party to beat a *Calderbank* offer will not, by itself, result in an award of costs against him/her. What must be shown is 'that the conduct of an appellant in rejecting the offer was unreasonable before the rejection becomes a relevant factor in the exercise of its discretion under [regulation 38]' (para 18). On the facts of that case, the EAT upheld a tribunal's award of £5,000 costs against the claimant where she had failed in her unfair dismissal and sex discrimination claims, and had not only turned down a 'generous' offer to settle the case but had persisted in alleging breaches of the provisions of the European Convention on Human Rights prohibiting torture and slavery, which the tribunal categorized as 'frankly ludicrous' and 'seriously misconceived'. In the circumstances, the EAT held that the tribunal was entitled to find that the rejection of the offer was unreasonable conduct of the proceedings justifying the award of costs that was made.

In *Power v Panasonic* (EAT 439/04, 9 March 2005) the EAT again stressed that the rule **11.69** in *Calderbank* has no place in the employment tribunal jurisdiction and cited *Kopel* with approval. However, where a party has obstinately pressed for some unreasonably high award despite its excess being pointed out and despite a warning that costs might be asked for against that party if it were persisted in, the tribunal could in appropriate circumstances take the view that the party had conducted the proceedings unreasonably. See also *Anderson v Cheltenham & Gloucester plc* (UKEAT/0221/13, 5 December 2013), where the EAT reiterated that whilst failure to beat an offer will not of itself justify an order for costs, the conduct in refusing an offer can be taken into account in determining whether a party had conducted the proceedings unreasonably.

It is worth considering *Iron and Steel Trades Confederation v ASW Limited* [2004] IRLR **11.70** 926, where Burton P said (at para 11):

> We do not encourage, indeed we would not welcome, a situation in which threats of costs are fired across the bows as a matter of course between the parties. There are many cases in which this will be seen almost to amount to emotional or financial blackmail, and certainly in any sort of race or sex discrimination cases it could be said, and has been I think in some cases said, that a threat of costs could amount to victimisation.

However, notwithstanding these cautionary words, a costs warning letter can be taken into **11.71** account in relation to whether a costs order should be made. Especially where the claimant is unrepresented, a carefully crafted warning letter may be of particular value in showing that it was unreasonable to proceed with the claim. That said, there is also a line of cases to the effect that the fact that an offer to settle was made is not an answer to a costs order made on grounds that the claim was misconceived. This is relevant in relation to offers which have been made to avoid time-consuming whistleblowing claims. In *Vaughan v Lewisham LBC No 2* [2013] IRLR 713 (EAT) it was held to be appropriate to make a costs order even though the claimant had not been put on notice that she was at risk as to costs, and nor had there been any application for a deposit order.[21] The claimant argued that because the respondents had attempted to settle the case it was not appropriate to make any award. However, it was held that this did not undermine the request for costs. The EAT said that it was notorious that the costs of defending a long claim against a persistent claimant can be such that from a purely commercial point of view it makes more sense to pay a substantial sum in settlement than to instruct lawyers.

---

[21] This was in part because the claimant had at no stage indicated that if she had been given any warning she would have discontinued her claim (para 19). Compare *Rogers v Dorothy Barley School* (UKEAT/0013/12, 14 March 2012) in which one of the reasons for not granting costs was that no warning had been given of such an application.

(3) Amount

11.72 Where it has been decided to make a costs order against a party, a tribunal or employment judge may make one of the following orders (see rule 78):

(a) an order for a specified sum not exceeding £20,000;
(b) an order for a specified sum agreed by the parties;
(c) an order that the whole or a specified part of the costs be determined by way of a detailed assessment in a county court in accordance with the CPR or, in Scotland, as taxed according to such part of the table of fees prescribed for proceedings in the sheriff court as shall be directed by the order;[22] or
(d) an order that the paying party pay the receiving party a specified amount as reimbursement of all or part of the tribunal fee.

11.73 It is unusual that an appeal court will allow an appeal unless the ET or EAT has adopted an incorrect legal principle in awarding or assessing costs: *Scott v Russell* [2013] EWCA Civ 1432.

(4) Wasted costs

11.74 Costs need not be awarded against the parties themselves. Tribunals can make a wasted costs order against a party's representative, which means legal or other representatives (rule 74(3)). The order may be made either in favour of another party, or in favour of the representative's own client (rule 80(2), (3)). The term 'wasted costs' means any costs incurred by a party as a result of any improper, unreasonable, or negligent act or omission or any costs incurred by such conduct which the tribunal considers it unreasonable for a party to pay (rule 80(1)). This is especially important in PIDA cases because allegations of serious wrongdoing might well be made and representatives need to be satisfied that there are proper bases on which to make such allegations.

11.75 The tribunal must ask itself three questions on such applications:

(1) Has the legal representative acted improperly, unreasonably, or negligently?
(2) Did such conduct cause the party to incur unnecessary costs?
(3) If so, is it unreasonable that the other party (or the representatives client) should pay those costs?

11.76 Guidance which has been set out for the equivalent High Court jurisdiction[23] is also applicable to the tribunal's wasted costs jurisdiction: see *Wilsons Solicitors v Johnson and others* (UKEAT/0515/10, 20 May 2011) at para 17. Improper conduct includes that which qualifies as very serious misdemeanors under the representative's professional code of conduct (*Medcalf v Weatherill and another* [2002] UKHL 27, [2003] 1 AC 120). 'Negligent' is to be used in the normal sense of failing to act with reasonable competence but also something akin to abuse of process (see *Persaud (Luke) v Persaud (Mohan)* [2003] EWCA Civ 394 and *Charles v Gillian Radford & Co* [2003] EWHC 3180 (Ch)). It is not sufficient to show that a hopeless case was pursued; it would need to be demonstrated that a party was abusing the process of the court in pursuing the case: *Ratcliffe Duce and Gammer v Binns t/a Parce Ferme and McDonald* (UKEAT/0100/08, 23 April 2008). In *Hafiz & Haque Solicitors v*

---

[22] See eg *Salinas v Bear Stearns* (EAT/0596/04, 21 October 2004) where an order for a detailed assessment of costs claimed to total £120,000 was upheld by Burton J; the claimant was found to have altered documents using typing correction fluid and was held to be dishonest and unreasonable in calling witnesses whose evidence was irrelevant.

[23] The leading authorities are *Ridehalgh v Horsefield* [1994] Ch 205 and *Medcalf v Mardell* [2003] 1 AC 120 (HL).

Mullick [2015] ICR 1085, the EAT held that the tribunal should engage in a two-stage process with a causative link so that the tribunal had to be satisfied that the representative had been guilty of an 'improper, unreasonable or negligent act or omission' and that costs were incurred as a result of that act.

11.77 Problems of privilege have arisen, for example, where a hopeless case has been pursued. A representative against whom the application is made cannot waive privilege on advice given unless the client permits this. The Court of Appeal has held that it cannot be inferred from those circumstances that the representatives have advised on the suitability of the course of action which has been taken. The task for the court is to ask whether no reasonably competent legal adviser would have evaluated the chances of success such as to continue with the action, but in many cases the judge will only be able to come to a conclusion adverse to the party's advisers if there has been a waiver of privilege and as a result he/she has seen their advice (*Dempsey v Johnstone* [2003] EWCA Civ 1134). In *Robinson v Hall Gregory Recruitment* [2014] IRLR 761 the EAT referred to the fact that the tribunal must consider in deciding whether to award wasted costs the possibility that issues of privilege might prevent a representative mounting a proper defence and that they should be given the benefit of the doubt. If instructed to do so, a representative could, and indeed was obliged to, argue a case which the representative considered hopeless and which he had advised the client was hopeless.

11.78 The wasted costs order may be one, or a combination, of the following, that the representative:

(a) pays costs to another party;
(b) pays costs to his/her own client; and/or
(c) pays any witness allowances of any person who has attended the tribunal by reason of the representative's conduct of the proceedings.

11.79 'Representatives' here means a party's legal or other representatives and any employee of such representatives (rule 80(2)). There are, however, excluded from wasted costs orders those representatives who do not act in pursuit of profit—principally law centres and Citizens' Advice Bureaux representatives—although those acting under conditional fee arrangements are deemed to be acting in pursuit of profit. Wasted costs orders may not be made against representatives who are the employees of a party but can be made in favour of a party regardless of whether he/she is legally represented.

11.80 As set out above (at paragraph 11.10), in many protected disclosure claims it will be important to exercise care at the case management stage in identifying and clarifying the issues. The failings of the claimant's representatives in this respect led to a wasted costs order being made in *Wilsons Solicitors v Johnson and others* (UKEAT/0515/10, 20 May 2011). Having been asked to provide further information in a claim brought by two claimants, which included claims under sections 47B and 103A ERA, the solicitors (Wilsons) served re-pleaded particulars of claim three days prior to a case management discussion (CMD). The employment judge considered that the pleading was still inadequate in several places, failed to give clarity on important issues such as the legal basis for asserting that there were protected disclosures, and failed to make clear which elements were new claims and required permissions to amend. Further, the representative from Wilsons was unable to assist in providing clarification at the CMD. As a result the CMD was aborted, and an order was made requiring the case to be re-pleaded. At a subsequent hearing, a wasted costs order was made against Wilsons. The decision may need to be treated with a degree of caution, since the EAT noted that no point had been taken before the tribunal to the effect that the employment judge could not assume that deficiencies in the pleading were the responsibility of Wilsons rather than their clients. Nor had attention been drawn to the authorities on the difficulties arising on such an application by reason of issues as to privilege. However, the EAT also noted (at para 30) that:

> The Judge's criticism . . . was of the defects in the pleadings and of Mr. Wilson's inability at the CMD to rectify those defects by clarifying the nature of his clients' case. No doubt in principle such failures could still be the fault of the client; but more typically they are the fault of the lawyer and result from failure to put the necessary work or thought into the preparation of the case. A judge will normally be well-placed to recognise failings of the latter kind (cf. the observations of the Court of Appeal in *Ridehalgh* at p. 270 C–E). The defects in the pleadings—both in their original and their amended form—were not of a kind which would typically flow from failures by the client: they were failures of analysis and accurate formulation.

(5) When can wasted costs orders be made?

11.81 An application for an order does not have to be made at the end of the case but the party's representative should be given notice in writing of the wasted costs proceedings and any order sought. The representative should be given a reasonable opportunity to make oral or written representations as to why the order should not be made; rule 77. The tribunal may have regard to the representative's ability to pay when considering whether to make an order or the amount; rule 84.

(6) Amount of wasted costs

11.82 There is no limit to the amount of a wasted costs order and the order should specify the amount to be paid or disallowed. The tribunal should give written reasons for any order, provided that a request for such reasons has been made within fourteen days of the date of the order.

I. Sending a Claim to the Regulator

11.83 Regulation 14 of Schedule 1 to the 2013 ET Rules of Procedure provides that if a claim contains an allegation that the claimant made a protected disclosure, the tribunal may, with the consent of the claimant, send a copy of the accepted claim to a regulator (being one of the regulators prescribed for the purposes of section 43F ERA[24]).

11.84 Paragraph 10.1 of the prescribed form provides that if the claimant's claim:

> consists of, or includes, a claim that you are making a protected disclosure under the Employment Rights Act 1996 (otherwise known as a 'whistleblowing' claim) please tick the box if you want a copy of this form, or information from it, to be forwarded on your behalf to a relevant regulator (known as a 'prescribed person' under the relevant legislation) by the tribunal staff.

The form would be clearer if it stated that the claim 'consists of or includes a claim that you made a protected disclosure'.

11.85 Annecdotal evidence suggests that in practice a positive indication often does not actually result in an investigaton by the regulator. Further, the provision might be thought to pose something of a dilemma for claimants and their lawyers. They may consider that the possibility that a regulator may become aware of the subject matter of their disclosure will provide an incentive to the respondent to make an offer of settlement *before* the issued

---

[24] As now set out in Schedule 1 to the Public Interest Disclosure (Prescribed Persons) Order 2014 (SI 2014/2418), as amended.

proceedings reach the stage of being heard. If the regulator is informed of that subject matter at the outset because the claimant has consented to this course then that incentive disappears. If, however, the claimant does not consent to disclosure being made to the regulator s/he might be cross-examined as to why consent was withheld. This might be relied upon as part of a case that the claimant did not hold a reasonable belief the disclosure was in the public interest.

J. Alternative Dispute Resolution

(1) Introduction

The alternative dispute resolution (ADR) options for employment and workplace cases are essentially conciliation, arbitration, and mediation. A tribunal 'shall wherever practicable and appropriate encourage the use by the parties of the services of ACAS, judicial or other mediation or other means of resolving their disputes by agreement'; rule 3. There is also a requirement to go through the early conciliation procedures introduced by the Enterprise and Regulatory Reform Act 2013. Central features of these processes are that they are voluntary, (hopefully) speedy, informal, private, independent of employment tribunals, and use the services of a neutral third party. Proving facts, presenting evidence, and making legal arguments are largely absent from most types of ADR and the focus shifts instead to exploring the issues and negotiating a settlement. The solutions available through ADR are not necessarily limited to the legal remedies. **11.86**

ADR may be of particular relevance in whistleblowing cases because of the desire of the employer to keep embarrassing matters away from the public realm of the tribunal. Further, the employee may wish not to be seen as a whistleblower—which may have the effect of limiting his/her job opportunities. The earlier the process commences, the better. **11.87**

The terms of ERA, section 43J are relevant to ADR and whistleblowing. This renders void any provision which purports to preclude the worker from making a protected disclosure (see further Chapter 14, paragraphs 14.124–14.129). **11.88**

There was concern that positive obligations to report what happens to criminal property and the restriction on concealing such property under sections 327 to 329 of the Proceeds of Crime Act 2002 (POCA) would cause difficulties in mediations because the parties to the mediation would feel restrained in what they could say. By section 328 'A person commits an offence if he enters into or becomes concerned in an arrangement which he knows or suspects facilitates (by whatever means) the acquisition, retention, use or control of criminal property by or on behalf of another person'. This is very wide, and concern on the part of mediators was heightened by the decision in *P v P (Ancillary Relief: Proceeds of Crime)* [2004] Fam 1, although it was argued on behalf of mediators that, even if lawyers were caught by POCA, mediators were not so included because they were not concerned in an arrangement. **11.89**

The central issue in *Bowman v Fels* [2005] EWCA Civ 226, [2005] 1 WLR 3083 was whether section 328 of the POCA applied to the ordinary conduct of legal proceedings or any aspect of such conduct—including, in particular, any step taken to pursue proceedings and to obtain a judgment. The Court of Appeal also considered whether POCA, section 328 applies to any consensual steps taken or settlement reached during legal proceedings and the extent to which the Act overrode legal professional privilege. **11.90**

The court concluded that: **11.91**

(a) Section 328 was 'not intended to cover or affect the ordinary conduct of litigation by legal professionals. That includes any step taken by them in litigation from the issue of proceedings and the securing of injunctive relief or a freezing order up to its final disposal by judgment. We do not consider that either the European or the United Kingdom legislator can have envisaged that any of these ordinary activities could fall within the concept of 'becoming concerned in an arrangement which ... facilitates the acquisition, retention, use or control of criminal property' (para 83).

(b) Proceedings or steps taken by lawyers in order to determine or secure legal rights and remedies for their clients would not involve them in 'becoming concerned in an arrangement which ... facilitates the acquisition, retention, use or control of criminal property', even if they suspected that the outcome of such proceedings might have such an effect (para 84). Therefore, the issue or pursuit of ordinary legal proceedings with a view to obtaining the court's adjudication upon the parties' rights and duties is not to be regarded as an arrangement or a prohibited act within POCA, sections 327 to 329. The policy reasons which persuaded the court to exclude settlements of existing or contemplated litigation from the POCA apply equally to mediations. Section 328 does not override legal professional privilege (paras 85–87 and 90).

(c) Privilege could only be overridden by express words or by necessary implication. There was nothing in the language of section 328 to suggest that Parliament expressly intended to override legal professional privilege and much stronger language would have been required for section 328 to be interpreted as bearing a necessary implication that legal professional privilege was to be overridden.

(2) The ADR options

(a) Conciliation

11.92 The Advisory, Conciliation and Arbitration Service (ACAS) provides an independent and impartial service to resolve statutory employment disputes. Once a claim has been made to an employment tribunal, the conciliation officer will make contact with the parties or their representatives. The role of the conciliation officer is to inform parties of their legal rights, examine the strengths and weaknesses of their case, and explore the options which appear open to them. The conciliation officer may encourage some bargaining to take place but if settlement is reached it is the parties and not the conciliation officer who determine the settlement.

11.93 The process does not normally involve any face-to-face meetings between the parties. Rather, conciliation officers relay the perspectives of one party to the other. Officers will not reveal information that one party wishes to keep from the other and information given to a conciliation officer in connection with conciliation is not admissible in evidence before a tribunal without the consent of the person who gave it.

(b) Arbitration

11.94 ACAS has responsibility for an arbitration scheme under the Employment Rights (Dispute Resolution) Act 1998 as a means to resolve claims of unfair dismissal. This has, however, been very little used.

(c) Mediation

11.95 The mediator, an independent neutral third party, assists disputing parties to reach a settlement. The mediator is not a judge or arbitrator of the dispute before him/her and will not seek to impose a solution. S/he is instead a facilitator. Like all ADR processes, mediation is voluntary, private, and informal. The process usually involves bringing the parties together for at least one face-to-face meeting, but the degree to which parties continue to meet in joint session thereafter will vary depending on the practice of the mediator and the willingness of the parties to have such joint meetings. In addition to the joint session, the mediator will speak to the parties privately and in confidence so that s/he can reveal to party B what took place at a private meeting with party A only if s/he has A's consent. Mediators may give an opinion on the merits of the dispute or make suggestions for settlement.

Mediation is flexible in terms of both process and outcomes and may be ideally suited **11.96** for problems concerned with relationships or behaviour, where the employee remains in employment, as will often be the case with whistleblowers. Mediated agreements can include protocols about future behaviour such as how complaints are to be aired in the future, a written apology, an explanation of what took place, and decisions about what might happen in the future. None of these are within the direct power of an employment tribunal or the court.

A mediation can be set up at short notice. The majority of mediations last no more than **11.97** one day.

Nothing said during mediation can be used against a party at a later time; the entire process **11.98** is strictly 'without prejudice' to their legal rights. If a satisfactory outcome is not reached through mediation, parties can still pursue a grievance or bring a claim to an employment tribunal (subject to the normal time limits).

The general principle as to the best time to mediate is 'the earlier the better', not just in **11.99** order that the issue does not become more bitter as time goes on, but also to save costs and time. However, it may be inappropriate to hold a mediation if further documents or information have to be provided by one party to enable the other party fully to understand the first party's allegations. In addition, part of the flexibility of mediation is that it can be used at any stage in a dispute and can run in parallel to a formal grievance or tribunal process and should not be used as an excuse to hold up an existing timetable. Sometimes, conversely, time is a healer and the optimum time to mediate will be some considerable time after a claim has been lodged. Therefore, the right time in each case will depend on a variety of factors.

The terms on which the mediation is to take place are usually outlined in a short document **11.100** ('the mediation agreement'), which must be agreed by the parties and the mediator. The mediation agreement sets out the practical details of the mediation, such as the paying parties, date, time, venue, selected mediator, etc. In mediated employment disputes in which the employee cannot afford to pay the mediator's costs, the employer frequently agrees to pay all the costs of the mediation. The agreement also establishes the legal features of the mediation, such as 'without prejudice', confidentiality, mediator immunity, and authority to settle. The document should be simple and straightforward so that all parties are willing to sign it. The mediation should be attended by those parties with first-hand knowledge of the issues and full authority to settle the dispute. If lawyers or other representatives do attend the mediation with their clients, it is important that they understand that their role is not to represent their client in the traditional sense, but rather to support them in seeking a solution going forward. Courtroom behaviour is wholly inappropriate in a mediation and usually achieves nothing. Unrepresented parties should consider bringing a 'friend' to the mediation; that is, someone who can play a supportive and largely observational role. Union representatives might also play such a role.

It is common for parties to submit to the mediator a brief written summary of the dispute **11.101** highlighting the key issues from each of their perspectives. This can help parties to focus on the real issues in dispute that they wish to address. In many disputes there will also be some relevant documentation which it is appropriate for the mediator to see in advance. The case summaries and relevant documents are then exchanged between the parties and copied to the mediator, at an agreed date before the mediation takes place. Parties may bring additional documents to the mediation for only the mediator to see or send such documents to the mediator before the mediation.

11.102 The parties will decide in advance how long they want the mediation to last. Even if the mediation is agreed at eight hours, parties are usually keen for it to continue on the same day if there has been no settlement at the end of the eight hours and one is in sight. If so, the mediation will continue by consent until either the dispute is resolved or it is agreed that there will be no resolution. Occasionally, mediations are adjourned after they have started if, during the course of the mediation, it is agreed that the parties require further information and the mediation cannot be resolved without that information.

(d) The settlement agreement

11.103 At the conclusion of the mediation, the mediator may assist the parties to prepare a list of the points they have agreed upon, although it is the parties' responsibility to draw up any such agreement. Once the agreement has been written, it must be signed. No agreement will be legally binding until it is in writing and signed by the parties or their authorized representatives in the form of a compromise agreement or ACAS COT3 form. It is important to ensure that the settlement which comes out of an employment mediation meets the criteria of compromise agreements within the ERA, including a statement that the employee has been independently advised by a relevant adviser.

12

WHISTLEBLOWING IN THE HEALTH AND FINANCIAL SERVICES SECTORS

The healthcare sector and the financial services sector have contributed to some of the **12.01** major influences on both legislative and case law developments and the practical approach to be taken to whistleblowing. In both sectors there has been a focus on the need to do more to encourage a climate in which those who are able to raise public interest concerns feel able to do so without fear of reprisal, and to ensure that their concerns are then heeded. These sectors have been in the vanguard in developing practical measures to achieve these goals. We focus in this chapter on the developments specific to each sector. In addition, in the light of criticisms made in the Francis report, 'Freedom to Speak Up', as to the limits of the specific whistleblowing legislation, we consider the scope for other avenues to obtain injunctive relief in the ordinary courts to prevent or bring to an end whistleblowing victimization.

A. The Health Sector

(1) Momentum for reform

12.02 The NHS is the UK's single largest employer, the largest employer in Western Europe and was ranked the fifth largest in the world in 2012[1] with a combined workforce of 1.7 million. The need for whistleblowing protection, its limits, and further steps that are required have been the subject of greater focus in this area than in any other.

12.03 Various reports have addressed the importance of whistleblowing protection in the health sector. Prior to Sir Robert Francis' 'Freedom to Speak Up', the most influential of these was Dame Janet Smith's Fifth report on the Shipman Inquiry (December 2004). Tracing the developments in the sector, the report noted that it was only in the early 1990s that the General Medical Council (GMC) made plain to doctors that their duty lay in making a report in any case where poor practice or performance might affect patient safety, and that this was not really heeded.[2] The first guidance to NHS staff about how to go about raising concerns was published in 1993. But it was flawed in various respects, including a lack of clarity as to how to make a disclosure and in taking a somewhat adversarial approach, akin to a grievance procedure. The focus was on whether the employee had substantiated the disclosure rather than on placing the onus on the recipient to investigate the concern.[3] The need to foster a climate of openness was then stressed in a Department of Health circular in 1999 which required that senior managers or non-executive directors be given specific responsibility for addressing concerns raised in confidence and which could be dealt with outside the usual line management chain.[4]

12.04 The Fifth report proceeded to make some specific proposals as to changes to the protected disclosure legislation. Of these perhaps the most notable was the suggestion that the requirement for disclosures to be made in good faith could be omitted. Almost a decade later, that suggestion was put into effect by the amendments relegating the good faith test to a remedy issue. Other proposals have not been implemented. In particular the proposal to introduce a reasonable suspicion test in place of the requirement for a 'reasonable belief' that the information tends to show a relevant failure, so as to encourage reporting of concerns where a worker has incomplete information,[5] has not been taken up. Dame Janet Smith's view was that whilst the reasonable belief test was appropriate for wider disclosures such as to the media, when applied to the test for a qualifying disclosure it might operate to discourage workers from reporting their concerns internally. Further, she argued that the requirements of section 43F ERA for protected disclosures to a regulator (that there be a reasonable belief that the information disclosed and any allegation contained in it are substantially true) are liable to lead to a reluctance to report concerns to regulators when the information is second hand (eg based on a strong rumour or suspicion), with the result that the regulators are likely to remain unaware of cases of which they should be aware.[6]

12.05 Overall, Dame Janet Smith accepted that there had been a move towards promoting an atmosphere of openness rather than blame, but emphasized the need for those in positions of leadership to commit to openness of reporting and noted that old attitudes had not by

---

[1] See http://www.telegraph.co.uk/news/uknews/9155130/NHS-is-fifth-biggest-employer-in-world.html.
[2] Shipman Fifth report, para 11.50.
[3] ibid, paras 11.51, 11.52.
[4] ibid, para 11.56–11.57.
[5] ibid, paras 11.109–11.113.
[6] See further the discussion in Chapter 3 at paras 3.103 and 3.104.

any means died out. Nevertheless, ten years after her report there was widespread recognition that there remained a deep-seated culture within parts of the NHS which tended to discourage staff from speaking up to raise their concerns. Staff believed that they would not be listened to if they did and might be subjected to retaliation. In January 2015 the Parliamentary Health Select Committee, in a report entitled 'Complaints and Raising Concerns', reached the damning conclusion that:

> The treatment of whistleblowers remains a stain on the reputation of the NHS and has led to unwarranted and inexcusable pain for a number of individuals. The treatment of those whistleblowers has not only caused them direct harm but has also undermined the willingness of others to come forward and this has ongoing implications for patient safety.

The shocking revelations of failures in care at Mid Staffordshire Foundation Trust acted as **12.06** a catalyst for fresh review of policy and legislation in this field. When, on 9 June 2010, the Secretary of State for Health, then Andrew Lansley, announced that Sir Robert Francis QC was to lead a public inquiry concerning the failures in care at Mid Staffordshire Foundation Trust, it was also acknowledged that further work was necessary to improve procedures to enable staff to raise concerns. The new measures included:

- guidance to NHS organizations that all their contracts of employment should include specific reference to whistleblowing rights;
- changes to the staff terms and conditions of service handbook (for those on Agenda for Change contracts);
- a promise of a full public consultation as to possible amendments to the NHS Constitution with regard to whistleblowing.

In October 2010 the Department of Health issued the consultation document and, follow- **12.07** ing on from this, in March 2012 a new edition of the NHS Constitution was published incorporating the following:

- the expectation for staff to raise concerns at the earliest opportunity;
- the pledge to support staff raising concerns;
- the legal right not to suffer a detriment.

On 6 February 2013 Sir Robert Francis QC published his findings from the Mid Staffordshire **12.08** public inquiry. He placed emphasis on the need for greater openness, transparency, and candour throughout the NHS, bringing into sharp focus the inadequacy of support and protections for staff raising concerns over patient safety. Following on from this, in response to continuing disquiet about the treatment of those who spoke up to raise concerns, Sir Robert Francis QC led a further review into how staff could be supported to raise concerns. The aim was to provide advice and recommendations to ensure that NHS staff feel that it is safe to raise concerns, and that they are confident that they will be listened to and that their concerns will be acted upon. The resulting report 'Freedom to Speak Up', published on 11 February 2015, provides a key point of reference for good practice in encouraging an open and honest reporting culture. The report wholeheartedly endorsed the observation of Dame Janet Smith in her Fifth Shipman report (at para 81) that:

> I believe that the willingness of one healthcare professional to take responsibility for raising concerns about the conduct, performance or health of another could make a greater potential contribution to patient safety than any other single factor.[7]

---

[7] *Fifth Report of the Shipman Inquiry—Safeguarding Patients: Lessons from the Past—Proposals for the Future*, Dame Janet Smith, 9 December 2004.

12.09   Sir Robert Francis concluded that there remained a culture within many parts of the NHS which 'deters staff from raising serious and sensitive concerns and which not infrequently has negative consequences for those brave enough to raise them'.[8] His report was followed by a number of further reports and consultations concerned with how to put its recommendations into practice. On 16 July 2015 the Government published 'Learning not blaming', endorsing the proposals to put in place Freedom to Speak Up Guardians in each Trust. That system has been implemented, supported by a National Guardian's Office, and a public consultation by the Care Quality Commission (CQC) as to how this should operate. A further public consultation by NHS Improvement preceded the introduction of a national template whistleblowing policy in April 2016. In addition, fresh guidance was issued by the Nursing and Midwifery Council ('Raising Concerns').

12.10   Meanwhile, on 19 March 2015, one month after 'Freedom to Speak Up', Sir Anthony Hooper provided a report commissioned by the GMC on the GMC's handling of cases involving whistleblowers. At the time of writing, steps to implement Sir Anthony's recommendations are being piloted. The objective is to reduce the scope for referrals of doctors to the GMC being deployed as a means of victimizing those who have raised public interest concerns. We consider this further at paragraphs 12.50 and 12.51 below.

(2) 'Freedom to Speak Up': legal context and intractable nature of the problem

12.11   Whilst the Francis review which led to 'Freedom to Speak Up' was not a public inquiry, and did not pass judgment on individual cases, Sir Robert noted that:

> There is nevertheless a remarkable consistency in the pattern of reactions described by staff who told of bad experiences. Whistleblowers have provided convincing evidence that they raised serious concerns which were not only rejected but were met with a response which focused on disciplinary action against them rather than any effective attempt to address the issue they raised. Whilst there may be some cases in which issues are fabricated or raised to forestall some form of justifiable action against them, this cannot be true of them all. I have concluded that there is a culture within many parts of the NHS which deters staff from raising serious and sensitive concerns and which not infrequently has negative consequences for those brave enough to raise them.[9]

12.12   As to the reasons why people might feel reluctant to speak up, whilst noting that there may be many reasons, the report concluded that:

> Two particular factors stood out from the evidence we gathered: fear of the repercussions that speaking up would have for an individual and for their career; and the futility of raising a concern because nothing would be done about it.

Those are themes that resonate beyond the NHS. But the findings were all the more striking given the steps that had already been taken to encourage staff to feel able to speak up on patient safety issues (which Sir Robert expressly noted that he took to include bullying and dysfunctional working relationships[10]) and the professional duties on health professionals to raise concerns.

(a) Professional duties to raise concerns and foster a suitable environment for raising concerns

12.13   One distinctive feature of the health sector is that the subject matter of the concerns which might arise is likely to also give rise not only to a right to report those concerns, but also a

---

[8] 'Freedom to Speak Up', Executive Summary, para 6.
[9] ibid.
[10] 'Freedom to Speak Up', para 1.18.

duty to do so and possibly also a duty to inform a patient as part of the duty of candour (as discussed in Chapter 13, at paragraphs 13.97–13.104). The professional duty required of all doctors registered with the GMC is reflected in its publication, *Good Medical Practice*, which came into effect on 22 April 2013. The GMC states that there are obligations on doctors:

- to 'promote and encourage a culture that allows all staff to raise concerns openly and safely' (para 24)
- if a patient is not receiving basic care to meet their needs, to immediately to tell someone who is in a position to act straight away (para 25(a))
- if patients are at risk because of inadequate premises, equipment, or other resources, policies, or systems, to raise a concern and make a record of the steps taken (para 25(b))
- if concerned that a colleague may not be fit to practise and may be putting patients at risk, and subject to first taking advice, to report this and make a record of the steps taken (para 25(c)).

Similarly, obligations to speak up are placed on registered nurses and midwives under their **12.14** professional code of conduct, including an obligation to 'raise and, if necessary, escalate any concerns . . . about patient or public safety, or the level of care people are receiving in your workplace or any other healthcare setting . . .' (para 16.1 of the Code published by the Nursing and Midwifery Council). Specific guidance on raising concerns was published in 2013, and updated in June 2015.[11] It provides that a nurse or midwife has a professional duty to report any concerns from their workplace about situations which put the safety of the people in their care at risk (para 1). The guidance states that failure to report concerns may bring that nurse's fitness to practice into question and put their registration at risk (para 2).

(b) NHS terms and conditions and the NHS constitution

Since July 2010, NHS standard terms and conditions, which, subject to narrow exceptions, **12.15** apply to all staff directly employed by NHS organizations, have specifically provided that:

> All employees working in the NHS have a contractual right and a duty to raise genuine concerns they have with their employer about malpractice, patient safety, financial impropriety or any other serious risks they consider to be in the public interest.
>
> (section 21.1); and

> NHS organisations must have local policies that emphasise that it is safe and acceptable for staff to raise concerns and set out clear arrangements for doing so. Such policies are often referred to as 'whistleblowing' or 'open practice' policies.
>
> (section 21.2)

Also since July 2010, the standard terms have recorded that the NHS Staff Council recom- **12.16** mends that local policies should include provision that it:

> . . . is a disciplinary matter either to victimise a genuine 'whistleblower' or for someone to maliciously make a false allegation. However, every concern should be treated as made in good faith, unless it is subsequently found out not to be.
>
> (section 21.3)

In addition, the NHS Constitution (first published in March 2012)[12] imposes a duty on all staff: **12.17**

> to raise any genuine concern you may have about a risk, malpractice or wrongdoing at work (such as a risk to patient safety, fraud or breaches of patient confidentiality), which may

---

[11] 'Raising Concerns: Guidance for nurses and midwives'.
[12] At the time of writing the Constitution was last updated on 14 October 2015.

affect patients, the public, other staff or the organisation itself, at the earliest reasonable opportunity.

12.18 In this context, the Francis Report noted encouraging signs that there was a genuine will to make progress. But the report also emphasized the intractable nature of the problem in fostering a culture where staff are able to feel confident in speaking up, and emphasized the need for further action to bring about cultural change, improved handling of cases, and further measures to support good practice.[13]

(3) 'Freedom to Speak Up': general criticisms of the protected disclosure legislation

12.19 With limited exceptions (considered in the following section), 'Freedom to Speak Up' focused on recommendations as to good practice aimed at fostering a culture in which concerns are welcomed and handled correctly, rather than changes to the ambit of protection provided by ERA's protected disclosure provisions. Annex A to the report summarizes recommendations focused on driving cultural change, handling of concerns, training, monitoring and provision of advice, and support for staff with concerns. Sir Robert expressed the view that the legislation was 'weak' (para 9.17) and was critical of its complexity (para 9.5). But in contrast to the approach adopted by Dame Janet Smith in the Shipman report, he made only very limited recommendations for change (considered in paragraphs 12.24–12.46 below).

12.20 In commenting on the phrase 'protected disclosure', it was noted in 'Freedom to Speak Up' (at para 2.2.9) that:

> The legislation does not provide an individual worker with guaranteed protection from suffering detriment if they make a protected disclosure . . .

It is not easy to see how any scheme of legislation could provide 'guaranteed protection'. In the all too frequent situation where performance management issues are raised after there has been public interest disclosure, it is still necessary to address the evidential question as to whether that disclosure was an influence in taking the action. The onus is on the employer to show the reason for the detrimental treatment (section 48(2) ERA)[14] and for the dismissal (subject to the employee first showing there is an issue warranting an investigation).[15] It would therefore be for the employer to explain the reasons for taking the management action. But plainly it would be quite wrong for a worker to be immune from action being taken on legitimate performance grounds which are unrelated to the disclosure merely because of the fact of having raised concerns.

12.21 Whilst guaranteed protection is not possible, there are some possible alternatives to strengthen protection that may merit consideration. One course, which was recommended by the Whistleblowing Commission established by PCaW (Recommendation 14), would be to apply the same test for whistleblowing dismissals as applies for detriments. That would entail applying a significant influence test rather than requiring that the reason or principal reason be the dismissal. It would also have the merit of avoiding anomalies that otherwise arise from the difference between detriment and dismissal cases (which could result in a worker's claim of termination of contract succeeding where an employee dismissal case fails).

---

[13] 'Freedom to Speak Up', paras 1.24 and 1.26.
[14] See Chapter 7, paras 7.191–7.201.
[15] See Chapter 9, paras 9.37–9.57.

One specific weakness highlighted in the protected disclosure legislation was the absence of **12.22** measures capable of preventing detriments occurring (para 2.2.9). We consider further (at paragraphs 12.62–12.86 below) the extent to which that gap might be filled by remedies in the ordinary courts.

The report expressed the view (at para 9.6) that there was no evidence that the potential for **12.23** a tribunal claim deters victimization. However, it seems rather unlikely that witnesses to the inquiry would have said that they had been deterred from victimizing whistleblowers by the possibility that the whistleblower might make such a claim. Nor was there any consideration of the potential impact of the provisions which have introduced individual liability for victimization of whistleblowers (combined with suitable training and education for staff as to the impact and effect of those provisions).

(4) 'Freedom to Speak Up': legislative reform

Whilst Sir Robert Francis did not recommend a wholesale review of the protected dis- **12.24** closure legislation, reforms were proposed in three areas: (a) extension of the class of prescribed persons, (b) amendments to the definition of workers, and (c) introducing protection for those have previously whistleblown when they apply for further employment in the NHS.

(a) Prescribed persons

The report noted that there were some surprising omissions from the list of prescribed per- **12.25** sons. In Sir Robert's view the list should be extended to cover a variety of bodies responsible for training. It was also desirable to include clinical commissioning groups and NHS England, as commissioners of services. Given the quasi market that operates within the NHS as between trusts and commissioning groups, it might be thought undesirable to extend the status of prescribed person to commissioning groups: the customer is thus accorded the status of regulator. But this misgiving is surely outweighed by the need to facilitate the raising of public interest concerns with commissioners.

The report recommended extending the list of prescribed persons to fill these gaps. Specifically, **12.26** it recommended including all relevant national oversight, commissioning, scrutiny, and training bodies, including NHS Protect, NHS England, NHS Clinical Commissioning Groups, Public Health England, Healthwatch England, local Healthwatch, Health Education England, Local Education and Training Boards, and the Parliamentary and Health Services Ombudsman. Not all of these recommendations have been implemented. But some additions were made by the Public Interest Disclosure (Prescribed Persons) Order 2014,[16] including designating Health Education England and the NHS Commissioning Board in relation to specified functions.

(b) Definition of workers—legislative and contractual extensions

In Chapter 6, we considered the ways in which protection is extended to various relation- **12.27** ships within the healthcare sector by section 43K (1)(ba), (bb), (c), and (cb) ERA. The Francis report recommended a further extension so as to cover all students studying for a career in healthcare rather than just student nurses. The Government's response of July 2015 (at para 78) stated an intention to enact this extension to cover all students studying for a career in healthcare when parliamentary time allows, though at the time of writing no such amendment has yet been introduced.

---

[16] As amended by the Public Interest Disclosure (Prescribed Persons) (Amendment) (No 2) Order 2015/1981.

12.28   If correctly decided, a gap in protection was revealed by the decision in *Day v Lewisham &*
Greenwich NHS Trust [2016] IRLR 415, where the EAT concluded that Health Education
England (HEE) is not the (or even an) 'employer' of a doctor in training. The issue arises
because of the nature of the arrangements where junior doctors undergo training in a programme organized by HEE. In each placement, junior doctors are contracted to work for an
employer, usually an NHS trust, who would be the employer under the protected disclosure
legislation. In *Day*, the EAT held that HEE's responsibility for appointing junior doctors to
the placement does not entail being an employer.[17]

12.29   The issue was addressed by an agreement made in September 2016 between the BMA and
HEE with the approval of the Department of Health and NHS Employers, and applicable to postgraduate trainee doctors and dentists. The mechanism for achieving protection
is for HEE to contract with local employers (typically an NHS trust) to confer the same
rights as if HEE was an employer for the purposes of the protected disclosure legislation.
The agreement expressly recognizes the right of such doctors to bring an action relying on
the Contract (Rights of Third Parties) Act 1999. It does not confer any greater rights than
those that would be available were HEE the doctor's employer under section 43K. It is also
provided, for the avoidance of doubt, that no trainee doctor shall have the right to claim
injunctive or equitable relief or to any relief or remedy which is not provided for by section
49 ERA against Health Education England in respect of the third party rights granted
under the Agreement.

12.30   The HEE agreement will terminate if there is legislation or a final court determination
giving junior doctors rights to bring a claim against HEE in the tribunal. In the meantime,
the agreement is necessarily a more cumbersome route than the straightforward course of an
extension of protection using the power in section 43K(4) ERA. Given that parties cannot
contract to confer jurisdiction on the employment tribunal, where a junior doctor wishes to
claim both against the local employer (eg the NHS trust) and HEE, she or he could not do
so in a single forum. There would need to be separate claims in the County or High Court
and the tribunal.

12.31   Pending a change in the law (or reversal of the EAT's decision in *Day*) the approach is
an innovative step aimed at proactively overcoming identified gaps in the legislation and
potentially provides a template for seeking to do so in other areas. That may be pertinent both within the NHS sector and beyond. Whilst the HEE Agreement fills one gap
in protection, as discussed in Chapter 6 there remain other gaps, such as in relation to
volunteers.

(c) Applicants for employment

12.32   Sir Robert's report suggested that the Government consider legislation to outlaw discrimination in recruitment against whistleblowers by NHS employers. Pursuant to this recommendation, section 49B ERA was inserted by the Small Business, Enterprise and Employment
Act 2015 (section 149(1), (2)). Rather than providing for protection against detriment done
to applicants for employment generally, this section confers a power to make regulations
prohibiting an 'NHS employer' from discriminating against an applicant because it appears
to that employer that the applicant has made a protected disclosure. There is provision to
permit an extended definition of NHS employer to include NHS public bodies such as the

---

[17]   At the time of writing, an appeal to the Court of Appeal is pending. See the discussion (and criticism)
of this decision in Chapter 6, paras 6.20–6.29, and the alternative interpretation advanced in *McTigue v*
University Hospital Bristol NHS Foundation Trust [2016] IRLR 742.

CQC or Monitor (section 49B(7) ERA). If implemented the provision would deal with blacklisting and other detriments where the reason for these is that the applicant made a protected disclosure. It would, in this specific context, address the lacuna in protection, by comparison to discrimination legislation, which arises by reason of there not yet being a relationship of employee or worker and employer. However, as yet no such regulations to implement these measures have been introduced. There are also important respects in which the provision is unsatisfactory, and/or raises serious questions as to why equivalent provision is not made beyond the NHS context. We consider this below.

Limit to NHS employers   The provision is limited to NHS employers. Given the focus of **12.33** Sir Robert Francis' review on the health sector it is perhaps understandable that the recommendation made in relation to applicants was limited to that sector. Less understandable is the Government's timid response. No persuasive reason has been advanced for the narrow approach taken of confining such protection to the NHS field.

In his report, Sir Robert highlighted several distinct features of the NHS in addition to its **12.34** sheer size: it has a very high public and political profile; it is immensely complex; it is heavily regulated; it consists of many autonomous decision-making units; and there is often intense pressure to emphasize the positive achievements of the service. It might also be said that there is a particular public interest in promoting integrity and safety in a service so central to the country's well-being and which exists as a monopoly employer. However, given the public policy considerations underlying protection of those who make public interest disclosures, none of those features appear to explain why protection of applicants should be confined to the NHS.

Perhaps more pertinently one of the issues emphasized by Sir Robert was that the NHS **12.35** seeks to unify a complex web of organizations as a unified service, and collectively operates as a monopoly employer, which may lead to a worker in the health sector effectively being excluded from employment. Sir Robert noted that in addition to formal mechanisms through the regulatory structure, there will also be informal networks which will share information on a non-attributable basis with the result that exclusion of a staff member from one employment, particularly a doctor or nurse, may mean that they cannot find work elsewhere (para 1.8). That may indeed mean that the impact of retribution is particularly acute. However, the NHS is not unique in this regard. In the financial services sector victimization by an employing firm may have a similar result. Workers in those fields where there is a fit and proper person requirement may be particularly susceptible to this. In any event, even aside from this, there is the risk of a stigmatizing effect, either from being the subject of misconduct or performance allegations or due to being branded a whistleblower, which may affect future job prospects: that is not a problem which is confined to the NHS.

It might be argued that the extension of protection to applicants who have made disclo- **12.36** sures to previous employers puts a prospective employer in difficulty because that prospective employer may be less able to investigate the circumstances of the disclosures than the employer to whom they were made. But that is unpersuasive. Protection applies against employers or former employers notwithstanding that the disclosure may have been made to a third party, whether under section 43C(1)(b) or sections 43D to H ERA, or because the disclosure was made to a previous employer: see *BP plc v Elstone and Petrotechnics Ltd* [2010] IRLR 558 (EAT). In any event, having properly accepted the principle that such protection should apply in the health sector, no good reason has been advanced for a different approach in other sectors.

Grafting on a discrimination model: Unnecessary complexity   Further, despite Sir **12.37** Robert Francis' criticisms of the complexity of the protected disclosure legislation, the decision to legislate separately for the health sector adds a further, and in our view unnecessary, layer of complexity. That is so not only in that separate provision is made for NHS employers/employees, but also that a framework modelled on the discrimination legislation is being grafted onto provisions that are founded on the concept of detriment. Section 49B(1) sets out a restriction on discriminating against applicants, and section 49B(3) ERA provides that:

> For the purposes of subsection (1), an NHS employer discriminates against an applicant if the NHS employer refuses the applicant's application or in some other way treats the applicant less favourably than it treats or would treat other applicants in relation to the same contract, office or post.

12.38 No explanation has been provided as to why it was thought necessary in this context to adopt the language of discrimination, whereas for any other sort of protected disclosure claim there is a test based on not subjecting the claimant to detriment by any act or deliberate failure to act on the ground of a protected disclosure. Related to this, section 49B(4) (c), (d) ERA contemplates that the regulations will make separate provision for the remedies associated with a breach of this provision, whereas there is an existing scheme already in place in relation to detrimental treatment.

12.39 The alternative and more straightforward approach would have been to extend protection to any person who applies for a position in which, if accepted, they would be a worker as defined in the legislation, and to include in a corresponding extension of the definition the person who would be the employer in the event that the application was accepted. That might in turn be subject to specific extensions such as contemplated in section 49B ERA to include NHS public bodies. But, whether or not restricted to the NHS sector, the grafting on of provisions in the language of the discrimination legislation makes little sense.

12.40 One illustration of the unnecessary uncertainty created by the adoption of a discrimination model is in relation to the issue as to whether, in determining if a detrimental act was on the ground of a protected disclosure, it is permissible to have regard to influence on the decision from someone who was not the decision-maker. As discussed in Chapter 7, there is some conflict on the authorities on this issue, and the decision in *Jhuti* suggests a difference of approach between that in the protected disclosure context and that applicable under the Equality Act 2010 (EqA), following *CLFIS (UK) Ltd v Reynolds* [2015] EWCA Civ 439, [2015] IRLR 562. The adoption of a discrimination model in section 49B ERA then in turn raises the further unwelcome prospect of a different approach to this as between section 49B ERA and the remainder of the protected disclosure legislation. We suggest that the preferable course as a matter of construction would be to adopt a uniform approach.

12.41 It is notable that in para 9.19 of 'Freedom to Speak Up' the proposal was put in broader terms. The report stated as follows:

> The evidence I have seen during the course of the Review indicates that individuals are suffering, or are at risk of suffering, serious detriments in seeking re-employment in the health service after making a protected disclosure. I am convinced that this can cause a very serious injustice: they are effectively excluded from the ability to work again in their chosen field. With that in mind, I think that consideration does need to be given to *extending discrimination law to protect those who make a protected disclosure from discrimination* either in the Employment Rights Act 1996 or the Equality Act 2010 or to finding an alternative means to avoid discrimination on these grounds. (emphasis added)

The suggestion of giving consideration to applying discrimination law to the status of being a whistleblower might therefore be read as being put in more general terms than being confined to protection of applicants for employment, albeit that it was said in the context of highlighting the difficulties faced by those seeking re-employment, and the particular proposal (at Action 20.1) referred specifically to discrimination in recruitment. A more general application of discrimination law principles would obviously have had a much greater impact than that actually adopted by the Government in the amendment to introduce section 49B. There would be advantages to such an approach. It would avoid the incongruence of the difference in approach as between the coverage of applicants and other whistleblowing claims. In addition to applying to applicants for employment, the discrimination provisions in the EqA also have broader provisions for secondary liability, through the provisions for instructing, causing, or inducing contraventions and aiding contraventions in sections 111 and 112 EqA. The application of those provisions would give greater scope to address the problem that detrimental treatment by reason of whistleblowing may be meted out by others within the service aside from the employer or those acting on behalf of the employer. Further, applying the discrimination model generally would avoid the anomalies that arise from the distinction between detriment and dismissal of employees. Those anomalies include (a) the difference in reversal of burden of proof compared to termination of the contract of a non-employee worker where there is insufficient qualifying service for ordinary unfair dismissal,[18] (b) the difference in available remedies,[19] and (c) that for dismissal of employees (but not other detriments) liability turns on the principal reason for dismissal rather that a material influence being sufficient.[20]

No individual liability   One further consequence of the decision to proceed by way of **12.42** a separate provision, rather than to amend the definition of worker and employer for the purposes of the detriment provisions, is that the provisions for individual liability do not apply. Again, the approach is unexplained. It might be said that there is some logic to this on the basis that typically the detriment in relation to an applicant will consist of not offering employment. In that respect it is plainly something done on behalf of and in the name of the employer, and is the mirror image of dismissal claims where there is also no provision for individual liability. We suggest, however, that this is unconvincing. First, in the general protected disclosure provisions individual liability is only excluded for unfair dismissal claims by employees, where it would cut across the unfair dismissal legislation. It is not excluded for other workers and, even in relation to employees, it is strongly arguable that it would not exclude a claim of detriment against the individual employee based on the distinct act of procuring a dismissal (as to which see the discussion of *Royal Mail Group Ltd v Jhuti* in Chapter 7). In any event, causing detriment against applicants might not be limited to refusing employment. It might for example take the form of breaching confidentiality in relation to the content of the job application or tipping off the current employer as to the fact that the application has been made.

Employer's perception   Section 49B ERA contemplates protection from discrimination **12.43** against an applicant 'because *it appears* to the NHS employer that the applicant has made a protected disclosure' (emphasis added). Protection is not limited to cases where the applicant has made a protected disclosure; it extends to a situation where it only appears to the prospective employer (who may be mistaken) that the applicant had made a protected disclosure. That may in turn reflect the influence of discrimination provisions under the EqA. In that context it is well established that there can be a claim based on the treatment of someone who is perceived to have a protected characteristic (see para 3.21 of the EHRC Employment Code). However, in contrast to the discrimination provisions (see section 13

---

[18] See Chapter 9, paras 9.46–9.48.
[19] Chapter 10, paras 10.63–10.70.
[20] Chapter 7, paras 7.82 and 7.83.

EqA), section 49B ERA stops short of permitting a claim based on association with someone else's protected disclosure rather than the prospective employer's belief that the applicant made the protected disclosure.

12.44 The inclusion of the test in section 49B ERA of whether 'it appears' a protected disclosure was made in turn begs the question of whether sections 47B and 103A ERA are similarly capable of being construed so as to cover this, and, if they are not, then why there should be a different and in some cases more favourable approach towards claims by applicants. The position may arise for example where a disclosure has been made anonymously or to a regulatory body and the employer mistakenly believes that a particular worker made the disclosure. To a large extent the policy considerations in favour of protecting that worker also apply in such a case just as much as they apply to protecting an applicant for employment. Detrimental treatment of the worker who is believed (albeit wrongly) to have made the disclosure is no less likely to have a chilling effect deterring others from reporting concerns than it would if the worker had in fact made the disclosure. It might be argued that in each case, section 47B and section 103A ERA focus on the state of mind of the person who carried out the detrimental act or failure to act. As such it can be said that an employer who wrongly believes that a worker has made a protected disclosure is acting on the grounds of the worker having made a disclosure, irrespective of whether that belief is correct.

12.45 However, there are some serious problems with this approach to construction. It may be said to drive a coach and horses through the structure of the legislation which requires careful focus on the elements of a protected disclosure, including consideration of whether the worker had a reasonable belief that the disclosure tended to show a relevant failure. That necessarily places the focus on the worker's state of mind to establish whether a protected disclosure was made. To take an extreme example, suppose a worker makes a disclosure of information indicating that unsafe medical practices are being followed but knowing full well that some of the information has been fabricated or exaggerated and as a result the worker does not have the requisite reasonable belief. To the employer receiving the information it may still appear that a protected disclosure has been made. It would run wholly contrary to the structure of the legislation for the worker's protected disclosure claim to succeed on the basis that it appeared to the employer that the worker had made a protected disclosure, and the worker was subjected to a detriment by reason of this apprehended state of affairs. That would be to circumvent the careful focus on the elements for the worker to qualify for protection.

12.46 It might be argued that in such a case, if a claim could succeed on the basis of the employer's perception even though a worker did not in fact make a protected disclosure, for example due to lacking a reasonable belief, this could be reflected by an adjustment made at the remedy stage. However, it is not the case that the approach in section 49B ERA of basing protection on where it 'appears to the NHS employer' that the applicant made a protected disclosure necessarily extends the scope of protection, so as to be wider than if it applied to detrimental treatment 'on the ground that' the applicant made a protected disclosure. The reasonable belief tests, both as to whether the information tends to show a relevant failure and as to whether disclosure is made in the public interest, deliberately place the focus on the worker's perspective and whether the worker's subjective belief is objectively reasonable. By contrast, the test in section 49B of whether 'it appears' that a protected disclosure was made places the focus on the employer's state of mind. It may open the door to an argument that there is no protection because it did not 'appear to' the employer that the worker had the requisite reasonable belief, or possibly even because the employer gave no thought to whether information disclosed amounted to a protected disclosure, or satisfied the elements for a protected disclosure. As such, that suggests that if there is a test of an apparent disclosure, it should apply as an additional basis of liability rather than (as drafted in section 49B ERA) applying instead of the test of detrimental act or failure to act on the grounds of a protected disclosure.

(5) The problem of pre-emptive/retaliatory whistleblowing and retaliatory employer complaint

As Sir Robert Francis noted in 'Freedom to Speak Up', the interaction between whistleblow- **12.47** ing and management of poor performance is a complex and controversial issue. On one hand victimization may take the form that those who have raised concerns suddenly find themselves subject to critical appraisals and poor performance concerns or other criticisms and complaints. On the other, employers expressed their frustration about weak performers who raise concerns as a deliberate attempt to thwart the performance-management process. That may be particularly pertinent in the NHS context because there is ample scope for a wide range of concerns and complaints to be framed in public interest disclosure terms. In his report Sir Robert Francis highlighted the interdependence of the many different elements of the NHS system (para 1.7). A consequence of this interdependence is that failings in any one part of the system may be said ultimately to have a bearing on patient safety and care and as such to entail public interest issues. That was also reflected in the view that concerns about oppressive or bullying and dysfunctional relationships were to be considered safety issues (para 1.18), and by the observation that poor performance is itself a safety issue (Executive Summary, para 34). Sir Robert warned of the dangers of failing to distinguish between a grievance and whistleblowing, but the line between the two will often be a blurred one.

The solution proposed by Sir Robert was to focus on investigating the concern on its merits. **12.48** Reflecting the amendment made to the protected disclosure legislation to relegate good faith to a remedy issue, he emphasized that the motive of a member of staff who raises a concern has no automatic association with the truth or falsity of what he or she reports (para 5.4.4). Sir Robert concluded (at para 5.4.5) that the best way to meet the possibility of false allegations was to investigate and establish whether they are true or false and to separate this from any existing processes in relation to the individual making the disclosure. He emphasized that there was no reason why the raising of a concern should ever impede the continuation of management of poor performance or disciplinary processes being undertaken for other genuine reasons. Indeed, he noted that poor performance is itself a safety issue (para 5.4.7). As against that, other than where there are exceptional circumstances, or where action in relation to an individual's performance was already underway or is unrelated to the concern raised, no disciplinary action directly associated with the concern should be considered or taken until the completion of the investigation and consequent identification of any required action (para 5.3.13).

Whilst that guidance makes sense in principle, both in the NHS field and beyond, its **12.49** application in practice may not be straightforward. This is particularly so where a worker speaks up to raise concerns as to the conduct of those who are involved in a disciplinary or performance process, where the risk of delaying the performance-management process may be both real and unavoidable if there is to be a fair investigation of the concerns that have been raised. In the meantime, it may be necessary for there to be a suspension in order to protect the public until the completion of the investigation of all concerns. It will, however, be important to be alert to the risk of interim suspension being used as a weapon against employees raising inconvenient concerns.

The issue was revisited from a different perspective in Sir Anthony Hooper's report of March **12.50** 2015, commissioned by the GMC. Sir Anthony's report grappled with the risk of health sector employers using a referral to the GMC as to a doctor's fitness to practise as retaliation against a doctor for raising concerns or simply as an inappropriate alternative to actually addressing the concerns. Sir Anthony proposed that when an NHS organization makes a referral to the GMC it should be encouraged at the same time to state whether the doctor had raised concerns as to patient safety or the integrity of the system. That would then provide context when investigating the issue referred to the GMC.

12.51 At the time of writing, this approach is being trialled by the GMC. It potentially has the merit of discouraging referrals made by way of retaliation for raising concerns. As against that there may be a risk that NHS organizations are deterred from reporting genuine concerns on the basis that they will be subjected to counter-criticisms of victimization (even if untrue). It may be that there is also some risk of encouraging staff who believe that they may be subject of a report to the GMC, to raise concerns with a view to deterring the employer from escalating the concern. Ultimately, though, we suggest the approach is a sensible one, provided there is clarity as to what the employer must disclose, so that all relevant facts are available for consideration.

(6) National Whistleblowing Policy

12.52 One recommendation made in the 'Freedom to Speak Up' report was to effect standardization of processes and policies across the NHS so that those who move between NHS organizations would be in no doubt as to how to raise a concern (paras 5.3.6–5.3.9). Following the report, the first national, integrated whistleblowing policy was published by NHS Improvement and NHS England. Its aim was to provide minimum standard terms and standardize the way that staff are supported to raise concerns within all the various NHS organizations.

12.53 The policy was published on 1 April 2016 and operates as a template which encapsulates the minimum standards. It contains the following important requirements:

- A Whistleblowing Guardian must be appointed (discussed below).
- Staff must be encouraged to speak up.
- Concerns unresolved by line management should be investigated.
- Investigations are led by an independent person and are evidence based.
- Any investigation report must examine lessons to be learnt and focus upon the goal of improving patient care.
- The whistleblower is kept fully informed throughout.
- The board are made aware of any strategic findings.
- The policy must be reviewed annually and improved where possible.

(7) Whistleblowing Guardians

12.54 One of the key recommendations made in 'Freedom to Speak Up', was that a National Guardian be appointed to support a network of 'Freedom to Speak Up Guardians' within NHS Trusts, who were to be responsible for developing a culture of openness in NHS trusts and NHS Foundation trusts in England. Sir Robert Francis envisaged that the Freedom to Speak Up Guardian should be only one of a range of people whom staff could approach for support. He recommended that a non-executive director act as an independent voice and board-level champion for those who raise concerns, and that there be an executive board lead to oversee processes and be accountable for the treatment of whistleblowers within the organization and possibly a lower-level nominated manager with whom concerns could be raised.

12.55 Linked to this, Sir Robert also recommended steps to move away from treating whistleblower cases as employment issues rather than safety or quality issues. To this end he suggested allocating responsibility for overseeing policy, procedure, and practice in this area to the executive board member with responsibility for safety and quality (para 5.3.12).

The recommendations as to Freedom to Speak Up Guardians were endorsed in the **12.56** Government's response of July 2015. Each trust was required to appointed a Guardian by 1 October 2016, a National Guardian's Office having been established in April 2016 to support them in their role and reinforce good practice. The Guardians are not responsible individually for the investigation of concerns, nor are they exercising an appellate function. They do have responsibility, however, to ensure and oversee the integrity, independence, and effectiveness of the trust's policies and procedures on whistleblowing. Perhaps the best guide to their role remains the summary set out in 'Freedom to Speak Up' (at para 7.2.11), where Sir Robert Francis described their role as that of a local champion to:

- ensure that any safety issue about which a concern had been raised is dealt with properly and promptly;
- intervene if there are any indications of recriminations against the person raising concerns;
- act as an 'honest broker' if someone was trying to delay performance action of any sort (which would appear to address the concern raised by some employers as to individuals raising concerns with a view to delaying performance-management steps—para 5.4.2);
- be involved in training staff to feel confident about speaking up, and about how to deal with concerns when raised;
- work with HR to address organizational culture;
- share best practice examples and facilitate learning;
- escalate concerns outside the organization, for example to the CQC, if they do not feel appropriate or timely action is being taken by the employer.

The standard National Whistleblowing Policy expressly provides that if raising a concern with **12.57** the line manager does not resolve the matter, or a worker does not feel able to raise it with them, then the Freedom to Speak Up Guardian is one of the people who can be contacted. As such, disclosure to the Guardian would fall squarely within section 43C(2) ERA.

As discussed further below (paragraphs 12.112–12.114) the approach has to an extent been **12.58** mirrored in the financial services sector with the implementation of a requirement for firms to each have a whistleblowers' champion. The development reflects a recognition of the need for positive steps to proactively encourage a culture which is conducive to reporting concerns and clear high-level responsibility for promoting this. It may be expected that it will be recognized as reflecting good practice beyond those specific sectors and that the trend will be replicated in other fields.

(8) Injunctions to restrain whistleblower victimization

(a) Limits of interim relief in the employment tribunal

As noted above, one of the weaknesses in the protected disclosure legislation identified **12.59** by Sir Robert Francis in 'Freedom to Speak Up' was the absence of any power to prevent an employer from imposing a detriment or to require that it be brought to an end (para 2.2.9) The Whistleblowing Commission set up by PCaW also highlighted this aspect. The only interim relief available in the employment tribunal is in relation to dismissal and, as discussed in Chapter 10, it is limited because of the high hurdle which applies before relief will be granted and also because it effectively applies only to continue remuneration until the determination of the case. As to final relief, reinstatement or re-engagement awards are rare, and are not enforceable other than by further financial award if the employer refuses to comply. Nor is interim relief available to prevent a threatened detriment.

12.60   The Whistleblowing Commission recommended the extension of interim relief to detriment cases. An example would be an order requiring that suspension from employment be brought to an end. Injunctive relief of this nature would, however, be significantly different to the interim relief currently available. In the event that an employer is not willing to reinstate the employee pending determination or settlement of the complaint, the tribunal merely continues the contract for the purposes of continuing pay and continuous employment: sections 129(3) and 130(1) ERA. As such, other than the financial consequence, the order does not compel the employer to act or cease to act in any way. By contrast, to be meaningful, interim relief to restrain or prevent a detriment of this nature[21] would indeed entail injunctive powers of the sort so far reserved for the ordinary courts, which have powers to enforce compliance, if necessary by contempt of court proceedings.

12.61   In the absence of legislative change to introduce wider tribunal powers to order such relief, the question arises as to whether the gap could be filled by a claim in the ordinary courts. We consider this next, focusing in particular on claims to restrain a breach of contract or claims by way of judicial review.

(b) Injunctions to restrain a breach of contract

12.62   In 'Freedom to Speak Up', Sir Robert Francis suggested (at para 9.6) that it would be 'extremely difficult' to obtain an injunction to prevent whistleblowing detriment occurring as it would be difficult to prove that detriment was going to happen. We suggest that this is too narrow a view and that it proceeds on the false premise that injunctive relief ceases to be of value once the detriment has started. It is clear, for example, that the courts have jurisdiction to grant injunctive relief to prevent an ongoing or threatened breach of contract, such as to restrain an employer from commencing or continuing disciplinary or capability proceedings where this would be in breach of contract[22] or to restrain an employer from instigating or continuing a suspension or to limit its scope.[23]

12.63   **Framing of the victimization as a breach of contract**   A complaint under the ERA's victimization or dismissal provisions can only be brought in the employment tribunal. However, it will often be possible to formulate a claim in contractual terms. In many cases it will be possible to place reliance on standard implied terms as to the duty not without reasonable cause or excuse to act in a manner likely to destroy or seriously damage the relationship of trust and confidence, or to exercise a discretion rationally and in good faith and consistently with its contractual purpose,[24] or to act fairly in the conduct of an internal disciplinary or similar process.[25] Ordinarily, the employer will retain a discretion over a range of possible reasonable options.[26] However, if it can be established that the

---

[21] There may be other instances where the detriment is financial in nature and the interim relief could restore the financial entitlements pending the hearing. But in those cases compensation is more likely to be an adequate remedy and so interim relief a less appropriate course.

[22] *West London Mental Health NHS Trust v Chhabra* [2014] IRLR 227 (SC).

[23] *Mezey v South West London and St George's Mental Health NHS Trust* [2007] IRLR 244 (CA).

[24] *Braganza v BP Shipping Ltd* [2015] ICR 449 (SC) at paras 30 and 53.

[25] *Chhabra v West London Mental Health NHS Trust* [2014] ICR 194 (SC) at para 37; *Al-Mishlab v Milton Keynes Hospital NHS Foundation Trust* [2015] EWHC 3096 at para 17. See also *Hendy v Ministry of Justice* [2014] IRLR 856 (where Mann J proceeded on the footing that a duty to proceed fairly could apply also to a non-contractual disciplinary policy or other process, though the claim failed on the facts). But in *Chakrabarty v Ipswich Hospital NHS Trust* [2014] EWHC 2735, at para 114, Simler J stated that she was not satisfied that there was a free-standing discrete implied term of fairness and that where the authorities contemplate a duty of fairness they do so in the context of the implied term of trust and confidence or on a narrower basis by reference to an implied term that disciplinary processes will be conducted fairly and without unjustified delay.

[26] ibid.

managerial action was an act of victimization for making a protected disclosure, that is liable to indicate that the decision was taken in bad faith or took into account irrelevant considerations.[27] Where, for example, disciplinary or capability proceedings are brought not on the basis of genuine concerns but as an act of victimization for raising a protected disclosure, it is unlikely that there would be difficulty in treating this as a plain breach of the implied contractual terms: see for example *Lew v Board of Trustees of United Synagogue* [2011] IRLR 664 (noting that if it was established that a capability procedure had been trumped up as another means of dismissing the claimant for reasons that did not go to any genuine concerns as to his capability, there would be a plain breach of contract). Similarly, such issues may arise in the event of allegations in the context of an MHPS[28] investigation being classified as conduct rather than capability (or a mixed capability and conduct issue), where it is said this was done as an act of victimization. This classification can be seriously damaging for a doctor, both by virtue of circumventing procedural safeguards[29] and in the light of para 10 of section III of MHPS which expressly provides that consideration must be given to a referral to the GMC in all cases where an allegation of misconduct has been upheld. Such a scenario might, for example, occur where allegations by a doctor that another is placing patient safety at risk, are countered with allegations against that doctor of poor clinical teamworking skills[30] and relationship breakdown. The argument that the classification is incorrect[31] and a breach of contract could be fortified by an argument that a circumvention of the correct process is victimization and ought to be restrained by way of an injunction.

As established by the House of Lords in *Johnson v Unisys Ltd* [2003] 1 AC 518 (HL), the **12.64** implied term of trust and confidence has no application to a decision to dismiss. Nor is there any implied duty to act in good faith or rationally in relation to the dismissal decision. However, there may be contractual provisions restricting the entitlement to dismiss. In *Edwards v Chesterfield Royal Hospital NHS Foundation Trust* [2012] 2 AC 22, the Supreme Court determined that, so as to maintain coherence with the unfair dismissal regime, contractual damages are not available for the manner of dismissal, as in the case of dismissal in breach of contractual disciplinary procedure. But that does not detract from the fact that dismissal in breach of such procedures would amount to a breach of contract which might in appropriate circumstances be restrained by injunctive relief (per Lord Dyson at para 44). Indeed, the absence of compensation for the manner of dismissal is one factor pointing towards injunctive relief as an appropriate remedy: *Chhabra v West London Mental Health*

---

[27] See eg *Frenkel Topping Ltd v King* (UKEAT/0106/15/LA, 21 July 2015) at para 36, where the fact that criticism of the claimant's performance was an act of detriment for making protected disclosures and not genuinely to do with performance, as well as the fact that it was contrary to the assurance of protection in the contractual whistleblowing policy, were important in making clear that the conduct was repudiatory.

[28] The national procedure known as 'Maintaining High Professional Standards in the Modern NHS'.

[29] Para 17 of s I of MHPS provides: 'In cases relating primarily to the performance of a practitioner, consideration should be given to whether a local action plan to resolve the problem can be agreed with the practitioner.' Para 2 of s IV of MHPS stipulates that: 'If the concerns about clinical performance cannot be resolved through local informal processes set out in Section I (paras 15–17) the matter must be referred to the NCAS before consideration by a performance panel (unless the practitioner refuses to have his or her case referred).'

[30] Section IV of MHPS sets out the procedures for dealing with issues of clinical performance. Para 3 provides that: 'Matters which may fall under the performance procedures include ... ineffective clinical team working skills.'

[31] The test for the correct classification is a practical one so as to accord with the purpose of the procedure, and it is for the court to decide the classification: See *Mattu v University Hospitals Coventry and Warwickshire NHS Trust* [2013] ICR 270). But the Court ought to be slow to interfere with the conclusion of an experienced case manager on classification, per Stanley Burnton LJ at para 34 and Elias LJ at para 88. See also eg *Fynes v St George's Hospital NHS Trust* [2014] EWHC 756, at para 81.

NHS Trust [2014] ICR 194 at para 39. The relief must, however, be sought before the termination of the employment contract: *Hale v Brighton and Sussex University Hospital NHS Trust* [2015] EWHC 833. As such, in the event of a purported dismissal alleged to be in breach of contract, it will be important to affirm the contract (*Geys v Societe Generale* [2013] 1 AC 523 (SC)) and crucially to take steps in good time.[32] Tactically it may be appropriate for the employee to write to the employer before any potential dismissal, requesting various procedural safeguards in line with any legitimately expected fair process, having regard to the size and resources of the employer, consistent with provisions of the ACAS Code and as provided by any contractual procedure. The employee may also request that s/he is given a fair warning of any dismissal in good time before that decision might be made (to improve prospects of obtaining interim relief).[33]

12.65 **Tests for granting relief**   At the stage of seeking interim relief, the first question is whether there is a serious issue to be tried, unless the relief would effectively dispose of the proceedings, in which case some further assessment of the merits is required.[34] If that hurdle is overcome it is then necessary to consider the issue of adequacy of damages and the balance of convenience. If those factors are evenly balanced, the court may favour relief which maintains the status quo pending trial, but the status quo is that which existed before alleged breach, rather than at the date of the hearing (unless due to delay in bringing the application a later date applies): see *Allfiled Ltd v Eltis and others* [2016] FSR 11 at paras 152–157.[35]

12.66 Orders for injunctions and specific performance are discretionary remedies, and will only be ordered if it is just and reasonable to do so: see eg *Powell v Brent LBC* [1988] ICR 176 (CA). Both in considering the balance of convenience, and in relation to whether final relief is appropriate, two factors in particular have been emphasized, both at the interim and final relief stage, as limiting the circumstances in which the court will intervene to grant injunctive relief or to order specific performance as between employee and employer.[36] First, the order should be workable, and ordinarily this entails that specific performance will not be ordered of a contract of personal service, where the relationship relies on continuing trust and confidence. Second, the courts will not intervene to micromanage internal disciplinary or other similar internal proceedings (*Chhabra*).

12.67 *Workability and loss of trust and confidence*   As to the first of these propositions, the orthodox position is that the court should not consider granting injunctive relief that has the effect of preserving the relationship of employer and employee unless mutual trust and confidence has survived between them: see for example *Lakshmi v Mid Cheshire Hospitals NHS Trust* [2008] IRLR 956 at para 49. That proposition is liable to be particularly problematic in the whistleblowing context if the disclosures have caused tensions in working relationships. However, the restriction on specific performance is subject to an exception where, due to the nature of the relief sought, and/or the extent to which trust and confidence remain, there is no difficulty in workability of the order. Typically that may arise where the relief is

---

[32] See also *Lauffer v Barking Havering and Redbridge University Hospital NHS Trust* [2009] EWHC 2360, discussed at 12.80 below.

[33] See eg *Kircher v Hillingdon Primary Care Trust* [2006] EWHC 21 where, in the context of considering what date was to be taken as the status quo for the purposes of preserving the position pending trial (as one relevant factor in the determination of whether to grant interim injunctive relief), the court (at para 66) took the status quo as being the date on which a letter was written asking for notice of any intention to dismiss so as to enable an application to be made for an injunction to prevent dismissal.

[34] *American Cyanamid Co v Ethicon Ltd* [1975] AC 396 (HL); *Lansing Linde Ltd v Kerr* [1991] 1 WLR 251 (CA).

[35] See also *Kircher v Hillingdon Primary Care Trust* [2006] EWHC 21.

[36] See eg *Powell; Ashworth v Royal National Theatre* [2014] IRLR 526 at paras 17–29.

sought to restrain an employer from dismissing without first complying with an applicable contractual procedure. This was the case, for example, in *Robb v Hammersmith and Fulham LBC* [1991] ICR 514. The claimant was employed as Director of Finance. He successfully sought an interim injunction to restrain the defendant from giving effect to his summary dismissal (which was not accepted as terminating his employment). The dismissal was on capability grounds (alleged inability to perform his duties properly) and there had been a failure to follow contractual capability and disciplinary procedures. It was no bar that trust and confidence in the claimant had been lost at that time as the capability procedure was still workable, and the claimant had given undertakings that he agreed to be treated as suspended on full pay during the procedure, to carry out no functions as Director of Finance, and not to go to the defendant's offices other than by prior arrangement at the claimant's reasonable request, and the defendant was able to appoint a temporary Director of Finance.[37]

Whilst decisions applying this approach have not generally involved any contention as to **12.68** detrimental treatment by reason of protected disclosures, they indicate the potential value of relief to secure procedural safeguards which may be important for a whistleblower so as to have the opportunity to establish that allegations are unfounded. The issue arose in the context of alleged whistleblowing in *Jesudason v Alder Hey Children's NHS Foundation Trust* [2012] EWHC 4265 (QB). The claimant was employed as a reader in paediatric surgery at the University of Liverpool. He also held a parallel honorary contract of employment with the defendant, an NHS foundation trust. Termination of his honorary employment with the defendant would be likely to lead to termination of his paid employment at the University. Mr Jesudason's colleagues, themselves surgeons or other medical practitioners at the defendant trust, had raised complaints about Mr Jesudason's behaviour. For his part Mr Jesudason had alleged, among other answers to those complaints, that they were made in retaliation for him raising matters which would qualify as protected disclosures. The HR manager commissioned a report on the situation from outside consultants who concluded that relationships in the paediatric surgical services team between current team members and Mr Jesudason had broken down and that they did not believe that any interventions would bring about a cohesive team and a shared approach. In the light of this, a meeting was convened that could have resulted in his dismissal. One of the defendant's contentions was that neither the (contractual) capability nor disciplinary procedures applied to a breakdown in relationships between colleagues. Interim injunctive relief was granted preventing the proposed hearing taking place other than in accordance with the capability procedure. It was held to be strongly arguable that the capability procedure applied since in substance the contention was that Mr Jesudason's colleagues could not work with him because of the way he worked, and due to his approach to team work, to discussion, and to disclosure of matters with which he was dissatisfied or about which he was concerned.[38] Relief was appropriate given the damage that he could otherwise have

---

[37] See to similar effect eg *Peace v City of Edinburgh Council* [1999] IRLR 417 (Court of Session) (interim interdict, ie injunction) restraining the employer from proceeding other than in compliance with collectively agreed disciplinary procedures which required all stages to take place before elected members of the authority—the procedure required no greater degree of control and cooperation in carrying out employment obligations than the parties were themselves prepared to accept); *Gryf-Lowczowski v Hinchingbrooke Healthcare NHS Trust* [2006] ICR 425 (an injunction to restrain termination pending disciplinary process was not barred by lack of trust and confidence as the claimant was not at work in the meantime).

[38] See also *Barros D'Sa v University Hospital Coventry and Warwickshire NHS Trust* [2001] EWCA Civ 983, concluding that an employer was not entitled to dispense with the disciplinary process (which required allegations to be subject first to investigation by an inquiry panel) on the grounds that trust and confidence had broken down.

suffered, whereas since he was not working at the trust in the meantime, there was no issue as to the workability of the order. The capability procedure would have entailed involvement of the National Clinical Assessment Service, and as such would have provided some independent safeguard.

12.69 It was also argued that the dismissal was a breach of contract by virtue of its being an act of victimization for making protected disclosures. It was also argued that the defendant trust's whistleblowing policy was contractual. The policy provided that the defendant would support staff raising genuine concerns and protect them from reprisals. It was argued on behalf of the claimant that in proceeding to a hearing the defendant was acting in breach of that policy by failing to protect the claimant from victimization, and that in any event by virtue of being an act of victimization, and contrary to the whistleblowing policy, proceeding to a hearing was in breach of the implied term of trust and confidence. For the defendant, it was disputed that the whistleblowing policy was contractual, and it was argued that in circumstances where Parliament had provided that employment tribunals were the sole forum for pursuing protected disclosure detriment claims under the ERA, it would be contrary to public policy for implied terms to provide for a contractual claim in the ordinary courts mirroring the statutory right. That argument might derive some support from the approach in *Johnson v Unisys Ltd* [2001] ICR 480. We suggest, however, that, having regard to the public interest in providing protection for those who raise public interest disclosures, and the obligation to protect freedom of expression under Article 10 (see Chapter 19), the contention that whistleblowing victimization could not be a breach of the implied term of trust and confidence is unconvincing. In the light of its conclusion that it was strongly arguable that the capability procedure applied, the court decided that it was not necessary for the court to address these arguments.

12.70 Aside from injunctive relief to require internal procedures to be followed, it may exceptionally be appropriate in other circumstances where the order is workable because the employee has either retained the employer's trust and confidence in full or in relevant respects. That was the case in *Powell v Brent LBC* [1988] ICR 176 (CA). The claimant had successfully applied for the post of Principal Benefits Officer. On the day after being informed of her appointment, one of the unsuccessful candidates challenged the decision, alleging that there had been a breach of the anti-discrimination policy. The defendant employer then sought to re-advertise the position and claimed that the appointment had not been confirmed and that the claimant should return to her former post. The claimant successfully sought an interim injunction to be permitted to continue in the new post until trial. The claimant had been doing the job for four months by this time and there was no lack of confidence in her ability to do the job. The court emphasized it would not grant relief unless it was just and reasonable to do so and there was sufficient confidence on the part of the employer in the claimant employee, judged in all the circumstances (including the nature of the work, the people with whom the work must be done, and the likely effect upon the employer and its operations).

12.71 The same approach applies where the relief sought is not to restrain dismissal, but some other step bearing on operation of the working relationship such as suspension from work. In *Mezey v South West London and St George's Mental Health NHS Trust* [2007] IRLR 244 (CA), where the court granted an injunction restraining the employer from suspending the claimant clinical psychologist arguably in breach of contract, there was no issue as to workability or trust and confidence. The context of the suspension was that there had been a series of reports into the circumstances surrounding one of the claimants' patients, a paranoid schizophrenic, having killed someone. It was only after the third of these reports that the claimant was suspended pending disciplinary proceedings. She accepted that it was appropriate pending the disciplinary hearing for her to abstain from diagnosis and treatment of patients. Since the relief sought concerned only non-clinical work, and there was no issue as to trust and confidence in her carrying out that work, there was no reason to withhold relief.

Micromanagement As set out above, in addition to the restrictions revolving around **12.72** enforcing a contract for personal service where trust and confidence has been lost, a further important discretionary factor concerns avoiding micromanagement of employment procedures. The court will generally not intervene merely in relation to minor irregularities: see *Chhabra v West London Mental Health NHS Trust* [2014] ICR 194 (SC) at para 39. Several aspects of this were summarized in *Al-Mishlab v Milton Keynes Hospital NHS Foundation Trust* [2015] EWHC 3096 at para 17:

1. Generally it is not appropriate for the court to intervene to remedy only minor irregularities in the course of disciplinary (or other internal) proceedings: *Chhabra* para 39. That requirement was met in *Chhabra*, where the evidence at its highest did not meet the contractual requirements for instituting disciplinary proceedings for gross misconduct.[39]

2. In an employment context, there is a power vested in the employer to manage employees, which in the first instance includes establishing the relevant facts: *Al-Mishlab*, para 16.

3. There is a public interest in allowing internal processes to run their course and courts should be slow to interfere if disputed issues can be sorted out and resolved within the framework of the internal procedure itself. Where the parties have agreed upon a process, the court should prima facie respect the contractual intention of the parties and allow the process to occur: *Al-Mishlab*, para 19.[40]

4. Further, there is a public interest that matters such as a decision upon the capability of a practitioner to work within the NHS should be taken by the mandated expert panel: *Al-Mishlab*, para 20.

In many cases those factors will make it inappropriate to proceed to seek injunctive relief **12.73** when internal proceedings are ongoing. Thus in a case where a worker claims that proceedings have been instituted by the worker's manager as an act of victimization, but the allegations were to be considered in accordance with an internal disciplinary process, it would ordinarily be appropriate for that procedure to run its course. It may be in part for that reason that, as yet, there is no reported case in which injunctive relief has been granted to restrain an employer from conduct, such as taking disciplinary action, on the basis that it would constitute victimization for a protected disclosure. As set out above, interim relief was sought on this basis in *Jesudason*, but ultimately the relief was granted on other grounds (that the employers had arguably followed an impermissible procedure).[41]

---

[39] See to similar effect *Mezey v South West London and St George's Mental Health NHS Trust* [2010] IRLR 512 (CA) where, on the basis of an independent report, the contractual requirements for convening a disciplinary panel were not met and nor had there been resort to an NCAS report as required, and an injunction was therefore granted restraining the employer from bringing disciplinary proceedings.

[40] See also *Makhdum v Norfolk and Suffolk NHS Foundation Trust* [2012] EWHC 4015 at paras 51–53; *Chakrabarty v Ipswich Hospital NHS Trust* [2014] EWHC 2735 at para 161; *Sarker v Worcestershire Acute Hospitals NHS Trust* [2015] EWHC 165 at paras 20–22.

[41] See also *Mattu* where the claimant, who ultimately succeeded in a claim of protected disclosure detriment, first sought a High Court declaration that his dismissal was invalid on the basis of having followed the wrong procedure. The High Court claim failed on the grounds that there had been no breach of the contractual disciplinary procedure. No whistleblowing argument was raised in the High Court proceedings.

(c) Judicial review

12.74 An alternative may in some cases lie in an application for judicial review, with a view (amongst other potential remedies) to quashing the decision which is alleged to be an act of victimization (eg dismissal or suspension) and obtaining other suitable relief. Whether that is available and appropriate turns on whether:

(a) the decision is amenable to judicial review;

(b) judicial review should be refused on the basis that there is a suitable alternative remedy—whether by virtue of a claim in the employment tribunal or for breach of contract; and

(c) the relief sought (eg injunctive relief) is such that it is appropriate for the court to order in its discretion.

12.75 The scope for such a claim was indicated, albeit not in a whistleblowing context, by the decision in *R (on the application of Shoesmith) v OFSTED* [2011] IRLR 679 (CA). The claimant, Ms Shoesmith, had been employed by Haringey LBC in the role of Director of Children's Services (DCS). This was an office established by statute (the Children Act 2004). During the period of her office there was a public and media outcry following the death of a baby (Baby P), who was the subject of a child protection plan devised by Haringey. At the instigation of the Secretary of State, an OFSTED report was prepared which was very critical. The claimant was not given any opportunity to coordinate comment on or to discuss the draft report. The Secretary of State then made a direction pursuant to his statutory powers replacing the claimant as DCS with a temporary secondment and also made public comments to the effect that he did not believe she should receive any compensation or pay off. Ms Shoesmith was suspended by Haringey, and called to a disciplinary hearing which resulted in her summary dismissal. She then brought judicial review proceedings. Notwithstanding that the claim related to termination of an employment contract, the decision was held to be amenable to judicial review and resulted (on appeal) in a declaration that her purported removal from her position by the Secretary of State, and her dismissal by Haringey, were unlawful due to procedural unfairness. There had been a predetermined dismissal, essentially making Ms Shoesmith a scapegoat to deflect public criticism (per Maurice Kay LJ at paras 125, 134–135). The fact of summary dismissal was relevant not only to the dismissal being wrongful, but also as contributing to the impression of unfair predetermination (para 125).

12.76 The effect of the decision that the dismissal was unlawful and void (paras 138 and 148) was that it was a nullity,[42] and the court determined that the claimant was at least entitled to a declaration, though further issues as to remedy were remitted (with the only remedy sought being compensation). The claimant's position was that as her employment had not been effectively terminated she was entitled to continue to receive her full contractual remuneration. That position derived support from the Privy Council decision in *McLauglin v Governor of Cayman Islands* [2007] 1 WLR 2839 (PC) (albeit in that case the claimant gave credit for sums received by way of mitigation).

12.77 **Amenability to judicial review** The court in *Shoesmith* stressed the importance of considering separately the issue as to whether the decision was amenable to judicial review and whether review should be refused due to the availability of an alternative remedy. So far as concerned amenability, the Court of Appeal placed emphasis on the fact that, whilst Ms Shoesmith was employed under a contract of employment, she was also an 'office holder', in that she held a position that was created, required, and defined by and under statute. In *R v East Berkshire Health Authority ex parte Walsh* [1985] ICR 152 (CA), Sir John Donaldson

---

[42] *McLauglin v Governor of Cayman Islands* [2007] 1 WLR 2839 (PC) at para 14.

MR (at 164) explained that employment by a public authority does not of itself inject the necessary element of public law so as to be amenable to judicial review, and that it was necessary for there to be special statutory restrictions on dismissal or other sufficient statutory underpinning. He explained the earlier decision in *Malloch v Aberdeen Corporation* [1971] 1 WLR 1578, in which an employee (a teacher) was also treated as an office holder, on the basis of statutory restrictions on dismissal. A narrow view of the scope for judicial review arising from a dispute over employment rights was also indicated by the approach in *R v Derby County Council ex parte Noble* [1990] ICR 808 (CA). The court emphasized the requirement for a sufficient public law element, and distinguished between decisions concerning purely private law matters, as in the case of a dispute over private rights under a contract of employment, as opposed to breach of a public duty (per Woolf LJ at 815D–F, McCowan LJ at 822B–D, Dillon LJ at 823E–H). However, the decision in *Shoesmith* suggests a broader approach. Whilst there was found to be a sufficient statutory underpinning to regard Ms Shoesmith as an officer, the decision did not proceed on the basis of any special statutory restrictions on her dismissal (beyond ordinary unfair dismissal protection). A submission that amenability to judicial review only arises where the power to dismiss is itself circumscribed by statute was expressly rejected (at para 91). In the context of the NHS, it will commonly arise that the relevant employing body is established by statute and that senior posts are filled by officers in the sense explained in *Shoesmith*, in that they are in positions created and required by statute.

Alternative remedy   The well-established general principle is that where other means   **12.78**
of address are conveniently and effectively available to a party they ought ordinarily to be used before resort to judicial review.[43] That may require consideration of internal routes for redress such as by a grievance or internal appeal, and the alternatives of a breach of contract claim.

Ordinarily, where there is an employment dispute, the safeguards that might be provided   **12.79**
by an action for judicial review will be provided in any event through the express or implied terms of the employment contract. Thus principles of natural justice are usually given effect through internal disciplinary or grievance policies and through the implied duty to act fairly in the conduct of an internal disciplinary or similar process: see for example *R v East Berkshire Health Authority ex parte Walsh* [1985] ICR 152 (CA). Similarly, public law standards are specifically applied in limiting managerial discretion by a duty to act rationally in and in good faith: *Braganza v BP Shipping Ltd* [2015] ICR 449 (SC).

However, there are at least three respects in which a claim in contract may not be suitable   **12.80**
or available. First, once an employee has been dismissed and the contract of employment terminated, the contractual claim is likely to be limited to a claim in damages, and to the loss if any during the notice period: see *Hale v Brighton and Sussex University Hospital NHS Trust* [2015] EWHC 833. By contrast, if a decision was unlawful in the public law sense the effect is that the decision is unlawful and void or if necessary may be quashed. The significance of this distinction is, however, reduced to some extent by the confirmation in *Geys v Société Générale* [2013] 1 AC 523 (SC) that in the event of purported terminated in breach of contract it is open to an employee to refuse to accept the breach and affirm the contract. That may then allow a window to seek any appropriate injunctive relief. The decision in *Lauffer v Barking, Havering and Redbridge University Hospital NHS Trust* [2009] EWHC 2360, where an injunction was granted after a purported dismissal on the ground of irrevocable loss of trust and confidence (but arguably in breach of a contractual

---

[43] *Shoesmith* [2011] IRLR 680 (CA) at para 92.

capability procedure), may be best understood on this basis. The interim relief was sought within a week of the purported dismissal, and though not analysed in those terms in the judgment, affirmation of the contract would appear to have been implicit in the contention that the dismissal was invalid.

12.81 A second potential advantage of judicial review proceedings lies in the effect of the decision in *Johnson v Unisys*. As noted above, the decision is to the effect that the implied terms of trust and confidence and to exercise discretion rationally and in good faith do not apply to the decision to dismiss. There was no argument in *Shoesmith* as to whether, in the interests of consistency, the same reasoning implemented in *Unisys v Johnson* should also be exercised when applying public law principles to employee office holders. But the Court of Appeal in *Shoesmith* referred to a line of cases, tracing back prior to *Ridge v Baldwin* [1964] AC 40 (HL), indicating that principles of natural justice do apply to a decision to dismiss an office holder. It may be expected that other public law restrictions would apply equally to a decision to dismiss. Thus, particularly where (as with the NHS) there is a whistleblowing policy which makes clear that victimization of those who blow the whistle is unacceptable, a decision to dismiss which is said to be such an act of victimization might be said to be an unlawful exercise of discretion as being contrary to substantive legitimate expectations and irrational.

12.82 A third potential advantage over contract claims applies to those cases where there is no contractual relationship. Thus, judicial review has been available in relation to decisions as to the dismissal on disciplinary grounds, or suspension from duty, of police officers[44] and prison officers.[45]

12.83 As to whether claims in the employment tribunal provide a suitable alternative remedy, to some extent the decision in *Shoesmith* may be said to be distinguishable because the alternative remedy in the tribunal was only for ordinary unfair dismissal where compensation would be capped, and any award quickly swallowed up by legal expenses.[46] The alternative remedy in a whistleblowing claim does not have that drawback as compensation is uncapped, and it also avoids the limitation of requiring sufficient qualifying service. There may still be factors which support a contention that it is not equally convenient and effective as a remedy. One aspect relates to the greater powers available on judicial review to quash the decision (eg to dismiss or suspend) and/or declare the employment on foot or order reinstatement (and to enforce such an order). It may be that in practice in some cases that benefit is more theoretical than real, because either the person victimized for blowing the whistle would not wish to return to employment or the court would not order specific performance of a contract for personal service. That might not however be the case where, for example, the purpose of quashing a dismissal is to require internal procedures to be followed and to give the whistleblower a chance to clear his or her name.

12.84 Further, in many claims of whistleblower victimization a claim may be framed in the alternative (a) on grounds that it was detrimental treatment by reason of protected disclosures and (b) that the detrimental treatment in any event was such as to give rise to an ordinary unfair dismissal claim. Thus, adapting the facts in *Shoesmith*, if her contention had been that she had been scapegoated for blowing the whistle, that complaint might have been advanced in the alternative to the claim based on breach of natural justice in dismissing

---

[44] *Chief Constable of the North Wales Police v Evans* [1982] 1 WLR 1155 (HL).
[45] *R v Secretary of State for the Home Department ex parte Benwell* [1985] QB 554 (dismissal); *R v Secretary of State for the Home Department ex parte Attard* [1990] COD 261 (suspension).
[46] Per Maurice Kay LJ para 99.

summarily. It is unlikely that the addition of a whistleblowing aspect of the claim would have led to a different decision as to whether the employment tribunal provided an alternative remedy. For the same reasons as the court found, the tribunal claim would not have provided an adequate remedy if the dismissal was found to be unfair but the protected disclosure claim did not succeed.

Mandatory orders   In contrast to the position on a protected disclosure claim in   **12.85** the employment tribunal, as well as the power to order compensation, the discretionary remedies available on a successful application for judicial review include a power to quash the decision which is challenged and/or declare it invalid, and a mandatory order (requiring performance) or prohibitory order or injunction (restraining action). It may be expected that the considerations which limit the Courts in ordering specific performance of employment contracts subject to limited exceptions would equally be material on an application for judicial review, particularly as those restrictions are founded on the need for the order to be workable: *Robb v Hammersmith and Fulham LBC* [1991] ICR 514 (Morland J) at 520E. However, the decision of Judge Behrens in *R (Kay) v Chief Constable of Northumbria (No 2)* [2010] ICR 974 provides some indication that an order for reinstatement may be available where this would not be the case in a breach of contract claim. The claimant was a probationary police constable who was charged with obtaining property by deception. The criminal charges were dismissed. Regulation 13 of the Police Regulations 2003 conferred a power on the Chief Constable to dispense with the services of a probationer if, amongst other things, it was considered that he was not likely to become an efficient or well-conducted constable. However, following a hearing conducted under regulation 13 of 2003 Regulations, the Chief Constable required the claimant to resign on the basis that he had doubts about her personal integrity and honesty. That decision was subsequently quashed on the basis that it had not been permissible to proceed under regulation 13, and that a full disciplinary hearing was required, under which the decision as to sanction would be determined by the disciplinary panel and not by the Chief Constable. Despite the fact that the Chief Constable continued to say that he had no confidence in the claimant, Judge Behrens made an order for reinstatement. He declined to give weight to the Chief Constable's view, on the basis of the absence of any objective basis for it since it resulted only from a procedurally flawed hearing, and the other evidence was to the contrary. The court concluded that reinstatement was required to put right a serious wrong.

In one sense the decision was exceptional, since the Chief Constable had no power to dis-   **12.86** miss for the alleged wrongdoing. That decision could only be made by the appropriate panel. As such the court was able to sidestep the concern as to the court usurping the role of the employer in reaching the decision. More broadly though, it might be regarded as reflecting the reality that in a large organization, such as in this case the Northumbria Police, it may be artificial to suggest that the order is not workable merely by reason of the assertion of the chief officer as to a lack of trust and confidence. That approach may be of considerable value if applied to the situation where a decision to dismiss a whistleblower can be treated as invalid by reason of being an act of victimization.

B. The Financial Sector

(1) Whistleblowing in the financial services sector

The financial crash of 2008 and the near collapse of the banking system directed atten-   **12.87** tion to the management of risk in the banking sector. Whereas in the health sector the focus of whistleblowing lies principally (though not only) on securing adequate standards of patient care, in the financial sector the focus is on fostering a culture which is conducive to raising public interest concerns as a necessary element of good corporate governance[47] and an important tool in deterring financial misconduct as well as reporting other wrongdoing.[48] In its report of 12 June 2013, 'Changing Banking for Good', the Parliamentary Commission on Banking Standards (PCBS) noted that the financial crisis and multiple conduct failures had exposed serious flaws in governance, and that poor governance and controls were illustrated by the rarity of whistleblowing, either within or beyond the firm. It noted that this had been the case even where, as in the case of Libor manipulation, prolonged and blatant misconduct had been evident. Indeed, the PCBS (at para 142 of its report) expressed its shock at the evidence it heard that 'so many people turned a blind eye to misbehaviour and failed to report it'. The PCBS (at para 151) emphasized the need for the financial sector to undergo a 'significant shift in cultural attitudes towards whistleblowing, from it being viewed with distrust and hostility to one being recognized as an essential element of an effective compliance and audit regime.'

12.88 In June 2013, the same month as the PCBS report, Public Concern at Work[49] published the results of its own study based on a sample of 320 cases of workers in the financial services sector, which concluded that in that sector, whistleblowers were more likely to be dismissed, less likely to raise a concern more than once or to approach higher management, and that compared to other areas there was a much higher likelihood that any concern would be raised in the first instance with the regulator (although the evidence heard by the PCBS indicated that far too often no concern was raised at all). That may in turn reflect a continuing culture in many organizations, similar to that identified in the health sector, which all too often leads staff to fear that if they raise concerns internally they will not be heeded and may be subjected to recriminations. The evidence to the PCBS was clear (at para 773) that whilst there were a number of different factors put forward as part of the explanation that employees did not raise the alarm, a common factor was that employees feared the consequences of speaking out.

12.89 Prompted by the PCBS report, there has been an overhaul of whistleblowing provisions within the financial services sector. In the light of the series of recommendations made by the PCBS, in February 2015 the Prudential Regulation Authority (PRA) and Financial Conduct Authority (FCA) issued a joint consultation paper, 'Whistleblowing in deposit-takers, PRA-designated investment firms and insurers'.[50] The consultation process culminated in PRA and FCA policy statements issued on 6 October 2015. The rules came partly into force from 7 March 2016 (in relation to the requirement to assign responsibilities to a whistleblowing champion) with the remaining elements being required by 7 September 2016. The requirements are mainly set out in an amended Chapter 18 of the FCA's Senior management arrangements, Systems, and Controls (SYSC) section of its handbook and

---

[47] One instance of the recognition of whistleblowing as a mark of good corporate governance, recognized at European Commission level, was when the Royal Bank of Scotland avoided fines from the Commission, because of its role in exposing others involved in the fixing of the Libor rate: http://www.theguardian.com/business/2014/oct/21/rbs-royal-bank-scotland-whistleblower-libor-rigging-fine.

[48] The evidence given to the Parliamentary Commission on Banking Standards (as recorded in its report, 'Changing Banking for Good', at para 778) noted that the fear of reporting for fear of retribution and damage to career prospects extending beyond financial misconduct, notably to cover fear of reporting sexual harassment.

[49] 'Silence in the City', PCaW. May 2013.

[50] PRA CP6/15 and FCA CP15/4. Available at https://www.fca.org.uk/static/documents/consultation-papers/cp15-04.pdf.

in a Supervisory Statement (SS39/15), entitled 'Whistleblowing in deposit-takers, PRA-designated investment firms and insurers', issued by the PRA in October 2015.[51]

In addition, effective whistleblowing procedures are required pursuant to EU obligations. **12.90** Council Regulation 596/2014 (the market abuse regulation) requires, by Article 32, that Member States must ensure that competent authorities must establish effective mechanisms to enable reporting of actual or potential infringements of the regulation, including protection against victimization in employment and protection of personal data both for the person reporting and the person about whom allegations are made. That is supplemented by Commission Implementing Directive 2015/2392, which sets out more detailed requirements including that the competent authorities have dedicated staff to handle reports of (market abuse) infringements (Article 3), and a requirement to publish information about whistleblowing arrangements including details of the confidentiality provided and that reports may be made anonymously (Article 4). In relation to setting out the confidentiality regime, there is also a requirement to make clear where confidentiality cannot be ensured, including where disclosure is necessary and proportionate under EU or national law in the context of subsequent judicial proceedings or to safeguard the right of defence of a reporting person. The regulation also provides that the procedures to protect against victimization are to include ensuring that the reporting person has access to comprehensive information and advice on the remedies and procedures available under national law to protect against unfair treatment (Article 8). Notably, it requires that the reporting person is to have access to effective assistance from competent authorities before any 'relevant authority' involved in their protection (ie including the employment tribunal), which is to include 'certifying the condition of whistle-blower of the reporting person in employment disputes' (Article 8(2)(b)).

Reform in relation to whistleblowing was accompanied by broader reforms in the banking **12.91** sector following the PCBS report, 'Changing Banking for Good'. This included changes introduced by the Banking Reform Act 2013, replacing the Approved Persons Regime[52] for banks, building societies, credit unions, and PRA-designated investment firms with a new regulatory framework for individuals. A Senior Managers Regime, and Senior Insurance Managers Regime, which came into force on 7 March 2016, were intended to ensure that senior managers would be held accountable for any misconduct falling within their area of responsibility. It was accompanied by a new Certification Regime which applies to other staff who could pose a risk of significant harm to the firm or any of its customers (such as through giving investment advice) and Conduct Rules setting out basic standards of behaviour. The detail of those provisions is beyond the scope of this book. It is relevant to place the whistleblowing reforms in context as one of many interconnected steps towards improving corporate governance and provide clearer lines of accountability and standards of behaviour.

(2) Coverage of the whistleblower provisions

The coverage of the new whistleblower provisions distinguishes between the anti-victimiza- **12.92** tion provision in SYSC 18.3.9 and the other whistleblowing provisions. SYSC 18.3.9 applies to all FCA-regulated firms and provides that:

> The FCA would regard as a serious matter any evidence that a firm had acted to the detriment of a whistleblower. Such evidence could call into question the fitness and propriety

---

[51] Available at http://www.bankofengland.co.uk/pra/Documents/publications/ss/2015/ss3915.pdf.
[52] Ie the system of approving individuals as being 'fit and proper' to carry out regulated activities: they must (a) meet the requirements of the FCA's 'fit and proper' test and follow its principles, (b) comply with the Statements of Principle and Code of Practice and (c) self-report anything that could affect their ongoing suitability to the and the authorised firm for whom they carry out regulated activities.

of the firm or relevant members of its staff, and could therefore, if relevant, affect the firm's continuing satisfaction of threshold condition 5 (Suitability) or, for an approved person or a certification employee, their status as such.

12.93 The provision is a potentially powerful deterrent. Whereas provision for individual liability under the ERA's protected disclosure provisions may lose its force if individuals expect to be reimbursed by their firm, the FCA regulatory powers hold the prospect that individuals found to have been involved in victimization would lose their ability to continue in a regulated function. However, the coverage of the remaining provisions is more limited. They affect UK deposit-takers (including banks, building societies, and credit unions) with assets of £250 million or greater, 'Solvency II insurers',[53] and investment firms which have been designated for supervision by the PRA deposit-takers (meaning banks, building societies, and credit unions) with assets over £250 million, Solvency II, insurers and PRA-designated investment firms. For all other FCA-regulated firms, the rules act as non-binding guidance[54] which is intended to reflect good practice.[55]

12.94 In essence, the major omissions from the scope of the new provisions were therefore (a) smaller deposit-takers (with assets of not more than £250 million), (b) UK branches of non-EEA deposit-takers and reinsurers, and (c) other firms regulated by the FCA such as stockbrokers, insurance brokers, consumer credit firms, and other (non-PRA-designated) investment firms. Broadly, the approach taken in the consultation response was to monitor effectiveness of the new rules for the larger deposit-takers, PRA-designated investment firms, and insurers before consulting on whether to expand their scope beyond being non-binding guidance. But given the strong findings of the PCBS as to the importance of good corporate governance for fostering a culture conducive to whistleblowing, the exclusions from any requirements other than non-victimization are not easy to justify.[56] If the provisions were considered overly prescriptive for smaller firms, it would have been open for the FCA at least to set out other minimum standards, such as to set out and publicize a whistleblowing policy with clear provisions such as in relation to how a concern can be raised, the right to raise concerns with the regulator, and an assurance that any victimization would not be tolerated.

12.95 In relation to UK branches, some limited proposals were advanced in further consultation papers issued in September 2016 by the FCA[57] and PRA.[58] Broadly, these focused on a proposed requirement that UK branches of overseas banks, PRA-regulated insurers, and PRA-regulated non-EEA deposit-takers[59] be required to inform their workers of the regulators' whistleblowing services. It is also proposed that where a non-EEA banking group has both a UK subsidiary (which would be caught by the UK regulatory requirements in relation to whistleblowing) and a UK branch, the staff of the branch be informed of the subsidiary's whistleblowing arrangements so as to have an additional route to raise

---

[53] That is, insurance and re-insurance firms within the scope of the Directive of the European Parliament and of the Council of 25 November 2009 on the taking-up and pursuit of the business of Insurance and Reinsurance (Solvency II) (No 2009/138/EC), and the Society of Lloyds and 'managing agents' as defined in the FCA handbook.

[54] PS15/24 para 1.5.

[55] See the FCA consultation of September 2016 (CP 16/25) at para 1.11.

[56] This is subject to a jurisdictional limit on being able to impose requirements on branches of EEA deposit-takers where the entity is based in another EEA state: see PRA consultation CP35/16 at para 2.4.

[57] CP 16/25, at https://www.fca.org.uk/sites/default/files/cp16-25.pdf.

[58] CP 35/16 at http://www.bankofengland.co.uk/pra/Documents/publications/cp/2016/cp3516.pdf.

[59] The PRA consultation paper notes that the PRA is not able to impose whistleblowing requirements on branches of EEA deposit-takers as this is a home state issue under the Capital Requirements Directive.

relevant concerns. However, it was proposed that other provisions of the FCA/PRA whistleblowing requirements, including that to establish internal whistleblowing channels, would not be applied. That was explained principally on the basis that it may not be possible to protect the worker against detriment, whether because the branches are often relatively small and so less able to protect the whistleblower's identity or because differences between the law of UK jurisdictions and that of a firm's home country could mean whistleblowers are unprotected and could potentially be put at risk by raising concerns. We suggest that this reasoning is unpersuasive. Those working at a UK branch will have PIDA protection. If staff are to be able to act as an early warning system it may well be important for there to be a route for them to be able to raise concerns without having to escalate matters to the regulator. Clarity as to how to raise concerns is in any event important.

(3) Internal whistleblowing arrangements

(a) Overview

The PRA supervisory statement (at para 2.1) sets out the following summary of the key **12.96** elements of the internal procedures that firms to whom these measures apply are required to implement. The procedures must:

- ensure the firm protects the confidentiality of whistleblowers, if the individual concerned requests this;
- ensure the firm is able to handle disclosures from people who wish to remain anonymous;
- assess and escalate concerns raised by whistleblowers within the firm as appropriate, and, where this is justified, to the FCA, PRA (or an appropriate law enforcement agency);
- track the outcome of whistleblowing reports;
- provide feedback to whistleblowers, where appropriate;
- prepare written procedures (e.g. staff handbooks);
- maintain appropriate records; and
- take all reasonable steps to ensure that no person under the firm's control engages in victimisation of whistleblowers, and take appropriate measures against those responsible for any such victimisation.

(b) Who and what is covered

There is a requirement on firms to 'establish, implement and maintain appropriate and **12.97** effective arrangements for the disclosure of reportable concerns by whistleblowers' (SYSC 18.3.1(1)). A 'reportable concern' is defined as a:

> concern held by any person in relation to the activities of a firm, including:
> (a) anything that would be the subject-matter of a protected disclosure, including breaches of rules;
> (b) a breach of the firm's policies and procedures; and
> (c) behaviour that harms or is likely to harm the reputation or financial well-being of the firm.

In making express reference to protected disclosures, the definition takes a different course **12.98** from that used in the NHS standard policy which refers more generally to a concern as to a risk, malpractice, or wrongdoing which is thought to harm the service being delivered or commissioned. The NHS approach may be thought to stick more closely to plain and easily understandable terms. No doubt, though, the difference reflects the fact that the definition of reportable concern in SYSC 18.3.1 forms part of the regulatory requirements rather than part of the whistleblowing policy itself to be established or adopted by each firm. Further, the definition in SYSC 18.3.1 is still deliberately wider in some respects than the definition of a protected disclosure.[60] The concern must be one related to the activities of the firm. It includes (but is not limited to) matters that could be the subject matter of a protected disclosure, but there is no reasonable belief test either as to the public interest or that the information tends to show a relevant failure (though it is expressly stated that nothing prevents action being taken against those who have made false and malicious disclosures[61]). In that respect it reflects the PCSB recommendation that there should be mechanisms for employees to raise concerns when they feel 'discomfort' about products or practices even when not making specific allegations about wrongdoing. That was noted as being of importance in response to the evidence that, as with the PPI scandal, staff were liable to have concerns or unease that there was something wrong without necessarily being able to make a specific allegation of wrongdoing.[62]

12.99 The arrangements are also deliberately not limited to disclosures raised by workers. They cover any person making the disclosure to the firm or to the FCA or the PRA in accordance with the internal arrangements set out, as well as workers making a disclosure in accordance with the ERA's protected disclosure provisions.

12.100 In the response to the consultation, the PRA and FCA took the view that the benefits of being able to handle all types of whistleblowing arrangements outweighed the risks of doing so. They envisaged that once raised there might then be a process to channel the matter through an appropriate route, such as for 'grievances, customer complaints, everyday differences of opinion'.[63] That in turn reflected the PCBS recommendation that whistleblowing concerns should be subject to an internal filter by the bank to identify those that should be treated as grievances, and banks should have the opportunity to conduct and resolve their own investigations of substantive whistleblowing allegations (ie these should not be dependent on whether a grievance is progressed).[64] That approach was expressly endorsed in the PRA's response to the consultation, noting that it would only expect a firm's whistleblowing function to deal with 'genuine reportable concerns'.[65] To that end, the PRA supervisory statement expressly reflects this (at para 2.4) in noting that it may be appropriate for some matters raised through the whistleblowing function to be dealt with by other areas, and that firms should be able to filter out genuine whistleblowing cases from those that could be better handled by other functions. In addition SYSC 18 provides that the internal procedures might clarify that alternative routes are appropriate in the first instance but that the whistleblowing procedure is available where the alternative routes have failed (SYSC 18.3.2(3)).

(c) Protection against victimization

12.101 As noted above, the protection against victimization of whistleblowers is the one provision which applies to all firms regulated by the FCA. The PRA Supervisory Statement further makes clear that the obligation is not merely a passive one. There is an obligation to take 'all reasonable steps' to ensure that no person under the firm's control engages in victimization of whistleblowers, as well as to take appropriate measures against those who engage in such victimization.

---

[60] As to whether a breach of FCA or PRA rules could amount to non-compliance with a legal obligation, see the discussion in Chapter 3 at para 3.120.

[61] SYSC 18.3.2(3)(b).

[62] 'Changing Banking for Good', paras 785–786.

[63] FCA response, para 2.7.

[64] 'Changing Banking for Good', para 792.

[65] PS24/15 at 3.5.

As a reflection of the fact that the policy decision that the whistleblower arrangements **12.102** are to be required to handle all types of disclosure (subject to being in relation to activities of a firm) and from all types of people, it necessarily applies more broadly than the protection under the whistleblowing legislation. SYSC 18.3.9 provides that the FCA would regard it as a serious matter, which could call into question the fitness and propriety of the firm or relevant members of staff, that a firm had acted to the detriment of a 'whistleblower'—in this context a whistleblower is any person who has disclosed or intends to disclose a reportable concern to a firm, the FCA or the PRA, or in accordance with the Part 4A of ERA (the protected disclosure provisions). It therefore covers (a) reportable concerns that may not be protected disclosures (due to, eg, lacking the requisite reasonable belief), (b) any person who is not covered by the legislation as a result of not being a worker, even within the extended definition (see Chapter 6), and (c) cases where someone 'intends to disclose' but has not yet done so, which again falls outside the legislation.

However, this still begs a question as to the extent of protection available to a whistleblower **12.103** in such a situation when not covered by the protected disclosure legislation. The FCA has a number of enforcement powers including the imposition of fines, the withdrawal of a firm's authorization, or the prohibition of an individual from operating in financial services.[66] It does not, however, have a power to award compensation. The PCBS recommended that the regulators should be empowered, in cases where as a result of an enforcement action it is satisfied that a whistleblower has not been properly treated by a firm, to provide compensation for that treatment without having to go to an employment tribunal.[67] However, that proposal has not been implemented.

(d) Anonymous and confidential disclosures

The procedures are expressly required to be able to deal not only with maintaining con- **12.104** fidentiality, but also with anonymous disclosures (SYSC 18.3.1(2)). However, the FCA's consultation response noted that it was open to firms to discuss with whistleblowers the advantages of disclosing their identity. That suggests that there may be a degree of persuasion to seek to encourage a whistleblower to reveal their identity on a confidential basis.

(e) Assessment and escalation

There is a requirement that the arrangements ensure that concerns can be effectively assessed **12.105** and, where appropriate, escalated (which may be to the FCA or PRA).[68] The obligation to ensure that concerns are 'effectively assessed' would implicitly seem to entail an obligation to carry out such investigation as is appropriate to enable this to be done.[69]

(f) Feedback

There is a specific requirement to provide feedback to the whistleblower about a reportable **12.106** concern where this is feasible and appropriate (SYSC 18.3.1(d)). That is important both so

---

[66] See the Decision Procedure and Penalties manual in the FCA handbook and the summary set out in the FCA's Enforcement Information Guide at https://www.fca.org.uk/publication/documents/enforcement-information-guide.pdf.

[67] 'Changing Banking for Good', para 805.

[68] SYSC 18.3.1(b); PRA Supervisory Statement para 2.1.

[69] An illustration of this, albeit in the context of a concern raised with the FCA rather than internally, is in the finding made by the Complaints Commissioner of a failure by the FCA appropriately to consider a concern where it had failed to carry out a sufficient investigation of the concern: see letter dated 11 May 2016, available at http://fscc.gov.uk/wp-content/uploads/FCA00101-FD-11-05-16.pdf.

as to foster a culture where the person raising the concern feels that they have been heeded and valued for making the disclosure, and to avoid the matter being unnecessarily escalated further. The nature of the feedback given may also have an important bearing on whether in relation to any subsequent disclosure the reasonable belief tests, or other elements of the tests for wider disclosures, were satisfied.

(g) Records and reports in relation to internal disclosures

12.107 There are specific recording and reporting requirements. These include:

- a requirement to record the reportable concerns made by whistleblower, the firm's treatment of the reports, and the outcome. This implemented a specific recommendation in the PCBS report (at para 793) that there should be a contemporaneous record of every whistleblowing complaint, regardless of outcome, with a view to the regulators periodically examining a firm's whistleblowing records. This would be directed both at the regulator informing itself about possible matters of concern and to ensure that firms are treating whistleblowers appropriately;
- a requirement that a report be made at least annually to the firm's governing body on the operation and effectiveness of the systems and controls in relation to whistleblowing. This need not be prepared by the whistleblowers' champion, but he or she is required to oversee its operation as part of the oversight role (see paragraph 12.119 below).[70] The report is required to maintain the confidentiality of the whistleblower (SYSC 18.3.1(f)(i)), and is not a public document but is to be available to the PRA and FCA on request;[71]
- a specific obligation to report to the FCA about each case the firm contested but lost before an employment tribunal where the claimant succeeded in a detriment or dismissal whistleblowing claim (18.3.1(f)(ii)).

12.108 The obligation to report the fact of having lost a whistleblowing tribunal claim implemented a recommendation made by the PCBS. No such specific obligation arises unless the claim has been lost at least in part on whistleblowing grounds, although in practice in most cases the firm will have made the FCA aware of the fact of the tribunal proceedings, and their subject matter.[72] The PCBS noted that it would then be for the regulator to consider whether to take any enforcement action against firms found to have acted in a manner inconsistent with regulatory requirements, and for the firm and whistleblowers' champion to show that they had acted appropriately.[73]

12.109 In any whistleblowing claim it may be important to keep in mind the scope of these obligations for the purposes of assessing the disclosure that should be given and if necessary requested in the proceedings. It may be important to identify what was said when the concern was raised and to whom the concerns were communicated and what steps were taken to deal with them.

(4) Informing staff of FCA and PRA whistleblowing services

12.110 In addition to the provisions relating to internal arrangements, there is a distinct obligation imposed on firms to communicate to their UK-based employees that they may disclose reportable concerns to the PRA or FCA and the methods for doing so (SYSC 18.3.6). This

---

[70] FCA response to consultation (PS15/24), below para 2.20, available at https://www.fca.org.uk/publication/policy/ps-15-24.pdf.

[71] PRA Supervisory Statement (SS39/15) para 4.2; FCA response to consultation (PS15/24), below para 2.20.

[72] See the ELA response of 22 May 2015 to the FCA and PRA consultation, at para 42.

[73] 'Changing Banking for Good', para 799.

must be set out in the employee handbook or its equivalent. It must also be made expressly clear that reporting to the PRA or FCA is not conditional on first having made a disclosure or report under the firm's own internal arrangements. As it was put in the October 2015 PRA response to consultation (at para 3.9): 'Firms may encourage speaking up internally by creating a culture that welcomes criticism: they should not seek to force people to raise concerns through one channel only'. Firms must also require their appointed representatives and tied agents to tell their UK-based workers that they may make protected disclosures to the FCA (SYSC 18.3.7).

The effect of these provisions would appear to be to remove the distinction altogether **12.111** between disclosures under sections 43C and 43F ERA. Disclosures to the regulator would appear to fall squarely within the provisions in section 43C(2) ERA as being by a procedure whose use is authorized by the employer. That is no less the case merely because it is a requirement under the SYSC. Whilst that effectively circumvents the requirement for a reasonable belief that the information and any allegation contained in it are substantially true (section 43F(1)(b)(ii) ERA), it may also be said to reflect the recognition of the particular need in this sphere to drive a change in culture (as reflected in the PCBS report). That said, it was not something that was considered in the FCA or PRA consultation response. Instead the response highlighted the importance of staff being made aware of their entitlement to approach regulators should they choose to do so, but did not consider the different legal test for protection. It may also entail the risk of reinforcing the trend that in this sector workers are more likely than in other areas to raise concerns only with the regulator rather than internally.

(5) Whistleblowers' champion

One of the notable recommendations contained in the PCBS report was that a non-execu- **12.112** tive member of the board should be given specific responsibility for the effective operation of a firm's whistleblowing regime. That recommendation is taken forward in SYSC 18.4 and the PRA Supervisory Statement. Each firm is expected to appoint a non-executive director as the 'whistleblowers' champion' (WC), though if there is not already a non-executive director there is no requirement to appoint one just for this purpose rather than appointing someone else to the role.[74] The WC is to have responsibility for overseeing the integrity, independence, and effectiveness of the firm's policies and procedures on whistleblowing, including, but not limited to, the protection against victimization. He or she must have a sufficient level of authority and independence within the firm and access to information and resources (including access to independent legal advice and training) in order to be able to carry out that responsibility.

The PCBS report envisaged that the person appointed would be personally accountable for **12.113** protecting whistleblowers against detrimental treatment. It further envisaged that should a whistleblower later allege detrimental treatment, it would be for the board member to satisfy the regulator that the firm acted appropriately.[75] That is not expressly stated in either SYSC 18 or in the PRA policy statement. Indeed, it might be seen as contrary to the collective responsibility of the board. The continuing importance of collective responsibility was one issue addressed by the PRA in its consultation of October 2015. It was emphasized that collective responsibility remains. One instance of this is that whilst the WC is responsible for ensuring a report on whistleblowing is put before the board on an annual basis, the whole

---

[74] Insurers who are subject to the provisions are required to appoint a director or senior manager to be the whistleblowing champion: SYSC 18.4.2.
[75] 'Changing Banking for Good', paras 788 and 791.

board would then need to consider the report and decide whether any action should then be taken as a result.[76]

12.114 A further concern raised during the consultation process was as to a requirement to assign tasks to the WC considered to be inappropriate for a non-executive director. This led to some revisions to the role as initially envisaged. Significantly, guidance to the effect that the WC was to be available to direct approaches was removed. Instead it was expressly provided that the WC need not have a day-to-day operational role handling disclosures from whistleblowers (SYSC 18.4.5 (2)), though the WC would need to consider how best to direct a whistleblower that does choose to contact the WC directly.[77]

(6) Settlement agreements

12.115 Under SYSC 18.5, those firms within scope for the whistleblowing provisions are required to include in any settlement agreement with a worker a term making clear that nothing prevents a worker from making a protected disclosure. Whilst this largely represents standard practice, the requirements go further in also placing a prohibition on requesting that the worker enter into warranties requiring them to disclose that they have either made a protected disclosure or know of no information which could form the basis of a protected disclosure. This is required since such a clause could deter the making of future protected disclosures for fear of being in breach of warranty. Equally, firms must not use other measures to prevent workers from making protected disclosures. As noted above, however, these provisions do not apply, other than as a guide to good practice, to deposit-takers with less than £250 million in assets. None of the reasons provided for limiting the scope of application of the whistleblowing provisions adequately explain that restriction in relation to settlement agreements.

(7) No duty to report concerns

12.116 The PCBS report recommended that all senior persons should have an explicit duty to be open with the regulators, including where that person becomes aware of possible wrongdoing, regardless of whether that person has a direct responsibility for interacting with the regulators.[78] However, in their consultation document the FCA and PRA proposed that no such obligation to report concerns should be imposed, and that view was confirmed in the response to the consultation. The FCA and PRA reasoned that such an obligation to speak up may place individuals in a position where they feel they face being penalized whatever course of action they take, and might lead worried employees to make defensive reports of little value that overwhelm whistleblowing services and damage their ability to function effectively. In this respect the approach differed significantly from that adopted in the health sector. The competing arguments in relation to a duty to speak up are considered further in Chapter 13.

(8) Financial incentives to report

12.117 Acting upon a recommendation in the PCBS report to do so,[79] the PRA and FCA conducted research into the impact of financial incentives in relation to reporting concerns. Their conclusion, as set out in a note dated July 2014,[80] was that financial incentives would

---

[76] PS24/15 at para 5.2.
[77] See also Chapter 6, paras 6.79 and 6.80, where the issue of whether a non-executive director is a worker for the purposes of the protected disclosure legislation is addressed.
[78] 'Changing Banking for Good', para 796.
[79] ibid, para 803.
[80] http://www.bankofengland.co.uk/pra/Documents/contact/financialincentivesforwhistleblowers.pdf.

be unlikely to increase the number or quality of disclosures received by the regulators. In November 2014, shortly after the publication of the FCA and PRA's conclusions, one study in the US concluded that in the thirty-five-year period from 1978 to 2012, some $21.27 billion had been collected in penalties due to the involvement of financial whistleblowers.[81] However, focusing on the period since the Dodd–Frank Act of 2010 in the US introduced powers to award a share of fines to whistleblowers, the research commissioned by the FCA and PRA concluded that there was not yet any empirical evidence of incentives leading to an increase in the number or quality of disclosures received by regulators.[82] The research also noted that incentives in the US benefit only the small number whose information leads directly to successful enforcement action resulting in the imposition of fines (from which the incentives are paid), and as such provide nothing for the vast majority of whistleblowers, and have been accompanied by a complex, and therefore costly, governance structure. The note further emphasized that incentives offered by regulators could undermine the introduction and maintenance by firms of effective internal whistleblowing mechanisms. The conclusion also accorded with that reached by the Government in its Call for Evidence on whistleblowing.

However, there remains a real tension between the approach to whistleblowers in the UK and that in other jurisdictions, perhaps most noticeably within the USA. Under the Dodd–Frank legislation, the Securities and Exchange Commission have rewarded corporate whistleblowers with awards ranging between 10 and 30 per cent of the money collected when the sanctions exceed $1 million. In successful claims the defendants are liable to pay fines of up to triple the loss caused by the malpractice. Payments to whistleblowers, which may be made regardless of their nationality,[83] may be very substantial. As of 30 August 2016, some $107 million had been awarded to thirty-three whistleblowers, with the largest payment to date being $30 million, awarded in 2014.[84] Those whistleblowers with disclosures relevant to both jurisdictions therefore have a clear incentive to raise matters in the US, where the rewards are substantially greater than in the UK. **12.118**

(9) Section 43FA ERA, and FCA and PRA annual reports on whistleblowing

Section 43FA ERA[85] confers on the Secretary of State a power to require a section 43F regulator to produce an annual report on disclosures. At the time of writing, no such regulations **12.119**

---

[81] *The Guardian*: 'Are financial whistleblowers worth it?' 19 November 2014: https://www.theguardian.com/money/us-money-blog/2014/nov/19/whistleblowers-helped-government-secure-21-billion-dollars-fines-study.

[82] *Qui tam* suits filed under the False Claims Act (which pre-dates the Dodd–Frank legislation) allow private citizens with information as to fraud against the United States to file a lawsuit on the government's behalf, and if the claim is successful to receive between 15 and 25 per cent of the government's recovery in a case in which the government is joined. Awards could be very substantial. For example in *United States ex rel. Merena v SmithKline Beecham Corp* 114 F. Supp. 2d 352 (E.D. Pa. 2000) three whistleblowing realtors were awarded 10 per cent of the total award in relation to one head of claims (reduced on appeal and remission from 17 per cent to reflect the fact that certain of the claims were primarily based on prior public disclosures), and 20 per cent on another, resulting in a total award for one of the claimants of $26m, in addition to $11m that had already been paid: see https://www.paed.uscourts.gov/documents/opinions/00D0679P.pdf.

[83] See eg *United States ex rel. Copeland v Lucas Western Inc et al* (D UT No. 93-C-831B), filed in September 1993 by Frederick Copeland. The Department of Justice's press release records that 'LWI pleaded guilty to 37 felony counts of making false certifications to the Department of Defense that 35 AMAD and two ADU gearboxes had been fully inspected in accordance with the applicable contractual requirements, when, in fact, they had not' (see <http://www.usdoj.gov/opa/pr/Pre_96/October95/523.txt.html>). In a settlement with a payment of $88 million to the United States, Mr Copeland, a British machinist at the company, received 21 per cent of the payment, namely $19,360,000.

[84] See SEC press release of 30 August 2016, announcing an award of in excess of $22 million to a whistleblower: https://www.sec.gov/news/pressrelease/2016-172.html.

[85] Inserted by the Small Business, Enterprise and Employment Act 2015, s 148(1), (2).

have yet been made. Nor does section 43FA identify the matters to be set out in the report, other than that it must not require detail to be given which would enable the workers who made the disclosure, or employers by or in respect of whom the disclosure was made, to be identified. However, FCA annual reports provide some indication of the matters liable to be covered by such reports. The annual reports of 2014/15[86] and 2015/16[87] provided information as to, amongst other things:

- A broad explanation of steps taken to improve the handling of whistleblowing cases, such as now offering feedback to all whistleblowers at the end of their case and creating a debriefing team for more complex issues, who can meet with whistleblowers if they wish to ensure the FCA understands the issues and circumstances being reported.[88]
- The number of cases handled by the whistleblowing team (showing a year-on-year increase, apart from one dip in 2011/12, from just 138 in 2007/08 to a peak of 1,340 in 2014/15, but then dropping back to 1,014—roughly the same level as 2013/14—in 2015/16). Notwithstanding the fall in numbers in 2015/16, the totals show a substantial increase since 2012/13 (when there were 657 cases), providing some support for the FCA's claim in its 2014/15 report that the figures highlight the greater importance placed on whistleblowing and increased awareness across the sector.
- An indication of the number of cases in which information was shared with external bodies such as the National Crime Agency, police forces, HMRC, and other UK and overseas regulators (over 260 cases in 2015/16).
- A breakdown between the number of cases which (a) had contributed to FCA enforcement activity or other intervention to protect consumers (only 19 cases in 2014/15 and 13 in 2015/16); (b) cases where intelligence was of significant value to the FCA and contributed to the discharge of its functions (235 in 2014/15 but only 89 in 2015/16); (c) cases where information was or may be of value to the FCA but was not currently actionable or did not meet regulatory risk thresholds (521 in 2014/15 but reducing to 242 in 2015/16); (d) cases where intelligence was of little value or unlikely to assist the FCA (100 in 2014/15 and 39 in 2015/16); and (e) cases not yet assessed (465 in 2014/15 and 631 in 2015/16).
- A breakdown of disclosures by sector.
- In 2014/15 there was also a breakdown by reference to the subject of disclosure (for example fitness and propriety, culture of organization, etc), but this was not retained in 2015/16.

---

[86] https://www.fca.org.uk/publication/corporate/annual-report-2014-15.pdf.
[87] https://www.fca.org.uk/publication/corporate/annual-report-2015-16.pdf.
[88] 2015/16 report, p 35.

PART II

THE OBLIGATION TO BLOW THE WHISTLE

13

OBLIGATIONS TO BLOW THE WHISTLE

The protected disclosure legislation does not impose any sanction upon an employee for **13.01** failing to blow the whistle. However, the public policy considerations which led to legislation protecting those who make protected disclosures, and in particular the disasters which might have been avoided had the whistle been blown, also justify imposing obligations of disclosure. This chapter considers the extent to which there may be a positive obligation upon employees to blow the whistle in particular circumstances, whether under the contract of employment, arising out of fiduciary obligations, or pursuant to specific statutory obligations.

A. *Bell v Lever Brothers*

In identifying the scope of duties of disclosure an important distinction has come to be **13.02** drawn between (a) duties of disclosure which might arise out of the fiduciary obligations of directors and of employees who are subject to such obligations, and (b) the disclosure obligations which otherwise might arise in certain circumstances under the contract of employment.[1] A further distinction, which has been the subject of reconsideration by the courts, has been drawn between disclosure of the wrongdoing of others (even if

---

[1] *Item Software (UK) Limited v Fassihi* [2004] EWCA Civ 1244, [2004] IRLR 928; *Tesco Stores Limited v Pook* [2004] IRLR 618; *Brandeaux Advisers (UK) Limited v Chadwick* [2011] IRLR 224 at paras 47 and 48. But as regards fiduciary duties of non-director employees, see the discussion of *Ranson v Customer Systems plc* [2012] IRLR 769 (CA) at para 13.72 below.

it implicates the employee making the disclosure) and disclosure of an employee's own wrongdoing. We address each of these matters below. In each case, however, the distinctions drawn have reflected in large part a need to distinguish the decision of the House of Lords in *Bell v Lever Brothers Limited* [1932] AC 161. The decision has held a baleful influence over this area of law for many decades, but the developing recognition that obligations of disclosure are sometimes appropriate has been facilitated by distinguishing the decision and, more recently, substantially confining it to its own facts in relation to duties of disclosure.

13.03 In *Bell v Lever Brothers*, Messrs Bell and Snelling entered into contracts of employment with Lever Bros, but were appointed as directors and respectively as chairman and vice-chairman of Lever's subsidiary company, Niger Company. Lever held over 99 per cent of the shares of Niger. Neither Bell nor Snelling was a director of Lever. During their appointments Bell and Snelling each made personal profits by speculating in Niger's business. However, before Lever became aware of this, the service contracts of Bell and Snelling were terminated and severance agreements were entered into with Lever Bros pursuant to which substantial severance payments were made by Lever to the employees. Upon becoming aware of the secret profits, Lever sought to recover the severance payments, arguing that Bell and Snelling were under an obligation to disclose their misdeeds in making the secret profits prior to the conclusion of the severance agreements and those agreements were voidable as a result of their failure to do so. This argument was accepted by the Court of Appeal but rejected by a majority of the House of Lords, which held that Lever was bound by the compromise in the absence on the part of the defendants (as found by the jury) of any fraudulent representation or of any fraudulent concealment. Lord Atkin said (at p 227):

> unless this contract can be brought within the limited category of contracts *uberrimae fidei* it appears to me that this ground of defence must fail. I see nothing to differentiate this agreement from the ordinary contract of service; and I am aware of no authority which places contracts of service within the limited category I have mentioned ... Nor can I find anything in the relationship of master and servant, when established, that places agreements between them within the protected category ... The servant owed a duty not to steal, but, having stolen, is there superadded a duty to confess that he has stolen? I am satisfied that to imply such a duty would be a departure from the well established duties of mankind and would be to create obligations entirely outside the normal contemplation of the parties.

13.04 Lord Thankerton similarly rejected the proposition that an employee had to confess his/her own wrongdoings to the employer. He said (at p 231):

> in the absence of fraud, which the jury has negatived, I am of opinion that neither a servant nor a director of a company is legally bound forthwith to disclose any breach of the obligations arising out of the relationship so as to give the master or the company the opportunity of dismissal ....

13.05 In *Item Software (UK) Limited v Fassihi* [2004] EWCA Civ 1244, [2004] IRLR 928, Arden LJ (at para 53) identified two material differences between the approaches of Lord Atkin and Lord Thankerton. First, Lord Thankerton equated the position of an employee with that of a director, whilst Lord Atkin left the position open, and the issue did not arise on the facts. Second, there were indications in Lord Atkin's speech that whether a duty of disclosure arose would depend on the particular circumstances.

13.06 In a number of subsequent cases, *Bell v Lever Brothers* has been distinguished in the context of considering the scope for a duty to make disclosure. In *Sybron Corp v Rochem limited* [1984] 1 Ch 112 (see below at paragraphs 13.10–13.16), the Court of Appeal distinguished *Bell* principally on the basis that it was concerned with whether an employee had a duty to confess his/her own wrongdoing. It was not therefore to be taken as authority as to whether an employee has a duty to report on the wrongdoing of others. As Stephenson LJ noted (at p 124), it was 'puzzling' that no one who dealt with *Bell v Lever Brothers* appeared to have considered whether Bell or Snelling had an obligation to report each other's wrongdoing. Indeed, Lord Atkin said in the course of his speech (at p 228) that:

> it is said that there is a contractual duty of the servant to disclose his past faults. I agree that the duty in the servant to protect his master's property may involve the duty to report a fellow servant whom he knows to be wrongfully dealing with the property.

In *Sybron Corp v Rochem*, Fox LJ further noted that *Bell v Lever Brothers* was also distin- **13.07** guishable on the basis that it related to past rather than ongoing wrongdoing, whilst Kerr LJ emphasized that *Bell v Lever Brothers* did not deal with a case where concealment of wrong- doing was fraudulent (because the claim of fraudulent concealment and misrepresentation was dismissed by the jury).

Subsequently, it has been emphasized that neither Bell nor Snelling were directors of Lever **13.08** Brothers (with whom the severance agreement was entered into), but of its subsidiary com- pany; and that it is therefore not authority as to whether there might be a fiduciary obliga- tion to disclose wrongdoing: *Fassihi; Tesco Stores Limited v Pook* [2004] IRLR 618. More generally, in *Fassihi* Arden LJ (with whose judgment Holman J and Mummery LJ agreed on this issue) emphasized that all that needed to be decided in *Bell v Lever Brothers* was that in their particular circumstances neither Bell nor Snelling owed a duty to disclose their misdeeds (including each other's misdeeds) to the employer. It did not therefore decide that there could never be such a duty on the part of the employee. Substantially this indicated that the decision could be confined to its own facts.

In *Fassihi*, Arden LJ proceeded to consider, without deciding, two alternative bases for saying **13.09** that employees might be obliged to disclose their own wrongdoing. We consider this further at paragraphs 13.59–13.65 below. In summary, consistent with the approach adopted in *Ranson v Customer Services plc* [2012] IRLR 769 (CA), we suggest that whether an implied duty to disclose arises (at least in relation to non-directors) turns upon the consideration of the particular circumstances of the employee's role and their express contractual obliga- tions. As such the decision in *Bell v Lever Brothers* may therefore no longer obstruct the path to development of positive obligations upon employees to disclose wrongdoing. However, this in turn begs the question as to the circumstances in which such obligations would be acknowledged.

B. Implied Reporting Obligations under the Contract of Employment

(1) Reporting wrongdoing of others

(a) Blowing the whistle on subordinates

As noted above, in *Sybron Corporation v Rochem Limited* [1984] 1 Ch 112 the Court of **13.10** Appeal emphasized that *Bell v Lever Brothers* did not stand in the way of an obligation to report on the wrongdoing of other employees. In *Sybron*, the employers sought to recover sums paid out to an ex-employee, Mr Roques, under a pension and life assurance scheme. Roques was employed by Gamlen Chemical Co (UK) Limited, a subsidiary of the Sybron Corporation group. He was the most senior employee for Gamlen's European operations and had power of hiring and firing over the whole of the European zone. Various employees of Gamlen and Sybron Corp secretly set up rival organizations to act in competition with

Sybron and Gamlen and traded through these rival companies whilst still employed by Sybron or Gamlen.

13.11   The judge found that the conspiracy would not have got off the ground if Roques had disclosed to Sybron that which, in the judge's view, he ought to have disclosed, namely the activities of his fellow conspirators and fellow employees. Instead, Roques had seen to it that nothing was passed to Sybron. He was not prepared to report what was going on and so to risk losing his pension. Before Sybron discovered what was happening, Roques duly retired and started to receive pension payments. When the conspiracy became apparent Sybron claimed that the pension payments were made under a mistake of fact. Sybron sought the return of them, alleging that the pension policies had been agreed, and the payments under them made because it was believed that Roques was entitled to his pension rights when in fact he was not: he could have been summarily dismissed for serious misconduct.

13.12   In these circumstances, the Court of Appeal upheld the finding that Roques had acted in breach of duty in not disclosing the wrongdoing, and had thereby induced a mistake of fact by Sybron, in implementing a pension agreement with Roques rather than exercising their rights in relation to the agreement. This was so irrespective of the fact that by reporting on others he would also have implicated himself in the wrongdoing.

13.13   The Court of Appeal recognized that there is no general rule that in every case an employee must disclose any information which s/he has about breaches of duty by fellow employees. Indeed, Stephenson LJ (at p 127) endorsed the view of the first instance judge (Walton J) that 'the law would do industrial relations generally no great service if it held that such a duty did in fact exist in all cases'.

13.14   As to where a duty to report arises, Stephenson LJ explained that:

> whether there is such a duty depends on the contract and on the terms of employment of the particular servant. He may be so placed in the hierarchy as to have a duty to report either the misconduct of his superior, as in *Swain v West (Butchers) Ltd* [1936] 3 All ER 261, or the misconduct of his inferiors, as in this case.

13.15   Stephenson LJ also endorsed the view expressed at first instance that:

> the duty must, in my view, depend upon all the circumstances of the case, and the relationship of the parties to their employer and *inter se*.
>
> . . . where there is an hierarchical system, particularly where the person in the hierarchy whose conduct is called into question is a person near the top who is responsible to his employers for the whole of the operation of a complete sector of the employers' business— here the European zone—then in my view entirely different considerations apply.
>
> . . . A person in a managerial position cannot possibly stand by and allow fellow servants to pilfer the company's assets and do nothing about it . . . Of course, this all depends upon the duties of the relevant employee under his contract of service. In the present case there was a well-recognised reporting procedure, whereunder the zone controller, Mr. Roques, was expected to make reports as to the state of matters in his zone every month.

13.16   *Sybron* may therefore be regarded as an extreme case. Roques occupied a very senior position in the employing organization, there was a recognized reporting structure under which he was required to make reports in relation to matters within his zone, and there was serious wrongdoing by subordinates within his zone which was clearly a matter which ought to have been dealt with in the monthly reports. Further, the wrongdoing was serious and, as Fox LJ emphasized (at p 129E–F), it was ongoing. Indeed, Kerr LJ emphasized, in the light of Roques' reporting duties, the circumstances amounted to fraudulent breach of his duties in covering up and deliberately concealing the conduct of his subordinates. The case therefore begs the question as to the extent to which the duty to report wrongdoing would extend to less extreme circumstances. Further, as made clear by the decision in *Ranson*, whilst seniority may carry with it responsibilities for the business or express reporting obligations, seniority does not of itself necessarily give rise to the obligation to disclose wrongdoing; in each case an analysis is required of the employee's role/job description and contractual terms vis-à-vis the matters alleged to be the subject of the duty of disclosure.

(b) Blowing the whistle on superiors

Senior employees Although in *Sybron* the Court of Appeal emphasized that Roques was required to report the misdeeds of his subordinates, it was his managerial status, with its attendant reporting duties, that was important. As acknowledged in *Sybron*, it is clear from the decision of the Court of Appeal in *Swain v West (Butchers) Limited* [1936] 3 All ER 261 that the duty to disclose misdeeds is not necessarily confined to reporting upon subordinates. Mr Swain was employed as the general manager of the employers' business and as such was responsible for the business as a whole except that he was subordinate to the managing director. However, he followed certain unlawful orders of the managing director involving the selling of incorrectly labelled meat. Swain was asked about this by the chairman of the employers and told that if he provided proof of the managing director's dishonesty he would not be dismissed. Swain provided the requisite information, thereby implicating himself in the fraud. He was then dismissed. **13.17**

The Court of Appeal held that Swain could not enforce the agreement that he would not be dismissed because he was already under an obligation to report the managing director's wrongdoing and there was therefore no consideration for the agreement with the chairman. The Court of Appeal emphasized that Swain's contract provided that he was to do all in his power to 'promote, extend and develop the interests of the company'. Of itself this might appear unremarkable. However, this was in a context where Swain, because of his seniority,[2] had control of the business and was responsible for seeing that it was conducted 'honestly and efficiently by all who came under his control' (per Greene LJ at 265). **13.18**

Again, in *RBG Resources plc (in liquidation) v Rastogi and others* [2002] EWHC 2782 (Ch), a senior employee was held to be arguably under an implied obligation to report the wrongdoing of (slightly) more senior colleagues. The fourth defendant, Mr Patel, was the 'Senior Vice-President—Structured Finance'. He was a very senior executive whose role included arranging bank borrowing. RBG's business (against which large amounts of money had been borrowed) was in fact largely fictitious and, some time prior to RBG's collapse, its auditors had resigned because of their misgivings about the audit trail. In an action brought by the liquidators in the name of the company, it was claimed that Patel owed his employer a duty to investigate and report on the wrongdoing of his co-defendants, who were each directors of the company. The question for the court was whether this case was arguable, since Patel's application was for summary judgment on the basis that it had no reasonable prospect of success. Laddie J dismissed the application and rejected the contention that there was a general rule that, before a duty to report wrongdoing on the part of fellow employees could be imposed, the defendant employee had to be in a supervisory position vis-à-vis those employees: **13.19**

> Whether or not Mr Patel was under a duty to report wrongdoing by his co-defendants is a matter of fact which is dependent upon a multitude of factors, including the terms of his contract of employment, his duties and his seniority in the company. One of the relevant factors will be the nature of the wrongdoing and its potential adverse effect on the

---

[2] In *Rochem*, Stephenson LJ at 815 stated 'He may be so placed in the hierarchy as to have a duty to report either the misconduct of his superior, as in *Swain v West (Butchers) Ltd* [1936] 3 All ER 261, or the misconduct of his inferiors, as in this case'.

company. Where, as here, the alleged wrongdoing went to the very survival of the company, it is more likely that the court would imply a duty to report.

13.20 Laddie J noted that in *Sybron* Stephenson LJ had indicated that such a duty might include a duty to report the wrongdoing of superiors and concluded (at para 40):

> at all material times, Mr Patel was a very senior executive of RBG concerned with arranging the bank borrowing . . . it is readily arguable that he was under a duty to report wrongdoing or suspected wrongdoing by others.

13.21 The decision also addressed the issues of to whom the wrongdoing should have been reported, and as to whether there was a duty to investigate, which we consider further below at paragraphs 13.85 and 13.86.

13.22 **Less senior employees**   In the case of less senior employees the courts are likely to be much more reluctant to find that there is a duty to report the misdeeds of superiors or colleagues at the same level. Such reluctance is evident in the decision of the majority of the EAT in *Ladbroke Racing Limited v King, Daily Telegraph*, 21 April 1989. Following the dismissal of a manager for gross misconduct, including falsification of records and removing money from the shop, an investigation was carried out into the conduct of his subordinates. This revealed that the subordinate employees had, on their manager's instructions, been involved in serious breaches of the rules including allowing unauthorized betting and failing to reconcile the cash. The employer's rules provided that it would not be an answer to a breach of those rules that this had been condoned over time by management. The subordinate employees were dismissed for their breaches of the rules and for failing to report the breaches of the rules by their manager. By a majority, the EAT held that the dismissal was unfair. There was no sufficiently clear express term upon which the employer could rely in order to impose an express duty to report the manager's misconduct. Nor was there a breach of the implied term of trust and confidence because this left a discretion in the employees and, in the EAT's view, the employees had not acted unreasonably in choosing not to report their manager's misconduct.

13.23 One difficulty in imposing an implied obligation of disclosure, even on junior employees, is the difficulty of reconciling this with the emphasis in *Sybron* that there is no general duty of disclosure on all employees. This was emphasized by Pumfrey J in *Cantor Fitzgerald International v Tradition (UK) Limited* (12 June 1998). A claim was brought by Tradition for infringement of copyright. It was alleged that Tradition's employed programmers had constructed a computer programme for Tradition which reproduced a code written for the claimant, their former employer. The employees had told Tradition that they were not copying the code. Tradition brought third-party proceedings against one of the employees (Mr Gresham) and sought leave to serve out of the jurisdiction. This was refused on the basis that there was no good arguable case. Tradition argued that the employee was under an implied duty to disclose the misconduct of his fellow employees in copying the code. Pumfrey J concluded that this was unlikely to succeed. There was nothing to distinguish Mr Gresham from the ordinary run of comparatively junior employees. He had no managerial responsibility and had worked under the direction of a director of Tradition who was principally responsible for any infringement of copyright.

(c) Blowing the whistle on employees of similar seniority

13.24 In *Sybron*, Stephenson LJ took the view (approving a dictum of Walton J at first instance that referred to *Bell v Lever Brothers*) that:

> it would be very difficult to have submitted, with any hope of success, that Messrs Bell and Snelling, having been appointed to rescue the affairs of their employers' African subsidiary in effect jointly, ought to have denounced each other.

This cannot, however, be taken as setting out any general principle that employees at a **13.25** similar level or in joint management do not have a responsibility to report as to each other's conduct. First, as also noted by Stephenson LJ, the issue as to whether there was an obligation to report on the wrongdoing of others was not addressed by the House of Lords in *Bell v Lever Brothers*, save for Lord Atkin's mention that there might be a duty to report on theft by a fellow employee. Second, the principles in *Sybron*, *Swain*, and *Rastogi* emphasize the need to consider all the circumstances, including management responsibilities, which might entail reporting duties. *Rastogi* was a case where the defendant was only slightly less senior than the directors about whom he should have reported. Indeed, rather than being of the same seniority, Bell was chairman of Niger Company and Snelling was vice-chairman, and Bell was entitled to a higher salary. In any event, it would be strange if a person in a managerial position had a responsibility to report on wrongdoing both by those more senior (as in *Swain*) and those less senior (as in *Sybron*) but not in respect of those at the same level.

(d) Express terms of the contract

The express terms of the contract may impose a clear obligation to disclose wrongdoing. **13.26** An obligation might also arise from the nature and circumstances of the employment, and from particular terms of employment other than an express reporting obligation. Indeed, in *Sybron* no reliance was placed on any express terms of the service agreement. However, as explained in *Ranson*, focus on the express terms (not limited to express reporting requirements) is crucial.

In *Swain* there was some emphasis on the express duty to 'promote, extend and develop the **13.27** interests' of the employer. Express contractual obligations to report were also emphasized in *Ranson* in explaining the obligation of disclosure imposed in *QBE Management Services (UK) Limited v Dymoke* [2012] IRLR 458. In *QBE* senior employees of the claimant agreed to set up a business venture together in competition with the employer and staffed by its current employees. There were clear breaches of contractual obligations in soliciting employees and brokers whilst still employed. In those circumstances Haddon-Cave J endorsed the view that the working assumption both for senior employees and directors should be that they ought to disclose any action which, if taken by others, would lead to competitive activity. He also held they should disclose their own action, once an irrevocable intention to compete was formed. However, that broad view is now to be read in the light of the emphasis in *Ranson* that the focus is not simply on seniority but on whether a duty to report can be spelled out from the nature of the role, contractual duties, and all the circumstances. In *Ranson* Lewison LJ highlighted that one of the defendants, Mr Dymoke, who was a senior employee but not a director, was subject to a contractual obligation to use his best endeavours to promote and protect the interests of the employer and a further obligation that he would 'fully and properly disclose to the Board . . . all of the affairs of the Group of which he is aware'. This was said (at para 55) to be the basis for the obligation to disclose his own activities in soliciting employees to defect en masse, his misuse of confidential information, and his solicitation of employees during his employment.

However, general wording such as was relied upon in *Swain* may not suffice. Indeed, **13.28** a similar obligation to that in *Swain* is likely to apply to most senior employees and directors (and would certainly have applied to Bell and Snelling). It remains necessary to consider this in the context of the employee's role, other terms, and all the circumstances. Thus in *Lonmar Global Risks Limited v West* [2011] IRLR 138 a duty of disclosure in relation to unlawful competitive activity did not arise despite a contractual obligation to use 'best endeavours to promote the general interests and welfare of the company'. Here the employees were salesmen, employed by a Lloyd's insurance and reinsurance broker to obtain and retain business from international brokers. They were found to have acted unlawfully in conducting business for a competitor whilst still employed and in one case by soliciting clients, but they were found not to have acted in concert and the general clause to promote the interests of the company was held not to be a sufficient basis for a duty to report their own misconduct. Hickinbottom J emphasized that such a general clause could not by itself impose wide-ranging duties to report wrongdoing and conduct that might be contrary to the employer's interests. But this was to be seen in the context that the employees were not part of senior management and had no management responsibilities or staff reporting to them. The decision may be compared with that in *Imam-Siddique v BlueBay Asset Management (Services) Limited* [2013] IRLR 344, where the claimant employee was employed as head of sales, and an express contractual obligation to act in the best interests of the employer was taken into account as one factor, though not of itself determinative, in the overall assessment of whether the employee was under an obligation to report that he had provided assistance to a prospective competitor who he was looking to join.

(e) Seriousness of the wrongdoing

13.29 The nature of the wrongdoing is likely to be highly important and may be crucial. If the wrongdoing is sufficiently serious this might of itself give rise to a duty of disclosure to the employer. An employee at any level would surely be expected to report if s/he was, for example, aware of a serious imminent health risk. In *Bell v Lever Brothers*, as we have seen, Lord Atkin (at p 228) suggested that there might be a duty on employees to protect the employer's property to the extent of reporting a theft by a fellow employee. Although Lord Atkin explained this by the basis of the duty to protect the employer's property, it might also have been explained on the implied duty of fidelity or that an employee who kept quiet about such a theft would thereby seriously damage the requisite mutual trust and confidence between employer and employee. Indeed, as we discuss below,[3] in *Lister v Hesley Hall Limited* [2001] UKHL 22, [2001] ICR 665 some of the speeches in the House of Lords contemplated an obligation even to confess one's own wrongdoing or the consequences of it in the context of particularly serious harm (sexual abuse), and in *The Zinnia* [1984] 2 Lloyd's Rep 211 seriousness of harm supported an implied disclosure obligation even in an arm's-length commercial context.

13.30 Where, however, the employee in a managerial position reasonably takes the view that the matter can be dealt with without disclosure to a more senior level, then it will be more difficult to argue (in the absence of an express term) that there was a duty to report the issue nonetheless. In the *Swain* case, discussed above, Swain was junior to the miscreant and there was no question of his being able to institute disciplinary action himself. However, even if a wrongdoing employee has been dismissed or disciplined, there might still be an obligation on the employee who is taking the disciplinary action to report on the reasons for having done so. If this is not properly communicated, the employer might be exposed to the risk of a claim for negligence if it subsequently provides a reference indicating that there is no reason to doubt the loyalty or probity of the ex-employee.

(f) Continuing wrongdoing

13.31 As noted above, in *Sybron* Fox LJ placed emphasis on the fact that the misconduct was continuing, whereas in *Bell v Lever Brothers* there was only a question as to past misconduct. It is apparent that Fox LJ regarded this as one factor to be weighed in the balance in favour of requiring disclosure rather than as necessarily being determinative. Certainly this may be

---

[3] At paras 13.66–13.69.

important. The seriousness of the matter and the urgency of disclosure to the employer will be all the more obvious in the case of ongoing misconduct.

13.32 The lesser importance of past wrongdoing may be seen as reflected in the decision in *Hands v Simpson Fawcett and Co Limited* (1928) 44 TLR 295. The claimant, whose contract with the defendants as a commercial traveller provided that he was to use a car for carrying samples, was convicted of driving the car 'to the common danger' and his licence was suspended for three months. The defendants dismissed him, arguing that the misconduct in driving the vehicle justified them in doing so, but further that he ought to have informed them that he had previously been convicted of being drunk in charge of a car and of dangerous driving. Both pleas failed. Finlay J said that the non-disclosure of the earlier motoring offences did not justify repudiation: this was not a contract like an insurance contract (with its implicit obligation of utmost good faith) requiring the claimant to state all the material facts.

13.33 There are, however, dangers in placing too much importance on whether the misconduct is ongoing. Irrespective of whether the misdeed has been completed, an employer might have an interest in rooting out the culprit. The misdeed might be such as to cast doubt on whether the culprit is a sufficiently trustworthy employee and there may be concern not only to prevent the same misconduct in future but also other misconduct. In *Camelot v Centaur Communications Limited* [1998] IRLR 80, for example, the Court of Appeal was faced with an application to disclose documents which would reveal the identity of an employee of Camelot who leaked a copy of Camelot's draft accounts to a journalist. There was no danger of a further leak of the same nature due to injunctions or undertakings which had already been given in relation to that information and the passage of time. However, the Court of Appeal accepted that an employee who was sufficiently disloyal or untrustworthy to make the initial disclosure could not be relied upon to refrain from revealing other confidential information such as, in the case of Camelot's employees, the names and addresses of lottery winners.[4]

13.34 Further, it is doubtful whether *Bell v Lever Brothers* can itself properly be regarded as a case which related solely to past misconduct. At the time when the severance agreements were entered into there were no longer any secret profits being made and the jury found that there was no deliberate concealment of the secret profits. However, Bell and Snelling held their senior positions at the time when they were engaged in making secret profits. The misconduct was then ongoing but it was not held that at that stage there was any duty to disclose the misconduct. If there had been such a duty, then it would have been strongly arguable that Lever Brothers had suffered loss of the sums paid by way of severance payments by reason of the breach of contract by Bell and Snelling.

13.35 Conversely, it seems very unlikely that the decision in *Sybron* would have been any different even if there was only past misconduct, for example because the wrongful competition had been brought to an end. Roques had a managerial responsibility, and also had an express obligation to report matters within his zone every month. As such he was certainly under an obligation to report the misconduct by other employees.

(g) Deliberate concealment

13.36 In *Bell v Lever Brothers* there was a specific finding by a jury that the non-disclosure of wrongdoing was not fraudulent. As noted above, in *Sybron* Kerr LJ drew attention to this

---

[4] See, further, Chapter 15 on informants.

as a point of distinction from *Bell*. In *Fassihi*, Arden LJ also referred to this consideration whilst noting that it was unnecessary to decide a point in relation to this.

13.37 Deliberate or fraudulent concealment is not, however, a prerequisite of liability. Where, as in *Sybron* and *Swain*, there is an express or implicit positive obligation arising from employment to report wrongdoing, for example due to a senior managerial role of the employee, there would then be a duty to exercise reasonable care and skill in relation to that duty. A breach of the duty might therefore arise from careless oversight rather than deliberate concealment. Further, as Lightman J observed in *BCCI v Ali (No 1)* [1999] IRLR 226, there is a logical difficulty in taking account of deliberate concealment. In the context of considering whether there was an obligation upon BCCI to disclose its fraud to its own employees, Lightman J noted (at para 16) that he could not see how questions of fraudulent concealment could arise unless BCCI was under a duty to disclose. Nevertheless, *Sybron* provides some support for the argument that dishonesty in taking deliberate steps to conceal information may be relied upon to indicate a positive obligation.

(h) Has there been a specific request?

13.38 Similarly, it might be important that an employee fails to supply information as to wrong-doing despite receiving a specific request. First, there may then be a positive representation that there is no further relevant information, rather than merely non-disclosure. Second, the obligation of disclosure may then be supported by the claim of a failure to obey lawful and reasonable instructions.

13.39 *Bell v Lever Brothers* was concerned with the duty on an employee to volunteer information concerning his own wrongdoing. As Lord Atkin put it, if the employer 'wishes to protect himself he can question his servant and will then be protected by the truth or otherwise of the answers' (at p 228). One approach might be for an employer to request that its employees periodically sign a statement confessing any breach or breaches of duty. Where the express terms of the contract impose a clear obligation to report wrongdoing this may also be significant, as to which see paragraphs 13.26–13.28 above.

13.40 Compromise agreements on termination in respect of senior employees often contain warranties that the employee has disclosed any prior breaches of duty of which s/he is aware. A false negative answer in this respect would ground an entitlement to set aside the resulting agreement. Similarly, in order to secure employment in the first place employees will usually be required to give, with varying degrees of formality and detail, information about themselves. Once again it would be open to an employer to avoid any contract formed on the basis of incorrect representations and, unsurprisingly, it has been held that a positive misrepresentation will be a good reason for dismissal. In *Birmingham District Council v Beyer* [1977] 1 IRLR 211 Mr Beyer was a well-known trade union activist. By October 1975 he was convinced (and no doubt correctly so, as Wood J said), that no large employer who recognized him or his name would give him a job unless he could be shunted off into some narrow and restricted field where his zeal could find no outlet. He therefore deceived the Birmingham Corporation into giving him a job by submitting a false name and a bogus reference. He was quickly identified and summarily dismissed on the grounds of gross misconduct. He tried unsuccessfully to gain other work with the Corporation until, in September 1976, he managed to slip past the barrier and, as an inconspicuous member of a three-man gang, was taken on by the Corporation at a site where his face and name were unknown to the local site agent. Within a couple of hours the intelligence system disclosed to the individual who had dismissed him a year earlier that Beyer was with the Corporation once more. Beyer was immediately dismissed on the ground that he was the man who had grossly deceived the Corporation a year earlier. Reversing the employment tribunal, the EAT said that dismissal for the previous year's deception was fair and Beyer was not unfairly dismissed.[5]

It is not though an essential factor in all cases that there be a specific request or instruction. **13.41** In *Sybron* there was indeed a duty to make monthly reports and in *Swain* the employee was expressly asked to blow the whistle on the managing director. However, it was made clear in *Swain* that the duty to report acts of which Swain was aware and which he knew were not in the interests of his employer arose irrespective of any specific request. This was reaffirmed in *Sybron* (per Stephenson LJ at p 126G).

(i) Is there someone with whom to raise concerns?

In *Rastogi* (see paragraph 13.19 above) it was argued that there was no duty to report wrong- **13.42** doing because the directors to whom the matter could be reported were implicated in the wrongdoing. This was rejected on the basis that there were members of the board against whom no accusations of wrongdoing had been made. Laddie J also held that there was an arguable duty to report to the company's auditors. He declined to consider (on the facts of the case before him) whether there was or might be a duty to report to the Serious Fraud Office, the police, or the company's solicitors.

The decision therefore illustrated that the fact that the concerns relate to the board does not **13.43** necessarily exclude a duty of disclosure if there is an appropriate outside body with whom to raise concerns. However, uncertainty about with whom a concern should be raised might point against the implication of a positive obligation. A clear whistleblowing policy would help to avoid this difficulty.[6]

(2) Implied contractual reporting obligations other than misdeeds

It is also apparent that where an employee has managerial functions s/he may be required **13.44** to report on matters other than the misdeeds of employees. In *Swain* Greer LJ noted that it was Swain's duty to report acts which he knew were not in his employer's interests. It appears to have been accepted that this flowed from Swain's overall responsibility for the business. Similarly, the speeches of Lords Steyn and Hobhouse in *Lister*, to which we refer below,[7] seem to assume a duty to report a sufficiently serious concern to the employer.

The issue has tended to arise in recent years in the context of whether there is a duty to **13.45** report on competitive threats, in particular in relation to departing employees. The leading guidance is now that in *Ranson v Customer Systems plc* [2012] IRLR 769 (CA), emphasizing a fact-sensitive approach focusing on the particular contractual obligations, the employee's role/job description, and all the circumstances. Consistently with this guidance, the position was summarized by Popplewell J in *Imam-Sadeque v BlueBay Asset Management (Services) Limited* [2013] IRLR 344 at para 133 as follows:

> The duty of fidelity may also require an employee to report to his employer a competitive threat of which he becomes aware, irrespective of whether he or any fellow employees are

---

[5] Statutory duties and absolutions from obligations to disclose on job applicants are contained in the Rehabilitation of Offenders Act 1974 Exemptions Order 1975 (SI 1975/1023) (as amended).

[6] See eg *Shinwari v Vue Entertainment Limited* (UKEAT/0394/14/BA, 12 March 2015) where the EAT (Simler J, at para 13) specifically noted that as part of its overall assessment of the facts the ET had found that all employees of the employer were under a positive obligation to report wrongdoing by fellow employees. Here the tribunal (upheld by the EAT) went on to reject a contention that a worker had been subjected to a detriment in revealing his identity to the person about whom he had made disclosures, since the reason for doing so was to provide that person with the evidence being relied against him in disciplinary proceedings.

[7] See para 13.67 below.

involved in that competitive threat. So too may an express term to act in the best interests of the company (cf *Swain v West (Butchers) Ltd* [1936] 3 All ER 261). Whether it does so is again fact sensitive, and will depend upon the terms of his contract of employment, the nature of his role and responsibilities, the nature of the threat, and the circumstances in which he becomes aware of it. A senior manager who becomes aware of a competitive threat to an aspect of the business for which he is responsible will normally come under such a duty, whereas a junior employee without such responsibility would not. The manager of a branch of a supermarket in the high street would normally be obliged to tell his superiors if he learned that a rival supermarket chain was proposing to open a store next door; whereas a junior employee working in the unloading bay would not.

13.46 In this case the employer, BlueBay, managed investments for institutions and high-net-worth individuals. Mr Imam-Sadeque was employed as head of sales. His employment contract provided that he was under an obligation to act in the best interests of BlueBay at all times. Shortly before entering into a compromise agreement for his departure and starting garden leave, he entered into discussions with a start-up asset management company, Goldbridge, which was proposing to enter into competition with BlueBay. Whilst still employed by BlueBay, he provided assistance in relation to Goldbridge's launch and in relation to its recruitment of another BlueBay employee, Mr Nixon. Shortly after starting garden leave, Mr Imam-Sadeque attended a meeting at BlueBay, where he falsely denied having helped recruit Mr Nixon to Goldbridge.

13.47 In the context of an issue as to whether Mr Imam-Sadeque was entitled to be treated as a 'good leaver', the court concluded that his duty of fidelity required that he inform BlueBay that Goldbridge intended to launch a start-up business in competition with BlueBay; that it had the necessary funding, resources, staff, and infrastructure in place to do so; and when it intended to launch. In so concluding the court stressed five factors as bearing on the scope of the duty of fidelity. First, his contractual terms required him to act in BlueBay's best interests at all times and imposed express restrictions on any activity contrary to BlueBay's interests. Second, Goldbridge was to be a direct competitor of BlueBay, targeting similar clients and offering similar investment products. It was not an answer that it would not be starting straight away. As Popplewell J put it, the supermarket manager who learns of the rival store to be built next door cannot wait until it has been completed, and started trading, before revealing his knowledge of it. Third, he was a senior employee of BlueBay and was highly remunerated. As to this, Popplewell J expressed the view (at para 138) that 'the scope of the duty imposed on someone at high managerial level in a multi-million pound business will involve a heavy burden not to do anything which might result in damage to the interests of that business'. Fourth, still focusing on the nature of Mr Imam-Sadeque's senior role, it was in an aspect of the business which was of very considerable importance to the success and profitability of BlueBay; he had responsibility for targeting and retaining clients. Finally, he was in a position to exert influence on the structure and operational implementation of Goldbridge's business plans in relation to this important area of activity. In addition, on the basis that the duty of fidelity entailed a duty of honesty, he was found to have acted in breach by virtue of the untruths told when questioned about recruiting Mr Nixon. Nor was the position altered by being on garden leave, given that the contract expressly provided that contractual terms continued to apply and a common purpose of garden leave is to secure loyalty to the employer until the termination date.

13.48 Whilst the decision framed the obligation to disclose in broad terms by reference to the employer's interest in learning of the competitive threat, it therefore focused on the employee's particular role and duties, and on the facts applied in the context of wrongdoing by the employee.

Similar considerations apply to the first instance decision of Mr Justice Langstaff in *Thomson* **13.49**
Ecology Limited v Apem Limited [2014] IRLR 184. Here the claimant employer ran a marine
biology laboratory. The employee was the most senior employee at the employer's Letchworth
premises, in overall charge of its operations and business. He left to work for a competitor,
APEM, and a large number of other biologists also did so. He had plainly acted in breach of
duty in that he admitted that whilst still employed he had discussed with APEM how they
might recruit the claimant's staff, informed the staff that APEM was looking to recruit and
provided APEM with salary details for employees who might contact them. In relation to the
scope of disclosure obligations, the court highlighted his role in charge of the claimant's operations at Letchworth, his obligations to manage the staff there, and his obligation to submit
reports on a fortnightly basis. Although the content of these reports was not specified, it was
to be taken as including how the business and staff were performing. In the circumstances
the court had little difficulty in finding a breach of a duty to disclose the competitive threat
notwithstanding that this arose on a summary judgment application.

More broadly, however, the court expressed agreement with the view of Openshaw J in **13.50**
UBS Wealth Management (UK) Ltd v Vestra Wealth Management [2008] IRLR 965 at para
24 that:

> I cannot accept that employees, in particular senior managers, can keep silent when they
> know of planned poaching raids upon the company's existing staff or client base and when
> these are encouraged or facilitated from within the company itself, the more so when they
> are themselves party to these plots and plans. It seems to me that would be an obvious
> breach of their duties of loyalty and fidelity.[8]

A broad approach was also adopted to a team move case by Wyn Williams J in *Kynixa* **13.51**
Limited v Hynes and others [2008] EWHC 1495 (QB), resulting in the imposition of a
duty to report such threats in the absence of a fiduciary duty. The employer, Kynixa, was
a specialist provider of rehabilitation and case-management services for individuals who
suffered injuries. The three defendants together comprised the senior management team of
Kynixa. They were each separately approached by and ultimately agreed to take up employment with a competitor. Two of the defendants were particularly senior, holding positions
of head of business development and a role equivalent to chief operating officer, and were
held to owe fiduciary duties. They were held to be in breach of those duties in failing to disclose the approaches to Kynixa once they became aware that their colleagues had also been
approached. This was on the basis that their duty to act in good faith in the best interests
of the company encompassed the duty to report this threat to its business, once they were
aware that each of them had been approached by the competitor.[9] The third defendant was
less senior and it was accepted that she did not owe relevant fiduciary duties. However, she
too was held to be under a duty to report the approaches once she became aware that the
other members of the senior management team had also been approached. This was not said
to arise from any specific reporting obligations arising from management of the business,
but from her duty of fidelity, arising due to her seniority. She was an important employee
who was part of the senior management team, and had access to the important information
which made the claimant's business a success. The judge commented (at para 283) that:

> A crucial aspect of the implied duty of fidelity is the concept of loyalty. The Third
> Defendant's actions were not consistent with that concept. I simply do not see how one

---

[8] See also *QBE Management Services (UK) Limited v Dymoke* [2012] IRLR 458 at para 172, also endorsing this dictum.
[9] This was said to be an application of Hart J's decision in *Midland Tool Limited v Midland International
Tooling Limited* [2003] 2 BCLC 523, which is discussed at para 13.80 below.

can be acting as a loyal employee when one knows that three senior employees (including oneself) may transfer their allegiance to a group of companies which includes a competitor and yet not only fail to divulge that knowledge but also say things which would have the effect of positively misleading the employer about that possibility.

13.52 This founded an obligation that was not dependent on reporting any wrongdoing. In that respect the decision was controversial, particularly insofar as it did not rest on identifying particular management responsibilities giving rise to the reporting obligation. To this extent this decision may need to be approached with some care. One important factor in such cases has been the element of employees' acting together. The decision may be contrasted with the conclusion in *Lonmar Global Risks Limited v West* [2011] IRLR 138. As discussed above (paragraph 13.28), employees who had acted unlawfully in conducting business for a competitor whilst still employed and in the case of one of them by soliciting clients, were found not to owe a duty to disclose their activities, given that they had not acted in concert and did not have management responsibility for other staff. Hickinbottom J suggested that the decision in *Kynixa* could be explained on the basis that the third defendant in *Kynixa* had positively misled her employer, rather than there merely being a non-disclosure. He added that, to the extent that dicta in *Kynixa* could be said to support a broad obligation on an employee, who owes no relevant fiduciary obligations and has not acted in concert with colleagues or otherwise unlawfully, to disclose that fellow employees are being recruited by a competitor, he disagreed with that proposition. There must be some additional factor, such as particular responsibilities, which gives rise to a reporting obligation.

13.53 Support for that view is provided by the decision on the facts in *Ranson*. Mr Ranson was employed in a senior sales role and responsible for 59 per cent of the employer's total revenue. Whilst still employed he made lawful preparations to set up a competing company and secure work for his prospective new business from another company, Diageo, knowing that his employer was seeking work from that company. He was held not to have acted in breach of duty in pursuing the opportunity on the basis that it was not on his 'patch' and so not part of his responsibility to pursue this for the employer. Having regard to the scope of Mr Ranson's responsibilities, even if pursuing this customer was a breach of duty, there was no obligation to report this.

13.54 There is, in any event, a danger in extrapolating from these cases a duty to disclose an approach by a competitor. Particular public policy considerations apply in such a case in relation to freedom of competition: see eg *Helmet Integrated Systems Limited v Tunnard* [2006] EWCA Civ 1735, [2007] IRLR 126 at para 27. By contrast, in other cases where such considerations do not apply, there may be other public policy considerations strongly supporting the imposition of disclosure obligations, as in the case of reporting a danger to health and safety.

13.55 However, considerable difficulty arises in relation to identifying the precise scope of the reporting obligation beyond the field of wrongdoing. There might also be difficult issues as to whether there is an obligation to disclose wrongdoing which tarnishes the image of the employer but is outside the work context. This problem could be partially resolved on the basis that in such marginal cases it would be for the manager in the first instance to assess, acting honestly in what s/he believes is in the employer's interests, whether the matters were such that s/he could deal with them without troubling superiors, or whether it would be necessary to take such matters further in order to protect the employer's interests. As we discuss further below (at paragraph 13.75 et seq), this would be consistent with the position in relation to duties of disclosure arising out of fiduciary obligations, where the fiduciary obligation is to act in the way the employee in good faith considers to be in the best interests of the company (*Fassihi*).

(3) Do employees have implied contractual obligations to disclose their own wrongdoing?

Traditionally *Bell v Lever Brothers* has been taken as authority for the proposition that, **13.56** whilst an employee may be obliged to blow the whistle on others, there is no obligation for an employee to disclose his/her own wrongdoing. However, this was qualified in *Item Software (UK) Limited v Fassihi* [2003] EWHC 3116, [2003] IRLR 769 (HC); [2004] EWCA Civ 1244, [2004] IRLR 928.

The directors of Item included Mr Dehghani, the managing director and the defendant, Mr **13.57** Fassihi, who was the sales and marketing director. A major part of Item's business was the distribution of software products for Isograph. Item decided to negotiate more favourable terms with Isograph. At the same time, Fassihi secretly approached Isograph with his own proposals which involved establishing his own company, RAMS, to take over the contract. Meanwhile, he encouraged Dehghani to press Isograph for terms which were more favourable to Item. Agreement was nearly reached by Dehghani with Isograph but the negotiations failed because Dehghani insisted on terms that Isograph was not prepared to accept. Isograph then terminated the contract by giving twelve months' notice. Item later discovered Fassihi's misconduct, and he was summarily dismissed. Item brought proceedings against Fassihi alleging, amongst other things, that he was in breach of duty in failing to disclose to Item his own wrongdoing in negotiating behind Item's back.

At first instance Nicholas Strauss QC, sitting as a High Court judge, suggested that *Bell v* **13.58** *Lever Brothers* was authority for the proposition that an employee is not obliged under his/ her contract of employment to disclose his/her own misconduct at or after the time it is committed, even where it is in the employer's interest to take action against the employee to prevent further misconduct or to secure the business or profit which the employee might have misappropriated. Nor is there a duty to disclose the misconduct where the employee later enters into a contract to vary or terminate his/her employment contract, even if the misconduct would be a material matter to take into account. The judge identified three bases for disapplying the general rule. First, as in *Sybron*, particular aspects of the employee's functions might require disclosure of relevant facts even if this involved the employee owning up to his/her own misconduct. Second, disclosure might be required in cases of fraudulent misconduct. Third, by virtue of his director's duties, Fassihi was obliged to disclose the secret profit made by appropriating the company's contract. In relation to the first ground, Fassihi's misconduct gave rise to a 'superadded' duty to disclose his own misconduct. He was involved in the negotiations between Item and Isograph and his contractual obligations of fidelity and care required him to disclose important information known to him which was relevant to those negotiations. If he had learned that a third-party rival distributor had been trying to sabotage the negotiations with Isograph, then it would have been his duty to tell Dehghani of this: the fact that the rival was himself did not relieve him of the duty. That it would also separately have been in Item's interest to know of the misconduct in order to deal with Fassihi would not have justified the imposition of a duty, but Fassihi was bound to disclose facts which were relevant to the ongoing negotiations with Isograph.

The Court of Appeal upheld the decision but focused on the fiduciary obligations to make **13.59** disclosure. However, in relation to ordinary contractual obligations, the Court of Appeal commented that *Bell v Lever Brothers* was not authority for the proposition that in no circumstances could an employee be under such an obligation. Arden LJ raised two possibilities:

(a) One route might be to conclude that no logical distinction can be drawn between an employee disclosing his/her own wrongdoing, and disclosing that of others, especially as the latter course might involve disclosing the employee's own wrongdoing.

(b) The second possibility was to rely upon the developing jurisprudence in relation to the obligation not without reasonable cause or excuse to act in a manner calculated or likely to destroy or seriously damage the requisite relationship of trust and confidence.

13.60 The second of these alternatives has not subsequently found favour. It was considered and rejected in *Ranson v Customer Services plc* [2012] IRLR 769 (CA). Lewison LJ noted that since this term is a default contractual obligation which is an incident of all employment contracts, it could not be a basis for identifying those cases where the duty of disclosure arose. Some of the difficulties arising from a generic obligation to disclose an employee's own wrongdoing were highlighted by Lightman J in *BCCI v Ali (No 1)* [1999] IRLR 226,[10] where it was held that BCCI was not under any duty to disclose to its employees the fraudulent manner in which it had been carrying on its business even though this conduct put at risk the employees' own reputation. Lightman J commented (at para 19) that:

> there is indeed much to be said for relaxing the rule which exempts employers and employees alike from any duty to disclose to the other their breaches of duty, for disclosure may be essential to enable the other party to take urgent steps to cure, control or mitigate the consequences of such breach; such disclosure may be necessary to protect the other's 'physical, financial and psychological welfare'. The price of any relaxation is however a high one. The T and C term is a mutual obligation of employer and employee. An employee's conduct may cast a stigma on an employer even as an employer's conduct may cast a stigma on an employee. Far from providing better protection for employees, the development represented by treating the T and C term as imposing duties of disclosure of wrongdoing may well be calculated to create more onerous burdens on employees than on employers. A duty on an employee to disclose eg that he took a day's sickness leave when not genuinely ill or used his employer's telephone or stationery for private use may be thought intolerable. A duty to confess wrongdoing whether on the part of employer or employee may be thought to require standards extravagant and unattainable in the workplace.

13.61 Lightman J referred to *University of Nottingham v Eyett* [1999] IRLR 87, in which Hart J rejected a submission that the implied trust and confidence term included a positive obligation on an employer to advise employees as to how best to exercise valuable pension rights under an employment contract. Hart J emphasized that such a term had potentially far-reaching consequences and that a cautious approach was therefore appropriate. It was necessary to consider how well such a positive obligation would cohere with the other default obligations implied by law. Lightman J considered that this pointed strongly against a duty to confess wrongdoing. Further, the approach in *Eyett* was endorsed by the Court of Appeal in *Crossley v Faithful & Gould Holdings Limited* [2004] EWCA Civ 293, [2004] ICR 1615. It was there emphasized that with most implied obligations it was obvious what an employer was required to do or not do. A proposed implied term to take reasonable care for the economic well-being of an employee was rejected in part because of considerable difficulty in seeing what the employer would be required to do. Equally, it might be contended that a duty to disclose wrongdoing would involve considerable uncertainty as to what must be disclosed and to whom, especially as there is no current obligation upon employers to introduce whistleblowing procedures.[11] Nor could this be answered on the basis that matters should be disclosed if they amount to protected disclosures. Aside from the uncertainty that might exist as to what is a protected disclosure, this does not necessarily provide an adequate touchstone since the legislation may cover only minor breaches of obligations as well as serious failures. Further, if a duty of disclosure was framed in terms of the duty of

---

[10] See para 13.37 above.
[11] In (2004) 33 ILJ 278 Prof David Lewis argued against introducing a general duty to report wrongdoing in the light of the uncertainty this would produce, and that instead express terms should be imposed

trust and confidence, this would have the limiting effect that the breach would necessarily be repudiatory (*Morrow v Safeway Stores plc* [2002] IRLR 9 (EAT)), whereas at present this may not necessarily be the case: see *Fulham Football Club (1987) Ltd v Tigana* [2004] EWHC 2585 (QB) at para 103.

The alternative basis advanced in *Fassihi* for a duty of disclosure was to reject the distinction **13.62** between an employer disclosing their own wrongdoing and disclosing that of others. Whilst that similarly may give rise to uncertainty, it avoids the pitfalls associated with being a default obligation arising irrespective of the circumstances. Consistent with that approach, Lewison LJ in *Ranson* emphasized the need in each case to focus on the employee's particular role, their job description, and express contractual terms, to identify whether an implied duty of disclosure (not necessarily limited to wrongdoing) arises and that this might entail a duty to disclose own wrongdoing.

The superadded duty found at first instance in *Fassihi* was also consistent with this approach, **13.63** essentially applying a similar analysis to that in *Sybron,* but in the context of disclosing the employee's own wrongdoing. Notwithstanding this, the extent of the duty to disclose one's own wrongdoing remains a controversial area. In *Hydra plc and another v Anastasi and others* [2005] EWHC 1559 (20 July 2005), and again in *Halcyon House Ltd v Baines* [2014] EWHC 2216 (per HHJ Seymour QC at para 236), *Bell v Lever Brothers* was relied on as authority that, in the absence of fiduciary obligations, employees are not obliged to disclose their own past misconduct or breaches of contract. As against that, in *Thomson Ecology Ltd v APEM Limited* [2014] IRLR 184, the implied duty of fidelity was held to require an employee to report his own wrongdoing in assisting a competitor to recruit, even if express contractual reporting obligations did not apply, due to the employee being on garden leave.[12]

We suggest that the better view, reflecting the dicta in *Ranson*, is that the same test applies, **13.64** focusing on the employee's role, terms of employment, and the circumstances, whether the duty applies to wrongdoing of others or own wrongdoing. Once the decision in *Bell v Lever Brothers* is acknowledged no longer to be a barrier, there is no good reason to draw the distinction in principle between confessing wrongdoing where no one else is involved, and reporting on the conduct of others. Rather, when it comes to taking into account the various factors which might be relevant, the fact that the disclosure is only about an employee's *own* wrongdoing would be relevant but might not be decisive. It may be important if the reporting obligation arises out of responsibility for subordinates in a hierarchical structure, where it might be more difficult to spell out a duty to report an employee's own misconduct. But it may be that the employee has reporting responsibilities for a particular part of the business of which the employee is a part, in which case spelling out a duty to report the wrongdoing need not necessarily pose a difficulty.

Further, lack of certainty as to when the duty arises may be said to be no greater than in **13.65** relation to whether there is a duty to disclose the wrongdoing of others. A duty to confess wrongdoing, whether on the part of the employer or the employee, might indeed require 'standards extravagant and unattainable in the workplace', as Lightman J suggested, if every

---

and accompanied by detailed procedures which make clear what is required of employees and provide protection against victimization for those who invoke them.

[12] See also *The Basildon Academies v Mr E Amadi* (UKEAT/0342/14/RN, 27 February 2015), in which Mitting J commented (at paras 21 and 22) that he took it now to be established that there was no rule of law that an employee could never owe a duty to disclose his own misconduct but, unsurprisingly, declined to imply a term that an employee must disclose to his employer an allegation of impropriety against him, however ill-founded. There was therefore no breach of contract where a cover supervisor failed to report to the college where he was employed unproven allegations of sexual assault made against him by a student.

wrongdoing had to be confessed. Such a duty to confess would become impossibly onerous if it applied in every case, by for example imposing a duty on an employee to confess taking a day's sick leave when not genuinely ill. However, there is already a need for the courts to ascertain in what circumstances and in relation to which wrongs an employee might owe a contractual duty to disclose the wrongdoing of others. The same process of reasoning could equally apply to ascertaining in what circumstances an employee should be required to disclose his/her own wrongs. There would be nothing extravagant in a requirement that an employee who, as in *Sybron*, is under an express or implied duty to report misconduct by reason of his/her position in the employer's organization, should be under a duty to report his/her own theft from the employer. Limits on the duty could be identified by reference to such matters as the position of the employee in the organization and the nature of the wrongdoing.

13.66 The irrationality of an immutable principle that employees need not disclose their own wrongdoing was perhaps tacitly recognized by some of the speeches of the House of Lords in *Lister v Hesley Hall Limited* [2001] UKHL 22, [2001] IRLR 472. The claimants had been boarders at the defendants' school for maladjusted and vulnerable boys. They were subjected to repeated acts of sexual abuse by a warden, Mr Grain. Many years later a police investigation led to Grain being convicted of a large number of offences against the claimants. The claimants then brought actions for damages for personal injury against the defendants on the basis that they were vicariously liable for the torts committed by Grain. The county court judge felt constrained[13] to accept the defendants' argument that they were not vicariously liable for the acts of Grain because those acts were outside the course of employment. However, the claimants still succeeded because the judge accepted that the employers were vicariously liable for Grain's failure to report his intentions to the defendants before the acts of sexual abuse were committed. The Court of Appeal held that if (as was the case in its view) the wrongful conduct was outside the course of employment, then the warden's failure to prevent or report that conduct was not within the scope of employment so as to make the defendants vicariously liable for that failure if they were not vicariously liable for the wrongful act itself. The House of Lords overruled earlier authority and allowed the claimants' appeal that the defendants were vicariously liable for the assaults.

13.67 The issue of liability in respect of the failure to disclose therefore became peripheral. Lord Steyn said (at para 29) that it was not necessary to express a view on the argument based on Grain's alleged breach of a duty to report his sexual intentions or the consequences of his misdeeds, but he noted that this line of argument might require further consideration. If an employee was aware of a physical injury sustained by a boy as a result of his conduct, it might be said to be part of his duties to report this fact to his employers. Lord Steyn questioned why, if that was so, the same would not be true of psychological damage caused by his sexual abuse of a boy. Lord Hobhouse (at para 62) noted that the judge had found that it was part of both the duty of the carers towards the claimants and of Grain towards his employers to report to them any incident which was relevant to the health and well-being of the claimants and that the Court of Appeal was mistaken in not attaching more validity to this way of putting the claimants' case. There was a whole succession of breaches of the duty to care for the claimants by Grain. The fact that the defendants might not have been liable for some of them did not alter the fact that the defendants would have been liable for the others. All it did was to put the former class of acts into the same category as acts done by some third party but of which, or of the consequences of which, Grain was aware. As the

---

[13] Because of the Court of Appeal's earlier decision in *Trotman v North Yorkshire County Council* [1999] IRLR 98.

trial judge had pointed out, there might have been a groundsman at the school and he might have been the abusing party; Grain might have discovered what had happened and the distress it had caused to the boys but then done nothing about it. The defendants might not be liable for what the groundsman did because he was employed to look after the grounds, not to have anything to do with the boys (or—he might have added—might have been employed by someone else). But the defendants would be liable for the breach of Grain who was employed to care for the boys and their welfare. The liability of the defendants might not be so grave or extensive as if Grain had been the abuser himself, but it would in principle be capable of existing. Lord Millett (at para 84) declined to base liability on Grain's failure to report his own wrongdoing to his employers, which was an 'artificial and unrealistic' approach. Even if such a duty did exist, on which he preferred to express no opinion, he thought that it would be a duty which was owed exclusively to the employers and not a duty for breach of which the employers could be vicariously liable. The same reasoning would not necessarily apply to the duty to report the wrongdoing of fellow employees, but it was not necessary to decide this.

The speeches in *Lister*, other than that of Lord Millett, therefore provide an indication that **13.68** an implied obligation to confess own wrongdoing, or the consequences of it, may sometimes arise, and that consideration of factors such as the other duties of the employees and, in particular, the seriousness of the concern, are likely to be important. In the context of arm's-length commercial contracts it has also been acknowledged that duties of disclosure might arise where these are required to avoid serious harm, even though the disclosure must be by the party who is in the wrong. In *The Zinnia* [1984] 2 Lloyd's Rep 211 there was a claim by shipowners against ship repairers following work done by the latter to reline the vessel's stern tube. In carrying out the repair, the repairers were supposed to use six-and-a-half sheets of Tufnol but instead they used only one-and-a-half sheets of Tufnol and five sheets of other material. The ship subsequently, and whilst in mid-voyage, suffered major damage in the engine room leading to dry-docking and loss and expense. Staughton J held that it had not been proved that the incorrect material had caused the damage but he accepted that the ship repairers owed a duty to inform the owners that part of the material used was not Tufnol. At p 218 he said:

> it is . . . a novel concept that a contractor who has broken his contract may be under a duty to inform the other party; I know of no authority to that effect and none was cited. At times, self-interest will suggest that course, if the defect can be remedied cheaply and might otherwise cause great loss. Motor manufacturers, on occasion, recall cars of a particular model for some modification . . . But at other times self-interest may point in the opposite direction. In the circumstances of this case, bearing in mind the unlikelihood of the stern tube being examined for four years unless a casualty occurred, the fact that the rules of the classification society had been infringed, and the possible danger to life at sea as well as very valuable property, I consider that [the repairers were] under a duty to inform the owners . . . I would say that the duty arose from an implied term in the contract, rather than as a part of a general contractual duty of care.

In practical terms, an obligation on an employee to report his/her own wrongdoing might **13.69** have little impact on the conduct of the employee. This was implicit in the concerns raised by Lord Millett in *Lister* as to a duty to confess one's own wrongdoing being 'artificial and unrealistic'. A person who is prepared to carry out a theft, for example, is unlikely to be willing to disclose his/her own wrongdoing merely because of a contractual obligation to do so. However, this concern was countered by Arden LJ (at para 66) in *Fassihi*, on the basis that 'two wrongs do not make a right: the fact that a director is unlikely to comply with a duty is not a logically sustainable reason for not imposing it if it is otherwise appropriate'. Further, the issue has often arisen in the context of seeking to set aside a contract such as a severance package. Where there has been a misrepresentation there is no difficulty since the employer would be entitled to rescind for misrepresentation. Indeed, this remedy could have been open in *Sybron* where the employee wrote misleading letters to his employer. In the absence of misrepresentation it may be necessary (as in *Bell v Lever Brothers*) to establish a duty of disclosure in order to prevent an employee, who was guilty of gross misconduct but concealed this from the employer, receiving a windfall from a severance payment made by the employer in ignorance of the employee's conduct.

(4) Conclusion as to the scope of the contractual duty of disclosure

13.70 While there will be many cases where there is obviously a duty to disclose misdeeds or other significant concerns, in other cases, as emphasized in *Sybron*, an assessment of all relevant circumstances will be necessary. The following matters, whilst not an exhaustive list, are likely to be of particular significance:

(a) the express terms of the contract;
(b) any works rules or policies clarifying the scope of the duty;
(c) any rules clarifying the procedure for raising concerns and to whom they are to be raised;
(d) whether there has been a request to the employee for disclosure;
(e) the seniority of the employee and his/her place in the employer's hierarchy;
(f) whether the employee has managerial responsibilities and the scope of those responsibilities;
(g) by whom any such wrongdoing was committed;
(h) the nature and seriousness of the wrongdoing or other matter to be disclosed;
(i) the degree of connection between the wrongdoing and the employment;
(j) whether the wrongdoing or other matter is of a continuing nature and/or is likely to continue unless reported;
(k) whether there has been deliberate concealment by the employee; and/or
(l) whether the wrongdoing has been by others.

C. Directors and Employees who owe Fiduciary Obligations

13.71 In some cases, in addition to their contractual obligations, employees also owe fiduciary obligations to their employer, which require separate consideration in relation to duties of disclosure. This will clearly be the case in relation to employees who are directors. It may also apply to very senior employees, having regard to the nature of their senior management obligations. Less senior employees might also acquire fiduciary obligations arising out of their specific obligations, where they can be regarded as having placed themselves in a position where they must act solely in the interests of the employer: see *Nottingham University v Fishel* [2000] ICR 1462.

13.72 However, as explained in *Ranson*, just as an analysis of the employee's contractual obligations, and the role/job description, is required to identify whether an implied contractual obligation of disclosure arises, similarly the same factors have to be considered to identify whether in particular respects the employee owes fiduciary obligations in the sense of an obligation to act solely in the employer's interests. To that end, in circumstances where an implied fiduciary obligation is found to arise, and to give rise to obligations of disclosure, there is also likely to be a contractual duty of disclosure, and the importance of identifying a fiduciary obligation is likely to lie only in the nature of the remedies available. Further, the court in *Ranson* cautioned against extrapolating from cases involving directors when considering the obligations arising in relation to non-director employees.

In relation to the core fiduciary duties, Elias J summarized the position in *Fishel* (at **13.73** paras 83–84):

> In *Bristol and West Building Society v Mothew* [1998] 1 Ch 1 at 18, Lord Millett elaborated on this analysis, and identified the duties which classically arise from such a fiduciary relationship:
>
> > 'A fiduciary is someone who has undertaken to act for or on behalf of another in a particular matter in circumstances which give rise to a relationship of trust and confidence. The distinguishing obligation of a fiduciary is the obligation of loyalty. The principal is entitled to the single-minded loyalty of his fiduciary. This core liability has several facets. A fiduciary must act in good faith; he must not make a profit out of his trust; he must not place himself in a position where his duty and his interest may conflict; he may not act for his own benefit or the benefit of a third person without the informed consent of his principal. This is not intended to be an exhaustive list, but it is sufficient to indicate the nature of fiduciary obligations. They are the defining characteristics of the fiduciary.'

So far as concerns directors, the position is provided for by the Companies Act 2006, which **13.74** sets out the following general duties, which are to be interpreted and applied in the same way as common law rules or equitable principles (section 170(4)):

(1) to act within powers: ie to act in accordance with the company's constitution and only to exercise powers for the purposes for which they were conferred: section 171;
(2) to act in good faith to promote the success of the company: section 172;
(3) to exercise independent judgment: section 173;
(4) to exercise reasonable care, skill, and diligence: section 174;
(5) to avoid conflicts of interest other than in relation to transactions or arrangements with the company: section 175;
(6) not to accept benefits from a third party unless there is no conflict of interest: section 176;
(7) to declare interest in proposed transactions or arrangements with the company: section 177.

In *Item Software (UK) Limited v Fassihi* [2004] EWCA Civ 1244, [2004] IRLR 928,[14] the **13.75** Court of Appeal emphasized the need to focus on the fiduciary obligation to act in what the fiduciary in good faith considers to be the best interests of his company. Arden LJ (at para 41) said that it was not correct that a fiduciary owed a separate and independent duty to disclose his/her own misconduct to his/her principal or, more generally, to disclose information of relevance and concern to the employer, because this would lead to a proliferation of duties and arguments about the breadth of those duties. Instead, the answer lay in the fundamental duty of loyalty. Fassihi could not reasonably have come to the conclusion that it was not in the interests of Item to know of his breach of duty and he could not fulfil his duty of loyalty except by telling Item about his setting up of RAMS, and his plan to acquire the Isograph contract for himself.

This approach is controversial insofar as it expands the scope for proscriptive, rather than **13.76** prescriptive, fiduciary duties.[15] It cuts through much of the difficulty with regard to directors. However, it should not be assumed that there is a duty upon a director to disclose all that the company would wish to know. That is going too far. First, the requirement is one of good faith—it is not a test of whether it is in fact in the interests of the employer that the information be disclosed but whether the employee in good faith considers this to be the case. That is subject to there having been actual consideration of the best interests of the company.

---

[14] See paras 13.05, 13.09, and 13.55–13.58.
[15] See *Attorney-General v Blake* [1998] Ch 439 at 455D–E (CA): 'equity is proscriptive, not prescriptive . . . It tells the fiduciary what he must do. It does not tell him what he ought to do'.

Otherwise the court should ask whether an intelligent and honest person in the position of a director would, in all the circumstances, have reasonably believed that the act or failure to act was for the benefit of the company: see *Madoff Securities International Limited (in Liquidation) v Raven* [2013] EWHC 3147 (Comm) at para 194; *Re HLC Environment Projects* [2013] EWHC 2876 (Ch) at para 92(b).

13.77 Prior to the decision in *Fassihi*, a more limited duty to confess to wrongdoing was recognized in the context of the prohibition on making a secret profit. This was considered in *Horcal Limited v Gatland* [1983] IRLR 459 (Glidewell J), [1984] IRLR 288 (CA). The defendant, Mr Gatland, was the managing director of the claimant building contractors. At a time when he was negotiating to purchase the company, he was telephoned by a customer about carrying out some work. Since he was in any event going to be taking over the company, he decided to keep the proceeds of the work for himself, whilst paying the expenses. However, the deal then changed and instead of buying the company he entered into an agreement pursuant to which he resigned and was paid for past services. At the time of the agreement he still intended to keep the profits from carrying out the work for the customer, but he did not receive the profits until after the agreement was entered into. At first instance the judge (Glidewell J) held that there was no breach of fiduciary duty at the time of entering into the agreement because, although he had decided to keep the profits, he had not yet received them. This finding was upheld by the Court of Appeal. However, Glidewell J held that if the profits had been received there would have been a duty to disclose this prior to entering the agreement. *Bell v Lever Brothers* was treated as distinguishable on the basis that only Lord Thankerton had dealt with duties of a director, and in any event neither Bell nor Snelling were directors of Lever Brothers with whom the severance agreement was entered into. In the Court of Appeal Goff LJ recorded the competing arguments as to whether there was a duty of disclosure prior to entering into the agreement, but did not express a concluded view because there had at that time been no breach of fiduciary duty. However, he commented that there was much force in the submission for the defendant that:

> putting fraud on one side, there is no general duty on directors or employees to disclose a breach of duty on their part. As I understood his argument he recognised that in the case of fiduciaries, such as directors, if they have failed to account for secret profits which they have made, then their failure to account must necessarily involve in consequence a failure to reveal a breach of duty which had given rise to that duty to account.

13.78 Whilst recognizing an implicit obligation of disclosure in relation to secret profit, beyond this, Goff LJ was sceptical as to whether there was a duty to disclose any breach of duty. He noted that this 'could lead to the extravagant consequence that a director might have to make . . . a "confession" as a prerequisite of such an agreement' (at para 16). That is now to be read subject to the application of the good faith test giving rise to a duty of disclosure as applied in *Fassihi*. Further, it follows from the approach in *Fassihi* that a disclosure duty may arise in circumstances other than wrongdoing, applying the touchstone of whether the disclosure is believed to be in the company's best interest. As explained in *GHLM Trading Limited v Maroo* [2012] 2 BCLC 369 (Newey J at para 195):

> it can be incumbent on a fiduciary to disclose matters other than wrongdoing. The 'single and overriding touchstone' being the duty of a director to act in what he considers in good faith to be in the best interests of the company (to quote from Etherton J in *Shepherds Investments Ltd v Walters* [2006] EWHC 836 (Ch), [2007] 2 BCLC 202, at paragraph 132), there is no reason to restrict the disclosure that can be necessary to misconduct. Were a director subjectively to consider that it was in the company's interests for something other than misconduct to be disclosed, he would, it appears, commit a breach of his duty of good faith if he failed to do so.

The scope of a director's duties will also depend upon how the business of the company is **13.79** organized and what part the director could reasonably be expected to play.[16] The scope of the director's responsibilities is therefore likely to be highly relevant. Equally, much may depend upon the nature and seriousness of the matter which it is alleged should have been disclosed. In particular, there is no breach of fiduciary duty in a director taking steps preparatory to setting up in competition after ceasing to be a director and accordingly it is difficult to see how a director's failure to disclose such steps could be a breach of a duty of disclosure, notwithstanding that disclosure would be in the employer's interest and the information is withheld out of self-interest.[17] Nor is there any duty upon a director to disclose that s/he has it in mind to act unlawfully and in breach of contract in the future before doing anything wrong.[18]

Disclosure obligations upon directors in respect of their own and other directors' wrongdo- **13.80** ing and anticipated wrongdoing are sometimes an important feature in claims in relation to loss caused by conduct preparatory to setting up in competition with the employer. In *Midland Tool Limited v Midland International Tooling Limited* [2003] 2 BCLC 523, directors of the claimant formed a plan to leave in concert and take many of the employees of the business with them to set up a rival undertaking. At para 89, having referred to *Balston Ltd v Headline Filters Ltd* [1990] FSR 385, Hart J said:

> a director's duty to act so as to promote the best interests of his company prima facie includes a duty to inform the company of any activity, actual or threatened, which damages those interests. The fact that the activity is contemplated by himself is, on the authority of *Balston*'s case, a circumstance which may excuse him from the latter aspect of the duty. But where the activity involves both himself and others, there is nothing in the authorities which excuses him from it. This applies, in my judgment, whether or not the activity itself would constitute a breach by anyone of any relevant duty owed to the company ... A director who wishes to engage in a competing business and not disclose his intentions to the company ought, in my judgment, to resign his office as soon as his intention has been irrevocably formed and he has launched himself in the actual taking of preparatory steps.

In *Shepherds Investments Ltd and another v Walters and others* [2007] IRLR 110 at para 108, **13.81** Etherton J commented that Hart J may have been 'too prescriptive' in saying that the director's obligation was to resign or disclose at the stage identified by Hart J. Etherton J did, however, agree with Hart J (at para 128) that it is the duty of a director to inform the company of any actual or threatened activity of another, whether or not s/he is involved, which damages the interests of the company, and whether or not that activity would in itself constitute a breach by anyone of any relevant duty owed to the company. The difficulty lies in deciding when the preparatory steps have reached such a stage as to trigger the duty to disclose.[19]

That, however, still requires some qualification. First, the test following *Fassihi* remains one **13.82** of whether disclosure is required by the duty to act in good faith in the best interests of the employer rather than being a free-standing duty. Second, there remains scope in applying that test for it to be applied with sensitivity to the particular circumstances. As explained by Rix LJ in *Foster Bryant Surveying Limited v Bryant* [2007] IRLR 425 (CA):

> while the principles remain unamended, their application in different circumstances has required care and sensitivity both to the facts and to other principles, such as that of

---

[16] *Framlington Group plc v Anderson* [1995] BCC 611 at 628H.
[17] *Balston Limited v Headline Filters Limited* [1990] FSR 385 at 412.
[18] *Horcal v Gatland* [1983] IRLR 459, Glidewell J; [1984] IRLR 288 (CA).
[19] See also *Kynixa Limited v Hynes and others* [2008] EWHC 1495 (QB) discussed at paras 13.51 and 13.52 above.

personal freedom to compete, where that does not intrude on the misuse of the company's property whether in the form of business opportunities or trade secrets. For reasons such as these, there has been some flexibility, both in the reach and extent of the duties imposed and in the findings of liability or non-liability. The jurisprudence also demonstrates, to my mind, that in the present context of retiring directors, where the critical line between a defendant being or not being a director becomes hard to police, the courts have adopted pragmatic solutions based on a common-sense and merits based approach.

13.83 The court therefore contemplated that considerations such as public policy against restraint of trade may be relevant. To this end, *Shepherds Investments* was explained in *Foster Bryant* on the basis that it involved the 'combination of disloyalty, active promotion of the planned business, and exploitation of business opportunity' whilst the directors remained in office, and was contrasted with other cases, such as *Balston*, where the resignations were not accompanied by disloyalty. In *Foster Bryant* the defendant director, Mr Bryant, had given notice of resignation and had in practice been excluded from discharging his role as a director (though he was still an employee) at the time of the alleged misconduct. He accepted an offer to work for a key customer of the claimant company to start after the end of his employment. The court rejected the contention that Mr Bryant should have rejected the offer of future work and pressed the customer to maintain its business with the claimant company. In effect the court, by focusing on the director's specific responsibilities (and the fact of his exclusion from the company) watered down the scope of the duty to act in good faith, and was instead willing to compare the conduct to legitimate preparation to compete.[20]

13.84 Further, as illustrated by the decision in *Brandeaux Advisers (UK) Limited v Chadwick* [2011] IRLR 224, following *Fassihi*, there is no longer a necessary distinction to be drawn between a director's own wrongdoing and that of others where there are relevant fiduciary duties. The claimants were members of the Brandeaux group. The defendant was a director of two of the claimants and head of compliance for the group. She sent a large number of emails, including highly confidential information, to her home address in order to arm herself with material in case of any disputes with the Brandeaux group or the regulators in the future. In so doing she was held to have acted in repudiatory breach of contract. The court emphasized the indiscriminate nature of the material which she had emailed to herself, and the fact that she was not 'involved in any whistle-blowing exercise' or any attempt to make disclosure to a regulator. Jack J expressed doubt as to whether the possibility of litigation with an employer could ever justify an employee transferring or copying confidential documents for his/her own retention. He also accepted, following *Fassihi*, that the defendant had acted in breach of her fiduciary duty in failing to report what she had done in emailing the confidential documents to her own private address. It was no bar to this finding that no other employee was involved in the wrongdoing.[21]

D. Duty to Investigate

13.85 In addition to the duty to disclose wrongdoing, in some cases it might be possible to establish that, due to the employee's duties, there is an obligation to investigate the wrongdoing.

---

[20] See also *First Subsea Limited v Balltec Limited* [2014] EWHC 866, where the fact that a director had been excluded from management of the business again shaped the content of the continuing fiduciary obligations.

[21] This was one step in an argument advanced by the claimant in support of reclaiming salary, in that disclosure would have led to her dismissal. That argument failed on the basis that no loss was shown since the company had the benefit of her work and the value of this was taken as being the salary which was paid.

This was addressed in *Rastogi* (see paragraph 13.19 above). The judge ruled that it was arguable that the fourth defendant, Mr Patel, was under an obligation to investigate and make inquiries as to whether there had been wrongdoing within the company. He said that there was no universal obligation to investigate, and the obligation to do so was likely to arise in fewer cases than those in which there was an obligation to report wrongdoing of which the employee became aware without investigation. Once again a major factor in deciding whether such an obligation existed would be the terms of the contract of employment and the duties which the employee had within the company. Patel was the, or one of the, interfaces with the auditors, and they had resigned, which was a very serious step which would not be taken lightly. He was accordingly under an arguable duty to make enquiries as to whether there was anything untoward in the way the company was carrying on its business.

The extent to which there may be a duty to investigate is necessarily fact-sensitive. However, **13.86** to the extent that the case law moves towards development of a duty to investigate in cases where there are serious concerns, this will throw into sharper relief the gap in protection under PIDA, where investigations leading up to a disclosure are not protected: *Bolton School v Evans* [2007] ICR 641 (CA).

E. Interface with PIDA

There may also be an issue in some circumstances as to the extent to which it is necessary **13.87** to modify the scope of the duty to disclose wrongdoing, or the remedies for breach, in light of the PIDA right not to be subjected to a detriment on the ground of, or to be dismissed by reason of, making a protected disclosure. These provisions would not have assisted the employee in *Swain*, notwithstanding that he was dismissed after disclosure of the misdeeds of the managing director, since the reason for the dismissal was Swain's misconduct rather than the disclosure.

The position would have been less straightforward if Swain had not himself been guilty **13.88** of serious misconduct, but had only been willing to make partial disclosure of the managing director's misconduct, perhaps due to concern about reprisals or implicating other colleagues. On the Court of Appeal's analysis, Swain was plainly obliged to make full disclosure of the wrongdoing. However, if he had been dismissed for failing to make full disclosure, he could now argue that it only became apparent to the employers that he had additional information to disclose by reason of the limited disclosure he made, and that it was limited disclosure which was the principal reason for the dismissal. This argument might be made with still greater force if, rather than having been asked for the information, Swain had voluntarily come forward to provide the partial disclosure and therefore exposed himself to the wrath of the employer for not disclosing more. The tribunal would need to consider, in addressing the 'reason why' question, whether the employer could demonstrate and be able to succeed on the basis that the dismissal was not by reason of the disclosure, but the misconduct in refusing to provide full information.

The protection provided by the Act, and its policy objectives, might be undermined if an **13.89** employer could justify victimization of an employee who comes forward to blow the whistle, but is reluctant to make fuller disclosure, on the grounds that the victimization was not due to the partial disclosure but due to breach of a duty to make fuller disclosure. By way of example, an employee may be under an express contractual obligation to report any incidences of theft of which s/he becomes aware. Pursuant to that duty, the employee may report that items have been taken from a shop where the employee is based. The disclosure might be made in the hope of encouraging the employer to improve procedures so as to deter a recurrence, but the employee may be reluctant to disclose the identity of the culprit(s). As a result of the employee's whistleblowing it might therefore be apparent to the employer that the disclosure is only partial, since the culprits have not been identified, and that the employee is therefore in breach of the express duty of disclosure. If an employer then imposed disciplinary action against the whistleblowing employee on the grounds of his/her failure to make fuller disclosure, the issue for the tribunal would be whether that was in fact the reason for the employer's action or whether the fact that the employee had made the initial disclosure was at least a materially significant influence. It would be relevant, for example, to consider how other employees were treated who could also have provided the fuller information sought, but had not made the initial disclosure. In approaching that issue a tribunal may be expected to have firmly in mind that if disciplinary action was permissible in such circumstances this could deter potential whistleblowers from coming forward and substantially undermine the purposes of the legislation.

F. Statutory and Regulatory Obligations to Disclose Information

13.90　In addition to contractual obligations of disclosure, the need for employees and professionals to blow the whistle on impropriety has been recognized by the implementation of specific statutory duties of disclosure. For example, section 70 of the Pensions Act 2004[22] imposes specific duties upon trustees and professional advisers to pension schemes to report what they have 'reasonable cause to believe' are relevant breaches of the law or other matters likely to be of material significance to the Pensions Regulator.

13.91　Similar obligations have also been imposed upon auditors of a person authorized under the Financial Services and Markets Act 2000, and who have been appointed pursuant to a statutory provision, to report matters to the Financial Conduct Authority (FCA). The auditor must make such a report where s/he reasonably believes that there is or has been or may be or may have been a contravention under the 2000 Act which relates to authorization under that Act or to the carrying out of any regulated activity or a requirement imposed by any other act which the FCA has power to prosecute.[23] Various statutory duties are also imposed upon employees, amongst others, to assist with or provide information in relation to investigations.[24]

13.92　Statutory duties to disclose also apply in contexts other than financial matters. Sections 330, 331, and 332 of the Proceeds of Crime Act 2002[25] make it a criminal offence for those who in the course of their employment acquire information that another person is engaged in laundering the proceeds of drug trafficking, but fail to disclose this to a constable as soon as reasonably practicable. Sections 19 and 20 of the Terrorism Act 2000[26] make similar provision in relation to failure to disclose financial assistance for terrorism. Employees also have a duty under regulation 14 of the Management of Health and Safety at Work Regulations (SI 1992/2051)[27] to inform the employer, and any other employee with specific

---

[22] Formerly s 48 of the Pensions Act 1995.

[23] Financial Services and Markets Act 2000 (Communications by Auditors) Regulations 2001 (SI 2001/2587).

[24] Building Society Act 1986, s 55(3); Companies Act 1985, s 434. The Financial Services and Markets Act 2000, ss 177 and 284 now provide for the same power to investigate collective investment schemes; Insolvency Act 1986, ss 218, 219, and 235; *Re Arrows* [1995] 2 AC 75 (HL).

[25] Formerly s 52(1) of the Drug Trafficking Act 1994.

[26] Formerly s 18A(1) of the Prevention of Terrorism (Temporary Provisions) Act 1989.

[27] Implementing in part Art 13 of Council Directive 89/391/EEC on the introduction of measures to encourage improvements in the safety and health of workers at work (OJ 1989 L183/1).

responsibility for health and safety, of any work situation which the employee ought to have considered to represent a serious and immediate threat to health and safety or a shortcoming in the employer's protection arrangements for health and safety, where the problem either affects that employee's health and safety or arises out of or in connection with that employee's activities at work and has not previously been reported to the employer or any other employee with specific responsibility for health and safety.

Additionally, in some other situations a duty is placed on members of a particular profession or group positively to report misconduct or incompetence when they become aware of the same. By way of example, in February 2012 the General Pharmaceutical Council (the regulator for pharmacists and pharmacy technicians) published 'Guidance on Raising Concerns' which builds on the regulatory requirements to take action to protect the well-being of patients and the public and to make the relevant authority aware of any policies, systems, and working conditions, or actions, professional performance, or health of others, if they may affect patient care or public safety. Paragraph 1 of the guidance sets out the obligation upon every pharmacy professional to raise any concerns about individuals, actions, or circumstances that may be unacceptable and that could result in risks to patients and public safety. The guidance warns (at para 1.4) that a failure to report any concerns about a colleague or others would be a breach of the regulator's standards of conduct, ethics, and performance and may call into question fitness to practise. **13.93**

A duty of medical professionals to raise concerns is set out in the General Medical Council's publication, *Good Medical Practice* (2013). This provides (at para 25(c)) that: **13.94**

> If you have concerns that a colleague may not be fit to practise and may be putting patients at risk, you must ask for advice from a colleague, your defence body or us. If you are still concerned you must report this, in line with our guidance and your workplace policy, and make a record of the steps you have taken.

It is notable that this refers to 'concerns' as triggering the duty, whereas an earlier edition set out a similar duty as arising where the medical professional had '*grounds to believe* that a doctor or other healthcare professional may be putting patients at risk' (emphasis added). In addition, there is a distinct 'duty of candour', which is considered in the following section. **13.95**

Whilst the various statutory and regulatory duties apply only in certain limited circumstances, they illustrate that where disclosure is particularly important it may be necessary to go beyond a permissive approach. However, as discussed in section H below, there are also some important potential drawbacks of imposing such a duty which need to be considered, as illustrated by the decision of the FCA and PRA, following a consultation process, not to impose such a duty (see paragraph 13.113 below). **13.96**

G. The Health Sector and the 'Duty of Candour'

Within the healthcare sector, a distinct but related principle has developed known as the 'duty of candour'. Essentially this means a responsibility to be honest with patients (or other duly authorized persons) when things go wrong, providing information and, where appropriate, an apology. The importance of this was reinforced by recommendations made in the first Francis Report (of February 2013) following the Inquiry into the failings at Mid-Staffordshire NHS Foundation Trust. These included recommending the introduction of a statutory duty of candour on health providers and individual health professionals. It overlaps with the purpose underlying public interest disclosures, in the sense that it involves making disclosures in relation to healthcare failures. However, it serves a distinct function in that it is focused on disclosure to the victims of the failing, rather than being a public **13.97** interest disclosure which may also involve disclosure with a view to averting an anticipated failing or may include disclosure of organizational failings identified, notwithstanding that harm had been avoided in a particular case.

13.98   So far as concerns individual healthcare professionals, the duty of candour has been addressed by way of regulatory requirements and guidance. Thus, paragraph 55 of *Good Medical Practice* (issued by the General Medical Council) imposes an obligation to be open and honest with patients if things go wrong, and if a patient under that healthcare professional's care suffers harm or distress, to (a) put matters right if possible, (b) offer an apology, or (c) explain fully and promptly what has happened and what the likely short-term and long-term effects will be. Equally, the 'Professional standards of practice and behaviour for nurses and midwives' (the relevant regulatory code) imposes a 'professional duty of candour' to raise concerns immediately upon coming across situations that put patients or public safety at risk. These regulatory obligations are supplemented by joint guidance issued by the Nursing and Midwifery Council and the General Medical Council.[28]

13.99   In addition, a statutory obligation was introduced upon healthcare service providers and registered managers by regulation 20 of the Health and Social Care Act 2008 (Regulated Activities) Regulations 2014. This includes a duty to act in an open and transparent way with relevant persons in relation to care and treatment provided to service users in carrying on a regulated activity. The provision applies the term 'notifiable safety incident' to certain types of serious incidents, such as those that in the reasonable opinion of a healthcare professional could or appear to have resulted in death or serious hardship. In relation to such an incident there is a notification duty to provide information about the incident and apologize.[29]

13.100   For the purposes of compliance with the requirements of the duty of candour, the registered person must have regard to guidance issued by the Care Quality Commission (CQC).[30] The guidance provides an explanation of the regulator's expectations with regards to the promotion of a culture that encourages candour, openness, and honesty at all levels through having policies and procedures in place and taking action to investigate and tackle bullying and harassment in relation to the duty of candour. The CQC expects providers to have a system in place to identify and deal with possible breaches of the professional duty of candour by staff who are professionally registered, including the obstruction of another in their professional duty of candour.

13.101   The concept and characteristics of a notifiable incident are not without difficulties of interpretation. In particular the question of whether the circumstances come within the reporting obligation is decided by the 'reasonable opinion of a health care professional'. There might be a range of opinions held by hypothetical professionals as to whether the circumstances applied. Does this mean a form of the *Bolam*[31] test is to be applied, such that *if* a healthcare professional could hold the view that the incident was notifiable then it is to be notified? Or does it mean that if a healthcare professional could reasonably conclude that the incident was *not* notifiable then no notification need be made? The first possibility

---

[28] 'Openness and honesty when things go wrong: the professional duty of candour.'

[29] It is an offence for a registered person to fail to comply with the notification requirements in regulation 20(2)(a) and (3) but it is a defence for a registered person to prove that they took all reasonable steps and exercised all due diligence to prevent the breach. A person guilty of that offence is liable, on summary conviction, to a fine not exceeding level 4 on the standard scale: Reg 23.

[30] See http://www.cqc.org.uk/content/regulation-20-duty-candour#guidance.

[31] *Bolam v Friern Hospital Management Committee* [1957] 1 WLR 582 (concerning standard of care in negligence cases).

seems to make the definition very wide: the second is not all that easy to reconcile with the wording used.

The difficulties of interpretation are not ameliorated by the CQC's Guidance; if anything **13.102** they are exacerbated. The Guidance states that:

> Where the degree of harm is not yet clear but may fall into [the categories defined in the regulation] in future, the relevant person must be informed of the notifiable safety incident in line with the requirements of the regulation.

This appears to widen the scope of the reporting obligation considerably. But it raises the **13.103** issue of how likely must be the possibility that the harm will occur. It may be recalled (as discussed in Chapter 3 at paragraph 3.93) that the state of the authorities in a whistleblowing context is for there to be a reasonable belief as to a likely future failure, the belief must be that the information tends to show that the failure is more likely than not to occur (*Kraus v Penna plc* [2004] IRLR 260 (EAT)). This risks setting the bar high for the whistleblower and may be thought to be antithetical to the desirability of exposing a risk of a deleterious consequence where the risk is significant but not, perhaps, probable. By contrast, in a duty of candour context, it might be thought that a requirement to tell a patient that it may turn out to be the case that they have been harmed by a mistake, even though it is not presently clear that is the case, is a debatable one.

It is also stated in the Guidance that providers are not required by the regulation to **13.104** inform a person using the service when a 'near miss' has occurred and the incident has resulted in no harm to that person. That *is* entirely consistent with an approach which focuses not on the desirability of avoiding a similar event in the future (or exacerbating the failure which has led to the harm-causing event) but on disclosing to the particular 'victim' the fact that the error has been made and that it has had deleterious consequences. This highlights an important distinction between the purpose of the duty of candour and the purpose underlying public interest disclosures. So far as concerns the duty of candour there is, arguably, no point in alarming a patient when no harm has been done. As against that, where the error has been an egregious one albeit there has been a lucky escape, it might be thought that the patient is entitled to know of that error in case it causes his or her confidence in the treating service provider to be damaged. In any event compliance with the duty of candour would not detract from the need to raise a concern through the whistleblowing policy where there are facts tending to indicate a risk of a recurrence.

H. Clarification by a Whistleblowing Policy

So as to ensure that employees are apprised of relevant statutory duties of disclosure, and **13.105** in the light of the difficulties that may arise in ascertaining whether there is a common law duty of disclosure in particular circumstances, it will often be in the employer's interest to seek to identify, as part of a whistleblowing policy, the following matters:

(a) which employees are required to disclose misdeeds of others;
(b) in relation to what types of misdeeds and what other matters there is a duty to blow the whistle;
(c) to whom disclosure should be made and what procedures exist for making the disclosure;
(d) the disciplinary sanction for a breach of the duty of disclosure; and
(e) the fact that an employee should not be victimized for making the disclosure. (See, more generally, Chapter 19.)

13.106 Some whistleblowing policies have embraced positive duties. By way of example, this is provided for by some local authority whistleblowing polices. Surrey County Council's policy states that 'Each person working for Surrey County Council needs to realise that they not only have the right, but also a duty to report any improper actions or omissions'.[32] Similarly, Hampshire County Council's policy records that 'All workers have a right and a duty to report concerns of malpractice that are in the public interest'.[33] Hounslow LBC's policy sets out under the heading 'duty to report' that it is the duty of all employees to raise 'any concerns about known, or possible, wrongdoing through this Policy'.[34]

13.107 In specific sectors or industries where there are likely to be matters which are of particular concern to the employer (eg banks and their statutory obligations regarding money laundering) the prudent course would be to set out specifically those who must disclose and what matters they must disclose, making it clear how they are to be disclosed and to whom. As the EAT explained in *The Distillers Company (Bottling Services) Limited v Gardner* [1982] IRLR 48 (where an employee was disciplined for failing to report theft of a case of whisky):

> if . . . this is a matter of great importance to the [employer], it would be reasonable to expect in their rules not merely a specific prohibition against misappropriation but a clear obligation placed upon employees who witness such behaviour to report it immediately. It is asking a lot of an employee to require him to report the misdemeanours of his colleagues, but if this is to be the rule it should . . . be very clearly spelled out.

13.108 This dictum was followed by the EAT in *Ladbroke Racing Limited v King, Daily Telegraph*, 21 April 1989. Delivering the majority judgment of the EAT, Wood J noted that if it were to be asserted that there was an express duty to report any breach of company rules, such a stipulation would have to be written clearly, if necessary in capital letters, in the staff handbook.

13.109 In addition to spelling out clearly the obligation to report certain matters, it is also likely to be important to identify the disciplinary consequences of failing to do so. This is particularly important if the employer is seeking to impose an onerous or unusual obligation, such as imposing wide obligations on employees with no managerial responsibility, or where there is regarded as having been gross misconduct.[35]

13.110 There may be significant advantages to the employer in including duties to blow the whistle in addition to setting out whistleblowers' rights and relevant procedures in a policy. In particular:

(a) if carefully drafted it would clarify the scope of the duty of disclosure;

(b) it might encourage a sense of corporate responsibility;

(c) it might encourage employees to bring serious matters to light where otherwise the temptation would be simply to ignore the matter;

(d) it would assist in entitling an employer to set aside a severance package or other agreement entered into with an employee guilty of (non-disclosed) wrongdoing; and

(e) it might entitle the employer fairly to impose a disciplinary sanction that would otherwise be regarded as too severe.

---

[32] See https://www.surreycc.gov.uk/__data/assets/pdf_file/0008/51929/Whistle-blowing-Policy.pdf.

[33] See http://documents.hants.gov.uk/corprhantsweb/WhistleblowingPolicy-V23-2015-07-WEBHF000 009845214.pdf.

[34] See http://www.hounslow.gov.uk/whistleblowingpolicy20141101.pdf.

[35] *Dalton v Burton's Gold Medal Biscuits Limited* [1974] IRLR 45 (NIRC).

However, the imposition of duties of disclosure is not without problems. In particular: **13.111**

(a) As noted in *Distillers* any express duty going beyond that which would be implied in the ordinary course would have to be very clearly spelled out. The wider the obligation sought to be imposed, the greater the difficulty there might be in identifying this and then in consistently applying it.

(b) There is a risk that workers will be overly cautious in reporting concerns, rather than exercising their own judgment, leading to a greater drain on management time.

(c) There is a risk of a focus on dealing with those who fail to speak up rather than on dealing with organizational failures when the whistle is blown and on encouraging a culture where workers feel safe in raising their concerns and are confident that notice will be taken of them if they do.

(d) Too wide an obligation upon employees carries the risk of the duties being too unspecific, damaging industrial relations, and causing friction and suspicion between employees.[36] If a defensive attitude is then encouraged this might undermine corporate responsibility rather than encouraging it.

(e) Even if there is a whistleblowing policy incorporating duties of disclosure, there may be difficulty where there is only partial disclosure or delayed disclosure. If a sanction is then imposed for failing to make full disclosure this might be regarded as being imposed by reason of the worker having made a protected disclosure and therefore amount to be unlawful victimization under PIDA.

(f) Workers who did not feel sufficiently confident to blow the whistle immediately may then be deterred from blowing the whistle subsequently for fear that they will be disciplined for not speaking up earlier.[37]

(g) The imposition of an obligation to raise concerns in an organization might be seen as suggesting that the organization needs to force staff to raise concerns in fear of the consequences, rather than because they believe that it is the right thing to do and that they will be protected in doing so. It may be suggested that a higher priority is to publicize whistleblowing channels, and to encourage a culture where workers feel safe in raising concerns, including making senior employers clearly accountable for any failure to deal with concerns where they are raised.

Again, the downside risks of imposing a duty to disclose were highlighted in a consultation   **13.112**
paper issued by the FCA and PRA in February 2015.[38]

> The FCA and the PRA are concerned a requirement on employees to speak up may place individuals in a position where they feel they face being penalised whatever course of action they take. It may also lead worried employees to make defensive reports of little value that overwhelm whistleblowing services and damage their ability to function effectively. Informal discussions with stakeholders such as firms, trade unions and trade bodies indicated such misgivings were shared by others. As a consequence, the FCA and the PRA take the view that the decision to speak up should remain a matter for the individual.

On this basis, following the outcome of the consultation, the decision was taken in the new   **13.113**
policy statement issued by the FCA and PRA on 6 October 2015 not to include a duty on staff to blow the whistle.[39]

---

[36] See *The Distillers Company (Bottling Services) Limited v Gardner* [1982] IRLR 48 at para 17.
[37] See PCaW, 'Speaking up for vulnerable adults: What the whistleblowers say' (April 2011).
[38] See http://www.bankofengland.co.uk/pra/Documents/publications/cp/2015/cp615.pdf.
[39] See para 2.24 of the Response to Consultation (https://www.fca.org.uk/publication/policy/ps-15-24.pdf).

13.114 Notwithstanding these concerns, since employees will in any event sometimes be under implied duties of disclosure, which may include statutory duties, a whistleblowing policy could usefully clarify the scope of such duties and the procedures to be followed. In addition, a whistleblowing policy could helpfully identify certain specific areas where a duty of disclosure is required. Careful identification of any duties of disclosure might be regarded as complementing PIDA, providing a rounded approach and encouraging whistleblowers to come forward and assuring of protection from reprisals for doing so and that the concerns raised will be taken seriously.

Part III

WHISTLEBLOWING OUTSIDE PIDA

14

OBLIGATIONS IN RESPECT OF CONFIDENTIAL OR PRIVATE INFORMATION AND PUBLIC INTEREST DISCLOSURE

A. Introduction

This chapter describes in broad terms the sources and nature of common law, equity-based, **14.01** and statutory protections in respect of confidential or private information. In each of those areas where public interest disclosures are concerned there is likely to be a need to determine how a tension between competing public interests, or between the public interest and private interests, is resolved. The approach to this has, to a substantial extent, been shaped by the need to give effect to the fundamental rights of privacy and freedom and expression contained in Articles 8 and 10 of the European Convention on Human Rights (ECHR), as applied by the Human Rights Act 1998 (HRA). One aspect has been the relatively recent identification of invasion of privacy as a common law tort. We address below those developments, and the nature, extent, and application of the public interest defence to enforcement of confidentiality and privacy rights.[1]

14.02 The main thrust of the protected disclosure provisions in the ERA is to protect a worker from the consequence of losing employment or suffering some other form of detriment by reason or on the grounds that the worker has made a protected disclosure. The PIDA provisions of the ERA impact upon or engage with the subject matter of this chapter in various ways:

(a) By section 43J ERA, under the heading 'Contractual duties of confidentiality', it is provided that any provision in an agreement between a worker and his/her employer (whether or not a worker's contract), including an agreement to refrain from instituting or continuing any proceedings under the ERA or any proceedings for breach of contract, is void insofar as it purports to preclude the worker from making a protected disclosure.[2]

(b) As we have seen, the fact that the information disclosed was or might be argued to be private or confidential is irrelevant to the question of whether the disclosure is a qualifying disclosure unless, as in the case of a breach of the Official Secrets Act, the breach of confidentiality also amounts to a criminal offence.[3] But duties of confidentiality may be highly relevant on the issue of whether the disclosure was a protected one if the employee wishes to invoke ERA, section 43G or 43H in contending that the disclosure was protected.[4]

(c) It has been suggested that the template established by the protected disclosure provisions is now of considerable relevance to the approach of the courts as to whether an injunction should be granted to restrain disclosure of information by a worker or former worker.[5]

(d) An employer may seek to argue that action by way of the imposition of a detriment or the dismissal of an employee following a disclosure was because the employee was or was perceived to be in breach of a duty of confidentiality in respect of the information disclosed rather than because the employee had blown the whistle (see Chapter 7, paragraphs 7.120–7.124).

(e) The making of a claim for an injunction or damages by an employer against an employee on the basis that the employee had breached a duty of confidence might itself constitute a 'detriment' under ERA, section 47B. This would depend on satisfying the tests for protection against detriment, which are considered in detail in Chapter 7.

---

[1] For an exhaustive, though now rather dated, treatment of this subject, see Cripps, *The Legal Implications of Disclosure in the Public Interest*, 2nd edn. London: Sweet & Maxwell, 1994.

[2] The section reflects the approach of, eg, Salmon LJ and Winn LJ in *Initial Services v Putterill* [1968] 1 QB 396 at pp 409–10 and 410–11: a contract which obliges an employee to keep secret a wrong that ought to be disclosed would be illegal on the ground that it was clearly contrary to the public interest. Other examples are cited by Toulson and Phipps, *Confidentiality*, 3rd edn. London: Sweet & Maxwell, 2012, Chapter 6, pp 133–60.

[3] In Chapter 3 at para 3.03.

[4] For more detail see Chapter 5 at paras 5.97 and 5.113.

[5] See the discussion of *Cream Holdings v Banerjee* [2004] UKHL 44, [2005] 1 AC 253 at para 14.50 below.

B. Obligations of Confidentiality/Privacy

(1) Contractual duties

A duty of confidentiality may arise as a matter of contract either by an express term or by an **14.03** implied term, although the case law does not always draw a very clear distinction between contractual duties and equitable duties (considered below) which may exist outside a contractual relationship.[6] The contract may impose duties, not only during the period of the active relationship between the parties, but also subsequently. During the employment an implied term protects as confidential a very wide range of information. The information does not have to be in the nature of a trade secret, but comprises all information of the employer not in the public domain which might be of advantage to a trade rival (see *Faccenda Chicken Ltd v Fowler* [1987] Ch 117; *Roger Bullivant v Ellis* [1987] ICR 464 at 473–75; *Lansing Linde v Kerr* [1991] 1 WLR 251 (CA)). The confidential information protected after employment by the implied terms of the contract is more limited. It covers trade secrets in the nature of secret formulae and highly confidential information of a non-technical nature which, if disclosed to a competitor, would cause real or significant harm (see *Lansing Linde v Kerr* (above) at 259–60, per Staughton LJ, and *Intelsec Systems Ltd v Grech-Cini* [2000] 1 WLR 1190 at 1205–06).

This distinction between duties during and after employment is illustrated graphically by **14.04** the decision of the Court of Appeal in *Brooks v Olyslager OMS (UK) Ltd* [1998] IRLR 590 (CA). After entering into a compromise agreement terminating his employment, Mr Brooks, who had been Olyslager's managing director, disclosed to an investment banker, who was interested in the company as a professional adviser and option holder, that the company was insolvent and that its budgets were considered too optimistic by its holding company. Olyslager argued that Mr Brooks was thereby in breach of the terms of the compromise agreement. The Court of Appeal upheld the trial judge who had ruled that Mr Brooks' disclosures were not a breach of any implied term of the agreement. Since the employment had ended there was no implied duty to keep secret information that was merely confidential, and no information akin to a trade secret had been disclosed by Mr Brooks.

Although there is little direct analysis of the point in the case law, it would seem logical **14.05** that similar principles as those applying to parties to employment contracts will apply to those where the relationship is that of hirer and independent contractor (see eg *Campbell v Frisbee* [2002] EWHC 328 (Ch), [2002] EMLR 31, where the contract was said to be one for services rather than of service).

In *Faccenda Chicken* (above) the Court of Appeal (at p 135) said that where the parties are, **14.06** or have been, linked by a contract of employment, the obligations of the employee are to be determined by the contract between him/her and his/her employer. This approach has its attractions: its principal difficulty is that if the employer is held to have repudiated the contract then all obligations of confidentiality under that contract will presumably come to an end. This issue was considered in *Campbell v Frisbee*, which we discuss below (at paragraph 14.120).

In order to grant relief, courts have required obligations of confidentiality, especially if relied **14.07** upon to impose obligations beyond implied obligations of confidentiality, to be identified

---

[6] There is a very helpful summary of cases and principles of the equitable and contractual strands of the law of breach of confidence in *Personal Management Solutions Ltd & Anor v Brakes Bros Ltd & Ors* [2014] EWHC 3495 (QB) at paras 161–77.

with particularity.[7] The decision of Mann J in *Tillery Valley Foods v Channel Four Television and another* [2004] EWHC 1075 (Ch), provides an illustration. Tillery produced chilled and frozen meals for NHS hospitals. A journalist obtained employment at Tillery's factory and carried out filming whilst employed there. Channel Four intended to broadcast some of his film and stated that it showed alleged practices, including employees routinely sneezing and coughing over food, employees eating on the production line, and improper re-heating procedures. Tillery sought an injunction to prevent the broadcasting of parts of a television programme in relation to its operation, at least until it could view and respond to what was contained in the programme. Clearly, as the judge remarked, these allegations were serious for Tillery and might have had a serious effect on its business. Tillery did not accept the truth of any of the allegations but the defendants said they intended to justify all the allegations and, because of the principle in *Bonnard v Perryman* [1891] 2 Ch 269,[8] Tillery could not, on the basis the allegation that the film was defamatory, obtain an interim injunction restraining the broadcast. Instead, Tillery sought to base the claim in the law of confidentiality. It argued that the activities of the journalist amounted to a breach of his duties of trust and confidence as an employee and that the film that he took amounted to confidential information. Tillery contended that Channel Four received and held the information in the form of the film knowing that it was confidential and so could be restrained from using it.

14.08   Mann J said that he was 'nowhere near satisfied' that the test under section 12(3) HRA was met (this required him to be satisfied that Tillery was likely to establish at trial that publication should not be allowed—see paragraphs 14.49 et seq below).[9] Tillery had not shown that it was likely that Channel Four had come into possession of information that was confidential. Mann J dismissed Tillery's argument that it was self-evident that where an employee filmed his/her workplace, working activities, and workmates, it was inevitably going to have the quality of confidential information. There would have to be something more to produce that effect.[10] The terms of the employee's/journalist's contract with Tillery did not assist Tillery either. Clause 15 of that contract read (under the heading 'Confidentiality'):

> You may not disclose figures or other information about the company's or client's business to anyone outside the company which may injure or cause loss to the company or customer. In the event of a request for information from the press or for information likely to be of interest to the press, the request must be referred to your managing director.
>
> Any information regarding any supplier's business must also be treated confidentially.

14.09   Mann J rejected the contention that this term created confidentiality where it would otherwise not exist. It was a contractual bar on disclosure applying to all information and did

---

[7] In many cases this is also tied to the 'cardinal rule that any injunction must be capable of being framed with sufficient precision so as to enable a person injuncted to know what it is he is to be prevented from doing': *Lawrence David v Ashton* [1989] ICR 123 at 132, per Balcombe LJ.

[8] That is, that where a defendant to a defamation action intends to plead justification it will only be in exceptional cases that an interim injunction will be granted to restrain publication. A claimant would not be able to obtain an interim injunction unless it was plain that the plea of justification was bound to fail. See also *Greene v Associated Newspapers Ltd* [2004] EWCA Civ 1462, [2005] QB 972.

[9] Mann J applied the Court of Appeal's ruling in *Cream v Banerjee* as to the proper construction of the subsection. The House of Lords subsequently arrived at a different conclusion: see paras 14.50 et seq below, although this would not have affected the decision that Mann J reached in *Tillery*.

[10] Mann J referred to the Australian authority of *Australian Broadcasting Corporation v Lenah Game Meats Pty Ltd* [2001] HCA 63, where the High Court of Australia held that the activities of a company which processed possum meat for export were not such as to attract the quality of being confidential for the purpose of the law protecting confidentiality.

not depend on the information in issue being confidential. Nor did it vest all information with the character of confidentiality it would not otherwise have had, either expressly or implicitly.

The fact that the obligation on the holder of the private or confidential information originates in contract will, however, have a bearing on whether the court is prepared to accept the defence that the disclosure of that information was in the public interest. We consider this aspect in paragraphs 14.119 to 14.121.

(2) Duties outside contract

It has been pointed out that the underlying conceptual basis of the action for breach of **14.10** confidence where the parties are not linked by a contract is not easy to identify.[11] Property, contract, bailment, trust, fiduciary relationship, good faith, and unjust enrichment have all been claimed as the basis of judicial intervention and these concepts have also been intermingled.[12] However, by 1969 and the leading case of *Coco v Clark* [1969] RPC 41, the law had become fairly clear: aside from cases where the parties were bound by contract, the gist of the cause of action for breach of confidence was that:

(1) private information had been disclosed by one person to another in circumstances importing an obligation of confidence even though no contract of non-disclosure existed (Megarry J in *Coco* at 47–48); and
(2) a party who received information in confidence was subject to an obligation in equity not to take unfair advantage of it (*Seager v Copydex Ltd* [1967] 1 WLR 923 at 931B–F (CA)).

In *Coco*, Megarry J put it this way (at p 47):   **14.11**

> In my judgment, three elements are normally required if, apart from contract, a case of breach of confidence is to succeed. First, the information itself, in the words of Lord Greene MR in *Saltman Engineering Co Ltd v Campbell Engineering Co Ltd* (1948) 65 RPC 203, 215, must have the necessary quality of confidence about it. Secondly, that information must have been imparted in circumstances importing an obligation of confidence. Thirdly, there must be an unauthorized use of that information to the detriment of the party communicating it.[13]

Now, as Lord Nicholls put it in *Campbell v MGN* [2004] UKHL 22, [2004] 2 AC 457 at   **14.12** para 14, the cause of action has shaken off the limiting constraint of the need for an initial confidential relationship. In *A-G v Guardian Newspapers Ltd (No 2)* [1990] 1 AC 109 (the *Spycatcher* case), Lord Goff stated the broad principles as follows:

> ... a duty of confidence arises when confidential information comes to the knowledge of a person (the confidant) in circumstances where he has notice, or is held to have agreed, that the information is confidential, with the effect that it would be just in all the circumstances that he should be precluded from disclosing the information to others. I have used the word 'notice' advisedly, in order to avoid the (here unnecessary) question of the extent to which actual knowledge is necessary, though I of course understand knowledge to include circumstances where the confidant has deliberately closed his eyes to the obvious.

---

[11] Cripps (n 1 above) p 17, citing Jones, 'Restitution of Benefits obtained in breach of another's confidence' (1970) 86 LQR 463.

[12] In *Vidal-Hall v Google Inc* [2015] EWCA Civ 311 (Court of Appeal (Civil Division) 27 March 2015), [2015] 3 WLR 409 it was suggested that there was no satisfactory or principled reason why misuse of private information should not be categorized as a tort rather than as an equitable obligation; it was a civil wrong with no equitable characteristics. The case is referred to in more detail below (paras 14.20 et seq).

[13] See the restatement to similar effect in *Vestergaard Frandsen A/S v Bestnet Europe Ltd* [2013] UKSC 31, [2013] 1 WLR 1556, Lord Neuberger at para 23.

The existence of this broad general principle reflects the fact that there is such a public interest in the maintenance of confidences, that the law will provide remedies for their protection.

> . . . in the vast majority of cases, in particular those concerned with trade secrets, the duty of confidence will arise from a transaction or relationship between the parties, often a contract, in which event the duty may arise by reason of either an express or an implied term of that contract. It is in such cases as these that the expressions 'confider' and 'confidant' are perhaps most aptly employed. But it is well-settled that a duty of confidence may arise in equity independently of such cases.

14.13 In *Campbell*, Lord Nicholls said that the continuing use of the phrase 'duty of confidence' and the description of the information as 'confidential' was 'not altogether comfortable' since information about an individual's private life would not, in ordinary usage, be called 'confidential'. The more natural description today was that such information is 'private' and the essence of the tort was better encapsulated now as 'misuse of private information'.[14] His Lordship also (at para 19) said that the values enshrined in Articles 8 and 10 of the European Convention on Human Rights were now part of the cause of action for breach of confidence and those articles

> call for a more explicit analysis of competing considerations than the three traditional requirements of the cause of action for breach of confidence identified in (*Coco v Clark*).

We consider the way the courts have approached the need for a 'more explicit analysis' below in paragraphs 14.15 et seq.

(3) A tripartite distinction

14.14 We would endorse the suggestion[15] that three broad types of breach of confidence cases can now be identified: 'commercial' confidentiality cases where the information sought to be protected is or is said to be of commercial value; 'privacy' claims in respect of rights to protect personal information;[16] and 'state confidences' arising from the activities of the state, local government, or other public or quasi-public entities.

(4) Protection of private or confidential information today: sources of obligations to maintain confidentiality

14.15 The relationships and situations which will engender a duty to respect private information are many and various. A duty of confidence is an aspect of the fiduciary duty of a director. Professionals owe duties of confidence. Friends or former friends may also be held to owe duties of confidence.[17] In addition to common law obligations, statutory obligations restrict the use or disclosure of information, including intellectual property rights and obligations as to processing of data pursuant to the Data Protection Act 1998.[18] We considered in Chapter 3 the specific relevance this potentially has in relation to ERA, section 43B(3), which provides that a disclosure is not a qualifying disclosure if the making of it is a criminal offence.

---

[14] And see *Google Inc*, n 12 above.

[15] *Employee Competition*, (Goulding, ed.) 3rd edn. Oxford: OUP, 2016, para 4.06.

[16] Albeit that the private information in question may have a commercial value to a newspaper which wishes to publish it.

[17] See eg *McKennitt v Ash* [2005] EWHC 3003 (QB), [2006] EMLR 10, and [2006] EWCA Civ 1714, [2007] 3 WLR 194.

[18] The detailed provisions of the Data Protection Act 1998 (DPA) are beyond the scope of this book. In *Campbell v MGN* [2002] EWHC 499 (QB) Morland J (at para 17) associated himself with the remark by counsel that the DPA was a 'thicket'. In the Court of Appeal in that case ([2002] EWCA Civ 1373 at para 75) Lord Phillips MR described the Act as 'a cumbersome and inelegant piece of legislation'.

(5) Privacy and Article 8 of the European Convention on Human Rights

Until recently the common law had not developed an overall remedy for the invasion of **14.16** privacy. However, the courts did protect the privacy of the individual and, indeed arguably, that of corporations.[19] This is a rapidly developing area of law, driven in large measure by the effect given to the European Convention on Human Rights through HRA. Article 8 of the Convention provides:

Right to respect for private and family life
1. Everyone has the right to respect for his private and family life, his home and his correspondence.
2. There shall be no interference by a public authority with the exercise of this right except such as is in accordance with the law and is necessary in a democratic society in the interests of national security, public safety or the economic well-being of the country, for the prevention of disorder or crime, for the protection of health or morals, or for the protection of the rights and freedoms of others.

The right in Article 8(1) is qualified by Article 8(2) and is to be balanced against the right contained in Article 10, which states:

Freedom of expression
1. Everyone has the right to freedom of expression. This right shall include freedom to hold opinions and to receive and impart information and ideas without interference by public authority and regardless of frontiers. This article shall not prevent States from requiring the licensing of broadcasting, television or cinema enterprises.
2. The exercise of these freedoms, since it carries with it duties and responsibilities, may be subject to such formalities, conditions, restrictions or penalties as are prescribed by law and are necessary in a democratic society, in the interests of national security, territorial integrity or public safety, for the prevention of disorder or crime, for the protection of health or morals, for the protection of the reputation or rights of others, for preventing the disclosure of information received in confidence, or for maintaining the authority and impartiality of the judiciary.

Accordingly, Article 8 operates as a protective mechanism for private information. The **14.17** touchstone of private life is whether in respect of the disclosed acts the person in question had 'a reasonable expectation of privacy'.[20] If the interest in privacy is engaged, the focus then shifts to the balance between Article 8 and Article 10. We consider below in paragraphs 14.32 et seq how that balance is applied.

The modern approach to identifying confidentiality/privacy was considered by Eady J **14.18** in *McKennitt v Ash* [2005] EWHC 3003 (QB), [2006] EMLR 10 in the context of an

---

[19] In *R v Broadcasting Standards Commission ex p BBC (Dixons)* [2001] QB 885 at 900, Lord Mustill said he found it difficult to see that privacy could apply to an 'impersonal corporate body'. Cf *Investigating Directorate v Hyundai Motor Distributors* (2000) 10 BCLR 1079 (Constitutional Court of South Africa) where the court took the view that a company could have privacy rights. Clayton and Tomlinson, *The Law of Human Rights*, 2nd edn. Oxford: OUP, 2008, para 22.22, also cite *R v Loveridge* [2001] 2 Cr App R 591 where *ex p BBC* was applied. We are not aware of a case where Art 8 has been prayed in aid by a company in a whistleblowing context, although it appears to have been assumed that Art 8 would apply in *Cream Holdings v Banerjee* discussed at paras 14.50 et seq. In *Tillery Valley Foods v Channel Four Television and another* [2004] EWHC 1075 (Ch), the claimant expressly declined to argue any right of action based upon privacy. In *Abbey v Gilligan* [2012] EWHC 3217 (QB), [2013] EMLR 12, Tugendhat J said that the information concerned a company and was not personal to the claimant so there was no reasonable expectation of privacy.
[20] Lord Nicholls in *Campbell v MGN* [2004] UKHL 22, [2004] 2 AC 457 at para 21.

application to restrain publication of a book containing revelations about the private life of Ms McKennitt. Summarizing the position, Eady J said (at paras 60, 61, and 63):

> Lord Hope observed in *Campbell v MGN Ltd* at [85], that
>
> '... a duty of confidence will arise whenever the party subject to the duty is in a situation where he knows or ought to know that the other person can reasonably expect his privacy to be protected. The difficulty will be as to the relevant facts, bearing in mind that, if there is an intrusion in a situation where a person can reasonably expect his privacy to be respected, that intrusion will be capable of giving rise to liability unless the intrusion can be justified'.

Reference was made to the 'three limiting principles' identified by Lord Goff in *Attorney General v Guardian Newspapers Ltd (No 2)* [1990] 1 AC 109 at 282:

1. The principle of confidentiality only applies to information to the extent that it remains confidential. .... once it has entered what is usually called the public domain (which means no more than that the information in question is so generally accessible that, in all the circumstances, it cannot be regarded as confidential) then, as a general rule, the principle of confidentiality can have no application to it.
2. The duty of confidence applies neither to useless information, nor to trivia.
3. Although the basis of the law's protection of confidence is that there is a public interest that confidences should be preserved and protected by the law, nevertheless that public interest may be outweighed by some other countervailing public interest which favours disclosure. This limitation may apply ... to all types of confidential information. It is this limiting principle which may require a court to carry out a balancing operation, weighing the public interest in maintaining confidence against a countervailing public interest favouring disclosure.

14.19   In the same case in the Court of Appeal,[21] Buxton LJ, having stated that there was no English domestic law tort of invasion of privacy, said that, in developing a right to protect private information, including the implementation in the English courts of Articles 8 and 10 of the European Convention on Human Rights, the English courts had had to proceed through the tort of breach of confidence, into which the jurisprudence of Articles 8 and 10 had to be 'shoehorned': *Douglas v Hello! (No3)* [2006] QB 125 (at para 53). As extended by jurisprudence,[22] Article 8 imposed not merely negative but also positive obligations on the state: to respect, and therefore to promote, the interests of private and family life. That meant that a citizen could complain against the state about breaches of his/her private and family life committed by other individuals. Section 6(1) and (3) HRA placed on the courts the obligations appropriate to a public authority.[23] Articles 8 and 10 were 'now not merely of persuasive or parallel effect but the very content of the domestic tort that the English court had to enforce'. In a case where the complaint is of the wrongful publication of private information, the court had to decide two things.

- First, is the information private in the sense that it is in principle protected by Article 8? If no, that is the end of the case.
- If yes, the second question arises: in all the circumstances, must the interest of the owner of the private information yield to the right of freedom of expression conferred on the publisher by Article 10?

---

[21] [2006] EWCA Civ 1714, [2008] QB 73.
[22] In particular *Marckx v Belgium* (1979) 2 EHRR 330; *X and Y v Netherlands* (1985) 8 EHRR 235.
[23] Buxton LJ referred to Baroness Hale of Richmond in *Campbell* (at para 132); Lord Phillips of Worth Matravers in *Douglas v Hello!* [2005] EWCA Civ 595, [2006] QB 125 at para 53; and in particular Lord Woolf in *A v B plc* [2002] EWCA Civ 337, [2003] QB 195 at para 4.

The era of 'shoehorning' of existing common law or equitable wrongs in order to protect **14.20** Article 8 rights has now passed with the Court of Appeal's decision and reasoning in *Vidal-Hall and others v Google Inc (Information Commissioner intervening)* [2015] EWCA Civ 311 [2016] QB 1003. In that case the claimants issued proceedings alleging that Google had obtained and used information relating to their internet usage and that this use amounted to a misuse of their private information and/or a breach of confidence and also a breach of section 13 of the Data Protection Act 1998.[24] The issue for the Court of Appeal was whether permission to serve the claim form out of the jurisdiction had been given correctly, and, more precisely, whether 'damage' had been sustained within the jurisdiction (as required by the jurisdictional gateway at paragraph 3.1(9) of CPR Practice Direction 6B). Google contended that a claim for misuse of private information was not 'made in tort' as required by the gateway. In the view of the Court of Appeal the remarks of Lord Nicholls in *Douglas v Hello* showed that actions for breach of confidence and actions for misuse of private information rested on different legal foundations. They protect different interests: secret or confidential information on one hand and privacy on the other, and the focus of the actions therefore is also different. In *Campbell*[25] at para 51, Lord Hoffmann had described the 'shift in the centre of gravity' when the action for breach of confidence was used as a remedy for the unjustified publication of personal information. The focus was not on the duty of good faith applicable to confidential personal information and trade secrets alike, but the protection of human autonomy and dignity—the right to control the dissemination of information about one's private life and the right to the esteem and respect of other people. There was now (in the view of the Court of Appeal in *Google*):

> [no] satisfactory or principled answer to the question why misuse of private information should not be categorised as a tort for the purposes of service out of the jurisdiction. Misuse of private information is a civil wrong without any equitable characteristics. We do not need to attempt to define a tort here. But if one puts aside the circumstances of its 'birth', there is nothing in the nature of the claim itself to suggest that the more natural classification of it as a tort is wrong.[26]

This did not create a new cause of action but simply gave the correct legal label to one that already existed.[27] The law of confidentiality had been developed to protect one aspect of invasion of privacy, the misuse of private information. This addressed the tension between the requirement to give appropriate effect to the right to respect for private and family life set out in Article 8 of the Convention and the common law's perennial need (for the best of reasons, that of legal certainty) to appear not to be doing anything for the first time.[28]

The identification of invasion of privacy as a common law tort was confirmed by the **14.21** Supreme Court in *PJS v News Group Newspapers Ltd* [2016] UKSC 26, [2016] AC 1081. The claimant (and appellant in the Supreme Court) was in the entertainment business and married to YMA, a well-known individual in the same business. They had two young children. The evidence filed showed that the claimant had had occasional sexual encounters with AB and then a three-way sexual encounter with AB and CD, AB's partner. Some years later AB and CD approached the editor of the *Sun on Sunday* and told him about the sexual encounters. The editor notified PJS of the paper's intention to publish the story and PJS brought proceedings to restrain the proposed publication on the grounds that it would breach confidence and invade privacy. Cranston J refused an interim injunction

---

[24] This gives effect to Parliament and Council Directive 95/46 EC.
[25] *Campbell v MGN Ltd* [2004] UKHL 22, [2004] 2 AC 457.
[26] *Google* at para 43.
[27] *Google* para 51.
[28] *Google* para 19.

but the Court of Appeal reversed that decision. Later News Group applied to the Court of Appeal to set aside the injunction on the grounds that, as the protected information was now in the public domain, the injunction served no useful purpose and was an unjustified interference with News Group's rights under Article 10 of the ECHR. The Court of Appeal acceded to the application but continued the interim injunction pending an application for permission to appeal to the Supreme Court. The Supreme Court proceeded on the assumption that a significant body of internet material identifying those involved by name, and reproducing details from an American publication about the alleged activities, still existed and would continue to do so for the foreseeable future. The content of the speeches of their Lordships (Lord Toulson dissented) allowing the appeal was concerned in large part with arguments as to whether the injunction should be continued where the information was now in the public domain (but where it related to a right to privacy as distinct from a right to confidentiality) and the issue of whether an injunction was any longer an effective remedy. However, the analysis clearly proceeded on the basis that the heads of claim are distinct, and at para 32 Lord Mance referred to 'the tort of invasion of privacy'.

C. The Public Interest Defence of 'Just Cause and Excuse' as a Defence to Actions for Breach of Duty in Respect of Confidences and Private Information

(1) Overview

14.22 A defence of 'just cause or excuse' may be founded on the basis that the disclosure was under compulsion of law, that there was express or implied consent of the person to whom the duty is owed to make disclosure, or that the disclosure was in the public interest.[29] It is the last of these defences which is the subject of this section. It applies to someone who is bound by statutory obligations of 'confidentiality' to the Crown contained in the Official Secrets Act 1989 as well as to common law obligations of confidentiality.

14.23 The public interest principle is invoked in a variety of situations which do not fit easily into notions of what constitutes 'whistleblowing'. The disclosure in *London Regional Transport v The Mayor of London* [2001] EWCA Civ 1491, [2003] EMLR 88 (which concerned the publication of an unedited report from accountants regarding a proposal for a public/private partnership for the London Underground), and Ms Ash's disclosure on aspects of the life and activities of Ms McKennitt (*McKennitt v Ash* [2006] EMLR 10), would not on first impression appear to belong in a survey of the law of whistleblowing, where the emphasis is on disclosures by employees of relevant failures, usually (but not always) in the organization which employs them. However, it is appropriate and necessary to have regard to these cases, which illuminate the nature of the essential balancing function for the courts based principally on Articles 8 and 10 of the ECHR, with the principle of proportionality read into them.

---

[29] *Tournier v National Provincial and Union Bank of England* [1924] 1 KB 461 at 473, per Bankes LJ (CA). The Freedom of Information Act 2000 (FOIA) may conceivably provide an additional defence in relation to information within its scope. See eg *HRH the Prince of Wales v Associated Newspapers Ltd* [2006] EWHC 522 (Ch), where in Prince Charles' action to prevent the further publication of his private diaries, the newspaper appears to have argued that the Prince had or might have filed with a public authority records of the tours to which the eight journals relate or, possibly, a copy of the eight journals. On the facts, however, Blackburne J noted this was 'speculation without the least evidential foundation'.

(2) Development of the public interest defence

(a) *The old 'iniquity' principle*

The defence that the disclosure or intended disclosure was or will be in the public interest **14.24** has developed from a principle which initially required that there be 'iniquity' to attract the defence. The starting point is *Gartside v Outram* (1857) 26 Ch 113 at 114, in which Wood V-C stated the general principle thus:

> there is no confidence as to the disclosure of iniquity. You cannot make me the confidant of a crime or a fraud, and be entitled to close up my lips upon any secret which you have the audacity to disclose to me relating to any fraudulent intention on your part: such a confidence cannot exist.

In *Initial Services Ltd v Putterill* [1968] 1 QB 396 at 405G–406B (CA), Lord Denning MR **14.25** increased the reach of the principle beyond 'crime or fraud', saying that:

> I do not think that it is so limited. It extends to any misconduct of such a nature that it ought in the public interest to be disclosed to others. . ... *In Weld-Blundell v Stephens* ([1919] 1 KB 520 at p 527) Bankes LJ rather suggested that the exception was limited to the proposed or contemplated commission of a crime or a civil wrong; but I should have thought that that was too limited. The exception should extend to crimes, frauds and misdeeds, both those actually committed as well as those in contemplation, provided always—and this is essential—that the disclosure is justified in the public interest . . .. The disclosure must, I should think, be to one who has a proper interest to receive the information. Thus it would be proper to disclose a crime to the police; or a breach of the Restrictive Trade Practices Act, 1956, to the registrar. There may be cases where the misdeed is of such a character that the public interest may demand, or at least excuse, publication on a broader field, even to the press.

Nevertheless, the widened category still appeared to require something akin to willful, or perhaps reckless, wrongdoing—'misdeeds'.

(b) *From iniquity to public interest*

In *Fraser v Evans* [1969] 1 QB 349[30] and *Lion Laboratories Ltd v Evans* [1985] QB 526 the prin- **14.26** ciple developed from the notion of the need to demonstrate 'iniquity' or something like it to the wider, though rather less precise, concept that the disclosure be in the 'public interest'.[31] In *Lion Laboratories*, where former employees of the plaintiff had taken documents which, they said, demonstrated that there was doubt as to the accuracy of the breathalysers manufactured by the plaintiff, Griffiths LJ said this:

> I am quite satisfied that the defence of public interest is now well established in actions for breach of confidence and, although there is less authority on the point, that it also extends to breach of copyright. . ... I can see no sensible reason why this defence should be limited to cases in which there has been wrongdoing on the part of the plaintiffs. I believe that the so-called iniquity rule evolved because in most cases where the facts justified a publication in breach of confidence, it was because the plaintiff had behaved so disgracefully or criminally that it was judged in the public interest that his behaviour should be exposed. No

---

[30] Where Lord Denning put it in wider terms (at pp 361–62):

> No person is permitted to divulge to the world information which he has received in confidence, unless he has just cause or excuse for doing so. . ... I do not look upon the word 'iniquity' as expressing a principle. It is merely an instance of just cause or excuse for breaking confidence. There are some things which may be required to be disclosed in the public interest, in which event no confidence can be prayed in aid to keep them secret.

[31] The progression was not seamless: see for example *Schering Chemicals Ltd v Falkman Ltd* [1982] QB 1 (CA), discussed in para 14.101 below.

doubt it is in such circumstances that the defence will usually arise, but it is not difficult to think of instances where, although there has been no wrongdoing on the part of the plaintiff, it may be vital in the public interest to publish a part of his confidential information. . . .. it is not an essential ingredient of this defence that the plaintiffs should have been guilty of iniquitous conduct.

Stephenson LJ (at pp 536–37) invoked Article 10 of the Convention:

The problem before the judge and before this court is how best to resolve, before trial, a conflict of two competing public interests. The first public interest is the preservation of the right of organisations, as of individuals, to keep secret confidential information. The courts will restrain breaches of confidence, and breaches of copyright, unless there is just cause or excuse for breaking confidence or infringing copyright. The just cause or excuse with which this case is concerned is the public interest in admittedly confidential information. There is confidential information which the public may have a right to receive and others, in particular the press, now extended to the media, may have a right and even a duty to publish, even if the information has been unlawfully obtained in flagrant breach of confidence and irrespective of the motive of the informer.[32]

14.27 As Eady J later explained in *McKennitt* (at para 95):

Nowadays the principle is not regarded as confined to unlawful activity, or even 'iniquity', and it is customary to address the question in terms of a broader 'public interest'. On the other hand, as Mr Browne has fairly pointed out, it is necessary to confine the concept of 'public interest', especially in this context, in a fairly disciplined way. . . . The *Lion Laboratories* case represented something of a departure, in the sense that the emphasis shifted away from the old 'iniquity rule' and on to the somewhat wider, albeit less precise, concept of 'public interest'.

So Gray J observed in *Maccaba v Lichtenstein* [2004] EHWC 1579 (QBD), [2005] EMLR 6 at para 7 that: 'Iniquity is nowadays regarded as no more than one aspect of a broader defence of public interest or just cause'.

14.28 This development was reflected in Lord Goff's third limiting principle in the *Spycatcher* case, *A-G v Guardian Newspapers (No 2)* (above)[33] which can be seen as completing the transition from the narrow requirement of iniquity to the broad principle of justification in the public interest. Lord Goff said this:

Embraced within this limiting principle is, of course, the so called defence of iniquity. In origin, this principle was narrowly stated, on the basis that a man cannot be made 'the confidant of a crime or a fraud': see *Gartside v Outram* (1857) 26 LJCh 113, 114, *per* Sir William Page Wood V-C. But it is now clear that the principle extends to matters of which disclosure is required in the public interest: see *Beloff v Pressdram Ltd* [1973] 1 All ER 241, 260, *per* Ungoed-Thomas J, and *Lion Laboratories Ltd v Evans* [1985] QB 526, 550, *per* Griffiths LJ. It does not however follow that the public interest will in such cases require disclosure to the media, or to the public by the media. There are cases in which a more limited disclosure is all that is required: see *Francome v Mirror Group Newspapers Ltd* [1984] 1 WLR 892. A classic example of a case where limited disclosure is required is a case of alleged iniquity in the Security Service.

---

[32] He also noted (at p 538) that there were cases in which the public interest is best served by an informer giving the confidential information, not to the press but to the police or some other responsible body, as was suggested by Lord Denning MR in *Initial Services Ltd v Putterill* [1968] 1 QB 396, 405–406, and by Sir John Donaldson MR in *Francome v Mirror Group Newspapers Ltd* [1984] 1 WLR 892, 898.

[33] See para 14.12 above.

The language used by their Lordships was imperative in tone, applying where disclosure **14.29** is required in the public interest. From this it may be suggested that no obligation of confidence exists in contract or in equity, insofar as the subject matter concerns a serious risk of public harm where the alleged obligation would prevent disclosure appropriate to avert that risk.

Viewed in this way the principle does not amount to a defence to a claim of breach of confidence but instead has the effect that there is no confidentiality to be breached in the first **14.30** place. The phraseology used in *Gartside* (above), by Lord Denning MR in *Initial Services*, and, for example, by Scott J in *In re A Company* discussed below, supports this contention. That said, if the principle is a defence, then the obligation lies on the defendant to establish the public interest in question. Cripps[34] suggests that the increasing popularity of the second or 'defence' basis for the principle may be attributable to judicial recognition of the desirability of allowing confidential material to be disclosed or intercepted on the basis of a reasonable belief that the course of action is in the public interest, even if that belief subsequently turns out to be unfounded: in such a case it cannot be said that an obligation of confidence never arose in the first place.

However, the corollary of the relaxation of the requirement to find 'iniquity' is that the **14.31** scope of the defence becomes somewhat amorphous. In *R v Department of Health, ex p Source Informatics Ltd* [2001] QB 424 the court referred to what Gummow J said at first instance in *Smith Kline and French Laboratories (Australia) Ltd v Department of Community Services and Health* [1990] FSR 617 at 663, as to the defence being

> not so much a rule of law as an invitation to judicial idiosyncrasy by deciding each case on an ad hoc basis as to whether, on the facts overall, it is better to respect or to override the obligation of confidence.

(3) The balancing of interests in domestic law today

We have seen how, in the *Lion Laboratories* case, Stephenson LJ referred to Article 10. The **14.32** balancing of interests of confidentiality or privacy on one hand, and freedom of expression on the other, now has to be applied in the context of the incorporation of the Convention rights in Article 10 and Article 8 into domestic law through the medium of HRA. The cases emphasize the importance of freedom of expression: see for example Lord Steyn in *R v Home Secretary, ex p Simms* [2000] 2 AC 11:

> The starting point is the right of freedom of expression. In a democracy it is the primary right: without it an effective rule of law is not possible. Nevertheless, freedom of expression is not an absolute right. Sometimes it must yield to other cogent social interests. . . .
>
> Freedom of expression is, of course, intrinsically important: it is valued for its own sake. But it is well recognized that it is also instrumentally important. It serves a number of broad objectives. First, it promotes the self-fulfilment of individuals in society. Secondly, in the famous words of Holmes J (echoing John Stuart Mill), 'the best test of truth is the power of the thought to get itself accepted in the competition of the market': *Abrams v United States* (1919) 250 US 616, 630, per Holmes J (dissenting). Thirdly, freedom of speech is the lifeblood of democracy. The free flow of information and ideas informs political debate. It is a safety valve: people are more ready to accept decisions that go against them if they can in principle seek to influence them. It acts as a brake on the abuse of power by public officials. It facilitates the exposure of errors in the governance and administration of justice of the country: see Stone, Seidman, Sunstein and Tushnet, *Constitutional Law*, 3rd edn. (1996), pp 1078–1086.

---

[34] Cripps (n 1) p 25, referring to Megarry V-C in *Malone v MPC* [1979] Ch 344 at 377.

However, in *Campbell v MGN*, Lord Hope concluded (at paras 85–86) that although some of the language has changed (notably focusing on the concept of proportionality), the process remains substantially the same as that stipulated in *Spycatcher*:

> The third limiting principle is particularly relevant in this case. This is the principle which may require a court to carry out a balancing operation, weighing the public interest in maintaining confidence against a countervailing public interest favouring disclosure.

> The language has changed following the coming into operation of the Human Rights Act 1998 and the incorporation into domestic law of article 8 and article 10 of the Convention. We now talk about the right to respect for private life and the countervailing right to freedom of expression. The jurisprudence of the European Court offers important guidance as to how these competing rights ought to be approached and analysed. I doubt whether the result is that the centre of gravity, as my noble and learned friend, Lord Hoffmann, says, has shifted. It seems to me that the balancing exercise to which that guidance is directed is essentially the same exercise, although it is plainly now more carefully focused and more penetrating. As Lord Woolf CJ said in *A v B plc* [2003] QB 195, 202, para 4, new breadth and strength is given to the action for breach of confidence by these articles.

14.33   This applied even though *Campbell* was not a 'whistleblowing' case in any usually accepted sense: there were major differences between it and the *Spycatcher* case in which Lord Goff gave the exposition to which Lord Hope was referring. Peter Wright was 'whistleblowing' in respect of irregularities he alleged had occurred in the security services. The information he was disclosing was nothing like the information about Naomi Campbell's treatment for drug addiction, the disclosure of which was the subject matter of her claim against the *Daily Mirror*.

14.34   In *Re S (A Child) (Identification: Restrictions on Publication)* [2004] UKHL 47, [2005] 1 AC 593 at para 17 Lord Steyn referred to the opinions in the House of Lords in *Campbell* as having illuminated the interplay between Articles 8 and 10 and continued (at para 17):

> . . . for present purposes the decision of the House on the facts of *Campbell* and the differences between the majority and the minority are not material. What does, however, emerge clearly from the opinions are four propositions. First, neither article has *as such* precedence over the other. Secondly, where the values under the two articles are in conflict, an intense focus on the comparative importance of the specific rights being claimed in the individual case is necessary. Thirdly, the justifications for interfering with or restricting each right must be taken into account. Finally, the proportionality test must be applied to each. For convenience I will call this the ultimate balancing test.

14.35   Further guidance as to the approach required by the concept of proportionality is provided by the decision in *London Regional Transport v Mayor of London* [2001] EWCA Civ 1491, [2003] EMLR 88. London Regional Transport sought to prevent publication by the Mayor of London of a report commissioned by accountants concerning the London Underground. Sullivan J held that it was genuinely in the public interest for a redacted version of the report to be published. He arrived at that conclusion having balanced 'the desirability in the public interest of upholding confidentiality agreements and the public interest in freedom of access to information': see para 42 of the Court of Appeal judgment. Walker LJ (para 50) clearly thought that the information in question raised very serious issues:

> The guiding principle is to preserve legitimate commercial confidentiality while enabling the general public (and especially the long-suffering travelling public of London) to be informed of serious criticism, from a responsible source, of the value for money evaluation which is a crucial part of the PPP for the London Underground. That is a very important public interest which goes far beyond the transitional purposes of the 1999 Act, and it is the interest which must go into the scales on proportionality.

Sedley LJ's judgment expressed full agreement with that of Robert Walker LJ. In Sedley **14.36**
LJ's view the discharge of the injunction by Sullivan J was justified on the straightforward
ground that there was nothing of genuine commercial sensitivity in the redacted version
of Deloitte's report and nothing therefore to justify the stifling of public information and
debate by the enforcement of a bare contractual obligation of silence. However, addressing
the issue as to how the balance was to be struck between the interest in confidentiality and
the Article 10 interest in disclosure (and thus, indirectly, responding to the danger suggested by Gummow J in *Smith Kline* referred to above) he said this:

> Article 10 of the European Convention on Human Rights is not just about freedom of expres-
> sion. It is also about the right to receive and impart information. Whether or not undertak-
> ings of confidentiality had been signed, both domestic law and Art. 10(2) would recognise the
> propriety of suppressing wanton or self-interested disclosure of confidential information; but
> both correspondingly recognise the legitimacy of disclosure, undertakings notwithstanding,
> if the public interest in the free flow of information and ideas will be served by it.

> The difficulty in the latter case, as Miss Appleby's argument has understandably stressed,
> is to know by what instrument this balance is to be struck.

> It lies in the methodical concept of proportionality. Proportionality is not a word found **14.37**
> in the text of the Convention: it is the tool—the *metwand*—which the court has adopted
> (from nineteenth-century German jurisprudence) for deciding a variety of Convention
> issues including, for the purposes of the qualifications to Articles 8 to 11, what is and is
> not necessary in a democratic society. It replaces an elastic concept with which political
> scientists are more at home than lawyers with a structured inquiry: does the measure meet
> a recognized and pressing social need? Does it negate the primary right or restrict it more
> than is necessary? Are the reasons given for it logical? These tests of what is acceptable
> by way of restriction of basic rights in a democratic society reappear, with variations of
> phrasing and emphasis, in the jurisprudence of (among others) the Privy Council, the
> Constitutional Court of South Africa, the Supreme Court of Zimbabwe, and the Supreme
> Court of Canada in its Charter jurisdiction (see *de Freitas v Ministry of Agriculture* [1999]
> 1 AC 69, 80 (PC)), the courts of the Republic of Ireland (see *Quinn's Supermarket v A-G*
> [1972] IR 1), and the Court of Justice of the European Communities (see Article 3b, Treaty
> on European Union; *Bosman* [1995] ECR I–4921, §110).

Central importance was therefore attached to the principle of proportionality. The claim- **14.38**
ants in *London Regional Transport* were a public authority, but Sedley LJ noted that, whilst
it did not necessarily follow from the court's own status as a public authority that all its
judgments had, without more ado, to be Convention-compliant, it did follow that where
the court is deciding whether or not to grant an injunction, its judgment had to respect
both the relevant Convention rights and their qualifications. Sedley LJ concluded by
saying this:

> In the present case, as one would hope in most cases, the human rights highway leads to
> exactly the same outcome as the older road of equity and common law. But it may be that
> it is in some respects better signposted, and it is therefore helpful that it has played a central
> role in the argument.

Prior to the development of the requirement to apply Article 10 of the Convention, in a **14.39**
case between private litigants the burden of proof appears to have been on the defendant to
show that disclosure is justified, whereas the government had the burden of establishing a
public interest in maintaining confidentiality.[35] This must now be read subject to the need

---

[35] See the *Spycatcher* case at p 328, per Lord Griffiths, at p 256, per Lord Keith, at p 270, per Lord
Griffiths, and at p 283, per Lord Goff.

to apply proportionality to both the interests in confidentiality and in free expression, with no presumption in favour of either interest.

14.40 Whilst it is possible to identify important considerations which are relevant both in the context of protected disclosures and to the public interest defence to breach of confidentiality, in the latter context ultimately these considerations must be filtered into an assessment of proportionality. The *London Regional Transport* case provides one example of this. A further example is provided by the decision in *Imutran Ltd v Uncaged Campaigns Ltd* [2001] 2 All ER 385, which illustrates this in relation to wider disclosures. This concerned a claim for an injunction in respect of the intended publication of leaked confidential documents regarding animal testing. Having referred to *Initial Services* and other authorities in relation to the public interest defence, Morritt V-C noted that these demonstrated that:

(a) the public interest in disclosure might outweigh the right of the claimant to protect his confidences; and

(b) the court will also consider how much disclosure the public interest required; the fact that some disclosure may be required does not mean that disclosure to the whole world should be permitted.

14.41 Morritt V-C proceeded by saying (at para 21) that:

> in addition the Human Rights Act 1998 requires the court, as a public authority, to take into account the right of freedom of expression conferred by Article 10 European Convention on Human Rights. . . .. The effect of that article for present purposes is that any injunction, which by definition is a restriction on the exercise of the right to freedom of expression, must be justified as being no more than is necessary in a democratic society.

Various factors were then identified:

(a) The information contained in the documents received by the defendants from the anonymous sender was by its nature confidential.

(b) There could be no doubt that the defendants knew that the information contained in those documents was confidential.

(c) The defendants knew that Imutran had not known or consented to its documents being removed from its possession.

(d) The circumstances as they existed did not justify the width of disclosure the defendants sought; the House of Lords had set up its ad hoc Select Committee to enquire into the very matters which concerned the defendants; the Home Secretary and the Council of the RSPCA had called for reports and documents had been made available to the Good Laboratory Practice Monitoring Authority (GLPMA) and the UK Xenotransplantation Interim Regulatory Authority (UKXIRA); there was 'no impediment sought or in place such as to inhibit any regulatory authority from investigating all the matters on which the defendants expressed concern'.

(e) When considering what was necessary in a democratic society and when paying particular regard to the importance of the right to freedom of expression, it was relevant to consider which is the democratically selected responsible body or bodies and who would be the informed audience:

(i) Parliament had considered the issue of animal experimentation in 1986 and had laid down a licensing and inspection system and a forum for and source of continuing consideration and advice in the Animal Procedures Committee; and

(ii) the RSPCA, the GLPMA, and the UKXIRA all had an interest in investigating one or more of the matters which concerned the defendants.

(f) The defendants' right to freedom of expression was an element in their democratic right to campaign for the abolition of all animal xenotransplantation or other experimentation, but they could continue to do that whether or not the injunction was granted. The issue was whether they should be free to do so with Imutran's confidential and secret documents. However:

(i) many of those documents were of a specialist and technical nature suitable for consideration by specialists in the field but not by the public generally; and

(ii) given the provisos to the injunction sought there would be no restriction on the ability of the defendants to communicate the information to those specialists connected with the regulatory bodies denoted by Parliament as having responsibility in the field.

In making this assessment Morritt V-C therefore took into account the nature of the information, the steps that it could be expected would be taken to deal with the concern aside from the disclosure, and the width of the disclosure and that it went beyond what might be considered to be the informed audience having regard to the nature of the information. He concluded that the injunction sought did not go further than was necessary in a democratic society. Whilst paying particular regard to the importance of the right to freedom of expression, the Vice-Chancellor nevertheless concluded that the balance of convenience favoured the grant of the injunction sought because: (a) if no injunction was granted the confidence would be destroyed, and even if Imutran succeeded at trial the consequential damages would be entirely unquantifiable even if the defendants were able to pay them; and (b) by contrast, if the defendants were successful at the trial they would then be able to publish anything they liked with the added benefit of knowing the views of the regulatory bodies and their experts and there was no suggestion that the delay in establishing their right would cause any damage. Whilst several of the considerations relied upon would have been material to whether there was a protected disclosure, the protected disclosure legislation cannot be said to have provided a key to balancing the competing interest. **14.42**

In *HRH Prince of Wales v Associated Newspapers Ltd* [2006] EWCA Civ 1776, [2008] Ch 57 Lord Phillips (giving the judgment of the court) noted (at paras 67–68) that: **14.43**

> There is an important public interest in the observance of duties of confidence. Those who engage employees, or who enter into other relationships that carry with them a duty of confidence, ought to be able to be confident that they can disclose, without risk of wider publication, information that it is legitimate for them to wish to keep confidential. . . .. It is a test of proportionality. But a significant element to be weighed in the balance is the importance in a democratic society of upholding duties of confidence that are created between individuals. It is not enough to justify publication that the information in question is a matter of public interest. To take an extreme example, the content of a budget speech is a matter of great public interest. But if a disloyal typist were to seek to sell a copy to a newspaper in advance of the delivery of the speech in Parliament, there can surely be no doubt that the newspaper would be in breach of duty if it purchased and published the speech.
>
> . . . For these reasons, the test to be applied when considering whether it is necessary to restrict freedom of expression in order to prevent disclosure of information received in confidence is not simply whether the information is a matter of public interest but whether, in all the circumstances, it is in the public interest that the duty of confidence should be breached. The court will need to consider whether, having regard to the nature of the information and all the relevant circumstances, it is legitimate for the owner of the information to seek to keep it confidential or whether it is in the public interest that the information should be made public.[36]

---

[36] See also *Northern Rock plc v Financial Times Ltd* [2007] EWHC 2677 (QB), where this passage was applied.

14.44 The court noted (at paras 68–69) that in applying the test of proportionality the nature of the relationships which gives rise to the duty of confidentiality might be important, and gave cautious support to what had been said in *Campbell v Frisbee* in this regard: [2003] ICR 141 at para 22 (see paragraph 14.120 below). In *HRH Prince of Wales* the Prince's hand-written travel journals recorded his views and impressions during overseas travel. These were disclosed, in breach of contract, by an employee to a newspaper which published extracts from them. The court (at para 71) noted the 'the strong public interest in preserving the con-fidentiality of private journals and communications within private offices', and concluded that the trial judge was correct to hold that Prince Charles had an unanswerable claim for breach of privacy. It added that when the breach of a confidential relationship was added to the balance, his case was 'overwhelming'.

(a) Interim relief prohibiting disclosure: the context in which the balancing act is carried out and the relevance of the PIDA template

14.45 It is important to bear in mind, when considering the way in which the courts balance the competing public interests of confidentiality on one hand and exposure of 'relevant failures' on the other, the context in which the decisions have been and usually will be made. There are relatively few cases of a public interest defence being tested at a full trial, and in practical terms the interim hearing will very often resolve the matter entirely. The strength of the defence is tested at an interim hearing with limited evidence and limited time to consider it. Most of the cases discussed in this chapter arose out of applications for interim injunctions.

14.46 The basic test for the consideration of whether interim relief should be granted is that set out by Lord Diplock in *American Cyanamid Co v Ethicon Ltd* [1975] AC 396. The court must be satisfied 'that there is a serious question to be tried'. It is no part of the court's function at this stage of litigation to try to resolve conflicts of evidence on affidavit or in witness statements, nor to decide difficult questions of law calling for detailed argument and mature consideration. Unless the applicant fails to show that s/he has 'any real prospect of succeeding in his claim for a permanent injunction at the trial', the court should proceed to consider where the balance of convenience lies. As to that, where other factors appear to be evenly balanced 'it is a counsel of prudence' for the court to take 'such measures as are calculated to preserve the status quo'.

14.47 However, the *American Cyanamid* approach is not of universal application. The law rec-ognizes that there is a category of case in which a more stringent threshold than serious arguable case is required. In *NWL Ltd v Woods* [1979] 1 WLR 1294 at 1307 Lord Diplock said this:

> Where . . . the grant or refusal of the interlocutory injunction will have the practical effect of putting an end to the action because the harm that will have been already caused to the losing party by its grant or its refusal is complete and of a kind for which money cannot constitute any worthwhile recompense, the degree of likelihood that the plaintiff would have succeeded in establishing his right to an injunction if the action had gone to trial, is a factor to be brought into the balance by the judge in weighing the risks that injustice may result from his deciding the application one way rather than the other.[37]

14.48 This is apposite in the context of the balance to be struck at an interim stage between dis-closure and non-disclosure[38] because a disclosure once made cannot be unmade. But in a

---

[37] See also *Lansing Linde Ltd v Kerr* [1991] 1 WLR 251 at 258A–C.
[38] See Morrit V-C in *Imutran Ltd v Uncaged Campaigns Ltd* [2001] 2 All ER 385 at para 15, and Sullivan J in *London Regional Transport v The Mayor of London* at para 55 at first instance, together with the Court of Appeal's judgment in the latter case: [2001] EWCA Civ 1491, [2003] EMLR 88 at para 44.

case where publication is involved (ie wider disclosure, discussed below) different principles apply in any event, to which we now turn.

Section 12 HRA makes special provision regarding the right to freedom of expression. **14.49** When considering whether to grant relief which, if granted, might affect the exercise of the Convention right to freedom of expression, section 12(4) provides that the court must have particular regard to the importance of this right. Section 12(3) imposes a threshold test which has to be satisfied before a court may grant interim injunctive relief:

> No such relief [which might affect the exercise of the Convention right to freedom of expression] is to be granted so as to restrain publication before trial unless the court is satisfied that the applicant is likely to establish that publication should not be allowed.

This provision was the subject of the House of Lords decision in *Cream Holdings Ltd and* **14.50** *others v Banerjee and another* [2004] UKHL 44, [2005] 1 AC 253, of the Court of Appeal in *K v News Group Newspapers Ltd* [2011] EWCA Civ 439 [2011] 1 WLR 1827, and, more recently, of the Supreme Court in *PJS v News Group Newspapers Ltd* [2016] UKSC 26, [2016] AC 1081. *Cream Holdings* was a group of companies running businesses that included nightclubs, dance festivals, the franchising of their brand name and logo, and merchandising clothes and other items. Lord Nicholls described them as 'an important business in Liverpool featuring both on general news pages and financial pages of newspapers'. Ms Banerjee was a chartered accountant and worked as the financial controller of one of the companies in the Cream group for three years from February 1998 to January 2001. Prior to that she worked for a firm of accountants and was responsible for dealing with the Cream group's financial affairs between 1996 and 1998. The second defendant was the publisher of Liverpool's *Daily Post* and the *Liverpool Echo*. In January 2001 Cream dismissed Ms Banerjee. When she left, she took with her copies of documents that she subsequently claimed showed illegal and improper activity by the Cream group. Ms Banerjee passed these copy documents to the *Echo* with additional information. She received no payment for this. In June 2002 the *Echo* published articles about alleged corruption involving one director of the Cream group and a local council official. The Cream group sought injunctive relief to restrain publication by the newspaper of any further confidential information given to it by Ms Banerjee. The defendants admitted that the information was confidential but contended that disclosure was in the public interest.

At first instance, Lloyd J granted interim injunctive relief, restraining disclosure of confi- **14.51** dential information except to criminal or regulatory authorities. He considered that, given the undoubted obligation of confidentiality inherent in Ms Banerjee's employment contract, the disputes of fact on some matters, and the possibility that Ms Banerjee's complaints of defaults by the Cream group might be met adequately by disclosure to certain regulatory authorities as distinct from publication at large by the press, the right course was to maintain the status quo and direct a speedy trial if desired.

The majority in the Court of Appeal, Simon Brown and Arden LJJ, dismissed the appeal. **14.52** However, this was reversed by the House of Lords, which concluded that the prospects of establishing at trial the interest in confidentiality were insufficient to justify maintaining the injunction.

The precise way in which the conclusion was reached must be a matter of inference **14.53** because the detail was set out in closed judgments. In the Court of Appeal, Sedley LJ (who dissented) placed the protected disclosure provisions in ERA at the centre of his reasoning. He identified that there was a public interest in the disclosure of the information. He also noted that there might be an interest in maintaining confidentiality given that the information was disclosed by a former employee, albeit he also referred to the principle that no confidence attaches to an iniquity. Sedley LJ considered that the protected disclosure provisions provided a 'template' to balance the competing principles in relation to confidentiality and the public interest and that employees would step outside that protection at their peril. This approach has obvious attractions. It would provide a set of clear principles which will squarely meet the criticism by Gummow J to which we have referred in paragraph 14.31 above.

14.54   Whilst Lord Nicholls (who gave the only speech in the House of Lords) agreed with the conclusion reached by Sedley LJ as to the correct result, he did not endorse Sedley LJ's observations as to the use of the protected disclosure legislation as a template. Lord Nicholls explained (at para 24) that:

> I am satisfied that in one particular respect the judge fell into error in any event. The error was identified by Sedley LJ and sufficiently explained by him at para 88[39] of his judgment [2003] Ch 650, 677, and para 1 of his 'private' judgment. I agree with him that the principal happenings the *Echo* wishes to publish are clearly matters of serious public interest. The graduated protection afforded to 'whistleblowers' by sections 43A to 43L of the Employment Rights Act 1996, inserted by the Public Interest Disclosure Act 1998, section 1, does not militate against this appraisal. Authorities such as the Inland Revenue owe duties of confidentiality regarding the affairs of those with whom they are dealing. The 'whistleblower' provisions were intended to give additional protection to employees, not to cut down the circumstances where the public interest may justify private information being published at large.

14.55   Lord Nicholls therefore emphasized the differing considerations that may arise in relation to whether the public interest might justify private information being published and whether to grant protection under the ERA's protected disclosure provisions. It was relevant to draw this distinction because the defendant had raised potential defences under the protected disclosure provisions as a reason to refuse relief. At first instance Lloyd J had identified the question arising in the case as being: 'whether Cream is likely to be able to succeed at trial despite the defendants' defences based on the public interest and the Public Interest Disclosure Act'.[40]

14.56   Whilst Sedley LJ referred to a worker stepping outside the protected disclosure provisions at his peril, Lord Nicholls' approach identified that a defence under the protected disclosure provisions would not necessarily resolve the balance of where the public interest lay. This mirrored the approach of Auld LJ in *Street v Derbyshire Unemployed Workers' Centre* [2004] EWCA Civ 964, [2005] ICR 97, who rejected a submission that the tests applied in relation to publishing confidential information were of relevance in relation to the meaning of good faith which, at that time, applied in the protected disclosure provisions.

14.57   Notwithstanding Lord Nicholls' caution that protected disclosure defences do not *necessarily* negate an interest in disclosure, factors material to a protected disclosure are, we would suggest, highly relevant when assessing the balance of public interest in relation to confidentiality. Whilst not necessarily determinative given the different imperatives as to whether the discloser should be protected on one hand and whether the information disclosed should be ventilated on the other, the factors taken into account with regard to protected disclosures are likely to be material considerations in relation to whether a public interest defence to confidentiality is made out. Indeed, this is unsurprising given that, without tying protection

---

[39] In para 88 Sedley LJ noted that the disclosure was essentially true (otherwise there would have been a defamation claim) and that there was a serious public interest in disclosure.

[40] See para 24 of the judgment of Simon Brown LJ in the Court of Appeal: [2003] EWCA Civ 103, [2003] Ch 650 at 662.

to common law confidentiality obligations, the legislation drew upon principles established in the body of case law principally in the context of confidentiality. In the survey of the case law that follows we consider how factors central to the protected disclosure legislation also play an important role in relation to confidentiality obligations.

We have already set out the facts of *PJS* (paragraph 14.21). The content of the speeches of their Lordships (Lord Toulson dissented) allowing the appeal was concerned in large part with arguments as to whether the injunction should be continued where the information was now in the public domain (but where it related to a right to privacy as distinct from a right to confidentiality) and the issue of whether an injunction was any longer an effective remedy. However, the following, more general, points should be noted.   **14.58**

Lord Mance (with whom Lord Neuberger, Lady Hale, and Lord Reed agreed) reasserted (and in doing so held that the Court of Appeal had erred in this respect[41]) that even at the interim stage neither Article 8 nor Article 10 has primacy over the other, but that where their values are in conflict what is necessary is an 'intense focus' on the comparative importance of the rights being claimed in each case. The justifications for interfering with or restricting each right must be taken into account and the proportionality test must be applied.[42] The exercise is one which, if undertaken on a correct basis, will not readily attract appellate intervention. Although the media were obviously entitled to criticize the conduct of individuals even where there was nothing illegal about it, that could not be a pretext for invasion of privacy by disclosure of alleged sexual infidelity which was of no real public interest in a legal sense. That had been confirmed by the ECtHR in *Armonience v Lithuania* [2009] EMLR 7, para 39, where the court had noted the 'fundamental distinction' between 'reporting facts ... capable of contributing to a debate in a democratic society and making tawdry allegations about an individual's private life'.[43] If Article 10 was engaged and capable in principle of protecting any form of expression, the case law demonstrated that this type of expression was 'at the bottom end of the spectrum of importance (compared, for example, with freedom of political speech or a case of conduct bearing on the performance of a public office)'. Accordingly 'any public interest in publishing such criticism must, in the absence of any other, legally recognised, public interest, be effectively disregarded in any balancing exercise' and was 'incapable by itself of outweighing such article 8 privacy rights as the appellant [enjoyed]'.   **14.59**

(b) *The types of information that can form the basis of a public interest defence: the categories corresponding to those covered by the protected disclosure provisions of ERA*

As described in Chapter 3, ERA, section 43B sets out the categories of information—'relevant failures' in the terminology used by the Act—the disclosure of which can attract the protection of the ERA's protected disclosure provisions (see Chapter 3, paragraph 3.02). In this section we consider the extent to which the public interest defence mirrors those categories, recognizing that it is clear that the public interest defence is of wider scope than the 'relevant failures' which form the subject matter of qualifying disclosures under the ERA. The identification of a type of information which potentially provides a defence to a breach   **14.60**

---

[41] By proceeding on the basis that s 12 'enhances the weight which article 10 rights carry in the balancing exercise' and 'raises the hurdle which the claimant must overcome in order to obtain an interim injunction'.

[42] Referring to *In re S (A Child) (Identification: Restrictions on Publication)* as discussed in para 14.34 and in particular Lord Steyn at para 17; *McKennitt v Ash* [2006] EWCA Civ 1714, [2008] QB 73 at para 47 (Buxton LJ) and *Mosley v News Group Newspapers Ltd* [2008] EWHC 687 (QB) at para 28 (Eady J).

[43] A similar distinction was drawn by the ECtHR in *Mosley v United Kingdom* [2012] EMLR 1 para 114 and *Couderc and Hachette Filipacchi Associes v France* App No 40454/07 paras 100–01.

of confidentiality is not the end of the matter. As we have seen and shall examine further, considerations of proportionality and the balancing of the interest in disclosure against any interest in privacy/confidentiality still require consideration.

14.61 **Crime** Information that a criminal offence has been, is being, or is likely to be committed is a legitimate subject of disclosure. *Gartside v Outram* (1856) 26 LJ Ch 113 concerned disclosure by an ex-employee of accounting and business information which it was alleged showed that the employer had been carrying on business in a fraudulent manner. Wood V-C held that this would be a good defence if the factual basis for it was made out at trial.

14.62 In *R v Chief Constable of North Wales, ex p AB* [1999] QB 396[44] the chief constable had a policy of disclosing information in relation to paedophile offenders who had been released from prison to those with a need to know for the protection of children and vulnerable adults. This policy was challenged by the applicants. Lord Woolf MR stated (at p 428) that disclosure should only be made when there is a pressing need for that disclosure.[45] However, we are not aware of any case which specifically considers whether there is a threshold which must be reached in terms of the seriousness of the apprehended criminal offence in order to engage the public interest defence.

14.63 **Failure to comply with a legal obligation** *Initial Services Ltd v Putterill* [1968] 1 QB 396 provides an example falling within the category of information that a person has failed, is failing, or is likely to fail to comply with any legal obligation to which s/he is subject. On resigning as sales manager of the claimant launderers, Mr Putterill removed documents belonging to the claimant which he passed to *Daily Mail* reporters. Relying upon these documents, the newspaper alleged that there was an unlawful price-fixing agreement and that the laundries had misled the public in claiming to have increased their prices to offset tax when in reality they were increasing their profits. Breach of the Restrictive Trade Practices Act 1956 was not a criminal offence and it was argued that the disclosure could only be justified in cases of information relating to crime and fraud. As we have seen, the Court of Appeal rejected this submission and refused to strike out the defence that the disclosures were made in the public interest and thus extended the scope of the defence which had been allowed in *Gartside*.

14.64 **Miscarriage of justice** The decision of the Court of Appeal in *Lion Laboratories Ltd v Evans* [1985] QB 526 provides an example of information that a miscarriage of justice has occurred, is occurring, or is likely to occur. The contention of the defendant ex-employees was that, unless there was full disclosure of the information in issue, there might have been unsafe convictions for drink-driving. The claimants manufactured breathalyser equipment. The defendants had been employed by the claimants as technicians. When their employment ended, they removed documents which cast doubt on the reliability of the equipment. These documents were passed on to the press. It was admitted that the documents were confidential but an interim injunction was overturned because of the public interest in the public being informed that the equipment might not be reliable.

14.65 **Health and safety concerns** As to information that the health or safety of any individual has been, is being, or is likely to be endangered, see *Hubbard v Vosper* [1972] 2 QB 84.

---

[44] Followed in *R (on the application of W) v Chief Constable of Northumbria* [2009] EWHC 747 (Admin), concerning the disclosure of a spent conviction of sexual assault to an employer, which was held to be proportionate and the public interest adjudged to outweigh W's rights.

[45] See the more recent case of *R (A) v B* [2010] EWHC 2361 (Admin), where Langstaff J, having considered the *Chief Constable of North Wales* case, ruled that the disclosure by the police of information was not justified.

Lord Denning MR (at p 96A–B) considered that, in relation to material on Scientology which had been published in breach of confidence, a public interest defence might be established at trial on the basis that it was dangerous material including 'medical quackeries of a sort which might be dangerous if practised behind closed doors'. Similarly, in *Church of Scientology of California v Kaufman* [1973] RPC 635 Goff J held that disclosure by a former student of Scientology was justified on the basis of possible danger to the public in the light of evidence that Scientology had caused some followers to become ill.[46]

Damage to the environment/concealing information   Equally, the public interest principle would plainly be wide enough to cover disclosures of information that the environment has been, is being, or is likely to be damaged or, specifically, information tending to show that one of the other relevant failures has been or is likely to be deliberately concealed.   **14.66**

(c)   The types of information that can form the basis of a public interest defence: categories of information not covered by the ERA's protected disclosure provisions where the courts have held that there is a public interest in disclosure

The scope for a public interest defence appears to extend beyond the categories of 'relevant failures' provided for by section 43B.   **14.67**

Breaches of rules of self-regulatory schemes   We have already observed in Chapter 3, paragraph 3.120, that for the purposes of protection under PIDA it may be difficult to identify a legal obligation which has been flouted where the matter complained of is a breach of a regulatory as opposed to directly legally enforceable scheme. However, in a common law context it would appear that disclosure of a breach of the rules of a self-regulatory scheme, particularly in the financial services sector, is capable of being justified (at least where the disclosure is to the relevant regulatory body). In *Re A Company* [1989] Ch 477, which is considered in more detail below,[47] the claimant company provided financial advice and management. It was alleged that the defendant, a former employee, had threatened that if he was not paid £10,000 as compensation for his having been dismissed he would report breaches of the Financial Investment Management Rules to the Financial Investment Management and Brokers' Regulatory Authority (FIMBRA) and would also report allegations of tax improprieties to the Inland Revenue. The defendant sought an injunction to prevent any disclosures being made using its confidential information. Scott J refused to grant an interlocutory injunction to this effect: the duty of confidentiality did not extend to a duty not to make disclosure to the appropriate regulatory body of a possible breach of that body's regulatory rules.   **14.68**

Similarly, in *Francome v Mirror Group Newspapers Ltd* [1984] 1 WLR 892 secret tapes were made of telephone conversations involving John Francome, a well-known jockey. The tapes were then sold to the press. An attempt was made to justify the apparent breach of Mr Francome's confidence on the basis that the tapes revealed breaches of the rules of racing. The Court of Appeal restrained publication until trial but held that there was a triable issue as to whether the publication could be justified.   **14.69**

Damage to financial interests of investors/the public   Damage to the financial interests of the public which might not involve breaches of a legal obligation may also be justified. In *Price Waterhouse v BCCI Holdings (Luxembourg) SA* [1992] BCLC 583 the Court of Appeal   **14.70**

---

[46] The decision of Talbot J in *Distillers Co (Biochemicals) Ltd v Times Newspapers Ltd* [1975] 1 QB 613 at 622 that negligence, even if it could be proved, could not be within the same class as crime, fraud, or misdeed so as to constitute an exception to the need to protect confidentiality, is out of line with other authority. See Cripps (n 1) p 102.

[47] At paras 14.91–14.98.

expressly recognized that the public interest in effective supervision of banking institutions could justify overriding a duty of confidence. Price Waterhouse had acted as auditors to the BCCI Group. After the collapse of the Group, the Bank of England and the Treasury set up a non-statutory enquiry into the supervision of BCCI. The Bank of England and the Serious Fraud Office served notices on Price Waterhouse to disclose various confidential documents and Price Waterhouse sought a declaration that it was entitled to disclose the documents. Millet J considered that in this case the public interest in preserving the confidentiality of the documents relating to Price Waterhouse's client—BCCI—was outweighed by the public interest in the effective supervision of authorized banking institutions, having regard to the need to protect depositors, and the public interest in ensuring that the inquiry into the adequacy of such supervision should have access to all relevant material.

14.71 In *London Regional Transport v Mayor of London* [2001] EWCA Civ 1491, [2003] EMLR 88, London Regional Transport sought to prevent publication by the Mayor of London, Ken Livingstone, of a report prepared by a firm of accountants, Deloitte's, concerning the London Underground. The report went into the supposed flaws in the methods used to assess the efficacy of the public–private partnership that was proposed for the Underground. London Regional Transport argued that, because of written confidentiality agreements which bound the Mayor and which applied to his receipt of the Deloitte's report, the court had no option but to prevent disclosure. At first instance, Sullivan J held that it was genuinely in the public interest for a redacted version of the Deloitte's report to be published. He reached that conclusion having balanced 'the desirability in the public interest of upholding confidentiality agreements and the public interest in freedom of access to information'. The Court of Appeal held that the judge was correct to have conducted such a balancing exercise and agreed with his conclusion.

14.72 **Where the public has been/will be misled** A series of cases suggest that disclosure could be justified in order to prevent the public being misled. In *Initial Services* (paragraph 14.63 above) it was alleged that the public had been misled into believing that laundry prices had been increased due to tax when in fact there was substantial additional profit being made. This was held to be a further arguable ground justifying disclosure of otherwise confidential material. Similarly, in *Scientology v Kaufman* (paragraph 14.65 above) (at p 654) one ground for resisting an injunction was that otherwise the public might be deceived into paying for 'nonsensical mumbo-jumbo' (being the judge's description of the teachings of the Church of Scientology). It was therefore in the public interest that there should be disclosure of the type of thing for which payment was being requested.

14.73 The theoretical possible breadth of this ground was illustrated by the controversial decision in *Woodward v Hutchins* [1977] 1 WLR 760 (CA). A former public relations officer and press agent wrote a series of articles about the activities of pop stars by whom he had been employed (via a management company). An interim injunction was refused. Although the injunction sought was too wide in any event since it covered information in the public domain, Lord Denning MR and Bridge LJ both emphasized that since the pop stars had invited publicity they could not complain if the truth was then told. The information in issue in *Woodward* tended to show that the image that the pop group had fostered was not a true image and it was in the public interest that it should be corrected. Of course in no sense did the alleged hypocrisy represent any form of danger to the public. It may be, however, that the decision turned not so much upon whether there was a defence to a claim for breach of confidence as a matter of law, but on whether the discretion of the court should be exercised in favour of granting the claimant an injunction. Bridge LJ left open the possibility that if the defendants could show that the information was true there would only be nominal damages awarded for breach of confidence. Further, Lawton LJ explained the decision on the basis that the breach of confidence was interwoven with the allegations of libel and that the ordinary principle in the case of libel was to allow publication where justification was alleged.

The decision in *Woodward* was followed in *Khashoggi v Smith* (1980) 124 SJ 149 (CA), **14.74** where the claimant sought unsuccessfully to restrain her former housekeeper from disclosing information about her private affairs, including allegations of criminal conduct. Roskill LJ accepted that the allegations about the claimant's private life could not be disentangled from the allegations of offences and that disclosure was therefore justified since there could not be any confidence where the information was to be exploited (by the press) for investigation into the alleged offences. However, he also held that the claimant had allowed herself into the public eye to such an extent that she 'ran the risk of the whole story being made public', in the sense of giving a full account of matters where only a partial or misleading account had previously been given.

In *Campbell v MGN* [2004] UKHL 22, [2004] 2 AC 457 it was conceded that the *Daily* **14.75** *Mirror* was entitled to publish the fact of Naomi Campbell's drug dependency and that she was seeking treatment because she had specifically given publicity to the very question of whether she took drugs and had falsely said that she did not. This created a sufficient public interest in the correction of the impression which she had previously given. Lord Nicholls observed (at p 467D), albeit the point was not in issue in *Campbell*, that:

> where a public figure chooses to present a false image and make untrue pronouncements about his or her life, the press will normally be entitled to put the record straight.

Langley J ruled to a similar effect when David and Victoria Beckham sought an interim **14.76** injunction against their former nanny, Abbie Gibson,[48] who had signed a confidentiality agreement. On behalf of Ms Gibson (and the *News of the World*) it was argued that because the Beckhams used their marriage as a marketing tool, the public was entitled to know what Ms Gibson and the newspaper contended was the reality of that marriage. Langley J appears to have accepted this argument.

However, the decision in *Woodward* may be seen as failing adequately to observe the distinc- **14.77** tion between what is interesting to the public and what is in the public interest to be made known.[49] In *Campbell v Frisbee* [2002] EWHC 328 (Ch), [2002] EMLR 31 it was argued before Lightman J that the disclosures were legitimate because they corrected a false impression that Ms Campbell had placed before the public, and reliance was placed on *Woodward*. Lightman J said that he did not see how it was seriously maintainable that the public had any interest in the content of the disclosures (most particularly that the claimant was cheating on her partner) or any need to know, or that the defendant had any such reason or justification for making her disclosures, and there was no real prospect of the court holding at the trial that the disclosure by the defendant could possibly be justified. In the Court of Appeal ([2002] EWCA Civ 1374, [2003] ICR 141) Lord Phillips MR said that Lightman J 'might well have been right to suggest that *Woodward* should no longer be applied'. Further, in *McKennitt v Ash* [2005] EWHC 3003 (QB), [2006] EMLR 10, Eady J noted the range of criticism of *Woodward* and expressed the view that for personal misbehaviour which was not unlawful to justify disclosure, 'a very high degree of misbehaviour must be demonstrated'.

---

[48] *Beckham v Gibson* (unreported, 23 April 2005).

[49] Per Lord Wilberforce in *British Steel Corporation v Granada Television Ltd* [1981] AC 1096 at 1168G (HL). In the same case Viscount Dilhorne (at p 1176C) was of the view that disclosure would not have been justified in order to establish that it was not true that there had been no government intervention in the steel strike.

In the Court of Appeal, Buxton LJ said (at para 68) that 'as an entirely general statement, divorced from its context' that might well go too far but agreed with Eady J that the conduct complained of in the case of the claimant fell well below the level that would justify complaint on the ground of hypocrisy. The point is ventilated most recently in the speeches in the Supreme Court's decision in in *PJS v News Group Newspapers Ltd* [2016] UKSC 26, [2016] AC 1081, discussed above in paragraph 14.21.

14.78 **Alleged immorality** In *Stephens v Avery* [1988] 1 Ch 449 the *Mail on Sunday* published an article containing details of a lesbian affair on the basis of information passed on by a third party in whom the claimant had confided. The claimant brought a claim for breach of confidence. The defendants applied to have the action struck out as disclosing no reasonable cause of action, or as being scandalous, frivolous, or vexatious on the basis that there could be no confidence in respect of information concerning grossly immoral conduct. The Master refused to strike out the proceedings and Sir Nicholas Browne-Wilkinson V-C upheld this decision. The defendants relied on the decision of Younger J in *Glyn v Weston Feature Film Co* [1916] 1 Ch 261 where the claimant alleged that an episode in her novel had been pirated in breach of copyright. Younger J refused to grant relief on various grounds including that the episode in question was:

> grossly immoral in its essence, in its treatment, and in its tendency. Stripped of its trappings, which are mere accident, it is nothing more nor less than a sensual adulterous intrigue. And it is not as if the plaintiff in her treatment of it were content to excuse or palliate the conduct described. She is not even satisfied with justifying that conduct. She has stooped to glorify the liaison in its inception, its progress, and its results; and she has not hesitated to garnish it with meretricious incident at every turn. Now it is clear law that copyright cannot exist in a work of a tendency so grossly immoral as this, a work which, apart from its other objectionable features, advocates free love and justifies adultery where the marriage tie has become merely irksome.

14.79 Browne Wilkinson V-C did not suggest that *Glyn* was incorrect as a matter of law: that which was grossly immoral might not attract the law's protection.

> But at the present day the difficulty is to identify what sexual conduct is to be treated as grossly immoral. In 1915 there was a code of sexual morals accepted by the overwhelming majority of society. A judge could therefore stigmatize certain sexual conduct as offending that moral code. But at the present day no such general code exists. There is no common view that sexual conduct of any kind between consenting adults is grossly immoral. I suspect the works of Elinor Glyn if published today would be widely regarded as, at the highest, very soft pornography.
>
> The sexual conduct of the plaintiff was not so morally shocking in this case as to prevent the third defendant, a major national Sunday newspaper, from spreading the story all over its front and inside pages. The submission on behalf of these defendants that the actions of the plaintiff in this case are so grossly immoral as to produce a tendency towards immoral conduct and thereby to be without the law lies ill in their mouths, since they have themselves spread the news of such conduct nationwide for their own personal profit.
>
> If it is right that there is now no generally accepted code of sexual morality applying to this case, it would be quite wrong in my judgment for any judge to apply his own personal moral views, however strongly held, in deciding the legal rights of the parties. The court's function is to apply the law, not personal prejudice. Only in a case where there is still a generally accepted moral code can the court refuse to enforce rights in such a way as to offend that generally accepted code.

14.80 The practical problem is therefore likely to be how to satisfy the court that there is in the twenty-first century a 'generally accepted moral code' with regard to the subject matter of the information in question, whatever it may be. There is a large overlap with the category discussed above, that is to say cases where it is argued that the public is being misled as to the 'probity' of the individual seeking to prevent disclosure. More generally, as observed in *Douglas v Hello! Ltd (No 1)* [2001] 2 All ER 289 at 329, by Keene LJ:

> breach of confidence is a developing area of the law, the boundaries of which are not immutable but may change to reflect changes in society, technology and business practice.

In *Mosley v News Group Newspapers Ltd* [2008] EWHC 1777 (QB), Max Moseley's claim **14.81** against the *News of the World* in relation to its article published under the heading 'F1 Boss Has Sick Nazi Orgy With Five Hookers', Eady J reviewed the principles and the authorities and made the following points:

- Sometimes there may be a good case for revealing the fact of wrongdoing to the general public; it will not necessarily follow that photographs of 'every gory detail' also need to be published to achieve the public interest objective.[50] Anyone indulging in sexual activity is entitled to a degree of privacy—especially if it is on private property and between consenting adults (paid or unpaid). 'Public figures' are entitled to a private personal life. The notion of privacy covers not only sexual activities but personal relationships more generally.
- If it really were the case (and it was not) that Mr Mosley had for entertainment and sexual gratification been 'mocking the humiliating way the Jews were treated', or 'parodying Holocaust horrors', there could be a public interest in that being revealed at least to those in the FIA to whom he was accountable since he had to deal with many people of all races and religions, and had spoken out against racism in the sport. If he really were behaving in that way that would, for many people, call seriously into question his suitability for his FIA role and it would be information which people arguably should have the opportunity to know and evaluate. Whilst it was probably right to acknowledge that private fantasies should not in themselves be subjected to legal scrutiny by the courts, when they are acted out, that is not necessarily so.
- Even if there was adultery and even if one happened to agree that it was 'depraved', it by no means followed that this was a matter of genuine public interest, as that was understood in the case law. Sexual conduct is a significant aspect of human life in respect of which people should be free to choose. That freedom is one of the matters which Article 8 protects: governments and courts are required to afford remedies when that right is breached.
- In deciding whether a right has been infringed, and in assessing the relative worth of competing rights, it is not for judges to make individual moral judgments or to be swayed by personal distaste. It is not simply a matter of personal privacy versus the public interest. The modern perception is that there is a public interest in respecting personal privacy. It is thus a question of taking account of conflicting public interest considerations and evaluating them according to increasingly well-recognized criteria.

PJS, which is more fully described above in paragraph 14.21 shows how far the law has **14.82** moved on since *Glyn*. In that case Lord Mance said that the Court of Appeal had erred in the reference it made to there being in the circumstances even a 'limited public interest' in the proposed story and in its introduction of that supposed interest into a balancing exercise. The Court of Appeal had relied upon a point made by an earlier Court of Appeal in *Hutcheson (previously 'KGM') v News Group Newspapers Ltd* [2011] EWCA Civ 808, [2012] EMLR 2 (CA) that the media are entitled to criticize the conduct of individuals even where

---

[50] Reference was made to *Theakston v MGN Ltd* [2002] EMLR 22 where the injunction restrained publication of photographs but not a verbal description.

there is nothing illegal about it. That, said Lord Mance, was 'obviously so'. But, he continued (at para 21),

> . . .criticism of conduct cannot be a pretext for invasion of privacy by disclosure of alleged sexual infidelity which is of no real public interest in a legal sense. It is beside the point that the claimant and his partner are in other contexts subjects of public and media attention— factors without which the issue would hardly arise or come to court. It remains beside the point, however much their private sexual conduct might interest the public and help sell newspapers or copy.

And at para 24, having referred to the various authorities Lord Mance said this:

> In these circumstances, it may be that the mere reporting of sexual encounters of someone like the claimant, however well known to the public, with a view to criticising them does not even fall within the concept of freedom of expression under article 10 at all. But, accepting that article 10 is not only engaged but capable in principle of protecting any form of expression, these cases clearly demonstrate that this type of expression is at the bottom end of the spectrum of importance (compared, for example, with freedom of political speech or a case of conduct bearing on the performance of a public office). For present purposes, any public interest in publishing such criticism must, in the absence of any other, legally recognised, public interest, be effectively disregarded in any balancing exercise and is incapable by itself of outweighing such article 8 privacy rights as the claimant enjoys.

14.83 **Conclusions as to the nature of the information that can form the basis of a public interest defence** The ERA's protected disclosure provisions set out a finite list of the categories of information which can form the subject of qualifying disclosures. The principle of public interest disclosure which we are considering in this chapter is more flexible and matters not listed in section 43B might attract its application. There is no reason whatsoever to suppose that the categories are closed or even that the courts will proceed on the basis that they should find a precedent in a previous case involving information of an analogous nature to that under consideration. That is not to say that the nature, importance, and seriousness of the 'harm' in issue are not relevant: they most certainly are, and the distinction between what is of interest to the public and what is of public interest to be made known remains important. Indeed, its importance is emphasized by the need to apply considerations of proportionality in when weighting competing public interests.

(d) The identity of the recipient: first tier disclosures

14.84 First tier disclosure is disclosure either to the employer or to a person other than the employer in respect of a relevant failure for which a person other than the employer has legal responsibility. No issue as to breach of *confidentiality* would arise upon disclosure to the employer in cases where the duty of confidentiality is owed to the employer or to the person other than the employer who is responsible for the apprehended failure. But issues might arise where the duty is owed to a third party. One instance would be where an employee discloses information about a previous employer to a new employer. Ordinarily these issues arise in the context of disclosing valuable business information to a competitor, rather than disclosing issues of public concern. However, issues analogous to those raised by the protected disclosure legislation might arise in a common law context.

14.85 The position can be illustrated by the example of an employee who provides the new employer with sensitive salary information belonging to the old employer, which s/he believes shows that the old employer has been defrauding HMRC. In terms of protected disclosure provisions, the key issues under ERA, sections 43B and 43C would be whether the disclosure was made in the reasonable belief that it was in the public interest to make it and whether there was a reasonable belief that the information tended to show a relevant failure. By contrast, the balancing of public interests permits a more flexible approach. A court would be expected to take into account that there are far more appropriate recipients of the information, such as HMRC, than a trade rival.

As against this, in many cases the considerations relevant to protected disclosures and the balance of public interest will be similar. In relation to ERA, section 43C(1)(b), where the disclosure is to the person with legal responsibility or the person whose conduct is primarily involved, there may well be a breach of confidence owed to the employer in making the disclosure. However, it is inherent within these categories, as it ordinarily is with the employer despite the example considered above, that the disclosure is to someone with a proper interest in receiving the information. As identified by Lord Denning in *Initial Services*, that is an important consideration in favour of disclosure. Again, however, it cannot be assumed that the approach to protected disclosures will necessarily be identical to the public interest balance. **14.86**

(e) Second tier/regulatory disclosures

As we noted in Chapter 5, a second tier disclosure to the appropriate prescribed person under section 43F will be made if s/he reasonably believes that: **14.87**

(i) the relevant failure falls within any description of matters in respect of which the person to whom the disclosure is made is the prescribed person; and

(ii) the information disclosed, and any allegation contained in it, are substantially true.

Rationale for protection   The favoured position of the whistleblower who makes disclosure to a regulator (as opposed to a wider class of recipient) is explicable on the basis that: **14.88**

(a) The regulators will have a statutory duty to investigate such matters and they can only perform their role if members of the public are prepared to come to them with information, free from the threat of retaliation. Further, the regulator is likely to have the expertise to investigate the allegations and to identify those matters that are of legitimate concern.

(b) The regulator can usually be relied upon to maintain confidentiality of the material once it is in his/her own domain, whether the allegation is right or wrong.

(c) The motivation of anyone revealing material to a regulator is likely to be one of concerned public interest because the regulator will not pay money for the material (although someone who makes such a disclosure might qualify for a Crimestoppers Trust award).

Importance of recipient of disclosure   The courts have always regarded the identity of the intended recipient as being important to the question of whether disclosure should be permitted. As noted above, this was emphasized by Lord Denning MR in *Initial Services* (at pp 405G–406B). In *Francome v Mirror Group Newspapers Ltd* [1984] 1 WLR 892, the Court of Appeal was sceptical as to whether disclosure to the press was justified but was more sympathetic to the claim that publication might be justified if it was made to the police or to the Jockey Club (which had supervisory powers in relation to racing) (per Sir John Donaldson MR at p 899A–C, and per Stephen Brown LJ at p 902B). **14.89**

In *A-G v Guardian Newspapers (No 2)* [1990] 1 AC 109 Lord Griffiths (at p 268A–C) similarly emphasized the importance of the recipient of the information, stating that even if the balance comes down in favour of publication, it did not follow that publication should be to the world through the media and, in certain circumstances, the public interest may be better served by a limited form of publication via authorities who would be under a duty not to abuse the confidential information and to use it only for the purpose of their inquiry. Lord Goff (at pp 282H–283B) also emphasized that more limited disclosure might sometimes be required, and in the Court of Appeal ([1988] 3 All ER 545 at 597) Lord Donaldson MR **14.90** explained this on the basis that the nature and degree of communication must be proportionate to the cause of or excuse for the disclosure. On this basis both Lord Goff and Lord Griffiths in *A-G v Guardian (No 2)* emphasized that, since in that case there were a number of avenues open for proper complaint, it was difficult to envisage a case in which it would be in the public interest for allegations of iniquity to be published in the media (although no issue arose as to what steps could be taken if other avenues of complaint failed to advance the matter).

14.91 **Approach to substantial belief in truth in relation to regulatory disclosures** The removal of the requirement of good faith brings the ERA's protected disclosure provsisions into closer conformity with the principles applied outside a PIDA context. In *Re A Company* [1989] Ch 477 the claimant employer carried on business in the supply of financial advice and financial management of clients' investment portfolios and was subject to the regulatory scheme imposed by FIMBRA, pursuant to the provisions of the Financial Services Act 1986. The defendant had been an employee of the claimant company in a fairly senior position. His duties had included those of being the company's compliance officer. FIMBRA was entitled at its discretion from time to time to make spot checks on companies subject to its regulatory umbrella for the purpose of ensuring compliance with its regulations. Scott J said that it would be expected that any details which came to the attention of FIMBRA in the discharge of its regulatory role would be kept confidential by FIMBRA.

14.92 Following the termination of his employment (but while a form of self-employed consultancy continued) a telephone conversation took place between the defendant and a senior executive of the company, the content of which was in dispute in the proceedings. The company said that the defendant sought to extract £10,000 under threat of reporting the claimant to FIMBRA for breaches of the FIMBRA regulations and to the Inland Revenue for tax irregularities. The defendant denied any such blackmail, saying that he had indicated that he intended to seek compensation for unfair dismissal and that £10,000 was the right amount for him to receive. He had then gone on to raise with the senior executive various misfeasances which represented, in his view, breaches of the FIMBRA regulations and tax improprieties.

14.93 The company obtained injunctions to restrain any disclosure to the authorities based upon the confidential information or confidential documents and for a search order to locate and remove all of the company's documents from the defendant's home. The question for Scott J was whether the injunction against disclosure should be continued given the defendant's expressed intention to communicate information to FIMBRA and to the Inland Revenue. The company argued that the injunction ought to be continued to trial subject only to an undertaking by the company itself to place before FIMBRA and the Inland Revenue respectively such documents as it might have relating to the specific matters identified by the defendant as being matters which he thought merited investigation.

14.94 Scott J did not think that this was the right approach. It was 'easy to agree' that details about the company's clients' personal affairs should be regarded as confidential information and should be so treated by all of the claimant's employees. If there were any question or threat of general disclosure by the defendant of confidential information concerning the way in which the company carried on its business or concerning any details of the affairs of any of its clients, there could be no answer to the claim for an injunction. However, intended disclosure was limited to FIMBRA, the regulatory authority, and, in relation to a particular case, to the Inland Revenue. Scott J continued:

> I ask myself whether an employee of a company carrying on the business of giving financial advice and of financial management to members of the public under the regulatory

umbrella provided by FIMBRA owes a duty of confidentiality that extends to barring disclosure of information to FIMBRA. It is part of the plaintiff's case, although not essential to its confidential information cause of action, that the defendant in communicating with FIMBRA will be motivated by malice. The defendant's professed intention is, in the plaintiff's view, associated with the blackmail attempt made by the defendant. At the present stage, and until cross-examination, I must accept that that may be true. It is not necessarily true. The defendant's explanation may be a genuine one. But the plaintiff's case may be true. It may be the case that the information proposed to be given, the allegations proposed to be made by the defendant to FIMBRA, and for that matter by the defendant to the Inland Revenue, are allegations made out of malice and based upon fiction or invention.

But if that is so, then I ask myself what harm will be done. FIMBRA may decide that the allegations are not worth investigating. In that case, no harm will have been done. Or FIMBRA may decide that an investigation is necessary. In that case, if the allegations turn out to be baseless, nothing will follow the investigation. And if harm is caused by the investigation itself, it is harm which is implicit in the regulatory role of FIMBRA. It may be that what is put before FIMBRA includes some confidential information. But that information would, as it seems to me, be information which FIMBRA could at any time obtain by the spot checks that it is entitled to carry out. I doubt whether an employee of a financial services company such as the plaintiff owes a duty of confidence which extends to an obligation not to disclose information to the regulatory authority FIMBRA.

14.95 Scott J considered that, so far as the Inland Revenue was concerned, the point was a narrower one as that authority was not concerned in any general way with the business of a financial services company, but with tax. If confidential details which did not relate to fiscal matters were disclosed to the Inland Revenue, that would be as much a breach of the duty of confidentiality as the disclosure of that information to any other third party. That said, it would be difficult to accept that disclosure would be a breach of such a duty if what was disclosed to the Inland Revenue related to fiscal matters which were the concern of the Inland Revenue.

14.96 Scott J then rejected a submission on behalf of the company that he could and should conduct some sort of preliminary investigation into the substance of the allegations proposed to be made by the defendant to FIMBRA and to the Inland Revenue respectively, for the purpose of deciding whether there was any case warranting investigation either by FIMBRA or by the Inland Revenue. The submission was based on what Lord Keith of Kinkel said in the *Spycatcher* case ([1990] 1 AC 109 at 262A):

As to just cause or excuse it is not sufficient to set up the defence merely to show that allegations of wrongdoing have been made. There must be at least a prima facie case that the allegations have substance.

14.97 Scott J said that Lord Keith's remark was made in the context of a disclosure which it was threatened would be made to the world at large, a disclosure which would have taken place in the national press. Where the disclosure which is threatened was no more than a disclosure to a recipient which had a duty to investigate matters within its remit, it was not for the court to investigate the substance of the proposed disclosure unless there was ground for supposing that the disclosure goes outside the remit of the intended recipient of the information. He continued:

... it is for FIMBRA, on receiving whatever information the defendant puts before it, to decide whether there is a matter for investigation. If there is not then I cannot see that any harm has been done to the plaintiff. If there is, then it is right for FIMBRA rather than the court to investigate. Similarly, it is not for the court but for the Inland Revenue, if information is placed before them by the defendant, to decide whether there is material that warrants investigation or explanation.

> . . . I think it would be contrary to the public interest for employees of financial services companies who thought that they ought to place before FIMBRA information of possible breaches of the regulatory system, or information about possible fiscal irregularities before the Inland Revenue, to be inhibited from so doing by the consequence that they might become involved in legal proceedings in which the court would conduct an investigation with them as defendants into the substance of the information they were minded to communicate.
>
> If it turns out that the defendant's allegations are groundless and that he is motivated by malice then, as it seems to me, he will be at serious risk of being found liable in damages for defamation or malicious falsehood. But that is for the future.

14.98   In the context of the application for prior restraint of disclosure to the prescribed person which was sought by the company against the defendant, there were therefore parallels with the approach of the protected disclosure provisions of the ERA. Scott J clearly thought that it was essential that the intended disclosure was to the correct regulator and that the intended disclosure to that regulator was limited to the information which was relevant to the failure which was or would be the concern of that particular regulator. Scott J was not prepared to investigate the issue of whether the defendant was acting in good faith (or whether the threatened disclosure was blackmail); this was irrelevant to the question of prior restraint and would be relevant only if the allegations turned out to be 'groundless', in which case the sanction would be that the defendant might be liable in damages for defamation or malicious falsehood. However (and here there is a departure from the approach dictated by the ERA's protected disclosure provisions), whilst the court would have entered into a factual enquiry as to whether the intended disclosure was to the appropriate regulator, Scott J was not prepared to enter upon such an enquiry with regard to whether there was a prima facie case of a relevant failure that should be disclosed to the appropriate regulator. There was, therefore, no threshold of reasonable belief that the information disclosed and any allegation contained it in be substantially true.

14.99   **Seriousness of wrongdoing**   Scott J did not expressly address the seriousness of the alleged irregularities as a factor to be brought into account as to whether disclosure to the regulator ought to be restrained. As we shall see, the seriousness of the failure or the harm involved will be an important factor in the assessment of whether disclosure to the wider public and the media should be permitted. But it has also been regarded as a factor in cases of disclosure to persons in the position of a 'regulator'. In *W v Edgell* [1990] Ch 359 (CA) the claimant suffered from paranoid schizophrenia and was detained in a secure hospital after killing five people. He applied to the mental health review tribunal and, to support his application, sought a report from the defendant who was an independent consultant psychiatrist. The defendant's report revealed that the claimant had a continuing interest in home-made bombs and expressed the opinion that the claimant was a continuing danger to the public. The claimant then withdrew his application and refused to consent to the defendant disclosing the report. Notwithstanding this, the defendant disclosed the report to the medical officer at the secure hospital and a copy was sent to the relevant Secretary of State. When the claimant's case was subsequently referred to a mental health review tribunal it became apparent that the report had been disclosed and the claimant applied for an injunction to restrain the defendant from communicating the contents of the report and requiring all copies to be delivered up. In refusing the injunction the Court of Appeal held that the public interest in confidentiality was outweighed by the public interest in protecting others against possible violence. The Court of Appeal emphasized the degree of danger to the public, as demonstrated by the nature of the crimes which the claimant had previously committed, and the fact that the disclosure had been made to the appropriate regulatory bodies, which needed to have all relevant information in relation to the claimant before considering his release from hospital.[51] Again, however, this involved taking into account a consideration, namely the seriousness of the wrongdoing, which is not part of the test for protection under ERA, section 43F.

(f) Third tier/wider disclosures

In relation to third tier/wider disclosures, ERA, section 43G in particular, and to a lesser extent section 43H, set out detailed criteria to be taken into account for there to be a protected disclosure. It is therefore in relation to disclosures within these categories that protected disclosure legislation provides the most significant assistance by way of a checklist of appropriate considerations to take into account.   **14.100**

Good faith and personal gain   Although good faith is no longer a liability stage test   **14.101** even for third tier disclosures, considerations pertaining to motive are retained by virtue of the requirement that the disclosure not be for personal gain (sections 43G(1)(c), 43H(1) (c)). Similarly, whilst good faith was not treated as significant in *Re A Company* (above) in relation to a second tier/regulatory disclosure, it tends to be of greater importance in relation to third tier disclosures. In *Schering Chemicals Ltd v Falkman Ltd* [1982] QB 1 (CA), it was alleged that confidential information had been used to make a film relating to the drug Primodos. The claimant company had withdrawn Primodos from the market after suspicions had arisen that it had caused abnormalities in newborn children. The Court of Appeal declined to discharge an injunction restraining the broadcast of the film. Shaw and Templeman LJJ appeared to consider it relevant that the motive of the person making the disclosure was financial, albeit there were other powerful reasons for granting the injunction quite apart from the motive of the discloser.

In *British Steel Corporation v Granada Television Ltd* [1981] AC 1096 Lord Fraser referred to   **14.102** weighing up the public interest for and against publication. He went on (at p 1202) to say that the informer's motives were in his opinion irrelevant. However, in *Francome v Mirror Group Ltd* [1984] 1 WLR 892 Lord Donaldson MR noted that it is almost unheard of for compliance with the moral imperative to make disclosure to (also) be in the financial interests of the person making the disclosure. Again, in *Initial Services* Lord Denning MR (at p 406G) suggested that differing considerations might apply depending on the motive for the disclosure. He commented that:

> I say nothing as to what the position would be if he disclosed it out of malice or spite or sold it to a newspaper for money or for reward. That indeed would be a different matter. It is a great evil when people purvey scandalous information for reward.

Even if there is a public interest defence in relation to confidentiality, if the disclosure is   **14.103** in bad faith the employee is likely to be in breach of the duty of fidelity and of the duty not without reasonable and proper cause to conduct him/herself in a manner calculated or likely to destroy or seriously damage the relationship of confidence and trust between the employee and employer.[52] Additionally, an employee who owes fiduciary duties would in general be required to account for secret profits made from his/her employment through acting other than bona fide in the best interests of the employer.

---

[51] See also *Woolgar v Chief Constable of the Sussex Police* [1999] 3 All ER 604, where an application to restrain disclosure by the police to the UK Central Council for Nursing, Midwifery and Health Visiting (the UKCC) of information given under caution failed and the court considered that the police were best placed to decide whether the information should be disclosed, but should first give notice to the person whose confidentiality was breached so that this could be challenged if appropriate.

[52] *Malik v BCCI SA* [1998] AC 20 (HL); *Byford v Film Finances Ltd* (EAT/804/86).

14.104 Similarly, there may be an obligation placed upon an employee to make restitution of any profits resulting from the disclosure if it is something which the employee had specifically contracted not to do. In *Woodward v Hutchins* [1977] 1 WLR 760 (CA), for example, although the Court of Appeal considered that publication by the press of material 'putting the record straight' as to the private lives of various pop stars should not be restrained, the conduct of the employee who leaked the story for reward was clearly regarded with distaste. As Lawton LJ put it (at p 75SF), 'persons like the first defendant cannot expect much in the way of admiration when they sell their employers' secrets for money'.

14.105 In any event, if the allegation proves to be false, the employee motivated by malice may also be liable in damages for defamation or malicious falsehood. The motive of the person responsible for the disclosure may also be taken into account when the court exercises its discretion as to costs.[53]

14.106 **Evidential basis** From the earliest cases, attention has been paid to the quality of the information upon which the disclosure is made or is proposed to be made. In *Gartside v Outram* (1856) 26 LJ Ch 113, it was said that it would not be sufficient for the employee to make the disclosure 'upon a mere roving suggestion'. In the *Spycatcher* case (above) Lord Keith referred to the need for there to be 'at least a prima facie case that the allegations have substance' (at p 787). This might be regarded as a broad equivalent to the statutory test in ERA, sections 43G and 43H that there must be a reasonable belief that the information disclosed and any allegation contained in it are substantially true, except that in contrast to the protected disclosure position, the test of substantiality is not here expressly tied to the belief of the person making the disclosure. In *Lion Laboratories Ltd v Evans* [1985] QB 526, Griffiths LJ emphasized that it was necessary at least that a fair reading of the documents disclosed to the press should cast doubt on the accuracy of the breathalyser equipment. Further, it was said to be necessary to evaluate the strength of the defence at the interlocutory stage since otherwise the defence of public interest could operate as a 'mole's charter' (at pp 550G–551A, G). The strength of the evidence required might also vary according to the importance of the public interest in preserving confidentiality in the particular case. In the context of the burden of proof required to remove the cloak of privilege on grounds of iniquity, for example, the balance of authority is that at least prima facie evidence that the allegation of fraud is well founded will be required before privilege is lifted.[54] The evidential burden will, however, vary according to the particular circumstances—including the public interest in confidentiality, the recipient of the disclosure, and the matters being disclosed. As Vinelott J explained in *Derby & Co Ltd v Weldon (No 7)* [1990] 1 WLR 1156 at 1173E—F:

> There is a continuous spectrum and it is impossible to, as it were, calibrate or express in any simple formula the strength of the case that the plaintiff must show in each of these categories. An order to disclose documents for which legal professional privilege is claimed lies at the extreme end of the spectrum.

14.107 The evidential burden was not a point expressly addressed in *Cream Holdings Ltd and others v Banerjee and another* [2004] UKHL 44, [2005] 1 AC 253 (see paragraph 14.50 above) save that (in the Court of Appeal) Sedley LJ noted that the proposed disclosure in that case was 'essentially true; otherwise the action would be in defamation'. In a case where the facts were disputed the court would presumably enter into *some* evaluation of the substantiality of the allegations, and the wider the disclosure and the greater the degree of confidentiality in issue, the higher the burden on the defendant to substantiate the allegations.

---

[53] See *Schering Chemicals Ltd v Falkman Ltd* (above para 14.101).
[54] See *Kuwait Airways Corpn v Iraqi Airways Co (No 6)* [2005] 1 WLR 2734 (CA).

Other responses inapplicable or exhausted   For the purposes of ERA, section 43G   **14.108**
one of the three gateway requirements in section 43(2) must be satisfied. One of these is
that the worker has previously made a disclosure of substantially the same information
to the employer or a prescribed person. The decision in *Cream v Banerjee* indicates that
similar considerations might also arise in relation to confidentiality. Sedley LJ placed
particular emphasis on the finding that Ms Banerjee had exhausted the responses that
could be given short of going to the press (albeit the detail had to be relegated to his
closed judgment).

Reasonableness of disclosure   Over and above these matters, ERA, section 43G contains   **14.109**
a general reasonableness test subject to the requirement to take into account specific considerations. The factors which must be taken into account are also liable to be material in
relation to a defence to confidentiality.

(g) The identity of the recipient to whom the disclosure is made

As noted above in the context of regulatory disclosures, the identity of the recipient is an   **14.110**
important consideration in the context of obligations of confidentiality.

(h) The seriousness of the relevant failure

This must be taken into account in relation to reasonableness under ERA, section 43G.   **14.111**
Further, if there is an exceptionally serious failure, section 43H applies. Clearly, the seriousness of the relevant failure will also be a highly important consideration in relation to
confidentiality and in some cases will be decisive. However, other factors might still need
to be taken into account. Thus, although the public interest in disclosing past or proposed
crimes will often be a determinative consideration, even in this context it has been recognized that other factors, such as the person to whom disclosure is made and any countervailing public interest in preserving confidentiality, need to be considered as well as the
nature of the crime.[55] Thus, even where a disclosure relates to serious criminal conduct,
there may, exceptionally, be a countervailing public interest which prevents confidentiality
being overridden. In *Bunn v BBC*[56] [1999] FSR 70, an application was made to restrain
the BBC from making reference in a television programme to an interview with the police
under caution by Mr Bunn, the former deputy managing director of Robert Maxwell
Group plc. The interview was said to show that Mr Bunn was engaged in a conspiracy to
defraud. The statement was also said to contain material which would enable the public
fairly to assess the workings and efficiency of the Serious Fraud Office (SFO) since it would
be relevant to whether the SFO had had sufficient material to proceed with the second
criminal trial relating to the fraud by Robert Maxwell and his companies. Lightman J held
that the statement made under caution was confidential in that it was only to be used for
the purposes of criminal proceedings. Although Lightman J refused the injunction on the
grounds that the information was already in the public domain and of delay, he held that
the public interest defence to the claim of breach of confidence would not have succeeded
because there was a countervailing public interest in an accused person being able to make

---

[55] See also *Initial Services Ltd v Putterill* [1968] 1 QB 396 at 405 (CA), where Lord Denning MR emphasized the overall qualification that disclosure must be justified in the public interest.

[56] Considered in *Mitchell v News Group Newspapers Ltd* [2014] EWHC 879 (QB) para 17, where
Tugendhat J noted (at para 17) that the courts have recognized that those who make statements to the
police, or give information as witnesses, may do so in circumstances where an equitable obligation of confidence is owed to them, and, where that is the case, then there are two competing public interests to be
balanced: on one hand the public interest of maintaining the confidentiality of those who make statements
to the police in the course of a criminal investigation, and on the other the public interest of ensuring that
as far as possible the courts try civil claims on the basis of all the relevant material and thus have the best
prospect of reaching a fair result.

full disclosure in a statement to the police without fear of that statement being used for extraneous purposes.

14.112　In *Cream v Banerjee*, Sedley LJ concluded that the principal matter which the *Echo* wanted to publish was 'incontestably a matter of serious public interest' and that the 'essential story' was one which, whatever its source, no court could properly suppress. However, as we have already noted, it appeared to be important to him that Ms Banerjee had exhausted other responses and Sedley LJ did not say that the matter was of 'exceptionally serious' public interest. Earlier cases such as *Initial Services* envisage that there may be a class of failure which requires disclosure to the public as a whole without reference to considerations of whether other routes of disclosure could or should have been followed already. If the protected disclosure provisions were to be a guide, this would indicate that the courts would have to be satisfied that the relevant failure is exceptionally serious, rather than merely serious, to allow general disclosure in a case where other routes have not been followed and would be applicable. However, whilst the seriousness of the matter is an important consideration, such a limitation would unduly restrict the weighing of the public interest in each case by reference to the test of proportionality, and run counter to Lord Nicholls' emphasis that the protected disclosure provisions are not intended to cut down the circumstances where the public interest may justify disclosure.

(i) Whether the relevant failure is continuing or is likely to occur in future

14.113　In *Schering Chemicals Ltd v Falkman Ltd* [1982] QB 1 (CA) one factor that clearly weighed with the court was that the drug which was the subject of the intended broadcast was no longer in production; there was thus no continuing risk of damage to the health of the user, whatever the risk might or might not have been when the drug was being used.

(j) Whether the disclosure is made in breach of a duty of confidentiality owed by the employer

14.114　Whether the disclosure is made in breach of a duty of confidentiality owed by the employer to any other person who is not mixed up in the wrongdoing is clearly relevant. In *Re A Company* [1989] 1 Ch 477 (albeit a second tier/regulatory case) Scott J said that details about the claimant's clients' personal affairs should be regarded as confidential information and should be so treated by all the claimant's employees: if there were any question or threat of general disclosure by the defendant of confidential information concerning any details of the affairs of any of its clients, there could be no answer to the claim for an injunction. However, the fact that third party confidences might be disclosed can only be a factor, not a bar. Many disclosures of relevant failures will involve at least some information being disclosed concerning third parties because they will be the 'victims' of the iniquity or the hazard. Of course, it will usually be possible for their identities to be protected even if the facts of their cases have to some extent to be revealed.

(k) Action which the employer or regulator might reasonably be expected to have taken

14.115　As noted above, the fact that disclosure on an internal or regulatory basis had apparently not succeeded in the *Cream v Banerjee* case was a key factor in Sedley LJ's view that the first instance decision should be reversed.

(l) Whether in making an internal disclosure the worker complied with an authorized procedure

14.116　We are not aware of any confidentiality case where a worker's compliance with a whistleblowing procedure has been a factor in a court's decision as to whether disclosure was in the public interest. However, its express inclusion in ERA, section 43G may be taken as indicative of its materiality to the overall assessment of whether the public interest is in favour of disclosure.

(m) The nature of the information

Whilst the protected disclosure provisions might be regarded as providing a checklist of **14.117** relevant considerations in relation to wider disclosure, it is clear that the checklist cannot be regarded as comprehensive. This follows from that fact that ERA, sections 43G and 43H themselves do not purport to identify all factors that might be relevant to the assessment of whether disclosure is reasonable. One factor which is omitted is the issue as to the degree of confidentiality or the nature of the privacy interest in relation to the information. This may, however, be an important consideration in assessing whether disclosure should be ordered in the public interest, and the need to consider this is in accordance with the requirement to apply proportionality.

(n) Privileged information

Where the information is not only confidential but is also subject to legal professional **14.118** privilege the public policy against disclosure is particularly strong. In this context the case law suggests that disclosure will only be justified in cases involving 'iniquity'. For these purposes, iniquity includes all forms of fraud and dishonesty but does not extend beyond dishonesty to include disreputable behaviour or a failure to maintain good ethical standards.[57] It is sufficient that the solicitor's advice is sought in furtherance of, or in relation to, the fraud or crime[58] or that the disclosure relates to evidence gathered by fraudulent or criminal conduct.[59] It is not necessary to show that the solicitor was aware of the iniquity. Even within the category of privileged communications, however, the court is required to weigh the public interest in confidentiality in the particular circumstances against the public interest in disclosing iniquity, having regard to the seriousness of the alleged iniquity and the circumstances in which the privilege is claimed.[60] The point also arises in relation to 'without prejudice privilege': it is only in the case of 'unambiguous impropriety' that disclosure to the court of communications covered by that privilege will be permitted, albeit that it may be easier to show unambiguous impropriety where the communication in issue was in the form of an improper threat as opposed to an admission of the truth.[61]

(o) The contractual/non-contractual dichotomy

An additional consideration might be the nature and source of the confidentiality obli- **14.119** gation. Confidential information may have differing degrees of importance and secrecy, ranging from trade secrets, which remain protected after the termination of employment, to lower levels of confidential information which are covered by implied confidentiality

---

[57] *Gamlen Chemical Co (UK) v Rochem (No 2)* (1980) 124 SJ 276 (CA), per Goff LJ; *Barclays Bank plc v Eustice* [1995] 1 WLR 1238 at 1248D, 1250D (CA), per Schiemann LJ; *Nationwide Building Society v Various Solicitors* [1999] PNLR 52, Blackburne J. But see *ISTIL Group and another v Zahoor and another* [2003] EWHC 165 (Ch), [2003] 2 All ER 252 (Lawrence Collins J) suggesting a wider power on public interest grounds to refuse injunctive relief to restrain use of privileged documents. The decision is criticized in Hollander, *Documentary Evidence*, 12th edn. London: Sweet & Maxwell, 2015, para 25-16.

[58] *Barclays Bank plc v Eustice* [1995] 1 WLR 1238 at 1251B–1252C, 1251E, per Schiemann LJ; *Nationwide Building Society v Various Solicitors* [1999] PNLR 52.

[59] *Dubai Aluminium Co v Al Alawi* [1999] 1 All ER 703 (Rix J).

[60] See *Derby v Weldon (No 7)* [1990] 1 WLR 1156 at 1173A–F, per Vinelott J; *Barclays Bank plc v Eustice* [1995] 1 WLR 1238 at 1249H–1250D, per Schiemann LJ where it was suggested that the cloak of privilege was less likely to be lifted where advice is sought as to something that has already been done and then for the purposes of imminent litigation, than where advice is sought in relation to prospective wrongdoing such as how to structure a fraudulent transaction. See also *Istil Group Inc and another v Zahoor and another* [2003] EWHC 165 (Ch), [2003] 2 All ER 252; and *Kuwait Airways Corporation v Iraqi Airways Corporation* [2005] EWCA Civ 286.

[61] *Savings & Investment Bank Ltd (In Liquidation) v Fincken* [2003] EWCA Civ 1630, [2004] 1 WLR 667, and *Ferster v Ferster* [2016] EWCA Civ 717.

obligations during employment. A related distinction may also be drawn between obligations arising under contract and other confidentiality obligations which impliedly arise from particular relationships.

14.120 This distinction was significant in *Campbell v Frisbee* [2002] EWCA Civ 1374, [2003] ICR 141. Ms Frisbee was employed by Naomi Campbell to provide management services under a weekly contract for services. Ms Frisbee supplied information to the *News of the World* which published an article about sexual encounters between Ms Campbell and Joseph Fiennes and the efforts made to keep secret the fact of these encounters—particularly from the man to whom Ms Campbell was engaged to be married. The newspaper paid Ms Frisbee £25,000 for the information. Ms Frisbee had orally agreed to keep confidential any information that she learnt about Ms Campbell in the course of her work and also had entered into a written confidentiality agreement in the form of a letter which included, in particular, that no information would be disseminated to the media without Ms Campbell's express written consent and that the confidentiality agreement would continue beyond the duration of the professional relationship between the parties. It was accepted by Ms Frisbee that it was an implied term of the confidentiality agreement that she would not divulge to the media or any third party any information, whether true or false, about Ms Campbell which Miss Frisbee claimed to have learnt in the course of working for Ms Campbell and also that, by reason of the relationship between them, Ms Frisbee owed to Ms Campbell a duty of confidence.

14.121 Ms Campbell claimed damages or an account of profits arising from breach of the confidentiality agreement and the duty of confidence. In her defence Ms Frisbee contended that there had been a course of unacceptable behaviour by Ms Campbell (including an alleged assault). This, she said, constituted a repudiation of her contract which she accepted, bringing their relationship to an end and thus discharging her from the confidentiality obligations. An alternative defence was that Ms Frisbee was entitled to disclose the information to the newspaper because it was in the public interest that this information should be published. Ms Campbell obtained summary judgment. Ms Frisbee appealed to Lightman J who dismissed her appeal ([2002] EWHC 328 (Ch), [2002] 2 EMLR 656) but his judgment was reversed by the Court of Appeal, which held that it was arguable that a duty of confidentiality expressly assumed under contract carried more weight, when balanced against the restriction to the right to freedom of expression, than a duty of confidentiality that was not buttressed by express agreement.[62] If that contractual obligation had been discharged by repudiation of the contract Ms Frisbee might have had a defence to the claim based upon the non-contractual claim, albeit the court appears to have been unenthusiastic about the possibility. These were considerations that do not arise under the express requirements in relation to protected disclosures, although they might be considered material as part of the overall test of reasonableness for wider disclosures.

(4) Conclusions in relation to the application of the PIDA provisions as a template

14.122 We have seen that considerations which are material to assessing whether there is a protected disclosure may also play an important role in relation to whether there is a public

---

[62] See also *London Regional Transport v The Mayor of London* [2001] EWCA Civ 1491, [2003] EMLR 88, referred to in *Campbell v Frisbee*, where the view was expressed that there was no distinction to be drawn between contractual and other duties of confidence; *Attorney-General v Parry and MGN Ltd* [2004] EMLR 223, where it was said to be well arguable that a contractual duty should be given greater weight, and *HRH Prince of Wales v Associated Newspapers Ltd* [2008] Ch 57 (CA) at para 69 where it was commented that 'the extent to which it a contract adds to the weight of duty of confidence arising out of a confidential relationship will depend upon the facts of the individual case'.

interest defence to confidentiality. It is clear, however, that the protected disclosure provisions are not being, and cannot be, applied simply as a 'pass or fail' test for protection. In particular:

(a) Such a test would be inconsistent with the central importance of proportionality in considering the balancing of the interests in confidentiality and disclosure. Within ERA, section 43G (wider disclosures) there is scope to give effect to proportionality in relation to the overarching reasonableness test. However, it is first necessary to satisfy a series of 'pass or fail' tests such as that the disclosure is not for personal gain.

(b) As emphasized by Lord Nicholls in *Cream v Banerjee* the issues which arise in relation to confidentiality are not the same as those arising in relation to whether the added protected disclosure protection should apply. The focus in relation to a protected disclosure is on whether the worker acted properly in making the disclosure. Thus, for example, reasonable belief for the purposes of a qualifying disclosure is judged from the worker's perspective on the basis of information available to the worker and his or her expertise: *Darnton v University of Surrey* [2003] IRLR 133, *Korashi v Abertawe Bro Morgannwg University Local Health Board* [2012] IRLR 4 at para 62. However, when the court considers whether disclosure is in the public interest for the purposes of deciding whether confidentiality is overridden, it need not (and should not) be confined to consideration of this from the worker's perspective.

(c) These differences are reflected in the wider public interest considerations which can justify disclosure or give rise to a defence and are not limited to the categories of relevant failures for the purposes of establishing a protected disclosure.

(d) In determining whether a disclosure is protected, the position is considered as at the time when the disclosure was made, albeit the truth of the allegations may be material in relation to whether there was a reasonable belief. Again, the court is not so confined when it comes to considering whether to restrain disclosure or whether disclosure would amount to a breach of confidence.

(e) In some cases it will not be possible to apply the protected disclosure provisions with any certainty in a confidentiality case because the person who made the disclosure will not be available to give evidence (and sometimes will not be identifiable). Thus, for example, where disclosure is made anonymously to a newspaper there may be no way, other than speculation, of testing whether any of the gateways in section 43G(2) ERA have been satisfied (eg earlier internal disclosure or fear of victimization or cover-up if the disclosure was made internally).

Whilst it does not give rise to a 'pass or fail' test, the protected disclosure legislation can, however, provide a helpful (though not necessarily exhaustive) checklist of important considerations to be taken into account, especially in relation to third tier/wider disclosures. **14.123**

D. Agreements Rendered Void

In one significant respect the ERA's protected disclosure provisions do modify contractual obligations, and this might be material in relation to obligations of confidentiality. Section 43J ERA provides an important mechanism for ensuring that those making protected disclosures cannot be silenced: **14.124**

(1) Any provision in an agreement to which this section applies is void in so far as it purports to preclude the worker from making a protected disclosure.

(2) This section applies to any agreement between a worker and his employer (whether a worker's contract or not), including any agreement to refrain from instituting or continuing proceedings under this Act or any proceedings for breach of contract.

14.125 As such, any clause or term in an agreement between a worker and his/her employer is void insofar as it purports to preclude the worker from making a protected disclosure as defined. The agreement may be in an employment contract, in a contract of a worker who is not an employee, or in any other agreement between a worker and employee. This section therefore outlaws 'gagging clauses', although only insofar as they apply to a protected disclosure.

14.126 Accordingly, insofar as it is established (or, in interim proceedings, likely to be established) that the making of a disclosure would be a protected disclosure, a contractual confidentiality obligation could not be a basis to restrain disclosure. Nor could there be a claim for contractual damages where the disclosure was a protected disclosure. Irrespective of the issue considered above (see paragraphs 14.119–14.121) as to the scope for non-contractual obligations to exist alongside contractual obligations, and whether they have less weight in the balancing exercise, it is difficult to conceive of circumstances where the court would restrain publication of information despite finding that a contractual restraint is void under ERA, section 43J.

14.127 It should also be noted that section 43J covers settlement agreements compromising tribunal proceedings. These very often contain confidentiality clauses as part-consideration for money paid in settlement. The employer might only be prepared to make a payment to an ex-employee if s/he can feel secure against the risk not only of further legal proceedings but also against his/her dirty linen being washed—or further washed—in front of an interested public. This may be of particular importance where the employer is concerned to prevent the employee contacting a prescribed regulator under section 43F. The provision would apply with equal strength and immediacy where a public body seeks to stop a worker contacting the sponsoring department under section 43E. However, confidentiality clauses in compromise agreements are in any event notoriously difficult to enforce, and even without section 43J it would have been difficult to obtain injunctive relief to prevent disclosure to a prescribed regulator or sponsoring department (see *Re A Company* [1989] 1 Ch 477).

14.128 In the event that an employee accepts a specific sum in return for not making a protected disclosure it is likely that (subject to a defence of change of position) the employer would be entitled to claim the return of that sum. Ordinarily, money paid under a void contract can be reclaimed by means of an action for money had and received.[63] In *Credit Suisse First Boston (Europe) Ltd v Padiachy* [1998] IRLR 504 in the context of a void term in relation to a transfer of undertaking, Longmore J said that he could see no answer to a claim for the return of the money paid in consideration for entering into a void restrictive covenant. The position is less straightforward if a sum is paid in part in return for a restriction on protected disclosures and in part for other obligations in the settlement agreement. That would give rise to the difficulty of establishing a total failure of consideration. In the context of ERA, section 203, in *Sutherland v Network Appliance Ltd* [2001] IRLR 12, the EAT held that the express words of section 203, which stipulates that 'any provision in an agreement . . . is void *in so far as it purports* . . . to exclude or limit the operation of any provision of this Act' (emphasis added) rendered void only those provisions within the agreement in question which infringed section 203. The rest of the agreement remained in existence and enforceable. However, the EAT expressly noted that this was not a case where the payor (who agreed and paid ostensibly for full and final settlement of all claims) asserted that it would be wrong that only some of those claims should turn out to be effectively compromised. It therefore did not address the issue which would arise if the employer did not wish the agreement to stand in the light of a confidentiality obligation being void in relation to protected disclosures by virtue of ERA, section 43J.

---

[63] *Guinness Mahon & Co Ltd v Kensington & Chelsea LBC* [1999] QB 215.

Finally in this discussion of section 43J we should note *Barton v Royal Borough of Greenwich* **14.129** (UKEAT 0041/14/0105, 1 May 2015), which indicates an important distinction between an agreement restricting making a protected disclosure (to which section 43J applies) and an instruction given by the employer but without any agreement (in which case section 43J would not apply). The claimant was, until his dismissal, employed by Greenwich as a tenancy relations officer and was also an elected shop steward as well as a health and safety representative. The claimant was contacted by a fellow employee who expressed concerns that his line manager had emailed a large number of documents to her home using the respondent's facilities. The fellow employee believed that these documents contained confidential or personal data about himself and that the line manager's personal email was not part of a secure system. The claimant then consulted the ICO website and telephoned the ICO advice line to clarify his understanding of the Data Protection Act. He followed this with an email to the ICO asking for general advice as to whether there was any urgent action that may be taken to retrieve and prevent further access to the material that he had been told had been sent to the home email address. The claimant also emailed his own managers suggesting that the colleague had provided information which appeared to show that 'hundreds of documents' had been sent to a home email address. This led to one of those managers, Mr O'Malley, saying to the claimant that he would be investigating all aspects of the issue and would take whatever actions were appropriate. He also told the claimant that, given that he was arranging for the matter to be investigated as soon as practicable, he was instructing the claimant not to contact the ICO or any other external body in relation to this issue without prior authorization from the claimant's line manager. The claimant did not comply with this instruction from Mr O'Malley and that led, eventually, to his dismissal. One of the points taken on the claimant's behalf in the ET and EAT was a challenge, by reference to section 43J ERA, to the legitimacy of the instruction. It was submitted that the instruction should be equated with an agreement that would be held to be void, in so far as it precluded the claimant from making a protected disclosure. The EAT gave the argument short shrift: what was in issue in this case was an instruction given by an employer rather than any provision in an agreement.[64] Section 43J was irrelevant.

E. Criminal Law

In this section we consider the principal criminal provision relating to 'confidentiality'[65] **14.130** under the Official Secrets Act 1989 ('OSA'). The provisions take on a particular significance in the context of the protected disclosure provisions by virtue of section 43B(3) ERA. This provides that if a person making the disclosure commits an offence in making it, then it is not a qualifying disclosure.

Under section 1(1) OSA a person who is or has been a member of the security and intelli- **14.131** gence services, or a person notified that s/he is subject to the provisions of this subsection, is guilty of an offence if without lawful authority s/he discloses *any* information, document, or other article relating to security or intelligence which is or has been in his/her possession by virtue of his/her position as a member of any of those services or in the course of his/her work while the notification is or was in force. 'Disclosing information relating to security or intelligence' includes making any statement which purports to be a disclosure of such information or is intended to be taken by those to whom it is addressed as being such a

---

[64] See para 69.
[65] For a consideration of other criminal provisions and a fuller treatment of the 1989 Act and the background to it, see Cripps (n 1 above) and Chapter 3.

disclosure. There is no requirement in section 1(1) that the disclosure be 'damaging' or be likely to cause damage. It is this provision which was directly in issue in *R v Shayler* which we consider below.

14.132 Under section 1(3) a person who is or has been a Crown servant or government contractor is guilty of an offence if, without lawful authority, s/he makes a *damaging disclosure* of any information, document, or other article relating to security or intelligence which is or has been in his/her possession by virtue of his/her position as such. A disclosure is damaging if it causes damage to the work of, or of any part of, the security and intelligence services; or if it is of information or a document or other article which is such that its unauthorized disclosure would be likely to cause such damage or which falls within a class or description of information, documents, or articles the unauthorized disclosure of which would be likely to have that effect.

14.133 Specific defences are provided by section 1(5): that the discloser proves that s/he did not know, and had no reasonable cause to believe, that the information, document, or article in question related to security or intelligence or, in the case of an offence under section 1(3), that the disclosure would be 'damaging'.

14.134 There are various provisions (referred to below) for members and former members of the security services to express concerns within the service and within the government and executive, and to seek permission to make wider disclosure of those concerns.

14.135 Section 2(1) of the 1989 Act provides that a person who is or has been a Crown servant or government contractor is guilty of an offence if without lawful authority he makes a damaging disclosure of any information, document, or other article relating to defence which is or has been in his possession by virtue of his position as such. By section 2(2) a disclosure is damaging if it damages the capability of, or of any part of, the armed forces of the Crown to carry out their tasks or leads to loss of life or injury to members of those forces or serious damage to the equipment or installations of those forces; or otherwise endangers the interests of the United Kingdom abroad, seriously obstructs the promotion or protection by the United Kingdom of those interests, or endangers the safety of British citizens abroad; or it is of information or of a document or article which is such that its unauthorized disclosure would be likely to have any of those effects. Subsection 3 of section 2 provides for a defence for a person charged with an offence under this section to prove that at the time of the alleged offence he did not know, and had no reasonable cause to believe, that the information, document, or article in question related to defence or that its disclosure would be damaging. Equivalent provisions are contained in section 3 in relation to damaging disclosures relating to international relations.[66]

14.136 In *R v Shayler* [2002] UKHL 11, [2003] 1 AC 247 the principal question for the House of Lords was whether, as a result of the coming into force of the HRA, there could be a defence to the offences under the OSA (but specifically section 1(1) of the OSA) that disclosure was necessary in the public interest to avert damage to life or limb or serious damage to property, or to expose serious and pervasive illegality or iniquity in the obtaining of warrants and surveillance of suspected persons, at common law. Moses J, and then the Court of Appeal, rejected this argument. The House of Lords ruled to similar effect holding that it was plain that the only defences were those expressed in the statute. Lord Bingham said (at para 20) that the sections left no room for doubt, and if they did, the 1988 White Paper,

---

[66] There are other provisions, not considered here, relating to crime and special investigation powers (s 4); information resulting from unauthorized disclosures or entrusted in confidence (s 5); and information entrusted in confidence to other states or international organizations (s 6).

was a legitimate aid to construction. It had expressly dealt with and rejected the idea of a public interest defence. That made the intention of Parliament clear beyond argument. The HRA did not alter this position. Article 10(1) of the European Convention, which contained the right to free expression, was subject to Article 10(2), which provides that freedom of expression could be restricted provided that restriction was prescribed by law and directed to one or more of the objectives specified in the article and shown by the state concerned to be necessary in a democratic society. 'Necessary' was not synonymous with 'indispensable'; nor did it have the flexibility of such expressions as 'admissible', 'ordinary', 'useful', 'reasonable', or 'desirable'.[67] Lord Bingham identified (at para 23) the questions to be considered:

(a) Did the interference with freedom of expression correspond to a pressing social need; was it proportionate to the legitimate aim pursued?
(b) Were the reasons given by the national authority to justify it relevant and sufficient under Article 10(2)?[68]

The OSA did restrict Shayler's right to free expression. But that restriction was directed to permissible objectives (ie national security, territorial integrity, public safety, and the prevention of disorder or crime). The questions were whether the restrictions were necessary, met a pressing social need, and were proportionate. **14.137**

Lord Bingham said that the acid test was whether, in all the circumstances, the interference with the individual's Convention right prescribed by national law was greater than was required to meet the legitimate object which the state sought to achieve. His Lordship noted that the ban on disclosure in the OSA was not absolute. A member or former member of the security and intelligence services had various means of recourse: **14.138**

(a) disclosure could be made to the staff counsellor, a high-ranking former civil servant, in respect of concerns relating to the work of the service which it had not been possible to allay through the ordinary processes of management–staff relations;
(b) concerns about the lawfulness of what the service had done or was doing could be disclosed to (among others) the Attorney-General, the Director of Public Prosecutions, or the Commissioner of Metropolitan Police, and these officers were subject to a clear duty, in the public interest, to uphold the law, investigate alleged infractions, and prosecute where offences appear to have been committed, irrespective of any party affiliation or service loyalty; and
(c) concerns about misbehaviour, irregularity, maladministration, waste of resources, or incompetence in the service could be disclosed to the Home Secretary, the Foreign Secretary, the Secretaries of State for Northern Ireland or Scotland, the Prime Minister, the Secretary to the Cabinet, or the Joint Intelligence Committee. Disclosure could also be made to the staff of the Comptroller and Auditor General, the National Audit Office, and the Parliamentary Commissioner for Administration.

A further safeguard was that a former member could seek authorization from his former superior or the head of the service to make a wider disclosure. Consideration of a request for authorization should never be a routine or mechanical process: it should be undertaken bearing in mind the importance attached to the right of free expression and the need for any restriction to be necessary, responsive to a pressing social need, and proportionate. If a request for permission was refused it could be the subject of an application for judicial review, and in any such application alleging violation of a Convention right the court will now conduct a much more rigorous and intrusive review than was once thought to be **14.139**

---

[67] Referring to *Handyside v United Kingdom* (1976) 1 EHRR 737 at para 48.
[68] *Sunday Times v United Kingdom* (1979) 2 EHRR 245 at para 62.

permissible,[69] with the application of the proportionality approach as opposed to the less intensive traditional approach.

14.140 Finally, section 9(1) of the OSA provides that the consent of the Attorney-General is required before any prosecution is instituted for an offence under (among other sections) sections 1(1) and 4(1) and (3). The Attorney-General would not give his consent to prosecution unless he judged prosecution to be in the public interest. He is unlikely to consent if the disclosure alleged is trivial or the information disclosed stale and notorious, or the facts are such as would not be thought by reasonable jurors or judges to merit the imposition of criminal sanctions. The consent of the Attorney-General is required as a safeguard against ill-judged, ill-founded, or improperly motivated or unnecessary prosecutions.

14.141 Whilst the tenor of Lord Hope's speech might be thought to have expressed a degree of misgiving with the absence of a general public interest defence within the OSA, he nevertheless agreed with Lord Bingham's conclusions, as did the rest of their Lordships. In effect, a member or former member of the security services has no right, even as a last resort and even in the face of the most serious iniquity, to make a general disclosure. There is, however, an extensive system of internal disclosure with the safeguard of judicial review to oversee its proper functioning.

14.142 *Shayler* only deals directly with offences under section 1(1) OSA in relation to security and intelligence. However, it seems clear that a similar approach would be applied to offences under the other sections—with one important caveat. As quoted by Lord Bingham in para 11 of his speech, having set out the reasons for rejecting the incorporation of a public interest defence the 1988 White Paper provided at para 61 as follows:

> So far as the criminal law relating to the protection of official information is concerned, therefore, the Government is of the mind that there should be no general public interest defence and that any argument as to the effect of disclosure on the public interest should take place within the context of the proposed damage tests where applicable.

We have referred to those provisions of the Act which do incorporate a 'damage test'. We are not aware of any further authority on the way in which the damage test would fall to be applied, but (as Lord Bingham pointed out at para 20) the White Paper is a legitimate aid to construction of those provisions.

14.143 In February 2017, the Law Commission published a consultation paper in relation to 'Protection of Official Data', including a review of the Official Secrets Acts. The Paper considered whether developments in ECtHR jurisprudence since *Shayler* (see Chapter 18) had affected the view that there is no requirement under Article 10 of the ECHR for a public interest defence to official secrets breaches, and concluded it had not. The Paper did not support the introduction of a public interest defence, as it was regarded as too uncertain and could open the floodgates; no information could be guaranteed to be safe and it would risk undermining trust between Ministers and Civil Servants. Instead it provisionally favoured a model involving the ability to raise concerns with an independent statutory commissioner who would be under a duty to investigate the allegation, and a statutory obligation on the relevant parties to assist. The paper also included a proposal to replace the Official Secrets Acts with a new Espionage Act, increasing the maximum sentence for offences that currently fall within the 1989 Act from 2 to 14 years, and consultation as to whether offences should cover disclosure of information relating to the economy in so far as it relates to the national interest.[70]

---

[69] Citing Lord Steyn in *R (Daly) v Secretary of State for the Home Department* [2001] 2 AC 532 at 546–48.
[70] The Law Commission Consultation Paper is available at http://www.lawcom.gov.uk/wp-content/uploads/2017/02/cp230_protection_of_official_data.pdf.

15

PROTECTION OF THE IDENTITY
OF INFORMANTS

A prospective whistleblower (in this context the expression 'informant' is more apposite) **15.01** may be deterred from making a disclosure if his/her identity will become apparent to the perpetrator of the wrongdoing or to someone associated with the perpetrator. There is a recognized public interest that there should be disclosures of wrongdoing and also in extending protection to informants. However, a balance has to be struck between the protection afforded to the informant and the rights of those who are the subject of the information disclosed.

A. Victimization

A whistleblower whose employer fails to take reasonable protective steps to prevent det- **15.02** rimental treatment by fellow employees or others by maintaining the confidentiality of the disclosure or otherwise may have a claim under ERA, section 47B against both their employer and/or the worker or agent responsible for detriment. There might also be a claim of unfair dismissal under section 103A if an employee leaves in circumstances amounting to constructive dismissal. We consider the ingredients which would need to be satisfied for such claims in Chapters 7 and 9. We also consider the ways in which these issues are approached through the use of whistleblowing procedures in Chapter 19.

B. Anonymity of Informants and the Fairness of Disciplinary and Dismissal Procedures

The difficulties which arise in relation to protecting the identity of an informant may be **15.03** particularly acute in the context of an employee making allegations against a colleague. Clearly, if the information received by the employer is from an anonymous and untraceable source then it will not be possible for the employer to disclose the identity of the informant. If, however, the informant gives evidence to the employer confidentially and wishes to remain anonymous to the alleged perpetrator, an employer risks a complaint by either the whistleblower or the perpetrator. In the context of disciplinary proceedings, the alleged perpetrator will need to have sufficient details of any allegation to be able to respond substantively and these details might of themselves reveal the identity of the whistleblower. Further, it may be argued that the employee who is being investigated cannot properly defend him or herself without knowing the identity of the accuser: they may want to try and demonstrate that the accuser has a malign motive.

15.04   Guidance has developed as to how a reasonable employer would be expected to proceed.[1] The starting point is *Linfood Cash and Carry Ltd v Thomson* [1989] IRLR 235. In that case the EAT (Wood J) set out guidance for employers in dealing with informant evidence against employees who are accused of misconduct (in that case theft) where the informants wish to remain anonymous:

1. The information given by the informant should be reduced into writing in one or more statements. Initially these statements should be taken without regard to the fact that in those cases where anonymity is to be preserved, it may subsequently prove to be necessary to omit or erase certain parts of the statements before submission to others—in order to prevent identification.[2]

2. In taking statements the following seem important:
   (a) date, time and place of each or any observation or incident;
   (b) the opportunity and ability to observe clearly and with accuracy;
   (c) the circumstantial evidence such as knowledge of a system or arrangement, or the reason for the presence of the informer and why certain small details are memorable;
   (d) whether the informant has suffered at the hands of the accused or has any other reason to fabricate, whether from personal grudge or any other reason or principle.

3. Further investigation can then take place either to confirm or undermine the information given. Corroboration is clearly desirable.

4. Tactful inquiries may well be thought suitable and advisable into the character and background of the informant or any other information which may tend to add or detract from the value of the information.

5. If the informant is prepared to attend a disciplinary hearing, no problem will arise, but if, as in the present case, the employer is satisfied that the fear is genuine then a decision will need to be made whether or not to continue with the disciplinary process.

6. If it is to continue, then it seems to us desirable that at each stage of those procedures the member of management responsible for that hearing should himself interview the informant and satisfy himself what weight is to be given to the information.

7. The written statement of the informant—if necessary with omissions to avoid identification—should be made available to the employee and his representatives.

8. If the employee or his representative raises any particular and relevant issue which should be put to the informant, then it may be desirable to adjourn for the chairman to make further inquiries of that informant.

9. Although it is always desirable for notes to be taken during disciplinary procedures, it seems to us to be particularly important that full and careful notes should be taken in these cases.

10. Although not peculiar to cases where informants have been the cause for the initiation of an investigation, it seems to us important that if evidence from an investigating officer is to be taken at a hearing it should, where possible, be prepared in a written form.

---

[1] Each case must be considered on its own particular facts however, and in *Sainsburys Supermarkets Ltd v Hitt* [2002] EWCA Civ 1588, [2003] IRLR 23 the Court of Appeal confirmed that the range of reasonable responses test (the need to apply the objective standards of the reasonable employer) apply to the investigation and procedure adopted as much as to the reasonableness of a decision to dismiss.

[2] In *Hussain v Elonex* [1999] IRLR 420, the Court of Appeal confirmed there is no general rule that an employee must be shown statements obtained regarding misconduct, but the emphasis was on whether they had received a full opportunity to respond to the allegations.

The *Linfood* guidance therefore envisaged that the information provided by the informant, **15.05** suitably edited to prevent his/her identity, should be supplied to the employee who is the subject of the allegations, and that management conducting a disciplinary hearing against the person subject to the allegations should themselves interview the informant. In some cases, however, this might be problematic. This was the situation considered by the EAT in *Ramsey v Walkers Snack Foods Ltd; Hamblet v Walkers Snack Foods Ltd* [2004] IRLR 754. The context was 'the necessity of obtaining information about dishonesty[3] in a factory in a close-knit community where the slightest whiff of cooperation with the management could have the most serious consequences'. The particular issues were:

(a) the unwillingness of informants to sign a statement unless it had been sufficiently edited so as to remove any risk of identifying the maker of the statement from its content; and
(b) the informants' unwillingness to be exposed to further questioning on their statements by managers within the investigatory and/or disciplinary process (other than the human resources officer who took the original statements) for risk of their identities being revealed with the resulting reprisals that they feared.

The EAT said that the employment tribunal had made 'the clearest of findings' that the **15.06** offer of anonymity given by the employer to the informants was not unreasonable in the circumstances of the case. The informants who had come forward had done so expressly on the basis that their identity would remain confidential. In those circumstances the tribunal found that the respondent genuinely and reasonably believed that no further information would be provided unless it was on an entirely confidential basis; and that was the offer made to the workforce. The tribunal found that the respondent genuinely and reasonably believed in the informant employees' expressions of fear. It was reasonable for that anonymity to be extended so that neither the decision-maker nor even the investigating officers were able to directly test that which the informants had to say, but had to rely substantially on the belief of the human resources officer that the informants were reliable and trustworthy. However, the employment tribunal heard evidence as to the approach of the human resources officer and the fact that she had explored the detail of their evidence with them. Also she knew the workforce well enough to cover the point made by Wood J in *Linfood* concerning the need to consider the character and background of the informants and whether there was likely to be any form of personal grudge in play.

The demands of anonymity meant that even in their original form the statements could not **15.07** contain the sort of detail that the *Linfood* guidelines suggested they should contain, but the tribunal had made the clearest of findings that the informants were not willing to put their name to paper unless there was sufficient editing.[4] In the circumstances the EAT upheld the

---

[3] In the form of theft from the production line.
[4] See also *Asda Stores Ltd v Thompson and others* [2002] IRLR 245 where the claimants applied to the employment tribunal for a disclosure order in respect of the witness statements taken from informants who had been promised anonymity. The employment tribunal granted the order but the EAT said that it was within the power of an employment tribunal to direct disclosure of documents in anonymized or redacted form, and the employment tribunal in that case should have made such a direction in order to conceal the identity of the witnesses and maintain the employer's promise of confidentiality to those who had made the statements. The case returned to the EAT on issues relating to the extent to which the employees' lawyers could participate in the redaction process: see [2004] IRLR 598. A promise of anonymity was again upheld in *Fairmile Kindergarten v MacDonald* (EAT/0069/05/RN, 20 January 2006) where the claimant was alleged to have struck a child. The child's parents were promised anonymity by the respondent's solicitor, who had compiled a report upon the basis of which the claimant had been dismissed. The employment judge ordered disclosure of the identities of the parents and their child. On the respondent's appeal (unfair dismissal and sex discrimination) the EAT (Lady Smith) held that it was not necessary for the claimant's claim that she knew those identities.

tribunal's finding that dismissals for theft were fair even though the statements given to the employees had been lacking in detail and the informants had not been questioned by management involved in the disciplinary process. The interest in encouraging the informants to come forward, and honouring the promise of anonymity, was found to be compelling.

15.08 In *Linfood* and *Ramsey* the essential elements of the alleged offence could be communicated to the accused without revealing the identity of the informant, albeit in *Ramsey* in particular the statements provided were lacking in detail. This was not the case in *Surrey County Council v Henderson* (EAT/0326/05, 23 November 2005), where fellow employees were said to have given information that the claimant had made threats of violence towards various parties. The claimant was not told the identity of persons who said that they had been threatened. His complaint of unfair dismissal was upheld by the employment tribunal but the EAT allowed the employer's appeal on the basis that the tribunal had applied the wrong test as to whether the dismissal was substantively fair. The question then arose as to whether the decision could be upheld on the basis that it was plainly and unarguably correct since, having not been given the basic details of the allegations, the employee had been given no opportunity to defend himself properly. The EAT said that it could see the force of those submissions. However, it noted that this was a new point since the previous cases relating to informants had not concerned a situation where it had not been possible to give the employee the basic details of the allegations due to the need to protect the informants. In those circumstances the EAT was not persuaded that such an outcome was so plain and obvious that it could affirm the decision of the tribunal, and the case was remitted.

15.09 In *A v B* [2010] IRLR 844 the EAT considered the position where the informant is a public authority, in that case the Police's Child Abuse Investigation Command (CAIC). The police gave information (verbally) to the employer (B) that the claimant (A) had visited child brothels in Cambodia. The allegations were then raised by B at a disciplinary hearing and notes of the meeting with the police officers were provided to A. A denied the allegations. The EAT confirmed that an employer is entitled 'to take the view that to continue to employ, in the position in question, a person who it had been officially notified was a child sex offender and a continuing risk to children, would—if he were subsequently exposed . . . — severely shake public confidence in it'. Underhill P stated that 'it sticks in the throat that an employee may lose his job, and perhaps in practice any chance of obtaining further employment, on the basis of allegations which he has had no opportunity to challenge in any court of law—or may indeed have successfully challenged'. An employer cannot simply take an uncritical view of the information received, and the EAT addressed the issue of what steps an employer must take. Given the seriousness of the allegation the employer should insist on a 'sufficient degree of formality and specificity' to the allegations. Nevertheless, should any employer receive official information it is 'subject to certain safeguards, [to] be entitled to treat that information as reliable'.

C. Forcing Disclosure of the Identity of Informants

(1) *Norwich Pharmacal*: general

15.10 In the cases discussed above the question for the tribunal was, in the end, whether the employer acted reasonably in dismissing the employee. An accused employee might also

---

The issue of whether or not the claimant had in fact struck the child was irrelevant; the issue was whether the respondent had acted on the basis of the information before it (the report of the solicitor) and whether it had done so reasonably. In these circumstances, the tribunal should have been slow to interfere with the promise of anonymity. The interests of justice did not require that it be breached.

have an interest in knowing the identity of his/her accuser in order to protect his/her reputation. An organization might have a legitimate interest in finding the source of a leak so that action can be taken against the employee who has been prepared to disclose confidential information before and may do so again.

The court's jurisdiction to force disclosure of the identity of an informant (and ancillary **15.11** information or documentation) takes its name from *Norwich Pharmacal Co v Commissioners of Customs and Excise* [1974] AC 133. The *Norwich Pharmacal* jurisdiction allows a claimant to seek disclosure from an 'involved' third party who had information enabling the claimant to identify a wrongdoer, so as to be in a position to bring an action against the wrongdoer where otherwise s/he would not be able to do so. In *Norwich Pharmacal* Lord Reid said:[5]

> if through no fault of his own a person gets mixed up in the tortious acts of others so as to facilitate their wrong-doing he may incur no personal liability but he comes under a duty to assist the person who has been wronged by giving him full information and disclosing the identity of the wrongdoers. I do not think that it matters whether he became so mixed up by voluntary action on his part or because it was his duty to do what he did. It may be that if this causes him expense the person seeking the information ought to reimburse him. But justice requires that he should co-operate in righting the wrong if he unwittingly facilitated its perpetration.

The required disclosure may take any appropriate form, not only by way of production of **15.12** documents, but also providing affidavits, answering interrogatories, or attending court to give oral evidence. The Civil Procedure Rules do not limit the powers of the court to order disclosure before proceedings have started or against a person who is not a party to proceedings.[6] Since *Norwich Pharmacal* the courts have extended the application of the basic principle:[7]

(a) It is not confined to circumstances where there has been tortious wrongdoing and is now also available where there has been contractual wrongdoing, where the disclosure is to enable the claimant to bring a claim against that third party: *P v T Ltd* [1997] 1 WLR 1309; *Carlton Film Distributors Ltd v VCI plc* [2003] FSR 47.

(b) It is not limited to cases where the identity of the wrongdoer is unknown: relief can be ordered where the identity of the claimant is known but where the claimant requires disclosure of crucial information in order to be able to bring its claim or where the claimant requires a missing piece of the jigsaw. This was used by victims of the phone hacking scandal: *Axa Equity & Law Life Assurance Society plc v National Westminster Bank* [1998] CLC 1177; *Aoot Kalmneft v Denton Wilde Sapte* [2002] 1 Lloyds Rep 417; *Various Claimants v News Group Newspapers* [2014] Ch 400; see also *Carlton Films*.

(c) Further, the third party from whom information is sought need not be an innocent third party—s/he may be a wrongdoer him/herself or have enabled the commission of the wrongdoing, perhaps by providing facilities to enable it to occur: *CHC Software Care v Hopkins and Wood* [1993] FSR 241; Hollander, *Documentary Evidence* (12th edn, London: Sweet & Maxwell, 2015, para 4-06). But the third party must be in some way involved in furtherance of the transaction identified as the relevant wrongdoing: *NML Capital Ltd v Chapman Freeborn Holdings Ltd* [2013] EWCA Civ 589.

(d) The relief is a flexible remedy capable of adaptation to new circumstances: *Ashworth Hospital Authority v MGN Ltd* [2002] UKHL 29, [2002] 1 WLR 2033 at 2049F (Lord Woolf).

---

[5] At p 175.
[6] Civil Procedure Rules ('CPR') 31.18.
[7] See Lightman J in *Mitsui & Co Ltd v Nexen Petroleum UK Ltd* [2005] EWHC 625 (Ch) at para 18.

(e) An application may need to balance rights to property against the Article 8 right to privacy: *Rugby Football Union v Consolidated Information Services Ltd (formerly Viagogo Ltd) (in liquidation)* [2012] UKSC 55, [2012] 1 WLR 3333.

15.13 The three conditions to be satisfied for the court to exercise the power to order are:

(a) a wrong must have been carried out, or arguably have been carried out, by an ultimate wrongdoer;

(b) there must be the need for an order to enable action to be brought against the ultimate wrongdoer; and

(c) the person against whom the order is sought must:

(i) be mixed up in and so have facilitated the wrongdoing; and

(ii) be able or likely to be able to provide the information necessary to enable the ultimate wrongdoer to be sued.[8]

15.14 If the three conditions are met there remains a discretion to be exercised. Lord Kerr in the *Rugby Football Union* case[9] identified the following:

17. The essential purpose of the remedy is to do justice. This involves the exercise of discretion by a careful and fair weighing of all relevant factors. Various factors have been identified in the authorities as relevant. These include:

(i) the strength of the possible cause of action contemplated by the applicant for the order: the *Norwich Pharmacal* case [1974] AC 133,199F–G, per Lord Cross of Chelsea, *Totalise plc v The Motley Fool Ltd* [2001] EMLR 750, para 27, per Owen J at first instance, *Clift v Clarke* [2011] EWHC 1164 (QB) at [14], [38], per Sharp J;

(ii) the strong public interest in allowing an applicant to vindicate his legal rights: the *British Steel* case [1981] AC 1096, 1175C–D, per Lord Wilberforce, the *Norwich Pharmacal* case [1974] AC 133, 182C–D, per Lord Morris of Borth-y-Gest, and p188E–F, per Viscount Dilhorne;

(iii) whether the making of the order will deter similar wrongdoing in the future: the *Ashworth* case [2002] 1 WLR 2033, para 66, per Lord Woolf CJ;

(iv) whether the information could be obtained from another source: the *Norwich Pharmacal* case [1974] AC 133, 199F–G, per Lord Cross, the *Totalise plc* case [2001] EMLR 750, para 27, *President of the State of Equatorial Guinea v Royal Bank of Scotland International* [2006] UKPC 7 at [16], per Lord Bingham of Cornhill;

(v) whether the respondent to the application knew or ought to have known that he was facilitating arguable wrongdoing: the *British Steel* case [1981] AC 1096, 1197A–B, per Lord Fraser, or was himself a joint tortfeasor, *X Ltd v Morgan-Grampian (Publishers) Ltd* [1991] 1 AC 1, 54, per Lord Lowry;

(vi) whether the order might reveal the names of innocent persons as well as wrongdoers, and if so whether such innocent persons will suffer any harm as a result: the *Norwich Pharmacal* case [1974] AC 133, 176B–C, per Lord Reid; *Alfred Crompton Amusement Machines Ltd v Customs and Excise Comrs (No 2)* [1974] AC 405, 434, per Lord Cross of Chelsea;

(vii) the degree of confidentiality of the information sought: the *Norwich Pharmacal* case [1974] AC 133, 190E–F, per Viscount Dilhorne;

---

[8] ibid at para 21.
[9] *Rugby Football Union v Consolidated Information Services Ltd (formerly Viagogo Ltd) (in liquidation)* [2012] UKSC 55, [2012] 1 WLR 3333.

(viii)   the privacy rights under Article 8 of the European Convention for the Protection of Human Rights and Fundamental Freedoms of the individuals whose identity is to be disclosed: the *Totalise plc* case [2001] EMLR 750, para 28;

(ix)   the rights and freedoms under the EU data protection regime of the individuals whose identity is to be disclosed: the *Totalise plc* case [zoo,] EMLR 750, at paras 18–21, per Owen J;

(x)   the public interest in maintaining the confidentiality of journalistic sources, as recognised in section 10 of the Contempt of Court Act 1981 and Article 10 of the European Convention for the Protection of Human Rights and Fundamental Freedoms: the *Ashworth* case [2002] 1 WLR 2033 para 2, per Lord Slynn of Hadley.[10]

The importance of full and frank disclosure, together with the need to establish a legitimate purpose when seeking a *Norwich Pharmacal* order, was underlined in *Orb ARL and others v Fiddler and another* [2016] EWHC 361 (Comm). The order concerned instructions given to a computer hacker to place child pornography onto a computer. An order that had been obtained was later discharged when it was established that there had been very serious failures when the order was obtained and a failure to comply with the duty to make full and frank disclosure of material facts had occurred. This was coupled with the finding that the evidence being sought was to discredit the party and obtain a 'litigation advantage' in relation to another action. The failure to state the actual intended use of the information was fatal and, given that that intended use was not one that engaged the policy justification for the order sought, it was discharged.   **15.15**

(2)   Protection of the identity of journalists' sources through section 10 of the Contempt of Court Act

Special protection is offered to the media against *Norwich Pharmacal* applications. Section 10 of the Contempt of Court Act 1981 (the 1981 Act) provides under the heading 'Sources of Information':   **15.16**

> No court may require a person to disclose, nor is any person guilty of contempt of court for refusing to disclose, the sources of information contained in a publication for which he is responsible, unless it be established to the satisfaction of the court that disclosure is necessary in the interests of justice or national security or for the prevention of disorder or crime.

Section 10 of the 1981 Act was enacted to reflect Article 10 of the European Convention on Human Rights (ECHR), which is set out in Chapter 14 (at paragraph 14.16), and decisions of the European Court of Human Rights (ECtHR) have continued to shape the approach to be taken. In particular, domestic decisions are now to be read in the light of the decisions of the ECtHR in *Goodwin v United Kingdom* (1996) 22 EHRR 123 and *Financial Times Ltd v United Kingdom* (2010) 50 EHRR 46.   **15.17**

In *Goodwin* the applicant, William Goodwin, was a journalist who had received a call from a source who had informed him of plans by a company (Tetra) to raise a £5 million loan and that the company had financial problems. The information derived from a draft of Tetra's confidential corporate plan, although Mr Goodwin's case was that he had no reason to believe this was the case when he was provided with the information. Tetra successfully obtained an injunction to prevent publication of any information derived from the corporate plan, supported by evidence that if the plan was to be made public it could result in a complete loss of confidence in the company on the part of its actual and potential creditors, customers, and suppliers. It also obtained an order for disclosure of Mr Goodwin's notes   **15.18**

---

[10]   See now also *The Financial Times v United Kingdom* [2010] EMLR 21 (paras 15.20–15.26 below).

from the telephone conversation, identifying his source, on the grounds that this was 'in the interests of justice' within the meaning of section 10 of the 1981 Act. Appeals to the Court of Appeal and House of Lords were rejected. It was emphasized (per Lord Bridge) that the threat of severe damage to the company could only be defused if the company could identify the source either as himself being the thief of the stolen copy of the plan or as a means to identification of the thief, and that the importance of protecting the thief was much diminished by the source's complicity in, at least, a gross breach of confidentiality. Lord Templeman added that Mr Goodwin should have recognized that the information was both confidential and damaging. Separately, Mr Goodwin was also ordered to pay a fine for contempt of court due to his failure to produce his notes.

15.19 The ECtHR concluded that there had been a violation of Article 10. The disclosure order and fine were prescribed by law (in the light of section10 of the 1981 Act) and pursued the legitimate aim of protecting Tetra's rights. But the interference with the Article 10 right did not meet the requirement in Article 10(2) that freedom of expression could only be subject to restrictions that are 'necessary in a democractic society'. The court emphasized that, given the importance for freedom of expression of protecting journalists' sources and the potential chilling effect of an order for disclosure, such an order could only be justified by an overriding requirement of public interest where there was a pressing social need, and it needed to be convincingly established. The national court had a margin of appreciation in assessing this, but it was circumscribed by the interest in ensuring and maintaining a free press; it had to be shown that the restriction was 'relevant and sufficient'. Here the purported need for the disclosure had to be seen in the context that there had already been an injunction restraining not only Mr Goodwin but also the publisher of the magazine concerned from publishing any information derived from the plan, which had the effect of substantially neutralizing the threat. The court acknowledged that this would not prevent the source directly alerting Tetra's customers and competitors to the information, and this could not be prevented without identifying the source. It also acknowledged that the company had a legitimate interest in unmasking a disloyal employee or collaborator in order terminate their association with the company. But the court added that it would not of itself be sufficient for a party seeking disclosure of a source to show merely that without disclosure it would be unable to exercise a legal right or avert a threatened wrong. Here the residual threat of further disclosure, and the interest in unmasking a disloyal employee were not, even considered cumulatively, sufficient to outweigh the public interest in the disclosure of the journalists' sources. There was therefore not a reasonable relationship of proportionality between the legitimate aim and the restriction on the Article 10 right.

15.20 The reasoning of the ECtHR therefore placed emphasis on the high threshold for requiring disclosure even in a case where it appeared there had been wrongdoing by the informant, and even without an additional element of the informant being a whistleblower in the sense of disclosing matters that would amount to a relevant failure for the purposes of section 43 ERA. The approach in *Goodwin* was followed in *Financial Times Ltd v United Kingdom* (2010) 50 EHRR 46, where the ECtHR again disagreed with the assessment of the UK court. Here an anonymous source (X) sent various newspapers and a news agency leaked documents concerning a possible takeover bid by Interbrew of a competitor in the brewing industry. The High Court had ordered delivery up of the leaked documents. That decision was upheld on appeal by the Court of Appeal, and the House of Lords refused permission to appeal, but the ECtHR found that the High Court's order had involved a violation of Article 10.

15.21 Since the newspapers themselves were not aware of the identity of the source, in this case the application was not aimed at directly disclosing the identity, but on provision of documents which it was hoped would assist in enabling the identification of the source. But the ECtHR made clear that there was no significance in this distinction. The same principles applied.

Again, the interference was prescribed by law and it pursued the legitimate aims of protect- **15.22** ing the rights of others and preventing the disclosure of information received in confidence. The court reiterated the principles set out in *Goodwin*, and highlighted that disclosure orders have a detrimental impact not only on the source in question, but on the newspaper against which the order is directed (whose reputation may be negatively affected in the eyes of potential sources) and on members of the public who have an interest in receiving informa- tion imparted through anonymous sources by the disclosure, and who are potential sources themselves. The ECtHR accepted that there may be no real damage to the public perception of the principle of non-disclosure of sources where it was overridden in circumstances where the source was clearly acting in bad faith with a harmful purpose and disclosed intentionally falsified information. But it added that courts should be slow to assume, in the absence of compelling evidence, that these factors were present in any particular case. Further, the con- duct of the source could never be decisive in determining whether a disclosure order ought to be made. It would merely be one, albeit important, factor to be taken into account in the balancing exercise required under Article 10(2).

The ECtHR proceeded to accept that there may be circumstances in which the source's **15.23** harmful purpose would in itself constitute a relevant and sufficient reason to make a disclo- sure order. But in the present case X's purpose could not be ascertained with the necessary degree of certainty. Pausing there, the same would generally also apply where disclosure was on a matter of public concern, since it would be difficult to establish that an unknown source had acted for nefarious reasons rather than for example to expose the issue of public concern. But nor did the ECtHR say that an order requiring disclosure of the source could only be justified if the source was shown to have acted for a nefarious purpose. There might be other countervailing considerations which would make the need to identify the source particularly pressing.

The ECtHR was also unimpressed by the suggestion that some of the documents had been **15.24** doctored. It had not been established with the required certainty that the documents sup- plied were not authentic. In any event inaccuracy of the information provided would only be one factor to take into account in the balance, as would steps taken by the journalists to verify the information.

Turning to the balancing exercise, the ECtHR noted that wherever an unauthorized leak **15.25** had occurred, a general risk of future unauthorized leaks would be present if the source of the leak remained undetected. Whereas in *Goodwin* the fact that an injunction against fur- ther disclosure had been obtained was relied upon as reducing the risk of further disclosure, here the fact that Interbrew did not seek an injunction was taken into account as a factor against ordering the disclosure sought. The court added that the aim of preventing further leaks would only justify an order for disclosure of the source in exceptional circumstances where no reasonable and less invasive alternative means of averting the risk posed were avail- able and where the risk threatened was sufficiently serious and defined to render the order necessary. The national court had accepted that there was no less invasive means since the company had retained Kroll (security and risk consultants) to assist in identifying X. But the ECtHR did not accept that view. It said it was based on inference only since the national court had not been given full details of the inquiries made by Kroll.

In all, taking into account the importance of the public interest in protecting journal- **15.26** ists' sources, the exceptional circumstances required for an order requiring journalists to reveal their source, the absence of sufficiently certain evidence as to X's purpose or that the documents were not authentic, the failure to seek injunctive relief, and the lack of convincing evidence of having pursued all less invasive means of identifying the source, the court concluded that Interbrew's interests in eliminating the threat of damage through future dissemination and obtaining damages for past breaches were not, even considered cumulatively, sufficient to outweigh the public interest in the protection of journalists' sources.

15.27 The approach in the ECtHR cases therefore indicates the exceptional and narrow circumstances in which an order would be made for revealing a journalist's sources even in the absence of the additional factor of the disclosure being on a matter of public concern such as would constitute a relevant failure within section 43C ERA. In both *Goodwin* and *Financial Times*, the interest in pursuing claims against the source was not sufficient to justify the order. However, the factors taken into account indicate a fact-sensitive balance of considerations is required, including having regard to the evidence of the purpose of the source (if it can be identified with sufficient certainty), the extent of harm caused, and the alternative less invasive measures to identify the source.

Whereas in *Goodwin* the interest in unmasking a disloyal employee was not sufficient to justify interference with the Article 10 right, it left open the possibility that, taking into account all the circumstances, including the nature of the information disclosed and any findings as to wrongdoing by the source, prospective harm arising from being unable to identify the employee could tip the balance in favour of ordering identification of the source. That was the conclusion reached by the Court of Appeal in *Camelot v Centaur Communications Ltd* [1998] IRLR 80 (CA). Taking into account the guidance in *Goodwin*, the Court of Appeal upheld an order of Maurice Kay J against a magazine ordering it to return documents which would lead to the identification of an employee of Camelot who had leaked confidential draft year-end accounts. Schiemann LJ (at paras 15–20) set out the following principles:[11]

(a) There is an important public interest in the press being able to protect the anonymity of its sources.

(b) The law does not, however, enable the press to protect that anonymity in all circumstances.

(c) When assessing whether an order forcing disclosure of the source should be made, a relevant but not conclusive factor is that an employer might wish to identify the employee so as to exclude him from future employment.

(d) Whether sufficiently strong reasons are shown in a particular case to outweigh the important public interest in the press being able to protect the anonymity of its sources will depend on the facts of the particular case.

(e) In making its judgment as to whether sufficiently strong reasons are shown in any particular case to outweigh the important public interest in protecting anonymity of press sources, the domestic court will give great weight to the judgments, in particular recent judgments, made by the European Court of Human Rights in cases where the facts are similar to the case before the domestic court.

15.28 The Court accepted that, whilst there was no continuing threat to Camelot by further disclosure of the draft accounts, there was unease and suspicion amongst the employees of the company which inhibited good working relationships. There was a risk that an employee who had proven untrustworthy in one regard might be untrustworthy in a different respect and reveal the name of, say, a public figure who had won a huge lottery prize. The decision in *Goodwin* was distinguished on this basis because there was a continuing threat of damage

---

[11] By reference to *X Ltd v Morgan Grampian (Publishers) Ltd* [1991] 1 AC 1 (HL); *Goodwin v United Kingdom* (1996) 22 EHRR 153 (ECHR).

of a type which did not feature significantly in *Goodwin* (and indeed the same could be said for the decision in *Financial Times*). Schiemann LJ emphasized that this was not a case of disclosing iniquity, nor was it a whistleblowing case (at para 23). He continued (at para 25) by saying that:

> there is a public interest in protecting sources. But it is relevant to ask, 'what is the public interest in protecting from disclosure persons in the position of the source in the present case?'. Is it in the public interest for people in his position to disclose this type of information? Embargoes on the disclosure of information for a temporary period are a common and useful feature of contemporary life. It does not seem to me that if people in the position of the present source experience the chilling effect referred to by the ECHR the public will be deprived of anything which it is valuable for the public to have.

15.29 The effect of disclosing the identity of one source who has leaked unimportant material might be to have a chilling effect on the willingness of other sources to disclose material which is important. However, 'the well-informed source is always going to have to take a view as to what is going to be the court's reaction to his disclosure in the circumstances of his case'.[12]

15.30 The decision in *Camelot* was followed by Neuberger J in *O'Mara Books Ltd v Express Newspapers plc* [1999] FSR 49 where stolen manuscripts of the book *Fergie—Her Secret Life* were found in the possession of two of the defendants and they were ordered to disclose their source. Again, an important element of the decision was that the source had not made a public interest disclosure. Neuberger J noted that whoever had stolen the manuscript had done so with a view to making a profit, and he noted that, given the content of the book, it was even harder than in *Camelot* to mount an argument that apparently unlawful disclosure was somehow in the public interest. Further, there was a likelihood that the source was an employee of either the publishers or their American printers. As in *Camelot* the existence of a dishonest employee was damaging to employer–employee relations and to relations between employees. There was also an obvious risk of the dishonest employee making further unlawful disclosures. As such, the only public interest against disclosure was the general public interest (underlying section 10 of the Contempt of Court Act) in encouraging freedom of expression, and, in the view of the court, the interests of justice were clearly in favour of disclosure.[13]

15.31 Neither *Camelot* nor *O'Mara* were concerned with the case of a whistleblower and the desirability of protecting a person who makes a disclosure in what they regard as the public interest. The issue did, however, arise in the later stages of the litigation culminating in the Court of Appeal's decision in *Mersey Care NHS Trust v Ackroyd (No 2)* [2008] EMLR 1 (CA), albeit in circumstances where although the source was found to have acted in what he or she believed to be the public interest, this belief was found to be misguided.

15.32 The litigation originated in the publication by the *Daily Mirror* of extracts from the 'PACIS' medical records of the Moors murderer, Ian Brady, who was being held at the hospital run by Ashworth (the hospital subsequently became the responsibility of Mersey Care NHS Trust). It was believed that the disclosure would have been by an employee, and the application was brought with a view to bringing disciplinary proceedings against, and dismissing, the employee. MGN declined to disclose its source. It was ordered by Rougier J to do so, and the order confirmed by the Court of Appeal[14] and subsequently the House of Lords,

---

[12] Schiemann LJ in *Camelot* at p 138.
[13] See also *John Reid Enterprises Ltd v Pell* [1999] EMLR 675 (Carnwarth J).
[14] [2001] 1 WLR 515 (CA).

in *Ashworth Hospital Authority v MGN Ltd* [2002] UHKL 29, [2002] 1 WLR 2033. Lord Woolf CJ (giving the leading speech) reiterated that, in accordance with *Goodwin*, both section 10 of the 1981 Act and Article 10 of the ECHR required that disclosure could only be ordered where it was necessary to meet a legitimate aim, was not disproportionate and met a 'pressing social need'. But here there were exceptional circumstances which justified the order, given the nature of the leak which involved confidential medical records from a high-security hospital, and the likelihood that the source was an employee of the authority. There was evidence that if staff felt that there was a possibility of what they reported entering the public domain, their reporting would be inhibited due to a concern as to putting patients and staff at risk. Further, whilst confidentiality of medical records would always be important, that was particularly so in relation to the class of patients being cared for at the hospital. As such there were strong countervailing concerns balancing the interest in protection of journalistic sources of a kind which were considerably more compelling than those considered in *Goodwin* and *Financial Times*.

15.33   When MGN provided the disclosure it transpired that Mr Ackroyd, an investigative journalist, was the *Mirror's* source. Ackroyd was in turn made the subject of an application for an order that he disclose *his* source(s), admitted to be 'at Ashworth', whose identity Ackroyd had promised not to disclose. Summary judgment on that application was overturned on appeal (in *Mersey Care Trust v Ackroyd (No 1)* [2003] EMLR 36), on the basis that there were potentially importance differences compared to the action against MGN which required consideration at trial. May LJ (at para 65) stated that he was prepared to assume, without deciding, that, if there were no wrongdoing by the source, because the source had a public interest defence to a claim against him by the hospital, then the *Norwich Pharmacal* jurisdiction would not be established for want of a wrongdoer. However, the Court of Appeal did not consider this issue further because it considered that the appeal succeeded on grounds that were available to Mr Ackroyd even if the source were a wrongdoer.

15.34   At the trial Tugendhat J accepted the principle suggested by the dicta of Lord Woolf and May LJ as to the need to establish wrongdoing by the source (*Mersey Care NHS Trust v Ackroyd (No. 2)* [2006] EMLR 12). Consistently with the approach in *Financial Times*, he further concluded that in a claim just for a disclosure order, the burden of proving that there was wrongdoing by the informant fell on the trust (the party seeking the order) even though in a claim against the informant the burden would probably have been upon the informer to establish a public interest defence. However, even allowing for that, there were evidential difficulties in ascertaining whether disclosure was in the public interest arising from the fact that the source's evidence was not before the court. As the judge noted (at para 70):

> the court may gain little assistance from the interpretation or use that the journalist or a subsequent publisher places on the information disclosed. The manner in which the story is reported, if it is reported, may or not be what the source intended. Journalists and publishers are not the puppets of their sources. They may not know, or may fail to understand, the source's purpose, and they may have purposes of their own which are different.

15.35   The court emphasized that the test of whether the source had a public interest defence for having disclosed medical records was an objective one. It was not enough that the source might have intended to act in what s/he thought was the public interest. Tugendhat J concluded that there was no such public interest defence available in relation to the disclosure of the medical records, having regard to the nature of the information disclosed and the failure to explain why there were no other persons in the NHS or the police to whom the disclosures could be made, or that internal or limited disclosure had been made and had not had the appropriate effect.

Whilst that approach might be viewed as in tension with the emphasis in *Financial Times* on **15.36** the importance of establishing any nefarious purpose with sufficient certainty, the conclusion that there had been wrongdoing by the source only meant that a threshold requirement for seeking the relief had been met. It did not determine the issue as to whether to do so was an appropriate exercise of discretion. In relation to this a relevant factor was that, although the public interest defence was not made out, the source had received no payment in return for the disclosure. Further, Tugendhat J accepted that the source's most probable purpose was to provide support for Brady's allegations of mistreatment (and indeed the hospital had subsequently accepted that Brady had been mistreated). Indeed, the judge concluded that Brady had probably encouraged or authorized the leak. As such, whilst there was a breach of duty to the hospital in the disloyal disclosure of the records, the facts did not indicate that there had been any breach of duty owed to Brady. These were factors against the order sought, as, whilst the wrongdoing of the source was regarded as serious, it was not as serious as it might have been.

Against this were to be weighed the interests in removing from innocent employees the **15.37** cloud of suspicion and the need to take disciplinary action against any employee responsible and to avoid the risk of a further disclosure. But the evidence was that there were very many people (not limited to 200 as had been thought earlier in the litigation) that could have been responsible. As such, taking this together with the passage of time (six years later), the issue as to a cloud of suspicion had less weight as any suspicion was so thinly spread. The risk of further disclosure was also affected by the finding that the source had probably acted out of a 'misguided attempt to act in the public interest', as, given how events had moved on since the events surrounding the alleged mistreatment of Brady, there was less likely to be a repeat.

In all, Tugendhat J concluded (and was upheld by the Court of Appeal) that it had not been established that there was a pressing social need for disclosure, given the vital public interest in the protection of a journalist's source. In other words, taking into account amongst other things that the source had acted in what he or she regarded as the public interest, the balance that had gone in favour of disclosure in the *Camelot* and *O'Mara* cases went the other way in the circumstances of *Mersey Care Trust*.

(3) *Norwich Pharmacal* and employers

Section 10 of the 1981 Act specifically concerns the position where there is a publication, **15.38** and as such is principally directed at requiring journalists to disclose their sources, and the particular emphasis on this as an important element of freedom of expression in a democratic society. Some different considerations therefore arise where the issue concerns information that has been provided to the employer. On the one hand, particularly where the information comes from a colleague, there is a heightened likelihood that the information amounts to a protected disclosure due to the lower threshold under section 43C ERA and as such a heightened public interest in maintaining confidentiality. As against that, adverse information provided to the employer may be particularly harmful to employees who are the subject of the allegation, and it may be relevant to have information as to the source in order to be able to provide a full answer.

Scott V-C dealt with a *Norwich Pharmacal* application in *P v T Ltd*[15] [1997] IRLR 405 **15.39** where P, a senior employee, was notified that his employer had received serious allegations about him from a third party. He was not told what the allegations were or by whom they

---

[15] Also reported as *A v Company B Ltd*.

were made other than that they related to gross misconduct in the way he had conducted himself with external contractors. The employer stated that it would not disclose more as to the nature of the allegations since this would disclose the identity of the informant and the employer considered that the informant's request for anonymity was reasonable. P was dismissed for gross misconduct. In subsequent proceedings the employer admitted unfair and wrongful dismissal but P also sought an order against the employer compelling it to disclose the precise nature of the allegations against him and the identity of the informant. Scott V-C made the order notwithstanding that no wrongdoing by the informant had yet been made out. There were potential claims of defamation (which would depend upon the information being false) and malicious falsehood (which would depend on the information being given maliciously). P could not establish that these claims could be made out unless the order was granted. Justice demanded that the order be made in order to give P a chance to clear his name.

15.40   Whilst the informant in *P v T Ltd* was an outside source, the same considerations would have been relevant if it had been another employee. However, there would then be the additional complication that by revealing the identity of the employee, the employer might be said to be subjecting the employee, who may have made a protected disclosure, to a detriment. That issue arose in *Shinwari v Vue Entertainment Ltd* (UKEAT/0394/14/BA, 12 March 2015), the facts of which are set out in Chapter 7 at paragraph 7.110. In summary, Mr Shinwari had made disclosures alleging bribery by an employee. His statement, revealing his identity, was then provided to the colleague for the purposes of disciplinary proceedings against the colleague. Mr Shinwari complained that the failure to keep his identity confidential amounted to a detriment on the grounds of a protected disclosure. But the EAT accepted that the employment tribunal had been entitled to find that the reason for disclosing his statement was to comply with the employer's long-standing and well-established disciplinary policy and practice that the witness statement relied upon to support the allegation of misconduct be disclosed to the employee facing the allegations, and that this was something separable from the disclosure itself.

15.41   Whilst that was a conclusion found to be available to the employer on the facts of that case, we suggest that it may need to be treated with some caution. It could also be said that the reason for revealing that a whistleblower had made the disclosure was indeed by reason of the very fact of making that disclosure. Equally, where there has been an assurance of confidentiality, or where the evidence could plausibly be provided without identifying the accuser, in accordance with the guidance in *Linfood*, tribunals may be expected to be less sympathetic to a distinction drawn between acting by reason of the protected disclosure, and acting for some other reason such as to comply with the disciplinary policy.

15.42   Whilst in *P v T Ltd* the court was willing to make a disclosure order, that is to be viewed in the context of the serious consequences, and unfairness, to the employee of withholding the information. Scott V-C clearly considered the situation to be extreme, and indeed said that the conduct of the employer in *P v T Ltd* was outrageous. The decision may be compared to that in *Noordeen v Hill and Health Research Authority* [2012] EWHC 2847. Here a consultant surgeon at the Royal National Orthopaedic Hospital applied for a *Norwich Pharmacal* order to identify the names of clinicians whom he believed had spoken to the chair of a research ethics committee, and had made adverse comments about his research study. He wished to identify the clinicians so as to bring defamation proceedings. Males J refused the order on the ground that there was no reasonable basis for concluding that an action in defamation would succeed, given the defence of qualified privilege and because it was time barred. But he held that he would in any event have refused relief in his discretion. In relation to this he held that similar principles applied to those in relation to journalist sources (where section 10 of the 1981 Act applied). As such, disclosure should only be ordered if there was a pressing social need. Aside from the issue of the strength of the case of wrongdoing by the third party, Males J (at para 53) placed emphasis on the risk of a chilling effect if it was necessary to reveal the identities; it would discourage people from volunteering to serve in the research ethics committee if they thought they would be drawn into legal proceedings simply became people raised concerns with them.[16] Further (at para 54) the public had an interest in such concerns being expressed to appropriate persons so that if necessary they could be properly investigated.[17]

---

[16] As to the particular importance attached under Article 10 to protecting free expression on matters of public concern, see eg *Thorgeirson v Iceland* (1992) 14 EHRR 843 (ECtHR), and the decisions considered in Chapter 18.

[17] See further, in relation to the issues addressed in this Chapter, the report on research led by researchers at the Information Law and Policy Centre at the Institute of Advanced Legal Studies on 'Protecting Sources and Whistleblowers in a Digital Age', published in February 2017 (available online at http://infolawcentre.blogs.sas.ac.uk/files/2017/02/Sources-Report_webversion_22_2_17.pdf). The report concludes that UK governmental action, notably the Investigatory Powers Act 2016, and the Digital Powers Bill, have or threaten to substantially weaken protection for sources, and that technological protection for sources has not kept pace with the ability of states and others to use technology to intercept or monitor communications. One of the (ten) recommendations is that there should be research on examining the merits of extending public interest defences for whistleblowers, which would extend beyond employment-related provisions.

16

WHISTLEBLOWING AND COPYRIGHT

16.01 A potential whistleblower who is considering speaking out will often be concerned to be able to provide evidence in support of his/her allegations. The employee may, for example, wish to make copies of research gathered in the course of employment if that research demonstrates a health and safety concern. Alternatively, the employee may wish to make and disclose copies of internal memoranda which evidence impropriety. In these circumstances, especially if there is a risk that s/he will be acting outside the protection of the protected disclosure legislation, the potential whistleblower may have to consider not only whether there is a risk of a claim of breach of confidence, but also a risk of a breach of copyright.[1]

A. Infringement

16.02 Copyright will be infringed where there is unlicensed use of a work, for example by copying or reproducing all or a substantial part of the work or by communicating the work to the public. Most documents (being original literary works) and photographs (artistic works) will be included as works within the meaning of the Copyright Designs and Patents Act 1988 (CDPA).[2] Ordinarily the author of a work will be the first owner of the copyright in that work.[3] However, where the work is made by an employee in the course of his/her employment, the employer will be the first owner of the copyright, subject to any agreement to the contrary.[4] In ascertaining whether work was carried out in the course of employment or in the course of duties, the court will have regard to whether the skill, effort, and judgement expended by the employee or officer in creating the work fell within the scope of

---

[1] In addition to general provisions relating to infringement of copyright, specific obligations apply in relation to data within the meaning of the Data Protection Act 1998 (DPA). Under s 55 it is an offence for a person knowingly or recklessly to obtain or disclose personal data (or the information contained in such data), or to procure the disclosure to another person of that information, without the consent of the data controller. However, it is a defence to show that the action was necessary for the purpose of preventing or detecting a crime or that disclosure was justified in the public interest.

[2] CDPA, ss 1 and 4.

[3] ibid, s 11.

[4] ibid, s 11(2).

the normal express or implied duties of the employee or officer or within any special duties assigned to him/her. The employer will not have copyright in the work merely because it was created in working hours and might be a useful accessory to the contracted work.[5] In addition, even where an employee creates a work other than in the course of his/her employment, the employer may be the owner of that work in equity if the work is created in breach of the employee's fiduciary duty to the employer.[6]

B. Defence of Fair Dealing

So far as the whistleblower is concerned, the most relevant defences are the public interest and the fair dealing defences. As to the fair dealing defence, the most relevant provisions are contained in CDPA, section 30, which has been amended by the Copyright and Related Rights Regulations 2003 (SI 2003/2498) and, with effect from 1 October 2014, by the Copyright and Rights in Performances (Quotation and Parody) Regulations 2014/2356 which added provisions in relation to use of quotations. Section 30 provides (with the amendments shown by the words in square brackets): **16.03**

(1) Fair dealing with a work for the purpose of criticism or review, of that or another work or performance of a work, does not infringe any copyright in the work provided that it is accompanied by a sufficient acknowledgment, [(unless this would be impossible for reasons of practicality or otherwise)[7]] [and provided that the work has been made available to the public[8]].

[(1ZA) Copyright in a work is not infringed by the use of a quotation from the work (whether for criticism or review or otherwise) provided that—
(a) the work has been made available to the public,
(b) the use of the quotation is fair dealing with the work,
(c) the extent of the quotation is no more than is required by the specific purpose for which it is used, and
(d) the quotation is accompanied by a sufficient acknowledgement (unless this would be impossible for reasons of practicality or otherwise).[9]]

[(1A) For the purposes of subsection (1) [and (1ZA)] a work has been made available to the public if it has been made available by any means, including:
(a) the issue of copies to the public;
(b) making the work available by means of an electronic retrieval system;
(c) the rental or lending of copies to the public;
(d) the performance, exhibition, playing or showing of the work in public;
(e) the communication to the public of the work,
but in determining generally for the purposes of [those subsections[10]] whether a work has been made available to the public no account shall be taken of any unauthorised act[11]].

(2) Fair dealing with a work (other than a photograph) for the purpose of reporting current events does not infringe any copyright in the work provided that (subject to subsection (3)) it is accompanied by a sufficient acknowledgment.

---

[5] *Stephenson Jordan & Harrison Ltd v MacDonald* [1952] RPC 10; *Noah v Shuba* [1991] FSR 14.
[6] *Service Corporation International plc v Channel Four Television Corporation* [1999] EMLR 83 at 91. See also *Nottingham University v Fishel* [2001] RPC 367.
[7] Inserted by SI 2014/2356, reg 3(3).
[8] Inserted by SI 2003/2498, reg 10(1)(a).
[9] Inserted by SI 2014/2356, reg 3(4).
[10] Inserted by SI 2014/2356, reg 3(5)(b).
[11] Inserted by SI 2003/2498, reg 10(1)(b).

(3) No acknowledgment is required in connection with the reporting of current events by means of a sound recording, film, [or broadcast where this would be impossible for reasons of practicality or otherwise[12]].

[(4) To the extent that a term of a contract purports to prevent or restrict the doing of any act which, by virtue of subsection (1ZA), would not infringe copyright, that term is unenforceable.[13]]

(1) 'Purpose'

16.04 The application of the fair dealing defence therefore depends on whether the purpose is criticism or review of that work or another work or performance of a work or reporting current events. In *Pro Sieben Media AG v Carlton UK Television Ltd* [1999] 1 WLR 605 (at 614A–D) the Court of Appeal explained that the subjective mental element is not of importance in ascertaining the 'purpose'. It is not sufficient that the person seeking to rely upon the defence of fair dealing subjectively intended the work to be for the purpose of criticism or review or for reporting current events, or sincerely believed that this was the effect of the work. Whether that is the purpose of the work is to be determined objectively, although the motive of the infringer of the copyright might be relevant in ascertaining whether there has been fair dealing.[14] The words 'in the context of' or 'as part of an exercise in' could be substituted for the phrase 'for the purpose of' without any significant alteration of meaning. The Court of Appeal concluded that the judge at first instance (see below) had wrongly decided that the use of copyright material was not for the purpose of criticism and review because he had focused too much on the purposes, intentions, and motives of those involved in the planning and production of the programme, and too little on the likely impact on the audience.

(2) Criticism or review of that or another work made available to the public

16.05 The fair dealing defence in CDPA, section 30(1) enables the potential whistleblower to use a copyright work only for the purpose of criticizing or review of that work or another work. The criticism can be strongly expressed, and even unbalanced, without forfeiting the fair dealing defence. Any remedy for malicious or unjustified criticism rests in an action for defamation, although the work must be genuinely concerned with criticism or review rather than an attempt to dress up an infringement in the guise of criticism or review.[15] Criticism of a work need not be limited to criticism of style. It can extend to criticism of the thoughts or ideas to be found in the work and its social or moral implications.[16] Ideas or philosophy underlying a certain style of, for example, journalism, as manifested in the works themselves, could be the subject of criticism which falls within section 30; there is no requirement that the criticism and review contained specific reference to the work in question.[17]

16.06 In *Pro Sieben Media AG v Carlton UK Television Ltd* [1998] FSR 43 Laddie J, at first instance, emphasized that it was not sufficient to use the copyright work for the purpose of criticizing something other than the work or another work. Laddie J explained that criticism of the work

---

[12] Inserted by SI 2003/2498 reg 10(1)(c).

[13] Inserted by SI 2014/2356, reg 3(6).

[14] See *England and Wales Cricket Board Ltd and Sky UK Ltd v Tixdaq Ltd and another* ([2016] EWHC 575 per Arnold J at para 75, confirming that this approach still applies following the implementation of the Information Society Directive 2001/29/EC, 22 May 2001 (on the harmonization of certain aspects of copyright and related rights in the information society).

[15] Per Robert Walker LJ in *Pro Sieben Media AG* (CA) at 613D; *Time Warner v Channel Four* [1994] EMLR 1 at 14, per Henry LJ.

[16] *Hubbard v Vosper* [1972] 2 QB 84 at 94F, per Lord Denning; at 98D, per Megaw LJ; *Time Warner v Channel Four TV* [1994] EMLR 1 at 15, per Henry LJ; *Pro Sieben Media AG* (CA) at pp 614H–615B.

[17] *Fraser-Woodward Ltd v (1) British Broadcasting Corporation (2) Brighter Pictures Ltd* [2005] FSR 36.

or another work need not be the only purpose and could be used as a springboard to attack something else. However, criticism of the work or another work must be a significant purpose. In *Pro Sieben* the defendant, as part of a series of programmes on chequebook journalism, made a programme including the case of Mandy Allwood who had become pregnant with eight children after undergoing fertility treatment. As part of the programme, the defendants used footage from a programme made by the claimant about Ms Allwood's case. Laddie J concluded that the use of the copyright footage by the defendant was for the purpose of criticism of the decision to pay for an interview rather than for the purpose of criticism of the claimant's programme. As such, he concluded that it was not a criticism or review of that work or another work as required by section 30(1). The Court of Appeal did not take issue with Laddie J's analysis that the criticism must be of the work or another work. However, it concluded that, on the facts, the use of the copyright footage was for the purpose of criticism or review of the claimant's report, and of other newspaper material, as the fruit of chequebook journalism. This was in turn used as an illustration of the theme that chequebook journalism is inimical to the truth.

16.07 In many cases this approach will be wide enough to provide protection to the whistleblower. In a case where a whistleblower seeks to rely on documentary evidence which has been copied and is to be disclosed in breach of copyright, it will often be possible to show that the whistleblower is criticizing the ideas or themes contained in those documents. In other cases, however, the whistleblower will not be criticizing either the work or the ideas contained in it. In *Lion Laboratories Ltd v Evans* [1985] 1 QB 526 (CA), for example, on leaving employment with the claimant, two of the defendants removed confidential internal memoranda which cast doubt on the accuracy of breathalyser equipment. This material was offered to a newspaper for publication. Although an allegation was made both of breach of confidence and breach of copyright, in refusing an interim injunction the Court of Appeal considered only the common law defence of public interest and not the statutory defence of fair dealing. The memoranda were to be used as evidence, but there does not appear to have been criticism either of those documents or of the ideas they contained. As discussed below (paragraph 16.23), the exception in relation to use of quotations may also be of relevance in this respect. In addition, if the documents had also suggested that the results should not be made public then the criticism of that sentiment, expressed in the document, would have qualified as criticism of the work.

16.08 It should be noted, however, that the amendments to sections 30(1) and 30(1A) of the CDPA made by the 2003 Regulations, as set out above, restrict the statutory defence of fair dealing with a work for the purposes of criticism and review, to a work that has been made available to the public. That is a potentially important restriction in the context of whistleblowing. Typically the role of a whistleblower will be as an insider able to raise an early alarm, by virtue of being able to have sight of what may be going on that is not available to the general public. That may involve concerns arising from sight of documents that raise matters of public concern but which are not available to the public. In that event the public interest defence may be crucial.

(3) 'Reporting current events'

16.09 A potential whistleblower may seek to show that disclosing documents in breach of copyright constitutes reporting current events within CDPA, section 30(2). The Act does not contain any definition of what constitutes a current event. Unless this is given a very liberal interpretation it might be difficult for a potential whistleblower to fall within the scope of this section. In many (but not all) cases the potential whistleblower will wish to bring to light matters which have not yet been placed in the public spotlight and, as such, on a narrow view might not be regarded as an 'event'. The whistleblower might also be concerned not merely about something which happened on a particular occasion but have an ongoing concern, such as failings in health and safety practice at the workplace.

16.10 It is clear that 'current events' should be given a liberal meaning, since it is prima facie in the public interest that the public should be informed regarding matters of public concern.[18] This view has received judicial support.[19] At first instance in *The NLA v Marks & Spencer plc* [1999] EMLR 369, Lightman J expressed the view that the report need not be made in the media or be open or accessible to the public. He added that the publication of a report or article in the press might itself constitute a current event, but the reporting of current events does not extend to publishing matters which are merely currently of interest but are not current events, or to publishing matters not previously known and of historical interest only. Publication of matters which are not current events can only be justified if reasonably necessary to understand, explain, or give meaning to a report of current events.[20]

16.11 The liberal approach as to what is 'current' was illustrated by the decision of Jacob J at first instance in *Hyde Park Residence v Yelland* (1999) EMLR 654. In August 1998 the *Daily Mirror* printed an article in which Mohamed Al-Fayed repeated an allegation that, shortly before their accident in August 1997, the Princess of Wales and Dodi Fayed had visited Mohamed Al-Fayed's Villa Windsor in Paris. He claimed that they had been accompanied by an Italian designer and were planning to get married and live in the house. The former chief security officer at Villa Windsor, Mr Murrell, had made two video stills which demonstrated that the couple had only been at the villa for 28 minutes. He took these to the *Sun* newspaper to support his claim that there had been only a short tour of the house by Diana and Dodi, and that there had been no discussion of any plans to live there. The *Sun* printed the story and published the stills. The security company which had employed Mr Murrell brought proceedings against him and the *Sun* for breach of confidence and breach of copyright. Both claims failed. It was argued that there could be no defence of fair dealing under section 30(2) of the CDPA since the event in question, being the tour of the villa, had taken place one year prior to publication. Jacob J emphasized that this was too narrow an approach. It was sufficient that the report was topical and, even aside from the fact that Mohamed Al-Fayed had recently repeated his allegations, the events at Villa Windsor were still very much under discussion. The decision of Jacob J was reversed by the Court of Appeal,[21] but the court accepted for the purposes of the appeal that the media coverage in question could be described as 'current events' when those words were construed liberally.[22] The Court of Appeal rejected the fair dealing defence on the basis that the dealing with the work was not fair. The guidance as to the scope of current events remains good law. Thus in *England and Wales Cricket Board Ltd and Sky UK Ltd v Tixdaq Ltd and another* [2016] EWHC 575 Arnold J (para 80), citing *Pro Sieben* and *Hyde Park v Yelland*, Arnold J noted that the events need not be very recent, particularly where the ramifications of an event continue to be a matter of public debate or concern.[23]

---

[18] See eg *Copinger and Skone James on Copyright*, 17th edn. London: Sweet & Maxwell, 2016, paras 9-32, 9-57.
[19] *Pro Sieben Media AG* (CA); *The NLA v Marks & Spencer plc* [1999] EMLR 369 at 381–82, per Lightman J; *England and Wales Cricket Board Ltd and Sky UK Ltd v Tixdaq Ltd and another* [2016] EWHC 575 per Arnold J at para 79.
[20] *The NLA v Marks & Spencer plc* [1999] EMLR 369 at 382. It should be noted that the decision of Lightman J was reversed in the Court of Appeal ([2000] 3 WLR 1256), but the court found it unnecessary to rule on the fair dealing defence. In the House of Lords ([2001] 3 All ER 977), the decision of the Court of Appeal was upheld, but no argument was heard on the defence of fair dealing.
[21] [2001] Ch 143.
[22] Per Aldous LJ at p 226.
[23] See also *Ashdown v Telegraph Group* [2001] EWCA Civ 1142, [2002] Ch 149, discussed at 16.33 to 16.37 below, where coverage of a meeting between the Prime Minister and the leader of an opposition party was regarded as arguably a publication concerning a current event, since it covered a matter of continuing public interest.

In other cases, the general approach has been to assess whether there has been a report as to **16.12** something which can legitimately be regarded as an 'event' having regard to the newsworthiness of the matter. In *Pro Sieben*, for example, the Court of Appeal, in concluding that media coverage of Ms Allwood's case was itself a current event, referred to the volume and intensity of media interest in the case. A similar approach appears to have been taken in *PCR Ltd v Dow Jones Telerate Ltd* [1998] FSR 170. The claimant issued reports concerning the status of cocoa crops around the world. The defendant, a specialist commodity news service, published articles containing substantial quotations from the reports. Lloyd J accepted that the fact that the reports had come out into the market, and their impact on the market, was 'news' and, as such, a current event. However, in *Associated Newspapers Group plc v News Group Newspapers Ltd* [1986] RPC 515 Walton J took the view that the publication of an exchange of letters between the Duke and Duchess of Windsor was not the sort of current event with which the statute was concerned.

In any event an artificially wide interpretation of what constitutes a current event may be **16.13** unnecessary if it is instead possible to rely on a public interest defence. The scope of such a defence is considered below.

(4) Sufficient acknowledgment—'identifying the author'

Subject to the exception in section 30(3) of the CDPA, there can be no fair dealing defence **16.14** under section 30 unless the infringing copy is accompanied by a 'sufficient acknowledgment'. As to this, section 178 provides that:

'sufficient acknowledgment' means an acknowledgment identifying the work in question by its title or other description, and identifying the author unless:
(a) in the case of a published work, it is published anonymously;
(b) in the case of an unpublished work, it is not possible for a person to ascertain the identity of the author by reasonable inquiry.

Accordingly, it is not sufficient to identify the copyright owner. The author must also be **16.15** identified.[24]

(5) 'Fair'

Even where a publication has been for one of the purposes set out in section 30 of the CDPA, **16.16** the dealing must be shown to be fair in all the circumstances. Fair dealing is a matter of degree to be assessed on the basis of fact and impression in each case.[25] The dealing must be fair for the approved purpose and the court will take into account such matters as the amount of the extract taken, its proportion to any criticism (where section 30(1) applies), the purpose of the infringement, and the motive of the person infringing the copyright.[26]

In *Ashdown v Telegraph Group Ltd* [2002] Ch 149, the Court of Appeal (at paras 70–71[27]), **16.17** whilst emphasizing that considerations of public interest are paramount, identified the three most important facts bearing on fairness, in descending order of importance, as being:

(1) whether the alleged fair dealing is in fact commercially competing with the proprietor's exploitation of copyright;

---

[24] *Express Newspapers plc v News (UK) Ltd* [1990] FSR 359.
[25] *Pro Sieben Media AG* (CA) at p 613B, per Robert Walker LJ; *Hubbard v Vosper* [1972] 2 QB 84 at 94C, per Lord Denning MR; at 98F, per Megaw LJ.
[26] See *Hubbard v Vosper* 1972] 2 QB 84 at 94B–C, per Lord Denning MR; *Associated Newspaper Group plc v News Group Newspapers Ltd* [1986] RPC 515 at 518; *BBC v BSB Ltd* [1992] Ch 141 at 157–58; *PCR Ltd v Dow Jones Telerate Ltd* [1998] FSR 170 at 185–86; *Pro Sieben Media AG* (CA); *Hyde Park Residence Ltd v Yelland* [2000] 3 WLR 215.
[27] Followed in *England and Wales Cricket Board Ltd and Sky UK Ltd v Tixdaq Ltd and another* [2016] EWHC 575 per Arnold J at paras 83–85, where it was noted that other relevant factors include the motive

(2) whether the work has already been published or otherwise exposed to the public; if unpublished there is ordinarily unlikely to be fair dealing but that may not be so where publication is in the public interest; and

(3) the amount and importance of the work which has been undertaken.

16.18 A further potentially relevant factor is the purpose for which the copyright has been infringed. This is likely to be particularly important in the context of whistleblowing. Where the copyright work is being used in conjunction with raising matters of public concern, copying of very substantial extracts may be fair dealing. For example, in *Hubbard v Vosper* [1972] 2 QB 84 (CA), Mr Vosper wrote a book critical of Scientology which contained substantial extracts from books and bulletins about Scientology by L Ron Hubbard. In holding that there was an arguable defence of fair dealing, and refusing an interim injunction, the Court of Appeal took account of the fact that Vosper claimed to be seeking to expose Scientology to the public and to criticize and condemn it. This was contrasted with an infringement of copyright in order to attack or compete with a trade rival. In such circumstances there is far less likelihood of establishing fair dealing,[28] albeit this is not an absolute bar to there being fair dealing.[29]

16.19 The circumstances in which the potential whistleblower obtains or discloses the infringing copyright may also be relevant. In *Beloff v Pressdram Ltd* [1973] 1 All ER 241 the claimant, who was the political and lobby correspondent for the *Observer*, wrote an internal memorandum to her editor stating that she had had a conversation with a named member of the government to the effect that, if the Prime Minister was to be run over by a bus, Mr Maudling would become Prime Minister. She then published an article criticizing *Private Eye*'s attitude to Maudling. *Private Eye* then published a reply attacking the claimant in personal terms and incorporating in full her internal memorandum. The Editor of the *Observer* purported to assign the copyright in the memorandum to the claimant and she then brought an action for infringement of copyright. Ungoed-Thomas J held that there was no valid assignment but, if there had been, no fair dealing defence would have been established. Publication of information which is known to have been leaked and which could not have been pursued without the leak was unjustifiable for the authorized purposes of criticism or review and was not fair dealing.

16.20 In *Time Warner Entertainments Company LP v Channel Four Television Corporation plc* [1994] EMLR 1 the Court of Appeal distinguished *Beloff* on the grounds that it related to an unpublished work. In *Time Warner* the Court of Appeal was concerned with whether there had been a breach of copyright in use of extracts from the film *A Clockwork Orange* which had already been released. The Court of Appeal emphasized that criticism and review of a work already in the public domain which might otherwise constitute fair dealing would seldom, if ever, be rendered unfair because of the method by which the copyright was obtained. This would, though, be of little comfort for the whistleblower or those seeking to publish the matters disclosed by the whistleblower where, as in the ordinary case, the whistleblower seeks to make public matters which are not already in the public domain.

16.21 However, the circumstances in which the copyright material is obtained and disclosed is merely one factor to be taken into account. It is in any event unlikely that it would be

---

for the disclosure and the nature of any accompanying material and the relation it bears to what has been taken from the copyright work.

[28] See also *Associated Newspaper Group plc v News Group Newspapers Ltd* [1986] RPC 515 at 518; *Pro Sieben Media AG* (CA); *Walter v Steinkopff* [1892] 3 Ch 489; *Weatherby v International Horse Agency & Exchange Ltd* [1910] 2 Ch 297.

[29] *BBC v BSB Ltd* [1992] Ch 141 at 158.

sufficient of itself to render dealing unfair where a whistleblower raises matters of public concern. This would be inconsistent with the public interest defence and with the judicial recognition that a distinction is to be drawn between whistleblowing cases and other disclosures: *Camelot v Centaur Communications Ltd* [1998] IRLR 80 (CA). As the Court of Appeal noted in *Time Warner*, if confidential material is improperly disclosed the remedy usually lies in an action for breach of confidence. The position is illustrated by the decision in *Hubbard v Vosper*. In rejecting the claim that there could be no fair dealing defence in relation to unpublished Scientology memoranda, the Court of Appeal recognized that there might be such general interest in the unpublished material that it is legitimate to criticize it, or the ideas contained in it, without there being any infringement of copyright.[30] Similar considerations may apply in relation to the suggestion in *Pro Sieben Media* that the motive of the alleged infringer may be relevant. By analogy with the approach in section 43B ERA as amended, of greater importance may be the question of whether the use of the material was, or was reasonably regarded as being, in the public interest.

16.22 However, decisions which relate to the fair dealing defence for the purposes of criticism or review in a work that has not been made available to the public will need to be revisited, or studied with care, having regard to the amendments to section 30(1) and (1A) inserted by the 2003 and 2014 Regulations, and set out above (at paragraph 16.03) and also by the need to construe the legislation compatibly with the Human Rights Act 1988.[31] The latter is likely to be of particular importance when disclosing matters of public concern.

(6) Use of a quotation

16.23 With effect from 1 October 2014, section 30 CDPA was amended so as to add a specific provision that a copyright work is not infringed by the use of a quotation, subject to compliance with the conditions in section 30(1ZA). The provision applies where the use of the quotation is for criticism or review 'or otherwise'. It has been suggested that the exception is narrow; the ejusdem generis principle of statutory construction indicates that the words 'or otherwise' contemplates purposes of a similar kind to the criticism or review.[32] But the exception may be material where a whistleblower wishes to cite from a document by way of evidence in support of the concerns being raised, rather than by way of criticism or review of the work itself, as discussed at paragraph 16.07 above by reference to the *Lion Laboratories* decision. The extent of the quotation would, however, need to be no more than required for the specific purpose for which it is used (section 30(1ZA)(c) CDPA). Further, and significantly, there must still be compliance with the requirement that the work has been made available for the public, as well as the usual requirement that the use of the quotation is fair dealing with the work and that the quotation is accompanied by a sufficient acknowledgment.

C. Public Interest Defence

16.24 Whilst it might be prudent for a potential whistleblower to seek to meet the requirements for a fair dealing defence, where matters of public concern are raised (within or akin to the relevant failures in section 43B ERA), the question may arise as to whether the whistleblower can rely on a defence of public interest to claims for copyright infringement. Section 171(3)

---

[30] Per Lord Denning MR at p 95A–B.
[31] See *Copinger and Skone James on Copyright*, 17th edn. London: Sweet & Maxwell, 2016, para 9-31; *Ashdown v Telegraph Group* [2002] Ch 149 at para 71, considered at 16.33 below.
[32] See *Copinger and Skone James on Copyright*, 17th edn. London: Sweet & Maxwell, 2016, at para 9-50.

of the CDPA specifically provides for the preservation of 'any rule of law preventing or restricting the enforcement of copyright, on grounds of public interest or otherwise'.

16.25 The scope of the public interest defence in relation to claims for breach of confidence is considered in Chapter 14. However, the Court of Appeal has observed that the basis of the court's jurisdiction to allow a public interest defence in copyright claims was not the same as that which arose in the defence of public interest in a breach of confidence action.[33]

16.26 The availability of a general common law public interest defence in the context of infringement of copyright has been recognized in a number of cases, at least since 1972. In *Beloff v Pressdram* (above) at p 259H, Ungoed-Thomas J explained that:

> fair dealing is a statutory defence limited to infringement of copyright only. But public interest is a defence outside and independent of statutes, not limited to copyright cases and is based on a general principle of common law.

16.27 Further recognition was given to the availability of a public interest defence to infringement of copyright in *A-G v Guardian Newspapers (No 2)* [1990] 1 AC 109 (HL). The House of Lords required the *Sunday Times* to account for the profits made in serialization of the book *Spycatcher* written by Peter Wright. Lord Keith explained that, in calculating profits, no account was to be taken of any sums paid to Peter Wright or his publishers for the copyright because no claim for these sums would have been enforceable. This was because there was no copyright in a work the publication of which was brought about contrary to the public interest.[34] Similarly, Lord Jauncey noted that there could be no enforceable copyright in *Spycatcher* since it 'reeked of turpitude'.[35]

16.28 In two whistleblowing cases involving allegations of infringement of copyright, reliance has been placed on the public interest defence and the court has not considered it necessary to refer to the fair dealing defence. It was on the basis of a common law public interest defence that an interim injunction was refused by the Court of Appeal in *Lion Laboratories* (paragraph 16.07 above). The judgment of Stephenson LJ (with whom O'Connor LJ agreed) might be explained on the basis that, although Stephenson LJ recognized that the courts would not restrain a breach of copyright where there was just cause or excuse for infringing the copyright, this was consistent with public interest being a factor relevant to discretionary injunctive relief rather than as a substantive defence. However, Griffiths LJ stated expressly that he considered that the defence of public interest applied to breach of copyright in addition to breach of confidence.

16.29 A substantive defence of public interest was also recognized in a whistleblowing context in *Service Corporation International plc v Channel Four Television Corporation* [1999] EMLR 83. One of the defendants, Mr Anderson, was employed by an operator and owner of funeral homes as a trainee funeral director. In fact during the period of his employment he worked undercover, and covertly made a film which purported to show corpses being subjected to disrespectful and abusive treatment and coffins containing corpses being used as rubbish bins. The claimants sought to restrain the showing of the film on Channel Four, claiming that it had been made in breach of confidence and as a result of trespass and also that the claimants owned the copyright in the film. Injunctive relief was refused. Unsurprisingly, in relation to the claim of infringement of copyright Lightman J concluded that there were good prospects of establishing a public interest defence at trial, raising questions not only as

---

[33] *Hyde Park Residence v Yelland* [2000] 3 WLR 215.
[34] Per Lord Keith at pp 262G–263A.
[35] At p 294D.

to the funeral home where the filming took place but also as to whether the state of affairs revealed might be prevalent in the claimants' funeral homes or in the industry generally.

There are other examples of cases in which the courts have recognized some form of public **16.30** interest defence in copyright cases.[36] In *Hyde Park Residence Ltd v Yelland* [2001] Ch 143, referred to at paragraph 16.11 above, the Court of Appeal held that the CDPA did not give to a court a general power to enable an infringer to use another's copyright in the public interest, although the court had an inherent jurisdiction preserved by section 171(3) to refuse to enforce an action for infringement of copyright where enforcement would offend against the policy of the law. The court held, by a majority of two to one (Mance LJ dissenting), that although it was not possible to define the circumstances in which a court would be entitled to invoke the jurisdiction, they had to derive from the work in question and not from the ownership of the copyright, and included, for example, circumstances in which the work in question either (a) was immoral, scandalous, or contrary to family life; or (b) was injurious to public life, public health and safety, or the administration of justice; or (c) incited or encouraged others to act in such a way. On the facts of the case, the Court of Appeal found that there was nothing in the circumstances which required the court to refuse to enforce the copyrights provided by the CDPA. As we discuss below, however, following the Human Rights Act 1998 (HRA), the Court of Appeal has preferred the dissenting view of Mance LJ as to the scope of the public interest defence.[37]

(1) The effect of the passing of the Human Rights Act 1998

Before the passing of the HRA, the public interest defence had been found to apply not **16.31** only in cases in which the defendant had infringed copyright in order to reveal some form of impropriety, but also to cases in which disclosure was otherwise held to be in the public interest.[38]

The passing of the HRA has created a tension between copyright protection and freedom **16.32** of expression. The authorities decided before it came into force need to be approached with caution, but the heightened importance afforded fundamental principles such as freedom of expression reinforces the approach in *Lion Laboratories* and *Service Corporation v Channel Four* of giving effect to a public interest defence where the infringement is tailored to the raising of matters of public concern.

The decision of the Court of Appeal in *Ashdown v Telegraph Group* [2001] EWCA Civ 1142, **16.33** [2002] Ch 149 must now be considered to be the leading case on the interaction between the right to freedom of expression in Article 10 of the European Convention on Human Rights and a claim for infringement of copyright and the remedies for infringement, and on the public interest defence.

The facts of the case were as follows. The claimant had kept diaries whilst he was the leader **16.34** of the Liberal Democrats. After he gave up the leadership, he prepared the material for publication and showed it in strict confidence to the press and publishing houses. Included in the material was a minute of an important political meeting in October 1997. A copy of the minute reached the political editor of the defendant newspaper, which published articles

---

[36] *Lion Laboratories v Evans* [1985] 1 QB 526 (CA) (see para 16.07 above); *Church of Scientology v Miller, The Times*, 23 October 1987; *Beggars Banquet Records Ltd v Carlton Television* (1993) EMLR 349; *ZYX Music GmbH v King* (1995) EMLR 281; *PCR Ltd v Dow Jones Telerate Ltd* [1998] FSR 170 (see para 16.12 above); *Service Corp. International v Channel Four Television Corp., Independent*, 14 May 1998.

[37] *Ashdown v Telegraph Group* [2001] EWCA Civ 1142, [2002] Ch 149 (see para 16.33 below).

[38] Eg *Lion Laboratories v Evans* [1985] 1 QB 526, CA (see para 16.07 above), and *PCR Ltd v Dow Jones Telerate Ltd* [1998] FSR 170 (see para 16.12 above).

about it, quoting verbatim from a substantial part of the minute. The claimant brought an action against the defendant claiming breach of confidence and copyright infringement, and seeking injunctions and damages or an account of profits. An application for summary judgment in respect of the copyright claim was resisted on the grounds that, when considering whether actionable breach of copyright had occurred, or any appropriate remedies for breach, the court should have regard to the Article 10 right to freedom of expression, which required the court to give individual consideration to the facts of each case in order to assess the impact of Article 10.[39] The judge at first instance granted the claimant's application for summary judgment.

16.35   The Court of Appeal held that rare circumstances could arise where the right to freedom of expression came into conflict with the protection afforded by the CDPA, and that in those circumstances the court was bound so far as possible to apply the CDPA in a manner that accommodated the right to freedom of expression, which made it necessary for the court to look closely at the facts of individual cases. In most cases it would be sufficient simply to decline the discretionary relief of an injunction, while recognizing that, if a newspaper considered it necessary to copy the exact words used by another, it should in principle indemnify the author for any loss caused, or account for any profit made, as a result of copying the work.

16.36   The Court of Appeal held that the circumstances in which the public interest defence to breach of copyright in section 171(3) of the CDPA might override copyright were not capable of precise categorization or definition. Since the coming into force of the HRA, there was the clearest public interest in giving effect to the right of freedom of expression in those rare cases where it trumped the rights in copyright conferred by the CDPA. While section 171(3) permitted the defence of public interest to be raised, it would be rare for the public interest to justify copying the form of a work to which copyright attaches. In reaching this conclusion, the Court of Appeal disagreed with the way in which the majority of the Court of Appeal in the *Hyde Park Residence* case sought to circumscribe the public interest defence as tightly as it did, and preferred the conclusions of Mance LJ in his dissenting judgment, in which he said that whilst the public interest defence for infringement of copyright and breach of confidence was not necessarily to be equated; 'the circumstances in which the public interest may override copyright are probably not capable of precise categorisation or definition'.

16.37   On the facts of the *Ashdown* case, the court rejected any fair dealing defence under section 30(1) or (2). The court also concluded (at para 66) that where part of the work was copied in the course of a report on current events, the fair dealing defence would normally afford the court all the scope that it needed properly to reflect the public interest. Here, applying the required liberal meaning of the test for reporting current events (see paragraphs 16.09–16.13 above), this arguably covered the publication even though it concerned a meeting some two years earlier. The meeting was between the Prime Minister and an opposition party leader during the then current Parliament and was to discuss possible close cooperation between those parties. That was a matter of continuing public interest. However, the extent of reproduction was not justified. It had been done for journalistic reasons to further the *Telegraph*'s commercial interests, and Article 10 of the European Convention did not require that the *Telegraph* should be able to profit from the use of Mr Ashdown's copyright without paying compensation. The fair dealing defence under s30(2) was therefore not made out. Since the public interest was weighed in the context of the fair dealing defence relating to current

---

[39] The impact of Article 10 is discussed further in Chapter 14, paras 14.16–14.21 and 14.32–14.59, and in Chapter 18.

events, that also dealt with the public interest defence under section 171(3). The appeal was therefore dismissed.

In the light of the *Ashdown* case, there are two ways of giving effect to the right of freedom **16.38** of expression in copyright cases. The first is by refusing injunctive relief, and leaving the copyright owner to his/her remedies by way of damages or an account of profits. This is not an application of the public interest defence. It is a question of applying the CDPA so as to accommodate the Article 10 right to freedom of expression.

The second way is to permit the use of the public interest defence under section 171(3). **16.39** This will be in rare cases only, where it is in the public interest for the copyright work to be reproduced without the reproducer being exposed to infringement proceedings. The Court of Appeal has made it clear that the defence is not limited to cases where copyright has been infringed in order to reveal acts of impropriety, and that the circumstances in which the public interest may override copyright are not capable of precise categorization or definition. The HRA requires the court to look at each case carefully on its own facts, though, as in *Ashdown*, it will not require separate consideration where it has been possible to weigh the public interest under the guise of the fair dealing defence.

The Court of Appeal expressed the view that the refusal of an injunction would usually be **16.40** sufficient to give effect to freedom of expression. However, it left over the issue as to the circumstances in which the courts will consider that this is not sufficient, and will allow the application of the public interest defence, with the effect of denying the copyright owner all statutory remedies for infringement of copyright. Commentators have suggested that, where the defendant is not a newspaper, but, for example, a person of limited means, and where a notional royalty for use of the copyright work would be unaffordable by the defendant, then the use of the public interest defence might be permitted.[40]

It has been suggested that cases in which the public interest defence succeeds despite **16.41** unavailability of other specific defences such as fair dealing will be rare.[41] Examples of cases in which the public interest defence in copyright claims has been squarely rejected by the courts since the introduction of the HRA include the following:

- *Imutran Ltd v (1) Uncaged Campaigns Ltd (2) Daniel Louis Lyons* [2001] 2 All ER 385 (concerning website publications by an animal rights group of material based on leaked documents of a pharmaceutical company).
- *HRH Prince of Wales v Associated Newspapers Ltd* [2006] EWHC 522 (Ch) (publication by the *Mail on Sunday* of articles based upon and containing extracts from the Prince of Wales' personal diary, which was likely to have been provided by a former employee).
- *Grisbrook v MGN Ltd* [2009] EWHC 2520 (Ch) (newspaper publisher's use of back catalogue of freelance photographer's photos; no sufficient public interest as there was already extension provision for such material to be made available to the public).
- *Unilever plc v Griffin* [2010] FSR 33 (alleged infringement of copyright by BNP using a jar of Marmite in a political broadcast). The court (per Arnold J at para 18) commented *obiter* that the public interest defence to copyright was 'somewhat limited'. However, this was said only in the context of an interim relief application and of considering defences that might be run at trial, and Arnold J added that it seemed to him that this was an area where there may be room for further development, particularly in a political context.

---

[40] See eg *Copinger and Skone James on Copyright*, 17th edn. London: Sweet & Maxwell, 2016, para 21-111.

[41] See *HRH Prince of Wales v Associated Newspapers Ltd* [2006] EWHC 522 (Ch) at para 180, following *Ashdown*.

16.42 The warning that the public interest defence will only apply in rare cases suggests that caution is needed as to whether the public interest defence embodied in section 171(3) of the CDPA will be successful in circumstances where a fair dealing defence is not available. In that regard, it must also be remembered that the fact that disclosure of copyright material would be of interest to the public is not the same as disclosure being in the public interest. However, the above line of cases cannot, we suggest, be seen as an indication of the likely approach where the use or disclosure is part of the proportionate raising of issues of public concern such as would fall within the protected disclosure regime. The decision in *Imutran* preceded that in *Ashdown* and proceeded on the basis that there was no public interest defence to breach of copyright. In *HRH Prince of Wales v Associated Newspapers* publication was to the public as a whole, and even if it could be said that there was a public interest in disclosure of the Prince of Wales's diaries, as opposed to it being a matter of interest to the public, it was not a matter of disclosure of matters of public concern akin to the categories of relevant failure in section 43B ERA. In granting summary judgment on the claim in breach of copyright (and of confidence), the Court therefore held that there were no specific clear public interest considerations over and above those available under the fair dealing defence. Similarly, in *Unilever* and *Grisbrook* there was wide disclosure to the public as a whole and nothing akin to a relevant failure within the meaning of section 43B ERA. In those circumstances it is unsurprising that the court was unwilling to accept that Article 10 considerations were sufficient to 'trump' the copyright owner's right to peaceful enjoyment of his/her property, without it being established that the infringement in question was actually necessary in the public interest.

16.43 The dicta in *Ashdown* and *HRH Prince of Wales* noting that it would be rare for a public interest defence to succeed on public interest grounds if fair dealing fails, did not address the situation where there is a strong Article 10 argument by virtue of raising matters of public concern akin to a section 43B ERA 'relevant failure', and where disclosure is made to those with a proper interest in receiving the information. As noted above, the fair dealing defence may not be suited to addressing such a situation. Notably that is so in relation to the limitation that the work subject to criticism or review, or from which quotations have been used, must have been made available to the public. Having regard to the policy of PIDA and the guidance in *Ashdown* (see paragraphs 16.36–16.40 above), as illustrated by *Lion Laboratories* and *Service Corporation v Channel Four*, it is still more likely that injunctive relief would be refused where it is sought to enforce copyright in circumstances where the infringement is part of or in support of a protected disclosure.[42]

D. Interrelation of Copyright Protection and PIDA

16.44 There is no express provision in PIDA addressing the extent to which a whistleblower is entitled to infringe copyright in order to supply evidence to support a protected disclosure. The evidence collected and disclosed, whether or not in breach of copyright, may form part of a qualifying disclosure being part of the information tending to show the relevant failure. Alternatively it may be relied upon by way of evidence in support of reasonable belief.

---

[42] See also *BBC v Hainey* [2012] SLT 476, where the (Scottish) High Court of Judiciary held that there was no infringement of copyright in the use of photographs taken by a mother of her child for the purposes of reporting criminal proceedings against the mother. This was primarily on the basis of permitted reporting of court proceedings but the court held (at para 25) that if it had been necessary to rely on a public interest defence it would have succeeded on the basis that the public interest in the proper and full reporting of the case was sufficient to 'trump' any right of the copyright owner.

The infringement may also take place in the course of preparation in advance of making a protected disclosure, as where material is copied as part of the investigations which are carried out by a worker to be satisfied that there is a reasonable belief in a relevant failure. As discussed in Chapter 7, it is clear that such preparatory steps and evidence gathering are not themselves protected by the protected disclosure regime, subject to causation arguments as to whether detriment imposed was really by reason of taking such preparatory steps rather than the disclosure itself: see *Bolton School v Evans* [2006] IRLR 500 (EAT) [2007] IRLR 140 (CA). It does not, however, follow that a public interest defence to a claim of copyright infringement would not be available where such preparatory steps are proportionate and taken in the course of making a disclosure as to a relevant failure.

Where the infringing copy is itself the means by which the requisite information is dis- **16.45** closed, if the requirements for a protected disclosure are met, the worker will have the right not to be subjected to a detriment by the employer for disclosing the protected information, notwithstanding that, in making the disclosure, or in order to be able to do so, copyright was infringed. Again, as discussed in Chapter 7, in principle it remains open to an employer to seek to distinguish between detriment or dismissal by reason of the disclosure itself and the manner of the disclosure being an infringement of copyright (see Chapter 7, paragraphs 7.120–7.124). But having regard to the policy underlying PIDA, the courts are likely to regard such a submission with scepticism.

17

DEFAMATION

17.01 In addition to facing disciplinary action, the whistleblower may find him/herself on the receiving end of a claim in defamation; a fate that may also await any media entity or third party which republishes his/her allegations. The full law of defamation is beyond the scope of this book so we focus here on those features that are of most relevance to the whistleblower.

17.02 The Defamation Act 2013 (which came into force on 1 January 2014) introduced a number of reforms as well as attempting to codify large parts of the common law. However, the Act does not fully consolidate the laws of defamation, and so cannot be considered in isolation from the case law which predates it. The Act is still very much in its infancy, and as such there remains considerable uncertainty as to how it will be interpreted and applied by the courts.

A. The Prima Facie Case

17.03 Any publication to third parties of material that refers to and is defamatory of a living and identifiable person gives rise to a prima facie cause of action in libel or slander.[1] Since the essence of whistleblowing is communication with another, publication to a third party will invariably occur and this appears to be the case even where publication has been by one employee or officer of a company to another and solely concerns the company's affairs.[2]

---

[1] The distinction between the two being, in essence, that publication in writing or some other permanent form will constitute libel while spoken or otherwise transient publication will generally constitute slander. Any legal person may bring a claim in libel or slander, including corporate bodies. There are, however, exceptions, including government departments and local authorities. See *Derbyshire CC v Times Newspapers* [1993] AC 534.

[2] *Riddick v Thames Board Mills* [1977] QB 881 (CA) (although note the dissenting judgment of Lord Denning MR).

A statement is, according to the traditional test, defamatory if it tends 'to lower the claimant **17.04** in the estimation of right thinking members of society generally',[3] and therefore prior to the enactment of the Defamation Act 2013 a whistleblower seeking to expose malpractice was likely to find it almost impossible to avoid publication of defamatory material. However, a new requirement of 'serious harm' was introduced in section 1 of the Act, which raises the bar for defamation claimants.

(1) Serious harm

While the Defamation Act 2013 does not include a definition as to what constitutes defam- **17.05** atory publication, it does provide that a statement is not defamatory 'unless its publication has caused or is likely to cause serious harm to the reputation of the claimant'.[4] Therefore, the court will no longer simply confine itself to considering the seriousness of the words complained of and the harmful tendency of that meaning, but may also have regard to all the relevant circumstances of publication, including factors such as the identity and number of publishees, the extent to which the allegations were treated as credible, and whether the allegations were made verbally or in a permanent form.

The effect of the requirement for serious harm may mean, for example, that allegations **17.06** which if made in the press would be actionable might not be when made, say, to a company director who, after investigation, concluded they were baseless. In each case the claimant will be required to demonstrate that the defamatory publication had caused or is likely to cause harm to his/her reputation.

Evidence of what has actually happened after publication will be particularly pertinent, as a **17.07** cause of action will not arise until serious harm is caused or becomes probable. If defamatory allegations are made but promptly retracted and corrected—or if the subject of the allegations is exonerated following an internal investigation—then this may be sufficient for a court to con-clude that serious harm has neither been caused nor is likely to be caused in the future.[5]

Except in the most obvious cases (for example, allegations of serious crime published in the **17.08** national media, where the court may draw an inference of serious harm), the claimant will be required to adduce evidence of serious harm, which may involve giving live evidence at a preliminary hearing.

The Defamation Act 2013 introduces a further requirement for any for-profit trading body **17.09** wishing to bring a claim, as such a body must show that a statement 'has caused or is likely to cause the body serious financial loss' in order to meet the test of serious harm.[6]

This requirement will greatly restrict the ability of a trading corporation to bring a def- **17.10** amation claim in respect of allegations contained in a disclosure to an employer or to a prescribed person or body, as the limited extent of publication may mean serious financial

---

[3] *Sim v Stretch* [1936] 2 All ER 1237. See also *Parmiter v Coupland* (1840) 6 M&W 105 (would the offending words 'injure the reputation of another by exposing him to hatred, contempt or ridicule'?) and *Youssoupoff v MGM Pictures Ltd* (1934) 50 TLR 581, CA (do the words cause the claimant to be 'shunned and avoided'?, although there is perhaps some doubt that this test would be applied today).

[4] This new test of 'serious' harm builds upon existing case law which sought to prevent trivial claims from being brought, and means that libel is no longer actionable without proof of damage, and that the legal presumption of damage will cease to play any significant role. See *Lachaux v Independent Print Ltd & Ors* [2016] 2 WLR 437, at para 60. It should be noted that the Court of Appeal's judgment in *Lachaux* is awaited.

[5] See *Cooke and Anor v MGN* [2015] 1 WLR 895 at para 21. However, the consensus is that this case turned upon its specific facts, and that it will be rare for a court to conclude that even a prompt and full apology will be sufficient to negate completely any serious harm caused or likely to have been caused.

[6] Section 1(2).

loss is not probable. The position may of course be different if allegations are published more widely, and in particular if they are repeated in the press.

17.11   As to the evidence which will be required to prove 'serious financial loss', this is likely to involve details as to the company's financial position before and after the offending publication,[7] and may include loss of sales, loss of customers, or an overall decline in business, which may well require the deployment of expert evidence. A claimant company can recover damages only for loss of profit (or increased losses); it does not necessarily follow that a reduction in 'net sales' translates into a loss of profit.[8]

17.12   Under section 1(2) it is sufficient to show that serious financial loss is 'likely', as opposed to actual financial loss. However, unless the gravity of the allegations and the circumstances of their publication are such that the court is willing to draw an inference of serious financial loss,[9] this new test is likely to present a significant hurdle to any for-profit body wishing to sue a whistleblower for defamation. Initial indications are that the courts will require very clear evidence of a causal link between the publication complained of and any loss of profits consequently claimed.[10]

17.13   Finally, the question arises as to the point in time at which a claimant must demonstrate that serious harm has actually been caused or is likely. Is it at the time of publication, or when issuing the claim form, or when the court determines the issue? While it was not necessary to his decision in *Lachaux v Independent Print Ltd*,[11] it was the view of Warby J that it should be the latter. Otherwise a claim would fail if actual damage had been caused by the time of the determination, but was not likely at the time of publication; and a claim would succeed if damage was likely at the time of publication even if it turned out that none was in fact caused.

(2) Reference, and intention of the publisher

17.14   Two further points in relation to the prima facie case should be noted. First, a defamatory statement can be held to refer to a person even when that person is not named.[12] Second, the fact that the whistleblower might not have intended to publish a defamatory statement and/ or to refer to a given individual will, in relation to the prima facie cause of action, be of no assistance as the law deems such matters irrelevant.

17.15   Once the claimant has discharged the task of establishing a prima facie case, the burden of proof shifts to the whistleblower (and to any republisher of the latter's allegations that might also be sued) to make out one of the recognized defences to libel proceedings.[13] These are now a dozen or so in number, but we will deal solely with those most likely to be of relevance in the whistleblowing context, namely truth, qualified and absolute privilege, and the statutory defence of publication on a matter of public interest.

---

[7] *(1) Undre (2) Down to Earth (London) Ltd v London Borough of Harrow* [2016] EWHC 931 (QB), [2017] EMLR 3 at para 46.

[8] ibid, para 49.

[9] As was the case in *Theedom v Nourish Training* [2015] EWCA 3769 (QB).

[10] See *Undre* (n 7, above).

[11] [2016] 2 WLR 437 at para 67.

[12] For example, a fellow employee responsible for the operation or management of a department about which allegations of malpractice are made by a whistleblower might be referred to, and thus defamed, even if s/he is not named.

[13] None of these is specifically designed to take account of whistleblowing and all have material shortcomings in that context. This perceived deficiency has led to as yet unsatisfied calls for the introduction of an additional statutory defence (see eg David Lewis, 'Whistleblowers and the Law of Defamation: Time for Statutory Privilege?' [2005] 3 Web Journal of Current Legal Issues).

B. Truth

Under section 2 of the Defamation Act 2013, 'it is a defence to an action for defamation for **17.16** the defendant to show that the imputation conveyed by the statement complained of is substantially true'. [14] Therefore, if a defendant is able to show that his/her allegations are true in substance and in fact s/he will, in all but the most exceptional circumstances, have an absolute defence to an action for defamation. For a plea of truth to be made out it is not necessary to establish the truth of every detail that formed part of the relevant allegations; only the sting or substance of the defamatory statement need be justified.[15] Further, a defence of truth may still succeed even if a statement contains more than one defamatory imputation but the defendant is able to prove the truth of only the most serious imputation(s).[16]

Nonetheless, there will inevitably be instances where a whistleblower is unable to provide **17.17** the court with sufficient particulars of the malpractice s/he has felt it necessary to disclose. In these circumstances, and in cases where the whistleblower subsequently finds his/her revelations to have been in error, his/her primary recourse will be to the alternative defence of qualified privilege.

C. Qualified Privilege

(1) The 'duty and interest' test

Where a statement is published in circumstances of qualified privilege this will provide a **17.18** defence to libel proceedings even though the statement is defamatory and untrue, unless the person making the statement was actuated by malice. A variety of circumstances might give rise to such privilege, but in cases of first tier disclosure a whistleblower will almost certainly be well advised to consider whether what is known as the 'duty and interest test' applies. This test was most succinctly expressed by Lord Atkinson in *Adam v Ward*:[17]

> A privileged occasion is an occasion where the person who makes a communication has an interest, or a duty, legal, social or moral, to make it to the person to whom it is made, and the person to whom it is made has a corresponding interest or duty to receive it. This reciprocity is essential.

In some cases of first tier disclosure there may be a legal duty to make the disclosure—either **17.19** to an appropriate regulatory body or to the employer. Even if there is no legal duty, an employee may be under a moral or social duty to blow the whistle. As to whether there is a social or moral duty, the test was enunciated by Lindley LJ in *Stuart v Bell*:[18]

> Would the great mass of right minded men in the position of the defendant have considered it their duty under the circumstances to make the communication?

---

[14] Section 2 of the Defamation Act replaced the common law defence of justification with a new statutory defence of truth. The explanatory notes to the Act make clear that this section is intended broadly to reflect the common law justification defence.

[15] See *Belt v Lawes* (1882) 51 LJQB 359 and *Sutherland v Stopes* [1925] AC 47.

[16] Section 2(3) of the Defamation Act 2013 provides 'If one or more of the imputations is not shown to be substantially true, the defence under this section does not fail, if, having regard to the imputations which are shown to be substantially true, the imputations which are not shown to be substantially true do not seriously harm the claimant's reputation'.

[17] [1917] AC 309 at 334. See also *Loveless v Earl* [1999] EMLR 530, CA where, in addition to requiring a common and corresponding interest, the Court of Appeal applied a test of whether the communication was 'warranted by any reasonable occasion or exigency'.

[18] [1891] 2 QB 341 at 350.

17.20 In many cases the legal, moral, or social duty will arise out of the whistleblower's position as an employee. In particular, the whistleblower may be able to rely on the *dictum* of Blackburn J in *Davies v Snead*[19] that the requisite duty arises:

> [w]here a person is so situated that it becomes right in the interest of society that he should tell to a third person certain facts.

17.21 As under the protected disclosure provisions inserted by PIDA, the identity of the recipient of the disclosure will be a very important consideration when determining the presence or otherwise of privileged circumstances. It is not sufficient that the whistleblower believes that the person to whom the disclosure is made has the requisite interest. In general the recipient must in fact have the requisite interest,[20] and where publication is made to a person not having such an interest qualified privilege will not apply.[21] That said, a publication may in certain circumstances be privileged notwithstanding the absence of the necessary reciprocity between the duty to make the disclosure and the interest in receiving the information; for example if it is made in the ordinary course of business, if it is otherwise reasonably necessary, or it is the only effective way of discharging a duty or protecting an interest.[22]

17.22 In relation to disclosure to another employee in a supervisory position or to an employer, the whistleblower will almost always be able to rely on the principle that there is a common interest as between employees in a business and between employees and the employer in the success of the business and the way it is carried on.[23] In most cases the common interest or duty is likely to be equally apparent in relation to other first tier disclosures, such as disclosure to an appropriate regulatory authority or disclosure to a trade union in order to obtain advice.

17.23 In the important but unreported case of *Halpin v Oxford Brookes University*[24] an unsuccessful attempt was made to exclude qualified privilege on the basis that the publication was made in breach of a contract of employment. The claimant was employed in the University's Business School and complained that he had been defamed in an internal memorandum circulated by the Head of the Business School which was critical of his performance. The head of the school plainly had an interest or duty in relation to the claimant's performance and the memorandum was circulated to others who had a corresponding duty or interest to receive the information. It was argued, however, that circulation of the criticisms without allowing the claimant to comment on them was a breach of the disciplinary procedure and constituted a repudiatory breach of his contract of employment. It was then suggested that since the communication was in breach of contract there could be no defence of qualified privilege. The Court of Appeal rejected this logic and, in doing so, emphasized the importance of employees being able to raise internally matters of concern to employing organizations. As Neill LJ explained:

> it remains an important public interest that people should be able to communicate freely and frankly on matters of mutual concern. It seems to me to be beyond argument therefore that managers in large organisations must be free to have free and frank discussions on all

---

[19] [1870] LR 5 QB 608 at 611.

[20] *Hebditch v MacIlwaine* [1894] 2 QB 54, CA.

[21] See eg *Watt v Longsdon* [1930] 1 KB 130 where publication by a company director of allegations concerning the sexual misconduct of an employee were held to be privileged when made to the chairman of the company but not to be privileged when made to the employee's wife. See also *Tench v G.W.Ry.* (1873) 33 UP Can QB 8 and *Mutch v Robertson* (1981) SLT 217.

[22] *Edmondson v Birch* [1907] 1 KB 371; *Pullman v Hill* [1891] 1 QB 524; *R v Lancs CC Police Authority, ex p Hook* [1980] QB 603.

[23] *Bryanston Finance v de Vries* [1975] QB 703, CA; *Hunt v G.N.Ry.* [1891] QB 189.

[24] Unreported, 30 November 1995 [1996] CLY 5658.

matters relating to the organisation in which the parties to the discussion have a proper mutual interest. The protection of the individual who may be defamed is that the privilege to communicate is qualified privilege only. It can be destroyed by malice. But I cannot accept that a manager can be prevented from expressing an honest and relevant opinion merely by reason of the fact that the matter or person discussed might have been dealt with in some other way.[25]

It should be noted that a particularly liberal approach to the defence of qualified privilege **17.24** has, for well over a century, generally been adopted where a defamatory statement consists of an allegation against a person with responsibilities to the public, provided that the allegation is made bona fide to a person with a proper interest in the subject matter.[26] This approach has only been reinforced by the advent of Article 10 of the European Convention on Human Rights guaranteeing freedom of expression[27] and by the series of cases that have followed in the wake of the decision of the House of Lords in *Reynolds v Times Newspapers Ltd*[28] which has now culminated in the enactment of a statutory public interest defence (see paragraph 17.34 below).

(2) Malice

Any plea of qualified privilege based on duty and interest or common interest will be **17.25** defeated where the claimant can show that, in publishing defamatory material, the defendant was actuated by malice. The defendant will have acted maliciously in this context if s/he used the privileged occasion for some purpose other than that for which the occasion was privileged.[29]

Thus, for example, if a whistleblower's dominant purpose was not to reveal malpractice but **17.26** to injure the claimant, the defence will not be available. This can be contrasted with the position under section 43B of the Employment Rights Act,[30] which focuses on whether the worker reasonably believed that making the disclosure was in the public interest, and where good faith falls to be considered only at the remedies stage.

The fact that the defendant did not believe that what s/he said was true should usually be **17.27** conclusive evidence of malice. The use of excessive language in the circumstances of the case

---

[25] For another case in which the relationship between defamation and rights under an employment contract was explored see *Friend v CAA* [1998] IRLR 253, where the Court of Appeal held that allegations made against an employee during the course of a formal disciplinary process concerning that individual were protected by the defence of *volenti non fit injuria* where the disciplinary procedure formed part of the employee's contractual terms of employment.

[26] For example *Couper v Lord Balfour of Burleigh* (1913) SC 492; *A v B* (1907) SC 1154; *Purcell v Sowler* [1891] 1 QB 474.

[27] In any claim for defamation, the court must engage in a two-way balancing exercise between the Article 8 rights of the claimant (protection of reputation) and the Article 10 rights of free speech of the defendant. The jurisprudence in this area has been better developed by the domestic courts in the context of privacy and breach of confidence cases; see the discussion in *Re S (A Child) (Identification: Restrictions on Publication)* [2005] 1 AC 593 at [17]. In the libel case of *Karpov v Browder and others* [2014] EMLR 8 (at para 47) it was suggested—and the court did not demur—that where a party acted in effect as a whistleblower, disclosing serious allegations of what it believes to be misconduct by a public authority, the court should afford a higher degree of protection to the defendant pursuant to Article 10. See also *Kharlamov v Russia* App No 27447/07 [2015] ECHR 27447/07, 8 October 2015, and *Aurelian Oprea v Romania* App No 12138/08 [2016] ECHR 85, 19 January 2016, considered in Chapter 18 paras 18.36–18.38.

[28] [1999] 3 WLR 1010. However, see also *Clift v Slough Borough Council* [2009] 4 All ER 756 where the provisions of the Human Rights Act 1998 were held to circumscribe 'traditional' qualified privilege.

[29] Per Lord Nicholls in *Cheng Albert v Tse Wai Chun Paul* (Court of Final Appeal, Hong Kong) FACV No 12 of 2000, [2001] EMLR 31, a decision followed by the High Court in *Sugar v Associated Newspapers Ltd* (unreported, 6 February 2001), QBD and in *Branson v Bower (No 2)* [2002] QB 737.

[30] As amended by s 17 of the Enterprise and Regulatory Reform Act 2013, see Chapter 4.

might itself be indicative of malice but there must be something so extreme in the words used to afford evidence that the publication was actuated by malice. Although recklessness as to the truth of what was being alleged will suffice to establish malice, it is not sufficient for a claimant to show that the defendant was careless, impulsive, or irrational in arriving at his/her belief or that s/he was improvident, credulous, or stupid.[31] If a defendant honestly believed his/her statement to be true, s/he does not lose the protection of qualified privilege because s/he had no reasonable grounds for so believing.

17.28 It is also important to distinguish between the objective test which is applied for ascertaining the meaning of what has been published and the subjective test for malice. It may be that, applying the objective test, the words published have a defamatory meaning and that the defendant had no honest belief in the truth of that meaning. However, there will be no malice if the defendant had an honest belief that the words have a different meaning which, at the time of publication, s/he honestly believed to be true.[32]

17.29 A large degree of latitude is thus given to those who publish in privileged circumstances and, in consequence, the likelihood of a plea of malice being successfully made out should not be exaggerated. The libel courts have generally shown a much greater reluctance to arrive at a finding of bad faith than have the employment tribunals when considering the question of motivation in the context of protected disclosures.

17.30 While an employment tribunal may be ready to draw an inference of bad faith,[33] for the purposes of the qualified privilege defence in libel the court will not make any finding of malice absent very clear evidence that an improper motive caused the defendant to publish the offending statement. Simply establishing that the defendant felt ill will towards the claimant will not be sufficient if it cannot also be shown that the publication was motivated by malice.[34] Indeed, in *Sugar v Associated Newspapers Ltd*,[35] Eady J, the then senior libel judge and a man having more than thirty years of experience as a libel practitioner, observed that he personally had come across only one case in which a finding of malice was made against a defendant.[36]

17.31 Once a defendant to a libel claim has established that the statement complained of was published on an occasion of privilege, the burden of proof then shifts to the claimant to prove the defendant was motivated by malice, rather than the defendant having to prove that s/he acted in good faith.

(3) Absolute privilege

17.32 Qualified privilege is so called because it is qualified by the requirement that the defendant's publication was not malicious. In contrast, the defence of absolute privilege affords complete protection to certain categories of communication regardless of the publisher's motives or state of mind at the material time. The rationale is that law recognizes that there are certain occasions where it is for the public benefit that a person can speak or write freely and that the public interest is sufficiently high that it should override the usual reputational protection granted by the laws of defamation.

---

[31] See the classic exposition on malice of Lord Diplock in *Horrocks v Lowe* [1975] AC 135 (HL) endorsed by Lord Nicholls in *Cheng Albert v Tse Wai Chun Paul* (n 29, above).

[32] *Loveless v Earl*, above n 17.

[33] See, for example, the case of *Phipps v Bradford Hospitals NHS Trust* (EAT/531/02, 30 April 2003), discussed at para 4.88, in Chapter 4, above.

[34] See eg the Australian case of *Cush v Dillon; Boland v Dillon* [2011] HCA 30.

[35] (Unreported, 6 February 2001), QBD.

[36] Although he himself subsequently doubled that figure with his finding of malice in *Lillie and Reed v Newcastle City Council* [2002] 146 SJLB 225.

There are a small number of cases where a whistleblower might benefit from a defence of **17.33** absolute privilege, for example where a statement is made to investigators where an official investigation is ongoing; see *Taylor v Director of the Serious Fraud Office*[37] and *Mahon v Rahn (No 2)*.[38] It has also been confirmed—albeit not until surprisingly recently—that defamatory allegations published to the police are absolutely privileged.[39]

D. Publication on a Matter of Public Interest

(1) Background

The Defamation Act 2013 (section 4) introduced a new defence of publication on a matter **17.34** of public interest where a defendant can show that:

(a) the statement complained of was, or formed part of, a statement on a matter of public interest; and

(b) the defendant reasonably believed that publishing the statement complained of was in the public interest.

This new defence is founded upon the principles expounded in the common law defence of so-called *Reynolds* qualified privilege,[40] which in turn was itself abolished by the Defamation Act 2013.[41]

In *Reynolds v Times Newspapers Ltd* ([1999] 3 WLR 1010) the House of Lords (while osten- **17.35** sibly adhering to the conceptual foundation of duty and interest qualified privilege) upheld what was effectively a public interest defence in cases of defamation. In cases where 'the public was entitled to know the particular information' (per Lord Nicholls at p 1020C)— an issue to be determined by reference to all the circumstances of the case and particularly to ten specific criteria[42] identified in the judgment of Lord Nicholls (at p 1027C–F)—the media would be protected where it published defamatory statements even if these should prove to be untrue. Although the public interest was at the heart of this defence, it was commonly referred to as a defence of responsible journalism.[43]

While it is not the purpose of this chapter to review fully the means by which a media entity **17.36** might seek to defend itself against a defamation claim arising out of its coverage of material originating with a whistleblower, the introduction of the new defence of publication on a matter of public interest will clearly have a significant impact upon cases resulting from third tier/wider disclosures.

However, before further considering this new defence in the context of publication by the **17.37** media (however loosely this term may be defined), it is worth noting that the Defamation Act 2013 in fact makes no express mention of responsible journalism, nor does it contain any apparent stipulation that the section 4 defence can be relied upon only in relation to allegations published in the media.

---

[37] [1999] 2 AC 177

[38] [2000] 1 WLR 2150 CA.

[39] *Westcott v Westcott* [2008] EWCA Civ 818, [2009] QB 407 per Ward LJ at para 32.

[40] Although the use of this phrase was frowned upon by the Court of Appeal in *Jameel v Wall Street Journal Europe* [2005] 4 All ER 356.

[41] Section 4(6).

[42] As set out at para 17.52.

[43] While the *Reynolds* defence was widely regarded as being a media defence, in *Seaga v Harper* ([2008] UKPC 9) the Privy Council held that in principle it could apply to a non-media publication. The case of *Seaga* concerned a Jamaican politician who gave a speech at a public meeting attended by the press, although the Privy Council went on to hold that the *Reynolds* defence failed on its facts.

17.38 As such, if a whistleblower were to face a defamation claim (whether brought in relation to a protected disclosure or to another defamatory publication) it would arguably be open to him/her to rely on the public interest defence, in addition to, or instead of, the traditional qualified privilege defence.

17.39 The official explanatory notes which accompany the Defamation Act 2013 state (at para 29) that the new defence is 'based on the existing common law defence established in *Reynolds v Times Newspapers* and is intended to reflect the principles established in that case and in subsequent case law', which of course include the principles of responsible journalism (albeit it was apparently accepted by the Privy Council that the *Reynolds* defence may not be strictly limited to the media).[44]

17.40 The Act (at section 4(4)) goes on to state that the court 'must make such allowance for editorial judgement as it considers appropriate' when determining whether the defendant reasonably believed publishing the statement was in the public interest, once again in apparent anticipation of the fact that this is a defence upon which journalists and media publishers will rely.

17.41 However, the explanatory notes to the Act also make clear (at para 33) that the question of making allowances for editorial judgement 'is not limited to editors in the media context', while the early case law on the public interest defence also indicates that it is of wider applicability.[45] As such, while the interpretation of the new defence is very much in its infancy, it certainly appears that whistleblowers may be able to avail themselves of it.

(2) The statement was, or formed part of, a statement on a matter of public interest

17.42 In contrast with the public interest test that applies in protected disclosure cases (which requires only that the worker *reasonably believes* that disclosure is made in the public interest),[46] a libel defendant must prove as a matter of fact that the statement was, or formed part of, a statement on a matter of public interest in order to avail himself of this defence.

17.43 The Defamation Act 2013 does not attempt to define what is meant by 'the public interest' on the basis that it is (according to the Explanatory Notes to the Act) 'well established in the English common law'.[47]

17.44 In the media context, it is expected that the courts will continue to be guided by the *Reynolds* case law in determining the public interest test which is to apply to the new defence. In its ruling in *Reynolds* the Court of Appeal stated that by matters of public interest they meant:[48]

> matters relating to the public life of the community and those who take part in it, including . . . activities such as the conduct of government and political life, elections and public administration . . . [and] more widely . . . the governance of public bodies, institutions and companies which give rise to a public interest in disclosure, but excluding matters which are personal and private, such that there is no public interest in their disclosure.[49]

---

[44] *Seaga v Harper* [2008] UKPC 9.

[45] *Economou v de Freitas* [2016] EWHC 1853 (QB) at para 139—see discussion below at paras 17.56 and 17.57.

[46] Section 43B Employment Rights Act 1996 as amended by s 17 of the Enterprise and Regulatory Reform Act 2013, see detailed discussion in Chapter 4.

[47] At para 30.

[48] *Reynolds v Times Newspapers Ltd* [2001] 2 AC 127 at 176–77 per Lord Bingham.

[49] For a discussion on the impact on protected disclosure of the meaning of the 'public interest' in other legal contexts, see discussion in Chapter 4 at para 4.36 onwards.

Defamation cases in which there has been found to be a public interest include protection of **17.45**
public health in relation to claims made by a high-profile nutritionist,[50] police corruption,[51]
corruption and cheating in sport,[52] involvement in serious crimes including the funding of
terrorism,[53] organized crime,[54] breach of the duties of trustees of charities,[55] and a wide variety
of allegations of corporate malpractice including overcharging customers, failing to conduct
proper checks on the qualifications and background of staff and making false claims as to
insurance cover,[56] allegations that a subcontractor employed child labour in India,[57] and the
misappropriation of corporate funds.[58]

It is worth noting that the new Act provides that the public interest defence may be available **17.46**
where the statement complained of was, 'or formed part of', a statement on a matter of public
interest. Therefore it is not necessary to show that the defamatory allegations themselves were
on a matter of public interest if it can instead be demonstrated that they formed part of a wider
public interest statement. In this situation, the question is likely to turn on whether it was reasonable to include the allegations complained of as part of the overall picture.[59]

Any whistleblower (or indeed, any other defendant) contemplating this defence would be wise **17.47**
to note the dicta of Lord Hoffmann in *Jameel (Mohammed) v Wall Street Journal SPRL*:[60]

> . . . the more serious the allegation, the more important it is that it should make a real
> contribution to the public interest element in the article.

In the most recent pre-Defamation Act 2013 cases on the *Reynolds* defence, the courts have **17.48**
been keen to stress that allowances should be made for editorial judgement when deciding
whether the defamatory details should have been included,[61] a consideration which is now
reflected in the second limb of the statutory defence.

(3) Reasonable belief of the defendant that publication was in the public interest

As noted above,[62] the second limb of the statutory defence represents an apparently sig- **17.49**
nificant departure from the *Reynolds* case law; in place of any express requirement that
journalism be responsible, there appears the provision that a defendant must establish that
s/he 'reasonably believed that publishing the statement complained of was in the public
interest'.[63]

This wording essentially mirrors the wording of section 43B ERA which states that for a **17.50**
disclosure to be protected it must entail 'disclosure of information which, in the reasonable
belief of the worker making the disclosure, is made in the public interest'.[64] The focus for

---

[50] *McKeith v News Group Newspapers* [2005] EMLR 32 (QB).
[51] See eg *Flood v Times Newspapers Ltd* [2012] 2 AC 273.
[52] See eg *Grobbelaar v News Group Newspapers Ltd* [2001] 2 All ER 437.
[53] *Jameel v Wall Street Journal Europe SPRL* (No 3) [2007] 1 AC 359.
[54] *Hunt v Times Newspapers* [2013] EWHC 1868 (QB).
[55] *Seray-Wurie v Charity Commission of England and Wales* [2008] EWHC 870 (QB).
[56] *GKR Karate (UK) Ltd v Yorkshire Post Newspapers Ltd* [2000] 1 WLR 2571 (CA).
[57] *James Gilbert Ltd v MGN Ltd* [2000] EMLR 680 (QB).
[58] *Hutcheson v News Group Newspapers Ltd* also known as *KGM v News Group Newspapers Ltd* [2010]
EWHC 3145 (QB).
[59] *Prince Radu of Hohenzollern v Houston* [2007] EWHC 2735 (QB) at para 14.
[60] UKHL 44; [2007] 1 AC 359 at [51].
[61] See eg Lord Dyson in *Flood v Times Newspapers* [2012] 2 AC 273 at para 194.
[62] See para 17.37.
[63] The Nicholls criteria were included in the original draft of the statutory defence, but were omitted
from the Bill as it passed.
[64] See the discussion in Chapter 4 at 4.76 onwards.

both tests is the effect of the publication or disclosure and whether the worker reasonably believed it to be in the public interest, rather than the worker's reasons for making the disclosure.

17.51 The requirement of 'reasonable belief' involves the court applying a two-stage test. First, did the defendant genuinely believe that publication was in the public interest? After this subjective question has been answered, the court must then go on to consider the objective question of whether it was reasonable in all the circumstances for the defendant to hold such a belief.

17.52 The reasonable belief element of this defence was newly introduced by the Defamation Act 2013, and did not form an explicit part of the *Reynolds* defence which preceded it. As noted above, the *Reynolds* defence instead required consideration of ten non-exhaustive criteria, the purpose of which was to determine whether publication was in keeping with the tenets of responsible journalism, as follows:

1. The seriousness of the allegation. The more serious the charge, the more the public is misinformed and the individual harmed, if the allegation is not true.
2. The nature of the information, and the extent to which the subject-matter is a matter of public concern.
3. The source of the information. Some informants have no direct knowledge of the events. Some have their own axes to grind, or are being paid for their stories.
4. The steps taken to verify the information.
5. The status of the information. The allegation may have already been the subject of an investigation which commands respect.
6. The urgency of the matter. News is often a perishable commodity.
7. Whether comment was sought from the plaintiff. He may have information others do not possess or have not disclosed. An approach to the plaintiff will not always be necessary.
8. Whether the article contained the gist of the plaintiff's side of the story.
9. The tone of the article. A newspaper can raise queries or call for an investigation. It need not adopt allegations as statements of fact.
10. The circumstances of the publication, including the timing.[65]

17.53 Now, in deciding both whether publication was in the public interest and whether the defendant held the requisite reasonable belief that publication was in the public interest, the Defamation Act 2013 simply states that 'the court must have regard to all the circumstances of the case'.[66]

17.54 In the context of publications by the media it is anticipated that the courts will continue to have regard to the *Reynolds* criteria in relation to the new statutory public interest defence, on the basis that they will be illuminative as to whether a defendant reasonably believed that publication was in the public interest. For example, if a journalist defendant has taken no steps to verify the information contained in an article and if there were obvious doubts as to the reliability of the source of the allegations complained of, it is likely to be difficult for a defendant to show that s/he reasonably believed that publication was in the public interest.

17.55 It should be noted, however, that there was considerable criticism from within media circles to the effect that the *Reynolds* criteria were being too strictly applied in court, such that the defence succeeded only on a relatively small number of occasions. The enactment of the public interest defence was intended to address this criticism by replacing the specific *Reynolds* criteria (which had in effect been treated as hurdles, each of which a publisher had

---

[65] *Reynolds v Times Newspapers Ltd and Others* [2001] 2 AC 127.
[66] Section 4(2).

to surmount) with broader public interest considerations. This is underlined by section 4(4) which expressly provides that the court 'must make such allowance for editorial judgement as it considers appropriate'[67] when determining whether it was reasonable for the defendant to believe that publishing the statement was in the public interest.

The fact that the specific test of reasonable belief is a new element to this defence means there **17.56** is little precedent from the libel courts as to how it will be interpreted and applied in practice, and in particular in non-media cases. Some guidance has, however, been provided in the first case to consider the public interest defence in detail—*Economou v de Freitas* [2016] EWHC 1853. The claim was brought against an individual whose allegations were published in the media, rather than against the media publishers. In his judgment Warby J set out a number of points in deciding the reasonableness of the defendant's belief, including:

> The 'circumstances' to be considered pursuant to s 4(2) are those that go to whether or not the belief was held, and whether or not it was reasonable. . . . The focus must therefore be on things the defendant said or knew or did, or failed to do, up to the time of publication. Events that happened later, or which were unknown to the defendant at the time he played his role in the publication, are unlikely to have any or any significant bearing on the key questions.[68]

Warby J also considered[69] that a number of features of the *Reynolds* defence were applicable **17.57** to the new statutory defence, including flexibility and adaptability to the circumstances of the individual case. He went on to set out a non-exhaustive list of circumstances relevant to the question of what enquiries and checks a defendant would need to have undertaken in any given case to demonstrate that his/her belief was reasonable:

> Among the circumstances relevant to the question of what enquiries and checks are needed, the subject-matter needs consideration, as do the particular words used, the range of meanings the defendant ought reasonably to have considered they might convey, and the particular role of the defendant in question.

While it appears that the new public interest defence should in principle be available to **17.58** whistleblowers, it remains unclear how it might apply to the whistleblower who has provided information to a media entity. For example, where the court finds publication of the relevant information to the world at large to have been in the public interest then it might be thought obvious that the whistleblower's original disclosure to the media was also in the public interest. However, while it seems the umbrella of the new public interest defence extends in principle to cover the media's sources against claims in defamation, it is easy to envisage arguments to the effect that the public interest test is not, in the circumstances of a particular case, satisfied by disclosure to the media rather than to, say, the appropriate regulatory body. In particular, a whistleblower may face an uphill battle to persuade a court that s/he 'reasonably believed' publication to have been in the public interest in circumstances where s/he had failed to avail him/herself of more appropriately restricted modes of disclosure.

It is also easy to contemplate circumstances in which the court would be only too keen **17.59** to deny a supposed whistleblower the protection it is willing to afford a media defendant that has conducted itself responsibly; most obviously where a 'whistleblower' has acted maliciously by making statements s/he knows to be untrue to a newspaper which unfortunately has had no reason to doubt the truth of what it is being told and has published accordingly.[70]

---

[67] Section 4(4).
[68] ibid, para 139(3) and (4).
[69] At para 240.
[70] It is the apparent and not the actual reliability of the source that is relevant. See *GKR Karate (UK) Ltd v Yorkshire Post Newspapers Ltd & others* [2000] 2 All ER 931.

17.60 One factor that is likely to minimize the number of occasions upon which this kind of interaction falls to be considered by the court is the media's continued entitlement generally to preserve the anonymity of its confidential sources. Although the Nicholls criteria required the court to assess the nature and extent of the defendant's inquiries prior to publication, the Court of Appeal held that, given the statutory protection afforded to a journalist who does not wish to disclose his/her source,[71] the identification of a source should not be a necessary element of a defence of responsible journalism[72] and the same will almost certainly be true of the new statutory defence. Thus if a whistleblower obtains an undertaking of confidentiality before s/he speaks with a journalist it is most unlikely (barring the application of the relevant exemptions under the Contempt of Court Act 1981) that the court will compel the latter to disclose his/her identity.

(4) Traditional qualified privilege versus publication on a matter of public interest

17.61 In light of the current uncertainty as to the precise scope of the statutory public interest defence, consideration should be given to whether the statutory defence may offer any advantages to a whistleblower over and above the traditional qualified privilege defence.

17.62 A key distinction between the two defences relates to the question of the motivation of the worker in publishing the statements complained of. The traditional qualified privilege defence can be defeated by establishing that the defendant was malicious in publishing the allegations complained of. Therefore if the claimant can show that the defendant's dominant motive was improper, the defence will fail.

17.63 In contrast with this, the question of motive is not a direct consideration in relation to the statutory public interest defence; provided that the defendant can demonstrate that s/he reasonably believed that publication was in the public interest, it will not matter if his/her primary motivation for publication was improper.

17.64 The facts giving rise to the case of *Street v Derbyshire Unemployed Workers' Centre*[73] illustrate a situation in which, if faced with a libel claim, the claimant may fail in a defence of qualified privilege but may succeed in relation to the public interest defence.

17.65 As discussed in Chapter 10 (paragraphs 10.112 et seq), in *Street* the claimant alleged that her manager had engaged in fraud to obtain funding for the centre where she worked. Although Ms Street was found to have made a qualifying disclosure (on the basis that she had a reasonable belief that the allegations she made were true), she was also found to have been motivated by personal antagonism towards her manager rather than by public interest considerations and therefore the disclosures were held not to be protected.[74] On these facts Ms Street may have been able to rely on the public interest defence if her manager had brought a claim for libel against her, but a defence of qualified privilege may well have failed.

17.66 As indicated above (at paragraph 17.29), however, the libel courts have generally been reluctant to reach findings of malice against a defendant. Further, the category of cases where a defendant can show that s/he reasonably believed that publishing was in the public interest—notwithstanding that his/her main motivation for publication was improper—is

---

[71] Section 10 of the Contempt of Court Act 1981.
[72] *Gaddafi v Telegraph Group* [2000] EMLR 431.
[73] [2005] ICR 97 (CA).
[74] The case of *Street* was determined before the Employment Rights Act was amended by s 17 of ERRA 2013 so that in *Street* the question of good faith fell to be considered when deciding whether the disclosure was protected, rather than simply at the remedies stage.

likely to be very narrow. As noted in Chapter 4,[75] where a court or tribunal finds that a worker has acted with ulterior motives rather than with the predominant purpose of exposing, preventing, or addressing wrongdoing, then it may well be difficult to persuade the court or tribunal that the whistleblower believed that making the disclosure was in the public interest, particularly where it is not obviously a matter of wider public interest.

E. The Public Interest Disclosure Act 1998

PIDA does not provide a whistleblower with specific protection against proceedings for defamation in relation to defamatory allegations contained within a protected disclosure.[76] **17.67**

However, if such proceedings were to be brought (or even threatened) by the employer, or indeed by a fellow worker or an agent of the employer, these might be regarded as subjecting the worker to a detriment within section 47B ERA as amended by ERRA.[77] **17.68**

This would not directly affect the ability of the defamed party to bring a claim; provided the cause of action was made out then the defamation claim would succeed unless the worker could make out one of the recognized defamation defences. However, if a co-worker, employer, or employer's agent were to contemplate bringing a defamation claim against a worker in respect of allegations contained in a protected disclosure it would certainly be prudent to weigh up their potential exposure to a compensation claim for detriment. **17.69**

Furthermore, it might be felt to be contrary to the underlying policy of the Act if a worker could be the subject of defamation proceedings despite having made a protected disclosure. On this basis a worker who makes a protected disclosure could argue that s/he should by definition also succeed in a defence of qualified privilege in relation to that disclosure, particularly as the duty and interest test mirrors the structure of PIDA to a substantial degree. However, and as discussed in detail above,[78] the two tests do differ in one respect in particular, in that the qualified privilege defence can be defeated if it can be shown that the defendant's publication was in bad faith, while the question of motive is no longer relevant when deciding whether a protected disclosure has been made. Therefore, it is certainly conceivable that a worker may succeed in establishing that s/he had made a protected disclosure, but then remain exposed to a libel claim if it could be established that s/he had a dominant improper motive for making the disclosure.[79] **17.70**

In any event, this specific point has not, as far as we are aware, yet been determined by the court. Similar uncertainty exists in relation to the converse position where a worker publishes a defamatory statement in circumstances that do not amount to a protected disclosure under PIDA. One example may be where a worker has sent an email to an employer making bare allegations against a colleague, but the worker failed to provide sufficient information for it to constitute a protected disclosure. It could be argued that qualified privilege should not apply in such circumstances on the basis that the Act encapsulates the balance struck by **17.71**

---

[75] See Chapter 4, para 4.81.

[76] Indeed PIDA makes no mention of the law of defamation.

[77] In *Royal Mail Group Ltd v Jhuti* [2016] ICR 1043 the EAT (at para 27) suggested that although there may now be a right to bring a claim for detriment against a fellow worker, the only remedy is a declaration, and there is no right to compensation. But as discussed in Chapter 8 (paras 8.73–8.77) this appears to have overlooked s 48(5) ERA.

[78] At paragraphs 17.25–17.31 and 17.62–17.66.

[79] As noted above at para 17.56, it appears from the case of *Economou v de Freitas* [2016] EWHC 1853 that non media entities – including, arguably, workers – may also be able to rely on the statutory public interest defence under s 4 Defamation Act 2013.

Parliament between the public interest in encouraging disclosure of matters of public concern and the interests of the employer and/or those others about whom the allegations are made. Against this it might be said that the Act does not, in any context, purport to define in comprehensive fashion the actions that might properly be taken by a whistleblower—or, for that matter, the circumstances in which an employer or a fellow worker can take action against a whistleblower.[80] For this and other reasons it does not necessarily follow that, provided the duty and interest test is satisfied, a defence of qualified privilege should fail merely because the worker would not have been entitled to the higher level of protection under PIDA.

F. Limitation

17.72   At common law the basic limitation period for bringing proceedings for defamation is, in comparison with other tort claims, relatively short: one year from the date of publication in relation to libel.[81]

17.73   The Defamation Act 2013, at section 1, now provides that the cause of action is not complete until serious harm has been caused or is likely to be caused.

17.74   The extent to which this affects the common law position in practice has been the subject of considerable debate.[82] For the purposes of advising a prospective defamation claimant it is certainly safest to proceed on the basis that proceedings should be issued within one year of the date of the publication complained of.

---

[80] For example, even where a disclosure is not protected an employee might still be protected against unfair dismissal—a point emphasized by Auld LJ in *Street v Derbyshire Unemployed Workers' Centre* [2005] ICR 97 (CA) at para 47.

[81] For slanders which were actionable only on proof of special damage the cause of action did not accrue until the damage was sustained.

[82] See eg: Richard Parkes, QC and Professor Alastair Mullis, *Gatley on Libel and Slander*, 12th edn, as amended by the First Supplement. London: Sweet & Maxwell, December 2013, p 789.

18

THE EUROPEAN CONVENTION ON HUMAN RIGHTS AND PUBLIC INTEREST DISCLOSURES BY WORKERS

A. Introduction

18.01 We have seen in Chapters 14 and 16 how rights contained in the ECHR, particularly Articles 8 and 10, have shaped the development of domestic law in relation to the protection of privacy and confidentiality, and protection of copyright, and the balance to be struck with rights in relation to freedom of expression and disclosures in the public interest. In Chapter 15 we saw how decisions of the European Court of Human Rights (ECtHR) have shaped the approach to be taken by the courts when considering an application to reveal the source of information, which may have been provided by a whistleblower, particularly journalists' sources.[1] Until fairly recently, there was relatively little direct guidance from the ECtHR on the approach to be taken in relation to public interest disclosures in the workplace in a context that would be covered by the ERA's protected disclosure provisions, where the employer dismisses a worker or subjects him/her to a detriment by reason of a protected disclosure. It was possible, as we did in previous editions of this book, to piece together from decisions in related areas, and from European Commission decisions, how these issues were likely to be addressed. But more recently, and notably since the decision in *Guja v Moldova* (2011) 53 EHRR 16, there have been a spate of decisions in this area from which a set of criteria has developed to assess whether it is proportionate to interfere with freedom of expression.

18.02 The developing jurisprudence in this area may have implications not only in relation to enforcing rights outside of PIDA, such as confidentiality or reputational rights,[2] but might also open scope for argument as to the proper interpretation or application of the PIDA rights themselves, having regard to:

- Section 2 of the Human Rights Act (HRA): the obligation on domestic courts and tribunals when determining questions which arise in connection with Convention rights; courts must take into account judgments of the ECtHR and opinions and decisions of the Commission where relevant to the proceedings.

---

[1] See Chapter 15, and the discussion of *Goodwin v United Kingdom* (1996) 22 EHRR 123 (ECtHR); *Financial Times Ltd v United Kingdom* (2010) 50 EHRR 46; and (extending beyond journalist's sources) *Noordeen v Hill and Health Research Authority* [2012] EWHC 2847.
[2] See eg *Karpov v Browder and others* [2014] EMLR 8 at para 47.

- Section 3 HRA: the obligation, so far as it is possible to do so, to read and give effect to primary legislation in a way which is compatible with Convention rights. See eg the summary of principles in *British Gas Trading Ltd v Lock and others* [2016] EWCA Civ 983 at paras 31–40: a conforming meaning may be given to domestic legislation even if this is contrary to its unambiguous meaning according to ordinary principles of interpretation, subject to a restriction on doing so (a) where words sought to be read in do not 'go with the grain of the legislation' or are inconsistent with a fundamental feature of it, and (b) where this would require courts to make choices, including policy choices, which are properly for the legislature and where they may have significant practical consequences.
- Section 6 HRA, which makes it unlawful for a public authority to act in a way which is incompatible with a Convention right.

18.03   We therefore address first the developing ECtHR jurisprudence on the approach to be taken to public interest disclosures in the employment context, before considering some potential implications for the domestic approach to protected disclosures.

B. Article 10 ECHR

18.04   The essential issue in the Convention case law in this area is whether the interference with the whistleblower's right to freedom of expression is justified. Article 10(2) requires that the interference be:

(a) prescribed by law; and
(b) necessary in a democratic society:
    (i)   in the interests of national security, territorial integrity, or public safety;
    (ii) for the prevention of disorder or crime;
    (iii) for the protection of health or morals;
    (iv) for the protection of the reputation or rights of others;
    (v)   for preventing the disclosure of information received in confidence; or
    (vi) for maintaining the authority and impartiality of the judiciary.

18.05   In addressing issues concerning interference with freedom of expression rights, the ECtHR has generally been willing to accept that the restriction is 'prescribed by law' and to accept that it is for national authorities to interpret and apply domestic law.[3] The key question is then whether the interference is 'necessary in a democratic society'. This requires first the identification of a legitimate aim, which might typically be protecting the employer's right to fidelity or confidentiality (or, as it is put in the ECtHR decisions, the employee's duty of loyalty, reserve, and discretion[4]), or protecting the employer's reputation or otherwise protecting the rights of the employer.[5] The question is then whether, having regard to that aim, the interference is 'necessary in a democratic society'.

---

[3] See the cases discussed in Section D below at paras 18.11 et seq and eg *Goodwin v United Kingdom* (1996) 22 EHRR 123 at 139–41 where the court applied this principle in finding that the possibility of a journalist being required to disclose his sources was sufficiently 'prescribed by law' even though the court had to carry out a balancing exercise between competing public interests and had to be satisfied that disclosure was 'in the interests of justice'.

[4] See *Guja v Moldova* (2011) 53 EHRR 16 App no 14277/0 and the line of cases discussed in Section D below at paras 18.11 et seq, following *Guja*.

[5] See eg *Heinisch v Germany* App no 28274/08, 21 July 2011, [2011] IRLR 922. Indeed interference need not even be for the purpose of protecting legally recognized rights: see *X v UK* (1979) 16 D & R 101: there is a legitimate interest in protecting the rights of others not to be offended by speech.

The ECtHR has explained on several occasions (eg *Barthold v Germany* (1985) 7 EHRR 383 at para 55) that:

> whilst the adjective 'necessary', within the meaning of Article 10(2) of the Convention, is not synonymous with 'indispensable', neither does it have the flexibility of such expressions as 'admissible', 'ordinary', 'useful', 'reasonable' or 'desirable'; rather it implies a 'pressing social need'. The Contracting States enjoy a power of appreciation in this respect, but that power of appreciation goes hand in hand with a European supervision which is more or less extensive depending on the circumstances; it is for the Court to make the final determination as to whether the interference in issue corresponds to such a need, whether it is 'proportionate to the legitimate aim pursued' and whether the reasons given by the national authorities to justify it are 'relevant and sufficient'.[6]

Thus, it must be shown that the interference: **18.06**

(a) corresponds to a 'pressing social need';
(b) is proportionate to the aim pursued or, as it is sometimes put,[7] there is a reasonable relationship of proportionality between the legitimate aim pursued and the means deployed to achieve that aim; and
(c) is justified by reasons which are relevant and sufficient.

The ECtHR has often emphasized that the exceptions contained in Article 10(2) are to be **18.07** 'narrowly interpreted' and must be 'convincingly established'.[8]

C. Council of Europe Recommendation

Before turning in more detail to the recent ECtHR jurisprudence, a useful starting point **18.08** is provided by the Council of Europe's Recommendation and Explanatory Memorandum (CM/Rec (2014)7) of 30 April 2014. This provides a helpful distillation of the following six criteria, drawn from the ECtHR decisions, as being key to whether the interference with Article 10 is to be regarded as 'necessary in a democratic society':[9]

i. whether the person who has made the disclosure had at his or her disposal alternative channels for making the disclosure;
ii. the public interest in the disclosed information.[10] The Court in *Guja v Moldova*[11] noted that 'in a democratic system the acts or omissions of government must be subject to the close scrutiny not only of the legislative and judicial authorities but also of the

---

[6] See to similar effect, in the whistleblowing context, *Guja v Moldova* (2011) 53 EHRR 16 at para 69.
[7] *Fressoz and Roire v France* (2001) 31 EHRR 2 at para 56, ECJ.
[8] See eg *Vogt v Germany; Handyside v United Kingdom* (1976) 1 EHRR 737 at para 49; *Lingens v Austria* (1986) 8 EHRR 407 at para 41; *Jersild v Denmark* (1994) 19 EHRR 1 at para 31; *Goodwin v United Kingdom* (1996) 22 EHRR 123 at para 40; *Kharlamov v Russia* App no 27447/07 [2015] ECHR 27447/07, 8 October 2015.
[9] Set out at paragraph 53 of the Explanatory Memorandum, in the order which the principles were set out in *Bucur and Toma v Romania* [2013] ECHR 14.
[10] In *Thorgeirson v Iceland* (1992) 14 EHRR 843 (not an employment case) the ECtHR expressly rejected the proposition that the wide limits of acceptable criticism in political discussion do not apply equally to other matters of public concern. In *Steel and Morris v United Kingdom* (2005) 41 EHRR 403 ('the Mac libel case') at para 88 the Court acknowledged the breadth of matters that are of public concern, stating (in the context of allegations on abusive and immoral farming and employment practices, deforestation, the exploitation of children and their parents through aggressive advertising and the sale of unhealthy food) that 'The Court has long held that "political expression", including expression on matters of public interest and concern, requires a high level of protection under Article 10.'
[11] *Guja v Moldova* App no 14277/04 (2011) 53 EHRR 16, considered further below.

media and public opinion. The interest which the public may have in particular information can sometimes be so strong as to override even a legally imposed duty of confidence';

iii. the authenticity of the disclosed information. The Court in *Guja v Moldova* reiterated that freedom of expression carries with it duties and responsibilities and any person who chooses to disclose information must carefully verify, to the extent permitted by the circumstances, that it is accurate and reliable. The Court in *Bucur and Toma v Romania*[12] bore in mind Resolution 1729 (2010) of the Parliamentary Assembly of the Council of Europe and the need to protect whistleblowers on the basis that they had 'reasonable grounds' to believe that the information disclosed was true;

iv. detriment to the employer. Is the public disclosure so important in a democratic society that it outweighs the detriment suffered by the employer? In both *Guja v Moldova* and *Bucur and Toma v Romania* the employer was a public body and the Court balanced the public interest in maintaining public confidence in these public bodies against the public interest in disclosing information on their wrongdoing;

v. whether the disclosure is made in good faith. The Court in *Guja v Moldova* stated that 'an act motivated by a personal grievance or a personal antagonism or the expectation of personal advantage, including pecuniary gain, would not justify a particularly strong level of protection';

vi. the severity of the sanction imposed on the person who made the disclosure and its consequences.

18.09 These principles were set out in the Explanatory Memorandum by way of elucidation of Principle 8 of the Council of Europe's Recommendation, that restrictions and exceptions to the rights and obligations of any person in relation to public interest reports and disclosures should be no more than necessary and, in any event, not be such as to defeat the objectives of the Recommendation (which included, in Principle 7, facilitating public interest reporting and disclosures). The above principles were identified as being relevant to cases where the disclosure was made in the public domain, meaning outside an employment or regulatory relationship. To that end, the Explanatory Memorandum stated (at para 51) that:

> For an individual who reports a concern about wrongdoing within the working relationship—to the employer or to a person designated by the employer to receive reports in confidence—there is usually little or no basis in law for an employer to take action against that person in any event. There is no breach of confidentiality or duty of loyalty.[13] Outside of the working relationship, however, it is recognised that the interest of employers to manage their organisations and to protect their interests (for example, intellectual property rights) must be balanced with the interest of the public to be protected from harm, wrongdoing or exploitation. This balancing must take into account other democratic principles such as transparency, right to information and freedom of expression, and the media, all of which tend to favour disclosure over restricting information. The phrase, 'no more than necessary', strikes the appropriate balance between the different competing interests.

18.10 We make the following introductory observations in relation to this summary:

- As we set out below, the ECtHR jurisprudence, and in particular the decision in *Langner v Germany* [2015] ECHR 803, points to the need for a degree of caution around this statement of the position concerning disclosures within the working relationship.

---

12 *Bucur and Toma v Romania* [2013] ECHR 14.
13 In a footnote here, the Explanatory Memorandum noted that:

> It is important that any rules on defamation do not hinder internal reports of suspected wrongdoing. In this regard, any action taken against anyone for misconduct as a result of an initial report should be based on the rules of natural justice and, as a result, there should be a full and fair investigation of the facts and an opportunity for the person to respond.

- Subject to that, the criteria have generally been formulated in the context of external disclosures, and as such the closest comparison is with section 43G ERA, with the more nuanced balancing exercises required for disclosures within that section.
- In at least one respect there is a fundamental difference from the approach in the ERA's protected disclosure provisions. Those provisions separate out from the issue of detriment or dismissal the question of whether the disclosure is protected. The question of whether there is protection is a prior question. By contrast, the ECtHR approach incorporates the sanction as one key factor to be taken into account in relation to whether there is unlawful interference with the Article 10 right.
- The ECtHR is engaged in a process of review of the decision of the national court, in relation to whether it has discharged its obligation to secure the Article 10 right—including positive obligations to do so where the detriment has been imposed by a private employer. That is a different perspective from that of the employment tribunal which is focused on the act or omission of the employer (or a respondent worker or agent), and a degree of caution is required in considering the decisions in the light of this. We address this further at paragraphs 18.24–18.29 below in the context of the decisions in *Matuz v Hungary* [2014] ECHR 1112, [2015] IRLR 74 and *Rubins v Latvia* [2015] ECHR 2, [2015] IRLR 319.

D. The Recent ECtHR Case Law

18.11 We turn to consider the key ECtHR decisions more closely. In *Guja v Moldova* (2011) 53 EHRR 16 (App No 14277/04), Mr Iacob Guja was dismissed from the Prosecutor General's Office (PGO) for leaking two letters (sent by a deputy Minister and the deputy Speaker in Parliament to the PGO) to a newspaper which, in his opinion, disclosed corruption and political interference in the PGO, involving interference by a high-ranking politician in pending criminal proceedings. Unsurprisingly, the ECtHR held that Mr Guja's dismissal for making the letters public amounted to an 'interference by a public authority' with his right to freedom of expression under the first paragraph of Article 10. The court said that it was ready to accept that the legitimate aim pursued was the prevention of the disclosure of information received in confidence.

18.12 Turning to the crucial question of whether the interference with Mr Guja's Article 10 rights was necessary in a democratic society, and in particular a proportionate relationship between the interference and the aim thereby pursued, the court first noted that Article 10 applies to the workplace. Weighed against this, employees owed their employer 'a duty of loyalty, reserve and discretion'. Indeed, the court commented that this was particularly so in the case of civil servants, given that their role by its nature demands loyalty, and they often have access to information which the government, for various legitimate reasons, may have an interest in keeping confidential or secret. However, the signalling by a civil servant or an employee in the public sector of 'illegal conduct or wrongdoing in the workplace should, in certain circumstances, enjoy protection'. This might be called for where the employee or civil servant concerned was the only person, or part of a small category of persons, aware of what was happening at work and was thus best placed to act in the public interest by alerting the employer or the public at large. Whether that was so, however, involved considering various factors. In particular the court highlighted the following considerations:

(a) Whether there was available to Mr Guja any other effective means of remedying the wrongdoing which he intended to uncover. Disclosure should be made in the first place to the person's superior or some other competent authority or body and it is only where this is 'clearly impracticable' that the information could, as a last resort, be disclosed to the public.

(b) The public interest involved in the disclosed information: the interest which the public may have in particular information can sometimes be so strong as to override even a legally imposed duty of confidence.[14]

(c) The authenticity of the information disclosed: it was open to the competent state authorities to adopt measures in order to react appropriately and without excess to defamatory accusations which were devoid of foundation or formulated in bad faith.[15] Freedom of expression carried with it duties and responsibilities and any person who chooses to disclose information must carefully verify, to the extent permitted by the circumstances, that it is accurate and reliable.[16]

(d) The court had to weigh the damage, if any, suffered by the public authority as a result of the disclosure in question and assess whether such damage outweighed the interest of the public in having the information revealed. In this connection, the subject matter of the disclosure and the nature of the administrative authority concerned may be relevant.[17]

(e) The motive behind the actions of the reporting employee: an act motivated by a personal grievance, a personal antagonism, or the expectation of personal advantage (including pecuniary gain) would not justify a particularly strong level of protection. It was important to establish that, in making the disclosure, the individual acted:
- in good faith; and
- in the belief that the information was true; and
- in the belief that it was in the public interest to disclose it; and
- in the belief that no other, more discreet, means of remedying the wrongdoing was available to him/her.

(f) Analysis of the penalty imposed on the applicant and its consequences is required.[18]

18.13 Applying those criteria, in upholding Mr Guja's complaint, the court took into account the following aspects:

(a) Whether there were alternative channels for making the disclosure: Neither the Moldovan legislation nor the internal regulations of the PGO contained any provision concerning the reporting of irregularities by employees, so there was no authority other than Mr Guja's superiors to which he could have reported his concerns and no prescribed procedure for reporting such matters. Despite having been aware of the situation for some six months the Prosecutor General had shown no sign of having any intention to respond, but instead gave the impression that he had succumbed to the pressure that had been imposed on his office. There was no satisfactory evidence to counter Mr Guja's submission that none of the proposed alternatives would have been effective in the special circumstances of the present case. In the circumstances, external reporting, even to a newspaper, could be justified.

(b) The information was of public interest: the letters disclosed by Mr Guja had a bearing on issues such as the separation of powers, improper conduct by a high-ranking politician, and the government's attitude towards police brutality. These are very important matters in a democratic society which the public have a legitimate interest in being informed about and which fall within the scope of political debate. It was in the public

---

[14] Referring to *Fressoz and Roire v France* App no 29183/95 (2001) 31 EHRR 2; and *Radio Twist, AS v Slovakia* App no 62202/00.

[15] Referring to *Castells v Spain*, Series A no 236, 23 April 1992, at para 46.

[16] See *Morissens v Belgium* App no 11389/85 (1988) D & R 56 at 127; and *Bladet Tromsø and Stensaas v Norway* App no 21980/93, ECHR 1999-III at para 65.

[17] See *Haseldine v United Kingdom* (18957/91) May 13, 1992.

[18] See *Fuentes Bobo* App no 39293/98, 29 February 2000 at para 49.

interest to maintain confidence in the independence and political neutrality of the prosecuting authorities of a state. The public interest in having information about undue pressure and wrongdoing within the PGO revealed was so important in a democratic society that it outweighed the interest in maintaining public confidence in the PGO. Open discussion of topics of public concern is essential to democracy and regard must be had to the great importance of not discouraging members of the public from voicing their opinions on such matters.

(c) Authenticity: It was common ground that the letters disclosed by the applicant to the newspaper were genuine (ie no issue arose as to the evidential basis of the disclosure).

(d) Damage suffered: whilst the letters sent to the newspaper were not written by officials of the PGO, the conclusion drawn by the newspaper that the PGO was subject to undue influence 'may have had strong negative effects on public confidence in the independence of that institution'.

(e) Mr Guja had acted in good faith.

(f) It had been open to the authorities to apply a less severe penalty; they chose to dismiss Mr Guja, which had negative repercussions on his career: it could also have a serious chilling effect on other employees from the PGO and discourage them from reporting any misconduct. Moreover, in view of the media coverage of the applicant's case, the sanction could have a chilling effect not only on employees of the PGO but also on many other civil servants and employees.

18.14 At first blush there may appear to be similarities here with the approach required by section 43G ERA, with its requirement to consider (amongst other matters) whether in all the circumstances it was reasonable to make the disclosure. Whilst the ECtHR applied a criterion of good faith, that is similar to the requirement under section 43G(1)(c) that the disclosure is not for the purposes of personal gain. However, there are important differences from section 43G:

(1) It is not clear whether any of the gateways to protection in section 43G(2) ERA would have been satisfied in *Guja* (though they might have been). The focus was on whether reporting internally would have been effective and the fact that individuals internally were aware of the issue, but not specifically on whether Mr Guja believed he would have been subjected to a detriment if he reported internally or that information would be concealed or destroyed or that he had made substantially the same discussion to his employer or other responsible body. It was part of Mr Guja's case (at para 62) that he had reasonable grounds for fearing that evidence would be concealed or disclosed if he disclosed his concerns to his superiors, but it is not clear that findings were made as to this and it was not mentioned in the court's reasoning.

(2) Given that disclosure in *Guja* took the form of leaking letters, under the ERA an argument might be expected that the disclosure was to be distinguished from the act of misusing internal documents,[19] albeit that here this was part of the disclosure.

(3) Section 43G ERA leaves no scope to take into account the severity of the sanction.

18.15 In *Heinisch v Germany* [2011] IRLR 922, the ECtHR built upon the approach in *Guja*. *Heinisch* concerned a geriatric nurse employed in a majority state-owned nursing home. She reported her employers to the prosecuting authorities because of the understaffing in the home. Heinisch ended up being dismissed. Although her claim of unfair dismissal was successful in the Berlin Labour Court, the Berlin Labour Court of Appeal quashed the

---

[19] See Chapter 7, paras 7.86–7.156. Cf *Bolton School v Evans* [2007] ICR 641 (CA), though this may be distinguished from the act of breaking into the school computer on the basis that in *Guja* the misuse of documents was part of the disclosure itself.

judgment of the Labour Court and found that the dismissal of 9 February 2005 had been lawful as the applicant's criminal complaint had provided a 'compelling reason' for the termination of the employment relationship without notice, as required under the Civil Code, and had made continuation of the employment relationship unacceptable. The Berlin Labour Court of Appeal held that Heinisch's criminal complaint was neither justified nor proportionate. Heinisch had never attempted to have her allegation of fraud examined internally and, moreover, she had intended to put undue pressure on her employer by provoking a public discussion of the issue. Heinisch could, said the Berlin Labour Court of Appeal, have awaited the outcome of an upcoming visit by the regulator instead of making a criminal complaint.

18.16 Having noted that German law did not contain specific protection for whistleblowing employees, the ECtHR made observations as to relevant European and international measures. In its Resolution no 1729 of 2010[20] on the protection of whistleblowers the Parliamentary Assembly of the Council of Europe had stressed the importance of whistleblowing as an opportunity to strengthen accountability, and bolster the fight against corruption and mismanagement, in both the public and private sectors. It had invited all Member States to review their legislation concerning the protection of whistleblowers. The ECtHR also noted that a number of international instruments addressed the protection of whistleblowers in specific contexts, in particular the fight against corruption, such as the Council of Europe's Criminal Law Convention on Corruption and Civil Law Convention on Corruption, or the United Nations Convention against Corruption.

18.17 The court noted that it was not disputed between the parties that the criminal complaint lodged by Heinisch had to be regarded as whistleblowing on the alleged unlawful conduct of the employer, which fell within the ambit of Article 10 of the Convention. It was also common ground between the parties that the resulting dismissal of the applicant and the related decisions of the domestic courts amounted to an interference with the applicant's right to freedom of expression.

18.18 The court accepted the contention that the interference with Heinisch's right to freedom of expression was 'prescribed by law'. There was no dispute between the parties that the interference pursued the legitimate aim of protecting the reputation and rights of others, namely the business reputation and interests of the employer.

18.19 It was therefore necessary to examine whether the interference was 'necessary in a democratic society'; in particular whether there was a proportionate relationship between the interference and the aim pursued. The court said that its task, in exercising its supervisory jurisdiction, was not to take the place of the competent national authorities but rather to review under Article 10 the decisions they delivered pursuant to their power of appreciation. However, this did not mean that the supervision was limited to ascertaining whether the state exercised its discretion reasonably, carefully, and in good faith. Instead, what the court had to do was look at the interference complained of in the light of the case as a whole and determine whether it was 'proportionate to the legitimate aim pursued' and the reasons relied upon by the national authorities to justify it were 'relevant and sufficient'. The court had to be satisfied that the national authorities applied standards which conformed to the principles embodied in Article 10 and that there was an acceptable assessment of the relevant facts. The review standard was therefore a fairly intense one.

---

[20] Now superseded by Recommendation CM/Rec (2014) 7.

As in *Guja* (above), the court noted that the signaling by an employee in the public **18.20** sector of illegal conduct or wrongdoing in the workplace should, in certain circumstances, enjoy protection. It reiterated the observation in *Guja* that this might be called for in particular where the employee or civil servant concerned was the only person, or part of a small category of persons, aware of what is happening at work and was thus best placed to act in the public interest by alerting the employer or the public at large. Whilst employees owe to their employer a duty of loyalty, reserve, and discretion, and (the court said) such a duty of loyalty may be more pronounced in the event of civil servants and employees in the public sector as compared to employees in private-law employment relationships, the court held that it also constituted a feature of private-law employment relationships.

The court examined the factors to be considered when assessing the proportionality of the **18.21** interference in relation to the legitimate aim pursued, essentially adopting (though re-ordering) the same criteria as in *Guja* (see paragraph 18.12 above). This was addressed under the following heads:

(1) *The public interest in the disclosed information*: The court held that dissemination of information about the quality or deficiencies of care for elderly people was of vital importance with a view to preventing abuse, and even more so when institutional care was provided by a state-owned company, where the confidence of the public in an adequate provision of vital care services by the state is at stake.

(2) *Whether there were alternative channels for making the disclosure*: The court stated that disclosure should be made in the first place to the person's superior or other competent authority or body and it is only where this is clearly impracticable that the information could, as a last resort, be disclosed to the public. The court therefore had to take into account whether Heinisch had any other effective means of remedying the wrongdoing. Where internal channels could not reasonably be expected to function properly, external whistleblowing should be protected. Here Heinisch had indicated on numerous occasions to her superiors that she was overburdened and had also alerted the management to a possible criminal complaint through her counsel. While the legal qualification of the employer's conduct as 'aggravated fraud' was used for the first time in the criminal complaint drafted by Heinisch's lawyer, Heinisch had nevertheless previously made internal disclosure of the factual circumstances on which her subsequent criminal complaint was based. The court said that it had not been presented with sufficient evidence to counter Heinisch's submission that any further internal complaints would not have constituted an effective means with a view to investigating and remedying the shortcomings in the care provided. In circumstances such as those in Heinisch's case, external reporting by means of a criminal complaint could be justified. It also observed, in response to a suggestion that Heinisch should and could have waited for external inspections to take place, that such external inspections appeared not to have resulted in any improvement.

(3) *The authenticity of the information disclosed*: The court commented that any person who chooses to disclose information must 'carefully verify, to the extent permitted by the circumstances, that it is accurate and reliable', in particular if owing an employee duties of loyalty. Here the allegations made by Heinisch were 'not devoid of factual background' and there was nothing to establish that she had knowingly or frivolously reported incorrect information even though she 'allowed herself a certain degree of exaggeration and generalisation'.

(4) *Whether the applicant acted in good faith*: The court did not have reason to doubt that Heinisch had acted in good faith and in the belief that it was in the public interest to disclose the alleged wrongdoing on the part of her employer to the prosecution authorities, and that no other more discreet means of remedying the situation was available to her. It was noted that rather than going directly to the media she had first gone to the public prosecution authorities with a view to initiating an investigation.

(5) *The detriment to the employer*: The allegations underlying Heinisch's criminal complaints, in particular those containing allegations of fraud, were certainly prejudicial to her employer's business reputation and commercial interests, and there was an interest in protecting the commercial success and viability of companies for the benefit of shareholders and employees, but also for the wider economic good (*Steel and Morris v United Kingdom* (2005) 41 EHRR 403). However, while state-owned companies also had an interest in commercial viability, the protection of public confidence in the quality of the provision of a vital public service by state-owned or administered companies is decisive for the functioning and economic good of the entire sector, and for this reason the public shareholder itself has an interest in investigating and clarifying alleged deficiencies in this respect, within the scope of an open public debate. The public interest in having information about shortcomings in the provision of institutional care for the elderly by a state-owned company was so important in a democratic society that it outweighed the interest in protecting the latter's business reputation and interests.

(6) *The severity of the sanction*: As the court put it, Heinisch had been subjected to the heaviest sanction possible under labour law (ie dismissal). This sanction not only had negative repercussions for her career but it could also have a serious chilling effect on other employees of the employer and discourage them from reporting any shortcomings in institutional care. Moreover, in view of the media coverage of Heinisch's case, the sanction could have a chilling effect not only on employees of the employer but also on other employees in the nursing service sector. This chilling effect worked to the detriment of society as a whole and also had to be taken into consideration when assessing the proportionality of, and thus the justification for, the sanctions imposed on Heinisch, who was entitled to bring the matter at issue to the public's attention. This was, said the court, particularly true in the area of care for the elderly, where the patients are frequently not capable of defending their own rights and where members of the nursing staff will be the first to become aware of unsatisfactory conditions in the care provided and are thus best placed to act in the public interest by alerting the employer or the public at large.

18.22 The court concluded that the interference with Heinisch's right to freedom of expression, in particular her right to impart information, was not 'necessary in a democratic society', taking into account the right to freedom of expression on matters of general interest, the right of employees to report illegal conduct and wrongdoing in the workplace, and duties and responsibilities of employees to their employers. Accordingly, the German courts had failed to strike a fair balance between the need to protect the employer's reputation and rights on one hand, and the need to protect the applicant's right to freedom of expression on the other: Heinisch's claim for compensation succeeded.

18.23 A series of cases have applied the approach in *Heinisch* and *Guja*.[21] In *Bucur and Toma v Romania* [2013] ECHR 14, one of the applicants (Constantin Bucur) worked in the telephone communications surveillance and recording department of a military unit of the Romanian Intelligence Service (the RIS). He came across several irregularities relating to phone tapping. These included that details of the person whose communications were being tapped, or the reason for doing so, were not properly recorded. In addition to the eavesdropping on a large number of journalists, telephones belonging to politicians and businessmen were being tapped, especially after high-profile events in the press. Bucur reported the irregularities to his colleagues and the head of department. He alleged that he was then

---

[21] *Bucur and Toma v Romania* [2013] ECHR 14; *Matuz v Hungary* [2014] ECHR 1112, [2015] IRLR 74; *Rubins v Latvia* [2015] ECHR 2, [2015] IRLR 319; *Langner v Germany* [2015] ECHR 803; *Aurelian Oprea v Romania* [2016] ECHR 85; *Soares v Portugal* [2016] ECHR 549.

reprimanded. Given the lack of interest shown by the people to whom he had reported his concerns he then contacted an MP, and was advised to hold a press conference. He did so, and criminal proceedings followed. The ECtHR upheld his complaint that there had been a breach of Article 10, applying the following criteria:

(a) *Whether there had been other means of imparting the information*: No official procedure existed. The irregularities discovered directly concerned his superiors and the court accepted that it was therefore unlikely that any (or any further) internal complaints would have led to an investigation and stopped the unlawful practices concerned. The court also took into account that he had contacted an MP who was a member of the parliamentary commission responsible for supervising the RIS and had been advised to hold a press conference and that a complaint to the RIS commission would serve no useful purpose. In addition, although Romania had passed whistleblower-protection laws, this was only after the events concerning Mr Bucur and so the new laws did not apply to him.

(b) *The public interest of the information divulged*: The court commented that the interception of telephone communications was particularly significant in a society that had been accustomed to a policy of close surveillance by secret services under the former Communist regime. In addition, civil society was affected by the information given that anyone could have their phone tapped. It was also significant that the disclosure concerned abuses by high-ranking officials and affected the democratic foundations of the state, and raised important issues for political debate in a democratic society.

(c) *The accuracy of the information made public*: The court considered that all the evidence tended to support Mr Bucur's conviction that there were no signs of any threat to national security that could justify the tapping, and there had been a lack of information provided by Romania to show that proper authorization had been given. The court accepted therefore that there were reasonable grounds to believe that the information he divulged was true.

(d) *The damage done to the RIS*: The general interest in the disclosure of information revealing illegal activities within the RIS was sufficiently important in a democratic society to prevail over the interest in maintaining public confidence in the RIS.

(e) *The good faith of Mr Bucur*: There was no ulterior motive. That was supported by the fact that he had not chosen to go to the press directly and before doing so had turned to a member of the parliamentary commission responsible for supervising the RIS.

In *Matuz v Hungary* [2014] ECHR 1112, [2015] IRLR 74, Mr Matuz was a journalist who **18.24** was employed by the Hungary state television company. He was the editor and presenter of a programme, 'Night Shelter', which involved interviews with figures of cultural life. He complained to the president of the television company that a new cultural editor had been censoring 'Night Shelter'. He then published a book on the alleged censorship, which contained extracts of interviews which had not been broadcast, and exchanges between the cultural editor and the editor-in-chief about suggested changes in the programme. In response Mr Matuz was summarily dismissed for breach of the confidentiality clause in his contract. Applying the criteria set out in *Guja*, the ECtHR upheld his complaint that this was in breach of Article 10, on the basis that the interference (that is to say his dismissal) was not necessary in a democratic society, applying *Guja*'s six criteria but adding one further consideration:

(a) *Public interest involved in disclosing the information*: here there was clearly a public interest in disclosure, given the importance of the independence of public service broadcasters. Mr Matuz's combined professional and trade union roles were also relevant in relation to this.

(b) *Authenticity of the information disclosed*: There was no suggestion here that the documents published in Mr Matuz's book had not been authentic or had been distorted or that there had been a lack of factual basis for the disclosure.

(c) *The damage, if any, suffered by the authority as a result of the disclosure*: The court stated that it was mindful of the potential damage to the reputation of the employer company, and to the breach of confidentiality, but as against that the substance in general had already been made accessible through an online publication and was known to a number of people.

(d) *The motive behind the actions of the reporting employee*: There was no challenge to Mr Matuz's good faith before the Hungarian courts.

(e) *Whether in the light of the duties owed to the employer the information was made public as a last resort following disclosure to the employer or other appropriate body*: So far as concerned the duty of loyalty/confidentiality owed to the employer, the court commented that having regard to the role played by journalists in society and their responsibility to contribute to and encourage public detail, these obligations did not apply with equal force to journalists. Duties of loyalty and restraint also needed to be weighed against the public character of the broadcasting company Mr Matuz worked for. Further, the book had only been published after Mr Matuz had felt prevented from remedying the perceived interference with his journalistic work internally within the television company; there was a lack of an effective alternative channel for his concern.

(f) *Severity of the sanction imposed*: the sanction was severe; Matuz had been dismissed.

(g) In addition to the above factors drawn from *Guja*, the court added that the fairness of the proceedings and the procedural guarantees afforded were also factors to be taken into account in assessing the fairness of the interference. Here the court had limited their analysis to finding that Mr Matuz had breached his obligations by publishing the book, and had not weighed the fact that he had been exercising his freedom-of-expression right in the public interest, or taken into account the content of the book or the context of its publication which was relevant to that issue.

18.25 As was apparent from the factors taken into consideration in *Matuz*, consideration of the fairness of the procedure did not refer only to the process followed internally by the employer, but also to the procedure in the courts. That was so because the obligation is placed on the state to secure the Article 10 freedoms. It is on that basis that positive obligations may arise even though the direct interference (or victimization) is by a private employer. In that important respect the exercise carried out by the ECtHR in the line of cases which has developed since *Guja* and *Heinisch* differs from that carried out by employment tribunals, and the conclusions reached also need to be treated with some care with that in mind.

18.26 The point was developed further by the ECtHR in *Rubins v Latvia* [2015] ECHR 2, [2015] IRLR 319. Andris Rubins was a professor and head of department in the faculty of medicine at Riga Stradina University, a Latvian state university. As a result of the merger of his department with another, his position was abolished. He was given an opportunity to agree changes to his contract and informed that if he did not he would be dismissed. He then sent an email to the rector of the University and members of the University's Senate, in which he criticized the University's leadership for lacking democracy and accountability. He also alleged that the University's finances were mismanaged, citing conclusions adopted by the state audit office. His email also contained personal criticisms of management, including saying that one pretended to be a God-fearing Catholic but had several children born out of wedlock. He then sent an email (referred to as 'the settlement email') to the rector which set out two versions of a settlement agreement. Version 1 was that the University would reverse its reorganization decision, that Mr Rubins would withdraw his appeals, and that certain 'plagiarists' would be moved or fired. Version 2, was that Mr

Rubins would leave his post in return for compensation (and he stated a figure) but that he would reserve his right to appeal 'while of course making everything public beforehand and attracting the attention of society'. He also said that 'I do not believe that in an election year, taking into consideration the latest news (the conclusion adopted by the state audit office on the illegalities at the University, plagiarism on the part of lecturers and professors of the University, etc), you would want to have additional tasks and trouble'. He added that if agreement was not reached by a specified date he would make all of his 'current information' public.

18.27   The proposals were rejected. The next day a national news agency (LETA) published his views about the alleged shortcomings in the University's management, stating that a small group of people had usurped all power and set up an authoritarian or even dictatorial regime. He was then dismissed on the grounds that the settlement email had amounted to serious misconduct, including inappropriate demands including threats and elements of blackmail. The finding of serious misconduct was upheld by the domestic courts.

18.28   The ECtHR concluded that there had been a violation of Article 10 ECHR. The crux of the employment dispute concerned the allegation that the manner of expression used by Mr Rubins in communicating with his employer was unethical. The court noted that insofar as the University acted in the area of private law, there was still an obligation on the state authorities to secure enjoyment of the Article 10 rights. The court accepted that the interference was prescribed by law and pursued a legitimate aim, being based on the domestic law that employees owed a duty of 'loyalty, reserve and discretion'. The court also noted that certain manifestations of the right to freedom of expression are not legitimate in the sphere of labour relations. However (by a majority) it concluded that the interference went beyond what is 'necessary in a democratic society'. The ECtHR analysed this by reference to four of the six factors listed in *Guja*: (a) public interest, (b) motive, (c) harm to reputation of others (corresponding to the criterion in *Guja* of damage to the public authority), and (d) severity of the measure. Of the other two categories identified in *Guja*, authenticity was addressed in the context of considering the public interest, and it may be that the issue as to whether the matter should have been raised internally first was not specifically mentioned because the case concerned essentially communications with the employer.

18.29   In relation to public interest, it was argued that there had been no public interest involved in the email because it had been a personal threat against the rector. Rejecting that argument, the court said that the email should not be assessed in isolation, and that attention had to be paid to what information Mr Rubins was going to disclose and did in fact disclose, which included shortcomings identified by the State Audit Office and an issue about cases of plagiarism at the University that had been confirmed by reports of a professional association. It also noted that the truthfulness and authenticity of these matters had not been contested and the information which had been published by LETA had not been contested in any defamation proceedings. It was also noted in relation to public interest that the University was a state-funded educational establishment. Yet the domestic court had not assessed the public interest in truthfulness of the information.

18.30   In relation to Mr Rubins' motive, the government argued that Mr Rubins had acted for selfish reasons, and had known that the requests made were unlawful, in that the rector did not have authority to annul Senate action. The court stated as follows (at para 87):

> The Court could understand the Government's argument regarding the applicant's motives as relevant if the case was one of the protection of whistle-blowers. However, the Court does not consider that to be the case. The Court examines whether in view of the applicant's freedom of expression exercised in the context of a labour dispute, the national courts

have carried out the appropriate balancing exercise. In this regard, the Government's arguments about the applicant's motives for the impugned statements are relevant for the assessment of the proportionality of the interference in the applicant's exercise of his freedom of expression.

18.31   The ECtHR therefore highlighted the distinction between the process such as that carried out by the employment tribunal in assessing a whistleblowing complaint, and that carried out in a complaint to the ECtHR. Here the court was not simply considering if the interference was justified. It was looking at whether sufficient had been done by the state to protect the Article 10 right, which in turn involved considering the adequacy of the assessment carried out. But in relation to that, motive was one factor to be weighed in the balance.

18.32   The ECtHR proceeded to identify three matters bearing on proportionality which the domestic court had failed to assess. First, the complaints had been prompted by the reorganization of the department, and Mr Rubins had first attempted to raise his concerns about this within the hierarchy. Second, the structure of the department was such that it was not wholly unreasonable to address the demands to the rector, given that he was the respondent to appeal proceedings, could convene the constituent assembly, had the right of suspensive veto in the Senate, and was the highest-ranking official in the University. Third, the amount requested by way of compensation was not unreasonable, as it was calculated by reference to his monthly income and the terms set out in his employment contract. The court did not decide that these provided justification, but said it could not speculate as to how the national court would assess these facts.

18.33   In relation to the criterion of harm to the reputation of others, the court emphasized that neither in the settlement email nor the subsequent publication was there any private information divulged that was damaging to the honour or dignity of Mr Rubins' colleagues or the employer. The government argued that disciplinary action was merited because of the use of insulting expressions in the professional environment. Again, the domestic court's assessment was crucial in relation to this. The ECtHR took a narrow approach to what appeared on the face of the earlier email in that it emphasized that the question of the email having contained insults was not analysed or found to be established by the domestic court. Whilst the earlier email could (as the ECtHR put it) 'raise certain questions', the national court had not assessed the language.

18.34   In relation to the severity of the measure, the court was unimpressed by the submission that the dismissal could not be considered a severe sanction because Mr Rubins had taken up a post in another university soon after, and his career had not been affected. Instead, the court emphasized that dismissal was the harshest sanction available and was liable to have a serious chilling effect on other employees.

18.35   In all, the ECtHR concluded that the reasons relied upon by the domestic court were not sufficient to show that the interference with the Article 10 right was proportionate to a legitimate aim. The decision is striking given the threats made by Mr Rubins. Indeed, in a forceful minority dissenting opinion by two judges (Judges Mahoney and Wojtyczek), it was argued that the public interest in disclosure of information on management shortcomings and plagiarism appeared very weak, particularly as Mr Rubins was willing to forego any such disclosure if he kept his job as head of department or received significant compensation, and it was evident that disclosure of information was being used as a bargaining tool. It was also emphasized that the truthfulness and authenticity of the disparaging information, to which the majority attached some importance, did not at all detract from its blackmailing character, in that he was using the threat to obtain the settlement he desired (albeit that he also required that certain plagiarists be moved or fired). The domestic court had indeed made findings that what Mr Rubins was seeking to achieve was the self-serving objective of preserving his job or obtaining financial compensation, rather than any objective of acting in the public interest. All in all, we suggest that the decision needs to be treated with some care, and may be best explained on the basis of criticisms of the adequacy of the analysis carried out by the domestic court (though the minority opinion also makes forceful criticisms in relation to this).

The importance of protecting expression on matters of public interest, and that this may **18.36** outweigh duties of good faith in the work environment, was again emphasized in *Kharlamov v Russia* (App No 27447/07) [2015] ECHR 27447/07, 8 October 2015, albeit in the particular context of academic freedom. Mr Kharlamov was a tenured professor in the Physics department at Orel State Technical University. He was unhappy that the Physics department was not consulted in relation to nomination of candidates for the University Senate. He made criticisms of this at a public conference, claiming that his rights and those of his colleagues had been breached, and that other employees had been removed from election to the Senate and that this amounted to discrimination, and that the Senate may not be considered a legitimate body. The University then brought a claim in defamation, claiming that the speech had undermined the professional reputation of the University and its academic Senate, and this was upheld by the domestic courts.

The ECtHR concluded that there had been a breach of Kharlamov's Article 10 rights. **18.37** The interference with free expression pursued a legitimate aim (protection of the rights and reputation of others) but it was not a proportionate interference. The test of whether the interference was necessary entailed consideration of whether it corresponded to a pressing social need, whether it was proportionate to the legitimate aim pursued, and whether the reasons given by the national authorities were relevant and sufficient. The court reiterated that employees owe a duty of 'loyalty, reserve and discretion' and that, in striking a fair balance, 'the limits of the right to freedom of expression and the reciprocal rights and obligations specific to the professional environment must be taken into account'. It also stressed that, at the same time, it was important not to lose sight of the academic context of the debate, and that '[t]he principle of open discussion of issues of professional interest must thus be construed as an element of a broader concept of academic autonomy which encompasses the academics' freedom to express their opinion about the institution or system in which they work' (para 27). Assessing the comments in their professional and academic context, the court was clear that the interference with free expression had been disproportionate and that the domestic court had overstepped the narrow margin of appreciation in matters of debate of public interest. It also took into account the following:

(a) Mr Kharlamov's comments had brought to light a matter of professional concern, namely opacity of the academic Senate selection. The composition of the ruling body of the University and its procedure to designate candidates for election was of central importance for the University staff, and discussion about this was an integral part of the organization of academic life and self-governance. The debate took place in public and was a matter of general interest.

(b) Under the Convention there is little scope for restrictions on debate on questions of public interest and very strong reasons are required to justify restrictions (para 29). The courts had failed to carry out a balancing exercise between the need to protect the University's reputation and Mr Kharlamov's right to impart information on issues of general interest concerning the organization of academic life. They also failed to take into account that the dignity of an institution (the University) could not be equated with the dignity of a human being (Mr Kharlamov) and did not necessarily have the same weight when assessing the impact on the rights of others.

(c) As to the validity or otherwise of the comments, the court stated that a distinction needed to be drawn between statements of fact (which are amenable to proof), and value judgements (which are not). But even for a value judgement there still needed to be a factual basis to support it. The correct classification fell, in the first instance, within the margin of appreciation for the national court. Here Mr Kharlamov had voiced his personal comment on a matter of public interest for the University staff. Having called four witnesses in the domestic proceedings in support of his case, he had shown that his value judgement had a sufficient factual grounding in relation to the absence of an open discussion of candidates for the academic Senate election. It was therefore irrelevant whether there had been formal compliance with the University's internal regulations.

(d) Although Mr Kharlamov used a degree of hyperbole and exaggeration, this was permissible, whilst engaging in debate on a matter of public interest, provided he did not overstep the limits of permissible criticism. The court accepted he had not overstepped the mark, given that he did not resort to offensive and intemperate language and did not go beyond a 'generally acceptable degree of exaggeration'.

18.38 To similar effect is the decision in *Aurelian Oprea v Romania* (App No 12138/08) [2016] ECHR 85, where there was found to be a breach of Article 10 in the upholding of a defamation claim and awarding substantial compensation against a university professor who had made public allegations of corruption against his own university. The defamation claim was brought by the deputy rector of the University, and the court balanced his Article 8 right to protect his reputation (pursuant to *Cumpana v Romania* [2004] ECHR 22238/96, paras 90–91) against the Article 10 right of the discloser. The court accepted that the applicant acted in good faith in the belief that it was in the public interest to disclose the alleged shortcomings of the University, and that whilst he allowed himself a certain degree of exaggeration and generalization, his allegations were 'not entirely devoid of factual grounds' and did not amount to a 'gratuitous personal attack' on colleagues. It also accepted that the applicant had raised his concerns internally with the rector, and also with the Ministry of Education, before disclosing them in the press. The court took into account that the deputy rector held important management positions in a state-financed university and as such had to tolerate a greater degree of public scrutiny than a private individual, that the criticisms concerned his behaviour and attitudes in his capacity as an official rather than in his private life, and that these had not caused any particular harm to him or adversely affected his career. Finally, it took into account the extent of the compensation (and liability to costs) that had been ordered.

18.39 Two further decisions, however, illustrate the scope for the fact-sensitive application of the *Guja* criteria to lead to a conclusion that there was a proportionate interference with the Article 10 right, even where there has been no breach of confidentiality. In *Langner v Germany* (App No 14464/11, 17 September 2015) [2015] ECHR 803, the ECtHR held that there had been no breach of Article 10 despite an employee having been dismissed for criticism made of an elected official and in circumstances that would seem to have fallen within section 43C ERA (if they had been capable of being pursued under the ERA's protected disclosure provisions). Mr Langner was head of a subdivision in charge of giving sanctions for misuse of housing property in the Dresden Housing Office. At a meeting of Housing Office staff, which was attended by the Deputy Mayor for Economy and Housing (who was responsible for the Housing Office), he accused the Deputy Mayor of having committed 'perversion of justice' by ordering the issue of an unlawful demolition permit for a block of flats. On 17 December 1998, in response to a request by his head of division to substantiate the allegations in writing, Mr Langner submitted a written response repeating the allegation. He was then dismissed. After his dismissal a local newspaper published a letter from him expressing the view that the Deputy Mayor lacked competence to resolve problems relating to housing issues. On appeal, the German Labour Court of Appeal concluded that the dismissal had been justified because Mr Langner seriously insulted and slandered the Deputy Mayor by accusing him of perversion of justice. The court found that the decision taken by the Deputy Mayor, which Mr Langner had criticized, had been lawful. Mr Langner's written submission of 17 December showed that he was willing to implement politically legitimate decisions if they concerned sanctions for misuse of property by house owners. In addition the Deputy Mayor could not be expected to maintain daily cooperation with Mr Langner after reading the letter describing him as incompetent. The court also considered that a lesser sanction was not available as Mr Langner would not have changed his stance and would have continued with a self-righteous attitude.

The ECtHR concluded that the decision was a proportionate means of pursuing the legiti-   **18.40**
mate aim of protecting the Deputy Mayor's honour and a professional work environment at the Housing Office, and therefore the reputation and rights of others. The court reiterated that employees have 'a duty of loyalty, reserve and discretion' to the employer and that this was particularly so in the case of the public service, which requires loyalty and discretion. Weighing up considerations relevant to proportionality, the court emphasized the following:

(a) At the time of the staff meeting, the decision which Mr Langner criticized had taken place almost two years before. The ECtHR appears therefore to have considered that, in weighing the public interest, it was permissible to give less weight to this than disclosure of recent wrongdoing or to prevent future or ongoing wrongdoing.

(b) Mr Langner had addressed his concerns neither to the Deputy Mayor's superior nor to the public prosecution. This appears to have been cited as a point against protection, in contrast to section 43C(1)(b) ERA which accords greater protection where the disclosure is made to the person responsible for the alleged wrongdoing.

(c) The issue was not closely related to the subject on the agenda of the staff meeting.

(d) Motive: The domestic court had decided that Mr Langner's statement was not aimed at uncovering an unacceptable situation within the Housing Office, but was motivated by Mr Langner's personal misgivings about the Deputy Mayor arising from the prospect of the impending dissolution of his subdivision. The court held that on this basis that case was to be distinguished from whistleblowing cases.

(e) Authenticity of the issue raised: The domestic court had found that the impugned decision of the Deputy Mayor had been lawful and that the accusations of perversion of justice were unfounded. It was also relevant that due to his role Mr Langner must have been well acquainted with the legal background and should have been aware of the implication of the term 'perversion of justice' in that it denoted intentional and criminal abuse of public authority. Reflecting this conclusion, the court was not satisfied that he had 'acquitted himself of the obligation to verify carefully whether his allegations were accurate'. The ECtHR stated that it considered 'the unfounded allegation of a serious crime rather a defamatory accusation than a criticism in the interest of the public'. The emphasis on the fact that Mr Langner was in a position to verify the allegations suggests some similarity with the reasonable belief test under ERA. One difference is that under section 43C ERA there is no requirement to establish a reasonable belief in the substantial truth of the allegation (as would apply for example to section 43G ERA). Nor did the court seek to separate out any information from mere allegations. But the court's reasoning tends to indicate that if the ERA protected disclosure provisions had applied, and assuming the disclosure fell within section 43C ERA, Mr Langner would still have failed the test for a qualifying disclosure of whether there was a reasonable belief that the information tended to show a relevant failure. In applying the qualifying disclosure test it would have been highly material that, as the ECtHR noted, Mr Langner must have been well acquainted with the legal background and therefore in a position to verify the allegations: see *Korashi v Abertawe Bro Morgannwg University Local Area Health Board* [2012] IRLR 4 (EAT). The ECtHR appears to have accepted that Mr Langner was in a position to check the basis for the allegations and, as such, it would seem to follow that he did not hold a reasonable belief that any facts disclosed tended to show a relevant failure. Further, under section 43C ERA, the findings that the allegations were in fact unfounded would have been a potentially important evidential tool to assist in assessing reasonableness of belief (though of course a belief might be reasonable but wrong).[22]

(f) When Mr Langner was given the opportunity to substantiate his allegations, he repeated them, and therefore it was not merely a spontaneous outburst.

(g) In relation to damage suffered by the employer, it was not only likely to damage the Deputy Mayor's reputation but also to interfere seriously with the working atmosphere within the Housing Office by undermining the Deputy Mayor's authority. Although the accusations were made during a staff meeting rather than publicly, not all those present had been staff members (eg there were union representatives) and there had been a risk that the allegations would become known to the wider public.

(h) Mr Langner had not acted in the context of an ongoing labour conflict and nor was he engaging in trade union activity. Again, these were matters viewed as relevant to weighing the public interest involved.

(i) Whilst dismissal was the heaviest sanction possible and it was difficult for Mr Langner to find alternative work, it was necessary because he was viewed as being likely to reproach the Deputy Mayor's conduct in the presence of other employees and the public, and given his written comments on 17 December and in the letter published in the local newspaper, that view was not unreasonable.

18.41 The most recent in the line of decisions applying the *Guja* approach is *Soares v Portugal* (App No 79972/12) [2016] ECHR 549. Soares was a chief corporal in the Portuguese National Republican Guard. He sent an email to the General Inspectorate of Internal Administration on the subject of 'Suspected misuse of money', in which he made reference to an alleged misuse by a superior—'MC'—about which he had heard in a conversation with colleagues. He asked the General Inspectorate to investigate the alleged facts, stating that he had become aware of the matter through rumours from members of the military who, he said, claimed that they had not reported the situation for fear of reprisals. He asked for secrecy during the investigation because he was also a member of the military. The email was passed on to the public prosecutor's office, which opened an investigation into Soares' allegations. However, eventually the public prosecutor's office discontinued the proceedings on the grounds that, following investigations by the criminal investigation police, it had found no evidence of the criminal offence denounced by Soares. An inquiry by the General Inspectorate of Internal Administration also conducted an inquiry into Soares' allegations but that was also discontinued. Finally, the General Command of the National Republican Guard started an internal inquiry into the allegations and heard from MC.

18.42 MC became aware of Soares' email and its content. Disciplinary proceedings were begun against MC but they were discontinued on the grounds that there was insufficient evidence to take disciplinary action. MC then lodged a criminal complaint before the Lousã public prosecutor's office, accusing Soares of defamation.

18.43 In due course the public prosecutor brought charges against Soares for aggravated defamation on the grounds that the statements made in his email called into question MC's

---

[22] See Chapter 3, paras 3.79–3.85.

honesty, honour, and professional reputation, which Soares had intentionally attacked. MC also lodged a claim for damages. Soares was convicted of aggravated defamation and sentenced to eighty day-fines, totaling €720. He was also ordered to pay €1,000 in damages to MC. Soares was also subjected to disciplinary proceedings which concluded with a finding that he had breached his duties.

Soares applied to the ECtHR. In deciding whether the domestic authorities had struck a fair **18.44** balance between on one hand Soares' right to freedom of expression under Article 10 and, on the other, the protection of reputation of MC (a right which, as an aspect of private life, is protected by Article 8[23]) the ECtHR noted that whilst Soares' allegations concerned an important question of public interest—the possible misuse of public money by a civil servant—his allegations were, as he admitted, based on a rumour. The accusation against MC that he had misused public money was a particularly serious one capable of affecting his reputation and, to an even larger extent, that of the National Republican Guard. Thus, even if Soares had intended to prompt an investigation, he had to have a factual basis on which to base his allegations. In fact he based them on a mere rumour and had no evidence to support them. The domestic courts' finding that he had not acted 'in good faith' was thus proportional and justified. The case was contrasted with that of *Bargão and Domingos Correia v Portugal* (nos. 53579/09 and 53582/09), where the applicants had believed that the information disclosed was true and were able to prove it (ibid, sections 41–42). By contrast, Soares, knowing that his allegations were based on a rumour, made no attempt to verify their authenticity before reporting them. Indeed, in the criminal proceedings against Soares the domestic courts were not even able to establish the existence of the rumour which had given rise to his allegations.

Furthermore, Soares was aware that he had internal channels within the hierarchy of the **18.45** National Republican Guard to which he could have reported the rumour—namely the commander of his territorial post or of the territorial unit where he had heard it. He did not convincingly explain why he did not disclose the allegations to a superior. By not doing so, Soares did not comply with the chain of command and, it was held, denied his hierarchical superior the opportunity to investigate the veracity of the allegations. Soares' case had to be distinguished from cases of justified information supplied to the superior (or 'whistle-blowing', an action warranting special protection under Article 10) such as *Guja* and *Heinisch*. The reasons advanced by the domestic courts in support of their decisions were 'relevant and sufficient', and the interference was not disproportionate to the legitimate aim pursued, namely, the protection of reputation. The interference could thus, in the view of the ECtHR, reasonably be considered 'necessary in a democratic society' within the meaning of paragraph 2 of Article 10 of the Convention. The decision may be regarded as harsh, and to have taken a very narrow view of whistleblowing. Indeed it may be viewed as entailing some risk of a chilling effect, given that the concern was not raised with the media but with an apparently appropriate body in the form of the General Inspectorate of Internal Administration. But it accorded with the approach under section 43F ERA, which also requires a substantial belief in the information disclosed and any allegation contained in it.

E. Positive Obligations to Secure Article 10 Rights

Whilst Article 10(1) proclaims that everyone has the right to freedom of expression, a com- **18.46** plaint can only be made if the interference has been by a public authority. This requirement

---

[23] The ECtHR referred to *Couderc and Hachette Filipacchi Associés v France* [GC], no 40454/07, § 91, 10 November 2015).

is satisfied where an employer relies upon the courts to provide a sanction against interference with free expression, such as by awarding an injunction or damages. It may, however, also be met on the basis of a failure by the state to comply with positive obligations to secure the rights in the Convention for everyone within its jurisdiction, as set out in Article 1 of the Convention. As the ECtHR explained in *Palomo Sanchez and others v Spain* [2011] IRLR 934, in the context of a complaint by employees of a private company who had been dismissed for publishing insulting leaflets (at paras 60 and 62):

> The applicants' dismissal was not the result of direct intervention by the national authorities. The responsibility of the authorities would nevertheless be engaged if the facts complained of stemmed from a failure on their part to secure to the applicants the enjoyment of the right enshrined in Article 10 of the Convention (see, mutatis mutandis, *Gustafsson*,[24] cited above, paragraph 45).
>
> . . .
>
> Whilst the boundary between the State's positive and negative obligations under the Convention does not lend itself to precise definition, the applicable principles are, nonetheless, similar. In both contexts regard must be had in particular to the fair balance that has to be struck between the competing interests of the individual and of the community as a whole, subject in any event to the margin of appreciation enjoyed by the State (see *Karhuvaara and Iltalehti*,[25] cited above, para 42).

18.47   As such the criteria relevant to the balancing exercise recognized in the line of cases following *Guja*, also apply in relation to positive obligations. There may, however, be some distinct considerations. Thus, as in *Heinisch* (see paragraphs 18.15–18.22 above) and *Rubins* (paragraphs 18.26–18.35 above) the public nature of the employer may be relevant to the public interest element of the disclosure. Conversely, the fact that private interests are involved, whether of an employer or its staff, may also be relevant. That was the case in *Palomo Sanchez*. The applicants had brought proceedings against their (private) employer seeking to secure recognition of their salaried-worker status, and had set up a trade union to defend their interests. A Barcelona employment tribunal partly upheld their claims. During the tribunal proceedings two colleagues appeared as witnesses for the employer. The union then published a newsletter with a cartoon on the cover showing a caricature of the human resources manager and the two colleagues, insinuating they were waiting their turn to engage in a sex act with the manager. Inside the newsletter were two articles, denouncing the fact that the two colleagues had given evidence, claiming that they earned their living by 'selling the workers in the courts'. One of the articles was entitled 'When you've rented out your arse you can't shit when you please'. The applicants were then dismissed on the grounds of serious misconduct consisting of impugning the reputations of the two witnesses and the HR manager. Their complaints about dismissal were rejected by the Spanish courts.

18.48   Whilst accepting that there could be positive obligations, the ECtHR also found that there was no violation of Article 10, taking into account that the role of the ECtHR was one of review of the domestic courts. In this case the ECtHR accepted that the Spanish courts/ tribunal had carried out a detailed analysis of the fact and reached a permissible conclusion that the drawing and the two articles were offensive and capable of harming the reputation of the HR manager and two witnesses. The ECtHR noted that a distinction was to be drawn between criticism and insults which may in principle attract sanctions. As such here the sanction of dismissal was in pursuit of a legitimate aim of protecting the individuals who had been targeted.

---

[24] *Gustafsson v Sweden* App no 15573/89 (1996) 22 EHRR 409 ECHR.
[25] *Karhuvaara v Finland* App no 53678/00 (2004) 41 EHRR 1154 ECHR.

Turning to whether the sanction was proportionate to the seriousness of the impugned **18.49** remarks, the court emphasized that the extent of acceptable criticism is narrower as regards private individuals than, for example, politicians or civil servants acting in the exercise of their duties. The court accepted that the dispute was not merely a private one, in that the publication was in the context of a labour dispute and raised matters of general interest for the workers of the employer company. But here the domestic court had balanced the nature of the publication and the offensiveness of the content and expressions used, with the reciprocal rights and duties in the employment context. It had been entitled to find that the cartoon and texts were intended more as an attack on colleagues for testifying than as a means of promoting trade union actions. The court also placed emphasis on the fact that labour relations must be based on mutual trust and that

> certain manifestations of the right to freedom of expression that may be legitimate in other contexts are not legitimate in that of labour relations . . . an attack on the respectability of individuals by using grossly insulting or offensive expressions is, on account of its disruptive effects, a particularly serious form of misconduct capable of justifying severe sanctions.[26]

Therefore, whilst Article 10 rights extended to the workplace, the balancing exercise could also encompass that context and the impact on work relationships of insulting language.[27]

Considerations liable to arise in relation to whether the state has been in breach of positive **18.50** obligations to secure Article 10 rights in relation to a private employment relationship, and the issue of balancing considerations of loyalty to the employer, are further illustrated by the Commission decision in *Rommelfanger v Federal Republic of Germany* (1989) 62 D & R 151. The applicant was employed in a Catholic hospital and was dismissed because he had expressed in a newspaper an opinion which was not in conformity with the position of the Church. He signed, together with fifty others, a letter to the weekly magazine, *Stern*, criticizing the attitude of leading personalities in medical organizations to abortion legislation which had been introduced some three years earlier. He was given notice of termination. He then appeared on television to defend his views. Mr Rommelfanger was initially successful in challenging the dismissal but the Federal Constitutional Court decided that the Labour Courts had not given sufficient weight to the principle of Church autonomy. The Commission held that the dismissal of the physician employee by a Roman Catholic foundation was an act of a private employer. The fact that in German law the Catholic Church could be regarded as a corporation in public law did not make the dismissal an act of the

---

[26] See also *Morissens v Belgium* (1988) 56 D & R 127; where a teacher made accusations of discrimination by her employers, the Commission noted that the applicant had accepted a responsible post in the provincial education service and that she had therefore accepted certain restrictions on the exercise of her freedom of expression as being inherent in her duties. Having regard to her professional responsibilities, the suspension of the applicant without pay was reasonably justified for the protection of the reputation of the teaching establishment where she worked and the reputation of her superiors. The Commission also emphasized that the teacher had chosen to make her accusations on television without providing any proof for her claims. Nor was there any suggestion that she had previously raised these matters internally and the Commission also took account of the absence of evidence in support of the allegations which the applicant made in relation to her employers.

[27] See also *Fuentes Bobo v Spain* (2000) 31 EHRR 1115, where the ECtHR held that the State could be under a positive obligation to secure Article 10 rights, and held that they had been infringed when a Spanish television producer and presenter was dismissed for making offensive remarks about the employer's management during two live radio broadcasts. The court took into account that he had been denouncing the mismanagement of the public entity and that though he used 'coarse and impolite words', these were first used by the radio presenters, and he had merely endorsed them during a rapid and spontaneous exchange and had almost been provoked by them. The court further took into account that none of those against whom the comments had been made had brought defamation proceedings, and that dismissal without compensation had been the most severe penalty available.

state. The Commission also held that the state would not be in breach of any positive obligation to protect the employee's free speech rights provided it ensured that 'there is a reasonable relationship between the measures affecting freedom of expression and the nature of the employment as well as the importance of the issue for the employer'.

18.51 The Commission accepted that Rommelfanger's right to freedom of expression was limited to some extent by the duty of loyalty to his employer. Having noted that the views he expressed on abortion were contrary to the convictions and value judgements which the Church considered to be essential to the performance of its functions in society, the Commission concluded that the requisite reasonable relationship between the expression and the nature of employment and the importance of the issue to the employer was satisfied and that as such there was no violation of Article 10. However, the matters raised by the whistleblower will often be closely related to the employment and will touch on matters of great importance to the employer. *Rommelfanger* may not be encouraging to the extent that it suggests that the freedom of expression can be restricted on those matters. But the decision preceded the *Guja* line of cases and the guidance as to the range of criteria to be taken into account and emphasis on the greater protection which is liable to be available when disclosing matters of public concern, especially where attempts to raise these internally have been or are likely to be unsuccessful.

F. Conclusion on the ECtHR Authorities and Implications

18.52 Whilst there are inevitable overlaps with the approach to protection of public interest disclosures in domestic law through the ERA, there are also important differences in approach and in scope. Those differences in turn offer the prospect of arguments that the domestic law should be interpreted or extended so as to comply with the obligation on Member States to secure Article 10 rights within their jurisdiction.

18.53 As to differences in scope or approach, we would highlight in particular the following aspects:

(1) The protected disclosure legislation in the ERA provides protection only for those that fall within the definition of a worker. By contrast, under Article 10 the obligation is to secure the rights for all within the jurisdiction, albeit that there has been emphasis on some specific factors highlighted in relation to the workplace. Notably, one factor to be weighed in the assessment of proportionality by way of the duties and responsibilities upon the employer has been the procedural guarantees afforded by the domestic courts: see *Matuz* and *Rubins*. As against that, particular work contexts, such as the academic, journalistic, or government context, have been viewed as furthering the public interest in freedom of expression, and the importance of employment has been given particular weight.

(2) In relation to external disclosures, there is some support for a more flexible approach than that dictated by the section 43G(2) gateways. As in relation to those gateways, and indeed section 43G(3)(a), consideration of the identity of the recipient of the disclosure and whether there could have been an internal disclosure or disclosure to a regulator are important factors. But there is some support for the approach that there could still be protection of an external disclosure in circumstances not falling within those gateways but where, more generally, internal disclosure would not be viewed as effective (see *Guja*, and the discussion at paragraph 18.14 above).

(3) In the ECtHR jurisprudence, motive for the disclosure continues to be emphasized as an important criterion. To some extent that may be aligned with the domestic approach

in section 43G ERA, with its reference to personal gain. Even in *Rubins*, where there was found to be interference with the Article 10 right, though not being a complete answer, motive was still identified as being a factor relevant to the overall assessment of the proportionality of interference with the Article 10 right. In *Langner* it was an important factor against protection in the context of what may arguably have amounted to an internal staff meeting (though there was some reference to the presence of outsiders). The disclosure was principally addressed to the Deputy Mayor, and in the ERA's protected disclosure provisions even if he was not the employer that would have fallen within section 43C(1)(b) (on the basis either of being the person solely or mainly responsible for the conduct or as relating to a matter for which he had legal responsibility).

(4) In the ECtHR jurisprudence, the severity of the sanction is part of the overall assessment of the proportionality of the interference. By contrast, in the ERA the question of whether the disclosure is protected is an anterior question before addressing the issue of detriment (or dismissal).

(5) The ECtHR jurisprudence focuses not only on the decision of the employer but also on the processes of the state in securing the Article 10 right. In cases where there has been an absence of specific domestic legislation, that has been a point noted in the assessment of the ECtHR, and as such the presence of the specific protected disclosure protection is likely to be an important factor in favour of the overall assessment that the Article 10 rights have been secured. As against that, where there are gaps in protection (such as volunteers or threats of future disclosures), and as such there is not a judicial assessment of the proportionality of the interference, that may still be an important consideration. Where the protected disclosure legislation does not apply it will be relevant to consider what if any other protection applies, and whether that is adequate.[28] The absence of coverage by the ERA protected disclosure provisions may entail that there are a lack of procedural safeguards or remedies which could, as in *Rubins*, contribute to a finding of a failure by the state to take sufficient steps to secure the rights under Article 10.

(6) The ECtHR jurisprudence has not drawn the clear distinction in the domestic legislation between disclosure of information and allegations, though there is some overlap with the approach that mere insults may not be protected, and a distinction between criticisms and mere insults.[29]

(7) More generally, notwithstanding the criteria that have been developed, the ECtHR's approach may be regarded as more flexible but also less certain and less clearly structured than the domestic legislation. The consequence is that whilst some of the criteria may be applied consistently with the domestic legislation, there remains some scope for argument. One aspect is taking into account the detriment to the employer as part of the overall assessment of proportionality. Under the domestic legislation there is ample scope to take this into account in relation to external disclosures. In relation to disclosures within sections 43C–43F the scope for this is less clear. Essentially, it would come into the equation not in relation to whether there was a disclosure (unless it went to the issue of whether there was no disclosure of information) but in applying the reason why test, for example if the action taken was by reason of the manner of the disclosure. But, notwithstanding the decision in *Langner*, we consider that the UK's domestic legislation already provides an appropriate balance by differentiating the approach that should be taken between different levels of disclosure, and there is scope for the application of Article 10 to reach the same conclusion. For example, the interference with the rights

---

[28] See eg the approach of the EAT in *Gilham v Ministry of Justice* (UKEAT 0087/16/LA, 31 October 2016).
[29] *Palomo Sanchez and others v Spain* [2011] IRLR 934.

of others is given less weight when there is no breach of confidentiality and the issue is raised internally (*Rubins*). Again, in relation to the authenticity of the information, the domestic legislation provides greater clarity as to the tests to be applied as to the discloser's reasonable belief for different levels of disclosure. The ECtHR case law in contrast is less clear as to how the authenticity criterion is applied, but we suggest it is unlikely that the domestic approach would be found to fall outside the margin of appreciation in this respect.

18.54 To date, whilst Article 10 rights may be relevant to the application of the fairness test in a case of ordinary unfair dismissal,[30] attempts to extend the scope of the protected disclosure legislation by reference to the ECtHR jurisprudence have not met with conspicuous success. Notably, as discussed in Chapter 6, in relation to the definition of workers, Article 10 arguments were deployed without success in *Day v Lewisham and Greenwich NHS Trust and another* [2016] IRLR 415 (EAT)[31] and *Gilham v Ministry of Justice* (UKEAT 0087/16/LA, 31 October 2016).[32] But it does not follow that such arguments will not be successful in future. The decision in *Gilham*, if rightly decided, may be distinguished from the position of other workers, on the grounds of the emphasis on the range of other remedies available to a district judge, and the conclusion that in many respects a district judge has a greater degree of protection than other workers (though it was also held that the requirement for a contractual relationship is a fundamental feature of the legislation). In *Day* (under appeal at the time of writing), the Article 10 argument was dealt with dismissively (at para 43) on the basis that in the two cases cited (*Heinisch* and *Matuz*) there had not been national legislation protecting whistleblowers, and that it was 'well within the margin of appreciation to be accorded to a member state that it should enact careful and detailed provisions as the United Kingdom Parliament has done in enacting Part IVA of the [ERA]'.

18.55 With respect, we suggest that is not a sufficient analysis. As noted above, the ECtHR has emphasized that states have only a narrow margin of appreciation where it impinges on disclosures on matters of public interest: see *Kharlamov*. Allied to this, it has adopted a series of criteria by reference to which to test whether the disclosure is proportionate to a legitimate aim. That suggests that it was not sufficient just to adopt the broad-brush approach of saying that there was legislation in place, without focusing on the gaps in protection, the remedies available for those who fall into those gaps having regard to the obligation on the state to secure the Article 10 rights, and indeed the fact that where a worker such as Mr Day fell into such a gap there was little by way of protection against victimization for making public interest disclosures. Langstaff J noted (at para 35) that it had been accepted by counsel for Mr Day that he could not contend for a general principle that a person making a protected disclosure should be protected against all or any detriment whatever the relationship with the person treating him detrimentally. But again, whether and to what extent the protection was required to be provided in order to comply with the positive obligations on the state needed to be tested by the criteria developed in the ECtHR case law. Further, in any event, as shown in *McTigue*, the legislation is capable of being construed so as to provide protection even without requiring a conforming interpretation in accordance with Article 10.[33]

---

[30] See *Hill v Governing Body of Great Tey Primary School* [2013] ICR 691 (EAT).

[31] See Chapter 6, paras 6.22–6.26.

[32] See Chapter 6, para 6.94–6.95.

[33] See also *Smania v Standard Chartered Bank* [2015] ICR 436 (EAT) and *Fuller v United Healthcare Services Inc & Anor* (UKEAT 0464/13/0409, 4 September 2014), discussed in Chapter 6 at paras 6.136–6.143 (in relation to territorial grasp of the protected disclosure legislation).

Reliance was also placed on the ECtHR jurisprudence, including the decision in *Heinisch*, **18.56** on behalf of the claimant in *Clyde & Co LLP and another v Bates van Winkelhof* [2014] 1 WLR 2047 (SC) in support of the argument that limited liability partners should fall within the definition of worker. Ultimately, the Supreme Court did not need to determine the Article 10 issue (see Chapter 6, paragraphs 6.13 et seq). But Lady Hale commented that:

> This argument raises what might be a difficult question. Under section 3(1) of the Human Rights Act 1998, we have a duty to read and give effect to legislation in a way which is compatible with the Convention rights (and this means that it may have a different meaning in this context from the meaning it has in others). While it is comparatively easy to see how this may be done in order to prevent the state from acting incompatibly with a person's Convention rights, in other words, to respect the negative obligations of the state, it is a little more difficult to assess whether and when this is necessary in order to give effect to the positive obligations of the state and thus to afford one person a remedy against another person which she would not otherwise have had. It is at this point that the LLP's argument that the 1996 Act gives better protection than is required under the Convention might be relevant.

We note in this respect that whether or not the ERA gives better protection than required **18.57** for those covered by it does not on its face appear to be a convincing answer if others who are not covered, despite being victimized for raising public interest disclosures, are left without recourse, having regard to the Article 1 obligation to secure the Convention rights for everyone in the jurisdiction.

Against that context, and having regard to sections 2, 3, and (where the respondent is a pub- **18.58** lic authority) 6 HRA (see paragraph 18.02 above), we suggest that there are various respects in which there is scope for argument that Article 10 and the ECtHR jurisprudence may be prayed in aid in relation to the protected disclosure provisions of the ERA, including in the following respects:

(1) Gaps in relation to who is covered, such as applicants for employment and volunteers. Those gaps may be said to be inconsistent with the obligation to secure the Article 10 rights for everyone within the jurisdiction. That view may derive some support from Council of Europe Recommendation CM/Rec(2014)/7 and the accompanying explanatory memorandum. Recommendation 3 is that the personal scope of protection should 'cover all individuals working in either the public or private sectors, irrespective of the nature of the working relationship and whether they are paid or not'. In relation to this, the explanatory memorandum comments (at para 45) that this would include trainees and volunteers. It adds that 'in certain contexts and within an appropriate legal framework, members States might also wish to extend protection to consultants, freelance and self-employed persons, and sub-contractors' on the basis that the underlying reason for recommending protection to whistleblowers is their economic vulnerability vis à vis the person for whom they depend for work.

(2) The distinction following the decision in *Cavendish Munro Professional Risk Management Ltd v Geduld* [2010] ICR 325 (EAT) between a disclosure of information and a mere allegation might be challenged. An allegation of wrongdoing may still be by way of raising the early alarm in the public interest, possibly with the expectation that supporting detail would be provided later. The failure to protect the worker who raises an allegation but is dismissed before being given the chance to provide the supporting information would seem to sit uneasily with an obligation to secure Article 10 rights.

(3) Similarly, and related to this, Article 10 may be relied upon to contend that the legislation should be construed to cover prospective future disclosures, for example where an employer, on learning that a worker has been gathering information about wrongdoing, dismisses for the principal reason that it is believed that the employee will make a protected disclosure in future.

(4) As discussed in Chapter 7, the domestic protected disclosure legislation permits a distinction to be drawn between the disclosure and the manner of the disclosure, or conduct associated with the disclosure. Whilst the ECtHR jurisprudence recognizes that the manner or terms in which what is said is relevant, and a distinction is to be drawn between criticism and insults,[34] they are matters weighed in the balance rather than being addressed as a matter of causation (in the 'reason why' sense). It might be argued that whether such a distinction should be permitted is to be tested by whether, applying the criteria developed in the ECtHR jurisprudence, there would be a breach of Article 10 in permitting it to be drawn.

(5) As discussed in Chapter 6 (paragraphs 6.136–6.143), Article 10 might be relied upon in relation to construing the territorial grasp of the legislation, so as to encompass cases where the relevant act of detriment or dismissal occurred in Great Britain, but where the application of the close connection test leads to the conclusion that the tribunal cannot consider the claim.

(6) In relation to external disclosures, it might be argued that the gateways for protection have the effect that some of the considerations which the ECtHR jurisprudence requires to be considered are left out of account, notably whether the sanction is proportionate. That might be the case, for example, where although a worker takes the view that raising the matter internally would be ineffective, the specific gateways in section 43G(2) ERA are not satisfied, and having raised a matter of public interest more widely (eg to the police or with an MP) he is then dismissed as a result. Under the ECtHR jurisprudence those considerations, and the reasons for taking the view that internal disclosure would be ineffective, would be factors to weigh in the balance, together with the identity of the recipient and the severity of the sanction. But under section 43G ERA, on its face the enquiry comes to an end if the gateway requirements in section 43G(2) are not satisfied. Nor would the worker have any fallback of protection through an ordinary unfair dismissal claim if there were insufficient qualifying service. That said, even if the approach in section 43G was found to be inconsistent with the ECtHR, it is not apparent that there could be a conforming interpretation (so as to change the gateways or otherwise to allow the severity of the sanction to be considered) which does not go against a fundamental feature of the legislation.[35]

---

[34] *Palomo Sanchez and others v Spain* [2011] IRLR 934 (ECtHR).

[35] As to the power to make a declaration of incompatibility (which does not lead to a remedy in the individual case) see s 4 HRA. Such a declaration could not be made by an employment tribunal, but could be made by the Court of Appeal.

PART IV

RULES, POLICIES, PROCEDURES, AND PROBLEMS

19

WHISTLEBLOWING PROCEDURES IN THE PUBLIC AND PRIVATE SECTORS: WHY THEY ARE NEEDED AND WHAT THEY SHOULD CONTAIN

> The essence of a whistleblowing system is that staff should be able to bypass the direct management line because that may well be the area about which their concerns arise, and that they should be able to go outside the organisation if they feel the overall management is engaged in an improper course.
>
> Committee on Standards in Public Life, Third Report (1996), page 48.

A. Why?

Whilst the enactment of PIDA provided encouragement for the introduction of whis- **19.01** tleblowing policies, more recent developments have provided fresh impetus for and renewed focus on the importance of adopting and implementing good policies and procedures. We considered those developments insofar as they have concerned the health and financial services sectors in Chapter 12. Legislative reform is also a significant driver to the adoption of effective policies. The introduction of vicarious liability and the statutory defence for employers set out in section 47B ERA (as discussed in Chapter 8) provides a direct incentive for employers to implement a proper whistleblowing policy and to comply with good practice. If it does not take these steps an employer is most unlikely to be able to show that all reasonable steps were taken to prevent victimization of a claimant whistleblower.

Meanwhile, guidance as to good practice has emerged from several sources. Most notably, in November 2013, the Whistleblowing Commission set up by Public Concern at Work (PCaW), published its report with a draft Code of Practice,[1] and, in March 2015, the then Department for Business Innovation and Skills (BIS), issued 'Whistleblowing Guidance for Employers and Code of Practice'.[2] These materials added to the good practice guidance published by the British Standards Institute's whistleblowing code of practice.[3]

19.02 There are several aspects to the benefits of implementing sound whistleblowing procedures so as to encourage staff to first raise concerns within the employing organization rather than externally:[4]

(1) It fosters a more healthy and accountable workplace where problems are likely to be 'nipped in the bud'.

(2) It encourages reporting that may act as an early warning system. Consider the *Herald of Free Enterprise* ferry disaster and the findings of Barry Sheen LJ; the *Piper Alpha* disaster and Lord Cullen's findings; the Clapham rail crash and Lord Hidden's inquiry; the *Matrix Churchill* affair; Beverly Allitt and the inquiry by Sir Cecil Clothier; Dame Janet Smith's *Shipman* inquiry; the BCCI inquiry by Lord Bingham; the Bank of England's report on the collapse of Barings. All of these events occurred despite people possessing critical information which, if it had been passed on and heeded, would have prevented the subsequent disaster.

(3) If encouragement, security, and a reporting structure for those raising concerns is provided, then not only is it more likely that a report will be raised but also that it will in the first instance be raised internally. The degree of control thus achieved provides the employer organization with every opportunity to address the concern, and minimizes the need for external involvement or the involvement of regulators.

(4) Perhaps most importantly, a procedure will ensure that the critical information reaches those who can act upon it. The existence and use by workers of a policy makes it more likely that the organization will recognize a qualifying disclosure without recourse to external advice.

(5) Workers considering becoming involved in malpractice are likely to be deterred by the existence of a policy which increases the likelihood of their colleagues raising suspicions.

(6) As we have noted, implementation of a whistleblowing procedure and associated good practice is likely to be an essential element in establishing the statutory defence to vicarious liability under section 47B ERA.

(7) A workforce where those in charge accept the commercial advantages and have implemented a whistleblowing procedure will be more likely to realize that concerns need to be addressed and handled appropriately, thereby also reducing the risk of litigation.

(8) If a worker makes an external disclosure without first having made the disclosure internally (and then waited for the matter to be addressed in accordance with the internal procedure) then the prospects of that external disclosure attracting protection are reduced. ERA, section 43G(3)(f) specifically provides that, in a case where the worker has previously made a disclosure of substantially the same information to the employer,

---

[1] See http://www.pcaw.org.uk/files/WBC%20Report%20Final.pdf.

[2] See https://www.gov.uk/government/uploads/system/uploads/attachment_data/file/415175/bis-15-200-whistleblowing-guidance-for-employers-and-code-of-practice.pdf.

[3] Available at http://www.bsigroup.com/en/sectorsandservices/Forms/PAS-19982008-Whistleblowing/Download-PAS-1998/.

[4] But, as discussed in Chapter 12 at para 12.110, in the financial services sector it must also be made expressly clear that reporting to the PRA or FCA is not conditional on first having made an internal report to the employer.

in assessing whether it was reasonable to make a wider disclosure the tribunal shall take into account whether the worker complied with any authorized procedure. Further, the failure to follow a well-established route for raising concerns may lead to adverse inferences being drawn as to whether the worker held a reasonable belief that disclosure was made in the public interest and (though now only an issue at the remedy stage) whether the disclosure was made in good faith.[5]

(9) For some organizations there will be an added advantage in the impression made on outsiders that the organization is following good practice, and that any concerns over malpractice within it are likely to be identified and addressed. This may be important in terms of fostering greater confidence among investors, in the marketplace and in those with whom the organization is dealing or wants to deal.

Additionally, section 7 of the Bribery Act 2010 now provides a strict liability offence for commercial organizations that fail to prevent bribery by any 'person associated' with the organization. The only defence is for the organization to establish that it possessed 'adequate procedures designed to prevent persons associated with Company from undertaking' bribery[6]. A properly resourced, fully implemented whistleblowing procedure would be an important ingredient in establishing a defence that adequate procedures were put in place.[7] The penalty for breach of section 7, upon summary conviction, is a sentence of up to 12 months' imprisonment and/or a fine not exceeding the statutory maximum. However, the maximum sentence on indictment is imprisonment for up to 10 years together with an unlimited fine. The EU levied fines in relation to cartels in excess of €12 billion between 2010 and 19 July 2016.[8] There are additional implications from both the United Kingdom and the EU of any conviction. Pursuant to regulation 57 of the Public Contracts Regulations 2015 (SI 2015/102) and regulation 80 of the Utilities Contracts Regulations 2016 (SI 2016/274), both of which enacted EU directives,[9] if the contracting authority is aware that the economic operator, or any member of the administrative, management, or supervisory body of that economic operator, or any person who has powers of representation, decision, or control in the economic operator, has been convicted of any of various offences listed, including conspiracy, corruption, bribery, or fraud, it will be ineligible and cannot be selected in tenders. **19.03**

In addition, as the discussion of the health and financial sectors in Chapter 12 shows there is now an increased emphasis on the importance of regulators playing a proactive role in seeing that employers take appropriate steps to foster a culture where whistleblowers are encouraged to raise concerns and are heeded when they do so. As proposed by PCaW's 'Report on the effectiveness of existing arrangements for workplace whistleblowing in the UK' (November 2013), an amendment was made to the ERA to give the Secretary of State power to require prescribed persons to report on the effectiveness of whistleblowing procedures within their industry (see section 43FA ERA),[10] and some regulators have taken **19.04**

---

[5] See eg *Muchesa v Central and Cecil Housing Care Support* (UKEAT/0443/07/ZT, 22 August 2008) where emphasis was placed on the claimant's failure to follow a whistleblowing policy, despite being aware of it, in support of a conclusion that disclosures were made without any genuine belief in their truth and not in good faith (see Chapter 3, para 3.70).

[6] Section 7(2) of the Bribery Act 2010, 'But it is a defence for C to prove that C had in place adequate procedures designed to prevent persons associated with C from undertaking such conduct'.

[7] See 'Managing Global Corruption' (2011) 161 NLJ 669; 'Uncovering misconduct' (2011) 123 Em LJ 22.

[8] See http://ec.europa.eu/competition/cartels/statistics/statistics.pdf.

[9] Directives 2004/18/EC [2004] OJ 134/114 and 2004/17/EC [2004] OJ L134/1.

[10] Inserted by Small Business, Enterprise and Employment Act 2015 (c. 26), ss 148(2), 164(1); SI 2015/2029, reg. 2(a) on 1 January 2016. At the time of writing no regulations have yet been introduced.

steps to do so in advance of this power being exercised.[11] It may be that this will provide an impetus for regulated organizations to be required to inform their prescribed regulators of the way in which they manage their internal policies, to enable the prescribed body to report on the effectiveness of procedures and ensure that workers are aware of their role. For example, as discussed in Chapter 12 (paragraph 12.107), one aspect of the overhaul in the FCA's approach is that there is a requirement for a report to be made at least annually to each regulated firm's governing body on the operation and effectiveness of the systems and controls in relation to whistleblowing and this is to be available to the PRA and FCA on request.[12] The scope for the FCA to examine procedures and their implementation is a material change to the existing system of oversight. It is against this backdrop that the steps advocated in this chapter has become even more important. However, whether a particular regulator will use a carrot or a stick to encourage compliance remains to be seen.

19.05   The importance of introducing effective whistleblowing policies was emphasized by the Committee on Standards in Public Life. Under the chairmanship of Sir Alistair Graham, the Committee stated:

> 4.31 Effective whistleblowing is . . . a key component in any strategy to challenge inappropriate behaviour at all levels of an organisation. It is both an instrument in support of good governance and a manifestation of a more open organisational culture. . . .
>
> 4.35 . . . Where an individual case reaches the point of invoking the Act then this represents a failure of the internal systems in some respect. Either the employee has failed to follow the procedure (for whatever reason) or the procedures themselves have failed. In our view, therefore, any case where the Act is invoked should initiate a review of the whistleblowing procedures in that organisation.[13]

These statements apply to any organization in the public, private, or voluntary sector.

19.06   The Committee on Standards provided the following recommendation:[14]

> Leaders of public bodies should reiterate their commitment to the effective implementation of the Public Interest Disclosure Act 1998 and ensure its principles and provisions are widely known and applicable in their own organisation. They should commit their organisations to following the four key elements of good practice i.e.
>
> (i)   ensuring that staff are aware of and trust the whistleblowing avenues;
> (ii) provision of realistic advice about what the whistleblowing process means for openness, confidentiality and anonymity;
> (iii) continual review of how the procedures work in practice; and
> (iv) regular communication to staff about the avenues open to them.

19.07   These recommendations provide good guidance for any organization in any sector. The Committee concluded that:

> the statutory framework (Public Interest Disclosure Act 1998) is a helpful driver but must be recognised as a 'backstop' which can provide redress when things go wrong not as a substitute for cultures that actively encourage challenge of inappropriate behaviour. We have recommended that leaders of public bodies should commit themselves to follow the elements of good practice.[15]

---

[11]   See Chapter 12, para 12.119.

[12]   PRA Supervisory Statement (SS39/15) para 4.2; FCA response to consultation (PS15/24), below para 2.20.

[13]   Tenth Report of the Committee on Standards in Public Life, *Getting the Balance Right: Implementing Standards of Conduct in Public Life*, Cm 6407; the report is available on the Committee's website, <http://www.public-standards.gov.uk>.

[14]   ibid, recommendation 38.

[15]   ibid, para 4.46.

The importance of implementing adequate whistleblowing arrangements has also been **19.08** highlighted at EU level in the Council of Europe's Recommendation CM/Rec(2014)7 and explanatory memorandum.[16] The explanatory memorandum comments (at paras 9 and 10) that:

9. Organisations that let those who work for them know that it is safe and acceptable for them to report concerns about wrongdoing are more likely to:
   a. be forewarned of potential malpractice;
   b. investigate it; and
   c. take such measures as are reasonable to remove any unwarranted danger.
   Thus implementing internal whistleblowing arrangements is increasingly understood to be part of establishing an organisational ethos of integrity, delivering high standards of public and customer service and managing risk in a responsible manner.

10. Furthermore, the emphasis on accountability and democratic principles is important. Employers, governments and citizens increasingly recognise that while encouraging whistleblowers to speak up averts harm and damage, it also improves public services and strengthens organisational responsibility and public accountability.

There have also been warnings at EU level, from the perspective of data protection rights, **19.09** of the dangers of a whistleblowing procedure drafted or implemented in an inappropriate way and lacking suitable safeguards, as we discuss at paragraphs 19.109–19.118 below. Introducing a whistleblowing policy should only be considered as a start. Further proactive steps are needed to foster a culture where workers feel able to raise their concerns internally, and, when raised, that those concerns are properly addressed. It is essential that the policy should ensure that the worker knows when and how to raise a concern and that the organization understands how to react. The organization needs to ensure that it is receptive to concerns and consistent and effective in the manner of its response to them. There needs to be a clear structure and guidance to managers as to how concerns will be raised internally, with the recipient of concerns knowing how to respond when a concern is received. The introduction of whistleblowing champions and whistleblowing guardians in the health and financial services sectors (discussed in Chapter 12) follows an important theme that shows procedures without either oversight, analysis, or review are likely to be less effective. There needs to be careful and ongoing consideration as to the effectiveness of procedures implemented in a workplace. The overseers need access to the board (in private organizations) on at least an annual basis. Organizations should consider their reports closely and support them in securing cultural change within the organization.

According to PCaW's review in 2010, outside of the financial services sector (where disclo- **19.10** sures are more likely to be made to a regulator[17]) around 80 per cent of claimants raise their concern with their employer before presenting their claims to a tribunal. That would tend to indicate that employers are usually given the first opportunity to address the concerns. Yet the escalating number of claims provides some indication that this opportunity is not being taken in an effective way. In 2010 PCaW published a review of whistleblowing over the previous decade.[18] This report highlighted that in 1999/2000 there were 157 PIDA claims, whereas by 2009 this had increased to 1,761 claims. PCaW's biennial review in October 2011 reported that there was a further rise to about 2,000 claims in the year to 31 March

---

[16] Available at http://www.coe.int/t/DGHL/STANDARDSETTING/CDcj/CDCJ%20 Recommendations/CMRec(2014)7E.pdf.
[17] PCaW, 'Where's whistleblowing now? 10 years of legal protection for whistleblowers', March 2010, p 6, available at http:// www.pcaw.org.uk.
[18] 'Where's Whistleblowing now?' op. cit. n 17.

2010, with total awards in that period of £2.3 million, bringing the total awarded under the legislation to just under £12 million. About a quarter of the cases proceeded to a hearing, of which 20 per cent (85 cases) were successful. The average award in successful claims was £58,000, compared to average awards of £18,584, £19,499, and £52,087 in race, sex, and disability discrimination cases respectively. This may reflect the continuing difficulties which those who blow the whistle may find in seeking alternative employment. PCaW's 2010 review recorded that only 28 per cent of individuals contacting its helpline stated that their employer did not have a whistleblowing procedure. From its research, PCaW stated that only one per cent of individuals who raised their concern with their employer or regulator went to the media. Further, 35 per cent of callers to PCaW had suffered reprisals for having raised concerns. The message, again, is that introduction of a whistleblowing procedure is a start, but more is required to ensure effective implementation.

B. How?

(1) Sources of guidance

19.11 A policy must be more than a tepid statement issued to tick a box under a compliance regime. We focus in this section on the elements of an effective whistleblowing procedure (or, more appropriately, a confidential reporting procedure). We recommend that this chapter be read together with the terms of the BSI Guide (Publicly Available Specification 1998:2008) ('PAS').[19] Other sources of helpful guidance include:

(1) Whistleblowing guidance published by the Government in March 2015;
(2) The Whistleblowing Commission's Code of Practice;
(3) 'Speak up for a Healthy NHS' (guidance published in 2010, written by PCaW, which was commissioned by the NHS Social Partnership Forum (NHS Employers, NHS trade unions, and the Department of Health));
(4) The template national whistleblowing policy for the NHS, published in April 2016;
(5) SYSC 18 in the FCA handbook (see Chapter 12); and
(6) Observations made by the National Audit Office in its report of 2014 as to the main criteria to be included in a whistleblowing policy.[20]

19.12 These guides provide a useful check and can be used as discussion points for any policy and procedure. But it remains important to tailor policies for the particular organization and take into account its structure and functions. A properly drafted procedure can ensure that focus is given to specific interests so that particular sources of possible wrongdoing or failure can be addressed. A care home needs a very different policy to a bank. This point was made in evidence submitted by Guy Dehn and Anna Myers of PCaW to the Committee on Standards in Public Life regarding the substance of whistleblowing procedures. They warned:

> of the dangers of a prescriptive 'one size fits all' approach to whistleblowing policies because of the wide differences in the size, function, and constitution of public bodies and because

---

[19] Available at <http://www.bsigroup.com/en/sectorsandservices/Forms/PAS-19982008-Whistleblowing/Download-PAS-1998/>.

[20] See, https://www.nao.org.uk/wp-content/uploads/2014/01/Government-whistleblowing-policies.pdf, referring to the main elements as (a) setting a positive environment for a whistleblowing policy: structure, commitment, clarity and tone from the top, offering an alternative to line management, reassuring potential whistleblowers and addressing concerns and providing feedback; (b) supporting whistleblowers; (c) openness, confidentiality, and anonymity, (d) access to independent advice; and (e) whistleblowing to external bodies, such as prescribed regulators.

the uncritical adoption of model procedures can lead to an unwitting tick-box approach to governance.[21]

Notwithstanding the need to be alert to the individual circumstances of the particular **19.13** organization, PCaW identified four key elements to any procedure:

(1) Ensuring that staff are aware of and trust the whistleblowing avenues. Successful promotion of awareness and trust depend upon the simplicity and practicality of the options available, and also on the ability to demonstrate that a senior officer inside the organisation is accessible for the expression of concerns about wrongdoing, and that where this fails, there is recourse to effective external and independent oversight.

(2) Provision of realistic advice about what the whistleblowing process means for openness, confidentiality and anonymity. While requests for confidentiality and anonymity should be respected, there may be cases where a public body might not be able to act on a concern without the whistleblower's open evidence. Even where the whistleblower's identity is not disclosed, 'this is no guarantee that it will not be deduced by those implicated or by colleagues'.

(3) Continual review of how the procedures work in practice. This is a key feature of the revised Code on Corporate Governance, which now places an obligation on the audit committees of listed companies to review how whistleblowing policies operate in practice. The advantage of this approach is that it ensures a review of action taken in response to the expression of concerns about wrongdoing; it allows a look at whether confidentiality issues have been handled effectively and whether staff have been treated fairly as a result of raising concerns.

(4) Regular communication to staff about the avenues open to them. Creative approaches to this include the use of payslips, newsletters, management briefings and intranets, and use too of Public Concern's helpline, launched in 2003 and available through subscription.[22]

Likewise the government guidance published in March 2015, whilst commenting that there **19.14** 'is no one-size-fits-all whistleblowing policy as policies will vary depending on the size and nature of the organization', sets out the following 'tips about what a policy should include':

- An explanation of what whistleblowing is, particularly in relation to the organization
- A clear explanation of the organization's procedures for handling whistleblowing, which can be communicated through training
- A commitment to training workers at all levels of the organization in relation to whistleblowing law and the organization's policy
- A commitment to treat all disclosures consistently and fairly
- A commitment to take all reasonable steps to maintain the confidentiality of the whistleblower where it is requested (unless required by law to break that confidentiality)
- Clarification that any so-called gagging clauses in settlement agreements do not prevent workers from making disclosures in the public interest
- An idea about what feedback a whistleblower might receive
- An explanation that anonymous whistleblowers will not ordinarily be able to receive feedback and that any action taken to look into a disclosure could be limited—anonymous whistleblowers may seek feedback through a telephone appointment or by using an anonymized email address
- A commitment to emphasize in a whistleblowing policy that victimization of a whistleblower is not acceptable. Any instances of victimization will be taken seriously and managed appropriately

---

[21] Tenth Report of the Committee on Standards in Public Life, Getting the Balance Right: Implementing Standards of Conduct in Public Life, Cm 6407, para 4.38.
[22] ibid, para 4.43.

- An idea of the time frame for handling any disclosures raised
- Clarification that the whistleblower does not need to provide evidence for the employer to look into the concerns raised
- Signposts to information and advice to those thinking of blowing the whistle, for example the guidance from the Government, Acas, Public Concern at Work, or Trade Unions
- Information about blowing the whistle to the relevant prescribed person(s).

19.15 The government guidance also included a Whistleblowing Code of Practice, setting out the following elements of good practice:

- Have a whistleblowing policy or appropriate written procedures in place
- Ensure the whistleblowing policy or procedures are easily accessible to all workers
- Raise awareness of the policy or procedures through all available means such as staff engagement, intranet sites, and other marketing communications
- Provide training to all workers on how disclosures should be raised and how they will be acted upon
- Provide training to managers on how to deal with disclosures
- Create an understanding that all staff at all levels of the organization should demonstrate that they support and encourage whistleblowing
- Confirm that any clauses in settlement agreements do not prevent workers from making disclosures in the public interest
- Ensure the organization's whistleblowing policy or procedures clearly identify who can be approached by workers that want to raise a disclosure. Organizations should ensure a range of alternative persons who a whistleblower can approach in the event a worker feels unable to approach their manager. If your organization works with a recognized union, a representative from that union could be an appropriate contact for a worker to approach
- Create an organizational culture where workers feel safe to raise a disclosure in the knowledge that they will not face any detriment from the organization as a result of speaking up
- Undertake that any detriment towards an individual who raises a disclosure is not acceptable
- Make a commitment that all disclosures raised will be dealt with appropriately, consistently, fairly, and professionally
- Undertake to protect the identity of the worker raising a disclosure, unless required by law to reveal it, and to offer support throughout with access to mentoring, advice, and counselling
- Provide feedback to the worker who raised the disclosure where possible and appropriate, subject to other legal requirements. Feedback should include an indication of timings for any actions or next steps

19.16 Whilst these elements might be regarded as largely a statement of the obvious, they also serve as broad headings by which to test the adequacy of procedures and it may be they will be regarded as such by tribunals in considering the application of the statutory defence under section 47B ERA.

(2) Key issues

19.17 We address these points further in commenting below on the following basic areas which any policy should consider:

(a) Preliminary matters
(b) Explaining why concerns should be raised
(c) Who can raise concerns?
(d) What concerns can be raised?
(e) Distinguishing whistleblowing and grievances
(f) To whom should reports be made?
(g) How should a report be made?

(h) When should the concern be raised?

(i) Confidentiality or anonymity?

(j) Protection against reprisal and exceptions from protection

(k) Process

(l) Advice or assistance

(m) Monitoring

(n) Review

(o) Advertising

(p) Training

We will now address each of these elements in turn.

(a) Preliminary matters

Before implementing any policy or procedure it is important to seek to consult with the **19.18** various stakeholders in both the creation and dissemination of that policy. Next, the organization should consider who, or which body, should 'lead' the arrangements for its development and introduction. As discussed in Chapter 12, the NHS has introduced 'guardians', and the financial services industry 'champions'. Whatever the nomenclature, there needs to be someone with oversight of the process who can report on its application at least annually: such reports may be required by regulators. It is important that any procedure, and communications about the policy, clearly show that senior, middle, and line managers support the use of the procedures, and that from the start the policy is seen as an initiative to which senior management subscribes. Further, it is advisable to involve personnel/human resources from an early stage in both the formulation of the policy and its integration, to ensure that it is consistent with other policies or procedures.

Consideration should be given to appropriate consultation steps, suitable to the organization **19.19** concerned, in relation to the proposed policies and processes. 'Speak up for a healthy NHS' comments that:

> Consulting with staff, managers and unions will provide you with an opportunity to think through policy messages, any issues arising, and the language of the policy. It is also an opportunity to decide what it should be called (for example some organisations prefer to call their policies 'Speak Up' or 'Raising Concerns' rather than 'Whistleblowing Policy') and how helpful staff think it would be, should they face a dilemma on how or whether to raise their concern.

Once the process and policy is determined and the foundations of senior management are in **19.20** place, the organization should seek to prepare and introduce the initiative through consultation and clear communication from multiple sources and not rely on mere line management distribution or instruction. Further considerations can be obtained from the PAS (4.1 to 4.2). The aim of the organization should not just be to instruct those who are to use the policy of its existence, but to enable the organization to inform, instruct, and gently educate all those who are to use the system of the importance of the policy for them as individuals as well as the organization as a whole.

(b) Explaining why concerns should be raised

The policy should convey a clear message about the commitment of senior managers and **19.21** the board to the policy and why workers are being encouraged to raise matters. It should set out clearly that they are protected in doing so and that it would be better to raise a concern and to be wrong than not to raise it at all. It may be a good idea to make clear at the start of the document that matters may be raised in confidence and that such confidences will be maintained as far as possible.

19.22 Ideally these introductory comments will be tailored to the particular organization. By way of example the template national whistleblowing policy begins with the following introduction:

> **Speak up—we will listen**
>
> Speaking up about any concern you have at work is really important. In fact, it's vital because it will help us to keep improving our services for all patients and the working environment for our staff.
>
> You may feel worried about raising a concern, and we understand this. But please don't be put off. In accordance with our duty of candour, our senior leaders and entire board are committed to an open and honest culture. We will look into what you say and you will always have access to the support you need.

(c) Who can raise concerns?

19.23 It is helpful to spell out in the policy who is able to raise concerns under the policy. Whether it is open to 'anyone' (for example under the FCA and PRA rules), or to specific categories of people, it must be clear. The legislation protects workers,[23] but a whistleblowing policy does not need to be confined in that way. It is good practice for the policy also to cover others who fall outside the legislation, such as volunteers or shareholders. The NHS template national whistleblowing policy, for example, provides that concerns can be raised by anyone who works in the NHS or an independent organization that provides NHS services, and states that this includes agency workers, temporary workers, students, volunteers, and governors.

19.24 It is our view that in most cases it will be appropriate also to consider widening the applicability of the policy to include those external to the organization and thereby including outsiders who may have critical information. These would include, for example, contractors and suppliers. One factor relevant to extending coverage is that the Bribery Act 2010 makes the commercial organization liable for the acts of those 'associated' with the organization, which is clearly wide enough to include contractors and consultants. Thought should be given to ensuring that contracting parties are aware of the procedure, that it applies to them, and how they should access it. This is of particular use in the public sector, for example by local authorities, given the number of agencies and organizations providing services for and to them. It would make commercial sense to ensure that those individuals know of the local authorities' procedures, and even to make having a whistleblowing policy a condition of the contract with the organization providing goods or services to the authority. It may be that those with whom the employing organization is contracting could be included and specifically sent a copy of the procedure. Alternatively, consideration may need to be given to the subcontractor's own whistleblowing arrangements. The PAS suggests (at para 4.3) that:

> Organizations that contract out significant parts of their business activities should consider how best to approach the work of subcontractors. The simplest options are to establish that (a) the subcontractor has its own effective whistleblowing arrangements or (b) the subcontractor agrees to promote the organization's whistleblowing contacts to its own staff where the concern relates to a threat or risk to the organization.

19.25 In Professor David Lewis's 2010 survey of confidential reporting procedures in the UK top 250 FTSE firms,[24] of those responding sixty-four of the 250 had a confidential reporting procedure, and it was noted that of these 83 per cent permitted their procedures to be used

---

[23] See Chapter 6.

[24] Research commissioned by SIA Global and available at <https://www.saiglobal.com/compliance/resources/expert-commentaries/david-lewis-hotline-research.htm>.

by the self-employed; 50 per cent allowed contractors, and 42 per cent permitted subcontractors or suppliers access to it.[25]

The case of *Montgomery v Universal Services Handling Ltd (in Liquidation)* (ET, Case No 2701150/03, 29 January 2004) is a good example, in the private sector, of the potential consequences of a whistleblowing procedure being constructed too narrowly. Mr Montgomery worked as a night driver, delivering perishable foodstuffs to American Airlines for export by air from Heathrow. The perishable items should have been X-rayed before loading, but Montgomery noticed that some consignments were not in fact passed through the X-ray machine despite its being certified that this had been done. He raised his concerns with colleagues and with his employer. About the same time the employer had taken the decision to reduce staffing levels and there was a lot of pressure to get work out and cut corners by avoiding the X-ray machine; indeed, a letter was sent to all staff telling them that the X-ray machines had to be bypassed, and staff had to 'like it or lump it'. Montgomery reported the practice to the Metropolitan Police at Heathrow who dismissed his concerns. He also raised his concern by sending a fax anonymously to the Department of Transport before going on holiday. When the practice continued, Montgomery notified Customs and Excise of what was happening, using its confidential reporting line. Nine days after contacting Customs and Excise, Montgomery refused to deliver a consignment of fresh flowers he knew had not been X-rayed. Before the start of his next shift he was telephoned by the operations manager and told not to return to work as he was being 'let go'. No reason for the dismissal was given at this time, although, at a later date, Montgomery received a letter stating that it was 'due to redundancy'. The ET had no hesitation in finding that the real reason for his dismissal was that he had made protected disclosures, not only to his employer but, on different occasions, to the Police, the Department of Transport, and Customs and Excise. It said that Montgomery had acted in an exemplary fashion to try to ensure the safety of air travellers and had brought blatant lapses of security practice to the attention of the appropriate authority. Given the freight was being placed on aircraft, the security implications had been considerable. But despite Mr Montgomery's attempts to raise concerns to prevent the wrongdoing from continuing, there had been no process to ensure the disclosures reached the organization most affected by the breach, namely the airlines taking on board the freight. It was not until long after the complaint was first made that American Airlines became aware that up to 300 tons had been presented as 'X-rayed', when in fact it had not been, and that action was taken. Putting aside the grave security issues, this is an example of why the potential use of contractual confidential reporting lines between, on the facts of this case Universal Services and the contractor American Airlines, should be seriously countenanced. The continuing security failings might have been avoided if (a) there had been a contractual requirement that staff working upon American Airlines freight receive a copy of a whistleblowing policy, and (b) such a policy entitled them to raise concerns direct with American Airlines. Such a mechanism would make those providing services more likely to be reluctant to cut corners or mislead the client for commercial gain. At the very least, however, a condition of a contract must be that the contractor has a whistleblowing policy.

19.26

Depending on the organization there may also be merit in opening up the confidential reporting system to customers, users, and other members of the public. For example, the City of London's procedure applies to 'all members of the public', 'employees', and 'contractors working for the City of London' including their 'employees and sub-contractors'. It therefore covers agency staff and those providing services under a contract with the City of

19.27

---

[25] Of those organizations that fully completed the questionnaire, more than 80 per cent stated that the procedure had been invoked.

London in their own premises, for example care homes. Whilst it does not apply to Police Officers this is because they have a separate, specific procedure to follow.[26]

19.28   Different considerations may arise in relation to complaints by members of the public which may merit maintaining a different route for raising concerns; however, it is the view of the authors that this does not necessarily rule out the procedure acting as a triage to allocate disclosures to the more appropriate part of the organization to address. In PAS 4.3 it states:

> It is not advisable for a whistleblowing policy to be expressly extended to members of the public or consumers in instances where, for example, a patient complains about a negligent surgeon, a passenger reports seeing a firm's truck dumping waste near a rail station or a passer-by sees a danger on a building site. This is because the issues of confidentiality, protection from reprisal and reporting lines either do not arise or operate in a markedly different way when the information comes from members of the public. While in almost all organizations, there will be some pre-existing arrangements for individual customer complaints or consumer feedback, it is both common sense and good governance that an organization is open and receptive to warnings of risks and malpractice that may be raised by consumer interests, shareholders, community or public interest groups and other stakeholders.

(d) What concerns can be raised?

19.29   Consideration should be given to what concerns are covered by the policy. We have seen in Chapter 12 the different approaches in relation to this taken by the NHS national whistleblowing policy and the FCA requirements in SYSC 18.3.1(1).[27] The NHS policy avoids referring to 'protected disclosures' in relation to the scope of matters that may be raised. It provides that a concern can be raised about any 'risk, malpractice or wrongdoing' thought to be harming the service delivered or commissioned, and follows this with some non-exhaustive examples. By comparison SYSC 18.3.1(1) defines a reportable concern as being a concern held in relation to the activities of the firm, including anything that could be the subject matter of a protected disclosure or a breach of the firm's policies and procedures or behaviour that harms or is likely to harm the reputation or financial well-being of the firm.

19.30   Both formulations are intentionally broader than the statutory definition of a protected disclosure: they are not limited to the specified categories of relevant failure in section 43B ERA. We suggest, though, that generally it will be preferable to use plain language and broad terms rather than defining the scope by reference to the legal language of protected disclosures. Indeed the reference to these in SYSC 18.3.1(1) is no doubt explained by its being part of a set of rules, rather than forming part of the whistleblowing policy itself to be issued by individual firms.

19.31   The protected disclosure legislation covers past acts, present acts, and likely future acts. It must be clear that the procedure covers them all.

(e) Distinguishing whistleblowing and grievances

19.32   The guidance provided in the policy should explain clearly that the confidential reporting procedure is distinct and separate from the grievance procedure. The ordinary grievance procedure provides the appropriate route where a worker has a complaint in relation to his/her own individual employment situation. A whistleblowing procedure provides the appropriate route where the worker has a concern about a risk, malpractice, or wrongdoing

---

[26] City of London Police Professional Standards Reporting—Standard Operating Procedure. See https://www.cityoflondon.gov.uk/about-the-city/how-we-make-decisions/budgets-and-spending/Documents/col-whistleblowing-policy.pdf.

[27] See Chapter 12, paras 12.97 and 12.99.

which concerns others.[28] Consistently with this, the template NHS national whistleblowing procedure for example provides that: 'This policy is not for people with concerns about their employment that affect only them—that type of concern is better suited to our grievance policy.'

The distinction between grievances and matters for the whistleblowing procedure is now **19.33** reflected in the ERA's protected disclosure provisions, by virtue of the introduction of the requirement for a reasonable belief that that disclosure was made in the public interest. The scope for disclosures of information as to apprehended breaches of a worker's own employment contract is therefore much reduced; see the more detailed discussion of this in Chapter 4.

There may, of course, be cases where there is an overlap between the two categories and **19.34** either procedure is appropriate because the wrongdoing affects the worker's own employment situation but also has a wider impact. However, drawing the distinction is necessary so that the concerns raised are appropriate for a procedure designed as an early warning system and for the investigation of essentially public interest concerns. The PAS comments that unless the organization's own arrangements make the distinction clear, it cannot assume or expect that employees will understand the difference. That is not to say, of course, that a concern which is raised that should more appropriately have been brought under another procedure should simply be rejected rather than redirected. As we saw in Chapter 12, the approach taken by the PRA and FCS had been to frame in wide terms the reportable concerns that can be raised under the whistleblowing procedures but on the basis that there should then be an internal filter to determine those that should be treated as grievances.[29] This was seen as preferable to producing a complex system, and as recognizing that the potential benefits of receiving all information that could prevent wrongdoing outweigh the disadvantages of not receiving any.

As has been done by the NHS, the PAS recommends that examples are provided to illus- **19.35** trate the distinction between the whistleblowing procedure and the grievance procedure. It also recommends that where the employee claims that s/he is being bullied or discriminated against and the organization has a policy specifically for bullying, discrimination, or harassment or, as the case may be, a grievance policy, then whichever of those policies is appropriate should be used rather than the whistleblowing policy. The PAS notes that where such issues are raised through the whistleblowing procedure, it may still be appropriate to treat a matter as a 'tip-off' and to investigate whether there is anything to suggest a wider problem, which may be evidenced by a high staff turnover, increased sickness rates, or found within other allegations raised in exit interviews. It also notes that where the issue is raised other than by an alleged victim it may well not be feasible to take action without the victim's evidence. An alleged victim may prefer to deal with the issue in other ways and may oppose interference by the employer (PAS 3.10).

Where the concern raised does amount to a grievance, there should also be compliance with **19.36** the ACAS Code of Practice on Disciplinary and Grievance Procedures, which requires a process of investigation, a hearing, and a decision with a right to appeal. A failure to follow this Code entitles employment tribunals to adjust any awards made in relevant cases by up to 25 per cent for unreasonable failure to comply with any provision of the Code.[30] As discussed in Chapter 10, paragraph 10.44, that raises some practical difficulty, because a

---

[28] See PAS 0.5 and 'Speak up for a Healthy NHS' (see para 19.11 above) p 11.
[29] See Chapter 12, para 12.100.
[30] Sections 207A TULRCA and 124A ERA.

grievance is widely defined in the Code as 'problems or complaints that employees raise with their employers'. On its face that would appear sufficiently broad to cover concerns on public interest matters not specific to the worker's own situation. As such, whilst there are arguments that the application of the Code should be more narrowly construed (see paragraph 10.44), in the absence of clear authority to that effect the sensible course is for the employer so far as is possible to abide by the requirements of the Code. Whilst there may be some differences of emphasis, in many cases that will accord with good practice in relation to arranging (or at least offering to arrange) a meeting to discuss the concern and to elicit details in relation to it (and permitting the employee to be accompanied should he or she so wish), providing feedback on the outcome, and offering a further avenue to escalate the concern at a higher level internally if not resolved.

(f) To whom should concerns be raised?

19.37   It is good practice to encourage staff to raise concerns initially through their line management where they feel able to do so. This is also the norm in practice. Professor David Lewis' research in 2006 noted that the majority of organizations in his survey made provision for reports to be initially to line managers,[31] and his 2010 survey of FTSE 250 firms identified that 68 per cent had line managers as the initial point of contact.[32]

19.38   However, an important aspect of an effective whistleblowing policy is to provide safe and readily accessible routes for raising concerns other than through direct line management. This may, for example, be a senior designated individual, or one of a range of individuals such as a head of a particular area (eg a regional manager) or of a particular function (eg head of the legal department or human resources), or non-executive directors, with a further more senior level of recourse in the event of dissatisfaction with the outcome. Indeed following a review of thirty-nine whistleblowing policies across government, the National Audit Office, in its 2014 report,[33] found that, despite there often being a strong performance in setting a positive environment for whistleblowing to occur, a common failing was that the policies failed to outline suitable alternatives to line managers when making a disclosure.[34]

19.39   Many organizations use a dedicated telephone hotline to report concerns, with the NHS using a freephone helpline and a website.[35] However, there are downsides to directing all concerns either to senior managers or to hotlines, rather than encouraging staff to raise their concerns first with line management where they feel able to do so. In many cases the quickest and most effective route will be to go through line management. There is also a risk that line management will be alienated if it is bypassed.

19.40   One of the recommendations of the Article 29 Data Protection Working Party (see paragraph 19.114 below) was to have a separate dedicated unit to receive the report. This reduces concern as to fairness in processing personal data[36] because it reduces to the minimum necessary the number of people who have access to the data. Furthermore, the unit is likely to develop expertise in dealing with disclosures.

---

[31]   Professor David Lewis, 'The contents of confidential reporting/whistleblowing procedures in the UK: some lessons from empirical research' (Middlesex University, 2006), para 7 of the conclusions.

[32]   See para 19.25 above.

[33]   See para 19.11 above.

[34]   The other common failings identified were failing to explain when the confidentiality of a whistleblower may be compromised, failing to mention the risks and limitations of disclosures outside the organization, and failing to highlight the benefits of seeking independent advice.

[35]   Of those responding to Professor Lewis's study into FTSE 250, 75 per cent used telephone hotlines.

[36]   For a decision on what is and is not personal data, see *R (on the application of the Department of Health) v Information Commissioner* [2011] EWHC 1430 (Admin), by Cranston J when determining whether detailed abortion statistics were personal data.

Whichever option is taken, it is important that names and contact details of those **19.41** with whom concerns can be raised are readily accessible and kept updated, and that those with responsibilities under the policy are trained on how to handle the concerns raised. The procedure also needs to be adequately resourced and capable of maintaining records, and there may need to be steps in place to ensure the person has sufficient ability and access to appropriate individuals either to investigate the matter or to ensure that the concern is properly directed to a route through which it can be properly investigated.

Careful consideration needs to be given not only to the preferred initial contact to whom the **19.42** report should be made, but also the hierarchy through which the concern may be escalated and to the range of alternatives. The government guidance emphasizes that it is important to ensure a range of alternative persons whom a whistleblower can approach in the event that a worker feels unable to approach their manager. Having more than one outlet reduces the risk of the worker feeling reluctant to raise the concern because of misgivings related to the identity of the person with whom the concern is to be raised, and allows the opportunity for review where the worker remains concerned. There are, however, benefits to not expanding the list of potential recipients of the disclosure too widely. Restricting the number of people who are aware of the disclosure and its content reduces the number of individuals who might be accused of victimizing the whistleblower. As noted above, it is also conducive to the development of expertise in handling concerns, including ensuring that the recipient will be better able to differentiate between serious concerns requiring immediate action and those that do not require such urgent investigation.

The Whistleblowing Commission's Code of Practice suggests that the policy should include **19.43** a list of persons and bodies with whom workers can raise concerns, which should be sufficiently broad to permit workers to raise concerns with: 'i. the worker's line manager; ii. more senior managers; iii. an identified senior executive and/or board member; and iv. relevant external organisations (such as regulators)'. The NHS template national whistleblowing policy provides an illustration of such a four-step process:

(1) In the first instance, workers etc are encouraged to raise concerns with their line manager (or lead clinician or tutor), but it is stated that if they do not feel comfortable doing so they can move straight to using any of the other options listed;
(2) If either raising the matter with line manager (or lead clinician or tutor) does not resolve the concern, or the worker does not feel able to raise it with them, it can be escalated to the Freedom to Speak Up Guardian[37] or the risk management team;
(3) If the worker etc still remains concerned, he or she can contact the (named) director with responsibility for whistleblowing;
(4) Concerns can also be raised with one of a list of external bodies.

As reflected in the fourth step above, if there are prescribed bodies applicable to the organi- **19.44** zation (eg Government departments), reference should be made to them in the policy and procedure, together with some guidance as to the circumstances when concerns may be raised with them. The FCA and PRA have specifically required that policies inform users of their right to inform the regulator, but they also go further in that they set out that a policy cannot restrict staff by seeking to ensure matters are raised internally before they can go externally to the regulator.[38]

---

[37] See Chapter 12. The policy explains that the Guardian acts as an independent and impartial source of advice to staff at any stage of raising a concern, with access to anyone in the organization, including the chief executive, or if necessary, outside the organization.
[38] See Chapter 12, para 12.110.

19.45 Some care is needed with the wording, where it is intended to avoid a disclosure to an external body being regarded as falling within ERA, section 43C(2) (ie a disclosure in accordance with a procedure authorized by the employer), and thereby circumventing the need to comply with the additional requirements for a disclosure under section 43F (for a prescribed regulator) or section 43G (wider disclosures). For example, 'Freedom to Speak Up' appended a model NHS policy (now superseded by the template national whistleblowing policy) which noted that there may be circumstances in which a report could properly be made to an outside body (and examples were given) and that this would be preferred to not raising the matter at all. The template national whistleblowing policy, however, having listed a range of people with whom concerns can be raised, also provides that if 'for any reason you do not feel comfortable raising your concerns internally, you can raise concerns' with one of a number listed external bodies (NHS Improvement, the Care Quality Commission, NHS England, and NHS Protect). It then sets out the matters in relation to which concerns can be raised with each body (eg to the CQC for quality and safety concerns). The effect would appear to be that a disclosure to one of those bodies about a concern of a type identified would fall within section 43C(2) ERA, rather than having to meet the requirements of section 43F.

19.46 Small organizations will need to consider which procedure would best suit the size and resources available. If it is a two-tiered organization with a shallow structure, then it may be sufficient to have statements and a policy stating that the person in charge (the managing director, for example) encourages and would support the raising of concerns. PAS recommends[39] further that smaller businesses should consider providing clear reference to external organizations who are suitable for external disclosures (for example, the prescribed person or a relevant regulator).

(g) How should a report be made?

19.47 It is not necessary for all disclosures to be in writing. A disclosure may be made face to face or on the telephone, at least in the first instance. It may be counterproductive to require that disclosures be submitted in writing, since this may lead to a greater reluctance to raise a concern. Raising the matter verbally in the first instance allows for the matters to be discussed, confidentially, before reports are written, and perhaps whilst matters are either imminent or fresh in the mind of the worker. This enables a dialogue to be created and for critical information to be fully understood. The recipient of an oral disclosure must be trained as to how to listen to concerns and elicit any necessary details. They also need to have training in record keeping. The worker should be encouraged to provide a written statement if she or he is willing and able to do so.

(h) When should the concern be raised?

19.48 Those in a position to raise concerns need to know when it is appropriate to use the procedure. Given that PIDA protects those who possess a reasonable belief as to information tending to show a relevant failure, even though the belief may prove to be wrong,[40] guidance should be provided to workers as to when they should raise concerns. Examples may be helpful to assist workers in understanding how much of an evidential basis they should have before they report concerns. It may be that merely overhearing allegations will be considered sufficient—provided they have some evidential credibility as opposed to mere 'tittle-tattle'.

19.49 Whereas a mere concern or allegation, with a disclosure of information, is insufficient for a qualifying disclosure,[41] whistleblowing policies are commonly drawn up in wider terms. To

---

[39] PAS 0.9.
[40] See Chapter 3 and the discussion of good faith in Chapter 10.
[41] *Cavendish Munro Professional Risk Management Ltd v Geduld* [2010] ICR 325 (EAT).

that end, the procedure in the FCA handbook (SYSC 18) applies to reporting of concerns.[42] Similarly, in the health sector, the template national whistleblowing policy simply refers to covering a 'concern' as to risk, malpractice, or wrongdoing. Subject only to a requirement that any concern be genuine, it urges the approach of: 'If in doubt, please raise it' (ie the concern) and states:

> Don't wait for proof. We would like you to raise the matter while it is still a concern. It doesn't matter if you turn out to be mistaken as long as you are generally troubled.

In order to encourage concerns to be raised at an early stage so that they can be investigated, **19.50** it may therefore be appropriate to spell out that the worker need not be certain, and that they will not suffer any adverse consequences unless it is later established that the information provided was known by the worker to be false.[43]

Some organizations and professional bodies make it a requirement that concerns be reported **19.51** (as discussed in Chapter 13). If this is the case it may be that the policy should distinguish specifically between those (usually) professionals and other workers to whom the requirement does not apply.

(i) *Confidentiality or anonymity?*

Open, confidential, and anonymous whistleblowing The PAS (at 3.5) draws a distinc- **19.52** tion between (a) 'open whistleblowing', (b) 'raising a concern confidentially', and (c) 'anonymous informing':

- Open whistleblowing—this is where the employee who has a whistleblowing concern feels it is safe and acceptable to raise the concern openly, such that those involved know what the issue is and who has raised it.
- Confidentiality—the identity of the whistleblower will be made known to the recipient of the report but their name will not be revealed without their consent subject to narrow exceptions (usually expressed in terms of whether it is required by law).
- Anonymous information—where the worker does not identify him or herself at any stage to anyone, even to the recipient of the report.

The PAS argues that it is essential that the whistleblowing policy covers clearly the issue of **19.53** how a whistleblowing concern can best be raised. The policy should provide clear information as to the difference between each process and the implications for the informer arising from either option. As noted in the PAS, open whistleblowing has a clear advantage in enabling the organization to assess the issues, to work out how to investigate, to obtain more information, enable the person subject to allegations to have a fair opportunity to respond, and therefore to minimize the risk of a sense of mistrust and injustice developing. That is also the approach taken in the Whistleblowing Commission's model procedure.

Equally, the PAS recognizes that staff may have good reason to feel anxious about identify- **19.54** ing themselves and that protection of confidentiality, if requested, may be important. More recently there has been a trend, at least in the UK, towards recognizing the value of permitting disclosures to be raised anonymously. We address the issues in relation to confidential reporting and anonymous informing further below.

Confidential whistleblowing Confidential reporting requires the informant to pro- **19.55** vide at least their name, if not their contact details. This enables the recipient to verify information, seek additional information, and, perhaps most importantly, it enables

---

[42] See Chapter 12, para 12.97.
[43] See eg the Whistleblowing Commission code of practice, para 5(c).

the informant to be protected on the basis that they are known to be the source of the report.

19.56 The government guidance comments that:

> There may be good reason why a worker wishes their identity to remain confidential. The law does not compel an organisation to protect the confidentiality of a whistleblower. However, it is considered best practice to maintain that confidentiality, unless required by law to disclose it. Managers dealing with whistleblowing concerns should be briefed to ensure they understand how to handle the disclosure and protect personal information.

19.57 The guidance therefore appears to contemplate that protection of confidentiality will be the default position. In that respect it differs from the PAS which suggests in terms that the default position should be that concerns are raised openly, albeit acknowledging that some organizations provide that where a concern is raised beyond line management the assumption is that the contact will be made in confidence. The key point, we suggest, is that where a disclosure is made on an open basis this should be a clear choice, where the worker has been made aware of the option of choosing to proceed on a confidential basis.

19.58 The government guidance adds that: 'It will help to manage the expectations of whistleblowers if the risk that some colleagues may still speculate who has raised the concern is explained to them'. This appears to be drawn from the guidance in the PAS to similar effect. The PAS proceeds to note that it is worth pointing out that where the employee has already voiced the concern to colleagues or their manager, others may assume they are the source of the disclosure. It argues that this is another example of why open whistleblowing is the best approach, and that often when an employee understands this, they will say that they do not want to invoke or retain confidentiality and will raise the concern openly (PAS 3.5.3).

19.59 Whilst the principle of offering confidentiality is relatively uncontroversial, more difficult issues are liable to arise in relation to the circumstances in which it is appropriate to reveal the identity of the whistleblower. In relation to this, the government guidance stipulates that it is best practice to 'Undertake to protect the identity of the worker raising a disclosure, unless required by law to reveal it and to offer support throughout with access to mentoring, advice and counselling.'

19.60 Similarly, the standard NHS whistleblowing policy provides an exception only where required by law. It provides:

> We hope you will feel comfortable raising your concern openly, but we also appreciate that you may want to raise it confidentially. This means that while you are willing for your identity to be known to the person you report your concern to, you do not want anyone else to know your identity. Therefore, we will keep your identity confidential, if that is what you want, unless required to disclose it by law (for example, by the police).

19.61 This formulation is therefore designed to go a little further towards managing expectations, but it still conveys an assurance that confidentiality will be maintained unless required by law or with consent.[44] Potential difficulties arise, however, in cases where maintaining confidentiality comes into conflict with enabling a person who is subject to the allegations a fair opportunity to answer the allegations. That might arise because there is a need for that person to know the identity of the whistleblower to be able effectively to challenge their

---

[44] See also the European Data Protection Supervisor, 'Guidelines on processing personal information within a whistleblowing procedure', providing guidance for EU institutions and bodies, which also states (at para 6) that there can be disclosure if the whistleblower maliciously makes a false statement, but only to judicial authorities.

credibility, or because supplying the supporting evidence will be likely to reveal the identity of the whistleblower.

Confidentiality for informants is discussed in Chapter 15 of this book. As set out at para- **19.62** graphs 15.04–15.09, guidance as to the approach expected of a reasonable employer was set out in *Linfood Cash & Carry v Thomson* [1989] IRLR 235, [1989] ICR 518 (EAT) and in a series of subsequent decisions. Broadly, the guidelines envisage measures to mitigate any unfairness from an informant's unwillingness to have their identity revealed or to give evidence. Whilst a tribunal should be slow to interfere with an employer's approach of respecting a promise of confidentiality, there may still be a difficulty in fairly dismissing if, for example, protecting the identity would mean that the accused employee is not given the basic details of the allegations (see paragraph 15.08).

To some extent that issue is addressed in the Council of Europe's Recommendation CM/ **19.63** Rec(2014)7 and explanatory memorandum. This suggests, at paragraph 71, that:

> The principle also recognises that protecting the identity of the whistleblower can occasionally conflict with the rules of fairness (for example, fair trial and the common-law notion of natural justice). Where it is impossible to proceed—for example, to take action against a wrongdoer or those responsible for the damage caused without relying directly on the evidence of the whistleblower and revealing his or her identity—the consent and co-operation of the whistleblower should be sought, and any concern that he or she might have about their own position addressed. In some cases it may be necessary to seek a judicial ruling on whether and to what extent the identity of the whistleblower can be revealed.

The guidance, therefore, whilst placing emphasis on seeking to proceed in the first place by **19.64** seeking to secure consent from the whistleblower, contemplates that it may be appropriate (though it suggests on the basis of a 'judicial ruling') to override confidentiality if it is necessary to proceed. That approach may be compared to the approach suggested in 'Speak up for a healthy NHS', which recommends managing expectations as to the issue that might arise in disciplinary proceedings in the following terms:

> With these assurances, we hope you will raise your concern openly. However, we recognise that there may be circumstances when you would prefer to speak to someone in confidence first. If this is the case, please say so at the outset. If you ask us not to disclose your identity, we will not do so without your consent unless required by law. You should understand that there may be times when we are unable to resolve a concern without revealing your identity, for example where your personal evidence is essential. In such cases, we will discuss with you whether and how the matter can best proceed.

This approach therefore contemplates that there may be a future stage where the worker **19.65** would be encouraged to consent to proceeding on an open basis, but does not flag up any circumstances in which confidentiality may be overridden beyond referring in general terms to where this is required by law.

This in turn begs a question as to whether it is preferable to provide in the policy at the out- **19.66** set further wording to qualify the assurance of confidentiality by making clear that confidentiality may not be maintained in exceptional circumstances where it is necessary in order fairly to address wrongdoing. We would, however, urge caution as to taking that approach. First, if the assurance of confidentiality is seen to be watered down, it may discourage workers from raising concerns, or lead to this only being done on an anonymous basis. Second, it departs from the formulation that has been adopted as in the government guidance, and has tended to be used in other policies and as such may be seen as a reflection of good practice, such as the NHS policy. Third, it may lead managers in applying the policy too readily to bypass the stage of seeking to encourage the worker to proceed by consent, and considering what safeguards can be put in place to seek to achieve a fair disciplinary process if consent is withheld. Further, whilst revealing the identity of the whistleblower against their wishes might not itself amount to a protected disclosure detriment,[45] if the worker is then subjected to detriment by co-workers, the ability to rely on the statutory defence may be lost if it is determined that not revealing the identity was a step that could reasonably have been taken to prevent the wrongdoing.

19.67 **Anonymous informers**   Whilst there has been a consensus as to the need to protect confidentiality of whistleblowers where requested, the issue of whether to permit or encourage anonymous whistleblowing has been far more controversial. There has been a tension between the approach under US legislation which requires a facility for anonymous informing, and the EU model where, for historical reasons, there has been a particular unease over an approach of encouraging people to come forward to inform on others anonymously and without an immediate recourse for the person subject to the allegations to respond. More recently, there has been a trend in the UK towards providing for there to be the opportunity for anonymous whistleblowing, and this is reflected in the government guidance. We address these developments below. It is, however, also important to keep in mind that the issue of whether anonymous whistleblowing should be permitted has been considered as part of a broader consideration of the application of data protection principles, and the protection of the rights of the subject to the disclosure (and others named in the disclosure) when processing personal data involved in the disclosure. Good practice guidance has been developed in relation to this, as discussed in paragraphs 19.109–19.118 below. As such the issue of whether there should be a facility for anonymous whistleblowing is not to be seen in isolation, but together with consideration of whether there are other safeguards in place within the whistleblowing procedure to prevent abuse.

19.68 *The US model: SOX and Dodd–Frank*   Under the US's Sarbanes–Oxley Act 2002 ('SOX'), the audit committee of publicly held US companies and their EU-based affiliates, and non-US companies listed on one of the US stock markets, are required to establish procedures for 'confidential, anonymous' reporting by employees of concerns in relation to accounting and auditing matters (SOX, section 301(4)). In addition, section 806 of SOX makes it illegal for companies to 'discharge, demote, suspend, threaten, harass, or in any other manner discriminate against' employees for using these procedures or for providing assistance to government and regulatory agencies in relation to inquiries into account irregularities. In addition, the Dodd–Frank Wall Street Reform and Consumer Protection Act 2010 ('Dodd–Frank') strengthened this protection and provides for substantial financial incentives for whistleblowers who disclose 'original information' to the regulator if it leads to successful enforcement action.

19.69 Section 929A of Dodd–Frank specifies that the whistleblower-protection provisions of SOX apply to employees of subsidiaries of publicly traded companies whose financial information is included in the consolidated financial statements of a publicly traded company, as well as the listed company itself. Notwithstanding that, the extent to which SOX and Dodd–Frank apply extraterritorially has been controversial. Being a matter of US law, detailed consideration is beyond the scope of this book. But in broad terms, limits on extraterritoriality have been recognized, at least in relation to the provisions concerning protection against retaliation. In *Carnero v Boston Scientific Corp* 433 F3d 1 (1st Cir 2006) the US Court of Appeals for the First Circuit held that the anti-relation provisions in section 806 of SOX did not apply in relation to a foreign employee who worked outside United States, whose complaint was made outside the US and who reported financial misconduct by a foreign subsidiary of a US company. This was followed by some lower-level decisions where there was found to be a sufficient nexus between the alleged wrongful conduct, the complainant, and the US to

---

[45] See *Shinwari* and the discussion in Chapter 7, paras 7.110–7.113.

lead to a different view.[46] However, the US Supreme Court has reiterated the presumption against extraterritorial effect in *Morrison v National Australian Bank Ltd* (130 S.Ct. 2869, 2877 (2010)), in the absence of a clear statutory indication of extraterritorial application, and rejected an argument that application could be premised on some effect on American securities markets or investors.

Following *Morrison*, in *Villanueva v Core Laboratories NV and Saybolt de Colombia Limitada* **19.70** (ARB No 09-108, ARB Dec. 22, 2011) the US Department of Labor Administrative Review Board, held (by a majority 3 to 2 decision) that the anti-retaliation protection in section 806 does not have extraterritorial application. The complainant was a Colombian national who worked in Colombia for a Colombian company that was an indirect subsidiary of a Dutch company whose shares traded on the New York Stock Exchange. The Board identified the following four factors to be considered in relation to whether there was a sufficient nexus with the US: (a) the location of the protected activity; (b) where the employee works and the location of the employer; (c) where the retaliatory act took place; and (d) the nationality of the laws allegedly violated, which the employee was punished for reporting. Applying those criteria, the claim failed because Mr Villaneuva worked in Colombia, submitted his internal report there in relation to tax avoidance schemes outside the US, and it concerned violations of foreign laws and did not identify any violations of US law. It was held not to be sufficient that the report had been made in emails sent to management in Houston and that the decision to dismiss him was alleged to have been made in the US as a result of those emails.[47]

However, these decisions do not necessarily affect the obligation under section 301(4) SOX **19.71** to implement confidential and anonymous reporting procedures. Failure to comply may result in heavy fines and possible delisting from the stock exchange. SOX does not distinguish between a confidential and anonymous procedure and accordingly it is appropriate for any organization which must comply with the SOX to operate procedures capable of dealing with both anonymous and confidential disclosures. There are equivalent provisions, providing for anonymous reporting, in the Nasdaq and New York Stock Exchange rules. Whether complying with the SOX requirements or otherwise, organizations must also consider the data protection provisions afforded to EU citizens, which regulate the use and export of data outside of the EU (see paragraphs 19.109–19.118 below).

The approach in France and other EU states   The requirement to permit anonymous **19.72** whistleblowing has been a source of controversy in some EU states. The tension between the SOX approach and the EU model came to a head in 2005 in France when two US organizations sought approval for their SOX helplines from the French data protection authority (CNIL[48]). CNIL declined permission, in part on the grounds that any procedure

---

[46] See eg *Walters v Deutsche Bank AG* (2009-SOX-70, ALJ 23 March 2009), finding that s 806 SOX protected an employee who worked in Switzerland for a Swiss subsidiary of a US company, where (a) the retaliatory decision and some of the protected activity occurred in the US, (b) the complainant employee spent some time working in the US, and (c) although the alleged securities law violation did not occur in the US, it had an adverse impact in the US.

[47] See also eg *Liu Meng-Lin v Siemens AG* (2d Cir, Docket No 13-4385, August 14, 2014) (decision of the United States Court of Appeals for the Second Circuit that anti-retaliation provisions of Dodd–Frank do not protect a foreign worker employed abroad by a foreign corporation where the events related to the disclosures occurred abroad); *Ulrich v Moody's Corp.* (US Dist LEXIS 138082 (SDNY 30 Sep 2014)) (dismissal by Southern District of New York court of claim by US citizen and former employee of Moody's Corporation based in Hong Kong, who claimed to have reported securities violations by the company by disclosing non-public information in Hong Kong, and that he was dismissed for doing so. The court concluded that despite being a US citizen the claim had little if any connection with the US as he resided in Honk Kong during his employment and the disclosure concerned non-public information disclosed in Hong Kong and other matters outside the US, and the allegation about retaliation orchestrated in the US was speculative.

[48] The French National Commission for Data Protection and Liberties.

advocating anonymous reporting would increase the risk of staff making false allegations that could injure the reputation of other workers.[49] It also considered that hotlines would give rise to a disproportionate level of collection and processing of personal data on French employees and that a more targeted procedure for reporting breach of company policies or applicable laws would be more appropriate. In addition, it emphasized that the employees mentioned in the reports, whether as wrongdoers or otherwise, would not be adequately informed, or informed in a timely manner, about the collection and processing of their personal data.

19.73 Since 2005, employers in France have had to register their whistleblowing schemes with the CNIL. In doing so they can either file a request for approval or obtain automatic approval by self-certifying that their whistleblowing scheme complies with pre-established conditions in the CNIL's single authorization (AU-004).[50] Initially this was limited to finance, accounting, banking, corruption, and compliance with SOX section 301(4) to establish confidential and anonymous reporting procedures in relation to questionable accounting and auditing matters. There was also a provision that information falling outside this scope, but which might affect the vital interests of the business or moral integrity of employees, could be sent to relevant persons in the company. This was deleted in 2010, following another ruling as to illegality of a whistleblowing procedure.[51] At the same time it was extended to cover prevention of anti-competitive practices and compliance with the Japanese Financial and Exchange Act (sometimes known as the Japanese SOX). It was extended again in January 2014 to cover discrimination and work harassment; compliance with health, hygiene, and safety measures in the workplace; and protection of the environment. Whilst anonymous reporting is not prohibited, it is clarified that companies should not encourage it, and it should be the exception. If an anonymous report is received, special precautions are required including that the person reviewing the report must assess whether it is appropriate to disclose the report internally before doing so, and whether the facts reported are sufficiently precise and serious.[52]

19.74 Concerns as to anonymous whistleblowing have also arisen in other EU countries. In the Fifteenth Report of the Article 29 Working Party on Data Protection, covering 2011,[53] the Working Party noted that an issue that had arisen in Iceland in relation to websites run by the Icelandic Directorate of Labour and Directorate of Internal Revenue. Icelandic citizens were given the opportunity anonymously to report their suspicion of tax evasion and related offences. The Icelandic data protection authority investigated the lawfulness of processing personal data related to this anonymous reporting and published decisions finding that an opportunity to report in this manner should not be explicitly provided because of non-compliance with data protection rights. It was considered that anonymous reporting was liable to result in inaccurate personal data being collected, and also that the guarantees given to those reporting on their anonymity were unreliable since telecommunications

---

[49] CNIL Decision 2005-110 of 26 May 2005 (Group McDonald's France), https://www.legifrance. gouv.fr/affichCnil.do?oldAction=rechExpCnil&id=CNILTEXT000017653326&%20 fastReqId=1321386284&fastPos=1.

[50] However, a whistleblowing scheme that falls within the scope of the self-certification may still be found to violate French law: *Benoist Girard (subsidiary of Stryker) v CHSCT* (Cour d'Appel Caen 3rd Chamber, Sept. 23, 2011).

[51] *CGT v Dassault Systemes*, Court of Cassation, Social Chamber, Decision No 2524 of December 8, 2009 (08-17.191).

[52] See Cooper and Martilla, 'Corporate Whistleblowing hotlines and EU data protection laws', Practical Law (2016), Thomson Reuters, p 6.

[53] Adopted on 3 December 2013, see http://ec.europa.eu/justice/data-protection/article-29/documenta- tion/annual-report/files/2013/15th_annual_report_en.pdf.

technology made it possible to track the reports. The conclusion was that even though an administrative authority could never prevent citizens completely from sending anonymous reports, it should not explicitly offer the opportunity to do so.[54]

Article 29 Data Protection Working Party The issue as to lawfulness of whistleblowing **19.75** hotlines, and steps needed to ensure a proportionate approach in relation to the management of data obtained and held, was addressed in the opinion of 1 February 2006, the Article 29 Data Protection Working Party.[55] The opinion (which is advisory rather than binding) was limited to the fields of accounting, internal accounting controls, auditing matters, the fight against bribery, banking, and financial crime, but the principles set out may be regarded as having wider application to cases where (as will inevitably be the case) processing of personal data is involved. The recommendations of the Working Party are considered in more detail at paragraphs 19.109 et seq below. Broadly, it concluded that whistleblowing hotlines could, subject to meeting other recommended safeguards, be permissible as being proportionate to legitimate aims. But it emphasized the disadvantages of anonymous reporting, in that:

> Anonymity might not be a good solution, for the whistleblower or for the organisation, for a number of reasons:
> — being anonymous does not stop others from successfully guessing who raised the concern;
> — it is harder to investigate the concern if people cannot ask follow-up questions;
> — it is easier to organise the protection of the whistleblower against retaliation, especially if such protection is granted by law, if the concerns are raised openly;
> — anonymous reports can lead people to focus on the whistleblower, maybe suspecting that he or she is raising the concern maliciously;
> — an organisation runs the risk of developing a culture of receiving anonymous malevolent reports;
> — the social climate within the organisation could deteriorate if employees are aware that anonymous reports concerning them may be filed through the scheme at any time.

The Working Party added that anonymous reports raise specific problems in relation to **19.76** data protection rules and in particular the requirement that personal data should only be collected fairly. However, it proceeded to set out conditions under which there could be anonymous reports. In particular:

• First, it expressed the view that the whistleblowing scheme should be built so as not to encourage anonymous reporting. It recommended that an anonymous report should only be accepted if the person reporting wants to remain anonymous after being informed of the option of confidentiality. To the extent that this required that the scheme should make clear that open or confidential reporting was the preferred route, this was relatively uncontroversial. However, Working Party went further, in suggesting that companies should not advertise the fact that anonymous reports should be made through the scheme. The suggestion of not making clear in the policy that there is the option of anonymous reporting does not sit well with obligations under SOX, and as set out below

---

[54] Decisions of the German employment court in 2005 (though turning on failure to consult the works council) and of the Swedish admistrative court in 2010 have also been seen as casting doubt over the legality of whistleblowing hotlines: see Cooper and Martilla, 'Corporate Whistleblowing hotlines and EU data protection laws', Practical Law (2016), Thomson Reuters.

[55] The Article 29 Data Protection Working Party was created under Art 29 of the Data Protection Directive and its remit is set out under Arts 29 and 30 of that Directive. It is comprised of a representative from each Member State's 'supervisory authority'; a representative from the European Data Protection Supervisor; and a representative of the European Commission; and it may make recommendations and provide opinions upon Codes of Practice (Article 30).

has not been taken up in UK good practice guidance. In addition, in a further opinion on 9 April 2014,[56] the Working Party included an example of a compliant whistleblowing scheme which included an explanation to staff that if they preferred they could use the scheme anonymously or identify themselves.

- The Working Party also recommended that anonymous reports should be subject to special caution, including examination by the first recipient of the report with regard to whether it is appropriate to admit within the scheme.
- A number of further recommendations were made as to suitable safeguards, which we consider at paragraphs 19.109 et seq below.

19.77 *Domestic guidance*   Consistently with the points made by the Article 29 Working Party (previous paragraph), disadvantages associated with anonymous informing were acknowledged by the PAS. It noted that:

> anonymity makes it difficult to investigate the concern and to deter misuse and impossible to liaise with the employee (to seek clarification or more information, to assure them or to give them feedback). As an example, in the case of Enron, the US company which collapsed in one of the biggest financial scandals in corporate history, the company had a highly rated anonymous reporting scheme which, though it was regularly promoted to staff, proved ineffective.

19.78 The PAS therefore recommended that whistleblowing policies should not actively encourage or solicit employees to raise concerns anonymously. It did recommend that where anonymous information was received under the whistleblowing scheme (whether or not it enables or promotes anonymous reports) this should be assessed to establish whether it is possible or prudent to follow it up. Similarly, whilst the Whistleblowing Commission's Code of Practice does not specify whether the policy should publicize the ability to raise concerns anonymously, it suggests that when receiving such a report, the organization should assess the information as best it can to establish whether there is substance to the concern and whether it can be addressed.

19.79 However, the government guidance provides in terms that it is good practice to have a facility for anonymous reporting. It adds that:

> Anonymous information will be just as important for organisations to act upon. Workers should be made aware that the ability of an organisation to ask follow up questions or provide feedback will be limited if the whistleblower cannot be contacted. It may be possible to overcome these challenges by using telephone appointments or through an anonymised email address.

19.80 The national template NHS whistleblowing policy similarly provides that concerns may be raised anonymously, and in the financial services sector SYSC 18.3.1 requires that the whistleblowing scheme must be able to handle not only confidential but also anonymous reporting. As noted in Chapter 12 (paragraph 12.104), the FCA consultation document suggested that when information is provided anonymously there may be a degree of persuasion of the informant to report openly or on an identified but confidential basis.

19.81 Clearly the government approach, and those in the NHS and financial services, reflects an assessment that it is better to have a facility to deal with the situation that without anonymous reporting concerns may not be raised at all. We suggest it is appropriate for the policy to state that there is the facility for anonymous reporting if that is the only basis on which the informant is prepared to proceed. Given the recent developments, there is a risk that a

---

[56] Opinion 06/2014 at Example 15 (http://ec.europa.eu/justice/data-protection/article-29/documentation/opinion-recommendation/files/2014/wp217_en.pdf).

policy which refuses to consider anonymous reports may be viewed as not following good practice, which may inhibit reliance on the statutory defence. However, it is also appropriate to make clear that open or confidential reporting is preferable, and to seek to explain to a person who raises concerns the advantages of proceeding on an open or confidential basis. It is also appropriate to explain that where the disclosure is provided on an anonymous basis that may make it more difficult to resolve the concern, though that problem may be ameliorated to some extent through a system which permits that communication to continue, whether over the telephone, through an anonymous messaging service, or via a third party. Further, the good practice guidance suggested below at paragraphs 19.109–19.118 in relation to addressing data protection issues are of particular importance in relation to anonymous reporting, given the heightened risk of unreliable information.

(j) Protection against reprisal and exceptions from protection

It is crucial that an organization makes a clear statement in support of concerns being raised **19.82** and that the organization will protect the whistleblower against suffering detriments as a consequence. The government guidance suggests that it should be made clear that victimization is not acceptable and that any instances 'will be taken seriously and managed appropriately'. We suggest that it may be appropriate to add that any such victimization may be treated as a serious disciplinary matter which may lead to dismissal.

Further, given the interest in encouraging the raising of concerns at an early stage, which **19.83** may be made on the basis of a suspicion only, the policy should make clear that the protection against reprisal applies irrespective of whether the concern is later determined to be not well founded. In the light of the amendment to the protected disclosure legislation in 2013, it is important that the policy does not provide an exception for cases where the disclosure was not made in good faith.[57]

A safer course is to focus on whether the information provided is known to be false or (as in **19.84** the NHS template policy) whether the concern raised is not genuinely held. SYSC 18.3.2(3)(b) provides that nothing prevents action being taken where the report is 'false and malicious'. But we suggest that there is a danger in that formulation that it might be read as applying to cases where the disclosure was made for an ulterior motive and is later found to have been false, rather than when it was known to be false at the time made. There is also a danger of encouraging a focus on motive, and a consequent risk of workers being discouraged from raising concerns. We suggest, therefore, that it is better to stick to focusing on whether the concern was not genuinely held and the information supplied known to be false.[58]

Some organizations have provided protection by way of an undertaking from the head of the **19.85** organization, for example the chief executive's undertaking within the Higher Education Funding Council for Wales set out in its Whistleblowing Policy.[59] This states:

> Provided that a member of staff raises a Qualifying Disclosure in good faith,[60] and follows the procedures set out in this policy, the Chief Executive makes the following commitment:

---

[57] See *Frenkel Topping Ltd v King* (UKEAT/0106/15/LA, 21 June 2015) where an employment tribunal's finding that a failure to amend a whistleblowing policy to remove the requirement that it be made in good faith entailed or contributed to a breach of contract, was held by the EAT to have been inadequately reasoned.

[58] See also *Audere Medical Services Ltd v Sanderson* (UKEAT/0409/12/RN, 29 May 2013), where the employer appears to have been led into error, and subjected the worker to a detriment for breach of a whistleblowing policy, where the policy impermissibly imposed a requirement that any concerns had to be raised internally in the first instance.

[59] Version 3.3, May 2013, para 23. See http://www.hefcw.ac.uk/documents/about_us/internal_policies/whistleblowing%20policy%203%203%20may%2013.pdf.

[60] But as noted above, in the light of the legislative changes in 2013, the exception should not be based on whether the disclosure was made in good faith.

- That the member of staff will not be disciplined or subjected to any other detriment to his or her career as a result, even if the concern turns out to be mistaken.
- that the identity of the whistleblower will be kept confidential for as long as the individual requires, whilst this is under HEFCW's control, subject to the requirements of criminal investigations, where applicable. (More detailed provisions as to confidentiality and anonymity are set out in this policy.)
- that HEFCW will take all other reasonable steps to protect members of staff from any harassment, victimisation or other personal detriment.
- that the member of staff will be informed of the action being taken in response to their concern and of the outcome (subject to any legal constraints).

19.86 The procedure should also provide for advice to be available for the worker as to what they should do if they consider they have suffered a detriment. It may be the worker is referred directly to the grievance procedure. However, there is some sense in keeping such matters within the remit of the confidential reporting system.

19.87 The worker should be asked to provide evidence and the necessary particulars: what, when, how, and who is responsible for an alleged detriment. A simple form for completion will focus the mind of the person who believes s/he is suffering a detriment.

19.88 By continuing to keep confidential reporting matters within this defined procedure, those responsible for dealing with such matters are more likely to be concerned and aware of the need to ensure that, if detriments have been suffered, they are quickly stopped and remedial action taken, or if they are considered not to have occurred, that the worker feels that his/her concerns have been taken seriously and that s/he has been listened to sympathetically. It is likely that those involved in the confidential reporting procedure will be better able to meet the requirements of ensuring the disclosure is addressed and reducing the risk that the worker will make an external disclosure.

(k) Process

19.89 The confidential reporting procedure should be prescriptive as to the process to be followed, making it clear when each step should be taken. The PAS advises against the inclusion of timescales, whereas the government guidance only provides for 'clear timescales for providing updates'. There is, however, much to be said for having guideline time estimates for each stage of the process even if it is also made clear that those guidelines may need to be departed from in some circumstances. The purpose of the timescales is to provide confidence to the individual reporting the matter that s/he will know by a defined date whether his/her concern is being treated seriously. Where that time frame will not be met, this should be explained and the individual who raised the concern should be appraised of the progress of any investigation.

19.90 The steps in the process should include the following:

1. *Clarification.* As noted above, the initial step may be for a concern to be raised verbally. That may be followed by putting the concerns into writing. Alternatively, it may be appropriate to write to the person raising the concern summarizing what has been reported so as to ensure that there is clarity in relation to this. Clarification may also be sought as to whether there is any further information to be provided, the quality of the evidence relied upon (such as whether it is first hand or hearsay), and whether confidentiality is sought (PAS 5.6). The government guidance of March 2015[61] states that the

---

[61] See eg the template national NHS policy which encourages raising of 'concerns' but adds: 'please be ready to explain as fully as you can the information and circumstances that give rise to your concern.'

policy should clarify that the whistleblower does not need to provide evidence for the employer to look into the concerns raised. That reflects the fact that it may be appropriate to encourage the worker to raise the concern at an early stage. But, clearly, where the worker does have further information or evidence it is important to ask for this so as to facilitate investigation.

2. *The investigation*:

   2.1 *Who investigates?* It is sensible to have a named person or level of individual responsible for the investigation. The person who is responsible for the investigation need not be the person who received the information and there is good reason to separate the two.

   2.2 *What does s/he investigate?* The initial investigation would usually be into whether there is any evidence to support the concerns raised. The investigation at this stage should typically focus not on who is responsible for the malpractice but whether there is malpractice. Focusing on this issue ensures that the organization considers the malpractice and not the personalities involved.

   2.3 *How should it be investigated?*

   (a) There may be two stages of investigation. The first stage could be to see whether there is any prima facie evidence of the malpractice reported. Once malpractice is thought to exist then a second stage can occur where the personalities are investigated. Some malpractice can be investigated initially without the need to interview other staff—if, for example, one is dealing with financial malpractice there should be independent evidence that supports the report. Other circumstances, such as the abuse of one resident by a member of staff, are clearly more difficult. Any investigation, however, should be in a manner containing procedural safeguards similar to a disciplinary investigation.

   (b) Some investigations may need to take place without the alleged perpetrator being aware, sometimes with external involvement from other organizations such as the police. The procedure should explain that this may occur to determine whether any grounds for further investigation have been found.

   (c) It should be stated that it may be necessary to suspend workers on full pay during the investigation and that such a suspension is not a disciplinary act.

3. *Acting on the investigation findings*:

   3.1 Depending on the size of the organization it may be necessary to make it clear to whom any investigation will report and what will be his/her remit. For example, if the initial investigation is restricted to malpractice the reporting process may begin with feedback to the nominated recipient of the information. If there appears to be malpractice then the matter may then be referred for disciplinary action, if necessary, or for further investigation into who is the perpetrator.

   3.2 Records should be kept.

   3.3 It is essential that whoever makes the decision to continue or discontinue any investigation is capable of accounting for that decision and that some explanation is provided to the worker who made the disclosure. Such feedback then allows a review or appeal and provides another opportunity for the allegation to be scrutinized.

4. *Decision*:

   4.1 Any investigation will involve a conclusion. There are three possible results: insufficient evidence and a further investigation; insufficient/no evidence and no further investigation; evidence of malpractice or other relevant failure.

   4.2 This decision must be reported to someone or a body responsible for this procedure.

   4.3 The decision must be communicated to the person who made the disclosure to enable him/her to provide feedback or appeal, or to seek a review.

5. *Feedback*:

    5.1 It is important that a worker receives feedback on his/her concerns. If no feedback is given, the worker is more likely to be inclined to make an external disclosure under s 43G (and be protected in doing so).

    5.2 It may not be possible to give feedback in relation to sanctions imposed, such as internal disciplinary action, due to the need to maintain confidentiality. If this is the case then such information as can be given should be given, even if only to confirm that the worker was right to raise concerns.

6. *Satisfaction*:

    6.1 The person making the disclosure must be provided with an opportunity to challenge or review any decision not to take matters further. For any such challenge to be credible it is recommended that the reporter receives a decision with reasons.

    6.2 If a three- or two-stage process is adopted, this enables a review and/or an appeal.

(l) Advice or assistance

19.91 Those reporting should be permitted to attend meetings and hearings with a colleague or a union representative. A good procedure would also provide the worker with some assistance as to whom s/he can contact internally and, if necessary, externally for support. With reference to the fact that not all concerns raised will be protected disclosures,[62] the template national whistleblowing policy points out that there are very specific criteria that need to be met to be 'covered by whistleblowing law' when raising a concern. It suggests, to help consider whether these criteria are met, seeking independent advice from either the whistleblowing helpline for the NHS and social care, Public Concern at Work, or a legal representative. An alternative would be to refer to a union legal advice line. Independent helpline referral is also recommended by the Committee on Standards in Public Life, the FCA, and the Institute of Chartered Accountants. Some NHS trusts in the United Kingdom specifically refer to their existence in their policy. Workers should be informed of their right to take independent legal advice.

19.92 Where the policy makes reference to a helpline for advice, it should also be made clear that (unlike in the case of a hotline) information given to a helpline will not mean that information has been given to the employer.

(m) Monitoring

19.93 It is essential that there be monitoring of the system and its effectiveness so that the organization can consider which areas could be improved. The criteria we have referred to above can also be used as a focus for areas for improvement. In order to facilitate efficient monitoring, records should be kept, in an anonymized format, setting out the following:

1. How was the whistleblower aware of the procedure?
2. Did s/he seek advice before raising a report?
3. Did s/he raise matters orally or in writing?
4. Had s/he raised the matter previously and, if so, to whom, and what was the outcome?
5. What is the subject matter of the report? It may be that options are given here, that is, by reference to the categories of relevant failure in ERA, section 43B.

The following information should also be maintained:

1. How long was the investigation?
2. What was the outcome?

---

[62] For example, there might not be a disclosure of 'information' or the threshold reasonable belief requirements might not be met.

3. Was the worker who made the disclosure satisfied with that outcome?

4. Have they raised any matters relating to detriments?

A further impetus for effective monitoring may be provided as a result of the introduction **19.94** of any regulations made pursuant to section 43FA ERA, relating to reports by regulators. As in the case of the financial services, that may prompt the requirement from regulators for records to be kept which are to be made available to the regulator on request.

In any event, it would be appropriate to allocate someone, preferably at board level (nor- **19.95** mally, but not necessarily, a non-executive director), with specific responsibility for the whistleblowing arrangements. In some cases, for example depending on the size of the orga- nization, the role of whistleblowing guardian or champion from the NHS or financial ser- vices sectors may provide a template.

(n) Review

In line with the proposed scope for regulators, any board or controlling mind of an orga- **19.96** nization would be advised to review the policy annually or biannually to consider its effec- tiveness, and this was recommended by the Committee on Standards in Public Life and has been proposed by other professional bodies such as the Institute of Chartered Accountants (in its guidance to audit committees[63]) (see PAS 6.2), the FCA, and PRA. Warning signs will be that the procedure is not used or that it is used wrongly by staff.

(o) Advertising

A whistleblowing policy is of no value unless those to whom it applies are aware of its exis- **19.97** tence. A continuing knowledge gap in relation to protected disclosure more generally was indicated by the Audit Commission report that:

> only 50 per cent of the employees in the local government and health bodies which have used the Commission's self-assessment tools were aware of the Public Interest Disclosure Act, and the protection this affords an employee making a disclosure concerning fraud and corruption.[64]

In 2011 a YouGov survey commissioned by PCaW indicated that 77 per cent of working **19.98** Britons were not aware of the whistleblowing protection. Further, 55 per cent of workers employed in organizations with whistleblowing policies either thought that their employer did not have such a policy or were unaware of it.[65] In 2015 a further PCaW-commissioned YouGov survey showed some improvement, but still indicated that 67 per cent of working Britons were unaware of whistleblowing protection, and that only 48 per cent said their employer had a whistleblowing policy.[66]

The government guidance of March 2015 sets out the following suggestions for promoting **19.99** the policy:

- Hold a staff session or in larger organisations require managers to hold smaller, consistent team meetings
- Make the policy accessible on the staff intranet

---

[63] Institute of Chartered Accountants in England and Wales, *Guidance for Audit Committees: Whistleblowing arrangements* (2004).

[64] See Tenth Report of the Committee on Standards in Public Life (n 15 above), para 4.42.

[65] See https://d25d2506sfb94s.cloudfront.net/cumulus_uploads/document/aecs67p0bl/YG-Archive-PCAW-whistleblowing-work-concerns-100611.pdf.

[66] See http://www.pcaw.co.uk/content/5-latest/2-blog/7-new-pcaw-report-and-yougov-survey-into-the-state-of-whistleblowing-in-the-uk/PCaW%20UK%20whistleblowing%20report%20and%20 YouGov%20survey%202015.pdf.

- Appoint a whistleblowers' champion to drive the commitment to valuing whistleblowing and protecting whistleblowers within the organisation
- Use promotional posters around the building
- Include the policy within induction packs for newcomers
- Set the policy out in staff handbooks and contracts.

19.100 PCaW suggests novel methods to advertise policies, such as the use of the employer's payslips to continually remind workers of the procedure. It is assumed that the procedure would be included within any induction checklist. Most organizations also now possess intranet manuals and guidance to which staff can be easily referred and through which they can use a whistleblowing procedure.

19.101 Regular reminders are important, through such methods as briefings and surveys, and through publishing summaries and responses showing how the arrangements have worked, identifying lessons learned that have been prompted by the reporting process and examples of where it has been operated successfully.

19.102 A good policy can also be highlighted to customers or clients. This shows the organization not only as open, but also as, perhaps, a safer organization with which to contract or deal.

(p) Training

19.103 The government guidance states that the policy should include a commitment to training workers at all levels of the organization in relation to whistleblowing law and the organization's policy on whistleblowing. In addition, training of those to whom concerns will be reported should be considered as essential. Training of managers and of the workforce as to the advantages of confidential reporting, whilst expensive, can be one of the most effective means of ensuring a change in a culture at an organization. If an organization is seeking to establish a defence under the Bribery Act 2010 it will need to have clear records of both the training of those designated officers who have a role in the procedure and clear records that those 'associated' with the commercial organization are aware of the existence of the policy and how to access it.

C. Data Protection

(1) The DPA and the Data Protection Directive/Regulation 2016/679

19.104 Whilst there is now a broad consensus as to the value and importance of whistleblowing procedures, there is also a requirement to comply with obligations in relation to processing of personal data. The issue was brought into focus by the opinion of the Article 29 Data Protection Working Party adopted on 1 February 2006, and further highlighted by decisions in some EU Member States that concluded that whistleblowing hotlines were unlawful (see paragraphs 19.72–19.76 above). At EU level, the issue has focused on the obligation under Directive 95/46EC ('the Data Protection Directive'), which sets out the principle that that Members States shall provide that personal data may be processed only if one of six exceptions apply. Most pertinently, Article 7 (f) provides an exception where:

> processing is necessary for the purposes of the legitimate interests pursued by the controller or by the third party or parties to whom the data are disclosed, except where such interests are overridden by the interests for fundamental rights and freedoms of the data subject which require protection under Article 1(1).[67]

---

[67] Referring to the obligation in Article 1(1) on States to: 'protect the fundamental rights and freedoms of natural persons, and in particular their right to privacy with respect to the processing of personal data'.

The Data Protection Directive is replaced with effect from 25 May 2018 by Regulation 2016/679 of 27 April 2016, which contains an exception in Article 6(f) in materially the same terms as Article 7(f) of the Data Protection Directive.

The Directive is implemented in the UK by the Data Protection Act 1998 (DPA). Data **19.105** controllers[68] must comply with the data protection principles (set out in Schedule 1 DPA),[69] being the following:

1. Personal data shall be processed fairly and lawfully and, in particular, shall not be processed unless—

   (a) at least one of the conditions in Schedule 2 is met, and

   (b) in the case of sensitive personal data, at least one of the conditions in Schedule 3 is also met.

2. Personal data shall be obtained only for one or more specified and lawful purposes, and shall not be further processed in any manner incompatible with that purpose or those purposes.

3. Personal data shall be adequate, relevant and not excessive in relation to the purpose or purposes for which they are processed.

4. Personal data shall be accurate and, where necessary, kept up to date.

5. Personal data processed for any purpose or purposes shall not be kept for longer than is necessary for that purpose or those purposes.

6. Personal data shall be processed in accordance with the rights of data subjects under this Act.

7. Appropriate technical and organisational measures shall be taken against unauthorised or unlawful processing of personal data and against accidental loss or destruction of, or damage to, personal data.

8. Personal data shall not be transferred to a country or territory outside the European Economic Area unless that country or territory ensures an adequate level of protection for the rights and freedoms of data subjects in relation to the processing of personal data.

As set out in the first principle therefore, and in section 4(3) DPA, minimum conditions to **19.106** be able to process personal data are set out in Schedule 2 DPA. As to this,

1. Mirroring Article 7(f) of the Data Protection Directive, one of the permissible conditions for processing personal data (see the first principle above) is that it is necessary for the purposes of legitimate interests pursued by the data controller (or by the third party or parties to whom the data is disclosed), except where the processing is unwarranted in any particular case by reason of prejudice to the rights, interests, or freedoms of the data subject.[70]

2. A further alternative is where the processing is necessary for compliance with any legal obligation to which the data controller is subject. This mirrors Article 7(c) of the Data Protection Directive (and Article 6.1(c) of its successor, Regulation 2016/679. That provision was narrowly construed by the Article 29 Working Party so as not to include an obligation imposed by a foreign legal statute or regulation, such as SOX. We suggest though that article 7(c) is applicable by virtue of the vicarious liability and statutory defence provisions in section 47B ERA, since it is only by complying with the requirement to take all reasonable steps to prevent the victimization that an employer can avoid

---

[68] Defined as being the person who (alone or jointly or in common with others) determined the purposes for which and the manner in which any personal data are, or are to be, processed (s 1(2) DPA).

[69] See also in relation to organizations with the NHS, the NHS Code of Practice: Confidentiality (Code of Confidentiality).

[70] Schedule 2 para 6.

liability for protected disclosure victimization of workers by other workers in the course of their employment.

19.107 Particular care is needed where processing of sensitive data is involved, as defined in section 2 DPA. This includes personal data consisting of the commission or alleged commission of any offence by the data subject (DPA, section 2(g)). In relation to this, minimum conditions are set out in Schedule 3 of the DPA, supplemented by secondary legislation. In particular:

1. Various circumstances in which the data may potentially be processed (subject to compliance with the data protection principles) are set out in the Data Protection (Processing of Sensitive Personal Data) Order 2000 (SI 2000/417). The most likely basis is Article 2(1) of the Schedule to the Order. This applies where the processing (a) is in the substantial public interest, (b) is necessary for the purposes of the prevention or detection of any unlawful act, and (c) must necessarily be carried out without the explicit consent of the data subject being sought so as not to prejudice those purposes.
2. In addition, para 2(1) of Schedule 3 DPA provides an exception where processing is necessary for the purposes of exercising or performing any right which is conferred or imposed by law on the data controller in connection with employment.[71] Again, that would appear to cover steps taken under a whistleblowing policy which are required to be able to rely on the statutory defence in section 47B ERA, though it would not cover processing sensitive personal data which is irrelevant to, for example, any wrongdoing reported.

19.108 The conditions in Schedules 2 and 3 of the DPA are only minimum conditions. It is still necessary to comply with the data protection principles, including the general obligation to process data fairly and lawfully. Further provisions in relation to the interpretation of these principles are set out in Part II of Schedule 1 DPA. As further addressed in the following section, that issue had been addressed at an EU level in the context of a tension between US legislation and the EU model, notably in relation to anonymous whistleblowing.

(2) Article 29 Data Protection Working Party Recommendations

19.109 Whilst there is little difficulty in showing that having a whistleblowing procedure pursues a legitimate aim, the key consideration is whether there are safeguards to ensure a proportionate approach in relation to the management of data obtained and held. That issue, and the lawfulness of whistleblowing hotlines, was addressed in the Article 29 Data Protection Working Party Opinion of 1 February 2006. The opinion was limited to the fields of accounting, internal accounting controls, auditing matters, the fight against bribery, and banking and financial crime, but the principles set out may be regarded as having wider application to cases where (as will inevitably be the case) processing of personal data is involved.

---

[71] See eg *Laverty v Police Service for Northern Ireland and another* [2015] NICA 75 where the Northern Ireland Police Service (PSNI) dismissed a police officer relying on information supplied by the Eire police service An Garda Siochana (AGS) in circumstances where AGS subsequently accepted that the information had been supplied without legal basis and therefore unlawfully. The court accepted that the processing of the information was necessary for (amongst other reasons) compliance with the legal obligation to conduct disciplinary proceedings against police officers and as such for exercising or performing a right or obligation conferred or imposed by law in connection with employment. The court further concluded that the data was processed fairly, taking into account that it was received innocently, that AGS provided it innocently (though it later transpired it was done in breach of legislation), and (which was said to be a necessary requirement) that the claimant knew the identity of PSNI as data controller, the purpose of processing the data, and information about the processing of the data, and taking into account the overall fairness of the use of the data including the nature of the wrongdoing and its relevance in proving that wrongdoing.

The Article 29 Working Party concluded that reliance could not be placed on Article 7(c) **19.110** of the Data Protection Directive (processing necessary to comply with a legal obligation) to comply with foreign law obligations (ie under SOX). However, the Working Party accepted that Article 7(f) was likely to apply (processing necessary for the purposes of the legitimate interests pursued by the data controller or a third party or parties), though it was emphasized that this requires a balance with the fundamental rights and freedoms of the data subject. Pursuant to the Data Protection Directive (as under the DPA), (a) personal data must be processed fairly and lawfully; (b) personal data must be collected for specified, explicit, and legitimate purposes and not be used for incompatible purposes; and (c) the processed data must be adequate, relevant, and not excessive in relation to the purposes for which they are collected and/or further processed.

The Article 29 Working Party returned to the issue of the approach to the exception for the **19.111** legitimate interests of the data controller in an Opinion (06/2014) of 9 April 2014.[72] Again it emphasized that Article 7(f) necessitates a balancing of the legitimate interest of the controller (or third party or parties to whom the data is disclosed) against the interests or fundamental rights of data subjects. It identified relevant factors as (a) the nature and source of the legitimate interest (such as whether the disclosure is in the public interest); (b) the impact on the data subjects (such sensitive personal data being processed, the reasonable expectations of the data subject, and the balance of power between data controller and data subject); and (c) the presence of additional safeguards.

One illustrative example offered by the Working Party was as follows:[73] **19.112**

Example 16: 'In-house' whistle-blowing scheme without consistent procedures

A financial services company decides to set up a whistle-blowing scheme because it suspects widespread theft and corruption amongst its staff and is keen to encourage employees to inform on each other. In order to save money, the company decides to operate the scheme in-house, staffed by members of its Human Resources department. In order to encourage employees to use the scheme it offers a cash 'no questions asked' reward to employees whose whistle-blowing activities lead to the detection of improper conduct and the recovery of monies.

The company does have a legitimate interest in detecting and preventing theft and corruption. However, its whistle-blowing scheme is so badly designed and lacking in safeguards that its interests are overridden by both the interests and right to privacy of its employees— particulary those who may be the victim of false reports filed purely for financial gain. The fact that the scheme is operated in-house rather than independently is another problem here, as is the lack of training and guidance on the use of the scheme.

The example was intended to illustrate the need in applying the balancing exercise to focus **19.113** on factors that might lead to unfairness to the subject of the disclosure. We suggest, however, that the example is to be treated with caution. Notably, the suggestion that the fact of operating the process in-house is an indicator of unfair processing is out of step with the common practice in the UK, and we suggest is overly restrictive.

In its 2006 report the Working Party set out a number of more specific proposals: **19.114**

1. Anonymous reports should not be encouraged but confidentiality should be maintained (see paragraphs 19.75–19.81 above).

---

[72] See http://www.dataprotection.ro/servlet/ViewDocument?id=1086.

[73] The Opinion also sets out a further example (Example 15) illustrating a whistleblowing scheme set up to comply with foreign obligations, noting that it may be explained that whistleblowers can raise concerns anonymously providing that there are 'sufficient safeguards, in accordance with guidance from the relevant regulatory authorities in the EU'.

2. A possible limit on the number of persons entitled to report alleged improprieties or misconduct through whistleblowing schemes or who may be incriminated through the scheme. (We do not think this is a helpful or necessary restriction. Indeed, as discussed above, and as exemplified by the approach in the financial services sector, good practice may be to broaden the category of those who may make public interest disclosures.)[74]

3. The permissible subject matter of the report should be tied to the corporate governance issues for which the report is established. (This proposal is to be seen in the context of the limited ambit of the Working Party's opinion. As discussed above, we suggest that an approach such as in the NHS policy which covers any 'risk, malpractice or wrongdoing' affecting the business or delivery of the service is appropriate. In practice, though, the scope of matters dealt with under such a policy is likely to be limited by personal grievances or complaints being dealt with separately as part of grievance or harassment procedures).

4. Personal data processed by a whistleblowing scheme should be deleted promptly and usually within two months of the completion of the investigation, unless legal proceedings or disciplinary measures are initiated against the incriminated person or the whistleblower.

5. Personal data relating to matters found to be unsubstantiated should be deleted without delay.

6. Data subjects should be informed about the existence, purpose, and functioning of the scheme.

7. The person accused in the report should be informed by the person in charge of the scheme as soon as reasonably possible after the data concerning him/her is recorded. By way of exception, where there is substantial risk that such notification would jeopardize the employer's ability to investigate effectively, notification may be delayed for as long as this risk exists.

8. The scheme should take the necessary steps to ensure that the information disclosed will not be destroyed.

9. The scheme should ensure compliance with the right, including the right of the person subject to the complaint, to access to the data and the right to rectify incorrect, incomplete, or outdated data. However, this should not include access to the identity of the person making the report except in cases of maliciously making a false statement.

10. A specific unit should ideally be set up within the employing organization dedicated to handling whistleblowers' reports and leading the investigation. It should comprise a limited number of specifically trained and dedicated people, and should be separate from other parts of the company including the human resources department. There should also be steps to ensure that concerns within the ambit of the scheme are specifically transmitted to this group.

11. Where the scheme is provided by external service providers, there should be appropriate measures to ensure that the providers adopt similar safeguards.

---

[74] See also the criticisms of the Working Party's recommendation in this respect by Professor David Lewis in 'Whistleblowing and data protection principles: is the road to reconciliation really that rocky?', (2011) European Journal of Law and Technology, Vol 2, No 1. On page 4, Professor Lewis argues (and we agree) that the Working Party's recommendation in this respect was fundamentally misconceived in that, as a matter of principle, whistleblowing schemes should encourage all staff, and perhaps relevant outsiders, to raise serious concerns and that this is consistent with empirical research in the UK showing that many employers in both the public and private sectors have whistleblowing procedures that can be invoked by non-employees such as agency workers, contractors, subcontractors, suppliers, customers, and members of the public (Lewis, D, 2006, 'The contents of whistleblowing/confidential reporting procedures in the UK: some lessons from empirical research', Employee Relations, Vol 28, No 1 pp 76–86).

The PAS records that: **19.115**

> The EU data protection authorities have confirmed that the additional obligations in their Guidance are not intended to apply to whistleblowing schemes—such as those described in this PAS—that do not promote anonymous reporting and that build in existing management, audit and compliance records.

However, whilst the advice was not directly applicable to confidential rather than anon-   **19.116** ymous reporting, the recommendations in subparagraphs (4) to (11) above are of some wider relevance in identifying material considerations in building appropriate safeguards into the scheme, albeit that some recommendations, such as deleting personal data within two months, may be considered unnecessarily restrictive.

(3) European Data Protection Supervisor Guidance

In addition, building on the Working Party's opinions, in July 2016 the European Data   **19.117** Protection Supervisor (EDPS) published 'Guidelines on processing personal information within a whistleblowing procedure'.[75] The Guidelines are specifically for EU institutions and bodies, but again are of more general relevance. The Guidelines include the following points which we suggest set out good practice:

- Whilst there is rightly a focus on protecting the confidentiality of the whistleblower, the person against whom an allegation has been made should be protected in the same way, since there is a risk of stigmatization and victimization within their organization. Further, they will be exposed to those risks even before they are aware that they have been incriminated and the alleged facts have been investigated and analysed (para 7).
- Therefore, internal access to the information processed as part the investigation of the allegations must be granted strictly on a need-to-know basis. Persons in charge of the management of reports could be subject to a reinforced obligation of secrecy (para 8).
- Personal information must be stored securely (para 8).
- Any whistleblowing-related personal information retained for statistical purposes should be made anonymous (para 9).
- Particular care is needed however where the personal sensitive information is not relevant to the concern raised. To that end, the EDPS Guidelines provide that internal rules or a policy should describe categories of sensitive information which should be avoided, such as racial or ethnic origin, political opinions, religious or philosophical beliefs, trade union membership, and data concerning health or sex life not relevant for the case (para 11).
- Where personal information is provided which is clearly of no interest and irrelevant to the allegations, this should not be further processed. The example is given of a whistleblower who reports suspected fraud but also discloses information about the whistleblower's health situation which it is clear is completely irrelevant to the reported wrongdoing. That information should not be further processed.
- It may be appropriate at an early stage to defer providing information to the person about whom the allegation is made, so as not to damage the investigation. But the reasons for doing so should then be documented, showing for example why there is a high risk that giving the information would hamper the procedure (para 20).
- In relation to access rights, an assessment must be made on a case-by-case basis and the reasons for the decision documented. When access is granted to the personal information

---

[75] Available at https://secure.edps.europa.eu/EDPSWEB/webdav/site/mySite/shared/Documents/ Supervision/Guidelines/16-07-18_Whistleblowing_Guidelines_EN.pdf.

of any concerned individual, the personal information of third parties such as informants, whistleblowers, or witnesses should be removed from the documents except in exceptional circumstances if the whistleblower authorizes the disclosure about himself, or it is required by any subsequent criminal law proceedings, or if the whisteblower maliciously makes a false statement (para 25).

- Personal information must not be kept for a longer period than necessary having regard to the purpose of the processing (para 27).

19.118 Further considerations arise where data is to be transferred outside the EU. Article 25 of the Data Protection Directive (and the 8th data protection principle in Schedule 1 to the DPA) prohibits transfer of data to a country outside the EU which does not ensure an adequate level of protection. So far as concerns data transfer to the US, the issue was considered in *Schrems v Data Protection Commission* (C-362/14), where the CJEU concluded that the 'International Safe Harbor Privacy Principles' that had been agreed between the EU and the US did not provide sufficient protection for data protection rights, and the Commission decision approving those arrangements was invalid. The decision in *Schrems* resulted in urgent adoption by Member States of the EU–US 'Privacy Shield', launched on 12 July 2016. Organizations are able to sign up to the Privacy Shield from 1 August 2016 provided they have implemented the necessary changes so as to comply with the new, stricter rules. However, the Article 29 Working Party has issued a detailed Opinion stating that the Privacy Shield still does not include certain key EU data protection principles and does not exclude indiscriminate collection of personal data from the EU by US intelligence agencies,[76] and it may be challenged before the CJEU, particularly in the light of ongoing concerns as to government surveillance. More generally, specific legal advice should be obtained before passing any personal data, including that collected under a whistleblowing scheme, from within the EEA to another country, and should ensure that any external organization that undertakes a whistleblowing function for or on behalf of the organization is compliant.

D. Financial Incentives?

19.119 In Chapter 12 (paragraphs 12.117 and 12.118), we considered the recent assessment of the merits of introducing financial incentives to encourage disclosures within the financial services industry. As noted there, awards can be made of 15 to 25 per cent of the Government's recovery from *qui tam* suits filed under the False Claims Act, which allows private citizens with information as to fraud against the US to file a lawsuit on the Government's behalf. The scope for financial sanctions has been extended by the Dodd–Frank Act of 2010. Whilst the False Claims Act only applies to financial fraud committed against the government, the Dodd–Frank Act applies to a much broader range of financial fraud committed by a business which is required to report to the US Securities and Exchange Commission (SEC) or US Commodity Futures Trading Commission (CFTC). A person with independent knowledge of a financial fraud committed by such a business, who reports the information to the SEC or the CFTC, may be entitled to between 10 and 30 per cent of any amount over $1 million recovered in a judicial or administrative action against the wrongdoer. Both sets of legislation have resulted in some very large awards, as noted in 12.117 and 12.118.

---

[76] Opinion 01/2016 of 13 April 2016: http://ec.europa.eu/justice/data-protection/article-29/documentation/opinion-recommendation/files/2016/wp238_en.pdf.

The approach of offering financial incentives has not been generally adopted in the United **19.120** Kingdom,[77] and, as noted in Chapter 12, it was rejected both in the financial services review and following the Government's Call for Evidence. Indeed, the protected disclosure legislation is framed as being to protect disclosures made in the public interest rather than for personal gain.[78] One criticism of a system that rewards informants for blowing the whistle on the basis of the value of the large-scale fraud they uncover is that a whistleblower might wait until the fraud has occurred before disclosing the wrongdoing to increase the potential sum from which they may receive a percentage.

There is nothing to prevent a contractual agreement within an organization in the UK to **19.121** enable internal whistleblowers the opportunity to receive a payment, perhaps even calculated as a share of any losses stopped. It would, however, require careful and specific drafting. The PAS recommends (at 5.10), and we agree, that, insofar as rewards are provided, this is better dealt with by way of after-the-event discretion in a particular case rather than being offered in advance as a matter of policy:

> *Rewards:* Sometimes a whistleblowing employee will sound the alarm on a matter that can save the organization substantial sums of money. Where this happens, some organizations may consider giving the employee a reward—be it a bonus, promotion or some other benefit. Rather than spell this possibility out in any procedure, the issue should be left to the discretion of the Board.

There is, we suggest, good reason for the caution expressed in the PAS over offering rewards to encourage whistleblowers to come forward. Whilst it has the attraction of encouraging the provision of information and discouraging workers from doing so only on an anonymous basis, it risks leading to suspicion as to the motives of those who raise concerns, with the potential for their credibility to be undermined. As such it may encourage attention on the whistleblower rather than on the message. The provision of incentives may also complicate any litigation under the ERA's protected disclosure provisions. An employer which had offered an incentive might be tempted to argue that the whistleblower did not hold a reasonable belief that the disclosure was made in the public interest or (albeit only a remedy issue for disclosures made since 25 June 2013) that it was not made in good faith. If it is a wider disclosure pursuant to section 43G ERA, then protection could fall foul of section 43G(1)(c) if it is made for 'personal gain'.[79] Indeed, as noted above (paragraph 19.112), in one of the examples appended to the A29 Working Party Report of 9 April 2014 (Example 16), the fact of offering cash rewards for information leading to detection of improper conduct and recovery of monies was one factor which the Working Party regarded as making the scheme badly designed and liable to infringe data protection rights, due to the risk of encouraging false claims for financial gain.

---

[77] But see *Virgo Fidelis Senior School v Boyle* [2004] IRLR 268 (EAT) in relation to the scope for awards of exemplary damages, discussed in Chapter 10, at 10.102–10.103.

[78] See the discussion of *Street v Derbyshire Unemployed Workers' Centre* [2004] EWCA Civ 964, [2005] ICR 97 in Chapter 5, at 5.52.

[79] ERA, s 43L provides that only rewards payable by or under any enactment are to be disregarded for the purposes of determining whether a disclosure was for purposes of personal gain.

Appendices

Case Study

THE SCENARIO

1. Adam was employed by Megaphones Ltd in a call centre as a team leader. His employment began on 1 November 2015. Megaphones has a whistleblowing policy which states that staff are encouraged to raise any concerns about Megaphones' business to their line manager or the HR Director, that victimization is not acceptable, and that any instances will be taken seriously and managed appropriately.

2. Adam had been managed by Derek with whom he got on well. Derek was then moved to another department and Belinda took over as Adam's manager. Adam applied for promotion but was unsuccessful. He sought feedback from his manager, Belinda, but this led to a vicious argument between them in which Belinda said that Adam was useless and Adam replied that Belinda was a hopeless manager.

3. Adam reported the incident to Belinda's manager, Carol, who was also the company's HR Director, telling her what had been said. He added that Belinda had been placing him and his team under unreasonable pressure. He said she should not be surprised if his team had to take time off work due to stress, given the 'disgusting' way that Belinda treated him and his team. Adam did not say he was raising this under the whistleblowing policy. Carol did not ask for any more details. However, she said Adam should leave the matter with her. During the period following the meeting Adam noticed some positive changes in Belinda's behaviour.

4. A month after the argument, Megaphones indicated that they were proposing to make a number of staff redundant. Adam told Belinda that the proposed redundancies could breach employment legislation. Belinda told him that this was not his concern.

5. Adam says that around the same time he became suspicious that Belinda was breaching the company's data protection policy. He stayed late one evening to investigate further. He found evidence that suggested that there had been a breach, printed out some company material and took it home. He told Carol of his suspicions and gave her a copy of the relevant material.

6. A month went by and so far as Adam could tell there was no investigation into his allegations about the breach of the data protection policy. Also, Belinda called him a 'slacker' and a 'sneak', and referred to him as 'the terrorist' in front of his team and peers at a gathering at the local pub after work for farewell drinks for one of their colleagues who was leaving Megaphones. Furthermore, Adam was the only team leader not to be offered overtime. As a result of these things, Adam had problems sleeping and developed nervous rashes.

7. Belinda complained about Adam to Megaphones' CEO. The CEO subsequently held a discussion about Adam with Carol in which he suggested that she consider instigating disciplinary proceedings against Adam. Carol decided to do so, and Adam was called to see Carol and was told that he faced a disciplinary hearing. The charge was that he breached the company's security policy by taking home copies of the material about his manager's activities.

8. As he came out of the meeting with Carol, Adam, who was feeling very anxious, saw Belinda who smiled and asked if he 'enjoyed' his meeting with Carol. Adam swore loudly at Belinda. The incident was overheard by various members of staff. Adam was immediately suspended and told that this was because of his outburst.

9. On 30 November 2016, Adam resigned with immediate effect. He claimed that he had been constructively dismissed.

10. Adam has always thought that Megaphones was a sweatshop with 'dodgy' employment practices that unfairly exploited its workers, and that as a company it used various shady financial practices. Immediately before his resignation he posted his concerns on an internet site, setting out examples to support his claims. He also set out his concern that his manager was breaching the company's data protection policy, referring to his findings when he stayed late to investigate the issue, and stated that she had been secretly profiting from private company information.

11. After he had resigned, he wrote to his MP about the same subjects.
12. Adam was offered a job by Loudspeakers Ltd. He contacted Derek, another manager at Megaphones, to ask whether he would provide a reference for him. Derek said he would be happy to do so. However, a day later he sent Adam a text saying that he had had a word with Carol and he had changed his mind and could not help Adam.

Introduction

Whistleblowing claims tend to be both very fact sensitive and potentially quite technical. In considering the questions below, which are mainly focused on disclosures to the employer, it is important to follow the structure of the relevant provisions of the Employment Rights Act 1996 (ERA).

The questions need to be asked in a structured way; usually

(a) is there a disclosure?; if so
(b) is the disclosure a qualifying disclosure?; if so
(c) is the qualifying disclosure protected?; if so
(d) detriment:
   • was there an act or a deliberate failure to act and by whom was it carried out?
   • is the act or deliberate failure to act to be treated as done by the employer?
   • does the act or deliberate failure to act cause detriment?
   • was the act done or was the deliberate failure on the ground of the qualifying protected disclosure?
   • does the employer have a defence under section 47B(1D) ERA?
   • does the worker or agent have personal liability (and does the defence under section 47B(1E) apply to any worker)?
(e) dismissal:
   • was there a dismissal?
   • if so, is the reason or principal reason that the employee made the protected disclosure?
(f) what is the remedy?

(1) Are there any protected disclosures?

1. For a protected disclosure to arise, there will first need to be a *qualifying* disclosure within ERA, section 43B ie:
   (a) a disclosure of information (which may include something drawn to the attention of, but already known by, the employer); a bare allegation or statement of position or of concern might not necessarily entail a disclosure of information: *Cavendish Munro Professional Risks Management Ltd v Geduld* [2010] ICR 325; but see *Kilraine v London Borough of Wandsworth* [2016] IRLR 422 (EAT).
   (b) which, in the reasonable belief of the worker making the disclosure:
      (i) tends to show there has been, is currently, or is likely to be a relevant failure (criminal offence, non-compliance with a legal obligation, miscarriage of justice, endangering of health and safety, damage to the environment, or cover-up of one of these); and
      (ii) is made in the public interest:[1] *Chesterton Global Ltd v Nurmohamed* [2015] IRLR 614 (EAT).
2. An appropriate structured approach is first to identify the information disclosed, ensure that the worker had a reasonable belief that it was in the public interest to make the disclosure, then to identify the relevant failure which the worker believed tended to be shown, then to assess whether they are sufficiently connected by the requisite reasonable belief.
3. In order to be protected, a qualifying disclosure will need to be made in accordance with any of ERA, sections 43C–43H.
4. Section 43C(1)(a) will obviously be relevant in this case. It requires the qualifying disclosure to be made to the employer (or to another person in accordance with a procedure authorized by the employer).
5. Adam's adviser will also need to consider sections 43F (disclosure to prescribed person) and 43G (disclosure in other cases).

---

[1] Applicable to disclosures made on or after 25 June 2013. For disclosures made before 25 June 2013, there would instead have been a requirement that the disclosure was made in good faith.

The following disclosures need to be considered:

(i) Adam reports the argument with Belinda to the HR Director (Carol)

6. There was a disclosure of information consisting at least of what Belinda said to Adam and the way she spoke to him in the context of having sought feedback. The contention that Belinda's treatment was 'disgusting' and was placing him and the team under unreasonable pressure might be argued only to be an allegation and a statement of opinion. Adam also arguably conveyed information as to his view of Belinda's conduct.

7. The next question would be to ascertain why Adam considered that information 'tended to show' a relevant failure and whether it was reasonable for him to hold that belief. It may be that Adam genuinely believed that the information tended to show a breach of a legal obligation, most probably consisting of a breach of his own employment contract (eg a breach of the implied term of trust and confidence) and/or a breach by Belinda of her duties (owed to Megaphones) as a manager under her own contract. He might have also considered that the information tended to show that health and safety of his team was being endangered. For the employer it could be said that Adam could not reasonably have believed this to be shown by the mere fact that this was Adam's view, without conveying any other facts to support that view. But context may be important. Here Adam was not asked for any more information and Carol's comment to leave the matter with her could reasonably support his belief that what he had said was sufficient.

8. Adam would also need to explain why he considered the disclosure to be in the public interest, and there would need to be an assessment of whether that belief was reasonable. On its face, the complaint about the way that Belinda spoke to Adam, and his being a poor manager, would appear to be more akin to a grievance, rather than a disclosure in the public interest. But the reference to unreasonable pressure on the team and the prospect of members of the team taking time off work with stress might allude to a broader public interest concern in raising the disclosure so as to prevent a harm to the health and safety of others (his team) and/or to prevent unfair exploitation of them. It is not necessarily a bar that only other employees of the employer are directly affected by the disclosure: see *Chesterton Global*.[2]

9. Nor is it a bar to success that Adam did not invoke the company's whistleblowing procedure, although that may be evidentially relevant in relation to whether it was believed that the disclosure was made in the public interest and whether he had a reasonable belief that what he was conveying tended to show a relevant failure.

10. The fact that Adam did not provide any details in support of his allegation as to the way that Belinda treated the team may be evidentially relevant in relation to whether he did hold a belief that disclosure was made in the public interest, and also be relevant to the assessment of whether that belief was reasonable. It could be said that if he genuinely held that belief he would have provided the information necessary to enable the issue properly to be addressed. But it would be necessary also to take into account the HR Director's statement that Adam should leave the matter with her, which might be relied upon to explain the failure to provide further information.

11. The disclosure was plainly made to the employer, and as such if there was a qualifying disclosure it would also be a protected disclosure.

(ii) Adam tells Belinda that the proposed redundancies could breach employment legislation

12. The first hurdle would be to show that there was a disclosure of information rather than a mere allegation, or a statement of concern. Here it would seem that the only information disclosed was the fact of the redundancies and the disclosure as to Adam's state of mind; that he held a concern as to lawfulness of the redundancies.[3]

13. On the basis of the (controversial) decision in *Kraus v Penna plc* [2004] IRLR 260, EAT,[4] Adam must establish that he reasonably believed that the information disclosed tended to show that it was probable, or more probable than not, that there would be a failure to comply; mere possibility is insufficient. In some cases, it might be that, although moderate language was used in saying only that there *could* be a breach, this was playing down the concern, and

---

[2] Under appeal at the time of writing.
[3] See *Goode v Marks and Spencer plc* (EAT/0442/09, 15 April 2010).
[4] But see the criticisms of the reasoning in *Kraus* in Chapter 3.

that it was believed, reasonably, that the information provided showed that non-compliance with a legal obligation was likely. But here Adam would face the difficulty that there was no further information provided. On the face of it, he was only voicing an opinion or making an allegation.

14. Even if it could be shown that there was a reasonable belief that there was a disclosure of information tending to show a past, present, or likely future relevant failure, it would still be necessary to satisfy the public interest test. One would need to consider Adam's explanation of why (if it was contended to be the case) he considered that the disclosure was made in the public interest, and to consider whether that was objectively reasonable.

(iii) Adam tells Carol of the alleged breach of the data protection policy

15. Again, the first issue will be to identify what information was disclosed other than the mere making of an allegation of a breach of the policy. Adam had provided what he regarded as relevant material to Carol. It will be necessary to consider what Adam told Carol and what the information was within that material which he believed to show a breach of a legal obligation or a criminal offence.

16. The relevant failure which Adam believed tended to be shown might be of a legal obligation (ERA, section 43B(1)(b)) by virtue of a breach of the Data Protection Act 1998 and/or the manager's contract of employment. It may also fall within the *criminal offence* provision in section 43B(1)(a). The fact that Adam carried out an investigation to test the matter, and the adequacy of that investigation, is likely to be relevant to whether any belief that there was a breach of a legal obligation/criminal offence was reasonable (but he might be disciplined for having done so—see below). It will also be relevant to consider to what extent, given the position he held, it was reasonable to expect Adam to carry out the investigation, or further investigation, himself. If it is possible to reach a conclusion as to whether or not Adam was right that Belinda was breaching the data protection policy, and that this amounted to breach of a legal obligation or criminal offence, this may also be relevant.[5] If he was wrong, in considering whether his belief was nevertheless reasonable it will be relevant to consider whether there were any features of Adam's role or experience that bear on whether he could be expected to know that the belief was ill-founded: see *Korashi v Abertawe Bro Morgannwg University Local Area Health Board* [2012] IRLR 4 (EAT).[6]

17. Again, in relation to the question of whether Adam held a reasonable belief that the disclosure was made in the public interest, it will first be necessary to understand the basis for his contention that this was the case. If for example the breach concerned the misuse of confidential data relating to customers or prospective customers, it might be that Adam could say that it was in the public interest that this be investigated. If the relevant failure amounted to a criminal offence that might provide further support for the contention that it was reasonable to believe that the disclosure was made in the public interest. Although not expressly stated at the time of making the disclosure to Carol, the subsequent allegation when posting information on the internet site, to the effect that Belinda had been making a secret profit from private company information, may be relevant as evidencing the issue which Adam had in mind (making a secret profit from private company information), and in turn have a bearing on whether it was genuinely believed that the disclosure was made in the public interest, and whether any such belief was reasonable.

18. It might be found that Adam did not make the disclosure in good faith as a result of the principal reason being an ulterior motive (eg hostility to Belinda or the dispute with her).[7] That would now be an issue going only to remedy (since the disclosure was made after 25 June 2013). It would not of itself establish that Adam did not hold a reasonable belief that the disclosure was made in the public interest. It would be evidentially relevant, but Adam could still reasonably believe that making the disclosure was in the public interest.[8]

---

[5] See Chapter 3, paras 3.79–3.85.

[6] See Chapter 3, para 3.67.

[7] See Chapter 10, paras 10.108 et seq. The test remains whether it was not in good faith rather than whether there was an ulterior motive, and it is ultimately a question of fact for the tribunal (see Chapter 10, paras 10.126–10.132).

[8] See the discussion in Chapter 4, paras 4.76–4.82.

(iv) Adam posts his concerns about Megaphones Ltd on an internet site

19. Again, the starting point in identifying whether this is a qualifying disclosure will be to identify what information was disclosed, and whether the information tended to show a past, ongoing, or likely future relevant failure. Here Adam has not merely expressed his concerns, but has provided examples in support. As such there would be information disclosed beyond merely information as to Adam's state of mind. It would then be necessary to consider whether he had a reasonable belief that this information tended to show the relevant failures. One relevant factor in relation to this would be the failure to raise these matters internally, so as to give the company the opportunity to answer, unless Adam could provide a convincing reason for not having done so. Other factors to be taken into account would include whether the examples given were correct or, if he had not witnessed them personally, whether it was reasonable in the circumstances to rely on the information he was given.

20. It is then necessary to consider whether Adam had a reasonable belief in his disclosure being in the public interest. Here the nature of the information disclosed appears to lend itself to a finding that this was the case.

21. If this is a qualifying disclosure, it is plainly not a protected disclosure within the scope of s 43C. In order to fall within section 43G (which potentially protects wider disclosure), the following requirements, which are extra to those for first tier disclosures, are necessary:
    (a) He reasonably believed the information disclosed and any allegation contained in it were substantially true.
    (b) He did not make the disclosure for personal gain.
    (c) One of the following were met:
       • when making the disclosure he reasonably believed that he would be subject to detriment if he disclosed to the employer; or
       • he reasonably believed relevant evidence would be concealed or destroyed if he disclosed to the employer; or
       • he had previously made a disclosure of substantially the same information to his employer.
    (d) It was reasonable for him to make the disclosure in all the circumstances.

22. In order to succeed Adam would therefore need to meet the higher hurdle of a reasonable belief that the information and allegations were substantially true. There is no suggestion of personal gain. As to whether Adam could satisfy one of the gateways in section 43G(2) ERA:
    22.1 In relation to the data protection allegations it may be possible to show that they had already been raised with the employer, and it may be that the substance of the concerns about profiting from private information were raised as part of that disclosure (thereby satisfying the condition in ERA, section 43G(2)(c)).
    22.2 In relation to the other matters, he had not previously made a disclosure of substantially the same information, in that there had been no previous disclosure about financial accounting, and the allegations as to running a sweatshop with 'dodgy' employment practices, and the supporting detail went substantially beyond the previous comments about the way in which Belinda treated her team.
    22.3 The exception for a reasonable belief that information would have been concealed or destroyed only applies if there is no person prescribed for the purposes of section 43F ERA. Here, depending on the nature of the information disclosed, it might fall within the description of matters prescribed for the Commissioners for HMRC (if the disclosures concern tax evasion), the Health and Safety Executive (health and safety of individuals at work), the Secretary of State for Business, Energy and Industrial Strategy (prescribed for fraud, and other misconduct, in relation to companies), the Information Commissioner (for compliance with data protection legislation), or members of the House of Commons (for any of the matters for which any other body is prescribed).
    22.4 Although Adam knew that his employment was about to terminate (because he was going to resign) it might be possible for Adam to show a reasonable belief that he would be subjected to a detriment by his (former) employer,[9] such as by being given a negative reference, if he made the disclosure to Megaphones. On the face of it, Adam's disclosure

---

[9] Section 43G(2)(b) refers to a detriment by his employer, but this includes a former employer—see s 230(1) ERA.

to the public would seem at least as likely to produce that result as keeping the disclosure within Megaphones (although if the company were publicly 'shamed' it might want to be seen to be rewarding Adam and not punishing him). But section 43G(2)(a) does not require that the detriment would be greater by making the internal disclosure than it would be if taking the disclosure more widely. Further, it would be relevant to take into account the previous treatment when Adam did raise matters internally, and whether it was reasonable for him to believe that he had been subjected to detrimental treatment that was influenced by the disclosures that he made.

23. In considering whether Adam's posting on the internet was reasonable in all the circumstances of the case for the purposes of section 43G ERA, it would be necessary at least to take into account the specific factors which are listed in section 43G(3). One important consideration would be whether there was a more targeted disclosure that would be appropriate to be made in the first instance before going public with it. Related to this, the failure first to make a disclosure about these matters either to the employer or in accordance with section 43F would be highly relevant (see section 43G(3)(e)). As against that, the continuing nature of the alleged wrongdoing believed to be taking place and, possibly, its seriousness, might weigh in favour of wider disclosure, particularly if Adam felt that it was important that the prospective staff and customers be warned about this, and if that was a reasonable view to hold. The information posted and the nature of the internet site are also part of the circumstances that fall to be considered.

24. In order to fall within section 43H it would be necessary for Adam to show, amongst other things, that the relevant failure was 'of an exceptionally serious nature'. This seems unlikely to be made out, and few claims have been upheld under section 43H.

(v) Adam writes to his MP about Megaphones Ltd

25. Although by the time he wrote to his MP Adam's employment had already ended, that is not a bar to his having made protected disclosures: see *Onyango v Berkeley (t/a Berkeley Solicitors)*.[10] There can be a claim based on post-termination detriment such as being given a negative reference.[11]

26. All members of the House of Commons are now prescribed individuals provided the disclosure relates to any of the matters described in the second column of the Schedule to the Public Interest Disclosure (Prescribed Persons) Order 2014. It would, however, still be necessary to meet the requirements for a qualifying disclosure, and a reasonable belief at the time of making the disclosure that the information disclosed, and any allegation contained in it, was substantially true.

(2) What are the acts/deliberate failures to act and what are the detriments in respect of which Adam should be claiming?

27. The right under section 47B is not to be subjected to any detriment by any act, or any deliberate failure to act, by his employer that took place *on the ground* that the worker has made a protected disclosure. In some cases, the doing of the act or the deliberate failure and the suffering of the detriment might be in effect the same thing (eg where disciplinary action is taken). In other cases the act/failure to act and the detriment may clearly be separate. It is the act or deliberate failure to act which must be on the ground of the protected disclosure, whereas the detriment must be caused by the act or deliberate failure to act: *Vivian v Bournemouth BC* (UKEAT/0254/10, 6 May 2011).[12]

28. There are the following acts or deliberate failures to act:
    (a) being called names by his manager in front of his team and peers;
    (b) not being offered overtime;
    (c) (possibly), the apparent failure to investigate (if it is found to have been deliberate);
    (d) the conduct of the CEO in encouraging Carol to instigate disciplinary proceedings against Adam;
    (e) Belinda's complaints to the CEO;

---

[10] [2013] IRLR 338. See Chapter 7, para 7.45.
[11] *Woodward v Abbey National plc (No. 1)* [2006] EWCA Civ 822, [2006] IRLR 677: see Chapter 7, paras 7.35–7.44.
[12] See Chapter 7, para 7.210.

(f) the instigation of the disciplinary proceedings;

(g) suspension;

(h) (possibly) a deliberate failure to support Adam as a whistleblower;

(i) Derek's withdrawal of the offer of a reference;

(j) Persuasion of Derek to withdraw the offer of a reference by Megaphones' management/ Carol.

29. There are the following detriments identified:

(a) loss of overtime;

(b) injury to feelings (including stress and anxiety); and

(c) (possibly) injury to health.

(d) being the subject of hostile name-calling, and the instigation of disciplinary proceedings and instruction to do so, and lack of support as a whistleblower. These are liable to be detrimental by their nature. The same may be true of suspension, despite this being an ostensibly neutral act.

(e) Derek's withdrawal of the offer of a reference and the impact of that on Adam's search for replacement employment.

(3) Potential respondents

30. Under section 47B ERA, the individual worker responsible for the alleged victimization may also be made a respondent to the claim. It may be important to give consideration to this, at least where the employer's statutory defence under section 47B(1D) might be relied upon, or where there is a risk of the employer entering into insolvency. Here it is therefore relevant to consider the following claims:

30.1 In relation to being called names and in relation to her complaints to the CEO—a claim against Belinda and Megaphones.

30.2 In relation to not being offered overtime—a claim against Belinda (or whoever else made the decision) and Megaphones.

30.3 In relation to the failure to investigate (if deliberate)—a claim against Carol and Megaphones.

30.4 In relation to the encouragement to instigate disciplinary proceedings—against the CEO and Megaphones.

30.5 In relation to the instigation of the disciplinary proceedings—against Carol, the CEO, and Megaphones.

30.6 In relation to suspension—against Carol and Megaphones

30.7 In relation to the alleged deliberate failure to support Adam—against Carol and Megaphones.

30.8 In relation to the withdrawal of the offer of a reference—against Derek, Carol, and Megaphones.

(4) Vicarious liability

31. In relation to most of the alleged acts of detrimental treatment, there is not likely to be any difficulty in establishing that they are acts done in the course of employment so as to give rise to vicarious liability (if they were done on the grounds of protected disclosures). There may be an issue as to this in relation to the name-calling, since it took place out of work. But as it was a work-related social occasion, it is still likely to be regarded as in the course of employment.[13]

(5) Were the acts/deliberate failures done on the ground of the disclosures?

32. Note that the test under section 47B is whether the act/deliberate failure to act was done *on the ground of* the protected disclosure. The ground on which the employer acts requires an analysis of the conscious or subconscious mental processes which caused the employer to act, as in victimization in sex/race discrimination cases. It is not sufficient to show that 'but for' the disclosure the act or omission would not have occurred, nor merely that the act or omission was 'related to' the disclosure.[14] The act/deliberate failure must in no sense whatsoever be on the

---

[13] See Chapter 8, paras 8.19–8.24.

[14] *London Borough of Harrow v Knight* [2003] IRLR 140, EAT.

grounds of a protected disclosure, which equates to a test that the protected disclosure must not be a significant influence; an influence is significant if it is material and more than trivial.[15]

33. Section 48(2) ERA provides that it is for the employer to show the ground on which any act, or deliberate failure to act, took place. Similarly, if Belinda, Carol, and/or the CEO are made individual respondents, the burden will be on them in relation to any claim against them to show the reasons for the act or deliberate failure to act (see section 48(5) ERA). It will be a question of fact for the tribunal to decide.

34. The following issues seem likely to arise in Adam's case on the 'reason why' question:

(a) Can the employer and Belinda prove any innocent explanation for the manager's name-calling, or otherwise prove that it was not by reason of any of the disclosures established to be protected disclosures (eg by showing that Belinda was not aware of the disclosures)? The reference to 'Sneak' in particular appears to be on the ground of whistleblowing.

(b) Can the employer/Belinda show the reason why Adam was not offered overtime, other than because of the whistleblowing, or in any event show that it was not by reason of whistleblowing?

(c) Has there in fact been an investigation into Adam's allegations? If not, is there a credible explanation why? In any event can it be shown that it was not by reason of having made protected disclosures?

(d) Was the CEO aware of the disclosures?

(e) What was the reason for the CEO becoming involved in giving instructions to instigate disciplinary proceedings? Would that be a normal part of his role?

(f) How have other staff who have breached the security policy been treated? Is there a credible explanation for any difference?

(g) Was any failure to support Adam deliberate (as opposed to merely insensitive or careless)? Was it based on hostility, conscious or subconscious, to Adam as a whistleblower? Reference might be made to Carol's responsibility as HR Director under the whistleblowing policy, as indicating that it can be inferred that she must have been aware of the need to take steps to ensure protection was provided, given the nature of the concerns raised, even though not formally invoking the whistleblowing policy.

(h) Why did Derek change his mind about the reference? What did Carol say to him? Why did she say what she said? Was there another reason for not giving Adam a reference apart from the fact that he had made protected disclosures?

35. In each case, if Megaphones (or, as the case may be, the individual respondent) cannot positively establish the reason for the act or deliberate failure to act, it is still open to it to show that the reason was not a protected disclosure. A failure to establish a positive reason may, however, make it more difficult to show this.

36. In relation to the discipline which was applied, the protection under the ERA is against detriment/dismissal on the ground of the disclosure itself, not for any activity by the worker that is connected to the disclosure. Thus, it would be open to the employer to seek to show that Adam was disciplined for breaching the security policy, provided it can be established that the decision to discipline was not materially influenced by a protected disclosure: see *Bolton School v Evans* [2006] EWCA Civ 1653, [2007] ICR 641 (CA).

37. In relation to Carol's part in instigating the disciplinary procedure, it may be possible to show that she did so because she was encouraged to do so by the CEO. But it would still be necessary to address whether any protected disclosures were a significant influence in her decision.

38. A further complication arises if it is found that, although it was Carol's decision to instigate the disciplinary proceedings and she was not herself influenced by any protected disclosures, the CEO was so influenced, and the CEO's encouragement to instigate disciplinary proceedings was a significant influence in her decision to do so. The same issue arises if Belinda's complaints to the CEO were by reason of Adam having made protected disclosures, but the CEO, though acting on those complaints, did not himself do so by reason of Adam's protected disclosures. There are conflicting lines of authority in relation to this (see Chapter 7, paragraphs 7.163–7.190).

39. One set of authorities suggests that the decision to instigate disciplinary proceedings is then to be regarded as having been on the grounds of a protected disclosure. But that has the difficulty

---

[15] *Fecitt and others v NHS Manchester* [2011] EWCA Civ 1190, [2012] ICR 372.

that, on the face of section 47B ERA, since it was Carol's decision made in the course of her employment, it would be an act for which she would have a liability despite the fact she did not herself do so by reason of any protected disclosures. She would not be able to rely on the defence under section 47B(1E) ERA as there was no statement made by the CEO that instigating disciplinary proceedings did not contravene the ERA.

40. But the better view, we suggest, is to distinguish the act by the CEO of encouraging the instigation of disciplinary proceedings from the decision (by Carol) to do so, and to say that (on the basis that Carol was herself not materially influenced by the disclosures) only the CEO's act of encouragement was on the grounds of the protected disclosures. On that basis the instigation by Carol of the disciplinary proceedings would not be an act or deliberate failure to act by reason of the protected disclosures. It would instead be a detriment caused by the CEO's act of encouraging Carol to instigate the disciplinary procedure, for which the CEO and Megaphone, but not Carol, might be liable.

(6) Employer's statutory defence

41. Megaphones might seek to rely upon the statutory defence in section 47B(1D) ERA that it took all reasonable steps to prevent the workers through whom it would be vicariously liable from doing the acts of victimization. That might come about, for example, by way of seeking to answer the claims arising from Belinda's conduct. Megaphones might seek to rely on its whistleblowing policy in support of the argument. But by itself that is unlikely to be sufficient. It would be necessary also to consider, for example, what steps were taken by way of training in relation to the policy. In addition, consideration would be needed of whether Adam was given the option of his concerns remaining confidential and whether confidentiality was maintained in relation to them, and, if they were brought to Belinda's attention, what steps were taken to emphasize to her the obligation not to subject Adam to a detriment by reason of the disclosures.

(7) Dismissal

42. Clearly, in relation to the (constructive) dismissal, Adam will be claiming that the reason or principal reason for dismissal was that he had made protected disclosures. Section 103A provides that a dismissal in such circumstances is automatically unfair. It is important to recognize that before getting to PIDA questions, Adam must prove that he has been constructively dismissed on the normal tests. That is subject to the caveat that if the employer subjected Adam to a detriment by reason of a protected disclosure, that of itself may lead to the conclusion that it was in breach of the implied term not without reasonable cause or excuse to act in a manner calculated or likely to destroy or seriously damage trust and confidence.[16] However, for these purposes it would be necessary to establish that the detrimental acts of Belinda, Carol, or the CEO are to be attributed to the employer without relying on the provisions in section 47B(1A) ERA (see Chapter 8, paragraphs 8.83–8.86).

43. In relation to the reason for dismissal, the focus is on the reason for the conduct in response to which Adam resigned. It is not sufficient for these purposes that protected disclosures were a significant influence. Instead it is necessary that they were the reason or principal reason. Further, since Adam had less than two years' service, the burden on proof would be on him to establish the reason for dismissal (see Chapter 9, paragraphs 9.46–9.48).

(8) What remedy can Adam claim?

44. Section 49 ERA provides that if a detriment claim is upheld the tribunal shall make a declaration to that effect and may make an award of compensation to be paid by the employer to the complainant in respect of the act or failure to act to which the complaint relates. In making an award of compensation the tribunal must have regard to the infringement to which the complaint relates and any loss caused by the breach.

45. Section 124(1A) provides that the limit on compensatory awards does not apply to a dismissal that is automatically unfair under section 103A.

---

[16] See Chapter 12, para 12.63.

46. Interim relief is available where the complaint is of unfair dismissal contrary to section 103A. But reinstatement or reengagement is unlikely to be of interest to Adam on the facts of this case.

Detriment under ERA, section 49(2)

47. Adam can claim in respect of:
    (a) financial loss (loss of overtime, loss consequent on the withdrawal of the reference);
    (b) injury to feelings, and/or
    (c) injury to health.
48. As discussed at paragraphs 39 and 40 above,[17] an issue may arise if a decision to dismiss (or, it would follow, decision to act in such a way as to give the employee grounds to treat him/herself as constructively dismissed) can be said to have been tainted because it was reached on the basis of information or an instruction from another person who supplied the information or gave the instruction then and who was acting by reason of protected disclosures. The decision in *Royal Mail Group Ltd v Jhuti* [2016] ICR 1043 (EAT) indicates that the employee has a claim under section 103A. Whether there can be a claim in detriment for the acts of the person who supplied the information or gave the instruction depends on whether that can properly be framed as entailing a detriment other than dismissal (section 48(2) ERA). This issue would need to be borne in mind in relation to claims against the CEO, Carol, and indeed Megaphones in relation to Adam's claim of (constructive) dismissal.
49. In relation to injury to feelings, the *Vento* guidelines are to be applied (see *Virgo Fidelis v Boyle* [2004] IRLR 268, EAT[18]). The award is compensatory not punitive, and as such it would be necessary to focus on detail of the impact on Adam. Although victimization for making a protected disclosure is serious, it is not inherently more serious than other prohibited discrimination, eg on grounds of race or sex (*Commissioner of Police of the Metropolis v Shaw* [2012] IRLR 291).
50. While not likely to be open to Adam, aggravated damages are potentially available depending on the particular circumstances including the way in which the complaint was handled. In *Boyle*, the EAT referred to a press release issued by the employer *after* the merits hearing in the tribunal as one of the factors in support of an award of £10,000 for aggravated damages, in addition to an award for injury to feelings of £25,000. The conduct of the employer was described as a 'travesty' and there was no apology or mitigation. There was no separate head of psychiatric damage claimed in that case. See the guidance in *Commissioner of Police of the Metropolis v Shaw*, suggesting that aggravated damages should be treated as a distinct subheading within injury to feelings, albeit that they may lift the total award out of the usual *Vento* range.
51. Exemplary damages are potentially available on normal principles, ie oppressive, arbitrary, or unconstitutional action by the servants of the government or where the respondent's conduct is calculated to make a profit for him/herself (see *Rookes v Barnard* [1964] AC 1129) but these do not apply here.

Dismissal

52. Adam can claim in respect of a basic award, and an uncapped compensatory award. While no injury to feelings can be claimed in relation to dismissal (*Dunnachie v Hull City Council* [2004] UKHL 36, [2005] 1 AC 226), in a constructive dismissal case injury to feelings may be awarded right up to the employee's resignation (rather than up to the point at which the employer's conduct becomes so serious that it amounts to a repudiatory breach). (See *Melia v Magna Kansei Ltd* [2006] IRLR 117.)
53. If the employer can establish that Adam made the disclosures otherwise than in good faith then compensation for detriment and dismissal can be reduced by up to 25 per cent. See Chapter 10, paragraphs 10.108–10.109.

(9) What is the relevance of Adam swearing at his manager?

54. The whistleblowing provisions of the ERA protect against detriment/dismissal on the ground of a protected disclosure rather than all conduct that is connected with the disclosure (see in a slightly different context *Bolton School v Evans*).

---

[17] See also Chapter 9 (para 9.27) and Chapter 7 (paras 7.163–7.190).
[18] Updated by *Da Bell v NSPCC* [2010] IRLR 19 (EAT).

55. The company may try to argue that, even if Adam succeeds with his claim for constructive dismissal, he would have been dismissed in any event and that any compensation should be reduced accordingly. Alternatively, the swearing might go to contributory fault (see *Perkin v St George's Healthcare NHS Trust* [2005] IRLR 934; *Friend v CAA* (cited in [1998] IRLR 253); *Aryeetey v Tuntum Housing Association* (UKEAT 0324/08, 8 April 2009).

56. Adam is likely to argue that a fair disciplinary hearing of the swearing charge would have taken into account all the circumstances, including the stress he had been under as a whistleblower and the provocation from his manager, and that a fair dismissal was unlikely to have resulted.

(10) Is Adam justified in posting the concerns on the internet and to his MP?

57. See discussion of the relevant disclosures at (1) above. There is a material difference between the posting on the internet and writing to his MP, as the latter is now a prescribed person. It may be argued that posting matters on the internet is relevant conduct in relation to compensation on the basis that it could have given rise to a fair dismissal: *Aryeetey v Tuntum Housing Association* (UKEAT 0324/08, 8 April 2009).

(11) Might Megaphones Ltd take any action against Adam?

58. Megaphones Ltd might be tempted to claim that the allegation regarding its financial accounting is defamatory, but unless Adam says that he will not seek to justify the same it is unlikely that Megaphones Ltd can gain an injunction. Alternatively, Megaphones Ltd might seek an injunction to restrain the misuse of confidential information but there is a public interest defence for Adam (see eg *Initial Services Ltd v Putterill* [1968] 1 QB 396; *A-G v Guardian Newspapers (No 2)* [1990] 1 AC 109). However, Megaphones might demand the return of all company documents, and, on the basis that the internet disclosure in relation to data protection indicates that Adam retained company documents, Megaphones might seek an Order for delivery up of its documents, the deletion of any soft copies, and details of any third parties to whom these were supplied.

APPENDIX 2

Appellate Whistleblowing Cases

Overview of ingredients of a claim

1. *Miklaszewicz v Stolt Offshore Ltd* [2002] IRLR 344 (Court of Session).
2. *London Borough of Harrow v Knight* [2003] IRLR 140 (EAT).
3. *Flintshire County Council v Sutton* (EAT/1082/02, 1 July 2003).
4. *Pinnington v Swansea City Council and another* [2005] ICR 685 (CA).
5. *Melia v Magna Kansei Ltd* [2005] ICR 874 (EAT); [2006] ICR 410 (CA).*Ltd*

Worker/section 43K ERA

6. *Croke v Hydro Aluminium Worcester Ltd* [2007] ICR 1303 (EAT).
7. *Hinds v Keppel Seghers UK Ltd* [2014] IRLR 754, [2014] ICR 1105 (EAT).
8. *Clyde & Co LLP v Bates van Winkelhof* [2014] UKSC 32, [2014] 1 WLR 2047 (SC).
9. *Sharpe v Bishop of Worcester* [2015] IRLR 663, [2015] ICR 1241 (CA).
10. *Day v Lewisham and Greenwich NHS Trust and Health Education England* [2016] IRLR 415 (EAT).
11. *McTigue v University Hospital Bristol Foundation Trust* [2016] IRLR 742 (EAT).
12. *Gilham v Ministry of Justice* (UKEAT 0087/16/LA, 31 October 2016).

Police

13. *Lake v British Transport Police* [2007] ICR 1293 (CA).

Judicial immunity

14. *Engel v The Joint Committee for Parking & Traffic Regulation Outside London (PATROL)* [2013] ICR 1086.
15. *P v Commissioner of Police for the Metropolis* [2016] EWCA Civ 2, [2016] IRLR 301.

Qualifying disclosure

16. *Sim v Manchester Action on Street Health* (EAT0085/01, 6 December 2001).
17. *Parkins v Sodexho* [2002] IRLR 110 (EAT).
18. *Welsh Refugee Council v Brown* (EAT/0032/02, 22 March 2002).
19. *Fincham v HM Prison Service* (EAT/0925/01 and EAT/0991/01, 19 December 2002).
20. *Butcher v Salvage Association* (EAT/988/01, 21 January 2002; [2002] EWCA Civ 867).
21. *Darnton v University of Surrey* [2003] IRLR 133 (EAT).
22. *Everett Financial Management Ltd v Murrell* (EAT/552/02, EAT/553/02, and EAT/952/02, 24 February 2003).
23. *Douglas v Birmingham City Council and others* (EAT/018/02, 17 March 2003).
24. *De Haney v Brent Mind and Lang* (EAT/0054/03/DA, 10 April 2003).
25. *Sir Robert McAlpine Ltd v Telford* (EAT/0018/03, 13 May 2003).
26. *Odong v Chubb Security Personnel* (EAT/0819/02, 13 May 2003).
27. *Kraus v Penna plc* [2004] IRLR 260 (EAT).
28. *Felter v Cliveden Petroleum Company* (EAT/0533/05, 9 March 2006).
29. *Boulding v Land Securities Trillium (Media Services) Ltd* (EAT/0023/06, 3 May 2006).
30. *Bolton School v Evans* [2006] IRLR 500 (EAT), [2007] ICR 641 (CA).
31. *Babula v Waltham Forest College* [2007] ICR 1045 (CA).
32. *Network Rail Infrastructure Ltd v Glencross* (UKEAT/0094/08, 16 May 2008).
33. *Muchesa v Central and Cecil Housing Care Support* (EAT/0443/07, 22 August 2008).
34. *Hibbins v Hesters Way Neighbourhood Project* [2009] IRLR 198 (EAT).
35. *Cavendish Munro Professional Risk Management Ltd v Geduld* [2010] ICR 325 (EAT).
36. *Goode v Marks and Spencer plc* (EAT/0442/09, 15 April 2010).

37. *BP plc v Elstone and Petrotechnics Ltd* [2010] ICR 879 (EAT).
38. *Easwaran v St George's University of London* (EAT/0167/10, 24 June 2010), [2011] EWCA Civ 181.
39. *Parker v Northumbrian Water* [2011] IRLR 652 (EAT).
40. *Ross v Eddie Stobart* (UKEAT/0085/10, 16 May 2011).
41. *Smith v London Metropolitan University* (EAT/0364/10, 21 July 2011).
42. *Freeman v Ultra Green Group Ltd* (UKEAT/0239/11, 9 August 2011).
43. *Royal Cornwall Hospitals NHS Trust v Watkinson* (UKEAT/0378/10, 17 August 2011).
44. *Korashi v Abertawe Bro Morgannwg University Local Health Board* [2012] IRLR 4 (EAT).
45. *Greenly v Future Network Solutions Ltd* (UKEAT/0359/13/JOJ, 19 December 2013).
46. *Millbank Financial Services Ltd v Crawford* [2014] IRLR 18 (EAT).
47. *Gebremariam v Ethiopian Airlines Enterprise t/a Ethiopian Airlines* [2014] IRLR 354 (EAT).
48. *Norbrook Laboratories (GB) Ltd v Shaw* [2014] ICR 540 (EAT).
49. *Northumberland Tyne & Wear NHS Foundation Trust v Geoghegan* (UKEAT/0048/13/BA, 29 January 2014), [2014] EWCA Civ 1094 (CA).
50. *Western Union Payment Services UK Ltd v Anastasiou* (UKEAT/0135/13/LA, 21 February 2014; UKEAT/0135/13/LA, 12 May 2014).
51. *Ibekwe v Sussex Partnership NHS Foundation Trust* (UKEAT/0072/14, 20 November 2014).
52. *Soh v Imperial College of Science, Technology and Medicine* (UKEAT/0350/14/DM, 3 September 2015).
53. *Kilraine v London Borough of Wandsworth* [2016] IRLR 422 (EAT).
54. *Wharton v Leeds City Council* (UKEAT/0409/14/DM, 6 October 2015).

Public interest

55. *Chesterton Global Ltd & Anor v Nurmohamed* [2015] IRLR 614 (EAT).
56. *Underwood v Wincanton plc* (UKEAT/0163/15/RN, 27 August 2015).
57. *Morgan v Royal Mencap Society* [2016] IRLR 428 (EAT).

Good faith

58. *Phipps v Bradford Hospitals NHS Trust* (EAT/531/02, 30 April 2003).
59. *Morrison v Hesley Lifecare Services Ltd* (EAT/0262/03 and EAT/0534/03, 19 March 2004).
60. *Street v Derbyshire Unemployed Workers' Centre* [2005] ICR 97 (CA).
61. *Lucas v Chichester Diocesan Housing Association Ltd* (UKEAT/0713/04/DA, 7 February 2005).
62. *Milne v The Link Asset and Security Company Ltd* (EAT/0867/04, 26 September 2005).
63. *Bachnak v Emerging Markets Partnership (Europe) Ltd* (EAT/0288/05, 27 January 2006).
64. *Roberts v Valley Rose* (UKEAT/0394/06, 31 May 2007).
65. *Clark v Clark Construction Initiatives Ltd* [2008] ICR 635, [2008] IRLR 364 (EAT).
66. *Aryeetey v Tuntum Housing Association* (UKEAT/0070/07, 12 October 2007, UKEAT 0324/08, 8 April 2009) and [2009] EWCA Civ 974, 1374, [2010] EWCA Civ 1088 (CA).
67. *Ezsias v North Glamorgan NHS Trust* [2007] ICR 1126 (CA), [2011] IRLR 550 (EAT).
68. *Mears v Medway Primary Care Trust* (UKEAT/0065/10, 7 December 2010), [2011] EWCA Civ 897.
69. *Korashi v Abertawe Bro Morgannwg University Local Health Board* [2012] IRLR 4 (EAT).
70. *Bleasdale v Healthcare Locums plc & Ors* (UKEAT/0324/13/LA, 15 April 2014).
71. *Nese v Airbus Operations Ltd* (UKEAT/0477/13/DA, 27 January 2015).
72. *Soh v Imperial College of Science, Technology and Medicine* (UKEAT/0350/14/DM, 3 September 2015).

Section 43C

73. *Douglas v Birmingham City Council and others* (EAT/018/02, 17 March 2003).
74. *Premier Mortgage Connections Ltd v Miller* (EAT/0113/07, 2 November 2007).

Section 43D

75. *Audere Medical Services Ltd v Sanderson* (UKEAT/0409/12/RN, 29 May 2013).
76. *Schaathun v Executive & Business Aviation Support Ltd* (UKEAT/0226/12/LA, 30 June 2015).

Sections 43F–H: reasonable belief that substantially true

77. *Muchesa v Central and Cecil Housing Care Support* (EAT/0443/07, 22 August 2008).

78. *Korashi v Abertawe Bro Morgannwg University Local Health Board* [2012] IRLR 4 (EAT).
79. *Barton v Royal Borough of Greenwich* (UKEAT/0041/14/DXA, 1 May 2015).
80. *Schaathun v Executive & Business Aviation Support Ltd* (UKEAT/0226/12/LA, 30 June 2015).

Section 43G: substantially the same internal disclosure

81. *ALM Medical Services Ltd v Bladon* (EAT/709/00 and EAT/967/00, 19 January 2001), [2002] ICR 1444 (CA).
82. *Goode v Marks and Spencer plc* (EAT/0442/09, 15 April 2010).
83. *Korashi v Abertawe Bro Morgannwg University Local Health Board* [2012] IRLR 4 (EAT).

Detriment

84. *Pinnington v The City and County of Swansea and another* [2005] ICR 685 (CA).
85. *Woodward v Abbey National plc (No. 1)* [2006] EWCA Civ 822, [2006] ICR 1436 (CA).
86. *Onyango v Adrian Berkeley t/a Berkeley Solicitors* [2013] IRLR 338 (EAT).
87. *Abertawe Bro Morgannwg University Health Board v Ferguson* [2013] ICR 1108 (EAT).

Vicarious liability

88. *Fecitt and others v NHS Manchester* [2011] ICR 476 (EAT), [2012] ICR 372 (CA).
89. *Panayiotou v Chief Constable of Hampshire Police* [2014] IRLR 500 (EAT).
90. *Shinwari v Vue Entertainment Ltd* (UKEAT/0394/14/BA, 12 March 2015).

Reason why question

91. *Brothers of Charity Services Merseyside v Eleady Cole* (EAT/0661/00, 24 January 2002).
92. *Aspinall v MSI Mech Forge Ltd* (EAT/ 891/01, 25 July 2002).
93. *Hossack v Kettering BC* (EAT/ 1113/01, 29 November 2002).
94. *London Borough of Harrow v Knight* [2003] IRLR 140 (EAT).
95. *Mama East African Women's Group v Dobson* (EAT/0219/05 and EAT/0220/05, 23 June 2005).
96. *Bolton School v Evans* [2006] IRLR 500 (EAT); [2007] ICR 641 (CA).
97. *Network Rail Infrastructure Ltd v Glencross* (UKEAT/0094/08, 16 May 2008).
98. *Redcar and Cleveland BC v Scanlon* (UKEAT/0369/06, 22 May 2007; UKEAT/0088/08, 20 May 2008).
99. *El-Megrisi v Azad University* (EAT/0448/08, 5 May 2009).
100. *Ezsias v North Glamorgan NHS Trust* [2007] ICR 1126 (CA), [2011] IRLR 550 (EAT).
101. *Fecitt and others v NHS Manchester* [2011] ICR 476 (EAT), [2012] ICR 372 (CA).
102. *Vivian v Bournemouth BC* (UKEAT/0254/10, 6 May 2011).
103. *Price v Surrey County Council and Governing Body of Wood Street School* (EAT/0450/10, 27 October 2011).
104. *Dunster v First Transpennine Express Ltd* (UKEAT/0570/10/ZT, 19 August 2011).
105. *Martin v Devonshires Solicitors* [2011] ICR 352 (EAT).
106. *Panayiotou v Chief Constable of Hampshire Police* [2014] IRLR 500 (EAT).
107. *Barclays Bank plc v Mitchell* (UKEAT/0279/13/JOJ, 11 February 2014).
108. *Westminster Drug Project v O'Sullivan* (UKEAT/0235/13/BA, 11 March 2014).
109. *Shinwari v Vue Entertainment Ltd* (UKEAT/0394/14/BA, 12 March 2015).
110. *Barton v Royal Borough of Greenwich* (UKEAT/0041/14/DXA, 1 May 2015).
111. *Salisbury NHS Foundation Trust v Wyeth* (UKEAT/0061/15/JOJ, 12 June 2015).
112. *Croydon Health Services NHS Trust v Beatt* (UKEAT 0136/15/JOJ, 19 January 2016).
113. *London Borough of Wandsworth v CRW* (UKEAT/0322/15/LA, 7 March 2016).

Time limits

114. *Meteorological Office v Edgar* [2002] ICR 149 (EAT).
115. *Arthur v London Eastern Railway Ltd (trading as One Stansted Express)* [2007] ICR 193 (CA).
116. *Tait v Redcar and Cleveland BC* (UKEAT/0096/08, 2 April 2008).
117. *Unilever UK plc v Hickinson and Sodexo Ltd* (EAT/0192/09, 24 June 2009).
118. *Vivian v Bournemouth BC* (EAT/0254/10, 6 May 2011).

119. *St. John Ambulance v Mulvie* (UKEAT/0129/11, 1 July 2011).
120. *Flynn v Warrior Square Recoveries Ltd* (UKEAT/0154/12/KN, 3 October 2012), [2014] EWCA Civ 68.
121. *Northumberland Tyne & Wear NHS Foundation Trust v Geoghegan* (UKEAT/0048/13/BA, 29 January 2014), [2014] EWCA Civ 1094 (CA).
122. *Theatre Peckham v Browne* (UKEAT/0154/13/RN, 24 June 2014).
123. *Canavan v Governing Body of St Edmund Campion Catholic School* (UKEAT/0187/13, 13 February 2015).
124. *McKinney v London Borough of Newham* [2015] ICR 495 (EAT).

Burden of proof

125. *London Borough of Harrow v Knight* [2003] IRLR 140 (EAT).
126. *Bachnak v Emerging Markets Partnership (Europe) Ltd* (EAT/0288/05, 27 January 2006).
127. *Kuzel v Roche Products Ltd* [2008] ICR 799 (CA).
128. *Redcar and Cleveland BC v Scanlon* (UKEAT/0369/06, 22 May 2007; UKEAT/0088/08, 20 May 2008).
129. *Whitelock & Storr and others v Khan* (EAT/0017/10/RN, 26 October 2010).
130. *Nunn v Royal Mail Group Ltd* [2011] ICR 162 (EAT), [2011] EWCA Civ 244.[1]
131. *Blitz v Vectone Group Holdings Ltd* (UKEAT/0253/10/DM, 29 November 2011).
132. *Ross v Eddie Stobart Ltd* (UKEAT/0068/13/RN, 28 June 2013).
133. *Blackbay Ventures Ltd (t/a Chemistree) v Gahir* [2014] IRLR 416, [2014] ICR 747 (EAT).
134. *Ibekwe v Sussex Partnership NHS Foundation Trust* (UKEAT/0072/14, 20 November 2014).
135. *Phoenix House Ltd v Stockman* [2016] IRLR 848 (EAT).

Jurisdiction

136. *Clyde & Co LLP v Bates van Winkelhof* [2014] UKSC 32, [2014] 1 WLR 2047 (SC).
137. *Fuller v United Healthcare Services Inc & Anor* (UKEAT/0464/13/BA, 4 September 2014).
138. *Smania v Standard Chartered Bank* [2015] IRLR 271 (EAT).
139. *Strickland v Kier Ltd & Ors* (UKEAT/0062/15/DM, 23 September 2015).

Case management

140. *ALM Medical Services Ltd v Bladon* (EAT/709/00 and EAT/967/00, 19 January 2001); [2002] ICR 1444 (CA).
141. *Secretary of State for Work and Pensions (Jobcentre Plus) v Constable* (UKEAT/0156/10, 30 June 2010).
142. *Price v Surrey County Council and Governing Body of Wood Street School* (EAT/0450/10, 27 October 2011).
143. *Blackbay Ventures Ltd (t/a Chemistree) v Gahir* [2014] IRLR 416, [2014] ICR 747 (EAT).

Striking out/determination prior to completion of evidence

144. *Boulding v Land Securities Trillium (Media Services) Ltd* (EAT/0023/06, 3 May 2006).
145. *Ezsias v North Glamorgan NHS Trust* [2007] ICR 1126 (CA), [2011] IRLR (EAT).
146. *Hudson v Oxford University* (UKEAT/0488/05, 26 July 2007).
147. *Sood v Christ the King School Governors* (UKEAT/0449/10, 20 July 2011).
148. *Pillay v Inc Research UK* (UKEAT/0182/11, 9 September 2011).
149. *Namoale v Balfour Beatty Engineering Services Ltd* (UKEAT/0126/12/DM, 29 November 2012).
150. *Short v Birmingham City Council & Ors* (UKEAT/0038/13/DM, 5 July 2013).
151. *Garcia v Market Probe Europe Ltd* (UKEAT/0024/13/BA, 5 November 2013).
152. *Greenly v Future Network Solutions Ltd* (UKEAT/0359/13/JOJ, 19 December 2013).
153. *Millbank Financial Services Ltd v Crawford* [2014] IRLR 18 (EAT).
154. *Robinson v Royal Surrey County Hospital NHS Foundation Trust & Ors* (UKEAT/0311/14/MC, 30 July 2015).
155. *Underwood v Wincanton plc* (UKEAT/0163/15/RN, 27 August 2015).
156. *Morgan v Royal Mencap Society* [2016] IRLR 428 (EAT).

---

[1] Refusing permission to appeal (Smith LJ).

Amendment

157. *Evershed v New Star Asset Management* [2010] EWCA Civ 870.
158. *Watkins v BBC* (UKEAT/0189/12/LA, 27 June 2012).
159. *Robinson v Royal Surrey County Hospital NHS Foundation Trust & Ors* (UKEAT/0311/14/MC, 30 July 2015).
160. *Makauskiene v Rentokil Initial Facilities Services (UK) Ltd* (UKEAT/0503/13/RN, 29 April 2014).

Interim relief

161. *Parkins v Sodexho* [2002] IRLR 110 (EAT).
162. *Dandpat v University of Bath* (UKEAT/0408/09, 10 November 2009), [2010] EWCA Civ 305.
163. *Raja v Secretary of State for Justice* (EAT/0364/09, 15 February 2010).
164. *Ministry of Justice v Sarfraz* [2011] IRLR 562 (EAT).
165. *Turullols v Revenue and Customs Commissioners* [2014] UKFTT 622 (First-tier Tribunal (Tax Chamber)).
166. *Parsons v Airplus International Ltd* (UKEAT/0023/16/JOJ, 4 March 2016).

Compensation

167. *Virgo Fidelis Senior School v Boyle* [2004] IRLR 268 (EAT).
168. *Melia v Magna Kansei Ltd* [2005] ICR 874 (EAT), [2006] ICR 410 (CA).
169. *Mama East African Women's Group v Dobson* (EAT/0219/05 and EAT/0220/05, 23 June 2005).
170. *Williams v North Tyneside Council* (UKEAT/0415/05, 31 January 2006).
171. *Aryeetey v Tuntum Housing Association* (UKEAT/0070/07, 12 October 2007, UKEAT 0324/08, 8 April 2009); and [2009] EWCA Civ 974, 1374, [2010] EWCA Civ 1088 (CA).
172. *AE Davidson-Hogg v Davis Gregory Solicitors, Mr T Howarth* (UKEAT/0512/09, 15 November 2010).
173. *Commissioner of Police of the Metropolis v Shaw* [2012] IRLR 291 (EAT).
174. *Local Government Yorkshire & Humber v Shah* (UKEAT/0587/11/ZT, 19 June 2012).
175. *Audere Medical Services Ltd v Sanderson* (UKEAT/0409/12/RN, 29 May 2013).
176. *Small v The Shrewsbury & Telford Hospitals NHS Trust* (UKEAT/0300/14/LA, 19 May 2015).
177. *Roberts v Wilsons Solicitors LLP and others* [2016] ICR 659 (EAT).
178. *Hamer v Kaltz Ltd* (UKEAT/0198/11/RN, 24 February 2012; UKEAT/0502/13/BA, 4 August 2014).

Costs

179. *Morrison v Hesley Lifecare Services Ltd* (EAT/0262/03 and EAT/0534/03, 19 March 2004).
180. *Milne v The Link Asset and Security Company Ltd* (EAT/0867/04, 26 September 2005).
181. *Clark v Clark Construction Initiatives Ltd* [2008] ICR 635, [2008] IRLR 364 (CA).
182. *HCA International Ltd v May-Bheemul* (UKEAT/0477/10/ZT, 6 May 2009).

Purposive approach

183. *ALM Medical Services Ltd v Bladon* (UKEAT/709/00, EAT/967/00, 19 January 2001) (EAT), [2002] ICR 1444 (CA).
184. *Virgo Fidelis Senior School v Boyle* [2004] IRLR 268 (EAT).
185. *El-Hoshi v Pizza Express Restaurants Ltd* (EAT/0857/03, 23 March 2004).
186. *Boulding v Land Securities* (EAT/0023, 3 May 2006).
187. *Croke v Hydro Aluminium Worcester Ltd* [2007] ICR 1303 (EAT).
188. *Ezsias v North Glamorgan NHS Trust* [2007] ICR 1126 (CA), [2011] IRLR 550 (EAT).
189. *Babula v Waltham Forest College* [2007] ICR 1045 (CA).
190. *BP plc v Elstone and Petrotechnics Ltd* [2010] ICR 879 (EAT).
191. *Audere Medical Services Ltd v Sanderson* (UKEAT/0409/12/RN, 29 May 2013).

Who is responsible? The 'Iago' conundrum

192. *The Co-operative Group Ltd v Baddeley* (UKEAT/0415/12/JOJ, 15 November 2013), [2014] EWCA Civ 658.

193. *Ahmed v City of Bradford Metropolitan District Council* (UKEAT/0145/14/KN, 27 October 2014).
194. *Royal Mail Group Ltd v Jhuti* [2016] IRLR 854 (EAT).
195. *Dr Brito-Babapulle v Isle of Wight NHS Trust* (UKEAT/0090/16/DM, 10 June 2016).

Disclosure of documents

196. *Gray v Merrill Lynch, Pierce, Fenner & Smith Ltd* (UKEAT/0058/16/DM, 16 March 2016).

Whistleblowing policies

197. *Audere Medical Services Ltd v Sanderson* (UKEAT/0409/12/RN, 29 May 2013).
198. *Frenkel Topping Ltd v King* (UKEAT/0106/15/LA, 21 July 2015).

Contractual terms rendered void

199. *Hamer v Katlz Ltd* (UKEAT/0198/11/RN, 24 February 2012; UKEAT/0502/13/BA, 4 August 2014).

Case Summaries

Overview of ingredients of a claim

1. Miklaszewicz v Stolt Offshore Ltd

[2001] IRLR 656 (EAT), [2002] IRLR 344 (Court of Session)

Key issue: coverage of pre-Act disclosures if dismissal post-PIDA.

Case summary: Protected disclosure in 1993, dismissal in 1999 after enactment of PIDA: did the ET have jurisdiction to entertain the s 103A complaint?

ET: no jurisdiction.

EAT (Lord Johnston): reversed decision. The dismissal was after the legislation came into force and the tribunal therefore had jurisdiction even though the protected disclosure was prior to the Act coming into force.

Court of Session, Inner House (Extra Division): dismissed the appeal from the Employment Appeal Tribunal.

Sections considered: ERA, ss 43A, 47B, 103A.

Cited by: *Pinnington v (1) City and County of Swansea and (2) Governing Body of Ysgol Crug Glas School* [2005] ICR 685; *BP plc v Elstone* [2010] ICR 879 (EAT); *Canavan v Governing Body of St Edmund Campion Catholic School* (UKEAT/0187/13, 13 February 2015).

2. London Borough of Harrow v Knight

[2003] IRLR 140 (EAT)

Key issue: meaning of 'on the ground that' and the burden of proof in relation to that issue.

Case summary: Mr Knight was a technical officer employed by the respondent. In February 1999 he raised concerns under the respondent's whistleblowing procedure that another officer might be complicit in breaches of health regulations by a business. The respondent appointed persons to investigate the allegations. By November 1999 Knight had become stressed and suffered a 'nervous breakdown'. The respondents failed to respond to any correspondence from him.

ET: held that the exacerbation of Knight's medical condition was 'related to the disclosure'. They accepted that he had suffered distress, especially when his letters were ignored both by the chief executive and the investigators. He had not gained from this disclosure; rather he had suffered a detriment which was 'directly related to the protected disclosure that he had made'. The tribunal concluded that the complaint under ERA, s 47B succeeded.

EAT (Mr Recorder Underhill QC): held that in order for liability in this case to be established, the tribunal has to find:

(1) a claimant has made a protected disclosure (or disclosures);
(2) that he had suffered some identifiable detriment (or detriments);

(3) that the council had 'done' an act or deliberate failure to act (for short, an 'act or omission') by which he had been 'subjected to' that detriment; and

(4) that this act or omission had been done by the council 'on the ground that' the claimant had made the protected disclosure identified at (1).

The act or omission identifiable from the tribunal's reasons was the respondent's failure to answer Knight's letters. The EAT accepted that the tribunal was entitled to find that the council subjected the claimant to that detriment because, following *Burton v de Vere Hotels Ltd*, [1997] ICR 1 at 10A–B, per Smith J, an employer subjects an employee to a detriment if s/he causes or allows the detriment to occur in circumstances where s/he can control whether or not it happens. [Note: this is no longer good law: see *Macdonald v Advocate General for Scotland and Pearce v Governing Body of Mayfield Secondary School* [2003] IRLR 512 (HL).] However, the tribunal erred in its approach to whether the act or omission was on the ground of the protected disclosure. As to this (at para 16):

> It is thus necessary in a claim under s 47B to show that the fact that the protected disclosure had been made caused or influenced the employer to act (or not act) in the way complained of: merely to show that 'but for' the disclosure the act or omission would not have occurred is not enough (see *Khan*). In our view, the phrase 'related to' imports a different and much looser test than that required by the statute: it merely connotes some connection (not even necessarily causative) between the act done and the disclosure.

Recorder Underhill also expressed the view that the effect of ERA, s 48(2) regarding the burden of proof for detriment was that if the employer failed to establish the reason, it did not necessarily follow that the reason was deemed to be a protected disclosure, but rather that the tribunal might have regard to this in drawing an inference (but need not do so).

As the ET had failed to consider on what ground the respondent had acted or failed to act the case had to be remitted.

Result: remitted for full hearing.

Detriment: Knight asserted three: (1) the loss of the opportunity to remain in the Department because he had failed to obtain the necessary professional qualification; (2) when the Council had wrongly disclosed confidential information to a third party with whom he was in litigation; (3) his nervous breakdown. The ET only found (3).

Sections considered: ERA, s 47B(1).

Damages awarded: remitted.

Cited by: *Theatre Peckham v Browne* (UKEAT/0154/13/RN, 24 June 2014); *Ibekwe v Sussex Partnership NHS Foundation Trust* (UKEAT/0072/14, 20 November 2014); *Blackbay Ventures Ltd (t/a Chemistree) v Gahir* [2014] IRLR 416 (EAT); *Barclays Bank plc v Mitchell* (UKEAT/0279/13/JOJ, 11 February 2014); *Flynn v Warrior Square Recoveries Ltd* (UKEAT/0154/12/KN, 3 October 2012); *Vivian v Bournemouth BC* (UKEAT/0254/10, 6 May 2011); *Fecitt and others v NHS Manchester* [2011] ICR 476 (EAT), [2012] ICR 372 (CA); *Unilever UK plc v Hickinson and Sodexo Ltd* (EAT/0192/09, 24 June 2009); *El-Megrisi v Azad University* (EAT/0448/08, 5 May 2009); *Kuzel v Roche Products Ltd* [2008] ICR 799 (CA); *Tait v Redcar and Cleveland BC* (UKEAT/0096/08, 2 April 2008); *Cumbria County Council v Carlisle-Morgan* [2007] IRLR 314 (EAT); *Bolton School v Evans* [2006] IRLR 500 (EAT), [2007] ICR 641 (CA); *Miller v 5m(UK)Ltd* (EAT/0359/05, 5 September 2005); *The Trustees of Mama East African Women's Group v Dobson* (EAT/0219/05 and EAT/0220/05, 23 June 2005); *Flintshire v Sutton* (EAT/1082/02, 1 July 2003); *Odong v Chubb Security Personnel* (EAT/0819/02, 13 May 2003); *South Central Trains Ltd v Rodway* [2005] ICR 75 (EAT); *De Haney v Brent Mind and Lang* (EAT/0054/03, 10 April 2003); *Everett Financial Management Ltd v Murrell* (EAT/552, EAT/553/02 and EAT/952/02, 24 February 2003).

3. Flintshire County Council v Sutton

EAT/1082/02/MAA, 1 July 2003

Key issue: detriment—failure to support by reason of protected disclosures.

Case summary: Mr Sutton was an audit manager with the respondent. He raised concerns regarding a payment purported to have been made on the grounds of 'redundancy' to someone who remained a member of the respondent's staff. The respondent investigated the matter. The investigation gave rise to a suggestion that serving officers were involved in falsifying documents. The County Secretary

(Mr Loveridge) instructed counsel to advise, but then instead of simply presenting his opinion to the full council, Mr Loveridge paraphrased it. Mr Sutton believed that Mr Loveridge passed off his own views as those of counsel. Sutton put his criticisms of Mr Loveridge to the respondent's *ultra vires* panel. He claimed he was then ostracized by Mr Loveridge. Other concerns arose and Sutton sent council members a memorandum accusing the respondent's Chief Offices of failing to comply with the council's financial regulations as to cooperation and providing records for internal audit. The memo was leaked to the press. Sutton then sent three further memos to council members raising concerns. In response to one of them, the deputy chief executive wrote to council members stating that it would be necessary to consider what action to take 'in response to the inappropriate and misleading memorandum' sent by Sutton. He also wrote to the Nolan Committee and Public Concern at Work referring to alleged failures by senior officers of the respondent to comply with financial regulations. He then went off work for an extended time suffering from stress. Ultimately, he resigned and claimed constructive dismissal. The trigger event was a refusal to reinstate sick pay, which was found to be an exception to the norm, but this was the culmination of a history of failure to provide support following his disclosures. The district auditor's involvement and report had only unreserved praise and no criticism of Sutton's pursuit of the various investigations and emphasized the very serious procrastination and delay which had taken place in dealing with his concerns.

ET: found the following were protected disclosures: (1) the four memoranda to the council were protected under ERA, s 43G (and there was no good reason to distinguish between the four memoranda making up the sequence); (2) a verbal challenge during a meeting was protected under s 43C; (3) disclosures made to the district auditor were protected under s 43F; and (4) the letters sent to outside bodies were protected under s 43G.

The tribunal further found that the respondent had acted or deliberately failed to act, subjecting Sutton to a detriment, in that it had failed to provide him with the support to which he was entitled. It further found that the failure to act had been on the ground of at least some of those disclosures (the four memoranda, the verbal challenge, and, to a lesser extent the disclosure to outside bodies except the district auditor).

The tribunal also rejected a limitation defence in relation to the s 47B claim, on the ground that the respondent's course of conduct in failing to give support to Sutton after the *ultra vires* panel meeting continued up to the termination of employment. Also there were a series of similar failures.

It also found that Sutton had been constructively unfairly dismissed under s 103A.

EAT (HHJ Peter Clark): upheld findings of detriment and s 103A dismissal by reason of protected disclosures to or about the council—ss 43C, 43F, 43G. As to s 43G, there was no need to show that precisely the same memoranda had been disclosed when making the earlier internal disclosure. The EAT commented of s 48(4)(b) (at para 46) that the 'near impenetrable language' was 'not ... the Parliamentary draftsman's finest hour'. However, nothing turned on this because on the facts the timing of the last detriment was such that the claim was in time.

In relation to constructive dismissal, there was an issue between the parties (para 28) as to whether a failure of the respondent to discharge the burden of showing the reason for dismissal meant that it had no reason or that it had not disproved an inadmissible reason. The EAT did not address this because the tribunal had concluded that the reason for the respondent's conduct which amounted to a repudiatory breach of the implied trust and confidence term was its 'perception of the Applicant as a problem because he had made the relevant protected disclosures' and those protected disclosures were therefore the reason or principal reason for the dismissal.

Result: appeal dismissed.

Detriment: serious procrastination and delay; failing to keep Sutton informed of decisions. Employment tribunal found that 'he did not receive the support from the Respondent to which he was entitled either in health or in sickness'.

Sections considered: ERA, ss 43A, 43B, 43C, 43F, 43G, 47B, 48(1A), 48(4)(b), 95(1)(c), 103A.

Damages awarded: remedies hearing had not occurred before appeal.

4. Pinnington v (1) City and County of Swansea and (2) Governing Body of Ysgol Crug Glas School

[2005] ICR 685 (CA)

Key issue: Was there a deliberate failure to act: ERA, s 47B.

Case summary: Mrs Pinnington was a nurse at a special needs school. She alleged that a policy of non-resuscitation of terminally ill children was being implemented at the school. An inquiry by the local council found no basis for the allegations. She was away from work on certificated sick leave from 17 September 1997 to 31 March 1998 suffering from stress and anxiety. She returned to work for a short period between 31 March and 29 April 1998 but then went off sick again and did not return prior to her dismissal. On 2 July 1998, after she had begun the second period away sick, she was suspended by the employer on the grounds of a breach of confidence about records relating to children at the school. Following a capability hearing (and thereafter an appeal) the claimant was dismissed with effect from 3 July 1999. PIDA only came into effect on the previous day, 2 July 1999. Later Mrs Pinnington was vindicated when the Secretary of State expressed concern over the resuscitation procedures operated at the school, by which time she was medically permanently unfit to return to work.

ET: held that the dismissal was fair and the principal reason for the dismissal of the claimant was capability due to illness, rather than the protected disclosures. No period earlier than 2 and 3 July 1999 was relevant because the protected disclosure provisions did not come into effect until 2 July 1999. Even in that short period she was prevented by ill health from going to work. It was not simply a question of her having been suspended and that suspension still being in force. She was unable to go to work because of her ill health.

EAT (HHJ McMullen QC): found that Pinnington had been fairly dismissed, despite the connection between the injury sustained by her and that injury being the reason for her dismissal. The tribunal had found as a fact that its reason was simply the lack of capability due to ill health of the claimant. The EAT commented (at para 91) that:

> An employer who responds to a complaint with a detailed and thorough investigation is, in our judgment less likely unfairly to dismiss the complainant for that reason.

The EAT, however, did remit an issue as to detriment regarding the failure to terminate Mrs Pinnington's suspension that continued for one day after PIDA was brought into force. This was the focus of the appeal to the Court of Appeal.

CA (Mummery, Clarke, and Wall LJJ): held that there was no issue to remit in relation to the two days that PIDA was in force during Mrs Pinnington's continuing suspension. For Mrs Pinnington it was argued that there was a 'deliberate failure to act' by not terminating the suspension, which had been in force since 2 July 1998. This was rejected by the Court of Appeal on the basis that whilst there was a failure to act, in the sense of the failure to terminate the suspension, this was not a deliberate failure. There was neither any evidence of a deliberate failure nor any basis upon which one could be inferred. Prior to PIDA coming into force it had already been decided that she would be dismissed on grounds of capability and it was unrealistic in those circumstances to expect that it should have considered, on 2 July, terminating the suspension.

Result: claim failed.

Detriment: two days' suspension; ostracism; ill health.

Sections considered: ERA, ss 47B, 43C, 43E, 43F, 43G, 98(1), 98(2), 98(3), 103A.

5. Melia v Magna Kansei Ltd

[2005] ICR 874 (EAT), [2006] ICR 410 (CA).

Key issues: (1) (in CA) what is the boundary between detriment and dismissal claims? (2) (in EAT) reduction of compensatory award for pre-dismissal conduct.

Case summary: Mr Melia worked as a senior designer for the respondent. He made a protected disclosure when he alleged that a colleague had assaulted him at work. Following the disclosure he was subjected to bullying. He was then suspended pending an investigation of an allegation against him of gross misconduct. In response, in November 2001, he resigned and claimed constructive dismissal. He claimed that his dismissal was by reason of his disclosure.

ET: concluded that he was subjected to a detriment on the ground that he made a protected disclosure and also that his (constructive) dismissal was automatically unfair under ERA, s 103A. However, prior to and unconnected with his dismissal, he had committed an act, namely the serious misuse of the respondent's computer system, which was a blameworthy act for which it was possible that he might have been fairly dismissed in any event.

The ET awarded £6,000 compensation for the detriment having concluded that it should only award injury to feelings up to June 2001, taking into account conduct prior to that which had been relied on by Melia as repudiatory of his contract. The repudiatory conduct which was directly tied to the dismissal was excluded from the ET's assessment.

EAT (Mr Justice Burton, President): increased the award in favour of the appellant by £600 to take into account two points on appeal (although the exact figure was agreed by the parties). First, whilst there was a deduction to Melia's award to take into account early payment of future benefits, there was no interest charged on payments in relation to past losses already sustained. Second, with regard to the exclusion of an award for legal fees incurred in drafting a compromise agreement. The EAT also upheld a reduction of 50 per cent in both the basic and compensatory award which had been made on the grounds that it was just and equitable to do so in the light of Melia's misconduct prior to dismissal. This reduction was made notwithstanding the tribunal's finding that the evidence of wrongdoing was:

> discovered after a concerted effort to find material which—as a result of the protected disclosure—could be used to ensure the termination of the claimant's employment, if possible without the need for any form of negotiated settlement.

The EAT (at para 55) noted the force of the submission that employers should not be permitted 'to scrabble around after a protected disclosure to try to find some misconduct which it could then use as a justification or excuse for dismissal, or at any rate by way of self-defence to claim against it'. Notwithstanding this, the EAT considered that there was no basis to interfere with the tribunal's decision on this issue. There was no appeal on this point.

CA (Chadwick and Wilson LJJ): Where a detriment occurs before the dismissal but forms part of the reason for the dismissal (ie because it is a repudiatory breach in response to which the employee resigns) compensation for that detriment could be awarded under ERA, s 47B(2). Section 47B(2) excludes detriment which can be compensated under the unfair dismissal provisions. If the detriment cannot be compensated under the unfair dismissal provisions, because it precedes dismissal and so is not a loss sustained in consequence of the dismissal, then there is nothing to take it out of s 47B. Within s 47B(2) the word 'dismissal' means the date on which dismissal occurs, and in relation to constructive dismissal this is the date of acceptance of the repudiatory breach.

Lady Justice Smith stated (at para 46):

> if an employee suffers a detriment due to making a protected disclosure and is then dismissed by the employer, the employee will be entitled to compensation for the detriment under s 47B of the Employment Rights Act up to the date of dismissal. That compensation may include compensation for personal injury and injury to feelings. He may also claim compensation for the consequences of unfair dismissal, including a compensatory award under s 123. But, say the respondents, the position is different with a case of constructive dismissal. There, the employee may only recover for the detriment he suffers until the time comes when the employer's conduct amounts to a repudiatory breach of the employment contract. If that were right, it would follow that an employee might suffer from gradually deteriorating and increasingly unlawful treatment by the employer, but if he does not resign immediately when the conduct has become bad enough to amount to a repudiatory breach, but waits some time before he accepts the breach, he will not be able to recover for the detriment he has suffered during that intervening period. I, for my part, cannot accept that Parliament should have intended so unjust a consequence.

Result: appeal dismissed—automatically unfair constructive dismissal.

Detriment: bullying.

Sections considered: ERA, ss 47B, 48, 49, 94, 95(1)I, 97(1), 103A, 123.

Damages awarded: £6,000 for the detriment; basic award of £840 and a compensatory award of £11,601.87 was made by the ET, and increased by the EAT by £600, of which £300 was for delay in Mr Melia receiving payment, which was permitted by the CA.

Cited by: *Romanowska v Aspirations Care Ltd* (UKEAT/0015/14/SM, 25 June 2014); *Vivian v Bournemouth BC* (UKEAT/0254/10, 6 May 2011); *Francois v Castle Rock Properties Ltd (t/a Electric Ballroom)* (UKEAT/0260/10, 5 April 2011); *Kuzel v Roche Products Ltd* [2007] ICR 945 (EAT); *Bolton School v Evans* [2006] IRLR 500 (EAT).

Worker

6. Croke v Hydro Aluminum Worcester Ltd

[2007] ICR 1303

Key issue: scope of extended definition of 'worker' under ERA, s 43K.

Case summary: Huxley (a recruitment consultancy) provided Mr Croke's CV to Hydro. Huxley then entered into a contract with Amerstar Ltd (of which Mr Croke was the sole director) for the provision by Amerstar Ltd of technical services by 'the consultant'. The consultant was named as Mr Croke. However, a term of the contract allowed Amerstar Ltd to substitute another consultant for Mr Croke subject to various criteria. Shortly thereafter Mr Croke attended an interview with Hydro and was offered work. Huxley later entered into a contract with Hydro for the supply of technical services. This contract again named the consultant as Mr Croke, and again contained a substitution clause. After Mr Croke fell out with certain Hydro staff, Hydro notified Huxley that it no longer wanted Mr Croke on site. Mr Croke was given notice of termination by both Hydro and Huxley. Mr Croke brought a claim under ERA, s 47B against Hydro.

ET: concluded that Mr Croke did not have protection due to his status. Mr Croke did in essence 'work for' Hydro, but he did not satisfy the definition of worker under ERA, s 230. On consideration of s 43K the ET concluded that although the section provided protection to an 'individual' whose services are provided to an end user by an agency, this was not the case here. Mr Croke's services as an individual were provided by Amerstar to Huxley, not to Hydro. Amerstar had no contract with Hydro. Mr Croke appealed on grounds including that s 43K was in fact satisfied both on the basis that he had been 'introduced' to Hydro by Huxley and also 'supplied'.

EAT (Mr Justice Wilkie): accepted that a purposive construction was appropriate, following the approach in the disability discrimination case of *MHC Consulting Services Ltd v Tansell* [2000] ICR 789 (CA) in which Mummery LJ (giving the judgment of the court) said:

> An interpretation which applies the section to the less common case, as well as to the standard case, is more consistent with the object of the section and of the Act of 1995 than an interpretation which does not do so. In a number of authorities the appellate courts have stressed the importance of giving the wide ranging provisions of the discrimination legislation a generous interpretation.
>
> . . .
>
> it is more probable that Parliament intended to confer than to deny protection from discrimination in cases where the supply of the employee was made by his company to the principal through an employment agency rather than direct to the principal.

In accepting this approach Wilkie LJ commented (at para 33) that:

> Whilst we agree with Mr Bowers that one has to be cautious before simply transplanting an approach appropriate to one set of legislative provisions to a wholly different set of legislative provisions we do not agree that this prevents our recognizing . . . that where statutory provisions are explicitly for the purpose of providing protection from discrimination or victimisation it is appropriate to construe those provisions so far as one properly can to provide protection rather than deny it.

As to the 'Introduction' argument: the ET failed to consider whether Huxley introduced Croke the individual to Hydro as a potential individual to do the work, albeit subsequently supplied through the corporate vehicle Amerstar. The EAT concluded that Huxley did 'introduce' Mr Croke to do that work.

As to the 'supplied' argument: adopting the purposive approach, the ET misdirected itself in concluding that Croke was not supplied to do that work by Huxley. The ET concluded that Croke 'worked for' Hydro by reference to the realities rather than the strict contractual position. 'Adopting that approach to the question, who 'supplied' Mr Croke to Hydro to do the work, the correct answer, in our judgment, is that it was Huxley'.

Result: appeal upheld.

Sections considered: ERA, ss 43K, 230.

Cited by: *Day v Lewisham and Greenwich NHS Trust and Health Education England* [2016] IRLR 415; *Hinds v Keppel Seghers UK Ltd* [2014] IRLR 754, [2014] ICR 1105; *BP plc v Elstone* [2010] ICR 589 (EAT); *Hibbins v Hesters Way Neighbourhood Project* [2009] ICR 319 (EAT).

7. Hinds v Keppel Seghers UK Ltd

[2014] IRLR 754, [2014] ICR 1105

Key issues: Was Hinds a worker?

Case summary: Hinds, a health and safety adviser, provided his services through 'Crown', his company of which he was the sole shareholder, a director, and an employee. The respondent, using 'First', a recruitment agency, sourced Hinds. The respondent interviewed and engaged him, but did not have a direct contractual relationship with Hinds who was therefore 'supplied' through two corporate entities—'Crown' and 'First'. Was he a worker?

ET: The ET noted the respondent's 'contractual requirement' that any individual contractor must provide services through intermediary companies. The contract also envisaged that the individual contractors (rather than any companies through which they supplied their services) would be subject to suitability checks. They found it was not in the parties' contemplation that any intermediary company could substitute anyone else for the individuals who had passed the suitability check. Therefore, whilst the terms on which 'First' engaged the claimant allowed for a substitute, the tribunal found the respondent did not envisage that happening. Further, the respondent set the specification for the work, and authorized changes to the claimant's hours (he could not dictate his hours). The claimant was obliged to report regularly to a manager within the respondent, and he was generally subject to the respondent's control, albeit he worked on his own and was not micromanaged.

EAT (Judge Eady QC): noted s 43K was 'explicitly introduced for the purpose of providing protection to those who have made protected disclosures'. Adopting a purposive construction, to provide protection rather than deny it, the EAT applied *Croke v Hydro Aluminium Worcester Ltd* para 33, noting the warning in *Redrow Homes (Yorkshire) Ltd v Wright* not to determine cases by reason of policy rather than the correct application of the law.

> 59. ... Section 43K is expressly stated to provide an extended meaning to terms such as 'worker'. ... It is plainly intended to extend this protection to a wider range of relationships than would be encompassed by the definitions of 'employee' or 'worker' with which employment lawyers are more familiar. Indeed, it is a provision that takes employment lawyers outside the comfort zone of the contractual approach normally required in determining employment status. The protection extends to relationships where there is no contract in existence between the parties (see Cox J in *Sharpe* at paragraph 237) and to cases where there might be no direct contract between the complainant and the user of her services but contracts between each of them and other parties, impacting upon (if not governing) their relationship. This might include a contract between the complainant and an employment agency where the complainant is engaged through her own service company (see *Croke*).
>
> 60. ... The focus [s 43K(1)(a)(i)] is on what happened in practice rather than on the contractual agreement.

Result: Hinds was found to be a s 43K(1)(a)(i) 'worker'. Note the case relied on *Sharpe* in the EAT, which was subsequently overturned by the Court of Appeal.

Sections considered: ERA, ss 43K(1), 43K(2), 230.

Cited by: *Day v Lewisham and Greenwich NHS Trust and Health Education England* (UKEAT/0250/15/RN, 9 March 2016), [2016] IRLR 415.

8. Clyde & Co LLP v Bates van Winkelhof

[2014] UKSC 32, [2014] 1 WLR 2047

Key issues: Can an LLP member be a worker?

Case summary: In November 2010, BvW reported to the LLP's money-laundering reporting officers that the managing partner of a Tanzanian law firm by which BvW was employed as joint venture between that firm and the LLP, had admitted paying bribes to secure work and to secure the outcome of cases. BvW claimed that these were 'protected disclosures'. She also claimed that she was subject to a number of detriments as a result, including suspending her, making allegations of misconduct against her, and ultimately expelling her from the LLP in January 2011. These claims were denied by the LLP.

ET: found that she was not a 'worker' (although she worked under a contract to do or perform personally work or services for the LLP), because she was 'in business in her own right receiving a share of the profits in relation to the work carried out'. However, the tribunal would have had jurisdiction to consider her claim even though she worked principally in Tanzania.

EAT (Judge Peter Clark): (1) Allowed BvW's appeal and held that she was a worker. She was an integral part of the LLP's business, she could not offer her services to anyone else, she was in a subordinate position, and the LLP was not her client. (2) Dismissed the LLP's appeal on the question of territorial jurisdiction. All that was required was for the tribunal to be satisfied that the claimant's connection with Great Britain was sufficiently strong to enable it to be said that Parliament would have regarded it as appropriate for the tribunal to deal with her claim and that the tribunal was entitled so to conclude.

CA (Elias LJ): considered the issue of subordination in the context of determining whether the LLP was a client or customer, rather than as an independent requirement in its own right. The LLP's appeal to the Court of Appeal was successful, but on a different ground than argued in the employment tribunal. The CA held that BvW could not be a worker for the purpose of s 230(3) because s 4(4) of the Limited Liability Partnerships Act 2000 provides:

> A member of a limited liability partnership shall not be regarded for any purpose as employed by the limited liability partnership unless, if he and the other members were partners in a partnership, he would be regarded for that purpose as employed by the partnership.

In relation to territorial jurisdiction, where (as here) the claimant lived and/or worked for at least part of the time in Great Britain, it was not necessary to carry out a comparative exercise between factors pointing towards a connection with Great Britain and factors pointing in favour of another jurisdiction. It was sufficient that the claimant's connection with Great Britain was sufficiently strong to be able to say that Parliament would have regarded it as appropriate for the tribunal to deal with the claim. Here the claimant principally worked in Tanzania, but during the eleven months that she was an equity member she spent seventy-eight days working in the respondent's London office. As such, the tribunal had been entitled to find that there was territorial jurisdiction for the Equality Act claim, and by implication the same would have applied to the whistleblowing claim if the tribunal had found that the claimant was a worker.

SC: There was no appeal against the territorial jurisdiction decision but BvW's appeal as to worker status was successful. Section 4(4) of the 2000 Act did not prevent her from being a worker, and, applying the plain wording of s 230 ERA, BvW worked under a contract to do or perform work or services formally, and the respondent was not a client or customer of a profession or business carried out by her. Giving the leading speech, Baroness Hale approved the approach in *Hospital Medical Group Ltd v Westwood* [2013] ICR 415, where Maurice Kay LJ pointed out (para 18), that neither the *Cotswold* 'integration' test nor the *Redcats* 'dominant purpose' test laid down a test of general application. Baroness Hale stated:

> 39. I agree with Maurice Kay LJ that there is not 'a single key to unlock the words of the statute in every case'. There can be no substitute for applying the words of the statute to the facts of the individual case. There will be cases where that is not easy to do. But in my view they are not solved by adding some mystery ingredient of 'subordination' to the concept of employee and worker. The experienced employment judges who have considered this problem have all recognised that there is no magic test other than the words of the statute themselves. As Elias J recognised in the *Redcats* case [2007] ICR 1006, a small business may be genuinely an independent business but be completely dependent on and subordinate to the demands of a key customer (the position of those small factories making goods exclusively for the 'St Michael' brand in the past comes to mind). Equally, as Maurice Kay LJ recognised in *Westwood's* case [2013] ICR 415, one may be a professional person with a high degree of autonomy as to how the work is performed and more than one string to one's bow, and still be so closely integrated into the other party's operation as to fall within the definition. As the case of the controlling shareholder in a company who is also employed as chief executive shows, one can effectively be one's own boss and still be a 'worker'. While subordination may sometimes be an aid to distinguishing workers from other self-employed people, it is not a freestanding and universal characteristic of being a worker.

> 40. ... the appellant falls within the express words of section 230(3)(b). ... she could not market her services as a solicitor to anyone other than the LLP and was an integral part of their business. They were in no sense her client or customer. I agree.

Result: The claimant was a worker. Case remitted to the employment tribunal to determine her claims.

Cited by: *Unite the Union v Nailard* [2016] IRLR 906 (EAT); *Windle v Secretary of State for Justice* [2016] ICR 721 (CA); *Roberts v Wilsons Solicitors LLP* [2016] ICR 659 (EAT); *Day v Lewisham and Greenwich NHS Trust* [2016] ICR 878 (EAT); *Reinhard v Ondra LLP* [2015] EWHC 1869; *Suhail v Barking Havering and Redbridge University Hospitals NHS Trust* (UKEAT/0536/13/RN, 11 June 2015); *Sharpe v Worcester Diocesan Board of Finance Ltd* [2015] ICR 1241 (CA); *Altus Group (UK) Ltd v Baker Tilly Tax and Advisory Services LLP* [2015] EWHC 12; *Pimlico Plumbers Ltd v Smith* (UKEAT/0495/12/DM, 21 November 2014); *Halawi v WDFG UK Ltd (t/a World Duty Free)* [2015] 3 ALL ER 543 (CA); *Macalinden (t/a Charm Offensive) v Lazarov* (UKEAT/0453/13/JOJ, 17 October 2014); *Plastering Contractors Stanmore Ltd v Holden* (UKEAT/0074/14/LA, 7 July 2014).

9. Sharpe v The Worcester Diocesan Board of Finance Ltd

[2015] IRLR 663, [2015] ICR 1241 (CA)

Key issues: Was Sharpe, an ordained minister in the Church of England working as Rector in the Benefice of Teme Valley South in the Diocese of Worcester, a worker?

Case summary: Sharpe claimed detriments and dismissal arising from protected qualifying disclosures. The preliminary hearing was to determine his status as a worker.

ET: Sharpe was not a worker; s 43K(1)(a)(ii) and the words 'the terms on which he is engaged to do the work' envisage terms that are capable of legal enforcement and imply the existence of a contract. His appointment was not through a contract. He was appointed under ecclesiastical law to an office. They found that to qualify as a s 43K(1)(a) worker one must have a contract with at least one of either the supplier/introducer or the end user of the services.

EAT (Mrs Justice Cox): Sharpe was a worker.

CA (Lady Justice Arden, Lord Justice Davis, and Lord Justice Lewison). Lady Justice Arden stated 'In the absence of a contract between the parties, neither s 43K(1)(a) or (b) can apply', the status and form of ecclesiastical office did not create a contractual relationship.

> 108. A rector assumes office not simply because he or she is selected at interview but because he or she is installed as rector. That is not to be discounted as just another ceremony. As a clergyman, Reverend Sharpe must as part of his installation demonstrate his commitment to follow his calling by making the oath of Canonical obedience in the presence of the bishop and his parishioners. In exchange for that, the Church provides him with the facilities to discharge his calling—stipend, housing, assistance with cars, and guidance on holidays and so on: there is an open offer by the appropriate organs of the Church to make those facilities available so there is no need for them to be discussed. They are taken as read. Any incumbent is expected to behave responsibly and given considerable freedom to take care of the souls of his parishioners in the way he considers appropriate. But, for a mixture of historical and ideological or theological reasons, the Church has little power of control over the way an incumbent discharges his functions or to remove him from his post. The reality is that that is not the point of the appointment. Put another way, by accepting office as rector he or she agrees to follow their calling. They do not enter into an agreement to do work for the purposes and benefit of the Church as a commercial transaction.

Sections considered: ERA, ss 43K, 203.

Cited by: *Gilham v Ministry of Justice* (UKEAT0087/16/LA, 31 October 2016); *McTigue v University Hospital Bristol NHS Foundation Trust* [2016] IRLR 742 (EAT); *Farmer v Heart of Birmingham Teaching Primary Care Trust* (UKEAT/0180/15/LA, 22 March 2016); *Day v Lewisham and Greenwich NHS Trust* [2016] ICR 878 (EAT); *Otuo v Morley* [2016] EWHC 46.

10. Day v Lewisham and Greenwich NHS Trust and Health Education England

UKEAT/0250/15/RN, 9 March 2016, [2016] IRLR 415

Key issues: Does the fact that a person is a worker of one employer (within s 230 ERA) have the effect that reliance cannot be placed on s 47K ERA in relation to a different employer?

Case summary: A training doctor, supplied by HEE to work for Lewisham in a training post as a specialist registrar in ACCS Emergency Medicine, claimed to have had his training post terminated because of a disclosure. Was he a worker under the extended definition under section 47K vis a vis HEE?

ET: decided it was arguable Dr Day met the requirements of s 43K(1)(a)(i) but he did not meet the terms of s 43K(1)(a)(ii). Dr Day argued that the terms on which he was engaged to do the work were in practice not substantially determined by him. This was accepted by HEE. However, s 43K(2)(a) also requires that the respondent must be the person who substantially determines or determined the terms on which s/he is or was engaged. Day failed to offer any clear factual basis for asserting that the terms were determined by HEE, and the ET held that they were not. It was not suggested that HEE was responsible for the 'Gold Guide', which set out the terms governing the training of doctors. As for the performance of clinical duties, HEE successfully argued that the documentary evidence showed Lewisham was substantially responsible for determining his terms and conditions of work.

EAT (Mr Justice Langstaff): Whilst a purposive approach should be taken, it did not entitle a court to ignore the words of the legislation. Section 43K cannot apply to someone who is already a worker defined by s 230(3) ERA in relation to a different person as 'employer'. The President was unpersuaded that the inclusion of that requirement was a 'belt and braces' and construed it as a condition precedent. Turning to the HEE he said:

> 44. He was not its employee, nor its worker. He was at the material time a worker for Lewisham. In so far as his complaint arose out of that work he could not, therefore, claim protection under section 43K. If forensic illustrations are to be drawn this is not a case of a gap within the boundaries of protection, but a case in which the relationship falls well outside those boundaries.

CA: Appeal outstanding. See different approach adopted in *McTigue* (case [11]).

Result: Not covered by s 47K.

Sections considered: ERA, ss 47K, 230.

Cited by: *McTigue v University Hospital Bristol NHS Foundation Trust* [2016] IRLR 742 (EAT).

11. McTigue v University Hospital Bristol Foundation Trust

[2016] IRLR 742 (EAT)

Key issues: Can an agency nurse who is a s 230(3) worker bring a claim against the principal pursuant to s 43K(1), and, if so, how is s 43K(1)(a)(ii) to be interpreted?

Case summary: McTigue was a nurse who was supplied by an agency, Tascor, to work at UHBFT. A preliminary hearing was held to determine whether McTigue was caught under the extended definition of s 43K or excluded by the condition precedent arising from the interpretation in *Day* as to the effect of the words 'who is not a worker as defined by section 230(3)'. Could she present a claim against UHBFT?

ET: The claimant had by the date of her hearing discontinued her claim against the agency (Tascor) leaving only UHBFT as the putative employer. The ET found that the requirement that the terms are 'substantially determined by the person alleged to be the employer' must require and mean that it decides the majority of the terms or the more significant ones'. It then found that because she could have presented a claim against Tascor, she could not satisfy the requirements of s 43K(1) because she was a worker for them, which excluded her ability to rely on s 43K to bring a claim against anyone else, here the principal.

EAT (Mrs Justice Simler DBE (President)): McTigue entered into a written contract with her agency dealing with remuneration, holiday, sickness, maternity, pension, discipline, grievance procedures, and notice, amongst other matters. The tribunal found that these formed 'a picture of a normal contractual arrangement as between an employer and employee'. In addition, McTigue was provided with an honourary appointment with UHBFT, in a simple and unsigned form—but importantly it authorized her to carry out the duties of and practise as a Forensic Nurse Examiner. UHBFT also provided a supervisor, who had to be informed of any absences. Mrs Justice Simler held that s 43K(1)(a)(ii) expressly recognizes that there can be more than one party who substantially determines the terms, and any attempt to limit the putative employer to the person who determined the majority of those terms is wrong. Further, she held the question is whether the terms of employment were 'in large part' determined by the putative employer. The tribunal had therefore erred in its construction. Any requirement that 'substantial' means 'majority' was wrong in law, and she explained (at para 22):

> there is no room for an interpretation of s 43K(1)(a)(ii) based on who determined 'the majority of the terms' or 'the most significant terms' as between the agency supplier and the end user. Where two parties (other than the individual) have between them determined the terms upon which an individual worked but have done so to different extents, each might nevertheless have substantially determined the terms.

UHBFT also tried to argue, relying on *Day*, that the fact that McTigue was a s 230(3) worker for the agency meant she could not present a claim against UHBFT. Rejecting that argument, Mrs Justice Simler noted that the claim by McTigue was only now against UHBFT (because it had been withdrawn against the agency). If UBHFT was not and could not be the employer under to s 230(3), then the condition precedent wording arising from s 43K(1) was not engaged; it was not engaged by some other party being the employer under s 230(3) ERA.

Result: The claimant could present a claim against the principal, in this case a hospital.

Sections considered: ERA, ss 47K, 203(3).

12. Gilham v Ministry of Justice

UKEAT 0087/16/LA, 31 October 2016

Key issue: whether a holder of judicial office was also worker.

Case summary: The claimant was a district judge. She made a detriment claim under s 47B ERA. It was agreed that she was an office holder. Was she also a worker within the meaning of s 230(3) ERA. Following *Sharpe v Bishop of Worcester* [2015] ICR 1241 (CA), in order for ERA, s 230(3) to apply there had to be a contract between the parties. The claimant argued that the relationship between district judges and the Ministry of Justice had the typical features of a contract that would fall within s 230(3), that is offer, acceptance, consideration, mutuality of obligation, and exchange of promises.

ET rejected this contention.

EAT (Simler J (P)) dismissed the appeal. There were no features of the method of the claimant's appointment, the duties or functions of her role, or the means by which she could be removed from it which supported the existence of a contract between her and the Ministry of Justice in addition to the office which she held. A district judge's appointment was by the Crown; the duties, functions, and authority of a district judge are defined by statute and by rules made under statutory authority and, to the extent that the terms of service went beyond this, they were incidental to the terms made by or under statute (and were not at all determined by private negotiation). Further, responsibility for welfare arrangements, training and guidance, and deployment of the judiciary rests with the Lord Chief Justice (rather than the Ministry of Justice or Lord Chancellor), and the Ministry of Justice had no power to end the relationship. These features provided a clear and complete explanation for the relationship between the parties, and as such there was no necessity to imply a contractual relationship. A fundamental feature of s 230(3) ERA is to define those within the scope of protection by reference to the existence of a contract, whether a contract of service or a contract for services. Parliament had extended the meaning of 'worker' (and associated terms) for the purposes of whistleblowing protection beyond that otherwise provided by s 230(3) ERA under s 43K(1). This extended protection afforded was carefully identified and delineated, preserving the general rule that a contractual relationship is required for 'worker' status, save only in a limited number of circumstances (for example agency and NHS arrangements) where the requirement to have a contract was replaced by a requirement to work for a person in particular circumstances or performing particular services. Parliament was or would have been entitled to conclude that extended protection is unnecessary to give effect to the claimant's Article 10 rights. Judicial office holders had a range of protections for the right not to suffer whistleblowing detriments. A district judge's position was therefore quite different from that of a worker or employee who did not benefit from such protections: in many respects, a district judge is protected to a greater degree than other workers. Where adequate safeguards were in place there could be no necessity to rewrite s 230(3)(b) so as to permit the specific route to a remedy provided by s 47B ERA. An extension of the meaning of worker in s 43K(1) is properly a question for Parliament.

Result: Appeal dismissed.

Sections considered: ERA, ss 43K(1), 230(3)(b).

Police

13. Lake v British Transport Police

[2007] ICR 1293

Key issues: whether police disciplinary board immune from suit.

Case summary: L made a disclosure of allegations against two other officers which resulted in them being arrested, but not charged. He claimed that charges subsequently made against him were as a result of his disclosures.

ET: determined that the claimant could not be permitted to attack the police disciplinary board in relation either to its proceedings or to its decision. The decision of the police disciplinary board was the subject of an appeal to the chief constable, and if the claimant could demonstrate that the chief constable's decision was made by reason of the fact that he had made a protected disclosure, the dismissal claim might still be able to succeed.

EAT (Judge Serota QC): dismissed the claimant's appeal against that finding, concluding that the scope of immunity from suit afforded to judicial and quasi-judicial bodies extended to the police disciplinary board.

Court of Appeal (Pill, Wall, Maurice Kay LJJ): reversed the decision of the EAT, noting that ERA, s 43KA extends protected disclosure protection to persons who hold the office of constable, otherwise than under a contract of employment. It provides that the constable shall be treated as an employee employed by the chief officer of police under a contract of employment. The proceedings before the police disciplinary board and the decision of the board could not form the basis of the s 103A claim since those proceedings and that decision were immune from suit. However, the claimant was not seeking to challenge the customary immunity from suit enjoyed by those engaged in proceedings in a judicial tribunal. He was seeking to advance the case in the ET which he had unsuccessfully put to the disciplinary board. The ET was not bound by the decision of the board and could make its own decision:

> 31. It may be unusual that a statutory appeals procedure, which has sole jurisdiction (subject to judicial review) in most cases where disciplinary action is taken against police officers, can in a section 47B(1)/section 103A case be followed by a claim to an employment tribunal but that, in my judgment, is the effect of the insertion of section 43KA into the 1996 Act. The right is conferred by statute and notions of judicial immunity do not defeat it. The court is concerned with an issue of jurisdiction and I express no views upon the merits of the claimant's claim.

Result: claim not struck out.

Sections considered: ERA, ss 47B, 43KA, 103A.

Cited in: *P v Metropolitan Police Commissioner* (UKEAT/0449/13 25 March 2014), [2016] IRLR 301 (CA).

Judicial immunity

14. Engel v The Joint Committee for Parking & Traffic Regulation Outside London (PATROL)

[2013] ICR 1086.

Key issue: Did a decision by the Chief Adjudicator of the Traffic Parking Tribunal not to allocate cases to a fee-paid Parking Adjudicator amount to a detriment for the purpose of section 47B ERA or was it within the scope of judicial immunity?

Case summary: Mr Engel was a parking adjudicator authorized to hear appeals against decisions of local enforcement authorities to uphold the imposition of penalty charges in respect of certain road traffic contraventions. The Chief Adjudicator was a judicial office holder and was entitled to judicial immunity and in respect of her discharge of those functions, the Joint Committee did not have vicarious responsibility. The Chief Adjudicator, in addition to being a judicial office holder discharging judicial functions, was an employee of the Joint Committee and did perform administrative or 'ministerial' functions. Whilst it was common ground that in appointing and reappointing an adjudicator, the Chief Adjudicator would not be exercising a judicial function and that a decision by the Joint Committee not to reappoint a person as an adjudicator or to remove him from office under reg. 17(3) of the relevant Regulations would also not be made in the exercise of judicial functions, the decision not to allocate personal or postal cases to Engel was made in the performance of the Chief Adjudicator's duties as a judicial office holder.

EAT dismissed appeal. The taking of disciplinary steps by the Chief Adjudicator against an adjudicator, other than a decision not to allocate personal or postal cases or both, would not be in the exercise of her judicial functions. Disciplinary proceedings had nothing to do with the resolution of disputes between parties to an appeal by an adjudicator. They concerned only the position of the adjudicator. This was contrasted with a listing or allocation decision, which would be the exercise of a judicial function. The EAT accepted that the decision not to allocate Mr Engel any personal or postal cases had the effect of suspending Mr Engel from work but it was not necessary to look at the purpose of the decision not to allocate. Even if the decision was taken as a free-standing disciplinary measure and even if it was taken for the improper purpose alleged by Engel of subjecting him to a detriment because of his protected disclosure, the decision would still be covered by judicial immunity. The principle of immunity for the exercise of judicial functions was ultimately a policy decision, which must be upheld even in extreme circumstances.

15. P v Commissioner of Police for the Metropolis

[2016] EWCA Civ 2, [2016] IRLR 301.

Key issue: Was the Police Misconduct Board immune from suit?

Case Summary: P, a serving Police Officer, was assaulted in 2010. As a consequence she suffered post-traumatic stress disorder (PTSD). She complained in an application to the employment tribunal that she did not have support at work to help her cope with the consequences of that condition, aggravated by the fact that just prior to 12 September 2011 she had worked excessively long hours. On that date, whilst 'in drink', as the EAT put it, she was involved in an incident which led to her arrest and dismissal. She asserted that her behaviour was heavily affected by her PTSD. An investigation led to a disciplinary charge before the Police Misconduct Board. She substantially accepted that she had been culpably guilty of the misconduct alleged, but relied on her good record as a police officer and her condition in mitigation. The Board nonetheless decided that she should be dismissed from the Force without notice. A claim of (ordinary) unfair dismissal was struck out because P had no right to bring such a claim. However, P also claimed that she had been subjected to disability discrimination contrary to section 15(1) of the Equality Act (EqA) and failure to make reasonable adjustments contrary to section 20 and 21 EqA. P's claim had been struck out: the ET accepted that the Metropolitan Police Misconduct Board was a judicial body which enjoyed immunity from suit.

Appeals to the Employment Appeal Tribunal and the Court of Appeal were dismissed. A further appeal to the Supreme Court will be heard in 2017. *Heath v Commissioner of Metropolitan Police* [2005] IRLR 270 followed. The police disciplinary hearing was a judicial proceeding in respect of which members of the panel had an absolute immunity in respect of complaints of unlawful sex discrimination. Application of *Trapp v Mackie* [1979] 1 WLR 377 (HL) and the four indicia of judicial proceedings set out in that case led to the conclusion that the ET and the EAT were justified in finding that the Board was a judicial body acting judicially: 'the essential features of the disciplinary hearing rendered it closely analogous to a judicial proceeding before a court of justice.'

Result: Appeal dismissed.

Qualifying disclosure

16. Sim v Manchester Action on Street Health

EAT/0085/01, 6 December 2001

Key issue: qualifying disclosure.

Case summary: Dr Sim was employed by an NHS Trust but seconded on most Tuesday nights to work as a night service doctor for the respondent charity (dealing with prostitutes). His time was paid for by the NHS Trust. When he did not attend, the charity did not complain or ask for sickness notes. The charity decided it no longer needed Dr Sim's services. He claimed unfair dismissal, saying he had been dismissed for raising concerns as to financial probity and safeguarding the health and safety of employees and clients of MASH. At a preliminary hearing, the ET held that his claim would fail as he was neither an employee nor a worker of the charity.

EAT (Mr Justice Lindsay (President)): was critical of the way in which the claim was framed: 'expressions such as "I believe" and "may be" hardly suffice as a true allegation' for s 103A. The EAT upheld the finding that the claimant was neither a worker nor an employee of the charity, rather being a seconded employee of the NHS Trust.

As to the elements of a qualifying disclosure the EAT said at paragraph 4:

> The subject matter of protected disclosures and to whom they must be made and by whom and in what state of mind are all matters carefully regulated by the Employment Rights Act Sections 43B and 43C and need to have their constituent parts set out and specified in a claim even if only in brief or summary form. Concern as to financial probity falls short, as it seems to us, without further allegation, of 43B(1)(b). Concerns as to safeguarding the health and safety of employees also fall short, in our view, unless further amplified, of 43B(1)(d). It is not said, either, to whom the disclosure was made—compare Section 43C.

Result: appeal dismissed.

Sections considered: ERA, ss 43K, 47B, 98, 103A, 230(3).

Cited by: *Duffin v Deloitte and Touche Wealth Management Ltd* (EAT/0453/03, 24 September 2003).

17. Parkins v Sodexho

[2002] IRLR 109 (EAT)

Key issues: (1) meaning of legal obligations for purposes of qualifying disclosure; (2) approach to assessing evidence on interim relief application.

Case summary: This claim concerned an application for interim relief that was refused with a costs order being made against Mr Parkins. The disclosure by Mr Parkins was with regard to (para 6):

> two areas of work and he complained, or says that he complained, on one of them where he had to use a buffing machine, that he did not have supervision on site and in the event of problems, he was instructed to telephone a supervisor off site in the evenings. He says now that that was a matter of health & safety and also gave rise to a breach of contract, which he properly complained of and as a result of his complaint he was dismissed.

ET: gave a narrow interpretation of s 43B when it found against Parkins, stating that:

> we do not consider that an allegation of breach of an employment contract in relation to the performance of duties comes within the letter or spirit of the statutory provision.

EAT (HHJ Altman): allowing the appeal, the EAT said (para 18):

> … we do not agree with the assertion of the Employment Tribunal, where they say that 'an allegation of breach of an employment contract, in relation to the performance of duties, does not come within the letter or spirit of the statutory provision'. We find it difficult to define the spirit of this sort of legislation or to be confident that we know about it, but it certainly comes within the letter of the provision, on a literal interpretation. It seems to us that we do not need to go beyond that.

The EAT also commented on the process to be undertaken in relation to interim relief (paras 25–27), emphasizing that it is a process of predicting the outcome at the final hearing. The ET had not adopted that approach but had instead purported to make a final decision, based on what was necessarily a cursory review of the evidences, as to the reason for dismissal.

Result: remitted the application for interim relief to a different tribunal—to be heard at the same time as the application for unfair dismissal.

Detriment: not an issue.

Sections considered: ERA, ss 43B, 103A, 129.

Damages awarded: remitted.

Cited by: *Morgan v Royal Mencap Society* [2016] IRLR 428 (EAT); *Millbank Financial Services Ltd v Crawford* [2014] IRLR 18; *Ministry of Justice v Sarfraz* [2011] IRLR 562 (EAT); *Raja v Secretary of State for Justice* (EAT/0364/09, 15 February 2010); *Cavendish Munro Professional Risks Management Ltd v Geduld* [2010] ICR 325 (EAT); *Felter v Cliveden Petroleum Co* (EAT/0533/05, 9 March 2006); *Milne v The Link Asset and Security Company Ltd* (EAT/0867/04, 26 September 2005); *Street v Derbyshire Unemployed Workers' Centre* [2005] ICR 97; *Kraus v Penna plc* [2004] IRLR 260 (EAT); *Odong v Chubb Security Personnel* (EAT/0819/02, 13 May 2003); *Douglas v Birmingham City Council and others* (EAT/018/02, 17 March 2003); *Darnton v University of Surrey* [2003] ICR 615 (EAT).

18. Welsh Refugee Council v Brown

EAT/0032/02, 22 March 2002

Key issue: reasonable belief for qualifying disclosure.

Case summary: The Welsh Refugee Council was funded by the Home Office. In her first week Mrs Brown received information from the finance officer of the council which indicated to her that a colleague (Y) was making dishonest expenses claims and procuring other dishonest payments. Mrs Brown then raised these concerns with a member of the management committee. The respondent then contended that Mrs Brown's appointment was 'invalid' because references had not been received and her employment was terminated. She claimed to have made a protected disclosure and that her dismissal was automatically unfair.

ET: found that, since there was no other rational reason for the dismissal, and points as to her conduct were contrived, the reason for dismissal was that Mrs Brown had made a disclosure to members of the respondents' management committee.

EAT (Mr Justice Holland): upheld the finding of automatically unfair dismissal (para 9):

> ... a finding that Mrs Brown had a reasonable belief for these purposes necessarily connotes two component matters; thus it necessarily connotes that she did in point of fact believe what she was saying, that is, it necessarily connotes a subjective finding to that extent. Second and further, it connotes a finding that that belief was reasonable, that is, it was a tenable belief neither eccentric nor fanciful, it is a belief that withstands objective assessment.

As to the basis for the reasonable belief (para 13):

> ... How could the grounds be other than reasonable as a basis for further disclosure, given the source of the information? What else should Mrs Brown as regional coordinator have done, other than pass the material forward? Should she have kept silent pending her own investigation before passing the matter forward?

The EAT then went on to comment of the appeal to the EAT that:

> At its best it was tactical. It could not possibly have been regarded as having any merit at all. The Council knew the grounds underpinning Mrs Brown's complaint. If it did not, it should have done. Given now two critical judgments, the first being that of the Employment Tribunal, the second being that of this Tribunal, cannot the Council now learn valuable lessons in the public interest that will help it devote its time and funds to its essential laudable purpose and will prevent it engaging in bad man management and hopeless litigation?

The council was also ordered to pay costs to Mrs Brown.

Result: automatically unfair dismissal.

Detriment: none pleaded.

Sections considered: ERA, ss 43A, 43B, 43C, 103A.

Damages awarded: appeal prior to remedy hearing.

Cited in*: Garcia v Market Probe Europe Ltd* (UKEAT/0024/13/BA, 5 November 2013); *Kraus v Penna* [2004] IRLR 260; *Odong v Chubb Security Personnel* (EAT/0819/02/DM, 13 May 2003).

19. Fincham v HM Prison Service

EAT/0925/01/RN and EAT/0991/01/RN, 19 December 2001

Key issue: qualifying disclosure—to what extent must a breach of a legal obligation or other relevant failure be spelled out?

Case summary: Ms Fincham was employed as operations support grade personnel and made allegations of harassment against two members of staff. Subsequently, her fixed term contract was not renewed.

EAT (Mr Justice Elias): stated (at paras 24, 30, and 32–33):

> The specific breaches of legal obligation relied upon were infringements of obligations under Health and Safety legislation, and the breach by the employer of the duty to respect the trust and confidence of the employee. We were referred to the decision of this Tribunal in *Parkins v Sodexho* [2002] IRLR 109, Judge Altman presiding, in which the Tribunal took a broad view

of what would constitute a legal obligation within the terms of this section. That Tribunal held that it would include breaches of the contract of employment and we agree with that.

. . .

... What the Tribunal is saying is that the statement does not tend to show that health and safety was likely to be endangered. We found it impossible to see how a statement that says in terms 'I am under pressure and stress' is anything other than a statement that her health and safety is being or at least is likely to be endangered. It seems to us, therefore, that it is not a matter which can take its gloss from the particular context in which the statement is made. It may well be that it was relatively minor matter drawn to the attention of the employers in the course of a much more significant letter. We know not. But nonetheless it does seem to us that this was a disclosure tending to show that her own health and safety was likely to endangered within the meaning of subsection [1(d) of section 43B ERA].

If an employee complains on various occasions about the conduct of other employees that is not of itself demonstrating any breach of any duty by the employer at all. Of course there can be a breach of trust and confidence resulting from a whole series of acts of inattention or carelessness or any inconsiderate behaviour by an employer over a period of time.

But there must in our view be some disclosure which actually identifies, albeit not in strict legal language, the breach of legal obligation on which the employer is relying. In this case the Tribunal found none. We have no reason to conclude that they erred in law in reaching that conclusion.

Result: remitted to a different ET.

Detriments: anxiety, demoralization; segregated at work; refused renewal of contract; refused promotion.

Sections considered: ERA, ss 47B, 43B(1)(b) and (d).

Cited in: *Western Union Payment Services UK Ltd v Anastasiou* (UKEAT/0135/13/LA, 21 February 2014; UKEAT/0135/13/LA, 12 May 2014).

20. Butcher v Salvage Association

EAT/988/01, 21 January 2002, [2002] EWCA Civ 867

Key issue: Whether disclosure tended to show a legal obligation or only a professional obligation.

Case summary: Mr Butcher, was employed as the respondent's chief financial officer. The chief executive disagreed with the way Mr Butcher presented financial reports to the respondent's governing committee. The committee preferred the chief executive's position. Mr Butcher raised a concern internally that in being asked to adopt the chief executive's approach to the financial reporting involved being asked to change figures and monthly management reports to the board in a way which he believed would be misleading. The governing committee rejected his complaint. He was subsequently dismissed and the employer contended that this was on the grounds of his continued under performance and inability to fulfill the requirements of his role.

ET: rejected the claim that it was a capability dismissal, but found it was for some other substantial reason being the irreconcilable differences between Mr Butcher and the Chief Executive. It found the dismissal procedurally and substantively unfair but reduced compensation by 50 per cent for contributory fault. The claim under s.103A was dismissed as there was no protected disclosure. After hearing expert evidence on the point, the ET concluded that Mr Butcher's concerns were about acting professionally and that it was 'purely contrived to seek to promote an issue as to professional ethics into a legal obligation'. Nor were the requirements of professional ethics incorporated into his contract since the accounts were only internal (so there was no question of misleading a third party or the board—who were aware of the issues), and in preparing the accounts in the way required he was acting on the instructions of the board and the governing committee.

EAT and CA (Peter Gibson LJ): The appeal on the protected disclosure issue was dismissed by the EAT at a preliminary hearing (and the appeal on the issue of contributory fault dismissed at the substantive appeal hearing), and permission to appeal was refused by the Court of Appeal ([2002] EWCA Civ 867). The Court of Appeal also rejected a submission that the ET should have first decided whether the dismissal was unfair and then decide whether the reason was that he had made a protected disclosure. On the contrary, the ET must (and did) first decide the reason for dismissal, and it had rejected the contention that it was the reason Butcher had advanced

Result: Unfair dismissal under s 98 ERA (but not by reason of protected disclosure). Compensation reduced by 50 per cent for contributory fault.

Sections considered: ERA, s 103A.

21. Darnton v University of Surrey

[2003] IRLR 133 (EAT)

Key issue: test of reasonable belief for qualifying disclosure.

Case summary: Mr Darnton, a full-time lecturer, fell out with the head of his school over working hours shortly after starting work at the university. Following a meeting to agree hours of work, he criticized the head over his 'ridiculous' management style. There then followed a deterioration in the relationship, with Darnton accusing the head of 'serious academic malpractice' regarding unrealistic time periods for marking. The relationship further deteriorated. Darnton then made enquiries about the grievance procedure and, during this, proposed the termination of his employment on terms. He complained about bullying and harassment. A compromise was entered into that included terms of a single payment together with an agreement that he continue as an 'associate lecturer' for one year doing work valued at £20,000. Darnton obtained a new post at another university. He believed the university was still bound to pay for the agreed work; the respondent did not. Darnton wrote to the respondent complaining and demanding more compensation. He contended that this letter contained protected disclosures.

ET: considered the letter so as to 'carefully, isolate from it the disclosures as opposed to the general complaints, demands for money and vituperation and decide whether in the reasonable belief of the [claimant] that the information tended to show either that a criminal offence had been committed or that the respondents had failed to comply with any legal obligation to which they were subject'. It found that there was no qualifying disclosure.

EAT (Judge Serota QC): remitted the claim back to the ET. The ET did not appear to have asked itself the question required by s 43B, namely whether, at the time of making the disclosure, in Darnton's reasonable belief the disclosure tended to show a relevant failure. It was submitted and accepted that in determining whether the information 'tends to show' a relevant failure, the ET should look at matters from the perspective of the worker, not on the basis of the facts it had found (para 32):

> We agree with the authors [of the first edition of this book] that, for there to be a qualifying disclosure, it must have been reasonable for the worker to believe that the factual basis of what was disclosed was true and that it tends to show a relevant failure, even if the worker was wrong, but reasonably mistaken.

The truth of the allegations would often be relevant to ascertaining reasonable belief, but all depends on the circumstances:

> We consider that as a matter of both law and common sense all circumstances must be considered together in determining whether the worker holds the reasonable belief. The circumstances will include his belief in the factual basis of the information disclosed as well as what those facts tend to show. The more the worker claims to have direct knowledge of the matters which are the subject of the disclosure, the more relevant will be his belief in the truth of what he says in determining whether he holds that reasonable belief.
>
> However, it is clear from the wording of the statute that the standard of belief in the truth of what is disclosed cannot be such as to require the employee making a qualifying disclosure, under s 43B, to hold the belief that both the factual basis of the disclosure and what it tends to show are 'substantially true'.

The EAT also endorsed the commentary in the predecessor to this book:

> We have derived considerable assistance from *Whistleblowing: the new law* by John Bowers QC, Jeremy Lewis and Jack Mitchell. The learned authors write, at p 19, under the heading 'Reasonable belief in truth':
> 'To achieve protection under any of the several parts of the Act, the worker must have a "reasonable belief" in the truth of the information as tending to show one or more of the six matters

listed which he has disclosed, although that belief need not be correct (section 43B(1)). This had led some to criticize the statute as giving too much licence to employees to cause trouble, since it pays no regard to issues of confidentiality in this respect. Nor need the employee actually prove, even on the balance of probabilities, the truth of what he is disclosing. This is probably inevitable, because the whistleblower may have a good "hunch" that something is wrong without having the means to prove it beyond doubt or even on the balance of probabilities. [An example is the Herald of Free Enterprise disaster where no one had the resources to check on the hunch which several employees had about the safety of the bow doors.[2]] The notion behind the legislation is that the employee should be encouraged to make known to a suitable person the basis of that hunch so that those with the ability and resources to investigate it can do so.

The control on abuse is that it must have been reasonable for the worker to believe that the information disclosed was true. This means, we think, that the following principles would apply under the Act:

(a) It would be a qualifying disclosure if the worker reasonably but mistakenly believed that a specified malpractice is or was occurring or may occur.
(b) Equally if some malpractice was occurring which did not fall within one of the listed categories, the disclosure would still qualify if the worker reasonably believed that it did amount to malpractice falling within one of those categories.
(c) There must be more than unsubstantiated rumours in order for there to be a qualifying disclosure. The whistleblower must exercise some judgment on his own part consistent with the evidence and the resources available to him. There must additionally be a reasonable belief and therefore some information which tends to show that the specified malpractice occurred . . .
(d) The reasonableness of the belief will depend in each case on the volume and quality of information available to the worker at the time the decision to disclose is made. Employment tribunals will have to guard against use of hindsight to assess the reasonableness of the belief in this respect in the same way as they are bound, in considering liability in unfair dismissal cases, to consider only what was known to the employer at the time of dismissal or appeal . . .'

Result: remitted.

Sections considered: ERA, ss 43B, 43C, 43(5), 43F, 43G, 43H, 43K.

Cited by: *Soh v Imperial College of Science, Technology and Medicine* (UKEAT/0350/14/DM, 3 September 2015); *Nese v Airbus Operations Ltd* (UKEAT/0477/13/DA, 27 January 2015); *Aryeetey v Tuntum Housing Association* (UKEAT/0070/07, 12 October 2007 and UKEAT 0324/08, 8 April 2009); *Hibbins v Hesters Way Neighbourhood Project* [2009] ICR 319 (EAT); *Muchesa v Central and Cecil Housing Care Support* (EAT/0443/07, 22 August 2008); *Babula v Waltham Forest College* [2007] ICR 1026 (CA); *Bolton School v Evans* [2006] IRLR 500 (EAT); *Street v Derbyshire Unemployed Workers' Centre* [2005] ICR 97; *Kraus v Penna plc* [2004] IRLR 260 (EAT); *Sir Robert McAlpine Ltd v Telford* (EATS/0018/03, 13 May 2003); *De Haney v Brent MIND* (EAT/0054/03, 10 April 2003).

22. Everett Financial Management Ltd v Murrell

EAT/552/3/02 and EAT/952/02, 18 December 2002

Key issues: (1) qualifying disclosure requires disclosure of information; (2) 'reason why' question; (3) affirmation.

Case summary: Mr Murrell claimed constructive dismissal caused by a protected disclosure. He was an equities dealer in the respondent's 'Elite Group'. He and 19 colleagues became concerned about a particular practice which they were required to carry out. They raised their concerns in a meeting and the next day they wrote a petition to directors seeking assurances that they were not 'engaged in any activity that is unlawful, could be construed as unlawful, in contravention of any SIB Principle/ Regulation or could jeopardise our individual personal registration'. The respondent invited Murrell to set out any issues that would 'be dealt with under EFML's public disclosure policy'. Murrell was

---

[2] This sentence was omitted from the passage quoted by the EAT.

then informed that he was to be removed from the Elite Group, losing various perks, including an assistant. A few days later he was issued with a final written warning. After a further few days Murrell was suspended. During his suspension his solicitors wrote to the respondent stating that the treatment he had received was because he had made a protected disclosure. Murrell was then invited to rejoin the Elite Group, which he accepted. Upon his return Murrell took issue over who was appointed as his assistant and then resigned.

ET: the majority concluded that he had been the object of victimization under s 47B. In giving Murrell 'an assistant who was known to be underperforming, EFML had set up Mr Murrell to fail and that it was therefore only a matter of time before EFML took further measures against him'.

The minority took the view that there was no protected disclosure because it did not specifically name or identify a practice which could be identified as making a disclosure for the purposes of the Act.

EAT (HHJ Burke QC): found that the agreement entered into after Murrell's solicitor's intervention was an 'unequivocal affirmation of the contract of employment'. However, neither party invited the EAT 'to remit this case to the Tribunal for determination of the critical issue as to when the affirmation... took place'. The EAT found that Murrell had affirmed the contract in full knowledge of all the alleged acts including the appointment of his assistant and accordingly 'as a matter of law the Tribunal cannot have held that there was a constructive dismissal on that date'. The EAT found that the unfair dismissal claim must be dismissed.

Regarding causation the EAT took issue with the ET for failing to set out why it concluded that the purported disclosure was a reason or the principal reason for the dismissal. It highlighted (para 40) that 'prima facie the five month gap in which no steps were taken against Mr Murrell contra-indicated a connection between the two episodes'.

The EAT also found that Murrell did not disclose any information falling within s 43B at all. It referred to the fact that a number of concerns had been raised on the previous day (which of itself could not be and was not suggested to have been a qualifying disclosure) and thereafter simply sought assurances. Merely expressing a concern and seeking reassurance that there was no breach of a legal obligation did not involve a disclosure of information within s 43B.

Result: Mr Murrell did not make a qualifying disclosure.

Detriment: providing an assistant who was not capable and thus setting the employee up to fail.

Sections considered: ERA, ss 47(b), 47B, 98(1), 98(2), 98(4), 103A.

Damages awarded: £301,115.83 by ET, nothing by EAT.

Cited by: *Norbrook Laboratories (GB) Ltd v Shaw* [2014] ICR 540.

23. Douglas v Birmingham City Council and Governing Body of Canterbury Cross School and Boyle

EAT/018/02, 17 March 2003

Key issues: (1) who is the employer for the purposes of ERA, s 43C?; (2) scope of 'legal obligation' for qualifying disclosure.

Case summary: Ms Douglas was an Afro-Caribbean school governor who claimed to have made a qualifying disclosure to the chair of the governing body and also to another governor. Her concern was that the head teacher had refused to replace a member of staff who was retiring. She claimed that this was a failure to comply with equal opportunities procedure. Her concerns were initially raised in confidence with a fellow governor (C). A subsequent disclosure was made to the chair of the governing body of her school.

ET: claim dismissed at a preliminary hearing on the basis that no disclosure was made.

EAT (HHJ McMullen QC): one disclosure made during a private conversation with another governor could not amount to a qualifying disclosure (paras 30–31):

> . . . Mrs Canning was being consulted for the purposes only of advice and the Applicant indicated that she would herself pursue the matter and did not want the matter to be handled on her behalf by Mrs Canning. The relationship was one of confidentiality and thus, at first sight and on close analysis thereafter, a statute which is designed in the public interest to protect disclosures ought not to apply to a private conversation between these two governors of the school.

Thus, the Applicant falls at the first hurdle, in our judgment, since what she is disclosing to Mrs Canning is done in a confidential manner and not to her qua employer. . .

The subsequent disclosure to the chair of the governing body of her school was to be regarded as to her employer within the extended meaning in s 43K(1):

She was supplied by a contract of employment, effected by the City Council, to do work for the Governing Body of the School. The terms on which she was engaged to do that work were in practice determined, not by her, but by the Governing Body or by the Council or by both of them.

It was found that an allegation that there had been a failure to follow the equal opportunities policy would be a failure of a legal obligation either because the school was enjoined to follow the policy or because a failure to follow it would result in a breach of the trust and confidence obligation (para 36):

An allegation that a head teacher is engaged in a practice which conflicts with that obligation is, it seems to us, indicating that she is failing to comply or likely failing to comply with a legal obligation—both within the equal opportunities policies, which we have no doubt in so far as they are apt, are incorporated into the contracts of employment; and the anti-discrimination legislation.

Result: appeal allowed.

Sections considered: ERA, ss 47B, 43K, 43A, 43B, 43C, 230.

24. De Haney v Brent Mind and Lang

EAT/0054/03/DA, 10 April 2003, [2004] ICR 348 (CA)

Key issue: qualifying disclosure.

Case summary: Ms De Haney alleged that she had been suspended and dismissed because she had made protected disclosures. One such disclosure was that she had complained that the appointment of a colleague had been in breach of the equal opportunities policy.

ET: dismissed claim on facts. It held that her allegation as to what was said did not amount to a qualifying disclosure because (a) she did not in terms allege race discrimination, (b) the appointment did not happen in the way she alleged, and (c) the allegation was added late as a 'makeweight'.

EAT (HHJ McMullen QC): upheld the finding of the ET. There was no qualifying disclosure, and if there had been a protected disclosure, that was the not the cause of the failure to make the claimant a permanent employee.

Court of Appeal: set aside the EAT's decision on the ground that the EAT panel was not properly constituted. Remitted to the EAT.

EAT (HHJ Serota): dismissed the appeal. The claimant had raised a concern about the appointment of a colleague in writing prior to her dismissal, but the allegation that her concerns in relation to this amounted to a protected disclosure was not contained in the claim form or De Haney's further particulars of her claim, but was first made in her witness statement. In those circumstances the EAT held that the ET had been entitled to find that the allegation was put in as a 'makeweight' and as such was not a qualifying disclosure (in that she did not hold the requisite reasonable belief).

Detriment: not invited to meetings; not considered for deputizing duties; failing to appraise.
Sections considered: ERA, ss 43A, 43B, 47B(1), 48(2), 103A.

25. Sir Robert McAlpine Ltd v Telford

EATS/0018/03, 13 May 2003

Key issue: admissibility of evidence; reasonable belief of relevant failure.

Case summary: It was Mr Telford's case that he had made a disclosure in November 1997 in relation to alleged corrupt payments to subcontractors, and that his subsequent resignation in 2000 was in response to acts of his employer in repudiatory breach (in particular a refusal of promotion in late 1999), the acts having been committed by reason of his earlier disclosure. There was no exchange of witness statements prior to the hearing. During Mr Telford's evidence in chief at the hearing an objection was made on the grounds that he was about to give evidence in relation to alleged fraud in 1998 and 1999 which was not relevant and as such inadmissible. In the ET hearing Mr Telford' advocate had thought that Mr Telford did not himself have any evidence of whether the alleged fraud had taken place. During the course of the EAT hearing it became clear for the first time that Mr Telford did in fact himself have evidence to give in relation to alleged fraud in 2000.

ET: repelled the objection for three reasons, the most significant of which was that since the claim had been brought as a s 103A claim the evidence of alleged fraud was relevant.

EAT (Burton J): first noted that evidence as to whether the alleged fraud that was the subject of his disclosure had occurred would be relevant to the issue of reasonable belief:

> 9(iv) Always of assistance in order to decide the question of reasonable belief, would be included the question as to whether, in fact, it was happening; because, if it was happening, then that would assist the Tribunal in deciding that his belief that it was happening was a reasonable one, although it would not of itself be determinative of that aspect, one way or the other.

The EAT then turned to whether evidence of alleged fraudulent activity subsequent to the disclosure in 1997 was admissible. It rejected an argument that this was relevant to reasonable belief (at para 25):

> 25. . . . He submits that in testing the reasonable belief of the applicant in November 1997, not only is the court enabled to look at what is strictly not probative, namely whether in fact that conduct was taking place, in order to assess the reasonableness of the belief (just as if it can be shown that it was not taking place it would be suggested that such belief was not reasonable) but in addition the Tribunal ought to be able to use, as a tool, the question as to whether somewhat different fraudulent conduct subsequently took place, in order to support the existence of a reasonable belief in November 1997. We do not consider that that is arguable.

The EAT accepted, however, that the evidence that there was continuing fraudulent activity after 1997 was arguably relevant in relation to causation, even if the claimant was not aware of it at the time, because it could form the basis of an argument or cross-examination that a fear of discovery led to the alleged detriment. But before allegations of that seriousness were permitted there should be (a) proper notice and (b) a proper foundation for the allegation. It was premature for the ET to allow the evidence, rather than enquiring as to the nature of the evidence and determining its admissibility.

Result: appeal upheld in part: objection to admissibility of evidence was well founded at the relevant time. Sequential exchange of statements ordered on the issue of alleged corruption.

Sections considered: N/A.**Cited by**: *Gray v Merrill Lynch, Pierce, Fenner & Smith Ltd* (UKEAT/0058/16/DM); *Aryeetey v Tuntum Housing Association* (UKEAT/0070/07, 12 October 2007).

26. Odong v Chubb Security Personnel

EAT/0819/02/TM, 13 May 2003

Key issues: qualifying disclosure: legal obligation and reasonable belief.

Case summary: Mr Odong was a security officer employed by the respondent. He was instructed to work in the relevant period for American Express. When Odong attended work, the guard finishing the previous shift instructed him to make regular checks in three rooms because of a 'danger of overheating which might lead to a fire'. Odong refused to perform the task as (a) he suspected the previous guard did not have authority to instruct him as to what he must do and (b) the rooms were marked 'No Entry'. Odong did not therefore carry out the checks. On the next day at the start of his shift there was a written instruction provided by a manager to perform the tasks and Odong duly obliged. American Express became aware of his refusal and instructed Chubb to remove him. Odong asserted that the direction of his colleague was unlawful and unauthorized. He asserted that he had made a protected disclosure to his colleague when he refused to perform the tasks. He claimed that he had suffered a detriment in (a) his removal from his posting to American Express and (b) the failure to post him elsewhere thereafter.

ET: found that Odong was removed because he failed to obey a reasonable instruction to conduct temperature checks. The tribunal dismissed the claim that his removal was due to his protected disclosure.

EAT (Mr Recorder Luba QC): allowed the appeal. It accepted that on the tribunal's findings of fact there was a qualifying disclosure under s 43(1)(b) for 'failing or likely to fail to comply with a legal obligation' in that Odong had doubted that the person who gave the instruction to enter the room to carry out the checks had the authority to do so (paras 13, 20 and 21):

> [Counsel] draws attention to the fact that there are several potential legal obligations which may have been infringed by Mr Bailey [who gave the instruction to carry out the checks]. First,

Mr Bailey may have been in breach of his own contract of employment with Chubb, if he was giving a fellow employee an unauthorised or illegitimate instruction. Second, insofar as Mr Bailey was acting as Chubb's representative in giving the instruction, the giving of an unauthorised instruction or an instruction beyond the terms of Mr Odong's contract of employment was a breach of that contract of employment. Thirdly, the instruction may have been in breach of legal obligations imposed by American Express Bank, as represented by the fact that they had described the rooms as 'No Entry' rooms. It is not necessary for Mr Odong to establish that, in fact, there was a failure to comply with any legal obligation in giving Mr Odong the instruction he was given. For the purposes of section 43B, it is sufficient if it was the reasonable belief of Mr Odong that the instruction was given in breach of legal obligations.

... on the basis of the recent authority of this Tribunal in *Parkins v Sodexho Ltd* ... that a breach of a term of a contract of employment is a sufficient breach, or a potentially sufficient breach, to come within section 43B(1)(b). In those circumstances, ... the Tribunal, having found the facts that it did find, must have been satisfied that the conditions of section 43B(1)(b) were made out and insofar as they thereafter rejected the proposition that that section was satisfied, they erred in law in doing so. As to the 'reasonable belief' component of the section 43B test, ... the finding by the Tribunal that Mr Odong believed that the employer's representative (Mr Bailey) had no authority to give the instruction. Although the Tribunal do not expressly find that this was a reasonable belief, nor do they find that it was an unreasonable belief. In those circumstances it seems to us that there was material found by the Tribunal capable of amounting to a protected disclosure for the purposes of 43A and 43B of the 1996 Act.

Result: remitted to ET.

Detriment: removal of his posting to American Express and the failure to post him elsewhere thereafter.

Sections considered: ERA, ss 43A, 43B, 47B.

27. Kraus v Penna plc

[2004] IRLR 260 (EAT)

Key issues: (1) meaning of 'likely' in ERA, s 43(1) re qualifying disclosure; (2) requirement for actual legal obligation (not merely reasonable belief of one) for s 43(1)(b).

Case summary: Mr Kraus alleged that the human resource services he provided under contract for R1 to R2 had been terminated because he had advised that proposed redundancies 'could' breach employment legislation and leave a vulnerability to unfair dismissal claims.

ET: no qualifying disclosure. ET justified in striking out the claim as misconceived.

EAT (Mr Justice Cox): the word 'likely' in s 43B(1)(b) requires more than a possibility or a risk that an employer might fail to comply with a relevant legal obligation. The information disclosed should, in the reasonable belief of the worker at the time it is disclosed, tend to show that it is probable or more probable than not that the employer will fail to comply with the relevant legal obligation. Therefore it was not sufficient merely to say that the company 'could' breach employment legislation (para 21). At its highest, therefore, Mr Kraus' belief was limited to the possibility or the risk of a breach of employment legislation, depending on what eventually took place. The EAT commented that it also bore in mind that, as Mr Kraus would know, consultation on the reorganization/redundancy programme would have to take place, which could affect the numbers of employees to be made redundant, and there may have been sufficient volunteers for redundancy so as to avoid the need for, or reduce considerably, any compulsory redundancies. Mr Kraus did not himself believe that the information he disclosed to Mr Bolton tended to show that a failure to comply with a legal obligation was 'likely', in the sense of 'probable' or 'more probable than not'. [3]

[Note: The EAT also held that the alleged legal obligation must in fact exist and it would not be sufficient that the employee believed that it existed but this has now been overturned by *Babula v Waltham Forest* [2007] IRLR 346 (CA).]

Result: no disclosure as no legal obligation—appeal dismissed.

---

[3] For criticism of this approach see Chapter 3 paras 3.92 et seq.

Detriment: the termination of the consultancy agreement.

Sections considered: ERA, ss 43A, 43B, 43C, 43K(1)(a), 43K(2)(a), 43L(3), 47B, 48(1A), 103A.

Overruled in part by: *Babula v Waltham Forest College* [2007] ICR 1026.

Cited by: *Western Union Payment Services UK Ltd v Anastasiou* (UKEAT/0135/13/LA, 21 February 2014; UKEAT/0135/13/LA, 12 May 2014); *Raja v Secretary of State for Justice* (UKEAT/0364/09, 15 February 2010); *Kirwan v First Corporate Shipping Ltd* (EAT/0066/07, 12 October 2007); *Felter v Cliveden Petroleum Company* (EAT/0533/05, 17 May 2006); *Boulding v Land Securities Trillium (Media Services) Ltd* (EAT/0023/06, 3 May 2006).

28. Felter v Cliveden Petroleum Company

EAT/0533/05, 9 March 2006

Key issues: whether there was a legal obligation (ERA, s 43B(1)(b)). Where there was a commercial contract between two commercial companies whether that contract contained an implied obligation requiring the executive chairman of one of them to inform the other when 50 per cent of the shareholding was sold by its owner to Chinese companies?

Case summary: Dr Felter was appointed director and executive chairman of an oil company, Cliveden SA. Cliveden owned eight geological basins, known as the 'Chad Convention', that were to be explored for oil. Fifty per cent of Cliveden's interest in the Chad Convention was sold to a Canadian corporation, Encana. The deal was negotiated by Dr Felter. An agreement was entered into between Encana and Cliveden. It was common ground between the parties, and recorded by the EAT (at para 25), that the agreement was 'impenetrable'. Subsequently, 50 per cent of Cliveden's shares were sold to two Chinese companies. It was alleged by Dr Felter that he had made a protected disclosure by advising the respondent that it was obliged to tell Encana of the share sale before it took place or immediately afterwards.

ET: found that there was no implied legal obligation or express obligation to tell Encanca.

EAT (HHJ McMullen QC): dismissed the appeal on the basis that following *Kraus v Penna* [2004] IRLR 260 the finding that there was no legal obligation was decisive of the issue. Notwithstanding the impenetrable nature of the agreements, and the difficult legal issues which arose as to what obligations should be implied under the agreement, there was no issue as to whether it was reasonable for Dr Felter to believe that there was a legal obligation. [Note: *Kraus v Penna* was overruled on this point in *Babula v Waltham Forest College* [2007] ICR 1026 (CA).]

Result: appeal dismissed.

Detriment: released from position as chairman and member of board.

Sections considered: ERA, ss 43B(1)(b), 47B, 103A.

29. Boulding v Land Securities

UKEAT/0023/06, 3 May 2006

Key issue: whether it was an error for the ET to accede to a submission of no case to answer on the grounds of lack of reasonable belief.

Case summary: Mr Boulding had responsibility relating to a generator. In October he delayed action on the generator on the grounds that various necessary actions had not been undertaken. He prompted a further delay in February and purported to make a qualifying disclosure by email. He was dismissed soon afterwards. He brought a claim under ERA, s 103A. After he had given his evidence the respondent made a submission of no case to answer on the grounds of lack of qualifying disclosure.

ET: upheld the submission of no case to answer. Although Mr Boulding had made the reports in the email in good faith, the ET found that he could not have had a reasonable belief that any breaches of regulation were likely to occur. It came to this conclusion principally on the grounds of the respondent's actions in response to his reports of the past and the power he had in his position to prevent any breaches in any event. The ET further awarded costs of £10,000 against Mr Boulding.

EAT (HHJ McMullen QC): found that the ET had failed to focus upon the central complaint made by the claimant in his email (relied on as the protected disclosure) that there would be non-compliance by his employer with the statutory CE marking regime. That was a commercial matter over which he had no power. It was the matter on which he took advice from the Institute of Directors. He took the trouble of finding the relevant regulations and presented them to his manager:

> It would be strange indeed and out of step with the regime of protection for an employee in such a situation not to have the statutory protection, as he saw it, although steps were being taken to provide documentation. No one had assured him that a CE marking was forthcoming. . ... The Tribunal had before it the components of a valid claim under s 43C all of which should be tested through evidence from the Respondent.

Although the burden of proof was on Mr Boulding to establish a protected disclosure, the ET had wrongly decided to cut short the case at half time. The finding as to what was likely to be a failure by the respondent could not be determined simply upon the evidence of the claimant. What people have done in the past in response to the claimant's earlier complaints would be relevant. But it was not the sole basis upon which it could be determined whether the claimant had a reasonable belief in the likelihood of a failure and (para 31):

> It is only in an exceptional case that a half-time submission in what is effectively a discrimination matter should be acceded to.

The EAT also commented (para 2) that:

> the legislation is to be made to operate to protect those whose employers and colleagues may regard as eccentric and misguided in their response to an irregularity at work.

And (para 24) that:

> . . . The approach in *ALM v Bladon* is one to be followed in whistle-blowing cases. That is, there is a certain generosity in the construction of the statute and in the treatment of the facts. Whistle-blowing is a form of discrimination claim (see *Lucas v Chichester* UKEAT/0713/04).

Result: case remitted to same ET for hearing to continue. Costs order set aside.

Sections considered: ERA, s 43B.

Cited by: *Western Union Payment Services UK Ltd v Anastasiou* (UKEAT/0135/13/LA, 21 February 2014); *Korashi v Abertawe Bro Morgannwg University Local Health Board* [2012] IRLR 4; *Dunster v First Transpennine Express Ltd* (UKEAT/0570/10/ZT, 19 August 2011).

30. Bolton School v Evans

[2006] IRLR 500 (EAT), [2007] IRLR 140 (CA)

Key issue: reason for dismissal/detriment: distinction between the making a protected disclosure and other conduct of the whistleblower.

Case summary: Mr Evans deliberately 'hacked' into the new computer system at the respondent school to test and demonstrate the validity of his concerns over data security. He was disciplined and then resigned in protest at this. He claimed that he had been constructively unfairly dismissed. He also asserted that he had permission to try to break into the system. The respondent argued that he had been dismissed not because he had disclosed matters of public interest but, rather, because he had without authority hacked into the computer system.

ET: found that the claimant had been automatically unfairly dismissed (constructive dismissal) and suffered a detriment. He had also been unfairly dismissed contrary to s 98 ERA. In relation to causation the ET adopted a purposive approach:

> . . . it would emasculate the public policy behind the legislation for us to accept the respondent's submission that the claimant was the subject of disciplinary action not because he had blown the whistle on a suspected failure to comply with the legal obligation but rather because he had hacked into the respondent's computer system without authority. To allow an employer to defeat a Public Interest Disclosure Act case in this way would be to drive a coach and horses through the intention of the legislature that whistleblowers should have employment protection. Doubtless, had the claimant approached Mr Edmundson, Mr Brooker or anyone else for that matter, and simply said that he had a belief that the security system was inadequate, and had he been subject to disciplinary action and brought a similar complaint as he now does, the respondent would have sought to argue that he did not have the basis for a reasonable belief. The respondent cannot have it both ways. In order to obtain sufficient evidence to found a reasonable belief, the Claimant had to do more than simply express misgivings about what had

happened over the summer of 2003. It is our view that the legislation must be construed purposively and the investigation undertaken by the employee to found his reasonable belief should not be divorced from the disclosure itself.

It is our judgment, therefore, that the claimant has established that the reason that disciplinary action was taken against him was because he made a protected disclosure.

Section 43B(3) ERA provides that a disclosure is not protected if the person making it commits a criminal offence in so doing. However, the EAT held that Evans did not lose protection on this basis because the Computer Misuse Act 1990 only established criminal liability for unauthorized access to computers, and the ET found that he was in fact authorized.

EAT (Mr Justice Elias): found that breaking into the computer system was not a disclosure. Informing relevant people that it could be broken into was a disclosure. Mr Evans was dismissed for breaking into the system, which was not a protected act. The EAT explained (paras 64–68) that a distinction was to be drawn between the making of the disclosure (which was protected) and the previous investigation (which was not protected):

> The Tribunal sought to justify its conclusion on policy grounds. It observed that if the Claimant had simply noted that the security system was inadequate and had been disciplined then the employers would have said that he had no reasonable grounds for his belief. The point is, however, it seems to us, that if he had done simply that there is no reason to suppose that he would have been subject to any disciplinary sanction at all. And even if he had, the law only protects him if he has reasonable grounds for his belief. It does not allow him to commit what would otherwise be acts of misconduct in the hope that he may be able to establish the justification for his belief.

> An employee cannot be entitled to break into his employer's filing cabinet in the hope of finding papers which will demonstrate some relevant wrongdoing which he can then disclose to the appropriate person. He is liable to be disciplined for such conduct, and that is so whether he turns up such papers or not. Provided that his misconduct is genuinely the reason for the disciplinary action, the employee will not be protected even if he does in fact discover incriminating papers. Success does not retrospectively provide a cloak of immunity for his actions, although he will then of course be protected with respect to the subsequent disclosure of the information itself.

> . . .

> Putting it simply, it seems to us that the law protects the disclosure of information which the employee reasonably believes tends to demonstrate the kind of wrongdoing, or anticipated wrongdoing, which is covered by section 43B. It does not protect the actions of the employee which are directed to establishing or confirming the reasonableness of that belief. The protection is for the whistleblower who reasonably believes, to put it colloquially if inaccurately, that something is wrong, not the investigator who seeks either to establish that it is wrong or to show that his concerns are reasonable.

The EAT also considered the case of *Kraus v Penna plc* [2004] IRLR 260 (EAT) and the requirement (subsequently disapproved by the CA in *Babula*) that where reliance is placed on s 43B(1)(b) there must be an actual legal obligation rather than merely a belief that one exists. As to this (paras 51–52):

> We do not think that the protection is lost merely because the employer may be able to show that, for reasons not immediately apparent to the employee, the duty will not apply or that he has some defence to it. The information will still, it seems to us, tend to show the likelihood of breach. It is potentially powerful and material evidence pointing in that direction even although there may be other factors which ultimately would demonstrate that no breach is likely to occur.

> There may indeed be cases where a relatively detailed appreciation of the relevant legal obligation is required before an employee can establish that he reasonably believed that the information tended to show that a breach of a legal obligation was likely. But it would undermine the protection of this valuable legislation if employees were expected to anticipate and evaluate all potential defences, whether within the scope of their own knowledge or not, when deciding whether or not to make that disclosure.

CA (Buxton, Lathan, and Longmore LJJ): Evans was disciplined for hacking into the computer system, not the disclosure. The court rejected an argument that the hacking could be regarded as part of the disclosure. The legislation did not attribute a special meaning to the word 'disclosure'. The tribunal's findings as to why the claimant was disciplined were a conclusive answer to the question of whether he was dismissed for making a protected disclosure.

Result: no protected disclosure.

Detriment: a warning.

Sections considered: ERA, ss 43A, 43B, 43C, 47B, 103A.

Damages awarded: at first instance £26,118.13 was awarded which included an award of £3,000 for injured feelings resulting from the detriment.

Cited by: *Barton v Royal Borough of Greenwich* (UKEAT/0041/14/DXA, 1 May 2015); *Hibbins v Hesters Way Neighbourhood Project* [2009] ICR 319 (EAT); *Babula v Waltham Forest College* [2007] ICR 1026 (CA); *Kuzel v Roche Products Ltd* [2007] ICR 945 (EAT).

31. Babula v Waltham Forest College

EAT/0635/05, 31 March 2006, [2007] ICR 1026 (CA)

Key issue: reasonable belief in relevant failure; meaning of 'likely'.

Case summary: Mr Babula joined the respondent college as a lecturer. He discovered that his predecessor had divided students into Islamic and non-Islamic groups and stated to the Islamic group that he wished that a September 11 incident would occur in London, indicating his happiness with the events in New York on 11 September 2001. The students and then Babula raised concerns with the college that these observations amounted to a 'threat to national security and a possible criminal offence of incitement to racial hatred'. He then reported the matter to the CIA and FBI, where he was advised to report his concerns to the local police. The claimant asserted that the disclosure tended to show a criminal offence of incitement to commit racial hatred under s 18 of the Public Order Act 1986.

ET: the Chairman at a preliminary hearing followed *Kraus v Penna plc* [2004] IRLR 260 (EAT) and struck out the claim. The underlying problem on the pleaded case was really one of religion rather than race and there was (at that time) no offence of inciting religious hatred.

EAT (HHJ Peter Clark): upheld the ET's finding in the light of *Kraus*.

Babula's pleaded case was that he reasonably believed that a criminal offence of incitement to racial hatred had been committed. That claim failed because the allegations only amounted to racial hatred. The disclosure that a lecturer had said that he wished to see a 9/11 incident in the United Kingdom was capable of amounting to threatening words, but the words were not capable of evincing an intention to stir up racial hatred, that is hatred against a racial group. The racial group against whom the 9/11 remark was directed was not made up of British citizens, but the group of students consisting of Jews and white Europeans and that group emerged from the division of the class into Islamic and non-Islamic students, a division based on religion, not race.

CA (Thorpe, Thomas and Wall LJJ): overturning *Kraus v Penna* in this respect, the reasonable belief test applies to whether the relevant legal obligation or criminal offence exists.

> 75. ... Provided his belief (which is inevitably subjective) is held by the tribunal to be objectively reasonable, neither (1) the fact that the belief turns out to be wrong, nor (2) the fact that the information which the claimant believed to be true (and may indeed be true) does not in law amount to a criminal offence, is, in my judgment, sufficient, of itself, to render the belief unreasonable and thus deprive the whistleblower of the protection afforded by the statute.
>
> ...
>
> 79. It is also, I think, significant that section 43B(1) uses the phrase 'tends to show' not 'shows'. There is, in short, nothing in section 43B(1) which requires the whistleblower to be right. At its highest in relation to section 43B(1)(a) he must have a reasonable belief that the information in his possession 'tends to show' that a criminal offence has been committed: at its lowest he must have a reasonable belief that the information in his possession tends to show that a criminal offence is likely to be committed. The fact that he may be wrong is not relevant, provided his belief is reasonable, and the disclosure to his employer made in good faith (section 43C(1)(a)).

80. ... The purpose of the statute, as I read it, is to encourage responsible whistleblowing. To expect employees on the factory floor or in shops and offices to have a detailed knowledge of the criminal law sufficient to enable them to determine whether or not particular facts which they reasonably believe to be true are capable, as a matter of law, of constituting a particular criminal offence seems to me both unrealistic and to work against the policy of the statute.

...

82. ... in my judgment, the word 'belief' in section 43B(1) is plainly subjective. It is the particular belief held by the particular worker. Equally, however, the 'belief' must be 'reasonable'. That is an objective test. Furthermore, like the appeal tribunal in *Darnton*, I find it difficult to see how a worker can reasonably believe that an allegation tends to show that there has been a relevant failure if he knows or believes that the factual basis for the belief is false. In any event, these are all matters for the employment tribunal to determine on the facts.

Result: remitted to a fresh tribunal.

Sections considered: ERA, s 43B(1)(a), (b), (f).

Cited by: *Underwood v Wincanton plc* (UKEAT/0163/15/RN 27 August 2015); *Chesterton Global Ltd & Anor v Nurmohamed* [2015] IRLR 614; *Barton v Royal Borough of Greenwich* (UKEAT/0041/14/DXA, 1 May 2015); *Soh v Imperial College of Science, Technology & Medicine* (UKEAT/0350/14/DM, 3 September 2015); *Western Union Payment Services UK Ltd v Anastasiou* (UKEAT/0135/13/LA, 21 February 2014); *Blitz v Vectone Group Holdings Ltd* (EAT 29 November 2011, UKEAT /0253/10/DM); *Korashi v Abertawe Bro Morgannwg University Local Health Board* [2012] IRLR 4; *Cavendish Munro Professional Risks Management Ltd v Geduld* [2010] ICR 325 (EAT); *Muchesa v Central and Cecil Housing Care Support* (EAT/0443/07, 22 August 2008); *Premier Mortgage Connections Ltd v Miller* (EAT/0113/07, 2 November 2007).

32. Network Rail Infrastructure Ltd v Glencross

UKEAT/0094/08, 16 May 2008

Key issues: qualifying disclosure; reason why question.

Case summary: Glencross was responsible for issuing overhead line permits. In March 2004 a colleague, Mr Taylor, was involved in an accident when he fell off a ladder whilst working with Glencross on the maintenance of overhead lines. The use of a ladder, instead of the correct piece of equipment, was a fast but dangerous way of doing the work. Taylor and Glencross were pressurized by their manager (Mr Arminger) to give false statements in which they untruthfully claimed that they had been issued with the correct equipment. In August 2005 Glencross provided a statement to Taylor's personal injury lawyer which contained a correct statement of what had happened. A manager than asked Mr Arminger to speak to Glencross and Taylor to tell them that if they changed their original statement they would be subject to disciplinary action. However, Glencross wrote to the manager on 12 January 2006 setting out a truthful account of the accident and raising other complaints about safety. Matters then deteriorated. Disciplinary action was taken in relation to other matters, and Glencross was summarily dismissed for the offence of having made a false statement in relation to Taylor's accident and then made corrective statements. On appeal the sanction in relation to the false statement was changed to a final written warning on the basis that there were mitigating circumstances. He received reprimands in relation to the other disciplinary matters. He returned to work and was then disciplined and ultimately dismissed purportedly in relation to a failure to follow certain safety procedures. An appeal was dismissed.

ET: found that Glencross's letter of 12 January 2006, in which he referred to having been put under undue pressure to make a false statement and threatened with dismissal, contained protected disclosures in that it tended to show that health and safety of an individual had been, was being, or was likely to be put in danger. He was dismissed and subject to detriment by reason of the protected disclosure.

EAT (Wilkie J): found that there was no error of law in the determination of dismissal by reason of a protected disclosure. The EAT rejected a submission that it was not relevant for the ET to make findings as to the 2004 accident and making of false statements and having changed them, as the truth of those allegations was highly relevant for reasonable belief for the purposes of a qualifying disclosure and for good faith. Although the ET had not expressly said that it disbelieved the dismissing officers as to their reasons for dismissal, and it would have been better if the ET had done so, this was implicit in its reasoning. The ET was entitled to look at the surrounding circumstances, including the change in attitude to Glencross and the differing treatment of incidents before and after the disclosure, in order to make findings as to the real reason for dismissal. However, the reasoning in relation to ERA, s 47B was deficient in failing to identify the detriment concerned and the process of reasoning by which it concluded the detriment was on the grounds of a protected disclosure.

Result: ET decision that claimant dismissed by reason of protected disclosure upheld; s 47B detriment claim remitted.

Sections considered: ERA, ss 43B, 43C.

Damages: £203,000 at first instance.

33. Muchesa v Central and Cecil Housing Care Support

[2008] EAT/0443/07, 22 August 2008

Key issues: reasonable belief and good faith; to what extent must an ET make express findings on the subjective elements of the test?

Case summary: Ms Muchesa was employed as a senior night carer at a residential care home (CCHCS). She made allegations to a daughter of a resident of seriously defective care. She also made calls to the police and social services alleging serious neglect and was subsequently suspended. She then lodged grievances alleging sexual harassment and race discrimination. She made very serious allegations about the care of residents. She brought claims including under ss 47B and 103A.

ET: found that the external disclosures were not qualifying disclosures. The alleged acts did not occur. Ms Muchesa did not have a reasonable belief that the disclosures made to the external recipients were substantially true.

EAT (HHJ Burke QC): held that the guidance in *Darnton* and *Babula* is applicable to the reasonable belief test in the context of reasonable belief in the substantial truth test for external disclosures. However, the ET was entitled to consider whether the complaints were true and to regard its view of this as an important tool to the resolution of the reasonable belief issue, especially as Ms Muchesa was complaining of matters of which she claimed to have direct knowledge. The ET was also entitled to have regard to objective factors such as the failure to use CCHS's whistleblowing procedure of which she was aware, her failure to ask a junior member of staff to witness the abuse of which she was complaining, her failure to require the attendance of the police herself, her failure to write up the incident in the communications book, and the significant amount of time she spent photocopying rather than attending to the problem which was at the root of her complaints. The ET was entitled to ask itself whether the actions or inactions of Ms Muchesa pointed not only towards the truth of her complaints but also to whether she genuinely believed in that truth. She had not behaved in the manner she would have behaved had she reasonably believed in the truth of the complaints.

In relation to good faith, the ET properly directed itself that lack of good faith involved more than lack of reasonable belief and that it required a predominant motive which was an ulterior motive unrelated to the statutory objectives, although (at para 41):

> there must have been, as a matter of commonsense, not a very great distance between a finding that Miss Muchesa did not reasonably believe in the truth of her allegations and a finding that she had not acted in good faith; but, whatever the extent of that distance, the Tribunal were fully aware of it and had expressly directed themselves as to it. . .

The failure of the ET to make express findings as to the internal disclosures was addressed under the process of questions being posed to the ET by the EAT, as endorsed by the Court of Appeal in *Barke v Seetec Business Technology Centre Ltd* [2005] ICR 1373.

Result: there were no qualifying disclosures; appeal dismissed; detailed costs assessment against Ms Muchesa (publicly funded).

Sections considered: ERA, ss 43B, 43C–F, 43G.

Cited in: *Soh v Imperial College of Science, Technology and Medicine* (EAT 3 September 2015, UKEAT/ 0350/14/DM).

34. Hibbins v Hesters Way Neighbourhood Project

[2009] IRLR 198 (EAT)

Key issue: whether the wrongdoing raised in the disclosure must be that of the employer or whether it can be that of some other person/organization.

Case summary: the claimant, a teacher, read a report in a local newspaper from which she identified a suspect in a rape case as a student she had interviewed for a course run by her employer. She passed information about him to the police. She claimed that in consequence she was branded a trouble-maker by her employer because her disclosures to the police had involved the employer in a criminal matter, and claimed that the disclosures were protected disclosures made in accordance with s 43H.

ET: concluded that she had not made a protected disclosure since the disclosure related to a third party, not her employer.

EAT (Mr Justice Silber): found there is no limitation in the statute on the people or entities whose apprehended wrongdoings could be the subject of qualifying disclosures because the wrongdoer is simply identified within s 43B as a 'person'.

Result: appeal allowed; case remitted for a different tribunal.

Sections considered: ERA, ss 43B, 43C.

Cited by: *BP plc v Elstone* [2011] ICR 879 (EAT).

35. Cavendish Munro Professional Risks Management Ltd v Geduld

[2010] ICR 325

Key issue: what is a 'disclosure of information'?

Case summary: Mr Geduld was a director, shareholder, and employee of CMPRM. Following mounting tensions between himself and other directors he was removed as a director. Mr Geduld wrote to CMPRM, via his solicitors. The letter alleged that there were issues as to the validity of a shareholders' agreement and as to unfair prejudice, and reserved his rights and put forward settlement proposals. He was dismissed the next day and claimed unfair dismissal under s 103A (having less than 12 months' service).

ET: found that the statement (as detailed above) was a 'disclosure of information' for the purposes of s 43B(1). It also went on to uphold the s 103A claim.

EAT (Mrs Justice Slade): found that there was no disclosure of information. A disclosure of information is to be distinguished from an allegation (para 20):

> That the Employment Rights Act 1996 recognises a distinction between 'information' and an 'allegation' is illustrated by the reference to both of these terms in section 43F. Although that section does not apply directly in the context of this case, nonetheless it is included in the section of the Act with which we are concerned. It is instructive that those two terms are treated differently and can therefore be regarded as having been intended to have different meanings. Further, that 'information' and 'an allegation' are different is clear from the victimisation provisions in the Sex Discrimination Act 1975 and in the Race Relations Act 1976.

As to the meaning of disclosure of information:

> 24 ... the ordinary meaning of giving 'information' is conveying facts. In the course of the hearing before us, a hypothetical was advanced regarding communicating information about the state of a hospital. Communicating 'information' would be 'The wards have not been cleaned for the past two weeks. Yesterday, sharps were left lying around'. Contrasted with that would be a statement that 'you are not complying with Health and Safety requirements'. In our view this would be an allegation not information.

> 25. In the employment context, an employee may be dissatisfied, as here, with the way he is being treated. He or his solicitor may complain to the employer that if they are not going to be treated better, they will resign and claim constructive dismissal. Assume that the employer, having received that outline of the employee's position from him or from his solicitor, then dismisses the employee. In our judgment, that dismissal does not follow from any disclosure of information. It follows a statement of the employee's position. In our judgment, that situation would not fall within the scope of the Employment Rights Act s.43.

26. The tribunal based its conclusion that Mr Geduld was dismissed because, through his solicitor's letter of 4 February 2008, he made a protected disclosure. In our judgment the letter sets out a statement of the position of Mr Geduld. In order to fall within the statutory definition of protected disclosure there must be disclosure of information. In our judgment, the letter of 4 February 2008 does not convey information as contemplated by the legislation let alone disclose information. It is a statement of position quite naturally and properly communicated in the course of negotiations between the parties.

The ET had also erred in relation to whether there was a disclosure:

27 ... The natural meaning of the word 'disclose' is to reveal something to someone who does not know it already. However s.43L(3) provides that 'disclosure' for the purpose of s.43 has effect so that 'bringing information to a person's attention' albeit that he is already aware of it is a disclosure of that information. There would no need for the extended definition of 'disclosure' if it were intended by the legislature that 'disclosure' should mean no more than 'communication'.

28. On the facts of this case, the solicitor's letter of 4 February 2008 was written as part of an ongoing unresolved dispute between the parties. It in effect was alleging that Mr Geduld was an oppressed minority shareholder and, in summary terms, stated the basis of that position. It did not disclose any facts; it merely summarised the basis of a position adopted by Mr Geduld.

29. It is not unusual that solicitors are asked to write on behalf of employees. If an employee is feeling badly treated, the solicitor may write to say that the employer is in breach of contract. There may be allegations over allocation of work or that the employee has been overlooked for a promotion. The solicitor may say, 'If the situation does not improve, we have advised our client that he can resign and claim constructive dismissal'. In those circumstances, in our judgment, no protected disclosure is made in such a letter. Similarly, if the individual met the employer without the intervention of the solicitor and made the same points, there would be no protected disclosure by that employee to the employer.

Result: appeal upheld; decision of ET set aside.

Sections considered: ERA, ss 43A, 43B, 43L.

Cited by: *Kilraine v London Borough of Wandsworth* [2016] IRLR 422; *Barton v Royal Borough of Greenwich* (UKEAT/0041/14/DXA, 1 May 2015); *Ahmed v City of Bradford Metropolitan District Council* (UKEAT/0145/14/KN, 27 October 2014); *Gebremariam v Ethiopian Airlines Enterprise t/a Ethiopian Airlines* [2014] IRLR 354 (EAT); *Western Union Payment Services UK Ltd v Anastasiou* (UKEAT/0135/13/LA, 21 February 2014); *Millbank Financial Services Ltd v Crawford* [2014] IRLR 18; *Norbrook Laboratories (GB) Ltd v Shaw* [2014] ICR 540; *Watkins v BBC* (UKEAT/0189/12/LA, 27 June 2012); *Local Government Yorkshire & Humber v Shah* (UKEAT/0587/11/ZT, 19 June 2012); *Blitz v Vectone Group Holdings Ltd* (EAT 29 November 2011, UKEAT /0253/10/DM); *Royal Cornwall Hospitals NHS Trust v Watkinson* (UKEAT/0378/10, 17 August 2011); *Freeman v Ultra Green Group Ltd (In Liquidation)* (EAT/0239/11, 9 August 2011); *Smith v London Metropolitan University* (EAT/0364/10, 21 July 2011); *Kennedy v Margarot Forrest Care Management* (UKEATS/0023/10, 26 November 2010); *Goode v Marks and Spencer plc* (EAT/0442/09, 15 April 2010).

36. Goode v Marks and Spencer plc

EAT/0442/09, 15 April 2010

Key issue: what is a 'disclosure of information'?

Case summary: M&S put forward a proposal ('the document of 11 July') to amend its enhanced redundancy scheme (said to be discretionary). Mr Goode told Mr Raichura (of M&S) that he thought the proposals were disgusting. He emailed *The Times* making other statements including that it could be a prelude to a wave of redundancies and his expectation that the staff representative group would not be able to counter their proposals. He was dismissed following his email to *The Times*. He claimed unfair dismissal, including under s 103A.

ET: found that Goode was dismissed for the email to *The Times*. However, the dismissal was fair. His comment to Raichura was not a 'disclosure of information'. In respect of the email to *The Times*, it found that he did not make a 'disclosure of information', he did not make a disclosure of 'substantially the same information', and further he did not reasonably believe that Raichura was likely to breach its legal obligations.

EAT (Wilkie J):

(1) The disclosure to Mr Raichura was at its highest only 'information' in the sense of being a statement of Goode's state of mind, namely that he was disgusted with the proposals (applying *Geduld*). Even viewing this in the context of the document of 11 July, there was nothing which anyone could reasonable believe tended to show a likely failure to comply with a legal obligation.

(2) As to disclosure to *The Times*, even if it was a qualifying disclosure it was not protected under s 43G. Goode's contention that he had previously made disclosure of substantially the same information to his employer (within s 43(G)(2)(c)(i)) was rejected. If the internal disclosure was not a qualifying disclosure, but the external disclosure was a qualifying disclosure, it could not be that the internal disclosure was of substantially the same information. The previous disclosure of disgust at the proposals was not substantially the same information.

(3) In any event there was no reasonable belief in a likely breach of a legal obligation given that the scheme was discretionary and there was to be consultation as to proposed changes to the scheme and nothing to indicate the consultation would be a sham.

Result: appeal dismissed.

Sections considered: ERA, ss 43B, 43C, 43G; TULRCA 1992, ss 188, 195.

Cited by: *Western Union Payment Services UK Ltd v Anastasiou* (UKEAT/0135/13/LA, 21 February 2014); *Norbrook Laboratories (GB) Ltd v Shaw* [2014] ICR 540; *Millbank Financial Services Ltd v Crawford* [2014] IRLR 18; *Korashi v Abertawe Bro Morgannwg University Local Health Board* [2012] IRLR 4 (EAT).

37. BP plc v Elstone and Petrotechnics Ltd

[2010] ICR 879

Key issue: definition of 'worker' in ERA, s 47B; whether a disclosure in a previous employment is covered.

Case summary: Mr Elstone was dismissed by Petrotechnics for making a disclosure to BP. Later he was engaged by BP. He was then dismissed by BP on the grounds of his earlier disclosure whilst working at Petrotechnics.

ET: concluded that a claimant does have to have been a 'worker' when s/he makes the disclosure, but not necessarily a worker of the company against which s/he later claims for detriment.

EAT (Mr Justice Langstaff): found that a worker is protected against detriment or dismissal by his/her current employer by reason of a protected disclosure whilst made in previous employment:

> the courts are obliged to take a purposive approach to the statutory provisions, so as to advance the protection of whistleblowers from later retribution by an employer. It is protection, rather than the identity of the employer, which is central to this.

Result: Elstone satisfied the definition of worker under s 47B; appeal and cross-appeal dismissed.

Sections considered: ERA, ss 43A, 43B, 43C, 47A, 47B.

Damages awarded: none.

Cited in: *Day v Lewisham and Greenwich NHS Trust and Health Education England* (UKEAT/0250/15/RN, 9 March 2016), [2016] IRLR 415.

38. Easwaran v St George's University of London

EAT/0167/10, 24 June 2010

Key issues: ERA, s 43B and reasonable belief in whether disclosure 'tended to show' a relevant failure.

Case summary: The claimant was a medical demonstrator. His work was mostly done in a dissecting room, which he complained was excessively cold. The windows in the room were kept open to counteract a risk from fumes from the formalin used for preservation. The claimant had an altercation with the dissecting room technician, Mr Dennis, who refused to close the windows due to the risk of the fumes building up. He then wrote a letter to management (Dr Murphy) complaining about Dennis having sworn at him. In the course of this he complained that the dissecting room was freezing, that this was a breach of basic health and safety requirements, and that this could affect his health adversely, eg due to a risk of pneumonia.

ET: held that there was no qualifying disclosure. There were a number of unsubstantiated expressions of opinion.

EAT (Underhill J): found that the ET had erred in mixing up the differing elements of a qualifying disclosure. It was important to separate out the elements:

> 19. . . . It is always desirable, and particularly so in the case of complex provisions of this kind, for employment tribunals carefully to analyse the separate elements in the statutory provision under consideration and then to consider in turn whether each has been met.

The relevant separate elements here were:

(a) Was there a disclosure of information? There was a disclosure that the room was very cold and that Dennis was not prepared to close the window in order to try to mitigate the problem.
(b) Did the claimant genuinely believe that the information tended to show a relevant failure? There was no finding as to a lack of such belief, and as it would have amounted to a finding of bad faith it would have had to be expressly set out.
(c) Was the belief reasonable? It was apparent from the ET's finding that it had concluded it was not a reasonable belief on the claimant's part that pneumonia was a condition caused by working in cold temperatures. It did not matter that the claimant may genuinely have believed what he said. Further (para 23) 'it is clear that the Tribunal saw this as a case where his anger with Mr Dennis led him into taking an extreme and unjustifiable position about the risk of pneumonia'.

CA: an application for permission to appeal was refused by Sedley LJ ([2011] EWCA Civ 181).

Result: appeal dismissed.

Detriment: N/A.

Sections considered: ERA, s 43B(1).

Damages: N/A.

Cited by: *Dr Brito-Babapulle v Isle of Wight NHS Trust* (UKEAT/0090/16/DM, 10 June 2016).

39. Parker v Northumbrian Water

[2011] IRLR 652 (EAT)

Key issues: qualifying disclosure relating to alleged miscarriage of justice; whether excluded as being collateral attack on earlier decision.

Case summary: Mr Parker objected when his employer introduced a new way of treating hours not worked on rostered shift days. He brought proceedings initially for deduction of wages then recast as a declaration of particulars of employment. Declarations as terms of employment were made at the conclusion of those proceedings. The Claimant was dismissed and brought a second claim for breach of contract, unlawful deduction of wages, and unfair dismissal, including for asserting a statutory right. He then sought to amend to include detriment and dismissal on the grounds that he had made a protected disclosure. The alleged protected disclosures included allegations that the employer had lied to the employment tribunal (and the EAT) in the first proceedings.

ET: the employment judge gave permission to add a protected disclosure dismissal claim. He initially refused the s 47B detriment claims on the grounds that they would be out of time and caught by the rule in *Henderson v Henderson* but on a review he accepted some detriment claims would not caught by this. However, noting the alleged protected disclosure involved an allegation of a miscarriage of justice by misleading the ET and the EAT in the first proceedings. He concluded that it was 'manifestly unjust and wrong in principle' to allow such a further attack on the previous proceedings. He therefore refused the amendment.

EAT (HHJ Hand QC): The EJ erred in his conclusion that the protected disclosure claim was excluded because it was a collateral attack on the previous proceedings. The issue in relation to whether there was a qualifying disclosure was as to the claimant's 'reasonable belief' that what he disclosed tended to show a miscarriage of justice. That was a different question to what had been determined in the previous proceedings and Parliament must be taken to have intended that protection would apply notwithstanding that it may involve criticism of the outcome in previous proceedings:

> 76. . . . a distinction must be made between an attempt through the medium of further litigation to resurrect the issue, which has already been the subject of an (adverse) decision,

on the one hand, and a complaint of mistreatment by an employer contrary to a statutory prohibition, which is triggered not by the actual decision but by the disclosure of information 'which ... tends to show' that something may be wrong with the decision, on the other hand. The former is a collateral attack and potentially an abuse of process; the latter is not. ...

77. ... The protection against abuse has been built into the statutory regime by the inclusion of the filter that the belief must be 'reasonable'.

The tribunal needs to consider whether Parker held a reasonable belief that the information he disclosed tended to show a miscarriage of justice. If it was held that he did not, whether due to the previous decision or otherwise, that would be a determination of the case on the merits. By contrast, where a case is barred on the basis of estoppel/abuse of process that prevents the case proceeding to a determination on the merits.

The EJ had also erred in the approach to excluding claims on the basis of the rule in *Henderson v Henderson*. He had proceeded on the basis that claims prior to the previous ET were barred, rather than applying a broader merits-based approach in determining whether his second claim was an abuse of process.

Result: deduction of wages claims were excluded to the extent that they relied upon issues decided in the first proceedings, but not otherwise. Section 47B detriment claims not excluded.

Sections considered: ERA, s 43B(1)(c), 47B.

40. Ross v Eddie Stobart

UKEAT/0085/10, 16 May 2011

Key issues: scope of ERA, s 43C(1)(b)(ii). Disclosure to regulatory authorities is not within s43C(1)(b). Burden where insufficient service for statutory rights.

Case summary: Ross worked as an HGV driver. Because of limits on working hours, he was required to stay at the depot on three days. However, the effect of the Road Transport (Working Time) Regulations 2005 ('RTR') was that the time when he was required to attend at the depot was to be included within working time. Ross raised with his manager and Vehicle and Operator Services Agency (VOSA) whether it was lawful to require him to remain on site on those days. He asserted this was a protected disclosure. He was subsequently dismissed after less than a year's service. He claimed that the dismissal was automatically unfair by reason of (amongst other matters) his protected disclosures and/or by reason of raising concerns as to health and safety.

ET: found that the claimant was dismissed because he was difficult to work with and had a poor attitude to his work colleagues.

EAT (HHJ Richardson): held that there was a protected disclosure to the claimant's employer, in that he brought to the attention of management facts which indicated that the employer had failed, was failing, or was like to fail to comply with a legal obligation.

The disclosure to VOSA did not fall within s 43C(1)(b)(ii), which is directed to where the recipient of the disclosure has legal responsibility for the matter:

38. ... the purpose of section 43C(1)(b)(ii) was to protect disclosure of a relevant failure if it was made to a person having legal responsibility for the matter. Suppose, for example, that an employee discovers that the employee of a contractor is breaking the law in a way for which the contractor bears responsibility. The employee will be protected under section 43C(1) if he tells his own employer (section 43C(1)(a)), the employee of the contractor (section 43C(1)(b)(i)) and the contractor (section 43C(1)(b)(ii)). In our judgment section 43C is not concerned with disclosure to regulatory authorities.

Further, the ET's finding as to the reason for dismissal could not stand as it was undermined by having misunderstood the claimant's case as to the effect of the RTR:

58. ... It is one thing to say that an employee is 'difficult to work with' where there is a genuinely grey area about a regulatory matter; another thing altogether to make the same finding if the employee is plainly right on a subject which the employer should know and understand. It is one thing to find that an employee 'has a poor attitude to work colleagues' if his complaints about vehicle safety are unjustified; another if he was broadly justified in asking for matters to be corrected before he left the depot.

[Note: A disclosure was made to VOSA, after the claimant had specifically asked if he could call them, but it does not appear to have been argued (as it might have been) that there was therefore a disclosure under s 43C(2).]

Result: matter remitted to be heard afresh. The remitted hearing subsequently failed, see note at *Ross v Eddie Stobart Ltd* (UKEAT/0068/13/RN, 28 June 2013).

Detriment: dismissal.

Sections considered: ERA, s 43C(1).

Damages: N/A.

Cited in: *Ross v Eddie Stobart Ltd* (UKEAT/0068/13/RN, 28 June 2013).

41. Dr Smith v London Metropolitan University

EAT/0364/10, 21 July 2011

Key issues: disclosure of information.

Case summary: Dr Smith was a senior lecturer in the theatre studies department. She was moved to the English literature department following a confrontation with colleagues. Concerned she was then required to take on teaching responsibilities beyond her qualifications, she claimed she was not contracted to teach them. She raised a grievance which was dismissed and her appeal rejected. She raised a further grievance asserting harassment and stress.

The claimant was dismissed for failing to carry out her duties. She claimed unfair dismissal, detriment and automatic unfair dismissal by reason of protected disclosures.

ET: found that the claimant's misconduct in failing to carry out her duties, rather than her grievances, were the reason for her treatment and dismissal. The ET considered that there was no qualifying disclosure in relation to being required to carry out duties as this involved no breach of a legal obligation (it is not clear how the reasonable belief test was applied).

EAT (Slade J): remitted the claim of ordinary unfair dismissal to consider issues of fairness in the investigation and whether dismissal for not carrying out duties was within the range of reasonable responses. However, there was no error in dismissing the protected disclosure claims because she had no qualifying disclosures because her grievances amounted to allegations rather than disclosures of information, and in any event the disclosures were not the reason for her treatment and dismissal.

Result: dismissal of protected disclosure claims upheld. Ordinary unfair dismissal claim remitted to ET.

Detriment: N/A.

Sections considered: ERA, 47B(1).

Damages: N/A.

Cited in: *Greenly v Future Network Solutions Ltd* (UKEAT/0359/13/JOJ, 19 December 2013); *Millbank Financial Services Ltd v Crawford* [2014] IRLR 18 (EAT); *Western Union Payment Services UK Ltd v Anastasiou* (UKEAT/0135/13/LA, 21 February 2014).

42. Freeman v Ultra Green Group Ltd

UKEAT/0239/11/CEA, 9 August 2011

Key issues: was there a disclosure of information. Does a contractual retirement date limit future loss of compensation?

Case summary: the tribunal erred in law in holding that words spoken at a meeting by the claimant did not amount to information.

ET: found the claimant (working in the investment field) had stated the following at a meeting on 20 July 2009:

> The calculated return on investment is 4.66 as I have based the financial model on the 100,000 hectares and I refuse to base it on 2 million hectares as ... directed. To use the bigger area without proper costing information and scrutiny will provide investors with false information and would be misleading.

The tribunal found that this was not a disclosure of information.

EAT (HHJ Richardson): held it was clearly a disclosure of 'information'. Noting there was no proper costing information or scrutiny for the basis to use 2 million hectares and that to use that basis would provide investors with false information and would be misleading.

It is also noteworthy that the ET stated that since the respondent operated retirement provisions derived from the Employment Equality (Age) Regulations 2006 ('the Age Regulations'), his compensation was limited to the date of retirement. HHJ Richardson said this was an error. The provisions excluding unfair dismissal apply only where the contract of employment terminates on the intended date of retirement, which was not the case here.

Result: appeal allowed, remitted to fresh tribunal.

Sections considered: ERA, s 43B.

43. Royal Cornwall Hospitals NHS Trust v Watkinson

UKEAT/0378/10, 17 August 2011

Key issues: disclosure of information.

Case summary: the claimant was the respondent's chief executive. He disclosed to the respondent's board an opinion obtained from counsel stating the respondent and the Primary Care Trust ('PCT') would be acting unlawfully if they did not conduct public consultation before relocating the provision of 'Upper GI' services ('the August Disclosure'). This information came to the attention of the South West Strategic Health Authority (SHA) which regarded it as 'a severe irritant'. The claimant was suspended and dismissed just before a meeting which, had he not been dismissed, he would have attended and reiterated the advice that to proceed without consultation was illegal.

ET: found that the dismissal was as a result of pressure applied by the SHA to the respondent as a result of the August Disclosure, and was automatically unfair under ERA, s 103A.

EAT (Silber J): held that there was no error in the finding of automatically unfair dismissal under s 103A. The August Disclosure was a protected disclosure in that:

(1) In the context of the long history of opposition on the part of the PCT and SHA to the need for consultation, the claimant had a reasonable belief when disclosing counsel's opinion that it tended to show a likely breach of a legal obligation.

(2) The EAT rejected the contention that the disclosure was a mere allegation rather than the making of a disclosure. It was giving information as to what had to be done by the respondent and the PCT to comply with their obligations.

Result: appeal dismissed. Claimant was unfairly dismissed under s 103A ERA.

Sections considered: ERA, s 43B(1)(b), 103A.

Damages: The Tribunal originally awarded £1.2 million which was reduced on review to £818,000 but by the time of the Appeal the damages award was just short of £900,000 (including interest).

Cited in: *Western Union Payment Services UK Ltd v Anastasiou* (UKEAT/0135/13/LA, 21 February 2014).

44. Korashi v Abertawe Bro Morgannwg University Local Health Board

[2012] IRLR 4 (EAT)

Key issues: reasonableness of belief for ERA, ss 43B(1), 43G(1)I, and 43G(1)(e).

Case summary: the claim, presented over a three-year period during 40 days of tribunal time, concerned, amongst other claims, the assertion that the claimant's disclosures regarding the competence of a colleague who was a consultant (Mr A) at the Trust resulted in his detriment. His disclosures were both internal and external to the GMC and the police.

ET: dismissed the PIDA claims.

EAT (McMullen QC): upheld the tribunal's decision. Noting the low threshold of s43(1)(a)–(e), the words 'tend to show' required a belief centred upon a subjective consideration of what was in the mind of the discloser, but which must be objectively reasonable. That assessment is however required to take account of the context:

> 62. ... Bringing it into our own case, it requires consideration of what a staff grade O&G doctor knows and ought to know about the circumstances of the matters disclosed. To

take a simple example: a healthy young man who is taken into hospital for an orthopaedic athletic injury should not die on the operating table. A whistleblower who says that that tends to show a breach of duty is required to demonstrate that such belief is reasonable. On the other hand, a surgeon who knows the risk of such procedure and possibly the results of meta-analysis of such procedure is in a good position to evaluate whether there has been such a breach. While it might be reasonable for our lay observer to believe that such death from a simple procedure was the product of a breach of duty, an experienced surgeon might take an entirely different view of what was reasonable given what further information he or she knows about what happened at the table. So in our judgment what is reasonable in s 43B involves of course an objective standard—that is the whole point of the use of the adjective reasonable—and its application to the personal circumstances of the discloser. It works both ways. Our lay observer must expect to be tested on the reasonableness of his belief that some surgical procedure has gone wrong is a breach of duty. Our consultant surgeon is entitled to respect for his view, knowing what he does from his experience and training, but is expected to look at all the material including the records before making such a disclosure. To bring this back to our own case, many whistleblowers are insiders. That means that they are so much more informed about the goings-on of the organisation of which they make complaint than outsiders, and that that insight entitles their views to respect. Since the test is their 'reasonable' belief, that belief must be subject to what a person in their position would reasonably believe to be wrong-doing.

As to s 43G the information and any allegations are believed to be substantially true, and this applies to each allegation. As not all allegations made to the GMC were believed by the claimant to be substantially true, the claim failed. It was noted that a reliance on a 'gist' that his colleague was not properly qualified was inadequate. To succeed the claimant must believe that each allegation was substantially true when it was made.

66. ... once one goes outside the immediate confines of the employment relationship and to an outsider, here the GMC, additional layers of responsibility are required upon the discloser. The information must in the reasonable belief of the discloser be substantially true. There is no obligation to make allegations but if they are made they too must in the reasonable belief of the discloser be substantially true. Both information and allegations must fit that criterion. Here on the facts found by the Tribunal they did not.

The ET also found the disclosure to the GMC had not been made in good faith, as the matters were not raised with the person who was investigating Korashi's claims internally and given this issue is 'a matter of impression for an Employment Tribunal that it must be rare indeed for an appellate court to have jurisdiction to intervene'.

The complaint to the police also fell outside s 43G, as Claimant could not have believed reasonably that he would suffer detriment by making the complaint to the police since there had been no previous detriment, and there was no evidence of a reasonable belief that the material would be concealed or destroyed. Further, the disclosure to the police was not substantially the same as was previously disclosed to the respondent or to the GMC. The EAT said if it had been necessary to determine whether it was reasonable in all the circumstances to make the disclosure to the police, the EAT would have been minded to say that it was not reasonable since the respondent's whistleblowing procedure required the claimant to operate first through that and he did not.

Result: the disclosures were not protected.

Detriment: Noting all detriments were out of time, save an allegation that he was 'required to attend the communications skills unit' upon returning to work, it was upheld that this was not a detriment, as an unjustified sense of grievance does not suffice.

Sections considered: ERA, ss 43B(1), 43G(1)(b), 43G(1)(e).

Cited in: *Phoenix House Ltd v Stockman* [2016] IRLR 848 (EAT); *Chesterton Global Ltd (t/a Chestertons) v Nurmohamed* [2015] ICR 920 (EAT); *Benney v Department for Environment, Food and Rural Affairs* (UKEAT/0245/13/SM, 06 February 2015); *Western Union Payment Services UK Ltd v Anastasiou* (UKEAT/0135/13/LA, 21 February 2014); *Millin v Capsticks LLP* (UKEAT/0225/12/MC, 16 August 2013); *Tansell v Henley College Coventry* [2013] IRLR 174; *Bal v Parallel Realisations 1 Ltd (In Administration)* (UKEAT/0215/12/DM, 25 October 2012).

45. Greenly v Future Network Solutions Ltd

UKEAT/0359/13/JOJ, 19 December 2013

Key issues: Whether there was an arguable disclosure of information; whether the claim could be struck out.

Case summary: The claimant claimed to have made protected disclosures concerning (a) failure to consult on changes to terms and conditions; (b) stopping paying for cabling, rod, and roping work and not correctly paying holiday pay; and (c) not paying the national minimum wage (NMW). He subsequently complained to HMRC of a breach of NMW regulations.

ET: The ET struck out the claims, except that which was based on the disclosure to HMRC, on the basis they were allegations and not disclosures of information, each being a complaint as to a reduction in pay under the transferee.

EAT (HHJ Eady QC): the ET had erred, as whether there had been a disclosure of information had to be determined at a full hearing to assess what had been said or written in context:

> 41. Whistle-blowing cases, as has previously been observed (see *North Glamorgan NHS Trust v Ezsias* [2007] ICR 1126) have much in common with discrimination cases; in particular, in that they tend to be fact-sensitive and involve similar public interest considerations. While there will obviously be exceptions, experience suggests that the evidence in such cases is generally viewed best as a totality at a full merits hearing, rather than trying to adjudicate on selected parts of the evidence at a preliminary stage.

Result: Appeal upheld, strike out prevented.

Sections considered: ERA, s 47B.

46. Millbank Financial Services Ltd v Crawford

[2014] IRLR 18

Key issues: Disclosure of information could relate to an omission.

Case summary: The claimant was employment as financial director designate. Shortly before the end of her six-month probationary period she was told that the period was being extended and there were some concerns about her performance. There was, however, no suggestion that she was going to be dismissed. She then sent a letter to senior management complaining of lack of feedback during her probationary period, and that she had not been told how long her probationary period would last. A week later she was dismissed. The employer applied to strike out on the basis that the letter contained no information.

ET: The letter might amount to a protected disclosure, and this was a matter for the substantive trial.

EAT (HHJ David Richardson): The facts conveyed may relate to an omission ('the wards have not been cleaned for the last two weeks') just as they may relate to a positive action ('sharps were left lying around'). Here the letter stated that there had been no feedback during the probationary period, no consultation with the person recruited to carry out the HR function, and no consultation with the director—just a single meeting at the end of the probation period with no plan of action and no idea how long the probation period would last. As such the letter went far beyond simply making an allegation or stating a position, and set out the factual basis of her complaint in considerable detail.

Result: Claim not struck out.

Sections considered: ERA, ss 43B, 43L(3), 103A.

47. Gebremariam v Ethiopian Airlines Enterprise (t/a Ethiopian Airlines)

[2014] IRLR 354 (EAT)

Key issues: Whether disclosure conveyed information.

Case summary: The claimant was employed by Ethiopian Airlines as a customer service reservation and ticket agent. She was informed in April 2011, soon after returning from a period of maternity leave, that she was to be dismissed on grounds of redundancy. Her appeal against the decision was upheld. But she resigned soon afterwards claiming constructive unfair dismissal, and also detriment on the grounds of protected disclosures.

ET: In relation to the protected disclosure detriment claim, the tribunal held that there was no qualifying disclosure but did not deal with this in its reasons.

EAT (Jeffrey Burke QC): One of the alleged protected disclosures was an email in which the claimant said (referring to the obligation to consult):

> It is sad to see the legal requirement has been breached again in this day and age. Anyway thank you for looking into the matter. I really appreciate for all your effort.

This was unarguably only an allegation and did not involve any disclosure of information. Two other disclosures did not give rise to any arguable claim, as the detriments had either occurred prior to the disclosure or were not something that could have been affected by the disclosure. The remaining two disclosures did give rise to potential detriment, and disclosed information relating to failure to carry out risk assessments relating to the claimant's pregnancy, and could be read as implicitly asserting a breach of a legal obligation to carry out that assessment; the absence of such an obligation did not negative there having been the requisite reasonable belief.

Result: In relation to protected disclosure, remitted in relation to two of the disclosures.

Sections considered: ERA, ss 43B(1).

48. Norbrook Laboratories (GB) Ltd v Shaw

[2014] ICR 540

Key issues: Can a disclosure occur through an amalgamation of communications?

Case summary: Shaw sent three emails to Norbrook; taken together did they amount to a qualifying disclosure within the meaning of section 43B(1)(d) of the Employment Rights Act 1996?

ET: In the first email Mr Shaw wrote to Mr Cuthbertson, the employer's health and safety manager, as follows: 'Could you please provide me with some advice on what my territory managers should do in terms of driving in the snow? Is there a company policy and has a risk assessment been done?' The employment judge held, at para 6:

> Leaving the story at that point it seems clear to me that this email could not be described as a disclosure of information, it is quite clearly taken by itself upon its face simply an inquiry about what territory managers should do and whether or not there was a company policy or a risk assessment in relation to driving in snowy conditions.

Mr Cuthbertson made some suggestions about driving in the snow. Mr Shaw emailed Mr Cuthbertson again on 30 November 2010 at 12:04: 'I was hoping for some formal guidance from the company. The team are under a lot of pressure to keep out on the roads at the moment and it is dangerous. Do I log this as the formal guidance?' On 6 December 2010 at 15:44 Mr Shaw sent an email to a different employee, a member of the human resources department:

> I am only after a simply [sic] policy statement to increase transparency and help build morale and goodwill within the team. As their manager I also have a duty to care for their health and safety. Having spent most of Monday and Friday driving through snow I know how dangerous it can be. In addition the time spent battling through the snow is unproductive; they can gain more sales by phoning customers. If they are not going to be paid then I have to put in contingencies for diverting calls to those team members still on the road. In the absence of any formal guidance I take full responsibility for the directions given to my team.

The judge concluded that in the course of the emails Mr Shaw was informing his employer that the road conditions were so dangerous that the health and safety of his team was being placed a risk, and this was a disclosure falling within section 43B(1)(d).

EAT (Slade J):

> 22. ... An earlier communication can be read together with a later one as 'embedded' in it, rendering the later communication a protected disclosure, even if taken on their own they would not fall within section 43B(1)(d) (*Goode*, para 37). Accordingly, two communications can, taken together, amount to a protected disclosure. Whether they do is a question of fact.

Result: Embedded communications can be a protected qualifying disclosure.

Sections considered: ERA, 43A, 43B.

49. Northumberland Tyne & Wear NHS Foundation Trust v Geoghegan

UKEAT/0048/13/BA, 29 January 2014; [2014] EWCA Civ 1094 (CA)

Key issues: The tribunal must grapple with the motivation for the respondent's acts or omissions.

Case summary: Dr Geoghehan, a consultant child and adolescent psychiatrist and child psychotherapist in the Northumberland Child and Adolescent Mental Health Service (CAMHS), a disabled person by reason of depression and attention deficit hyperactivity disorder (ADHD), alleged that the respondent subjected her to detriment for making twenty public interest disclosures.

ET: Each disclosure relayed 'information' as described in *Geduld*. Each complaint was fact-specific and contained sufficient information for the person or persons to whom the disclosure was made to be able to identify the subject matter of that disclosure. Each was made to her employer [43C(1)(a)] and in good faith. There had been a breakdown in the working relationship between the claimant and others, and there was no evidence her disclosures were motivated by ill will or bad faith. The tribunal concluded that the cumulative effect of the claimant's protected disclosures reinforced the respondent's refusal to manage the claimant sensitively and sympathetically or to implement its own stress at work and diversity and equality policies. The respondent's discriminatory treatment of the claimant was influenced by her numerous protected disclosures, finding a causal connection between the protected disclosures and the respondent's acts or omissions.

EAT (HHJ David Richardson): allowing the appeal, the EAT found that the tribunal's reasons did not deal with the specific issues it had to decide. For example, in January 2010 the claimant asked Mr D for special leave pending an investigation; Mr D wished her to work elsewhere at the respondent rather than grant special leave, a pleaded detriment. There were issues (1) whether some disclosures to Mr D were made in good faith, (2) whether refusing special leave was a detriment, and (3) whether it was by reason of any protected disclosure. Acknowledging it is serious to make a finding that an acting chief executive had subjected an employee to a detriment, these issues were not addressed in any specific way in the tribunal's reasons, noting the tribunal found him to be truthful as a witness, and yet rejected his reason for his actions without any explanation.

Result: remitted to a fresh tribunal.

CA (Lord Justice Vos): Permission stage only, permission granted on the grounds that it was arguable the EAT overreacted to the limited decision and did not take the decision as a whole. Cost capping order under Part 52.9A CPR that the claimant would not be at risk of an adverse costs order if she lost the substantive appeal.

Detriment: Her isolation by both senior and junior work colleagues and the exacerbation of her mental condition: (i) Dr C subjecting the claimant to hostility from 2007 to 2010 and in particular on 23 July 2007, 16 January 2008 and 19 August 2009 . . . (iii) Dr J referring the claimant to NCAS in 2009; (iv) Mr D removing the claimant from her team at the end of January 2010; (v) Mr D denying the claimant's request for special leave in 2010; (vi) the respondent tolerating an environment in which Mrs F, Mrs C, and Mrs S were able to and did undermine the claimant's role as a senior clinician and criticized her for requiring reasonable adjustments to be made to her working practices/arrangements from 2007 to 2010.

Sections considered: ERA, ss 43C(1)(a), 47B(1).

50. Western Union Payment Services UK Ltd v Anastasiou

UKEAT/0135/13/LA, 21 February 2014; UKEAT/0135/13/LA, 12 May 2014

Key issues: The distinction between an allegation or opinion and information; whether the legal obligation in issue has to be identified; whether the direct perpetrators of the detriment complained of must act with knowledge of and on the ground of the worker's protected disclosures.

Case summary: Mr Anastasiou was employed as a senior manager by Western Union, assisting on a project to open branches offering a cash transmission service. In the course of an interview with his employer's in-house lawyer as part of an investigation as to whether statements made by the employer to the stock market as to the likely number of branches to be opened within the next year should have been made, Mr Anastasiou expressed the view that the statements should not have been made because he did believe that the level of roll-out could be achieved.

ET (EJ Glennie presiding): Mr Anastasiou was subjected to detriments because of the view he had expressed. There was no evidence that those employees who had actually subjected Mr Anastasiou to detriment had been aware of the making of the protected disclosure. His case was that those employees had been instructed to subject him to detriment(s).

EAT (Judge Eady QC): It was not necessary for Mr Anastasiou to identify the legal obligations that were engaged and had or might have been broken by the making of the statements to the stock market. The context had to be considered. That context (the fact that Mr Anastasiou was being interviewed by the employer's in-house counsel about the statements to the stock market) made the relevant legal obligation (sufficiently) apparent.

The EAT also rejected the contention that all that Mr Anastasiou had done was disclose his opinion that the projections as to branch openings should not have been given to the stock market by the employer. The distinction between an opinion and information can be a fine one to draw and there were circumstances in which the statement of a position could involve the disclosure of information, and vice versa. In this case the context showed that Mr Anastasiou was not merely expressing an opinion but was conveying information.

The EAT accepted that there might be cases where there was an organizational culture or chain of command such that the final actor might not have personal knowledge of the protected disclosure but where it nevertheless still materially influenced the treatment of the complainant worker. However, in such cases it would still be necessary for the ET to explain how it had arrived at the conclusion that this is what had happened and the EAT concluded that that explanation had not been given in that case: accordingly the case was remitted.

Result: The matter was remitted back to the tribunal.

Detriments: (1) Sidelining claimant from accounts; (2) Making enquiries into claimant's expenses claims; (3) Referring the results of enquiries and other alleged financial irregularities to a disciplinary hearing; (4) Intervening in claimant's bankruptcy petition.

Sections considered: ERA, ss 43B(1), 47B, 103A.

51. Ibekwe v Sussex Partnership NHS Foundation Trust

UKEAT/0072/14, 20 November 2014

Key issues: Where no evidence is adduced to explain a potential detriment, will the claim necessarily succeed?

Case summary: The employer failed to deal with a detriment, namely a grievance raised by the claimant regarding her disability. In failing to respond to the detriment, the respondent had acted unreasonably, but did it make that failure a detriment?

ET: EJ Hodgson noted that the respondent failed to deal with an alleged grievance; however, the ET found the issue was not pursued before the claim was issued. Whilst the failure could be seen as unreasonable, the ET found there was nothing whatsoever to suggest it had anything to do with the protected disclosure. Whilst the lack of action provides some evidence of a managerial failure, there was insufficient evidence that any protected disclosure caused the delay. The ET stated: 'the Claimant does not win by default if the Respondent fails to establish a reason. There remains an evidential burden and there is no evidence to find the action was on the relevant ground.'

EAT (Judge Peter Clark): The complaint was that the respondent did not recognize her as a disabled person. But the real question was whether the failure to deal with her complaint was causatively linked to the protected disclosure. The finding of the tribunal was not in error.

The EAT also rejected a submission that a grievance letter submitted by the claimant did not convey information and was a mere allegation. Whether or not the letter amounted to a grievance, it conveyed information that the respondent was failing to acknowledge her conditions and to recognize her as a disabled person, and thus was not complying with its duties to her under discrimination legislation.

Result: Appeal dismissed.

Detriment: Failing to address a grievance.

Sections considered: ERA, ss 47B, 48(2).

Cited: *Cavendish Munro Professional Risks Management Ltd v Geduld* [2010] IRLR 38, para 24, [2010] ICR 325, per Slade J; *Fecitt and others v NHS Manchester* [2012] ICR 372 (CA); *London Borough of Harrow v Knight* [2003] IRLR 140; *Kuzel v Roche Products Ltd* [2007] IRLR 309, [2007] ICR 945.

52. Soh v Imperial College of Science, Technology and Medicine

UKEAT/0350/14/DM, 3 September 2015

Key issues: (a) Distinction between reasonable belief in a relevant failure and reasonable belief in information tending to show a relevant failure; (b) Whether disclosures were made in bad faith, and relevance of motive.

Case summary: The claimant, who was a lecturer employed by the respondent college, was given a performance warning after adverse feedback from students about her lectures. She raised a grievance against the Head of Department (Professor Alford) after being warned she might fail her probationary period. In a probationary review, one of her two academic advisers (Dr McPhail) exaggerated the extent to which he had met the claimant to discuss her teaching. The panel recommended that her appointment not be confirmed. The claimant then raised a grievance against Dr McPhail. An investigation had cleared Dr McPhail of malpractice. Disciplinary proceedings were brought against the claimant for making vexatious allegations (that he spoon-fed his students, which she indicated meant he had given them the exam questions). The claimant contended that her comments about students being spoon-fed were protected disclosures and that she believed that there was a legal obligation upon lecturers not to undermine the integrity of the examination system.

ET: The disclosures were made in good faith, but the claimant lacked a reasonable belief that they tended to show a relevant failure. The claimant did not believe that Dr McPail was undermining the integrity of the exam system. She believed that it was wrong and unfair to call him a good teacher on the basis of his receiving good feedback scores, and the claimant a bad teacher because she received bad student feedback, but that was not a breach of a legal obligation.

EAT (HHJ David Richardson):

1. The EAT erred in its conclusion as to reasonable belief, and that issue was remitted. The ET had to ask itself whether the claimant herself believed that the information she was disclosing tended to show that the examination system was being undermined, and whether that belief was reasonable. It did not clearly address either of these questions. It instead addressed the different question of whether the claimant reasonably believed that the examination system was being undermined (not whether the information tended to show this). That might be an important evidential tool but it is not in itself conclusive. As the EAT explained (at para 47):

> There is ... a distinction between saying, 'I believe X is true', and, 'I believe that this information tends to show X is true'. There will be circumstances in which a worker passes on to an employer information provided by a third party that the worker is not in a position to assess. So long as the worker reasonably believes that the information tends to show a state of affairs identified in section 43B(1), the disclosure will be a qualifying disclosure for the purposes of that provision.

2. The ET had been entitled to find that the disclosure was made in good faith. The fact that a disclosure is made in response to a complaint, or in this case in order for the claimant to defend herself against disciplinary action, does not mean it is made in bad faith. As the EAT explained (at para 58):

> The fact that a disclosure of information was made by a worker seeking to defend herself against an adverse assessment of her performance does not necessarily mean that the disclosure was made other than in good faith. There is no halfway house between 'good faith' and 'bad faith'; the one is the converse of the other. 'Bad faith' connotes some degree of impropriety in the making of the disclosure. On the ET's findings the disclosure was not made out of spite towards Dr McPhail but rather to illustrate why some lecturers might be more popular with students than others, hence rendering the SOLE [system of online evaluation] marks an unfair way of assessing a lecturer's performance. The ET correctly applied the words of the statute; it had regard to the guidance in *Street*, and we do not think it erred in law.

The EAT also concluded that a finding of ordinary unfair dismissal could not stand. The ET should have considered whether it was reasonable for the disciplining officer to conclude that the claimant had intended to make an allegation of cheating against Dr McPhail and whether if so it was reasonable to conclude that the allegation was vexatious. Instead the ET had substituted its own findings on those issues.

Result: Remitted to a freshly constituted employment tribunal.

Sections considered: ERA, ss 43A, 43B.

53. Kilraine v London Borough of Wandsworth

[2016] IRLR 422 (EAT)

Key issues: Whether disclosure contained information. Whether reasonable belief as to existence of a relevant legal obligation. Whether claimant entitled to rely on s 43C(1)(b), having only relied on s 43C(2) before the employment tribunal.

Case summary: Ms Kilraine worked as an education achievement project manager. She claimed to have made four protected disclosures during her employment and to have been subjected to detriment as a result. She was ultimately suspended pending a disciplinary investigation. The suggestion was that she had raised unfounded allegations against a number of colleagues on a number of occasions. That suspension remained in place until her dismissal by reason of redundancy.

ET (Employment Judge Zuke): Kilraine's first disclosure, in which she asserted discrimination by Ofsted inspectors, was to a director of a private company which was not her employer. Her claim was that the disclosure fell within section 43C(2) on the basis that the respondent's whistleblowing policy authorized the disclosure. The tribunal rejected the argument as there was nothing in the policy which specifically referred to the Ofsted complaint procedure. In relation to a second disclosure, the detrimental act alleged was suspension, and the claim in relation to that was held to be out of time and in any event had nothing to do with the protected disclosure.

The third disclosure relied upon was a report in 2009 to the Assistant Director of Children's Services to the effect that the local authority (the employer) was failing in its legal obligation in respect of bullying and harassment. The fourth alleged disclosure was a report to the human resources officer at the education directorate that Kilraine's line manager had not supported her when she raised a safeguarding issue in relation to a school. The tribunal held that these were not qualifying disclosures as they did not contain any information, and in relation to the fourth disclosure the claimant had not held a reasonable belief in the asserted legal obligation.

EAT (Mr Justice Langstaff): In relation to the first disclosure, Kilraine argued that the tribunal had overlooked 43C(1)(b)(ii), raised in Further and Better Particulars. However, the employment tribunal had not erred in referring only to section 43C(2) as the submission made by counsel for the claimant focused entirely upon that subsection.

In relation to the second disclosure, the tribunal had erred in that the suspension, linked to disciplinary proceedings, was an act extending over time. But the decision was upheld on the basis of the finding of fact that the suspension had nothing to do with the protected disclosure.

In relation to the third and fourth disclosures, the EAT (at para 30) warned of the need for caution in applying the distinction between information and a mere allegation:

> I would caution some care in the application of the principle arising out of *Cavendish Munro*. The particular purported disclosure that the Appeal Tribunal had to consider in that case is set out at paragraph 6. It was in a letter from the claimant's solicitors to her employer. On any fair reading there is nothing in it that could be taken as providing information. The dichotomy between 'information' and 'allegation' is not one that is made by the statute itself. It would be a pity if tribunals were too easily seduced into asking whether it was one or the other when reality and experience suggest that very often information and allegation are intertwined. The decision is not decided by whether a given phrase or paragraph is one or rather the other, but is to be determined in the light of the statute itself. The question is simply whether it is a disclosure of information. If it is also an allegation, that is nothing to the point.

However, here the ET had been entitled to find that the third alleged disclosure did not contain information. It had included the assertion that:

> Since the end of last term, there have been numerous incidents of inappropriate behaviour towards me, including repeated sidelining, and all of which I have documented.

The EAT rejected a contention that this provided information that there had been incidents of inappropriate behaviour. It noted that if the word 'inappropriate' was taken away from the above passage, then it said nothing at all specific. As such it did not convey any information at all. Langstaff J added, however, that if he was wrong in that conclusion, it was in any event difficult to see how what was said alleged a criminal offence, a failure to comply with a legal obligation, or any other relevant failure, as it was far too vague: '"Inappropriate" may cover a multitude of sins', and what was said had to show or tend to show something that comes within the section.[4]

In relation to the fourth disclosure, the ET had erred in finding it did not disclose information. As well as making an allegation as to being belittled by her manager when raising a safeguarding issue, it provided some detail in relation to the lack of support provided to Kilraine. However the ET's decision was upheld on the basis of its finding that Kilraine did not hold a reasonable belief that there was any legal duty to which her line manager was subject. There was some documentation before the ET referring to s 11 of the Children Act 2004 and s 175 of the Education Act 2002, but those provisions did not impose a relevant duty on Kilraine's line manager. The tribunal's conclusion that Kilraine did not hold the requisite reasonable belief was a finding of fact which it was entitled to reach.

Result: No protected disclosure. A point not taken before ET could not be advanced before EAT.

Sections considered: ERA, ss 43(2), 43C(1)(b)(ii), 43C(2)(1)(b).

54. Wharton v Leeds City Council

UKEAT/0409/14/DM, 6 October 2015

Key issues: Whether claimant's disclosures were capable of being qualifying disclosures.

Case summary: The claimant was employed as an assistant community curator by the respondent local authority. He was not confirmed in his post following his probationary period, and was therefore dismissed. The respondent claimed this was due to performance concerns. He claimed to have made protected disclosures which were the reason for his dismissal. In further particulars he contended that the museum service was prioritizing the achievement of funding targets at the expense of its stated aims, and was neglecting to utilize available equality data to plan and coordinate its engagement work as stipulated in the strategic plan, which was underpinned by Arts Council England (ACE) funding. He claimed that his disclosures pointed to a major organization deliberately and knowingly designing a project that would not meet the relevant aims, and that to accepted ACE funding knowing this indicated a significant failure to act with integrity.

ET: At a preliminary hearing, without hearing oral evidence, the tribunal dismissed the claims on the basis that the disclosure was not capable of amounting to a protected disclosure as, although there was a disclosure of information, it did not tend to show the alleged relevant failure (here a breach of the funding agreement between the respondent and another public body), and nor could the claimant have held a reasonable belief that there had been such a breach as he had not seen the funding agreement.

EAT (Mr Justice Lewis): Allowing the appeal, the ET had erred by not addressing the question of whether there was an implicit link between (a) the claimant's job description, the bid for funding, and the strategic plan, and (b) the arrangements between ACE and the respondent for funding. The claimant had raised a concern about his job description, and that ACE had a duty of care to ensure that public funds were used for their intended purpose. There was just enough information to raise the possibility that the claimant was saying in effect that there was an agreement between ACE and the respondent, that documents like his job description were intended to reflect that agreement, and that a failure to comply with his job description involved a failure by the respondent to comply with its obligations under the funding agreement.

It was also an error to find that not having seen the funding agreement necessarily meant that the claimant lacked a reasonable belief. The claimant could have reached that belief if, rightly or wrongly, he believed that the job description, funding bid, or strategic policies were incorporated in or reflected obligations contained in the funding agreement.

---

[4] Presumably, meaning on the facts here that there could not have been a reasonable belief that any information tended to show a relevant failure.

The ET also erred in failing to address the question of whether the claimant had disclosed information tending to show (in the claimant's reasonable belief) that the respondent had concealed information about the alleged breach.

Result: Appeal allowed; remitted to freshly constituted tribunal.

Detriment: Dismissal.

Sections considered: ERA, s 43B(1).

Public interest

55. Chesterton Global Ltd & Anor v Nurmohamed

[2015] IRLR 614

Key issues: Whether disclosure, affecting only employees of the employer, was (in the claimant's reasonable belief) made in the public interest.

Case summary: N made a disclosure about accounts that affected up to one hundred senior managers. Was this in the public interest?

ET: They found:

> 147. We are not aware of any case law in existence as yet, which identifies the proper meaning of public interest. In the circumstances we have had to consider for ourselves what it might mean. It is clear to us that it cannot mean something which is of interest to the entirety of the public since it is inevitable from the kind of disclosures which arise from time to time such as disclosures about hospital negligence or disclosures about drug companies that only a section of the public would be directly affected. With this in mind, it is our view that where a section of the public would be affected, rather than simply the individual concerned, this must be sufficient for a matter to be in the public interest.

EAT (Mr Justice Supperstone): Citing the Committee debate on the Bill and the comments by Mr Norman Lamb, the Parliamentary Under-Secretary of State for Business, Innovations and Skills (the promoter of the Bill):

> Therefore there is no need to disallow claims based on an individual's contract, as suggested in the amendment. Indeed, although our aim is to prevent the opportunistic use of breaches of an individual's contract that are of a personal nature, there are also likely to be instances where a worker should be able to rely on breaches of his own contract where those engage wider public interest issues. In other words, in a worker's complaint about a breach of their contract, the breach in itself might have wider public interest implications.

The EAT agreed with the tribunal's judgment, stating:

> 28. ... the question for consideration under section 43B(1) of the 1996 Act is not whether the disclosure per se is in the public interest but whether the worker making the disclosure has a reasonable belief that the disclosure is made in the public interest.
>
> ...
>
> 34. ... applying the Babula approach to section 43B(1) as amended, the public interest test can be satisfied where the basis of the public interest disclosure is wrong and/or there was no public interest in the disclosure being made provided that the worker's belief that the disclosure was made in the public interest was objectively reasonable.

Result: Disclosure regarding one hundred people, who were in the same employment, was reasonably believed to be in the public interest.

Detriment: not recorded in the judgment.

Sections considered: ERA, s 43B(1).

Cited by: *Underwood v Wincanton plc* (UKEAT/0163/15/RN, 27 August 2015); *Morgan v Royal Mencap Society* [2016] IRLR 428 (EAT).

56. Underwood v Wincanton plc

UKEAT/0163/15/RN 27 August 2015

Key issues: Could there be a reasonable belief that a disclosure concerning allocation of overtime between colleagues was made in the public interest?

Case summary: First instance decision preceded before *Chesterton*. Appeal allowed on the basis that *Chesterton* should be followed and a disclosure could be in the public interest when it concerned a dispute with the employer.

ET: The claimant raised a joint grievance with four employees over the allocation of overtime. However, they asserted the issue did not concern just them but a number of workers at that site. The tribunal initially issued a show cause notice for the claimant to show why this aspect of the claim should not be struck out (though other alleged protected disclosures were permitted to proceed to a full hearing). The claim was then struck out on the basis that it was only a dispute between the claimant and her fellow employees and therefore it was not in the public interest.

EAT (Recorder Luba QC): Providing a 'benevolent approach', the disclosure alleged unfair distribution of overtime hours between drivers at the same depot. Following *Chesterton* it was not appropriate to strike out on the basis that the detriment only affected employees of the particular employer. In any event there was arguably a broader issue, in that within the complaint there was arguably a contention that overtime was being withheld from those drivers who were seen as being difficult over the safety and roadworthiness of their vehicles.

Result: Remitted to the tribunal to determine at a full hearing.

Detriment: allocation of overtime.

Sections considered: ERA, s 43B(1)(b); Employment Tribunals (Constitution and Rules of Procedure) Regulations 2013, Rule 37(1)(a).

57. Morgan v Royal Mencap Society

[2016] IRLR 428 (EAT)

Key issues: Was there arguably a reasonable belief that a disclosure about health and safety dangers primarily to the claimant was made in the public interest?

Case summary: M raised health and safety concerns with the Assistant Service Manager about her cramped working area adversely affecting her injured knee.

ET (EJ Freer): The claimant asserted that the public would be shocked to know of her working conditions, following her broken knee that occurred at work. She further asserted the public would be equally appalled to know that she was victimized for expressing her concerns over health and safety. Finally she also asserted others could be affected by similar conditions. The judge held it could not have be in the claimant's reasonable belief that these matters amount to ones within the public interest.

EAT (Mrs Justice Simler DBE (President)): Despite the finding, no reference was made to the specific beliefs asserted by the claimant as to how the public interest was engaged. Such matters were not something that should be determined summarily, particularly where they depend upon evidence about how other workstations were organized, how other employees might or might not be affected by cramped conditions, and what the claimant's belief was about all of that. Those are questions of fact and degree that will be affected by the evidence and might in the particular circumstances of this case demonstrate that the claimant's own alleged complaint had wider public interest implications in the context of other members of the workforce or in the other ways that she asserted it was engaged.

Result: Remitted to tribunal for full hearing.

Sections considered: ERA, 43B(1)(a) to (f).

Good faith

58. Phipps v Bradford Hospitals NHS Trust

EAT/531/02, 30 April 2003

Key issue: good faith.

Case summary: Mr Phipps was employed by the respondent as a consultant surgeon. He wrote to the medical director raising concerns as to treatment of patients with breast cancer. A few months later he was dismissed, purportedly for misconduct, but, Phipps contended, actually because of the disclosure he had made.

ET: found that the disclosure was not made in good faith. Instead, in writing his letter to the medical director, Phipps was seeking to demonstrate that his position was not to be challenged lightly by the medical director. He was dismissed by reason of conduct unrelated to the disclosure. The procedure was unfair but a 100 per cent reduction was made on the basis that he would certainly have been fairly dismissed if a fair procedure was followed. Also there was 90 per cent contributory fault.

EAT (HHJ Peter Clark): dismissed the appeal. The tribunal made an error of fact in stating that the letter containing the protected disclosure had not been reviewed by Phipps' union when it had. But that was not sufficient to overturn the findings. There were ample other bases for the tribunal's finding that the disclosure was not in 'good faith' including that: (a) the issue raised had already been the subject of a report and discussion within the respondent, (b) immediately prior to writing the letter he had had a meeting with the medical director following an investigation of interpersonal relationships and Phipps was suspicious of him, and (c) the failure to set out information in the letter or subsequently to enable the respondent to investigate.

Further, there was no error in the tribunal's finding as to the reason for dismissal or as to reductions from the award.

Result: procedurally unfairly dismissed but 100 per cent reduction for likelihood of dismissal in any event and 90 per cent contributory fault.

Detriment: none.

Sections considered: ERA, ss 47B, 103A.

59. Morrison v Hesley Lifecare Services Ltd

UKEAT/0262/03/DM and UKEAT/0534/03/DM, 19 March 2004

Key issue: good faith.

Case summary: Mr Morrison was a special support assistant in a school for children exhibiting challenging behaviour. He had received warnings, verbal warnings about repeated incidents of inappropriate language to and about students. Whilst he raised a grievance contained protected disclosures. He was subsequently given a written warning after his line manager complained of harassment. Mr Morrison then made various threats through his solicitors against the respondent and to the Social Services Directorate. When he then resigned he claimed to have been constructively dismissed.

ET: rejected Morrison's case based on protected disclosures since 8 January 2001. It found that Morrison had not received any detrimental treatment due to the disclosure on 8 January 2001 and doubted his good faith. As to the subsequent disclosures, the ET made findings that he did not have a reasonable belief in the substantial truth of what was disclosed and again expressed doubt as to good faith. It found that he latched on to the whistleblowing protection 'as a weapon in the campaign he has waged against the respondent', having been advised by counsel that a constructive dismissal claim was unlikely to succeed (privilege in the advice having been waived).

The tribunal dismissed his claim and ordered him to pay the respondent's costs. The costs order was made on the ground that his claim had not been brought in good faith. The ET did not deal with the alleged protected disclosures in November and December 2000. In response to questions from the EAT, the ET explained that it did not understand Morrison to be relying on these as discrete protected disclosures.

EAT (HHJ McMullen QC): dismissed the appeal, noting (at para 26) that findings on issues such as reasonable belief or good faith are 'peculiarly fact sensitive'. Morrison was not permitted to rely on the alleged protected disclosures in November and December 2000 on the basis that he had not raised them as protected disclosures before the tribunal. The costs order was upheld, noting (at paras 20, 32) that:

20. First, the Applicant's Counsel had advised that he could not discern the elements of a repudiatory breach of contract. The Applicant regarded the protection which the law affords to whistle blowers as a weapon in a campaign he has waged against the Respondent. He sought to carry out at an Employment Tribunal the function of a public enquiry into the running of the Respondent's establishments. That is an approach which the Tribunal found to be inappropriate.

. .

32. He was acting in bad faith in pursuing a campaign against the Respondent.. . . a claim for Public Interest Disclosure protection will not succeed even if there is reasonable belief in the truth of the matter put forward if it is put forward out of personal antagonism. We bear in mind that this legislation is designed to protect people who no doubt would be regarded as officious, at best and bloody minded at worst. It is in the public interest that people be protected if they make disclosures meeting the specific conditions, and do so in good faith reasonably believing the material before them. It is not Parliament's intention to protect those who simply wage a campaign against their employer. The finding by the Tribunal based upon both the conduct of the proceedings and upon the lack of good faith is an ample basis upon which the Tribunal could exercise its discretion when asked by the Respondent to award costs.

CA (Mummery LJ): refused permission to appeal ([2004] EWCA Civ 1209).

Result: no public interest disclosure.

Detriment: not set out.

Sections considered: ERA, s 43C (good faith), s 103A.

Damages awarded: none.

60. Street v Derbyshire Unemployed Workers' Centre

[2004] ICR 213 (EAT), [2005] ICR 97 (CA)

Key issue: meaning of 'good faith'.

Case summary: Mrs Street was an administrator for the respondent, which was partly funded by a borough council (BC). She raised concerns with the management committee of the respondent and wrote to the treasurer of the council making allegations against the respondent's coordinator including: setting up a secret account so as to conceal the true level of the Centre's assets for the purposes of obtaining funding which was means-tested, that the manager had made trips abroad for the benefit of other organizations during his working time, that he had frequently instructed the claimant to work for other organizations in her working time for the Centre, and that he had shown double standards in the implementation of the Centre's equal opportunities policy. The allegations were investigated and the coordinator exonerated. The respondent initiated disciplinary proceedings against Street for breach of trust and gross misconduct.

ET: found that the disclosures were qualifying disclosures within s 43(1)(b). It held that Mrs Street possessed a reasonable belief in the truth of the allegations and that the disclosure to a member of the management committee of the respondent was a disclosure to her employer. The disclosure to the treasurer of BC was considered under s 43G. The tribunal found that the conditions of s 43G, other than good faith, were satisfied. The disclosure to the treasurer was reasonable given that the BC was a major funder of the respondent. However, none of the disclosures were protected disclosures because they were not made in 'good faith' and had instead been made due to 'personal antagonism' towards the coordinator.

EAT (HHJ McMullen QC): held that there was nothing inconsistent with a finding of 'reasonable belief' in the truth and raising a matter with 'ulterior' intentions.

There is nothing inconsistent in an applicant holding such a belief that the material is true and yet promoting it for reasons which are based upon personal antagonism. It seems to us that what Lord Denning had in mind, albeit in a different context [*Secretary of State for Employment v ASLEF (No 2)*] . . . was that the motive for which a person does a particular act can change its character from good to bad, and so here . . . It is not, in our view, the purpose of the Public

Interest Disclosure Act to allow grudges to be promoted and disclosures to be made in order to advance personal antagonism. It is, as the title of the statute implies, to be used in order to promote the public interest. The advancement of a grudge is inimical to that purpose ...

CA (Auld, Wall, and Jacob LJJ): the claimant sought to assert that an ulterior motive would have to be both malicious and predominant to amount to bad faith. Public Concern at Work, as an interested party, submitted that if an ulterior motive can vitiate the requirement of good faith, even where the disclosure is made honestly, it should only have that effect where: (1) it is so 'wicked or malicious' that it approaches 'dishonesty'; and (2) it is the predominant motive for the disclosure. The respondent submitted that the requirement of good faith must mean that the disclosure should be made for the purpose of disclosing one or more of those wrongdoings, not for some other ulterior motive such as personal antagonism, to the person the subject of the disclosure, as the ET had found in this case. The Court of Appeal held that 'good faith' is more than just a reasonable belief in the truth. If the dominant or predominant reason for raising the concern was not in the public interest the tribunal can find that it was not made in good faith.

Auld LJ said (paras 53 and 56):

In considering good faith as distinct from reasonable belief in the truth of the disclosure, it is clearly open to an employment tribunal, where satisfied as to the latter, to consider nevertheless whether the disclosure was not made in good faith because of some ulterior motive, which may or may not have involved a motivation of personal gain, and/or which, in all the circumstances of the case, may or may not have made the disclosure unreasonable. Whether the nature or degree of any ulterior motive found amounts to bad faith, or whether the motive of personal gain was of such a nature or strength as to 'make the disclosure for purposes of personal gain' or 'in all the circumstances of the case' not reasonable, is equally a matter for its assessment on a broad basis ...

... it seems more in keeping with the declared public interest purpose of this legislation, fair and a more useful guide to employment tribunals in conducting this sometimes difficult, sometimes straightforward, exercise—depending on the facts—to hold that they should only find that a disclosure was not made in good faith when they are of the view that the dominant or predominant purpose of making it was for some ulterior motive, not that purpose.

Lord Justice Wall said (para 68):

... good faith is a question of motivation, and as a matter of general human experience, a person may well honestly believe something to be true, but, as in the instant case, be motivated by personal antagonism when disclosing it to somebody else. . ... Motivation, however, is a complex concept, and self-evidently a person making a protected disclosure may have mixed motives. He or she is hardly likely to have warm feelings for the person about whom (or the activity about which) disclosure is made. It will, of course, be for the tribunal to identify those different motives, and nothing in this judgment should derogate from the proposition that the question for the tribunal at the end of the day as to whether a person was acting in good faith will not be: did the applicant have mixed motives? It will always be: was the complainant acting in good faith? In answering this question, however, it seems to me that tribunals must be free, when examining an applicant's motivation, to conclude on a given set of facts that he or she had mixed motives, and was not acting in good faith. If that is correct, how is it to be done? I can see no more satisfactory way of reaching such a conclusion than by finding that the applicant was not acting in good faith because his or her predominant motivation for disclosing information was not directed to remedying the wrongs identified in s 43B, but was an ulterior motive unrelated to the statutory objectives.

Result: appeal dismissed.

Detriment: not relevant.

Sections considered: ERA, ss 43A, 43B, 43C, 43E, 43F, 43G, 98(1), 98(2), 103A.

Damages awarded: none.

Cited by: *Soh v Imperial College of Science, Technology and Medicine* (UKEAT/0350/14/DM, 3 September 2015); *Nese v Airbus Operations Ltd* (UKEAT/0477/13/DA, 27 January 2015); *Bleasdale v Healthcare Locums plc & Ors* (UKEAT/0324/13/LA, 15 April 2014); *Korashi v Abertawe Bro Morgannwg University Local Health Board* [2012] IRLR 4 (EAT); *Local Government Yorkshire & Humber v Shah* (UKEAT/0587/11/ZT, 19 June 2012); *Ezsias v North Glamorgan NHS Trust* [2011]

IRLR 550 (EAT); *Ministry of Justice v Sarfraz* [2011] IRLR 562 (EAT); *Meares v Medway Primary Care Trust* (UKEAT/0065/10, 7 December 2010); *Aryeetey v Tuntum Housing Association* (UKEAT 0324/08, 8 April 2009); *Hibbins v Hesters Way Neighbourhood Project* [2009] ICR 319 (EAT); *Muchesa v Central and Cecil Housing Care Support* (EAT/0443/07, 22 August 2008); *Clark v Clark Construction Initiatives Ltd* [2008] ICR 635 (EAT); *Babula v Waltham Forest College* [2007] ICR 1026 (CA); *Bolton School v Evans* [2007] ICR 641 (CA); *Bachnak v Emerging Markets Partnership (Europe) Ltd* (EAT/0288/05, 27 January 2006); *The Trustees of Mama East African Women's Group v Dobson* (EAT/0219/05 and EAT/0220/05, 23 June 2005); *Lucas v Chichester Diocesan Housing Association* (EAT/0713/04, 7 February 2005); *Morrison v Hesley Lifecare Services Ltd* (EAT/0262/03 and EAT/ 0534/03, 19 March 2004).

61. Lucas v Chichester Diocesan Housing Association Ltd

UKEAT/0713/04/DA, 7 February 2005

Key issue: burden of proof for good faith.

Case summary: Ms Lucas's position whilst employed by the respondent was funded by the Brighton and Hove Corporation. She raised concerns over financial irregularities involving M. Ms Lucas was confronted by M who stated she was 'extremely angry' about the allegation. Later M informed Ms Lucas that her hours and pay were to be reduced. She then raised her concerns with an employee of Brighton and Hove Corporation. M wrote to Ms Lucas informing her of her dismissal because her 'strained relationship' was having an 'adverse effect' on the project.

ET: Ms Lucas claimed automatic unfair dismissal contrary to s 103A. The ET held that she had acted in bad faith.

EAT (HHJ McMullen QC): There is a 'heavy burden' to show disclosure in bad faith. Such an allegation must be clearly put to a claimant. The ET had no ground to determine that a 'deeply worsening relationship' and an assertion that the claimant had raised her concern in 'spite' as opposed to the promotion of public interest was sufficient to found a case of 'bad faith'. This assertion had not been put in the ET3 or in cross-examination and appeared first within the respondent's written legal argument. To find 'bad faith' there must be cogent evidence. Where there is an allegation of 'bad faith' it must be made explicitly and in advance and must be put to a claimant (para 39):

> Where an allegation is made that the disclosure was not made in good faith, the evidence as a whole must be cogent, for bad faith is a surprising and unusual feature of working relationships, and as Lord Nicholls said in *In Re H (Minors) (Sexual Abuse: Standards of Proof)* [1996] AC 563 at 586: 'The more serious the allegation the more cogent is the evidence required . . . to prove it'.

Result: case remitted to the same ET to determine whether Ms Lucas was dismissed because she had made the disclosure.

Detriment: reduction in hours.

Sections considered: ERA, ss 103A, 43B, 43C.

Damages awarded: remitted.

Cited by: *Bleasdale v Healthcare Locums plc & Ors* (UKEAT/0324/13/LA, 15 April 2014); *Korashi v Abertawe Bro Morgannwg University Local Health* Board [2012] IRLR 4 (EAT); *Dunster v First Transpennine Express Ltd* (UKEAT/0570/10/ZT, 19 August 2011); *Mears v Medway Primary Care Trust* (UKEAT/0065/10, 7 December 2010); *Roberts v Valley Rose* (UKEAT/0394/06, 31 May 2007); *Boulding v Land Securities* (EAT/0023, 3 May 2006); *Bachnak v Emerging Markets Partnership (Europe) Ltd* (EAT/0288/05, 27 January 2006); *The Trustees of Mama East African Women's Group v Dobson* (EAT/0219/05 and EAT/0220/05, 23 June 2005); *Doherty v British Midland Airways Ltd* (UKEAT/0684/04, 7, 8 February 2005) applied *Lucas* in the context of dismissal for trade union activities.

62. Milne v The Link Asset and Security Company Ltd

EAT/0867/04, 26 September 2005

Key issues: no 'good faith', no 'reasonable belief', and no causal link between the disclosure and the resignation.

Case summary: Mr Milne was a broker and manager for the respondent. The respondent operated an optional trust benefit tax (EBT) scheme. Milne joined the scheme then raised concerns about it. Milne was suspended and disciplined regarding his conduct elsewhere. He resigned and claimed constructive dismissal.

ET: found that although it was highly critical of the respondent's process, there was no breach of fundamental term of Milne's contract and therefore no dismissal. It also found that although Milne had genuine concerns about the EBT scheme, he did not have a genuine belief as to its illegality. The whistleblowing claim was 'opportunistic' and the claim was brought to put pressure on the respondent through litigation. Milne was ordered to pay £5,000 to the respondent towards its costs.

EAT (Mr Justice Silber): held that there was no error of law in the tribunal's finding that there was no constructive dismissal.

In relation to whistleblowing, there were some references indicating that the claim was being considered under s 43(1)(a) (criminal offence) rather than s 43(1)(b) (legal obligation) but the ET probably did appreciate that it was dealing with a claim under s 43(1)(b). It was argued that this was significant because of the differing mental elements. For s 43(1)(b) it was only necessary to believe that the tax scheme was unlawful, not that there was a criminal *mens rea*. Also it was argued that the claimant was permitted to have a concern as to his own financial position because that was the nature of the scheme's illegality.

However, the EAT held that the matter was concluded by the tribunal's findings of fact that Milne lacked the requisite reasonable (or indeed genuine) belief. In addition, the disclosure was not the reason for resignation—the ET was entitled to place emphasis on the fact that this was not raised during the disciplinary process or when he resigned.

Result: no whistleblowing claim; costs order against Milne of £5,000.

Detriment: none.

Sections considered: ERA, ss 43A, 43B, 103A.

Damages awarded: none.

Cited by: *Camden and Islington Mental Health and Social Care Trust v Atkinson* (UKEAT/0058/07, 20 August 2007).

63. Bachnak v Emerging Markets Partnership (Europe) Ltd

EAT/0288/05, 27 January 2006

Key issue: burden of proof for good faith.

Summary: Mr Bachnak, an investment officer was dismissed by EMP(E) Ltd, and subsequently brought an unfair dismissal claim. Among other things, he alleged that he had been dismissed as a result of making a number of 'protected disclosures' to his employer regarding the way in which the company was conducting its investment business. Bachnak claimed dismissal under ERA, s 103A.

ET: rejected Bachnak's 'whistleblowing' claim, holding that some of his disclosures had not been made in 'good faith' and thus were not 'protected disclosures' within the meaning of either s 43C or s 43G. Since the disclosures were not 'protected', s 103A did not apply. In any event, the tribunal found, there was no causal link between Bachnak's disclosures and his dismissal, which was carried out for reasons of misconduct. The tribunal went on to uphold Bachnak's alternative claim of 'ordinary' unfair dismissal under s 98, since the employer had failed to follow a fair procedure. It decided, however, that it would not be just and equitable to award compensation because Bachnak had contributed to his own dismissal by 100 per cent.

Bachnak appealed, contending that the burden should have been on EMP(E) Ltd to prove that he had acted in bad faith in making his disclosures. The tribunal, he submitted, had erred in proceeding on the basis that the burden of proof in this regard was neutral.

EAT (HHJ Peter Clark): having referred to the decisions in *Lucas v Chichester Diocesan Housing Association Ltd* (EAT/0713/04) and *GMB v Fenton* (EAT/0484/04, EAT/0798/02, and EAT/0046/03) agreed with Bachnak that the burden is on the employer to show that an employee made the relevant disclosures in bad faith. It thus rejected the tribunal's tentative suggestion that the burden was neutral. It also held that the onus of showing the reason for dismissal is on the employer once a protected disclosure is established.

Despite the tribunal's error over the burden as to good faith, the EAT declined to overturn the tribunal's decision on this issue. The tribunal had made firm findings of fact on the basis of the evidence presented to it, and its decision was in no way dependent on the burden of proof. Having heard the witnesses and considered the documentary evidence, the tribunal had found that two of Bachnak's disclosures had been made to strengthen his hand in negotiations for a new contract with EMP(E) Ltd. One had been made after Bachnak had been summoned to a meeting for copying documents without permission. The other had followed his suspension, and had been intended to put pressure on his employer not to dismiss him. These were findings of fact as to Bachnak's motive which were open to the tribunal to make and with which the EAT would not interfere. Bachnak had been acting out of personal interest in making the disclosures and not out of public interest. The EAT therefore dismissed his appeal.

Result: no protected disclosure.

Detriment: none.

Sections considered: ERA, s 103A.

Damages awarded: none.

Cited in: *Local Government Yorkshire & Humber v Shah* (UKEAT/0587/11/ZT, 19 June 2012).

64. Roberts v Valley Rose Ltd t/a Fenbank Nursing Home

UKEAT/0394/06/DA, 31 May 2007

Key issues: when and how must bad faith be put to a claimant?

Case summary: the claimant was an experienced registered nurse, working at the respondent nursing home. She was dismissed on various grounds of misconduct. She claimed that she had been dismissed and subjected to detriments by reason of protected disclosures.

ET: upheld 20 acts of misconduct against the claimant and found that the principal reason for her dismissal and her treatment was nothing to do with whistleblowing but was her gross misconduct. One of the disclosures related to treatment of a resident. The ET found that the claimant had acted in bad faith in that she had falsely alleged an injury as part of a vendetta against one of the nurses.

EAT (HHJ McMullen QC): On the appeal it was alleged that there was a failure to comply with the guidance in *Lucas* as to making the issues known in advance. The ET3 had only stated in broad terms that the allegations were not made in good faith and given a different ground (that she did not have 12 months' service). The EAT held that the allegations had been sufficiently raised in advance. The broad allegation in the ET3 put the claimant on notice that she would have to defend an allegation of bad faith. The materials relevant to the allegation in fact made were exchanged in standard disclosure, and the allegation was set out in a witness statement (albeit served only five days before the hearing) and there was then cross-examination on the point and, following the claimant's evidence and the commencement of the respondent's evidence, the claimant was recalled and gave rebuttal evidence. As such there was an opportunity to rebut the allegation, and an attempt to do so: 'There was disclosure in advance of the allegation of bad faith and there was an opportunity provided to the Claimant to fight back'. This was in contrast to *Lucas* where the allegation was first made in closing submissions.

Result: appeal dismissed.

Detriment: none found.

Sections considered: ERA, s 103A.

Damages: N/A.

65. Clark v Clark Construction Initiatives Ltd

[2008] ICR 635 (EAT)

Key issues: good faith; costs.

Case summary: the claimant was a building contractor. He arranged for the incorporation of the respondent (CCI), and was its managing director and sole shareholder. CCI became responsible for building a large block of flats that was being developed by a company controlled by Mr and Mrs Grew. Mr Grew took a shareholding in CCI and later the remaining shares were transferred to him. The relationship between the claimant and the Grews broke down after he refused to attend a trial to give evidence for the Grews in a dispute in relation to the flats and he later alleged they had tried to persuade him to lie in court. The claimant was given a verbal warning and then summarily dismissed. He claimed that he was dismissed by reason of protected disclosures.

ET: considered only one of the alleged protected disclosures, being an allegation that the Grews had effected a transfer of the flat in circumstances where the claimant's signature had been forged. It found that this was made in bad faith in that it was advanced as a negotiating tactic. Nor had the claimant been dismissed by reason of the disclosure. The ET therefore dismissed the protected disclosure claims and made a costs award against the claimant. The ordinary unfair dismissal claim was dismissed on the basis that there was no sufficient service because the claimant had not been an employee whilst he was the sole shareholder.

EAT (Mr Justice Elias P): upheld the finding on ordinary unfair dismissal. There was no appeal on the findings as to the one protected disclosure considered by the ET, but the case was remitted to the ET to consider the other protected disclosures. The finding as to costs was also remitted to be reconsidered in the light of the findings as to the other protected disclosures. However, but for this the costs order would have been upheld. The EAT stated (para 114):

> ... the Tribunal was in our view entitled to conclude that it was unreasonable to bring the particular protected disclosure claim that failed. The Claimant was in a position to know that he had not made the complaint to the employers in good faith, in the sense that it was not for a purpose which the law is willing to protect. That is not something that would only have become obvious after the evidence had been heard. It followed that the Claimant was seeking to recover compensation notwithstanding that he ought to have known that the claim would not succeed. This in our view justified the Tribunal in concluding, as we think it implicitly plainly did, that the conduct was unreasonable. We do not accept that an experienced tribunal would think that costs could be awarded simply where the claim was misconceived.

CA: rejected a further appeal limited to the ordinary unfair dismissal claim ([2009] ICR 718).

Result: case remitted to a fresh tribunal to determine these outstanding issues.

Detriment: N/A.

Sections considered: ERA, ss 43C, 103A.

Damages: N/A.

66. Aryeetey v Tuntum Housing Association

UKEAT/0070/07, 12 October 2007, UKEAT 0324/08, 8 April 2009

Key issues: whether post-dismissal disclosures made in bad faith can reduce or extinguish a compensatory award.

Case summary: the Claimant was dismissed on 26 July 2005 from his post as the respondent's finance director by its chief executive. He made disclosures, initially internally and then to the housing corporation (which was prescribed for the purposes of ERA, s 43F), on 11 April 2005, alleging breach of internal financial procedures by the chief executive and as to interference with his investigation into this. He brought a number of claims including that he was unfairly dismissed by reason of protected disclosures.

ET (liability): found that the claimant had suffered detriments and was then automatically unfairly dismissed (ERA, s 103A) by the respondent by reason of protected disclosures. His compensation was reduced by 25 per cent on account of contributory fault. This took into account that whilst the letter to the housing corporation on 11 April 2005 was the trigger for the suspension and dismissal and was a protected disclosure, in a subsequent letter to the housing corporation on 25 April 2005 (after being suspended) he had accused the chief executive of dishonesty. The ET found the context was that: 'by now he was beleaguered and had been unfairly treated and could see his dismissal round the corner. He threw caution to the winds in what was an attempt to get the Housing Corporation to investigate; the aim obviously being that this would ward off his dismissal'.

EAT (liability) (Ansell J): rejected an argument that the ET had erred in placing reliance in relation to Aryeetey's reasonable belief on an accountant's report. The report exonerated the chief executive of dishonesty but found that there had indeed been breaches of financial regulations by him and therefore vindicated Aryeetey's concerns. Aryeetey was not aware of the report at the time of his disclosures. The respondent was aware of its full contents before the conclusion of the disciplinary process but refused to supply a copy to Aryeetey. Following *Darnton v University of Surrey* [2003] ICR 615 (EAT) and *Sir Robert McAlpine v Telford* (EATS/0018/03, 13 May 2003) the EAT commented (para 42):

> It seems to us that the Tribunal were quite entitled to assess the issues of good faith and belief as against what the accountants eventually found, particularly in the light of the Respondent's reluctance to permit sight of the full report.

The EAT also upheld the approach to contributory fault.

ET (remedy): found, at a subsequent remedies hearing, that following his dismissal the claimant had engaged in a sustained campaign to show that the respondent's chief executive was dishonest. After the liability hearing, he pressurized the housing corporation for an inquiry. It found no evidence of dishonesty. He then wrote to the police (with copies to other bodies) alleging that the respondent was guilty of fraudulent accounting and possibly of theft. The police found no evidence of any criminal practices. The ET held that the claimant's motive was a vendetta and that the claimant could not have had a reasonable belief in the truth of the accusation that the chief executive was dishonest and he had become unreasonably obsessed and gone over the borderline from good faith into bad faith in persisting with his allegations. Therefore, the ET considered that if the claimant had remained in the employ of the respondent then at least by the time of his letter to the police of 16 April 2007, the respondent would not have been acting unfairly in dismissing him for persisting in making the disclosures as he had written to the police showing 'his obsession to destroy [the chief executive of his employers]'. Therefore, he was awarded no compensation for the period after 16 April 2007.

EAT (remedy) (Mr Justice Silber): considered that the tribunal was entitled to find in relation to compensation that the later disclosure by the claimant which was 'motivated by vendetta and an obsession to destroy the Chief Executive entitled them to determine that by the time he complained to police he could not have a reasonable belief in the truth of the accusation that the Chief Executive was dishonest', and thereby concluded that he would suffer no losses as he would have been dismissed from shortly after that date.

Court of Appeal: permission to appeal was refused ([2009] EWCA Civ 974, 1374, [2010] EWCA Civ 1088).

Result: automatically unfair dismissal and the claimant suffered detriments. Compensation awarded but reduced on the basis of contributory fault and then extinguished by pursuing a 'vendetta' which would have entitled the respondent to dismiss.

Detriment: the ET found two detriments: (a) he was asked to apologize to the chief executive (para 15.3 of the liability decision); (b) that he was suspended on 20 April 2005 (para 22.4 of the liability decision).

Sections considered: ERA, ss 47B, 103A.

Damages: loss up to 16 April 2007; £6,000 injury to feelings.

67. Ezsias v North Glamorgan NHS Trust

[2007] ICR 1126 (CA), [2011] IRLR 550 (EAT)

Key issues: good faith; reason why question; approach to striking out protected disclosure claims.

Case summary: Mr Ezsias, a surgeon, made a number of complaints about colleagues. He contended that he was victimized and harassed by senior manager for raising these concerns which he claimed were protected disclosures. Matters came to a head as a result of a breakdown in his relationship with two colleagues, who later became consultants. They claimed that their clinical competence had been unfairly questioned by Ezsias. An internal report was critical of the frequency and unrelenting nature of Ezsias' complaints. Following the report Ezsias was not prepared to resolve the interpersonal difficulties with colleagues noted in the report. He continued to make complaints about colleagues. Nine senior members of the department signed a petition expressing concerns as to lack of progress in resolving issues in relation to Ezsias. They asked for their concerns to be addressed as a formal grievance. Ezsias was then suspended. The matter was investigated by a senior human resources professional who reported an irretrievable breakdown in working relationships between Ezsias and his colleagues and that this was largely down to Ezsias. In response Ezsias was dismissed on the grounds of the irretrievable breakdown in relationships. Ezsias claimed ordinary unfair dismissal and under

ERA, s 103A. The tribunal found the report into the working relationship to be 'comprehensive, thorough and extremely detailed'.

CA (Ward, Maurice Kay, Moore-Bick LJJ): the case was initially struck out but this was reversed by the EAT, whose decision was affirmed by the CA. The CA stated (per Maurice Kay LJ at paras 30–32):

30. Whistleblowing cases have much in common with discrimination cases, involving as they do an investigation into why an employer took a particular step, in this case dismissal.

31. The claimant will often run up against the same or similar difficulties to those facing a discrimination applicant. There is a similar but not the same public interest consideration. In *Anyanwu v South Bank Students' Union* [2001] UKHL 14, [2001] IRLR 305 Lord Steyn said at paragraph 24:

'For my part such vagaries in discrimination jurisprudence underline the importance of not striking out such claims as an abuse of process except in the most obvious and plainest cases. Discrimination cases are generally fact sensitive and their proper determination is always vital in our pluralistic society. In this field perhaps more than any other the bias in favour of the claim being examined on the merits or de-merits of its particular facts is a matter of high public interest.'

. . .

32. In my judgment the same or a similar approach should generally inform whistleblowing cases, subject always of course to the kind of exceptional case to which I have referred. If she had had it in mind the chair of the employment tribunal would surely not have concluded as she did. She ought not to have done so in any event.

ET: did not deal individually with all 75 alleged protected disclosures. It found that all the complaints were part of Ezsias' campaign against certain colleagues, and as such were not made in good faith. In any event the disclosures were not the reason for his dismissal, which was due to the breakdown in relationships with his colleagues. In relation to ordinary unfair dismissal, the ET found that the breakdown in relationships amounted to some other substantial reason and that Ezsias was the author of his own misfortune, and that the dismissal was fair.

EAT: dismissed the appeal. In relation to s 103A it was argued that there was a failure to determine what lay behind the petition by his colleagues and whether it was motivated by protected disclosures against them. However, the EAT accepted (para 33) that it was the way Ezsias treated his colleagues, and the manner in which he expressed his concerns, rather than any concerns on their part as to what he was disclosing, which caused the breakdown of the relationships. The EAT (para 37) also approved the ET's approach in declining to address all of the protected disclosures individually in circumstances where it concluded that the disclosures were not made in good faith. Nor did the ET have to make findings as to all 75 complaints to make findings as to why the working relationships broke down.

Result: claims of ordinary unfair dismissal, and dismissal by reason of protected disclosure, dismissed.

Sections considered: ERA, s 103A.

Damages: none.

Cited by (CA, [2007 ICR 1126): cases involving protected disclosures: *Daly v Northumberland Tyne and Wear NHS Foundation Trust* (UKEAT/109/16/JOJ, 7 July 2016); *Morgan v Royal Mencap Society* [2016] IRLR 428 (EAT); *Robinson v Royal Surrey County Hospital NHS Foundation Trust & Ors* (UKEAT/0311/14/MC, 30 July 2015); *McKinney v London Borough of Newham* [2015] ICR 495 (EAT); *Greenly v Future Network Solutions Ltd* (UKEAT/0359/13/JOJ, 19 December 2013); *Namoale v Balfour Beatty Engineering Services Ltd* (UKEAT/0126/12/DM, 29 November 2012); *Short v Birmingham City Council & Ors* (UKEAT/0038/13/DM, 5 July 2013); *Pillay v Inc Research UK Ltd* (UKEAT/0182/11, 9 September 2011); *Nageh v David Game College Ltd* (UKEAT/0112/11, 22 July 2011); *Sood v Christ the King School Governors* (UKEAT/0449/10, 20 July 2011); *Hudson v Oxford University* (UKEAT/0488/05 and UKEAT/0142/06, 26 July 2007).

Other cases: *Lockey v East North East Homes Leeds* (UKEAT/0511/10, 14 June 2011); *Roberts v Carlin* (UKEAT/0183/09, 17 December 2010); *A v B* [2011] ICR D9 (CA); *Evans v Parasol Ltd* [2011] ICR 37 (CA); *Clifton v Lloyds TSB Bank plc* (UKEAT/0347/09, 4 March 2010); *Igboaka v Royal College of Pathologists* (UKEAT/0036/09, 3 December 2010); *Beswick Paper Ltd v Britton* (UKEAT/0104/

09, 9 October 2009); *Gordon v Ford Motor Co* (UKEAT/0089/09, 12 June 2009); *Verma v Harrogate & District NHS Foundation Trust* (UKEAT/0155/09, 21 May 2009); *Knight v Treherne Care & Consultancy Ltd* (UKEAT/0384/08, 15 April 2009); *Coutinho v Rank Nemo (DMS) Ltd* (UKEAT/0315/08, 16 September 2008); *Shestak v Royal College of Nursing* (UKEAT/0270/08, 14 August 2008); *Ahari v Birmingham Heartlands and Solihull Hospitals NHS Trust* (UKEAT/0355/07, 1 April 2008); *Iya-Nya v British Airways plc* (UKEAT/0302/07, 17 January 2008); *Alstom Transport v Tilson* (UKEAT/0532/07, 4 December 2008); *Jatto v Godloves Solicitors* (UKEAT/0300/07, 26 October 2007); *Jansen van Rensburg v Kingston upon Thames RLBC* (UKEAT/0096/07, 16 October 2007); *Moorse v NTL Group Ltd* (UKEAT/0258/07, 26 July 2007).

68. Meares v Medway Primary Care Trust

[2011] EWCA Civ 897 (CA)

Key issues: good faith; when addressing good faith and where there are mixed motives, whether the tribunal must determine the predominant motive.

Case summary: the claimant was employed as a nurse. She reacted angrily when issues were raised by her immediate boss, Mrs Cable, as to her being late for work. She wrote a letter in response to her line manager which raised allegations of bullying and harassment. The letter was found by the ET to be 'written in a tone which was extremely abrupt to the point of rudeness, aggressive and quite extraordinary given that it was written to her line manager' (para 6). Later the claimant resigned because she had been accused of lack of performance and poor timekeeping but had been given no particulars to back that up.

ET: held that the disclosure was not made in good faith because it was motivated by personal antagonism towards Mrs Cable.

EAT: upheld the findings as to lack of good faith. The EAT rejected a submission that it was a necessary requirement for a tribunal to spell out all various motives that may impact on a decision. It is open to a tribunal simply to find that a disclosure was not in good faith by reason of an ulterior motive that it identifies as being the sole or predominant motive. The EAT also rejected a submission as to failing to put an allegation of bad faith to the claimant both at the hearing and sufficiently in advance. Provided a reasonable opportunity is made available for the claimant to rebut a suggestion of lack of good faith, the critical time before which the allegation must be made is before the tribunal begins to consider the decision after the end of evidence and submissions. If the claimant had been at a disadvantage by the allegation being raised for the first time in submissions, it would have been open to her to ask for an adjournment or to call further evidence to deal with the point. Indeed the EAT commented that it would have expected that the claimant's counsel would have done so. Further, although express reference to want of good faith was first made in submissions, questions had been put in cross-examination to the claimant as to her motives for making the disclosure. This was the substantive basis for challenging want of good faith, and it was therefore far more helpful to ask this than simply asking about good faith which may have simply begged the question as to what was meant by this. The claimant had therefore been given a fair chance to answer the allegation in evidence, and had also had the final word in submissions, so there was no procedural unfairness.

CA (Rimer LJ): refused permission to appeal:

16. The question the statute poses is whether the disclosure was made in good faith. It does not ask for a description and evaluation of other motives there may have been. The ET in Street had not apparently engaged in any such exercise in finding a lack of good faith and its decision was upheld: it had investigated the motive, found it was antagonism and had concluded that it did not meet the statutory requirement of good faith.

. . .

21. . . . The ET plainly did consider the decision in Street (see paragraph 33) and its paragraph 34 findings show that it found on the evidence that personal antagonism was either the sole or predominant motive. There was no requirement upon it to explain what other motives might have been in play, or what proportion of the overall motivation they respectively represented, a task which would in practice be an unrealistic one.

Result: appeal dismissed.

Detriment: N/A.

Sections considered: ERA, s 43C.

Damages: N/A.

Cited by: *Bleasdale v Healthcare Locums plc & Ors* (UKEAT/0324/13/LA, 15 April 2014); *Korashi v Abertawe Bro Morgannwg University Local Health Board* [2012] IRLR 4 (EAT).

69. Korashi v Abertawe Bro Morgannwg University Local Health Board

[2012] IRLR 4 (EAT)

See Case 44.

70. Bleasdale v Healthcare Locums plc & Ors

UKEAT/0324/13/LA, 15 April 2014

Key issues: Ulterior motive, no protected disclosures.

Case summary: Ms Bleasdale ('B') was the founder of HCL, a board member and its Executive Vice-Chairman. The Chief Financial Officer, Ms Jarvis, admitted to falsifying the accounting figures so as to present HCL in a far healthier position than was the case. She also implicated B. Disciplinary proceedings were brought in relation to three charges relating to false accounting, and a further charge relating to sale of a database. B asserted the principal reason for her dismissal was her disclosures, and brought claims of detriment and automatic unfair dismissal. The employment tribunal rejected all claims. It concluded that B had been fairly dismissed, and that the alleged protected disclosures were not the reason for dismissal, and some of them had not been made in good faith. The appeal was only against the findings of ordinary and s 103A unfair dismissal (not the detriment claim).

EAT (HHJ Peter Clark): Rejecting the appeal, the ET had been entitled to find that the dismissals were by reason of conduct rather than the alleged protected disclosures, and were fair. The appeal against the finding that certain of the disclosures had not been made in good faith was also dismissed. The case as to lack of good faith had been sufficiently put to B in that (a) arising out of the pleadings it had been identified as an issue as the case management discussion and in the list of issues, (b) it was put in cross-examination, and (c) it was dealt with in closing submissions. The ET was entitled to infer that the disclosures were made for an ulterior motive in that on B's case she learned of Ms Jarvis' wrongdoing from her on 9 January 2011, yet she waited until 13 January 2011 to make the first of a tranche of disclosures. It was open to the ET to find that she did so to further her own cause.

Result: Disclosures not made in good faith but for ulterior motive, to further her own cause.

Sections considered: ERA, 103A.

71. Nese v Airbus Operations Ltd

UKEAT/0477/13/DA, 27 January 2015

Key issues: Whether claimant's conduct subsequent to a disclosure could be relevant to whether it was made in good faith

Case summary: The claimant was employed by Airbus as a composite and metallic stress engineer. He reported to a Mr Hewson, and together there were responsible for liaison with a company (FACC) subcontracted by RSP to do part of the development of aircraft components. The claimant and Mr Hewson both reported to a Ms Dee, who in turn reported to Mr Watts. Following a meeting with RSP, the claimant became concerned as to its ability to carry out the required work. He sent an email to Mr Hewson and Ms Dee with his concerns. Later, on 26 September 2011, he met with Ms Dee and raised his technical concerns and concerns about how Mr Hewson had acted in a meeting with RSP and that he was concealing the lack of progress made by FACC. Having investigated this, Ms Dee concluded that the concerns were not well founded, and she fed this back to the claimant. The claimant took the view that Ms Dee was complicit with Mr Hewson in concealing safety issues and lack of progress by RSP. However, (as the ET found) it would have been apparent to him following a technical review meeting on 5 October 2011, if not before, that there was no concealment. Later in October 2011 the claimant met with Mr Watts and repeated the allegations of concealment on the part of Mr Hewson and that safety was being put at risk. Mr Watts assured him that senior management were aware of what was going on and nothing was being concealed. Subsequently, after a performance review in which Ms Dee was involved, the claimant submitted a grievance against

Mr Hewson, Ms Dee, and Mr Watts, in which he accused them of concealing unsatisfactory work of FACC and subjecting him to retaliation for not participating in their breach of ethics. Following an investigation, the grievance was rejected, and that conclusion was upheld on appeal. Disciplinary proceedings then followed on the basis that his comments in the appeal indicated he did not genuinely believe the safety allegations. He was dismissed for gross misconduct on the basis of pursuing serious allegations despite knowing that they were not based on fact and were untrue, and the decision was upheld on appeal. He brought claims including of protected disclosure detriment and dismissal, relying on as protected disclosures his disclosures (1) to Ms Dee at the meeting on 26 September 2011, (2) to Mr Watts in October 2011, and (3) in his grievance.

ET: Whatever might have been the position in relation to the first disclosure, there was no reasonable basis for the claimant's concerns after the stress audit meeting on 28 September 2011, and still less after the technical review meeting on 5 October 2011. Despite this the claimant had reiterated the same allegations to Mr Watts and in his grievance, without any reasonable grounds. Those disclosures were therefore made without the requisite reasonable belief and not in good faith, being instead made out of anger and mistrust of Mr Hewson and the other managers. The first disclosure was also found not to have been made in good faith, taking into account the way that (albeit subsequent to the first disclosure) the allegations were pressed when there was no basis for them. Nor were there any detriments by reason of any alleged protected disclosures. Dismissal was for gross misconduct, by reason of the lack of good faith in raising serious allegations, and in particular what the respondent took to be an acknowledgement in the course of the grievance appeal hearing that the concerns were not genuine. Claims of ordinary unfair dismissal, race discrimination, and breach of contract were also dismissed.

EAT (HHJ Eady QC): Rejecting the appeal, in respect of the second and third disclosures the tribunal made permissible findings of fact that they were made not in good faith and without a reasonable belief. The claimant sought to argue that allegations as to safety issues were only referred to by way of context for the disclosures as to alleged victimization, but the ET was entitled to find that was not the case, and in relation to good faith that the disclosures were not made on reasonable grounds and were motivated by anger and mistrust of Mr Hewson and other managers.

In relation to the first disclosure, the EAT rejected a contention that it was impermissible to take into account what had occurred after that disclosure. HHJ Eady QC explained (at para 59) that:

> I think you can look at what happens later as evidence of somebody's motivations at an earlier stage. It is something which occurs in discrimination cases, for example, when drawing inferences of an employer's motivation. Given that the Claimant continued to repeat the same points even after there was no reasonable basis for so doing, given all the assurances that had been given, an employer and an ET might well draw the inference that he never really believed those matters originally and had a different motivation for making the allegations.

The EAT did accept that the ET had not made a sufficiently clear finding that the first disclosure was not made in good faith or without a reasonable belief, rather than only expressing doubt about this. But nothing turned on this as the ET was entitled to find that the dismissal (which was the only detriment subject to the appeal) was due to continued reiteration of serious allegations (subsequent to the first disclosure) after the assurances, which were made absent good faith, which was a decision on the facts that was open to the ET.

Result: Appeal dismissed; no protected disclosure and fair dismissal due to misconduct.

Sections considered: ERA, ss 43B(1), 43C(1), 103A.

72. Soh v Imperial College of Science, Technology and Medicine

UKEAT/0350/14/DM, 3 September 2015

See Case 52.

Section 43C

73. Douglas v Birmingham City Council and others

EAT/018/02, 17 March 2003

See Case 23.

74. Premier Mortgage Connections Ltd v Miller

UKEAT/0113/07, 2 November 2007

Key issues: the recipient of the disclosure; whether disclosure can be made to someone who formerly had legal responsibility for the apprehended relevant failure.

Case summary: the Claimant, Ms Miller, made a disclosure to a former director of the employer, alleging misappropriation of funds by a current director. She claimed the misappropriation had begun whilst the former director was still a director. This felt outside ERA, s 43C subject to reasonable belief test.

ET: found that the disclosure to the former director (Mr Day) was a qualifying disclosure under ERA, s 43B(1)(a), (b). It was made to a person with legal responsibility within s 43C(1)(b)(ii) on the basis that Ms Miller believed that the wrongdoing had been ongoing whilst Mr Day was still a director.

EAT (HHJ Richardson): held that disclosure to a former director was not within s 43C, since a former director had no legal responsibility for the matter. There must be a reasonable belief in ongoing legal responsibility. Disclosure could be made to a single serving director, notwithstanding that directors have joint and several liability. The disclosure must relate solely or mainly to a matter for which the director has responsibility, not a matter for which s/he has sole or main responsibility. The matter was remitted to consider the reasonable belief test:

29. ... Suppose that a teacher, employed by a school, takes his children on an adventure holiday, organised by a specialist firm. He hears that an employee of the specialist firm has told a child to ignore a safety precaution. The teacher may report the matter to his own school and if the report is in good faith it will be protected by virtue of section 43(1)(a). He may complain about it to the employee of the specialist firm who in his belief told the child to ignore the safety precaution: that will be protected by section 43(1)(b)(i) if it is in good faith, so long as the teacher reasonably believes that the matter was wholly or mainly about his conduct. Finally, he may report the matter to the man's employer, so long as he reasonably believes that the matter solely or mainly relates to health and safety and that the firm has legal responsibility for the safety of the undertaking; that will be protected by section 43(1)(b)(ii).

30. ... section 43C is directed to protecting a disclosure which the employee reasonably believes is made to the person who has ongoing legal responsibility for dealing with it at the time the disclosure is made. The language of the statute is in the present tense.

31. ... Suppose a worker in the course of his work for his own employer visits a factory which he believes has for some years been operated in a way which is hazardous. A disclosure made in good faith to his own employer will be protected. A complaint made in good faith to any person actually operating the factory in a hazardous way will be protected. A disclosure made to the current health and safety director of the factory will be protected. But we see no reason why a disclosure to a former director of the company which owns the factory should be protected, even if the worker thought he was once legally responsible for safety. We see no indication of any statutory purpose in drawing the protection afforded by section 43C as widely as this.

32. That, however, is not the end of the matter. Section 43C does not only protect a worker where the worker is correct in thinking that a person has legal responsibility for a matter. It also protects a worker where the worker reasonably believes that to be the case, even if the worker is wrong.

...

36. ... A worker cannot always be expected to have in mind the precise terms of the other person's legal responsibility. The belief, if reasonable, need not necessarily be correct. He must, of course, make the disclosure in good faith.

...

38. It will, we think, be rare that a worker will have a reasonable belief that information he is disclosing relates solely or mainly to a matter for which an ex-director still has legal responsibility. An ex-director is not generally legally responsible for errors and omissions which take place after he ceases to be director, and we can see no reason why an employee should generally think that he is. Each case, however, turns on its own facts.

Result: matter remitted to the tribunal to consider whether Miller reasonably believed that the relevant failure related solely or mainly to a matter for which Mr Day had legal responsibility at the time when she made the disclosure.

Sections considered: ERA, ss 43C(1)(b)(ii), 103A.

Section 43D

75. Audere Medical Services Ltd v Sanderson

UKEAT/0409/12/RN, 29 May 2013

Key issues: Whether disclosure to PCaW was within section 43D ERA; contributory fault; interaction of whistleblowing policies and protected disclosure provisions.

Case summary: The respondent is a company specializing in decontamination equipment, maintenance, and validation. It had a whistleblowing policy which said that divulging information to an outside body without first raising it internally by an employee might result in disciplinary proceedings. Mr Sanderson was employed by the respondent as a hospital technician, based at Nuffield Orthopaedic Centre, on the site of Nuffield Hospital Trust. He was found to be a challenging, and at times confrontational employee. An officer of the trust complained to one of the respondent's directors about the claimant's appearance (described as scruffy and smelly), his use of bad language, and his attitude. Subsequently, Mr Sanderson had a conversation with an officer of the respondent from which he understood that he had been instructed by one of the directors to overcharge the client by charging for nine hours work on a job that was only expected to take two hours. He contacted the NHS Control Fraud office (without disclosing his concerns) and was referred by them to Public Concern at Work (PCaW), to whom he then reported the perceived fraud. Shortly afterwards, Mr Sanderson was called to a disciplinary hearing. The charges included the poor performance and poor conduct and unfavourable feedback from the client. It also included a charge of 'breach of the public interest disclosure policy' in that the claimant had admitted at a grievance hearing that he had 'notified external bodies' of a concern prior to informing the respondent. Following a disciplinary hearing, Mr Sanderson was dismissed. The letter of dismissal specifically referred to breach of the whistleblowing policy, and stated that it was clear that trust and confidence between Mr Sanderson and the respondent had gone.

ET: The ET accepted that the disclosure to PCaW was a protected disclosure within section 43D ERA, as a disclosure in the course of obtaining legal advice, and that it was the principal reason for dismissal. It noted that PCaW's website stated that it is a legal advice centre for assistance designated by the Solicitors Regulation Authority. No issue was taken by the parties disputing that PCaW was a legal adviser, and the case proceeded on the assumption that it was. However, the ET held that it was 'illogical' to make any reduction for contributory fault because it was a case of automatically unfair dismissal.

EAT (HHJ Serota QC): There was no error in the ET's finding that dismissal was by reason of a protected disclosure. However (as the respondent conceded), the ET erred in failing to consider a reduction for contributory fault. That issue was remitted to a differently constituted tribunal.

In relation to the respondent's whistleblowing policy, the EAT commented (at para 8) that:

> the Respondent's whistle-blowing policy attempts to go too far. We find that it purports to override or restrict the statutory provisions and not only does it try to do that, but it tries to impose a sanction for people doing [sic] acting accordingly.

The EAT noted that this was at odds with section 43J ERA, which renders a provision in an agreement void insofar as it purpose is to preclude a worker from making a protected disclosure.

Result: Remitted to a fresh tribunal.

Sections considered: ERA, ss 43, 43D, 43J, 103A.

Damages: c. £11,500 (but remitted).

76. Schaathun v Executive & Business Aviation Support Ltd

UKEAT/0226/12/LA, 30 June 2015

Key issues: Causation—need to consider different ways in which employer may have become aware. Approach to striking out—ET failed to consider disclosures to a legal advisor in accordance with section 43D or to a prescribed person in accordance with section 43F

Case summary: The respondent carried out and managed the maintenance of private and corporate jet aircraft. Ms Schaathun (S) had been in a personal relationship with the respondent's founder, Mr Abbott. S was the Company Secretary. At a time when the relationship was in difficulties, she started investigating her suspicion that he had been putting personal expenditure through the company account. In December 2008, Mr Abbott discovered various papers S had collected to investigate this. S was also angry that Mr Abbott had entered the part of the house they shared which she thought was her space. S moved out on 18 December 2008, and on the following day was removed as Company Secretary. S alleged that between December 2008 and March 2009 she made protected disclosures:

- to solicitors and to the Environment Agency, about the storage of hazardous substances at the respondents' premises and that chocks had been removed from under aircraft wheels;
- to solicitors and HMRC, about the use of the her tax allowance for the respondent's dividends;
- to Mr Abbott about a tax evasion scheme;
- to solicitors, alleging Mr Abbott was putting personal expenses through the respondent's accounts; and
- to solicitors and the Civil Aviation authority (CAA), alleging that Mr Abbott was maintaining and flying aircraft whilst under the influence of alcohol.

ET: The ET rejected the claim of automatic unfair dismissal under s 103A ERA and found that the reason for the dismissal was the breakdown of the relationship with Mr Abbott and the irretrievable breakdown of trust arising from the events in December 2008. It concluded that S's disclosure to HMRC, a prescribed body, was not protected because S did not inform the employer about the matters disclosed before doing so. It found the dismissal was procedurally unfair, but that a fair procedure would have resulted in her dismissal in any event by the same date as she was in fact dismissed. The ET struck out several of the alleged disclosures on the basis that S admitted that she had not informed Mr Abbott about them and so they could not have contributed to the decision to dismiss her.

EAT (Mrs Justice Slade DBE): The ET fell into error in several respects:

1. It found that S had made a qualifying disclosure to HMRC in relation to being asked to make a misleading tax return, but it erred in concluding that this was not a protected disclosure as it had not been shown to Mr Abbott (which was required for a disclosure under sections 43D or 43F).
2. It erred in finding that because the disclosures to the HMRC were not shown to Mr Abbott, they were not relevant to the reason for dismissal, as the ET failed to consider whether the respondent became aware of them by other means.
3. The ET also erred in striking out protected disclosure allegations without considering sections 43D and 43F, and there were also concerns as to the way the EJ had conducted the proceedings (which gave the impression that he was cross-examining S), with the effect that the dismissal of the s 103A claim was set aside.

Result: Remitted to a fresh tribunal.

Sections considered: ERA, ss 43, 43D, 43F, 103A.

Reasonable belief that substantially true (ss 43F–H)

77. Muchesa v Central and Cecil Housing Care Support

[2008] EAT/0443/07, 22 August 2008

See Case 33.

78. Korashi v Abertawe Bro Morgannwg University Local Health Board

[2012] IRLR 4 (EAT)

See Case 44.

79. Barton v Royal Borough of Greenwich

UKEAT/0041/14/DXA, 1 May 2015

Key issues: (a) Test of reasonable belief for a qualifying disclosure and substantial belief in truth for s 43F. (b) Could request to the ICO for employment advice arising from an instruction not to contact the ICO be within s 43F? (c) Can two disclosures be aggregated?

Case summary: Mr Barton was informed by a colleague (Mr Oree) that a manager had sent hundreds of emails home. Barton raised it with the ICO and sought advice as to whether there was any urgent action that could be taken in relation to this ('the first disclosure'). He then raised this with his employer, who instructed him not to contact the ICO without the prior authority of his line manager. Barton then called the ICO ('the second disclosure') to seek advice as to what he should do about the instruction not to communicate with them. In fact, the information that Mr Barton provided to the ICO was wrong, in that the manager had emailed only eleven documents to her home email and that email was password protected, and it was not inappropriate for her to have sent them to the home email address. The Council took the view that Mr Barton's second contact with the ICO in breach of the instruction given to him was a serious breach of duty. He was already subject to a final written warning in relation to an unrelated matter. He was dismissed for breach of the instruction in relation to contacting the ICO, taken together with one other matter.

ET: The first disclosure to the ICO was a qualifying disclosure, which disclosed information based on what Mr Barton had been told by his colleague. As to whether Mr Barton had the requisite reasonable belief, the tribunal noted that Mr Barton had not sought to verify this information before contacting the ICO, and that he was aware that there was no immediate urgency as to contacting the ICO. But the tribunal accepted that Mr Barton had a long association with Mr Oree acting as his representative and on the face of it he had no reason to doubt Mr Oree's complaint, and Mr Oree had appeared very concerned about the matter. In all, although the tribunal considered the point to be finely balanced, it accepted that Mr Barton had the requisite reasonable belief for a qualifying disclosure. But it held that he did not meet the requirement of showing a reasonable belief for the purposes of s 43F ERA that the information disclosed and any allegation contained in it was substantially true. This entailed a higher threshold than for a qualifying disclosure, and Mr Barton did not meet that threshold since he had 'jumped the gun' in circumstances where he knew and/or could fairly easily have found out there was no real urgency and that there was time to seek some verification of the allegation made by Mr Oree before contacting the ICO.

In relation to the second disclosure to the ICO, the ET concluded that there was no qualifying disclosure. The only information conveyed was the instruction given not to contact the ICO. Although Mr Barton believed that his employer did not have the power to issue the instruction, this was not a reasonable belief, as he had taken no steps to evaluate the legality of the instruction before calling the ICO, there had been no urgency to call the ICO before checking this, and he had made no request when he did call the ICO to speak to anyone with experience in employment matters. The tribunal also held that the second disclosure did not fall within s 43F since the Information Commissioner was only a prescribed person in respect of matters specified in the schedule to the Public Interest Disclosure (Prescribed Persons) Order.[5] This related to data protection compliance, and not to employment law advice on whether a contract of employment had been breached.

EAT (Judge Serota QC): Dismissing the appeal, the EAT warned that a disclosure that does not qualify cannot become qualified by associating it with one that does (ie associating the two calls to the ICO). Each disclosure must be considered separately in accordance with the decision in *Bolton School v Evans.*

Result: Telephoning the ICO was not a protected disclosure. Note that *Norbrook* was not referred to before the EAT.

Sections considered: ERA, ss 47B, 47F.

80. Schaathun v Executive & Business Aviation Support Ltd

UKEAT/0226/12/LA, 30 June 2015

See Case 76.

Section 43G: substantially the same disclosure

81. ALM Medical Services Ltd v Bladon

[2002] IRLR 807, [2002] EWCA Civ 1085 (CA)

First appeal of PIDA case to Court of Appeal.

---

[5] Now SI 2014/2418.

Key issues: (1) test for substantially the same disclosure for ERA, s 43G(2) (EAT); (2) case management (CA).

Case summary: Mr Bladon, a registered nurse, was employed by ALM from 14 June 1999 until 6 September 1999. He made disclosures concerning patient care and wellbeing, first by telephone to the personal assistant of the managing director. He was asked to put these concerns in writing and he did so by fax to the managing director on 22 August 1999. On 31 August 1999 Bladon spoke to the Nursing Home Inspectorate of the local authority, which carried out an investigation on 1 September 1999. The Inspectorate wrote to the respondent on 8 September 1999. Following a disciplinary hearing the day before, Bladon received a written warning on 10 September 1999. On 16 September 1999 he was summarily dismissed. On 20 September 1999 Bladon presented an ET1 claiming 'unfair dismissal (Protected Disclosure)' based on the alleged detriment of the written warning and on his dismissal. He was represented by Unison.

The respondent's ET3 stated that Bladon's dismissal 'had nothing whatsoever to do with his allegations to the Nursing Inspectorate'. They claimed that he was dismissed for serious breaches of contract regarding the proper discipline of a care assistant and a failure to investigate properly an incident of possible non-accidental injury to a resident. They also relied on shortcomings in his professional attitude to staff and that, while on leave from the respondent, he was supplied to another home of the respondent without the management's knowledge. It was then claimed that he had acted in bad faith in making statements to staff on 15 September 1999 to the effect that he intended 'to close the [respondent] down for good' and that he wanted the staff there to provide him with 'information and written statements citing any failings at Arundel Lodge for him to use as extra ammunition for his case against ALM'.

ET: held that Bladon had been dismissed as a consequence of making a protected disclosure. The tribunal did not accept the respondent's explanation of the dismissal and concluded that the protected disclosures were the principal reason for the dismissal of Bladon.

The tribunal awarded £10,000 for the detriment (ie the written warning for having made a protected disclosure to the Inspectorate), and, for his automatically unfair dismissal, £13,075.06 compensation.

It was held that the disclosures related to the danger to the health or safety of a patient (s 43B(1)(d)), to a failure or likely failure to comply with a legal obligation (s 43B(1)(b)), and possibly to the potential commission of a criminal offence (s 43B(1)(a)); that they were made in good faith (s 43C(1)) and in the reasonable belief that the information communicated (which was substantially the same in the disclosures to both the employer and the Inspectorate) was true (ss 43C(1)(a) and 43C(1)(b) respectively), with the motive of achieving an investigation, which took place and substantiated most of the allegations. The tribunal found that Bladon had acted reasonably in contacting Social Services nine days after his fax to the managing director without waiting for him to return from holiday.

EAT: during a preliminary hearing on 19 January 2001 the EAT determined not to allow ALM's appeal to proceed to a full hearing on the ground that it had no reasonable prospect of success. At this stage the focus of the appeal was on the conclusions of the ET as to whether Bladon had a reasonable belief in the matters raised with the Inspectorate. It was alleged that the tribunal erred in holding that the information disclosed to the Inspectorate was substantially the same as the information disclosed to the employer; and that it was perverse in holding that it was reasonable for Mr Bladon to make the disclosure to the Inspectorate. Whilst an application was made to amend the grounds of appeal to allege bias on the part of the chairman and for permission to adduce fresh evidence, this was refused. In relation to the phrase 'substantially the same' in s 43G(2), EAT said (para 31):

> it would, in our judgment, be wholly inappropriate for tribunals to embark upon an exercise of nice and detailed analysis of the disclosure to the employer, compared with the disclosure to the outside body, for the purpose of deciding whether the test in section 43G(2)(c) has been made out. The correct approach, in our judgment, is for tribunals to adopt a commonsense broad approach when decided whether or not the disclosure is 'substantially the same'.

CA (Sir Andrew Morritt (Vice Chancellor), Mummery, and Rix LJJ): on the application for permission to appeal, ALM sought to rely on additional grounds: an allegation that the chairman of the ET, accused of conducting the hearing in an unfair manner, did not disclose his prior association with Unison (on the ground that he was a partner and later a consultant with Unison's solicitors).

Lord Justice Mummery, on 22 November 2001, requested the chairman to write a letter to the court commenting on the allegation of bias. The chairman's reply, dated 3 January 2002, made it clear that the proceedings in the ET were legally flawed by the decision not to permit ALM to call relevant evidence which it wished to put to Bladon in cross-examination. Mummery LJ said (para 22):

> In order to reduce the risk of this happening in another case, I would suggest that there should be directions hearings in protected disclosure cases in order to identify the issues and ascertain what evidence the parties intend to call on those issues.

Mummery LJ also commented (para 2):

> The self-evident aim of the provisions is to protect employees from unfair treatment (ie victimisation and dismissal) for reasonably raising in a responsible way genuine concerns about wrongdoing in the workplace. The provisions strike an intricate balance between (a) promoting the public interest in the detection, exposure and elimination of misconduct, malpractice and potential dangers by those likely to have early knowledge of them, and (b) protecting the respective interests of employers and employees. There are obvious tensions, private and public, between the legitimate interest in the confidentiality of the employer's affairs and in the exposure of wrong.

Result: rehearing by a fresh tribunal.

Detriment: final written warning; value: £10,000 (pre-*Virgo Fidelis* decision).

Sections considered: ERA, ss 43B(1)(a), (b), (c), 43C(1)(a), (b), 103A.

Damages: Compensatory award—£13,075.06.

Cited by: *Chesterton Global Ltd & Anor v Nurmohamed* [2015] IRLR 614; *Pybus v Geoquip Ltd* (UKEAT/0093/10, 13 April 2011); *Evershed v New Star Asset Management* [2010] EWCA Civ 870 (CA); *Dandpat v University of Bath* (UKEAT/0408/09 and others, 10 November 2009); *Netintelligence Ltd v McNaught* (UKEATS/0057/08, 3 March 2009); *Hibbins v Hesters Way Neighbourhood Project* [2009] ICR 319 (EAT); *Chelsea Football Club plc v Smith* (UKEAT/0262/08, 23 June 2008); *Digby v East Cambridgeshire DC* [2007] IRLR 585 (EAT); *La Vertue v Ilex Energy Consultants Ltd* (UKEAT/0520/05, 16 February 2006); *Street v Derbyshire Unemployed Workers' Centre* [2005] ICR 97; *Boulding v Land Securities Trillium (Media Services) Ltd* (EAT/0023/063, 3 May 2006); *The Trustees of Mama East African Women's Group v Dobson* (EAT/0219/05 and EAT/0220/05, 23 June 2005); *Lucas v Chichester Diocesan Housing Association* (EAT/0713/04, 7 February 2005); *Pinnington v Swansea City Council* (UKEAT/0561/03, 28 May 2004); *Ganatra v London North Business Into Education Ltd* (EAT/0498/04 and EAT/0499/04); *Arthur v London Eastern Railway Ltd* [2006] EWCA Civ 1358 (CA).

82. Goode v Marks and Spencer plc

[2010] EAT/0442/09, 15 April 2010

See Case 36.

83. Korashi v Abertawe Bro Morgannwg University Local Health Board

[2012] IRLR 4 (EAT)

See Case 44.

Detriment

84. Pinnington v The City and County of Swansea and another

[2005] ICR 685 (CA)

See Case 4.

85. Woodward v Abbey National plc

[2005] ICR 1750 (EAT); [2006] ICR 1436 (CA)

Key issue: employer liable for detriment imposed after employment.

Case summary: the claimant was employed in risk management by Abbey National. She contended that she raised concerns as to bad investments out of which large commissions were being paid, and that she was shouted down and then made redundant.[6] Her dismissal was in 1994 (ie prior to PIDA) and she brought claims of unfair dismissal and sex discrimination that were settled in 1996. She then claimed that some years after the termination of her employment, she was caused detriment by her ex-employers including by their not providing a reference for her due to her having been a whistleblower and/or as acts of sex discrimination (including victimization).

EAT (Mr Justice Burton (President)): found that the ET and the EAT did not have jurisdiction to consider a claim regarding her post-termination detriment.

Court of Appeal (Ward, Maurice Kay, Wilson LJJ): claims could be brought for post-termination detriment.

In relation to other discrimination statutes, post-termination victimization claims could be brought: *Rhys-Harper v Relaxion Group plc* [2003] ICR 867 (HL). The same applied here. Ward LJ (with whom Maurice Kay LJ and Wilson LJ agreed), observed that:

> Victimisation is established by showing inter alia the discrimination of the employee by 'subjecting him to any other detriment'—see s 6(2) of the 1975 Act and s 4(2) of the 1976 and 1995 Acts. Under s 47B of the ERA a worker likewise has the right 'not to be subjected to any detriment'. Although the language and the framework might be slightly different, it seems to me that the four Acts are dealing with the same concept, namely, protecting the employee from detriment being done to him in retaliation for his or her sex, race, disability or whistle-blowing. This is made explicit by the long title to the Public Interest Disclosure Act 1998, which is, as I have already set out:

> 'An Act to protect individuals who make certain disclosures of information in the public interest; to allow such individuals to bring action in respect of victimisation.'

> All four Acts are, therefore, dealing with victimisation in one form or another. If the common theme is victimisation, it would be odd indeed if the same sort of act could be victimisation for one purpose, but not for the other.

The various tests suggested in *Rhys-Harper* in relation to whether relief should be afforded after termination of employment were summarized by Ward LJ in *Woodward* (at para 53 and referring in brackets to paragraph numbers in *Rhys-Harper*):

(1) for Lord Nicholls, the employment relationship triggered the employer's obligation not to discriminate in all the incidents of the employment relationship whenever they arise, provided the benefit in question arises between the employer or former employer as such and the employee or former employee as such (44, 45);

(2) for Lord Hope the test was whether there is still a continuation of the employment relationship (114, 115);

(3) for Lord Hobhouse the test was one of proximity: does the conduct complained about have a sufficient connection with the employment (139) or a substantive and proximate connection between the conduct complained of and the employment by the alleged discriminator (140);

(4) for Lord Rodger, one must look for a substantive connection between the discriminatory conduct and the employment relationship, with the former employer discriminating qua former employer (205);

(5) for Lord Scott, it depends on whether the relationship between employer and employee brought into existence when the employee entered into the employer's service is still in existence (200) or is still continuing notwithstanding the termination of the employment (204).

In other words Lord Hope and Lord Scott seem to tie the application of the Act to the continuance of the employment relationship whereas the majority look for a connection (variously described) between the former employee as such and the former employer as such.

On each of these tests references would be covered. More remote claims would still be problematic. Further, the Court of Appeal expressly left over the question as to whether the protected disclosure must precede the termination of employment.

---

[6] See [2011] EWCA Civ 179 at para 5.

Result: CA reversed the EAT and ruled that *Fadipe v Reed Nursing Personnel* [2005] ICR 1760 could not stand with the decision of the House of Lords in *Rhys-Harper*. The case was remitted, but the ET then dismissed all claims, and that decision was upheld on appeal: see *Woodward v Santander UK plc* [2010] 834 (EAT) and (refusing permission to appeal) [2011] EWCA Civ 179 (upholding the exclusion of without prejudice negotiations in relation to refusing to give a reference as part of the 1996 settlement as it was not unambiguous impropriety).

Detriment: poor reference after termination.

Sections considered: ERA, ss 48, 47B.

Damages awarded: none. Remitted back to the ET and then all claims dismissed.

Cited by: *Onyango v Adrian Berkeley T/A Berkeley Solicitors* [2013] IRLR 338; *Blitz v Vectone Group Holdings Ltd* (EAT 29 November 2011; UKEAT /0253/10/DM); *Fecitt v NHS Manchester* [2011] ICR 476 (EAT); *Gayle v Sandwell and West Birmingham Hospitals NHS Trust* (UKEAT/0338/09, 16 April 2010) (race and trade union victimization); *BP plc v Elstone* [2010] ICR 879 (EAT); *Hibbins v Hesters Way Neighbourhood Project* [2009] ICR 319 (EAT); *Coutinho v Rank Nemo (DMS) Ltd* [2009] ICR 1296 (CA) (race victimization); *Croke v Hydro Aluminium Worcester Ltd* [2007] ICR 1303 (EAT); *Cumbria County Council v Carlisle-Morgan* [2007] IRLR 314 (EAT).

86. Onyango v Adrian Berkeley T/A Berkeley Solicitors

[2013] IRLR 338

Key issues: Post-termination disclosure and detriment—jurisdiction.

Case summary: O made a protected disclosure *after* he had left his employment. He claimed this led to accusations of forgery and dishonesty which were then investigated by the Solicitors Regulatory Authority.

ET: The ET held that they did not have jurisdiction to hear the claim of detriment because the protected disclosure had been made after his employment terminated.

EAT (HHJ Peter Clark): Focusing upon section 47B, HHJ Clark stated that the detriment must occur and be causatively linked to the protected disclosure; it follows that it must come later in time than the disclosure. Since the detriment may arise post termination, the EAT concluded there was no warrant for requiring that the disclosure be made during the period of the employment.

Result: Appeal succeeded, case remitted.

Detriment: Allegations of fraud and dishonesty.

Sections considered: ERA, s 43B.

87. Abertawe Bro Morgannwg University Health Board v Ferguson

[2013] ICR 1108 (EAT)

Key Issue: Was it necessary for a respondent to have a duty to act in a particular way in order that a failure to do so could constitute subjecting the claimant to a detriment?

Case Summary: The claimant GP disclosed concerns to the respondent health board that one of her partners in the practice of which they were both members had acted wrongly in relation to prescribing a drug. Section 43K(1)(ba) meant that the claimant was a worker vis-à-vis the health board. The detriments complained of were that the health board had:

- failed properly to investigate the GP's concerns, preventing her from fulfilling her obligations to the General Medical Council;
- failed to treat the GP's identity as whistleblower with due confidentiality, releasing her name and her report to her GP partners;
- failed to act in accordance with its own whistleblowing policy so as to prevent the GP from being subjected to reprisals from her colleagues in her GP practice;
- forced the GP to take voluntary leave as an alternative to suspension, and had inappropriately maintained that enforced voluntary leave;
- forced the GP to be subjected to an investigation.

The respondent applied to strike out the claim, contending that there had to be an obligation or duty to act in the way in which it was alleged there had been a failure to act. This application was rejected by the ET.

EAT: dismissed the appeal. In s 47B the expression 'subjected to' did not necessarily extend so far as to cover a failure to fulfil an expectation that the respondent would act in a particular way. It would do so only if the respondent had the ability or power to have acted. If the respondent had a choice as to how it behaved, and it could exercise that choice by not taking action when it otherwise could have done so legitimately, that was capable of being a deliberate failure to act. If it were established as a deliberate failure which, applying the words of the section, subjected the claimant doctor to any detriment, she would succeed in a claim if it were also shown that the respondent had deliberately decided not to act as it did on the ground that she had made a protected disclosure.

Result: Appeal dismissed.

Relevant Section: ERA, s 47B.

Vicarious liability

88. Fecitt and others v NHS Manchester

[2012] ICR 372 (CA), [2011] IRLR 111 (EAT)

Key issues: vicarious liability and reason for detriments.

Case summary: The claimants were registered nurses working at a walk-in centre. They raised concerns to their line manager regarding a colleague (Mr Swift) that he had exaggerated his clinical experience and qualifications—which they reasonable believed to be a danger to health and safety. The respondent admitted that they had made protected disclosures. As a consequence Mr Swift became seriously ill. An investigation into Mr Swift concluded that as he had acknowledged his wrongdoing, no action would be taken. He lodged a claim of bullying and harassment against one of the claimants (Ms Fecitt). This went to a hearing even though he withdrew his complaint. There were no findings of bullying but concerns expressed about her management style. Relations deteriorated and staff at the walk-in centre became split between those who supported him and those who supported the claimants. Mr Swift was suspended. Ms Fecitt made a formal complaint under the whistleblowing procedure. A report found that she had been justified in raising the concerns and that there was a lack of robust management. Ms Fecitt suffered various detriments including an anonymous call in which an unknown male had threatened to burn down her home if she did not drop her complaint, and her picture was displayed on Facebook. The claimants raised a grievance. Only one (Ms Hughes) pursued this to a hearing. This concluded that she was subjected to unpleasant treatment by their colleagues and management could have done more (and the ET held that the same conclusion would have been reached in relation to all claimants if there had been a decision on their grievances). The respondent then removed managerial responsibilities from Ms Fecitt, and then redeployed her and another claimant (Ms Woodcock) and gave no further work to another claimant (Ms Hughes). An internal human resources email referred to her expressly as a troublemaker.

ET: The claims were dismissed. Any failure on the part of the employer to take sufficient steps to protect the claimants from being subjected to a detriment was not 'because' they had made protected disclosures and was not therefore 'on the ground that' they had made the protected disclosures. The decision to redeploy Ms Fecitt and Ms Woodcock was because it was the only feasible way of resolving the problem and was not 'on the ground that' they had made protected disclosures. The decision not to provide work to Ms Hughes was not because she had made protected disclosures but because management had already formed a negative view of her and partly to redress the dysfunctional state of the centre.

EAT (Judge Serota QC): The ET erred in failing to deal with vicarious liability of the respondent for treatment of the claimants by its employees. The ET also erred in relation to whether the acts or deliberate failures to act were on the grounds of protected disclosures. The respondent must show where claimants have suffered a detriment that it is 'in no sense whatever' associated with the protected disclosures.

Court of Appeal: (Mummery, Elias, and Davis LJ): appeal allowed and ET decision that no breach of s 47B restored. In this important decision, the Court first determined that *Cumbria County Council v Carlisle-Morgan* [2007] IRLR 314 (EAT) had been wrongly decided. Vicarious liability only applies in relation to legal wrongs of employees. Since individual workers (rather than the employer) have no personal liability under the protected disclosure provisions, nor can there be any vicarious liability under those provisions. In the course of victimizing a colleague for making a protected disclosure, a worker may commit some other wrong such as unlawful harassment. But if so the vicarious liability is for that wrong, rather than a breach of the protected disclosure provisions.

With regard to whether the act or deliberate act was on the grounds of a protected disclosure, the test is whether the protected disclosure was a material influence in the sense of being more than a trivial influence. Although the Court of Appeal preferred this formulation to that adopted by the EAT, it regarded it as reflecting the same EU derived principles as had been applied in discrimination legislation in that the protected disclosure should be no material influence at all. Elias LJ commented that when considering the explanations of employers:

> where the whistleblower is subject to a detriment without being at fault in any way, tribunals will need to look with a critical—indeed sceptical—eye to see whether the innocent explanation given by the employer for the adverse treatment is indeed the genuine explanation. The detrimental treatment of an innocent whistleblower necessarily provides a strong prima facie case that the action has been taken because of the protected disclosure and it cries out for an explanation from the employer.

However the Court concluded that the protected disclosures were not a material influence. The employer had been acting in response to the dysfunctional situation in the workplace, and the fact that this had come about as a result of the protected disclosures did not mean that the protected disclosures could be regarded as a material influence.

The Court of Appeal were invited by the intervener in the case, Public Concern at Work, to apply a wider approach so as to ensure that whistleblowers are more fully protected. However the Court concluded that the language of the legislation did not allow for this.

Result: appeal allowed and employment tribunal decision restored.

Detriment: threat of arson; placing pictures on Facebook; failing to provide work and moving to different areas.

Sections considered: ERA, s 47B.

Cited (EAT decision) by: *Day v Lewisham and Greenwich NHS Trust and Health Education England* (UKEAT/0250/15/RN, 9 March 2016), [2016] IRLR 415; *Salisbury NHS Foundation Trust v Wyeth* (UKEAT/0061/15/JOJ, 12 June 2015); *Ahmed v City of Bradford Metropolitan District Council* (UKEAT/ 0145/14/KN, 27 October 2014); *Blackbay Ventures Ltd (t/a Chemistree) v Gahir* [2014] IRLR 416 (EAT); *Barclays Bank plc v Mitchell* (UKEAT/0279/13/JOJ, 11 February 2014); *Price v Surrey County Council and another* (EAT/0450/10, 27 October 2011); *Dunster v First Transpennine Express Ltd* (UKEAT/0570/10/ZT, 19 August 2011); *Mahood v Irish Centre Housing Ltd* (UKEAT/0228/10, 22 March 2011) at para 45.

89. Panayiotou v Chief Constable of Hampshire Police

[2014] IRLR 500

Key issues: A distinction can be drawn between the fact of making a protected disclosures and other features which, although related to that, are separable and not protected.

Case summary: Mr Panayiotou made protected disclosures to senior officers concerning the attitude of other officers in respect of race, and treatment of victims of rape, child abuse, and domestic violence. Following an investigation, Panayiotou was found to be largely correct in his concerns. However, he then began to campaign for the Force to take the actions that he believed appropriate.

ET: Mr Panayiotou had started a campaign for actions to be taken when the Force did not take what he believed to be appropriate action. His actions 'were sufficient to try and to exhaust the patience of any organization' (para 62). He had taken up 'huge amounts' of management time, made 'very lengthy complaints' (one running to twenty-two pages). The Force was determined to rid itself of him and did so in a manner that was not fair, but was not in any sense whatsoever connected with his disclosures (para 66).

EAT (Mr Justice Lewis): Upholding the ET's decision, the EAT held that it had been entitled to draw a distinction between making disclosures and the manner in which Panayiotou pursued the issues, including what the ET found was his 'relentless' campaign:

> 47 ... the tribunal is seeking to distinguish between the fact of making protected disclosures and the fact that the employee had 'become completely unmanageable' because of the way in which he would not accept any answer other than that which he considered appropriate and the exasperation and time taken in dealing with that situation. ...

52. ... authorities demonstrate that, in certain circumstances, it will be permissible to separate out factors or consequences following from the making of a protected disclosure from the making of the protected disclosure itself. The employment tribunal will, however, need to ensure that the factors relied upon are genuinely separable from the fact of making the protected disclosure and are in fact the reasons why the employer acted as it did.

Result: Appeal dismissed, the distinction was a proper one to be made.

Sections considered: ERA, ss 47B, 103A.

90. Shinwari v Vue Entertainment Ltd

UKEAT/0394/14/BA, 12 March 2015

Key issues: Vicarious liability.

Case summary: S witnessed a colleague selling complimentary tickets to members of the public. S was offered a £5 bribe; S took the money but only as evidence to hand to managers (which he later did) and not as a bribe. S's complaints included a failure (a) to keep confidential that he was the source of information (by providing a copy of his witness statement to the colleague accused of wrongdoing); (b) to protect him and keep him safe in the workplace; (c) to move him to a safe working environment other than simply to Shepherd's Bush, too close to the former cinema; and (d) to stop the bullying and harassment he suffered at the hands of colleagues, resulting in his ostracism and isolation then reduced hours of work.

ET: The disclosure of S's statement (the source of the problems) was not on the ground of the protected disclosure, it was also not a breach of contract, but for 'wholly legitimate reasons anticipated by and authorised by its disciplinary policy'.

EAT (Mrs Justice Simler): Referring to *Martin v Devonshire* the EAT noted the proper distinction between the fact of making a protected disclosure and the consequences, which were related to but separable from those disclosures. The reason for disclosing the claimant's witness statement to the colleague accused of the wrongdoing was the legitimate reason, consistent with the respondent's disciplinary policy, that an individual who was to be disciplined should be provided with the evidence on which the disciplinary action would be based.

Result: Appeal dismissed.

Sections considered: ERA, 47B(1), 48(2).

Reason why question

91. Brothers of Charity Services Merseyside v Eleady Cole

EAT/0661/00, 24 January 2002

Key issue: drawing inferences concerning reason for dismissal.

Case summary: Mr Eleady-Cole was a full-time support worker in a hostel operated by the respondent. He raised concerns regarding his fellow workers' use of pornographic material and illegal substances at the residence. This disclosure was made through a telephone system (EAP) that was not confidential. Eleady-Cole was not confirmed in post at the expiry of his probationary three-month period. The respondent relied upon his conduct in other areas to support its decision not to confirm him in post.

ET: The disclosure by a non-confidential telephone support service that passed on information to the respondent fell within ERA, s 43C(2). Taking into account a sudden change in attitude to the claimant after making his disclosure, the ET concluded that he was dismissed by reason of his protected disclosure.

EAT (Mr Commissioner Howell QC): upheld the finding that the disclosure was within s 43C(2). However, the appeal was allowed, in part on the basis that the tribunal's approach to drawing inferences had strayed too far into considering reasonableness rather than the reason for dismissal (paras 25, 30, 31):

The Tribunal's explanation for how they came to draw the inferences they did relied too much on surmise as to what the reasons might have been in the absence of what they considered reasonable explanations, and too little on a reasoned explanation of their own having regard to specific findings of fact that ought to have been made. . . .

Under Section 103A where a finding of unfair dismissal in circumstances such as those in this case necessarily involves a finding that the reasons put forward by the employer were not genuine and that evidence given before the Tribunal was untruthful, it is incumbent on the Tribunal to base its conclusions on clear findings as to the primary facts about which of the persons before it were responsible for what happened, and to explain clearly how those findings lead causally to the conclusion that the protected disclosure had been the true reason for the employee's dismissal.

Result: remitted to a freshly constituted ET to consider the reason for dismissal.

Sections considered: ERA, ss 43C, 103A.

Damages awarded: none at this stage.

Cited by: *De Haney v Brent Mind and Lang* (EAT/0054/03, 10 April 2003).

92. Aspinall v MSI Mech Forge Ltd

EAT/891/01, 25 July 2002

Key issue: 'reason why' test.

Case summary: the respondent makes fork lift truck arms. In 1999 Mr Aspinall was injured at work. He asked a colleague to make a video of a production process for evidence in support of his personal injury claim and his colleague agreed. The video was given to the claimant's solicitors. It was subsequently disclosed to the respondent's insurer's solicitors. The respondent did not view the video. The respondent was concerned that the video showed a secret and confidential process used by the company. During an investigation Aspinall was pressed to identify the name of his colleague who had made the video. He considered that he had been threatened that if he did not reveal the name he would be sacked. He returned to work to find his clocking-in card missing and as a consequence he resigned, giving no reasons. He then immediately started work in a new job for which he had applied and been interviewed before the disciplinary process was completed. He claimed unfair dismissal. On the day of the hearing the tribunal permitted the claim to be amended to include a claim under ERA, s 103A.

ET: found that Aspinall left employment for his own reasons so there was no dismissal. The company's actions were taken because of a breach of confidentiality rather than a disclosure about health and safety. The disappearance of the clocking-in card occurred without any involvement of the respondent. The claim that he was warned that he would be sacked was rejected and there was nothing upon which such a belief could reasonably have been entertained.

EAT (HHJ Reid QC): upheld the finding that there was no constructive dismissal. The EAT commented *obiter* that it had reservations as to the concession that the mere making of a video, as opposed to showing it to someone else, was a protected disclosure. In any event any detriment was solely by reason of the breach of confidentiality rather than any disclosure, applying a test that the protected disclosure must be causative in the sense of being 'the real reason, the core reason, the *causa causans*, the motive for the treatment complained of', to borrow the words of Lord Scott in the race relations case of *Chief Constable of West Yorkshire Police v Khan* [2001] ICR 1065 at 1083 (HL). [Note: *Aspinall* disapproved on this point in *Fecitt v NHS Manchester* [2011] ICR 476 (EAT)].

Sections considered: ERA, ss 43B(1)(d), 47BA, 103A.

Issues considered: late amendment to include PIDA claim; 'reason why' question.

ET determined that making of a video could be a disclosure under s 43B(1)(d), but this was doubted by EAT.

Result: No automatically unfair dismissal.

Detriment: not pleaded.

Damages awarded: none.

Disapproved (on reason why question) in: *Fecitt v NHS Manchester* [2011] ICR 476 (EAT).

93. Hossack v Kettering BC

EAT/1113/01, 29 November 2002

Key issue: 'reason why'; is it permissible to discipline/dismiss for concerns evidenced by a protected disclosure?

Case summary: Ms Hossack was appointed policy research officer to provide assistance to the Conservative Group of the respondent council. She was commissioned to draw up a report on the sale by the council of property for a councillor to submit to the district auditor. The report drafted by her and handed to the councillor (Freer) alleged the commission of criminal offences and made suggestions of wrongdoing. The councillor insisted that these references be removed before it was submitted to the district auditor. Ms Hossack wrote to the district auditor, which was alleged to be a protected disclosure under ERA, s 43F. The councillor became aware of this letter and requested her dismissal. She was dismissed and brought claims under s 47B and s 103A.

ET: found that the reason for the dismissal was not the protected disclosure but Ms Hossack's inability to distinguish her role as a research officer employed by the council to assist the Conservative Group from the role of an elected member of the group or its leader, as a result of which Freer lost all confidence in her and could no longer work with her. It was not the substantive issues that she raised with the district auditor which were a matter of concern to Freer, but the tone of the letter, which indicated that the claimant 'saw herself as "the tail wagging the dog"'.

EAT (Mr Justice Wall): upheld the decision of the EAT and found that the ET was entitled to find that the dismissal was not for disclosure, but was due to Ms Hossack's inability to understand that her role was not a political one, and some of her comments made in her disclosures were evidence of this.

> 37. In our judgment, it is not an accurate analysis of the Respondent's behaviour in this case to assert that the Appellant was dismissed for the manner in which she made the disclosure.
>
> . . .
>
> 39. The manner in which the Appellant went about the protected disclosure was a manifestation of her inability to understand her advisory role.
>
> . . .
>
> 41. We see the force of Mr McGrath's anxiety that a differentiation between the content of a disclosure and the manner in which it is made could, if not carefully analysed, emasculate the legislation. Plainly, any Tribunal approaching a protected disclosure will need to be alert to that danger. In our judgment, however, this Tribunal was so alert, and its conclusions are not only, in our view, correct in law, they also accord with common-sense and in no way offend against either the spirit or the letter of the legislation.

Result: appeal dismissed; no automatic unfair dismissal.

Sections considered: ERA, ss 43A, 47B, 103A.

Damages awarded: none.

Cited by: *Blitz v Vectone Group Holdings Ltd* (UKEAT /0253/10/DM, 29 November 2011); *Vaseghi v Brunel University* (EAT/0757/04 and EAT/0222/05, 3 November 2005) at paras 15 and 16 (claim of race and trade union victimization). See also *Martin v Devonshires Solicitors* [2011] ICR 352 (EAT); Blackbay Ventures Ltd (t/a Chemistree) v Gahir [2014] IRLR 416 (EAT).

94. London Borough of Harrow v Knight

[2003] IRLR 140 (EAT)

See Case 2.

95. Mama East African Women's Group v Dobson

EAT/0219/05/ and EAT/0220/05, 23 June 2005

Key issues: (1) When a claimant has made a protected disclosure what is the correct test to determine whether the dismissal was for that reason? (2) What is the assessment of compensation when the employer seeks to limit the compensation for unfair dismissal on the basis of treatment by others that may have been avoided but for its own failure to protect the employee from the consequences of her disclosure?

Case summary: Ms Dobson was an English teacher to Somali women in Sheffield. Her disclosure alleging child mistreatment (criminal offence) took place on 10 May and she was dismissed on 24 May following the investigation by the respondent, which concluded that there was no evidence of mistreatment.

ET: looked at the reasons set out in the dismissal letter which advanced three bases for the dismissal. (1) false allegation; (2) not following the procedure; (3) breach of confidentiality. The respondent accepted that, but for the disclosure, Ms Dobson would not have been dismissed. The tribunal commented that the respondent's assertion that she had committed 'unprofessional conduct' by reporting 'unfounded' allegations was not sufficient for an employer in the social context of this legislation to avoid its connection to the protected activity. The reason or the principal reason the tribunal found was that Dobson had raised a disclosure.

The respondent appealed in relation to Dobson's award contending that she would have been dismissed in any event as her students had lost confidence in her, because they were aware of her having raised her concern.

EAT (HHJ McMullen QC): held that the reason or principal reason for the dismissal was the disclosure. An ET must make clear findings as to what is in the mind of the person who dismisses. The reasons advanced by the respondent were inextricably linked to the disclosure (in this case the manner in which it was raised and the lack of substance). To permit such reasons to be fair would undermine the purpose of the legislation. In relation to the award a respondent cannot use its own failure (here to maintain confidentiality and thus the loss in confidence) to reduce any award to which the claimant was entitled.

Result: automatically unfair dismissal. [Note: The decision is now to be read in the light of the decision in *Bolton School v Evans* where the EAT rejected a similar policy argument by the ET and drew a distinction between the disclosure and the associated previous conduct: see further the discussion in Chapter 7.]

Detriment: none.

Sections considered: ERA, ss 103A, 123.

Damages awarded: £12,035.76 for unfair dismissal and damages of £489.62 for wrongful dismissal.

Cited by: *Melia v Magna Kansei Ltd* [2006] ICR 410 (CA); *Redcar and Cleveland BC v Scanlon* (UKEAT/0369/06, 22 May 2007) (stating at para 17 that it was superseded in part by the decision in *Kuzel v Roche Products*).

96. Bolton School v Evans

[2006] IRLR 500 (EAT), [2007] ICR 641 (CA)

See Case 30.

97. Network Rail Infrastructure Ltd v Glencross

UKEAT/0094/08, 16 May 2008

See Case 32.

98. Redcar and Cleveland BC v Scanlon

EAT/891/01, 25 July 2002; UKEAT/0369/06, 22 May 2007; UKEAT/0088/08, 20 May 2008

Key issue: reason why.

Case summary: the claimant wrote a letter of 16 March 2003 complaining about the respondent council's director of finance (Mr Richardson). The letter was found to contain protected disclosures in relation to breach of the council's policies and procedures and breach of discrimination policy in relation to appointments made by the council. Mr Richardson later brought disciplinary proceedings against the claimant purportedly on grounds related to the performance of her duties unrelated to the protected disclosures. Ultimately a decision to dismiss was taken by the council's chief executive.

ET (1st hearing): the letter of 16 March 2003 contained protected disclosures. The allegation in relation to policies and procedures of the council related to legal obligations by virtue of incorporation into contracts of employment and breach of discrimination legislation. In relation to good faith, the ET rejected a contention that the allegations had been made out of personal antagonism to Richardson. The claimant saw it as a genuine issue of principle that policies designed to ensure equal opportunities should not be set aside on the basis of expedience. Some of the intemperate language used in her letter reflected both the strength of her feelings on the matter 'as well as her zealotry'. She had acted in good faith 'despite her lack of tact and diplomacy'. It was no answer that she had raised the issue with the director of finance, and then the chief executive, rather than using the whistleblowing policy. The disciplinary action taken against the claimant was wholly disproportionate notwithstanding that there were some proper areas for concern. The ET concluded, having regard to the change in Richardson's attitude following the claimant's disclosures, the disproportionate action taken, and the consistent failure on the council's part to have regard to matters substantially in the claimant's favour and to treat her fairly in the disciplinary process, that the action taken against her culminating in dismissal constituted sex discrimination, victimization, and that the dismissal was by reason of her protected disclosure (the complaints in the letter of 16 March 2003 being both protected acts under the Sex Discrimination Act 1975 and protected disclosures). There was found to be a 20 per cent contribution to dismissal.

EAT (HHJ Birtles): remitted the matter to the ET due to a failure properly to apply the test of the reason for dismissal or whether the action was by reason of the protected acts. There had been a reference to whether there was a causal connection with the protected disclosures/protected acts and a focus on the reasons of Richardson, whereas the chief executive was the dismissing officer.

ET (remitted hearing): found again that the dismissal was by reason of the protected disclosure and sex discrimination victimization by reason of the protected acts. Although the claimant had not realized this at the time she made her complaint against Richardson, he had been acting with the full approval and concurrence of the chief executive. By challenging Richardson she had unwittingly challenged the chief executive. That was the reason that ultimately led to the dismissal and explained the conduct of the chief executive throughout the disciplinary process. The respondent had failed to prove otherwise.

EAT (Wilkie J): found that there was no error by the ET at the remitted hearing. It had properly applied the approach in *Kuzel v Roche Products* in relation to the shifting burden of proof. In relation to the 'reason why' question the ET had properly applied *Chief Constable of West Yorkshire v Khan* [2001] IRLR 830 (HL) and asked itself why the chief executive acted as he did, and what consciously or unconsciously was his reason. It concluded that the cause was the whistleblowing complaint. Nor had the ET gone beyond the scope of its remit in relation to the findings of fact. Rooting itself on the findings of primary fact from the first hearing, it was a permissible and necessary approach, in order to identify the chief executive's thought processes, to then consider what inferences were properly to be drawn from those primary findings of fact.

Sections considered: ERA, s 103A, Sex Discrimination Act 1975, s 4(1).

Result: findings of protected disclosure dismissal and sex discrimination victimization ultimately upheld following remitted hearing.

Detriment: dismissal.

99. El-Megrisi v Azad University

[2009] EAT/0448/08, 5 May 2009

Key issues: ERA, s 103A; need to consider cumulative impact of disclosures.

Case summary: the claimant raised various concerns regarding the immigration status of staff and students. He was dismissed and claimed under ERA, ss 47B and 103A. The tribunal should consider the cumulative effect of protected disclosures on the employer's decision to dismiss.

ET: found that the dismissal which was purportedly due to redundancy was in fact 'a manufactured means to disguise the real reason for the Claimant's dismissal'. It was significant that the perceived redundancy situation arose immediately after the latest and most formal representation by the claimant of her continuing concerns about staff and student work permits or visas and their immigration status. The ET found that 'no Polkey deduction can arise where we find, as we do, that the Respondent dismissed the Claimant because they thought she was a nuisance who would not willingly undertake the questionable tasks, amongst others, that were assigned to her'. The ET concluded that the claimant was dismissed because the respondent thought that she was 'an obstructive nuisance and a trouble maker' and upheld the claim for ordinary unfair dismissal but dismissed the claim under s 103A.

EAT (Underhill J):

The ET erred in failing to consider the claim of detriment under s 47B. It would be sensible for the ET to require particulars:

> to clarify more precisely what particular acts she says were done on the grounds that she had made the protected disclosures pleaded, what detriment she says she suffered from those acts, and what compensatable loss or damage she says that she suffered as a result: the detriment and the damage may be self-evident once the acts complained of are identified, but that will not necessary be so . . . .

In relation to section 103A, the ET erred in focusing on the last disclosure. Where there was a history of disclosures which were, as here, found to have operated cumulatively, it was wrong to seek to identify how much each could be said to have contributed to the dismissal. Instead, the question was whether their cumulative impact was the principal reason for the dismissal—which it was on the basis of the ET's own findings. On the facts, the finding of a s 103A dismissal did not have a financial impact because the compensatory award was only £16,000. But the EAT accepted that having a finding that was dismissed for raising concerns rather than just because she was a nuisance, was a matter of practical value.

Result: remitted in relation to s 47B.

Detriment: undermining her role; being shadowed; a threat that if the claimant was 'uncooperative' her life would be made 'difficult'.

Sections considered: ERA, ss 47B, 103A.

Damages: total award without any detriment was £16,000 but included a 50 per cent uplift under the Employment Act 2002.

Cited in: *Blackbay Ventures Ltd (t/a Chemistree) v Gahir* [2014] IRLR 416 (EAT).

100. Ezsias v North Glamorgan NHS Trust

[2007] ICR 1126 (CA), [2011] IRLR 550 (EAT)

See Case 67.

101. Fecitt and others v NHS Manchester

[2011] ICR 476 (EAT), [2012] ICR 372 (CA).

See Case 88.

102. Vivian v Bournemouth BC

UKEAT/0254/10, 6 May 2011

Key issues: ERA, s 47B; when time begins to run; whether detriment on grounds of a protected disclosure.

Case summary: V raised a grievance against her line manager of bullying. The ET accepted that this amounted to a protected disclosure. The conclusion of the grievance was that there was insufficient evidence and a decision to separate V from the staff about whom she complained. V was placed in a redeployment pool, refused to cooperate, asserting it was the perpetrator who should be moved. As no alternative employment she was dismissed.

ET: found that the process of dealing with the formal allegation of bullying was completed when V was informed that it would not be progressed any further. V did not present a claim within three months of that date. Despite access to union and legal advice it was therefore reasonably practicable to present the claim and it was out of time.

EAT (Slade J): dismissing the appeal, held that the three-month time period runs from the date of the act complained of, not from the detriment alleged to be suffered as a result. Where the act or failure is part of a series of acts or failures, the three-month period runs from the last of them.

Result: appeal dismissed.

Sections considered: ERA, ss 47B, 103A.

Cited by: *Korashi v Abertawe Bro Morgannwg University Local Health Board* [2012] IRLR 4.

103. Price v Surrey County Council and Wood Street School Governing Body

EAT/0450/10, 27 October 2011

Key issue: Resignation due to inadequate response to disclosures, not the disclosure itself.

Case summary: Price, an office assistant, raised a complaint of bullying, an accepted protected disclosure. After a long delay her grievance was rejected. An independent investigation concluded no bullying but stated it was a finely balanced decision. When informed of the outcome and the rejection of her appeal against the dismissal of her grievance, she resigned.

ET: Price was constructively unfairly dismissed. The tribunal found that the letter stating there was no evidence of bullying, in the face of an investigation that showed this assertion to be untrue, amounted to a repudiatory breach of contract. But they found there was no link, causal or otherwise, to her protected disclosures.

EAT (Carnwarth LJ): upheld the ET's decision. The ET was entitled to find that the resignation was due to the inadequacy of the response to her protected disclosures, rather than by reason of the protected disclosures themselves.

The EAT emphasized that the list of issues should clearly identify the central issues and should avoid mixing up these (and indeed the relevant sub-issues) with the detailed factual allegations in relation to the case. In this case the list of issues failed to discriminate between the significant and the 'utterly trivial' factual issues in the case. The emphasis on a long list of individual detriments, together with the inclusion of many allegations that were peripheral or exaggerated or unsustainable, had added considerably to the length of the case and to the difficulty for the tribunal in 'seeing the wood for the trees'.

Result: unfair dismissal under s 98 ERA, but protected disclosure claims dismissed.

Sections considered: ERA, ss 47B, 103A.

104. Dunster v First Transpennine Express Ltd

UKEAT/0570/10/ZT, 19 August 2011

Key issues: Causation and potentially contradictory findings.

Case summary: D, a train conductor, complained about an injury from a train driving over bumpy track. D wrote to her union disclosing health and safety concerns and then refused to collect revenue at the bumpy part of the track. She was suspended.

ET: Found that the reason for her suspension was not her disclosure but her actions. They did comment on inferences, saying

> 5.31 ... There is no overt or direct evidence to establish such a reason. We accept that such evidence will rarely be forthcoming, and have therefore also considered the sequence of events as a whole to see if they reveal any pattern of underlying adverse behaviour towards the Claimant, from which we might draw an inference of some underlying, hidden motive, not apparent from simply examining each incident on its own. Indeed, the Claimant's case is that there was here a hidden agenda, in effect a conspiracy amongst the Respondent's employees, to punish her for the disclosure.

The ET concluded such that her case would require a wide-reaching conspiracy which was ultimately unlikely.

EAT (HHJ McMullen QC): The tribunal had applied the correct test, and was entitled to find that 'the incident had nothing whatsoever to do with any earlier disclosure'.

Result: Appeal dismissed.

Sections considered: ERA, ss 43A, 43B, 43C, 47B, 48(2), 98(4), 103A.

105. Martin v Devonshires Solicitors

[2011] ICR 352

Key issues: Reason why—wholly or partially because of a protected act?

Case summary: Allegations of sex discrimination against two partners in the firm of solicitors. Those allegations were untrue. M did not appreciate that they were untrue, in part because of her mental health difficulties. The fact that she had made protected acts by making complaints of sex discrimination formed part of the facts that led to her dismissal. The reason why the employer dismissed her, however, was not the making of those complaints but rather the fact that the complaints involved false allegations which were serious and were repeated and which she refused to accept were untrue. The reason for the dismissal was that she was mentally ill and that there were management problems to which that gave rise.

EAT (Underhill J): 'the question in any claim of victimization is what was the "reason" that the respondent did the act complained of: if it was, wholly or in substantial part, that the claimant had done a protected act, he is liable for victimization' (para 22). But if 'as a matter of common sense and common justice ... the reason for the dismissal was not the complaint as such but some feature of it which can properly be treated as separable' (para 23), then there is no liability. Underhill J provided three examples where he suggested the reason would be the manner of the complaint. First, if employee in making a complaint of discrimination does it through means of the violent racial abuse of the manager; Second, if a genuine complaint was accompanied with threats of violence. Third, where it is made by ringing the Managing Director at home at 3 o'clock in the morning.

Cited by: *Lambert v Secretary of State for the Home Department* (UKEAT/0074/16/BA, 28 September 2016); *Ladiende v Royal Mail Group Ltd* (UKEAT/0197/15/DA, 27 May 2016); *Kowalewska-Zietek v Lancashire Teaching Hospitals NHS Foundation Trust* (UKEAT/0269/15/JOJ, 21 January 2016); *Bham v 2gether NHS Foundation Trust* (UKEAT/0417/14/DXA, 07 August 2015); *Shinwari v Vue Entertainment Ltd* (UKEAT/0394/14/BA, 12 March 2015); *Vernon v Azure Support Services Ltd* (UKEAT/0192/13/SM, 07 November 2014); *Ahmed v Bradford MDC* (UKEAT/0145/14/KN, 27 October 2014); *Panayiotou v Kernaghan* [2014] IRLR 500 (EAT); *Olayemi v Athena Medical Centre* (UKEAT/0221/11/MC, 8 April 2014); *Blackbay Ventures Ltd (t/a Chemistree) v Gahir* [2014] ICR 747 (EAT); *Veolia Environmental Services UK v Gumbs* [2014] Eq LR 364 (EAT); *Gebremariam v Ethiopian Airlines Enterprise (t/a Ethiopian Airlines)* [2014] IRLR 354 (EAT); *Thames Honda Ltd v Purkis* (UKEAT/0265/13/RN, 10 January 2014); *Gillingham Football Club Ltd v McCammon* [2014] Eq LR 4 (EAT); *Woodhouse v West North West Homes Leeds Ltd* [2013] IRLR 773 (EAT): *X v Y* (UKEAT/0322/12/GE, 04 June 2013); *Heafield v Times Newspapers Ltd* [2013] Eq LR 345 (EAT); *Miller v Interserve Industrial Services Ltd* [2013] ICR 445 (EAT); *Pasab Ltd (t/a Jhoots Pharmacy) v Woods* [2013] IRLR 305 (CA); *North Bristol NHS Trust v Harrold* (UKEAT/0549/11/CEA, 19 September 2012); *Hewage v Grampian Health Board* [2012] ICR 1054 (SC); *Royal Bank of Scotland Plc v Morris* [2012[Eq LR 406 (EAT); *Hawkins v Atex Group Ltd* [2012] ICR 1315 (EAT); *Arriva London South Ltd v Nicolaou* [2012] ICR 510 (EAT); *Blitz v Vectone Group Holdings Ltd* (EAT 29 November 2011, UKEAT /0253/10/DM); *Dunster v First Transpennine Express Ltd* (UKEAT/0570/10/ZT, 19 August 2011); *Fecitt v NHS Manchester* [2012] ICR 372 (CA); *Korashi v Abertawe Bro Morgannwg University Local Health Board* [2012] IRLR 4 (EAT); *Habashi v Crown Prosecution Service* (UKEAT/0554/10/CEA, 10 July 2011); *Wilcox v Birmingham CAB Services Ltd* [2011] Eq LR 810 (EAT); *Bury MBC v Hamilton* [2011] ICR 655 (EAT).

106. Panayiotou v Chief Constable of Hampshire Police

[2014] IRLR 500 EAT

See Case 89.

107. Barclays Bank plc v Mitchell

UKEAT/0279/13/JOJ, 11 February 2014

Key issues: What is required for causation?

Case summary: M had her drink spiked by a colleague. M reported it to the police. Barclays was aware of this but she did not make a formal report to Barclays. When she complained at having to work with him, she was advised to consider moving regions or obtaining a new job.

ET: The advice to move arose from a statement that M did not want to be in the same hotel as the colleague. Those making the suggestion had known M had accused her colleague of spiking her drink. But the ET found she had disclosed that she was 'frightened' of him. The ET found this established a direct link between her problem with her colleague and the decision to suggest moving. On that basis it upheld the claim of detriment on the grounds of a protected disclosure.

EAT (HHJ Peter Clark): Allowing the appeal, it is not enough that the disclosure is linked to the management problem leading to the detrimental treatment. 'What is required ... is a clear finding that the disclosure(s) materially caused or influenced the employer to act as he did. . .. [I]t was not the fact of the earlier disclosures which influenced the suggestion she a move to another region; rather it was the her announcement she could not be in the same room as' her colleague. The finding by the tribunal that 'We are satisfied that the trigger for this meeting . . . was the fact that Miss Mitchell did not want to be in the same hotel as him' did not answer this issue. It was unclear whether that was the sole reason for the eventual outcome of the meeting, a suggested transfer, or not. As this was not clear, the issue was remitted.

Result: Remitted to a fresh tribunal.

Sections considered: ERA, ss 47B, 48(2).

108. Westminster Drug Project v O'Sullivan

UKEAT/0235/13/BA, 11 March 2014

Key issues: Detriment of termination of worker's contract found on the basis that protected disclosure was a material influence. Appealed raising manner of disclosure.

Case summary: WDP were commissioned by the LB Enfield Drug and Alcohol Action Team (DAAT) to provide support to drug users involved in the criminal justice system. Ms O'Sullivan (S) worked as a community care assessor. S forwarded an email from the husband of a client (CO) direct to DAAT. There followed an argument between S and her line manager, Mr Welsh, when he reminded her how uncomfortable he felt with her contacting DAAT, as it was outside her remit. Over a week later Mr Welsh told his line manager (Ms McLean) of concerns over S's punctuality. Subsequently S arrived at work very late. S gave an explanation which Mr Welsh checked, and on his understanding he found it to be false. Following a further dispute over whether Mr Welsh should have checked up on her explanation, the claimant was dismissed.

ET: S was a worker, but not an employee of the respondent. The claim was therefore one of detriment under s 47B ERA. Mr Welsh's relationship with S had broken down and he found her difficult to manage due to (a) her late arrival on a particular occasion and her reaction to her whereabouts being questioned, (b) his concerns that she was going beyond her job description and not accepting his authority, and (c) her having made a protected disclosure to DAAT in CO's case. It found that it was the fact that S had contacted CO that triggered Mr Welsh's decision to complain to Ms McLean (on the same day). The ET concluded that Ms McClean would have discussed the subject of the protected disclosure with Mr Welsh, and that it materially influenced the decision to dismiss.[7] The claim under s 47B therefore succeeded.

EAT (HHJ Shanks): It is permissible to draw a distinction between the fact and manner of the disclosure. Here the case could have been run on the basis that insofar as S's dismissal was related to a protected disclosure, it was caused by the manner of the disclosure and associated conduct about which Mr Welsh was legitimately concerned. But that was not how the case was run before the ET, and it was now too late, on appeal, to raise that distinction. The distinction between the fact and manner of the disclosure had not been brought to the ET's attention, and there had been no cross-examination about the manner of the disclosures. The ET had found that S had been genuinely worried about the health and safety of the clients (including CO) and felt she had to inform those who were in a position to do something about it. If the respondent wanted to run a case that she was making disclosures in an inappropriate manner, an attack on her good faith might have been expected. The ET was entitled to draw an inference that the fact of the dismissal materially influenced the decision.

Result: Appeal dismissed; disclosure was a material influence on detriment.

Detriment: Termination of contract.

Sections considered: ERA, ss 43B(1), 43C(1), 47B, 48(2).

109. Shinwari v Vue Entertainment Ltd

UKEAT/0394/14/BA, 12 March 2015
See Case 90.

---

[7] Note that the finding of material influence would not have been sufficient if S had been an employee; it would have been necessary to find that the protected disclosure was the principal reason for dismissal.

110. Barton v Royal Borough of Greenwich

UKEAT/0041/14/DXA, 1 May 2015

See Case 79.

111. Salisbury NHS Foundation Trust v Wyeth

UKEAT/0061/15/JOJ, 12 June 2015

Key issues: Constructive dismissal: was it a s 103A dismissal? Need for a critical analysis of employer's explanation for conduct amounting to a repudiatory breach, even where no fair reason is put forward for the dismissal.

Case summary: The claimant, a nursing assistant, raised concerns as to the behaviour of the Operating Department Practitioner on his team (ODP1) in relation to the misuse of anaesthetic drugs. He first raised this in 2001 with the general manager of Main Theatres, Mrs Hope. The claimant said he had seen ODP1 inhaling a substance from a bottle in the operating theatre. The claimant regarded ODP1 as a friend, and found it difficult to report the conduct, but did so in the interests of public safety. Mrs Hope spoke to ODP1 about this. He denied the allegation and it was taken no further at that time. In 2012 the claimant raised further concerns about ODP1 (which were found to be protected disclosures), saying he had seen ODP1 crawling on the floor comatose. Another ODP (ODP2), who was a friend of ODP1 sought to carry out an investigation with a view to exonerating ODP1. The claimant informed Mrs Hope of this. She told ODP2 to desist. ODP2 acted aggressively towards the claimant. When the claimant complained about this to Mrs Hope, she told him to put this in writing. The claimant was then moved temporarily from night shift to day shift. He was told this was to avoid the hostile situation with ODP2, but the claimant found it humiliating and embarrassing. He then went off sick. The respondent investigated the allegations against ODP1, but failed to interview the claimant (his name having not been put forward to the investigator by Mrs Hope). The allegation about ODP2's conduct was not investigated. The investigation concluded that there was no direct evidence to support the allegation of anaesthetic drug misuse by ODP1. The claimant was notified of the outcome of the investigation by letter, which is when he realized that he had not been called to be part of the investigation. The letter was also sent to other members of staff. It ended with the comment that 'unfounded gossip undermining [ODP1's] return to work' would not be tolerated. The claimant took this as a veiled warning to him. On returning to work after the Easter holiday, it was apparent that the outcome of the investigation was generally known and being discussed. The claimant felt that he had been made to look a liar. He therefore tendered his resignation.

ET: By failing to investigate his complaint under the bullying and harassment policy, unilaterally moving him from night shifts to day shifts, and ignoring his difficulties arising, the respondent conducted itself in a manner likely to destroy or seriously damage the relationship of confidence and trust with the claimant. This was a repudiatory breach going to the root of the contract. His disclosures were found to be 'at the root' of the events. The ET noted that whilst others had complained about ODP1's behaviour in 2012, the claimant was the only person who had raised concerns a year earlier and the only person to be removed from his shift. Given the absence of a credible explanation for that treatment, the EJ drew an inference, on the balance of probabilities, that Mrs Hope did not want the claimant working among the staff on the night shift while the investigation was undertaken, nor did she want the claimant to give his evidence to the investigation. The ET found the claimant's protected disclosure was the reason or at least the principal reason for what had occurred that led to the claimant's resignation.

EAT (Judge Eady QC): A distinction was to be drawn between dismissal being by reason of or principally by reason of a dismissal and:

- a protected disclosure merely being an influence on the decision (such as would suffice for a detriment claim);
- a 'but for' test; it is not sufficient that the dismissal would not have occurred but for the protected disclosure;
- a separable feature such as the manner of in which the disclosure was made; and
- the way in which the employer responds to the dismissal (citing *Price v Surrey County Council and Governing Body of Wood Street School* [2011] UKEAT/0450/10/SM, 27 October 2011).

Further, in a constructive dismissal claim the focus is on the employer's reason for the conduct amounting to a repudiatory breach of contract which caused the employee to resign. The tribunal has to ask what was the reason why the employer behaved in the way that gave rise to the fundamental breach of contract. Here the conduct which gave rise to the fundamental breach was (a) moving the claimant without consultation from the night to the day shift, (b) ignoring the difficulties that had arisen from the sudden move, (c) continuing not to investigate and resolve his complaint of bullying, (d) leaving him 'temporarily' working on the day shift, (e) not including him in the investigation into ODP1, and (f) sending the letter to the claimant and other staff about ODP1's return, which might have been read as a veiled threat. It was for the ET to decide what weight to give to each of those factors, but a reasonable reading of the ET's decision was that the main factors were the move onto the day shift and the exclusion of the claimant from the investigation. The key issue for the tribunal was therefore what was the reason or principal reason for that conduct. It was insufficient that but for the disclosures none of these events would have occurred. The ET had properly kept this in mind, and the need to focus on the principal reason.

Since the employer had not put forward a potentially fair reason for dismissal, it was unfair. But that did not mean it was by reason of protected disclosures. The respondent had put forward some evidence by way of explanation of its conduct. So far as concerned the shift move, Mrs Hope was concerned about a volatile situation and took the view that there was a need for an experienced ODP to work on the night shift. Since ODP1 was likely to be suspended, she did not want to move ODP2 as well. The ET failed to engage with that explanation, and to state whether it was accepted or rejected, and if rejected why.

In relation to the claimant's exclusion from the investigation process, the ET appeared to have identified Mrs Hope's desire to save face by avoiding disclosure of the 2011 disclosure and how she failed to deal with it. The EAT noted that, whilst this was not laudable conduct on Mrs Hope's part, it could be said to be something other than the protected disclosure itself, notwithstanding that the disclosure would have provided the context. However, it was not possible to tell from the tribunal's reasoning whether that was what it found or how it would then impact on its assessment of the reason or principal reason for dismissal.

The EAT therefore allowed the appeal on the basis that the ET had failed to conduct the necessary critical analysis of the respondent's reason for its conduct and failed properly to explain its finding and reasons in that regard.

In deciding to remit to a differently constituted tribunal, the EAT took into account that there was something to be said for it being preferable for the matter to be heard by a full ET with lay members.

Result: Remitted back to a differently constituted ET.

Sections considered: ERA, ss 47B, 103A.

112. Croydon Health Services NHS Trust v Beatt

UKEAT/0136/15/JOJ, 19 January 2016

Key Issue: Approach to the burden of proof in a claim for dismissal by reason of making protected disclosure.

Case Summary: The claimant was employed by the respondent as a consultant cardiologist. He was dismissed after a six-day disciplinary hearing. The panel concluded that the claimant should be summarily dismissed for gross misconduct. His appeal was unsuccessful. In the ET the claimant contended that the reason or principal reason for his dismissal was that he had made protected disclosures. He further contended that the disciplinary process prior to dismissal, the dismissal itself, the internal appeal process, and acts of post-termination victimization were unlawful, as being detrimental treatment on the grounds of his having made protected disclosures.

EAT (HHJ Clark): the overarching question was which narrative, in whole or in part, the ET accepted: the respondent's case that the claimant had misconducted himself in circumstances where, following a fair and impartial process, he was dismissed for that reason; or the claimant's case that the whole disciplinary process was a 'sham exercise' designed to rid the trust of a distinguished medical practitioner because he had blown the whistle. The employment tribunal said that the respondent had shown a potentially fair reason to dismiss and the chair of the panel had stated (in evidence) that he dismissed for conduct. Further, the tribunal appeared to accept that the investigation had been balanced and the conduct of the disciplinary hearing was 'quasi judicial in nature'. However, the tribunal then went on to place their own view of the strength or weakness of the allegations against the claimant, and concluded that on all the evidence the respondent had 'not shown that the reason for dismissal was misconduct'. The tribunal then expressed a finding as to 'how little an understanding of the facts' the chair of the appeal had. Having referred themselves to *Kuzel*, the ET concluded that 'the Respondent's evidence of conduct be rejected' and 'that the reason put forward by the Claimant, that he was dismissed for making protected disclosures, was the principal factor operating on the decision maker's mind'. The ET said they reached that conclusion

> on the basis of the consistency of the Claimant's evidence in respect of the events of the 9 June and his concerns expressed about patient safety after that date. We conclude that the Claimant was dismissed for escalating his concerns about health and safety concerns . . ..

The EAT allowed the appeal and remitted the case to a fresh tribunal. Instead of determining 'the set of facts known to the employer, or it may be beliefs held by him, which cause him to dismiss the employee' as required by *Abernethy v Mott, Hay and Anderson*, the ET had embarked on its own assessment of the conduct charges upheld by the disciplinary and appeal panels, found them less than compelling, and then moved to the conclusion that the protected disclosures, rather than conduct, were the reason for dismissal. What was 'signally missing' was an analysis leading to the conclusion that the evidence of both the chairs of the panels was false and a deliberate attempt to mislead the ET as to the true reason for dismissal.

Result: Case remitted to a fresh tribunal.

Sections referred to: ERA, s 103A.

113. London Borough of Wandsworth v CRW

UKEAT/0322/15/LA, 7 March 2016

Key Issue: Approach to burden of proof and finding of 'reason or principal reason' under s 103A ERA: whether a dismissal could be fair for s 98 purposes yet automatically unfair for s 103A purposes.

Case Summary: The claimant, a black British woman of Caribbean descent, was employed by the respondent local authority as a worker at a residential unit for severely disabled young people. Disciplinary action was taken against the claimant for matters characterized as acts of gross misconduct, ultimately leading to her dismissal. Another worker, SRW, who was white, was relied on by the claimant as a comparator. The ET found that the concerns relating to SRW, which had been raised by the claimant with the respondent, also raised matters of potential risk to the young people at the unit, although in SRW's case the incidents alleged gave rise to questions of inappropriate behaviour and potential sexual abuse rather than, as in the claimant's case, the risk of physical harm. The ET found that the allegations involving SRW were serious. Whilst, however, the claimant had been suspended, SRW had initially faced no further action. The claimant had formally put her concerns relating to SRW into writing and there was some attempt to look at matters further, but—as the ET found—no proper investigation at that stage. The claimant reported matters to the police. That led to an investigation by the respondent during which SRW was redeployed into a neighbouring unit. Subsequently, SRW was subjected to the disciplinary process, albeit that the charges against him were limited to those he admitted and were characterized as misconduct rather than—as was the case in respect of the claimant—gross misconduct.

Both the disciplinary hearings in respect of the claimant and SRW took place before a Mr Benaim. Mr Benaim found the three charges against the claimant proven and concluded she should be summarily dismissed. The claimant's appeal was dismissed. Mr Benaim found two matters proved against SRW and concluded that SRW had been guilty of misconduct that was serious and warranted a written warning.

The ET considered there was considerable discrepancy in tone, process, and substance between the way the claimant was treated as compared to SRW. The ET accepted Mr Benaim's characterization of SRW's failings as 'procedural breaches' but concluded the same term could apply to the claimant's defaults. The ET was very concerned about the lack of seriousness attached to the incidents involving SRW, as to the way in which the charges against him had been limited to the two matters he had admitted and the unexplained failure to see the reputational risk as being as great in his case as that of the claimant. In the circumstances, the ET considered that the burden of proof was reversed and it was therefore appropriate to look to the respondent for a non-racial explanation. It did not consider that adequate explanations had been given for some of the considerable differences in treatment and concluded that it was appropriate to infer that one of the reasons for or an effective cause of the difference in treatment between the claimant and SRW in the disciplinary proceedings in terms of the process followed and the sanctions applied was race.

In considering the whistleblowing complaint, the ET rejected Mr Benaim's assertion that he had not considered the claimant was a whistleblower. It accepted that the facts of the allegations against the claimant had warranted investigation and disciplinary action, but, set against the treatment by the respondent of SRW, the ET considered that SRW had been treated far more leniently and less formally by the respondent. The ET concluded that the reason for this was because SRW was accused of conduct which was extremely sensitive and which had considerable potential for adversely affecting the respondent's reputation, and to which the relevant management of the respondent did not wish to draw attention. The respondent only launched a formal investigation into these matters when they had to, after the claimant had made it clear that she would pursue matters further. Although there might be a distinction between adopting a light touch towards SRW because of the nature of the allegations against him and being punitive or formal towards the claimant because she had raised those allegations, the ET concluded the latter was the case because the claimant was seen by the respondent as someone who was raising uncomfortable issues in relation to SRW which the respondent did not wish to address properly. Having regard to the very different treatment of SRW, the claimant's disclosures were the principal reason why the respondent subjected the claimant to such a serious misconduct charge and suspended her, and then found that dismissal was the appropriate penalty. Thus the claimant's automatically unfair dismissal complaint under s 103A was well founded.

The ET then went on to consider the claim for 'ordinary' unfair dismissal. It accepted that the referral of the claimant to discipline was justified given the allegations in question: the respondent had reasonable grounds for its belief and there had been adequate investigation. The ET revisited its earlier findings in respect of SRW, but said it did not consider that the disparity of treatment between these two cases took the sanction imposed on the claimant outside the range of reasonable responses, given that the claimant had not acknowledged her wrongdoing or given reassurance to the respondent that the conduct would not be repeated. The ET said it was satisfied that this conclusion did not undermine or conflict with the conclusion in relation to the whistleblowing as it had found in effect that, on the balance of probabilities, absent the background of the claimant's whistleblowing disclosures, this employer would have treated the claimant less harshly and would not have dismissed her for the agreed misconduct.

EAT (HHJ Eady QC) allowed the respondent's appeal. The ET had found that the claimant's whistleblowing was the principal reason why the respondent subjected her to such a serious misconduct charge and then found that dismissal was the appropriate penalty. Having reached that conclusion, the ET needed go no further: the dismissal was for a prohibited, automatically unfair reason. The ET had in fact asked itself the same question for s 98 purposes and concluded the dismissal was fair. It had not done so simply on an alternative basis but expressly found that the dismissal had been fair under s 98(2) for a reason or principal reason (here, conduct) that was capable of being fair. These conclusions were inconsistent and there was no way of remedying that inconsistency.

In respect of the claim of race discrimination, the ET had found that the respondent had not adequately explained the difference in treatment. The respondent's evidence as to why it had treated the claimant in the way it did had apparently been accepted, at least in part, by the ET for the purposes of the unfair dismissal claim. That gave rise to an inconsistency in the ET's findings. Whilst the ET was looking at this question under two different statutory regimes and the answers would not necessarily be the same, where there was an apparent inconsistency in conclusions there had to be adequate reasoning so the parties could understand the ET's findings in each respect. The ET needed to explain which aspect of the reasoning was tainted by race; to scrutinize the mind of the respective decision-takers and state which part of the process was rendered unlawfully discriminatory.

Result: The matter was remitted back to the tribunal.

Sections considered: ERA, ss 98 and 103A.

Time limits

114. Meteorological Office v Edgar

[2002] ICR 149

Key issue: coverage for pre-PIDA protected disclosures; whether a claimant could rely on a protected disclosure that pre-dated the coming into force of PIDA.

Case summary: on 11 March 1999 (prior to PIDA coming into force) Mr Edgar made a formal complaint of bullying and harassment to the respondent. This complaint was investigated and a report produced that was favourable to Edgar. The person against whom the complaint had been made was disciplined. Following a period of sick leave said to have been caused by this treatment Edgar returned to work to be informed that he was being relocated away from the BBC Weather Centre. This decision, he claimed, had a detrimental effect on his career and earning capacity.

ET and EAT: the time for bringing a complaint ran from the date of the detrimental act or omission complained of.

Detriment: relocation.

Sections considered: ERA, s 48(1)(a).

Damages: N/A.

Cited by: *Miklaszewicz v Stolt Offshore Ltd* [2002] IRLR 344 (Court of Session).

115. Arthur v London Eastern Railway Ltd (t/a One Stansted Express)

[2007] ICR 193 (CA)

Key issues: ERA, s 48(3)—'a series of similar acts or failures'; PHR—strike out.

Case summary: the claimant was an on train member of staff. He made disclosures to the police and to the respondent (LER) regarding assaults he suffered whilst working. He claimed that he suffered various detriments and failures to act by LER. Some were within and some outside of the three-month time limit. He sought to present them all as a 'series of similar acts or failures'. What was required to link separate detriments?

ET: at a PHR, dismissed, without hearing any evidence, earlier detriments on the grounds that they were not part of a series of similar acts or failures.

EAT (Judge Reid QC): upholding the ET, stated (paras 11,12) that series 'connotes some factual linkage between events. It is not simply some concatenation of similar acts or failures.... [It] necessarily connotes a temporal element to it; one event following on after another.... [I]t is necessary that there should be a significant degree of linkage between the events'.

CA (Mummery, Sedley, and Lloyd LJJ): allowing the appeal, held that the ET had erred in determining the time point in the way it did, solely on the basis of legal argument without hearing any evidence or making any findings of fact. Per Mummery LJ:

35. In order to determine whether the acts are part of a series some evidence is needed to determine what link, if any, there is between the acts in the three-month period and the acts outside the three-month period. We know that they are alleged to have been committed against Mr Arthur. That by itself would hardly make them part of a series or similar. It is necessary to look at all the circumstances surrounding the acts. Were they all committed by fellow employees? If not, what connection, if any, was there between the alleged perpetrators? Were their actions organised or concerted in some way? It would also be relevant to inquire why they did what is alleged. I do not find 'motive' a helpful departure from the legislative language according to which the determining factor is whether the act was done 'on the ground' that the employee had made a protected disclosure. Depending on the facts I would not rule out the possibility of a series of apparently disparate acts being shown to be part of a series or to be similar to one another in a relevant way by reason of them all being on the ground of a protected disclosure.

36. ... It will in many cases be better to hear all the evidence and then decide the case in the round, including limitation questions, on the basis of all the evidence: see, for example, *Comr of Police of the Metropolis v Hendricks* [2003] ICR 530, particularly paras 48 and 49, regarding the approach to multiple acts alleged to extend over a period.

Per Sedley LJ:

40. [Respondent counsel's] initial insistence that, to come within the statutory formula, acts or failures must be physically alike drove her to this position: that if the suspected whistleblower had repeatedly found that salt had been put in his tea, his time for bringing proceedings would be three months from the most recent occasion; but that if he had first

had salt put in his tea, then had chewing gum left on his chair, then had his bicycle tyres deflated, it would not. One has only to imagine the ministerial answer to a parliamentary question on the point from that under-used aid to construction, the industrious back-bencher, to appreciate that this is unlikely to have been Parliament's intention.

41. I see the force of Lloyd LJ's reasoning about the redundancy of the requirement of similarity if it extends to the grounds on which hostile acts were done as distinct from the acts themselves. But on this issue I agree with Mummery LJ, because the alternative is a construction which demands uniformity in a situation which, as the legislature will have known, is typically multiform. In the second example I have given, which is a classic tale of harassment at work, the only link may be the inferred motive of the aggressors. . ... While I agree with Mummery LJ that, on what is in substance a strike-out application, the search for a shared motive may be entirely unhelpful, when the evidence has been heard and considered it is possible that a series of apparently unconnected acts will all be found—using the statutory language—to have been done to the claimant on the ground that he had made a protected disclosure. The difference between such a finding and a finding of detrimental acts linked by a common motive may be no more than semantic. In either such case I would consider it within the statutory purpose to treat the history as constituting a series of similar acts.

Per Lloyd LJ:

44. . ... it cannot be enough for the complainant to say that the acts in question are all similar in that they were all done on the relevant ground. Any act which can be relied on under section 47B of the Employment Rights Act 1996 must, by definition, have been done 'on the ground that' the complainant had made a protected disclosure. More generally, all the various complaints which may be presented to an employment tribunal under section 48 are defined as involving an allegation that the employer has done an act 'on the ground that' something set out in the particular section has happened (or, in section 47C, that the act has been done 'for a prescribed reason'). That being so, if it were sufficient similarity to assert that all the acts had been done on the particular ground, the use of the word 'similar' would add nothing, and the section could simply have said 'a series of acts'. All acts would be in time so long as one was and all could be said to be part of a series.

45. Mummery LJ would not rule out the ground on which the act is done as the linking feature of similarity: . . . I respectfully disagree on this.

Result: remitted to a fresh tribunal.

Detriment: regarded as a troublemaker; delays in payment of pay in lieu; manner of internal grievance; failure to respond to medical advice.

Sections considered: ERA, ss 47B, 47C.

Damages: N/A.

Cited by: *Nageh v David Game College Ltd* (UKEAT/0112/11, 22 July 2011); *St John Ambulance v Mulvie* (UKEAT/0129/11, 1 July 2011); *Weare v HBOS plc* (UKEAT/0300/08, 28 October 2008); *Tait v Redcar and Cleveland BC* (UKEAT/0096/08, 2 April 2008); *Iya-Nya v British Airways plc* (UKEAT/0302/07, 17 January 2008); *Outokumpu Stainless Ltd v Law* (UKEAT/0199/07, 4 October 2007); *Lyfar v Brighton and Hove University Hospitals Trust* [2006] EWCA Civ 1548 (CA).

116. Tait v Redcar and Cleveland BC

UKEAT/0096/08, 2 April 2008

Key issues: whether claim was in time.

Case summary: the claimant was a parking enforcement manager. He passed on information from a member of the public that a manager (Mr Gittens) had been involved in corruptly cancelling penalty notices. The claimant was suspended by Gittens a month later following a complaint by a parking attendant whom he managed. The disciplinary process continued for some months but, on 29 September 2005, he was told that the disciplinary investigation was to stop immediately and no disciplinary action would be taken. He returned to work in January 2006, but to a self-contained project rather than to his old role. He found the situation difficult and his health suffered. He brought ET proceedings on 25 April 2006, claiming that the refusal to restore him to his old role was a dismissal which he claimed was by reason of protected disclosures, and also alleged detriments by reason of protected disclosures.

ET: upheld the claims of ordinary unfair dismissal but not of dismissal by reason of protected disclosure. It also dismissed the claims of detriment under ERA, s 47B as being out of time. There was no appeal against the findings in relation to dismissal.

EAT (Underhill J): held that there was no error in finding that the detriment claims were out of time. The act of suspension was 'an act extending over a period' within the meaning of ERA, s 48(3)(a). However, it had come to an end when the claimant received a letter informing him that the disciplinary action against him was to stop 'immediately' because from that moment he was no longer under a disciplinary suspension. That occurred more than six months before the institution of proceedings. There was no subsequent act or deliberate failure to act on the ground of a protected disclosure. Even if the request to stay at home after being told that the disciplinary investigation had ended could be regarded as a continuation of the suspension, it was for a different purpose. Therefore, the claim was out of time.

Result: appeal dismissed.

Detriment: alleged suspension; out of time.

Sections considered: ERA, ss 47B(1), 48.

Damages: N/A.

Cited by: *Weare v HBOS plc* (UKEAT/0300/08, 28 October 2008).

117. Unilever UK plc v Hickinson and Sodexo Ltd

EAT/0192/09, 24 June 2009

Key issues: ERA, s 47B and time limits; whether detriment was a continuing act.

Case summary: Mr Hickinson worked in security at Unilever for Sodexho. Unilever asked for him to be removed for making covert recordings of staff at Unilever. He was later dismissed after being unable to find another assignment. His claim was presented within three months of his dismissal, but more than three months after the removal from the site.

ET: held that the claim was in time as the removal from the site set in train the series of event which resulted in his dismissal and was a continuous act.

EAT (Judge Reid QC): held that the ET had erred in failing to distinguish the act of removal from the site and its consequences. The s 47B claim was therefore out of time. The position would have been different if there had been continued pressure from Unilever after removal from the site.

Result: claim against Unilever dismissed.

Detriment: removal from Unilever site.

Sections considered: ERA, ss 47B(1), 48(3)(A), 48(4)(a).

Damages: N/A.

118. Vivian v Bournemouth BC

UKEAT/0254/10, 6 May 2011

See Case 102.

119. St. John Ambulance v Mulvie

UKEAT/0129/11, 1 July 2011

Key issues: ERA, s 47B and time limit.

Case summary: Mr Mulvie resigned from his employment with St John Ambulance on 12 February 2010, and presented a claim, including under ERA, s 47B, on 4 May 2010. The last act or deliberate failure to act alleged was when he was told by a letter from the respondent's solicitors on 12 January 2010 that the respondent was not going to revert to him further in relation to the resolution of his concerns relating to his protected disclosures, that they were a matter for the respondent to consider internally, and offering instead to discuss Mr Mulvie's other concerns in a mediation.

ET: concluded that the issue of whether s 47B detriment claims were in time should be determined at the full merits hearing.

EAT (Keith J): held that the detriment claims were out of time, subject to whether time could be extended. Since the last of a series of detriments occurred more than three months before presentation of the claim, the time point did not need to be put off to the substantive trial. If there had been a continuing act of failing to deal with the claimant's grievances, that situation was brought to an end by the communication of a definitive decision on 12 January. As such there was no detriment less than three months prior to the presentation of the claim. The fact that on the claimant's case he continued to be sidelined until his resignation did not affect this, as the relevant act/deliberate failure to act was to be distinguished from its consequences.

Result: appeal allowed and the issue of whether there could be an extension of time for s 47B was remitted to the ET.

Detriment: refusing to deal with grievance and sidelined.

Sections considered: ERA, ss 47B, 48(3).

Damages: N/A.

120. Warrior Square Recoveries Ltd v Flynn

UKEAT/0154/12/KN, 3 October 2012; [2014] EWCA Civ 68

Key issues: Time limits.

Case summary: F, a senior broker, made a disclosure suggesting money had been misappropriated. In 2006 he was invited to a disciplinary hearing because of an untrue allegation of fraud. The hearing was adjourned and never came to a conclusion before formally being withdrawn. However, the claimant fell sick and never went back to work. He remained in employment until 21 May 2010 when he resigned. On 22 September 2010 he claimed that he had suffered a detriment by reason of making a public interest disclosure.

ET (EJ Davidson): The purported disclosure was made in December 2005. The claimant asserted his detriment was the threat of disciplinary action and legal action for defamation. The respondent's case was that those threats were lifted by at the latest 30 November 2009. The ET noted that the claimant had been consistent and persistent in his view that these threats were still present and, in his mind, repeated by the respondent's actions. The ET concluded that if the claimant was correct, then the detriment continued and his claim was within time.

EAT (Mr Justice Langstaff (President)): Allowing an appeal, and substituting a finding that the claim was out of time, the EAT emphasized that it is essential that, where time is in issue, the tribunal must identify any act, or the deliberate failure to act; and the date of that act, or the date of that failure to act, must then be established. Where the latest act, or the deliberate failure to act, is out of time, the claim is out of time unless the claimant can show that it was not reasonably practicable for him to present a complaint before the end of that period. The employment judge erred in failing to identify what was the act, or deliberate failure to act, causative of detriment. Instead the EJ appeared to have confused a continuing detriment with a continuing cause. As no argument was made at the ET or EAT that it was not reasonably practicable for the claim to be made in time, the EAT substituted a finding that the claim was out of time.

CA: When giving permission to appeal ([2013] EWCA Civ 917), Rimer LJ noted the only possible argument was that an application for subject access disclosure, whose purpose was to provide information as to whether or not the defamation claim was being pursued and which was not complied with within a forty-day time limit, could be another deliberate failure, occurring less than three months prior to the tribunal proceedings being issued, and so potentially providing a gateway detriment. However, on the substantive appeal, the court concluded that the only case presented to the employment judge had been based on allegations of detriment consisting of the threats of disciplinary proceedings and an action in defamation. The EAT had correctly concluded that in reality those threats had not endured. Accordingly the appeal was dismissed.

Result: Claim out of time.

Sections considered: ERA, ss 47B, 48.

Cited by: *McKinney v Newham LBC* [2015] ICR 495 (EAT).

121. Northumberland Tyne & Wear NHS Foundation Trust v Geoghegan

UKEAT/0048/13/BA, 29 January 2014; [2014] EWCA Civ 1094, (CA)

See Case 49.

122. Theatre Peckham v Browne

UKEAT/0154/13/RN, 24 June 2014

Key issues: Last detriment not pleaded and wrongly determined; application of *Fecitt*.

Case summary: If a gateway detriment is out of time, what happens to those remaining?

ET (EJ Corrigan): considered six alleged detriments and found in the claimant's favour only on detriments 2, 5, and 6. Detriment 6 was the only one within the primary time limit. The tribunal held that it formed the last of a series of acts and that the entire claim was in time. This 'gateway' detriment was challenged on appeal.

EAT (HHJ Burke QC):

The tribunal had not erred in finding that there was a detriment in seeking to persuade the claimant to agree to terminate her employment. The respondent had chosen, in a situation of stalemate between two employees, to seek to persuade the claimant to bring her employment to an end when that had not been done with the other employee. A reasonable worker could regard that as a detriment. However, the tribunal had failed to address the respondent's case that it had been seeking to remedy a dysfunctional situation produced by the dispute between the claimant and a colleague, which a mediation had been unable to remedy. The tribunal had adopted a 'historical' approach of relying on the fact that the detrimental treatment flowed from the grievance, rather than an analytical approach of focusing on the reason for the detrimental treatment—and whether it was the protected disclosure or the dysfunctional situation.

However, the ET had erred in relation to detriment 6 in that it had not been pleaded and therefore could not be relied upon. The claim as a whole therefore failed as there was no detrimental act or deliberate failure to act, and nor was there any evidence that it was not reasonably practicable to bring the claim in time.

Result: Once the gateway detriment was removed, the others were out of time and there was no prospect of her establishing that it was not reasonably practicable for her to present her claim in time.

123. Canavan v Governing Body of St Edmund Campion Catholic School

UKEAT/0187/13/DA, 13 February 2015

Key issues: claimant ordered to produce schedule of claims. Months after the claim she produced 'Further Information'. A year later she produced 'Amended Particulars'. The amended versions included new claims, including detriments for protected disclosures and for trade union activities together with post-ET1 claims.

Case summary: Employment judge applied the statutory time limits to the disclosures relied upon rather than to the detriments which the claimant alleged she had suffered by reason of making those protected disclosures.

ET: Employment Judge Dean refused the application to amend applying Selkent principles. Various parts of the claim were disallowed.

EAT (HHJ Jeffrey Burke QC):

> [25] ... in considering time limits in a protected disclosure case, the tribunal should consider the point of time at which the alleged dismissal or detriment is said to have occurred and not the point of time at which the disclosure or disclosures relied upon were made.
>
> . . .
>
> [56] ... the judgment of the Court of Appeal in *Hendricks* and in *Arthur*[8] put difficulties in the way of an employer who seeks victory on a series of acts issue at an interlocutory stage. There

---

[8] That is, *Arthur v London Eastern Railways Ltd* ([2007] ICR 193 (CA)).

may be cases in which the facts are clear enough for a decision to be made at that stage; they are not likely to be frequently met; see the Judgment of Lloyd LJ in *Arthur* at paragraph 43.

Result: Some claims properly struck out, but those based on the date of the disclosure were wrongly struck out.

Sections considered: ERA, s 48(3);

Cited: *ASLEF v Brady* ([2006] IRLR 576) at para 55; *Fuller v London Borough of Brent* [2011] EWCA Civ 267, [2011] IRLR 414; *Arthur v London Eastern Railways Ltd* ([2006] EWCA Civ 1358, [2007] IRLR 58, [2007] ICR 193); *Commissioner of Metropolitan Police v Hendricks* [2003] ICR 530; *Miklaszewicz v Stolt Offshore Ltd* [2002] IRLR 344, 2002 SC 232, 2002 SLT 103; *Tait v Redcar and Cleveland Borough Council* (EAT 0096/08, 2 April 2008); *Nageh v David Game College Ltd* (EAT 0112/11, 22 July 2011).

124. McKinney v London Borough of Newham

[2015] ICR 495 (EAT)

Key issues: When does time start to run for a detriment; the date of the decision, or the date of receipt of decision that is the detriment? ERA, s 97(1)(b) or s 48(3).

Case summary: When did time start? Was it (a) when the respondent reached the decision to reject the claimant's third-stage grievance on 8 October 2010, following a hearing on 6 October; or (b) when the claimant learned of that decision on 14 October, on receipt of the respondent's outcome letter dated 8 October? The date of 8 October rendered the form ET1 lodged on 11 January 2011 out of time; if 14 October was the relevant date, it was in time.

EAT (HHJ Peter Clark): Time started to run from the date the detrimental act was done, not when the complainant acquired knowledge of it.

Result: The claim was out of time. Time starts from the date of the decision, not when it was known to the claimant.

Sections considered: ERA, ss 48(3), 97(1)(b), 123.

Burden of proof

125. London Borough of Harrow v Knight

[2003] IRLR 140 (EAT)

See Case 2.

126. Bachnak v Emerging Markets Partnership (Europe) Ltd

EAT/0288/05, 27 January 2006

See Case 63.

127. Kuzel v Roche Products Ltd

[2008] ICR 799 (CA)

Key issues: burden of proof for automatic unfair dismissal under ERA, s 103A.

Case summary: Dr Kuzel, head of regulatory affairs at RPL, claimed that she was dismissed for protected disclosures. RPL asserted that she was dismissed for 'some other substantial reason' regarding her relationships with her line manager and a senior colleague.

ET: concluded that her dismissal was unfair and not for the reason advanced by RPL, but because of her manager's loss of temper and not by reason of a protected disclosure. There was sufficient evidence in encouraging Dr Kuzel in the actions she was taking, and in the absence of criticisms from the employer for pursuing these issues, to negate a finding that the dismissal was by reason of the protected disclosures, even if there was a difference of style between Dr Kuzel and the respondent.

EAT (Peter Clark J): remitted the issue to the ET on the basis that it had placed the burden on Dr Kuzel. The EAT set out the approach to be followed (para 47):

> (1) Has the claimant shown that there is a real issue as to whether the reason put forward by the employers, some other substantial reason, was not the true reason? Has she raised some doubt as to that reason by advancing the section 103A reason? (2) If so, have the employers proved their

reason for dismissal? (3) If not, have the employers disproved the section 103A reason advanced by the claimant? (4) If not, dismissal is for the section 103A reason. In answering those questions it follows: (a) that failure by the employers to prove the potentially fair reason relied on does not automatically result in a finding of unfair dismissal under section 103A; (b) however, rejection of the employers' reason coupled with the claimant having raised a prima facie case that the reason is a section 103A reason entitles the tribunal to infer that the section 103A reason is the true reason for dismissal, but (c) it remains open to the employers to satisfy the tribunal that the making of the protected disclosures was not the reason or principal reason for dismissal, even if the real reason as found by the tribunal is not that advanced by the employers; (d) it is not at any stage for the claimant (with qualifying service) to prove the section 103A reason.

CA (**Mummery, Arden, Longmore LJJ**): whilst approving the approach to be followed as set out by the EAT, the CA allowed the appeal and affirmed the decision of the ET. The burden of proof as to the reason for dismissal is on the respondent but it may discharge that either by showing a legitimate reason for dismissal or by showing that the reason was not in any event a protected disclosure.

Per Mummery LJ (with whom Arden LJ and Longmore LJ agreed):

46. The summary of the submissions shows how worked up lawyers can get about something like the burden of proof. In some situations, such as being charged with a criminal offence, there is plenty to get worked up about. It is very important indeed. In many areas of civil law, however, the burden of proof is not a big thing. Discrimination law is an exception, because discrimination is so difficult to prove. In the case of unfair dismissal, however, there has never been any real problem for the tribunals in practice. The danger is that in cases like this something so complicated will emerge that the sound exercise of common sense by tribunals will be inhibited.

. . .

57. I agree that when an employee positively asserts that there was a different and inadmissible reason for his dismissal, he must produce some evidence supporting the positive case, such as making protected disclosures. This does not mean, however, that, in order to succeed in an unfair dismissal claim, the employee has to discharge the burden of proving that the dismissal was for that different reason. It is sufficient for the employee to challenge the evidence produced by the employer to show the reason advanced by him for the dismissal and to produce some evidence of a different reason.

. . .

61. . . .An employer who dismisses an employee has a reason for doing so. He knows what it is. He must prove what it was.. . .

. . .

65. The 1996 Act presupposes that there can only be one reason or principal reason for the dismissal within the meaning of the Act. The tribunal found that the principal reason was Mr Doherty's loss of temper and failing to follow advice. Dr Kuzel's criticisms of the reasons cannot advance her ground of appeal because, if they are correct, it just means that Roche have failed to establish any potentially fair reason for the dismissal. In coming to its conclusion the tribunal did not require Dr Kuzel to prove the reason for dismissal. It simply concluded that this reason put forward by her was not 'made out'. It was not 'made out' because the tribunal decided that Roche had disproved it.

Result: no automatic unfair dismissal; tribunal decision stands.

Detriment: N/A.

Sections considered: ERA, s 103A.

Damages: N/A.

Cited by: *Royal Mail Group Ltd v Jhuti* [2016] IRLR 854; *Serco Ltd v Dahou* [2016] EWCA Civ 832, [2017] IRLR 81; *Croydon Health Services v Beatt* (UKEAT/0136/15/JOJ, 19 January 2016); *Corrigan v University of Bolton* (UKEAT/0408/14/RN, 21 December 2015); *Basildon and Thurrock NHS Foundation Trust v Weerasinghe* [2016] ICR 305 (EAT); *Arriva London South Ltd v Graves* (UKEAT/ 0067/15/DA, 03 July 2015); *Schaathun v Executive & Business Aviation Support Ltd* (UKEAT/0226/12/ LA, 30 June 2015); *Salisbury NHS Foundation Trust v Wyeth* (UKEAT/0061/15/JOJ, 12 June 2015); *Brailsford v John Reid and Sons (Strucsteel) Ltd* (UKEAT/0036/15/MC, 21 May 2015); *Barton v Greenwich*

RLBC (UKEAT/0041/14/DXA, 01 May 2015); *Azam v Ofqual* (UKEAT/0407/14/JOJ, 19 March 2015); *Marshall v Game Retail Ltd* (UKEAT/0276/13/DA, 13 February 2015); *Ahmed v Bradford MDC* (UKEAT/0145/14/KN, 27 October 2014); *Co-operative Group Ltd v Baddeley* [2014] EWCA Civ 658; *Bleasdale v Healthcare Locums Plc* (UKEAT/0324/13/LA, 15 April 2014); *Healey v Wincanton Plc* (UKEAT/0400/13/LA, 07 February 2014); *Ross v Eddie Stobart Ltd* (UKEAT/0068/13/RN, 28 June 2013); *CSC Computer Sciences Ltd v McAlinden* (UKEAT/0252/12/LA, 11 December 2012); *Parekh v Brent LBC* [2012] EWCA Civ 1630; *Renton v Cantor Fitzgerald Europe* (UKEAT/0236/10/JOJ, 18 July 2012); *Learning Trust v Marshall* [2012] Eq LR 927 (EAT); *Blitz v Vectone Group Holdings Ltd* (EAT 29 November 2011, UKEAT /0253/10/DM); *Price v Surrey County Council and another* (EAT/0450/ 10, 27 October 2011); *Freeman v Ultra Green Group Ltd (In Liquidation)* (UKEAT/0239/11, 9 August 2011); *Cromwell Garage Ltd v Doran* (UKEAT/0369/10, 8 April 2011); *Ministry of Justice v Sarfraz* [2011] IRLR 562 (EAT); *Fecitt v NHS Manchester* [2011] ICR 476 (EAT); *Nunn v Royal Mail Group Ltd* [2011] ICR 162 (EAT); *Whitelock & Storr v Khan* (UKEAT/0017/10, 26 October 2010); *Bradford and Bingley plc v McCarthy* (UKEAT/0458/09, 5 February 2010); *Wilson v Health and Safety Executive* [2010] ICR 302 (CA); *J v DLA Piper UK LLP* [2010] ICR 1052 (EAT); *St Alphonsus RC Primary School v Blenkinsop* (UKEAT/0082/09, 18 May 2009); *El-Megrisi v Azad University* (EAT/0448/08, 5 May 2009); *Woodhouse School v Webster* [2009] ICR 818 (CA); *Redcar and Cleveland BC v Scanlon* (UKEAT/ 0369/06, 22 May 2007; UKEAT/0088/08, 20 May 2008); *Network Rail Infrastructure Ltd v Glencross* (UKEAT/0094/08, 16 May 2008).

128. Redcar and Cleveland BC v Scanlon

UKEAT/0369/06, 22 May 2007; UKEAT/0088/08, 20 May 2008

See Case 98.

129. Whitelock & Storr and others v Khan

EAT/0017/10/RN, 26 October 2010

Key issues: s 103A and reason for dismissal.

Case summary: Whitelock & Storr are a firm of solicitors. Khan was a solicitor employed by them undertaking a criminal duty solicitor role. An issue arose over the non-payment of a bonus due to financial problems at the firm. Khan raised a grievance seeking payment and raising other matters, such as the adequacy of training for another employee and the state of the premises. Before the grievance procedure had concluded, Khan threatened that he would not sign up for new duty solicitor slots beginning in a few months, stating that he did not intend to sign for them until being paid his outstanding bonus. Khan was paid his outstanding bonus. However, unbeknown to the firm, he had by that time signed the duty solicitor form for the benefit of another firm. Later the firm invited Khan to a disciplinary meeting regarding letters discovered on his computer which included one dealing with his intention not to provide the benefit of the duty solicitor slots he had signed, together with other allegations. During a ten-minute disciplinary meeting, Khan alleged that the disciplinary process was as a consequence of his grievance, stated that he was leaving the firm, and refused to answer questions. Khan was dismissed for using the firm's facilities to assist a rival firm.

ET: Found his grievance to be a protected disclosure and was the reason for his dismissal. The tribunal found that the dismissal was not on the basis that he had attempted to transfer duty solicitor slots because Khan was unable to do so, but was in response to his grievance, finding that there was 'no evidence supporting the conclusion they reached'.

EAT (HHJ Ansell): The tribunal was found to have failed to apply the guidance in *Kuzel* because it did not consider the respondent firm's reason for dismissal before considering whether the real reason was the disclosure. The EAT remitted the case because the tribunal had looked more into the ability of Khan to transfer the duty solicitor slots as opposed to properly examining what was in the mind of the firm when it made its decision to dismiss Khan. The mere fact that they were misguided as to whether the slots could be transferred was not relevant. If that was the reason, irrespective of whether they were mistaken in their view, their belief that there had been a transfer of the slots (and not any protected disclosure) was the reason for the dismissal.

Result: claim remitted to fresh tribunal.

130. Nunn v Royal Mail Group Ltd

[2011] ICR 162 (EAT)

Key issues: automatic unfair dismissal; burden of proof.

Case summary: during a disciplinary process, N was accused of deliberately misleading his manager for which he was disciplined and then demoted together with a reduction in salary. He lodged a grievance and a complaint to the ET over the deduction of wages. The proceedings were settled, but his grievance was not upheld. He refused to accept the demotion and was dismissed. He claimed that he was automatically unfairly dismissed for asserting a statutory right by bringing the ET proceedings or for making protected disclosures in those proceedings.

ET: found that he was dismissed for refusing to accept the sanction of demotion. The manager who demoted and dismissed him had no knowledge of the ET proceedings. The demotion and dismissal of the claimant were not by reason of any protected disclosure.

EAT (Judge Ansell): found that there was no error of law by the ET, acknowledging *Kuzel* he confirmed that PIDA claims required a different approach to discrimination claims.

> 18. ... In discrimination claims, there is clearly a necessity to exercise a degree of care in relation to the establishment of primary facts. In order to set up the shifting burden of proof, the court is urged to look carefully in relation to what inferences can be drawn from those facts particularly as the basic information will often be in the hands of the employer rather than the employee. However, in unfair dismissal claims, the burden is on the employer, there being no need for the employee to set up sufficient facts for that burden to exist. Obviously, a tribunal, in assessing what reasons the employer is putting forward, will have in mind what the employee is saying about the reason, and will need to test the employer's witnesses in relation to those matters that point to a reason other than that that the employee is putting forward. But, at the end of the day, it is a matter for the tribunal to come to a view as to whether, on the balance of probabilities, the employer has satisfied them as to the reason. In this particular case, the question very much turned on the credibility of Mr Willis. The tribunal were in the best position to assess him and his state of knowledge in June 2008. We can see no criticism in the approach the tribunal took.

CA (Smith LJ): refused permission to appeal ([2011] EWCA Civ 244).

Result: appeal dismissed.

Sections considered: ERA, s 103A.

131. Blitz v Vectone Group Holdings Ltd

UKEAT /0253/10/DM, 29 November 2011

Key issues: Can the ET rely on a statement, without cross-examining its author, to dismiss a claim for a detriment done by the non-attending witness?

Case summary: Eight claims were issued after four weeks of employment. A rare case where a Continuity of Employment Order was made, but the claim subsequently failed.

ET: B issued demands on his new employer. These included refusing to stay at a hotel, his inappropriate tone in his communications, and criticizing a colleagues' working hours by email addressed to her and the CEO. The ET found that once he had received information he immediately sought legal advice and tendered his resignation from his directorship to the CEO. The ET could not reasonably conclude that the issues he had received were 'of such significance and such urgency' to warrant his resignation forthwith, without any attempt to obtain an explanation. He demonstrated a lack of proportion, proper consideration for others, or lack of an understanding of what he had been employed to do. The ET found that his detriment was not on the grounds of his disclosure, notwithstanding that the respondent called no witnesses, and instead relied upon the witness statement of the claimant's former line manager (Mr Wilson).

EAT (Judge Serota QC): The ET's decision was that the real reason for the respondent's conduct was its dissatisfaction with the claimant's performance and a lack of trust in his judgement. Although the tribunal is not obliged to treat hearsay evidence strictly in accordance with the Civil Evidence Act, as made clear in rule 14(2) of sch 1 of the 2004 ET Rule of Procedure (now contained in rule 41 of sch 1 of the 2013 Rules), it is nowadays commonplace for employment tribunals to receive hearsay evidence in witness statements or other documents. The ET had also noted the claimant himself relied upon the statements of two witnesses who were not called to give evidence. Judge Serota QC stated that it was clear the ET 'carried out the appropriate weighing exercise and set Mr Wilson's evidence clearly in the matrix of the contemporaneous documents and the Claimant's own evidence'.

CA (Elias LJ): Refusing permission to appeal, Elias LJ commented (at para 9) that whilst it would be 'a rare case where an employer can establish a reason for dismissal without providing a witness to appear before the Tribunal', here the tribunal was not simply left with hearsay evidence contained in Mr Wilson's witness statement. It also had a number of contemporaneous documents and the evidence from the claimant himself, and it had expressly rejected parts of his evidence.

Result: Appeal dismissed.

Detriment: The claimant alleged: (i) failure to pay expenses; (ii) holding disciplinary hearings on the grounds that he had made protected disclosures; (iii) failure to respond to his request for time off for Jewish holidays; (iv) failure to reply to a number of letters; (v) late payment of salary and contravention of the Continuation of Contract Order; (vi) failure to update the claimant's PAYE coding; (vii) failure to pay monthly instalments in respect of salary pursuant to the CCO via BACS; and (viii) the provision of the services of the headhunter while he was still employed.

Sections considered: ERA, ss 43A, 43B, 43C, 47B, 100(1)(e), 103A, 128. Civil Evidence Act, s 4(2).

Cited by: *Blackbay Ventures Ltd (t/a Chemistree) v Gahir* [2014] IRLR 416 (EAT).

132. Ross v Eddie Stobart Ltd

UKEAT/0085/10, 16 May 2011

See Case 40.

133. Blackbay Ventures Ltd (t/a Chemistree) v Gahir

[2014] IRLR 416, [2014] ICR 747 (EAT)

Key issues: guidance for all whistleblowing claims. Relationship deteriorated because G questioned procedures and practices. Detriment and automatic unfair dismissal claims succeed.

Case summary: The claimant was employed as a pharmacist. Her duties included monitoring and securing compliance with statutory requirements and guidance issued by the General Pharmaceutical Council. Two days after starting work she sent an email to her employer raising health and safety issues and concern about the employer's failure to comply with its legal obligations. The employer's superintendent pharmacist replied in detail six days later and emailed its other pharmacists with revised instructions to address matters raised by a report from a professional standards inspector. The claimant replied on the same day expressing her concern as to a failure to comply with the statutory requirements. She also sent a copy to the inspector. The superintendent pharmacist sent a further reply addressing each point. The following day the claimant's request for time off in lieu of overtime was refused. She sent a letter of complaint to the superintendent pharmacist which she circulated to the other employees. She was dismissed on the next day on the grounds of 'mutual unsuitability'.

ET: upheld the claims of dismissal by reason of protected disclosures, and detriment consisting of stress suffered as a result of employer's failure to deal with the issues she had raised.

EAT (Judge Serota QC): overturned the finding of detriment but upheld the s 103A dismissal finding. As to dismissal, although the tribunal's decision might seem surprising given that the employer responded promptly to address the issues raised, there was material on which the ET could conclude that the protected disclosures were the principal reason for dismissal.

In relation to detriment, the tribunal had failed to determine when the 'deliberate' decision to subject the claimant to a detriment was taken. There was no finding as to any conscious decision to take no action. In the absence of evidence to the contrary, the respondent could only be taken to have decided on a deliberate failure to act when the period expired when it might have been expected to do the failed act if it was to be done (s 48(4)(b) ERA). Here the bulk of the complaints, and the more serious ones, were in an email of 31 August 2010, and the dismissal was only 3 September 2010. It was difficult to see what detriment the claimant could claim to have suffered during that short time even if the tribunal could have decided that there was a deliberate decision to take no action despite having apparently been satisfied that the concerns were promptly addressed. The EAT also noted that it could not understand how simple inaction could amount to a detriment, given that the claimant's job necessarily required her to draw attention to breaches of obligations placed by law on pharmacists. Nor could it see how she could reasonably have held a justified sense of grievance for the limited time she claimed to have suffered stress when her concerns were being promptly and fully addressed. In all, the decision in relation to detriment was plainly wrong and perverse.

The EAT also (at para 98) set out the following general guidance on the approach when considering protected disclosure detriment claims:

1. Each disclosure should be separately identified by reference to date and content.
2. The alleged failure or likely failure to comply with a legal obligation, or matter giving rise to the health and safety of an individual having been or likely to be endangered as the case may be, should be separately identified.
3. The basis upon which each disclosure is said to be protected and qualifying should be addressed.
4. Each failure or likely failure should be separately identified.
5. Save in obvious cases, if a breach of a legal obligation is asserted the source of the obligation should be identified and capable of verification by reference, for example, to statute or regulation. It is not sufficient as here for the employment tribunal to simply lump together a number of complaints, some of which may be culpable, but others of which may simply have been references to a checklist of legal requirements or do not amount to disclosure of information tending to show breaches of legal obligations. Unless the ET undertakes this exercise it is impossible to know which failures or likely failures were regarded as culpable and which attracted the act or omission said to be the detriment suffered. If the ET adopts a rolled-up approach it may not be possible to identify the date when the act or deliberate failure to act occurred, as logically that date could not be earlier than the latest act or deliberate failure to act relied upon and it will not be possible for the appeal tribunal to understand whether, how, or why the detriment suffered was as a result of any particular disclosure; it is of course proper for an employment tribunal to have regard to the cumulative effect of a number of complaints, providing always they have been identified as protected disclosures.
6. The employment tribunal should then determine whether or not the claimant had the reasonable belief referred to in s 43 B1 of ERA 1996 under the 'old law' whether each disclosure was made in good faith; and under the 'new' law introduced by s 17 Enterprise and Regulatory Reform Act 2013 (ERRA), whether it was made in the public interest.
7. Where it is alleged that the claimant has suffered a detriment, short of dismissal it is necessary to identify the detriment in question and, where relevant, the date of the act or deliberate failure to act relied upon by the claimant. This is particularly important in the case of deliberate failures to act because unless the date of a deliberate failure to act can be ascertained by direct evidence, the failure of the respondent to act is deemed to take place when the period expired within which he might reasonably have been expected to do the failed act.
8. The employment tribunal under the 'old law' should then determine whether or not the claimant acted in good faith, and under the 'new law' whether the disclosure was made in the public interest.

Result: Detriment dismissed on Appeal; dismissal upheld.

Detriment: failing to 'address the issues' raised in disclosures or 'deal with them adequately' amounted to a detriment.

Sections considered: ERA, ss 43B(1)(b), 43L(3), 47B, 48(4)(b), 103A.

Cited: *Martin v Devonshires Solicitors* [2011] ICR 352; *London Borough of Harrow v Knight* [2003] IRLR; *Hossack v Kettering Borough Council* (UKEAT/1113/01).

134. Ibekwe v Sussex Partnership NHS Foundation Trust

UKEAT/0072/14, 20 November 2014

See Case 51.

135. Phoenix House Ltd v Stockman & Anor

[2016] IRLR 848

Key issue: the burden of proof in a detriment claim

Case Summary: The claimant received a twelve-month written warning for misconduct from the respondent's manager, Ms Taylor. The employment tribunal had held that Ms Taylor's decision to issue the warning had been influenced by the claimant having made a protected disclosure. Ms Taylor had not given evidence but Ms Bond of the respondent's HR department gave evidence that she had advised Ms Taylor that a twelve-month sanction (as opposed to the previous norm of six months) was imposed as a new normal (general) practice. The employment tribunal noted that Ms Taylor did not give evidence to explain why she accepted the advice of Ms Bond and observed that Ms Bond's account of her application of a twelve-month sanction 'was uncorroborated by supporting evidence'. The tribunal concluded that because the sanction imposed lasted longer than the normal period set out in the respondent's disciplinary policy the relevant facts from which an inference that the sanction had been influenced by the making of the protected disclosure or the protected act were established. It then went on to find that because Ms Taylor had not given evidence and because Ms Bond's account was uncorroborated, the respondent had not discharged the burden of proof imposed on them of demonstrating the absence of a connection between the two.

The EAT (Mitting J): The tribunal's approach was incorrect. The crucial issues were whether (a) Ms Taylor had accepted the advice of Ms Bond (which by inference the employment tribunal found she had) and (b) whether or not that advice was given for the reasons stated by Ms Bond. It was not necessary for there to be corroboration of Ms Bond's evidence. If the tribunal accepted Ms Bond's evidence as to her reason for giving the advice, it followed that that advice was not affected by the making of protected disclosures. That was the key factual question which the tribunal needed to address. Instead, the employment tribunal had 'ducked the single most important question to answer' in the context. It was not permissible to do so.

In relation to a second detriment—the sending of a meeting invitation letter from Ms Bond to the claimant—the EAT held that a similar error had been made. It was not possible to decide an issue which depended on the truthfulness or otherwise of a single witness, by falling back on the burden of proof rather than deciding that question. The employment tribunal did not adequately discharge its duty to find relevant facts about the supposed detriment.

Result: The matter was remitted back to the tribunal.

Detriments (1) Final written warning (2) Invitation to disciplinary meeting.

Sections considered: ERA, s 48(2).

Jurisdiction

136. Clyde & Co LLP v Bates van Winkelhof

[2014] UKSC 32, [2014] 1 WLR 2047

See Case 8.

137. Fuller v United Healthcare Services Inc & Anor

UKEAT/0464/13/BA, 4 September 2014

Key issues: Jurisdiction.

Case summary: The claimant—a US citizen, working for a US company and paid in US dollars—was assigned to a subsidiary incorporated in the UK, spending half his time in the UK. While he was in London, he continued with his previous US role of senior strategic leadership, advice, and assessment of new potential world markets, and lived in accommodation rented for him by the respondent, whilst also retaining his home in Texas. Whilst in the US he was informed by telephone of the termination of his assignment in London and was effectively recalled to the USA. He was then dismissed when no suitable post could be found.

ET: Overwhelmingly the strongest connection was with the US. The claimant's contract referred to his base as the US, an analysis of his detailed work log indicated that his employment in London 'did not constitute a true break with the substantive nature of his previous work, nor did it sever any of the continuities or realities of his existing US employment'. There was not a sufficiently strong connection with the UK, and UK employment law, to fall within the grasp of unfair dismissal protection. The contractual position had not been overtaken by events when the claimant took up the assignment in the UK. Further, he had been dismissed in the USA.

EAT (**Lady Stacey**): Upholding the ET's decision, the EJ was entitled to find that the employment relationship was overwhelmingly American in nature and that the work carried out in the UK did not alter that, and there was no reason to apply a different test for s 103A ERA. The claimant had not given up his base in the USA, despite carrying out some work in the United Kingdom and in other countries.

Result: UK has no jurisdiction.

Sections considered: ERA, s 103A.

138. Smania v Standard Chartered Bank

[2015] IRLR 271

Key issues: Jurisdiction—is it wider under PIDA than for ordinary unfair dismissal? What is the reach of Article 10 of the European Convention on Human Rights ('ECHR') and Article 11 of the EU Charter of Fundamental Rights ('the Charter')?

Case summary: S is not a British national, but Italian. His relevant employment was in Singapore. He was dismissed in Singapore. He resided in Singapore. He paid tax in Singapore. His contract of employment was governed by the law of Singapore. Although S had lived in Great Britain before being recruited to work in Singapore, the only link with the United Kingdom and its employment law was the fact that the Bank had its headquarters in Great Britain. The operation in Singapore, though large, was a branch of the Bank, and not a separate legal entity.

ET: having considered *Lawson v Serco Ltd* [2006] ICR 250 (HL), *Duncombe v Secretary of State for Children, Schools and Families (No 2)* [2011] ICR 1312 (SC), and *Ravat v Halliburton Manufacturing and Services Ltd* [2012] ICR 389 (SC) the ET decided there was basis to find that a different test should apply in relation to other provisions of ERA, including those relating to dismissal and detriment in relation to whistleblowing. The UK tribunal did not have jurisdiction.

EAT (Langstaff J): Upholding the ET's decision, no adequate basis had been shown for a different approach to territorial jurisdiction for the whistleblowing provisions. Reference to the European Convention of Human Rights and Article 11 of the EU Charter of Fundamental Rights did not assist as, so far as material, they did not apply outside the territory of contracting states and so did not apply to employment in Singapore.

Result: No jurisdiction.

Sections considered: ERA, s 103A.

139. Strickland v Kier Ltd & Ors

UKEAT/0062/15/DM, 23 September 2015

Key issues: Is there a wider test for jurisdiction for whistleblower?

Case summary: Between Sept 1997 and Oct 2007, S was employed by Kier, living and working in the UK. In 2007 he took employment in the Middle East with another construction business. Whilst living in Dubai in 2008 S had discussions with Kier to return to their employment in the Middle East. Later he was offered and accepted the post of Area Commercial Manager based in the Dubai office on the terms set out in writing. He commenced that employment and he continued to work under that contract, as amended as to salary, in Dubai and Saudi Arabia, until his resignation in June 2013.

EAT (HHJ Peter Clark): the ET had asked itself the correct question, namely did S have a closer connection with the countries in which he worked than with Britain and British employment law? There is no wider test of territorial grasp for whistleblowers than for ordinary unfair dismissal.

Result: No jurisdiction, no wider test.

Case management

140. ALM Medical Services Ltd v Bladon

EAT/709/00, EAT/967/00, 19 January 2001; [2002] ICR 1444 (CA)

See Case 81.

141. **Secretary of State for Work and Pensions (Jobcentre Plus) v Constable**

UKEAT/0156/10, 30 June 2010

Key issues: entitlement to proper particulars of protected disclosure claim.

Case summary: The claimant, who had been employed as a job reviewer in a job centre, alleged that he had been dismissed by reason of protected disclosures. In his ET1 he alleged that his manager had actively encouraged him to sign off job vacancies regardless of whether the applicant was actively seeking work. The ET refused an application for further particulars.

EAT: held that the ET had erred in failing to require particulars of (a) what the protected disclosure was that had been made, (b) to whom, when, and how he made the alleged disclosure, and (c) how that disclosure was alleged to have led to his dismissal. The respondent needed to know what the case was against it and who to call as witnesses and should not be required to call evidence effectively in relation to the whole employment period in the hope that it dealt with the claimant's case.

Result: further particulars ordered.

142. **Price v Surrey County Council and Wood Street School Governing Body**

EAT/0450/10, 27 October 2011

See Case 103.

143. **Blackbay Ventures Ltd (t/a Chemistree) v Gahir**

[2014] IRLR 416 (EAT)

See Case 133.

Striking out/determination prior to completion of evidence

144. **Boulding v Land Securities Trillium (Media Services) Ltd**

EAT/0023/06, 3 May 2006

See Case 29.

145. **Ezsias v North Glamorgan NHS Trust**

[2011] IRLR (EAT), [2007] ICR 1126 (CA)

See Case 67.

146. **Hudson v Oxford University**

EAT/0488/05, 26 July 2007

Key issues: strike out of PIDA claims; ERA, ss 103A and 47B.

Case summary: Mr Hudson was employed by Oxford University (OU) at the Museum of History and Science. He created a collections database. A disagreement arose over the intellectual property in that work. This resulted in his being denied access by OU to it. The disputes involved the various committees set up by OU. Hudson was dismissed. He claimed that his dismissal was linked to disclosures he made. He also sought to include claims of detriment.

During the internal disciplinary process when the claimant was suspended and awaiting the hearing of his appeals against dismissal, OU's chief administrator wrote a letter, dated 9 September 2003, stating that there was no prospect of him returning to work in the light of his allegations. OU contended that this was inadmissible as it was headed 'without prejudice'.

ET: two pre-hearing reviews were held. At the first, Hudson's ordinary unfair dismissal claim was struck out as having no reasonable prospect of success. At the second, his claim under ERA, s 103A was struck out also as having no reasonable prospect of success. Claims of detriment under s 47B were struck out as being out of time or having no reasonable prospect of success. A breach of contract claim was struck out on grounds of lack of jurisdiction.

EAT (Mrs Justice Cox): held that the ET had erred in summarily dismissing the claims. Notwithstanding that there had been 'an elaborate and quasi-independent disciplinary and appeals procedure', the chairman had erred in effectively deciding the substantive issues against the claimant on the papers, without permitting Hudson to advance his case. There were fact-sensitive disputes which needed to be determined on the evidence by the tribunal as an 'industrial jury'.

The letter of 9 September 2003 was admissible since it was not an attempt to compromise the dispute and, even if it had been, it would have fallen within the unambiguous impropriety exception. The EAT accepted a submission (para 75) that:

> 75. ... the contents of the letter, in declaring that there was no prospect of the Claimant returning to work for the Respondents in any capacity, given his 'unfounded allegations' (i.e. the fact that he had made protected disclosures), amounted to unambiguous impropriety and therefore fell within the recognised exception to the 'without prejudice' rule referred to, in the discrimination context, in *BNP Paribas v Mezzotero* [2004] IRLR 508. The addition of the words 'without prejudice' amounted to an inappropriate attempt to cloak discriminatory and improper conduct by the Respondents under the veil of without prejudice correspondence. It therefore fell outside the protection afforded by the rule. The Claimant's case is that this letter supports his allegations as to the real reason for his dismissal, namely that he had made these protected disclosures, and the letter is therefore properly admissible in the circumstances.
>
> . . .
>
> 79. In so concluding we have had regard in particular (a) to the decision of the EAT in the *BNP Paribas* case, in the context of alleged sex discriminatory remarks said to have been made without prejudice but held to fall within the exception to the rule; and (b) to the observations of the Court of Appeal in *Ezsias* (at paragraphs 30–32) as to the similarities between whistleblowing cases and discrimination cases, both of which require a careful investigation into why an employer took a particular step, e.g. dismissal; and as to the public interest in the proper determination of such claims by Tribunals on all the available evidence.

Result: remitted.

Sections considered: ERA, s 103A.

Damages: N/A.

147. Sood v Christ the King School Governors

UKEAT/0449/10, 20 July 2011

Key issues: strike out of whistleblowing claims.

Case summary: Complaint of over 174 allegations in a large number of areas including detriments and automatically unfair dismissal ERA, s 103A.

ET: held that where there is a 'substantive' claim of direct discrimination the alternative claim of victimization, based on the same factual allegations, ought to be struck out.

EAT (HHJ Peter Clark): held that discrimination claims (including 'whistleblowing' claims; see *Ezsias v N Glamorgan NHS Trust* [2007] ICR 1126) should be not be struck out as having no reasonable prospect of success, save in the most plain and obvious case. There was no basis for the ET's approach. The question as to whether, if the individual factual allegation is proved, the act complained of was on the grounds of prohibited discrimination or by reason of the claimant having done a protected act is a matter for the fact-finding tribunal to determine after hearing all the evidence. A further issue is as to whether there would in any event be any saving of time or expense in striking out claims at a preliminary stage given the possibility that arguably out of time allegations (such as particular allegations of discrimination or detriment) might still be relied upon as background evidence.

Result: detriment and whistleblowing dismissal claims not struck out.

Sections considered: ERA, ss 47B, 103A.

148. Pillay v Inc Research UK

UKEAT/0182/11/ZT, 9 September 2011

Key issues: application of *Ezsias v N Glamorgan NHS Trust* [2007] ICR 1126 restrictions on strike out where no qualifying period.

Case summary: Mr Pillay was a project manager within the clinical data management department. He claimed that he was dismissed after making protected disclosures. He had less than a year's service at the time of dismissal.

ET: held that the disclosure (accepted as being a protected disclosure) related to the claimant being told to perform a task he had not been trained for. He raised the fact that the respondent was in breach of provisions which had the force of law and which required the respondent to ensure that certain tasks were only performed by individuals qualified by education, training, and experience to undertake them. The ET at the PHR concluded that there was no evidence from which a tribunal could infer any causal connection between the claimant's alleged disclosure and the fact of his dismissal. It therefore struck out the claim as having no reasonable prospect of success.

EAT (HHJ Richardson): held, following *Ezsias*, that the claim should not to have been struck out before hearing evidence. There was no exception from the principles in *Ezsias* for a case where the claimant did not have the qualifying period for an ordinary unfair dismissal claim. There would still need to be an investigation as to why the employee was dismissed.

Result: case remitted to full hearing.

Sections considered: ERA, s 43B(1)(b).

149. Namoale v Balfour Beatty Engineering Services Ltd

UKEAT/0126/12/DM, 29 November 2012

Key issues: Strike out for no prospect of success; deposit order for little reasonable prospect of success.

Case summary: N was one of four men disciplined for breach of the safety regime. But unlike the others, he had made complaints about the others' breaches.

ET: EJ Hughes noted the claim of automatically unfairly dismissal by reason of a health and safety disclosure and/or a public interest disclosure arose from when N raised concern over a piece of electrical work being improperly isolated. His concern was overruled and the work went ahead. He then claimed he was disciplined and dismissed because that work had been undertaken. EJ Hughes considered that even if the claimant succeeded in establishing that he made a protected disclosure, it was 'unlikely that he would succeed in establishing the necessary causal link between that disclosure and the disciplinary action and/or dismissal' because other people who had allegedly raised concerns were also disciplined and/or dismissed.

EAT (HHJ McMullen QC): whilst in deciding against N the EJ had properly taken his case at its highest, the fatal weakness was her approach to causation and its relationship between N and the three other people. The EJ's reliance on the fact that four people were said to be engaged in the unsafe practice and all four were disciplined missed the point. Only the claimant asserted protected acts, so it was wrong to categorize their circumstances as the same. Further, the other men were not disciplined by the respondent for raising health and safety issues, but for not following the health and safety regime. N's case was different in that he claimed he had been treated in the same manner, but because he *objected* to the breaches, not because he was responsible for them.

Result: Case restored.

Sections considered: ERA, s 103A.

150. Short v Birmingham City Council & Ors

UKEAT/0038/13/DM, 5 July 2013

Key issues: Strike out or deposit?

Case summary: Preliminary hearing whether the claimant, as a result of what were accepted for the purposes of the PHR to be protected disclosures, was dismissed and subjected to detriment (1) by instructing enquiry agents to investigate whether S was working and earning money by giving hypnotherapy treatment from home, at a time when she was on paid sick leave; and (2) as a result instituting disciplinary proceedings against her, leading to her dismissal.

EAT (HHJ Peter Clark): Referring closely to *A v B* [2011] ICR 9, strike-out could not be justified and needed to be dealt with at a substantive trial.

Result: Deposit ordered, case not struck out.

Detriment: Investigation, instituting disciplinary proceedings.

Sections considered: ERA, ss 47B, 103A.

151. Garcia v Market Probe Europe Ltd

UKEAT/0024/13/BA, 5 November 2013

Key issues: Had the claimant pleaded a protected disclosure detriment claim?

Case summary: The claimant drafted his own claim.

ET: Whilst he set out a claim with a complaint entitled 'detrimental treatment', it was considered to be a breach of contract; he was advised to consider whether a fresh claim should be made.

EAT (Mr Justice Mitting): The complaint was sufficient to be a protected disclosure detriment claim. Under the heading 'my claim for detrimental treatment', he had stated that he had sustained detrimental treatment and been dismissed because he had made a complaint against his supervisor as he had refused to record all of his hours and had therefore wrongfully been blamed for not attending a booked shift. He added that he had sustained detrimental treatment only because he was ascertaining his legal right concerning legal obligations owed by his employer. The EAT commented that the claim form should be 'read generously' and if as here it contained enough information to indicate a claim of protected disclosure detriment, that should go to trial.

Result: Case remitted to a Tribunal to determine his PIDA claim.

Detriment: Removed shifts.

152. Greenly v Future Network Solutions Ltd

UKEAT/0359/13/JOJ, 19 December 2013

See Case 45.

153. Millbank Financial Services Ltd v Crawford

[2014] IRLR 18

See Case 46.

154. Robinson v Royal Surrey County Hospital NHS Foundation Trust & Ors

UKEAT/0311/14/MC, 30 July 2015

Key issues: Amendment, strike out, and parameters of preliminary hearings

Case summary: claimant pleaded 'other complaints'. At a PHR she set out those as PIDA claims, but did not particularize them.

ET (EJ Salter): At a preliminary hearing Robinson (R) asserted a detriment being a collusive arrangement made by managers to remove her from employment culminating in a capability hearing.

EAT (Judge Eady QC): R had put her case differently before two different EJs, but both ways contained no particularity. The ET had no obligation to invite R formally to amend her claim or to assume she was making such an application. It only needed to address the claim as pleaded. Further, having considered the claim as outlined at the hearing, the ET was then entitled to conclude the claim had no reasonable prospect of success, having gone through the various layers of implausibility inherent in the case. 'Where a claim is so implausible, it can be right that it be struck out: an ET is not obliged to let every matter proceed, however improbable.'

Result: Claim struck out.

Sections considered: ERA, s 123.

155. Underwood v Wincanton plc

UKEAT/0163/15/RN, 27 August 2015

See Case 56.

156. Morgan v Royal Mencap Society

[2016] IRLR 428 (EAT)

See Case 57.

Amendment

157. Evershed v New Star Asset Management

[2010] EWCA Civ 870

Key issues: amendment of claim to include PIDA claim; whether new facts were required.

Case summary: Mr Evershed was employed as a fund manager. He claimed unfair dismissal on the basis that he had raised a grievance complaining about bullying and harassment of himself and his colleagues which created an intolerable working environment. He was suspended on the ground that he was 'emotionally disturbed and unfit to manage money'. He applied to amend to add an allegation that the treatment he received was in response to making protected disclosures. It was claimed to be a relabelling exercise.

ET: the application to amend was refused (at a PHR) on the basis that it was not mere relabelling, there had been no grievance raised in relation to a protected disclosure claim, the request to amend was out of time, and Evershed had been represented by solicitors at the time of his termination of employment and there was no explanation why the claim was omitted, and there would be prejudice to the respondent in allowing the amendment.

EAT (Mr Justice Underhill (President)): held that the ET had erred by failing properly to analyse the extent to which the proposed amendment would extend the scope of the issues and the evidence. The EAT allowed the amendment as the new claim would not involve a substantial increase in the scope of the factual inquiry, the application was made at an early stage in the proceedings, and even though the equivalent free-standing claim would have been out of time, it would only have been so by a short time. Whilst there would be prejudice to the respondent in having to meet the new claim which could significantly increase its liability, that was balanced by the equal and opposite prejudice to Evershed in being deprived of the opportunity to advance the claim.

Court of Appeal (Sedley, Rimer LJJ, Sir Scott Baker): upholding the decision of the EAT, Rimer LJ accepted that the amendment would not raise wholly new factual allegations, and therefore the appeal would be allowed. It was true that there were different ingredients to the protected disclosure claim, having regard to the elements of a qualifying disclosure. But that did not entail wholly new evidence to address those elements.

Result: amendment granted.

Detriment: N/A.

Sections considered: ERA, ss 43B, 43C, 103A.

Damages: N/A.

Cited by: *Olayemi v Athena Medical Centre and another* (UKEAT/0613/10 and 0614/10, 20 April 2011) (Mr Record Luba QC). (*Evershed v New Star* distinguished: ET decision to refuse amendment to add protected disclosure claim to existing sex discrimination and unfair dismissal claim upheld where the claim was made late and would substantially expand the relevant evidence: (para 56):

> *Evershed* was a case in which the necessary additional material constituted one email in relation to which there was no dispute as to whether it was sent or received. Here there are some 24 to 30 documents, not all of them sent to the Respondent, and in relation to which there is a dispute about their receipt. Moreover, and most pertinently, *Evershed* was a case in which the unfair dismissal claim itself raised the question of the state of the mind of the employee, whereas no such consideration or concern arose in the underlying complaint made by Dr Olayemi in this case.

158. Watkins v BBC

UKEAT/0189/12/LA, 27 June 2012

Key issues: Whether application to amend should be permitted to include a claim of protected disclosure detriment.

Case summary: As originally pleaded, the claimant asserted protected disclosure detriments in not being allocated further work; he had previously undertaken ad hoc work for the respondent. An application to strike out the claims had been refused. At no stage during the pre-hearing review or the following case management discussion did W indicate he might seek to rely upon further incidents of protected disclosure detriment (which would have necessitated an amendment of his ET1 and particulars of claim). He later made that application, seeking to add two new grounds of detriment; that the respondent had breached a legal obligation in his contract (a) by the unfair allocation of shifts favouring other workers, and (b) by delaying an investigation into a grievance that he had raised regarding bullying.

ET: EJ Lewis focused on the prejudice the respondents would suffer in having to face an additional claim. The respondents had prepared their defence on the basis of a different case. Although there was an overlap of facts, there were also substantial differences. The proposed amendment cast the net much wider in terms of the content of the claimant's emails. The respondents' solicitors may need to re-interview witnesses to whom they had already spoken. They may wish to amend their ET3.

EAT (HHJ Serota): accepted it was too simplistic to say that the proposed amendment was merely an amendment to the existing claim and just another example of PID victimization merely designed to alter the basis of the existing claim. It was a wholly new allegation even if it could be said to arise out of matters already pleaded, and it raised a new distinct head of complaint and was not simply a relabelling exercise of facts already pleaded. In addition to new detriments it also relied on new protected disclosures and required new matters to be investigated. The judge was entitled to have regard to the balance of hardship that might be caused by the loss of the hearing date, and was best placed to say whether the hearing might have to be extended and the trial date lost.

Result: Appeal refused, no amendment permitted, *Selkent* applied.

159. Robinson v Royal Surrey County Hospital NHS Foundation Trust & Ors

UKEAT/0311/14/MC, 30 July 2015

Sections considered: ERA, ss 43A, 43B(1), 47B.

See Case 154.

160. Makauskiene v Rentokil Initial Facilities Services (UK) Ltd

UKEAT/0503/13/RN, 29 April 2015

Case summary: On 1 November 2012 the claimant presented an ET1. She ticked boxes to indicate that she was bringing claims for unfair dismissal and race discrimination. The tribunal listed the case for a two-day hearing in April 2013. There was no prior case management discussion. The claimant attended the hearing in person with a translator. The hearing was ineffective as a final hearing. A substantial amount of time was spent defining the issues: the respondent said the reason for dismissal was conduct and the claimant disputed that reason and said that the dismissal was an act of race discrimination. The employment judge gave further case management directions and listed the case for hearing between 15 and 18 October 2013. On 31 July 2013 the claimant's representative wrote to the tribunal on behalf of the claimant with an application for permission to amend the ET1 claim form 'to add the label of detriment and dismissal on the ground of having made protected disclosures', stating that the addition of the label relied on the facts already pleaded. The letter then contained a table which identified as disclosures six grievances or complaints which had been mentioned in the timeline to which the claimant had previously made reference in support of her claims of unfair dismissal and race discrimination. Twenty detriments which it was said the claimant had suffered by reason of the disclosures had also been mentioned in the timeline.

An employment judge refused the application. He said that the amendment sought to bring a protected disclosure claim which was the bringing of a new claim, although a claim that referred to events already pleaded. That claim was 'a long way out of time'. The application was very late, some months after a hearing at which a considerable amount of time had been spent seeking to analyse the claimant's case and draw up a comprehensive list of issues and after the date of exchange of witness statements. There would be prejudice to both sides depending on the result. Whilst it would not be like starting the case again, the respondent would suffer substantial additional costs because numerous protected disclosures had been asserted, which would need analysing, and consideration would need to be given as to whether any allegation of bad faith was being made. The tribunal's length of time to deliberate would be significantly extended. After balancing all the factors, the employment judge refused the application for leave to amend.

On a reconsideration (with a narrower alternative case on amendments excluding most of the proposed detriment claims) the employment judge acknowledged that there was some link between the facts pleaded and the issue of protected disclosure detriment. The respondent would in any event need to prove the reason or principal reason for the claimant's dismissal and there was already a race discrimination claim in respect of the claimant's suspension and dismissal. The respondent would 'not have to adduce wholly different evidence'. Only one disclosure would need to be considered, rather than the six in the original application; and only two detriments (including dismissal), both of which formed part of the race discrimination claims, rather than twenty allegations of detriment. The implications of the length of the hearing would be minor, rather than major. However, the application was made at a late stage and long after a list of issues had been completed at a lengthy discussion of the issues in the case. On balance and 'by a narrow margin' the employment judge confirmed his original decision.

EAT: It was important to draw a distinction between the claim of unfair dismissal and the claims of detriment by reason of public interest disclosure. The dismissal was expressly connected by the respondent with an email to one of the respondent's customers which was intended to be relied upon as a disclosure by the claimant. The factors which the employment judge relied on did apply with the same force to the unfair dismissal claim as they did in relation to detriment because the reason for dismissal was bound to be in play at the final hearing. As in the case of *New Star Asset Management Holdings v Evershed*, allowing the amendment would not materially increase the amount of evidence required for the unfair dismissal claim.

The detriment claim was different: this involved taking grievances from the claimant's timeline, asserting that they were public interest disclosures, and asserting that other matters complained of in the timeline were detrimental treatment by reason of the public interest disclosure. The claim of public interest detriment, if allowed, would go back a very long time prior to dismissal. The employment judge did not err in law in rejecting the application to amend in respect of the detriment claim.

Result: Appeal allowed in respect of amendment to add s 103A claim, but disallowed in respect of s 47B claim.

Interim relief

161. Parkins v Sodexho

[2002] IRLR 110 (EAT)

See Case 17.

162. Dandpat v University of Bath

UKEAT/0408/09, 10 November 2009; [2010] EWCA Civ 305 (CA)

Key issues: procedure at interim hearings; definition of 'likely'.

Case summary: The claimant claimed to have been constructively dismissed and that the principal reason for the conduct on the part of the university which entitled him to resign was that he had made protected disclosures. He applied for interim relief. The application was rejected by the ET without hearing oral evidence or seeing witness statements.

ET: concluded that it did not appear that the unfair dismissal claim based on ERA, s 103A stood a 'pretty good chance of success'. The tribunal was of the opinion that a tribunal panel was unlikely to find that the claimant's reason for resigning was connected with his having made any disclosure or the consequences of having done so, and it dismissed the application for interim relief.

EAT (Underhill (P)):

(1) The ET was entitled to determine the matter on the basis of submissions and contemporary documents without hearing oral evidence or seeing witness statements.

(2) It was sufficient for the ET to indicate the essential gist of its reasoning, being that on its reading of the resignation letter it was unlikely that the claimant would be able to show that he had resigned in response to conduct the principal reason for which was a protected disclosure.

(3) There were good reasons of policy for setting the test for interim relief comparatively high since if relief is granted the respondent is irretrievably prejudiced because it would be obliged to treat the contract as continuing, and pay the claimant, until the conclusion of proceedings.

CA: unusually three different Lord Justices considered the appeal on three separate occasions. In refusing permission to appeal Arden LJ ([2010] EWCA Civ 305) endorsed the EAT's reasoning. The same conclusion was reached at a further hearing, where Smith LJ noted that 'Proceedings for an interim order are supposed to be summary proceedings, designed to be conducted quite quickly at an early stage so as to preserve the applicant's position pending a full hearing. It is not intended that there should be a full hearing of the evidence such as would enable the tribunal to make findings of fact as to which witnesses are truthful, accurate and reliable'.

Result: interim relief not awarded.

Sections considered: ERA, ss 128, 129.

Cited by: *Chesterton Global Ltd & Anor v Nurmohamed* [2015] IRLR 614; *Ministry of Defence v Sarfraz* [2011] IRLR 562 (EAT) (which noted that *Dandpat* was perhaps the most significant of the recent cases and it expressly addressed and rejected a submission that *Taplin v C Shippam Ltd* [1978] IRLR 450 (EAT) should be revisited following the decision of the House of Lords in *SCA Packaging v Boyle* [2005] ICR 156, and since permission to appeal was refused by the Court of Appeal on two separate occasions—first by Arden LJ and secondly by Smith LJ).

163. Raja v Secretary of State for Justice

EAT/0364/09, 15 February 2010

Key issues: practical approach to interim relief; burden of proof; an applicant for interim relief had to show a 'pretty good chance' that s/he would succeed at trial.

Case summary: Mr Raja was employed as a prison officer at a young offender's institution. He claimed unfair dismissal on the grounds of protected disclosure and/or health and safety and also that his dismissal was on the grounds of race and disability. It was alleged that all the complaints in relation to race and disability also amounted to protected disclosures.

ET: rejected the claim on the basis that interim relief is intended to apply to claims where there is a clear and simple conflict between the parties' assertions that can be addressed in an emergency. The employment judge (EJ) concluded that a complicated, long-running dispute about race discrimination, disability, and arrangements for return to work was not suitable for this type of emergency order. He said that if he had not refused the application, he would have struck it out as having no reasonable prospect of success and being vexatious because it was inappropriate to pursue such an application when it was clear from the ET1 that over many months there had been a dispute between employer and employee over a range of issues.

EAT (HHJ Birtles): held that the EJ had erred in rejecting the application without considering the substance of the application, merely on the basis that interim relief was designed for clear and simple conflicts. Once a claimant satisfies the procedural requirements in ERA, s 128 s/he is entitled as of right to have the application heard. Further, the EJ could not properly have formed a view on the application without reading the bundle of documents and evidence before her. She should have asked the parties to direct her attention to those parts of the evidence relevant to the interim relief application.

    The test in *Taplin v C Shippam Ltd* [1978] IRLR 450 remains good law, ie 'likely' to succeed means a 'pretty good chance'. The tribunal must not attempt to decide the issue as if it were a final issue. Nor is there any additional hurdle such as a need to show that the case is exceptional.

Result: remitted to a fresh employment judge.

Sections considered: ERA, s 129(1).

Damages: N/A.

Cited by: *Ministry of Defence v Sarfraz* [2011] IRLR 562 (EAT).

164. Ministry of Justice v Sarfraz

[2011] IRLR 562 (CA)

Key issues: interim relief; burden.

Case summary: Mr Sarfraz was a legal adviser to the magistrates' court in Gloucester. He submitted a lengthy grievance (23 pages, 85 allegations). The ET upheld an application for interim relief (providing for his contract to continue in force pending the tribunal hearing).

EAT (Mr Justice Underhill (P)): held that the employment judge had erred in failing to consider the question whether the claimant's belief that he was disclosing information that tended to show a breach of legal obligations on the part of the employer was reasonable. It was therefore appropriate for the EAT to make its own assessment to save time and expense and since such applications are to be decided as speedily as possible, and that at the interim stage the question of reasonableness of the claimant's belief must be depend largely on an examination of the disclosures themselves in the light of the correspondence and other available contemporary and documentary evidence. The EAT concluded that it was not likely that the claimant would succeed at the final hearing. It could not be said to be likely that the tribunal would conclude that the claimant held a reasonable belief that the grievances disclosed a breach of legal obligations by the employer, which would only arise if there was a breach of the term of trust and confidence or if the conduct amounted to harassment.

As to the appropriate test (at para 16): 'likely' does not mean simply 'more likely than not'—that is at least 51 per cent—but connotes a significantly higher degree of likelihood'.

Result: appeal allowed; interim order quashed.

Detriment: N/A.

Sections considered: ERA, ss 44A, 43B, 43C.

165. Turullois v Revenue and Customs Commissioners

[2014] UKFTT 622 (First-tier Tribunal (Tax Chamber))

Key issues: Whether salary payments made pursuant to an interim relief order were emoluments from employment liable to income tax.

Case summary: The claimant successfully applied for an interim relief order, claiming that she was dismissed by reason of making protected disclosures. The claimant therefore continued to receive salary payments. At the substantive hearing, she succeeded in an ordinary unfair dismissal and wrongful dismissal claim, but not in her protected disclosure dismissal claim. A settlement was reached immediately prior to a remedies hearing. The claimant then claimed repayment of tax which had been deducted from the first £30,000 of the salary paid pursuant to the interim relief order.

First-tier tribunal: It was only as a result of termination of employment that the claimant had become entitled to claim interim relief. The order did not reinstate the employment, but only provide an entitlement to receive certain payments and benefits equivalent to those she would have received if the employment had continued. The interim relief payments were therefore not emoluments from employment and so were taxable only to the extent that they exceeded £30,000.

Result: Claimant entitled to repayment of tax deducted on first £30,000 of salary under interim relief order.

166. Parsons v Airplus International Ltd

UKEAT/0023/16/JOJ, 4 March 2016

Key Issue: extent of the employment judge's duty to give reasons on an application for interim relief

Case summary: The claimant commenced worked as Compliance Manager for the respondent. After five weeks she was dismissed with immediate effect as (in the respondent's words) a 'cultural misfit'. The claimant presented a claim under s 103A and an application for interim relief. At the hearing by agreement the employment judge did not hear oral evidence but had two witness statements from the claimant and one each from two employees of the respondent. The EJ dismissed the application, holding that although the claimant had a 'good arguable case' it could not be said that she had a 'pretty good chance of success', and that the application failed on the issue of causation.

EAT: the claimant argued that the EJ had not, in her reasons for judgment, given any express consideration to the fact that the claimant had raised concerns relating to the respondent's disclosure as to non-compliance with the Companies Act on the day before she was dismissed. The claimant contended that this temporal proximity between disclosure and dismissal made her case on causation very strong, and that this should have been considered and referred to by the EJ. However, the EAT accepted that the evidence showed that the events of the day before dismissal were not relied on as strongly at the interim relief hearing as they were on appeal, and it was not entirely clear that what the claimant said on that occasion necessarily amounted to a protected disclosure. Seen in that context and bearing in mind 'the limited obligation to give reasons falling on a Judge hearing an interim relief application' the EAT did not think that the omission to refer to this point indicated any kind of error of law by the EJ.

Result: Appeal dismissed.

Sections considered: ERA, s 128.

Compensation

167. Virgo Fidelis Senior School v Boyle

[2004] IRLR 268 (EAT)

Key issues: (1) quantum for injury to feelings in protected disclosure case; (2) scope for aggravated and exemplary damages.

Case summary: Mr Boyle made a protected disclosure by writing a letter making explicit allegations against various members of the school staff to the Diocese, London Borough of Croydon and the Convent de Notre Dame de Fidelité in France. He was bullied leading to inadequate cover and the onset of stress-related injuries.

ET: held that the claim for detriment and automatic unfair dismissal was made out. It awarded £47,755 in damages.

EAT (HHJ Ansell): held that the guidelines in *Vento v Chief Constable of West Yorkshire Police (No 2)* [2003] IRLR 102 (CA) applied. Awards should be compensatory, albeit that the seriousness of the wrong normally affects the amount of harm (para 45):

> ... we are firmly of the view that the Tribunal were in error in not having regard to the *Vento* guidelines, albeit that detriment suffered by 'whistle-blowers' should normally be regarded by Tribunals as a very serious breach of discrimination legislation. [But see *Commissioner of Police of the Metropolis v Shaw* (UKEAT/0125/11/ZT, 29 November 2011), noting that, though serious, whistleblowing victimization is not inherently more serious than other prohibited discrimination.]

The injury to feelings award was therefore reduced to £25,000 (reflecting that it was a very serious case) with no separate award for psychiatric damage.

As to aggravated damages (paras 64–65), it was clear from the ET's decision that it would have made such an award if it thought that it had the power to do so. The ET described the employer's conduct as a 'travesty' and noted the absence of any apology or mitigation, and the governors described the original disclosure letter as 'totally reprehensible, unprofessional and unethical'. The EAT therefore made an award of £10,000 by way of aggravated damages.

The EAT reviewed the cases on exemplary damages, starting with *Rookes v Barnard* [1964] AC 1129 (HL) which:

> identified the two circumstances in which exemplary damages might be available, namely (1) in the case of oppressive arbitrary or unconstitutional action by the servants of the Government and (2) where the defendant's conduct had been calculated by him to make a profit for himself. They defined those damages where the object was to punish or deter and which were distinct from aggravated damages, whereby the motives and conduct of the defendant aggravating the injury to the plaintiff would be taken into account in assessing compensatory damages. Lord Devlin made it clear in the course of his speech at page 412D–I that the fact that the injury to a claimant had been aggravated by the malice or by the doing of the injury would not normally be justification for an award of exemplary damages, aggravated damages would be sufficient in that type of case.

Whilst noting that awards of exemplary damages could be made if the above conditions were satisfied in a protected disclosure case, the EAT declined to make an award (paras 78–81). It noted that 'in the majority of cases aggravated damages would be sufficient to mark the employer's conduct'. In any event despite the close relationship with Croydon LBC, the school was not acting as servants or agents of the executive in exercising its disciplinary powers and despite the proper criticisms of the respondent there was not a sufficient basis to say that there was oppressive, arbitrary, or unconstitutional action.

Result: *Vento v Chief Constable of West Yorkshire Police (No 2)* applied; award of £25,000 for injury to feelings and £10,000 aggravated damages.

Detriment: disciplining of the claimant.

Sections considered: ERA, ss 47B, 48, 103A, 123.

Damages awarded: £47,755; £45,000 for injury to feelings; reduced as above on appeal.

Cited by: *Rowe v London Underground Ltd* (UKEAT/0125/16/JOJ, 17 October 2016); *Phoenix House Ltd v Stockman* [2016] IRLR 848 (EAT); *Santos Gomes v Higher Level Care Ltd* [2016] ICR 926 (EAT); *Small v Shrewsbury and Telford Hospitals NHS Trust* (UKEAT/0300/14/LA, 19 May 2015); *Fecitt v NHS Manchester* [2011] ICR 476 (EAT); *Ministry of Defence v Fletcher* [2010] IRLR 25 (EAT); *Pinnington v Swansea City and County Council and another* [2005] ICR 685 (CA); *Commissioner of Police of the Metropolis v Shaw* (UKEAT/0125/11/ZT, 29 November 2011); *Pinnington v Swansea City Council* [2005] ICR 685 (CA).

168. Melia v Magna Kansei Ltd

[2005] ICR 874 (EAT), [2006] ICR 410 (CA)

See Case 5.

169. Mama East African Women's Group v Dobson

EAT/0219/05 and 0220/05, 23 June 2005

See Case 95.

170. Williams v North Tyneside Council

UKEAT/0415/05/CK, 31 January 2006

Key issue: quantification of loss.

Case summary: Miss Williams claimed that she was unfairly constructively dismissed on three grounds (ERA, ss 100C, 103A, and 104). She claimed that as a consequence of making a protected disclosure she suffered a detriment. The protected disclosure related to the bullying and harassment by her manager, Mr Pringle. Miss Williams raised her concerns as a grievance. She suffered the following detriments: the respondent refused to accept the grievance; Pringle refused to speak to her; she was cold-shouldered by colleagues; and she was not invited to meetings. During an adjournment the respondent admitted liability in respect of all Miss Williams' claims.

ET: found that Miss Williams had unreasonably 'taken herself outside the world of work' when she enrolled on a four-year university course.

EAT (HHJ Burke QC): held that the tribunal's finding was of a failure to mitigate loss but it erred in failing to calculate when Miss Williams would reasonably have obtained a new job and what losses she sustained up to that time or, indeed, what if any loss would have continued after that time if her new employment had not been on terms that were as favourable as the employment from which she was dismissed.

Regarding pension losses, the tribunal stated:

> Employment Tribunals are entitled to adopt a pragmatic and proportionate approach to the calculation of pension loss; and it would be wholly impracticable and disproportionate when only a short period was in issue for detailed and difficult or even actuarial calculations to be embarked upon.

Regarding aggravated damages Miss Williams relied on four allegations: (1) the respondent did not carry out a full and fair investigation into her allegations; (2) it offered no form of apology; (3) it made allegations against her credibility, professional standing, and capability; (4) it discussed her case with her previous employers. The tribunal erred in only considering damages for the actions during the hearing and not the other grounds for contending that there should be aggravated damages.

Result: remitted to the same tribunal to consider the issue as to mitigation of loss (when acting reasonably, would Miss Williams have obtained alternative employment and what loss was incurred?) and the issues as to aggravated damages.

Detriments: the ET found that life had been made very unpleasant for Miss Williams over the previous six to seven weeks in that the respondent refused to accept the grievance; Pringle refused to speak to her; she was cold-shouldered by colleagues; and she was not invited to meetings.

Sections considered: ERA, ss 47B, 100C, 103A, 104.

Damages awarded: detriment—£5,000 for injury to feelings; £2,257.17 as a compensatory award. (But the award was remitted for reconsideration.)

171. Aryeetey v Tuntum Housing Association

UKEAT/0070/07, 12 October 2007; UKEAT 0324/08, 8 April 2009

See Case 66.

172. Ms AE Davidson-Hogg v Davis Gregory Solicitors, Mr T Howarth

UKEAT/0512/09/ZT, 15 November 2010

Key issues: dismissal for protected disclosure; compensatory award reduced as tribunal found that claimant would have been dismissed in any event; whether interest is payable on an injury to feelings award under PIDA.

Case summary: the claimant, a legal executive, only worked with DGS for 13 days until she was unfairly dismissed on 8 November 2006. She was to be admitted as a solicitor had she not been dismissed. The ET found that the claimant had difficulties in her working relationships with colleagues and her employment would have come to an end in any event by resignation or fair dismissal on 16 January 2007.

ET: upheld the claims under ERA, s 47B of detriment during employment and post-employment victimization in the form of material provided to the claimant's former employer, and for dismissal under s 103A. As for interest the tribunal found:

> 22. We make no award of interest on the awards for injury to feelings or personal injury as we conclude that the major causal factor (supported by the medical evidence) was the dismissal, arising out of the detriment for having made a protected disclosure. An award of interest on damages for personal injury or injury to feelings is made pursuant to the Employment Tribunals (Interest on Awards in Discrimination Cases) Regulations 1996. An award made pursuant to a breach of s 47B does not come within the ambit of those Regulations.

EAT (HHJ McMullen QC):

(1) There was no error in limiting loss on the basis that the claimant's employment would have ended in any event on 16 January 2007.

(2) In principle the manner of dismissal could cause continuing loss, eg psychological injury could make it more difficult to find alternative work. But that was not the case here.

(3) The ET should have assessed loss taking into account that if the claimant had remained in work to the end of her probation period on 16 January, she would have moved into the different status of a solicitor and her position in the labour market could have been markedly different. This was remitted to the ET to assess.

Result: remitted to the same ET to determine whether loss after 16 January occurred, on the footing that by then the claimant would have been admitted as a solicitor with access to higher paid work and to assess interest.

Detriment: not set out.

Sections considered: ERA, ss 47B, 103A.

Damages: claimant awarded basic award of £1,160, compensatory award of £5,083.94, £10,000 for injury to feelings, £9,000 for damages by way of personal injury, psychological, and psychiatric damage, and financial loss arising out of that in the sum of £1,504.50; and aggravated damages of £5,000.

173. Commissioner of Police of the Metropolis v Shaw

UKEAT/0125/11/ZT, 29 November 2011, [2012] IRLR 291

Key issue: aggravated damages.

Case summary: Shaw (a police officer) was subjected to false allegations (relating to setting up his own business) on the grounds of making protected disclosures. He was suspended and disciplinary proceedings were initiated but the charges were later withdrawn. He left the unit where he had worked because he could no longer stand the atmosphere. The disciplinary action was initiated because more senior officers in his unit, about whom he had raised allegations of misconduct, wanted to remove him from the unit because they believed he was about to put his complaints about them on a more formal basis. Shaw suffered no financial loss.

ET: At a remedies hearing, Shaw was awarded compensation of £37,000, comprising injury to feelings of £17,000 and aggravated damages of £20,000, and awarded £1,000 in costs. There was no personal injury claim.

EAT (Mr Justice Underhill): Reducing the award to £30,000 in total, the EAT accepted that whistleblower detriment claims should be assessed as discrimination cases. Whilst *dicta* in *Virgo Fidelis Senior School v Boyle* [2004] ICR 1210 (EAT) indicated that whistleblowing victimization is very serious, it is not inherently more serious than other discrimination prohibited under the Equality Act 2010 such as race or sex discrimination.

The EAT reviewed the principles applicable to awards of aggravated damages. Such awards are compensatory only, being awarded for aggravating the injury to feelings caused by the wrongful act. Circumstances which give rise to the award are (a) the manner in which the wrong was committed, or (b) the motive for it, or (c) the respondent's conduct subsequent to the wrongdoing but in relation to it. These matters are only relevant to an award of aggravated damages if the claimant was aware of them. In relation to conduct subsequent to the wrongdoing, tribunals should be aware of the risks of awarding compensation in respect of conduct which has not been properly proved or examined in evidence and allowing the scope of the hearing to be disproportionately extended by considering distinct allegations of subsequent misconduct.

Generally, 'the more heinous the conduct the greater the impact is likely to have been on the claimant's feelings'. But the tribunal should be cautious that it is awarding compensation rather than punishing the misconduct. With some reservations, the EAT concluded that a distinct figure could continue to be attributed to aggravated damages rather than subsuming it within injury to feelings. That would enable the *Vento* guidelines to continue to be used for the non-aggravated element of the injury to feelings award. Aggravated damages should be a distinct sub-heading within injury to feelings so as to emphasize the compensatory element. Tribunals should assess whether the totality of the injury to feelings award, including aggravated damages, was fair and proportionate in relation to the totality of suffering caused to the claimant. Tribunals should identify the main considerations which have led them to make the overall award for injury to feelings, specifying any aggravating or mitigating features to which they attach particular weight.

Here the award was out of line with the conventional scale of aggravated damages awards. These were mainly in the range of £5,000 to £7,500, and it was also exceptional for the aggravated damages to exceed the ordinary injury to feelings. There were indications that the tribunal had taken into account matters which were part of the complaint rather than aggravating features, and also matters of which the claimant was not aware. The EAT reduced the total award to £30,000, of which £22,500 was attributed to 'core' injury to feelings and £7,500 to aggravating of it. It took into account Shaw's loss of faith in the Metropolitan Police to whom he had devoted his career, that he had moved to another unit which was less satisfying work, that for several months he was subjected to unjustified disciplinary allegations which caused him to worry for his reputation, that he was humiliated in being escorted from the office on the occasion of his suspension, that after being cleared he continued to feel ostracized and stigmatized as an outsider, that no action was taken against those who victimized him and he received no apology. He had suffered serious physical and psychological symptoms of stress and taken time off sick. This was therefore a case of serious injury to feelings affecting his wellbeing on a long term basis. But it fell short of the most serious cases such as where there is a prolonged campaign of discriminatory bullying. Other mitigating factors were that in the end there was no disciplinary sanction and no permanent or public damage to his reputation and he was within a few years of retirement in any event.

Result: compensation reduced to £30,000 (injury to feelings plus aggravated damages).

Cited by: *Rowe v London Underground Ltd* (UKEAT/0125/16/JOJ, 17 October 2016); *Roberts v Wilsons Solicitors LLP* [2016] ICR 659 (EAT); *Gulati v MGN Ltd* [2016] FSR 12; *Newcastle upon Tyne Hospitals NHS Foundation Trust v Bagley* [2012] Eq LR 634 (EAT); *Niekrash v South London Healthcare NHS Trust* (UKEAT/0252/11/JOJ, 07 March 2012).

174. Local Government Yorkshire & Humber v Shah

UKEAT/0587/11/ZT, 19 June 2012

Key issues: Top bracket *Vento* and can a worker receive an uplift under section 207A of TULR(C)A?

Case summary: Appeal against *Vento* finding. Claimant dismissed for protected qualifying disclosure. Is there an ACAS uplift for a worker? What is the impact of *Da'Bell*?

ET (EJ Wade):. Finding no separate award for psychiatric injury, they found for injury to feelings that the Respondent's actions had a devastating effect on the Claimant, her family, domestic, private and professional life, both at the time of the detriments suffered and on an ongoing basis. That impact had not been lessened by subsequent actions of the Respondent, neither by the very robust defence, nor in not responding to her letter since the liability judgment. The Tribunal has decided that it is just and equitable to award £25,000 by way of injury to feelings.

EAT (HHJ Serota): Applying *Vento* and *Da'Bell* they upheld the tribunal's sensible prediction on the likelihood of future employment, which remained a matter of impression and judgement. It confirmed that there is no ACAS adjustment for a worker. The tribunal was entitled to find that losses would extend beyond a fixed-term secondment. Finally, the injury to feelings award was not perverse.

Result:(a) no ACAS adjustment for worker; (b) *Da'Bell* might need to be uplifted for inflation.

Detriment: termination of worker contract.

Sections considered: 207 TULR(C)A.

Damages awarded: £25,000 injury to feelings, in the top band of *Vento*.

175. Audere Medical Services Ltd v Sanderson

UKEAT/0409/12/RN, 29 May 2013

See Case 75.

176. Small v The Shrewsbury & Telford Hospitals NHS Trust

UKEAT/0300/14/LA, 19 May 2015

Key issues: Could/should stigma damages be awarded? (Stigma—*Smith v Manchester* 'disadvantage in the labour market' award).

Case summary: Having found S had lost his agency role because of a protected disclosure, but that S would have been dismissed in any event before the remedy hearing, was S entitled to an award for stigma damages? Stigma damages were not sought during the ET remedy hearing and the question was whether it should have been applied in any event, or could be raised subsequently.

ET: The tribunal accepted that with S as an interim worker his career was dependant on the outcome of his last job; he is only as good as his last reference, proven perhaps by his six interviews following 576 applications for work. His dismissal was therefore career-ending. They found had he not been dismissed, he would have continued as a project manager, but he would have been dismissed on a later date. They did not award damages beyond the second date.

EAT (Mr Justice Langstaff (President)): confirmed there was no need to plead stigma losses and, whilst it is good practice to plead it expressly, where there is a claim for a *Smith v Manchester* award, it should be made and argued. The tribunal had held that the failure to provide a reference was realistically to remove him from the work environment. This led to a question as to whether that was a further wrong done to him for which he may be compensated in the proceedings. As to this, there were likely to be further findings of fact which needed to be made. However, in the absence of any argument, it was not appropriate to expect the tribunal to anticipate and grant an award for stigma damages or for his difficulties on the labour market arising purely as a result of the discriminatory act or the dismissal, because such claims are far from commonplace; indeed they are unusual.

Result: Appeal dismissed.

177. Roberts v Wilsons Solicitors LLP and others

[2016] IRLR 586; [2016] ICR 659

Key issues: the approach to attribution of loss in a claim for compensation under ERA s 49(2); operation of the cap on compensation for workers in s 49(6) ERA where the detriment takes the form of dismissal.

Case summary: The claimant was a solicitor and member of the respondent LLP. He was also the managing partner and compliance officer. He produced a report into an allegation of bullying against a colleague. Before the meeting at which that report was due to be discussed, a majority of the other members of the LLP informed the claimant that they would not attend the meeting. Subsequently the LLP voted to remove the claimant from the position of managing partner and compliance officer. The claimant notified his acceptance of these steps as a repudiatory breach of the LLP agreement and stated that he regarded the LLP agreement as terminated. The LLP denied the alleged repudiatory breaches and asserted that the claimant continued as a member because he had not provided a valid resignation notice. The claimant ceased work and brought proceedings in the ET, claiming compensation for detriment suffered by him as a worker as a result of the making of protected disclosures. Following the claimant's ceasing work the LLP voted to expel him.

The claimant's claim of detriment was struck out by the ET on the basis that, following *Flanagan v Liontrust Investment Partners LLP* [2016] 1 BCLC 177, the doctrine of automatic termination following acceptance of a repudiatory breach did not apply in a case involving an LLP with more than two members. On appeal to the EAT the claimant accepted that *Flanagan* applied and was correct, but contended that the tribunal should not have struck out the claim without applying s 49(2) ERA, and that it would be just and equitable in all the circumstances to award him compensation.

EAT: (Simler J (P)) allowed the appeal. The word 'attributable' in s 49(2) ERA did not import a requirement that the infringement or unlawful act had to be the proximate cause of loss. A loss may be attributable to a particular act whether that act is closest in time to the loss or not, and two or more consecutive (or concurrent) acts may combine to bring about a particular consequence or loss. Proximity by itself is not the determining factor. It is a question of fact and judgment in every case for the tribunal whether a particular consequence or loss is attributable to a particular unlawful act or infringement, or to something else, or both, and if so, to what extent. The 'but for' test was not applicable either. 'Attributable' is an ordinary English word that is well understood and is capable of being applied flexibly by tribunals on a broad common-sense basis. The statutory test imposed by s 49(2)(b) provides that in deciding what compensation should be awarded, tribunals have discretion to determine what is just and equitable in all the circumstances. They must have regard to the infringement itself, in other words the nature and gravity of that infringement; and second, they must have regard to the loss attributable to the act or failure to act which infringed the individual's rights.

That the claimant's purported resignation was not effective for the purposes of LLP law did not determine the question of what loss was attributable to the unlawful detriments on which he relied. If the unlawful 'victimization' of the claimant by the LLP made his position untenable and led him to withdraw his labour, thereby exposing him to the likelihood of expulsion, it was hard to see why that consequence should as a matter of law (or inevitable fact) be regarded as too indirect or unnatural to attract compensation in accordance with the statutory test. In seeking to recover termination related losses in such circumstances an LLP member would have to prove loss attributable to the infringing act, and might face formidable difficulties in proving this. The LLP member also had to persuade a tribunal that it was just and equitable to award compensation having regard to the infringing act (its nature and seriousness) and any loss proved to be attributable to it.

As to the cap contained in s 49(6) ERA on the recovery of damages for a worker where the detriment to which the worker is subjected is the termination of his or her contract (so as to be no greater than if the worker was an employee claiming unfair dismissal), if and to the extent that s 49(6) is interpreted as preventing a worker who is claiming dismissal contrary to s 47B from obtaining a head of loss such as injury to feelings that would not be available to an employee who is successful in establishing unfair dismissal, s 49(6) makes clear that it only applies where 'the detriment to which the worker is subjected is the termination of his worker's contract'. In a case where a worker suffers detriment prior to termination, an award of injury to feelings can be claimed in respect of that detriment but not in respect of the termination. An LLP member whose sole detriment complaint is about termination or expulsion cannot recover for injury to feelings on this basis. An LLP member, permitted to claim for post-termination losses based on detriment other than termination, can obtain injury to feelings compensation in relation to the earlier detriments (just as any other worker can) but not in relation to the detriment of termination, and is accordingly in no better position than any other worker (or employee).

Result: The matter was remitted back to the tribunal.

Detriments: Removal of claimant from position as managing partner and compliance officer

Sections considered: ERA ss 49(2) and 49(6).

178. Hamer v Kaltz Ltd

UKEAT/0198/11/RN, 24 February 2012 UKEAT/0502/13/BA, 4 August 2014

Key issues: were the rulings of the ET on contributory fault and *Polkey* reduction consistent and permissible? Was the dismissal of the claimant for breach of a contractual term which was rendered void by s 43J ERA?

Case summary: The claimant had been employed as the administration manager of the respondent. Following a disciplinary meeting she was dismissed for gross misconduct. Her internal appeal against that decision was unsuccessful. The ET held however that the principal reason for the dismissal was that the claimant had made a protected disclosure, and that her dismissal had, in consequence, been unfair. The particular subject of the claimant's protected disclosure was the amount of salary being paid to a Mr White, another employee. The claimant made a disclosure relating to his salary because she believed that Mr White was receiving an amount of pay, while on paternity leave, that was less than he had had a right to receive. The ET rejected by majority the claimant's claim that, absent the legal effect of her being dismissed for making a protected disclosure, her dismissal had been unfair. However, the tribunal also decided that the respondent had had a genuine belief on reasonable grounds, and after a reasonable investigation, that the misconduct alleged against the claimant had been established. It held that on the material available to the respondent, dismissal was within the range of reasonable responses open to such an employer. With regard to the claimant's breach of contract claim the tribunal said that the principal reason for dismissal was the disclosure of confidential payroll information concerning Mr White. The respondent's disciplinary rules classed this as gross misconduct. The ET therefore concluded that her notice pay claim must fail because she was lawfully summarily dismissed under her contract.

At a remedies hearing the claimant was awarded £33,941.20 for (automatically) unfair dismissal.

On appeal the respondent argued that the ET had misdirected itself to the effect that, as a matter of law and/or legal principle, it could not or should not take account of an employee's conduct in a case of unfair dismissal that is automatically unfair by reason of a protected disclosure. Even if the ET did not err by way of misdirection, nevertheless its conclusion that there was no conduct on the part of the claimant for it to take into account was inconsistent with its findings on the ordinary unfair dismissal claim and the rejection by it of the wrongful dismissal claim because these were premised on the proposition that there must have been at least some misconduct on the part of the claimant. A further criticism of the ET was that it did not address properly the question of whether the claimant would have been, or was likely to have been, dismissed in any event.

First EAT: held that there had been no misdirection. However, the EAT noted that the protected disclosure was not the only matter on which the respondent had based and pursued disciplinary proceedings. There were two other (non-protected) disclosures and another two instances of misconduct, and the majority found that the claimant was 'being disciplined for her insubordination towards a director and had disclosed confidential payroll information'. One of the non-protected disclosures of confidential information was admitted by the claimant and in respect of the other non-protected disclosure of confidential information her denial was counteracted by a statement from another staff member. In the EAT's view it was incumbent upon the ET in reaching its finding that there was no culpable or blameworthy conduct on the part of the employee to explain how the other conduct was immaterial on the question of compensation. There was also an unexplained inconsistency in that the ET dismissed the wrongful dismissal claim on the grounds that there had been gross misconduct justifying summary dismissal, but when it came to assessing compensation the ET had found that there had been no relevant misconduct on the claimant's part. The EAT reached much the same conclusion on the *Polkey* point. The remedies judgment made no mention of the respondent's case that even if the protected disclosure was put to one side the claimant faced two disciplinary charges for misconduct and two further allegations of unauthorized disclosure. A tribunal might nevertheless be entitled not to make a *Polkey* reduction, but it was obliged to give the reasons for not doing so.

Second ET: The matter was remitted to the same ET which decided at a further remedies hearing that the claimant should receive no compensatory award because she would inevitably have been dismissed on the same date as she in fact had been. The tribunal also imposed a 10 per cent reduction in the basic award for conduct. Both sides appealed.

EAT: the ET's reasoning as to wrongdoing in relation to the wrongful dismissal claim was inadequate; the disclosure in question which was found to justify dismissal was a protected disclosure and as such any contractual provision giving an entitlement to dismiss for making that disclosure was void under s 43J ERA. In any event it was not obvious why an honest, reasonable disclosure of a matter of concern to a line manager would be a repudiatory breach of contract in itself.

As to unfair dismissal, the EAT observed that the ET had found by a majority, applying ordinary unfair dismissal principles, that the dismissal was fair. However, they appeared to have left out of account the finding that the principal reason for dismissal was the making of a protected disclosure. If a tribunal finds the principal reason is proscribed, it makes no sense to rule separately on ordinary unfair dismissal unless it is done expressly on an alternative basis in case the employment tribunal is wrong about s 103A. In this case, the ET expressed its conclusions on ordinary unfair dismissal first and it was unclear on precisely what basis it made its finding on ordinary unfair dismissal.

As to the *Polkey* reduction, the majority had ruled at the second remedies hearing that it was inevitable that the claimant was going to be dismissed lawfully in any event and the compensatory award should therefore be extinguished. A reduction of 10 per cent on the basic award was made. But it was impossible to understand, from the ET's reasons, how it concluded that it was inevitable that the respondent, if it acted fairly, would have dismissed the claimant on the very same day absent the principal reason for dismissal. The ET had concluded, in its liability reasons, that the respondent had not regarded the other complaints against the claimant as serious and had maintained this finding when it came to assess contributory conduct. The appeal was therefore allowed on the *Polkey* issue and the conclusion that an appropriate reduction to the compensatory award was 40 per cent was substituted with a further deduction of 10 per cent for contributory fault.

Result: Dismissal by reason of protected disclosure. Reduction in compensatory award of 40 per cent, and further reduction of 10 per cent to both basic and compensatory awards.

Sections covered: ERA, ss 43J, 103A, 122(2), 123(1), (6).

Costs

179. Morrison v Hesley Lifecare Services Ltd
EAT/0262/03 and EAT/0534/03, 19 March 2004

See Case 59.

180. Milne v The Link Asset and Security Company Ltd
EAT/0867/04, 26 September 2005

See Case 62.

181. Clark v Clark Construction Initiatives Ltd
[2008] ICR 635 [2008] IRLR 364

See Case 65.

182. HCA International Ltd v May-Bheemul

UKEAT/0477/10/ZT, 23 March 2011

Key issue: costs where belief in relevant failure was not objectively reasonable.

Case summary: the claimant, a finance coordinator, expressed concern that other employees used her login and password in breach of security. She later also alleged financial irregularities and, ultimately, fraud. She became ill and later claimed that she had been constructively dismissed on grounds of her protected disclosures.

ET: in raising her concern that staff had used her name and password to book shifts in breach of their confidentiality and security agreements, the claimant made protected disclosures. Regarding her disclosures of fraud and financial irregularities, although the claimant genuinely believed the allegations, her view was not objectively reasonable. She was not subjected to a detriment by reason of these disclosures. The respondent's application for costs was dismissed.

EAT (Cox J): the appeal was confined to the decision to reject the application for costs. It was argued that it was perverse not to award costs to the successful party where the losing party's central allegation (in this case being subject to detriments) when the central allegation was not established and is held to be wrong. The EAT firmly rejected that submission. As the claimant's initial concerns did amount to protected disclosures and she did have an honest and genuine belief in the later allegations notwithstanding that her belief was found not to be objectively reasonable:

> 42. . . . . the objective unreasonableness of genuine belief, and a consequent failure on a Claimant's part to establish the necessary legal elements of the claim, does not equate to unreasonable conduct of the proceedings.

Other factors, including a without prejudice offer and having subsequently reported matters to external agencies, did not on the facts of the case require a costs order.

Result: refusal of costs order upheld.

Detriment: none.

Sections considered: Employment Tribunal Rules, Sch 1, r 40.

Damages awarded: none.

Cited by: *Arrowsmith v Nottingham Trent University* [2011] EWCA Civ 797.

Purposive approach

183. ALM Medical Services Ltd v Bladon

UKEAT/709/00, EAT/967/00, 19 January 2001 (EAT); [2002] ICR 1444 (CA)

See Case 81.

184. Virgo Fidelis Senior School v Boyle

[2004] IRLR 268 (EAT)

See Case 67.

185. El-Hoshi v Pizza Express Restaurants Ltd

EAT/0857/03, 23 March 2004

Key issue: affirmation of contract; policy approach in whistleblowing context.

Case summary: Mr El-Hoshi claimed constructive dismissal. The respondent admitted that El-Hoshi had made a protected disclosure but took issue with whether he had suffered a detriment and whether that was as a result of the disclosure. As a fall-back position it asserted in any event that the contract had been affirmed after any alleged breach.

ET: held that while El-Hoshi was off work he constantly submitted sick notes covering the whole of the period. These were expressly in relation to depression. The tribunal held that his depression was due to the detriment. It decided that, while El-Hoshi had a legitimate claim for being subjected to a detriment, he was not constructively dismissed, for he had affirmed the contract.

EAT (HHJ McMullen QC): held that El-Hoshi did not affirm the contract by virtue of delaying his resignation by three months, during which he submitted sick notes and received statutory sick pay. His illness was due to the detriment that had been inflicted upon him and the delay was therefore caused by that detriment.

> We also take the view that we have taken against the background of the protection given to 'whistle-blowers'. The reaction of this manager, to humiliate the Applicant, was bound to cause an effect upon the Applicant's health. This legislation is there to protect those people who raise issues of concern and which are acknowledged to be in the public interest. It would be an odd result if an employee who raised an issue were to find himself or herself dismissed, even constructively dismissed. Public policy is to protect and take a liberal view of employees who raise these issues and who pass the thresholds in Part IVA of the Employment Rights Act 1996 entitling them to claim that they are legitimate whistle-blowers.

Result: remitted to the ET to consider damages for unfair dismissal.

Detriment: being rostered to work four nights in the kitchen.

Sections considered: ERA, s 47B(1).

Damages awarded: £9,640.75 (injury to feelings £3,500) before award for unfair dismissal.

Cited by: *Newcastle City Council v Spires* (UKEAT/0334/10, 22 February 2011).

186. Boulding v Land Securities

EAT/0023/0306, 3 May 2006

See Case 29.

187. Croke v Hydro Aluminum Worcester Ltd

[2007] ICR 1303 (EAT)

See Case 6.

188. Ezsias v North Glamorgan NHS Trust

[2007] IRLR 603 (CA), [2011] IRLR 550 (EAT)

See Case 67.

189. Babula v Waltham Forest College

[2007] ICR 1045 (CA)

See Case 31.

190. BP plc v Elstone and Petrotechnics Ltd

[2010] ICR 879 (EAT)

See Case 37.

191. Audere Medical Services Ltd v Sanderson

UKEAT/0409/12/RN, 29 May 2013

See Case 75.

Who is responsible? The 'Iago' conundrum

192. The Co-operative Group Ltd v Baddeley

UKEAT/0415/12/JOJ, 22 February 2013, 15 November 2013; [2014] EWCA Civ 658

Key issues: The mental process of the person responsible for the detriment or dismissal.

Case summary: The claimant raised his belief that pharmaceutical stock was being sold without a licence. He was subsequently investigated and dismissed.

CA (Laws, Ryder, and Underhill LJJ): The identification of the decision-makers in this case gave rise to further questions as to whether 'the actual decision-maker acts for an admissible reason but the decision is unfair because ... the facts known to him or beliefs held by him have been manipulated by some other person involved in the disciplinary process who has an inadmissible motivation—for short, an Iago situation'.

Underhill LJ considered that the motivation of a manipulator could in principle be attributed to the employer, where the manipulator was a manager with some responsibility for the investigation. On the facts of the case as found, the two protagonists were found not to be 'innocent dupes but knowing participants'. However, there was no proper reasoning to support this finding. Motivation to support a view held by a colleague could be materially different to motivation being *because* he was a whistleblower.

Result: Case remitted to a fresh tribunal.

Sections considered: ERA, ss 47B, 103A.

193. Ahmed v City of Bradford Metropolitan District Council

UKEAT/0145/14/KN, 27 October 2014

Key issues: Relevance of influence over the person making the impugned decision.

Case summary: Ahmed was in danger of redundancy, subject to an alternative post being found. When he was seeking to be redeployed, his line manager wrote a bad reference because of a protected qualifying disclosure. His application was rejected because of the recipient of the reference relying on it, unaware of the motivation behind it and the disclosure.

ET (EJ Starr): Mr Rashid (who relied on the reference) and who made the decision, did so with no knowledge of the protected acts or protected disclosures.

EAT (Judge Serota QC): The motivation of the manipulator *could* in principle be attributed to the employer, at least where he was a manager with some responsibility for the investigation. The tribunal should have applied *Fecitt* to the claimant's non-appointment to the post. The evidence strongly suggested that the reference, tainted as it was, had more than a trivial influence and it was a means of manipulating the redeployment process.

The EAT criticized the ET for separating the motivation for writing the reference (found to be with the intent that he should cease to be employed and not be re-employed) from the reliance by Mr Rashid upon it. The fact that Mr Rashid did not realize he was being misled did not sanitize the effect of the reference and did not exonerate Bradford as the employer from a decision where they had been influenced by an infected reference that came into existence as a result of a protected disclosure. Standing back the tribunal found that the claimant was dismissed not by reason of redundancy but because the decision to dismiss was clearly influenced by the response to a protected disclosure.

> 49 ... In my opinion where employee X does an act which amounts to a detriment to employee Y by reason of a protected disclosure, such as by giving an unfair and negative reference, with the intention that it should lead to the Claimant suffering a further detriment at the hands of employee Z, or might reasonably be found to have been so intended, the employer will be liable for the second detriment if it can be shown to have been infected by the first discriminatory act and had materially influenced the imposition of the second detriment imposed by Z upon Y.

Result: remitted to the tribunal.

Detriment: It was argued as a s 103A, whereas it should have been argued as a s 47B.

Sections considered: EAR, ss 47B, 103A.

194. Royal Mail Group Ltd v Jhuti

[2016] IRLR 854 (EAT)

Key issues: The person who dismissed Jhuti was misled, by the claimant's line manager. The line manager did this because of the disclosure. Is the employer liable despite the innocence of the dismissing manager?

Case summary: Jhuti was employed as a probationary media specialist for just over a year. She believed a manager she was shadowing had offered an incentive discount to a company in breach of internal and regulatory rules. Having raised this by email to the head of her team, Mr Widmer, she met him at a service station on 13 November 2013, where the focus was upon her understanding of the incentive discount scheme, rather than her account of what had occurred and the potential for fraud. She was then told she had made a mistake and advised to send an email retracting her concerns. The meeting left Jhuti distressed, shaking, and in tears. She sent the email as suggested. Thereafter she was set an 'ever changing unattainable list of requirements' to drive her out of her job, together with an instruction to compile a list of clients from previous employers. This resulted in performance management. Jhuti raised grievances, including one in which she made reference to her previous disclosures, and said that Mr Widmer was looking to 'manage me out of the business for his own gain' and that his judgement and actions towards her were clouded 'since I raised my issue'. Jhuti became ill. Royal Mail made offers of three month's salary, and then a year's salary, for her to leave. They were not accepted. Pauline Vickers was then appointed to review the claimant's performance, although her grievances were excluded. She was provided, however, with documents containing references to 'cheating the business and the public, to which the claimant did not wish to be a party'. Ms Vickers spoke to Jhuti's manager who provided his version of events, but she did not meet with Jhuti. Ms Vickers dismissed Jhuti. Her appeal, whilst delayed to look into the disclosures, still resulted in her dismissal.

ET: The tribunal found that the claimant had made a protected disclosure in (both individually and collectively) emails to Mr Widmer on 8 and 12 November 2013, which had then been repeated in her combined grievance and appeal against dismissal on 13 September 2014. In consequences Jhuti was subjected to the following detriments:

- Bullying and harassment by Mr Widmer at and following a meeting at the service station on 13 November, including imposing ever changing and unobtainable requirements on her, which amounted to 'setting up a paper trail which set her to fail'.
- As a facet of this, issuing her with a performance plan which included a requirement for her to provide key contacts in previous employments.

However, the ET found that the fact that Jhuti had made protected disclosures was not part of Ms Vickers' reasoning in deciding to dismiss. Instead the decision was based on Ms Vickers' genuine belief that Jhuti was a poor performer. Following the reasoning in *CLFIS v Reynolds* [2015] ICR 1010, the tribunal concluded that for the dismissal claim to succeed, Ms Vickers must have been motivated by the protected disclosure, and that it was not sufficient that her decision to dismiss was based on someone else's motivation. Therefore the principal reason was not the disclosure.

EAT (Mitting J): Allowing the appeal, the ET erred in applying *CLFIS v Reynolds* as there was no read across from discrimination principles, particularly as the Equality Act 2010 has no equivalent to s 47B(2) ERA (which excludes a claim of detriment consisting of dismissal of an employee). Mitting J explained (at para 34) that:

A man can manipulate what a person believes as to his reason just as well as he manipulates what a person believes as to the fairness of decisions which flow from having that reason. . . .. I am satisfied that, as a matter of law, a decision of a person made in ignorance of the true facts whose decision is manipulated by someone in a managerial position responsible for an employee, who is in possession of the true facts, can be attributed to the employer of both of them.

This applied in the present case given Mr Widmer's role in bringing about the dismissal, taking into account:

1. He was Jhuti's line manager responsible for Jhuti's induction, supervision, and allocating duties to her and reporting on her performance.
2. She made protected disclosures to him, which he realized were serious and of significance to him, to those senior to him, and to the respondents generally.
3. She was deliberately subjected to detriments by him from the moment that she made the disclosure until he ceased to be her line manager.
4. His temporary replacement, Mr Reed, displayed no difference in approach from that adopted by Mr Widmer.
5. Mr Widmer 'was setting up a paper trail which set her to fail'.
6. He succeeded.
7. He lied to Ms Vickers about the disclosures made by Jhuti by 'explaining disingenuously that this was an issue which had been raised but that the claimant had told him that she had got her wires crossed' and by giving her email to him of 13 November 2013 to Ms Vickers, but not the earlier emails of 8 and 12 November 2013.
8. Ms Vickers was deprived of information for unexplained reasons by Human Resources, who did not give her copies of the emails of 6 February and 25 and 26 February 2014, and by the decision to separate the grievance from performance issues.

The EAT concluded that it is not 'only the mind of Ms Vickers which needs to be examined to discern the reasons for dismissal' but the reasons of her line manager 'also must be taken into account'. Once Mr Widmer's involvement was taken into account, this led inevitably to the conclusion that the dismissal was unfair by reason of the protected disclosures.

Note: At para 27 the EAT commented that there is no provision for payment of compensation by an employee who subjects a claimant to a detriment. But this appears to have overlooked s 48(5) ERA.

Result: Dismissal automatically unfair. Counsel were invited to address how the matter should proceed.

Detriment: See ET findings above.

Sections considered: ERA, ss 47B, 103A.

195. Dr Brito-Babapulle v Isle of Wight NHS Trust

UKEAT/0090/16/DM, 10 June 2016

Key issue: Had the ET adopted the correct approach in considering the respondent's grounds for subjecting the claimant to a detriment?

Case summary: The claimant held a locum position with the respondent NHS Trust. The employment tribunal accepted that some (though not all) of the matters she relied upon amounted to protected disclosures. She asserted two detriments: failure to pay her on-call hours after 28 October 2013, and failing to afford her a hearing prior to dismissal.

ET: The tribunal accepted that these were detriments, but concluded that neither of them was on the grounds of the protected disclosures. So far as concerned the payment for on-call hours, the tribunal accepted that the explanation for the decision to do so was that the decision-maker (K) was given incorrect HR advice to the effect that it was not the policy to pay for on-call time which had not actually been worked. The ET stated that it could not accept the basis for that advice, but nonetheless it provided a reason for the decision (which it accepted) which was not the protected disclosure. Indeed K's evidence was unchallenged as to the reason for her decision.

EAT: it was not sufficient to focus on K's mental processes. In order to ascertain whether the protected disclosures were a significant influence, it was also necessary to consider the mental processes of the individual within HR who had given the erroneous advice which in turn let to the decision to refuse the on call payments. The issue was therefore remitted.

Result: Issue as to adviser's reason for giving advice remitted.

Sections referred to: ERA, s 48.

Disclosure of documents

196. Gray v Merrill Lynch, Pierce, Fenner & Smith Ltd

UKEAT/0058/16/DM, 16 March 2016

Key issues: Can the respondent refuse disclosure of documents relevant to the protected disclosure?

Case summary: Claimant dismissed for redundancy, alleging it was for a protected disclosure. Claimant sought disclosure of documents relevant to the disclosure.

EAT (Judge Eady QC): There were two strands to disclosure: documents relevant to the alleged protected disclosure and those relevant to a redundancy exercise that was being challenged as a sham. The protected disclosure turned on an allegation as to the improper use of inside information. The EAT accepted that information relating to the number of bids made and their timing, whether successful or not, was relevant to the question of whether the claimant had a reasonable belief that information disclosed tended to show a relevant failure. The ET erred and they were a properly disclosable category of documents.

Result: Tribunal erred, disclosure ordered.

Sections considered: ERA 103A; Rule 31 of the Employment Tribunals (Constitution and Rules of Procedure) Regulations 2013, Civil Procedure Rules 1998, Rule 31.6.

Whistleblowing policies

197. Audere Medical Services Ltd v Sanderson

UKEAT/0409/12/RN, 29 May 2013

See Case 75.

198. Frenkel Topping Ltd v King

UKEAT/0106/15/LA, 21 July 2015

Key issues: Whether detriment on ground of protected disclosures amount to a repudiatory breach of contract. Whether failure to amend contractual whistleblowing policy to reflect that good faith is no longer a requirement could be a breach of contract.

Case summary: The claimant was a solicitor employed as a welfare benefits case worker by the respondent. She resigned, claiming constructive unfair dismissal by reason of protected disclosures and protected disclosure detriment.

ET: The claimant had made two protected disclosures in early January 2014, and suffered detriment on the grounds of these disclosures in being subjected to unfair and inappropriate criticisms in two meetings on 17 February 2014 (one being a meeting with the Managing Director and Finance Director, and the second meeting involving criticism of her in front of her team and others). She had been constructively dismissed, and the dismissal was unfair, but was not by reason of the protected disclosures. Several matters were found to constitute or contribute to a repudiatory breach, including (but not limited to) (a) the conduct found to be subjecting her to a detriment on ground of her protected disclosures, and (b) operating a whistleblowing policy which, despite the legislative change made to the protected disclosure legislation in 2013 (relegating good faith to a remedy requirement), continued to provide that:

> if the procedure has not been invoked in good faith (eg for malicious reasons or in pursuit of a personal grudge), then it will make you liable to immediate termination of engagement or such lesser disciplinary sanction as may be appropriate in the circumstances.

The tribunal concluded that the provisions had deterred the claimant from making a further protected disclosure (by reporting concerns to the Financial Conduct Authority), and that the failure to provide a proper and up-to-date policy in compliance with the law amounted to a breach of the implied term of trust and confidence.

EAT (Langstaff J (P)): The findings in relation to most of the matters found to be a repudiatory breach were not sufficiently reasoned. However, the appeal was dismissed, because the conduct on 17 February 2014 was by itself a repudiatory breach and it was sufficient that this was part of the reason for resignation: *Wright v North Ayrshire Council* [2014] IRLR 4, [2014] ICR 77 (EAT). The EAT accepted that unfair and inappropriate criticism of performance need not necessarily be sufficient to be repudiatory. But here there were two further factors which made it clear that the conduct could not have been other than repudiatory. First it was repeated in that there were two separate episodes on 17 February, and on the second the claimant was effectively humiliated in front of others at the workplace in that she was criticized in front of her team and others. Further, her critics were the Managing Director and the Finance Director. The second aggravating element was that the reason for doing this had nothing to do with the claimant's performance, and was simply that she had raised a disclosure (which amounted to a protected disclosure). In addition, the contractual whistleblowing policy advertised that employees were free, without any threat, to raise such disclosures, and the employer was therefore not honouring what had been said in that respect.

The EAT rejected as inadequately reasoned the ET's further conclusion that the failure to amend the whistleblowing policy was itself a breach or a repudiatory breach of contract, whilst noting how that might have been argued (at para 41):

> As to the question of the whistleblowing policy, we have great difficulties with the Tribunal's finding in respect of this. It asserts that a delay in changing the terms of the contract to accord with the applicable law amounted, first of all, to a breach of contract and, secondly, to one so serious that it might justify the employee in resigning. The breach is said to be a breach of the implied term. Unless the implied term is to be considered as an incident of the contract of employment, to be implied as a matter of law whatever the contract happens to say, this becomes a difficult argument since the contract itself laid down what the procedures were. Act of Parliament aside (and none was relied on) the employer could hardly be in breach of contract because of what the contract itself provided. A more developed argument might be to the effect that the contract became unlawful and void in this respect once the law had changed, that that then gave room for the implied term of trust and confidence to operate as a proper implied term, since it would no longer be contrary to the express terms of the contract, and that the delay in making the change was such that it was to be treated more seriously than it might otherwise have been. The Tribunal engaged in no consideration of this kind, nor was such an argument put to it.

The EAT added that whilst it is not uncommon for fear of detrimental treatment to have a chilling effect, there was no adequate reasoning as to why the particular wording of the unamended policy deterred the claimant from making a further disclosure. It was not the claimant's case that she would be making the disclosure other than in good faith, and there was no more reason to suppose that the employer would accuse her of lack of good faith than, for example, claiming that she lacked a reasonable belief.

Result: Appeal dismissed; disclosure was a material influence on detriment.

Detriment: Constructive dismissal and being subjected to unfair and inappropriate criticisms which were not genuinely due to performance.

Sections considered: ERA, s 43B(1).

Contractual terms rendered void

199. Hamer v Katlz Ltd

UKEAT/0198/11/RN, 24 February 2012; UKEAT/0502/13/BA, 4 August 2014

See Case 178.

APPENDIX 3

Precedents

FORM 1

CIVIL PROCEDURE RULES 1998 PART 25 PROVIDES THE RULES IN RELATION TO
INTERIM REMEDIES TOGETHER WITH THE PRACTICE DIRECTIONS 25A.

DELIVERY UP ORDER	**IN THE HIGH COURT OF JUSTICE QUEEN'S BENCH DIVISION**

BEFORE THE HONOURABLE MR/MRS JUSTICE 'X'

CLAIM No:

BETWEEN: DATED:

BIG BUCKS PLC   APPLICANT

- AND -

THE DAILY RAG LTD   RESPONDENT

NAME, ADDRESS, AND REFERENCE OF RESPONDENT:

THE DAILY RAG

1 SLEAZY STREET

LONDON P4P ER5

PENAL NOTICE

IF YOU THE DAILY RAG LTD DISOBEY THIS ORDER YOU MAY BE HELD TO
BE IN CONTEMPT OF COURT AND MAY BE IMPRISONED, FINED OR HAVE
YOUR ASSETS SEIZED.

ANY OTHER PERSON WHO KNOWS OF THIS ORDER AND DOES ANYTHING
WHICH HELPS OR PERMITS THE RESPONDENT TO BREACH THE
TERMS OF THIS ORDER MAY ALSO BE HELD TO BE IN CONTEMPT OF
COURT AND MAY BE IMPRISONED, FINED, OR HAVE THEIR ASSETS SEIZED.

THIS ORDER

An Application was made on _____ by Counsel for the Applicant, [and attended by Counsel for
the Respondent] to Mr/Mrs Justice _____ who heard the application. The Judge read the witness
statements listed in Schedule A and accepted the undertakings set out in Schedule B at the end of
this Order.

As a result of the application **IT IS ORDERED** that:

1. Until [ ] or further Order of the Court, the Respondent shall be restrained whether by its directors,
   officers, employees or agents or any of them, or otherwise howsoever:
   1.1 from making any use (to include the passing to any third party) of the report to the Board
       ('the Report'), referred to in the issue dated 29 July 2016 of The Daily Rag or any of its
       content and
   1.2 from defacing, deleting any part of, or otherwise altering or tampering with the format or
       appearance of any and all documents and records which are the property of the Applicant.
2. The Respondent must immediately hand over to the Applicant's solicitors any of the listed items,
   which are in his possession or under his control, save for any computer or hard disk integral to any
   computer. Any items the subject of a dispute as to whether they are listed items must immediately

be handed over to the Applicant's solicitors for safe keeping pending the resolution of the dispute or further order of the court. The Respondent must hand over:

2.1 the Report or any extracts from it and all documents containing information derived from the Report.

2.2 all documents and records (in hard copy, digital or electronic form) which are the property of the Applicant.

PROVISION OF INFORMATION

3. The Respondent shall swear an affidavit within [two] days of the date of this Order:

3.1 confirming compliance with paragraph 2 of this Order.

3.2 to the extent that any copy of the Report or any other document belonging to the Applicant was, but is no longer, in the possession of the Respondent, and has not been returned to the Applicant, stating what has become of it.

3.3 stating when, how and to whom the Report or any of its contents has been disclosed by the Respondent.

3.4 identifying the person or people who disclosed the Report to the Respondent and what other information relating to the Applicant, or property belonging to the Applicant, was disclosed by that person or people to the Respondent and stating when and how the disclosure was made.

PROHIBITED ACTS

4. Except for the purpose of obtaining legal advice, the Respondent must not directly or indirectly inform anyone of these proceedings or of the contents of this order, or warn anyone that proceedings have been or may be brought against him by the Applicant until 4.30 pm on [date] or further order of the Court.

5. Until 4.30 on the return date the Respondent must not destroy, tamper with, cancel or part with possession, power, custody or control of the listed items otherwise than in accordance with the terms of this order.

COSTS

6. The costs of the Applicant's application shall be the Applicant's costs in the case.

RESTRICTIONS ON SERVICE

7. This order may only be served between [_____] am/pm and [_____]am/pm [and on a weekday].

EFFECT OF THIS ORDER

8. A Respondent who is an individual who is ordered not to do something must not do it himself or in any other way. He must not do it through others acting on his behalf or on his instructions or with his encouragement.

9. A Respondent which is a corporation and which is ordered not to do something must not do it itself or by its directors, officers, employees or agents or in any other way.

VARIATION AND DISCHARGE OF THIS ORDER

10. Anyone served with or notified of this Order may apply to the Court at any time to vary or discharge this Order (or so much of it as affects that person) but they must first inform the Applicant's solicitors [at least 48 hours beforehand]. If any evidence is to be relied upon in support of the application, the substance of it must be communicated in writing to the Applicant's solicitor in advance.

INTERPRETATION OF THIS ORDER

11. In this Order the words 'he', 'him', or 'his' include 'she' or 'her' and 'it' or 'its'.

12. Where there are two or more Respondents then (unless the contrary appears):

12.1 a reference to 'the Respondent' means both or all of them;

12.2 a requirement to serve on 'the Respondent' means on each of them; however, the order is effective against each Respondent on whom it is served; and

12.3 an Order requiring 'the Respondent' to do or not to do anything applies to all Respondents.

COMMUNICATIONS WITH THE COURT

All communications to the Court about this Order should be sent, where the Order was made in the Queen's Bench Division, to Room WG08, Royal Courts of Justice, Strand, London WC2A 2LL quoting the case number.

The telephone number is 0207 947 6010.

The offices are open between 10 am and 4.30 pm Monday to Friday.

SCHEDULE A

WITNESS STATEMENTS

The Applicant relied on the following witness statements—

Name   number of witness statement   date of statement   filed on behalf of

1.
2.

SCHEDULE B

The listed items:

1. The report to the Board or any extracts from it and all documents containing information derived from the Report.
2. All documents and records (in hard copy, digital or electronic form) which are the property of the Applicant.

SCHEDULE C

UNDERTAKINGS GIVEN TO THE COURT BY THE APPLICANT

1. If the court later finds that this order has caused loss to the Respondent, and decides that the Respondent should be compensated for that loss, the Applicant will comply with any order the court may make. Further, if the carrying out of this order has been in breach of the terms of this order or otherwise in a manner inconsistent with the Applicant's solicitors' duties as officers of the court, the Applicant will comply with any order for damages the Court may make.
2. [The Applicant will—
   2.1 on or before [date] cause a written guarantee in the sum of £[ ] to be issued from a bank with a place of business within England or Wales, in respect of any order the court may make pursuant to (1) above, and
   2.2 immediately upon issue of the guarantee, cause a copy of it to be served on the Respondent, and
   2.3 maintain pending further order the sum of £[ ] in an account controlled by the Applicant's solicitors.]
3. As soon as practicable the Applicant will issue and serve a claim form [in the form of the draft produced to the court][claiming the appropriate relief].[1]
4. The Applicant will [swear and file an affidavit][cause an affidavit to be sworn and filed][substantially in the terms of the draft affidavit produced to the court][confirming the substance of what was said to the court by the Applicant's Counsel/Solicitor].[2]
5. The Applicant will serve upon the Respondent [together with this order][as soon as practicable]—
   5.1 copies of the [witness statements][affidavits] and exhibits containing the evidence relied upon by the Applicant, and any other documents provided to the court on the making of the application;
   5.2 the claim form; and
   5.3 an application notice for continuation of the order.
6. [Anyone notified of this Order will be given a copy of it by the Applicant's legal representatives.]
7. The Applicant will not, without permission of the court, use any information or documents obtained as a result of carrying out this order nor inform anyone else of these proceedings except for the purposes of these proceedings (including adding further Respondents) or commencing civil proceedings in relation to the same or related subject matter to these proceedings until after the return date.

---

[1] Applicable if the Order was sought prior to issuing the claim.
[2] Applicable if the application was without notice.

8. If this order ceases to have effect (for example, if the Respondent provides security or the Applicant does not provide a bank guarantee as provided for above) the Applicant will immediately take all reasonable steps to inform in writing anyone to whom he has given notice of this order, or whom he has reasonable grounds for supposing may act upon this order, that it has ceased to have effect.

9. [The Applicant will not without the permission of the court use any information obtained as a result of this order for the purpose of any civil or criminal proceedings, either in England and Wales or in any other jurisdiction, other than this claim.]

10. [The Applicant will not without the permission of the Court seek to enforce this order in any country outside England and Wales [or seek an order of a similar nature including orders conferring a charge or other security against the Respondent or the Respondent's assets].

SCHEDULE D

UNDERTAKINGS GIVEN BY THE APPLICANT'S SOLICITORS

1. The Applicant's Solicitors will serve upon the Respondent [together with this order][as soon as possible]—
   1.1 a service copy of this order;
   1.2 the claim form (with the Defendant's response pack) or, if not issued, the draft produced to the court;
   1.3 an application notice for hearing on the return date;
   1.4 copies of the witness statements and exhibits containing the evidence relied upon by the Applicant;
   1.5 a note of any allegations of fact made orally to the court where such allegation is not contained in the affidavits or draft affidavits read by the judge;
   1.6 a copy of any other documents provided to the court on the making of the application; and
   1.7 a copy of the skeleton argument produced to the court by the Applicant's [Counsel/solicitors].

2. The Applicant's solicitors will answer at once to the best of their ability any question whether a particular item is a listed item.

3. Subject as provided below the Applicant's solicitors will retain in their own safe keeping all items obtained as a result of this order until the court directs otherwise.

4. The Applicant's solicitors will retain the originals of all documents obtained as a result of this order (except original documents which belong to the Applicant).

NAME AND ADDRESS OF APPLICANT'S LEGAL REPRESENTATIVES

The Applicant's legal representatives are—

[name, address, reference, fax and telephone numbers both in and out of office hours and email]

FORM 2

PARTICULARS OF CLAIM

Confidentiality/informant/delivery up

IN THE HIGH COURT OF JUSTICE   Claim Number:

QUEEN'S BENCH DIVISION   ––––––––––

Between:

BIGBUCKS PLC

Claimant

- and -

THE DAILY RAG LTD

Defendant

PARTICULARS OF CLAIM

The Parties

1. At all times material to this action:
   1.1 the Claimant has been a public limited company which has been authorized to run a game of chance, and
   1.2 the Defendant was the proprietor and publisher of a weekly magazine bearing the title *'News that is fit to print'* ('the Magazine').

The Draft Statement

2. The Claimant's financial and accounting year ends on 31 March. In preparation for publication on 1 June 2016 of a preliminary financial statement, the Claimant prepared a report to the board ('the Report').
3. The Report and its contents:
   3.1 constituted confidential information the property of the Claimant which was only to have been disseminated to third parties with the authority of the Claimant; and
   3.2 had been passed in confidence to the Board of the Claimant for the sole purpose of enabling them:
      (a) to audit the Claimant's draft accounts;
      (b) otherwise and generally to advise, as appropriate, on the contents of such document.

Copyright

4. Further, the Report is an original literary work which was prepared by employees of the Claimant in the course of their employment with the Claimant and accordingly the Claimant is the first owner of the copyright in the Report.

Unauthorized Disclosure of the Report

5. On a date of which the Claimant is unaware, but which fell prior to 28 June 2016, an individual or individuals ('the Informant(s)') whose identity is unknown to the Claimant, acting without the authority or knowledge of the Claimant, wrongfully caused and/or permitted a copy of the Draft Statement to be passed to a journalist employed by the Defendant ('the Journalist').

Equitable Duty of Confidence Owed by the Defendant

6. The Journalist received the copy of the Report in circumstances where it was obvious that the Report had been disclosed in breach of an equitable duty of confidence owed to the Claimant.
7. Accordingly upon receipt of the Report the Defendant was under a duty not to use any part of the Report or divulge any part of its contents without the Claimant's consent.

Receipt and Publication of the Report by the Defendant

8. Following the receipt by the Defendant of the Report, in the issue of the Magazine dated 29 June 2016 (published and/or distributed on the 1 July 2016) the Defendant published an article written by the Journalist under the heading *'Big Buck's chief's pay soars as lottery gives less and less to charity'* ('the Article'). The Article made express reference to (parts of) the Report as having been the source for the conclusions drawn by the Journalist and included extracts from the Draft Statement.

Breach of Confidence

9. Accordingly the Defendant has acted in breach of its equitable duty of confidence.

Infringement of Copyright

10. Further:
    10.1 by making unauthorized use of the Draft Statement, including printing extracts from the Report, the Defendant has infringed the Claimant's copyright in the Report.
    10.2 the Defendant has in its possession custody or control in the course of its business, infringing copies of the Claimant's copyright work, the Report.

Wrongful Interference with Property

11. Further, the Defendant has failed or refused to return the copy or copies of the Report supplied to it without authority, notwithstanding a demand made for the return of such copies in a facsimile message dated 28 June 2016. Accordingly the Defendant has wrongfully interfered with the Claimant's property.

Duty of Disclosure

12. Further and in any event, the Defendant has become mixed up in, and has facilitated, the wrong-doing of the Informant(s). Accordingly the Defendant is under a duty to assist the Claimant by providing full information of matters within its knowledge relating to such wrongdoing, including information as to the identity of the Informant(s). The Claimant contends that such disclosure is in the interests of justice within the meaning of that phrase in section 10 of the Contempt of Court Act 1981. In particular:
    12.1 it is likely that the Informant(s) is or are employed by either the Claimant or the Auditors and, as such, the Claimant and the Auditors have a legitimate interest in identifying a disloyal employee who will have access to confidential information of the Claimant and the Auditors.
    12.2 it is in any event necessary to identify the Informant(s) so as to prevent further wrongful disclosures of confidential information.

Threat of Further Use of the Report

13. Unless restrained by this Honourable Court, the Defendant threatens and intends to make further use of the Report and/or parts of it in breach of its equitable duty of confidence to the Claimant and by way of infringement of the Claimant's copyright interest in the Report.

Loss and Damage/Account of Profits

14. By reason of the matters set out above the Claimant has suffered loss and damage. Alternatively, and at the election of the Claimant, the Defendant is liable to account to the Claimant for the profits earned by reason of its breach of the equitable duty of confidence and infringement of copyright.

15. Further, the Claimant claims interest pursuant to the equitable jurisdiction of the Court, alternatively pursuant to section 35A of the Senior Courts Act 1981, on such sums as are found to be due to the Claimant at such rate and for such period as the Court shall think fit.

AND the Claimant claims:

(1) An injunction restraining the Defendant, whether by its directors, officers, employees or affects or any of them, or otherwise howsoever:
    i. from making any use (to include the passing to a third party) of the Report or any of its content; and
    ii. from infringing the Claimant's copyright interest in the literary work constituted by the Draft Statement; and

751

iii. from defacing, deleting any part of, or otherwise altering or tampering with the format or appearance of any and all documents and records which are the property of the Claimant.

(2) An Order for the delivery up to the Claimant of all property belonging to the Claimant in its possession including:

    i. the Report and any extracts from it and all documents containing information derived from the Report, alternatively destruction upon oath of all such documents.

    ii. all documents and records (in hard copy, digital, or electronic form) which are the property of the Claimant.

(3) An Order for disclosure by the Defendant of the identity of the Informant(s) and of the precise circumstances in which each and every piece of confidential information, or other property of the Claimant, received by the Defendant from the Informant(s) came to its attention and into its possession.

(4) Damages consequential upon the Defendant's wrongful interference with the Claimant's property.

(5) An Inquiry into the damages which have been, and may be, suffered by the Claimant by reason of the Defendant's wrongful use of confidential information the property of the Claimant and infringement of copyright.

(6) Alternatively, and at the election of the Claimant, an Account of profits made by the Defendant with the assistance of confidential information the property of the Claimant and/or by reason of the Defendant's infringement of copyright.

(7) Payment of the amount certified in answer to such Inquiry or Account as set out above.

(8) Interest pursuant to section 35A of the Senior Courts Act 1981 as above.

(9) Such further or other relief as the Court shall consider appropriate.

The Claimant believes the facts stated in this Particulars of Claim are true.

Signed: . . ..

Position or office held:

Date: . . ..

STATEMENT OF VALUE

FORM 3

The Grievance Letter

Mr T. Leaf
The Manor House
The Manor
London D0D GY1

Chairman
Big Bucks plc
Swell Place
Righteous Lane
London GR8 P4D

12 July 2016

GRIEVANCE

Dear Mr V. Rich,

I am writing following your decision to dismiss me summarily on 10 July 2016.

You dismissed me on the ground that I had made a disclosure of a confidential report to the Magazine the *Daily Rag.*

I informed you during the disciplinary hearing that I had disclosed the report dated 1 June 2016 to the Magazine. All gambling cards are sold with the following information upon them—'You may lose, but 10 pence of every pound you spend goes to charity'.

I was asked on 1 June 2016 to photocopy a report that was to be handed to the Board of Directors that afternoon. This report clearly set out that Big Bucks intend only to provide 8 pence to Charity, the remaining 2 pence being used to fund the Chief Executive's pay rise.

Given that the Board saw this report and as far as I am aware did nothing, I took a copy of that report and gave it to the *Daily Rag.*

I believe that my giving that report to the *Daily Rag* was a protected disclosure and that I suffered a detriment in being dismissed without you following the company's disciplinary procedure and that as you have dismissed me because of that disclosure my dismissal is automatically unfair.

I look forward to hearing from you.

T. Leaf.

FORM 4

Response to Grievance Letter

Chairman
Big Bucks plc
Swell Place
Righteous Lane
London GR8 P4D

Mr T. Leaf
The Manor House
The Manor
London D0D GY1

20 August 2016

Dear Mr Leaf,

Thank you for your letter dated 12 July 2016.

We have investigated your grievance. The report dated 1 June 2016 [the Report] was a confidential report and is an original literary work which was prepared by employees of the Claimant in the course of their employment with the Claimant and accordingly the Claimant is the first owner of the copyright in the Report.

The Report was disclosed by someone unknown to the *Daily Rag*. We issued court proceedings against the *Daily Rag* and they were ordered by a High Court Judge to inform us who had provided them with a copy of the Report on 5 July 2016. In a statement written for the Court dated 4 July 2016, the journalist Mr V. Hugo stated that it was you who provided the Report to the *Daily Rag*.

We initiated a disciplinary investigation and we followed our disciplinary procedure. We do not accept that we failed to follow the disciplina ry procedure. In such circumstances we do not believe you suffered a detriment by reason of your disclosure.

During the Disciplinary Hearing on 10 July 2016 that you attended with your Union Representative, you admitted removing the Report and providing it to the *Daily Rag*. Given that the Report contained confidential information of highly commercially sensitive information it was determined that you had acted in breach of the implied term within your contract of trust and confidence.

We note that you did not use our Whistleblowing procedure and seek to raise your concern with Father Ted as provided for in that procedure.

Finally it was stated within Mr V. Hugo's statement that he paid you £15,000 for the Report by a cheque made out to you from the *Daily Rag* dated 28 June 2016 which was cashed on 1 July 2016.

We note that you do not state specifically which legal obligation was being breached in the Report. We deny that you made a protected disclosure. We also believe that, in providing the Report to the *Daily Rag* in circumstances where you were paid, you did not believe (reasonably or otherwise) that you were making your disclosure in the public interest.

Yours truly,

V Rich.
Chairman, Big Bucks plc

FORM 5

EMPLOYMENT CLAIM

The Employment Tribunal now use a digital form available from https://www.gov.uk/employment-tribunals/make-a-claim

Before issuing a claim you must inform ACAS of your intention to make a claim to a Tribunal by completing an Early Conciliation Notification, see https://ec.acas.org.uk/; however, this does not apply if your claim is for Interim Relief.

If required, once you have received your Early Conciliation Certificate from ACAS, you can submit our Employment Tribunal Form.

It is a statutory requirement that the Employment Tribunal's form is used.[3]

It is a statutory requirement that you include your Early Conciliation Certificate Number in this form, otherwise it will be rejected.

A fee is payable, currently the issuing fee for a whistleblowing claim is £250 and a hearing fee is £950. A claimant may be entitled to a reduction in fees.

If the claim is only in relation to a detriment suffered then the claim must be described under the 'reasons for the claim' and 'other complaints' in section 9.1 of the form. If the claim is also for unfair dismissal then the necessary information for that claim will need to be placed in box 5.1.

The following example sets out a sample Grounds of Complaint (as required on Page 8, Question 8.2) of a claim of unfair dismissal and detriment for having made a protected disclosure.

IN THE LONDON CENTRAL EMPLOYMENT TRIBUNAL

Claim No xxxxx

BETWEEN:

TREVOR LEAF

Applicant

- and –

BIG BUCKS PLC

Respondent

GROUNDS OF COMPLAINT
(Particulars for paragraph 8.2 of the Employment Tribunal Claim Form)

---

1. I started working for Big Bucks on 6 January 2016 as an assistant in the photocopying room.
2. Big Bucks operate a gambling card sold nationally. The purchasers buy the card in the hope of winning money. It is sold with the following statement that is also used in advertising: 'You may lose, but 10 pence of every pound you spend goes to charity'.
3. On 1 June 2016 I was asked to photocopy a report. The report was drafted by Big Bucks' internal auditor and it stated that Big Bucks over the past year had only given 8 pence of every pound to Charity, the remaining 2 pence being used to fund the Chief Executive's pay rise.
4. All gambling cards are sold with the following information upon them: 'You may lose, but 10 pence of every pound you spend goes to charity'.
5. I read the report as I was copying it and I was very upset by its contents. It was clear to me from the contents of the report that Big Bucks were misleading the public over the amount of money they

---

[3] Employment Tribunal (Constitution and Rules of Procedure) Regulations, Schedule 1 The Employment Tribunal's Rules of Procedure. A claim shall be started by presenting a completed claim form (using a prescribed form) in accordance with any practice direction made under regulation 11, namely one issued by the Presidents of the Employment Tribunals (SI 2013/1237 Sch 1 r 8(1)).

provided to charity. I believe that the report showed that Big Bucks breached a legal obligation to customers who purchased the card. I believe the report contained evidence of false accounting, theft, or misappropriation of charitable assets and/or evidence of a material application of charitable funds for a non-charitable purpose. I believed the contents of the report were true as it was written by the Financial Director.

6. I believed that if I had raised the matter with Big Bucks they would have dismissed me.[4]

7. I also believed that if I had raised my concerns with Big Bucks they would have destroyed the report.[5]

8. As the entire Board knew of the contents of the Report I didn't know who else to go to and so I called the *Daily Rag* and they told me they would expose Big Bucks to stop them.

9. During my disciplinary hearing Big Bucks stated they were dismissing me because of my disclosure to the *Daily Rag*.

10. I believe that my giving that Report to the *Daily Rag* was a protected disclosure in accordance with section 43G of the Employment Rights Act 1996 and that my dismissal was automatically unfair in that I was dismissed by reason of this disclosure.

11. Further, I was subjected to detrimental treatment other than dismissal on the grounds of my protected disclosure in that:

    1.1 Big Bucks' disciplinary procedure states that reasonable notice will be given of any disciplinary allegations and that no person can be summarily dismissed unless the decision is made by the Chief Executive and the Chairman of Big Bucks.

    1.2 I was given very little prior warning that a disciplinary hearing was to be held.

    1.3 The decision to dismiss me was taken by the Chairman alone who attended the disciplinary hearing and the Chief Executive was not in attendance.

    1.4 I believe I suffered a detriment as a consequence of my disclosure set out above by the manner in which the disciplinary procedure was carried out.

---

[4] Section 43G(2)(a).
[5] Section 43G(2)(b).

FORM 6

Response to a Claim

The Employment Tribunal now use an online from found at https://www.employmenttribunals.service.gov.uk/forms/form/172/en/response_to_claim

Or it can be downloaded at

http://hmctsformfinder.justice.gov.uk/HMCTS/GetForm.do?court_forms_id=3133

It is now a statutory requirement that the Employment Tribunal's form are used.

It is important to respond to the Details of Claim (questions 8.1 and 8.2) and any Additional Information in the Claim (question 15). Often in will be worth having a short summary at the outset. The following is a sample response to the complaint in Form 5 above.

IN THE LONDON CENTRAL EMPLOYMENT TRIBUNAL

Claim No xxxxx

BETWEEN:

TREVOR LEAF

Applicant

- and –

BIG BUCKS PLC

Respondent

GROUNDS OF RESISTANCE

(Particulars for paragraph 6.1 of the Response Form)

Summary

1. The Claimant was employed by the Respondent from 6 January 2016 until his summary dismissal on 10 July 2016. He was dismissed for gross misconduct following a disciplinary hearing at which he admitted supplying a copy of a confidential report from the Respondent's internal auditor ('the Report') to the *Daily Rag*. It is denied that the Claimant made any protected disclosure. His claims of dismissal and detriment by reason of protected disclosures are denied.

2. Unless otherwise stated, references below to paragraph numbers are to the Grounds of Complaint.

Background

3. Paragraphs 1 and 2 are admitted. On commencement of his employment with the Respondent, the Claimant was supplied with a copy of the Respondent's whistleblowing procedure. A copy is also available on the company's intranet.

4. As to paragraph 3:

    4.1 It is admitted that on 1 June 2016 the Claimant was requested to photocopy a Report. The Report constituted confidential information of the Respondent which was only to have been disseminated to third parties with the authority of the Respondent. It is admitted that the Report stated that, over the past year, so far the Respondent had only given 8 pence to charity. It is denied that the Report stated any remaining 2 pence had been used to fund the Chief Executive's pay rise.

    4.2 The Respondent first became aware of a disclosure of the Report when it was published on 29 June 2016 by the *Daily Rag* by the Journalist Mr V. Hugo under the heading 'Big Bucks' chief's pay soars as lottery gives less and less to charity'.

    4.3 As a consequence of this article the Respondent issued proceedings against the *Daily Rag* who consequently, pursuant to an Order of the High Court, disclosed the circumstances of the Claimant's disclosure of the Report. Included within the information was the fact that the Claimant had been paid £15,000 for the Report.

5. As to paragraph 4, it is admitted that all gambling cards are sold with the following information upon them: 'You may lose, but 10 pence of every pound you spend goes to charity'. During the disciplinary meeting the Claimant accepted that he had disclosed the Report to the *Daily Rag*.

Alleged protected disclosure

6. As to paragraphs 5 to 8:

    6.1 It is denied that the Report shows that the Respondent was misleading the public about the amount of money it provided to charity. Nor did the Report show that Big Bucks breached a legal obligation to customers who purchased the card or at all.

    6.2 It is not admitted that the Claimant believed that the report contained evidence of false accounting, theft, or misappropriation of charitable assets and/or evidence of a material application of charitable funds for a non-charitable purpose and the Claimant is put to strict proof of the same. Insofar as the Claimant did hold such a belief, this was not a reasonable belief. It was available to him to verify any such belief by raising the matter under the Respondent's whistleblowing procedure, which he chose not to do.

    6.3 It is admitted that the Report was drafted by the Financial Director.

    6.4 It is denied that the Claimant made a qualifying disclosure. As to this:

        6.4.1 He did not have a reasonable belief that any information he disclosed tended to show a relevant failure;

        6.4.2 It is not admitted that the Claimant held a genuine belief that the disclosure was made in the public interest. Having regard to the substantial payment made by the *Daily Rag* to the Claimant, it may be inferred that the disclosure was made in his own private interest. Further, if the Claimant had genuinely been pursuing the public interest he would first have sought to verify the matter by utilizing the Respondent's whistleblowing procedure. To the extent that the Respondent believed it was in the public interest to make the disclosure to the *Daily Rag* before first raising the matter internally so as to verify his stated belief, it is denied that this was a reasonable belief.

    6.5 Further, even if the Claimant made a protected disclosure, it is denied that it was a protected disclosure in accordance with section 43G ERA (or otherwise). In particular:

        6.5.1 It is denied that he held a reasonable belief as to the substantial truth of the information he disclosed and allegations he made

        6.5.2 The disclosure was made for the purposes of personal gain.

        6.5.3 He did not satisfy any of the conditions in section 43G(2) ERA. The Claimant appears to rely (in paragraphs 6 and 7) on sections 43G(2)(a) or (b) ERA. As to these:

            (a) It is not admitted that the Claimant held a belief that he would be subjected to a detriment if he made the disclose to the Respondent, but in any event any such belief was not reasonable. The Respondent's whistleblowing procedure makes clear that the company encourages staff to raise with it in the first instance any concerns that they have as to any matter relating to the Respondent's business, and that detrimental treatment of any person raising such concerns will not be tolerated and will be regarded as a serious disciplinary offence. It is also made clear that concerns may be raised under the procedure on a confidential basis.

            (b) It is not admitted that the Claimant believed that the Respondent would destroy the Report, and it is denied that any such belief was reasonable.

        6.5.4 In all the circumstances of the case, it was not reasonable for the Claimant to make the disclosure. The Claimant did not raise the matter with an appropriate person, and the *Daily Rag* was not such a person. Further, as set out above, it was available for him to use the Respondent's whistleblowing procedure but he failed to do so.

    6.6 Further, the Report is the Claimant's property. Even if there was a protected disclosure, the misappropriation of the Report was a separable act distinct from the protected disclosure.

    6.7 Paragraph 8 is denied except that no admissions are made as to what the *Daily Rag* told the Claimant.

Claim of dismissal by reason of protected disclosure

7. As to paragraph 9, the Claimant was dismissed because of his breach of confidence, and theft of the Respondent's property (ie the Report) that was sold to the *Daily Rag*. His conduct amounted to a serious breach of his duty of fidelity to the Respondent, and a breach of the implied term that he would not, without reasonable cause or excuse, act so as to destroy or seriously damage the relationship of trust and confidence. The Respondent was therefore entitled to dismiss him without notice. His dismissal was not by reason of any protected disclosure.

8. Paragraph 10 is denied.

Claim of detriment by reason of protected disclosure

9. As to paragraph 11:

   9.1 For the reasons set out above it is denied that the Claimant made a protected disclosure. Nor was he subjected to any detrimental treatment by reason of the alleged protected disclosure.

   9.2 Paragraph 11.1 correctly sets out certain terms of the Respondent's disciplinary procedure.

   9.3 Paragraph 11.2 is denied. The Claimant was given sufficient notice of the disciplinary hearing in all the circumstances, and was represented at the hearing by his union representative.

   9.4 Paragraph 11.3 is denied save that the Chief Executive did not attend the disciplinary hearing. The Chairman discussed the proposed decision with the Chief Executive before it was made. The Chief Executive agreed the decision to dismiss the Claimant. The non-attendance of the Chief Executive was due to other commitments and not by reason of the Claimant's disclosure.

   9.5 Further, insofar as in paragraph 11 the Claimant contends that he suffered the detriment of dismissal by reason of the matters alleged, pursuant to section 47B(2), the claim can only be raised as part of the claim of unfair dismissal.

INDEX

Index